Synthesizes and integrates rigorous and relevant strategy material

The book offers a mix of classic and contemporary content—strategy material that has stood the test of time (e.g., Porter's five forces model, the resource-based view) as well as up-to-date strategy material and current research (e.g., dynamic capabilities, the triple bottom line). It also includes student-accessible coverage of strategic management research drawn from both academic journals and best-selling business books. In every chapter, one section provides a critical evaluation, based on empirical research, of a specific theory or concept as it relates to competitive advantage.

 Uses up-to-date examples and discusses current topics within a global context

The book's current examples illustrate how companies apply strategy concepts in today's business world. Examples throughout the book and in the boxed Strategy Highlights reflect the global nature of competition and the importance of emerging economies. Additionally, a number of the in-text examples relate to sustainable strategy with a focus on "green" products and issues.

 Presents core concepts, frameworks, and techniques in a comprehensive yet concise way

While not compromising on the quality and grounding expected by instructors, the text is written in a student-friendly and engaging manner. This textbook will be an *enjoyable read* for students—clear, concise, and filled with examples from companies students know—while also providing the content and value-add that instructors expect.

 Offers high-quality cases, well integrated with textbook chapters

Instructors have varying needs for top-notch, up-to-date cases that are well-integrated with textbook content. This book offers three types of cases, to suit diverse needs. The **ChapterCases** (which begin and end each chapter) frame chapter content, and 12 **MiniCases** (following Chapter 12) present short case scenarios. Both types of case materials were researched and written by Frank T. Rothaermel. In addition, the book offers 30 **full-length Cases** (in the *Cases and Concepts* version of the book, or available through McGraw-Hill's custom-publishing *Create™* program). Half of these cases were researched and written by Frank Rothaermel specifically for the book, and half were selected from high-quality sources such as HBS Premier Cases, Darden, and Ivey. The full-length cases are supported with Case Teaching Notes, Case PowerPoints, and video cases, all developed by Professors Marne L. Arthaud-Day (Kansas State University) and Robert Porter (University of Central Florida), in close collaboration with Frank Rothaermel. All three types of case materials are **closely connected to chapter content**, for optimal teaching and learning, and all cases come with a set of questions.

FOR THE LATEST INFORMATION AND CURRENT UPDATES TO THE TEXTBOOK AND CASES, PLEASE VISIT THE AUTHOR AT:

www.ftrStrategy.com

A full complement of ancillaries—all with the same look and feel, the same voice, and the same high quality as the book itself

McGraw-Hill *Connect® Management* is the **leading online assignment and assessment system for business courses**. This web-based solution enhances your efforts to make your classroom a place for **meaningful, engaging learning**. With *Connect Management*, you can track student progress with just a few clicks of the mouse, save time through automatic grading, and generate an unparalleled array of reports.

For students, *Connect* improves learning and retention by helping students prepare for class, master concepts, and review for exams.

The Instructor's site in Connect:

- Houses **powerful tools and features** that facilitate development and grading of assignments.

- Generates an unparalleled array of reports that enable instructors to **assess learning outcomes** for accreditation purposes.

- Offers **teaching notes**, including lecture outlines and exams, PPT slide guidance, small-group exercises, suggestions for end-of-chapter answers and discussion points, and notes on topic extensions in Connect interactive applications.

- Includes a rich online **Test Bank**, with 100–150 test questions per chapter, including both **multiple-choice** and **short-answer** questions.

- Provides **PowerPoint® slides** that build upon and extend coverage from the book, with **embedded video links**, optional small-group exercise slides, and notes on topics covered in *Connect* Interactive Applications.

And, to save you time, assessment of student responses **flows easily into your grade book.**

The Student's site in Connect:

- Includes a minimum of three unique **instantly graded *Interactive Applications*** per chapter that ask students to apply strategic management concepts to real-world scenarios.

Included in the Interactive Applications are:

- An **interactive video case** in every chapter, covering a key chapter learning objective. Contemporary video topics include business in China, pricing of water, use of solar energy, and global forces affecting the future of business.

- **Drag-and-drop interactive assignments** that allow students to actively engage the material for deeper understanding of key tools and applications presented in the chapters.

- **Chapter quizzes** for student review in preparation for course exams.

- **Templates for strategic financial analysis** and a "How to do a case analysis" guide, complete with financial ratios used to compare performance between firms.

- A **financial review activity**—for students who wish to *refresh* or *extend* their working knowledge of major financial measures in a strategic framework.

All ancillary content in **Connect Management** was developed by Professor Anne W. Fuller, from California State University, Sacramento, in close collaboration with Frank T. Rothaermel.

Strategic Management

CONCEPTS & CASES

Strategic Management

FRANK T. ROTHAERMEL

Georgia Institute of Technology

STRATEGIC MANAGEMENT: CONCEPTS AND CASES

Published by McGraw-Hill/Irwin, a business unit of The McGraw-Hill Companies, Inc., 1221 Avenue of the Americas, New York, NY, 10020. Copyright © 2013 by The McGraw-Hill Companies, Inc. All rights reserved. Printed in the United States of America. No part of this publication may be reproduced or distributed in any form or by any means, or stored in a database or retrieval system, without the prior written consent of The McGraw-Hill Companies, Inc., including, but not limited to, in any network or other electronic storage or transmission, or broadcast for distance learning.

Some ancillaries, including electronic and print components, may not be available to customers outside the United States.

This book is printed on acid-free paper.

1 2 3 4 5 6 7 8 9 0 DOW/DOW 1 0 9 8 7 6 5 4 3 2

ISBN   978-0-07-811273-7
MHID   0-07-811273-7

Vice president and editor-in-chief: *Brent Gordon*
Editorial director: *Paul Ducham*
Executive editor: *Michael Ablassmeir*
Executive director of development: *Ann Torbert*
Development editor II: *Laura Griffin*
Editorial coordinator: *Andrea Heirendt*
Vice president and director of marketing: *Robin J. Zwettler*
Marketing director: *Amee Mosley*
Senior marketing manager: *Michelle Heaster*
Vice president of editing, design, and production: *Sesha Bolisetty*
Lead project manager: *Harvey Yep*
Buyer II: *Debra R. Sylvester*
Designer: *Matt Diamond*
Senior photo research coordinator: *Jeremy Cheshareck*
Photo researcher: *Allison Grimes*
Senior media project manager: *Bruce Gin*
Cover design: *MicroArts Pvt Limited* (http://microarts.biz/)
Interior design: *Matt Diamond*
Typeface: *10/12 Times Roman*
Compositor: *Laserwords Private Limited*
Printer: *R. R. Donnelley*

Library of Congress Cataloging-in-Publication Data

Rothaermel, Frank T.
    Strategic management : concepts & cases / Frank T. Rothaermel.
    p. cm.
    Includes index.
    ISBN-13: 978-0-07-811273-7 (alk. paper)
    ISBN-10: 0-07-811273-7 (alk. paper)
    1. Strategic planning. 2. Management. I. Title.
HD30.28.R6647 2013
658.4'012--dc23

                                                                 2011038165

Dedication

To my eternal family for their love, support, and sacrifice:
Kelleyn, Harris, Winston, Roman, and Adelaide

—Frank T. Rothaermel

FRANK T. ROTHAERMEL
Georgia Institute of Technology

Frank T. Rothaermel (PhD) is the Angel and Stephen M. Deedy Professor in the College of Management at the Georgia Institute of Technology. He is an Alfred P. Sloan Industry Studies Fellow, and also holds a National Science Foundation (NSF) CAREER award, which "is a Foundation-wide activity that offers the National Science Foundation's most prestigious awards in support of . . . those teacher-scholars who most effectively integrate research and education . . ." (NSF CAREER Award description).

Frank's research interests lie in the areas of strategy, innovation, and entrepreneurship. To inform his research, he has conducted extensive field work and executive training with leading corporations such as Amgen, Daimler, Eli Lilly, GE Energy, GE Healthcare, Kimberly-Clark, Microsoft, McKesson, and NCR, among others. *Bloomberg Businessweek* named Frank one of Georgia Tech's Prominent Faculty in its national survey of business schools. The Kauffman Foundation views Frank as one of the world's 75 thought leaders in strategic entrepreneurship and innovation.

Frank has published over 25 articles in leading academic journals such as the *Academy of Management Journal, Academy of Management Review, Organization Science, Strategic Management Journal*, and others. Some of his academic articles are highly cited. Frank currently serves (or has served) on the editorial boards of the *Academy of Management Journal, Academy of Management Review, Strategic Management Journal*, and *Strategic Organization*. He regularly translates his research findings for practitioner audiences in articles in *Forbes, MIT Sloan Management Review, The Wall Street Journal*, and elsewhere.

He has received several recognitions for his research, including the Sloan Industry Studies Best Paper Award, the Academy of Management Newman Award, the Strategic Management Society Conference Best Paper Prize, the DRUID Conference Best Paper Award, and the Israel Strategy Conference Best Paper Prize, and he is the inaugural recipient of the Byars Faculty Excellence Award. Frank has extensive teaching experience at a number of institutions and programs, including Georgia Tech, Georgetown University, Michigan State University, and the University of Washington. He has received multiple teaching awards at the undergraduate and MBA levels.

Frank holds a PhD degree in strategic management from the University of Washington, an MBA from the Marriott School of Management at Brigham Young University, and an MA in economics from the University of Duisburg, Germany. He was a visiting professor at the University of St. Gallen, Switzerland, and an Erasmus Scholar at Sheffield Hallam University, UK. Professor Rothaermel is a member of the Academy of Management, the Industry Studies Association (Founding Member), and the Strategic Management Society.

PREFACE

The vision for this book is to provide students with core concepts, frameworks, and analysis techniques in strategy that will not only integrate their functional course offerings but also help them to become managers who make better strategic decisions. It is a research-based strategy text for the issues that managers face in a globalized and turbulent 21st century, blending theory, empirical research, and practical applications in a student-accessible form.

The competition in the strategy textbook market can be separated into two overarching categories: traditional strategy textbooks, which are the first-generation books (from the 1980s), and more recent research-based strategy textbooks, which are the second-generation books (from the 1990s). This new textbook aims to be different—a third-generation strategy textbook, positioned to compete successfully with the primary first- and second-generation incumbents. The third-generation approach you will find in this book combines the student accessibility and application-oriented frameworks found in first-generation books with the strategy research in the second-generation books.

In this book, I synthesize and integrate theory, empirical research, and practical applications in a unique combination of rigor and relevance. With a single strong voice, the book weaves together classic and cutting-edge theory with in-chapter cases and strategy highlights, to demonstrate how companies gain and sustain competitive advantage. The strategic intent for the book is to combine quality and value with user-friendliness. The mental model I used throughout the process of writing and developing the project is Apple Inc.'s innovation approach, which tightly integrates different competencies to launch novel, but highly user-friendly products. I view this book, the different options for accompanying cases, and the additional instructor and student resources in much the same way.

In particular, this book is based on the following principles, each of which provides a value-added dimension for instructors or students, or both:

- **_Synthesis and integration of rigorous and relevant strategy material._** For example, the book includes strategy material that has stood the test of time (such as the resource-based view and Porter's five forces model) as well as up-to-date strategy material and current research (such as the dynamic capabilities perspective and the triple bottom line).

  The book also includes _student-accessible coverage_ of strategic management research. It draws on articles published in the leading academic journals (for instance, _Strategic Management Journal, Academy of Management Journal/Review, Organization Science, Management Science, Journal of Management_, and so on). Although academic theory and empirical research form the foundation of the text, I also have integrated insights from leading practitioner outlets (such as _Harvard Business Review, Sloan Management Review, California Management Review_) to enhance the application of concepts. To weave in current examples and developments, I draw on _The Wall Street Journal, The Economist, Bloomberg Businessweek, Fortune, Forbes,_ and others. In sum, theory is brought to life via the embedded examples within each framework and concept.

- **_The comprehensive yet concise presentation of core concepts, frameworks, and techniques._** Although comprehensive, the book does not include every single idea ever introduced to the strategy field. Many students don't read the assigned readings in their strategy textbooks because the books contain too much information, presented in a disjointed fashion. Many strategy books read more like a literature review, without addressing _what_ the research findings mean and _why_ they are important for managers. This jumble prevents students from seeing the bigger strategic picture: They may see the trees, but they fail to see the forest. In contrast, this textbook will be an *enjoyable read* for students—clear, concise, and filled with examples from companies today's students know—while at the same time providing the content and value-add that instructors expect. *It's one book with one voice!*

■ ***Combination of traditional and contemporary chapters.*** As a review of the chapter-contents listing will demonstrate (see the contents listing on pages xxxix–xlv), the book includes the traditional chapters needed in the core strategy course. In addition, it includes three contemporary *standalone chapters* that reviewers have identified as providing additional value: Chapter 2 offers an overview of the strategic management process and the importance of vision, mission, and values, before the book addresses the topics of external and internal analysis. Chapter 5 neatly ends the analysis section of the book by providing five approaches to measuring firm performance and assessing competitive advantage. Chapter 7 addresses the important topics of innovation and strategic entrepreneurship as aspects of business strategy. For more information about those chapters, see the discussion in the upcoming "Unique Features and Pedagogy" section.

■ ***Up-to-date examples and discussion of current topics within a global context.*** The book has been written for today's students to reflect the turbulence and dynamism that they will face as managers. I have drawn on up-to-date examples to illustrate how companies apply strategy concepts in today's business world. Although this text contains a standalone chapter on *Global Strategy*, examples throughout the book reflect the global nature of competition and the importance of emerging economies such as the BRIC countries. Additionally, a number of the examples relate to sustainable strategy with a focus on "green" products and issues.

I also have drawn topics and examples from recent and current bestsellers, such as *Co-opetition; Hypercompetition; Innovator's Dilemma (and Solution); Predictably Irrational; The Long Tail; Wisdom of the Crowds; Built to Last; How the Mighty Fall; Why Smart Executives Fail;* and *The World Is Flat,* among others. I have included these ideas to expose students to topics that today's managers talk about. Being conversant with these concepts from business bestsellers will help today's students interview better and effortlessly join the discourse in the corporate world.

Having spoken to hundreds of students across the world, I want to minimize the frustration they express in seeing the same, out-of-date examples in so many of their (generic and boiler-plate) business-school textbooks.

■ ***Use of the AFI strategy framework.*** The book demonstrates that "less is more" through a focused presentation of the relevant strategy content using *Analysis, Formulation*, and *Implementation* as a guiding framework. This model (see Exhibit 1.9 on page 20) integrates process schools of strategy (based on organization theory, psychology, and sociology) with content schools of strategy (based on economics). Process and content can be viewed as the "yin and yang" of strategy. Current strategy textbooks typically favor one or the other but do not integrate them, which leads to an unbalanced and incomplete treatment of strategic management. The AFI strategy strives for beauty through balance, which is lacking in most current strategy texts on the market. The model also emphasizes that gaining and sustaining competitive advantage is accomplished in an iterative and recursive fashion. The framework offers a repository for theoretical strategy knowledge that is well translated for student consumption, and it provides a toolkit for practicing managers.

■ ***High-quality cases, well integrated with textbook chapters.*** We all know that cases are a key ingredient in teaching strategy. My interactions with colleagues, reviewers, and focus group participants in the course of writing and developing this book indicate varying instructor needs for top-notch, up-to-date cases that are well-integrated with the content presented. Thus, the book offers three types of cases: **ChapterCases,** which begin and end each chapter; an additional 12 **MiniCases** (following Chapter 12), all based on original research; and 30 full-length **Cases** (in the *Cases and Concepts* version of the book or available through McGraw-Hill's custom-publishing *Create™* program).

The ChapterCases frame the chapter topic and content. The MiniCases provide a decision scenario that a company's manager might face, and they offer dynamic opportunities to apply strategy concepts in one or two class sessions. The full-length Cases, with more complex story lines, can be used for longer, more in-depth class discussion and case analysis and for bigger course projects (for example, term case papers). All cases come with a set of questions to stimulate class discussion or provide guidance for written assignments. The instructor resources offer sample answers that apply chapter content to the cases. For more description of each type of case, see the upcoming "Unique Features and Pedagogy" section.

Several of the leading strategy textbooks outsource their cases (and other supporting materials) to third parties without much, if any, quality control or integration with the concepts presented in the text. I have taken pride in authoring *all* of the ChapterCases and MiniCases, and in authoring or co-authoring half of the full-length Cases. This additional touch not only allows quality control but also ensures that chapter content and cases use one voice and are closely interconnected. In addition, I have maintained strict quality control for both Cases and Case Teaching Notes.

■ ***Direct applications of strategy to students' careers and lives.*** The examples in the book discuss products and services from companies with which students are familiar. Use of such examples aids in making strategy relevant to students' lives and helps them internalize strategy concepts and frameworks.

In addition, at the end of each chapter's homework materials is an innovative text feature, titled *my*Strategy, which personalizes strategy concepts through direct application of the chapter topic to students' lives. For example, questions asked in these sections include: *What is your positioning strategy in the job market? How will you differentiate yourself, and at what cost?* and *How much is an MBA worth to you?* These and similar questions are intended to help students think through strategic issues related to their budding careers.

UNIQUE FEATURES AND PEDAGOGY

As mentioned, the book contains three standalone chapters that set it apart from the competition. While some competitors may highlight one or the other topic, none has these three standalone chapters:

■ **Chapter 2,** *The Strategic Management Process*—This chapter allows for a thorough discussion of the strategic management process, including the role of vision, mission, and values; strategic intent; customer versus product-oriented missions; the combination of intended and emergent strategies; and the importance of long-term success in anchoring a firm in ethical values.

■ **Chapter 5,** *Competitive Advantage and Firm Performance*—This chapter looks at three traditional approaches to measure performance: economic value creation, accounting profitability, and shareholder value creation. It also looks at two holistic approaches: the balanced scorecard and the triple bottom line. Each of the five approaches is linked to a separate learning objective, enabling instructors to easily cover as many of the approaches as desired for their course and its goals. As the concluding chapter in Part 1, this chapter helps anchor the analysis content and prepares students with tools for the formulation chapters that follow.

■ **Chapter 7, *Business Strategy: Innovation and Strategic Entrepreneurship*—**Driven by Schumpeter's "perennial gale of creative destruction," competition seems more heated than ever, with innovation playing a key role in gaining and sustaining competitive advantage. This chapter addresses various aspects of innovation, beginning with the industry life cycle and the modes of competition, and business-level strategies at various stages in the life cycle. Using tools and concepts of strategic management, it explores four types of innovation, as well as the Internet as a disruptive force, paradigm changes, and hypercompetition. This chapter especially will engage students and provide much food for thought in their jobs and careers.

ChapterCases

Each chapter opens with a short case highlighting a strategic issue that a well-known company faced and relates that company to a concept to be taught in the chapter:

■ The Premature Death of a Google Forerunner at Microsoft (Chapter 1, p. 3)
■ Teach For America: Inspiring Future Leaders (Chapter 2, p. 31)
■ Build Your Dreams (BYD) to Sidestep Entry Barriers (Chapter 3, p. 55)
■ From Good to Great to Gone: The Rise and Fall of Circuit City (Chapter 4, p. 85)
■ Assessing Competitive Advantage: Google vs. Microsoft (Chapter 5, p. 113)
■ Trimming Fat at Whole Foods Market (Chapter 6, p. 139)
■ From Encyclopedia Britannica to Encarta to Wikipedia (Chapter 7, p. 171)
■ Refocusing GE: A Future of Clean-Tech and Health Care? (Chapter 8, p. 201)
■ Facebook: From Dorm Room to Dominant Social Network (Chapter 9, p. 237)
■ Hollywood Goes Global (Chapter 10, p. 269)
■ Zappos: An Organization Designed to Deliver Happiness (Chapter 11, p. 301)
■ HP's CEO Mark Hurd Resigns amid Ethics Scandal (Chapter 12, p. 333)

The end of each chapter returns to the ChapterCase. Here, we ask students to reconsider the case, applying concepts and information presented in the chapter, along with additional information about the focus company. Questions in the "*Consider This . . .*" section serve as good jumping-off points for class discussion.

Gaining & Sustaining Competitive Advantage Critical Analyses

Each chapter contains a section that puts one specific theory or concept "under the magnifying glass." The purpose is to critically evaluate if and how the theory or concept is linked to competitive advantage, the overarching goal in strategic management. In these sections, marked with a magnifying glass icon, we combine strategic management research with real-world observations. The list:

■ Stakeholders (Chapter 1, p. 18)
■ Mission Statements and Competitive Advantage (Chapter 2, p. 36)
■ Five Forces in Airlines vs. Soft Drinks (Chapter 3, p. 68)
■ How to Protect a Competitive Advantage (Chapter 4, p. 102)
■ Assessing Competitive Advantage: Google vs. Microsoft, Continued (Chapter 5, p. 123)
■ The Dynamics of Competitive Positioning (Chapter 6, p. 161)
■ Hypercompetition (Chapter 7, p. 191)

- Corporate Diversification (Chapter 8, p. 221)
- Mergers and Acquisitions (Chapter 9, p. 241)
- Regional Clusters (Chapter 10, p. 289)
- Organizational Culture and Competitive Advantage (Chapter 11, p. 319)
- Corporate Social Responsibility (Chapter 12, p. 341)

Strategy Highlight Boxes

Every chapter contains between one and four *Strategy Highlight* boxes. These in-chapter examples apply a specific concept to a specific company. They are right-sized for maximum student appeal—long enough to contain valuable insights, and short enough to encourage student reading. Examples:

- Threadless: Leveraging Crowdsourcing to Design Cool T-Shirts (Chapter 1, p. 17)
- Starbucks's CEO: "It's Not What We Do!" (Chapter 2, p. 44)
- UBS Relents to Pressure by U.S. Government (Chapter 3, p. 57)
- How Nintendo Focused on the Casual Gamer (Chapter 4, p. 95)
- Interface: The World's First Sustainable Company (Chapter 5, p. 128)
- Ryanair: Lower Cost than the Low-Cost Leader! (Chapter 6, p. 148)
- GE's Reverse Innovation: Disrupt Yourself! (Chapter 7, p. 186)
- ExxonMobil Diversifies into Natural Gas (Chapter 8, p. 218)
- Pixar and Disney: From Alliance to Acquisition (Chapter 9, p. 247)
- Does GM's Future Lie in China? (Chapter 10, p. 275)
- *USA Today:* Leveraging Ambidextrous Organizational Design (Chapter 11, p. 312)
- GE's Board of Directors (Chapter 12, p. 346)

To see all of the Strategy Highlight boxes, by chapter, go to the detailed Contents list beginning on page xl.

*my*Strategy Applications

Near the end of the chapter, immediately before the chapter endnotes, is a feature titled *my*Strategy, which applies strategy concepts from the chapter to students' lives. You may choose to make this feature a regular part of the course, or you may prefer to let students explore these items outside of the regular coursework. In whatever way they are used, the *my*Strategy features demonstrate opportunities to personalize strategy as students plan or enhance careers following completion of the strategy course and their degrees. Examples:

- How to Position Yourself for Career Advantage (Chapter 1, p. 25)
- How Much Are Your Values Worth to You? (Chapter 2, p. 51)
- Is My Job the Next One Being Outsourced? (Chapter 3, p. 80)
- Looking Inside Yourself: What Is My Competitive Advantage? (Chapter 4, p. 110)
- How Much Is an MBA Worth to You? (Chapter 5, p. 134)
- Different Value and Cost Drivers—What Determines *Your* Buying Decisions? (Chapter 6, p. 166)
- Do You Want to Be an Entrepreneur? (Chapter 7, p. 196)
- How Diversified Are You? (Chapter 8, p. 230)
- What Is Your Network Strategy? (Chapter 9, p. 262)
- Should There Be More H1-B Visas? (Chapter 10, p. 295)

- For What Type of Organization Are *You* Best-Suited? (Chapter 11, p. 328)
- Are You Part of Gen-Y, or Will You Manage Gen-Y Workers? (Chapter 12, p. 362)

MiniCases

Following the book's final chapter are an additional 12 original MiniCases; most are one or two pages in length. With suggested links to related chapters, the MiniCases include a handful of attached discussion questions (with suggested responses available to instructors in the online instructor's resources). These MiniCases are short enough to be assigned as add-ons to chapters, either as individual assignments or as group work, or to be used for class discussion. They are:

- Michael Phelps: Strategizing for Gold (MiniCase 1, p. 367)
- Strategy and Serendipity: A Billion-Dollar Bonanza (MiniCase 2, p. 369)
- Home Depot's Eco Options Boost Profit Margins (MiniCase 3, p. 370)
- Starbucks: Re-creating Its Uniqueness (MiniCase 4, p. 371)
- GE under Jack Welch vs. Jeffrey Immelt (MiniCase 5, p. 372)
- JetBlue: Losing the Magic Touch? (MiniCase 6, p. 374)
- Which Automotive Technology Will Win? (MiniCase 7, p. 375)
- Core Competencies From Circuit City to CarMax (MiniCase 8, p. 377)
- P&G's New Corporate Strategy: "Connect+Develop" (MiniCase 9, p. 379)
- The Wonder from Sweden: Is IKEA's Success Sustainable? (MiniCase 10, p. 383)
- Sony's Silos Prevent Collaboration Across Divisions (MiniCase 11, p. 385)
- PepsiCo's Indra Nooyi: "Performance with a Purpose" (MiniCase 12, p. 387)

For further information about the book's features, see the **Features Walkthrough,** beginning on page xv.

ACKNOWLEDGMENTS

Any list of acknowledgments will almost always be incomplete, but I would like to thank some special people without whom this book would not have been possible. First and foremost, my wife Kelleyn, and our children: Harris, Winston, Roman, and Adelaide. Over the last few years, I have worked longer hours than when I was a graduate student to conduct the research and writing necessary for this text and accompanying case studies and other materials. I sincerely appreciate the sacrifice this has meant for my family.

I was also fortunate to work with McGraw-Hill, and the best editorial and marketing team that one can imagine: Michael Ablassmeir (Executive Editor), Paul Ducham (Editorial Director), Ann Torbert (Executive Director of Development), Laura Griffin (Development Editor II), Anke Weekes-Braun (Executive Marketing Manager), Michelle Heaster (Senior Marketing Manager), and Harvey Yep (Lead Project Manager, EDP). This book was created through a parallel new product development process: All functions from basic research to marketing were involved from the start, including top management support, which made all the difference. Mike's vision to create a third-generation strategy text drove this project. It felt like an entrepreneurial venture, given that all parameters were up for discussion. Paul's support and candid input from the get-go made this a better book. Ann is the best content development editor one can imagine; her dedication to this project and her unwavering drive for quality made this book what it is today. Laura made sure that all of the many pieces would fall into place, and Harvey made the impossible possible: meeting our publication date! Anke has a keen understanding of market needs, and her ability to effectively communicate with customers (and authors), and to make complex events such as focus groups successful, are clearly unique—so much so that she was promoted to a new role. Michelle Heaster smoothly picked up the marketing reins and has ably guided the project as it goes to market. Thank you to senior management at McGraw-Hill/Irwin B&E who assembled this fine team.

I was fortunate to work with Anne W. Fuller (Georgia Tech PhD, and assistant professor at California State University, Sacramento) on the end-of-chapter material, the instructor resource manual, the *Connect Management* material (on which Anne is a digital co-author), the PowerPoint presentations that accompany the textbook, chapter videos, and the Test Bank. Anne has been a terrific contributor from the very beginning, combining strong academic training with more than 20 years of professional management experience at Motorola in the United States and China.

I was also fortunate to work with Marne L. Arthaud-Day (Indiana University PhD, and associate professor at Kansas State University) on the full-length cases and Case Teaching Notes, the "How to Conduct a Case Analysis" section (page 390) and case matrix, the PowerPoint presentations that accompany the cases, and the case videos. Marne's excellence in teaching was reflected in her careful reviews critiquing each chapter, upon which I invited her to work with me on the full-length case studies. Marne is the co-author on multiple full-length case studies. Thanks, too, to Robert Porter (PhD University of Central Florida) for his fine work on the Case Teaching Notes.

Over the years, I have been privileged to work with Karyn Lu, a superb copyeditor, on my scholarly research papers and on this project. Karyn has been much more than a copyeditor, she has been a sounding board for ideas and has helped to make the delivery of the content as user-friendly as possible. Karyn was also instrumental in launching the social media support for professors and students on www.ftrStrategy, Facebook, and Twitter for this book, a novel addition in the strategy textbook market.

I would also like to thank Carol Jacobson (of Purdue University) for providing solid content and editorial suggestions on numerous chapters.

The Georgia Institute of Technology provided a conducive intellectual environment and superb institutional support to make this project possible. I thank Angel and Stephen M. Deedy for generously funding the professorship that I am honored to hold. I'm grateful for Dean Salbu and Senior Associate Dean Narasimhan for providing the exceptional leadership that allows faculty to fully focus on research, teaching, and service. I have been at Georgia Tech for now more than eight years, and could not have had better colleagues— all of whom are not only great scholars but also fine individuals whom I'm fortunate to have as friends: Dan Breznitz, Marco Ceccagnoli, Annamaria Conti, Stuart Graham, Matt Higgins, David Ku, Jay Lee, John McIntyre, Alex Oettl, Henry Sauermann, and Jerry Thursby and Marie Thursby. At Georgia Tech, we have a terrific group of current and former PhD students, many of whom had a positive influence on this project, including: Shanti Agung, Drew Hess (University of Virginia), Kostas Grigoriou, Nicola McCarthy, German Retana, Jose Urbina, and Wei Zhang.

I'd also like to thank my students at Georgia Tech, both in the full-time day MBA and the executive MBA programs, as well as the executive MBA students from the ICN Business School in Nancy, France, on whom I beta-tested the materials. Their feedback helped fine-tune the content and delivery. I'm also grateful for professors and students at the undergraduate level who beta-tested various chapters and/or cases: Joshua Aaron at East Carolina University; Brent Allred at The University of William & Mary; Melissa Appleyard at Portland State University; Marne Arthaud-Day at Kansas State University; Bindu Arya at the University of Missouri-St. Louis; Danielle Dunne, formerly at Binghamton University, SUNY, now at Fordham University; Anne Fuller at California State University, Sacramento; Elouise Mintz at Saint Louis University; Chandran Mylvaganam at Northwood University; Louise Nemanich at Arizona State University; Frank Novakowski at Davenport University; Richard Quinn at The University of Central Florida; Beverly B. Tyler, North Carolina State University; and Joel West, formerly at San Jose State University, now at Claremont Graduate University. Their willingness to use the materials as they were being developed, and to gather student opinions, provided lots of useful feedback.

Last, but certainly not least, I wish to thank the reviewers and focus group attendees who shared their expertise with us, from the very beginning when we developed the prospectus to the final text and cases that you hold in your hands. The reviewers have given us the greatest gift of all—the gift of time! These very special people are listed starting on page xxxii.

I have long yearned to write a textbook that shows students and managers how exciting strategic management can be, but that at the same time presents the recent developments in the field, including the rigor upon which concepts and frameworks are now built, to make better strategic decisions in a turbulent and dynamic world. I'm fortunate that I had the support of many people to make this vision become a reality, and I'm truly grateful.

Frank T. Rothaermel
Georgia Institute of Technology

Web: http://ftrStrategy.com
Twitter: @ftrStrategy
Facebook: http://on.fb.me/r8kczS

CHAPTER ORGANIZATION AND REVIEWERS' COMMENTS

In addition to the traditional chapters needed in the strategy course, *Strategic Management* includes three separate, standalone chapters (Chapters 2, 5, and 7) that address topics that add value for your course and your students. Following the final chapter (in both versions of the book—*Concepts & Cases and Concepts-only*) is a set of 12 author-written MiniCases.

PART 1
Strategy Analysis

CHAPTER 1   What Is Strategy and Why Is It Important?

CHAPTER 2   The Strategic Management Process

CHAPTER 3   External Analysis: Industry Structure, Competitive Forces, and Strategic Groups

CHAPTER 4   Internal Analysis: Resources, Capabilities, and Activities

CHAPTER 5   Competitive Advantage and Firm Performance

". . . includes relevant, current examples from the business world while taking a focused approach in introducing and discussing the concept of strategy."

CH 1

Bindu Arya, University of Missouri–St. Louis

"The approach is fresh, direct, and serious . . . it did not dilute the theoretical base of the information. The inclusion of the discussion of 'what strategy is not' helps frame the course from the start."

Isaiah O. Ugboro,
North Carolina A&T State University

"Rothaermel's coverage of scenario planning is probably the best I have seen."

CH 2

James W. Bronson,
University of Wisconsin-Whitewater

"This is a terrific chapter: well-integrated, proceeding from the 'outside' in PESTEL to the 'inside.' The use of frameworks is exceptionally strong; they are developed well and applied well."

CH 3

Melissa M. Appleyard, Portland State University

"I found this chapter riveting, and one of the most comprehensive and clear textbook explanations of the resource-based view I have seen. It does an outstanding job of explaining the RBV in a very practical way."

 CH 4

Stephen V. Horner, Arkansas State University

PART 2
Strategy Formulation

"This is an excellent chapter to discuss competitive advantage both conceptually and operationally. . . . Outstanding."

 CH 5

Chris Papenhausen,
University of Massachusetts, Dartmouth

"The value-cost figures and accompanying discussions are very good, whereas other textbooks have often overlooked and underemphasized these points."

 CH 6

Carol Jacobson, Purdue University

"This chapter is a great addition! The examples are extremely current and relevant to the student population. . . . If we as strategy professors can do something

 CH 7

valuable for our students, it is to show them the power of innovation and try to get them to think about future possibilities and strategic directions."

Tammy G. Hunt,
University of North Carolina, Wilmington

"All theoretical notions are illustrated with real-world examples of domestic and international firms, which the students would find particularly helpful. . . . The real-world examples and corresponding theoretical concepts are in lock-step and well integrated, which is its key strength."

CH 8

Deepak Sethi, Old Dominion University

"This chapter provides one of clearest and most easily comprehended discussions of alliances, mergers and networks that I have read in the past 12 years." **CH 9**

Richard A. Quinn, University of Central Florida

"Great chapter. Would not change a thing. Gives content regarding why international context is becoming more important." **CH10**

Linda F. Tegarden, Virginia Tech

"This is one of the best organizational design chapters that I have read. It provides more integration between strategy and structure than I have seen in other texts. The chapter's exhibits are **CH11**

integral to the value-added for this chapter—and truly exceptional. I feel like the students will greatly benefit from this understanding and it provides a more holistic approach to the concept of fitting structure to strategy under strategic management."

Jill A. Brown, Lehigh University

"This chapter did a great job covering all three topics of governance, ethics, and leadership. Many texts have these concepts in different chapters, which is too much. This chapter combines them in a logical manner that makes sense, provides the appropriate attention to each, and ties them all together." **CH12**

Brent B. Allred, The College of William & Mary

Unparalleled Integration

The author's **AFI framework** (**A**nalysis, **F**ormulation, **I**mplementation) focuses content and organizes the book's "less is more" approach. The framework's unique integration of the *process* schools of strategy (based on organization theory, psychology, and sociology) with the *content* schools of strategy (based on economics) provides students with a balanced and complete treatment of strategy not found in other books for the course.

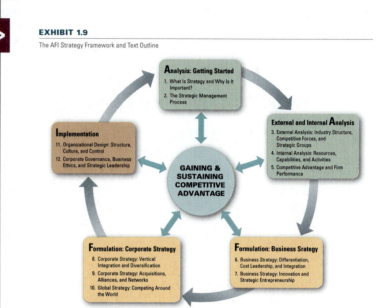

EXHIBIT 1.9

The AFI Strategy Framework and Text Outline

"... has a well-conceived **textbook structure**, and also it has a **well balanced approach** among theories, practices, and applications."

Seung Bach, California State University, Sacramento

Cohesive and Interconnected

With a single strong voice, the author weaves together classic and cutting-edge theory with in-chapter cases and strategy examples. Unlike other texts that often outsource cases, Rothaermel took pride in authoring *all* of the *ChapterCases* and *MiniCases*, and in authoring or co-authoring half of the full-length *Cases*.

"The cases, written to align with the text's vocabulary, are a definite plus. . . . The book offers a **new, refreshing approach to the field of strategic management**. Its presentation stays true to important strategic concepts and related topics while providing contemporary explanations, examples and relevant illustrations of them."

Frank Novakowski, Davenport University

> "The author packs in a lot of information relative to the amount of text. The charts are useful rather than just filler to achieve a predetermined ratio of text to graphics."
>
> *Bryan Mecklenburg, student at Davenport University*

Added Value for Instructors and Students

In a presentation that is comprehensive yet concise, rigorous yet relevant, the author includes classic and cutting-edge strategy material in a student-accessible format. By addressing *what* the research findings mean and *why* they are important for managers and by eliminating excess detail and outdated examples, the book helps students see the bigger strategic picture.

In addition, a key aspect of the author's vision is to provide value-added dimensions for both instructors and students, including:

FLEXIBILITY FOR INSTRUCTORS: The author has crafted the book to provide maximum teaching flexibility. Each chapter is sufficiently self-contained that it can be taught in any order. This flexibility supports teaching the content of the course in modules and other high-flex delivery approaches.

AN ENJOYABLE READ FOR STUDENTS: Filled with examples from companies today's students know, the book conveys to students how exciting strategic management can be and prepares them for the realities of strategic management in the turbulent 21st century.

> "The examples were relatable to everyday life, and the **read was 'easy'** compared to my other [strategy] textbook. No filler info . . . straightforward."
>
> *Lindsey Helgeson, student at Saint Louis University*

> "[This text] does an outstanding job framing the **pivotal strategic management theories,** capturing their essence and translating them into practice."
>
> *Marta Szabo White, Georgia State University*

> "I really like how the author has brought in so many **current stories involving major companies** and how those firms have struggled to develop and implement strategies to gain a sustainable competitive advantage. **This brings the concepts to life**."
>
> *Stephen F. Hallam, The University of Akron*

Rigorous, Relevant, and Balanced

A MIX OF CLASSIC AND CONTEMPORARY CONTENT: The book includes strategy material that has stood the test of time (the resource-based view, Porter's five forces model, etc.), as well as up-to-date strategy material and current research (dynamic capabilities perspective, and the triple bottom line, etc.). The book also includes student-accessible coverage of strategic management research drawn from both academic journals and best-selling business books.

UNDER THE MAGNIFYING GLASS SECTIONS: Each chapter contains a section that puts one specific theory or concept **"under the magnifying glass."** Combining strategic management research with real-world observations, these sections critically evaluate if and how the theory or concept is linked to competitive advantage.

Corporate Diversification

Corporate managers pursue diversification to gain and sustain competitive advantage. But does corporate diversification indeed lead to superior performance? To answer this question, we can evaluate the performance of diversified companies. The critical question to ask when doing so is whether the individual businesses are worth more under the company's management than if each were managed individually.

Research shows that the diversification-performance relationship is a function of the underlying type of diversification. A cumulative body of research indicates an inverted U-shaped relationship between the type of diversification and overall firm performance, as depicted in Exhibit 8.9.[59] High and low levels of diversification are generally associated with lower overall performance, while moderate levels of diversification are associated with higher firm performance. This implies that companies that focus on a single business, as well as companies that pursue unrelated diversification, often fail to achieve additional value creation. Firms that compete in single markets could potentially benefit from economies of scope by leveraging their core competencies into adjacent markets.

Firms that pursue unrelated diversification are often unable to create additional value, and thus experience a diversification discount in the stock market: the stock price of such highly diversified firms is valued at less than the sum of their individual business units.[60] In contrast, companies that pursue related diversification are more likely to improve their performance, and thus create a diversification premium: the stock price of related-diversification firms is valued at greater than the sum of their individual business units.[61]

Why is this so? At the most basic level, a corporate diversification strategy enhances firm performance when its value creation is greater than the costs it incurs. Exhibit 8.10 (next page) lists the sources of value creation and costs for different corporate strategies, for vertical integration as well as related and unrelated diversification. For diversification to enhance firm performance, it must do at least one of the following:

- Provide economies of scale, and thus reduce costs.
- Exploit economies of scope, and thus increase value.
- Reduce costs *and* increase value.

GAINING & SUSTAINING COMPETITIVE ADVANTAGE

>> LO 8-8
Explain when a diversification strategy creates a competitive advantage, and when it does not.

EXHIBIT 8.9
The Diversification-Performance Relationship

Source: Adapted from L. E. Palich, L. B. Cardinal, and C. C. Miller (2000), "Curvilinearity in the diversification-performance linkage: An examination of over three decades of research," *Strategic Management Journal* 21: 155–174.

> "The writing style is considerably 'down-to-earth' in terms of **meeting students where they are intellectually and bringing them along into more complex understanding** of competitive advantage and firm performance."

Stephen V. Horner, Arkansas State University

"The writing style . . . is a tonic for the strategic management student and faculty member. My [current] text takes a blunderbuss and shoots it against the barn wall, listing and covering everything the authors can think of; Rothaermel uses a competition grade rifle to pinpoint and logically focus the given area of concern."

Dr. Gene Simko, Leon Hess Business School, Monmouth University

 **Relevant**

Written to meet the needs of today's students, the book prepares them for the turbulence and dynamism that they will face as managers in the 21st century. *Strategic Management* consistently:

ENGAGES AND INTERESTS GEN-Y STUDENTS through use of up-to-date examples.

BRINGS THEORY TO LIFE THROUGH EMBEDDED EXAMPLES within each framework and concept.

INCLUDES TOPICS FROM RECENT AND CURRENT BESTSELLERS, exposing students to topics that today's managers talk about.

"**Excellent examples**—e.g., Facebook/Myspace; Amazon/Apple; Pixar/Disney, and **interesting discussion** [in Chapter 9] of why M&A may not increase value. . . . The content is **rich, and easy to read.**"

Dorothy Brawley, Kennesaw State University

"[My favorite aspects of this text are the] **more in-depth examples** of more **modern companies**. There was more **application to balance the theory** than in the traditional text used—and more recent examples."

Stacy Litchford, MBA student at The College of William & Mary

Fascinating Cases and Engaging Features
That Get Students Thinking . . .

CHAPTERCASES frame the chapter topic and content and focus on **companies and industries of interest to student**s, such as Google, Microsoft, Teach for America, GE, Whole Foods, Wikipedia, Facebook, Hollywood movies, and Zappos.

>>

> "Timely/relevant info about an interesting problem at an interesting company."
>
> *K. Matis, student at The College of William and Mary*

CHAPTERCASE 3

Build Your Dreams (BYD) to Sidestep Entry Barriers

THE BIG THREE—GM, Ford, and Chrysler—dominated the U.S. car market throughout most of the 20th century. As the competition in the industry became increasingly global, foreign car makers entered the U.S. market mainly by importing vehicles from overseas plants. Among the first were German carmakers Volkswagen, Daimler, and BMW as well as Japanese carmakers Honda, Toyota, and Nissan. The foreign entrants intensified competition, threatened the market share of the Big Three, and led to political pressure to impose import restrictions in the 1980s. The new players responded by building U.S. plants in order to avoid import restrictions. More recently, Korean car makers Hyundai and Kia have begun making and selling cars in the United States.

Although globalization and deregulation paved the way for significant new entry into the U.S. auto market, the worldwide car manufacturing industry has been exposed to few new entrants. In fact, no new major car manufacturers have emerged in the last couple of decades in part because automobiles powered by internal combustion engines are made out of thousands of precisely engineered parts; few industrial products, excluding commercial airplanes, are as complex as cars. Car manufacturers also require large-scale production in order to be cost-competitive. These facts create seemingly insurmountable barriers to entry into car manufacturing.

Thus, it would seem that an unknown startup from an emerging economy, attempting to enter the car industry during the deepest economic recession since the Great Depression, would surely be a fool's errand.

Yet Wang Chuanfu, founder and chairman of the Chinese technology startup Build Your Dreams (BYD) begs to differ. His strategy is to use new technology to sidestep entry barriers. BYD began its life as a battery company in 1995 and is now leveraging this expertise into electric vehicles. Unlike complex gasoline engines, electric cars are powered by simple motors and gearboxes that have very few parts. Electric vehicles are therefore much cheaper and more straightforward to build.

BYD's claim to fame is a lithium ferrous phosphate battery on which cars can run 250 miles on a single three-hour charge. Already one of the fastest growing independent automakers, BYD is selling plug-in hybrids and all-electric vehicles in China, Africa, the Middle East, and South America. It plans to sell cars in the U.S. and other Western countries in the near future.

Legendary investor Warren Buffett found BYD interesting enough to put in some $230 million for a 10 percent equity stake. Consumers may flock to BYD cars as well. Not only are they "green" cars, but their sticker price is anticipated to be about half that of the Chevy Volt (whose starting price is $40,000). Other companies entering the car industry by leveraging new battery technology include Tesla Motors and Fisker Automotive, both in California, as well as Think Global in Norway and Lightning Car in the United Kingdom. Sparks are sure to fly as the car industry becomes more competitive in the 21st century.[1]

After reading the chapter, you will find more about this case, with related questions, on page 77.

55

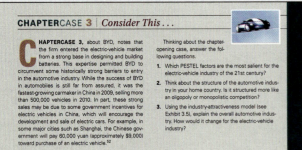

CHAPTERCASE 3 | *Consider This . . .*

CHAPTERCASE 3, about BYD, notes that the firm entered the electric-vehicle market from a strong base in designing and building batteries. This expertise permitted BYD to circumvent some historically strong barriers to entry in the automotive industry. While the success of BYD in automobiles is still far from assured, it was the fastest-growing carmaker in China in 2009, selling more than 500,000 vehicles in 2010. In part, these strong sales may be due to some government incentives for electric vehicles in China, which will encourage the development and sale of electric cars. For example, in some major cities such as Shanghai, the Chinese government will pay 60,000 yuan (approximately $9,000) toward purchase of an electric vehicle.[52]

Thinking about the chapter-opening case, answer the following questions.

1. Which PESTEL factors are the most salient for the electric-vehicle industry of the 21st century?

2. Think about the structure of the automotive industry in your home country. Is it structured more like an oligopoly or monopolistic competition?

3. Using the industry-attractiveness model (see Exhibit 3.5), explain the overall automotive industry. How would it change for the electric-vehicle industry?

>>

"Consider This . . ." sections
use additional information, plus concepts and information from the chapter, to extend and complete the ChapterCase example.

Questions in the "Consider This . . ." section are good **jumping-off points for class discussion.**

"The 'Strategy Highlights' are interesting."

Matthew DeRemer, student at University of Central Florida

Strategy Highlight Boxes

These engaging boxes apply a specific concept to a specific company. Each box is:

RIGHT-SIZED FOR MAXIMUM STUDENT APPEAL—long enough to contain valuable insights, yet short enough to encourage student reading.

FOCUSED ON COMPANIES THAT STUDENTS KNOW—Threadless, Sony, Starbucks, Nintendo, Toyota, Apple, GE, ExxonMobil, Pixar, GM, Walmart, W.L. Gore, USA Today, among others.

STRATEGY HIGHLIGHT 7.3

From King Gillette to King of Incremental Innovation

In 1903, entrepreneur Mr. King C. Gillette invented and began selling the safety razor with a disposable blade. This radical innovation launched the Gillette company (now a brand of Procter & Gamble). To sustain its competitive advantage, Gillette not only made sure that its razors were inexpensive and widely available (thus introducing the "razor and razor blade" business model),[31] but it continuously improved its razor blades. In a classic example of incremental innovation, Gillette kept adding an additional blade with each new version of its razor until the number had gone from one to six![32] Though this innovation strategy seems predictable, it worked: Gillette's top-selling razor today, the Fusion, holds about 45 percent market share and brings in annual revenues of more than $1 billion. Moreover, with each new razor introduction, Gillette is able to push up its per-unit cartridge price. A four-pack of razors for the new Fusion Proglide retailed for $17.99 when introduced in 2010.[33]

Forming Strategic Intent

Strategic intent is the staking out of a desired leadership position in the long term that far exceeds a company's current resources and capabilities.[4] Challenging goals that stretch an individual or an organization can lead to higher performance.[5] Many Japanese competitors set ambitious stretch goals of global leadership (reflected in their missions) and made them a reality: Canon "beat Xerox," Komatsu "encircled Caterpillar," and Honda became "a second Ford." (Today this may not sound like a desirable goal, but it was in the 1970s when Honda began its quest for global leadership.) Currently, Chinese companies such as Baidu, BYD, and Lenovo aspire to world leadership. These companies set their ambitious goals when they were only a fraction the size of the companies they were chasing. Indeed, they were so small that initially the market leaders did not even recognize them as potential competitors; many had never competed outside their domestic markets. Yet all made global leadership their mission, with goals so ambitious they exceeded the firms' existing resources and capabilities by a large margin. Effective use of stretch goals created at all levels of the organization an obsession with winning that is sustained over several decades.[6]

STRATEGY HIGHLIGHT 5.1

Interface: The World's First Sustainable Company

Interface, Inc. is a leader in modular carpeting, with annual sales of roughly $1 billion. What makes the company unique is its strategic intent to become the world's first *fully sustainable* company. In 1994, founder Ray Anderson set a goal for the company to be "off oil" entirely by 2020. That included not using any petroleum-based raw materials or oil-related energy to fuel the manufacturing plants.

According to Collins and Porras in *Built to Last*, their classic study of high-performing companies over long periods of time, this is a "BHAG"—*a big hairy audacious goal*. BHAGs are bold missions declared by visionary companies and are a "powerful mechanism to stimulate progress."[28] Weaning Interface off oil by 2020 is indeed a BHAG. Many see the carpet industry as an extension of the petrochemical industry, given its heavy reliance on

fossil fuels and chemicals in the manufacturing, shipping, and installation of its products.

Today, Interface is a leader in both modular carpet and sustainability. The company estimates that between 1996 and 2008, it saved over $400 million due to its energy efficiency and use of recycled materials. Its business model is changing the carpet industry. Speaking of sustainability as a business model, Mr. Anderson stated in 2009:

> Sustainability has given my company a competitive edge in more ways than one. It has proven to be the most powerful marketplace differentiator I have known in my long career. Our costs are down, our profits are up, and our products are the best they have ever been. Sustainable design has provided an unexpected wellspring of innovation, people are galvanized around a shared higher purpose, better people are applying, the best people are staying and working with a purpose, the goodwill in the marketplace generated by our focus on sustainability far exceeds that which any amount of advertising or marketing expenditure could have generated—this company believes it has found a better way to a bigger and more legitimate profit—a better business model.[29]

A Global Context

In addition to the standalone chapter on global strategy, examples throughout the book reflect the **global nature of competition** and the importance of emerging economies such as the BRIC countries.

Additionally, a number of the examples relate to sustainable strategy with a **focus on "green" products and issues**.

A Variety of End-of-Chapter Features Meet Varying Course Needs

Chapter summaries link key chapter content to the chapter's learning objectives.

End-of-chapter materials also include a list of **key terms** introduced in the chapter.

>>

> "I do not typically use the end-of-chapter material for the textbooks I use, but I got excited about the **excellent material provided** and believe I would use this material in my class."
>
> *Brent B. Allred, The College of William & Mary*

Discussion Questions offer a broad scope for classroom settings and uses.

Social/Ethical Issues and Questions enliven class discussion.

Small Group Exercises allow for different pedagogical approaches and offer opportunities to break up long class periods or promote group work outside of class.

All end-of-chapter features have been **beta-tested** in various classroom settings and different levels (undergraduate, MBA, and executive MBA).

<<

> "The chapter review questions are good, and the project ideas are good especially for those who are relatively new to the course."
>
> *Isaiah O. Ugboro, North Carolina A&T State University*

Strategy Term Project >>

Breaks a long-term project into a series of **focused, targeted tasks.**

Requires **data collection and analysis**, using the tools and concepts from each chapter.

Provides an extended, "hands-on" project, ideal for use by **individual students or small groups.**

Fulfills the **AACSB requirement** for an integrative management exercise.

Strategy Term Project

MODULE 2: MISSION, GOALS, AND THE STRATEGIC MANAGEMENT PROCESS

1. Search for a mission statement for the firm. Not all organizations publish such a statement, so alternatively you can look for enduring principles and values upon which the firm seems to be anchored. This information is often available at the firm's website (though it may take some searching) or is contained in its annual reports. You may also interview a manager of the firm or contact "investor relations."

2. Identify the major goals of the company.

3. Does the firm seem to have any longer-term challenging or stretch goals that would serve as its strategic intent?

4. Trace any changes in strategy that you can identify over time. Try to determine whether the strategic changes of your selected firm are a result of intended strategies, emergent strategies, or some combination of both.

Strategy Term Project

MODULE 4: INTERNAL ANALYSIS

In this section, you will study the internal resources, capabilities, core competencies, and value chain of your selected firm.

1. A good place to start with an internal firm analysis is to catalog the assets a firm has. Make a list of the firm's tangible assets in the firm. Then, make a separate list of the intangible assets you can identify.

3. Identify the core competencies that are at the heart of the firm's competitive advantage. (Remember, a firm will have only one, or at most a few, core competencies, by definition.)

4. Use the strategic activity system framework to diagram the important and supportive activities the firm has that are key to delivering and sustaining the firm's value proposition. (For an example, refer to Exhibits 4.7 and 4.8 showing the activity system of the Vanguard Group.)

> ## "The *my*Strategy module is a very cool feature, and the questions used to develop this are excellent."

Parthiban David, Kogood School of Business, American University

---

*my*Strategy

FOR WHAT TYPE OF ORGANIZATION ARE *YOU* BEST-SUITED?

As noted in the chapter, firms can have very distinctive cultures. Recall that Zappos has a standing offer to pay any new hire $2,000 to quit the company during the first month. Zappos makes this offer to help ensure that those who stay with the company are comfortable in its "create fun and a little weirdness" environment.

You may have taken a personality test such as Myers-Briggs or The Big Five. These tests may be useful in gauging compatibility of career and personality types. They are often available for both graduate and undergraduate students a...

the following questions, think about your next job and your longer-term career plans.

1. Review Exhibit 11.3 and circle the organizational characteristics you find appealing. Cross out those factors you think you would not like. Do you find a trend toward either the mechanistic or organic organization?

2. Have you been in school or work situations in which your values did not align with those of your peers or colleagues? How did you handle the situation? Are there certain values or norms important enough for you to consider as you look for a new job?

3. As you consider your career after graduation, which control and rewards system discussed in the concluding section of the chapter would you find most motivating? Is this different from the controls used at...

*my*Strategy

LOOKING INSIDE YOURSELF: WHAT IS MY COMPETITIVE ADVANTAGE?

Here, we encourage you to take what you have learned about competitive advantage and apply it to your personal career. Spend a few minutes looking at yourself to discover *your own* competitive advantage.

1. Write down your own personal strengths and weaknesses. What sort of organization will permit you to really leverage your strengths and keep you highly engaged in your work (person–organization fit)? Do some of your weaknesses need to be mitigated through additional training or mentoring from a more seasoned professional?

2. Personal capabilities also need to be evaluated over time. Are your strengths and weaknesses different

today from what they were five years ago? What are you doing to make sure your capabilities are dynamic? Are you upgrading skills, modifying behaviors, or otherwise seeking to change your future strengths and weaknesses?

3. Are some of your strengths valuable, rare, and costly to imitate? How can you organize your work to help capture the value of your key strengths (or mitigate your weaknesses)?

4. In this chapter, we discussed that the strategic activity system happening inside the firm can be a vital source of sustainable competitive advantage. If you are currently or previously employed, consider how your professional activities can help reinforce the key value-added activities in your department or organization.

*my*Strategy Boxes

Apply strategy concepts to students' lives.

Show students **how to internalize** strategy as they plan or enhance their careers.

Setting a "Gold Standard" for High-Quality Cases

Three Types of Cases—*ChapterCases*, *MiniCases*, and *Cases*—inform, instruct, and inspire students and meet varying classroom needs:

 CHAPTERCASES (all written by the author) begin and end each chapter, framing chapter content and bringing concepts to life.

 Twelve original, Author-Written MINICASES

- Provide a decision scenario that a company's manager might face.

- Include discussion questions and are linked to specific chapters.

- Are short enough to be assigned as add-ons to chapters as individual assignments or group work and can also be used for discussion.

 30 Full-Length CASES

Half of the book's Cases were written or co-written by the author specifically for use with the book, ensuring that chapter content and cases are closely interconnected.

The full-length Cases:

- Are preceded by "How to Conduct a Case Analysis," including a full set of financial ratios.

- Can be used for longer, more in-depth class discussion, case analysis, or term case papers.

- Are accompanied by a full set of *Case Teaching Notes*, written by Professors Marne L. Arthaud-Day of Kansas State University and Robert Porter of the University of Central Florida, in collaboration with Frank T. Rothaermel. Cases are also accompanied by **high-quality videos**.

Cases are available in the *Cases & Concepts* version of the book, or through McGraw-Hill's custom-publishing *Create™* program.

"This type of mini-case, with the kinds of questions added at the bottom, is exactly what I like to use. I find these types of cases, in addition to opening vignettes, are right on especially for undergrads . . . they want to get to the heart of the matter rather quickly."

Michael D. Santoro, College of Business and Economics, Lehigh University

---

MINICASE 1 | **Michael Phelps: Strategizing for Gold**

MICHAEL PHELPS, nicknamed MP, won an unprecedented eight gold medals at the Beijing Summer Olympics, and while doing so set seven new world records. Eight short days in August 2008 changed Olympic history and Michael Phelps's life forever, making MP one of the greatest athletes of all time. Immediately after the event, *The Wall Street Journal* reported that Phelps would be likely to turn the eight gold medals into a cash-flow stream of more than $100 million through a vari...

...ctivities.[1] The ... were product ...orsements: His ...ncluded AT&T ...g's, Omega, ...Stone, Speedo, ...rt. Other offers ...c and the mun- ...movies, sculp- ...his muscled ...ings, dog food (given Michael's ...bulldog, Herman), commemorative ...rims, and even bobblehead dolls. ...P was diagnosed with attention defi- ...sorder (ADHD). Doctors prescribed ...him release his energy. It worked! ...2008, Michael Phelps attended the ...igan, studying marketing and man- ...lready competed quite successfully ...Summer Olympics, where he won ...old and two bronze. Right after the ...then-19-year-old sat down with his ...lisle, and his long-time swim coach, ...map out a detailed strategy for the ...e explicit goal was to win nothing ...edal in each of the events in which ...n Beijing, thus preparing the launch ...rdom.[2]

...vas responsible for getting MP into ...cal shape he needed for Beijing and ...l toughness required to break Mark ...rd of seven gold medals won in the ...mpic Games. Peter Carlisle, mean- ...f a detailed strategy to launch MP

as a world superstar during the Beijing Games. While MP spent six hours a day in the pool, Carlisle focused on exposing MP to the Asian market, the largest consumer market in the world, with a special emphasis on the Chinese consumer. The earliest tie-in was with a Hong Kong–based manufacturer of MP3 players and other consumer electronics, Matsunichi, with whom MP became affiliated right after the 2004 Athens Games. MP made several other visits to China during the 2005–2007 period, among them the "Visa Friendship Lanes Tour" to promote the Special Olympics.

MP's wide-ranging presence in the real world was combined with a huge exposure in the virtual world. Phelps posts and maintains his own Facebook page, with millions of "phans" whose click-through rivaled the site of President Barack Obama in popularity. MP is also a favorite of YouTube and other online blogs (e.g., Swimroom.com), garnering worldwide exposure to an extent never before achieved by an Olympian.[3] The gradual buildup of Phelps over a number of years enabled manager Peter Carlisle to launch MP as a superstar right after he won his eighth gold medal at the Beijing Games. By then, MP had become a worldwide brand.

Clearly, a successful strategy rests on leveraging unique resources and capabilities. Accordingly, some suggest that MP's success can be explained by his unique physical endowments: his long thin torso, which reduces drag; his arm span of 6 feet 7 inches (204 cm), which is disproportionate to his 6-foot-4-inch (193 cm) height; his relatively short legs for a person of his height; and his size-14 feet which work like flippers due to hypermobile ankles.[4] While MP's physical attributes are a *necessary* condition for winning, they are *not sufficient*. Many other swimmers, like the Australian Ian Thorpe (who has size-17 feet) or the German "albatross" Michael Gross (with an arm span of 7 feet or 213 cm), also brought extraordinary resource endowments to the swim meet. Yet neither of them won eight gold medals in a single Olympics.

367

CASE 4 | **Better World Books: Social Entrepreneurship and the Triple Bottom Line**

Better World Books collects and sells books online to fund literacy initiatives worldwide. We're a self-sustaining, triple-bottom-line company that creates social, economic, and environmental value for all our stakeholders.

—WWW.BETTERWORLDBOOKS.COM

Frank T. Rothaermel
Georgia Institute of Technology

Marne L. Arthaud-Day
Kansas State University

Konstantinos Grigoriou
Georgia Institute of Technology

T IS ALMOST MIDNIGHT. David Murphy, President and CEO of Better World Books (BWB), sits at his desk, buried beneath market research and financial reports. BWB was founded as a "B corporation," one that is committed in its incorporation documents to meeting a triple bottom line of financial, social, and environmental performance. While traditional firms focus primarily on satisfying their shareholders, BWB recognizes that it has a responsibility to all stakeholders, including its employees, literacy partners, and "Mother Earth." Over the past few years, BWB has grown significantly, from a small, niche player frequenting college campuses to one of the most widely recognized social-entrepreneurship firms in the United States. As testament to its success, the company generated an estimated $45 million in revenues for 2010.[1,2] It has also raised close to $9 million for charities, saved countless books from landfills, and advanced literacy around the globe.

Although BWB's investors are happy with the venture's initial performance, they are demanding to know how Mr. Murphy plans to scale up BWB to ensure future growth and continued triple-bottom-line results. Glancing at the lights outside his office window, Mr. Murphy wonders how much more growth BWB's social-entrepreneurship model can sustain. Competition in the online book market has grown intense in recent years, both from companies like Amazon and eBay and from individual booksellers who

now populate such online marketplaces. Because of its social emphasis, BWB also competes with other socially minded enterprises like Books4Cause, which follows a strikingly similar business model. Meanwhile, the supply of used, printed books is likely to shrink due to the increasing popularity of e-book readers like the Kindle. Mr. Murphy wonders if BWB will need to expand to other products or foreign markets to ensure its survival. With challenges arising from all sides, he is not quite sure how to address these issues when meeting with BWB's investors the next morning.

BWB's History, 2003–2010

INCEPTION. As students attending Notre Dame University, Xavier Helgesen and Christopher "Kreece" Fuchs dreamed of jumping on the Internet bandwagon. In 1999, they developed a user-generated content application in which students could rate teacher evaluations. The application quickly spread to other universities. Unfortunately, the dot-com bust halted their plans, and the pair was forced to sell the company at only a small profit.

Once again searching for a way to make some money, Fuchs and Helgesen went to sell their old textbooks to the campus bookstore. They left disappointed when the bookstore offered no more than a few dollars to buy back books that had cost them over $150. Believing that the books were worth significantly more, they decided to reach out to a wider audience and listed their books for sale on the Internet. Much to their delight, the pair found that Internet customers were willing to pay much higher prices: Books for which the bookstore was not offering even a dollar were selling for $50 online![3] Eager to take advantage of this business opportunity, they asked their friends for their old textbooks and sold those as well.

C18

McGraw-Hill *Create*™

With McGraw-Hill's state-of-the art *Create*™ search engine, it is easy to find, arrange, and **personalize content**—whether from this textbook and its resources or from different sources—to create a customized book, perfect for your course, and at an affordable price.

For more information, contact your local McGraw-Hill sales rep or visit www.mcgrawhillcreate.com.

Blackboard® integration. . . Your life, simplified

Now you and your students can access McGraw-Hill's Connect® and Create™ right from within your Blackboard course—all with **one single sign-on**.

Not only do you get single sign-on with Connect and Create, you also get **deep integration of McGraw-Hill content and content engines** right in Blackboard.

When a student completes an integrated Connect assignment, the grade for that assignment automatically (and instantly) feeds your Blackboard grade center.

A solution for everyone—whether your institution is already using Blackboard or you just want to try Blackboard on your own, we have a solution for you. McGraw-Hill and Blackboard can now offer you easy access to industry leading technology and content, whether your campus hosts it, or we do.

The **Best** of **Both Worlds**

www.domorenow.com

Instructor Resources

Multiple resources, authored by Professor Anne W. Fuller, California State University, Sacramento, are available to make your teaching life easier:

- The **Instructors Manual (IM)** includes thorough coverage of each chapter as well as time-saving features such as a chapter outline including hyperlinks to later content in the chapter, a suggested lecture outline, teaching tips, PowerPoint references, video links and references, and answers to all end-of-chapter exercises.

- The **PowerPoint (PPT)** slides provide comprehensive lecture notes, video links, and company examples not found in the textbook, in an animated format for greater classroom interest.

- The **Test Bank** includes 100–150 questions per chapter, in a range of formats and with a greater-than-usual number of comprehension and application (or scenario-based) questions. It's tagged by learning objective, Bloom's Taxonomy levels, and AACSB requirements.

All of these instructors' resources have been copyedited and accuracy-checked to ensure a good fit with the textbook.

The **DVD** that accompanies the text includes videos that cover concepts from chapters as well as highlight cases. It offers video clips from sources such as Big Think, Stanford University's Entrepreneurship Corner, *The Economist, The* McKinsey *Quarterly,* MSNBC, NBC, and PBS. Videos are also conveniently referenced in the Instructor's Manual and Case Teaching Notes.

The **Online Learning Center (OLC)** is located at www.mhhe.com/ftrstrategy.

- At the **instructors' portion** of the OLC, which is password-protected, instructors can access all of the teaching resources described above, a Case Matrix relating cases back to concepts within the chapters, and comprehensive Case Teaching Notes, including case financial analysis.

- At the **students' portion** of the OLC, students can take chapter quizzes to review concepts, review chapter PowerPoint slides, and watch videos that relate back to concepts covered in this chapter and/or cases. Students can easily upgrade to a richer set of Premium Online Resources right on this site.

Tegrity Campus

 Tegrity Campus makes class time available 24/7 by automatically capturing every lecture in a searchable format for students to review when they study and complete assignments. With a simple one-click start-and-stop process, you capture all computer screens and corresponding audio. Students can replay any part of any class with easy-to-use browser-based viewing on a PC or Mac.

Tegrity Campus's unique search feature helps students efficiently find what they need, when they need it, across an entire semester of class recordings. Help turn all your students' study time into learning moments immediately supported by your lecture.

To learn more about Tegrity, watch a two-minute Flash demo at http://tegritycampus.mhhe.com.

Simulations

- McGraw-Hill has two current strategy simulations—Business Strategy Game and GLO-BUS—that can be used with the textbook.
- For more information, contact your local McGraw-Hill sales representative.

McGraw-Hill Customer Care Contact Information

At McGraw-Hill, we understand that getting the most from new technology can be challenging. That's why our services don't stop after you purchase our products. You can e-mail our Product Specialists 24 hours a day to get product-training online. Or you can search our knowledge bank of Frequently Asked Questions on our support website. For Customer Support, call **800-331-5094,** e-mail **hmsupport@mcgraw-hill.com,** or visit **www.mhhe.com/support.** One of our Technical Support Analysts will be able to assist you in a timely fashion.

Assurance of Learning Ready

Many educational institutions today are focused on the notion of *assurance of learning,* an important element of many accreditation standards. *Strategic Management* is designed specifically to support your assurance of learning initiatives with a simple yet powerful solution.

Each chapter in the book begins with a list of numbered learning objectives, which appear throughout the chapter as well as in the end-of-chapter assignments. Every Test Bank question for *Strategic Management* maps to a specific chapter learning objective in the textbook. Each Test Bank question also identifies topic area, level of difficulty, Bloom's Taxonomy level, and AACSB skill area. You can use our Test Bank software, *EZ Test* and *EZ Test Online*, or *Connect Management* to easily search for learning objectives that directly relate to the learning objectives for your course. You can then use the reporting features of *EZ Test* to aggregate student results in a similar fashion, making the collection and presentation of Assurance of Learning data simple and easy.

AACSB Statement

McGraw-Hill/Irwin is a proud corporate member of AACSB International. Understanding the importance and value of AACSB accreditation, *Strategic Management* recognizes the curricula guidelines detailed in the AACSB standards for business accreditation by connecting selected questions in the Test Bank to the general knowledge and skill guidelines in the AACSB standards.

The statements contained in *Strategic Management* are provided only as a guide for the users of this textbook. The AACSB leaves content coverage and assessment within the purview of individual schools, the mission of the school, and the faculty. While *Strategic Management* and the teaching package make no claim of any specific AACSB qualification or evaluation, we have within *Strategic Management* labeled selected questions according to the six general knowledge and skills areas.

THANK YOU . . .

This book has gone through McGraw-Hill/Irwin's thorough development process. Over the course of several years, it has benefited from numerous developmental focus groups and hundreds of reviews by hundreds of reviewers across the country. The author and publisher wish to thank the following people who shared their insights, constructive criticisms, and valuable suggestions throughout the development of this project. Your contributions have improved this product.

Product-Development Focus Groups

Fall 2009

Melissa M. Appleyard
Portland State University

Marne Arthaud-Day
Kansas State University

Bindu Arya
*University of Missouri,
St. Louis*

Tim Blumentritt
Kennesaw State University

Jill A. Brown
Lehigh University

Anne W. Fuller
*California State University,
Sacramento*

Devi R. Gnyawali
Virginia Tech

Steve Gove
Virginia Tech

Stephen F. Hallam
The University of Akron

Duane Helleloid
University of North Dakota

George Hruby
Cleveland State University

John G. Irwin
Troy University

Jerry Kopf
Radford University

Bruce C. Kusch
*Brigham Young University,
Idaho*

K. Blaine Lawlor
*University of West
Florida*

Marty Lawlor
*Rochester Institute of
Technology*

John Lawrence
University of Idaho

David Leibsohn
*California State University,
Fullerton*

Richard T. Mpoyi
*Middle Tennessee State
University*

Chandran Mylvaganam
*Northwood University,
Michigan*

Chris Papenhausen
*University of Massachusetts,
Dartmouth*

Luis A. Perez-Batres
Central Michigan University

JoDee Phillips
Kaplan University

Jim Sena
*California Polytechnic
State University, San Luis
Obispo*

Anju Seth
Virginia Tech

Lise Anne D. Slatten
*University of Louisiana at
Lafayette*

Thuhang Tran
*Middle Tennessee State
University*

Beverly B. Tyler
*North Carolina State
University*

Arvids A. Ziedonis
University of Oregon

Fall 2010

Seung Bach
*California State University,
Sacramento*

Dorothy Brawley
Kennesaw State University

Anne W. Fuller
*California State University,
Sacramento*

Tim Heames
West Virginia University

Grant Miles
University of North Texas

Elouise Mintz
Saint Louis University

Frank Novakowski
Davenport University

Srikanth Paruchuri
The Pennsylvania State University

Richard A. Quinn
The University of Central Florida

Simon Rodan
San Jose State University

Michael D. Santoro
Lehigh University

Deepak Sethi
Old Dominion University

Eugene S. Simko
Monmouth University

Linda F. Tegarden
Virginia Tech

Isaiah O. Ugboro
North Carolina A&T State University

Joel West
Claremont Graduate University

Marta Szabo White
Georgia State University

Market-Development Focus Groups

Summer 2011

Brent B. Allred
The College of William & Mary

Betty S. Coffey
Appalachian State University

Anne Cohen
University of Minnesota, Twin Cities

Darla Domke-Damonte
Coastal Carolina University

Stephen Drew
Florida Gulf Coast University

David Duhon
The University of Southern Mississippi

J. Michael Geringer
California Polytechnic State University, San Luis Obispo

Mahesh P. Joshi
George Mason University

Paul Mallette
Colorado State University

Michael Merenda
University of New Hampshire

Michael Pitts
Virginia Commonwealth University

Robert Porter
The University of Central Florida

Deepak Sethi
Old Dominion University

Fall 2011

Moses Acquaah
University of North Carolina at Greensboro

Garry Adams
Auburn University

David Baker
Kent State University

Geoff Bell
University of Minnesota Duluth

Heidi Bertels
University of Pittsburgh

David Epstein
University of Houston Downtown

Kevin Fertig
University of Illinois at Urbana-Champaign

Susan Fox-Wolfgramm
Hawaii Pacific University

Tammy Hunt
University of North Carolina Wilmington

Syeda Inamdar
San Jose State University

Jon Lehman
Vanderbilt University

David Leibsohn
California State University, Fullerton

David Major
Indiana University

Michael Miller
University of Illinois at Chicago

Chandran Mylvaganam
Northwood University

Louise Nemanich
Arizona State University

Ronaldo Parente
Florida International University

Keith Perry
San Jose State University

Vasudevan Ramanujam
Case Western Reserve University

Gary Scudder
Vanderbilt University

Thomas Shirley
San Jose State University

Eugene Simko
Monmouth University

Jing'an Tang
Sacred Heart University

Kim K.J. Tullis
University of Central Oklahoma

Isaiah Ugboro
North Carolina A&T State University

Jia Wang
California State University, Fresno

Margaret White
Oklahoma State University

Marta White
Georgia State University

Zhe Zhang
Eastern Kentucky University

Reviewers

Joshua R. Aaron
East Carolina University

Todd M. Alessandri
Northeastern University

Brent B. Allred
The College of William & Mary

Semiramis Amirpour
University of Texas at El Paso

Melissa M. Appleyard
Portland State University

Marne Arthaud-Day
Kansas State University

Bindu Arya
University of Missouri, St. Louis

Seung Bach
California State University, Sacramento

Dennis R. Balch
University of North Alabama

Edward R. Balotsky
Saint Joseph's University

Kevin Banning
Auburn University

Tim Blumentritt
Kennesaw State University

William C. Bogner
Georgia State University

Dorothy Brawley
Kennesaw State University

Michael G. Brizek
South Carolina State University

James W. Bronson
University of Wisconsin, Whitewater

Jill A. Brown
Lehigh University

Kenneth H. Chadwick
Nicholls State University

Clint Chadwick
The University of Alabama in Huntsville

Betty S. Coffey
Appalachian State University

Susan K. Cohen
University of Pittsburgh

Parthiban David
American University

Arthur J. Duhaime III
Nichols College

Danielle Dunne
Fordham University

Alan Ellstrand
University of Arkansas

Michael M. Fathi
Georgia Southwestern State University

Kevin Fertig
University of Illinois at Urbana-Champaign

Robert S. Fleming
Rowan University

Daniel Forbes
University of Minnesota

Isaac Fox
University of Minnesota

Steven A. Frankforter
Winthrop University

Anne W. Fuller
California State University, Sacramento

Venessa Funches
Auburn University at Montgomery

Jeffrey Furman
Boston University

J. Michael Geringer
California Polytechnic State University, San Luis Obispo

Debbie Gilliard
Metropolitan State College of Denver

Michelle Gittelman
Rutgers University

Devi R. Gnyawali
Virginia Tech

Sanjay Goel
University of Minnesota Duluth

Steve Gove
Virginia Tech

Michael Gunderson
University of Florida

Craig M. Gustin
American InterContinental University

Stephen F. Hallam
The University of Akron

Jon Timothy Heames
West Virginia University

Richard A. Heiens
University of South Carolina Aiken

Duane Helleloid
University of North Dakota

Andrew M. Hess
University of Virginia

Ken Hess
Metropolitan State University

Phyllis Holland
Valdosta State University

Stephen V. Horner
Arkansas State University

George Hruby
Cleveland State University

Tammy G. Hunt
University of North Carolina Wilmington

John G. Irwin
Troy University

Carol K. Jacobson
Purdue University

Scott Johnson
Oklahoma State University

Necmi Karagozoglu
California State University, Sacramento

J. Kay Keels
Coastal Carolina University

Franz Kellermanns
The University of Tennessee

Jerry Kopf
Radford University

Bruce C. Kusch
Brigham Young University, Idaho

K. Blaine Lawlor
University of West Florida

Marty Lawlor
Rochester Institute of Technology

John Lawrence
University of Idaho

Jun Lin
State University of New York (SUNY), New Paltz

Joseph Mahoney
University of Illinois at Urbana-Champaign

Paul Mallette
Colorado State University

Daniel B. Marin
Louisiana State University

Louis Martinette
University of Mary Washington

Anthony U. Martinez
San Francisco State University

David McCalman
University of Central Arkansas

Jeffrey McGee
The University of Texas at Arlington

Grant Miles
University of North Texas

Elouise Mintz
Saint Louis University

Gwen Moore
University of Missouri, St. Louis

James P. Morgan
Webster University, Fort Leonard Wood Campus

Richard T. Mpoyi
Middle Tennessee State University

Chandran Mylvaganam
Northwood University, Michigan

Louise Nemanich
Arizona State University

Frank Novakowski
Davenport University

Kevin O'Mara
Elon University

Chris Papenhausen
University of Massachusetts, Dartmouth

James M. Pappas
Oklahoma State University

Srikanth Paruchuri
The Pennsylvania State University

Christine Cope Pence
University of California, Riverside

Luis A. Perez-Batres
Central Michigan University

JoDee Phillips
Kaplan University

Michael W. Pitts
Virginia Commonwealth University

Richard A. Quinn
The University of Central Florida

Annette L. Ranft
The University at Tennessee

Gary B. Roberts
Kennesaw State University

Simon Rodan
San Jose State University

Yassir M. Samra
Manhattan College

Michael D. Santoro
Lehigh University

Jim Sena
California Polytechnic State University, San Luis Obispo

Deepak Sethi
Old Dominion University

Mark Sharfman
University of Oklahoma

Eugene S. Simko
Monmouth University

Faye A. Sisk
Mercer University, Atlanta

Lise Anne D. Slatten
University of Louisiana at Lafayette

Garry D. Smith
Mississippi State University

James D. Spina
University of Maryland

Linda F. Tegarden
Virginia Tech

Thuhang Tran
Middle Tennessee State University

Isaiah O. Ugboro
North Carolina A&T State University

Bruce Walters
Louisiana Tech University

Andrew Ward
Lehigh University

Vincent Weaver
Greenville Technical College

Laura Whitcomb
California State University, Los Angeles

Marta Szabo White
Georgia State University

Ross A. Wirth
Franklin University

Michael J. Zhang
Sacred Heart University

Yanfeng Zheng
The University of Hong Kong

Arvids A. Ziedonis
University of Oregon

Beta Testers

Instructors

Joshua R. Aaron
East Carolina University

Brent B. Allred
The College of William & Mary

Melissa M. Appleyard
Portland State University

Marne Arthaud-Day
Kansas State University

Bindu Arya
University of Missouri, St. Louis

Danielle Dunne
formerly Binghampton University, SUNY (now at Fordham University)

Anne W. Fuller
California State University, Sacramento

Elouise Mintz
Saint Louis University

Chandran Mylvaganam
Northwood University, Michigan

Louise Nemanich
Arizona State University

Frank Novakowski
Davenport University

Richard A. Quinn
The University of Central Florida

Beverly B. Tyler
North Carolina State University, Raleigh

Joel West
formerly San Jose State University (now at Claremont Graduate University)

Students

Over 400 students at various colleges and universities beta-tested parts of this textbook and shared their feedback. Special thanks to the following, who gave permission to include their names in the book.

Chelsea Aaberg
University of Missouri, St. Louis

Erin Allan
University of Missouri, St. Louis

Nolan Andelin
Arizona State University

Amy L. Ariss
Arizona State University

Christopher Bain
The University of Central Florida

Patrick Battillo
Arizona State University

Neha Bhatnagar
The College of William & Mary

Collin Breuhaus
Saint Louis University

Jennifer Brinkerhoff
The College of William & Mary

Chelsea Brooks
The University of Central Florida

Bethany Brown
Binghamton University

Michael Camey
The University of Central Florida

Gonzalo Carrillo
North Carolina State University

Tania Chackumkal
Saint Louis University

Meredith Chalk
Saint Louis University

Kerry Conaty
Saint Louis University

Zachary Davis
The University of Central Florida

Matthew DeRemer
The University of Central Florida

Lauren Dickerson
The University of Central Florida

Leah Ducey
Saint Louis University

Sumair Dugan
The University of Central Florida

Patrick Earley
Saint Louis University

Tony Fantozzi
University of Missouri, St. Louis

John Frankenhoff
The College of William & Mary

Nicole Friedman
Binghamton University

Jacob Galper
The University of Central Florida

Talia Gholson
University of Missouri, St. Louis

Tyler Greer
North Carolina State University

Scott Gumieny
Davenport University

Nicole Hansen
Portland State University

Lindsey Helgeson
Saint Louis University

David Herendeen
University of Missouri, St. Louis

Ashly Hughes
Arizona State University

David Hurdle
Arizona State University

Sodeth Im
Arizona State University

Stephen Kincaid
Saint Louis University

Juliya Korenchenkova
The University of Central Florida

Robert Lancaster
The College of William & Mary

Shawn Larson
Northwood University

Iris Lau
Binghamton University

Tak Lay
Arizona State University

Sanggyu Lee
Binghamton University

Angela Licata
University of Missouri, St. Louis

Laura Linton
The University of Central Florida

Stacy Litchford
The College of William & Mary

Ashley Marlow
The University of Central Florida

Blaire Martin
The University of Central Florida

Jonathan Martin
Saint Louis University

Joshua Martinez
The University of Central Florida

K. Matis
The College of William & Mary

Jennifer Maxson
Saint Louis University

Jill Mazur
The College of William & Mary

Lindsay McClure
The University of Central Florida

Stephen McGillivray
The College of William & Mary

Jonathan McGovern
The University of Central Florida

Bryan Mecklenburg
Davenport University

Steven Miller
The University of Central Florida

Aretia Dian Moir
Portland State University

Sudha Movva
The College of William & Mary

Eric Murray
Arizona State University

Alejandra M. Nauman
North Carolina State University

Dmitriy Ostrobrod
Binghamton University

Joseph Owen
Binghamton University

Timi Oyeleke
The University of Central Florida

Richard Ratkai
The University of Central Florida

Kirthi Ravi
The College of William & Mary

Rebecca Reibel
Northwood University

Amanda Rodriguez
The University of Central Florida

Suela Shaho
The University of Central Florida

Zachary Shapiro
Binghamton University

Amit Sharma
The College of William & Mary

Greg Smith
Arizona State University

Matthew Smith
The University of Central Florida

Andrea Smith
Binghamton University

Darshini Swamy
The College of William & Mary

Mariela Tchobanova
Arizona State University

David Tepper
Davenport University

C. Thornton
The College of William & Mary

Osman Alican Turhan
Binghamton University

James A. Unti
Arizona State University

Rachel Wheeler
North Carolina State University

Caroline Williams
North Carolina State University

Cho Ting Wong
Binghamton University

Anda Wood
The College of William & Mary

David Wright
North Carolina State University

Yiming Xu
Binghamton University

Linfeng Zhang
Northwood University

CONTENTS IN BRIEF

CONTENTS

(Full-length cases marked with a ♦ were authored or co-authored specifically for this book by Frank T. Rothaermel.)

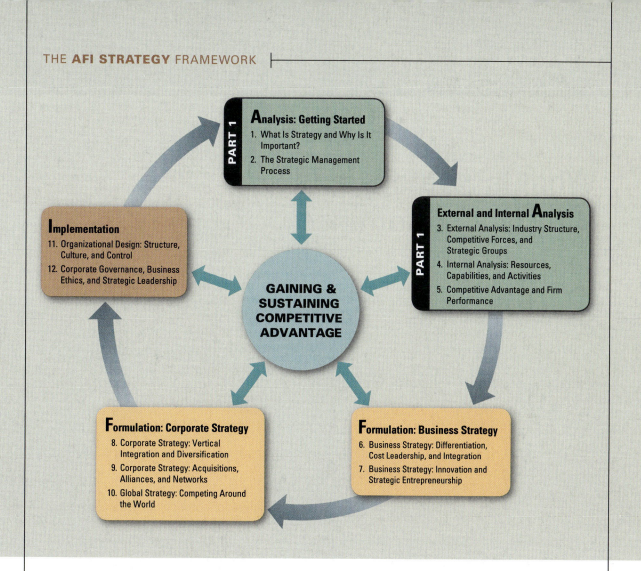

PART 1
Strategy Analysis

CHAPTER 1

What Is Strategy and Why Is It Important?

LEARNING OBJECTIVES

After studying this chapter, you should be able to:

LO 1-1 Define competitive advantage, sustainable competitive advantage, competitive disadvantage, and competitive parity.

LO 1-2 Define strategy and explain its role in a firm's quest for competitive advantage.

LO 1-3 Explain the role of firm effects and industry effects in determining firm performance.

LO 1-4 Describe the role of corporate, business, and functional managers in strategy formulation and implementation.

LO 1-5 Outline how business models put strategy into action.

LO 1-6 Describe and assess the opportunities and challenges managers face in the 21st century.

LO 1-7 Critically evaluate the role that different stakeholders play in the firm's quest for competitive advantage.

The Premature Death of a Google Forerunner at Microsoft

I N 1998, 24-year-old Sergey Brin and 25-year-old Larry Page founded Google. They met as graduate students in computer science at Stanford University, where they began working together on a web crawler, with the goal of improving online searches. What they developed was the PageRank algorithm, which returns the most relevant web pages more or less instantaneously and ranks them by how often they are referenced on other important web pages. A clear improvement over early search engines such as AltaVista, Overture, and Yahoo, all of which indexed by keywords, the PageRank algorithm is able to consider 500 million variables and 3 billion terms. What started as a homework assignment launched the two into an entrepreneurial venture when they set up shop in a garage in Menlo Park, California.

Today, Google is the world's leading online search and advertising company, with some 70 percent market share of an industry estimated to be worth more than $25 billion a year, and that is growing quickly. Though Yahoo is a distant second with less than 20 percent share, in 2008 Microsoft's CEO Steve Ballmer offered to buy the runner-up for close to $50 billion to help his company gain a foothold in the paid-search business where Google rules. Yahoo turned down the offer.

What haunts Ballmer is that Microsoft actually had its own working prototype of a Google forerunner, called Keywords, more than a decade earlier.

Scott Banister, then a student at the University of Illinois, had come up with the idea of adding paid advertisements to Internet searches. He quit college and drove his Geo hatchback to the San Francisco Bay Area to start Keywords, later joining an online ad company called LinkExchange. In 1998, Microsoft bought LinkExchange for some $265 million (about one two-hundredth the price it would later offer for Yahoo). LinkExchange's managers urged Microsoft to invest in Keywords. Instead, Microsoft executives shut down LinkExchange in 2000 because they did not see a viable business model in it. One LinkExchange manager actually approached Ballmer himself and explained that he thought Microsoft was making a mistake. But Ballmer said he wanted to manage through delegation and would not reverse a decision made by managers three levels below him. Thus ended Microsoft's first online advertising venture.

In 2003, Microsoft got a second chance to enter the online advertising business when some of its mid-level managers proposed buying Overture Services, an innovator in combining Internet searches with advertisements. This time, Ballmer, joined by Microsoft's co-founder Bill Gates, decided not to pursue the idea because they thought Overture was overpriced. Shortly thereafter, Yahoo bought Overture for $1.6 billion.

Having missed two huge opportunities to pursue promising strategic initiatives that emerged from lower levels within the firm, Microsoft has been playing catch-up in the paid-search business ever since. In the summer of 2009, it launched its own search engine, Bing. Microsoft's new search engine will also power Yahoo searches, after the two announced a strategic alliance. These two strategic moves helped Microsoft increase its share in the lucrative online search business to roughly

25 percent, up from just over 8 percent. It remains an open question whether this is sufficient, however, to challenge Google's dominance. In particular, Bing's increase in market share of online searches is obtained at the expense of Yahoo's, and not Google's, market share.[1]

After reading the chapter, you will find more about this case, with related questions, on page 21.

▲ **HOW DID A STARTUP** by two college students outperform Microsoft, one of the world's leading technology companies, in online search and advertising? Why is Google successful in the online search business while Yahoo is struggling? For that matter, why is any company successful? What enables some firms to gain and then sustain their competitive advantage over time? Why do once-great firms fail? How can a firm's managers influence performance?

Answering these questions requires integrating the knowledge you've obtained in your studies of different business disciplines (such as accounting, finance, economics, marketing, operations, IT management, organizational behavior, and human resource management) to understand what leads to superior performance. **Strategic management,** the topic of this course and this book, is the integrative management field that combines analysis, formulation, and implementation in the quest for competitive advantage. The AFI strategy framework shown on the part-opening page (page 1) embodies this view of strategic management. In this chapter, we lay the groundwork for the study of strategic management by introducing some foundational ideas about strategy and competitive advantage, and by looking at the components of the AFI framework.

WHAT STRATEGY IS: GAINING & SUSTAINING COMPETITIVE ADVANTAGE

>> LO 1-1
Define competitive advantage, sustainable competitive advantage, competitive disadvantage, and competitive parity.

The desire to perform better than our competitors applies to nearly every area of our lives. Universities compete for the best students and professors. Startup firms compete for financial and human capital. Existing companies compete for future growth, and employees compete for raises and promotions. University professors compete for research grants, and college students for jobs and graduate school admission. Political candidates compete for votes, and charities for contributions.

In every competitive situation, the winners are generally those with the better strategy. In general terms, *strategy* is the planned and realized set of actions a firm takes to achieve its goals. For instance, the general manager of the Oakland A's, Billy Beane, applied a sophisticated analysis to formulate and implement a new strategy.[2] Beane began by devising new metrics to assess a player's potential and performance more accurately. These metrics, in turn, allowed the Oakland A's to field a low-cost team that could compete against much richer rivals in Major League Baseball. Taken together, strategy governs the ubiquitous quest for superior performance.

What Is Competitive Advantage?

A firm that formulates and implements a strategy that leads to superior performance relative to other competitors in the same industry or the industry average has a **competitive advantage.** Google has a competitive advantage over Microsoft, Yahoo, and others competing in the online search and advertising business. A firm that is able to outperform its competitors or the industry average over a prolonged period of time has a

sustainable competitive advantage.[3] It appears that Google has a sustainable competitive advantage, because it has outperformed its rivals consistently over time. Yet, past performance is no guarantee of future performance. Microsoft, Yahoo, and others are working hard to neutralize Google's competitive advantage.

In both business and sports, strategy is about outperforming one's rivals. Identifying the winner in a sporting event, however, is relatively easy. In 2011, the University of Connecticut Huskies won the NCAA basketball championship, beating the Butler University Bulldogs 54-41 in the title game. We could say that the UConn Huskies gained a temporary competitive advantage. To answer the question of who has a *sustainable* competitive advantage, however, is a bit trickier. Here, we need to look at the recent history of tournaments. If we say, for example, that 10 years is an appropriate time period over which to assess the sustainability of competitive advantage (2002–2011), then we find that seven teams were victorious: the University of Connecticut, the University of Florida (Gators), and the University of North Carolina at Chapel Hill (Tar Heels) each two times; and Duke University, the University of Kansas, Syracuse University, and the University of Maryland each one time. We could argue that over this 10-year period the Huskies, the Gators, and the Tar Heels enjoyed a sustainable competitive advantage over other NCAA teams. Since competitive advantage needs to be assessed relative to other competitors, we can only say that the Huskies, Gators, and Tar Heels, although outperforming the other contenders, performed at a similarly high level. This example shows that assessing competitive advantage, let alone sustainable competitive advantage, is not an easy task.

In business, we have no *absolute* measure of performance for competitive advantage as we do for height or weight or NCAA tournament victories. Rather, we compare performance to a benchmark, either the performance of other firms in the same industry or an industry average. If a firm underperforms its rivals or the industry average, for instance, it has a **competitive disadvantage.** A 15 percent return on invested capital (RoIC) may sound like superior firm performance, but in the energy industry where the average RoIC has been above 20 percent the last few years, it is actually a competitive disadvantage. In contrast, if a firm's RoIC is 5 percent in a commodity industry like steel, where the industry average is 1–2 percent, then the firm has a competitive advantage. Should two or more firms perform at the same level, they have **competitive parity.**

If other companies can easily imitate a firm's source of competitive advantage, then any edge the firm gains is short-lived. But if the advantage is difficult to understand or imitate, the firm can sustain it over time. Patents, for example,

---

strategic management An integrative management field that combines analysis, formulation, and implementation in the quest for competitive advantage.

competitive advantage Superior performance relative to other competitors in the same industry or the industry average.

sustainable competitive advantage Outperforming competitors or the industry average over a prolonged period of time.

competitive disadvantage Underperformance relative to other competitors in the same industry or the industry average.

competitive parity Performance of two or more firms at the same level.

often protect certain products from direct imitation for a period. Pfizer's Lipitor, a patent-protected cholesterol-lowering drug, is the best-selling prescription drug ever, grossing some $14 billion dollars in revenues each year between 2006 and 2009.[4] This highly successful product contributed to a competitive advantage for Pfizer, accounting for roughly one-third of its total annual revenues.[5] The patent on Lipitor expired in 2010, however, allowing generic drug makers to copy the drug and offer it at much lower prices, eroding Pfizer's competitive advantage.

What Is Strategy?

>> **LO 1-2**
Define strategy and explain its role in a firm's quest for competitive advantage.

Strategy describes the goal-directed actions a firm intends to take in its quest to gain and sustain competitive advantage.[6] The firm that possesses competitive advantage provides superior value to customers at a competitive price or acceptable value at a lower price. Profitability and market share are the consequences of superior value creation. Henry Ford was driven by his ambition to mass-produce a reliable car at a low cost. Larry Page and Sergey Brin were motivated to create a better search engine. For Ford, Page, and Brin, and numerous other businesspeople, making money was the *consequence* of providing a product or service consumers wanted. The important point here is that strategy is about creating superior value, while containing the cost to create it. The greater the difference between value creation and cost, the greater the economic contribution the firm makes, and thus the greater the likelihood for competitive advantage.

Strategy is not, however, a zero-sum game—it's not always the case that one party wins while all others lose. Many strategic successes are accomplished when firms or individuals cooperate with one another.[7] Even direct competitors cooperate occasionally, to create win–win scenarios. When competitors cooperate with one another to achieve strategic objectives, we call this **co-opetition**.[8] The new Cell microprocessor, which powers the PlayStation 3 game console, was the result of a collaborative effort among IBM, Toshiba, and Sony—companies that directly compete with one another in other markets.

We've noted that to gain a competitive advantage, a firm needs to provide either goods or services consumers value more highly than those of its competitors, or goods or services similar to the competitors' but at a lower price. The essence of strategy, therefore, is being different from rivals and thus unique. Managers accomplish this difference through *strategic positioning,* staking out a unique position in an industry that allows the firm to provide value to customers, while controlling costs.

Strategic positioning requires trade-offs, however. As a low-cost retailer, JCPenney has a clear strategic profile and serves a specific market segment. Upscale retailer Neiman Marcus also has built a clear strategic profile by providing superior customer service to a specific (luxury) market segment. While the companies are in the same industry, their respective customer segments overlap very little, if at all, and thus they are not direct competitors. To keep it that way, their managers must make conscious trade-offs that enable both to strive for competitive advantage in the same industry.

strategy The goal-directed actions a firm intends to take in its quest to gain and sustain competitive advantage.

co-opetition Cooperation by competitors to achieve a strategic objective.

As emphasized by Michael Porter of Harvard Business School, strategy is as much about deciding what *not* to do, as it is about deciding what to do. Because the supply of resources is not unlimited, managers must carefully consider their business strategy choices in their quest for competitive advantage. Trying to be everything to everybody would be a recipe for inferior performance. For example, to ward off successful low-cost entrants like Southwest Airlines (SWA), Continental and Delta added low-cost Continental

Lite and Delta's Song to their core hub-and-spoke businesses. Their managers fell prey to the illusion that they could straddle a low-cost leadership position (already well-executed by SWA) and their existing differentiation strategy of serving a large number of destinations. Both new ventures failed because they left Continental and Delta *stuck in the middle*, leading to inferior performance in both markets. (We'll consider different business strategies in more depth in Chapter 6.)

Strategy as a Theory of How to Compete

A firm's strategy can be seen as its managers' theory about how to gain and sustain competitive advantage. A *theory* answers the questions, what causes what and why?[9] It's a contingent statement based on assumptions about how the world works. Based on the law of gravity, for example, we can predict what will happen if you drop something out the window—without your having to do it to find out. As the old adage goes, nothing is more practical than a good theory. Based on their assumptions about competitive conditions—that is, the relative value of their firm's resources and capabilities as compared to those of their collaborators and competitors, predictions about the actions that competitors may initiate, and the development of trends in the external environment—managers express their theory of how to gain and sustain competitive advantage in the strategy they set for the firm.[10] As we will see in Chapters 3 and 4, a firm can gain competitive advantage by leveraging its internal resources, capabilities, and relationships to exploit opportunities in its external environment.

Strategy as a *theory of how to compete* provides managers with a roadmap to navigate the competitive territory. The more accurate the map, the better strategic decisions managers can make. In the competitive world, managers test their theories in the marketplace. Positive feedback validates managers' strategic assumptions: "iPhone sales vastly exceeded expectations, so it must have been the right product at the right time." Negative feedback allows managers to adjust their assumptions: "The Apple Newton flopped [in 1993], so its price—over $1,000 in today's dollars—and bulkiness weren't right for the PDA market at that time." The Newton's failure, however, laid the foundation for later successes such as Apple's iPhone and the iPad. Competitors also learned from the Newton debacle: They subsequently introduced improved products, including Palm's Pilot, Handspring's Visor, and RIM's BlackBerry, at a lower price. A firm's relative performance in the competitive marketplace provides managers with the necessary feedback to assess how well their strategy works in their quest for competitive advantage. *The strategic management process, therefore, is a never-ending cycle of analysis, formulation, implementation, and feedback.*

Walmart became the world's largest retailer in part due to founder Sam Walton's accurate assumptions about the connection between low retail prices in underserved rural and suburban areas and high volume, thus generating the ability to be the low-price leader in mass-merchandising.[11] His insight of how to do things differently in the retail industry created a competitive advantage for his firm. Later, Walmart reinforced its competitive advantage with a revolutionary IT system that tracks sales in real time and allows just-in-time deliveries. For the year 2008, one of the worst stock performance years on record, the Dow Jones Industrial Average fell 34 percent, yet Walmart's shares actually rose 18 percent, outperforming the average of the 30 blue-chip firms by 52 percentage points. The reason? When managers align their assumptions closely with competitive realities, they can draft and implement a successful strategy that yields superior firm performance. Walmart's cost leadership strategy became even more valuable in a time of economic hardship.

In contrast, when managers' theories of how to gain and sustain competitive advantage do not reflect reality, their firm's strategy will destroy rather than create value and will lead to inferior performance. The U.S. auto manufacturers Chrysler, Ford, and GM have fallen on hard times partly because their managers built their strategies around the flawed assumptions that gasoline prices would remain low and U.S. drivers would continue to want big trucks and sport utility vehicles. These were also the only vehicles that U.S. car manufacturers, given their inflated cost structure, could sell at a profit. The Ford F-150 pickup truck is the most-sold vehicle of all time in the United States, and the Hummer (about 8 miles per gallon) was once one of GM's most profitable vehicles. When gas prices rose above $4 per gallon in the summer of 2008 (up from less than $2.50 a gallon just a year earlier), consumer preferences for more fuel-efficient and "green" cars increased.

Meanwhile, in Japan where gas prices have always been high, Toyota's managers had begun to think as early as the 1990s about how fuel efficiency and possible regulation would influence consumer behavior. So while Toyota provided large SUVs and pickup trucks to meet U.S. market demand, it also developed hybrid vehicles to compete in an environment of increased regulation, higher gas prices, and heightened consumer concerns about the ecological impact of gas-guzzling cars. In 1997, Toyota launched the Prius (60 miles per gallon), which has since sold more than 2 million units. Because the strategies of U.S. car manufacturers were based on flawed assumptions and each manufacturer had long-term resource commitments that were not easily reversible, U.S. car manufacturers did not have a competitive fuel-efficient (or hybrid) vehicle.[12] The poor financial performance that followed was the logical consequence of a strategy that no longer fit the competitive realities. In 2009, both GM and Chrysler filed for bankruptcy. Engineering a shrewd strategic turnaround, Ford (which, by the way, did not receive a government bailout) is experiencing a resurgence.[13]

firm effects The results of managers' actions to influence firm performance.

industry effects The results attributed to the choice of industry in which to compete.

Industry vs. Firm Effects in Determining Performance

Managers' actions tend to be more important in determining firm performance than the forces exerted upon the firm by its external environment. Thus, **firm effects**—the results of managers' actions to influence firm performance—tend to have more impact than **industry effects**—the results attributed to the choice of industry in which to compete.[14] Based on a number of empirical studies, academic researchers found that the industry a firm is in determines about 20 percent of a firm's profitability, while the firm's strategy within a given industry explains between 30–45 percent of its performance.[15] These findings are depicted in Exhibit 1.1. Although a firm's industry environment is not quite as important as the firm's strategy within its industry, they jointly determine the firm's overall performance.

Astute managers create superior performance through strategy.

EXHIBIT 1.1

Industry, Firm, and Other Effects Explaining Superior Firm Performance

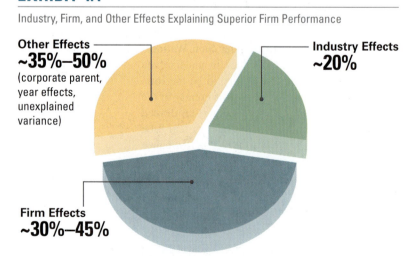

Other Effects
~35%–50%
(corporate parent, year effects, unexplained variance)

Industry Effects
~20%

Firm Effects
~30%–45%

They leverage a company's strengths while mitigating its weaknesses. They turn external threats into opportunities. Strategy generally requires making important trade-offs (think low-cost Kia versus luxury Ferrari in the car industry). Indeed, some of the biggest advances in competitive positioning have been accomplished when managers resolved apparent trade-offs. Toyota introduced lean manufacturing to resolve the trade-off between quality and cost. This process innovation allowed Toyota to produce higher-quality cars at a lower unit cost, and to perfect the mass customization of cars. Lean manufacturing, over time, has become a necessary but not sufficient condition for competitive advantage in the auto industry. Today, if a carmaker can't produce high-quality, mass-customized cars at low cost, it is not even in the game. More recently, Toyota stumbled as questions arose whether the company could maintain its stellar quality record while growing so fast. Korea's Hyundai stepped into this void, offering cars that surpass Toyota in quality while attempting to provide luxury similar to Lexus vehicles.[16] Hyundai's managers carved out a strong strategic position for the company by focusing on resolving the trade-offs between luxury, quality, and cost. The ups and downs in the car industry clearly show that competitive advantage is transitory. It is a difficult quest to gain competitive advantage; it is even more difficult to sustain it. The tools of strategic management aid managers in this important challenge.

>> **LO 1-3**
Explain the role of firm effects and industry effects in determining firm performance.

What Strategy Is *Not*

To gain a deeper understanding of what strategy is, it is helpful to know what strategy is *not*.[17] You will hear many people today refer to a host of different plans and activities as pricing strategy, Internet strategy, alliance strategy, operations strategy, IT strategy, brand strategy, marketing strategy, HR strategy, and so on. While all these elements may be *part* of a firm's functional strategy to support its business model (see the next section), we will reserve the term *strategy* for describing the firm's overall efforts to *gain and sustain competitive advantage*.

Nor is competitive benchmarking "strategy." Best-in-class practices such as just-in-time inventory, enterprise resource planning (ERP) systems, and Six Sigma quality initiatives all fall under the umbrella of *tools* for operational effectiveness. Being best-in-class is a sufficient but not a necessary condition for competitive advantage. Take this idea to its extreme in a quick thought experiment: If all firms in the same industry pursued Six Sigma in the same fashion, all would have identical cost structures and none could gain a competitive advantage. Indeed, competition would be cut-throat because all firms would be more or less the same, but very efficient. Everyone would be running faster, but nothing would have changed in relative strategic positions.

Rather than focusing on copying a competitor, the key to successful strategy is to combine a set of activities to stake out a unique position in an industry. Competitive advantage has to come from performing activities differently than rivals do. Operational effectiveness, marketing skills, and other functional expertise, along with best practices, contribute to a unique strategic position, but by themselves they are not a substitute for strategy. Exhibit 1.2 summarizes the concept of strategy.

EXHIBIT 1.2

What Is Strategy?

Definition: *Strategy is the quest to gain and sustain competitive advantage.*

- It is the managers' theories about how to gain and sustain competitive advantage.

- It is about being different from your rivals.

- It is about creating value while containing cost.

- It is about deciding what to do, and what *not* to do.

- It combines a set of activities to stake out a unique position.

- It requires long-term commitments that are often not easily reversible.

FORMULATING STRATEGY ACROSS LEVELS: CORPORATE, BUSINESS, AND FUNCTIONAL MANAGERS

>> LO 1-4
Describe the role of corporate, business, and functional managers in strategy formulation and implementation.

Strategy formulation concerns the choice of strategy in terms of *where* and *how* to compete. To understand the interdependencies across different levels, it is helpful to break down strategy formulation into three distinct levels: corporate, business, and functional.

Corporate strategy involves decisions made at the highest level of the firm about *where* to compete. *Corporate executives* need to decide in which industries, markets, and geographies their company should compete, as well as how they can create synergies across business units that may be quite different. They are responsible for setting overarching strategic goals and allocating scarce resources, among the different business divisions, monitoring performance, and making adjustments to the overall portfolio of businesses when needed. Corporate executives determine the scope of the business, deciding whether to enter certain industries and markets and whether to sell certain divisions. The objective of corporate-level strategy is to increase overall corporate value. Over the last 20 years, due to a new corporate-level strategy, IBM's CEO Sam Palmisano and his predecessors have transformed IBM from a hardware company to a global IT services firm. It even sold its PC unit to Lenovo, a Chinese high-tech company as part of the transformation process.

Exhibit 1.3 shows that corporate strategy is formulated at headquarters, and that *business strategy* occurs within **strategic business units,** the standalone divisions of a larger conglomerate, each with its own profit-and-loss responsibility. *General managers* in strategic business units (SBUs) must answer the strategic question of *how* to compete in order to achieve superior performance within the business unit. Currently, for example, IBM has four strategic business units or divisions: hardware, software, technology services, and financing. General managers are responsible for formulating a strategic position for their business unit. The technology services SBU at IBM is led by a senior vice president, who has profit-and-loss responsibility for IBM's technology services worldwide. The same goes for the heads of the other three SBUs at IBM.

strategic business unit (SBU) A standalone division of a larger conglomerate, with its own profit-and-loss responsibility.

EXHIBIT 1.3

Strategy Formulation and Implementation Across Levels: Corporate, Business, and Functional Strategy

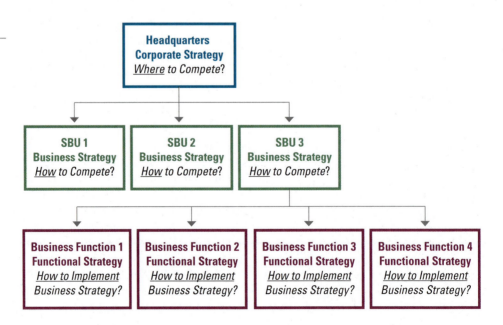

Within each SBU are various business *functions* such as accounting, finance, human resources, information technology, product development, operations, marketing, and customer service. Each *functional manager* is responsible for decisions and actions within a single functional area that aid in the implementation of the business-level strategy. A manager in IBM's product-development function, for example, may be responsible for encouraging new product offerings. The set of functional strategies enables the general managers of the SBUs to pursue their respective business-level strategy, which in turn needs to be in line with the overall corporate-level strategy.

Functional managers, who are closer to the final products, services, and customers than managers at higher levels, may sometimes be able to come up with strategic initiatives that may influence the direction of the company. One functional manager at IBM, for instance, suggested entry into the life sciences field.[18] In 2000, she saw a business opportunity for IBM, in which application of high-performance computing and information technology could solve thorny problems that accompanied data-intensive work such as decoding human genomes and furthering personalized medicine. IBM's general and corporate managers supported this strategic initiative, dubbed "information-based medicine."[19] This new business opportunity generated more than $5 billion in revenue by 2006.

BUSINESS MODELS: PUTTING STRATEGY INTO ACTION

We've said that strategy denotes the managers' theories of how to compete, but theory alone is useless if it is not put into action. The translation of strategy into action takes place in the firm's **business model,** which details the firm's competitive tactics and initiatives. Simply put, the firm's business model explains how the firm intends to make money. If it fails to translate a strategy into a profitable business model, the firm will cease to exist. To come up with a business model, the firm first transforms its theory of how to compete into a blueprint of actions and initiatives that support the overarching strategy. In a second step, the organization implements this blueprint through structures, processes, culture, and procedures.

>> **LO 1-5**
Outline how business models put strategy into action.

The so-called *razor–razor-blade business model* is a famous example. The idea is to give away or sell for a small fee the product and make money on the replacement part needed. As the name indicates, it was invented by Gillette, which gave away its razors and sold the replacement cartridges for relatively high prices. The razor–razor-blade model is found in many business applications today. For example, HP charges very little for its laser printers but imposes high prices for its replacement cartridges.

Similarly, telecommunications companies provide a basic cell phone at no charge or significantly subsidize high-end smartphones when you sign up for a two-year wireless service plan. They combine the razor–razor-blade model with the *subscription-based business model,* which was first introduced by magazines and newspapers. They recoup the subsidy provided for the smartphone by requiring customers to sign up for lengthy service plans. The leading provider of audio books, Audible, a subsidiary of Amazon, also uses a subscription-based business model.

The opening case foreshadows the up-and-coming battle between Google and Microsoft as each moves progressively on to the other's turf. Although Google started out as an online search and advertising company, it now offers software applications (Google Docs, word processing, spreadsheet, e-mail, interactive calendar, and presentation software) and operating systems (Chrome OS for the web and Android for mobile applications), among many other online products and services. In contrast, Microsoft began its life by offering an operating system (since 1985, called Windows), then moved into software applications with its

business model
Organizational plan that details the firm's competitive tactics and initiatives; in short, how the firm intends to make money.

EXHIBIT 1.4

Competing Business
Models: Google vs.
Microsoft

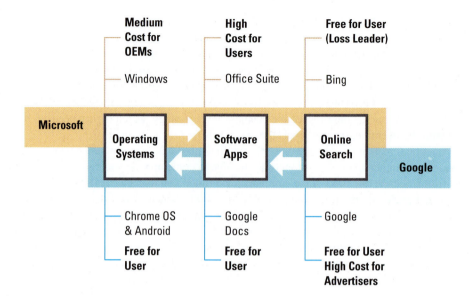

Office Suite, and now into online search and advertising with Bing. Thus, the stage is set for a clash of the technology titans.

In fighting this battle, Google and Microsoft pursue very different business models, as shown in Exhibit 1.4.[20] Google offers its applications software Google Docs for free to induce and retain as many users as possible for its search engine. Although Google's flagship search engine is free for the end user, Google makes money from sponsored links by advertisers. The advertisers pay for the placement of their ad on the results pages and every time a user clicks through an ad (which Google calls a "sponsored link"). Thus, many billion mini-transactions add up to a substantial business. As indicated in Exhibit 1.4, Google uses part of the profits earned from its lucrative online advertising business to subsidize Google Docs. Giving away products and services to induce widespread use allows Google to benefit from *network effects*—the increase in the value of a product or service as more people use it. Thus, Google can charge advertisers for highly targeted and effective ads, allowing it to subsidize other product offerings that compete directly with Microsoft.

Microsoft's business model is almost the reverse of Google's. Initially, Microsoft focused on creating a large installed base of users for its PC operating system (Windows). It now holds some 90 percent market share in operating system software worldwide. Once the users are locked into a Microsoft operating system (which generally comes preloaded with the computer they purchased), they then want to buy applications that run seamlessly with the operating system. The obvious choice for most users is Microsoft's Office Suite (containing Word, Excel, PowerPoint, Outlook, and Access), but they need to pay several hundred dollars for the latest version. As shown in Exhibit 1.4, Microsoft uses the profits from its application software business to subsidize its search engine Bing, which is—just like Google's—a free product offering for the end user. Given Bing's relatively small market share, however, and the tremendous cost in developing the search engine, Microsoft, unlike Google, does not make any money from its online search offering; rather, it is a big money loser. The logic behind Bing is to provide a countervailing power to Google's dominant position in online search. The logic behind Google Docs is to create a threat to Microsoft's dominant position in application software. These strategies create *multi-point competition* between the two technology firms.[21] Taken together, Google and Microsoft compete with one another for market share in several different product categories through quite different business models.

STRATEGY IN THE 21ST CENTURY

As the adage goes, change is the only constant—and the rate of change appears to be increasing.[22] Changing technologies spawn new industries, while others die out. Managers today face an increasingly competitive world and a truly global marketplace. These trends, rapid technological change and increasing globalization, dramatically affect how to formulate and implement an effective strategy in the 21st century. Here we expand on the impact of key trends (accelerating technological change, a truly global world, and future industries) that will affect strategy making in the 21st century.

>> LO 1-6
Describe and assess the opportunities and challenges managers face in the 21st century.

Accelerating Technological Change

The rate of technological change has accelerated drastically over the last hundred years. Exhibit 1.5 shows how many years it took for different technological innovations to reach 50 percent of the U.S. population (either through ownership or usage). As an example, it took 84 years for half of the U.S. population to own a car, but only 28 years for half the population to own a TV. The pace of the adoption rate of recent innovations continues to accelerate. It took 19 years for the PC to reach 50 percent ownership, but only 6 years for MP3 players to accomplish the same diffusion rate.

What factors explain rapid technological diffusion and adoption? One factor is that initial innovations like the car, airplane, telephone, and use of electricity provided the necessary infrastructure for newer innovations to diffuse more rapidly. Another reason is the emergence of new business models that make innovations more accessible. For example, Dell's direct-to-consumer distribution system improved access to low-cost PCs, and Walmart's low-price, high-volume model utilized its sophisticated IT logistics system to fuel explosive growth. In addition, satellite and cable distribution systems facilitated the ability of mass media such as radio and TV to deliver advertising and information to a wider audience. The speed of technology diffusion has accelerated further with the emergence of the Internet, social networking sites, and viral messaging.

The life experience of the Gen-Y population reflects the accelerated pace of technology diffusion. New technologies are a natural part of their lives, like eating and breathing. The

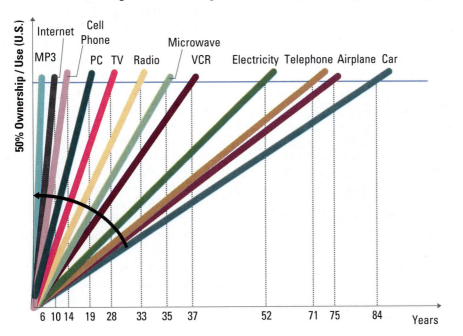

EXHIBIT 1.5

Accelerating Speed of Technological Change

Source: Data from U.S. Census Bureau; Consumer Electronics Association; *Forbes;* and National Cable and Telecommunications Association.

Gen-Y cohort came of age during the boom of the Internet; its members are accustomed to constant connectivity and to rapid technological change. By the time they graduate from college, the average Gen-Y student has spent over 10,000 hours playing video games and over 20,000 hours watching TV.[23] The Gen-Y cohort is sometimes called *digital natives*—people who grew up with the Internet and other advanced technologies and who need no help to adapt to new technologies.[24] Those who did not grow up with the Internet and other advanced technologies, and so have taken longer to adapt to them, are called *digital immigrants*. We discuss the strategic implications of innovation and technological change in Chapter 7.

A Truly Global World

New York Times columnist and author Thomas Friedman used his book title, *The World Is Flat,*[25] to describe a truly global marketplace in which goods, services, capital, knowledge, ideas, and people move freely across geographic boundaries in search of greater opportunities. Advances in information technology and transportation have led to the "death of distance."[26]

Due to falling trade and investment barriers, companies are now part of a global economy made up of several key markets. Combining 27 member states and more than 500 million people, the European Union (EU) is the world's largest economy.[27] Sixteen EU countries are almost a fully integrated bloc with unified economic and monetary policies, using the euro as a common currency.[28] China, with more than 1.4 billion people, is the most populous country in the world, and India, with 1.2 billion people, is the world's largest democracy. Together with Brazil and Russia, they make up the *BRIC countries,* which have more than 40 percent of the world's population and occupy more than a quarter of the world's landmass. This group of fast-growing, emerging economies could one day eclipse the richest countries in the world.

Many U.S. companies have become global players. The technology giant IBM employs 425,000 people and has revenues of roughly $100 billion. Although IBM's headquarters is in Armonk, NY, the vast majority of its employees (more than 70 percent) actually work outside the United States. IBM, like many other U.S.-based multinationals, now earns the majority of its revenues (roughly two-thirds) outside the United States (as shown in Exhibit 1.6).[29] IBM's revenues in the BRIC countries have been growing at between 20 and 40 percent per year, while they have grown by only about 1 to 3 percent in developed markets such as the United States. IBM's goal is to obtain 35 percent of its total revenue from fast-growing emerging economies such as the BRIC countries by 2015. To capture these opportunities, IBM (along with many other multinational companies) has been reducing the U.S. headcount while increasing employment in emerging economies such as India.[30]

While many multinational companies like Coca-Cola, Procter & Gamble, and

EXHIBIT 1.6

Geographic Sources of IBM Revenues, 2010

Source: 2010 IBM Annual Report.

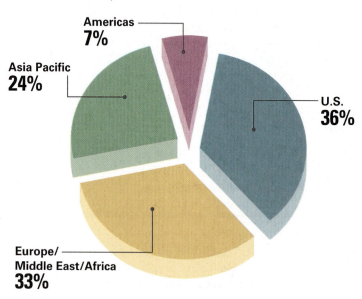

Americas **7%**

Asia Pacific **24%**

U.S. **36%**

Europe/ Middle East/Africa **33%**

Sony tend to focus on more affluent customers, some 4 billion people on the planet live on less than $2,000 a year (or $5.50 a day).[31] Recently, scholars have shown that this so-called **bottom of the pyramid** of the global economy—the largest but poorest socioeconomic group of the world's population—can yield significant business opportunities, which—if satisfied—could improve the living standard of the world's poorest.[32] Muhammad Yunus, winner of the 2006 Nobel Peace Prize, founded Grameen Bank in Bangladesh to provide small loans (so-called *microcredit*) to impoverished villagers. Loans provided funding for their entrepreneurial ventures so that villagers could help themselves climb out of poverty. As a follow-up business, Grameen Telecom now offers a microloan combined with a cell phone for local entrepreneurs. Other businesses have also found profitable business opportunities at the bottom of the pyramid. In India, Arvind Mills offers jeans in a ready-to-make kit that costs only a fraction of the high-end Levi's. The Tata Group, a widely diversified multinational conglomerate headquartered in Mumbai, India, in 2009 introduced its Nano car, the lowest-priced car in the world.[33] Although the Nano sells for less than $2,500 ("one lakh" rupees), sales of hundreds of millions of them can add up to a substantial business. Given its importance, we take up global strategy in Chapter 10.

Future Industries

Tomorrow's winners are the ones that focus today on making investments to build a position in up-and-coming industries. Given current trends, several industries promise significant potential for value creation (and thus career opportunities), among them health care, the green economy, and Web 2.0.[34]

HEALTH CARE. In 2010, U.S. health care spending reached $2.5 trillion, or 16 percent of total economic activity, making it the largest industry in the country.[35] With aging baby boomers making up the largest age demographic in the United States, the growth of the health care industry, estimated at 7 percent annually, will far outstrip the growth rate of the overall economy. As a consequence, by 2019 the health care sector is estimated to be 20 percent of total U.S. economic activity.

Not only are baby boomers a large part of the U.S. population, most of the wealth is also concentrated in this group. As baby boomers age, they will demand more professional health care, wellness and enhancement services such as Botox treatments, liposuction, and laser eye surgery. Important medical breakthroughs in biotechnology, nanotechnology, and genomics will allow health care providers to offer individualized medicine to support longer and healthier living. For example, 23andMe, an entrepreneurial venture founded by Anne Wojcicki and Linda Avey, leverages the convergence of IT, genomics, and biotechnology to allow customers to understand their own unique genetic makeup in terms of health, traits, and ancestry. After having one's personal DNA tested, 23andMe will provide an individualized profile of how that genetic makeup is related to the probability of developing any of over 100 different diseases and conditions.

Given the opportunities in the health care industry, GE announced its *healthymagination* initiative, in which it will invest $6 billion to attempt to solve strategic trade-offs in health care by increasing access, improving quality, and lowering costs.[36] Patterned after its successful *ecomagination* program, this initiative allows GE to draw on the expertise of its various business units. It is intended to refocus GE on its industrial strength, but in a way that looks to emerging opportunities.

Although the health care sector of the economy seems to provide significant business opportunities in the future due to favorable demographics in the U.S. and most developed economies, managers must also consider impending threats such as more government regulation. While more Americans will be required to have health insurance, the

bottom of the pyramid The largest but poorest socioeconomic group of the world's population.

reimbursements for specific procedures are likely to go down. This will decrease the incentives for firms to make investments in this industry and for students to become nurses or medical doctors. Health care providers, moreover, face the challenge of squaring a circle when required by law to provide more access, equal- or higher-quality care, and lower cost. One possible way to resolve this trade-off is innovation in products and processes, a topic that we will take up in Chapter 7.

GREEN ECONOMY. The vast majority of today's economic activity around the globe is powered by carbon-based sources of energy such as oil, coal, and natural gas. Yet, these carbon-based energy sources are finite, and they come with a cost that businesses and consumers do not bear. Such a cost, which economists call **externalities,** represents the side-effects of production and consumption that are not reflected in the price of the product. The externalities of carbon-based energy are CO_2 emissions, which some researchers suggest are linked to air pollution and global warming,[37] and ecological disasters such as the BP oil spill in the Gulf of Mexico.[38]

Moreover, fossil fuels are a finite, non-renewable resource. Oil prices spiked to almost $150 a barrel in the summer of 2008, pushing up gas prices in the U.S. to over $4 a gallon from $1.25 (inflation-adjusted) in the late 1990s. The increase in oil prices over time occurred in a roller coaster fashion as shown in Exhibit 1.7. The global trend line of oil prices, however, is pointing upwards as supplies dwindle and energy demand increases, especially in the rapidly developing countries. Higher oil prices and increasing public awareness of the externalities produced by the burning of fossil fuels have led to a search for renewable energy sources that are more ecologically friendly.

The *green and clean-tech economy* describes future business opportunities in renewable energy, energy conservation, efficient energy use, and energy technology.[39] The goal is to develop a sustainable global economy that the earth can support indefinitely.[40] Several governments across the world such as Germany, Denmark, Israel, and Spain provide incentives to induce businesses to invest in the green economy, and thus create sustainable jobs. The U.S.

externalities Side-effects of production and consumption that are not reflected in the price of a product.

EXHIBIT 1.7

Conceptual Depiction of Oil Prices and Predicted Trend

Source: Adapted from Shai Agassi's presentation at TED, February 2009, www.ted.com/talks/lang/eng/shai_agassi_on_electric_cars.html.

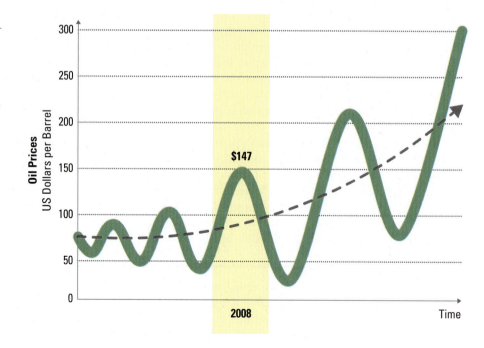

plans to invest $150 billion over the next decade to help jump-start a green economy. It hopes to create five million new jobs that pay well, can't be outsourced, and reduce America's dependence on middle-eastern oil.[41] In the meantime, China is fast becoming the world's leading producer of solar panels, having driven the prices for such panels down by almost 50 percent within just a year.[42] If the size of the current energy industry is any indication, the green and clean-tech economy is likely to be a multi-trillion dollar business. This of course creates opportunities for existing companies such as ABB, GE Energy, Philips, and Siemens, as well as entrepreneurs, in their quest to make an eco-system of energy innovation become a reality.[43]

Again, a note of caution is in order: Although the green economy receives significant media attention, most green energy sources are not yet cost-competitive with old-line coal and oil. This is partly due to the fact that market prices do not include externalities. Some studies also indicate that world oil reserves will be sufficient for another 100 years or more.[44] Moreover, the U.S. has the largest proven coal reserves worldwide (roughly 30 percent), and is most likely to use those to provide the base load for its energy consumption. Famed investor Warren Buffett shares this perspective: his Berkshire Hathaway company acquired Burlington Northern railroads for over $26 billion.[45] Railroads are the most cost-effective way of transporting commodities such as coal, steel, wheat, lumber, and consumer goods over long distances. Burlington Northern moves coal from where it is mined to population-rich states that receive much of their power from coal-fired plants. As in any business situation, managers must carefully consider both opportunities and threats when making strategic decisions.

STRATEGY HIGHLIGHT 1.1

Threadless: Leveraging Crowdsourcing to Design Cool T-Shirts

Threadless, a community-centered online apparel store (www.threadless.com), was founded in 2000 by Jake Nickell, then a student at the Illinois Institute of Art, and Jacob DeHart, then a student at Purdue University, with $1,000 as startup capital. After Jake had won an online T-shirt design contest, the two entrepreneurs came up with a business model to leverage user-generated content. The idea is to let consumers "work for you" and thus turn consumers into *prosumers,* a hybrid between producers and consumers.

Members of the Threadless "community" do most of the work, which they consider fun: They submit T-shirt designs online, and community members vote on which designs they like best. The designs receiving the most votes are put in production, printed, and sold online. Threadless leverages crowdsourcing, a process in which a group of people voluntarily perform tasks that were traditionally being completed by a firm's employees. Rather than outsourcing its work to other companies, Threadless outsources its T-shirt design to its website community. The Web 2.0 concept of leveraging a firm's own customers to help produce better products is explicitly included in Threadless's business model.

WEB 2.0. In the early days of the Internet, websites more or less passively displayed information. Examples of the "old" WWW (World Wide Web) are initial versions of companies' websites that merely displayed information such as their logo, hours, phone numbers, address, and a brief overview of the company. The term *Web 2.0* was coined to denote interactivity, with the goal of harnessing the collective intelligence of web users.[46] The idea was that the more people participate, the better the resulting websites and in turn the better the resulting products and services. Web 2.0, therefore, relies on network effects.[47] As an example, the more people use Google's search engine, the better the search engine gets as it continuously fine-tunes its PageRank algorithm. Many companies are devising ways to utilize social networking to strengthen customer relationships and thus the basis for competitive advantage. Amazon, Netflix, YouTube, Facebook, Flickr, and Threadless are but a few examples of Web 2.0 applications that benefit from network effects. Strategy Highlight 1.1 shows how the online startup Threadless uses Web 2.0 technology to craft an innovative business model.

crowdsourcing A process in which a group of people voluntarily performs tasks that were traditionally completed by a firm's employees.

Threadless's business model translates real-time market research and design contests into quick sales. Threadless produces only T-shirts that were approved by its community. Moreover, it has a very good understanding of market demand because it knows the number of people who participated in each design contest. In addition, when scoring each T-shirt design in a contest, Threadless users have the option to check "I'd buy it." These features give the Threadless community a voice in T-shirt design and also coax community members into making a pre-purchasing commitment. Threadless does not make any significant investments until the design and market size are determined, thus basically minimizing its downside. Not surprisingly, Threadless has sold every T-shirt that it has printed. Moreover, it has a cult-like following and is outperforming established companies such as Old Navy and Urban Outfitters with their more formulaic T-shirt designs.[48]

GAINING & SUSTAINING COMPETITIVE ADVANTAGE

>> **LO 1-7**
Critically evaluate the role that different stakeholders play in the firm's quest for competitive advantage.

STAKEHOLDERS

Each chapter contains a section entitled *Gaining & Sustaining Competitive Advantage,* in which we put one specific theory or concept under the magnifying glass to critically evaluate if and how it is linked to competitive advantage, the overarching goal in strategic management. To accomplish this, we combine strategic management research with real-world observations. We conclude this chapter by looking at stakeholders and their relationship to competitive advantage.

Successful business strategies generate value for society. When firms or individuals compete in their own self-interest while obeying the law and acting ethically, they ultimately create value. In so doing, they make society better.[49] Value creation lays the foundation for all the important benefits successful economies can provide: education, public safety, and health care, among others. Superior performance allows a firm to reinvest some of its profits to accrue more resources and thus to grow. This in turn provides more opportunities for employment and fulfilling careers. In the chapter opener, we saw that Google created tremendous value, and with it career opportunities. In contrast, strategic mistakes can be expensive. Conservative estimates of the ill-fated AOL TimeWarner merger suggest it destroyed about $100 billion of shareholder value and with it many employment and career opportunities.

Competitive advantage, therefore, not only is of interest to the CEO or shareholders, but also directly affects every person who has an interest in a company. These persons are stakeholders—individuals or groups who can affect or are affected by the actions of a firm.[50] They have a claim or interest in the performance and continued survival of the firm. As shown in Exhibit 1.8, *internal stakeholders* include stockholders, employees (including executives, managers, and workers), and board members. *External stakeholders* include customers, suppliers, alliance partners, creditors, unions, communities, and governments at various levels (local, state, federal, and supranational in the case of the European Union). As Exhibit 1.8 indicates, all stakeholders make specific contributions to the firm, which in turn provides different types of inducements to different stakeholders. The firm, therefore, has a multifaceted exchange relationship with a number of diverse internal and external stakeholders. (Given the importance of stakeholders to firm performance, we take up this topic again in Chapter 12 when studying strategy implementation.)

Some stakeholders can exert a powerful influence on firms. In some instances, firms are able to *create* a competitive advantage but fail to *capture* it because of actions of their stakeholders.[51] This sounds like a contradiction, doesn't it? It is not. Consider this: Once a firm has created a competitive advantage, a battle can ensue over how the spoils of that competitive advantage are split among the firm's different stakeholders.[52] In the U.S. car industry, the United Auto Workers (UAW) had such a stronghold on GM, Chrysler, and Ford that some argue they were a major factor in creating a competitive disadvantage

stakeholders
Individuals or groups who can affect or are affected by the actions of a firm.

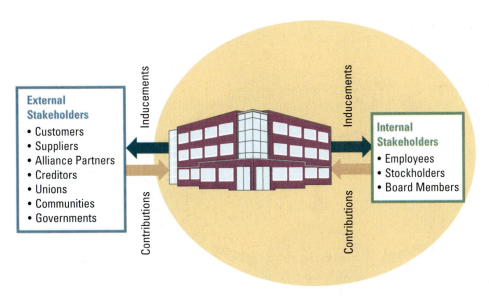

EXHIBIT 1.8

Internal and External
Stakeholders in an
Exchange Relationship
with the Firm

(although management signed the labor contracts with the unions).[53] In the investment banking industry, employees are powerful stakeholders. Skilled human capital is one of the most important resources in investment banking (as in other professional services such as management consulting and law firms). As a consequence of their strong position, the combined annual bonuses of investment banks' employees frequently exceed the bank's net income. In 2007, the year before the financial meltdown, the net income of the big-five U.S. investment banks combined (Bear Sterns, Goldman Sachs, Lehman Brothers, Merrill Lynch, and Morgan Stanley) was a little over $10 billion, and the total of the bonuses paid to the employees was close to $40 billion.[54] During 2008, the worst year in terms of stock performance since the Great Depression, the big-five investment banks lost $25 billion, but still paid bonuses that exceeded $25 billion.[55] These data show that although investment banks clearly have valuable resources (namely, employees) that can create competitive advantage, those same resources are powerful stakeholders that can capture the value they create. By capturing that value, the employee stakeholders left less value for other stakeholders, such as stockholders or customers.

These examples show that although some stakeholders have a strong influence in helping a firm gain and sustain competitive advantage, they also capture much of the value created because these key employees realize how critical they are in creating the value in the first place. Not all stakeholder groups are created equal, and their differential power influences how the economic value created is distributed among different stakeholder groups. If some stakeholders are able to extract significant value, the firm's competitive advantage may not be realized when comparing overall firm performance to that of competitors. 🔍

THE AFI STRATEGY FRAMEWORK

A successful strategy details a set of goal-directed actions that managers intend to take to improve or maintain overall firm performance. Building strategy is the result of three broad management tasks:

1. Analyze (A)
2. Formulate (F)
3. Implement (I)

EXHIBIT 1.9

The AFI Strategy Framework and Text Outline

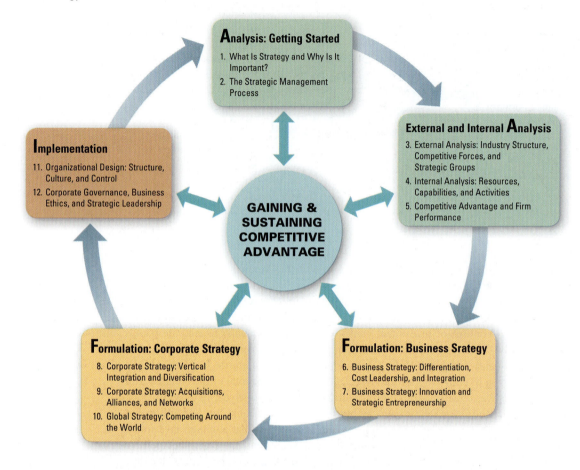

These are the pillars of research and knowledge about strategic management. Although we will study each task one at a time, they are highly interdependent and frequently happen simultaneously. A firm cannot really formulate a strategy without thinking about how to implement it, for instance, and while implementing a strategy, managers are constantly analyzing the need to adjust to changing circumstances. We've captured those relationships in the **AFI strategy framework,** shown in Exhibit 1.9. This model links the three interdependent management tasks—analyze, formulate, and implement. What we want our model to do is explain and predict differences in firm performance. This information will allow managers to conceive of and implement a strategy that can improve its performance and result in competitive advantage.

In each of the three broad management tasks, managers focus on specific *questions*, listed next. (We address those questions in specific chapters, as indicated.)

AFI strategy framework A model that links three interdependent strategic management tasks—analyze, formulate, and implement—that, together, help firms conceive of and implement a strategy that can improve performance and result in competitive advantage.

Strategy analysis (*A*):

- The strategic management process: *What are our vision, mission, and values? What is our process for "making" strategy (how does strategy come about)?* (Chapter 2)
- External analysis: *What effects do forces in the external environment have on strategy and competitive advantage?* (Chapter 3)

- Internal analysis: *What effects do our internal resources and capabilities have on strategy and competitive advantage?* (Chapter 4)
- Firm performance: *How can we measure competitive advantage?* (Chapter 5)

Strategy formulation (*F*):

- Business strategy: *How should we compete?* (Chapters 6 and 7)
- Corporate strategy: *Where should we compete?* (Chapters 8 and 9)
- Global strategy: *Where and how should we compete around the world?* (Chapter 10)

Strategy implementation (*I*):

- Organizational design: *How should we organize to put the formulated strategy into practice?* (Chapter 11)
- Corporate governance, business ethics, and strategic leadership: *What type of strategic leadership and corporate governance do we need? How do we anchor our decision in business ethics?* (Chapter 12)

The AFI strategy framework shown in Exhibit 1.9 will be repeated at the beginning of each of the book's parts, to help show where we are in our study of the firm's quest to gain and sustain competitive advantage.

CHAPTERCASE 1 | *Consider This . . .*

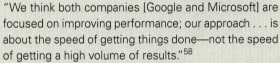

ON THE OPENING PAGE of the chapter, ChapterCase 1 provides background information about a quest for competitive advantage taking place in the Internet-search market. Microsoft's Bing picked up a new partner—Facebook—in its continuing journey to unseat Google from the top of the search engine business. In terms usually reserved for a hot new Silicon Valley startup, Facebook's CEO, Mark Zuckerberg, announced the company's surprising decision to partner with the "really scrappy . . . underdog" Bing, rather than the incumbent Google. Zuckerberg stated, "When you're an incumbent in an area . . . there is a tension between innovating and trying new things versus what you already have."[56] Perhaps the announcement shouldn't have been such a surprise. After all, in 2007 Microsoft did invest $240 million, for an ownership share of less than 2 percent, in privately held Facebook.[57]

Microsoft and Facebook are rolling out a variety of features to make "search more social." If, say, you are looking for a new restaurant in your area, Bing searches can include data on what your Facebook friends have "liked." A view of Microsoft's attempt to unseat Google can be found from Bing director Lisa Gurry, who notes, "We think both companies [Google and Microsoft] are focused on improving performance; our approach . . . is about the speed of getting things done—not the speed of getting a high volume of results."[58]

Thinking about this chapter's opening case, answer the following questions.

1. Google was not the first search engine on the Internet, but it has been the most successful for a decade. What is Google's competitive advantage?

2. LinkExchange was created in 1996 by Sanjay Madan and Tony Hsieh (more recently with Zappos) and, as noted in the case, was purchased by Microsoft in 1998. Why was Microsoft not interested in keeping the Keywords project in 2000?

3. What strategy and business model is Microsoft using today with Bing to try to succeed in the Internet-search business?

Take-Away Concepts

This chapter defined strategy and competitive advantage and set the stage for further study of strategic management, as summarized by the following learning objectives and related take-away concepts.

LO 1-1 Define competitive advantage, sustainable competitive advantage, competitive disadvantage, and competitive parity.

>> Competitive advantage is always judged relative to other competitors or the industry average.

>> To obtain a competitive advantage, a firm must either create more value for customers while keeping its cost comparable to competitors, or it must provide value equivalent to competitors but at lower cost.

>> A firm able to dominate competitors for prolonged periods of time has a sustained competitive advantage.

>> A firm that continuously underperforms its rivals or the industry average has a competitive disadvantage.

>> Two or more firms that perform at the same level have competitive parity.

LO 1-2 Define strategy and explain its role in a firm's quest for competitive advantage.

>> Strategy is the set of goal-directed actions a firm intends to take in its quest to gain and sustain competitive advantage.

>> An effective strategy requires that strategic trade-offs be recognized and addressed—e.g., between value creation and the costs to create the value.

>> Managers' strategic assumptions are an outflow of their theory of how to compete. Successful strategy requires three integrative management tasks—analysis, formulation, and implementation.

>> When managers align their assumptions closely with competitive realities, they can create and implement successful strategies, resulting in value creation and superior firm performance.

>> When managers' theories about how to gain and sustain competitive advantage do not reflect reality, their firm's strategy will destroy rather than create value, leading to inferior firm performance.

LO 1-3 Explain the role of firm effects and industry effects in determining firm performance.

>> A firm's performance is more closely related to its managers' actions (firm effects) than to the external circumstances surrounding it (industry effects).

>> Firm and industry effects, however, *are interdependent and thus both are relevant in determining firm performance.*

LO 1-4 Describe the role of corporate, business, and functional managers in strategy formulation and implementation.

>> Corporate executives must provide answers to the question of *where* to compete (in industries, markets, and geographies), and *how to create synergies* among different business units.

>> General (or business) managers must answer the strategic question of *how to compete* in order to achieve superior performance. They must manage and align all value-chain activities for competitive advantage.

>> Functional managers are responsible for *implementing business strategy* within a single functional area.

LO 1-5 Outline how business models put strategy into action.

>> To put a firm's strategy into action, a business model must: (1) translate the firm's strategy into competitive tactics and initiatives, and (2) implement the strategy through effective structures, processes, culture, and procedures.

LO 1-6 Describe and assess the opportunities and challenges managers face in the 21st century.

>> The competitive landscape of the 21st century is characterized by ever-faster technological change in a truly global marketplace.

>> Examples of industries that seem likely to provide good future opportunities are health care, the green economy, and Web 2.0.

LO 1-7 Critically evaluate the role that different stakeholders play in the firm's quest for competitive advantage.

>> Stakeholders are individuals or groups that have a claim or interest in the performance and continued survival of the firm; they make specific contributions for which they expect rewards in return.

>> Internal stakeholders include stockholders, employees (including executives, managers, and workers), and board members.

>> External stakeholders include customers, suppliers, alliance partners, creditors, unions, communities, and governments at various levels.

>> Some stakeholders are more powerful than others, and may extract significant rewards from a firm, so much that any firm-level competitive advantage may be negated.

Key Terms

AFI strategy framework *(p. 20)*

Bottom of the pyramid *(p. 15)*

Business model *(p. 11)*

Competitive advantage *(p. 4)*

Competitive disadvantage *(p. 5)*

Competitive parity *(p. 5)*

Co-opetition *(p. 6)*

Crowdsourcing *(p. 17)*

Externalities *(p. 16)*

Firm effects *(p. 8)*

Industry effects *(p. 8)*

Stakeholders *(p. 18)*

Strategic business unit (SBU) *(p. 10)*

Strategic management *(p. 4)*

Strategy *(p. 6)*

Sustainable competitive advantage *(p. 5)*

Discussion Questions

1. How is a strategy different from a business model? How is it similar?

2. Threadless (in Strategy Highlight 1.1) is an example of a firm building on its customer base to use new products and also to participate in the design and vetting of popular designs. In the summer of 2010, Dell Computer announced a partnership with Threadless for designs on its laptop computers. For a small additional fee (and an extra day's delay in shipping), you can get a Threadless design etched on your new Dell laptop.[59] Why do you think Dell is keen on offering this service? What other firms use this crowdsourcing technique? Where else might this type of business model show up in the future?

3. As noted in the chapter, research found that firm effects are more important than industry effects. What does this mean? Can you think of situations where this might not be true?

4. This chapter introduces three different levels appropriate for strategic considerations (see Exhibit 1.3). In what situations would some of these levels be more important than others? How should the organization ensure the proper attention to each level of strategy as needed?

Ethical/Social Issues

1. Given that traditional U.S. firms such as IBM have over 70 percent of their employees and almost two-thirds of revenues come from outside the United States, what is an appropriate definition of a "U.S. firm"? Is there any special consideration a firm should have for its "home country"?

2. Corporate leaders are responsible for guiding the firm's strategies. Their goal is to help the firm gain and sustain a competitive advantage and thus

a profit for the shareholders. What responsibility do company managers have for other consequences of their strategies? For example, should Walmart try to mitigate the negative impact its arrival in communities can have on small locally owned stores? Why or why not? Explain.

Small Group Exercises

SMALL GROUP EXERCISE 1

The chapter argues that Microsoft and Google have quite different business models. In 2009, Microsoft revenues were $58.4 billion, an amount that was down 3 percent from 2008 levels (the first annual decline in Microsoft's history). Google had sales of $23.6 billion—an increase of 9 percent over its 2008 levels.[60]

Form a group of three or four students and spend 5 to 10 minutes discussing one of the following questions. (Your instructor may assign the question.)

1. Is this revenue downturn a sign that Microsoft is in trouble or just a result of the recession over the period? Should Microsoft change any of its strategies based on this information?

2. While Google increased sales, 97 percent of its revenues came from advertising. Is this a problem going forward? Should it change any of its strategies?

3. Apple and IBM are two firms in the competitive landscape. Should Microsoft (Google) be more proactive in addressing these competitors?

SMALL GROUP EXERCISE 2

Corporations are starting to become more aware of blogging on the Internet. Blogging can be a factor that can increase buyers' ability to have either positive or negative effects on a firm.

In one well-publicized case, journalist/blogger Jeff Jarvis of www.buzzmachine.com blogged about problems with a Dell computer he purchased. His site was inundated with others who also had poor experiences with Dell. The "Dell hell" uproar resulted in Dell not only calling Mr. Jarvis and resolving his problem but opening its own blog www.dell.com/blogs. Additionally, some time later Mr. Jarvis visited Dell's headquarters and wrote an article for *BusinessWeek* entitled "Dell Learns to Listen."[61]

1. Use a search engine to find large companies that include a blog on their official website. (Keywords "fortune 500 blogs" will steer you to many lists of such companies.)

2. What seems to be the primary purpose of most of the blogs you found?

3. Does the blog seem to be updated regularly?

4. Does the blog allow users to post comments or questions to the firm? If so, do any of the questions get answered by the company?

Strategy Term Project

PROJECT OVERVIEW

The goal of the strategy term project is to give you practical experience with the elements of strategic management. Each end-of-chapter assignment requires data collection and analysis relating the material discussed in the chapter to the firm you select here for study throughout the course. At the end of each chapter, we make additional stages of a strategic analysis available. The goal of this term-long project is to give you a tangible application of many of the concepts discussed in the text. By the end of the project, you will not only have practice in using key strategic management components and processes to increase your understanding of the material, but you also will be able to conduct a complete strategic management analysis of any company.

MODULE 1: INITIAL FIRM SELECTION AND REVIEW

In this first module, you will identify a firm to study for this project. We suggest you select one company and use it for each module in this term project. Choose a firm that you find interesting or one that is part of an industry you would like to know more about. Throughout the modules, you will be required to obtain and analyze a significant amount of data about the firm. Therefore, a key criterion is also to choose a firm that has data available for you to gather.

The primary approach to this project is to select a publicly held firm. Many large firms such as Apple, Coca-Cola, and GE have been widely reported on in the business and popular press, and a wealth of information is available on them. Other medium-sized public firms such as GameStop, Netflix, and Under Armour can be used as example firms for this project. One cautionary note: For firms that are less than three years public or in industries that are not well-defined, it will take some additional reflection to properly identify such items as competitors and suppliers. But if it is a firm you are truly motivated to study, the effort can be quite rewarding.

Relevant data on all public firms can be freely obtained using web services such as Edgar (www.sec.gov/edgar.shtml). Annual reports for firms also are a treasure-trove of information. These reports and other quarterly update materials are often available from the firm's own website (look for "about us" or "investor relations" tabs, often located at the bottom of the company's website). Additionally, most university and public libraries have access to large databases of articles from many trade publications. (Factiva and ABI/Proquest are two examples.) Company profiles of a variety of publicly listed firms are available at reliable websites such as Hoovers.com and finance.yahoo.com. Also, many industries have quite active trade associations that will have websites and publications that can also be useful in this process. Your local librarian can likely provide you some additional resources that may be licensed for library use or otherwise not available online. Examples of these are Value Line Ratings & Reports and Datamonitor.

A second approach to this project is to select a smaller firm in your area. These firms may have coverage in the local press. However, if the firm is not public, you will need to ensure you have access to a wide variety of data from the firm. If this is a firm for which you have worked or where you know people, please check ahead of time to be sure the firm is willing to share its information with you. This approach can work well, especially if the firm is interested in a detailed analysis of its strategic position. But to be successful with this project, be sure you will have access to a broad range of data and information (perhaps including interviews of key managers at the firm).

If you are in doubt on how to select a firm, check with your instructor before proceeding. In some instances, your instructor will assign firms to the study groups.

For this module, answer the following questions:

1. Provide a brief history of the company.

2. List the top management of the firm and note what experience and leadership skills they bring to the firm. If a larger conglomerate, list both corporate and business managers.

3. What is the principal business model of the firm? (How does the firm make most of its profits?)

*my*Strategy

HOW TO POSITION YOURSELF FOR CAREER ADVANTAGE

As the chapter discussed, firm-level decisions have a significant impact on the success or failure of organizations. Industry-level effects, however, can also play a role. Many considerations go into deciding what career choices you make during your working life. The chapter notes that some sectors (such as health care, the green economy, and Web 2.0) are expected to grow faster than others.

At the top of the next page is a sample of revenue growth rates in various industries for a recent five-year period.

Sample Five-Year Growth Rates (2005–2009)[62]

Industry Name	Change in Sales	Industry Name	Change in Sales
Power	54.51%	Medical supplies	12.87%
Petroleum (production)	44.64%	**Total market average**	**12.79%**
Pharmacy services	43.68%	Apparel	0.50%
Insurance (property/casualty)	37.60%	Retail stores	0.49%
Advertising	35.99%	Banking	0.00%
Biotechnology	35.06%	Semiconductor equipment	−16.66%
Pharmaceuticals	24.88%	Homebuilding	−30.52%
Natural gas (diversified)	24.54%	Public/private equity	−32.41%
E-commerce	20.32%	Insurance (life)	−71.81%
Securities brokerage	16.20%		
Telecommunication services	16.05%		
Entertainment technology	15.99%		
Computer software/services	15.26%		
Internet	13.71%		
Chemical (diversified)	13.52%		

1. If you are about to embark on a new career, what effect should the likelihood of industry growth play in your decision?

2. Why could growth rates be an important consideration? Why not?

Endnotes

1. This ChapterCase is based on the following sources: "Yahoo to buy Overture for $1.63 billion," CNET News, July 14, 2003; "Microsoft bid to beat Google builds on a history of misses," *The Wall Street Journal,* January 16, 2009; "Yahoo tie-up is latest sign tide turning for Microsoft's Ballmer," *The Wall Street Journal,* July 30, 2009; "Bingoo! A deal between Microsoft and Yahoo!" *The Economist,* July 30, 2009; and "Google, Microsoft spar on antitrust," *The Wall Street Journal,* March 1, 2010.

2. For an in-depth discussion, see Lewis, M. (2003), *Moneyball: The Art of Winning an Unfair Game* (New York: Norton).

3. Porter, M. E. (1980), *Competitive Strategy: Techniques for Analyzing Competitors* (New York: The Free Press).

4. Top 15 Global Products (2009), *IMS Health,* www.imshealth.com.

5. Ibid.

6. This section draws on: Porter, M. E. (1996), "What is strategy?" *Harvard Business Review,* November–December: 61–78; and Porter, M. E. (1980), *Competitive Strategy.*

7. Dyer, J. H., and H. Singh (1998), "The relational view: Cooperative strategy and sources of interorganizational competitive advantage," *Academy of Management Review* 23: 660–679; and Rothaermel, F. T., and A. Hess (2010), "Innovation strategies combined," *MIT Sloan Management Review,* Spring: 12–15.

8. Brandenburger, A. M., and B. J. Nalebuff (1996), *Co-opetition* (New York: Currency Doubleday); and Gnyawali, D., J. He, and R. Madhavan, (2006), "Impact of co-opetition on firm competitive behavior: An empirical examination," *Journal of Management* 32: 507–530.

9. Christensen, C. M., and M. E. Raynor (2003), "Why hard-nosed executives should care about management theory," *Harvard Business Review,* September: 1–10.

10. Drucker, P. (1994), "The theory of business," *Harvard Business Review,* September–October: 95–105.

11. Duke, M. T. (2010), presentation at the Georgia Institute of Technology, April 1, 2010.

12. For more details, see Rothaermel, Frank T., with V. P. Singh (2013), "Tesla Motors and U.S. Auto Industry," case study, in Rothaermel, F. T., *Strategic Management* (Burr Ridge, IL: McGraw-Hill).

13. "Ford touts its small-car resurgence," *The Wall Street Journal,* January 11, 2010; and "Epiphany in Dearborn. How Ford turned a crash into a profit—without a government bail-out," *The Economist,* December 9, 2010.

14. Hansen, G. S., and B. Wernerfelt (1989), "Determinants of firm performance: The relative importance of economic and organizational factors," *Strategic Management Journal* 10: 399–411; and McGahan, A. M., and M. E. Porter (1997), "How much does industry matter, really?" *Strategic Management Journal* 18: 15–30.

15. The remaining 35–50 percent of variance in a firm's profitability is due to corporate-parent effects, year effects, and unexplained variation. This interesting debate unfolds in the following articles, among others: Rumelt, R. P. (1991), "How much does industry matter?" *Strategic Management Journal* 12: 167–185; and McGahan, A. M., and M. E. Porter (1997), "How much does industry matter, really?" *Strategic Management Journal* 18: 15–30.

16. See recent J.D. Power's quality reports, for example, as presented in "Ford touts its small-car resurgence," *The Wall Street Journal,* January 11, 2010.

17. This discussion is based on Porter, M. E. (1996), "What is strategy?" *Harvard Business Review,* November–December: 61–78.

18. This example is drawn from O'Reilly, C. A., B. Harreld, and M. Tushman (2009), "Organizational ambidexterity: IBM and emerging business opportunities," *California Management Review* 51: 75–99.

19. This is a play on the acronym IBM, which stands for International Business Machines.

20. This discussion is based on Anderson, C. (2009), *Free: The Future of a Radical Price* (New York: Hyperion).

21. Chen, M. J. (1996), "Competitor analysis and interfirm rivalry: Toward a theoretical integration," *Academy of Management Review* 21: 100–134; Gimeno, J. (1999), "Reciprocal threats in multimarket rivalry: Staking out 'spheres of influence' in the U.S. airline industry," *Strategic Management Journal* 20: 101–128; and Gimeno, J., and C. Y. Woo (1999), "Multimarket competition, economies of scale, and firm performance," *Academy of Management Journal* 42: 239–259.

22. Drucker, P. (1992), *The Age of Discontinuity: Guidelines to Our Changing Society* (New York: Transaction Publishers); D'Aveni, R. (1994), *Hypercompetition. Managing the Dynamics of Strategic Maneuvering* (New York: The Free Press); Friedman, T. L. (2005), *The World Is Flat. A Brief History of the Twenty-first Century* (New York: Farrar, Straus and Giroux); Esty, D. C., and A. S. Winston (2006), *Green to Gold. How Smart Companies Use Environmental Strategy to Innovate, Create Value, and Build Competitive Advantage* (Hoboken, NJ: Wiley); and Friedman, T. (2008), *Hot, Flat, and Crowded: Why We Need a Green Revolution—and How It Can Renew America* (New York: Farrar, Straus, and Giroux).

23. Prensky, M. (2001), "Digital natives, digital immigrants." From *On the Horizon,* Vol. 9, No. 5, October, MCB University Press.

24. Ibid.

25. Friedman, T. L. (2005), *The World Is Flat.*

26. Cairncross, F. (1997), *The Death of Distance: How the Communications Revolution Will Change Our Lives* (London, U.K.: Orion Business Books); and Kotha, S., V. Rindova, and F. T. Rothaermel (2001), "Assets and actions: Firm-specific factors in the internationalization of U.S. internet firms," *Journal of International Business Studies* 32: 769–791.

27. The 27 EU member states are Austria, Belgium, Bulgaria, Czech Republic, Cyprus, Denmark, Estonia, Finland, France, Germany, Greece, Italy, Ireland, Latvia, Lithuania, Luxembourg, Hungary, Malta, the Netherlands, Poland, Portugal, Romania, Slovakia, Slovenia, Spain, Sweden, and the United Kingdom. (Source: www.europa.eu.)

28. The Eurozone countries are Austria, Belgium, Finland, France, Germany, Greece, Italy, Luxembourg, Malta, the Netherlands, Portugal, Slovakia, Slovenia, and Spain. The euro is used by five other European countries that are not part of the Eurozone. In total, some 327 million Europeans are using the euro. Another 175 million people worldwide use currencies that are pegged to the euro, making it the second largest reserve currency in the world after the U.S. dollar. (Source: www.europa.eu.)

29. IBM annual reports. Various years.

30. "IBM to cut U.S. jobs, expand in India," *The Wall Street Journal,* March 26, 2009.

31. Peng, M. (2009), *Global Strategy,* 2nd ed. (Mason, OH: South-Western Cengage).

32. Prahalad, C. K., and S. Hart (2002), "The future at the bottom of the pyramid," *Strategy+Business* 26: 54–67; Prahalad, C. K. (2004), *The Future at the Bottom of the Pyramid* (Upper Saddle River, NJ: Wharton School Publishing); and Hart, S. (2005), *Capitalism at the Crossroads* (Upper Saddle River, NJ: Wharton School Publishing).

33. "The new people's car," *The Economist,* March 26, 2009.

34. For an in-depth discussion of future industries and its strategic as well as career implications, see: Reich, R. (2000), *The Future of Success. Working and Living in the New Economy* (New York: Knopf); Canton, J. (2006), *The Extreme Future. The Top Trends that Will Reshape the World in the Next 20 Years* (New York: Penguin); and Shuen, A. (2008), *Web 2.0: A Strategy Guide* (Sebastopol, CA: O'Reilly Media).

35. "Health-care providers pledge to try to curb costs," *The Wall Street Journal,* May 11, 2009.

36. "GE launches 'healthymagination'; Will commit $6 billion to enable better health focusing on cost, access and quality," *GE Press Release,* May 7, 2009. See also: www.healthymagination.com.

37. See data compiled by NASA's Goddard Institute for Space Studies and reports by the Intergovernmental Panel on Climate Change (IPCC).

38. "BP hit by doubts over ability to pay for costs of oil spill," *The Wall Street Journal,* June 9, 2010.

39. King, A., and M. Lenox (2002), "Does it really pay to be green?" *Journal of Industrial Ecology* 5: 105–117.

40. Hart, S. (1997), "Beyond greening: Strategies for a sustainable world," *Harvard Business Review,* January–February.

41. "The change we need," *The Wall Street Journal,* November 3, 2008.

42. "China races ahead of U.S. in drive to go solar," *The New York Times,* August 25, 2009.

43. Esty, D. C., and A. S. Winston (2006), *Green to Gold*; and Friedman, T. (2008), *Hot, Flat, and Crowded.*

44. "Another century of oil? Getting more from current reserves," *Scientific American,* October 2009.

45. "Buffett bets big on railroads," *The Wall Street Journal,* November 4, 2009.

46. Shuen, A. (2008), *Web 2.0.*

47. For an in-depth discussion on network effects see: Arthur, W. B. (1989), "Competing technologies, increasing returns, and lock-in by historical events," *Economic Journal* 99: 116–131; Arthur, W. B. (1990), "Positive feedbacks in the economy," *Scientific American* 262: 92–99; Arthur, W. B. (1996), "Increasing returns and the new world of business," *Harvard Business Review:* 100–109; and Shuen, A. (2008), *Web 2.0.*

48. This Strategy Highlight is based on: Rothaermel, F. T., and S. Sugiyama (2001), "Virtual Internet communities and commercial success: Individual and community-level theory grounded in the atypical case of TimeZone.com," *Journal of Management* 27: 297–312; Hippel, E. von (2005), *Democratizing Innovation* (Cambridge, MA: MIT Press); Howe, J. (2008), *Crowdsourcing. Why the Power of the Crowd Is Driving the Future of Business* (New York: Crown); Ogawa, S., and F. T. Piller (2006), "Collective Customer Commitment: Reducing the risks of new product development," *MIT Sloan Management Review* 47 (Winter): 65–72; Shuen, A. (2008), *Web 2.0*; and Surowiecki, J. (2004), *The Wisdom of Crowds. Why the Many Are Smarter than the Few and How Collective Wisdom Shapes Business, Economies, Societies, and Nations* (New York: Doubleday).

49. Smith, A. (1776), *An Inquiry into the Nature and Causes of the Wealth of Nations,* 5th ed. (published 1904) (London: Methuen and Co.).

50. Freeman, E. R. (1984), *Strategic Management: A Stakeholder Approach* (Boston, MA: Pitman); Freeman, E. R., and J. McVea (2001), "A stakeholder approach to strategic management," in Hitt, M. A., E. R. Freeman, and J. S. Harrison (eds.), *The Handbook of Strategic Management* (Oxford, U.K.: Blackwell), pp. 189–207; and Phillips, R. (2003), *Stakeholder Theory and Organizational Ethics* (San Francisco, CA: Berrett-Koehler).

51. Coff, R. (1999), "When competitive advantage doesn't lead to performance: Resource-based theory and stakeholder bargaining power," *Organization Science* 10: 119–133.

52. Freeman, E. R. (1984), *Strategic Management;* and Phillips, R. (2003). *Stakeholder Theory and Organizational Ethics.*

53. Lieberman, M., and R. Dhawan (2005), "Assessing the resource base of Japanese and U.S. auto producers: A stochastic frontier production function approach," working paper, UCLA Anderson School of Management.

54. "On street, new reality on pay sets in," *The Wall Street Journal,* January 31, 2009.

55. "Goldman Sachs staff set for bumper bonuses as bank earns $38 million per day," *The Guardian,* July 31, 2009.

56. Carr, A., "Facebook friends an 'underdog,' Microsoft," *Fast Company,* October 13, 2010.

57. "Bing upgrades draw upon Facebook, other partners," Associated Press, San Francisco, December 15, 2010.

58. Carr, A., "'Underdog' Bing talks Facebook partnership, Google rivalry," *Fast Company,* December 17, 2010.

59. Saadi, S., "Crowdsourcer Threadless' life beyond T-shirts," *Bloomberg BusinessWeek*, September 16, 2010.

60. Data compiled from company annual reports 2009.

61. Jeff, J. (2009), *What Would Google Do?* (New York: Collins Business); and "Dell learns to listen: The computer maker takes to the blogosphere to repair its tarnished image," *BusinessWeek,* October 29, 2007.

62. Compiled from Value Line Data by Dr. A. Damodaran, NYU, http://pages .stern.nyu.edu/~adamodar/.

CHAPTER 2

The Strategic Management Process

LEARNING OBJECTIVES

After studying this chapter, you should be able to:

LO 2-1   Explain the role of vision, mission, and values in the strategic management process.

LO 2-2   Describe and evaluate the role of strategic intent in achieving long-term goals.

LO 2-3   Distinguish between customer-oriented and product-oriented missions and identify strategic implications.

LO 2-4   Critically evaluate the relationship between mission statements and competitive advantage.

LO 2-5   Explain why anchoring a firm in ethical values is essential for long-term success.

LO 2-6   Compare and contrast strategic planning, scenario planning, and strategy as planned emergence, and discuss strategic implications.

Teach For America: Inspiring Future Leaders

TEACH FOR AMERICA is a nonprofit organization that recruits college graduates and professionals to teach for two years in socially and economically disadvantaged communities in the United States. The idea behind Teach For America was developed by then 21-year-old Wendy Kopp as her senior thesis at Princeton. Kopp was convinced young people today are searching for meaning in their lives by making a positive contribution to society.

The genius of Kopp's idea was to turn on its head the social perception of teaching—to make what appeared to be an unattractive, low-status job into a high-prestige professional opportunity. Kopp established a mission for the organization she had in mind: to *eliminate educational inequality by enlisting our nation's most promising future leaders in the effort.* Her underlying assumption was that significant numbers of young people have a desire to take on meaningful responsibility in order to have a positive impact on the lives of others. To be chosen for TFA is a badge of honor. In 2010, TFA received some 46,000 applications for only about 4,500 positions across the country (paying the same as all other first-year teachers, ranging from $30,000 to $51,500 a year). This translates to a mere 12 percent acceptance rate, comparable to being accepted to study at Harvard (a little less than 10 percent), Stanford (12 percent), or MIT (14 percent).[1]

After reading the chapter, you will find more about this case, with related questions, on page 47.

▲ **PERSUADING** highly qualified teachers to take up jobs in inner-city Detroit or Los Angeles and some rural areas in West Virginia or the Mississippi Delta region has been an elusive goal for many decades. How did an undergraduate student accomplish what the Department of Education, state and local school boards, and the national Parent-Teacher Association could not accomplish, despite trying for decades and spending billions of dollars in the process? First, Kopp established a clear mission that appealed to a large number of young people. Second, she made the hiring process highly selective and turned down many who might easily qualify for teaching jobs. Making TFA highly selective changed the social perception of teaching in underprivileged areas. Suddenly, it was an honor (and great résumé builder) to be chosen for TFA. In Chapter 2, we move from thinking about why strategy is important to considerations of how firms and other organizations define their vision, mission, and values and then translate them into strategic intent and plans.

VISION, MISSION, AND VALUES

>> LO 2-1
Explain the role of vision, mission, and values in the strategic management process.

In this chapter, we study the strategic management process, which describes the method by which managers conceive of and implement a strategy that can lead to a sustainable competitive advantage. The strategic management process follows the analyze-formulate-implement (AFI) strategy framework introduced in Chapter 1.

Discovering a firm's vision and mission and defining its values are the first steps in the strategic management process. For new organizations, like TFA, the founders usually begin with a driving vision that they must further shape into statements about what they want to accomplish and how they will do so. For existing firms, this step is about fine-tuning their vision and mission as well as reaffirming their values. To begin the strategic management process, managers ask the following questions:

- What do we want to accomplish ultimately? What is our *vision?*
- What are we about? What is our *mission?*
- How do we accomplish our goals? What are our *values?*

To answer questions about vision, mission, and values, managers need to *begin with the end in mind.* Think of building a house. The future owner must communicate her vision to the architect, who draws up a blueprint of the home. The process is iterated a couple of times until all the homeowner's ideas have been translated into the blueprint. Only then does the building of the house begin. The same holds for strategic success. Thus, success is created twice: first by creating, through strategic analysis, a clear mental model of what the firm wants to accomplish, and second by formulating and implementing a strategy that makes this vision a reality. An effectively communicated strategy should guide everyone in the organization.

Visionary Organizations

A vision is a statement about what an organization ultimately wants to accomplish. It captures the company's aspiration. An effective vision pervades the organization with a sense of winning and motivates employees at all levels to aim for the target, while leaving room for individual and team contributions. Employees in visionary companies tend to feel like part of something bigger than themselves. An inspiring vision helps employees find meaning in their work. Monetary rewards form only one part of what motivates people. An effective vision allows employees to reap intrinsic rewards by making the world a better place through their work activities.[2] This in turn is highly motivating for employees, leading to higher organizational performance.[3] Basing actions on its vision, a firm will build the necessary resources and capabilities through continuous organizational learning, including learning from failure, to translate into reality what begins as a "stretch goal."

Vision statements should be forward-looking and inspiring to provide meaning for employees when pursuing the organization's ultimate goals. Take Teach For America (TFA), whose vision is that *"one day, all children in this nation will have the opportunity to attain an excellent education."* It effectively and clearly communicates what TFA ultimately wants to accomplish; it provides an inspiring target to aim for. Exhibit 2.1 contains TFA's vision, mission, and values.

It's not surprising that vision statements can be inspiring and motivating in the not-for-profit sector. Many people would find meaning in wanting to help children attain an excellent education (TFA) or wanting to be "always there," touching the lives of people in need (American Red Cross). But what about for-profit firms? The main difference is the metric by which we assess successful performance. TFA measures its organizational success by the effects its teachers have on student performance. In the for-profit sector,

EXHIBIT 2.1

Teach For America: Vision, Mission, and Values

Vision	One day, all children in this nation will have the opportunity to attain an excellent education.
Mission	Eliminate educational inequality by enlisting our nation's most promising future leaders in the effort.
Values	**Relentless Pursuit of Results:** We assume personal responsibility for achieving ambitious, measurable results in pursuit of our vision. We persevere in the face of challenges, seek resources to ensure the best outcomes, and work toward our goals with a sense of purpose and urgency.
	Sense of Possibility: We approach our work with optimism, think boldly, and greet new ideas openly.
	Disciplined Thought: We think critically and strategically in search of the best answers and approaches, reflect on past experiences and data to draw lessons for the future, and make choices that are deeply rooted in our mission.
	Respect and Humility: We value all who are engaged in this challenging work. We keep in mind the limitations of our own experiences and actively seek out diverse perspectives.
	Integrity: We ensure alignment between our actions and our beliefs, engage in honest self-scrutiny, and do what is right for the broader good.

Source: www.teachforamerica.org

companies typically measure financial performance. Chapter 5 explores the various perspectives by which to measure performance and capture the multifaceted nature of competitive advantage.

Forming Strategic Intent

Strategic intent is the staking out of a desired leadership position in the long term that far exceeds a company's current resources and capabilities.[4] Challenging goals that stretch an individual or an organization can lead to higher performance.[5] Many Japanese competitors set ambitious stretch goals of global leadership (reflected in their missions) and made them a reality: Canon "beat Xerox," Komatsu "encircled Caterpillar," and Honda became "a second Ford." (Today the latter may not sound like a desirable goal, but it was in the 1970s when Honda began its quest for global leadership.) Currently, Chinese companies such as Baidu, BYD, and Lenovo aspire to world leadership. These companies set their ambitious goals when they were only a fraction the size of the companies they were chasing. Indeed, they were so small that initially the market leaders did not even recognize them as potential competitors; many had never competed outside their domestic markets. Yet all made global leadership their mission, with goals so ambitious they exceeded the firms' existing resources and capabilities by a large margin. Effective use of stretch goals created at all levels of the organization an obsession with winning that has been sustained over several decades.[6]

Strategic intent allows managers to operationalize their vision because it is not only forward-looking and future-oriented but also helps in identifying steps that need to be taken to make a vision become reality. Creating and executing strategy to achieve a strategic fit with *today's* environment is like driving a car while looking only in the rearview mirror. The focus should be how to create competitive advantage *tomorrow*. In fact, rather than

>> **LO 2-2**
Describe and evaluate the role of strategic intent in achieving long-term goals.

---

strategic management process
Method by which managers conceive of and implement a strategy that can lead to a sustainable competitive advantage.

vision A statement about what an organization ultimately wants to accomplish; it captures the company's aspiration.

strategic intent The staking out of a desired leadership position that far exceeds a company's current resources and capabilities.

Winning Through Strategic Intent

In the aftermath of World War II, an obscure Japanese technology startup firm named Tokyo Tsushin Kogyo K.K. began its life by repairing shortwave radios and inventing an electric rice cooker. Its lead scientist, Masaru Ibuka, thought a portable radio based on transistors might be possible. He conferred with scientists from Bell Labs, the U.S. firm that invented the transistor. They told him a transistor radio was not technologically feasible. Undeterred, Ibuka asked Japan's Ministry of International Trade and Industry (MITI) to obtain a license for the transistor from Bell Labs so he could build the portable radio. MITI turned him down, believing the fledgling firm could not commercialize such cutting-edge technology given its lack of track record and resources.

Ibuka persisted, however. Finally, in 1953 he secured permission to license the transistor. He then created an explicit strategic intent for his firm, focusing on being first to market with an innovative portable transistor radio of the highest possible quality.

Ibuka faced long odds: Radios then were enclosed in large pieces of decorative furniture; at that time, "Made in Japan" was synonymous with poor quality; and by the mid-1950s, Bell Labs scientists had already won two Nobel Prizes for physics. The idea that a Japanese startup working out of makeshift quarters in Tokyo could beat Bell Labs in commercializing the transistor radio seemed preposterous. But Ibuka inspired his hungry engineers to pursue their strategic intent. In 1957, they introduced the world's first pocket transistor radio, the TR-55. It sold 1.5 million units and catapulted the firm to leadership in consumer electronics. In 1958, the company changed its Japanese name to Sony Corporation.

Over time, Sony continually honed its core competency in miniaturization, which allowed it to create the Walkman, Discman, and MP3 players. More recently, though, Sony has fallen on hard times. Blamed on a silo mentality, it was not able to capitalize on its MP3 player or its electronic readers and has lost market share to Apple.[7]

attempting a strategic fit between a firm's resources and capabilities and today's external industry environment, strategic intent creates an extreme misfit by setting ambitious goals and then challenging managers and employees across all organizational levels to close the gap by building the resources and capabilities necessary to accomplish these goals. It does matter where you are today, but more importantly, it matters where you want to go tomorrow. Strategy Highlight 2.1 illustrates the powerful effects that strategic intent can have. It also demonstrates, however, what can happen when a firm accomplishes its strategic intent but then fails to set new stretch goals.

Mission Statements

Building on the vision, organizations establish a **mission,** which describes what an organization actually does—the products and services it plans to provide and the markets in which it will compete. Effective mission statements work through metaphors that help employees make appropriate decisions when faced with day-to-day situations, which sometimes can be novel or stressful.

Let's look at Disney's mission, which is *to make people happy.*[8] Disney's translation of this mission to employees who work at a Disney theme park is that they are not mere employees, they are cast members. Similarly, visitors to the park are not customers, they are audience members, there to enjoy a show. This metaphor has important implications for employees' behavior, beginning before they are even hired. Rather than interviewing for a job, for instance, they audition for a role, like cast members in a play. Thus any time a Disney park employee is in uniform, he or she is actually "on stage," delivering a performance. Even street sweepers (often college students on break) are part of the cast. Because they have the closest contact with guests, they are trained in great detail and are evaluated not only on personal neatness and job performance, but also on their knowledge about rides, parades, and restaurant and restroom locations. Like cast members in the theater, Disney employees pull off daily "the show must go on" performances that allow them to fulfill Disney's mission to make people happy.

CUSTOMER-ORIENTED MISSIONS. Disney's mission is aimed at its customers. *A customer-oriented mission* defines a business in terms of providing solutions to customer needs. Companies that have customer-oriented missions ("We are in the business of providing solutions to professional communication needs") tend to be more flexible when adapting to changing environments. In contrast, companies that have product-oriented missions ("We are in the typewriter business") tend to be less flexible and thus more likely to fail. Companies with customer-oriented missions are more likely to maintain strategic flexibility over time.

It is important not to confuse customer-oriented missions with listening to your customer. They are not the same thing! Customer-oriented missions identify a critical need but leave open the means of how to meet this need. It is critical not to define *how* a customer need will be met—because the future is unknowable, and innovation might provide new ways to meet needs that we have not thought of today. Even if customer needs are constant, the organization's mission should be flexible because the *means* of meeting those needs can change over time.

Think about the customer need for personal mobility. About 100 years ago, this need was met by horse-drawn buggies, horseback riding, or by trains for long distances. But Henry Ford had a different idea; he is famous for saying, "If I had listened to my customers, I would have built a better horse and buggy."[9] In contrast, Henry Ford's original mission was *to make the automobile accessible to every American.* He succeeded, and the automobile changed how mobility was achieved. Fast-forward to today: Ford Motor Company's mission is *to provide personal mobility for people around the world.* It does not even mention the automobile. Clearly, Ford is focusing on the consumer need for personal mobility while leaving open the door for how exactly it will fulfill this need. Today, it's with traditional cars and trucks propelled by gas-powered internal combustion engines, with some hybrid electric vehicles in its lineup. In the near future, however, Ford is likely to provide vehicles powered by alternative energy sources like electric power or hydrogen, among other new energy sources. In the far-reaching future, perhaps Ford will even get into the business of individual flying devices. If so, its mission would still be relevant and compel its managers to engage in this future market; a product-oriented mission would not allow for such a degree of strategic flexibility.

PRODUCT-ORIENTED MISSIONS. *Product-oriented missions* define a business in terms of a good or service provided rather than in terms of the customer need to be met. As noted, customer-oriented missions provide greater strategic flexibility than product-oriented missions. The strategic decisions of U.S. railroad companies show the potential shortcomings of defining a business based on a product-oriented mission. Railroads are in the business of moving goods and people from point A to point B by rail. When they started, their short-distance competition was the horse or horse-drawn carriage; there was little long-distance competition (such as ship canals and good roads) to cover the U.S. from coast to coast. Not surprisingly, the early U.S. railroad companies saw their mission as *being in the railroad business,* clearly a product-based definition. Due to their monopoly, especially in long-distance travel, they initially made big money. Indeed, many early fortunes were made in the railroad business. Leland Stanford, who made his fortune as president of the Central and Southern Pacific Companies, later founded and endowed Stanford University with a gift that equals approximately $500 million today (about half his total wealth).

The railroad companies' monopoly did not last. Technological innovations changed the transportation business dramatically. After the introduction of the automobile and the commercial jet, consumers had a wider range of choices, such as trucks and airplanes, to meet their long-distance transportation needs. Rail companies were slow to respond, however, and did not re-define their business in terms of services provided to the consumer. Had they seen themselves as *serving the* full range of *transportation needs of people across America* (a customer-oriented mission), they might have become successful forerunners of modern logistics companies like FedEx or UPS. Recently, the railroad companies seem to

>> **LO 2-3**
Distinguish between customer-oriented and product-oriented missions and identify strategic implications.

mission Description of what an organization actually does—what its business is—and why it does it; can be customer-oriented or product-oriented.

be learning some lessons: CSX Railroad is now re-defining itself as a green-transportation alternative with an ad campaign claiming it can move one ton of freight 423 miles on one gallon of fuel. Yet, its mission remains product-oriented: *to be the safest, most progressive North American railroad.*

Although a product-centric view can potentially limit a company's strategic options, it can also help a company to refocus. Shell Canada provides an example of how dealing with the question, "*What are we about?*" led to a refocusing of the company and as a consequence, superior performance.[10] Although the majority owner was Royal Dutch Shell, Shell Canada was more or less independent; its shares were traded on the Toronto Stock Exchange. In the 1980s, Shell Canada was a widely diversified business with interests not only in oil and gas exploration and distribution, but also in activities ranging from chemicals to forestry. Although it had performance comparable to the industry average, Shell Canada's executives began to focus on the firm's mission during this time. After some soul searching, the company's managers realized that Shell Canada was at its heart a *low-cost producer of oil and gas.* With this new clarity of mission, Shell Canada began to sell off its peripheral businesses to refocus on oil and gas. In 2007, Royal Dutch Shell bought, at a cost of $8.7 billion, the remaining 22 percent of shares that it didn't already own. By refocusing on oil and gas, Shell Canada was able to apply its core competency to increase the value created for customers, and to do this at a low cost. Its mission statement helped Shell Canada focus on the activities that yielded the greatest returns.

GAINING & SUSTAINING COMPETITIVE ADVANTAGE

>> LO 2-4
Critically evaluate the relationship between mission statements and competitive advantage.

MISSION STATEMENTS AND COMPETITIVE ADVANTAGE. So, we must ask, do mission statements help firms gain and sustain competitive advantage? The results are mixed: Having a clearly defined mission helps in some cases, actually hurts in others, and sometimes has no effect on performance, as the following examples demonstrate. (Note that although visions and missions are not entirely synonymous as discussed earlier, many managers use the terms interchangeably.)

Positive Association Between Mission Statements and Competitive Advantage. Researchers have found that visionary companies—those whose stated missions clearly capture the company's aspirations—such as 3M, Hewlett-Packard (HP), Merck, Nordstrom, and Procter & Gamble (P&G)—financially outperformed their peers by a wide margin.[11] An investment of $1 in the general stock market fund in 1926 (equivalent to the Dow Jones Industrial Index today) by 1990 would have grown to $415. Yet, an investment of $1 in a hypothetical stock fund composed of companies researchers identified as visionary would have grown over the same time period to $6,356. This implies visionary companies outperformed average companies by more than 1,400 percent. For visionary companies, superior financial performance is a byproduct of living up to their missions. Merck's mission, for example, is to *preserve and improve human life.*[12] The words of founder George W. Merck still form the basis of Merck's corporate philosophy today: "We try to never forget that medicine is for the people. It is not for profits. The profits follow, and if we have remembered that, they have never failed to appear. The better we have remembered it, the larger they have been."[13]

Negative Association Between Mission Statements and Competitive Advantage. Sometimes a firm's mission statement can hurt its financial performance. Better World Books (BWB), for example, is an online bookstore that focuses on economic, social, and environmental goals. (As we will discuss in Chapter 5, the combination of economic, social, and environmental concerns that can lead to a sustainable strategy is called the *triple-bottom line.*) BWB's stated mission is to *collect and sell books online to fund literacy initiatives worldwide.*[14] Initially, BWB's founders—recent graduates from Notre Dame University—decided to donate 50 percent of the firm's revenues to various non-governmental organizations (NGOs) that promote literacy. After a while, the founders realized that the way they operationalized their mission was threatening the future viability of the venture. They decided they had to reduce their donation commitment from 50 percent of revenues to between 7 and 10 percent. BWB provides an example in which a firm's mission and competitive advantage can be negatively associated, especially when competitive advantage is understood more narrowly as superior financial performance. (We will explore more about the triple-bottom line concept and competitive advantage in Chapter 5.)

No Association Between Mission Statements and Competitive Advantage.

In some cases, mission statements have little or no effect on performance and competitive advantage. Intel Corporation, one of the world's leading silicon innovators, provides an illustrative case. Intel's early mission was to be *the pre-eminent building-block supplier of the PC industry.* Intel designed the first commercial microprocessor chip in 1971 and set the standard for microprocessors in 1978; during the personal computer (PC) revolution in the 1980s, microprocessors became Intel's main line of business. Intel's customers were OEMs (original equipment manufacturers) that produce consumer end-products, such as computer manufacturers HP, IBM, Dell, and Compaq.

In the Internet age, however, the standalone PC as the end-product has become less important. Customers now want to stream video and share photos online. Such activities consume a tremendous amount of computing power. To reflect this shift, Intel in 1999 changed its mission to focus on being *the preeminent building-block supplier to the Internet economy.* Later, in 2008, Intel fully made the shift to a customer-oriented mission: Its current mission statement is to *delight our customers, employees, and shareholders by relentlessly delivering the platform and technology advancements that become essential to the way we work and live.* Part of this shift can be explained by a hugely successful "Intel Inside" advertising campaign in the 1990s that made Intel a household name worldwide.

Intel accomplished superior firm performance over decades through *continuous adaptation* to changing market realities. Yet its formal mission statement lagged the firm's transformations. Intel regularly changed its mission statement *after* it had accomplished successful transformation.[15] In such a case, mission statements and firm performance are clearly not related to one another.

Taken together, what empirical research shows is that sometimes mission statements and firm performance are *associated* with one another. What is less clear, however, is whether these relationships are *causal*—whether an effective mission statement *leads* to competitive advantage. The upshot is that an effective mission statement can lay the foundation upon which to craft a strategy that creates economic value, leading to competitive advantage. (You will learn more about *economic value creation* in Chapter 5, when studying competitive advantage in more depth.)

To be effective, firms do need to back up their mission statements with **strategic commitments,** actions that are costly, long-term oriented, and difficult to reverse. Boeing's decision to develop the 787 Dreamliner, for example, is a multibillion-dollar, multidecade strategic commitment.[16] Without such commitments, the firm's mission statement is just words. Eventually, both employees and external stakeholders may perceive the hollowness of the mission statement and realize that, however good the statement, it will not result in competitive

strategic commitments
Actions that are costly, long-term oriented, and difficult to reverse.

advantage without strategic actions to back it up. Moreover, if the vision-mission-values are not in coherence with each other, then a firm's strategy will necessarily be compromised. Effective alignment is key when translating a mission statement into strategic actions. 🔍

Living the Values

>> LO 2-5
Explain why anchoring a firm in ethical values is essential for long-term success.

Organizational values are the ethical standards and norms that govern the behavior of individuals within a firm or organization (and within society). Strong ethical values, in turn, have two important functions: First, they form a solid foundation on which a firm can build its mission and long-term success. They also are the guardrails put in place so the company can stay on track when pursuing its mission in its quest for competitive advantage.

Employees tend to follow values practiced by strategic leaders. Without commitment and involvement from top managers, any statement of values remains a meaningless public relations exercise. Employees find out very quickly by observing executives' day-to-day decisions whether they are guided by an unchangeable and ethical core that is reflected in the company's mission, or whether they merely pay lip service to its values. True values must be lived with integrity, especially by the top management team. Unethical behavior by top managers is like a virus that spreads quickly throughout the entire organization.

The values espoused by a company provide answers to the question, *How do we accomplish our goals?* They help individuals make choices that are both ethical and effective in advancing the company's goals. For instance, John Hammergren, Chairman and CEO of McKesson, a $110 billion health care company, sees a direct relationship between the company's performance and its values: "At McKesson, we are guided by a common set of values: integrity, customer-first, accountability, respect, and excellence. We call them our ICARE Shared Principles, and they serve as the framework for who we are and how we interact with each other and our customers. These ethics and behavior models are the cornerstones on which we have built our business and our culture."[17] The key issue is the extent to which these ICARE Shared Principles are used in everyday business situations. Do they really guide employee behavior, or are they just a part of public relations?

At McKesson, employees incorporate the ICARE Shared Values into their daily activities. For example, the employees of McKesson's U.S. Pharmaceutical Distribution center worked long overtime hours after the tragedies of hurricanes Katrina and Rita when assisting the Federal Emergency Management Agency (FEMA). One functional-level manager, credits this experience for helping workers to gain a deeper appreciation of the impact their work has on the well-being of thousands of people in need. It also helped families understand the importance of what McKesson's employees do for a living.[18]

Google's values also guided some tough strategic decisions.[19] In 2006, Google entered the Chinese market with a customized search engine (google.cn) to service some 400 million new online customers. This was a self-censored version of its regular search engine (google.com) to comply with China's restrictions on free speech. At that time, Google felt the good that access to its searches, albeit censored, would bring to the Chinese people would outweigh its discomfort with censorship. By 2010, Google felt it could no longer continue to provide self-censored searches; it alleged that the firm was the target of sophisticated hacker attacks, accessing some of its users' Gmail accounts, including those of Chinese human rights activists. Google decided it would no longer censor its searches in China, thus risking having its search engine shut down by the Chinese government. Google's strong values—such as "democracy on the web works," "you can make money without doing evil," and "the need for information crosses all borders"—guided this decision, which had potentially far-reaching strategic consequences.[20] Google now runs its China website on a server in Hong Kong. After several months of negotiations, the Chinese government renewed Google's

organizational values Ethical standards and norms that govern the behavior of individuals within a firm or organization.

license to do business in China.[21] Yet, Google's exit from mainland China further strengthened Baidu's lead with an almost 75 percent share of one of the fastest-growing online markets worldwide.[22] Baidu is a domestic Chinese company founded by Robin Li.

In contrast, when a firm does not have strong organizational values to inform the behavior of its top managers or other employees, major stakeholder value destruction is likely to follow. In the following examples, managers acted unethically and illegally:

- Using a giant Ponzi scheme, Bernie Madoff, with the help of several employees in his investment securities firm, defrauded high-profile institutional and individual investors such as bank HSBC, Banco Santander, Human Rights First, the International Olympic Committee, film producer and CEO of DreamWorks Animation Jeffrey Katzenberg, actor Kevin Bacon, and Nobel Peace Prize winner Elie Wiesel. Madoff's fraud totaled an estimated $65 billion. He was sentenced to 150 years imprisonment and fines of more than $170 billion.[23]

- At one time, it was hailed as one of "America's Best Companies to Work For," with more than 22,000 employees and over $100 billion in annual revenues. Enron's mission statement touted integrity as one of its key values. Yet, Enron's top-level executives were systematically defrauding investors, employees, customers, and other stakeholders. Enron's collapse in 2001 remains one of the biggest bankruptcies in U.S. history. Former Enron president Jeffrey Skilling was convicted of fraud and insider trading and is currently serving a 25-year term in a federal prison. The Enron shockwaves also sank Arthur Andersen, formerly the largest of the big five accounting firms, because of its role as an accomplice in the accounting scandal. Some 30,000 Andersen accountants and consultants lost their livelihoods.[24]

STRATEGIZING FOR COMPETITIVE ADVANTAGE: HOW IS STRATEGY "MADE"?

Since we now have a basic understanding of what strategy is and why it is important (discussed in Chapter 1) as well as vision, mission, and values, we can think about how strategy is made. How does strategy come about? When strategizing for competitive advantage, managers rely on three different approaches that can complement one another: (1) strategic planning, (2) scenario planning, and (3) strategy as planned emergence.

>> **LO 2-6**
Compare and contrast strategic planning, scenario planning, and strategy as planned emergence, and discuss strategic implications.

Strategic Planning

With the tremendous growth of corporations in the prosperous decades following World War II, corporate executives began to use **strategic** (or **long-range**) **planning** to manage firms more effectively and enhance their performance. Top executives and scholars alike understood strategic planning to be a rational, top-down process through which they could program future success.[25] One scholar wrote during this time: "Long-range planning is one of the really new techniques left to management that can give a company a major competitive advantage."[26]

With strategic planning, all strategic intelligence and decision-making responsibilities are concentrated in the office of the CEO who, much like a military general, leads the company strategically through competitive battles. Five-year plans, revisited regularly, predict future sales based on anticipated future growth. Strategic planners provide careful analyses of internal and external data and apply it to all quantifiable areas: prices, costs, margins, market demand, head count, and production runs. Top executives tie the allocation of the annual corporate budget to the strategic plan and monitor ongoing performance accordingly. In this process, the formulation of strategy is separate from implementation, and thinking about strategy is separate from doing it.

strategic (long-range) planning
A rational, top-down process through which management can program future success; typically concentrates strategic intelligence and decision-making responsibilities in the office of the CEO.

Shell's Future Scenarios

Shell predicts that in 2025 most of our energy will continue to be generated from fossil fuels but 20 percent will come from alternative energy sources like wind, solar, and hydro power. Shell managers thus focus more on fossil fuels in their scenario analysis than on renewable technologies.

Given Shell's past success in using scenario planning, one ought to pay attention to its predictions. Shell can claim a number of accurate predictions to its credit. In the 1960s, with the price of a barrel of crude oil around $10 (compared to a record high of close to $150 in the summer of 2008), managers at Shell began to formulate strategic plans for a future with a strong OPEC (the cartel of oil-exporting countries) and an accompanying drastic rise in oil prices. When the price of crude oil suddenly surged to over $80 a barrel in the late 1970s, Shell was well-positioned to take advantage of this new situation; other oil companies were scrambling to adjust. Shell activated one of its alternative strategic plans that detailed how to obtain crude oil from North Sea drilling, to which the firm had already secured the rights.

In the early 1980s, Shell made strategic preparations to take advantage of another apparently far-fetched scenario when it speculated that communism might fail, bringing down the powerful Soviet Union and ending Soviet artificial restrictions on the supply of natural gas. As a consequence of these strategies, Shell moved from eighth place to become the second-largest oil company in the world.[30]

Top-down strategic planning works reasonably well when the environment does not change very much, because it rests on the assumption that we can predict the future from the past. One major shortcoming of the strategic planning approach is that we cannot know the future. Unforeseen events can make even the most scientifically developed and best formalized plans obsolete. Moreover, as seen in Chapter 1, the rate of change appears to be increasing, which further undercuts the effectiveness of strategic planning.

Scenario Planning

Given that the only constant is change, should managers even use strategic planning? The answer is yes, but they also need to expect that unpredictable events will happen. We can compare strategic planning in a fast-changing environment to the operations of a fire department.[27] There is no way to know where and when the next emergency will arise, nor can we know its magnitude beforehand. Nonetheless, fire chiefs put contingency plans in place to address a wide range of emergencies along different dimensions. In the same way, **scenario planning** asks the "what if" questions. It is a strategy-planning activity in which managers envision different scenarios to anticipate plausible futures. As General (and later President) Eisenhower wisely said, "In preparing for battle, I have always found that plans are useless, but planning is indispensable."[28]

In scenario planning, managers envision different what-if scenarios: New laws might restrict carbon emissions or expand employee health care. Demographic shifts may alter the ethnic diversity of a nation, while changing tastes or economic conditions will affect consumer behavior. How would those changes affect a firm and how should it respond? Typical scenario planning addresses both optimistic and pessimistic futures. For instance, strategy executives at UPS recently identified six issues as critical to shaping its future competitive scenarios: (1) the price of oil; (2) climate change; (3) trade barriers (such as "buy American" or "buy Chinese" clauses in new laws around the world); (4) the emerging BRIC (Brazil, Russia, India, and China) economies; (5) political instability; and (6) online commerce worldwide.[29] Managers then formulated strategies they can activate and implement should one of the envisioned scenarios play a more significant role. Strategy Highlight 2.2 shows how the energy company Shell has used scenario planning to significantly improve its performance.

Exhibit 2.2 shows how to use the AFI strategy framework for scenario planning, to create strategic plans that are more flexible, and thus more effective, than the more static strategic planning approach.

In the *analysis stage,* managers brainstorm to identify possible future scenarios. Input from several different hierarchies within the organization and from different functional areas such as R&D, manufacturing, and marketing and sales is critical. UPS executives

scenario planning
Strategy-planning activity in which managers envision different what-if scenarios to anticipate plausible futures.

EXHIBIT 2.2

Scenario Planning
in the AFI Strategy
Framework

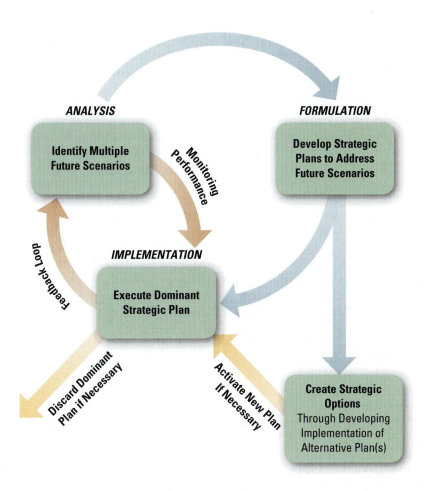

considered how they would compete if the price of a barrel of oil was $35, or $125, or even $200. Managers may also attach probabilities (highly likely vs. unlikely, or 85 percent likely vs. 2 percent likely) to different future states.

Managers often overlook pessimistic future scenarios. For example, many were caught off-guard by the recent economic downturn. Managers should consider negative scenarios more carefully, for example, how to obtain liquidity when credit and equity markets are tight. This was a serious problem during the 2008–2009 world financial crisis. An exporter like Boeing or Harley-Davidson would want to analyze the impact of shifts in exchange rates on sales and production costs—what if the euro depreciated to $1 per euro, or the Chinese yuan depreciated rather than appreciated?

In the *formulation stage,* management teams develop different strategic plans to address possible future scenarios. This kind of what-if exercise forces managers to consider contingency plans in the formulation stage, before events occur. Each plan relies on the entire set of analytical tools (which will be introduced in upcoming chapters) to capture the firm's internal and external environments and to answer several key questions:

■ What resources and capabilities do we need to compete successfully in each future scenario?

■ Which strategic initiatives should we put in place to respond to each?

■ How can we shape our expected future environment?

By formulating responses to the scenario analysis stage, managers achieve strategic flexibility by building a portfolio of future options. They continue integrating additional information over time, which in turn influences future decisions. Finally, they transform the most viable options into full-fledged strategic plans to be activated when needed.

In the *implementation stage,* managers activate the dominant strategic plan, the option they think most closely matches reality. If reality changes, managers can quickly retrieve and implement any of the alternate plans developed in the formulation stage. The firm's performance in the marketplace provides feedback to the managers concerning the viability of the dominant strategic plan. If the performance feedback is positive, managers continue to pursue the dominant strategic plan, while fine-tuning it in the process. If the performance feedback is negative, managers consider whether modifying the dominant strategic option will enhance firm performance or whether they are better off activating one of the alternative strategic plans.

To conduct successful scenario planning, managers need current information. The network-equipment giant Cisco Systems has invested huge sums in technology to generate just this kind of data.[31] Cisco's senior executives can track daily customer order data from its sales teams around the globe with up-to-the-minute accuracy. Walmart's CEO Mike Duke indicates that he too is using real-time sales data tracking, enabling top executives to monitor daily sales of each of the over 8,500 Walmart stores worldwide in real time.[32] With these real-time data systems, managers can identify emerging trends in each region and market segment long before they materialize in financial data. This in turn allows them to fine-tune their functional strategy with unprecedented accuracy and speed.

The circular nature of the scenario-planning model in Exhibit 2.2 highlights the continuous interaction between analysis, formulation, and implementation. Through this interactive process, managers can adjust and modify their actions as new realities emerge. The interdependence among analysis, formulation, and implementation also enhances organizational learning and flexibility.

"DON'T SEPARATE STRATEGIC ANALYSIS FROM STRATEGIC ACTION!" Critics of strategic planning and scenario planning, most notably Henry Mintzberg of McGill University, argue that strategic *planning* is not the same as strategic *thinking.*[33] In fact, Mintzberg suggests the strategic planning process often is too regimented and confining and does not allow for strategic thinking. Managers doing strategic planning may fall prey to an *illusion of control*—the hard numbers in a strategic plan can convey a false sense of security. To be successful, say these critics, a strategy should be based on an inspiring mission, and not on hard data alone. They advise that managers should focus on all types of information sources, including "soft" sources that can generate new insights, such as personal experience or the experience of front-line employees. The important work, say the critics of strategic planning, is to synthesize *all available input* into an overall strategic mission, which should then guide the firm's strategy.

Indeed, some companies *choose* not to articulate a corporate or business strategy. Rather, they focus on consistency in strategic actions across all levels of the organization.[34] For example, Nucor Corporation had 2010 sales of $16 billion and employed 22,500 people (fewer than 100 of them in its corporate headquarters), making it the largest steel maker in the United States.[35] Nucor has been profitable for several *decades* and has never laid off an employee for lack of work. Its employees are among the highest paid in the industry (two-thirds of their compensation is performance-related), and it has the lowest labor cost per ton of steel produced. Yet Nucor has no written strategic plan, no written mission statement, and no written goals and objectives. It does, however, have a strong organizational culture based on peer control combined with a set of clear operational rules supporting its functional-level strategy.[36]

How can a company like Nucor be so successful without an overarching strategic plan? Because lack of a *written strategic plan* does not indicate lack of a strategy. We can deduce a firm's strategy from the pattern of its actions.[37] Indeed, everything Nucor's managers and employees do across all levels of the organization indicate its strategy of cost leadership (providing an acceptable standard of product quality or value to the customer at the lowest cost to produce it). The absence of an explicitly formulated plan may give Nucor flexibility to more quickly react to changes in the marketplace. In addition, it may make Nucor's strategy less transparent and its future strategic moves less obvious to competitors. All this contributes to protecting and sustaining Nucor's competitive advantage.

Strategy as Planned Emergence: Top-Down *and* Bottom-Up

We now come to the third approach to strategizing for competitive advantage. In contrast to the two rational planning approaches just discussed, another view considers less formal and less stylized approaches to the development of strategy.

A strategic initiative is any activity a firm pursues to explore and develop new products and processes, new markets, or new ventures. Strategic initiatives can come from anywhere. They could be the result of top-down planning by executives, and they also can emerge through a bottom-up process. Strategic initiatives can emerge from deep within a firm through *autonomous actions* by lower-level employees, from random events, and maybe even luck.[38] Consider the following examples, in which the impulse for strategic initiatives emerged from the bottom up.

- Google's Vice President Marissa Mayer reports that 50 percent of the firm's new products come from the *20 percent rule,* which allows all employees to spend one day a week (20 percent of the workweek) on ideas of their own choosing. Examples of innovations that resulted from the 20 percent rule include Gmail, Google News, and Orkut.[39]

- A mid-level engineer at General Electric in 2001 proposed buying Enron Wind, a division that was up for sale as part of Enron's bankruptcy proceedings. CEO Jack Welch's response was that GE wouldn't touch anything with the name Enron on it, given its large-scale accounting fraud. When the mid-level engineer kept insisting, after being rejected several times, GE's leadership relented and bought Enron Wind for $200 million. It turned out to be a huge success, with revenues over $6 billion in 2009, and it opened up other significant opportunities for GE in the alternative-energy industry such as its *ecomagination* initiative. GE's shift from a product-oriented company ("*We bring good things to life*") to a more consumer-oriented one ("*Imagination at work*") was part of the leadership change from Jack Welch to Jeffrey Immelt, who approved the investment in Enron Wind.[40]

A firm's actual strategy, therefore, is often a combination of its top-down strategic intentions (which typically are expressed in written strategic plans) and bottom-up emergent strategy.[41] An emergent strategy describes any unplanned strategic initiative undertaken by mid-level

---

dominant strategic plan The strategic option that managers think most closely matches reality at a given point in time.

strategic initiative Any activity a firm pursues to explore and develop new products and processes, new markets, or new ventures.

emergent strategy Any unplanned strategic initiative undertaken by mid-level employees of their own volition.

STRATEGY HIGHLIGHT 2.3

Starbucks's CEO: "It's Not What We Do!"

Diana, a Starbucks store manager in southern California, received several requests a day for an iced beverage offered by a local competitor. After she received more than 30 requests one day, she tried the beverage herself. Thinking it might be a good idea for Starbucks to offer a similar iced beverage, she requested that headquarters consider adding it to the product lineup. Diana had an internal champion in Howard Behar, then one of Starbucks's top executives. Mr. Behar presented this strategic initiative to the Starbucks executive committee on which he sat, but it was voted down in a 7:1 vote. Starbucks's CEO Howard Schultz commented, "We do coffee, we don't do iced drinks."

Diana, however, was undeterred. She started experimenting with a blender to re-create this specific drink. Satisfied with her results, she began to offer the drink in her store. When Howard Behar visited Diana's store, he was shocked to see this new drink on the menu—all Starbucks stores were supposed to offer only company-approved drinks. But Diana told him the new drink was selling well.

Howard Behar flew Diana's team (and her blender) to Starbucks headquarters in Seattle, to serve this new drink to the executive committee. They liked the drink, but still said no. Then Behar pulled out the sales numbers that Diana had carefully kept. The drink was selling like crazy: 40 drinks a day the first week, 50 drinks a day the next week, and then 70 drinks in the third week after introduction. They had never seen such growth numbers. These results persuaded the executive team to give reluctant approval to introduce the drink in all Starbucks stores. You've probably by now guessed the drink—Starbucks's Frappuccino. Frappuccino is now a billion-dollar business for Starbucks, and at one point brought in more than 20 percent of Starbucks's total revenues (which were $11 billion in 2010).[43]

As the Starbucks example shows, companies can benefit from an attitude of "expect the unexpected, and react to it strategically"! Strategy can be planned, but sometimes important strategic initiatives simply emerge from the bottom up.

employees of their own volition.[42] If successful, emergent strategies have the potential to influence and shape a firm's strategy. Strategy Highlight 2.3 provides further evidence for the notion that successful emergent strategies are sometimes the result of *serendipity* combined with the tenacity of lower-level employees.

MINTZBERG'S PLANNING FRAMEWORK. To reflect the reality that strategy can be planned *or* can emerge from the bottom up, Mintzberg developed a more integrative and complete framework for strategy-making, shown in Exhibit 2.3.

According to this more holistic model, the strategy process may begin with a top-down strategic plan. Based on external and internal analyses, top-level executives design an **intended strategy**—the outcome of a rational and structured, top-down strategic plan. This is the first important step in strategy-making. However, in today's complex and uncertain world, unpredicted events can have huge effects. Very few people predicted, for example, that easy credit would lead to a housing bubble. The bursting of that bubble in 2008 rendered obsolete the best-laid strategic plans of financial, mortgage and insurance companies like Bank of America, Citigroup, Fannie Mae, Freddy Mac, and AIG. Indeed, most of these venerable institutions and many other firms would have faced bankruptcy were it not for a government bailout of $10 trillion.[44]

Unpredicted changes don't have to be cataclysmic, however, to be disruptive. Apple's hugely popular iPod and iPhone upset the strategic plans of a number of companies including Nokia, Sony, and RIM (the maker of the BlackBerry), forcing them to respond. Apple is trying to repeat this feat with its iPad, which could lead to industry convergence in computing, telecommunications, and media.[45] When unexpected events have dramatic strategic implications, part (or all) of a firm's strategic plan becomes an **unrealized strategy** and falls by the wayside.

Sometimes new ideas for strategic initiatives pop up in unusual ways. In these instances, astute managers combine serendipity and bottom-up emergent strategy into a successfully **realized strategy.** An unexpected event at the largest rail carrier in the world, Japan Railways, led to diversification from railroads into bottled water.[46] This may sound far-fetched, but here is how it happened: Japan Railways was constructing a new bullet train through the mountains north of Tokyo, requiring many tunnels. In one

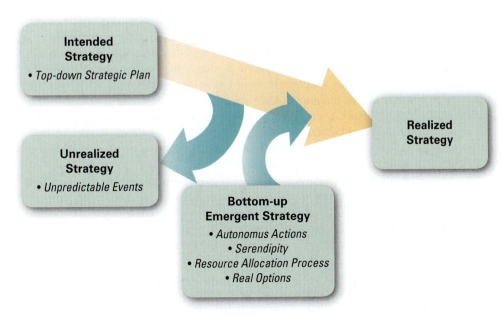

EXHIBIT 2.3

Realized Strategy
Is a Combination of
Top-down Intended
Strategy and
Bottom-up Emergent
Strategy

Source: Adapted from
H. Mintzberg and A. McHugh
(1985), "Strategy formation in
an adhocracy," *Administrative
Science Quarterly* 30: 162.

of the mountains, persistent flooding caused huge problems. Engineers responded by drawing up complex plans to drain the water. Meanwhile, workers inside the tunnel were making good use of the water—they were drinking it. A maintenance worker suggested the water should not be pumped away but rather bottled and sold as premium drinking water because it tasted so fresh. Its source was snow pack, purified and filtered in the slow percolation process through the mountain's geological layers and enhanced on the way with healthy amounts of calcium, potassium, and magnesium. Eventually, Japan Railways set up vending machines on 1,000 railroad platforms in and around Tokyo, and home delivery of water, juices, and coffee followed. The employee's proposal had turned an expensive engineering problem into a multimillion-dollar business. Because Japan Railways was willing to define its business as broader than just being in railroads, it was able to capture the emergent strategy and diversify into drinking water.

Bottom-up strategies can also emerge as a consequence of the firm's *resource alloca-tion process (RAP).*[47] The core argument linking the RAP and strategy is that the way a firm allocates its resources can be critical in shaping its realized strategy.[48] Intel Corp.'s famous rule to "maximize margin-per-wafer-start" illustrates this concept.[49] Intel was founded in 1968 to produce DRAM (dynamic random-access memory) chips. From the start, producing these chips was the firm's top-down strategic plan, and initially it worked well. However, in the 1980s, Japanese competitors brought better-quality chips to the market at lower cost, threatening Intel's position and strategic plan. Intel was able, how-ever, to pursue a strategic transformation due to the way it set up its RAP. In a sense, Intel was using functional-level strategies to drive business and corporate strategies. In particular, during this time Intel had only a few "fabs" (fabrication plants to produce silicon-based products). It would have taken several years and billions of dollars to build additional fabs.

intended strategy The outcome of a rational and structured top-down strategic plan.

unrealized strategy Part or all of a firm's strategic plan that falls by the wayside due to unexpected events.

realized strategy Combination of intended and emergent strategy.

Since Intel's production capacity was constrained, it had implemented the decision rule to "maximize margin-per-wafer-start." Each time functional managers initiated a new production run, they were to consider the profit margins for DRAM and for semiconductors (the "brains" of personal computers), and then to produce *whichever product* delivered the higher margin. Following this simple rule, front-line managers shifted Intel's production capacity away from the low-margin DRAM business to the higher-margin semiconductor business. The firm's focus on semiconductors thus emerged from the bottom up, based on resource allocation and without top-management planning. Indeed, by the time top-management finally approved the de facto strategic switch, the company's market share in DRAM had dwindled to less than 3 percent.[50]

Taken together, the Japan Railways and Intel examples demonstrate that a firm's realized strategy is frequently a combination of top-down strategic intent and bottom-up emergent strategies, as Exhibit 2.3 shows. Strategy-making has thus been called by some *planned emergence,* in which organizational structure and systems allow bottom-up strategic initiatives to emerge and be evaluated and coordinated by top management.[51]

A word of caution is in order: Not all emergent strategies are successful. As the story of Microsoft's Keywords in Chapter 1 shows, promising strategic initiatives can emerge from deep within the company, but top managers must have a system in place that allows them to judge whether to support those initiatives and allow them to influence and shape the firm's overall strategy. Although Microsoft missed the opportunity to lead in online search and advertising, it has a history of adapting successfully to quickly evolving environments. Mid-level Microsoft employees envisioned and developed both Internet Explorer (the leading web browser with more than two-thirds market share) and the Xbox videogame system to address threats posed by Netscape and Sony's PlayStation.

Implications for the Strategist

What approach can managers take to ensure that potentially high-impact strategic initiatives receive due consideration? When new ideas emerge, managers can go beyond standard evaluation metrics like net present value (NPV) and apply a *real options perspective.*[52] Both NPV and real options are tools taught in corporate finance. They provide critical information when a firm is making strategic decisions.

Though widely used, the net present value calculation is often inappropriate to assess the potential of highly uncertain strategic initiatives: It applies a high discount rate on the net present value of future cash flows, to reflect the high risk of these initiatives. At the same time, it ignores the potentially huge upside of such strategic initiatives. Applying net present value calculations, therefore, frequently leads to a premature death of strategic initiatives such as the Keywords project within Microsoft. Since there was no viable business model for it, shutting it down—based on an NPV calculation—was a rational decision.

In contrast, applying a real-options perspective to strategic decision making would break down a large investment decision into a set of smaller decisions that are staged sequentially over time. This approach allows the firm to obtain additional information in planned stages. At each stage, the firm evaluates a *real option,* which is the right, but not the obligation, to make a business decision. (Real options are sometimes called *strategic options,* to differentiate them from *financial options.*) Unlike the final "go or no-go" decision that an NPV calculation requires, applying a real-options framework allows managers to break down a big decision into smaller, stepped decisions based on a sequence of option payments over time. The idea is to keep the firm's alternatives open so that more information can reveal itself. Basically, managers are keeping open the possibility of changing the scope or timing of projects and other strategic initiatives, or even abandoning them altogether, as new information emerges.

Some cost is always involved in a real-options approach, but it's often less cost than a full-bore investment in a project that will not pan out. This approach reduces the uncertainty that surrounds the value of a bottom-up strategic initiative. Moreover, it prevents prematurely closing down a strategic initiative that is of high potential, but whose potential is revealed only at a later date. For example, rather than shutting down the Keywords initiative, Microsoft could have invested some money in it, to see if a business opportunity would arise.

A profitable business model in online search was demonstrated by Yahoo and later by Google. Microsoft's CEO Ballmer now attempts to apply a real-options perspective to emerging strategic initiatives: "The biggest mistakes I claim I've been involved with is where I was impatient—because we didn't have a business yet in something, we should have stayed patient. If we'd kept consistent with some of the ideas, we might have been in paid search. We are letting more flowers bloom."[53] Basically, the idea is not to shut down strategic experiments prematurely to foreclose future options. This approach requires not only application of a real-options perspective, but also recognition of strategy as planned emergence.

Here, we conclude our discussion of the strategic management process, which marks the end of the "getting started" portion of the AFI framework. The next chapter moves us into the analysis part of the framework—where we begin by studying the important topics of external and internal analysis, followed by consideration of how competitive advantage can be measured.

CHAPTERCASE 2 | *Consider This...*

IN FEBRUARY 2011, Teach For America (TFA) celebrated its 20th anniversary. In those 20 years, it has grown into a $212 million organization that attracted 12 percent of all Ivy League seniors in its 2010 application pool.[54] Studies show that TFA teachers have a stronger positive effect on high-school students' test scores than regular certified teachers—and that the performance difference was especially pronounced in math and science.[55]

A recent publication by TFA notes that teacher effectiveness is improved when teachers have course objectives that are "student-achievement based, measureable, and rigorous." Such course objectives are, in effect, mission statements. According to TFA, a poorly worded objective might be "The teacher will present a lesson on ordering fractions with different denominators." An improved objective would be "The student will be able to order fractions with different denominators."[56]

1. What role (if any) do you think TFA's vision statement may have had in the success of the organization?

2. How has TFA succeeded in recruiting so many Ivy League students into teaching in the lowest-performing regions of the United States?

3. Do you think TFA could have been just as successful if it had been structured as a traditional for-profit company?

Take-Away Concepts

This chapter explained the role of vision, mission, and values in the strategic management process and gave an overview of how strategy is made, as summarized by the following learning objectives and related take-away concepts.

LO 2-1 Explain the role of vision, mission, and values in the strategic management process.

>> A vision captures an organization's aspirations. An effective vision inspires members of the organization.

>> A mission statement describes what an organization actually does—what its business is—and why it does it.

>> Values define the ethical standards and norms that should govern the behavior of individuals within the firm.

>> Success is created twice: first by creating a mental model of what the firm wants to accomplish, and second by formulating and implementing a strategy that makes this vision a reality.

LO 2-2 Describe and evaluate the role of strategic intent in achieving long-term goals.

>> Strategic intent finds its expression in stretch goals that exceed the firms' existing resources and capabilities by a large margin.

>> Effective use of strategic intent creates at all levels of the organization an obsession with winning that can help companies ascend to global leadership.

LO 2-3 Distinguish between customer-oriented and product-oriented missions and identify strategic implications.

>> Customer-oriented missions define business in terms of providing solutions to customer needs.

>> Product-oriented missions define a business in terms of a good or service provided.

>> Customer-oriented missions provide managers with more strategic flexibility than product-oriented missions.

LO 2-4 Critically evaluate the relationship between mission statements and competitive advantage.

>> Mission statements can help a firm achieve superior performance, but mission statements by themselves do not directly affect firm performance.

>> To be effective, mission statements need to be backed up by hard-to-reverse commitments.

LO 2-5 Explain why anchoring a firm in ethical values is essential for long-term success.

>> Ethical core values enable employees to make day-to-day decisions that are guided by correct principles.

>> Strong ethical values are the guardrails that help keep the company on track when pursuing its mission and its quest for competitive advantage.

LO 2-6 Compare and contrast strategic planning, scenario planning, and strategy as planned emergence, and discuss strategic implications.

>> Top-down strategic (long-range) planning works reasonably well when the environment does not change much.

>> In scenario planning, managers envision different what-if scenarios and prepare contingency plans that can be called upon when necessary.

>> Strategic initiatives can be the result of top-down planning by executives or can emerge through a bottom-up process from deep within the organization.

>> A firm's realized strategy is generally a combination of its top-down intended strategy and bottom-up emergent strategy, resulting in planned emergence.

Key Terms

Dominant strategic plan *(p. 42)*

Emergent strategy *(p. 43)*

Intended strategy *(p. 44)*

Mission *(p. 34)*

Organizational values *(p. 38)*

Realized strategy *(p. 44)*

Scenario planning *(p. 40)*

Strategic commitments *(p. 37)*

Strategic initiative *(p. 43)*

Strategic intent *(p. 33)*

Strategic management process *(p. 32)*

Strategic (long-range) planning *(p. 39)*

Unrealized strategy *(p. 44)*

Vision *(p. 32)*

Discussion Questions

1. What characteristics does an effective mission statement have?

2. What is strategic intent? How can it be useful for goal setting and achievement?

3. In what situations is top-down planning likely to be superior to bottom-up emergent strategy development?

4. Based on discussions in this chapter, which railroad firm seems more prepared to use planned emergence, CSX or Japan Railways? Why?

5. Discuss how scenario planning can be used to prepare a firm for future events. Can some industries benefit more than others from this type of process?

Ethical/Social Issues

1. As noted in the "Living the Values" section, over 50,000 people lost their jobs and many their life savings in the Enron debacle. Some of those at Enron who were closely involved in the scandal, such as Jeffrey Skilling (CEO) and Andrew Fastow (CFO), are serving significant prison sentences. What responsibility do lower-level executives bear for not reporting such questionable practices by the firm's leadership? Why do you think only one employee initially came forward to report the irregularities and help with the investigation?

2. In the circumstance when an emergent idea arises that appears to mid-level managers to have strong merits yet conflicts with an existing intended strategy from the top managers, how would you suggest the organization decide which idea to push forward into a plan of action and thus contribute to a realized strategy? What would you do in this situation if you were (a) a mid-level manager or (b) an executive?

Small Group Exercises

SMALL GROUP EXERCISE 1

The National Aeronautics and Space Administration (NASA) is leading the public space program in the United States. Its vision is "to advance U.S. scientific, security, and economic interests through a robust space exploration program." Its mission is "to pioneer the future in space exploration, scientific discovery, and aeronautics research." To accomplish its vision and mission, in 2006 NASA specified a set of six strategic goals to be accomplished over the next 10 years:

1. Fly the Shuttle as safely as possible until its retirement, not later than 2010.

2. Complete the International Space Station in a manner consistent with NASA's International Partner commitments and the needs of human exploration.

3. Develop a balanced overall program of science, exploration, and aeronautics consistent with the redirection of the human spaceflight program to focus on exploration.

4. Bring a new Crew Exploration Vehicle into service as soon as possible after Shuttle retirement.

5. Encourage the pursuit of appropriate partnerships with the emerging commercial space sector.

6. Establish a lunar return program having the maximum possible utility for later missions to Mars and other destinations.

NASA's quest to accomplish these goals is grounded in its values of (1) safety, (2) teamwork, (3) integrity, and (4) mission success. In NASA's strategic plan, each of the six strategic goals is broken down into a number of detailed sub-goals. These goals are accompanied by a detailed list of expected outcomes that enables NASA to measure its progress and report its accomplishments back to its stakeholders. Michael Griffin, the NASA Administrator when the strategic plan was devised, said that "By pursuing the goals of the Vision for Space Exploration, NASA will contribute to American leadership in defining and pursuing the frontiers that expand humankind's reach, and we will help keep our nation at the cutting edge of science and technology. We also will work with other nations to do those things that fulfill the dreams of humankind, dreams that always have included the desire to see what lies beyond the known world."[57]

1. How is NASA including its mission and values in its strategic planning to make its goals become reality?

2. Do you think a 10-year planning horizon is realistic? Why or why not?

3. Do you agree with Michael Griffin's interpretation of the expected results of pursuing NASA's mission? Discuss why or why not.

SMALL GROUP EXERCISE 2

In many situations, promising ideas emerge from the lower levels of an organization only to be discarded before they can be tested and implemented. It was only due to extraordinary tenacity (and indeed disregard) for the policy of selling only corporate-approved drinks that permitted the Frappuccino to "bloom" within Starbucks (see Strategy Highlight 2.3). Some scholars have suggested that companies should set aside up to 2 percent of their budgets for *any* manager with budget control to be able to invest in new ideas within the company.[58] (Someone with a $100,000 annual budget to manage would be able to invest $2,000 in cash or staff time toward such a project. Multiple managers could go in together for somewhat larger funds or time amounts.)

Through such a process, the organization can generate a network of "angel investors." Small funds or staff time can be invested into a variety of projects. Approval mechanisms would be easier for these small "seed stock" ideas, to give them a chance to develop before going for bigger funding at the top levels of the organization.

What would be some problems that would need to be addressed to introduce this "angel network" idea into a firm? Use a firm someone in your group has worked for or knows well to discuss possible issues of widely distributing small funding level approvals across the firm.

Strategy Term Project

MODULE 2: MISSION, GOALS, AND THE STRATEGIC MANAGEMENT PROCESS

1. Search for a mission statement for the firm. Not all organizations publish such a statement, so alternatively you can look for enduring principles and values upon which the firm seems to be anchored. This information is often available at the firm's website (though it may take some searching) or is contained in its annual reports. You may also interview a manager of the firm or contact "investor relations."

2. Identify the major goals of the company.

3. Does the firm seem to have any longer-term challenging or stretch goals that would serve as its strategic intent?

4. Trace any changes in strategy that you can identify over time. Try to determine whether the strategic changes of your selected firm are a result of intended strategies, emergent strategies, or some combination of both.

*my*Strategy

HOW MUCH ARE YOUR VALUES WORTH TO YOU?

How much are you willing to pay for the job you want? This may sound like a strange question, since your employer will pay you to work, but think again. Consider how much you value a specific type of work, or how much you would want to work for a specific organization because of its values.

A recent study shows scientists who want to continue engaging in research will accept some $14,000 less in annual salary to work at an organization that permits them to publish their findings in academic journals, implying that some scientists will "pay to be scientists." This finding appears to hold in the general business world, too. In a recent survey, 97 percent of Stanford MBA students indicated they would forgo some 14 percent of their expected salary, or about $11,480 a year, to work for a company that matches their own values with concern for stakeholders and sustainability. According

to Monster.com, an online career service, about 92 percent of all undergraduates want to work for a "green" company. These diverse examples demonstrate that people put a real dollar amount on pursuing careers in sync with their values.

On the other hand, certain high-powered jobs such as management consulting or investment banking pay very well, but their high salaries come with strings attached. Professionals in these jobs work very long hours, including weekends, and often take little or no vacation time. These workers "pay for pay" in that they are often unable to form stable relationships, have little or no leisure time, and sometimes even sacrifice their health. People "pay for"—make certain sacrifices for—what they value, because strategic decisions require important trade-offs.[59]

1. What values are (were) most important to you in your career choice?

2. How much less salary would (did) you accept to find employment with a company that is in line with your values?

Endnotes

1. This ChapterCase is based on the following sources: Frankl, V. E. (1984), *Man's Search for Meaning* (New York: Washington Square Press); Kopp, W. (2001), *One Day, All Children…: The Unlikely Triumph of Teach For America and What I Learned Along the Way* (Cambridge, MA: Perseus Book Group); Xu, Z., J. Hannaway, and C. Taylor (2008), "Making a difference? The effect of Teach For America on student performance in high school," *Urban Institute,* March 27; and data from the U.S. Census Bureau, www. hernandezcollegeconsulting.com/ ivy-league-admission-statistics-2009/.

2. Frankl, V. E. (1984), *Man's Search for Meaning.*

3. Xu, Z., J. Hannaway, and C. Taylor (2008), "Making a difference? The effect of Teach For America on student performance in high school."

4. This section is based on: Hamel, G., and C. K. Prahalad (1989), "Strategic intent," *Harvard Business Review* (May–June): 64–65; and Hamel, G., and

C. K. Prahalad (1994), *Competing for the Future* (Boston, MA: Harvard Business School Press).

5. Locke, E. A., and G. P. Latham (1990), *A Theory of Goal Setting and Task Performance* (Englewood Cliffs, NJ: Prentice Hall).

6. Hamel, G., and C. K. Prahalad (1989), "Strategic intent," *Harvard Business Review*; and Hamel, G., and C. K. Prahalad (1994), *Competing for the Future.*

7. This Strategy Highlight is based on: Heath, C., and D. Heath (2007), *Made to Stick. Why Some Ideas Survive and Others Die* (New York, NY: Random House), pp. 93–95; and www.sony.net/ SonyInfo/CorporateInfo/History/history. html.

8. The Disney and Subway discussion is based on: Heath, C., and D. Heath (2007), *Made to Stick,* pp. 60–61.

9. "The three habits…of highly irritating management gurus," *The Economist,* October 22, 2009.

10. Author's interviews with Blaine Lawlor, former staff analyst at Shell Canada, and now a strategic management professor at the University of West Florida, November 6–7, 2009.

11. Collins, J. C., and J. I. Porras (1994), *Built to Last: Successful Habits of Visionary Companies* (New York: Harper Collins). Collins and Porras define visionary companies as follows: "Visionary companies are premier institutions—the crown jewels—in their industries, widely admired by their peers and having a long track record of making a significant impact on the world around them" (p. 1).

12. www.merck.com.

13. George W. Merck, address to the Medical College of Virginia, Richmond, VA (December 1, 1950), quoted in Collins, J. C., and J. I. Porras (1994), *Built to Last,* p. 48.

14. Rothaermel, F. T., K. Grigoriou, and V. Eberhardt (2013), "Better World Books: Social Entrepreneurship and the Triple Bottom Line," case study, in Rothaermel, F. T., *Strategic Management* (Burr Ridge, IL: McGraw-Hill).

15. Burgelman, R. A., and A. S. Grove (1996), "Strategic dissonance," *California Management Review* 38: 8–28; and Grove, A. S. (1996), *Only the Paranoid Survive: How to Exploit the Crisis Points that Challenge Every Company* (New York: Currency Doubleday).

16. Dixit, A., and B. Nalebuff (1991), *Thinking Strategically: The Competitive Edge in Business, Politics, and Everyday Life* (New York: Norton); and Brandenburger, A. M., and B. J. Nalebuff (1996), *Co-opetition* (New York: Currency Doubleday).

17. www.mckesson.com.

18. Ibid.

19. The original statement about Google's new approach to China is at http://googleblog.blogspot.com/2010/01/new-approach-to-china.html. Other sources: "Google threat jolts China web users," *The Wall Street Journal,* January 13, 2010; and "Flowers for a funeral," *The Economist,* January 14, 2010.

20. Google's values are at www.google.com/corporate/tenthings.html.

21. "China renews Google's license," *The Wall Street Journal,* July 11, 2010.

22. "How Baidu won China," *Bloomberg BusinessWeek,* November 11, 2010.

23. "Q&A on Madoff case," *The Wall Street Journal,* March 12, 2009.

24. "Watch out! If your mission statement is a joke, Enron may be the punchline," *Entrepreneur Magazine,* May 2002; and McLean, B., and P. Elkind (2003), *The Smartest Guys in the Room. The Amazing Rise and Scandalous Fall of Enron* (New York: Portfolio).

25. This discussion is based on: Mintzberg, H. (1993), *The Rise and Fall of Strategic Planning: Reconceiving Roles for Planning, Plans, and Planners* (New York: Simon & Schuster); and Mintzberg, H. (1994), "The fall and rise of strategic planning," *Harvard Business Review* (January–February): 107–114.

26. Payne, B. (1956), "Steps in long-range planning," *Harvard Business Review* (March–April): 97–106.

27. Grove, A. S. (1996), *Only the Paranoid Survive*.

28. As quoted in Rothaermel, F. T. (2008), "Competitive advantage in technology intensive industries," *Advances in the Study of Entrepreneurship, Innovation, and Economic Growth* 18: 203–226.

29. Personal communication with UPS strategy executives during onsite visit in corporate headquarters, June 17, 2009.

30. This Strategy Highlight is based on: deGeus, A. P. (1988), "Planning as learning," *Harvard Business Review* (March–April); Grant, R. M. (2003), "Strategic planning in a turbulent environment: Evidence from the oil majors," *Strategic Management Journal* 24: 491–517; Willmore, J. (2001), "Scenario planning: Creating strategy for uncertain times," *Information Outlook* (September); and "Shell dumps wind, solar, and hydro power in favour of biofuels," *The Guardian,* March 17, 2009.

31. "Managing in the fog," *The Economist,* February 26, 2009.

32. Duke, M. T. (CEO of Walmart) (2010), presentation at Georgia Institute of Technology, April 1; and Walmart–Corporate Fact Sheet (walmart-stores.com).

33. Mintzberg, H. (1993), *The Rise and Fall of Strategic Planning;* and Mintzberg, H. (1994), "The fall and rise of strategic planning."

34. Inkpen, A., and N. Choudhury (1995), "The seeking of strategy where it is not: Toward a theory of strategy absence," *Strategic Management Journal* 16: 313–323.

35. www.nucor.com.

36. See discussion on Nucor in Chapter 11, "Organizational Design: Structure, Culture, and Control."

37. Mintzberg, H., and J. A. Waters (1985), "Of strategies, deliberate and emergent," *Strategic Management Journal* 6: 257–272.

38. Arthur, B. W. (1989), "Competing technologies, increasing returns, and lock-in by historical events," *Economic Journal* 99: 116–131; and Brown, S. L., and K. M. Eisenhardt (1998), *Competing on the Edge. Strategy as Structured Chaos* (Boston, MA: Harvard Business School Press).

39. Mayer, M. (2006), "Nine lessons learned about creativity at Google," presentation at Stanford Technology Ventures Program, May 17.

40. John Rice (GE Vice Chairman, President & CEO, GE Technology Infrastructure) (2009), presentation at Georgia Institute of Technology, May 11.

41. Mintzberg, H., and A. McHugh (1985), "Strategy formation in an adhocracy," *Administrative Science Quarterly* 30: 160–197.

42. Ibid.; and Hill, C. W. L., and F. T. Rothaermel (2003), "The performance of incumbent firms in the face of radical technological innovation," *Academy of Management Review* 28: 257–274.

43. Based on Howard Behar (retired President, Starbucks North America and Starbucks International) (2009), Impact Speaker Series Presentation, College of Management, Georgia Institute of Technology, October 14. See also Behar, H. (2007), *It's Not About the Coffee: Leadership Principles from a Life at Starbucks* (New York: Portfolio).

44. "U.S. taxpayers risk $9.7 trillion on bailout programs," *Bloomberg News,* February 9, 2009.

45. "The book of Jobs," *The Economist,* January 28, 2010.

46. This example is based on Robinson, A. G., and S. Stern (1997), *Corporate Creativity: How Innovation and Improvement Actually Happen* (San Francisco, CA: Berret-Koehler Publishers).

47. Bower, J. L. (1970), *Managing the Resource Allocation Process* (Boston, MA: Harvard Business School Press); Bower, J. L., and C. G. Gilbert (2005), *From Resource Allocation to Strategy* (Oxford, UK: Oxford University Press); Burgelman, R. A. (1983), "A model of the interaction of strategic behavior, corporate context, and the concept of strategy," *Academy of Management Review* 8: 61–71; and Burgelman, R. A. (1983), "A process model of internal corporate venturing in a major diversified firm," *Administrative Science Quarterly* 28: 223–244.

48. Bower, J. L., and C. G. Gilbert (2005), *From Resource Allocation to Strategy.*

49. Burgelman, R. A. (1994), "Fading memories: A process theory of strategic business exit in dynamic environments," *Administrative Science Quarterly,* 39: 24–56.

50. Burgelman, R. A., and A. S. Grove (1996), "Strategic dissonance," *California Management Review* 38: 8–28.

51. Grant, R. M. (2003), "Strategic planning in a turbulent environment: Evidence from the oil majors," *Strategic Management Journal* 24: 491–517; Brown, S. L., and K. M. Eisenhardt (1997), "The art of continuous change: Linking complexity theory and time-based evolution in relentlessly shifting organizations," *Administrative Science Quarterly* 42: 1–34; Farjourn, M. (2002), "Towards an organic perspective on strategy," *Strategic Management Journal* 23: 561–594; Mahoney, J. (2005), *Economic Foundation of Strategy* (Thousand Oaks, CA: Sage); and Burgelman, R. A., and A. S. Grove (2007), "Let chaos reign, then rein in chaos – repeatedly: Managing strategic

dynamics for corporate longevity," *Strategic Management Journal* 28: 965–979.

52. Dixit, A. K. S., and R. Pindyck (1994), *Investment Under Uncertainty* (Princeton, NJ: Princeton University Press); Amram, M., and N. Kulatilaka (1998), *Real Options: Managing Strategic Investment in an Uncertain World* (Boston, MA: Harvard Business School Press); McGrath, R. G., and I. C. MacMillan (2000), "Assessing technology projects using real options reasoning," *Research Technology Management* 43: 35–49; Hill, C. W. L., and F. T. Rothaermel (2003), "The performance of incumbent firms in the face of radical technological innovation"; and Adner, R., and D. A. Levinthal (2004), "What is not a real option: Considering boundaries for the application of real options to business strategy," *Academy of Management Review* 29: 74–85.

53. "Microsoft bid to beat Google builds on a history of misses," *The Wall Street Journal,* January 16, 2009.

54. "What They're Doing After Harvard," *The Wall Street Journal,* July 10, 2010.

55. Xu, Z., J. Hannaway, and C. Taylor (2008), "Making a difference? The effect of Teach For America on student performance in high school."

56. "Teaching as leadership: The highly effective teachers' guide to closing the achievement gap," Jossey-Bass, February 3, 2010.

57. "2006 NASA Strategic Plan," NASA (www.nasa.gov).

58. Hamel, G. (2007), *The Future of Management* (Boston, MA: Harvard Business School Publishing).

59. This *my*Strategy vignette is based on Stern, S. (2004), "Do scientists pay to be scientists?" *Management Science* 50(6): 835–853; and Esty, D. C., and A. S. Winston (2009), *Green to Gold: How Smart Companies Use Environmental Strategy to Innovate, Create Value, and Build Competitive Advantage,* revised and updated (Hoboken, NJ: John Wiley).

CHAPTER 3

External Analysis: Industry Structure, Competitive Forces, and Strategic Groups

LEARNING OBJECTIVES

After studying this chapter, you should be able to:

LO 3-1   Apply the PESTEL model to organize and assess the impact of external forces on the firm.

LO 3-2   Apply the structure-conduct-performance (SCP) model to explain the effect of industry structure on firm profitability.

LO 3-3   Apply the five forces model to understand the profit potential of the firm's industry.

LO 3-4   Describe the strategic role of complements in creating positive-sum co-opetition.

LO 3-5   Understand the role of industry dynamics and industry convergence in shaping the firm's external environment.

LO 3-6   Apply the strategic group model to reveal performance differences between clusters of firms in the same industry.

Build Your Dreams (BYD) to Sidestep Entry Barriers

THE BIG THREE—GM, Ford, and Chrysler—dominated the U.S. car market throughout most of the 20th century. As the competition in the industry became increasingly global, foreign car makers entered the U.S. market mainly by importing vehicles from overseas plants. Among the first were German carmakers Volkswagen, Daimler, and BMW as well as Japanese carmakers Honda, Toyota, and Nissan. The foreign entrants intensified competition, threatened the market share of the Big Three, and led to political pressure to impose import restrictions in the 1980s. The new players responded by building U.S. plants in order to avoid import restrictions. More recently, Korean car makers Hyundai and Kia have begun making and selling cars in the United States.

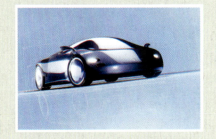

Although globalization and deregulation paved the way for significant new entry into the U.S. auto market, the worldwide car manufacturing industry has been exposed to few new entrants. In fact, no new major car manufacturers have emerged in the last couple of decades in part because automobiles powered by internal combustion engines are made out of thousands of precisely engineered parts; few industrial products, excluding commercial airplanes, are as complex as cars. Car manufacturers also require large-scale production in order to be cost-competitive. These facts create seemingly insurmountable barriers to entry into car manufacturing.

Thus, it would seem that an unknown startup from an emerging economy, attempting to enter the car industry during the deepest economic recession since the Great Depression, would surely be a fool's errand.

Yet Wang Chuanfu, founder and chairman of the Chinese technology startup Build Your Dreams (BYD) begs to differ. His strategy is to use new technology to sidestep entry barriers. BYD began its life as a battery company in 1995 and is now leveraging this expertise into electric vehicles. Unlike complex gasoline engines, electric cars are powered by simple motors and gearboxes that have very few parts. Electric vehicles are therefore much cheaper and more straightforward to build.

BYD's claim to fame is a lithium ferrous phosphate battery on which cars can run 250 miles on a single three-hour charge. Already one of the fastest growing independent automakers, BYD is selling plug-in hybrids and all-electric vehicles in China, Africa, the Middle East, and South America. It plans to sell cars in the U.S. and other Western countries in the near future.

Legendary investor Warren Buffett found BYD interesting enough to put in some $230 million for a 10 percent equity stake. Consumers may flock to BYD cars as well. Not only are they "green" cars, but their sticker price is anticipated to be about half that of the Chevy Volt (whose starting price is $40,000). Other companies entering the car industry by leveraging new battery technology include Tesla Motors and Fisker Automotive, both in California, as well as Think Global in Norway and Lightning Car in the United Kingdom. Sparks are sure to fly as the car industry becomes more competitive in the 21st century.[1]

After reading the chapter, you will find more about this case, with related questions, on page 77.

▲ **THE BYD STORY** illustrates that the structure of an industry has a direct bearing on a firm's performance. Industry structure captures important economic characteristics such as the number and size of competitors, whether the offering is an undifferentiated commodity like steel or a highly differentiated service like management consulting, and the height of entry and exit barriers. Having been protected by high entry barriers for a long time, GM, for example, once held more than a 50 percent U.S. market share; it was highly profitable for many decades, until about 1980. Ford and Chrysler also did well during this period.

The BYD ChapterCase also illustrates that competitive forces in an industry have an impact on firm performance. Globalization led to extensive entry by foreign car manufacturers, increasing the number of competitors in the U.S. auto industry, and with it, competitive rivalry. The Japanese automakers, for example, were successful in the U.S. market because their cars were generally of better quality, their production systems were more efficient, and they were more responsive to changes in customer preferences. Today, advances in battery technology allow startups like BYD to enter the electric car segment (or strategic group), thereby circumventing high entry barriers into the broad automotive market. With more firms vying for a smaller pie in the U.S. auto market, competitive intensity is sure to increase.

In this chapter, we turn our attention to what is considered the firm's *external environment:* the industry in which the firm operates and the competitive forces that surround the firm from the outside.

THE PESTEL FRAMEWORK

>> LO 3-1
Apply the PESTEL model to organize and assess the impact of external forces on the firm.

We now take a first look at the firm's external environment. Understanding the forces in the external environment allows managers to mitigate threats and leverage opportunities.

As Exhibit 3.1 shows, a firm is embedded in different layers in its environment. The firm falls into a *strategic group,* the set of companies that pursue a similar strategy within a specific industry. The strategic group, in essence, consists of the firm's closest competitors. Just outside the strategic group is the industry in which the company operates. Industries differ along important structural dimensions such as the number and size of competitors in an industry and the type of products or services offered. Industries, in turn, are embedded in the larger macro environment, in which a wide variety of forces exert their influence

EXHIBIT 3.1

The Firm Embedded in Its External Environment: Global World, PESTEL Forces, Industry, and Strategic Group

on industries, strategic groups, and firms. Depending on the firm's strategy, these forces can affect its performance in a positive or negative fashion. We now turn to studying each of these environmental layers in detail, moving from a firm's general environment to its task environment. That is, we will work from the outer to the inner ring in Exhibit 3.1.

For purposes of discussion, we can group the forces at the most macro level into six segments—*political, economic, sociocultural, technological, ecological,* and *legal,* which form the acronym PESTEL. Although many of the PESTEL factors are interdependent, the PESTEL model provides a relatively straightforward way to categorize and analyze the important external forces that might impinge upon a firm. As markets have opened up and international trade has increased exponentially in recent decades, the PESTEL forces have become more global. These forces are embedded in the global environment and can create both opportunities and threats, so it pays to monitor them closely.

Political Factors

The political environment describes the processes and actions of government bodies that can influence the decisions and behavior of firms.[2] Governments, for example, can affect firm performance by exerting political pressure on companies, as described in Strategy Highlight 3.1.

Economic Factors

The economic factors in the external environment are largely macroeconomic, affecting economy-wide phenomena. Managers need to consider how the following five macroeconomic factors can affect firm strategy:

- Growth rates
- Interest rates
- Levels of employment
- Price stability (inflation and deflation)
- Currency exchange rates.

GROWTH RATES. The overall economic *growth rate* is a measure of the change in the amount of goods and services produced by a nation's economy. It indicates what stage of the business cycle the economy is in—that is, whether business activity is expanding (boom) or contracting (recession). In periods of economic expansion, consumer and business demand are rising, and competition among firms frequently decreases. Basically, the rising tide of economic growth "lifts all boats." During these economic boom cycles, businesses expand operations to satisfy demand and are more likely to be profitable.

STRATEGY HIGHLIGHT 3.1

UBS Relents to Pressure by U.S. Government

UBS, a venerable Swiss banking institution with global business activities, experienced the significant implications that political factors can have on the bottom line. The U.S. government alleged that by advertising its "tax savings" advantages to U.S. clients, UBS aided wealthy Americans in siphoning off billions of dollars to a safe haven that the IRS cannot touch. The government requested from UBS the names of 52,000 U.S. citizens who it suspected were tax evaders.

Initially, UBS declined to release names, citing Swiss banking laws and regulations that guarantee privacy of customers. However, UBS was in a lose–lose situation: If it resisted the IRS, it risked losing its U.S. banking license. If it disclosed names of its customers, it would break the traditional Swiss banking secrecy and potentially violate Swiss law, which makes it a felony to improperly disclose client information. In 2009, after multiple rounds of intense negotiations, UBS finally relented to significant pressure by the U.S. government and released the names of 4,450 U.S. citizens who are suspected to have evaded taxes.

This incident marks a watershed for UBS and the entire Swiss banking system. Banking secrecy has formed the basis for a sustained competitive advantage in the financial industry for over 75 years. Estimates suggest that foreigners hold assets worth some $2 trillion in Switzerland, which could be withdrawn if banking secrecy is not guaranteed.[3]

PESTEL model
A framework that categorizes and analyzes an important set of external forces (political, economic, technological, ecological, and legal) that might impinge upon a firm. These forces are embedded in the global environment and can create both opportunities and threats for the firm.

Occasionally, boom periods can overheat and lead to speculative bubbles. Between 1995 and 2000, for example, the United States witnessed such a bubble, propelled by new companies seeking to capture business opportunities on the Internet. The market for dot-com companies was characterized by "irrational exuberance,"[4] with the NASDAQ stock index peaking at its all-time high of 5,132 points on March 10, 2000. Hundreds of dot-com businesses were founded during this time, but very few survived the burst of the bubble. Among the survivors are today's powerhouses of the Internet economy including Google, Amazon, and eBay.

In the early 2000s, the United States saw yet another bubble—this time in housing.[5] Easy credit, made possible by the availability of subprime mortgages and other financial innovations, fueled an unprecedented demand in housing. Real estate, rather than stocks, became the investment vehicle of choice for many Americans, in the common belief that house prices could only go up. The housing bubble burst in the fall of 2008. Many financial institutions had to write off billions of dollars in toxic or worthless mortgage assets. All of the large U.S. financial institutions, including Bank of America, Citigroup, Wells Fargo, and insurance giant AIG, ended up being bailed out by taxpayers. With the bursting of the housing bubble, the economic recession of 2008–2009 began, affecting in some way nearly all businesses in the United States and worldwide.

Periods of economic boom and bust are natural occurrences in free-market systems. Austrian economist Joseph Schumpeter argued that such uproar is the "music of capitalism"[6]—a healthy and normal thing to expect in free-market economies. Indeed, shrewd managers *initiate* strategic successes during periods of economic downturn. During a recessionary period in 2001, Apple boosted spending on research and development to design and develop the iPod. When the economy picked up again, Apple was ready to launch the iPod combined with iTunes services, a highly profitable strategic move.[7] More recently, Apple launched the iPad in early 2010, following the severe 2008–2009 recession.

INTEREST RATES. Another key macroeconomic variable for managers to track is *interest rates*—the amount that savers are paid for use of their money and the amount that borrowers pay for that use. The economic boom during the early years in the 21st century, for example, was fueled by cheap credit. Low interest rates have a direct bearing on consumer demand. When credit is cheap (because interest rates are low), consumers buy homes, automobiles, computers, and even vacations on credit. All this demand fuels economic growth. During periods of low interest rates, firms can easily borrow money to finance future growth. Borrowing at lower rates lowers their cost of capital, enhancing their competitiveness. These effects reverse, however, when interest rates are high. Consumer demand slows down; credit is harder to come by, and firms thus find it more difficult to borrow money to support operations and might defer expansions.

LEVELS OF EMPLOYMENT. The state of the economy directly affects the *level of employment*. In boom times, unemployment is low, and skilled human capital becomes a scarce and thus more expensive resource. In economic downturns, unemployment rises. As more people search for employment, skilled human capital is abundant and wages usually fall.

A period of high unemployment could be a good time for firms to expand or upgrade their human capital base. Although U.S. companies generally lay off people during recessions, some Japanese companies, such as Toyota, prefer to use the downturn to train their workers on the latest manufacturing techniques.[8] Clearly, this strategy is a short-term expense for Toyota, yet it positions the company well when the economy picks up again.

PRICE STABILITY. *Price stability*—the lack of change in price levels of goods and services—is rare. Therefore, companies will often have to deal with changing price levels. The price level is a direct function of the amount of money in any economy. When there is too much money in an economy, we tend to see rising prices—*inflation.* Indeed, a popular economic definition of inflation is "too much money chasing too few goods and services."[9] Inflation tends to go along with higher interest rates and lower economic growth.

Deflation describes a decrease in the overall price level. A sudden and pronounced drop in demand generally causes deflation, which in turn forces sellers to lower prices to motivate buyers. Because many people automatically think of lower prices from the buyer's point of view, a decreasing price level seems at first glance to be attractive. However, deflation is actually a serious threat to economic growth because it distorts expectations about the future.[10] For example, once price levels start falling, companies will not invest in new production capacity or innovation because they expect a further decline in prices. Deflation also cools demand: "Why should I purchase something today if it is likely to cost less tomorrow?" Both lower demand and lower investment in turn will deepen any recession. If an economic downturn is especially severe and prolonged, a recession may turn into a *depression.*

CURRENCY EXCHANGE RATES. The *currency exchange rate* determines how many dollars one must pay for a unit of foreign currency. It is a critical variable for any company that either buys or sells products and services across national borders. If the U.S. dollar is weak, for example, it takes more dollars to buy one euro. This in turn makes U.S. exports like Boeing aircraft or John Deere tractors cheaper in Europe. By the same token, European imports like BMW automobiles become more expensive for U.S. buyers. This process reverses when the dollar appreciates against the euro.

The important point here is that the currency exchange rate is partly a function of the interest rates in the United States versus the European Union, with higher interest rates leading to stronger currencies. The *balance of trade,* which is the difference between a nation's exports and imports, is an even more important factor in determining foreign exchange rates. For example, Americans consume a lot more Chinese goods than Chinese consume American products. This imbalance implies that the U.S. runs a huge balance of trade deficit with China, which in turn puts downward pressure on the U.S. dollar.

In summary, economic factors affecting business are ever-present and rarely static. Managers need to fully appreciate the power of these factors, in both domestic and global markets, in order to assess their effects on firm performance.

Sociocultural Factors

Sociocultural factors capture a society's cultures, norms, and values. Because sociocultural forces not only are constantly in flux but also differ across groups, managers need to closely monitor such trends and consider the implications for firm strategy. Changing sociocultural factors create opportunities as well as threats. In recent years, for example, a growing number of U.S. consumers have become more health-conscious about what they eat. This trend led to a boom for the sandwich store Subway and the organic grocery store Whole Foods. At the same time, traditional fast-food companies like McDonald's and Burger King and grocery chains like Albertsons and Publix all had to scramble to provide healthier choices in their product offerings. Similarly, Coca-Cola was slow in spotting the trend toward noncarbonated and healthier drinks, like bottled water and natural juices. In contrast, long-time rival Pepsi seized upon this opportunity more quickly, capturing market share from Coca-Cola.[11]

Demographic trends are also important sociocultural forces. They capture characteristics in a population related to age, gender, family size, ethnicity, sexual orientation, religion, and socioeconomic class. Like other sociocultural factors, demographic trends present opportunities but can also pose threats. For example, as baby boomers begin to retire in larger numbers, business may see opportunities from an increased demand for health care and wellness services. To finance their retirement, however, baby boomers will begin to drain their retirement savings accounts, which may cause a decline in demand for investment services.

Technological Factors

Technological factors capture the application of knowledge to create new processes and products. Recent innovations in process technology include lean manufacturing, Six Sigma quality, and biotechnology. Recent product innovations are the electric vehicle and the iPad.

Technological progress is relentless and seems to be picking up speed over time.[12] Think about the Internet or advancements in biotechnology and nanotechnology. Shopping online has radically altered business and consumer behavior. U.S. online retail sales accounted for 6 percent of total retail sales or $140 billion in 2008, and are expected to reach 8 percent by 2013.[13] The largest U.S. online retailers (or *e-tailers*) are Amazon, Staples, Office Depot, Dell, and Hewlett-Packard (HP).[14] Leveraging the biotechnology revolution, newcomers like Genzyme or Biogen are now full-fledged pharmaceutical companies.[15] The revolution in nanotechnology is just beginning, but promises major upheaval in a vast array of industries ranging from tiny medical devices to new-age materials for earthquake-resistant buildings.[16]

Given the importance of a firm's innovation strategy to competitive advantage, we discuss the effect of technological factors in detail in Chapter 7.

Ecological Factors

Ecological factors concern broad environmental issues such as the natural environment, global warming and sustainable economic growth. Managers can no longer separate the natural and the business worlds; they are inextricably linked.[17] BP's infamous oil spill in the Gulf of Mexico following the explosion on the Deepwater Horizon drilling rig may cost the company an estimated $40 billion.[18] Moreover, the perceived failure of BP's CEO Tony Hayward to manage the crisis cost him the CEO position, and he was replaced by Bob Dudley. Ecological factors also highlight the importance of a triple-bottom-line approach to a sustainable competitive advantage as discussed in Chapter 5.

Legal Factors

The *legal environment* captures the official outcomes of the political processes as manifested in laws, mandates, regulations, and court decisions. These in turn can have a direct bearing on a firm's bottom line. In 2009, for example, U.S. chipmaker Intel was found not to comply with the antitrust regulations of the European Union, which levied a $1.45 billion fine against Intel for alleged abuse of monopoly power.[19] Intel holds some 80 percent market share in semiconductors worldwide.[20] Its primary rival, U.S. chipmaker AMD, alleged that Intel leveraged its position as the largest supplier in the market to provide deep discounts to large computer manufacturers, to keep them from using AMD chips. EU regulators concluded that Intel's actions harmed millions of consumers by keeping the price of computer chips above competitive levels.

Regulatory changes tend to affect entire industries. The California Air Resource Board (CARB) in 1990 passed a mandate for introducing zero-emissions cars, which stipulated that 10 percent of new vehicles sold by car makers must be zero-emissions by 2003.[21] This mandate not only accelerated research in alternative energy sources for cars, but also led to the development of the first fully electric production car, GM's EV1. GM launched the car in California and Arizona in 1996. Competitive models followed, with the Toyota RAV EV and the Honda EV. In this case, regulations in the legal environment fostered innovation in the automobile industry.

Companies are not only influenced by forces in their environment but can also influence the development of those forces. The California mandate on zero-emissions, for example, did not stand. Several stakeholders, including the car and oil companies, fought it through lawsuits and other actions. CARB ultimately relented to the pressure and abandoned its zero-emissions mandate. When the mandate was revoked, GM recalled and destroyed its EV1 electric vehicles and terminated its electric-vehicle program. This decision turned out to be a strategic error that would haunt GM a decade or so later. Although GM was the leader among car companies in electric vehicles in the mid-1990s, it did not have a competitive model to counter the Toyota Prius or the Honda Insight when their sales took off in the early 2000s. The Chevy Volt (a plug-in hybrid), GM's first major competition to the Prius and the Insight, was delayed by several years because GM had to start its electric-vehicle program basically from scratch. Not having an adequate product lineup during the early 2000s, GM's U.S. market share dropped below 20 percent in 2009 (from over 50 percent a few decades earlier), the year it filed for bankruptcy.

This example demonstrates that it may be possible to influence the development of forces but it may not be the best use of management time and resources. GM's strategic decision to fight the regulatory outcome rather than change the product lineup also ignored changing trends in the sociocultural environment (a growing number of customers wanted low-emission cars) and the importance of the ecological environment. This goes to show that strategic decisions have long-term consequences that are not easily reversible.

UNDERSTANDING DIFFERENCES IN INDUSTRY PERFORMANCE: THE STRUCTURE-CONDUCT-PERFORMANCE MODEL

From the external PESTEL forces, we move one step closer to the firm and come to the industry in which a firm functions. An industry makes up the supply side of the market, while customers make up the demand side. An **industry,** therefore, is a group of companies offering similar products or services. In the $300 billion management-consulting industry, each of the major competitors such as Accenture, Boston Consulting Group, and McKinsey offers similar consulting services.[22] Our purpose in looking at the firm's industry is to understand differences in industry performance.

The **structure-conduct-performance (SCP) model** is a theoretical framework, developed in industrial-organization economics, that explains differences in industry

>> **LO 3-2**

Apply the structure-conduct-performance (SCP) model to explain the effect of industry structure on firm profitability.

---

industry A group of companies offering similar products or services. It makes up the supply side of the market, while customers make up the demand side.

structure-conduct-performance (SCP) model A framework that explains differences in industry performance. It identifies four different industry types:

(1) perfect competition, (2) monopolistic competition, (3) oligopoly, and (4) monopoly. Fragmented industries tend to be less profitable than consolidated ones.

EXHIBIT 3.2

Industry Structures
along the Continuum
from Fragmented to
Consolidated

Perfect Competition
- Many small firms
- Firms are price takers
- Commodity product
- Low entry barriers

Monopolistic Competition
- Many firms
- Some pricing power
- Differentiated product
- Medium entry barriers

Oligopoly
- Few (large) firms
- Some pricing power
- Differentiated product
- High entry barriers

Monopoly
- One firm
- Considerable pricing power
- Unique product
- Very high entry barriers

Fragmented
Low Profitability

Consolidated
High Profitability

performance.[23] According to the SCP model, the underlying *industry structure* determines *firm conduct,* which concerns the firm's ability to differentiate its goods and services and thus to influence the price it can charge. Industry structure and firm conduct combine to determine firm performance.

Exhibit 3.2 shows different industry types along a continuum from fragmented to consolidated structures. At one extreme, *fragmented industry structures* consist of many small firms and tend to generate low profitability. At the other end of the continuum, *consolidated industry structures* are dominated by a few firms, or even just one firm, and tend to be highly profitable. The SCP model categorizes industry structure into four main industry types: (1) perfect competition, (2) monopolistic competition, (3) oligopoly, and (4) monopoly. Here, we discuss each of the four different industry types and describe the differences.

Perfect Competition

A *perfectly competitive* industry is characterized as fragmented and has many small firms, a commodity product, ease of entry, and little or no ability for each individual firm to raise its prices. The firms competing in this type of industry are approximately similar in size and resources. Consumers make purchasing decisions solely on price, because the commodity product offerings are more or less identical. The resulting performance of the industry shows low profitability. Under these conditions, firms in perfect competition have difficulty achieving even a temporary competitive advantage and can achieve only competitive parity. While perfect competition is a rare industry structure in its pure form, markets for commodities such as natural gas, copper, and iron tend to approach this structure.

Many Internet entrepreneurs learned the hard way that it is difficult to beat the forces of perfect competition. Fueled by eager venture capitalists, about 100 e-tailers such as *pets. com, petopia.com,* and *pet-store.com* had sprung up by 1999, at the height of the Internet bubble.[24] Cut-throat competition ensued, with online retailers selling products below cost. To make matters worse, at the same time category-killers like PetSmart and PetCo expanded rapidly, opening some 2,000 brick-and-mortar stores in the United States and Canada. As a consequence, most e-tailers of pet supplies went out of business. Applying the SCP model could have predicted that online pet supply stores are unlikely to be profitable: Many small firms offering a commodity product in an industry that is easy to enter would be unable to increase prices and generate profits. The ensuing price competition led to an industry shakeout, with online retailers exiting the industry and the large brick-and-mortar retailers still standing.

Monopolistic Competition

A *monopolistically competitive* industry is characterized by many firms, a differentiated product, some obstacles to entry, and the basis for raising prices for a relatively unique product while retaining customers. The key to understanding this industry structure is that the firms now offer products or services that have unique features.

The computer hardware industry is one example. Many firms compete in this industry, and even the largest firms like Apple, Dell, or HP have less than 20 percent market share. Moreover, while products of one competitor tend to be similar to products of a rival, they are not identical. As a consequence, managers selling a product with unique features tend to have some ability to raise prices. When a firm is able to differentiate its product or service offerings, it carves out a niche in the market in which it has some degree of monopoly power over pricing, thus the name "monopolistic competition." Firms frequently communicate the degree of product differentiation through advertising.

Although undifferentiated agricultural products are commodities leading to a perfect competitive market structure, some farmers have noted the demographic trend toward organic food and recognized the opportunity to respond by differentiating their products. The demand for organic milk far outstrips supply, and allows dairy companies to command a 50–100 percent price premium over non-organic milk. The dairy producers now enjoy some pricing power as a result of their differentiated, rather than commodity, product.

Oligopoly

The term *oligopoly* comes from the Greeks and means "few sellers." An *oligopolistic* industry is becoming more consolidated with few (large) firms, differentiated products, high barriers to entry, and some degree of pricing power. The degree of pricing power depends, just as in monopolistic competition, on the degree of product differentiation.

One of the key features of an oligopoly is that the competing firms are *interdependent*. With only a few competitors, the actions of one competitor influence the behavior of the other competitors. Each competitor in an oligopoly, therefore, must consider the strategic actions of the other competitors. This type of industry structure is often analyzed using *game theory,* which attempts to predict strategic behaviors by assuming that the moves and reactions of competitors can be anticipated.[25] Due to their strategic interdependence, companies in oligopolies have an incentive to coordinate their strategic actions to maximize their joint performance. Although explicit coordination such as price fixing is illegal in the United States, tacit coordination such as "an unspoken understanding" is not.

The express-delivery industry is an example of an oligopoly. The main competitors in this space are FedEx and UPS. Any strategic decision made by FedEx (e.g., to expand delivery services to ground delivery of larger-size packages) directly affects UPS; likewise, any decision made by UPS (e.g., to guarantee next-day delivery before 8:00 a.m.) directly affects FedEx. Other examples of oligopolies include the soft drink industry (Coca-Cola vs. Pepsi), airframe manufacturing business (Boeing vs. Airbus), home-improvement retailing (The Home Depot vs. Lowe's), toys and games (Hasbro vs. Mattel), and detergents (P&G vs. Unilever).

Companies in an oligopoly tend to have some pricing power if they are able to differentiate their product or service offerings from those of competitors. *Non-price competition* is the preferred mode of competition. What does that mean? It means competing by offering unique product features or services rather than competing on price. When one firm in an oligopoly cuts prices to gain market share from its competitor, the competitor typically will respond in kind and also cut prices. This process initiates a price war, which can be especially detrimental to firm performance if the products are close rivals.

In the early years of the soft drink industry, for example, whenever Pepsi was lowering prices, Coca-Cola followed suit. These actions resulted only in reduced profitability for both competitors. In recent decades, the managers of Coca-Cola and Pepsi have repeatedly demonstrated that they learned this lesson. They shifted the basis of competition from price cutting to new-product introductions, product innovation, and lifestyle advertising. Any price adjustments are short-term promotions. By leveraging innovation and advertising, managers from Coca-Cola and Pepsi have moved to non-price competition, which in turn allows them to charge higher prices and to improve industry and company profitability.[26]

Monopoly

An industry is a *monopoly* when there is only one (large) firm supplying the market. "Mono" means *one,* and thus a monopolist is the only seller in a market. The firm may offer a unique product, and the challenges to moving into the industry tend to be high. The monopolist has considerable pricing power. As a consequence, firm (and thus industry) profitability tends to be high.

In some instances, the government will grant one firm the right to be the sole supplier of a product or service. This is often done to incentivize a company to engage in a venture that would not be profitable if there was more than one supplier. For example, public utilities incur huge fixed costs to build plants and to supply a certain geographic area. Public utilities supplying water, gas, and electricity to businesses and homes are frequently monopolists. Georgia Power is the only supplier of electricity for over 2 million customers in the Southeastern United States. Philadelphia Gas Works is the only supplier of natural gas in the city of Philadelphia, PA, serving some 500,000 customers. These are so-called *natural monopolies,* for which the governments involved believe the product or service would not be supplied by the market if there were not a monopoly. In the past few decades, however, more and more of these natural monopolies have been deregulated in the United States, including airlines, telecommunications, railroads, trucking, and ocean transportation. This deregulation allowed competition to emerge, which theoretically should lead to lower prices, better service, and more innovation.

While natural monopolies appear to be disappearing from the competitive landscape, so-called *near monopolies* are of much greater interest to strategists. These are firms that have accrued significant market power. In the process, they are changing the industry structure in their favor, generally from monopolistic competition or oligopolies to near monopolies. These near monopolies are firms that have accomplished product differentiation to such a degree that they are in a class by themselves, just like a monopolist. As highlighted in the legal ruling discussed earlier, the European Union views Intel, with its 80 percent market share in semiconductors, as a near monopoly. This is an enviable position in terms of the ability to extract profits, although a monopoly position may attract the anti-trust regulators and lead to legal repercussions.

COMPETITIVE FORCES AND FIRM STRATEGY: THE FIVE FORCES MODEL

>> **LO 3-3**
Apply the five forces model to understand the profit potential of the firm's industry.

Building on the SCP model, Michael Porter developed the highly influential **five forces model**.[27] As Exhibit 3.3 shows, Porter's model identifies five key competitive forces that managers need to consider when analyzing the industry environment and formulating strategy:

1. Threat of entry
2. Power of suppliers
3. Power of buyers
4. Threat of substitutes
5. Rivalry among existing competitors

Porter's model aims to enable managers not only to understand their industry environment but also to shape their firm's strategy. As a rule of thumb, the stronger the five forces, the lower the industry's profit potential—making the industry less attractive to competitors. The reverse also is true: The weaker the five forces, the greater the industry's profit potential—making the industry more attractive. The model's perspective is that of the manager of an existing (incumbent) firm competing for advantage in an established industry. Managers need to position their company in an industry in a way that relaxes the constraints of strong forces and leverages weak forces. We next discuss each of the five competitive forces in detail, and will take up the topic of competitive positioning in Chapter 6 when studying business-level strategy.

EXHIBIT 3.3

Porter's Five Forces Model

Source: Michael E. Porter, "The five competitive forces that shape strategy," *Harvard Business Review,* January 2008.

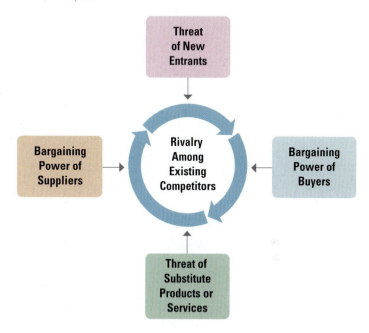

Threat of Entry

Entry barriers are obstacles that determine how easily a firm can enter an industry. High entry barriers can correspond to high industry profitability, assuming there is no excess capacity in the industry. Take the example of BYD in the ChapterCase. Entry barriers into the broad automobile industry seem almost insurmountable because of the engineering competence needed for manufacturing gasoline-powered engines and the need for large-scale production. Many industry analysts argue that to be viable, a car company must be able to produce and sell some 5 million cars per year.[28] This fact explains in part why Chrysler, selling less than 2 million vehicles per year, was bought out in part by Fiat, an Italian carmaker, itself a small company selling an estimated 2.5 million vehicles per year.

Given the industry structure in the automobile business and the economic downturn of 2008–2009, entering the auto manufacturing industry right now doesn't seem advisable. Yet BYD is joining the fray. How can it sidestep such insurmountable entry barriers? The answer: Technology is leveling the playing field. Mr. Wang, founder and chairman of BYD, explains his strategic intent: "It's almost hopeless for a latecomer like us to compete with GM and other established automakers with a century of experience in gasoline engines. With electric vehicles, we're all at the same starting line."[29] Actually, BYD may even have a head start because of its deep experience in batteries, selling them to technology giants like Motorola, Nokia, and Samsung. This example shows how managers can use technological innovation to avoid entry barriers into the broad industry and build a position in a smaller strategic group.

This shift in the external environment, in turn, has significant competitive implications for the existing firms in the automobile industry. Having new firms such as BYD and Tesla

five forces model
A framework proposed by Michael Porter that identifies five forces that determine the profit potential of an industry and shape a firm's competitive strategy.

entry barriers
Obstacles that determine how easily a firm can enter an industry. Entry barriers are often one of the most significant predictors of industry profitability.

Motors enter the industry leads to higher competitive intensity. Incumbent firms such as GM and Nissan are responding to the new entrants by introducing innovations of their own such as the Chevy Volt and the Nissan Leaf. Consumers are likely to benefit from an increase in competitive intensity if more innovative and efficient products are introduced with lower prices. Only time will tell if the new entrants will mature to be full-fledged industrial enterprises and become strong enough to push some incumbents out of the industry.

The height of entry barriers is also relevant to *potential competitors*—those that are not yet competing in the industry but have the capability to do so if they choose. The likelihood of entry is determined by the level of capital investment required to enter the industry and the expected return on investment. For example, in the Southeastern United States, TV cable company Comcast has entered the business for residential and commercial telephone services and Internet connectivity (as an ISP, Internet service provider), thus emerging as a direct competitor for AT&T and Bell South, who merged. The new AT&T responded to Comcast's threat by introducing U-verse, a product combining high-speed Internet access with cable TV and telephone service, all provided over its super-fast fiber-optic network. In turn, Comcast acquired a majority stake in NBC Universal, combining delivery and content.[30]

The Power of Suppliers

The bargaining power of suppliers captures pressures that industry suppliers can exert on an industry's, and therefore a company's, profitability. Inputs into the production process include raw materials and components, labor (may be individuals or labor unions, when the industry faces collective bargaining), and services. Powerful suppliers can raise the cost of production by demanding higher prices or delivering lower-quality products. As an example, the United Autoworkers (UAW) union is a powerful stakeholder that extracts significant profits from competitors in the auto industry like GM, Ford, and Chrysler by successfully demanding restrictive work rules and generous health care and retiree benefits. As an indication of UAW power, it owned the majority of Chrysler and almost one half of GM following their bankruptcy reorganizations.[31]

Suppliers are powerful relative to the firms in the industry if there are only few substitutes available for the products and services supplied. For example, crude oil is still a critical input in many industries, and oil suppliers are fairly powerful in raising prices and squeezing industry profitability where products and services rely heavily on oil inputs such as fertilizers or plastics. Suppliers are also in a more powerful position when the extent of competition among suppliers is low, which often goes along with a small number of large suppliers. Supplier power is further enhanced when the supplied product is unique and differentiated or when the companies in the industry face significant switching costs. Supplier power is also strengthened when suppliers provide a credible threat of *forwardly integrating* into the industry (i.e., moving into their buyers' market), or when the companies in the industry buy only small quantities from the suppliers.

Power of Buyers

The bargaining power of buyers concerns the pressure buyers can put on the margins of producers in the industry, by demanding a lower price or higher product quality. When buyers successfully obtain price discounts, it reduces a firm's top line (revenue). When buyers demand higher quality and more service, it generally raises production costs. Strong buyers can therefore reduce industry profitability and with it, a firm's profitability.

The buyers of an industry's product or service may be individual consumers—like you or me when we decide which provider we want to use for our wireless devices. In many areas, you can choose between several providers—AT&T, Sprint, or Verizon. Although we might be able to play different providers against one another when carefully comparing their individual service plans, as individual consumers we generally do not have significant buyer power. On the other hand, large institutions like businesses or universities have significant buyer power when deciding which provider to use for their wireless services, because they are able to sign up or move several thousand employees at once.

Buyers have strong bargaining power when they purchase in large quantities and control many access points to the final customer. Walmart, for example, can exert tremendous pressure on its suppliers to lower prices and to increase quality—or it will choose to not place the suppliers' products on its shelves. Walmart's buyer power is so strong that many suppliers co-locate offices directly next to Walmart's headquarters in Bentonville, Arkansas; such proximity enables Walmart's managers to test the supplier's latest products and negotiate prices.

Buyer power also increases when the buyer's switching costs are low. Having multiple suppliers of a product category located close to its headquarters helps Walmart demand further price cuts and quality improvements. Walmart can easily switch from one supplier to the next. This threat is even more pronounced if the products sold to buyers are non-differentiated commodities in the perception of the end consumer; for example, Walmart can easily switch from one producer of plastic containers (e.g., Rubbermaid) to another (e.g., Sterlite) by offering more shelf space to the producer that offers the greatest price cut or quality improvement.

Buyers also tend to be quite powerful when they are the only customer buying a certain product. Many modern defense technologies rely on the latest innovations, but frequently these products are bought by only one buyer, the U.S. Department of Defense (DoD).[32] Being the sole buyer implies that the DoD has considerable bargaining power to demand lower prices and higher quality. In many cases, however, this is balanced by the fact that there is only one supplier, like Lockheed Martin, of a type of specialized military equipment.

Buyers are also powerful when they can credibly threaten backward integration. *Backward integration* occurs when a buyer moves upstream in the industry value chain, into the seller's business. This situation is commonly observed in the auto-component supply industry, in which car manufacturers like GM, Ford, or BMW have the capability to backward-integrate in order to produce their components in-house if their demands for lower prices and higher product quality are not met by their suppliers.

In sum, powerful buyers have the ability to extract a significant amount of the value created in the industry, leaving little or nothing for producers.

Threat of Substitutes

The threat of substitutes is the idea that products or services available from *outside the given industry* will come close to meeting the needs of current customers. The existence of substitutes that have attractive price and performance characteristics results in low switching costs, increasing the strength of this threat. For example, if the price of coffee increased significantly, customers might switch to tea or other caffeinated beverages to meet their needs.[33] Other examples of substitutes are: video conferencing vs. business travel; e-mail vs. express mail; plastic vs. aluminum containers; gasoline vs. biofuel; and landline telephone services vs. Voice over Internet Protocol (VoIP, offered by Skype or Vonage).

Rivalry among Existing Competitors

Rivalry among existing competitors describes the intensity with which companies in an industry jockey for market share and profitability. It can range from genteel to cut-throat. As shown in Exhibit 3.3, the forces discussed earlier—threat of entry, power of buyers and suppliers, and the threat of substitutes—all put pressure on the rivalry among existing competitors. The stronger the forces, the stronger the expected competitive intensity, which in turn limits the industry's profit potential. When intense rivalry among existing competitors brings about price discounting, industry profitability clearly tends to erode. When non-price competition such as pressure to innovate, increased advertising, and improved service is the primary basis of competition, costs will increase, which may have some impact on industry profitability. However, when these moves create products that respond closely to customer needs and willingness to pay, then average industry profitability tends to increase because producers are able to raise prices and thus increase revenues.

The rivalry among existing competitors is also a function of industry's **exit barriers,** the obstacles that determine how easily a firm can leave an industry. An industry with low exit barriers is more attractive, because underperforming firms can exit more easily, reducing the competitive pressure on the existing firms as excess capacity is removed.

Exit barriers are comprised of both economic and social factors. They include costs that must be paid regardless of whether the company is operating in the industry or not (fixed costs). A company exiting an industry may still have contractual obligations to suppliers, such as an obligation to the suppliers of labor that could include health care and retirement benefits as well as severance pay. GM's health care and retirement costs are contractual obligations that would accrue regardless of whether GM produces and sells any vehicles. Some of these costs were restructured during GM's time in Chapter 11 bankruptcy (which allows companies to continue to operate while providing temporary relief from its creditors). Although GM's healthcare cost per vehicle sold remains above that of its foreign competitors, it is now reduced to about $330 per vehicle instead of $1,500 pre-bankruptcy.[34]

Social factors include things like emotional attachments to certain geographic locations. In Michigan, entire communities depend on GM, Ford, and Chrysler. If any of those carmakers were to exit the industry, communities would suffer. During the 1980s and 1990s, massive layoffs at GM factories devastated the economy of Flint, Michigan. Many more communities were affected during GM's 2009 bankruptcy, which resulted in the closing of more than a dozen manufacturing plants and thousands of dealerships.[35] Other social and economic factors include ripple effects through the supply chain. When one major player in an industry shuts down, its suppliers are affected adversely, potentially leading to further layoffs.

When managers understand the strength or weakness of the five forces that affect the competition in an industry, they are better able to position the company in a way that protects it from the strong forces and exploits the weak forces. The goal is of course to improve the firm's ability to achieve a competitive advantage. To summarize our discussion of the five forces, Exhibit 3.4 provides you with a checklist that you can apply to any industry when assessing the underlying five competitive forces. The key take-away from the five forces model is that *the stronger (weaker) the forces, the lower (greater) the industry's ability to earn above-average profits, and correspondingly, the lower (greater) the firm's ability to gain and sustain a competitive advantage.* The airline and soft drink industries provide illustrative examples.[36]

exit barriers
Obstacles that determine how easily a firm can leave an industry.

GAINING & SUSTAINING COMPETITIVE ADVANTAGE

Five Forces in Airlines vs. Soft Drinks

Let's put the five forces model under the magnifying glass, to critically evaluate what it can tell us about how companies gain and sustain competitive advantage. To do so, we will contrast two industries—airlines and soft drinks.[37]

Airlines have been one of the least profitable industries for decades, with an average return on invested capital (ROIC) of 5.9 percent between 1992 and 2006. Michael Porter

EXHIBIT 3.4

The Five Forces
Competitive Analysis
Checklist

THE THREAT OF ENTRY IS HIGH WHEN:

>> Customer switching costs are low.

>> Capital requirements are low.

>> Incumbents do not possess:

■ Proprietary technology

■ Established brand equity

>> New entrants expect that incumbents will not or cannot retaliate.

THE POWER OF SUPPLIERS IS HIGH WHEN:

>> Incumbent firms face significant switching costs when changing suppliers.

>> Suppliers offer products that are differentiated.

>> There are no readily available substitutes for the products or services that the suppliers offer.

>> Suppliers can credibly threaten to forward-integrate into the industry.

THE POWER OF BUYERS IS HIGH WHEN:

>> There are a few large buyers.

>> Each buyer purchases large quantities relative to the size of a single seller.

>> The industry's products are standardized or undifferentiated commodities.

>> Buyers face little or no switching costs.

>> Buyers can credibly threaten to backward-integrate into the industry.

THE THREAT OF SUBSTITUTES IS HIGH WHEN:

>> The substitute offers an attractive price–performance trade-off.

>> The buyer's cost of switching to the substitute is low.

THE RIVALRY AMONG EXISTING COMPETITORS IS HIGH WHEN:

>> There are many competitors in the industry.

>> The competitors are roughly of equal size.

>> Industry growth is slow, zero, or even negative.

>> Exit barriers are high.

>> Products and services are direct substitutes.

---

calls airlines a "zero star" industry, because each of the five forces is strong, leading to inferior industry performance. The nature of rivalry among airlines is incredibly intense, because the consumer views each airline's service to be undifferentiated and makes decisions mainly based on price. Thanks to Internet travel sites such as Orbitz and Travelocity, real-time price comparisons are effortless. Low switching costs and nearly perfect information combine to strengthen buyer power. Entry barriers are relatively low, resulting in a number of new airlines popping up. To enter the industry (in a small way, serving a few select cities), a prospective new entrant needs only a couple of airplanes (which can be rented), a few pilots and crew members, some routes connecting city pairs, and gate access in those cities. The supplier power is strong, with providers of aircraft engines such as GE, Rolls-Royce, or Pratt & Whitney, aircraft maintenance companies such as Goodrich, labor unions, and airports controlling gate access—all bargaining away the profitability of airlines. To make matters worse, substitutes are also readily available: If prices are seen as too high, customers can drive their cars or use the train or bus. As an example, the route between Atlanta and Orlando (roughly 400 miles) used to be one of the busiest and most profitable ones for Delta. Given the increasing security delays at airports, more and more people now prefer to drive. Taken together, the competitive forces are quite unfavorable for generating a profit potential in the airline industry: low entry barriers; high supplier power; high buyer power due to instant price information provided by websites, combined with low customer switching costs; and the availability of low-cost substitutes. This unfavorable environment leads to intense rivalry among existing firms and low industry profitability.

In contrast, soft drinks have been one of the most profitable industries for decades, with an average ROIC of 37.6 percent between 1992 and 2006. Michael Porter calls soft drinks a "five star" industry; by that, he means that each of the five forces is weak, leading to superior industry performance. The nature of competition between Pepsi and Coke is benign for the most part, focusing on non-price factors such as lifestyle advertising and product innovation rather than on price. The barriers to entry are high, because of the strong brand equity enjoyed by Coke and Pepsi, which has been built up over many decades. In addition, bottling is a capital-intensive activity. Consumers tend to be loyal to "their" cola, identifying themselves as Coke or Pepsi drinkers. The power of suppliers is quite limited: Arguably the most valuable input (e.g., Coke's secret formula) is provided by the soft drink companies, while the other inputs are commodities (e.g., water, aluminum cans, plastic bottles, and others). Likewise, the power of buyers is weak, because intermediate customers like bottling franchises and distributors are locked into long-term exclusive contracts with the soft drink companies, and the final end consumer market is extremely fragmented. Not even Walmart is able to force significant price discounts from Coca-Cola or Pepsi, focusing instead on offering its private-label cola Sam's Choice. Favorable competitive forces indicate a significant profit potential in the soft drink industry that the dominant players Coke and Pepsi are well positioned to capture.

Applying the five forces to the airline and soft drink industries shows the model's usefulness in evaluating the effects the industry environment can have on a firm's ability to gain and sustain competitive advantage. 🔍

ADDING A SIXTH FORCE: THE STRATEGIC ROLE OF COMPLEMENTS

>> LO 3-4
Describe the strategic role of complements in creating positive-sum co-opetition.

As valuable as the five forces model is for explaining the profitability and attractiveness of industries, some have suggested extensions of it. Intel's former chairman and CEO, Andy Grove, as well as strategy scholars, suggested that the value of the Porter's five forces model could be further enhanced if one also considers the availability of complements.[38]

complement
A product, service, or competency that adds value to the original product offering when the two are used in tandem.

complementor
A company that provides a good or service that leads customers to value your firm's offering more when the two are combined.

A **complement** is a product, service, or competency that adds value to the original product offering when the two are used in tandem.[39] Complements increase demand for the primary product, thereby enhancing the profit potential for the industry and the firm. A company is a **complementor** to your company if customers value your product or service offering more when they are able to combine it with the other company's product or service.[40]

Firms may choose to provide the complements themselves or work with another company to accomplish this. Several examples illustrate this point:

■ The French tire company Michelin and car manufacturers such as Ford and GM are complementors. Of course, people need tires for their cars, but more importantly, people who drive more need to replace their tires more often. Thus, Michelin has been publishing (since the early 1900s) the highly acclaimed Michelin guidebooks for travel and tourism, which encourage people to drive more and hopefully buy more Michelin tires.

- Claiming that Xerox office paper is specially designed to work best with its complex copying machines, and thus reducing downtime caused by jamming and other problems, Xerox is now one of the leading suppliers of office paper.

- Illegal music downloads created a powerful substitute for CD record sales, which plummeted with the availability of file-sharing software to facilitate illegal downloads. Seeing a strategic opportunity, Apple established the iTunes music store to complement its iPod music player. Apple makes money by selling the hardware (iPods), while providing the complement (iTune software) for free. That combination allows you to load your iPod with thousands of songs that can be selected from more than 14 million offered at the iTunes music store at a reasonable price (beginning at $0.69 each). Similarly, when Apple launched the iPad, it had already established relationships with several major publishing houses as complementors to fill its iBook online store with millions of e-books. Moreover, since the iPad runs on the same operating system as the iPhone, the over 400,000 apps for the iPhone are also available for the iPad through Apple's iTunes online store.

EXHIBIT 3.5

Determining Industry Attractiveness

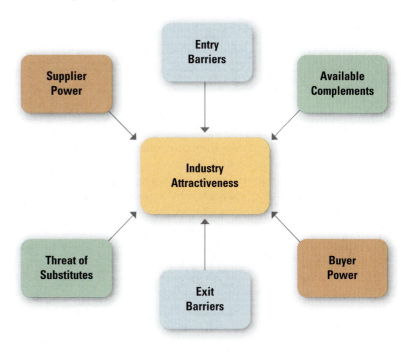

Industry attractiveness, in terms of profit potential, is therefore determined by *three distinct pairs of two forces* (as shown in Exhibit 3.5): (1) supplier and buyer power, (2) entry and exit barriers,[41] and (3) available complements and the threat of substitutes. A complete competitive analysis needs to consider not only Porter's five forces, but also the availability of complements. A successful manager, therefore, should search out complementors and encourage collaboration with them. Rather than seeing competition as a zero-sum game, those who prefer the five-forces-plus-complements model suggest that industry competition can be a positive-sum game. They use the term *co-opetition* to describe cooperative interactions among competitors, which results in success for each of the players—a larger pie for everyone involved.[42]

Strategy Highlight 3.2 (next page) shows how Microsoft—with Intel as complementor—was able to dominate the personal computer software industry for several decades.

CHANGES OVER TIME: INDUSTRY DYNAMICS

Although the five-forces-plus-complements model is useful in understanding an industry's profit potential, it provides only a point-in-time snapshot of a moving target. With it (and other static models), one cannot determine the speed of the change in an industry or the

>> **LO 3-5**
Understand the role of industry dynamics and industry convergence in shaping the firm's external environment.

Microsoft's Attractive OS Software Business: How Much Longer?

Microsoft dominates the industry for PC operating system (OS) software with a 90 percent market share. How can this be? Microsoft's strategy shaped the industry structure in its favor. Its installed base of Windows operating systems on existing computers and its long-term relationships with original equipment manufacturers (OEMs) like Dell and Lenovo create tremendous entry barriers for newcomers. The buyer power of OEMs in turn is low, given the fact that the successful combination of Microsoft's Windows and Intel's processors has produced the *Wintel standard* in the PC industry.

Perhaps most important, consumer switching costs are high. Once users have learned a specific software application program such as MS Word, they are much less likely to use a product from a different vendor. Supplier power is also low, because writing computer code has become a commodity. The threat of comparable substitutes that deliver similar or higher performance benefits, including compatibility among different software programs, is low.

Finally, Intel's semiconductor chips are the perfect complement to Microsoft's operating system. Every time Microsoft releases a new operating system, demand for Intel's latest processor goes up, because new operating systems require more computing power. Due to the complementary nature of their products, Microsoft's and Intel's alternating advances have created a *virtuous cycle*. The competitive forces of the PC operating system software industry and Microsoft's positioning in the industry combine to make the PC-OS software industry very attractive for Microsoft.

Yet, the Wintel standard is not without competition. Linux provides a free, open-source alternative. Red Hat, a software company, has created an $800 million business by distributing and servicing customized Linux versions for many major corporations. In addition, *cloud computing*—the move to distributed computing over the Internet—is also gaining momentum. All these forces threaten the dominance of the Wintel standard in certain segments of the industry and thus undermine the value of Microsoft's dominance in the PC-OS software industry.

rate of innovation. This drawback implies that managers need to repeat their analysis over time, to create a more accurate picture of their industry. It is therefore important that managers consider industry dynamics.

Different conditions prevail in different industries at different times, directly affecting the firms competing in these industries and their profitability. Exhibit 3.6 depicts industry performance as measured by average annual growth in profitability over the five-year time period between 2003 and 2008.[43] It is immediately apparent that industries differ widely in their average profitability. The average annual growth in profitability for metals such as aluminum and steel was almost 58 percent. How can this be? The 2003–2008 period was a boom period, characterized by high demand for metals in fast-growing economies such as China and India, to keep up with new construction and infrastructure projects. In second place were Internet service providers and online retailers with about 55 percent growth in average annual profitability. During this period, many people shifted purchases online, patronizing companies such as Amazon, eBay, and Zappos. On the other hand, the average growth in profitability of general merchandisers like Target, Sears, Macy's, and Kohl's was barely above 1 percent, coming in last.[44] As could be predicted by applying the SCP and five-forces-plus-complements models, significant differences exist in industry performance.

Industry structures, moreover, are not stable over time. Rather, they are dynamic. Since a consolidated industry tends to be more profitable than a fragmented one, firms have a tendency to change the industry structure in their favor, making it more consolidated through (horizontal) mergers and acquisitions. Having fewer competitors generally equates to higher industry profitability. Thus, industry incumbents have an incentive to reduce the number of competitors in the industry. For example, the U.S. banking industry has experienced major consolidation, and banking giants like Citigroup, Bank of America, and Wells Fargo have emerged. In a similar fashion, there used to be the Big Eight in the accounting and professional services industry, handling the audits of publicly traded and well-to-do private companies. Today, only the Big Four remain: PricewaterhouseCoopers, Deloitte, Ernst & Young, and KPMG.

Sometimes oligopolistic industry structures break up and become more fragmented. This generally happens when there are external shocks to an industry such as deregulation, new legislation, technological innovation, or globalization. The emergence of the Internet moved the stock brokerage business from an

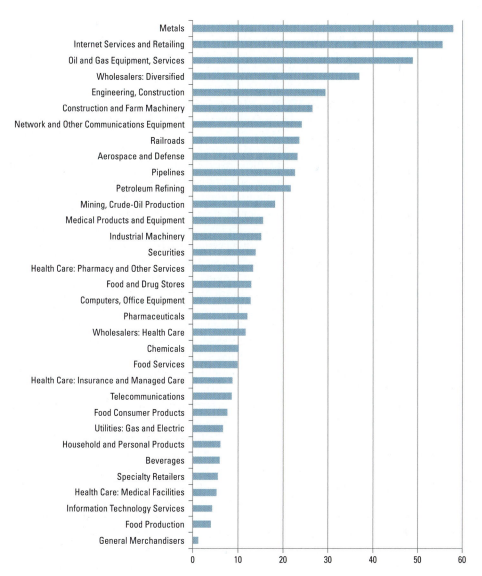

EXHIBIT 3.6

Average Annual
Growth in Industry
Profitability, 2003–2008

Source: Data from *Fortune,*
May 4, 2009.

oligopoly controlled by full-service firms like Merrill Lynch and Morgan Stanley to monop-olistic competition with many generic online brokers such as Ameritrade, E*TRADE, and Scottrade that offer trades at low prices.

Another dynamic to be considered is **industry convergence,** a process whereby for-merly unrelated industries begin to satisfy the same customer need. Industry convergence is often brought on by technological advances. For years, the many players in media indus-tries have been converging due to technological progress in IT, telecommunications, and digital media. Media convergence unites computing, communications, and content, thereby causing significant upheaval across previously distinct industries. Content providers in industries such as newspapers, magazines, TV, movies, radio, and music are all scrambling to adapt. Many standalone print newspapers are closing up shop, while others try to figure out how to offer online news content for which consumers are willing to pay.[45] As a conse-quence of media convergence, annual online ad spending is predicted to reach $62 billion in 2011, overtaking print advertising ($60 billion) and closing in fast on TV advertising ($80 billion).[46] Internet companies such as Google, Yahoo, and Twitter are changing the

industry convergence A process whereby formerly unrelated industries begin to satisfy the same customer need.

industry structure by constantly morphing their capabilities and thus forcing old-line media companies like News Corp., Time Warner, and Disney to adapt. For example, Amazon's Kindle e-reader, Apple's iPad, or Sony's e-reader provide a new form of content delivery that has the potential to make print media obsolete.

EXPLAINING PERFORMANCE DIFFERENCES WITHIN THE SAME INDUSTRY: STRATEGIC GROUPS

>> **LO 3-6**
Apply the strategic group model to reveal performance differences between clusters of firms in the same industry

In further analyzing the firm's external environment, we now move to firms *within the same industry,* to explain performance differences. As noted early in the chapter, a firm occupies a place within a strategic group, a set of companies that pursue a similar strategy within a specific industry in their quest for competitive advantage (see Exhibit 3.1).[47] Strategic groups differ from one another along important dimensions such as expenditures on research and development, technology, product differentiation, product and service offerings, pricing, market segments, distribution channels, and customer service. Applying the idea of strategic groups to the automobile industry featured in ChapterCase 3, one could identify (1) an old-line internal-combustion engine strategic group such as GM, Ford, Chrysler, Toyota, and Honda, and (2) an electric-car strategic group composed of new entrants such as BYD and Tesla Motors. The distinction between the two groups would highlight the underlying technology and market segment.

To explain differences in firm performance within the same industry, scholars offer the strategic group model, which clusters different firms into groups based on a few key strategic dimensions.[48] They find that even within the same industry, the performance of firms differs depending on strategic group membership. For example, the two auto-industry strategic groups just mentioned have different performance results. Some strategic groups tend to be more profitable than others. This difference implies that firm performance is determined not only by the industry to which the firm belongs but also by its strategic group membership.

The distinct differences across strategic groups reflect the strategies that firms pursue. Firms in the same strategic group tend to follow a similar strategy, whereas firms in a different strategic group follow a different strategy. Companies in the same strategic group, therefore, are direct competitors. Thus, the rivalry among firms of the same strategic group is generally more intense than the rivalry between strategic groups: *intra-group rivalry exceeds inter-group rivalry.* The number of different business strategies pursued within an industry determines the number of strategic groups in that industry. In most industries, strategic groups can be identified along a fairly small number of dimensions. In many instances, two strategic groups are in an industry: one that pursues a low-cost strategy and a second that pursues a differentiation strategy. (We'll discuss each of these generic business strategies in detail in Chapter 6.)

strategic group The set of companies that pursue a similar strategy within a specific industry.

strategic group model A framework that explains firm differences in performance in the same industry by clustering different firms into groups based on a few key strategic dimensions.

Mapping Strategic Groups

To understand competitive behavior and performance within an industry, we can map the industry competitors into strategic groups. When mapping strategic groups, it is important to focus on several factors:

- Identify the most important strategic dimensions (such as expenditures on research and development, technology, product differentiation, product and service offerings, pricing, market segments, distribution channels, and customer service).

- Choose two key dimensions for the horizontal and vertical axes, which expose important differences among the competitors.

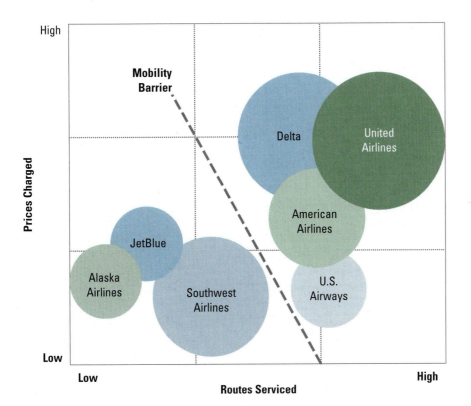

EXHIBIT 3.7

Strategic Groups and the Mobility Barrier in the U.S. Airline Industry

- The dimensions chosen for the axes should not be highly correlated.
- Position on the graph the firms in the strategic group, indicating each firm's market share by the size of the bubble by which it is represented.[49]

The U.S. airline industry provides an illustrative example. Exhibit 3.7 maps the companies active in the industry. The two strategic dimensions are the prices charged and the routes serviced. As a result of this mapping, two strategic groups are apparent: low-cost, point-to-point airlines versus differentiated airlines using a hub-and-spoke system (meaning the airline designates a geographic hub, upon which travelers between airports not connected by direct flights converge to change planes and continue to their final destination). The low-cost, point-to-point airlines are clustered in the lower-left corner; they include Alaska Airlines, JetBlue, and Southwest Airlines (SWA, which bought AirTran Airways in 2010). They cluster together on this plot because they tend to offer low ticket prices but generally service a smaller number of routes.

The differentiated airlines offering full service using a hub-and-spoke route system are the so-called legacy carriers, including American, Delta, United, and U.S. Airways. They tend to cluster in the upper-right corner: Their ticket prices tend to be somewhat higher, and they tend to offer many more routes than the point-to-point low-cost carriers, made possible by use of the hub-and-spoke system. This functional-level strategy allows the legacy airlines to offer many different destinations. For example, Delta's main hub is in Atlanta, GA.[50] If you were to fly from Seattle, Washington, to Miami, Florida, you would stop to change planes in Delta's Atlanta hub on your way.

The strategic-group mapping in Exhibit 3.7 allows some more insights:

- *The competitive rivalry is strongest between firms that are within the same strategic group.* The closer firms are on the strategic-group map, the more directly and intensely they are competing with one another. The mega-airlines Delta (merged with NWA in 2010) and United (merged with Continental, also in 2010) are competing head-to-head not only in the U.S. domestic market but also globally. We would expect strategists at United to monitor closely the actions of Delta, whose strategic decisions have the strongest impact on United's profitability (and vice versa). In contrast, U.S. Airways (which flies mainly on the East Coast, with some international routes) and Alaska Airlines (mainly West Coast and Alaska) are not direct competitors.

■ *Strategic groups are affected differently by the external environment.* During times of economic downturn, for example, the low-cost airlines tend to take market share away from the legacy carriers. Moreover, given their higher cost structure, the legacy carriers are often unable to be profitable during recessions (at least on domestic routes). This implies that external factors like recessions or high oil prices favor the companies in the low-cost strategic group.

■ *Strategic groups are affected differently by the competitive forces.* Let's look at three of the five competitive forces discussed earlier. *Barriers to entry,* for example, are higher into the hub-and-spoke (differentiated) airline group than into the point-to-point (low-cost) airline group. Following deregulation in 1978, many airlines entered the industry, but all of these new players used the point-to-point system. Since hub-and-spoke airlines can offer worldwide service and are protected from foreign competition by regulation, they often face weaker *buyer power,* especially from business travelers. While the hub-and-spoke airlines compete head-on with the point-to-point airlines when they are flying the same or similar routes, the *threat of substitutes* is stronger for the point-to-point airlines. This is because they tend to be regionally focused and thus also compete with car, train, or bus travel, which are viable substitutes.

■ *Some strategic groups are more profitable than others.* Historically, airlines clustered in the lower-left corner tend to be more profitable. Why? Because they create similar, or even higher, value for their customers in terms of on-time departure and arrival, safety, and fewer bags lost while keeping ticket costs below those of the legacy carriers. The point-to-point airlines are able to offer their services at a lower cost and a higher perceived value, thus creating the basis for a competitive advantage.

Mobility Barriers

Although some strategic groups tend to be more profitable and therefore more attractive than others, movement between groups is restricted by **mobility barriers.** These are industry-specific factors that separate one strategic group from another.[51]

The two groups identified in the U.S. airline industry map in Figure 3.7 are separated by the fact that the group using a hub-and-spoke operational model offers international routes, while the point-to-point airlines do not. Offering international routes necessitates the hub-and-spoke model. Indeed, the international routes tend to be the only remaining profitable routes left for the legacy carriers. This economic reality implies that if carriers in the lower-left cluster, such as SWA or JetBlue, would like to compete globally, they would likely need to change their point-to-point operating model to a hub-and-spoke model. Or, they could select a few profitable international routes and service them with long-range aircraft such as Boeing 787s or Airbus A-380s. To add international service to the low-cost model would require significant capital investments, and a likely departure from a well-functioning business model. Reinforcing the mobility barriers, moreover, are regulatory hurdles such as securing landing slots at international airports around the world. From the perspective of the legacy carriers whose profits tend to be generated

mobility barriers
Industry-specific factors that separate one strategic group from another.

primarily from international routes, the mobility barriers protect this profit sanctuary for the time being.

The strategic group model has two important shortcomings. First, just like the five forces model, it is static. It provides a snapshot of what is actually a moving target and thus does not allow for consideration of industry dynamics. Second, it does not help us understand fully *why* there are performance differences among firms in the *same* strategic group. To better understand differences in firm performance, we must look *inside the firm* to study its resources, capabilities, and activities. We do this in the next chapter.

CHAPTERCASE 3 | *Consider This . . .*

CHAPTERCASE 3, about BYD, notes that the firm entered the electric-vehicle market from a strong base in designing and building batteries. This expertise permitted BYD to circumvent some historically strong barriers to entry in the automotive industry. While the success of BYD in automobiles is still far from assured, it was the fastest-growing carmaker in China in 2009, selling more than 500,000 vehicles in 2010. In part, these strong sales may be due to some government incentives for electric vehicles in China, which will encourage the development and sale of electric cars. For example, in some major cities such as Shanghai, the Chinese government will pay 60,000 yuan (approximately $9,000) toward purchase of an electric vehicle.[52]

Thinking about the chapter-opening case, answer the following questions.

1. Which PESTEL factors are the most salient for the electric-vehicle industry of the 21st century?

2. Think about the structure of the automotive industry in your home country. Is it structured more like an oligopoly or monopolistic competition?

3. Using the industry-attractiveness model (see Exhibit 3.5), explain the overall automotive industry. How would it change for the electric-vehicle industry?

Take-Away Concepts

This chapter demonstrated various approaches to analyzing the firm's *external environment,* as summarized by the following learning objectives and related take-away concepts.

LO 3-1 Apply the PESTEL model to organize and assess the impact of external forces on the firm.

>> A firm's macro environment consists of a wide range of political, economic, sociocultural, technological, ecological, and legal (PESTEL) factors that can affect industry and firm performance.

These external forces have both domestic and global aspects.

>> The political environment describes the influence government bodies can have on firms.

>> The economic environment is mainly affected by five factors: growth rates, interest rates, levels of employment, price stability (inflation and deflation), and currency exchange rates.

>> Sociocultural factors capture a society's cultures, norms, and values.

>> Technological factors capture the application of knowledge to create new processes and products.

>> Ecological factors concern a firm's regard for environmental issues such as the natural environment, global warming, and sustainable economic growth.

>> Legal environment factors capture the official outcomes of the political processes that manifest themselves in laws, mandates, regulations, and court decisions.

LO 3-2 Apply the structure-conduct-performance (SCP) model to explain the effect of industry structure on firm profitability.

>> The structure-conduct-performance (SCP) model is a framework that helps to explain differences in industry performance.

>> A perfectly competitive industry is characterized by many small firms, a commodity product, low entry barriers, and no pricing power for individual firms.

>> A monopolistic industry is characterized by many firms, a differentiated product, medium entry barriers, and some pricing power.

>> An oligopolistic industry is characterized by few (large) firms, a differentiated product, high entry barriers, and some degree of pricing power.

>> A monopoly exists when there is only one (large) firm supplying the market. The firm may offer a unique product, the barriers to entry are high, and the monopolist has considerable pricing power.

LO 3-3 Apply the five forces model to understand the profit potential of the firm's industry.

>> Five competitive forces shape an industry's profit potential: (1) threat of entry, (2) power of suppliers, (3) power of buyers, (4) threat of substitutes, and (5) rivalry among existing competitors.

>> The stronger a competitive force, the greater the threat it represents.

>> The weaker the competitive force, the greater the opportunity it presents.

>> A firm can shape an industry's structure in its favor through its strategy.

LO 3-4 Describe the strategic role of complements in creating positive-sum co-opetition.

>> Co-opetition (co-operation among competitors) can create a positive-sum game, resulting in a larger pie for everyone involved.

>> Complements increase demand for the primary product, enhancing the profit potential for the industry and the firm.

>> Industry attractiveness can be determined by three pairs of two forces: (1) supplier and buyer power, (2) entry and exit barriers, and (3) available complements and the threat of substitutes.

>> Attractive industries for co-opetition are characterized by high entry barriers, low exit barriers, low buyer and supplier power, a low threat of substitutes, and the availability of complements.

LO 3-5 Understand the role of industry dynamics and industry convergence in shaping the firm's external environment.

>> Industries are dynamic—they change over time

>> Different conditions prevail in different industries, directly affecting the firms competing in these industries and their profitability.

>> In industry convergence, formerly unrelated industries begin to satisfy the same customer need. It is often brought on by technological advances.

LO 3-6 Apply the strategic group model to reveal performance differences between clusters of firms in the same industry.

>> A strategic group is a set of firms within a specific industry that pursue a similar strategy in their quest for competitive advantage.

>> Rivalry among firms of the same strategic group is more intense than the rivalry between strategic groups: intra-group rivalry exceeds inter-group rivalry.

>> Movement between strategic groups is restricted by mobility barriers—industry-specific factors that separate one strategic group from another.

Key Terms

Complement *(p. 70)*

Complementor *(p. 70)*

Entry barriers *(p. 65)*

Exit barriers *(p. 68)*

Five forces model *(p. 64)*

Industry *(p. 61)*

Industry convergence *(p. 73)*

Mobility barriers *(p. 76)*

PESTEL model *(p. 57)*

SCP (structure-conduct-performance) model *(p. 61)*

Strategic group *(p. 74)*

Strategic group model *(p. 74)*

Discussion Questions

1. Why is it important for an organization to study and understand its external environment?

2. How do the five competitive forces in Porter's model affect the profitability of the overall industry? For example, in what way might weak forces increase industry profits, and in what way do strong forces reduce industry profits?

3. What is a strategic group? How can studying such groups be useful in industry analysis?

4. How do mobility barriers affect the structure of an industry? How do they help us explain firm differences in performance?

Ethical/Social Issues

1. Strategy Highlight 3.1 discussed Swiss bank UBS's release of over 4,000 names of U.S. citizens suspected of not paying U.S. taxes. The government's case was helped immensely by a former employee at UBS who cooperated with prosecutors on details of how such transactions occur. The "whistleblower," a U.S. citizen, has been lauded for his help in the investigation. Yet, in January 2010 he also began serving a 40-month prison sentence for his own guilty plea for helping his clients at UBS evade taxes.[53] Some in the industry believe such a surprisingly long prison term, despite his cooperation with investigators, will dramatically reduce motivation for other potential whistleblowers to come forward.

   a. What is the proper role for a multinational firm in cases where government regulations across countries are in conflict?

   b. What is the responsibility of individual employees to their employers and to their government, when there seems to be a conflict?

Small Group Exercises

SMALL GROUP EXERCISE 1 (ETHICAL/SOCIAL ISSUES)

Your group is a team of Genentech (www.gene.com) sales representatives. You are meeting to discuss methods to promote additional sales of the drug Avastin which has been FDA approved to treat several metastatic cancers. Sales of Avastin were over $4 billion in 2008 in the United States alone, so it is already a market success. However, there is a controversy among doctors and some patient groups surrounding the costs and benefits of the drug. The *New England Journal of Medicine* reported that Avastin could extend the life of colorectal cancer patients by 4.7 months at a cost of nearly $50,000. The annualized cost of treatments for a number of diseases is $100,000 for a delay in the patient's death of several months.

As part of a sales team for one of the most expensive and widely marketed drugs, your task is to consider the approach to take with doctors who may be reluctant to prescribe Avastin due to the high cost of the treatment for the benefits received.[54]

SMALL GROUP EXERCISE 2

One industry with an impact on both undergraduate and MBA students is textbook publishing. Traditional printed textbooks are being challenged by the growing demand for electronic versions of these materials. As noted in the chapter, e-readers such as the Amazon Kindle and Apple iPad are examples of devices that are likely to drive industry convergence. Millions of e-readers are sold each year.[55]

Also, improvements abound in the availability of inexpensive and lightweight "netbooks" as a hardware complement to the demand for e-textbook media with a traditional keyboard. Netbooks, created in 2007, are smaller, lighter, and less-powerful than typical laptop computers. They tend to run reduced-features operating systems and often use applications from the Internet ("cloud computing") rather than hosting all the software on the device itself. In 2010, the price for a netbook was typically under $200 in the United States.

Use the five forces model to think through the various impacts such technology shifts may have on the textbook industry. Include in your response answers to the following questions.

1. How should managers of a textbook-publishing company respond to such changes?

2. Will the shifts in technology be likely to raise or lower the textbook industry-level profits? Explain.

Strategy Term Project

MODULE 3: EXTERNAL ANALYSIS

In this section, you will study the external environment of the firm you have previously selected for this project.

1. Are any changes taking place in the macro environment that might have a positive or negative impact on the industry in which your company is based? Apply the PESTEL framework to identify which factors may be the most important in your industry. What will be the effect on your industry?

2. Apply the five forces model to your industry. What does this model tell you about the nature of competition in the industry?

3. Identify any strategic groups that might exist in the industry. How does the intensity of competition differ across the strategic groups you have identified?

4. How dynamic is the industry in which your company is based? Is there evidence that industry structure is reshaping competition, or has done so in the recent past?

*my*Strategy

IS MY JOB THE NEXT ONE BEING OUTSOURCED?

The outsourcing of IT programming jobs to India is now commonly understood after years of this trend. However, more recently some accounting functions have also begun to flow into India's large technically trained and English-speaking work force. For example, the number of U.S. tax returns completed in India rose a startling 1,600 percent in the three years from 2003 to 2005 (25,000 in 2003 to 400,000 in 2005). Some estimate that millions of U.S. tax returns will be prepared in India within the next few years.

Outsourcing in the accounting functions may affect the job and career prospects for accounting-oriented business school graduates. Tax accountants in Bangalore, India, are much cheaper than those in Boston or Baltimore. Moreover, tax accountants in India often work longer hours and can therefore process many more tax returns than only U.S.-based CPAs and tax accountants during the crunch period of the U.S. tax filing system.[56]

1. Which aspects of accounting do you think are more likely to resist the outsourcing trends just discussed? Think about what aspects of accounting are the high-value activities versus the routine standardized ones. (If it's been a while since you took your accounting courses, reach out for information to someone in your strategy class who is an accounting major.)

2. What industries do you think may offer the best U.S. (or domestic) job opportunities in the future? Which industries do you think may offer the greatest job opportunities in the global market in the future? Use the PESTEL framework and the five forces model to think through a logical set of reasons that some fields will have higher job growth trends than others.

3. Do these types of macro environmental and industry trends affect your thought process about selecting a career field after college? Why or why not? Explain.

Endnotes

1. This ChapterCase is based on: "Technology levels playing field in race to market electric car," *The Wall Street Journal*, January 12, 2009; "Bright sparks: Electric propulsion provides some excitement amid the gloom," *The Economist*, January 15, 2009; and "GM hopes Volt juices its future," *The Wall Street Journal*, August 12, 2009.

2. For a detailed treatise on how institutions shape the economic climate and with it, firm performance, see: North, D. C. (1990), *Institutions, Institutional Change, and Economic Performance* (New York, Random House).

3. "UBS customers shielded by Swiss law, bank says," *The Wall Street Journal*, February 23, 2009; "Swiss to relax bank secrecy laws," *The Wall Street Journal*, March 14, 2009; "Picking on the Swiss," *The Wall Street Journal*, July 15, 2009; and "UBS to give 4,450 names to U.S.," *The Wall Street Journal*, August 20, 2009.

4. This phrase was used in a speech to the American Enterprise Institute on December 5, 1996, by the former Chairman of the Federal Reserve Bank, Alan Greenspan, to describe the mood in the equity markets.

5. Lowenstein, R. (2010), *The End of Wall Street* (New York: Penguin Press).

6. McCraw, T. (2007), *Prophet of Innovation: Joseph Schumpeter and Creative Destruction* (Cambridge, MA: Belknap Press).

7. "R&D spending holds steady in slump," *The Wall Street Journal*, April 6, 2009.

8. "Toyota keeps idled workers busy honing their skills," *The Wall Street Journal*, October 13, 2008.

9. "Professor Emeritus Milton Friedman dies at 94," University of Chicago press release, November 16, 2006.

10. Lucas, R. (1972), "Expectations and the neutrality of money," *Journal of Economic Theory* 4: 103–124.

11. Yoffie, D. B., and Y. Wang (2009), *Cola Wars Continue: Coke and Pepsi in 2006*, Harvard Business School Case Study 9-706-447.

12. Bettis, R., and M. A. Hitt (1995), "The new competitive landscape," *Strategic Management Journal* 16 (Special Issue): 7–19; Hill, C. W. L., and F. T. Rothaermel (2003), "The performance of incumbent firms in the face of radical technological innovation," *Academy of Management Review* 28: 257–274; and Afuah, A. (2009), *Strategic Innovation: New Game Strategies for Competitive Advantage* (New York: Routledge).

13. "Bleak Friday," *The Economist*, November 26, 2009.

14. "E-commerce," *The Economist*, October 8, 2009.

15. Rothaermel, F. T., and C. W. L. Hill (2005), "Technological discontinuities and complementary assets: A longitudinal study of industry and firm performance," *Organization Science* 16: 52–70.

16. Rothaermel, F. T., and M. Thursby (2007), "The nanotech vs. the biotech revolution: Sources of incumbent

productivity in research," *Research Policy* 36: 832–849; and Woolley, J. L., and R. M. Rottner (2008), "Innovation policy and nanotech entrepreneurship," *Entrepreneurship Theory and Practice* 32: 791–811.

17. Anderson, R. C. (2009), *Confessions of a Radical Industrialist: Profits, People, Purpose—Doing Business by Respecting the Earth* (New York: St. Martin's Press); and Esty, D. C., and A. S. Winston (2009), *Green to Gold: How Smart Companies Use Environmental Strategy to Innovate, Create Value, and Build Competitive Advantage*, revised and updated (Hoboken, NJ: John Wiley).

18. "Nine questions (and provisional answers) about the spill," *Bloomberg BusinessWeek*, June 10, 2010; and "Obama v BP," *The Economist*, June 17, 2010.

19. "Intel fine jolts tech sector," *The Wall Street Journal*, May 14, 2009.

20. "Intel's market share rises on AMD problems," *CNET News*, April 24, 2007.

21. The GM example is based on: Rothaermel, F. T., with V. Singh (2009), "Tesla Motors and the U.S. Auto Industry," Georgia Institute of Technology Case Study.

22. "Giving advice in adversity," *The Economist*, September 25, 2008.

23. This discussion is based on: Bain, J. S. (1968), *Industrial Organization* (New York, NY: John Wiley); Scherer, F. M., and D. Ross (1990), *Industrial Market Structure and Economic*

Performance, 3rd ed. (Boston, MA: Houghton-Mifflin); Carlton, D. W., and J. M. Perloff (2000), *Modern Industrial Organization,* 3rd ed. (Reading, MA: Addison-Wesley); and Allen, W. B., K. Weigelt, N. Doherty, and E. Mansfield (2009), *Managerial Economics: Theory, Application, and Cases,* 7th ed. (New York: Norton).

24. Besanko, D., E. Dranove, M. Hanley, and S. Schaefer (2010), *The Economics of Strategy,* 5th ed. (Hoboken, NJ: Wiley).

25. Dixit, A., S. Skeath, and D. H. Reiley (2009), *Games of Strategy,* 3rd ed. (New York: Norton).

26. Yoffie, D. B., and Y. Wang (2009), *Cola Wars Continue.*

27. The discussion in this section is based on: Porter, M. E. (1979), "How competitive forces shape strategy," *Harvard Business Review,* March–April: 137–145; Porter, M. E. (1980), *Competitive Strategy: Techniques for Analyzing Industries and Competitors* (New York: Free Press); and Porter, M. E. (2008), "The five competitive forces that shape strategy," *Harvard Business Review,* January.

28. "Fiat nears stake in Chrysler that could lead to takeover," *The Wall Street Journal,* January 20, 2009.

29. "Technology levels playing field in race to market electric car," *The Wall Street Journal,* January 12, 2009.

30. "Comcast, GE strike deal; Vivendi to sell NBC stake," *The Wall Street Journal,* December 2, 2009.

31. "The UAW in the driver's seat," *The Wall Street Journal,* April 30, 2009.

32. If there is only one buyer in the market, that market organization is a *monopsony.*

33. Whether a product is a substitute (complement) can be estimated by the cross-elasticity of demand. The cross-elasticity estimates the percentage change in the quantity demanded of good X resulting from a 1 percent change in the price of good Y. If the cross-elasticity of demand is greater (less) than zero, the products are substitutes (complements). For a detailed discussion, see: Allen, W. B., K. Weigelt, N. Doherty, and E. Mansfield (2009), *Managerial Economics.*

34. "Detroitosaurus wrecks," *The Economist,* June 6, 2009.

35. Ibid.

36. This discussion is based on: "An Interview with Michael E. Porter: The Five Competitive Forces that Shape Strategy," Harvard Business Publishing video (June 30, 2008).

37. This section is based on: Porter, M. E. (2008), "The five competitive forces that shape strategy"; "An Interview with Michael E. Porter: The Five Competitive Forces that Shape Strategy," Harvard Business Publishing video; author's interviews with Delta executives; and Yoffie, D. B. (2006), *Cola Wars Continue: Coke and Pepsi in 2006,* Harvard Business School Case Study 5-706-514, teaching note.

38. Brandenburger, A. M., and B. Nalebuff (1996), *Co-opetition* (New York: Currency Doubleday); and Grove, A. S. (1999), *Only the Paranoid Survive* (New York: Time Warner).

39. Milgrom, P., and J. Roberts (1995), "Complementarities and fit strategy, structure, and organizational change in manufacturing," *Journal of Accounting and Economics* 19(2-3): 179–208; and Brandenburger, A. M., and B. Nalebuff (1996), *Co-opetition.*

40. In this recent treatise, Porter also highlights positive-sum competition. See Porter, M. E. (2008), "The five competitive forces that shape strategy," *Harvard Business Review,* January.

41. Michael Porter subsumes exit barriers under intensity of rivalry.

42. Porter, M. E. (2008), "The five competitive forces that shape strategy."

43. Profits are shown after taxes; after extraordinary credits or charges, if any, that appear on the income statement; and after cumulative effects of accounting changes. Source: *Fortune,* May 4, 2009.

44. Note that several industries actually had negative profitability over the 2003–2008 time period: Entertainment (−35.1 percent); Wholesalers: Electronics and office equipment (−33.8 percent); Automotive retailing and services (−29.2 percent); Hotels, casinos, and resorts (−20.7 percent); Insurance: Life, health (mutual) (−18.3 percent); Energy (−15.6 percent);

Motor vehicles and parts (−11.8 percent); Home equipment and furnishings (−10 percent); Insurance: Life, health (stock) (−9.3 percent); Insurance: Property and casualty (stock) (−6.2 percent); Commercial banks (−5 percent); Diversified financials (−1.8 percent). Source: *Fortune,* May 4, 2009.

45. "Reading between the lines," *The Economist,* March 26, 2009; and "New York Times is near web charges," *The Wall Street Journal,* January 19, 2010.

46. "Online ads to overtake U.S. newspapers," *Financial Times,* August 7, 2007.

47. Hunt, M. S. (1972). *Competition in the Major Home Appliance Industry, 1960–1970,* Unpublished doctoral dissertation, Harvard University; Hatten, K. J., and D. E. Schendel (1977), "Heterogeneity within an industry: Firm conduct in the U.S. brewing industry," *Journal of Industrial Economics* 26: 97–113; and Porter, M. E. (1980), *Competitive Strategy: Techniques for Analyzing Industries and Competitors* (New York: Free Press).

48. This discussion is based on: Hunt, M. S. (1972), *Competition in the Major Home Appliance Industry, 1960–1970;* Hatten, K. J., and D. E. Schendel (1977), "Heterogeneity within an industry: Firm conduct in the U.S. brewing industry"; Porter, M. E. (1980), *Competitive Strategy;* Cool, K., and D. Schendel (1988), "Performance differences among strategic group members," *Strategic Management Journal* 9: 207–223; Nair, A., and S. Kotha (2001), "Does group membership matter? Evidence from the Japanese steel industry," *Strategic Management Journal* 22: 221–235; and McNamara, G., D. L. Deephouse, and R. Luce (2003), "Competitive positioning within and across a strategic group structure: The performance of core, secondary, and solitary firms," *Strategic Management Journal* 24: 161–181.

49. In Exhibit 3.7 United Airlines is the biggest bubble, because it merged with Continental in 2010, creating the largest airline in the U.S. Delta is the second-biggest airline in the U.S. after merging with Northwest Airlines in 2008.

50. American's hub is at Dallas–Fort Worth; Continental's is at Newark, NJ; United's is at Chicago, IL; and U.S. Airways's is at Charlotte, North Carolina.

51. Caves, R. E., and M. E. Porter (1977), "From entry barriers to mobility barriers," *Quarterly Journal of Economics* 91: 241–262.

52. "Buffett to visit BYD in China amid declining sales, disputes," *Bloomberg BusinessWeek,* September 22, 2010.

53. "Crying foul, ex-UBS banker starts prison term," *The Wall Street Journal,* January 9, 2010.

54. Mayer, R. J. (2004), "Two steps forward in the treatment of colorectal cancer," *New England Journal of Medicine* 350: 2406–2408; "A cancer drug shows promise, at a price that many can't pay," *The New York Times,* February 15, 2006; and Arthaud-Day, M. L., F. T. Rothaermel, and W. Zhang (2013), "Genentech: After the Acquisition by Roche," case study, in Rothaermel, F. T., *Strategic Management* (Burr Ridge, IL: McGraw-Hill).

55. "E-Readers everywhere: The inevitable shakeout," *Bloomberg BusinessWeek,* January 11, 2010.

56. The *my*Strategy exercise is based on: Friedman, T. (2005), *The World Is Flat: A Brief History of the Twenty-first Century* (New York: Farrar, Strauss & Giroux); and ValueNotes (2006), "Offshoring tax return preparations to India," *November,* p. 118.

CHAPTER 4

Internal Analysis: Resources, Capabilities, and Activities

LEARNING OBJECTIVES

After studying this chapter, you should be able to:

LO 4-1 Distinguish among a firm's resources, capabilities, core competencies, and firm activities.

LO 4-2 Differentiate between tangible and intangible resources.

LO 4-3 Describe the critical assumptions behind the resource-based view.

LO 4-4 Apply the VRIO framework to assess the competitive implications of a firm's resources.

LO 4-5 Identify competitive advantage as residing in a network of firm activities.

LO 4-6 Outline how dynamic capabilities can help a firm sustain competitive advantage.

LO 4-7 Identify different conditions that allow firms to sustain their competitive advantage.

LO 4-8 Conduct a SWOT analysis.

From Good to Great to Gone: The Rise and Fall of Circuit City

CIRCUIT CITY WAS at one time the largest and most successful consumer-electronics retailer in the United States. Indeed, Circuit City was so successful that it was included as one of only 11 companies featured in Jim Collins's 2001 best-seller *Good to Great.* To qualify for this august group of high performers, a company had to attain "extraordinary results, averaging cumulative stock returns 6.9 times the general market in the 15 years following their transition points."[1]

Indeed, Circuit City was the best-performing company on Collins's good-to-great list, outperforming the market 18.5 times during the 1982–1997 period.

How did Circuit City become so successful? The company was able to build and refine a set of core competencies (a unique set of activities that the firm excels at) that enabled it to create a higher economic value than its competitors. In particular, Circuit City created world-class competencies in efficient and effective logistics

expertise: It deployed sophisticated point-of-sale and inventory-tracking technology, supported by IT investments that enabled the firm to connect the flow of information among geographically dispersed stores. This expertise in turn allowed detailed tracking of customer preferences and thus enabled Circuit City to respond quickly to changing trends. The company also relied on highly motivated, well-trained sales personnel to provide superior service and thus build and maintain customer loyalty. These core competencies enabled Circuit City to implement a "4S business model"—service, selection, savings, and satisfaction—that it applied to big-ticket consumer electronics with an unmatched degree of consistency throughout the United States.

Perhaps even more important during the company's high-performance run, many capable competitors were unable to replicate Circuit City's core competencies. Further underscoring Circuit City's superior performance is the fact, as Jim Collins described it, that "if you had to choose between $1 invested in Circuit City or $1 invested in General Electric on the day that the legendary Jack Welch took over GE in 1981 and held [that investment] to January 1, 2000, you would have been better off with Circuit City—by [a factor of] six times."[2] In the fall of 2008, however, Circuit City filed for bankruptcy. What happened?[3]

After reading the chapter, you will find more about this case, with related questions, on page 106.

▲ **ONE OF THE KEY** messages of this chapter is that a firm's ability to gain and sustain competitive advantage is partly driven by **core competencies**—unique strengths that are embedded deep within a firm. Circuit City's core competencies lost value because the firm neglected to upgrade and protect them and was thus outflanked by Best Buy and online retailers like Amazon.[4] Moreover, Circuit City's top-management team was also distracted

core competencies
Unique strengths embedded deep within a firm.

by pursuing noncore activities such as the creation of CarMax,[5] a retail chain for used cars, a foray into providing an alternative to video rentals through its proprietary DivX DVD player,[6] and an attempted merger with Blockbuster (which filed for bankruptcy in 2010).

Perhaps the biggest blunder that Circuit City's top-management team committed was to lay off 3,000 of the firm's highest-paid sales personnel. The layoff was done to become more cost-competitive with Best Buy and, in particular, the burgeoning online retailers. The problem was that the highest-paid salespeople were also the most experienced and loyal ones, better able to provide superior customer service. It appears that laying off key human capital—given their valuable, rare, and difficult-to-imitate nature—was a supreme strategic mistake! Not only did Circuit City destroy part of its core competency, it also allowed its main competitor—Best Buy—to recruit Circuit City's top salespeople. With that transfer of personnel to Best Buy went the transfer of important tacit knowledge underlying some of Circuit City's core competencies, which in turn not only mitigated Circuit City's advantage but also allowed Best Buy to upgrade its core competencies. In particular, Best Buy went on to develop its innovative "customer-centricity" model, based on a set of skills that allowed its store employees to identify and more effectively serve specific customer segments.[7] (Best Buy now faces its own challenges competing with online retailers such as Amazon, highlighting the dynamic nature of the competitive process.)

INTERNAL ANALYSIS: LOOKING INSIDE THE FIRM FOR CORE COMPETENCIES

>> **LO 4-1**
Distinguish among a firm's resources, capabilities, core competencies, and firm activities.

In this chapter, we study analytical tools to explain why differences in firm performance exist even within the *same* industry. For example, why did Best Buy outperform Circuit City in the electronics retail industry? Since both companies competed in the same industry and thus faced the same external opportunities and threats, the source for the observable performance difference must be found *inside the firm.*

Exhibit 4.1 depicts how we move from the firm's external environment to its internal environment. To formulate and implement a strategy that enhances the firm's chances of gaining and sustaining competitive advantage, the firm must have certain types of resources and capabilities that combine to form core competencies. These in turn are leveraged through the firm's activities. The goal should be to develop resources, capabilities, and competencies that create a *strategic fit* with the firm's environment. Rather than creating a static fit, the firm's internal strengths should change with its external environment in a *dynamic* fashion. Upon completion of this chapter, you will have a deeper understanding of the sources of competitive advantage that reside within a firm.

It's time to introduce a more formal definition of **core competencies.** These are unique strengths, embedded deep within a firm, that allow a firm to differentiate its products and services from those of its rivals, creating higher value for the customer or offering products and services of comparable value at lower cost. The important point here is that competitive advantage can be driven by core competencies.[8] Core competencies that are not continuously nourished will eventually lose their ability to yield a competitive advantage, as did Circuit City's. Without upgrading and ongoing improvement to core competencies, competitors are more likely to develop equivalent or superior skills, as did Best Buy. This insight will allow us to explain differences between firms in the same industry. It also will help us identify strategies with which firms gain and sustain a competitive advantage and weather an adverse external environment.

core competencies
Unique strengths, embedded deep within a firm, that allow a firm to differentiate its products and services from those of its rivals, creating higher value for the customer or offering products and services of comparable value at lower cost.

Core competencies are built through the interplay of resources and capabilities. Exhibit 4.2 shows this relationship. *Resources* are assets such as cash, buildings, or intellectual property that a company can draw on when crafting and executing a strategy. Resources

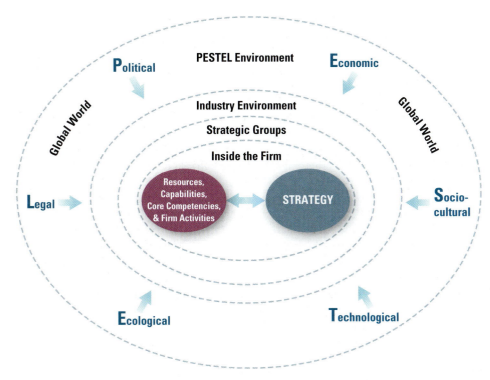

EXHIBIT 4.1

Creating a Strategic
Fit to Leverage a Firm's
Internal Strengths
to Exploit External
Opportunities

can be either tangible or intangible. *Capabilities* are the organizational and managerial skills necessary to orchestrate a diverse set of resources and to deploy them strategically. Capabilities are by nature intangible. They find their expression in a company's structure, routines, and processes. *Activities* enable firms to add value by transforming inputs into goods and services. In the interplay of resources and capabilities, resources reinforce core competencies, while capabilities allow managers to orchestrate their core competencies.

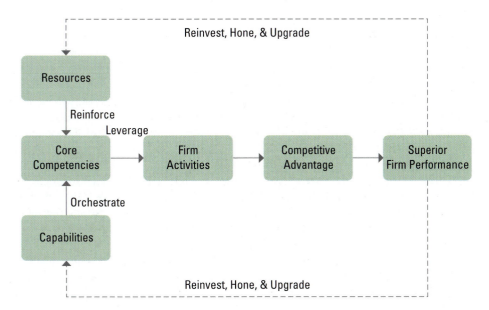

EXHIBIT 4.2

Linking Resources,
Capabilities, Core
Competencies,
and Activities to
Competitive Advantage
and Superior Firm
Performance

Strategic choices find their expression in firm activities, which leverage core competencies for competitive advantage. The arrows leading back from performance to resources and capabilities indicate that superior performance in the marketplace generates profits that can be reinvested into the firm (retained earnings) to further hone and upgrade a firm's resources and capabilities in its pursuit of competitive advantage and improved profitability.

Company examples of core competencies abound: Honda's life began with a small two-cycle motorbike engine. Through continuous learning over several decades, and often from lessons learned from failure, Honda built the core competency to design and manufacture small but powerful and highly reliable engines for which it now is famous. This core competency results from superior engineering know-how and skills carefully nurtured and honed over several decades. Today, Honda engines can be found everywhere: in cars, SUVs, vans, trucks, motorcycles, ATVs, boats, airplanes, generators, snow blowers, lawn mowers and other yard equipment, and so on. Due to their superior performance, Honda engines have been the only ones used in the Indy Racing League (IRL) since 2006. (Not coincidentally, 2006 was also the first year in its long history that the Indy 500 was run without a single engine problem.) One way to look at Honda is to view it as a company with a distinct competency in engines and a business model of finding places to put its engines. That is, underneath the products and services that make up the visible side of competition lies a diverse set of competencies that make this happen. These core competencies reside deep within the firm, implying that companies compete as much in the product and service markets as they do in developing and leveraging core competencies.

In a similar way, Sony's strategy in the consumer electronics industry was to first build the resources and capabilities to successfully commercialize a pocket radio. This success laid the foundation for Sony's core competency in the miniaturization of electronic technology and was subsequently applied to the Sony Walkman, followed by its MP3 Player. In the same industry (mobile devices), Apple has demonstrated core competency in user-friendly product design, which challenges Apple engineers to empathize with customers and deploy engineering knowledge in innovative and category-defining products like the iPod, iPhone, and iPad. Apple products have long been seen as engineered for users' enjoyment, resulting in a "cult-like following" among Apple users. Exhibit 4.3 identifies the core competencies of a number of companies, with application examples.

THE RESOURCE-BASED VIEW

>> **LO 4-2**
Differentiate between tangible and intangible resources.

To gain a deeper understanding of how resources and capabilities can be a source of competitive advantage, we turn to the resource-based view of the firm to provide a model that systematically aids in identifying core competencies.[9] As the name suggests, this model sees resources as key to superior firm performance. It defines resources broadly to include all assets that a firm can draw upon when formulating and implementing strategy. If a resource exhibits certain attributes (which we'll discuss next) that resource enables the firm to gain and sustain a competitive advantage.

As Exhibit 4.4 (page 90) illustrates, resources fall broadly into two categories: tangible and intangible. Tangible resources have physical attributes and are visible. Examples of tangible resources are capital, land, buildings, plant, equipment, and supplies. Intangible resources have no physical attributes and thus are invisible. Examples of intangible resources are a firm's culture, its knowledge, brand equity, reputation, and intellectual property.

Let's take Google as an example. Its tangible resources ("fixed assets"), valued at $5 billion, include its headquarters ("The Googleplex") in Mountain View, California, and numerous server farms (clusters of computer servers) across the globe. The Google brand, an intangible resource, is valued at over $100 billion (#1 worldwide)—which is twenty

EXHIBIT 4.3

Company Examples of Core Competencies and Applications

Company	Core Competencies	Application Examples
Amazon	Providing one of the largest selections of items online, combined with superior IT systems and customer service.	Expansion to cover most electronic media, digital downloads, e-readers as well as apparel, toys, electronics, and tools. Offering cloud computing services.
Apple	Leveraging industrial design to integrate hardware and software in innovative and category-defining mobile devices that take the user's experience to a new level.	iMac, iPhone, iPod, iPad, iTunes, Apple TV.
Coca-Cola	Leveraging one of the world's most recognized brand names (based on its original "secret formula") into a diverse lineup of soft drinks and other beverages.	Coke Zero, Diet Coke, Fanta, Fresca, Sprite, Dasani, Powerade, etc.
ExxonMobil	Discovering and exploring fossil-fuel–based energy sources globally.	Oil and gas.
General Electric	Designing and implementing efficient management processes, training leaders, leveraging industrial engineering.	Energy, health care, airplane jet engines, finance.
Google	Developing proprietary search algorithms.	Gmail, Goog411, Google Maps/Earth, AdWords, AdSense, Google Books, Google Scholar.
IKEA	Designing modern functional home furnishings at low prices offered in a unique retail experience	Fully furnished room setups, practical tools for all rooms, do-it-yourself.
Netflix	Providing Internet subscription services for televised media combined with superior algorithms to track individual customer preferences.	Online subscription, streaming, connection to game consoles.
Nike	Designing and marketing innovative athletic shoes and apparel.	Footwear, clothes, equipment.
Starbucks	Providing high-quality beverages and food, combined with superior customer service in a friendly and welcoming environment.	Customized handcrafted (coffee) beverages; warm/cold, seasonal, and fruit drinks; comfortable and convenient ambience in retail outlets; free Wi-Fi Internet connections (unlimited).
UPS	Providing superior supply chain management services at low cost.	Package tracking and delivery, transportation, ecommerce, consulting services.

resource-based view A model that sees resources as key to superior firm performance. If a resource exhibits VRIO attributes (see the section "The VRIO Framework" on page 91), the resource enables the firm to gain and sustain a competitive advantage.

tangible resources Resources with physical attributes, which thus are visible.

intangible resources Resources that do not have physical attributes and thus are invisible.

Resources

Tangible	Intangible
Physical Attributes, Visible	No Physical Attributes, Invisible
• Capital	• Culture
• Land	• Knowledge
• Buildings	• Brand Equity
• Plant	• Reputation
• Equipment	• Intellectual Property
• Supplies	• Patents
	• Copyrights
	• Trademarks
	• Trade Secrets

EXHIBIT 4.4

Tangible and Intangible Resources

times higher than the value of its tangible assets.[10] This relationship is even more skewed if we look at Apple. Its brand (#6 worldwide) is valued at over $63 billion, while its tangible assets are valued at a mere $2 billion.[11]

Competitive advantage is more likely to spring from intangible rather than tangible resources. Tangible assets, like buildings or computer servers, can be bought on the open market by any comers who have the necessary cash. However, a brand name must be built, often over long periods of time. Google accomplished its enormous brand valuation fairly quickly due to its ubiquitous Internet presence, while the next four companies on the list of the most valued brands—Microsoft, Coca-Cola, IBM, and McDonald's—took much longer.[12]

Google's headquarters provides examples of both tangible and intangible resources. The Googleplex is a piece of land with a futuristic building, and thus a tangible asset. The *location* of the company in the heart of Silicon Valley is an intangible resource that provides access to a valuable network of contacts and gives the company several benefits. It allows Google to tap into a large and computer-savvy work force and access to graduates and knowledge spillovers from world-class universities such as Stanford and the University of California, Berkeley, which adds to Google's technical capabilities.[13] Another benefit stems from Silicon Valley's designation as having the largest concentration of venture capital in the United States, which is beneficial because venture capitalists tend to look first for local investments.[14] Google received initial funding from the famous venture capital firms Kleiner Perkins Caufield & Byers and Sequoia Capital, both located in Silicon Valley.

Two Critical Assumptions

>> **LO 4-3**
Describe the critical assumptions behind the resource-based view.

Two assumptions are critical in the resource-based model: (1) *resource heterogeneity* and (2) *resource immobility*.[15] What does this mean? In the resource-based view, a firm is assumed to be a bundle of resources and capabilities. The first critical assumption—**resource heterogeneity**—is that bundles of resources and capabilities differ across firms. The insight that the resource-based view brings to strategy is that the resource bundles of firms competing in the *same* industry (or even the same strategic group) are unique to some extent and thus differ from one another. For example, although Southwest Airlines (SWA) and Alaska Airlines both compete in the same strategic group, they draw on different resource bundles. SWA's employee productivity tends to be higher than that of Alaska Airlines, because the two companies differ along human and organizational resources. At SWA, job descriptions are informal and employees pitch in to "get the job done." Pilots may help load luggage to ensure an on-time departure; flight attendants clean airplanes to help turn them around at the gate within 15 minutes from arrival to departure. This allows SWA to keep its planes flying for longer and thus lowers its cost structure, savings which SWA passes on to passengers in lower ticket prices.

The second assumption—**resource immobility**—is that resources tend to be "sticky" and don't move easily from firm to firm. Because of that stickiness, the resource differences that exist between firms are difficult to replicate and, therefore, can last for a long time. For example, SWA has enjoyed a sustained competitive advantage, allowing it to outperform its competitors over several decades. That resource difference is not due to a lack of imitation attempts, though. We mentioned (in Chapter 1) that Continental and

Delta both attempted to copy SWA, with Continental Lite and Song airline offerings, respectively. Neither Continental nor Delta, however, was able to successfully imitate the resource bundles and firm capabilities that make SWA unique. The important point is that resource bundles are different across firms, and these differences can persist for long periods of time. These assumptions are critical to explaining superior firm performance in the resource-based model.

Note, by the way, that the critical assumptions of the resource-based model are fundamentally different from the way in which a firm is viewed in the perfectly competitive model introduced in Chapter 3. In perfect competition, all firms have access to the same resources and capabilities, ensuring that any advantage that one firm has will be short-lived. That is, when resources are freely available and mobile, competitors can move quickly to acquire resources that are utilized by the current market leader. Although some commodity markets approach this situation, most other markets include firms whose resource endowments differ from one another. The resource-based view thus provides useful insights to firms in their quest for competitive advantage.

The VRIO Framework

We are now in a position to evaluate a firm's resource endowments and to answer the question of what resource attributes underpin competitive advantage. In the resource-based model, certain *types of resources* are seen as key to superior firm performance.[16] For a resource to be the basis of a competitive advantage, it must be *valuable (V), rare (R), costly to imitate (I),* and the firm must *organize (O) to capture the value of the resource.* Following the lead of Jay Barney, one of the pioneers of the resource-based view of the firm, we call this model the **VRIO framework.**[17] A firm can gain and sustain a competitive advantage only when it has resources and capabilities that satisfy the VRIO criteria.

Exhibit 4.5 captures the VRIO framework. You can use this decision tree to decide if the resource or capability under consideration fulfills the VRIO requirements. As you study

>> **LO 4-4**
Apply the VRIO framework to assess the competitive implications of a firm's resources.

EXHIBIT 4.5

Applying the Resource-Based View: A Decision Tree Revealing Competitive Implications

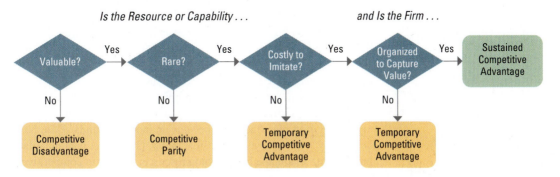

resource heterogeneity
Assumption in the resource-based view that a firm is a bundle of resources and capabilities that differ across firms.

resource immobility
Assumption in the resource-based view that a firm has resources that tend to be "sticky" and that do not move easily from firm to firm.

VRIO framework A theoretical framework that explains and predicts firm-level competitive advantage. A firm can gain a competitive advantage if it has resources that are valuable (V), rare (R), and costly to imitate (I); the firm also must organize (O) to capture the value of the resources.

the following discussion of each of the VRIO attributes, you will see that the attributes accumulate. Only if a firm's managers are able to answer "yes" four times to the attributes listed in the decision tree is the resource in question a core competency that underpins a firm's sustainable competitive advantage.

VALUABLE (V). A resource is valuable if it helps a firm increase the perceived value of its product or service in the eyes of consumers, either by adding attractive features or by lowering price because the resource helps the firm lower its costs. By raising the perceived value of the product, the resource increases the firm's revenues, in turn increasing the firm's profitability (assuming costs are not increasing). If the resource allows the firm to lower its cost, it also increases profitability (assuming perceived value is not decreasing).

Honda's competency in designing and producing efficient engines increases the perceived value of its products for consumers. That competency, supported by its lean manufacturing system, enables quality to be designed and built directly into the product and also helps Honda lower its costs. Thus, Honda's ability in designing and building engines is a valuable resource.

In our quest for competitive advantage, we next need to find out if the resource is also rare.

RARE (R). A resource or capability is rare if only one or a few firms possess the resource or can perform the capability in the same unique way. If the resource or capability is common, it will result in perfect competition where no firm is able to maintain a competitive advantage. A firm is on the path to competitive advantage only if it possesses a valuable resource that is also rare. As Toyota built its initial position as a global auto manufacturer, its lean manufacturing system was a valuable and rare resource. As the leading innovator in developing an efficient and effective approach to manufacturing, Toyota was the first carmaker to resolve a trade-off that had existed for many decades: to lower production costs *and* maintain the high quality of essentially "mass-customized" cars. Looking again at Exhibit 4.5, we can see the result of a resource being both valuable and rare: During the time period when lean manufacturing was a valuable and rare resource, Toyota was able to gain a *temporary competitive advantage.*

Tiffany & Co. has developed a core competency—elegant jewelry design and craftmanship—that is valuable, rare, and costly for competitors to imitate. Since the mid-1800s, its trademarked Tiffany Blue Box® has stood as a symbol of its sustained competitive advantage.

However, as knowledge about lean manufacturing diffused throughout the car industry, Toyota was not able to sustain its competitive advantage. *Knowledge diffusion* can occur through benchmarking studies, new methods taught in college courses, and consultants. After some time, use of lean manufacturing to produce mass-customized cars with high quality and low cost became a necessary but not sufficient condition for competitive advantage. Once lean manufacturing became an industry standard, the best firms could do was to achieve competitive parity. Over time, lean manufacturing had become a valuable but common resource, leading to competitive parity.

COSTLY TO IMITATE (I). A resource is costly to imitate if firms that do not possess the resource are unable to develop or buy the resource at a reasonable price. If the resource in question is valuable, rare, and costly to imitate, then it is an internal strength and a core competency (again, see Exhibit 4.5). If the firm's competitors fail to duplicate the strategy based on the valuable, rare, and costly-to-imitate resource, then the firm can achieve a temporary competitive advantage. Apple's core competencies in user-friendly product design (e.g., iPod, iPhone, and iPad) and complementary and user-friendly services (e.g., Apps, iTunes, and iBooks) are valuable, rare, and costly-to-imitate capabilities. Although Sony clearly has a strength in inventing and developing innovative and high-quality mobile devices (e.g., Walkman, Discman, MP3 player, e-book Reader, portable PlayStation PSP), it lacks Apple's design, integration, and marketing competencies, which are costly and difficult for Sony (and others) to imitate. The combination of the three resource attributes ($V + R + I$) has allowed Apple to enjoy a competitive advantage for many years.

A firm that enjoys a competitive advantage, however, attracts significant attention from its competitors, who will attempt to negate a firm's resource advantage. A competing firm can succeed in this effort through directly imitating the resource in question (*direct imitation*) or through working around it to provide a comparable product or service (*substitution*). Later in this chapter, we will discuss the need to continuously upgrade and reinforce the resources and capabilities that provide the basis for competitive advantage.

Take Crocs Shoes, the maker of a plastic clog, as an example. Launched in 2002 as a spa shoe at the Ft. Lauderdale, Florida, boat show, Crocs experienced explosive growth selling tens of millions of pairs each year and reaching over $650 million in revenue in 2008. Crocs are worn by people in every age group and walk of life, including celebrities such as Heidi Klum, Adam Sandler, Matt Damon, and Brooke Shields. To protect its unique shoe design, the company owns several patents. However, numerous cheap imitators of Crocs have sprung up to copy its colorful and comfortable plastic clog. Despite its patents and celebrity endorsements, other firms were able to more or less directly copy the shoe, taking a big bite into Crocs's profits. Indeed, Crocs's share price plunged from a high of $74.75 on October 31, 2007, to $0.94 on November 20, 2008. This example illustrates that competitive advantage cannot be sustained if the underlying capability (i.e., creating molds to imitate the shape, look, and feel of the original Crocs shoe) can easily be replicated and can thus be directly imitated. Any competitive advantage in a fashion-driven industry, moreover, is notoriously short-lived if the company fails to continuously innovate or build such brand recognition that imitators won't gain a foothold in the market. Crocs Shoes was more or less a "one-trick pony." Nike, on the other hand, was able to do both—continuously innovate *and* build tremendous brand recognition—and thus provides a counter-example of how to avoid losing a competitive advantage through direct imitation.

The second avenue of imitation is through *substitution,* which often entails some kind of work-around. The commercialization of the CAT scanner provides a classic example, in which substitution allowed a second mover not only to mitigate the innovator's advantage but also to gain and even sustain a competitive advantage. Based on internal research, the British conglomerate EMI developed and launched the computed axial tomography (CAT) scanner.[18] This technology, for which EMI received several patents, can take

---

valuable resource One of the four key criteria in the VRIO framework; a resource is valuable if it allows the firm to take advantage of an external opportunity and/or neutralize an external threat.

rare resource One of the four key criteria in the VRIO framework; a resource is rare if the number of firms that possess it is less than the number of firms it would require to reach a state of perfect competition.

costly to imitate resource One of the four key criteria in the VRIO framework; a resource is costly to imitate if firms that do not possess the resource are unable to develop or buy the resource at a comparable cost.

three-dimensional pictures of the human body and is considered to be the most important breakthrough in radiology since the discovery of X-rays. The invention of the CAT scanner also paved the way for follow-up innovations like nuclear magnetic resonance imaging (MRI). Despite its initial success, EMI lost out quickly to GE Medical Systems (GEMS). How can the innovator with a patent-protected technology lose out to a follower? GEMS was able to reverse-engineer EMI's CAT scanner to produce a model that worked around EMI's patents. Moreover, GEMS was able to leverage important complementary resources such as financing, large-scale manufacturing, and a wide distribution and marketing network. While EMI clearly possessed a valuable and rare resource, it was not able to protect itself from GE's substitution attempt.

Substituting for a firm's valuable and rare resource can also be accomplished through *strategic equivalence.* Take the example of Jeff Bezos launching and developing Amazon.com. Prior to inception, the retail book industry was dominated by a few large chains and many independent mom-and-pop bookstores. Bezos realized that he could not compete with the big-box book retailers directly and needed a different business model. The emergence of the Internet allowed him to come up with a new distribution system that negated the need for retail stores (and thus high real-estate costs). Bezos's new business model of ecommerce not only substituted for the traditional (fragmented) supply chain in book retailing, but also allowed Amazon to offer lower prices due to its lower operating costs.

ORGANIZED TO CAPTURE VALUE (O). The final criterion of whether a rare, valuable, and costly-to-imitate resource can form the basis of a sustained competitive advantage depends not on the resource or capability but on the *firm's ability* to capture the resource's value. To fully exploit the competitive potential of its resources and capabilities, a firm must be **organized to capture value**—that is, it must have in place an effective organizational structure and coordinating systems. (We will study organizational design in detail in Chapter 11.)

Before Apple, Dell, or Microsoft had any significant share of the personal computer market, Xerox PARC invented and developed an early word-processing application, the graphical user interface (GUI), the Ethernet, the mouse as pointing device, and even the first personal computer—all of which laid the foundation of the desktop-computing industry.[19] Due to a lack of appropriate organization, however, Xerox failed to appreciate and exploit the many breakthrough innovations made by its Palo Alto Research Center (PARC) in computing software and hardware. Xerox failed to exploit the value of these important resources because they did not fit within its business focus on photocopiers. Under pressure in its core photocopier business from Japanese low-cost competitors, Xerox's top management was busy looking for innovations in the photocopier business. The organization of the company's innovation system did not allow it to appreciate the competitive potential of the valuable and rare resources generated at PARC. The organizational problems were accentuated by the fact that Xerox headquarters is on the East Coast in Norwalk, Connecticut, while PARC was on the West Coast in Palo Alto, California. Nor did it help that development engineers at Xerox headquarters had a disdain for the scientists engaging in basic research at PARC.

In the resource-based view, for a firm to gain and sustain a competitive advantage, its resources and capabilities need to interact in such a way as to create unique core competencies. Ultimately, though, only a few competencies may turn out to be *core* competencies that fulfill the VRIO requirements.[20] A company cannot do everything equally well and must carve out a unique identity for itself, making necessary trade-offs.[21] Strategy Highlight 4.1 demonstrates application of the VRIO framework.

organized to capture value One of the four key criteria in the VRIO framework; the characteristic of having in place an effective organizational structure and coordinating systems to fully exploit the competitive potential of the firm's resources and capabilities.

value chain The internal activities a firm engages in when transforming inputs into outputs; each activity adds incremental value. Primary activities directly add value; support activities add value indirectly.

How Nintendo Focused on the Casual Gamer

Video gaming is big business—revenues were over $22 billion in 2009 and are expected to grow to more than $60 billion in 2013. The leading game consoles are Sony's PlayStation 3, Microsoft's Xbox 360, and Nintendo's Wii. Sony and Microsoft tend to compete on stronger technological prowess, a larger library of games, and deeper pockets of cash. On the other hand, Nintendo has over the years created and nurtured a valuable, rare, and hard-to-imitate resource: a deep understanding of the casual gamer that has enabled Nintendo to develop products that respond to the casual gamer's preferences.

While early home video games were played by die-hards, mostly teenage and college-age young men who spent hours playing Halo or Grand Theft Auto, Nintendo began courting the casual gamer with the introduction of its Game Boy line of handheld devices in 1990, followed by the Nintendo DS in 2004 and the DS3 in 2011. The line of handheld game consoles expanded the market by appealing to younger players and other customers who were not hard-core video-game aficionados.

With the introduction of its Wii game console, Nintendo's knowledge of the "casual gamer" became a *valuable* resource. The Wii console has the unique feature of a wireless handheld pointing device that can detect movements in three dimensions. The Wii remote allows players to imitate real-life movements like swinging a tennis racket or hurling a bowling ball. This unique feature allows Nintendo to court a broader demographic, thereby continuing to expand Nintendo's knowledge of its customer base and strengthening its basis for competitive advantage. With the introduction of the Wii game console, Nintendo became the market leader in game consoles: It has sold some 52 million Wii consoles worldwide, which equates to some 49 percent market share. As of 2010, Microsoft has sold about 31 million Xbox 360 consoles (29 percent market share), and Sony sold 23 million PlayStation 3 consoles (22 percent market share). (Those sales and market shares will continue to change, of course, as the companies jockey for competitive advantage.)

Nintendo's deep knowledge about the casual gamer is also *rare,* as Sony and Microsoft have largely ignored this market segment. It is *difficult to imitate* as well, since that knowledge has been built over such a long period of time. Similar to Apple, Nintendo tightly integrates hardware and software to enhance the user experience, and thus it is *organized* to exploit its deep knowledge of the casual gamer. That knowledge of its customer is therefore a VRIO resource, allowing it to gain a competitive advantage in the hotly contested video-game market. Yet, the competition is not standing still. In November 2010, Microsoft introduced *Kinect* for its Xbox 360, which—similar to the feature in Wii—allows users to interact without a controller because it responds to voice commands and gestures.[22]

THE VALUE CHAIN AND ACTIVITY SYSTEMS

The **value chain** describes the internal activities a firm engages in when transforming inputs into outputs.[23] Each activity the firm performs along the chain adds incremental value—raw materials and other inputs are transformed into components that are finally assembled into finished products or services for the end consumer. The value chain concept can be applied to basically any firm, from those in old-line manufacturing industries to those in high-tech ones or even service firms.

Primary and Support Activities

The value chain transformation process is composed of a set of distinct activities, shown in Exhibit 4.6 (next page). The value chain is divided into primary and support activities. The **primary activities** add value directly as the firm transforms inputs into outputs—from raw materials through production phases to sales and marketing and finally customer service.

>> **LO 4-5**
Identify competitive advantage as residing in a network of firm activities.

primary activities
Firm activities that add value directly by transforming inputs into outputs as the firm moves a product or service horizontally along the internal value chain.

EXHIBIT 4.6

The Value Chain: Primary and Support Activities

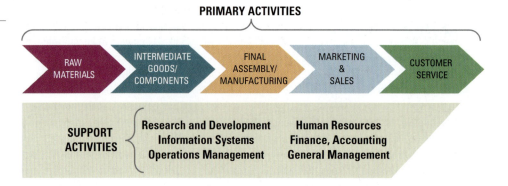

Other activities, called **support activities,** add value indirectly. These activities—such as research and development (R&D), information systems, operations management, human resources, finance, accounting, and general management—*support* each of the primary activities.

In the value chain perspective, resources and capabilities are needed to perform the firm's activities. While the RBV model helps to identify the integrated set of resources and capabilities that are the building blocks of core competencies, the value chain perspective helps managers to see how competitive advantage flows from the firm's *system of activities.* In the value chain perspective, the distinct activities a firm engages in are therefore the basic units of competitive advantage. It is important to note, however, that competitive advantage at the firm level is the outcome of the interplay among *all* of the firm's activities, not just a selected few. To create competitive advantage, a firm must be operationally efficient and also able to leverage its unique system of activities. Michael Porter emphasizes that the essence of strategy is to *choose* what activities to engage in and, more importantly, what *not* to do.[24] Companies that attempt to be too many things to too many customers often will be at a competitive disadvantage. The goal is to combine activities into a complex system that creates competitive advantage and also protects from imitation.

As an example, let's again look at the question, "What core competency underlies Southwest Airlines's superior performance?" To answer that question through the lens of the value chain perspective, we need to identify (1) a set of activities and (2) how SWA coordinates and orchestrates them to form a coherent low-cost strategy. SWA uses activities such as frequent and reliable departures, limited in-flight passenger service, low ticket prices, short-haul point-to-point flights using secondary airports, flying only one type of aircraft (which reduces pilot training time and maintenance cost), high aircraft utilization, and a lean, highly productive, and highly motivated ground and gate crew. Each core activity, in turn, is supported by a number of other activities. For example, the core activity of a lean, highly productive, and highly motivated ground and gate crew is supported by stock compensation plans and flexible contracts and work hours. Ideally, the activities pursued are consistent with one another, and complement and reinforce one another. The interconnected system of a firm's activities is more than the sum of its parts. Competitive advantage, therefore, can be embedded in a complex system of value-adding activities.

A **strategic activity system** conceives of a firm as a network of interconnected activities.[25] Strategic activity systems are socially complex. While one can easily observe several elements of a strategic activity system, the capabilities necessary to orchestrate and manage the network of activities cannot be so easily observed and therefore are difficult to imitate. Let's assume firm A's activity system, which lays the foundation of its competitive advantage, consists of 25 interconnected activities. Attracted by firm A's competitive

support activities Firm activities that add value indirectly, but are necessary to sustain primary activities.

strategic activity system The conceptualization of a firm as a network of interconnected activities.

advantage, competitor firm B closely monitors this activity system and begins to copy it through direct imitation. Moreover, firm B is very good at copying; it achieves a 90 percent accuracy rate. Will firm B, as the imitator, be able to copy firm A's activity system and negate its competitive advantage? Far from it. Firm A's activity system is based on 25 *interconnected* activities. Because each of firm A's 25 activities is copied with a 90 percent accuracy, firm B's overall copying accuracy of the entire system is $0.9 \times 0.9 \times 0.9 \ldots$, repeated 25 times. The probabilities quickly compound to render copying an entire activity system nearly impossible. In this case, firm B's "success" in copying firm A's activity system is $0.9^{25} = 0.07$, meaning that firm B's resulting activity system will imitate firm A's with only a 7 percent accuracy rate. Thus, the concept of the strategic activity system demonstrates the difficulty of using imitation as a path to competitive advantage.

Dynamic Strategic Activity Systems

In order for a firm to sustain competitive advantage, strategic activity systems need to evolve over time. This is because the external environment changes and also because a firm's competitors get better in developing their own activity systems and capabilities. Managers need to adapt their firm's strategic activity system by upgrading value-creating activities that respond to changing environments. To gain and sustain competitive advantage, managers may add new activities, remove activities that are no longer relevant, and upgrade activities that have become stale or somewhat obsolete. Each of these changes would require changes to the resources and capabilities involved.

For an example, let's look at The Vanguard Group's strategic activity system.[26] Vanguard is one of the world's largest investment companies, with about $1.4 trillion of assets under management. It serves individual investors, financial professionals, and institutional investors such as state retirement funds. Vanguard's mission is "to help clients reach their financial goals by being the world's highest-value provider of investment products and services."[27] Since its founding in 1929, Vanguard has emphasized low-cost investing and quality service for its clients. Vanguard's average expense ratio (as a percentage of total net assets) is 0.20 percent, generally the lowest in the industry.[28]

Vanguard pursued its mission in 1997 through its unique set of interconnected activities depicted in Exhibit 4.7 (next page). The six larger (blue) ovals depict Vanguard's strategic core activities: strict cost control, direct distribution, low expenses with savings passed on to clients, offering of a broad array of mutual funds, efficient investment management approach, and straightforward client communication and education. These six strategic themes were supported by clusters of tightly linked activities (smaller brown circles), further reinforcing the strategic activity network.

The needs of Vanguard's customers, however, have changed since 1997. Exhibit 4.8 shows Vanguard's strategic activity system in 2011. Again, the large ovals symbolize Vanguard's strategic core activities that help it realize its strategic position as the low-cost leader in the industry. However, the system evolved over time as Vanguard's management added a new core activity—customer segmentation—to the six core activities already in place in 1997 (still valid in 2011). Vanguard's managers put in place the customer-segmentation core activity, along with two new support activities, to address a new customer need that could not be met with its older configuration. Its 1997 activity system did not allow Vanguard to continue to provide quality service targeted at different customer segments at the lowest possible cost. The 2011 activity-system configuration allows Vanguard to customize its service offerings: It now separates its more traditional customers, who invest for the long term, from more active investors, who trade more often but are attracted to Vanguard funds by the firm's high performance and low cost.

EXHIBIT 4.7

The Vanguard Group's
Activity System in 1997

Source: Adapted from
N. Siggelkow (2002),
"Evolution toward fit,"
*Administrative Science
Quarterly* 47: 146.

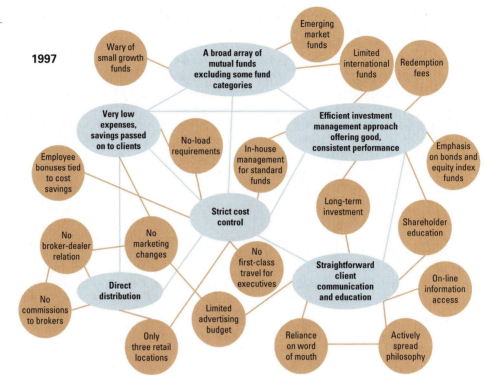

EXHIBIT 4.8

The Vanguard Group's
Activity System in 2011

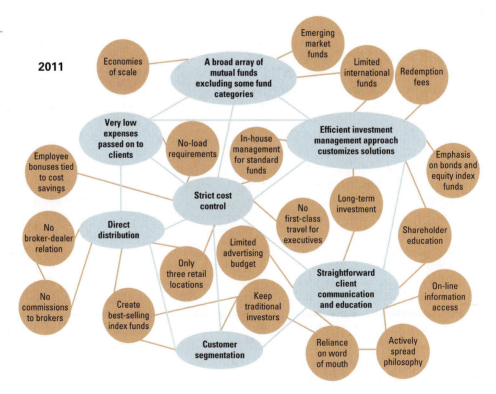

The core activity Vanguard added to its strategic activity system was developed with great care, to ensure that it not only fit well with its existing core activities but also further reinforced its activity network. For example, the new activity of "Create best-selling index funds" also relies on direct distribution; it is consistent with and further reinforces Vanguard's low-cost leadership position. As a result of achieving its "best-selling" goal, Vanguard is now one of the largest investment-management companies. This allows Vanguard to benefit from economies of scale (e.g., cost savings accomplished through a larger number of customers served and a greater amount of assets managed), further driving down cost. In turn, by lowering its cost structure, Vanguard can offer more customized services without raising its overall cost. Despite increased customization, Vanguard still has one of the lowest expense ratios in the industry. Even in a changing environment, the firm continues to pursue its strategy of low-cost investing combined with quality service. If firms add activities that don't fit their strategic positioning (e.g., if Vanguard added local retail offices in shopping malls, thereby increasing operating costs), they create "strategic misfits" that are likely to erode a firm's competitive advantage.

In summary, a firm's competitive advantage can result from its unique network of activities. The important point, however, is that a static fit with the current environment is not sufficient; rather, a firm's unique network of activities must evolve over time to take advantage of new opportunities and mitigate emerging threats. The goal of achieving such a *dynamic* fit lies—as the name suggests—at the heart of the dynamic capabilities perspective, which we'll discuss next.

THE DYNAMIC CAPABILITIES PERSPECTIVE

Dynamic capabilities describe a firm's ability to create, deploy, modify, reconfigure, upgrade, or leverage its resources in its quest for competitive advantage.[29] For a firm to sustain advantage over time, any fit between its internal strengths and the external environment must be dynamic. That is, the firm must be able to change its resource base and activity system as the external environment changes. Dynamic capabilities are essential in order to gain and sustain competitive advantage. Vanguard's dynamic capabilities, for example, helped it to reconfigure and adjust its activity system to sustain its advantage over time.

>> **LO 4-6**
Outline how dynamic capabilities can help a firm sustain competitive advantage.

Not only do dynamic capabilities allow firms to adapt to changing market conditions, they also enable firms to *create market changes* that can strengthen their strategic position. Apple's dynamic capabilities allowed it to redefine the market for portable music through its iPod, generating environmental change to which Sony and others had to respond. With its iPhone, Apple redefined the market for smartphones, again creating environmental change to which competitors like RIM, Nokia, HP, or Motorola must respond. More recently, Apple's introduction of the iPad attempts to redefine the media market, forcing competitors to respond. Dynamic capabilities are especially relevant for surviving and competing in markets that shift quickly and constantly, such as the high-tech space in which firms like Apple compete.

In the **dynamic capabilities perspective,** competitive advantage is the outflow of a firm's capacity to modify and leverage its resource base in a way that enables it to gain and sustain competitive advantage in a constantly changing environment. The firm may create, deploy, modify, reconfigure, or upgrade resources so as to provide value to customers and/or lower costs in a dynamic environment. The essence of this perspective is that competitive advantage is not derived from static resource or market advantages, but from a dynamic reconfiguration of a firm's resource base. Today, consumers value reliable, gas-powered engines made by Honda. If consumers start to value electric motors more (because they produce zero emissions), the value of Honda's engine competency will decrease. If this

dynamic capabilities perspective A model that emphasizes a firm's ability to modify and leverage its resource base in a way that enables it to gain and sustain competitive advantage in a constantly changing environment.

IBM's Dynamic Strategic Fit

In 2010, IBM generated 80 percent of its $99 billion of revenues from software sales and service. About 150,000 people now work in IBM Global Services, up from a mere 7,600 in 1992. Exhibit 4.9 depicts IBM's product scope in 1993 (the year its transformation began) and in 2010. Revenues from computing hardware declined from 50 percent to 18 percent, while revenues from software and services increased from 33 to 80 percent. Compared with 1993, total revenues are up by almost 70 percent. How did the company transform itself so radically?

IBM—nicknamed Big Blue—helped kick-start the PC revolution in 1981 by setting an open standard in the computer industry with the introduction of the IBM PC running on an Intel 8088 chip and a Microsoft operating system (MS-DOS). Ironically, in the years following, IBM nearly vanished after experiencing the full force of that revolution, because its executives believed that the future of computing lay in mainframe and mini-computers that would be produced by fully integrated companies. However, with an open standard in personal computing, the entire industry value chain disintegrated, and many new firms entered into its different stages. Intel entered as a provider of microprocessors and Microsoft as a provider of operating system and application software. This in turn led to a strategic misfit for IBM, which resulted in a competitive *dis*advantage.

By the early 1990s, the great U.S. computing icon was near bankruptcy. IBM's stock price had dropped to levels not seen in a decade, and more than 60,000 employees were laid off by the firm once known for offering lifetime employment. At the time, it was the biggest layoff in U.S. history. Lou Gerstner, an executive from consumer-products company RJR Nabisco, became IBM's CEO in 1993. Gerstner was not only an industry outsider, he was the first CEO of IBM not promoted from within. At the time, IBM was a stodgy hardware company. Rather than breaking up IBM into independent businesses, Gerstner refocused the company on satisfying market needs, which demanded sophisticated IT *services*.

Keeping IBM together as one entity allowed Gerstner to integrate hardware, software, and services to provide sophisticated solutions to customers' IT challenges. IBM was also quick to capitalize on the emergence of the Internet to add further value to its business solutions. The IBM of today is an agile and nimble global IT-services company.[30]

happens, BYD (the Chinese automaker introduced in Chapter 3), which morphed from a battery maker to a car company, might gain an advantage over Honda. While Honda views itself as an engineering-driven automotive company, startup BYD views its core competency as batteries, which in turn can be leveraged into strong strategic position in electric-power systems for cars, cell phones, laptops, cameras, medical devices, and so on. Imitation by competitors is especially difficult in such a case because it requires hitting a moving target.

Dynamic capabilities are especially relevant in markets that are constantly shifting. Given the accelerated pace of technological change, in combination with deregulation, globalization, and demographic shifts, dynamic markets today are the rule rather than the exception. Strategy Highlight 4.2 shows how IBM developed dynamic capabilities to reposition itself from a hardware company to a global IT-services firm.

IBM's successful turnaround is the result of the dynamic capabilities that its management team built, painstakingly, from its crisis in 1993 on. But how exactly do firms develop dynamic capabilities? Dynamic capabilities describe the firm's ability to reconfigure its resource base and to create external market change for others. Notice that we refer here not to the tangible resources themselves but to the ability to change those resources; thus, dynamic capabilities are an *intangible* resource.

One way to think about developing such intangible resources is to distinguish between resource stocks and resource flows.[31] **Resource stocks** are the firm's current level of

EXHIBIT 4.9

IBM Product Scope in 1993 and 2010 ($ in billions)

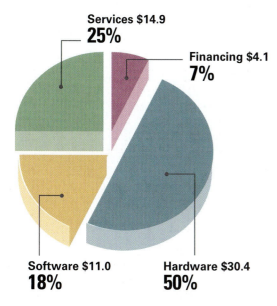

IBM 1993 Product Scope (total revenues $60bn)

Services $14.9
25%

Financing $4.1
7%

Software $11.0
18%

Hardware $30.4
50%

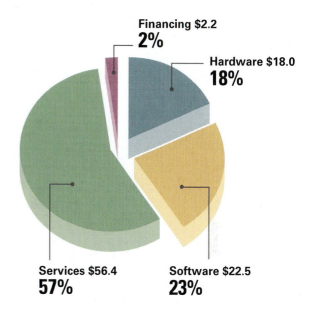

IBM 2010 Product Scope (total revenues $99bn)

Financing $2.2
2%

Hardware $18.0
18%

Services $56.4
57%

Software $22.5
23%

Source: Data from IBM Annual Reports, 1993 and 2010.

intangible resources. **Resource flows** are the firm's level of investments to maintain or build a resource. A helpful metaphor to explain the differences between resource stocks and resource flows is a bathtub that is being filled with water (see Exhibit 4.10, next page).[32] The amount of water in the bathtub indicates a company's level of a specific intangible resource stock—such as its dynamic capabilities, new-product development, engineering expertise, innovation capability, reputation for quality, and so on. Intangible-resource stocks are built through investments over time. This is represented in the drawing by the different faucets, from which water flows into the tub. These different faucets indicate investments the firm can make in different intangible resources. Investments in building an innovation capability, for example, differ from investments made in marketing expertise. Each investment flow would be represented by a different faucet. We saw that Vanguard and IBM both made specific investments in their resources over time, such as recruiting and retaining the best human capital and investing in R&D, among other activities.

How fast a tub fills depends on how much water comes out of the faucets and how long the faucets are left open. Intangible resources are built through continuous investments and experience over time. Many intangible resources, such as Hyundai's reputation for quality or Ritz-Carlton's excellence in customer responsiveness, take a long time to build. Organizational learning also fosters the build-up of intangible-resource stocks.

How fast the bathtub fills, however, also depends on how much water leaks out of the tub. The outflows represent a reduction in the firm's intangible-resource stocks. Resource

resource stocks The firm's current level of intangible resources.

resource flows The firm's level of investments to maintain or build a resource.

EXHIBIT 4.10

The Bathtub Metaphor:

The Role of Inflows and Outflows in Building Stocks of Intangible Resources

Source: Figure based on metaphor used in I. Dierickx and K. Cool (1989), "Asset stock accumulation and sustainability of competitive advantage," *Management Science* 35: 1504–1513.

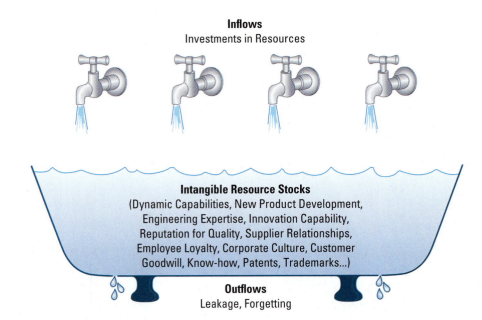

Inflows
Investments in Resources

Intangible Resource Stocks
(Dynamic Capabilities, New Product Development, Engineering Expertise, Innovation Capability, Reputation for Quality, Supplier Relationships, Employee Loyalty, Corporate Culture, Customer Goodwill, Know-how, Patents, Trademarks...)

Outflows
Leakage, Forgetting

leakage might occur through employee turnover, especially if key employees leave. Significant resource leakage can erode a firm's competitive advantage (as was the case for the Circuit City key employees who were let go and ended up at Best Buy). A reduction in resource stocks can occur if a firm does not engage in a specific activity for some time and forgets how to do this activity well.

GAINING & SUSTAINING COMPETITIVE ADVANTAGE

>> **LO 4-7**
Identify different conditions that allow firms to sustain their competitive advantage.

HOW TO PROTECT A COMPETITIVE ADVANTAGE

We will now consider whether specific internal conditions exist—above and beyond core competencies—that might help a firm protect and sustain its competitive advantage. Although no competitive advantage can be sustained indefinitely, several conditions can offer some protection to a successful firm by making it costly for competitors to imitate the resources or capabilities that underlie its competitive advantage: (1) better expectations of future resource value (or simply luck), (2) path dependence, (3) causal ambiguity, and (4) social complexity.[33] If one, or any combination, of these conditions is present, a firm may strengthen its basis for competitive advantage, increasing its chance to be sustainable over a longer period of time.

Better Expectations of Future Resource Value

Sometimes firms can acquire resources at a low cost, which lays the foundation for a competitive advantage later when expectations about the future of the resource turn out to be more accurate. Take a real estate developer, for example. One important decision she must make is to decide when and where to buy land for future development. Her firm may gain a competitive advantage if she buys a parcel of land for a low cost in an undeveloped rural area 30 miles north of San Antonio, Texas. Several years later, an interstate highway is built right near her firm's land. With the highway, suburban growth explodes as many new neighborhoods and shopping malls are built. Her firm is now able to develop this particular piece

Bill "Lucky" Gates

Taking a closer look at the richest man in the world shows that the co-founder of Microsoft, Bill Gates, was lucky on more than one occasion (as he himself freely admits). He was lucky to be born as William H. Gates III, into a well-to-do Seattle family. His father was a prominent attorney and co-founder of what is today the law firm K&L Gates LLC (one of the largest law firms in the world). His mother hailed from a banker's family in Nebraska. As a graduate from the University of Washington, Mrs. Mary Gates worked as a teacher and was active in civic affairs.

Young Bill was lucky to be enrolled in Lakeside School, an exclusive preparatory school in Seattle. In 1968, when Bill was in eighth grade, the Mothers Club at Lakeside School used proceeds of a rummage sale to buy a computer terminal along with time-share programming from GE. Suddenly, Lakeside School had more computer power than many premier research universities at that time. Bill fell in love with programming and spent every free minute he had on the computer, writing software programs. In 1973, he enrolled at Harvard, where he met Steve Ballmer, who later became Microsoft's CEO. The first minicomputer, the MITS Altair 8800, appeared on the cover of *Popular Electronics* magazine in January 1975. Paul Allen and Bill Gates wrote the Altair BASIC program and sold it to MITS of Albuquerque, New Mexico. In the same year,

19-year-old Bill Gates dropped out of Harvard and founded Microsoft with 22-year-old Paul Allen.

Microsoft's biggest break came in 1980 when IBM asked Microsoft to write the operating system for its PC. How did IBM, the world leader in computing, know about a fledgling startup? Here Bill Gates was lucky again. Mary Gates was the first woman to chair the United Way's national executive committee, and IBM's CEO, John Akers, also served on the charity's prestigious board. At one of the board meetings, Mr. Akers shared with Mrs. Gates the fact that IBM was looking for an operating system for its soon-to-be released PC that would set the standard in the industry. Mrs. Gates in turn suggested that her son's company would be the right partner.

The only catch was that Bill Gates didn't have an operating system that would meet IBM's needs, but he knew that a small computer outfit in Seattle had developed an operating system called Q-DOS, short for "quick and dirty operating system." On short notice, Bill Gates borrowed $50,000 (approximately $130,000 in today's value) from his father to buy Q-DOS from Seattle Computer Products, who did not know that IBM was looking for an operating system. Gates then turned around and sold a license of what is now MS-DOS to IBM, but he did not transfer the copyright to the operating system as part of the sale because he correctly believed that other hardware vendors would want to adopt IBM's open standard.[34] As discussed in Chapter 3, Microsoft later leveraged MS-DOS into industry dominance.

of property to build high-end office or apartment buildings. The value creation far exceeds the cost, and her firm gains a competitive advantage. The resource has suddenly become valuable, rare, and costly to imitate, allowing the developer's firm a competitive advantage. Other developers could have bought the land, but once the highway was announced, the cost of the developer's land and that of adjacent land would have risen drastically, reflecting the new reality and thus negating any potential for competitive advantage. In this case, the developer had better expectations than her competitors of the future value of the resource (the land she purchased). If this developer can repeat such "better expectations" over time, she will have a sustained competitive advantage.

Sometimes, better expectations result from luck, at least initially. The role of luck is illustrated in Strategy Highlight 4.3, about Bill Gates and Microsoft.

Path Dependence

Path dependence describes a process in which the options one faces in a current situation are limited by decisions made in the past.[35] Often, early events—sometimes even random ones—have a significant effect on final outcomes. For example, the U.S. customary system

path dependence
A situation in which the options one faces in the current situation are limited by decisions made in the past.

of measurements using miles, pounds, gallons, and so on was established in the 1820s. Today, the United States is the only industrial nation in the world not using the metric system as the official method of measurement, putting it at a disadvantage in some cross-border transactions and negotiations.

Other examples of path dependence highlight the notion that time cannot be compressed at will. Honda and Sony provide illustrative examples: Both companies took many decades to build their respective core competencies in high-powered efficient engines and electronic miniaturization. A competitor cannot imitate or create these competencies quickly, nor can one go out and buy a reputation for quality or innovation on the open market. These types of valuable, rare, and costly-to-imitate resources must be built and organized effectively over time, often through a painstaking process that may even include learning from failure.

Causal Ambiguity

Causal ambiguity describes a situation in which the cause and effect of a phenomenon are not readily apparent. We've defined strategy as the managers' theory of how to compete for advantage. This definition implies that managers need to have some kind of understanding about causes for superior and inferior performance. Understanding the underlying reasons of observed phenomena is far from trivial, however. Everyone can see that Apple has had several hugely successful innovative products such as the iMac, iPod, and iPhone. These successes stem from Apple's set of *V, R, I, O* core competencies that supports its ability to continue to offer a variety of innovative products.

However, a deep understanding of exactly *why* Apple has been so successful is very difficult. Even Apple's managers themselves may not be able to clearly pinpoint the sources of their success. Is it the visionary role that CEO Steve Jobs played? Is it the rare skills of its uniquely talented design team within Apple? Is it the timing of the company's product introductions? Or is it Apple's Chief Operating Officer who adds superior organizational skills and puts all the pieces together when running the day-to-day operations? If the link between cause and effect is ambiguous for Apple's managers, it is that much more difficult for others seeking to copy this valuable resource.

Social Complexity

Social complexity describes situations in which different social and business systems interact with one another. There is frequently no causal ambiguity as to how the *individual* systems such as supply chain management or new product development work in isolation. They are often managed through standardized business processes such as Six Sigma or ISO 9000. Social complexity, however, emerges when two or more such systems are *combined.* Copying the emerging complex social systems is difficult for competitors because neither direct imitation nor substitution is a valid approach. The interactions between different systems create too many possible permutations for a system to be understood with any accuracy. The resulting social complexity makes copying these systems difficult, if not impossible, resulting in a valuable, rare, and costly-to-imitate resource that the firm is organized to exploit.

A simple thought experiment can illustrate this point. A group with three people has three relationships, connecting every person directly with one another. Adding a fourth person to this group increases the number of direct relationships to six. Just introducing one more person then doubles the number of relationships to 12.[36] This gives you some idea of how complexity might increase when we combine different systems with many different parts.

A firm may be able to protect its competitive advantage (even for long periods of time) when its managers have consistently better expectations about the future value of resources, it has accumulated a resource advantage that can be imitated only over long periods of time, or when the source of its competitive advantage is causally ambiguous or socially complex. It is also important to note that while Bill Gates got a lucky break when starting Microsoft, luck cannot be sustained over time. Microsoft leveraged its initial break into a dominant position for several decades through an effective strategy (see Strategy Highlight 3.2). 🔍

PUTTING TOGETHER INTERNAL AND EXTERNAL ANALYSIS: THE SWOT ANALYSIS

We've now reached a significant point in the book: Combining tools for external analysis from Chapter 3 with the frameworks for internal analysis introduced in this chapter allows you to begin formulating a strategy that matches the firm's internal resources and capabilities to the demands of the external industry environment. Ideally, managers want to leverage a firm's internal strengths to exploit external opportunities, while mitigating internal weaknesses and external threats. This allows them to formulate a strategy that is tailored to their company, creating a unique fit between the company's internal resources and the external environment. If a firm achieves a dynamic fit, it is likely to be able to sustain its advantage over time.

>> **LO 4-8**
Conduct a SWOT analysis.

We synthesize insights from an internal analysis of the company's *strengths* and *weaknesses* with those from an analysis of external *opportunities* and *threats,* using the well-known SWOT analysis. Internal strengths (S) and weaknesses (W) concern resources, capabilities, and competencies. Whether they are strengths or weaknesses can be determined by applying the VRIO framework. External opportunities (O) and threats (T) are in the firm's general environment and can be captured by a PESTEL analysis.

A SWOT analysis allows managers to evaluate a firm's current situation and future prospects by simultaneously considering internal and external factors. It is one of the most popular tools used. The SWOT analysis encourages managers to scan the internal and external environments, looking for any relevant factors that might affect the firm's current or future competitive advantage. The focus is on internal and external factors that can affect—in a positive or negative way—the firm's ability to pursue its strategic goals. Ideally, a shrewd manager solicits input for the SWOT analysis from different perspectives and hierarchal levels within the organization. In Exhibit 4.11 (next page), the vertical axis is divided into factors that are *external to the organization* (the focus of Chapter 3) and the horizontal axis into factors that are *internal to the organization* (the focus of this chapter).

The gathering of information for a SWOT analysis allows managers to link internal factors (strengths and weaknesses) to external factors (opportunities and threats). The principal question to ask (as displayed in the northwest quadrant of Exhibit 4.11) is, "How can the firm use its strengths (the resource base and core competencies) to take advantage of an

---

causal ambiguity A situation in which the cause and effect of a phenomenon are not readily apparent.

social complexity A situation in which different social and business systems interact with one another.

SWOT analysis A framework that allows managers to synthesize insights obtained from an internal analysis of the company's strengths and weaknesses (S and W) with those from an analysis of external opportunities and threats (O and T).

Strategic Questions	Strengths	Weaknesses
Opportunities	*How can managers use strengths to take advantage of opportunities?*	*How can managers overcome weaknesses that prevent the firm from taking advantage of opportunities?*
Threats	*How can managers use strengths to reduce the likelihood and impact of threats?*	*How can managers overcome weaknesses that will make threats a reality?*

EXHIBIT 4.11

Addressing Strategic Questions within the SWOT Analysis

external opportunity in order to improve the performance of the firm?" Looking further ahead, managers need to consider additional resources and capabilities that may be needed in order to take advantage of external opportunities and mitigate threats. Considering these issues allows managers to match current and future resources and capabilities to the external environment.

You have now acquired the toolkit with which to conduct a complete strategic analysis of a firm's internal and external environments. In the next chapter, we consider various ways to measure competitive advantage. That chapter will complete Part 1, on strategy analysis, in the AFI framework.

CHAPTERCASE 4 *Consider This . . .*

EMPLOYEES AT CIRCUIT CITY stores and even at the headquarters in Richmond, Virginia, were shocked and devastated when the firm actually ceased operations in March 2009. More than a year after the closing, former headquarters workers note that the firm had a good, hardworking, and family-friendly atmosphere. They believed to the end that, in the worst case, another firm would buy Circuit City and perhaps reduce its size but not permanently close the business.[37]

1. Why did Circuit City lose its competitive advantage?

2. What could Circuit City's management have done differently?

3. What is the future of Best Buy as the leader in big-box electronic retailing? What resources and capabilities will positively impact its future?

Take-Away Concepts

This chapter demonstrated various approaches to analyzing the firm's *internal environment,* as summarized by the following learning objectives and related take-away concepts.

LO 4-1 Distinguish among a firm's resources, capabilities, core competencies, and firm activities.

>> Core competencies are unique, deeply embedded, firm-specific strengths that allow firms to

differentiate their products and services to create more value for consumers than their rivals or to offer products and services of acceptable value at lower cost.

>> Resources are assets that a company can draw on when crafting and executing strategy. Capabilities are the organizational skills necessary to orchestrate a diverse set of resources to deploy them strategically. Activities enable firms to add value by transforming inputs into goods and services.

LO 4-2 Differentiate between tangible and intangible resources.

>> Tangible resources have physical attributes and are visible.

>> Intangible resources have no physical attributes and are invisible.

>> Competitive advantage is more likely to be based on intangible resources.

LO 4-3 Describe the critical assumptions behind the resource-based view.

>> The resource-based view makes two critical assumptions: resource heterogeneity (resources differ across firms) and resource immobility (resources are sticky).

LO 4-4 Apply the VRIO framework to assess the competitive implications of a firm's resources.

>> For a firm's resource to be the basis of a competitive advantage, it must have VRIO attributes: valuable (V), rare (R), and costly to imitate (I). The firm must also be able to organize (O) in order to capture the value of the resource.

LO 4-5 Identify competitive advantage as residing in a network of firm activities.

>> Each primary activity the firm performs should add incremental value directly by transforming inputs into outputs. Support activities sustain primary activities.

>> A network of primary and supporting firm activities can create a strategic fit that can lead to competitive advantage.

>> A strategic activity system conceives of a firm as a network of interconnected activities. Firms need to upgrade their value activities over time, in response to changes in the external environment and to moves of competitors.

LO 4-6 Outline how dynamic capabilities can help a firm sustain competitive advantage.

>> To sustain a competitive advantage, any fit between a firm's internal strengths and the external environment must be dynamic. This is accomplished through the ability to create, deploy, modify, reconfigure, or upgrade the resource base.

LO 4-7 Identify different conditions that allow firms to sustain their competitive advantage.

>> Several conditions make it costly for competitors to imitate another firm's resource or capability that underlie its competitive advantage: (1) better expectations of future resource value (or simply luck), (2) path dependence, (3) causal ambiguity, and (4) social complexity.

LO 4-8 Conduct a SWOT analysis.

>> Formulating a strategy that increases the chances of gaining and sustaining a competitive advantage is based on synthesizing insights obtained from an internal analysis of the company's strengths (S) and weaknesses (W) with those from an analysis of external opportunities (O) and threats (T).

>> A SWOT analysis by itself is insufficient to guide strategy formulation.

Key Terms

Causal ambiguity *(p. 104)*
Core competencies *(p. 85, 86)*
Costly to imitate resource *(p. 92)*
Dynamic capabilities perspective *(p. 99)*
Intangible resources *(p. 88)*
Organized to capture value *(p. 94)*

Path dependence *(p. 103)*
Primary activities *(p. 95)*
Rare resource *(p. 92)*
Resource-based view *(p. 88)*
Resource flows *(p. 101)*
Resource heterogeneity *(p. 90)*
Resource immobility *(p. 90)*
Resource stocks *(p. 100)*

Social complexity *(p. 104)*
Strategic activity system *(p. 96)*
Support activities *(p. 96)*
SWOT analysis *(p. 105)*
Tangible resources *(p. 88)*
Valuable resource *(p. 92)*
Value chain *(p. 95)*
VRIO framework *(p. 91)*

Discussion Questions

1. Why is it important to study the internal resources, capabilities, and activities of firms? What insights can be gained?

2. Strategy Highlight 4.2 explains IBM's major transformation from a hardware to a services-oriented company. List the major dynamic capabilities that enabled IBM to make this change. Can you think of other firms that have been successful at a major transition such as this?

3. The resource-based model identifies four criteria that firms can use to evaluate whether particular resources and capabilities are core competencies and can, therefore, provide a basis for competitive advantage. Are these measures independent or interdependent? Explain. If (some of) the measures are interdependent, what implications does that fact have for managers wanting to create and sustain a competitive advantage?

Ethical/Social Issues

1. As discussed in this chapter, resources that are valuable, rare, and costly to imitate help create a competitive advantage. In many cases, firms try to "reverse-engineer" a particular feature from a competitor's product for their own uses. It is commonplace, for example, for cell phone manufacturers to buy the newest phones on the market and take them apart to see what new components/features the new models have implemented.

   However, as the competition between Google (www.google.com) and Baidu (www.ir.baidu.com) over Internet searches in China makes clear, this sort of corporate behavior does not stop with hardware products. Baidu is a 10-year-old firm that has allegedly adapted many of the search tools that Google uses. Baidu however modifies its searches inside China (its major market) to accommodate Chinese-government guidelines. In protest over these same guidelines, in 2010 Google left the Chinese market and is running its Chinese search operations from Hong Kong.[38]

   It is legal to take apart publicly available products and services and try to replicate them and even develop work-arounds for relevant patents. But is it ethical? If a key capability protected by patents or trademarks in your firm is being reverse-engineered by the competition, what are your options for a response?

2. The chapter mentions that one type of resource flow is the loss of key personnel who move to another firm. Assume that the human resources department of your firm has started running ads and billboards for open positions very near the office of your top competitor. Your firm is also running Google ads on a keyword search for this same competitor. Is there anything unethical about this activity? Would your view change if this key competitor had just announced a major layoff?

Small Group Exercises

SMALL GROUP EXERCISE 1

Brand valuations were mentioned in the chapter as a potential key intangible resource for firms. Some product brands are so well-established the entire category of products (including those made by competitors) may be called by the brand name rather than the product type. In your small group, develop two or three examples of this happening in the marketplace. In any of the cases noted, does such brand valuation give the leading brand a competitive advantage? Or does it produce confusion in the market for all products or services in that category?

SMALL GROUP EXERCISE 2

An enhancement on the basic SWOT analysis is to consider both *current* as well as *potential* conditions.[39] That is, conduct the SWOT in two stages: First, list the elements that are current strengths, weaknesses, opportunities, and threats; then repeat the process with the focus on potential strengths, weaknesses, opportunities, and threats. This two-stage process provides a perspective of the possible dynamic changes facing the organization.

Try this two-step approach on a firm of your group's choice (e.g., the firm that you use for your strategy term project) or use a firm assigned by the instructor.

CURRENT CONDITIONS

Strengths

1. _____
2. _____
3. _____
4. _____

Weaknesses

1. _____
2. _____
3. _____
4. _____

Opportunities

1. _____
2. _____
3. _____
4. _____

Threats

1. _____
2. _____
3. _____
4. _____

POTENTIAL CONDITIONS

Strengths

1. _____
2. _____
3. _____
4. _____

Weaknesses

1. _____
2. _____
3. _____
4. _____

Opportunities

1. _____
2. _____
3. _____
4. _____

Threats

1. _____
2. _____
3. _____
4. _____

Strategy Term Project

MODULE 4: INTERNAL ANALYSIS

In this section, you will study the internal resources, capabilities, core competencies, and value chain of your selected firm.

1. A good place to start with an internal firm analysis is to catalog the assets a firm has. Make a list of the firm's tangible assets in the firm. Then, make a separate list of the intangible assets you can identify.

2. Now extend beyond the asset base and use the VRIO framework to identify the competitive position held by your firm. Which, if any, of these resources are helpful in sustaining the firm's competitive advantage?

3. Identify the core competencies that are at the heart of the firm's competitive advantage. (Remember, a firm will have only one, or at most a few, core competencies, by definition.)

4. Use the strategic activity system framework to diagram the important and supportive activities the firm has that are key to delivering and sustaining the firm's value proposition. (For an example, refer to Exhibits 4.7 and 4.8 showing the activity system of the Vanguard Group.)

5. Perform a SWOT analysis for your firm. Remember that strengths and weaknesses (S, W) are internal to the firm, and opportunities and threats (O, T) are external. Refer to Small Group Exercise 2 earlier for an enhanced version of the SWOT analysis.

*my*Strategy

LOOKING INSIDE YOURSELF: WHAT IS MY COMPETITIVE ADVANTAGE?

H ere, we encourage you to take what you have learned about competitive advantage and apply it to your personal career. Spend a few minutes looking at yourself to discover *your own* competitive advantage.

1. Write down your own personal strengths and weaknesses. What sort of organization will permit you to really leverage your strengths and keep you highly engaged in your work (person–organization fit)? Do some of your weaknesses need to be mitigated through additional training or mentoring from a more seasoned professional?

2. Personal capabilities also need to be evaluated over time. Are your strengths and weaknesses different today from what they were five years ago? What are you doing to make sure your capabilities are dynamic? Are you upgrading skills, modifying behaviors, or otherwise seeking to change your future strengths and weaknesses?

3. Are some of your strengths valuable, rare, and costly to imitate? How can you organize your work to help capture the value of your key strengths (or mitigate your weaknesses)?

4. In this chapter, we discussed that the strategic activity system happening inside the firm can be a vital source of sustainable competitive advantage. If you are currently or previously employed, consider how your professional activities can help reinforce the key value-added activities in your department or organization.

Endnotes

1. Collins, J. (2001), *Good to Great: Why Some Companies Make the Leap . . . and Others Don't* (New York: HarperCollins), p. 3.

2. Ibid., p. 33.

3. This ChapterCase is based on: Collins, J. (2001), *Good to Great;* and Collins, J. (2009), *How the Mighty Fall: And Why Some Companies Never Give In* (New York: HarperCollins).

4. For an insightful discussion of Circuit City's rise and fall, see: Collins, J. (2001), *Good to Great;* and Collins, J. (2009), *How the Mighty Fall.*

5. For a detailed discussion of CarMax, see Mini Case 8.

6. Jim Collins describes the DivX DVD player concept as follows: "Using a special DVD player, customers would be able to 'rent' a DVD for as long as they liked before playing it, using an encryption system to unlock the DVD for viewing. The advantage: not having to return a DVD to the video store before having had a chance to watch it." See J. Collins (2009), *How the Mighty Fall*, pp. 30–31.

7. Rothaermel, F. T., M. L. Arthaud-Day, and N. McCarthy (2013), "Best Buy After Circuit City," case study in Rothaermel, F. T. (2013), *Strategic Management* (Burr Ridge, IL: McGraw-Hill).

8. Prahalad, C. K., and G. Hamel (1990), "The core competence of the corporation," *Harvard Business Review,* May–June.

9. This discussion is based on: Amit, R., and P. J. H. Schoemaker (1993), "Strategic assets and organizational rent," *Strategic Management Journal* 14: 33–46; Barney, J. (1991), "Firm resources and sustained competitive advantage," *Journal of Management* 17: 99–120; Peteraf, M. (1993), "The cornerstones of competitive advantage," *Strategic Management Journal* 14: 179–191; and Wernerfelt, B. (1984), "A resource-based view of the firm," *Strategic Management Journal* 5: 171–180.

10. "Top 100 Most Valuable Global Brands 2009," report by Millward Brown, WPP.

11. Ibid.

12. Ibid.

13. For a discussion on the benefits of being located in a technology cluster, see: Saxenian, A. L. (1994), *Regional Advantage: Culture and Competition in Silicon Valley and Route 128* (Cambridge, MA: Harvard University Press); and Rothaermel, F. T., and D. Ku (2008), "Intercluster innovation differentials: The role of research universities," *IEEE Transactions on Engineering Management* 55: 9–22.

14. Stuart, T., and O. Sorenson (2003), "The geography of opportunity: Spatial heterogeneity in founding rates and the performance of biotechnology firms," *Research Policy* 32: 229–253.

15. This discussion is based on: Amit, R., and P. J. H. Schoemaker (1993), "Strategic assets and organizational rent"; Barney, J. (1991), "Firm resources and sustained competitive advantage"; Peteraf, M. (1993), "The cornerstones of competitive advantage"; and Wernerfelt, B. (1984), "A resource-based view of the firm."

16. This discussion is based on: Amit, R., and P. J. H. Schoemaker (1993), "Strategic assets and organizational rent"; Barney, J. (1991), "Firm resources and sustained competitive advantage"; Barney, J., and W. Hesterly (2009), *Strategic Management and Competitive Advantage,* 3rd ed. (Upper Saddle River, NJ: Pearson Prentice Hall); Peteraf, M. (1993), "The cornerstones of competitive advantage"; and Wernerfelt, B. (1984), "A resource-based view of the firm."

17. Barney, J. (1991), "Firm resources and sustained competitive advantage"; and Barney, J., and W. Hesterly (2009), *Strategic Management and Competitive Advantage,* 3rd ed.

18. Ceccagnoli, M., and F. T. Rothaermel (2008), "Appropriating the returns to innovation," *Advances in Study of Entrepreneurship, Innovation, and Economic Growth* 18: 11–34.

19. Chesbrough, H. (2006), *Open Innovation: The New Imperative for Creating and Profiting from Technology* (Boston, MA: Harvard Business School Press).

20. Prahalad, C. K., and G. Hamel (1990), "The core competence of the corporation."

21. Porter, M. E. (1996), "What is strategy?" *Harvard Business Review,* November–December: 61–78.

22. This Strategy Highlight is based on: Asia Case Research Centre (2009), "Nintendo's disruptive strategy: Implications for the video game industry," *The University of Hong Kong* (HKU814); *Los Angeles Times,* http://latimesblogs.latimes.com/technology/nintendo/; and www.vgchartz.com/.

23. This discussion is based on: Porter, M. E. (1985), *Competitive Advantage: Creating and Sustaining Superior Performance* (New York: Free Press); Porter, M. E. (1996), "What is strategy?"; and Siggelkow, N. (2001), "Change in the presence of fit: The rise, the fall, and the renaissance of Liz Claiborne," *Academy of Management Journal* 44: 838–857.

24. Porter, M. E. (1996), "What is strategy?"; and Porter, M. E. (2008), "The five competitive forces that shape strategy," *Harvard Business Review,* January.

25. Porter, M. E. (1996), "What is strategy?"

26. This discussion draws on: Porter, M. E. (1996), "What is strategy?"; and Siggelkow, N. (2002), "Evolution toward fit," *Administrative Science Quarterly* 47: 125–159.

27. https://personal.vanguard.com/us/content/Home/WhyVanguard/AboutVanguardWhoWeAreContent.jsp.

28. "Funds: How much you're really paying," *Money,* November 2005; and https://personal.vanguard.com/us/content/Home/WhyVanguard/AboutVanguardWhoWeAreContent.jsp.

29. This discussion is based on: Eisenhardt, K. M., and M. Martin (2000), "Dynamic capabilities: What are they?" *Strategic Management Journal* 21: 1105–1121; and Helfat, C. E., S. Finkelstein, W. Mitchell, M. A. Peteraf, H. Singh, D. J. Teece, and S. G. Winter (2007), *Dynamic Capabilities: Understanding Strategic Change in Organizations* (Malden, MA: Blackwell).

30. This Strategy Highlight is based on: Gerstner, L. V. (2002), *Who Says Elephants Can't Dance?* (New York: HarperBusiness); Grove, A. S. (1996), *Only the Paranoid Survive: How to Exploit the Crisis Points that Challenge Every Company and Every Career* (New York: Currency Doubleday); Harreld, J. B., C. A. O'Reilly, and M. Tushman (2007), "Dynamic capabilities at IBM: Driving strategy into action," *California Management Review* 49: 21–43; and IBM Annual Reports (diverse years).

31. Dierickx, I., and K. Cool (1989), "Asset stock accumulation and sustainability of competitive advantage," *Management Science* 35: 1504–1513.

32. Ibid.

33. This discussion is based on: Barney, J. (1986), "Strategic factor markets: Expectations, luck, and business strategy," *Management Science* 32: 1231–1241; Barney, J. (1991), "Firm resources and sustained competitive advantage," *Journal of Management* 17: 99–120; Dierickx, I., and K. Cool (1989), "Asset stock accumulation and sustainability of competitive advantage"; and Mahoney, J. T., and J. R. Pandian (1992), "The resource-based view within the conversation of strategic management," *Strategic Management Journal* 13: 363–380.

34. This Strategy Highlight is based on: Manes, S., and P. Andrews (1994), *Gates: How Microsoft's Mogul Reinvented an Industry and Made Himself the Richest Man in America* (New York: Doubleday); and Gladwell, M. (2008), *Outliers. The Story of Success* (New York: Little, Brown, and Company).

35. Arthur, W. B. (1989), "Competing technologies, increasing returns, and lock-in by historical events," *Economics Journal* 99: 116–131; and Dierickx, I., and K. Cool (1989), "Asset stock accumulation and sustainability of competitive advantage."

36. More formally, the number of relationships (r) in a group is a function of its group members (n), with $r = n(n - 1)/2$.

The assumption is that two people, A and B, have only one relationship (A $\longleftrightarrow$ B), rather than two relationships (A $\rightarrow$ B and A $\leftarrow$ B). In the latter case, the number of relationships (r) in a group with n members doubles, where $r = n(n - 1)$.

37. *A Tale of Two Cities: The Circuit City Story*, film documentary by Tom Wulf, released November 2010.

38. "How Baidu won China," *Bloomberg BusinessWeek,* November 11, 2010.

39. This Small Group Exercise is drawn from: Blumentritt, T. (2009), *A Primer on the SWOT Analysis.* Teaching Note, Kennesaw State University.

CHAPTER 5

Competitive Advantage and Firm Performance

LEARNING OBJECTIVES

After studying this chapter, you should be able to:

LO 5-1   Describe and evaluate economic value creation when measuring competitive advantage.

LO 5-2   Describe and evaluate accounting profitability when measuring competitive advantage.

LO 5-3   Describe and evaluate shareholder value creation when measuring competitive advantage.

LO 5-4   Describe and evaluate the balanced-scorecard approach for assessing competitive advantage.

LO 5-5   Describe and evaluate the triple-bottom-line approach when assessing competitive advantage.

LO 5-6   Compare and contrast different approaches to measuring competitive advantage, and derive managerial implications.

Assessing Competitive Advantage: Google vs. Microsoft

WE BEGAN OUR JOURNEY into strategic management (in Chapter 1) by looking at Google's success in online search and advertising and Microsoft's challenges in catching up. Google holds some 70 percent market share and has outperformed its rivals for a number of years. Although it is relatively easy to pick a winner in a narrowly defined market segment, we also saw—when comparing Google's and Microsoft's business models in Chapter 1—that both firms compete with one another in a number of different markets and thus are exposed to multipoint competition. We discussed the quest to gain and sustain competitive advantage as managers' ability to formulate and implement a strategy that leads to superior firm performance.

Competitive advantage thus is defined and assessed at the *firm level*. In order to measure the firm's overall performance, we need tools to assess performance across all of the firm's different business activities. While that idea is straightforward enough, it is far from clear which performance metric is best.

Exhibit 5.1 (next page) compares Google and Microsoft using common performance metrics. Based on *revenues* and *net income*, Microsoft ($66 bn in revenues and $21 bn in net income) outperformed Google ($28 bn and $8 bn, respectively) by a wide margin. In the first quarter of 2011, Microsoft's market value (market capitalization, or "market cap") was $241 billion, while Google's was $196 billion.

But is this a valid comparison? Using *absolute* numbers such as these is like comparing apples and oranges: With 23,331 employees, Google is much smaller than Microsoft, which has 89,000 employees. When we adjust revenues, net income, and market value by the number of employees, so that the measures represent performance *per employee* (see the bottom row in Exhibit 5.1), we see Google outperforming Microsoft by a wide margin on each of the three performance dimensions.

After reading the chapter, you will find more about this case, with related questions, on page 130.

▲ **COMPARING THE PERFORMANCES** of Google and Microsoft makes it clear that understanding and measuring competitive advantage presents some challenges. Looking at *absolute* firm-level measures such as revenues, net income, and market capitalization, we concluded that Microsoft outperformed Google. When we adjusted these measures for size (in this case, size as measured by performance per employee), we saw Google outperforming Microsoft. As you know from your coursework in finance and accounting, it is also possible to use various other measures to analyze firm performance. For example, financial ratios adjust for firm size and thus are often preferred over absolute measures when tracking firm performance.

EXHIBIT 5.1

Comparing Google and Microsoft along Different Performance Dimensions

(Top row: absolute values; bottom row: ratios.)

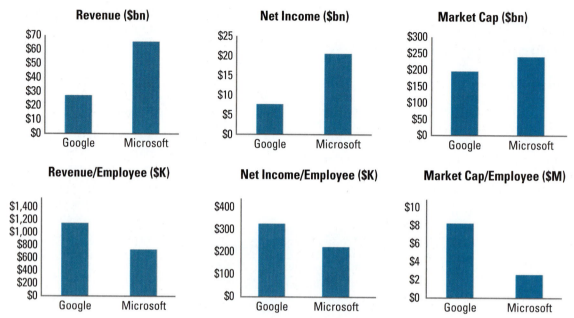

Source: Data gathered from companies' SEC filings. All data are as of December 31, 2010, except market capitalization, which is as of January 2011.

Competitive advantage leads to superior firm performance. Gaining and sustaining competitive advantage is the goal of strategic management. To explain and predict differences in firm performance, therefore, we must think hard about how to best measure it. We devote this chapter to studying how to measure performance. In particular, we introduce different frameworks and a diverse set of measures to capture the multifaceted nature of competitive advantage. These various tools will facilitate a critical evaluation of a firm's performance and help determine whether it has a competitive advantage.

MEASURING COMPETITIVE ADVANTAGE

If competitive advantage is always *relative*—measured in relation to other firms—then how do we know when a firm has competitive advantage? How do we measure competitive advantage? Surprisingly, these apparently simple questions do not have simple answers. Strategic management researchers have debated them intensely for at least 25 years.[1]

To answer these key questions, we will develop a *multidimensional perspective* to measuring competitive advantage. That is, we will apply not only the standard economic, accounting, and financial metrics, but also a wider set of performance metrics, some of which are qualitative rather than quantitative. Let's begin by focusing on the three standard dimensions by asking:[2]

1. How much *economic value* does the firm generate?
2. What is the firm's *accounting profitability?*
3. How much *shareholder value* does the firm create?

These performance dimensions tend to be correlated, particularly when considered over longer time periods. That is, economic value and accounting profitability tend to be reflected in the firm's stock price.

Economic Value Creation

Let's first consider performance through the dimension of *economic value.* Three factors are critical when evaluating any good or service a firm offers in the marketplace: (1) *value* (V), (2) *price* (P), and (3) *cost* (C).

Value denotes the dollar amount (V) a consumer would attach to a good or service. Simply put, how much are you willing to pay for it? Value captures a consumer's willingness to pay. (Economists call this amount the *reservation price.*) If the value you attach to a good or service is greater than the *price* charged (P), you are likely to purchase it. The cost (C) to produce the good or service matters little to the consumer, but it matters a great deal to the producer (supplier) of the good or service. The difference between a buyer's willingness to pay for a product or service and the firm's cost to produce it is the economic value created. A firm has a competitive advantage when it is able to create more economic value than its rivals.

Let's assume, for example, you are hungry and you value (V) a pizza at $12. You thus are willing to pay a price (P) of $10 for the pizza that your local bistro offers, even though you realize it probably costs less than $10 to produce it. Suppose the bistro's total cost (C) is in fact $7. The difference between value ($V = \$12$) and cost ($C = \$7$) is the economic value created by the entrepreneur who runs the bistro, in this case, $V - C = \$12 - \$7$, or $5. The economic value created is sometimes also called the *economic contribution.*

The difference between the price charged (P), and the cost to produce (C), is the entrepreneur's profit or (in economics) producer surplus. In our example, the profit is $P - C = \$10 - \$7 = \$3$. The entrepreneur captures this amount as profit. As the consumer, you capture the difference between what you would have been willing to pay (V) and what you paid (P) as something called consumer surplus. In our example, the consumer surplus is $V - P = \$12 - \$10$, or $2.

As you can see from the pizza example, economic value created therefore also equals the sum of consumer and producer surplus (that is, profit):

Economic value created $= \$12 - \$7 = \$5$

Consumer surplus $+$ Producer surplus $= \$2 + \$3 = \$5$

The relationship between consumer and producer surplus is the reason trade happens: Both transacting parties capture *some* of the overall value created. (Note, though, that the distribution of the value created between parties need not be equal to make trade worthwhile.) Thus, in an economic context, strategy is about (1) *creating economic value* and (2) *capturing as much of it as possible.*

From an economic point of view, revenues are a function of the value created for customers and the price of the good or service, which together drive the volume of

>> **LO 5-1**

Describe and evaluate economic value creation when measuring competitive advantage.

---

value The dollar amount (V) a consumer would attach to a good or service; the consumer's *maximum willingness to pay;* sometimes also called *reservation price.*

economic value created Difference between value (V) and cost (C), or ($V - C$); sometimes also called *economic contribution.*

profit (producer surplus) Difference between price charged (P) and the cost to produce (C), or ($P - C$).

consumer surplus Difference between the value a consumer attaches to a good or service (V) and what he or she paid for it (P), or ($V - P$).

goods sold. Thus, economists define a firm's profit (Π) as total revenues (TR) minus total costs (TC):

$$\Pi = TR - TC, \text{ where } TR = P \times Q, \text{ or price times quantity sold}$$

Total costs include both fixed and variable costs. *Fixed costs* are independent of consumer demand—e.g., the cost of capital to rent the bistro space and buy the pizza oven and other equipment. *Variable costs* change with the level of consumer demand—e.g., flour, tomato sauce, cheese, and other pizza ingredients as well as labor and utilities. Because the cost of capital and the cost of the bistro are fixed, the bistro becomes more profitable as the bistro entrepreneur sells more pizzas and thus spreads her fixed costs over a larger sales volume.

Also, if the economic value created ($V - C$) by the pizzeria across the street is only $4, then the bistro entrepreneur has a competitive advantage because $5 > $4. (For simplicity, assume there are no other pizza parlors or delivery services nearby.)

Exhibit 5.2 graphically illustrates how these concepts fit together. On the left side of the graph, V represents the value of the product to the consumer, as captured in the consumer's *maximum willingness to pay*. In the center bar, C is the cost to produce the product or service (the unit cost). It follows that the difference between the consumers' maximum willingness to pay and the firm's cost ($V - C$) is the *economic value created*. The price of the product or service (P) is indicated in the dashed line. The economic value created ($V - C$), as shown in Exhibit 5.2, is split between producer and consumer: ($V - P$) is the value the consumer captures (*consumer surplus*), and ($P - C$) is the value the producer captures (*producer surplus*, or *profit*).

Competitive advantage goes to the firm that achieves the largest difference between V, the consumer's willingness to pay, and C, the cost to produce the good or service. The reason is that a large difference between V and C gives the firm two distinct pricing options: (1) It can charge higher prices to reflect the higher product value and thus increase its profitability. Or (2) it can charge the same price as competitors and thus gain market share. Given this, the strategic objective is to maximize ($V - C$), or the economic value created.

opportunity costs
The value of the best forgone alternative use of the resources employed.

One last aspect of how to measure economic value merits mention: When economists measure economic value created, they include opportunity costs. **Opportunity costs** capture the value of the best forgone alternative use of the resources employed. The bistro entrepreneur, for example, faces two types of opportunity costs: (1) forgone wages she could be earning if she was employed elsewhere and (2) the cost of capital she invested in her bistro, which could instead be invested in, say, the stock market or U.S Treasury bonds. At the end of the year, the bistro entrepreneur considers her business over the last 12 months. She made an *accounting profit* of $60,000, calculated as total revenues minus expenses (which include all historical costs but not opportunity costs). But she also realizes she has forgone $40,000 in salary she could have earned at another firm. In addition, she knows she could have earned $25,000 in interest if she had bought U.S. Treasury bills with a 5 percent return instead of investing $500,000 in her business. The opportunity cost of operating the bistro was $65,000 ($40,000 + $25,000). Therefore, when considering all

EXHIBIT 5.2

Competitive Advantage and Economic Value Created: Looking at Different Components

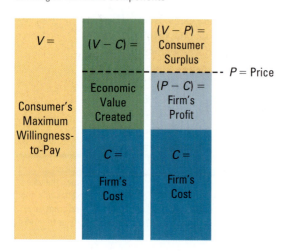

costs, including opportunity costs, she actually experienced an economic loss of $5,000 ($60,000 − $65,000). She should stay in business only if she values her independence more than $5,000 or thinks business will be better next year.

Understanding economic value creation gives us a good start toward measuring competitive advantage, but we must remember the following:

- *Determining the value of a good in the eyes of consumers is not a simple task.* One way to tackle this problem is to look at consumers' purchasing habits for their revealed preferences, which indicate how much each consumer is willing to pay for a product or service. In our pizza example, the value (V) you placed on the pizza—the highest price you were willing to pay, or your reservation price—was $12. If the entrepreneur is able to charge the reservation price ($P = \$12$), she captures all the economic value created ($V − C = \$5$) as producer surplus or profit ($P − C = \$5$).

- *The value of a good in the eyes of consumers changes based on income, preferences, time, and other factors.* If your income is high, you are likely to place a higher value on some goods (e.g., business-class air travel) and a lower value on other goods (e.g., Greyhound bus travel). In regard to preferences, you may place a higher value on a ticket for the final game of the NCAA basketball tournament if your school is playing in it than if it is not. As an example of time value, you place a higher value on an airline ticket that will get you to a business meeting tomorrow than on one for a planned trip to take place eight weeks from now. Airlines know this too, so they tend to charge you a higher price when you book your ticket closer to the departure date. (This pricing strategy again reverses a few short hours before departure if seats are still available: Remaining seats are then often sold at a discount as "stand-by" tickets, to obtain incremental revenues. However, given airlines' use of sophisticated yield-management algorithms in recent years, fewer last-minute stand-by tickets are now offered.)

- *To measure firm-level competitive advantage, we must estimate the economic value created for all products and services offered by the firm.* This estimation may be a relatively easy task if the firm offers only a few products or services. However, it becomes much more complicated for diversified firms like General Electric, Unilever, or the Tata Group (an Indian conglomerate) that may offer hundreds or even thousands of different products and services across many different industries and geographies. While the performance of individual strategic business units (SBUs) can be assessed along the dimensions described here, it becomes more difficult to make this assessment at the corporate level. Yet, assessing corporate-level performance is critical in order to justify the existence of diversified conglomerates (more on this in our discussion on diversification strategy in Chapter 8).

The economic perspective—in particular, the concept of economic value created—gives us one useful way to measure competitive advantage. This approach is conceptually quite powerful, and it lies at the center of many strategic management frameworks (such as the generic business strategies we discuss in the next chapter). However, it falls short when managers are called upon to operationalize competitive advantage. When the need for "hard numbers" arises, managers and analysts frequently rely on accounting data to assess firm performance. We now turn to *accounting profitability,* as a second traditional way to measure competitive advantage.

Accounting Profitability

When assessing competitive advantage by measuring accounting profitability, we use standard metrics derived from publicly available accounting data such as income statements

>> **LO 5-2**
Describe and evaluate accounting profitability when measuring competitive advantage.

and balance sheets.[3] Public companies are required by law to release these data, which must comply with the generally accepted accounting principles (GAAP) set by the Financial Accounting Standards Board (FASB) and be audited by certified public accountants.[4] Publicly traded firms are required to file the Form 10-K (or 10-K report) annually with the U.S. Security and Exchange Commission (SEC), a federal regulatory agency.[5] The 10-K reports are the primary source of companies' accounting data. As a result of the Enron scandal, which also led to the collapse of Enron's accounting firm Arthur Andersen, accounting data released to the public in the United States must now comply with more stringent legislation (the Sarbanes-Oxley Act of 2002), which in turn enhances the data's usefulness.

Though not perfect, accounting data enable us to conduct direct performance comparisons between different companies. Some of the profitability metrics most commonly used in strategic management are *return on assets* (*ROA*), *return on equity* (*ROE*), *return on invested capital* (*ROIC*), and *return on revenue* (*ROR*). In Table 1 in the "How to Conduct a Case Analysis" module at the end of the book, you will find a complete presentation of accounting measures (profitability, activity, leverage, liquidity, and market measures), how they are calculated, and their benefits and shortcomings. These will be useful for you when working through your strategy term project or analyzing different case studies and business situations. (You may want to bookmark the table.)

To visualize competitive advantage in accounting terms, let's take a look at the top 10 companies in the *Fortune 500* (based on December 31, 2010, accounting data). The *Fortune 500* is an annual list of the 500 largest U.S. companies by revenues. Exhibit 5.3 shows the top performers in terms of profits (net income). Given this metric, Exxon Mobil, with over $19.3 billion in profits, was the most successful company, followed by Microsoft ($14.6 bn), Walmart ($14.3 bn), and Procter & Gamble ($13.4 bn).

Although the performance of these companies is impressive in absolute terms, things look quite different when we compare their *relative* profitability in terms of return on revenue, which gives us a size-adjusted measure of profitability. Return on revenue (ROR) measures the profit earned per dollar of revenue, expressed in percentages. Exhibit 5.4 shows the top 10 performers in terms of return on revenue. Liberty Media, a multimedia conglomerate, shows by far the highest ROR, at 62.1 percent, followed by pharmaceutical companies, Bristol-Myers Squibb and Merck, with 49.1 percent and 47.0 percent RORs, respectively. Interestingly, when we compare the top 10 companies based on profits in Exhibit 5.3 and the top 10 based on ROR in Exhibit 5.4, only one company (Merck) appears in both rankings.

Although it is useful to see the top performers at any given point in time, we can improve the analysis further on two dimensions: First, since strategy is about gaining *and sustaining* competitive advantage, we need to go beyond a single year, which can at best provide a snapshot. Second, since we need to assess competitive advantage relative to a firm's competitors (or the industry average), we need to look at companies in the same industry. These added dimensions allow us to compare apples to apples.

EXHIBIT 5.3

Top 10 *Fortune 500* Companies by Profits (in $ million)

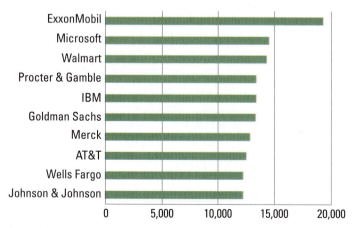

Source: Data from *Fortune,* http://money.cnn.com/magazines/fortune/fortune500/2010/, as of December 31, 2010.

Exhibit 5.5 shows the performance of four large pharmaceutical companies—Abbott, Johnson & Johnson (J&J), Merck—across the 2005–2009 time period based on return on assets (ROA). Over this five-year period, none of the firms was able to sustain a competitive advantage. Pfizer had the lead in 2005 through 2007 but was outperformed by J&J and Merck since 2007. Exhibit 5.5 clearly shows that is it difficult to gain competitive advantage, and even more difficult to sustain it. *Competitive advantage is transitory!*

Although accounting data tend to be readily available and we can easily transform them to assess competitive performance, they also exhibit some important limitations:

- *All accounting data are historical data and thus backward-looking.* Accounting profitability ratios show us only the outcomes from past decisions, and the past is no guarantee of future performance. Dell Computer, for example, clearly outperformed its competition based on accounting data in the first few years of the 21st century, but more recently it has been outperformed by Apple and Hewlett Packard. Also, as you probably already noticed in the earlier exhibits, there is a significant time delay until accounting data become publicly available. Some strategy scholars have even gone so far as to suggest that using accounting data to make strategic decisions is like driving a car by looking in the rearview mirror.[6]

- *Accounting data do not consider off–balance sheet items.* Off–balance sheet items, such as pension obligations (quite large in some U.S. industries) and operating leases in the retail industry, can be significant factors. For example, one retailer may own all its stores, which would properly be included in the firm's assets; a second retailer may lease all its stores, which would *not be* listed as assets. All else being equal, the second retailer's return on assets (ROA) would be higher. We address this shortcoming by adjusting accounting data to obtain an *equivalent* economic capital base, so that we can compare companies with different capital structures.

EXHIBIT 5.4

Top 10 *Fortune 500* Companies by Return on Revenue (ROR)

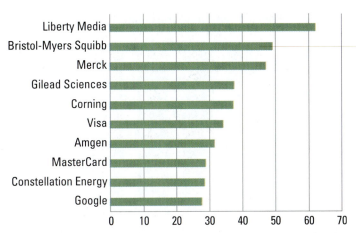

Source: Data from *Fortune,* http://money.cnn.com/magazines/fortune/fortune500/2010/, as of December 31, 2010.

EXHIBIT 5.5

Firm Performance in the Pharmaceutical Industry by Return on Revenue (ROR)

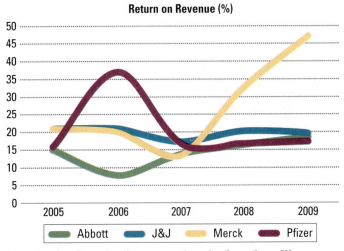

Source: Data from *Fortune,* http://money.cnn.com/magazines/fortune/fortune500.

EXHIBIT 5.6

The Declining Importance of Book Value in a Firm's Stock Market Valuation, 1980–2010

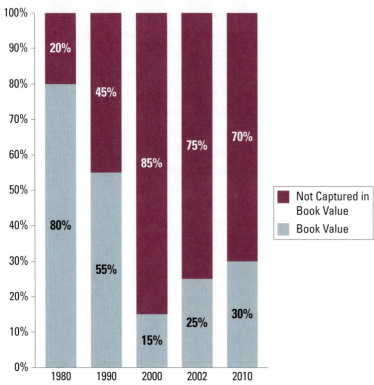

Book Valuation as Part of Total Market Valuation, S&P 500

Legend:
- Not Captured in Book Value
- Book Value

Source: Data from Compustat, 1980–2010.

■ *Accounting data focus mainly on tangible assets, which are no longer the most important.*[7] Although accounting data capture some intangible assets, such as the value of intellectual property (patents, trademarks, and so on) and customer goodwill, many key intangible assets are not captured. Competitively important assets in the 21st century tend to be intangibles such as innovation and quality, which are not included in a firm's balance sheets. For example, Hyundai's reputation for quality and Honda's core competency in designing highly reliable engines are not balance sheet items.

Indeed, intangibles that are not captured in accounting data such as a firm's reputation for quality and innovation or superior customer service have become much more important in firm stock market valuations over the last few decades. Look at Exhibit 5.6 which shows the firm's book value (accounting data that capture the firm's actual costs of assets minus depreciation) as part of a firm's total stock market valuation (number of outstanding shares times share price). The firm's book value captures the historical cost of a firm's assets, whereas market valuation is based on future expectations for a firm's growth potential and performance. For the firms in the S&P 500, the importance of a firm's book value has declined dramatically over time, while the importance of intangibles that contribute to growth potential and are not captured in a firm's accounting data has increased commensurately (see Exhibit 5.6). In 1980, about 80 percent of a firm's stock market valuation was based on its book value, and 20 percent was based on the market's expectations concerning the firm's future performance. This almost reversed by 2002 (in the aftermath of the Internet bubble), when firm valuations were based only 25 percent on assets captured by accounting data. The important take-away is that intangibles that are not captured in firms' accounting data have become much more important to a firm's competitive advantage (about 70 percent in 2010, for example).

Key financial ratios based on accounting data give us one more tool with which to assess competitive advantage. In particular, they help us measure *relative* profitability, which is useful when comparing firms of different size over time. While not perfect, they are an important starting point when analyzing the competitive performance of firms (and thus are a critical tool for case analysis).

We next turn to *shareholder value creation,* as a third traditional way to measure competitive advantage.

Shareholder Value Creation

Shareholders—individuals or organizations who own one or more shares of stock in a public company—are the legal owners of public companies. From the shareholders' perspective, the measure of competitive advantage that matters most is the return on their **risk capital,**[8] which is the money they provide in return for an equity share, money that they cannot recover if the firm goes bankrupt. In September 2008, the shareholders of Lehman Brothers, a global financial services firm, lost their entire investment of about $40 billion when the firm declared bankruptcy.

>> **LO 5-3**
Describe and evaluate shareholder value creation when measuring competitive advantage.

Investors are primarily interested in a company's **total return to shareholders,** which is the return on risk capital, including stock price appreciation plus dividends received over a specific period. Unlike accounting data, total return to shareholders is an *external* performance metric. It essentially indicates how the stock market views all available information about a firm's past, current state, and expected future performance (with most of the weight on future growth expectations). The idea that all available information about a firm's past, current state, and expected future performance is embedded in the market price of the firm's stock is called the *efficient-market hypothesis.*[9] In this perspective, a firm's share price provides an objective performance indicator.

All public companies in the United States are required to report total return to shareholders annually in the statements they file with the Securities and Exchange Commission (SEC). In addition, companies must also provide benchmarks, usually one comparison to the industry average and another to a broader market index (which is relevant for more diversified firms).[10] Since competitive advantage is defined in relative terms, these benchmarks allow us to assess whether a firm has a competitive advantage. In its annual reports, Microsoft, for example, compares its performance to two stock indices: the NASDAQ computer index and the S&P 500. The computer index includes over 400 high-tech companies traded on the NASDAQ, such as Apple, Dell, Intel, Oracle, and Google. It provides a comparison of Microsoft to the computer industry—broadly defined. The S&P 500 provides a comparison to the wider stock market beyond the computer industry. In its 2010 annual report, Microsoft shows that it *out*performed the S&P 500 over the last five years but *under*performed in comparison to the NASDAQ computer index.[11]

Effective strategies to grow the business can increase a firm's profitability and thus its stock price.[12] Indeed, investors and Wall Street analysts expect continuous growth. A firm's stock price generally increases only if the firm's rate of growth exceeds investors' expectations, because investors discount into the present value of the firm's stock price whatever growth rate they foresee in the future. If a low-growth business like Nucor (in steelmaking) is expected to grow 2 percent each year but realizes 5 percent growth, its stock price will appreciate. In contrast, if a fast-growing business like Dell in the early 2000s is expected to grow by 20 percent annually but delivers "only" 18 percent growth, its stock price will fall.

Investors also adjust their expectations over time. Since the business in the slow-growth industry surprised them by delivering higher than expected growth, they adjust their expectations upward. The next year, they expect this firm to again deliver 5 percent growth. On the other hand, if the industry average is 20 percent a year in the high-tech business, the firm that delivered 18 percent growth will again be expected to deliver at least the industry average growth rate; otherwise, its stock will be further discounted.

In Exhibit 5.5, we compared the performance of four leading pharmaceutical companies (Abbott, Johnson & Johnson, Merck, and Pfizer) based on ROA for the 2004–2009 time period. In Exhibit 5.7 (on next page), we compare the same companies over the same period using as a performance metric *normalized stock returns,* in which we compare the

risk capital Capital provided by shareholders in exchange for an equity share in a company; it cannot be recovered if the firm goes bankrupt.

total return to shareholders Return on risk capital that includes stock price appreciation plus dividends received over a specific period.

EXHIBIT 5.7

Normalized Stock
Returns for Abbott,
Johnson & Johnson
(J&J), Merck, and
Pfizer, 2005–2010
(2005 = base year)

Source: Companies' stock
price data.

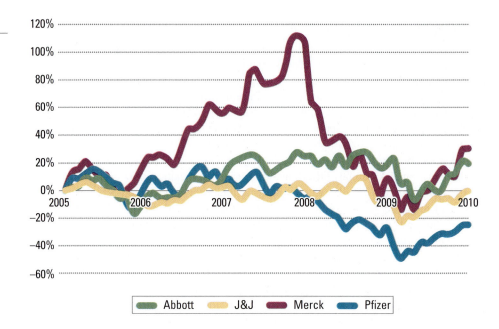

percentage change to a base year. The year 2005 is the base year, and we plot the percentage change in stock appreciation or depreciation over time. The percentages on the vertical axis are percentage changes relative to the 2005 stock price. In contrast to Exhibit 5.5, we now see that Merck had at least a temporary competitive advantage over the other three firms during 2006–2008. Pfizer, on the other hand, appeared to have experienced a competitive disadvantage since 2008, underperforming the other three companies.

Although measuring firm performance through total return to shareholders has many advantages, it is not without problems, as the 2008–2009 global financial crisis made abundantly clear:

- *Stock prices can be highly volatile, making it difficult to assess firm performance, at least in the short term.* This volatility implies that total return to shareholders is a better measure over the long term due to the "noise" introduced by market volatility, external factors, and investor sentiment.

- *Overall macroeconomic factors such as the unemployment rate, economic growth or contraction, and interest and exchange rates all have a direct bearing on stock prices.* Thus it can be difficult to ascertain the extent to which a stock price is influenced more by external macroeconomic factors (as discussed in Chapter 3) or the firm's strategy.

- *Stock prices frequently reflect the psychological mood of investors, which can at times be irrational.* Stock prices can overshoot expectations based on economic fundamentals amidst periods like the Internet boom, during which former Federal Reserve Chairman Alan Greenspan described investors' buoyant sentiments as "irrational exuberance."[13] Similarly, stock prices can undershoot expectations during busts like the 2008–2009 worldwide financial crisis, during which investors' sentiment was described as "irrational gloom."[14]

Assessing Competitive Advantage: Google vs. Microsoft, Continued

Using what we've so far learned about measuring competitive advantage, let's continue to look at Google vs. Microsoft, which are becoming more direct competitors (as discussed in ChapterCase 1). Which of the two has competitive advantage? Since we can find good financial data for this purpose, let's focus on assessing the competitive advantage of each in terms of accounting profitability and shareholder value creation.

Since Microsoft is many times larger than Google and thus records a higher net income ($20.6 bn vs. $7.9 bn in 2010) it has a higher ROA and ROE, as shown in Exhibit 5.8. Note, though, that high-tech companies like Google and Microsoft have relatively few tangible assets. This in turn limits the usefulness of accounting profitability when assessing competitive advantage. Key to their performance are intangible assets such as Google's ability to invent proprietary search and data-management algorithms and Microsoft's ability to develop proprietary software code for its Windows operating system. When we compare these two companies on ROA and ROE (as shown in Exhibit 5.8), we can see that Microsoft outperformed Google in 2010. This finding, however, demonstrates the importance of intangible over tangible assets. Both firms rely on intangibles that are not captured in a firm's accounting data for performance.

In ChapterCase 5, we made the argument that Google had at least a temporary competitive advantage over Microsoft, based on the three size-adjusted performance metrics shown in Exhibit 5.1 (revenue per employee; net income per employee; and market cap per employee). Exhibit 5.9 (next page) validates this assessment. It shows the normalized stock price performance of Google, Microsoft, and the NASDAQ-100 index over the 2005–2010 time period. The NASDAQ-100 is an index of the 100 largest nonfinancial companies listed on this U.S. stock exchange. In addition to Google and Microsoft, it includes many other high-tech companies, such as Adobe, Amazon, Apple, Cisco, Dell, Intel, Logitech, and Yahoo. Google outperformed both Microsoft and the NASDAQ-100 by a wide margin, reaching over 250 percent stock price appreciation in 2008 and over 200 percent in 2010 (compared with its 2005 stock price).

Google and Microsoft are direct competitors on only some dimensions, although their competitive overlap in various market segments seems to be increasing. Google is a software company focusing on the information industry; the vast majority of its revenues (approximately 97 percent) stem from online advertising. Microsoft dominates the personal computer world with its Windows operating system and Office application software suite. Google outperformed by a wide margin the NASDAQ-100 (represented by the purple line at the bottom of Exhibit 5.9); Microsoft's stock performance seems to correlate with the NASDAQ-100. When applying shareholder value creation as a yardstick, our conclusion

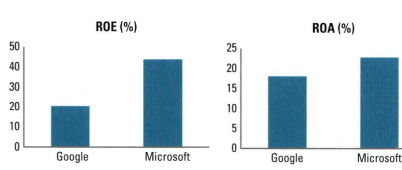

EXHIBIT 5.8

Comparing Google and Microsoft Using Return on Equity (ROE) and Return on Assets (ROA)

Source: Data obtained from companies' SEC filings, as of December 31, 2010.

EXHIBIT 5.9

Normalized Stock Returns for Google, Microsoft, and NASDAQ-100, 2005–2010 (2005 = Base Year)

Source: Companies' stock price data. MSN money, http://moneycentral.msn.com

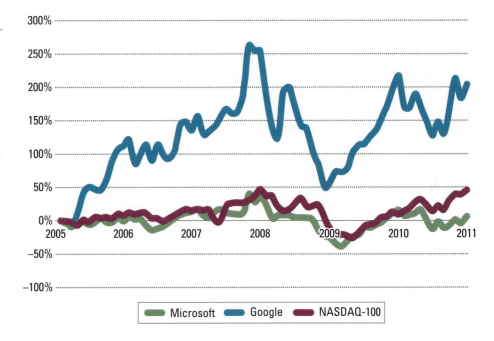

is thus that Google is experiencing a (sustained) competitive advantage, while Microsoft is experiencing a (sustained) competitive disadvantage compared with Google, and competitive parity when compared with the industry average.

You may have noticed that the information/software industry depicted in Exhibit 5.9 appears to be more volatile and to perform at a higher level than the pharmaceutical industry depicted in Exhibit 5.7. At their respective performance peaks, Google reached over 250 percent stock appreciation, while Merck accomplished over 100 percent. As we discussed in Chapters 3 and 4, there are pronounced differences in firm performance not only within the same industry, but also across different industries.

We've now completed our consideration of the three standard dimensions for measuring competitive advantage—economic value, accounting profitability, and shareholder value. Although each provides unique insights for our assessment of a firm's performance, one drawback is that they are more or less one-dimensional metrics. Focusing on just one performance metric when assessing competitive advantage, however, can lead to significant problems, because each metric has its shortcomings, as listed earlier. We now turn to two conceptual frameworks—the balanced scorecard and the triple bottom line—that attempt to provide a more holistic perspective on firm performance.

THE BALANCED SCORECARD

>> LO 5-4
Describe and evaluate the balanced-scorecard approach for assessing competitive advantage.

Just as airplane pilots rely on a number of instruments to provide constant information about key variables such as altitude, airspeed, fuel, position of other airplanes in the vicinity, and destination in order to ensure a safe flight, so should managers rely on multiple yardsticks to more accurately assess company performance in an integrative way. Kaplan and Norton proposed a framework to help managers achieve their strategic objectives more effectively.[15] Called the balanced scorecard, this approach harnesses multiple internal and external performance metrics in order to balance both financial and strategic goals.

Exhibit 5.10 depicts the balanced-scorecard framework. Managers using the balanced scorecard develop strategic objectives and appropriate metrics by answering four key questions that Kaplan and Norton, during a yearlong research project with a number of different companies, identified as the most salient.[16] Brainstorming answers to these questions (ideally) results in a set of measures that give managers a quick but also comprehensive view of the firm's current state. The four key questions are:

EXHIBIT 5.10

A Balanced-Scorecard Approach to Creating and Sustaining Competitive Advantage

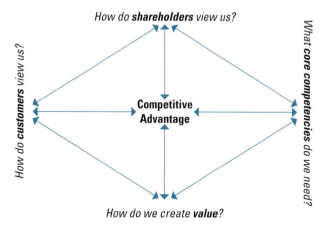

1. *How do customers view us?* The customer's perspective concerning the company's products and services is linked directly to its revenues and profits. The perceived value of a product determines how much the customer is willing to pay for it. The question, "How do customers view us?" is therefore directly linked to how much economic value a firm can create. If the customer views the company favorably, she is willing to pay more for a certain product or service, enhancing its competitive advantage (assuming production costs are well below the asking price).

    To learn how customers view a company's products or services, managers collect data to identify areas to improve, with a focus on speed, quality, service, and cost. In the air-express industry, for example, managers learned from their customers that many don't really need next-day delivery for most of their documents and packages; rather what they really cared about was the ability to track the shipments. This discovery led to the development of steeply discounted 2nd-day delivery by UPS and FedEx, combined with sophisticated online tracking tools.

2. *How do we create value?* Answering this question challenges managers to come up with strategic objectives that ensure future competitiveness, innovation, and organizational learning. It focuses on the business processes and structures that allow a firm to create economic value. One useful metric, for example, is the percentage of revenues obtained from new-product introductions. 3M, for example, requires that 30 percent of revenues must come from products introduced within the last four years.[17] A second metric, aimed at assessing a firm's external learning and collaboration capability, is to stipulate that a certain percentage of new products must originate from outside the firm's boundaries.[18] Through its Connect and Develop program, the consumer products giant Procter & Gamble has raised the percentage of new products that originated (at least partly) from outside P&G, from 15 to 35 percent.[19]

3. *What core competencies do we need?* This question focuses managers internally, to identify the core competencies needed to achieve their objectives, and the accompanying business processes that support, hone, and leverage those competencies. Robert Clarke, former president of performance development at Honda, argues that Honda is at its heart an engine company (not a car company).[20] Beginning with motorcycles in 1948, Honda nurtured this core competency over many decades, and today is leveraging it to reach stretch goals in the design, development, and manufacture of small airplanes.

4. *How do shareholders view us?* The final perspective in the balanced scorecard is the shareholders' view of financial performance. Some of the measures in this area rely on

balanced scorecard
Strategy implementation tool that harnesses multiple internal and external performance metrics in order to balance financial and strategic goals.

accounting data such as cash flow, operating income, ROE, and, of course, total returns to shareholders. Understanding the shareholders' view of value creation leads managers to a more future-oriented evaluation.

Taken together, the four balanced-scorecard questions are directly linked to economic value creation: They help managers increase the perceived value of their goods and services in the marketplace. By relying on both an internal and an external view of the firm, the balanced scorecard combines the strengths provided by the individual approaches to assessing competitive advantage discussed earlier: economic value creation, accounting profitability, and shareholder value creation.

Advantages of the Balanced Scorecard

The balanced-scorecard approach is popular in managerial practice because it has several advantages. In particular, the balanced scorecard allows managers to:

- Communicate and link the strategic vision to responsible parties within the organization.
- Translate the vision into measureable operational goals.
- Design and plan business processes.
- Implement feedback and organizational learning in order to modify and adapt strategic goals when indicated.

The balanced scorecard can accommodate both short- and long-term performance metrics. It provides a concise report that tracks chosen metrics and measures and compares them to target values. This approach allows managers to assess past performance, identify areas for improvement, and position the company for future growth. Including a broader perspective than financials allows managers and executives a more balanced view of organizational performance—hence its name. In a sense, the balanced scorecard is a broad diagnostic tool. It complements the common financial metrics with operational measures on customer satisfaction, internal processes, and the company's innovation and improvement activities.

Let's look at FMC Corporation, a chemical manufacturer employing some 5,000 people in different SBUs and earning over $3 billion in annual revenues, as an example of how to implement the balanced-scorecard approach.[21] To achieve its mission of becoming "the customer's most valued supplier," FMC's managers initially had focused solely on financial metrics such as return on capital employed (ROCE) as performance measures. FMC is a multibusiness corporation with several standalone profit-and-loss strategic business units; its overall performance was the result of both over- and underperforming units. FMC's managers had tried several approaches to enhance performance, but they turned out to be more or less ineffective. Perhaps even more significant, short-term thinking by general managers was a major obstacle in the attempt to implement a business strategy.

Searching for improved performance, FMC's CEO decided to adopt a balanced-scorecard approach. It enabled the managers to view FMC's challenges and shortcomings from a holistic, company perspective, which was especially helpful to the general managers of different business units. In particular, the balanced scorecard allowed general managers to focus on market position, customer service, and new-product introductions that could generate long-term value. Using the framework depicted in Exhibit 5.10, general managers had to answer tough follow-up questions such as: How do we become the customer's most valued supplier, and how can my division create this value for the customer? How do we become more externally focused? What are my division's core competencies and contributions to the company goals? What are my division's weaknesses?

Implementing a balanced scorecard allowed FMC's managers to align their different perspective to create a more focused corporation overall. General managers now review progress along the chosen metrics every month, and corporate executives do so on a quarterly basis. Although successful for FMC, implementing a balanced-scorecard approach is not a one-time effort, but requires continuous tracking of metrics and updating of strategic objectives, if needed. It is a continuous process, feeding performance back into the strategy process to assess its effectiveness (see Chapter 2).

Disadvantages of the Balanced Scorecard

Though successfully implemented by many businesses, the balanced scorecard is not without its critics.[22] It is important to note that the balanced scorecard is a tool for *strategy implementation,* and not for *strategy formulation.* It is up to a firm's managers to formulate a strategy that will enhance the chances of gaining and sustaining a competitive advantage. In addition, the balanced-scorecard approach provides only limited guidance about which metrics to choose. Different situations call for different metrics. All of the three approaches to measuring competitive advantage—economic value creation, accounting profitability, and shareholder value creation—in addition to other quantitative and qualitative measures, can be helpful when using a balanced-scorecard approach.

Once the metrics have been selected, the balanced scorecard tracks chosen metrics and measures and compares them to target values. It does not, however, provide much insight into how metrics that deviate from the set goals can be put back on track. Some argue that the balanced scorecard is sometimes seen as not much more than a set of metrics that are tracked over extended periods of time, thus not really providing any new approach.[23]

When implementing a balanced scorecard, managers need to be aware that a failure to achieve competitive advantage is not so much a reflection of a poor framework but of a strategic failure. The balanced scorecard is only as good as the skills of the managers who use it: They first must devise a strategy that enhances the odds of achieving competitive advantage. Second, they must accurately translate the strategy into objectives that they can measure and manage within the balanced-scorecard approach.[24]

THE TRIPLE BOTTOM LINE

In the 21st century, managers are frequently asked to maintain and improve not only the firm's economic performance but also its social and ecological performance. Non-economic factors can have a significant impact on a firm's financial performance, not to mention reputation and goodwill. BP's infamous oil spill in the Gulf of Mexico put the company on the brink of collapse and threatened to destroy fauna and flora along the U.S. shoreline from Texas to Florida, as well as the livelihood of hundreds of thousands of people in the tourism and fishing industries. BP's estimated damages could be as high as $40 billion; the loss of reputation and goodwill is likely to be much higher.[25] Ironically, with an extended moratorium on deepwater drilling and more stringent regulation, the oil industry—especially smaller companies—were also threatened in their survival.

In contrast, being proactive along non-economic dimensions can make good business sense. In anticipation of industry regulation in terms of "extended producer responsibility," which requires the seller of a product to take it back for recycling at the end of the its life, the German carmaker BMW was proactive. It not only lined up the leading car-recycling

>> **LO 5-5**
Describe and evaluate the triple-bottom-line approach when assessing competitive advantage.

EXHIBIT 5.11

The Triple Bottom Line

The simultaneous pursuit of performance along social, economic, and ecological dimensions provides a basis for a sustainable strategy.

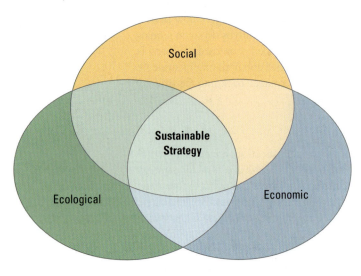

triple bottom line
Combination of economic, social, and ecological concerns that can lead to a sustainable strategy.

companies but also started to redesign its cars using a modular approach. The modular parts allow for quick car disassembly and reuse of components in the after-sales market (so-called "refurbished or rebuilt auto parts").

Three dimensions—*economic, social, and ecological*—make up the **triple bottom line.** As Exhibit 5.11 suggests, achieving results in all three areas can lead to a sustainable strategy. Like the balanced scorecard, the triple bottom line takes a more integrative and holistic view in assessing a company's performance.[26] Using a triple-bottom-line approach, managers audit their company's fulfillment of its social and ecological obligations to stakeholders such as employees, customers, suppliers, and communities in as serious a way as they track its financial performance.[27] In this sense, the triple-bottom-line framework is related to *stakeholder theory,* an approach to understanding a firm as embedded in a network of internal and external constituencies that each make contributions and expect consideration in return (see discussion in Chapters 1 and 12). For an example of how Interface uses a triple-bottom-line approach to gain and sustain a competitive advantage, read Strategy Highlight 5.1.

Interface: The World's First Sustainable Company

Interface, Inc., is a leader in modular carpeting, with annual sales of roughly $1 billion. What makes the company unique is its strategic intent to become the world's first *fully sustainable* company. In 1994, founder Ray Anderson set a goal for the company to be "off oil" entirely by 2020. That included not using any petroleum-based raw materials or oil-related energy to fuel the manufacturing plants.

According to Collins and Porras in *Built to Last,* their classic study of high-performing companies over long periods of time, this is a "BHAG"—a *big hairy audacious goal.* BHAGs are bold missions declared by visionary companies and are a "powerful mechanism to stimulate progress."[28] Weaning Interface off oil by 2020 is indeed a BHAG. Many see the carpet industry as an extension of the petrochemical industry, given its heavy reliance on

fossil fuels and chemicals in the manufacturing, shipping, and installation of its products.

Today, Interface is a leader in both modular carpet and sustainability. The company estimates that between 1996 and 2008, it saved over $400 million due to its energy efficiency and use of recycled materials. Its business model is changing the carpet industry. Speaking of sustainability as a business model, Mr. Anderson stated in 2009:

> Sustainability has given my company a competitive edge in more ways than one. It has proven to be the most powerful marketplace differentiator I have known in my long career. Our costs are down, our profits are up, and our products are the best they have ever been. Sustainable design has provided an unexpected wellspring of innovation, people are galvanized around a shared higher purpose, better people are applying, the best people are staying and working with a purpose, the goodwill in the marketplace generated by our focus on sustainability far exceeds that which any amount of advertising or marketing expenditure could have generated—this company believes it has found a better way to a bigger and more legitimate profit—a better business model.[29]

IMPLICATIONS FOR THE STRATEGIST

In this chapter, we discussed how to measure competitive advantage using three traditional approaches: economic value creation, accounting profitability, and shareholder value. We then introduced two conceptual frameworks to help us understand competitive advantage in a more holistic fashion: the balanced scorecard and the triple bottom line. Exhibit 5.12 summarizes the concepts we've discussed about how to measure competitive advantage.

>> **LO 5-6**
Compare and contrast different approaches to measuring competitive advantage, and derive managerial implications.

Several managerial implications emerge from our discussion of competitive advantage and firm performance:

- Both *quantitative and qualitative* performance dimensions matter in judging how effective a firm's strategy is. Those who focus on just one metric risk being blindsided by poor performance on another. Rather, managers need to rely on a more holistic perspective when assessing firm performance, measuring different dimensions over different time periods.

- Since the goal of strategic management is to integrate and align each business function and activity to obtain superior performance at the company level, competitive advantage is best measured by criteria that reflect *overall company performance* rather than the performance of specific parts. While the functional managers in the marketing department may (and should) care greatly about the success or failure of their recent ad campaign, what the *general* manager cares most about is not specifics at the functional level but performance implications at the firm level. Thus, metrics that aggregate upward and reflect overall firm performance are most useful to assess the effectiveness of a firm's strategy.

- Since no *best* strategy exists—only *better* ones (better in comparison with others)—we must interpret any performance metric relative to those of competitors and the industry average. True performance can be judged only in comparison to other contenders in the field, not on an absolute basis.

This concludes our discussion of competitive advantage and firm performance and of Part 1 on strategy analysis. In Part 2 of the book, we turn our attention to the topic of strategy formulation. There, in Chapters 6 and 7, we focus on business strategy (*"how to compete"*), and in Chapters 8 and 9 we study corporate strategy (*"where to compete"*). Chapter 10, which concludes Part 2, looks at global strategy (*"where and how to compete around the world"*).

EXHIBIT 5.12

How Do We Measure Competitive Advantage?

Competitive advantage is reflected in superior firm performance.

- ›› We always assess competitive advantage relative to a benchmark, either using competitors or the industry average.

- ›› When maintained over time, competitive advantage is *sustainable*.

- ›› Competitive advantage is a multifaceted concept.

- ›› We can assess competitive advantage by measuring economic value, accounting profit, or shareholder value.

- ›› The balanced-scorecard approach harnesses multiple internal and external performance dimensions to balance a firm's financial and strategic goals.

- ›› More recently, competitive advantage has been linked to a firm's triple bottom line, the ability to maintain performance in the economic, social, and ecological contexts.

CHAPTERCASE 5 | *Consider This . . .*

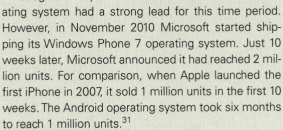

IT WOULD SEEM that Google and Microsoft will be competing in a variety of areas for many years to come. Though they have approached the market from different directions, they are now key competitors in areas such as Internet search, computer applications, and computer operating systems. One particularly interesting area of competition may be in the mobile device operating system. Smartphone shipments, by operating system, for the third quarter of 2010 are shown in the nearby table.[30]

Google's operating system had a strong lead for this time period. However, in November 2010 Microsoft started shipping its Windows Phone 7 operating system. Just 10 weeks later, Microsoft announced it had reached 2 million units. For comparison, when Apple launched the first iPhone in 2007, it sold 1 million units in the first 10 weeks. The Android operating system took six months to reach 1 million units.[31]

U.S. Smartphone Market Shipments by Operating System		
3rd Quarter 2010, Units in millions		
OS Vendor	**Units**	**% share**
Android (Google open system)	9.1	43.6
Apple (iPhone)	5.5	26.2
RIM (BlackBerry)	5.1	24.2
Microsoft	0.6	3.0
Others	0.6	3.0
Total	20.9	100.0

Source: Canalys estimates, Canalys 2010.

1. The chapter discusses three perspectives of competitive advantage. If Microsoft is successful in claiming a significant share of the burgeoning smartphone market, will the economic, accounting, or shareholder perspective be affected first? Which firm's performance would be the most affected by this type of market shift?

2. What *qualitative* elements are important for these firms? How would you rate Google and Microsoft on these aspects?

Take-Away Concepts

This chapter demonstrated three traditional approaches for measuring firm performance and competitive advantage and two conceptual frameworks designed to provide a more holistic perspective on firm performance.

LO 5-1 Describe and evaluate economic value creation when measuring competitive advantage.

>> Three components are critical to evaluating any good or service: value (V), price (P), and cost (C). In economics, cost includes opportunity cost.

>> Economic value created is the difference between a buyer's willingness to pay for a good or service and the firm's cost to produce it ($V - C$).

>> A firm has a competitive advantage when it is able to create more economic value than its rivals.

>> To measure firm-level competitive advantage, we estimate the economic value created for all products and services offered by the firm.

LO 5-2 Describe and evaluate accounting profitability when measuring competitive advantage.

>> To measure accounting profitability, we use standard metrics derived from publicly available accounting data.

>> Commonly used profitability metrics in strategic management are return on assets (ROA), return on equity (ROE), return on invested capital (ROIC), and return on revenue (ROR).

>> All accounting data are historical and thus backward-looking. They do not consider off–balance sheet items such as an innovation competency. They focus mainly on tangible assets, which are no longer the most important.

LO 5-3 Describe and evaluate shareholder value creation when measuring competitive advantage.

>> The measure of competitive advantage that matters from the shareholders' perspective is the return on (risk) capital.

>> Investors are primarily interested in total return to shareholders, which includes stock price appreciation plus dividends received over a specific period.

>> Total return to shareholders is an external performance metric; it indicates how the market views all available information about a firm's past, current state, and expected future performance.

>> Stock prices can be highly volatile, which makes it difficult to assess firm performance. Overall macroeconomic factors have a direct bearing on stock prices. Also, stock prices frequently reflect the psychological mood of the investors, which can at times be irrational.

LO 5-4 Describe and evaluate the balanced-scorecard approach for assessing competitive advantage.

>> The balanced-scorecard approach provides a more integrative view of competitive advantage.

>> Its goal is to harness multiple internal and external performance dimensions to balance financial and strategic goals.

>> Managers develop strategic objectives for the balanced scorecard by answering four key questions:

1. How do customers view us?
2. How do we create value?
3. What core competencies do we need?
4. How do shareholders view us?

LO 5-5 Describe and evaluate the triple-bottom-line framework when assessing competitive advantage.

>> Sustainable strategy refers to a firm's ability to maintain its performance in the economic, social, and ecological context—called the triple bottom line.

LO 5-6 Compare and contrast different approaches to measuring competitive advantage, and derive managerial implications.

>> Both quantitative and qualitative criteria matter when assessing the effectiveness of a firm's strategy.

>> Competitive advantage is best measured by criteria that reflect performance of the company overall; the goal of strategic management is to integrate and align each functional-level activity to obtain superior performance at the company level.

>> Any performance metric must be interpreted relative to competitors and the industry average.

Key Terms

Balanced scorecard *(p. 124)*

Consumer surplus *(p. 115)*

Economic value created *(p. 115)*

Opportunity costs *(p. 116)*

Profit (or producer surplus) *(p. 115)*

Risk capital *(p. 121)*

Total return to shareholders *(p. 121)*

Triple bottom line *(p. 128)*

Value *(p. 115)*

Discussion Questions

1. Domino's Pizza was 50 years old in 2010. Visit the company's business-related website (www.dominos-biz.com) and read the company profile under the "Investors" tab. Does the firm focus on the economic, accounting, or shareholder perspective in describing its competitive advantage in the profile?

2. Shareholder perspective is perhaps the most widely employed measure of competitive advantage for publicly traded firms. What are some of the

disadvantages of using shareholder value as the sole point of view for defining competitive advantage?

3. Interface, Inc., is discussed in Strategy Highlight 5.1. It may seem unusual for a business-to-business (B2B) carpet company to be using a triple-bottom-line approach for its strategy. What other industries do you think could productively use this approach? How would it change customers' perceptions if it did?

Ethical/Social Issues

1. You work as a supervisor in a manufacturing firm. The company has implemented a balanced-scorecard performance-appraisal system and a financial bonus for exceeding goals. A major customer order for 1,000 units needs to ship to a destination across the country by the end of the quarter, which is two days away from its close. This shipment, if it goes well, will have a major impact on both your customer-satisfaction goals and your financial goals.

   With 990 units built, a machine breaks down. It will take two days to get the parts and repair the machine. You realize there is an opportunity to load the finished units on a truck tomorrow with paperwork for the completed order of 1,000 units. You can have an employee fly out with the 10 remaining parts and meet the truck at the destination city once the machinery has been

repaired. The 10 units can be added to the pallet and delivered as a complete shipment of 1,000 pieces, matching the customer's order and your paperwork. What do you do?

2. The chapter mentions that accounting data do not consider off–balance sheet items. A retailer that owns its stores will list the value of that property as an asset, for example, while a firm that leases its stores will not. What are some of the accounting and shareholder advantages of leasing compared to owning retail locations?

3. How does this issue play out when comparing brick-and-mortar stores to online businesses (e.g., Best Buy versus Amazon; Barnes & Noble versus Amazon; Blockerbuster versus Netflix)? What conclusions do you draw?

Small Group Exercises

SMALL GROUP EXERCISE 1

As discussed in the chapter, a balanced scorecard views the performance of an organization through four lenses: customer, innovation and learning, internal business, and financial. According to surveys from Bain & Company (a consulting firm), in recent years about 60 percent of firms in both public and private sectors have used a balanced scorecard for performance measures. (See www.thepalladiumgroup.com for examples.)

With your group, create a balanced scorecard for the business school at your university. You might start by looking at your school's web page for a mission or vision statement. Then divide up the four perspectives among the team members to develop some key elements for each one. It may be helpful to remember the four key balanced-scorecard questions from the chapter:

1. How do customers view us? (Hint: First discuss the following: Who are the customers? The students? The companies that hire students? Others?)

2. How do we create value?

3. What core competencies do we need?

4. How do shareholders view us? (For public universities, the shareholders are the taxpayers who invest their taxes into the university. For private universities, the shareholders are the people or organizations that endow the university.)

SMALL GROUP EXERCISE 2

In the electronics retail industry, Circuit City filed for bankruptcy in the spring of 2009, but Best Buy continues on. (See ChapterCase 4, page 85) Financial data for Best Buy and Circuit City are provided in the table on the next page.

Using the financial ratios presented in Table 1 in the "How to Conduct a Case Analysis" module (at the end of the book, p. 390):

1. Calculate some of the key profitability, activity, leverage, liquidity, and market ratios for Best Buy and Circuit City.

2. Can you find signs of performance differentials between these two firms that may have indicated problems at Circuit City in 2007?

Key Financial Data for Best Buy and Circuit City

In Millions of US$ (except for per share items)	Best Buy Y/E Mar. 2008	Best Buy Y/E Mar. 2007	Circuit City Y/E Mar. 2008	Circuit City Y/E Mar. 2007
Total revenue	40,023.00	35,934.00	11,743.69	12,429.75
Cost of revenue, total	30,477.00	27,165.00	9,318.17	9,501.44
Gross profit	9,546.00	8,769.00	2,425.52	2,928.32
Selling/general/admin. expenses, total	7,385.00	6,770.00	2,770.10	2,841.62
Total operating expense	37,862.00	33,935.00	12,097.27	12,409.43
Operating income	2,161.00	1,999.00	−353.58	20.33
Income before tax	2,228.00	2,130.00	−353.58	20.33
Income after tax	1,413.00	1,378.00	−321.35	−10.18
Net income	1,407.00	1,377.00	−319.9	−8.28
Diluted weighted average shares	452.9	496.2	165.13	170.45
Dividends per share – common stock	0.46	0.36	0.16	0.12
Diluted normalized EPS	3.12	2.79	−1.69	0.83
Cash and equivalents	1,438.00	1,205.00	296.06	141.14
Short-term investments	64	2,588.00	1.37	598.34
Cash and short-term investments	1,502.00	3,793.00	297.42	739.48
Accounts receivable – trade, net	549	548	330.6	382.56
Total receivables, net	549	548	488.71	425.28
Total inventory	4,708.00	4,028.00	1,573.56	1,636.51
Total current assets	7,342.00	9,081.00	2,439.72	2,883.51
Property/plant/equipment, total – gross	5,608.00	4,904.00	2,485.60	2,221.33
Accumulated depreciation, total	−2,302.00	−1,966.00	−1,448.28	−1,300.30
Goodwill, net	1,088.00	919	118.03	121.77
Intangibles, net	102	81	18.4	19.29
Long-term investments	605	318	–	–
Other long-term assets, total	315	233	132.46	61.69
Total assets	12,758.00	13,570.00	3,745.93	4,007.28
Accounts payable	4,297.00	3,934.00	912.09	922.21
Accrued expenses	1,348.00	1,322.00	317.51	380.22
Other current liabilities, total	935	985	364.5	404.44
Total current liabilities	6,769.00	6,301.00	1,605.69	1,714.03
Total long-term debt	627	590	57.05	50.49
Total debt	816	650	68.63	57.65
Other liabilities, total	838	443	544.43	451.52
Total liabilities	8,274.00	7,369.00	2,242.76	2,216.04
Common stock, total	41	48	84.43	85.34
Additional paid-in capital	8	430	319.57	344.14
Retained earnings (accumulated deficit)	3,933.00	5,507.00	981.11	1,336.32
Total equity	4,484.00	6,201.00	1,503.17	1,791.24
Total liabilities and shareholders' equity	12,758.00	13,570.00	3,745.93	4,007.28
Total common shares outstanding	410.58	480.65	168.86	170.69

Strategy Term Project

MODULE 5: COMPETITIVE ADVANTAGE PERSPECTIVES

1. Based on information in the annual reports or published on the firm's website, summarize what the firm views as the reasons for its successes (either past or expected in the future). Search for both quantitative and qualitative success factors provided in the report.

2. Does the firm seem most focused on the economic, accounting, or shareholder perspective of its competitive advantage? Give quotes or information from these sources to support your view.

3. Many firms are now including annual corporate social responsibility (CSR) reports on their websites. See whether your firm does so. If it does not, are there other indications of a triple-bottom-line approach, including social and ecological elements, in the firm's strategies?

*my*Strategy

HOW MUCH IS AN MBA WORTH TO YOU?

The *my*Strategy box at the end of Chapter 2 asked how much you would be willing to pay for the job you want—for a job that reflects your values. Here, we look at a different issue relating to worth: How much is an MBA worth over the course of your career?

Alongside the traditional two-year full-time MBA program, many business schools also offer evening MBAs and executive MBAs. Let's assume you know you want to pursue an advanced degree, and you need to decide which program format is better for you (or you want to evaluate the choice you already made). You've narrowed your options to either (1) a two-year full-time MBA program, or (2) an executive MBA program at the same institution that is 18 months long with classes every other weekend. Let's also assume the price for tuition, books, and fees is $30,000 for the full-time program and $90,000 for the executive MBA program.

Which MBA program should you choose? Consider in your analysis the value, price, and cost concepts discussed in this chapter. Pay special attention to opportunity costs attached to different MBA program options.

Endnotes

1. This debate takes place in the following discourses, among others: Schmalensee, R. (1985), "Do markets differ much?" *American Economic Review* 75: 341–351; Rumelt, R. P. (1991), "How much does industry matter?" *Strategic Management Journal* 12: 167–185; Rumelt, R. P. (2003), "What in the world is competitive advantage?" *Policy Working Paper 2003-105,* UCLA; Porter, M. E. (1985), *Competitive Advantage: Creating and Sustaining Superior Performance* (New York: Free Press); McGahan, A. M., and M. E. Porter (1997), "How much does industry matter, really?" *Strategic Management Journal* 18: 15–30; McGahan A. M., and M. E. Porter (2002), "What do we know about variance in accounting profitability?" *Management Science* 48: 834–851; Hawawini, G., V. Subramanian, and P. Verdin (2003), "Is performance driven by industry-or firm-specific factors? A new look at the evidence," *Strategic Management Journal* 24: 1–16; McNamara, G., F. Aime, and P. Vaaler (2005), "Is performance driven by industry- or firm-specific factors? A reply to Hawawini, Subramanian, and Verdin," *Strategic Management Journal* 26: 1075–1081; Hawawini, G., V. Subramanian, and P. Verdin (2005), "Is performance driven by industry-or firm-specific factors? A new look at the evidence: A response to McNamara, Aime, and Vaaler," *Strategic Management Journal* 26: 1083–1086; and Misangyi, V. F., H. Elms, T. Greckhamer, and J. A. Lepine (2006), "A new perspective on a fundamental debate: A multi-level approach to industry, corporate, and business unit effects," *Strategic Management Journal* 27: 571–590.

2. Rumelt, R. P. (2003), "What in the world is competitive advantage?"

3. For a discussion see: McGahan, A. M., and M. E. Porter (2002), "What do

we know about variance in accounting profitability?"

4. "The term 'generally accepted accounting principles' has a specific meaning for accountants and auditors. The AICPA Code of Professional Conduct prohibits members from expressing an opinion or stating affirmatively that financial statements or other financial data 'present fairly . . . in conformity with generally accepted accounting principles,' if such information contains any departures from accounting principles promulgated by a body designated by the AICPA Council to establish such principles." Source: www.fasb.gov.

5. All listed companies on U.S. stock exchanges must file periodic reports with the SEC, which in turn makes them publicly available at their website, http://www.sec.gov/edgar.shtml. These reports are a treasure trove for your strategy term project, case analyses, and other tasks.

6. Hamel, G., and C. K. Prahalad (1994), *Competing for the Future* (Boston, MA: Harvard Business School Press).

7. Baruch, L. (2001), *Intangibles: Management, Measurement, and Reporting* (Washington, DC: Brookings Institution Press).

8. Friedman, M. (2002), *Capitalism and Freedom,* 40th anniversary edition (Chicago, IL: University of Chicago Press).

9. Fama, E. (1970), "Efficient capital markets: A review of theory and empirical work," *Journal of Finance* 25: 383–417; Beechy, M., D. Gruen, and J. Vickrey (2000), "The efficient market hypothesis:" A survey Research Discussion Paper, Federal Reserve Bank of Australia.

10. Alexander, J. (2007), *Performance Dashboards and Analysis for Value Creation* (Hoboken, NJ: Wiley-Interscience).

11. In its 2010 annual report, Microsoft provides the following comparison: Over a five-year period (June 2005–June 2010), $100 invested in (1) Microsoft stock would have grown to $100.77; in (2) the S&P 500, it would have been worth $96.09; in (3) the NASDAQ index, composed primarily of computer-related companies, it would have grown to $119.38. While outperforming the wider market, Microsoft significantly underperformed when compared to the broader computer industry. Source: Microsoft 2010 Annual Report, www.microsoft.com/investor/reports/ar10/10k_dl_dow.html.

12. This section draws on: Christensen, C. M, and M. E. Raynor (2003), *The Innovator's Solution: Creating and Sustaining Successful Growth* (Boston, MA: Harvard Business School Press).

13. Speech given by Alan Greenspan on December 5, 1996, at the American Enterprise Institute.

14. "Irrational gloom," *The Economist,* October 11, 2002.

15. Kaplan, R. S., and D. P. Norton (1992), "The balanced scorecard: Measures that drive performance," *Harvard Business Review,* January–February: 71–79.

16. Ibid.

17. Govindarajan, V., and J. B. Lang (2002), *3M Corporation,* case study, Tuck School of Business at Dartmouth.

18. Rothaermel, F. T., and A. M. Hess (2010), "Innovation strategies combined," *MIT Sloan Management Review,* Spring: 12–15.

19. Huston, L., and N. Sakkab (2006), "Connect & Develop: Inside Procter & Gamble's new model for innovation," *Harvard Business Review,* March: 58–66.

20. Clarke, R. (2009), "Failure: The secret to success," at http://dreams.honda.com/#/video_fa; and see also: Prahalad, C. K., and G. Hamel (1990), "The core competence of the corporation," *Harvard Business Review,* May–June.

21. Kaplan, R. S. (1993), "Implementing the balanced scorecard at FMC Corporation: An interview with Larry D. Brady," *Harvard Business Review,* September–October: 143–147.

22. Norreklit, H. (2000), "The balance on the balanced scorecard — a critical analysis of some of its assumptions," *Management Accounting Research* 11: 65–88; Jensen, M. C. (2002), "Value Maximization, Stakeholder Theory, and the Corporate Objective Function," in *Unfolding Stakeholder Thinking* Andriof, J., et al. (eds.), (Sheffield, UK: Greenleaf Publishing).

23. Lawrie, G., and I. Cobbold (2002), "Development of the 3rd generation balanced scorecard: Evolution of the balanced scorecard into an effective strategic performance management tool," 2GC Working Paper, 2GC Limited, Albany House, Market Street, Maidenhead, Berkshire, SL6 8BE UK.

24. Kaplan, R. S., and D. P. Norton (1992), "The balanced scorecard: Measures that drive performance"; Kaplan, R. S., and D. P. Norton (2007), "Using the balanced scorecard as a strategic management system," *Harvard Business Review,* July–August.

25. "After the leak. The gusher in the gulf may soon be sealed. BP's woes will be harder to cap," *The Economist,* July 22, 2010; and "BP's spill costs look manageable 8 months later," *Associated Press,* December 29, 2010.

26. Anderson, R. C. (2009), *Confessions of a Radical Industrialist: Profits, People, Purpose—Doing Business by Respecting the Earth* (New York: St. Martin's Press).

27. Norman, W., and C. MacDonald (2004), "Getting to the bottom of 'triple bottom line reads: line,'" *Business Ethics Quarterly* 14: 243–262.

28. Collins, J. C., and J. I. Porras (1994), *Built to Last: Successful Habits of Visionary Companies* (New York: HarperBusiness), p. 93.

29. Anderson, R. C. (2009), *Confessions of a Radical Industrialist,* p. 5; TED talk, "Ray Anderson on the business logic of sustainability," www.ted.com; and Perkins, J. (2009), *Hoodwinked: An Economic Hit Man Reveals Why the World Financial Markets Imploded—and What We Need to Do to Remake Them* (New York: Crown Business), p. 107.

30. Bilton, N. (2010), "The race to dominate the smartphone market," *The New York Times,* November 1, 2010.

31. Hardy, E. (2011), "Microsoft has sold more than two million Windows Phone 7 devices," January 27, 2011, www.brighthand.com.

Analysis: Getting Started
1. What Is Strategy and Why Is It Important?
2. The Strategic Management Process

External and Internal Analysis
3. External Analysis: Industry Structure, Competitive Forces, and Strategic Groups
4. Internal Analysis: Resources, Capabilities, and Activities
5. Competitive Advantage and Firm Performance

Implementation
11. Organizational Design: Structure, Culture, and Control
12. Corporate Governance, Business Ethics, and Strategic Leadership

GAINING & SUSTAINING COMPETITIVE ADVANTAGE

Formulation: Corporate Strategy
PART 2
8. Corporate Strategy: Vertical Integration and Diversification
9. Corporate Strategy: Acquisitions, Alliances, and Networks
10. Global Strategy: Competing Around the World

Formulation: Business Strategy
PART 2
6. Business Strategy: Differentiation, Cost Leadership, and Integration
7. Business Strategy: Innovation and Strategic Entrepreneurship

PART 2
Strategy Formulation

CHAPTER **6**

Business Strategy: Differentiation, Cost Leadership, and Integration

LEARNING OBJECTIVES
After studying this chapter, you should be able to:

LO 6-1   Define business-level strategy and describe how it determines a firm's strategic position.

LO 6-2   Examine the relationship between value drivers and differentiation strategy.

LO 6-3   Examine the relationship between cost drivers and cost-leadership strategy.

LO 6-4   Assess the benefits and risks of cost-leadership and differentiation business strategies vis-à-vis the five forces that shape competition.

LO 6-5   Explain why it is difficult to succeed at an integration strategy.

LO 6-6   Evaluate value and cost drivers that may allow a firm to pursue an integration strategy.

LO 6-7   Describe and evaluate the dynamics of competitive positioning.

Trimming Fat at Whole Foods Market

WHEN FOUR YOUNG ENTREPRENEURS opened a small natural-foods store in Austin, Texas, in 1980, they never imagined it would one day turn into an international supermarket chain with stores in the United States, Canada, and the United Kingdom. Thirty years later, with the acquisition of a close competitor, Wild Oats, Whole Foods now has over 300 stores, employs some 60,000 people, and earned $10 billion in revenue in 2010. Its mission is to offer the finest natural and organic foods available, maintain the highest quality standards in the grocery industry, and remain firmly committed to sustainable agriculture. Clearly, the customers the company wanted to serve were ready for Whole Foods!

Whole Foods is a high-end grocery store. In addition to natural and organic foods, it also offers a wide variety of prepared foods and luxury food items, such as $400 bottles of wine. The decision to sell high-ticket items incurs higher costs for the company because such products require more expensive in-store displays and more highly skilled workers, and many fresh items require high turnover. In order to delight its customers with a superior shopping experience, Whole Foods has developed an innovative human resource program, which focuses on happy employees, continuing education, and self-directed teams. Whole Foods has been included in *Fortune*'s list of the "Best Companies to Work For" every year

of its existence. Whole Foods is also active in a number of social causes, donating 5 percent of its net profits to charities every year.

Given its unique strategic position as an upscale grocer offering natural, organic, and luxury food items, Whole Foods enjoyed a competitive advantage during the economic boom through early 2008. But as consumers became more budget conscious during the recession of 2008–2009, the company's financial performance deteriorated. Competitive intensity also increased markedly because basically every supermarket chain now offers organic food.

To revitalize Whole Foods, co-founder and CEO John Mackey decided to "trim fat" on two fronts: First, the supermarket chain refocused on its mission to offer wholesome and healthy food options. In Mackey's words, Whole Foods had been selling "a bunch of junk," including candy. Mackey is passionate about helping U.S. consumers overcome obesity in order to help reduce heart disease and diabetes. Given that, the new strategic intent at Whole Foods is to become the champion of healthy living not only by offering natural and organic food choices, but also by educating consumers with its new Healthy Eating initiative. Whole Foods Market now has "Take Action Centers" in every story to educate customers on many food-related topics like genetic engineering, organic foods, pesticides, and sustainable agriculture.

Second, Whole Foods will trim fat by reducing costs. For example, it has expanded its private-label product line by 5 percent; it now includes over 2,300 products at lower prices. Moreover, to attract more customers who buy groceries for an entire family or group, Whole Foods now offers volume discounts to compete with Costco, the largest membership club chain in the U.S. To offer its private-label line and volume-discount packages, Whole Foods needs to rely more on low-cost suppliers and enhance its logistics system to cover larger geographic areas more efficiently. It remains to be seen if Whole Foods can increase the value gap by improving its differentiated appeal that allows it to command premium prices, while keeping its cost structure in check at the same time.[1]

After reading the chapter, you will find more about this case, with related questions, on page 163.

▲ **THE WHOLE FOODS STORY** raises a number of interesting issues that we will address in this chapter. At the business level, Whole Foods differentiates itself from competitors by offering top-quality foods obtained through sustainable agriculture. This strategy implies that Whole Foods focuses on increasing the perceived value created for customers, which allows it to charge a premium price. This strategy proved successful initially. Over time, though, in response to both changing external and internal factors, the strategy needed to be fine-tuned to fit the changing environment. Whole Foods needed to take a fresh look at reinvigorating its business-level strategy in order to better serve its particular market and strengthen its competitive position.

The first strategic initiative featured in the ChapterCase—becoming the champion of healthy living—therefore aims at further enhancing its differentiated appeal. Whole Foods needs to staff its education centers with higher-qualified personnel than found in other grocery stores, but this in turn drives up its cost structure. To reduce pressure on the profit margin, Whole Foods's CEO John Mackey knows that he must control the company's cost structure, which is higher than that of other grocers and has been rising. Whole Foods Market also is attempting to improve its logistics capabilities in order to offer private-label and large packages at a profit. The expectation is that the strategic initiatives featured in the ChapterCase will enhance Whole Foods's strategic profile, and thus help it regain its competitive advantage.

This chapter, the first in Part 2 on strategy formulation, takes a close look at business-level strategy and how to compete for advantage.

BUSINESS-LEVEL STRATEGY: HOW TO COMPETE FOR ADVANTAGE

>> **LO 6-1**
Define business-level strategy and describe how it determines a firm's strategic position.

Business-level strategy details the actions managers take in their quest for competitive advantage when competing in a single product market.[2] It may involve a single product or a group of very similar products that use the same channel. It concerns the broad question, "How should we compete?" To formulate an appropriate business-level strategy, managers must answer the "who-what-why-and-how" questions of competition:

- *Who*—which customer segments—will we serve?
- *What* customer needs, wishes, and desires will we satisfy?
- *Why* do we want to satisfy them?
- *How* will we satisfy our customers' needs?[3]

To formulate an effective business strategy, managers need to keep in mind that a firm's competitive advantage is determined jointly by industry characteristics and firm characteristics (see Exhibit 6.1). The more attractive an industry is, the more profitable it is. As discussed in Chapter 3 industry attractiveness can be assessed using the structure-conduct-performance (SCP) framework and the five forces model plus the availability of

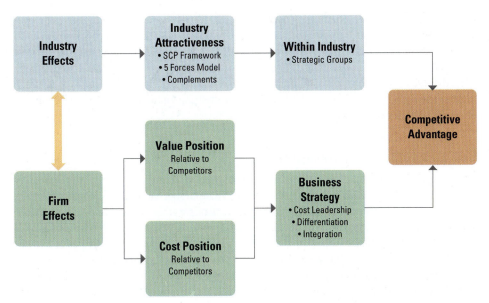

EXHIBIT 6.1

Industry and Firm
Effects Jointly
Determine Competitive
Advantage

complements. Managers need to be certain that the business strategy is aligned with the five forces that shape competition. They can evaluate performance differences among clusters of firms in the same industry by conducting a strategic-group analysis. The concepts introduced in Chapter 4 allow us to look inside firms and explain why they differ based on their resources, capabilities, and activities.

At the firm level, performance is determined by value and cost positions relative to competitors. Whole Foods, as the leading supermarket chain of natural and organic foods, has a strong value position in comparison to its competitors. On the other hand, its relative cost position is weaker due to its higher cost structure, thereby reducing its ability to compete solely on price.

Strategic Position

We noted (in Chapter 5) that a firm's competitive advantage is based on the difference between the *perceived value* a firm is able to create for consumers (V), captured by how much consumers are willing to pay for a product or service, and the total cost (C) the firm incurs to create that value. The greater the economic value created ($V - C$), the greater the firm's competitive advantage. Therefore, to answer the business-level strategy question of how to compete, managers have two primary competitive levers at their disposal: value (V) and cost (C).

A firm's business-level strategy determines its strategic position—its strategic profile based on value creation and cost—in a specific product market. A firm stakes out a valuable and unique position that allows it to meet customer needs while creating as large a gap as possible between the value the firm's product creates and the cost required to produce it. Higher value tends to require higher cost. Thus, to achieve a desired strategic position, managers must make strategic trade-offs—situations that require choosing

---

business-level strategy The actions managers take in their quest for competitive advantage when competing in a single product market.

strategic position A firm's strategic profile based on value creation and cost. The goal is to create as large a gap as possible between the value the firm's product or service creates and the cost required to produce it ($V - C$).

strategic trade-offs Situations that require choosing between a cost or value position, necessary because higher value tends to require higher cost.

between a cost or value position. Managers must address the tension between value creation (which tends to lead to higher cost) and the pressure to keep cost in check so as not to erode the firm's economic value creation. (The difference between value creation and cost is sometimes called the *value gap*.) A business strategy is more likely to lead to a competitive advantage if it allows firms to either *perform similar activities differently,* or *perform different activities* than their rivals that result in creating more value or offering similar products or services at lower cost.[4]

Generic Business Strategies

There are two fundamentally different generic business strategies—*differentiation* and *cost leadership*. A differentiation strategy seeks to create higher value for customers than the value that competitors create, by delivering products or services with unique features while keeping cost at the same or similar levels. A cost-leadership strategy, in contrast, seeks to create the same or similar value for customers by delivering products or services at a lower cost than competitors, enabling the firm to offer lower prices to its customers.

These two strategies are called *generic strategies* because they can be used by any organization—manufacturing or service, large or small, for-profit or not-for-profit, public or private, U.S. or non-U.S.—in the quest for competitive advantage, independent of industry context. Differentiation and cost leadership require distinct strategic positions in order to increase a firm's chances to gain and sustain a competitive advantage.[5] Because value creation and cost tend to be positively correlated, there exist important trade-offs between value creation and low cost.

Different generic strategies can lead to competitive advantage, even in the *same industry.* For example, Rolex and Timex both compete in the market for wristwatches, yet they follow different business strategies. Rolex follows a differentiation strategy: It creates a higher value for its watches by making higher-quality timepieces with unique features that last a lifetime and that bestow a perception of prestige and status upon their owners. Customers are willing to pay a premium for these attributes. Timex, in contrast, follows a cost-leadership strategy: It uses lower cost inputs and efficiently produces a wristwatch of acceptable quality, highlights reliability and accuracy, and prices its timepieces at the low end of the market. The issue is not to compare Rolex and Timex directly—they compete in different market segments of the wristwatch industry. Both can achieve a competitive advantage using diametrically opposed business strategies. Rather, the idea is to compare Rolex's strategic position with the next-best differentiator (e.g., Ebel), and Timex's strategic position with the next-best low-cost producer (e.g., Swatch).

When considering different business strategies, managers also must define the scope of competition—whether to pursue a specific, narrow part of the market or go after the broader market.[6] In the preceding example, Rolex focuses on a small market segment: affluent consumers who want to present a certain image. Timex offers watches for many different segments of the mass market.

Now we can combine the dimensions describing a firm's strategic position (*differentiation vs. cost*) with the scope of competition (*narrow vs. broad*). As shown in Exhibit 6.2, by doing so we get the two major generic (or broad) business strategies (*cost leadership* and *differentiation*), shown as the top two boxes in the matrix, and what are termed the *focused* version of each (shown as the bottom two boxes in the matrix). The focused versions of the strategies—focused cost-leadership strategy and focused differentiation strategy—are essentially the same as the broad generic strategies *except* that the competitive scope is narrower. The manufacturing company BIC pursues a focused cost-leadership strategy, offering disposable pens and cigarette lighters at a very low price (often free promotional give-aways by companies), while La Fraicheur pursues a focused differentiation strategy, offering exquisite luxury wine coolers priced at up to 100,000 euros a piece.

The automobile industry provides an example of the *scope of competition.* Alfred P. Sloan, long-time president and CEO of GM, defined the carmaker's mission as providing *a car for every purse and purpose.* GM was one of the first to implement a multidivisional structure in order to separate the brands into divisions, allowing each brand to create its unique strategic position within the broad automotive market. The position varies even with a brand. For example, the current Chevy product lineup ranges from the low-cost-positioned Aveo, starting at a price of about $12,000, to the highly differentiated Cadillac Escalade SUV priced at roughly $70,000.

Tesla Motors, maker of electric cars, offers a highly differentiated product and pursues only a small market segment. It pursues a *focused differentiation strategy.* Currently, Tesla focuses on well-heeled, environmentally conscious consumers. It offers its Roadster for a base price of about $110,000, and in 2012 is planning to launch the Model S—a four-door sedan. With only those two products, the company does not plan to sell more than 20,000 vehicles a year,[7] equal to less than 0.20 percent U.S. market share of auto sales. Tesla Motors is pursuing a focused-differentiation strategy, focusing on a narrow market segment of customers who are willing to pay a premium price.

EXHIBIT 6.2

Strategic Position and Competitive Scope: Generic Business Strategies

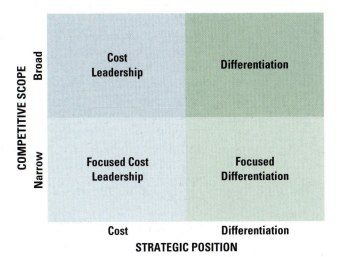

Source: Adapted from M. E. Porter (1980), *Competitive Strategy. Techniques for Analyzing Industries and Competitors* (New York: Free Press).

DIFFERENTIATION STRATEGY: UNDERSTANDING VALUE DRIVERS

The goal of a generic differentiation strategy is to add unique features that will increase the perceived value of goods and services in the minds of the consumers so they are willing to pay a higher price. Ideally, a firm following a differentiation strategy aims to achieve in the minds of consumers a level of value creation that its competitors cannot easily match. The focus of competition in a differentiation strategy tends to be on unique product features, service, and new product launches, or on marketing and promotion rather than price. For example, the carpet company Interface is a leader in sustainability and offers innovative products such as its Cool Carpet, the world's first carbon-neutral floor covering.

>> **LO 6-2**
Examine the relationship between value drivers and differentiation strategy.

---

differentiation strategy Generic business strategy that seeks to create higher value for customers than the value that competitors create, by delivering products or services with unique features while keeping the firm's cost structure at the same or similar levels.

cost-leadership strategy Generic business strategy that seeks to create the

same or similar value for customers by delivering products or services at a lower cost than competitors, enabling the firm to offer lower prices to its customers.

scope of competition The size—narrow or broad—of the market in which a firm chooses to compete.

focused cost-leadership strategy Same as the cost-leadership strategy except with a narrow focus on a niche market.

focused differentiation strategy Same as the differentiation strategy except with a narrow focus on a niche market.

Interface's customers reward it with a willingness to pay a higher price for its environmentally friendly products.[8]

A company that uses a differentiation strategy can achieve a competitive advantage as long as its economic value created $(V - C)$ is greater than that of its competitors. Panel (a) in Exhibit 6.3 shows that firm B, a differentiator, achieves a competitive advantage over firm A. Firm B not only offers greater value than firm A, but also achieves *cost parity* (meaning it has the same costs as firm A). However, even if firm B fails to achieve cost parity (which is often the case since higher value tends to go along with higher costs in terms of higher-quality raw materials, research and development, employee training to provide superior customer service, and so on), it can still gain a competitive advantage if its economic value creation exceeds that of its competitors. This situation is depicted in Panel (b) of Exhibit 6.3. In both situations, firm B's economic value creation, $(V - C)_B$, is greater than that of firm A $(V - C)_A$. Firm B, therefore, achieves a competitive advantage because it can charge a premium price, reflecting its higher value creation.

Although increased value creation is a defining feature of a differentiation strategy, managers must also control cost. If cost rises too much as the firm creates more value, the value gap shrinks, negating any differentiation advantage. Rising costs have lowered Starbucks's profitability in recent years, for example. To combat a squeeze on margins, Starbucks's managers are now applying lean manufacturing techniques to streamline processes and lower the firm's cost structure.[9]

Although a differentiation strategy is generally associated with premium pricing, managers have an important second pricing option. When a firm is able to offer a differentiated product or service and can control its costs at the same time, it is able to gain market share from other firms by charging a similar price but offering more perceived value. By leveraging its differentiated appeal of superior customer service and quality in delivery, for example, Marriott offers a line of different hotels, such as its flagship Marriott full-service business hotel equipped to host large conferences, Residence Inn for extended stay, Marriott Courtyard for business travelers, and Marriott Fairfield Inn for inexpensive leisure and family travel.[10] Although these hotels are roughly comparable to competitors in price, they generally offer a higher perceived value. This difference between price and value allows Marriott to gain market share and post superior performance.

EXHIBIT 6.3

Differentiation Strategy: Achieving Competitive Advantage

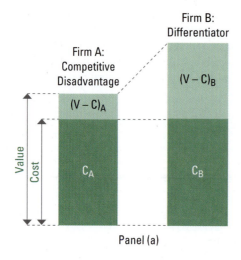

Panel (a)

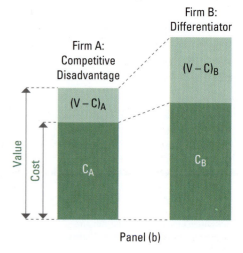

Panel (b)

Value Drivers

Managers can adjust a number of different levers to improve a firm's strategic position. These levers either increase perceived value or decrease costs. Here, we will study the most salient *value drivers* that managers have at their disposal.[11] They are:

- Product features
- Customer service
- Customization
- Complements

These value drivers are related to a firm's expertise in and organization of different internal value chain activities (a concept first introduced in Chapter 4). Although these are the most important value drivers, no such list can be complete. Applying the concepts introduced in this chapter should allow managers to identify other important value and cost drivers unique to their business.

When attempting to increase the perceived value of the firm's product or service offerings, managers must remember that the different value drivers contribute to competitive advantage *only if* their increase in value creation (ΔV) exceeds the increase in costs (ΔC). The condition of $\Delta V > \Delta C$ must be fulfilled if a differentiation strategy is to strengthen a firm's strategic position and thus enhance its competitive advantage.

PRODUCT FEATURES. One of the obvious but most important levers that managers can adjust are the product features and attributes, thereby increasing the perceived value of the product or service offering. For example, a BMW M3 comes with many more performance features than a Honda Accord. Adding unique product features allows firms to turn commodity products into differentiated products that command a premium price. By following its *philosophy of making products that are easy to use for the widest spectrum of possible users,*[12] OXO differentiates its kitchen utensils through its patent-protected ergonomically designed soft black rubber grips.

CUSTOMER SERVICE. Managers can increase the perceived value of their firms' product or service offerings by focusing on customer service and responsiveness. For example, the online retailer Zappos earned a reputation for superior customer service by offering free shipping both ways: to the customer and for returns.[13] Zappos's managers didn't view this as an additional expense but rather as part of their marketing budget. There seemed to be a good return on investment as word spread through the online shopping community. Competitors took notice, too: In the summer of 2009, Amazon bought Zappos for over $1 billion.[14]

L. L. Bean was founded in 1912 to sell the water-proof "Maine Hunting Shoe"®—a unique product that came with a guarantee of 100 percent satisfaction. The company built its business on superior customer service and customer satisfaction. Today, L. L. Bean's policy of "Shipped for Free. Guaranteed to Last." continues to focus on these strengths.

The hotel industry provides a second example of superior customer service. Following its credo, "We are Ladies and Gentlemen serving Ladies and Gentlemen," the Ritz-Carlton has become one of the world's leaders in providing a personalized customer experience based on sophisticated analysis of data gathered about each guest, including past choices. It offers personalized customer service that few hotel chains can match.

To excel at customer service, managers must be able to identify unmet customer needs and find ways to satisfy them or exceed customer expectations. As discussed in Strategy Highlight 6.1 (next page), the creation of Toyota's luxury brand Lexus illustrates how superior customer service can increase perceived product value.

Toyota: From "Perfect Recall" to "Recall Nightmare"

When Toyota launched its Lexus brand in 1989, it faced a steep uphill battle. The luxury car segment was dominated by Mercedes-Benz, which combined high performance with style and cutting-edge engineering. Other strong players in the luxury car segment included BMW and Cadillac.

Lexus needed a perfect launch of its new line of luxury vehicles to stand a chance against the strong competitors in the market. Yet its LS400 line required a recall a little more than a year after launch. Lexus's initial quality problems could have spelled an early doom for the new brand, whose slogan is "The Relentless Pursuit of Perfection." To address this serious threat, the brand's managers decided to go the extra mile. Rather than broadly announcing the recall in the media as is customary, it called each owner individually and advised bringing the car in for the recommended repair. When owners picked up their cars after the repair, they found their Lexus had been detailed and the gas tank filled. If owners lived far from a Lexus dealership, the company flew mechanics to the customer's location. In less than three weeks, Lexus was able to resolve the recall problems on all its 8,000 LS400 vehicles sold in the United States. The media dubbed Lexus's effort "a perfect recall."

By exceeding customer expectations, Lexus managers turned a serious threat into an opportunity and established the brand's reputation for superior customer service. Lexus's response was especially well received because customers who buy a brand-new and unknown luxury brand tend to be opinion leaders. They influence other consumers by sharing their product evaluation through word of mouth (or today, by viral messaging online). Only two years after its launch, Lexus was ranked first on vehicle quality and customer satisfaction by J.D. Power & Associates, a leading information-services firm. In the same year (1991), Lexus became the top-selling luxury brand in the United States. It has been one of the top-selling brands ever since.

However, after being a leader in quality for almost 20 years, Toyota faced the largest recall in automotive history in early 2010 when it called back more than eight million vehicles due to an alleged faulty accelerator pedal and alleged problems with the onboard electronics system. Rather than a nimble and brash new entry in the U.S. automotive market, Toyota was now the largest car manufacturer in the world. To defend its reputation as a quality leader it again needed to exhibit superior customer responsiveness. But satisfying more than eight million customers was much more challenging than pleasing the 8,000 original Lexus customers.[15]

CUSTOMIZATION. Customization allows firms to go beyond merely adding differentiating features to tailoring products and services for specific customers. Advances in manufacturing and information technology have even made feasible **mass customization**—the manufacture of a large variety of customized products or services done at a relatively low unit cost.[16] Customization and low cost were once opposing goals—you could have one or the other, but not both. Today, some companies are able to conquer this trade-off by using the Internet. You can design your own T-shirts at threadless.com or create customized sneakers at nike.com. BMW allows you to design your customized vehicle online and then follow the manufacturing progress in real time.

COMPLEMENTS. When studying industry attractiveness in Chapter 3, we identified the availability of complements as an important force determining the profit potential of an industry. Complements add value to a product or service when they are consumed in tandem. Finding complements, therefore, is an important task for managers in their quest to enhance the value of their offerings.

The introduction of AT&T U-verse is a recent example of managers leveraging complements to increase the perceived value of a service offering.[17] AT&T's U-verse service bundles high-speed Internet access, phone, and TV services. Service bundles can be further

mass customization
The manufacture of a large variety of customized products or services at relatively low unit cost.

enhanced by DVR capabilities that allow users to pause live TV, to record up to four live TV shows at once, and to access video on demand. A DVR by itself is not very valuable, but included as a "free" add-on to subscribers, it turns into a complement that significantly enhances the perceived value of the service bundle. Leveraging complementary products allowed AT&T to break into the highly competitive television services market, significantly enhancing the value of its service offerings.

By choosing the differentiation strategy as the strategic position for a product, managers focus their attention on adding value to the product through its unique features that respond to customer preferences, customer service during and after the sale, or an effective marketing campaign that communicates the value of the product's features to the target market. While this positioning involves increased costs (for example, higher-quality inputs or innovative research and development activities), customers will be willing to pay a premium price for the product or service that satisfies their needs and preferences. In the next section, we will discuss how managers formulate a cost leadership strategy.

COST-LEADERSHIP STRATEGY: UNDERSTANDING COST DRIVERS

The goal of a cost-leadership strategy is to reduce the firm's cost below that of its competitors. The *cost leader,* as the name implies, focuses its attention and resources on reducing the cost at which it is able to offer a product or service (and still make a profit in the long term). The cost leader optimizes all of its value chain activities to achieve a low-cost position. Although staking out the lowest-cost position in the industry is the overriding strategic objective, a cost leader still needs to offer products and services of acceptable value.

>> LO 6-3
Examine the relationship between cost drivers and cost-leadership strategy.

A cost leader can achieve a competitive advantage as long as its economic value created $(V - C)$ is greater than that of its competitors. Panel (a) in Exhibit 6.4 shows that firm B, a cost leader, achieves a competitive advantage over firm A because firm B not only has lower cost than firm A, but also achieves *differentiation parity* (meaning it creates the same value as firm A). Thus, firm B's economic value creation, $(V - C)_B$, is greater than that of firm A $(V - C)_A$. As an example, GM and Korean car manufacturer Hyundai offer some models that compete directly with one another, yet Hyundai's cars tend be produced at lower cost but provide a similar value proposition.

What if firm B fails to create differentiation parity? Such parity is often hard to achieve since value creation tends to go along with higher costs, and firm B's strategy is aimed at lower costs. Firm B can still gain a competitive advantage as long as its economic value

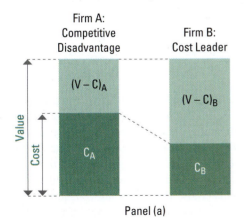

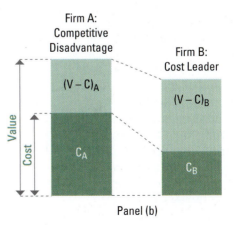

Panel (a)   Panel (b)

EXHIBIT 6.4

Cost-Leadership Strategy: Achieving Competitive Advantage

Ryanair: Lower Cost than the Low-Cost Leader!

Southwest Airlines is a classic example of a company pursuing a cost-leadership strategy.[18] Ryanair is pursuing a similar strategy in Europe. Headquartered in Dublin, Ireland, Ryanair proudly calls itself "the nastiest airline in the world" because of its relentless effort to drive down costs. In fact, Ryanair is the lowest-cost airline in the world. It flies some 200 Boeing 737 aircraft over more than 850 routes across Europe and North Africa, dozens of them priced as low as $8.

How can this be possible? Ryanair is the epitome of a no-frills airline: the seats don't recline, they have no seat-back pockets (safety cards are printed on the back of the seat in front of you), life jackets are in the overhead compartment, and the older planes have no window shades. These choices lower aircraft-purchase costs or allow faster cleaning and turnaround. Ryanair has explored other ideas to further reduce costs, such as removing two toilets to add six more seats, charging for the use of toilets, charging a premium for overweight passengers, having passengers carry their luggage to and from the airplane, and so on.

Although Ryanair's tickets are cheap, "extras" such as pillows, blankets, and a bottle of water require an additional fee. It costs $8 to check in online, but if you forget to do so, Ryanair will happily check you in at the airport for $65. Your first checked bag costs $15, the second $30. Ryanair offers many other amenities, and its website has been described as a bazaar: You can book a hotel room, rent a car, get a credit card, buy insurance, and even gamble. In flight, attendants sell merchandise such as digital cameras ($137.50) and MP3 players ($165). If you want to contact Ryanair, you can't via the website or e-mail; instead, you must use a premium-rate phone line. It is estimated that more than 20 percent of Ryanair's revenues flow from such ancillary services, unusual for an airline.

Ryanair is the epitome of unbundling air travel into its many components. Traditionally, air travel was sold at one price, which included "free" checking of bags as well as meals served on board. However, the extremely price-conscious traveler who can plan ahead to avoid the surcharges can still fly cheaply across Europe.[19]

creation exceeds that of its competitors. This situation is depicted in Panel (b) of Exhibit 6.4: even with lower value (no differentiation parity) but lower cost, firm B's economic value creation, $(V - C)_B$, still is greater than that of firm A $(V - C)_A$. For example, as the low-cost leader, Walmart was able to take market share from Kmart, which filed for bankruptcy in 2002. In the early 2000s, Dell dominated Apple, Compaq, Gateway, HP, and others in the computer industry by utilizing a low-cost strategy.

In both situations in Exhibit 6.4, firm B's economic value creation is greater than that of firm A. Firm B achieves a competitive advantage in both cases. Either it can charge similar prices as its competitors and benefit from a greater profit margin per unit, or it can charge lower prices than its competition and gain higher profits from higher volume. Both variations of a cost-leadership strategy can result in competitive advantage.

While companies successful at cost leadership must excel at controlling costs, this doesn't mean they can neglect value creation. Hyundai signals the quality of its cars with a 10-year, 100,000-mile warranty, the most comprehensive in the industry. Walmart offers products of acceptable quality, including many brand-name products. Within the airline industry, Strategy Highlight 6.2 shows how Ryanair has been able to devise and implement a cost-leadership strategy.

Cost Drivers

The most important *cost drivers* that managers can manipulate to keep their costs low are:

- Cost of input factors
- Economies of scale
- Learning-curve effects
- Experience-curve effects

However, this list is only a starting point; managers may consider other cost drivers, depending on the unique situation.

COST OF INPUT FACTORS. One of the most basic advantages a firm can have over its rivals is access to lower-cost input factors such as raw materials, capital, labor, and IT services. The South African company De Beers has long held a very strong position in the market for diamonds because it tightly controls the supply of raw materials. The aluminum producer Alcoa has access to lower-cost bauxite mines in the United

States, which supply a key ingredient for aluminum. GE, through its GE Capital division, has a lower cost of capital than other industrial conglomerates such as Siemens, Philips, or ABB. To lower labor costs for some types of tasks, some U.S. companies decide to outsource jobs to India, known for its low-cost call centers, data processing and accounting services, and medical-image reading.[20]

ECONOMIES OF SCALE. Larger firms might be in a position to reap **economies of scale,** decreases in cost per unit as output increases. This relationship between unit cost and output is depicted in the first (left-hand) part of Exhibit 6.5: Cost per unit falls as output increases up to point Q_1. A firm whose output is closer to Q_1 has a cost advantage over other firms with less output. In this sense, bigger is better.

EXHIBIT 6.5

Economies of Scale, Minimum Efficient Scale (MES), and Diseconomies of Scale

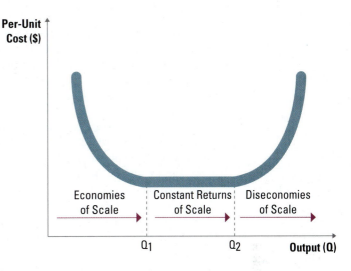

In the airframe-manufacturing industry, for example, reaping economies of scale and learning are critical for cost-competitiveness. Thus, Boeing chose not to compete with Airbus in the market for superjumbo jets; rather, it chose to focus on a smaller, fuel-efficient airplane (the 787 Dreamliner, priced at roughly $155 million) that allows for long-distance point-to-point connections. Each market segment is large enough to allow for significant scale and learning effects for only one manufacturer. Boeing can expect to reap significant economies of scale and learning. By early 2010, it had received almost 900 orders for the Dreamliner, a record number for any airplane.[21] At the same time, Airbus had delivered 26 A380 super jumbos (sticker price, $335 million), with a total of 202 orders on its books.[22]

What causes per-unit cost to drop as output increases (up to point Q_1)? Economies of scale allow firms to:

- Spread their fixed costs over a larger output.
- Employ specialized systems and equipment.
- Take advantage of certain physical properties.

Spreading Fixed Costs over Larger Output. Larger output allows firms to spread their fixed costs over more units. For example, between 2007 and 2009, Microsoft spent approximately $25 billion on R&D, a significant portion of it on its new Windows 7 operating system.[23] This R&D expense was a fixed cost Microsoft had to incur before a single copy of Windows 7 was sold. However, once the initial version of the new software was completed, the marginal cost of each additional copy was basically zero, especially for copies sold in digital form online. Given that Microsoft dominates the operating system market for personal computers with more than 90 percent market share, it expects to sell several hundred million copies of Windows 7, thereby spreading its huge fixed cost of development over a large output. Microsoft's large installed base of Windows operating systems throughout the world provides it with competitive advantage, because it can leverage its economies of scale to drive down the per-unit cost for each additional copy of Windows 7.

economies of scale Decreases in cost per unit as output increases.

Employing Specialized Systems and Equipment. Larger output also allows firms to invest in more specialized systems and equipment such as enterprise resource planning (ERP) software or manufacturing robots. To be cost-competitive in today's market, for example, industry experts believe a car manufacturer must produce at least five million vehicles per year.[24] GM introduced the Chevy Volt in late 2010, the first plug-in hybrid vehicle that is estimated to get 230 mpg fuel efficiency. It is priced at about $40,000, almost twice as expensive as a Toyota Prius that has been on the market longer and presumably has more scale efficiencies. Yet GM is counting on selling the Chevy Volt in large numbers so that economies of scale will kick in and drive down its production costs, and, therefore, lower the price to the end consumer.[25]

Taking Advantage of Certain Physical Properties. Economies of scale also occur because of certain physical properties. One such property is known in engineering as the *cube-square rule:* The volume of a body such as a pipe or a tank increases disproportionately more than its surface. This same principle makes big box retail stores such as Walmart, Target, and the French retailer Carrefour cheaper to build and run. They can also stock much more merchandise and handle inventory more efficiently. These and other scale benefits combine to explain the rise of superstores that are often 200,000 square feet or more. Other retailers that have leveraged the superstore concept to emerge as category killers are Toys R Us, Home Depot, Barnes and Noble, and Best Buy. Their huge size makes it difficult for department stores or small retailers to compete on cost and selection.

Look again at Exhibit 6.5. The output range between Q_1 and Q_2 in the figure is considered the **minimum efficient scale (MES)** in order to be cost-competitive. Between Q_1 and Q_2, the returns to scale are constant. It is the output range needed to bring the cost per unit down as much as possible, allowing a firm to stake out the lowest-cost position achievable through economies of scale. If the firm's output range is less than Q_1 or more than Q_2, the firm is at a cost disadvantage. For example, chipmaker AMD cannot muster the scale in production that Intel enjoys and thus is not able to drive down its cost as much. This puts AMD at a competitive disadvantage.

The concept of minimum efficient scale applies not only to production processes but also to managerial tasks such as how to organize work. Due to investments in specialized technology and equipment (e.g. electric arc furnaces), Nucor is able to reach MES with much smaller batches of steel than larger, fully vertically integrated steel companies using older technology. Nucor's optimal plant size is about 500 people, which is much smaller than at larger integrated steel makers like U.S. Steel (which often employs thousands of workers per plant).[26] Of course, minimum efficient scale depends on the specific industry: The average per-unit cost curve, depicted conceptually in Exhibit 6.5, is a reflection of the underlying production function, which is determined by technology and other input factors.

Benefits to scale cannot go on indefinitely, though. Bigger is not always better; in fact, sometimes bigger is worse. Beyond Q_2 in Exhibit 6.5, firms experience **diseconomies of scale**—increases in cost as output increases. Why? As firms get too big, the complexity of managing and coordinating raises the cost, negating any benefits to scale. Large firms tend to become overly bureaucratic, with too many layers of hierarchy, and thus grow inflexible and slow in decision making. To avoid problems associated with diseconomies of scale, Gore Associates, maker of Gore-Tex fabric, Glide dental floss, and many other innovative products, breaks up its company into smaller units. Managers at Gore Associates found that employing about 150 people per plant allows them to avoid diseconomies of scale. Gore's Ben Hen states: "We put 150 parking spaces in the lot, and when people start parking on the grass, we know it's time to build a new plant."[27]

minimum efficient scale (MES) Output range needed to bring down the cost per unit as much as possible, allowing a firm to stake out the lowest-cost position that is achievable through economies of scale.

diseconomies of scale Increases in cost per unit when output increases.

Finally, there are also physical limitations to scale. Airbus is pushing the envelope with its A380 aircraft, which can hold more than 850 passengers and fly up to 8,200 miles (enough to travel non-stop from Boston to Hong Kong at about 600 mph). The goal, of course, is to drive down the cost of the average seat-mile flown (CASM, a standard cost metric in the airline industry). It remains to be seen whether the A380 superjumbo will enable airlines to reach minimum efficient scale or will simply be too large to be efficient. For example, boarding and embarking procedures must be streamlined in order to accommodate more than 850 people in a timely and safe manner. Many airports around the world will need to be retrofitted with longer and wider runways to allow the superjumbo to take off and land.

Scale economies are critical to driving down a firm's cost and thus strengthening a cost-leadership position. Although managers need to increase output to operate at a minimum efficient scale (between Q_1 and Q_2 in Exhibit 6.5), they also need to be watchful not to drive scale beyond Q_2, where they would encounter diseconomies. Monitoring the firm's cost structure closely over different output ranges allows managers to fine-tune operations and benefit from economies of scale.

LEARNING CURVE. Learning by doing can also drive down cost. As individuals and teams engage repeatedly in an activity, whether writing computer code, developing new medicines, or building submarines, they learn from their cumulative experience.[28] In the business world, *learning curves* were first documented in aircraft manufacturing as the United States ramped up production in the 1930s, prior to its entry into World War II.[29] Every time production was doubled, the per-unit cost dropped by a predictable and constant rate (approximately 20 percent).[30] This important relationship is captured in Exhibit 6.6, where different colors denote different levels of learning curves: 90 percent (purple), 80 percent (green), and 70 percent (blue). As learning occurs, you move down the learning curve. The steeper the learning curve, the more learning takes place. For example, a 90 percent learn-

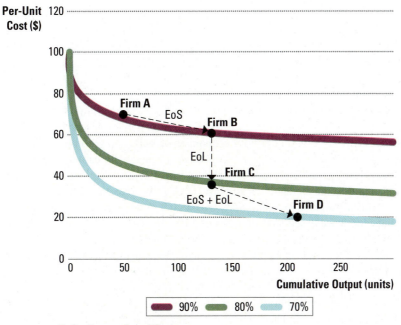

EXHIBIT 6.6

Gaining Competitive Advantage Through Leveraging Learning and Experience Curve Effects

EoS = Economies of Scale
EoL = Economies of Learning

ing curve indicates that per-unit cost drops 10 percent every time output is doubled. A 70 percent learning curve indicates a 30 percent drop every time output is doubled.

It is not surprising that a learning curve was first observed in aircraft manufacturing. An aircraft is an extremely complex industrial product; a modern commercial aircraft can contain more than one million different parts, compared with a few thousand for a car. The more complex the production process, the more learning effects we can expect. As cumulative output increases, managers learn how to optimize the process and workers improve their performance through repetition. Learning curves are a robust phenomenon that has been observed in many industries, not only in manufacturing processes like building airplanes, cars, ships, and semiconductors, but also in alliance management, pizza franchising, and health care.[31] For example, physicians who perform only a small number of cardiac surgeries per year can have a patient mortality rate five times higher than physicians who perform the same surgery more frequently.[32]

There are some important differences between economies of scale and learning effects.[33] In some production processes (e.g., a simple one-step process in the manufacture of steel rods), effects from economies of scale can be quite significant, while learning effects are minimal. In contrast, in some professions (brain surgery or the practice of estate law), learning effects can be substantial, while economies of scale are minimal. Managers need to understand the difference in order to calibrate their business-level strategy. For example, if a firm's cost advantage is due to economies of scale, a manager should be less concerned about employee turnover (and thus a potential loss in learning) and more concerned with drops in production runs. In contrast, if the firm's low-cost position is based on complex learning, managers should be much more concerned if a key employee (e.g., a star analyst at an investment bank or a star researcher at a pharmaceutical company) was to leave.

EXPERIENCE CURVE. The concept of an *experience curve* attempts to capture both economies of scale and learning effects.[34] In this perspective, economies of scale allow movement down a *given* learning curve based on current production technology. By moving further down a given learning curve than competitors, a firm can gain a competitive advantage. For example, Exhibit 6.6 shows that firm B is further down the purple (90 percent) learning curve than firm A. Firm B leverages economies of scale to gain an advantage over firm A.

As we know, however, technology and production processes do not stay constant. If firm C is able to implement a new production process (such as lean manufacturing), it initiates an entirely new and steeper learning curve. In Exhibit 6.6, firm C is able to gain a competitive advantage over both firms A and B through economies of learning by jumping down to the green (80 percent) learning curve, reflecting the new and lower-cost production process introduced. However, combining both economies of scale and learning effects, firm D is breaking away from firm C, gaining a competitive advantage. By capturing both economies of scale and learning effects, firm D is able to implement a cost-leadership strategy and enjoy a competitive advantage over firms A, B, and C. Taken together, learning by doing allows a firm to lower its per-unit costs by moving down a given learning curve, while leveraging experience based on economies of scale *and* learning allows the firm to leapfrog to a steeper learning curve, thereby further driving down its per-unit costs.

By choosing the cost leadership strategy, managers must focus their attention on lowering the overall costs of producing the product or service while maintaining an acceptable level of quality that will serve the needs of the customer. Cost leaders appeal to the price-conscious buyer, whose main criterion is the price of the product or service. By attending to the reduction of costs in each functional area (or value activity), managers aim to be the low-cost provider with the ability to offer the lowest price in the market. As successful cost leaders like Walmart illustrate, the low-cost producer with high volume can be a very profitable business.

BUSINESS-LEVEL STRATEGY AND THE FIVE FORCES: BENEFITS AND RISKS

The five forces model introduced in Chapter 3 helps managers assess the forces—threat of entry, power of suppliers, power of buyers, threat of substitutes, and rivalry among existing competitors—that make some industries more attractive than others. With this understanding of industry dynamics, managers use one of the generic business-level strategies to protect themselves against the forces that drive down profitability.[35] The business-level strategies introduced in this chapter allow firms to carve out strong strategic positions that enhance the likelihood of gaining and sustaining competitive advantage. Exhibit 6.7 details the relationship between competitive positioning and the five forces. In particular, it highlights the benefits and risks of cost-leadership and differentiation business strategies, which we discuss next.

> **>> LO 6-4**
> Assess the benefits and risks of cost leadership and differentiation business strategies vis-à-vis the five forces that shape competition.

EXHIBIT 6.7

Competitive Positioning and the Five Forces: Benefits and Risks of Cost-Leadership and Differentiation Business Strategies

Competitive Force	Cost Leadership		Differentiation	
	Benefits	**Risks**	**Benefits**	**Risks**
Threat of entry	• Protection against entry due to economies of scale	• Erosion of margins • Replacement	• Protection against entry due to intangible resources such as a reputation for innovation, quality, or customer service	• Erosion of margins • Replacement
Power of suppliers	• Protection against increase in input prices, which can be absorbed	• Erosion of margins	• Protection against increase in input prices, which can be passed on to customers	• Erosion of margins
Power of buyers	• Protection against decrease in sales prices, which can be absorbed	• Erosion of margins	• Protection against decrease in sales prices, because well-differentiated products or services are not perfect substitutes	• Erosion of margins
Threat of substitutes	• Protection against substitute products through further lowering of prices	• Replacement, especially when faced with innovation	• Protection against substitute products due to differential appeal	• Replacement, especially when faced with innovation
Rivalry among existing competitors	• Protection against price wars because lowest-cost firm will win	• Focus of competition shifts to non-price attributes • Lowering costs to drive value creation below acceptable threshold	• Protection against competitors if product or service has enough differential appeal to command premium price	• Focus of competition shifts to price • Increasing differentiation of product features that do not create value but raise costs • Increasing differentiation to raise costs above acceptable threshold

Source: Based on M. E. Porter, "The five competitive forces that shape strategy," *Harvard Business Review,* January 2008; and M. E. Porter (1980), *Competitive Strategy: Techniques for Analyzing Industries and Competitors* (New York: Free Press).

Benefits and Risks of the Cost-Leadership Strategy

A cost-leadership strategy is defined by obtaining the lowest-cost position in the industry while offering acceptable value. The cost leader, therefore, is protected from other competitors because of having the lowest cost. If a price war ensues, the low-cost leader will be the last firm standing; all other firms will be driven out as margins evaporate. Since reaping economies of scale is critical to reaching a low-cost position, the cost leader is likely to have a large market share, which in turn reduces the threat of entry.

A cost leader is also fairly well isolated from threats of powerful suppliers to increase input prices, because it is more able to absorb price increases through accepting lower profit margins. Likewise, a cost leader can absorb price reductions more easily when demanded by powerful buyers. Should substitutes emerge, the low-cost leader can try to fend them off by further lowering its prices to reinstall relative value with the substitute. For example, Walmart tends to be fairly isolated from these threats. Walmart's cost structure combined with its large volume allows it to work with suppliers in keeping prices low, to the extent that suppliers are often the party who experiences a profit margin squeeze.

Although a cost-leadership strategy provides some protection against the five forces, it also carries some risks. If a new entrant with new and relevant expertise enters the market, the low-cost leader's margins may erode due to loss in market share while it attempts to learn new capabilities. For example, Walmart faces challenges to its cost leadership: Target (which until 2000 was the Dayton-Hudson Company) has had success due to its superior merchandising capabilities. The Dollar Store has drawn customers who prefer a smaller format than the big box of Walmart. The risk of replacement is particularly pertinent if a potent substitute emerges due to an innovation. Powerful suppliers and buyers may be able to reduce margins so much that the low-cost leader could have difficulty covering the cost of capital, and thus lose the potential for a competitive advantage.

The low-cost leader also needs to stay vigilant to keep its cost the lowest in the industry. Over time, competitors can beat the cost leader by implementing the same business strategy, but more effectively. While keeping its cost the lowest in the industry is imperative, the cost leader must not forget that it needs to create an acceptable level of value. If continuously lowering costs leads to a value proposition that falls below an acceptable threshold, the low-cost leader's market share will evaporate. Finally, the low-cost leader faces significant difficulties when the focus of competition shifts from price to non-price attributes.

Target has been able to compete with Walmart by building equivalent skills in efficient logistics expertise, thus achieving cost parity. At the same time, Target outdoes Walmart in product selection, merchandising, and store layout so that its stores offer a higher-quality shopping experience for the customer, thus creating higher value.

Benefits and Risks of the Differentiation Strategy

A differentiation strategy is defined by finding a strategic position that creates higher perceived value while controlling costs. The successful differentiator is able to stake out a unique strategic position, where it can benefit from imperfect competition (as discussed in Chapter 3), and thus command a premium price. Such a position reduces rivalry among competitors.

A successful differentiation strategy is likely to be based on unique or specialized features of the product, on an effective marketing campaign, or on intangible resources such as a reputation for innovation, quality, and customer service. A rival would need to improve the product features as well as build a similar or more effective reputation in order to gain market share. Thus, the threat of entry is reduced: Competitors will find such intangible advantages time-consuming and costly, and maybe impossible, to imitate. If the source of the differential appeal is intangible rather than tangible (e.g., reputation rather than observable product and service features), a differentiator is even more likely to sustain its advantage.

Moreover, if the differentiator is able to create a significant difference between perceived value and current market prices, the differentiator will not be so threatened by increases in input prices due to powerful suppliers. Although an increase in input factors could erode margins, a differentiator is likely able to pass on price increases to its customers as long as its value creation exceeds the price charged. Since a successful differentiator creates perceived value in the minds of consumers and builds customer loyalty, powerful buyers demanding price decreases are unlikely to emerge. A strong differentiated position also reduces the threat of substitutes, because the unique features of the product have been created to appeal to customer preferences, keeping them loyal to the product. For example, Apple has built strong differentiated appeal for its products. As Apple creates new customer needs (even if customers are initially unaware of the need), it launches new products. Users of an iPhone are loyal to the product and unlikely to switch to a rival's offering.

The viability of a differentiation strategy is severely undermined when the focus of competition shifts to price rather than value-creating features. This can happen when products become commoditized (the original IBM personal computer) and an acceptable standard of quality has emerged across rival firms (IBM clones). A differentiator also needs to be careful not to overshoot its differentiated appeal by adding product features that raise costs but not the perceived value in the minds of consumers. Finally, a differentiator needs to be vigilant that its costs of providing uniqueness do not rise above the customer's willingness to pay.

It is important to note that none of the business-level strategies depicted in Exhibit 6.2 is inherently superior. The success of each is context-dependent and relies on two factors:

■ How well the strategy leverages the firm's internal strengths while mitigating its weaknesses; and

■ How well it helps the firm exploit external opportunities while avoiding external threats.

There is no single correct generic strategy for a specific industry. The deciding factor is that the chosen business strategy provides a strong position that attempts to maximize economic value creation and is effectively implemented.

INTEGRATION STRATEGY: COMBINING COST LEADERSHIP AND DIFFERENTIATION

Competitive conditions in an industry may require firms to develop skills in lowering costs as well as adding uniqueness—particularly in globalized industries. For example, success may require lowering costs in order to compete with firms in countries with lower labor costs and may require adding special features to respond to local customer preferences in individual country markets. Since either increasing perceived value or lowering production costs can increase a firm's competitive advantage, it is tempting to conclude that managers should be focusing on *both efforts*. To accomplish this, they would need to integrate two different strategic positions: differentiation and low cost.[36] As we will show, managers should not pursue this strategy unless competitive conditions require this position, because it is a complex strategy to execute due to the conflicting requirements of each generic strategy.

Integration Strategy at the Business Level

A successful **integration strategy** requires that trade-offs between differentiation and low cost are reconciled. This is often difficult because differentiation and low cost are distinct

>> **LO 6-5**
Explain why it is difficult to succeed at an integration strategy.

integration strategy
Business-level strategy that successfully combines differentiation and cost leadership activities.

strategic positions that require the firm to effectively manage internal value chain activities that are fundamentally different from one another. For example, a cost leader would focus research and development on process technologies in order to improve efficiency, but a differentiator would focus research and development on product technologies in order to add uniqueness. If successful, an integration strategy allows a firm to offer a differentiated product or service at low cost.

The startup Leopard Cycles, founded in 2004, shows how to address the necessary trade-offs inherent in an integration strategy. A customized road-race bicycle like those ridden by professionals such as Lance Armstrong, Alberto Contador, or Meredith Miller was once an expensive proposition that could cost up to $20,000.[37] Combining the latest flexible-manufacturing techniques with Internet-enabled technologies, Leopard Cycles offers mass-customized race bicycles built with advanced materials such as carbon fiber. Leopard Cycles describes how it addresses the trade-off between value and cost as follows: "Being the low-cost producer is mutually exclusive with exotic materials; however we're a firm believer that you don't have to be the most expensive to be the best."[38] This position implies that an integration of low cost and product differentiation enables companies to increase the perceived value of their products, while keeping the cost increase in check. Leopard Cycles prices its customized road-race bikes between $1,500 and $2,500, only about 15 percent of what one would have paid for such a specialized bicycle just a few years before.

Being successful at an integration strategy doesn't imply that the firm must be the highest value creator *and* the lowest-cost producer in its respective industry. Whether an integration strategy can lead to competitive advantage, however, depends on the *difference* between value creation (V) and cost (C), and thus on the magnitude of economic value created ($V - C$). The goal of an integration strategy is to have a larger economic value created than that of your competitors. This is what Avon has accomplished in the cosmetics industry. Exhibit 6.8 compares the value and cost positions of three cosmetics companies: L'Oreal, Avon, and Revlon. Each of these companies has succeeded in carving out a well-defined strategic position within the cosmetics world: L'Oreal is a differentiator; Revlon is a cost leader; Avon is an integrator.

EXHIBIT 6.8

Avon's Attempt at Achieving Competitive Advantage by Pursuing an Integration Strategy

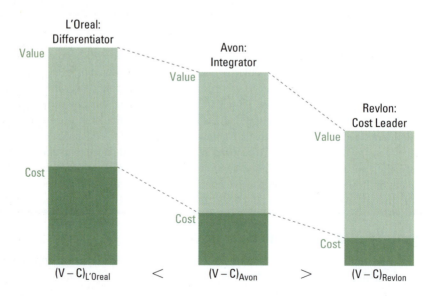

Avon has been able to raise the perceived value of its products while lowering its production costs. Under the leadership of its CEO, Andrea Jung, it began to pursue an integration strategy in 2002 by investing over $100 million in R&D and building a new research facility.[39] Avon's R&D investments were intended to increase the perceived value of its products, by developing cosmetics that look good *and* are good for the skin. In the same year, she began to lower Avon's cost structure by investing more than $50 million into optimizing its supply chain.[40] Avon's shift from a differentiation strategy to an integration strategy seems to be successful: Its profits rose 180 percent from 2002 ($3.9 billion) to 2010 ($10.9 billion). The key point is that Avon has achieved the highest economic value by following an integration strategy [in Exhibit 6.8, $(V - C)_{L'Oreal} < (V - C)_{Avon} > (V - C)_{Revlon}$]. When successful, investments in differentiation and low cost are not substitutes but are complements, providing important spill-over effects.

Although quite difficult to execute, a successfully implemented integration strategy allows firms two pricing options: First, the firm can charge a higher price than the cost leader, reflecting its higher value creation and thus generating greater profit margins. Second, the firm can lower its price below that of the differentiator (because of its lower cost structure); it thus can gain market share and make up the loss in margin through increased sales. An integration strategy is difficult to implement, though. It requires the reconciliation of fundamentally different strategic positions—differentiation and low cost—which in turn require distinct internal value chain activities (see Chapter 4) that allow the firm to increase value *and* lower cost at the same time.

Value and Cost Drivers of Integration Strategy

For an integration strategy to succeed, managers must resolve trade-offs between the two generic strategic positions—low cost and differentiation. Some possible levers they can use to overcome these challenges include quality, economies of scope, innovation, and the firm's structure, culture, and routines. These are critical: They allow managers to simultaneously *increase* perceived value and *lower* cost. Although we discuss each of these value and cost drivers individually, they are *interdependent*. For example, innovations like lean manufacturing contribute to better quality and customer service, which reinforce one another and thus enhance the brand of a product or service.

>> **LO 6-6**
Evaluate value and cost drivers that may allow a firm to pursue an integration strategy.

QUALITY. The quality of a product denotes its durability and reliability. Quality not only can increase a product's perceived value, but also can lower its cost. Through techniques like total quality management, companies design and build products with quality in mind, while increasing their differentiated appeal. By building in better quality, companies lower the cost of both production and after-sale service requirements. Thus, quality is a two-pronged activity: It raises economic value creation $(V - C)$ by simultaneously increasing V and lowering C.

ECONOMIES OF SCOPE. We saw that economies of scale allow a firm to lower its per-unit cost as its output increases. The concept economies of scope describes the savings that come from producing two (or more) outputs at less cost than producing each output individually, even though using the same resources and technology. Starbucks, for example, is already set up to boil purified water for its hot coffee beverages; thus, it reaps economies of scope when it offers tea in addition to coffee. As a result, Starbucks lowers its cost structure by sharing its production assets over multiple outputs, while increasing its menu and thus its differentiated appeal.

economies of scope
Savings that come from producing two (or more) outputs at less cost than producing each output individually, despite using the same resources and technology.

INNOVATION. Broadly defined, *innovation* describes any new product and process, or any modification of existing ones.[41] Innovation is frequently required to resolve existing trade-offs when companies pursue an integration strategy. As we saw earlier, Leopard Cycles leveraged the innovation of flexible manufacturing systems to create customized road-race bicycles of high quality at low cost. This innovation enabled managers to solve the trade-off between customization and cost, and also to increase the quality of the product, further enhancing its differentiated appeal.

Similarly, international furniture retailer IKEA orchestrates different internal value chain activities to reconcile the tension between differentiation and cost leadership in order to carve out a unique strategic position. In particular, IKEA uses innovation in furniture design, engineering, and store design to solve the trade-offs between value creation and production cost. Josephine Rydberg-Dumont, President of IKEA Sweden, highlights how difficult resolving this trade-off is: "Designing beautiful-but-expensive products is easy. Designing beautiful products that are inexpensive and functional is a huge challenge."[42] IKEA leverages its deep design and engineering expertise to offer furniture that is stylish and functional and that can be easily assembled by the consumer. IKEA also focuses on lowering cost by displaying its products in a warehouse-like setting, thus reducing inventory cost. Customers serve themselves, and then transport the furniture to their homes in IKEA's signature flat-packs for assembly. In this way, IKEA is able to pursue an integration strategy, leveraging innovation to increase the perceived value of its products, while simultaneously lowering its cost.

Given its importance in a firm's quest for competitive advantage, we'll discuss innovation as a business strategy in depth in Chapter 7.

STRUCTURE, CULTURE, AND ROUTINES. A firm's structure, culture, and routines are critical when pursuing an integration strategy. The challenge that managers face is to structure their organizations so that they both control cost *and* allow for creativity that can lay the basis for differentiation. Doing the two together is hard to accomplish. Achieving a low-cost position requires an organizational structure that relies on strict budget controls, while differentiation requires an organizational structure that allows creativity and customer responsiveness to thrive, which typically necessitates looser organizational structures and controls.

The goal for managers who want to pursue an integration strategy should be to build an **ambidextrous organization,** one that enables managers to balance and harness different activities in trade-off situations.[43] Here, the trade-offs to be addressed involve the simultaneous pursuit of low cost and differentiation strategies. Notable management practices that companies use to resolve this trade-off include flexible and lean manufacturing systems, total quality management, just-in-time inventory management, and Six Sigma.[44] Other management techniques that allow firms to reconcile cost and value pressures are the use of teams in the production process and decentralized decision making at the level of the individual customer.

Ambidexterity describes a firm's ability to address trade-offs not only at one point but also over time. It encourages managers to balance *exploitation* (applying current knowledge to enhance firm performance in the short term) with *exploration* (searching for new knowledge that may enhance a firm's future performance).[45] For example, while Intel focuses on maximizing sales from its *current* cutting-edge microprocessors, it also has several different teams with different time horizons working on *future* generations of microprocessors.[46] In ambidextrous organizations, managers constantly analyze their existing business processes and routines, looking for ways to change them in order to resolve trade-offs across internal value chain activities and time.[47] Given the importance of

ambidextrous organization An organization able to balance and harness different activities in trade-off situations.

a firm's structure, culture, and routines to gaining and sustaining competitive advantage, we dedicate Part 3 of this book, Strategy Implementation, to discussing this important topic in detail.

Although appealing in a theoretical sense, an integration strategy is actually quite difficult to translate into reality. The reason is that differentiation and cost leadership are distinct strategic positions that require important trade-offs.[48] Many firms that attempt to pursue an integration strategy fail because they end up being *stuck in the middle:* They succeed at neither a differentiation nor a cost-leadership strategy. In a world of strategic trade-offs, increasing value and lowering cost have opposite effects. Improved product features, customer services, and customization all result in higher cost, while offering a no-frills product reduces perceived value. Thus, it happens quite often that a firm can't do both but must choose to be *either* a differentiator *or* a cost leader.

When a firm is unsuccessful in pursuing an integration strategy and ends up stuck in the middle, the result is a competitive *disadvantage.* For example, the DaimlerChrysler merger was motivated by the integration of the differentiation advantage based on Daimler's engineering prowess and the low-cost manufacturing expertise of Chrysler. The resulting cars were a disaster. They were neither differentiated nor low cost. Daimler lost some $35 billion in the ill-fated merger.

We now have finished our discussion of value and cost drivers and how they are used to formulate and implement business-level strategies—differentiation, cost leadership, and integration. Exhibit 6.9 provides a summary of these drivers and their effects. In particular, the exhibit highlights drivers that uniquely affect either value creation or low cost (used for

EXHIBIT 6.9

Value and Cost Drivers

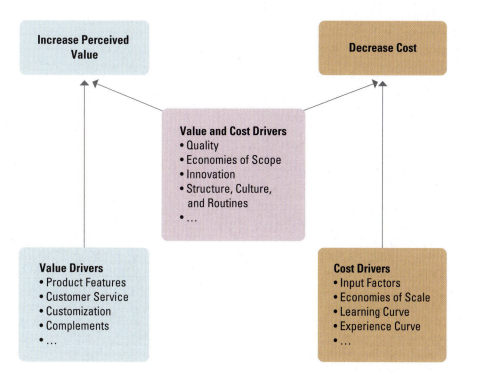

differentiation *or* cost leadership strategies) and drivers that simultaneously increase value while lowering cost (used for integration strategies).

Integration Strategy at the Corporate Level

In Chapter 1, we noted that it is helpful to break down strategy formulation into three distinct levels: corporate, business, and functional (see again Exhibit 1.3). Up to this point in this chapter, we have addressed what managers can do at both the business and functional levels to enhance the chances that an integration strategy will succeed. Another option is to reconcile the trade-offs that arise from pursuing an integration strategy at the corporate level. Corporate-level strategy concerns the overall competitiveness of a multibusiness company, sometimes called a **conglomerate.** In particular, corporate-level strategy concerns decisions about which industries a company should compete in and which types of business-level strategies each unit ought to pursue to maximize overall shareholder value. Conglomerates and other companies may decide to coordinate an integration strategy at the corporate, rather than the business, level.

The Tata Group of India provides an example. A widely diversified multinational conglomerate, headquartered in Mumbai, India, it is active in industries ranging from tea, to hospitality, steel, IT, communications, power, and automobiles.[49] In June 2008, Tata Motors attracted attention in the automotive world when it bought Jaguar and Land Rover from Ford for $2.3 billion. With this purchase, Tata hopes to leverage the prestige Jaguar and Land Rover brands to offer differentiated products.

In the spring of 2009, the Indian Tata Motors attracted even more attention when it unveiled its Tata Nano car. The Nano is the lowest-priced car in the world. It accommodates passengers just over six feet tall, goes from zero to 60 mph in 30 seconds, and gets 67 mpg, beating the Toyota Prius for fuel consumption. The Tata Nano, clearly a no-frills car, exemplifies a focused low-cost strategy. The rear hatch can't be opened, it doesn't have a radio or glove compartment, and its top speed is a little over 60 mph. Nonetheless, at about 50 percent cheaper than the next-lowest-cost car, the Tata Nano is likely to find tens of millions of customers in the fast-growing Indian and Chinese markets. (However, keep this in mind about any cost-leadership strategy: If the product or service does not provide acceptable value, it will not matter how low the price is. Although the Tata Nano is arguably the lowest-priced car in the world, if its reliability, performance, and safety features are unacceptable to customers, the car likely will not sell at company expectations.)

The Tata Group is attempting to carve out different strategic positions in its different divisions. The luxury division of Tata Motors, with the Jaguar and Land Rover brands, is pursuing a *focused* differentiation strategy; the Nano car division is pursuing a *focused* cost-leadership strategy. Although their respective strategic profiles are basically the opposite of one another (differentiation vs. low-cost), both business-level strategies are aimed at a *specific* segment of the market. Jaguar and Land Rover are both considered luxury brands in their respective categories, while the Nano is clearly a low(est)-cost offering, focused on a very specific market niche. Indeed, the Nano focuses on *non-consumption:*[50] Buyers of the Nano will not replace other vehicles, but will be first-time car buyers moving up from bicycles and mopeds. By offering the Nano, Tata is able to bring millions of new car buyers into the market and thus increase the size of the automobile market. Taken together, Tata's corporate strategy seems to be attempting to integrate different strategic positions, pursued by different strategic business units, each with its own profit and loss responsibility.[51] We will study corporate strategy in detail in Chapters 8 and 9.

conglomerate
An organization that combines two or more business units, often active in different industries, under one overarching corporation.

THE DYNAMICS OF COMPETITIVE POSITIONING

Strategic positions, moreover, are not fixed, but can—and need to—change over time as the environment changes. For example, eBay, the successful pioneer in online auctions, decided to retreat from competing in online retailing.[52] Although the company will continue to compete in the online-marketplace for used and overstocked goods, it will no longer compete in the retail market for *new* goods. This strategic shift allows eBay to avoid competing head-on with the online retail giant Amazon, which has morphed into a full-fledged online shopping mall. To further increase the focus on its core business, eBay sold its Skype Internet phone business to a group of private investors.[53] With these strategic moves, eBay returned to its core competency as the web's leading auction house, reaffirming a focused differentiation strategy.

>> **LO 6-7**
Describe and evaluate the dynamics of competitive positioning.

Companies that successfully implement one of the generic business strategies (differentiation or cost leadership) are more likely to attain competitive advantage. To do so, companies seek to reach the so-called **productivity frontier,** which is the value-cost relationship that captures the result of performing best practices at any given time.[54] Firms that exhibit effectiveness and efficiency reach the productivity frontier; others are left behind. Moreover, the productivity frontier represents possible strategic positions the firm can take relating to value creation and low cost. A firm's business strategy determines which strategic position it aspires to along the productivity frontier.

To illustrate this concept, let's look at the competitive dynamics in the mobile devices industry (including portable computers, phones, and other handheld devices) by highlighting the different competitive positions of Apple, HP, and Dell over time. At a given time, the horizontal axis in Exhibit 6.10 indicates best practice in cost leadership, and the vertical axis indicates best practice in differentiation.[55] Combining both cost leadership and differentiation, the company that seeks an integration strategy stakes out a position in the center part in the best-practice frontier (somewhere between the axes). The dashed line shows the productivity frontier in 2005. Both Apple and Dell had carved out strong strategic positions—Apple as differentiator and Dell as cost leader—and as a consequence, both enjoyed superior performance.

productivity frontier
Relationship that captures the result of performing best practices at any given time; the function is convex (bowed outward) to capture the trade-off between value creation and production cost.

Both were able to move to the productivity frontier because their strategic positions were clearly formulated and well-executed. In contrast, HP was "stuck in the middle" in 2005; when compared with Apple and Dell respectively, it could offer neither value-creating differentiation nor low cost. HP had acquired Compaq in 2002 for $25 billion. This merger, which created the world's largest computer PC manufacturer, was intended to stake out a strategic position as integrator, providing "high-tech at low cost." By 2005, however, HP was not able to reconcile the cost-differentiation trade-off, and thus was unable to reach the productivity frontier. HP's board replaced CEO Carly

EXHIBIT 6.10

The Dynamics of Competitive Positioning: Apple, HP, and Dell

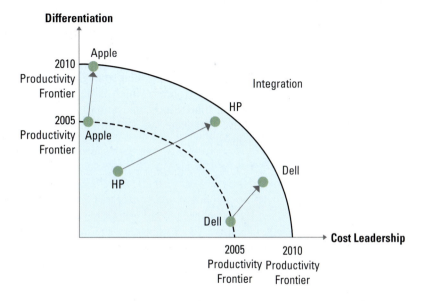

Fiorina with Mark Hurd (who in turn was replaced by Leo Apotheker in 2010, who in turn was replaced by Meg Whitman in 2011; see ChapterCase 12).

Fast-forward to 2010 . . . There, the competitive dynamics look quite different. Continued product and process innovations as well as improvements in functional strategies (e.g., more-efficient supply chain management and more-effective marketing—think of Apple's reinvented retail outlets) further pushed out the productivity frontier, now indicated by the solid line. Under Steve Jobs's leadership, Apple's successful innovations (iPhone, iTunes, iPad, iBookstore) and operational effectiveness allow the firm to maintain a strong strategic position as a differentiator, and thus sustain its competitive advantage.

On the other hand, by 2010 Dell's strategic position as cost leader appeared no longer as valuable as in the early 2000s, because one of the key competitive success factors in 2010 became product differentiation. Thus, Dell was attempting to change its strategic position, moving from its extreme cost-leadership strategy toward more differentiation. In 2007, founder Michael Dell returned from retirement to take over as CEO. In 2008, Dell hired an industrial designer from Nike to come up with colorful futuristic designs for its product offerings.[56] In 2009, Dell purchased Perot Systems, an IT service provider, for $3.9 billion to further enhance its differential appeal and to better compete with HP, which acquired EDS, another IT service provider, for $13 billion in 2008.[57] Yet, Dell is learning first-hand that reconciling the trade-offs inherent in pursuing low cost and differentiation simultaneously is non-trivial. As Exhibit 6.10 shows, although Dell is moving toward the differentiation axis, it had not reached the productivity frontier in 2010, and thus was experiencing a competitive disadvantage.

Under the leadership of CEO Mark Hurd, HP made significant progress toward reducing cost, by trimming its work force by about 10 percent, while also increasing the differential appeal of its product and service offerings. This performance allowed HP to move closer toward the productivity frontier, and to stake out a more clearly defined strategic position as an integrator.

In summary, strategic positioning is critical to gaining competitive advantage. Well-formulated and implemented generic business strategies (i.e., low cost *or* differentiation) enhance the firm's chances of obtaining superior performance. In some instances, a few exceptional firms might be able to reconcile the significant trade-offs between increasing value and lowering production cost by pursuing both business strategies simultaneously. These integration strategies tend to be successful only if a firm is able to rely on an innovation that allows it to reconcile the trade-offs mentioned (such as Toyota in the 1980s and 1990s with its lean-manufacturing approach, before that approach diffused widely).

Given the dynamics of competitive positioning, firms cannot stand still but must constantly refine and improve their strategic position over time. The goal is to not fall behind the productivity frontier, which is defined by the theoretically possible best practice at any given time. Since innovation is such an essential part of business strategy and competitive advantage, we now turn to discussing innovation in much more detail in the next chapter.

CHAPTER CASE **6** | *Consider This . . .*

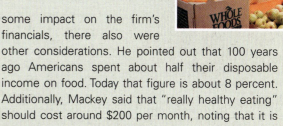

WHOLE FOODS continues to seek ways to differentiate itself from the competition. As the ChapterCase noted, the firm spends 5 percent of its net profits on a variety of charities, and it also provides opportunities for patrons to contribute to such causes.

In September 2010, Whole Foods enhanced a "back-to-school" project it started in 2009. It set a goal to put 300 salad bars in public schools within a 50-miles radius of any Whole Foods store. The firm solicited contributions from customers for this cause. In February 2011, Whole Foods announced the fund-raising had surpassed the original $750,000 goal. With over $1.4 million in collections, the company expanded the program to more than 500 elementary, middle, and high schools across the United States. Whole Foods is also expanding its in-store educational efforts with "wellness clubs" in some stores in the summer of 2011. These dedicated areas of the store give customers a chance to learn first-hand about healthy cooking and eating.[58]

In an interview on the impact of the recent recession, CEO John Mackey noted that while there was some impact on the firm's financials, there also were other considerations. He pointed out that 100 years ago Americans spent about half their disposable income on food. Today that figure is about 8 percent. Additionally, Mackey said that "really healthy eating" should cost around $200 per month, noting that it is the processing of foods that drives up food prices. The least-expensive way to eat, Mackey advised, is by sticking with whole grains, beans, seasonal plants and produce, and proper home cooking.[59]

1. What value drivers is Whole Foods using to remain differentiated in the face of Walmart and other competitors now selling organic foods? (Looking back at Exhibit 6.9 may be useful.)

2. Given the discussion in the ChapterCase about Whole Foods trimming its cost structure, does the firm risk being "stuck in the middle"? Why or why not?

3. What other methods could Whole Foods use to successfully drive its business strategy?

Take-Away Concepts

This chapter discussed two generic business-level strategies (*differentiation* and *cost-leadership*), some factors that companies can use to drive those strategies, and *integration strategy,* the attempt to find a competitive advantage by reconciling the trade-offs between the two generic business strategies, as summarized by the following learning objectives and related take-away concepts.

LO 6-1 Define business-level strategy and describe how it determines a firm's strategic position.

>> Business-level strategy determines a firm's strategic position in its quest for competitive advantage when competing in a single industry or product market.

>> Strategic positioning requires that managers address strategic trade-offs that arise between value and cost, because higher value tends to go along with higher cost.

>> Differentiation and cost leadership are distinct strategic positions.

>> Besides selecting an appropriate strategic position, managers must also define the scope of competition—whether to pursue a specific market niche or go after the broader market.

LO 6-2 Examine the relationship between value drivers and differentiation strategy.

>> The goal of a differentiation strategy is to increase the perceived value of goods and services so that customers will pay a higher price for additional features.

>> In a differentiation strategy, the focus of competition is on non-price attributes.

>> Some of the unique value drivers managers can manipulate are product features, customer service, customization, and complements.

>> Value drivers contribute to competitive advantage only if their increase in value creation (ΔV) exceeds the increase in costs (ΔC).

LO 6-3 Examine the relationship between cost drivers and cost-leadership strategy.

>> The goal of a cost-leadership strategy is to reduce the firm's cost below that of its competitors.

>> In a cost-leadership strategy, the focus of competition is on lowest-possible price, while offering acceptable value.

>> Some of the unique cost drivers that managers can manipulate are the cost of input factors, economies of scale, and learning and experience curve effects.

>> No matter how low the price, if there is no acceptable value proposition, the product or service will not sell.

LO 6-4 Assess the benefits and risks of cost leadership and differentiation business strategies vis-à-vis the five forces that shape competition.

>> The five forces model helps managers use generic business strategies to protect themselves against the industry forces that drive down profitability.

>> Differentiation and cost-leadership strategies allow firms to carve out strong strategic positions, not only to protect themselves against the five forces, but also to benefit from them in their quest for competitive advantage.

>> Exhibit 6.7 lists benefits and risks of each business strategy.

LO 6-5 Explain why it is difficult to succeed at an integration strategy.

>> A successful integration strategy requires that trade-offs between differentiation and low cost be reconciled.

>> Integration strategy often is difficult because the two distinct strategic positions require internal value chain activities that are fundamentally different from one another.

>> When firms fail to resolve strategic trade-offs between differentiation and cost, they end up being stuck in the middle. They then succeed at neither strategy, leading to a competitive disadvantage.

LO 6-6 Evaluate value and cost drivers that may allow a firm to pursue an integration strategy.

>> To address the trade-offs between differentiation and cost leadership at the business level, managers may leverage quality, economies of scope, innovation, and the firm's structure, culture, and routines.

>> The trade-offs between differentiation and low cost can either be addressed at the business level or at the corporate level.

LO 6-7 Describe and evaluate the dynamics of competitive positioning.

>> Strategic positions need to change over time as the environment changes.

>> Best practices determine the productivity frontier at any given time.

>> Reaching the productivity frontier enhances the likelihood of obtaining a competitive advantage.

>> Not reaching the productivity frontier implies competitive disadvantage if other firms *are* positioned at the productivity frontier.

Key Terms

Ambidextrous organization (p. 158)

Business-level strategy (p. 140)

Conglomerate (p. 160)

Cost-leadership strategy (p. 142)

Differentiation strategy (p. 142)

Diseconomies of scale (p. 150)

Economies of scale (p. 149)

Economies of scope (p. 157)

Focused cost-leadership strategy (p. 142)

Focused differentiation strategy (p. 142)

Integration strategy (p. 155)

Mass customization (p. 146)

Minimum efficient scale (MES) (p. 150)

Productivity frontier (p. 161)

Scope of competition (p. 142)

Strategic position (p. 141)

Strategic trade-offs (p. 141)

Discussion Questions

1. What are some drawbacks and risks to a broad generic business strategy? To a focused strategy?

2. How do economies of scale and economies of scope differ?

3. How can a firm attempting to have an integrated business-level strategy manage to avoid being "stuck in the middle"?

4. In Chapter 4, we discussed the internal value chain activities a firm can perform in its business model (see Exhibit 4.6). The value chain priorities can be quite different for firms taking different business strategies. Create examples of value chains for three firms: one using cost leadership, another using differentiation, and a third using an integration business-level strategy.

Ethical/Social Issues

1. Suppose Procter & Gamble (P&G) learns that a relatively new startup company Method (www. methodhome.com) is gaining market share with a new laundry detergent in West Coast markets. In response, P&G lowers the price of its Tide detergent from $15 to $9 for a 32-load bottle only in markets where Method's product is for sale. The goal of this "loss leader" price drop is to encourage Method to leave the laundry detergent market. Is this an ethical business practice? Why or why not?

2. A company such as Intel has a complex design and manufacturing process. This should lead Intel management to be concerned with the learning curves of employees. What practices would foster or hinder the hiring, training, and retention of key employees?

Small Group Exercises

SMALL GROUP EXERCISE 1

Ryanair (see Strategy Highlight 6.2) is noted as a firm that can make a profit on an $8 ticket by imposing numerous fees and surcharges.

1. Generally an ethical business practice is to disclose fees to potential customers to permit effective cost comparisons. Log onto www.ryanair. com and determine if Ryanair has transparent disclosure of these fees.

2. If you were a competitor in the European market, such as Aer Lingus or Lufthansa, how would you compete against Ryanair knowing your cost structure would not allow price parity?

SMALL GROUP EXERCISE 2

1. In the next column is a list of prominent firms. Place each firm you know (or research online) in one of the five categories of generic business-level strategies—broad cost-leadership, focused cost-leadership, broad differentiation, focused differentiation, and integration. Explain your choices.

2. What are some common features for firms you have placed within each category?

Ann Taylor	McKinsey & Co.
BIC	Nike
Big Lots	Patek Philippe
Black & Decker	Porsche
Clif Bar	Rhapsody
Coca-Cola	Rolls-Royce
Dollar Stores	Ryanair
Google	Samuel Adams
Goya Foods	Singapore Airlines
Greyhound Lines	Target
Kia Motors	Toyota
Lands' End	Vanguard
Liberty Mutual	Victoria's Secret
Louis Vuitton	WellPoint
Martin Guitars	Zara

Strategy Term Project

MODULE 6: BUSINESS STRATEGY

In this module, we will look at the business model your selected company uses and analyze its business-level strategy to see if it is appropriate for the strategic position. If your firm is a large multibusiness entity, you will need to choose one of the major businesses (strategic business unit, or SBU) of the firm for this analysis. In prior chapters, we collected information about this firm's external environment and some of its internal competitive advantages. Using this information and any other you have gathered, address the following questions.

1. Does your selected business have differentiated products or services? If so, what is the basis for this differentiation from the competition?

2. Does your firm have a cost-leadership position in this business? If so, can you identify which cost drivers it uses effectively to hold this position?

3. What is your firm's approach to the market? If it segments the market, identify the scope of competition it is using.

4. Using the answers to the preceding questions, identify which generic business strategies your firm is employing. Is the firm leveraging the appropriate value and cost drivers for the business strategy you identified? Explain why or why not.

5. As noted in the chapter, each business strategy is context-dependent. What do you see as positives and negatives with the selected business strategy of your firm in its competitive situation?

6. In Chapter 3, we identified strategic groups in the industry relevant to your firm. Review the firms listed in the same strategic group as your selected firm. See if there is a similarity with the generic business strategy used by each. In most strategic groups, there will be market and some strategy similarities across the firms.

7. What suggestions do you have to improve the firm's business strategy and strategic position?

*my*Strategy

DIFFERENT VALUE AND COST DRIVERS— WHAT DETERMINES *YOUR* BUYING DECISIONS?

Differentiation positioning versus low-cost strategies can be particularly pronounced in the retailing sector. As noted in the ChapterCase, Whole Foods is a differentiated grocery store that is finding it necessary to respond to low-cost leaders, such as Walmart, that have entered the organic food market. Additionally, Whole Foods must contend with a possibly shrinking market segment of customers who will pay extra for organic foods in an economic downturn. Some customers who might enjoy going to Whole Foods are finding they get more for their money at a traditional grocer such as Publix or Safeway.

What role does the awareness of a firm's strategy have on your buying decisions? Will you select (or stay away from) certain brands due to their position on global warming or certain social causes? Or are price and availability the real drivers of your purchasing dollars?

What if you needed to buy a pair of casual shoes? You have budgeted $60 for this purchase. You are in a local store and you have found two pairs of shoes you like. They are both $55. One is made by a company whose shoes you have purchased before, and you found the shoes durable and comfortable. The other pair is made by a newer company; you've never owned their products but a friend of yours told you a bit about the company before class a few weeks ago. (He also had been shopping for shoes.) The following is a brief write-up on each company. Which shoes do you buy?

1. G.H. Bass was founded in 1876 in Wilton, Maine, and over its storied history has largely maintained a differentiated position of high quality and comfortable casual shoes. The Bass Weejun loafer was introduced in the U.S. in 1936 and has continued to propel the firm as one of America's top-selling shoe brands. They also retail in Europe, Asia, and South America.

2. TOMS shoes was launched in 2006 in Venice, California, with a canvas shoe design adapted from Argentina, the alpargata. The shoes are sold via the company's website www.tomsshoes.com and also through a limited number of retail stores in the U.S., Europe, parts of Asia, and South America. From the start, TOMS has included a social aspect to the firm. For every pair of shoes purchased, TOMS sends one free pair to a child who can't afford to buy shoes. The firm also sponsors "shoe drops" and will sometimes have celebrity participants in the free-shoe-distribution events. In September 2010, the company's "One for One" program surpassed one million pairs of shoes provided to children in need.[60]

Endnotes

1. This ChapterCase is based on: "Frank talk from Whole Foods' John Mackey," *The Wall Street Journal,* August 4, 2009; "As sales slip, Whole Foods tries to push health," *The Wall Street Journal,* August 5, 2009; and "The conscience of a capitalist," *The Wall Street Journal,* October 3, 2009, www.wholefoodsmarket.com.

2. This discussion is based on: Porter, M. E. (1980), *Competitive Strategy: Techniques for Analyzing Industries and Competitors* (New York: Free Press); Porter, M. E. (1985), *Competitive Advantage: Creating and Sustaining Superior Performance* (New York: Free Press); Porter, M. E. (1996), "What is strategy?" *Harvard Business Review,* November–December; and Porter, M. E. (2008), "The five competitive forces that shape strategy," *Harvard Business Review,* January.

3. These questions are based on: Abell, D. F. (1980), *Defining the Business: The Starting Point of Strategic Planning* (Englewood Cliffs, NJ: Prentice-Hall); Porter, M. E. (1996), "What is strategy?"; and Priem, R. (2007), "A consumer perspective on value creation," *Academy of Management Review* 32: 219–235.

4. Porter, M. E. (1996), "What is strategy?"

5. The discussion of generic business strategies is based on: Porter, M. E. (1980), *Competitive Strategy: Techniques for Analyzing Industries and Competitors*; Porter, M. E. (1985), *Competitive Advantage: Creating and Sustaining Superior Performance*; Porter, M. E. (1996), "What is strategy?"; and Porter, M. E. (2008), "The five competitive forces that shape strategy."

6. To decide if and how to divide up the market, you can apply the market segmentation techniques you have acquired in your marketing and micro-economics classes.

7. Elon Musk in "Uber Entrepreneur: An Evening with Elon Musk," Churchill Club, Mountain View, CA, April 7, 2009 (available at ForaTV: http://fora.tv/2009/04/07/Uber_Entrepreneur_An_Evening_with_Elon_Musk).

8. Anderson, R. C., and R. White (2009), *Confessions of a Radical Industrialist: Profits, People, Purpose—Doing Business by Respecting the Earth* (New York: St. Martin's Press).

9. "Latest Starbucks buzzword: 'Lean' Japanese techniques," *The Wall Street Journal,* August 4, 2009.

10. Christensen, C. M., and M. E. Raynor (2003), *The Innovator's Solution: Creating and Sustaining Successful Growth* (Boston, MA: Harvard Business School Press).

11. The interested reader is referred to the strategy, marketing, and economics literatures. A good start in the strategy literature is the classic work of M. E. Porter: Porter, M. E. (1980), *Competitive Strategy: Techniques for Analyzing Industries and Competitors*; Porter, M. E. (1985), *Competitive Advantage: Creating and Sustaining Superior Performance*; and Porter, M. E. (2008), "The five competitive forces that shape strategy."

12. www.oxo.com/about.jsp.

13. "Amazon opens wallet, buys Zappos," *The Wall Street Journal,* July 23, 2009.

14. Hsieh, T. (2010), *Delivering Happiness: A Path to Profits, Passion, and Purpose* (New York: Business Plus).

15. This strategy highlight is based on: Gladwell, M. (2000), *The Tipping Point: How Little Things Can Make a Big Difference* (New York: Little, Brown and Company); Liker, J. (2003), *The Toyota Way* (Burr Ridge, IL: McGraw-Hill); Dawson, C. (2004), *Lexus: The Relentless Pursuit* (Hoboken, NJ: Wiley); Collins, J. (2009), *How the Mighty Fall and Why Some Companies Never Give In* (New York: HarperCollins); "Toyota recall spreads to Europe, China," *The Wall Street Journal,* January 28, 2010; "Car maker's fixes may not solve issue," *The Wall Street Journal,* February 24, 2010; and "Recall dims Japan's export outlook," *The Wall Street Journal,* February 24, 2010.

16. Davis, S. M. (1987), *Future Perfect* (Reading, MA: Addison-Wesley).

17. www.att.com/u-verse/.

18. See a discussion of Southwest Airlines's business activities in Chapter 5.

19. This strategy highlight is based on: Anderson, C. (2009), *Free: The Future of a Radical Price* (New York: Hyperion); "Walmart with wings," *BusinessWeek,* November 27, 2006; "Snarling all the way to the bank," *The Economist,* August 23, 2007; and "Ryanair's O'Leary: The duke of discomfort," *Bloomberg Businessweek,* September 2, 2010, www.ryanair.com.

20. Friedman, T. (2005), *The World is Flat: A Brief History of the Twenty-First*

Century (New York: Farrar, Strauss and Giroux).

21. "Boeing looks beyond Dreamliner's first flight," *The Wall Street Journal,* December 15, 2009, www.boeing.com.

22. www.airbus.com/en/aircraftfamilies/a380/home/.

23. Kevin Turner, COO Microsoft. Keynote Speech at Microsoft's Worldwide Partner Conference, New Orleans, July 15, 2009.

24. "Fiat nears stake in Chrysler that could lead to takeover," *The Wall Street Journal,* January 20, 2009.

25. "GM hopes Volt juices its future," *The Wall Street Journal,* August 12, 2009.

26. "Nucor's new plant project still on hold," *Associated Press,* July 23, 2009, www.nucor.com.

27. Gladwell, M. (2002), *The Tipping Point: How Little Things Can Make a Big Difference* (New York: Back Bay Books) p. 185.

28. Levitt, B., and J. G. March (1988), "Organizational learning," in Scott, W. R. (ed.), *Annual Review of Sociology* 14: 319–340 (Greenwich, CT: JAI Press).

29. For insightful reviews and syntheses on the learning curve literature, see: Yelle, L. E. (1979), "The learning curve: Historical review and comprehensive survey," *Decision Sciences* 10: 302–308; and Argote, L., and G. Todorova (2007), "Organizational learning: Review and future directions," in Hodgkinson, G. P., and J. K. Ford (eds.), *International Review of Industrial and Organizational Psychology* 22: 193–234 (New York: Wiley).

30. Wright, T. P. (1936). "Factors affecting the cost of airplanes," *Journal of Aeronautical Sciences* 3: 122–128.

31. This discussion is based on: Darr, E. D., L. Argote, and D. Epple (1995), "The acquisition, transfer and depreciation of knowledge in service organizations: Productivity in franchises," *Management Science* 42: 1750–1762; King, A. W., and A. L. Ranft (2001), "Capturing knowledge and knowing through improvisation: What managers can learn from the thoracic surgery board certification process," *Journal of Management* 27: 255–277; Zollo, M., J. J. Reuer, and H. Singh (2002), "Interorganizational routines

and performance in strategic alliances," *Organization Science* 13: 701–713; Hoang, H., and F. T. Rothaermel (2005), "The effect of general and partner-specific alliance experience on joint R&D project performance," *Academy of Management Journal* 48: 332–345; Rothaermel, F. T., and D. L. Deeds (2006), "Alliance type, alliance experience, and alliance management capability in high-technology ventures," *Journal of Business Venturing* 21: 429–460; Pisano, G. P., R. M. Bohmer, and A. C. Edmondson (2001), "Organizational differences in rates of learning: Evidence from the adoption of minimally invasive cardiac surgery," *Management Science* 47: 752–768; Edmondson, A. C., R. M. Bohmer, and G. P. Pisano (2001), "Disrupted routines: Team learning and new technology implementation in hospitals," *Administrative Science Quarterly* 46: 685–716; Thompson, P. (2001), "How much did the liberty shipbuilders learn? New evidence from an old case study," *Journal of Political Economy* 109: 103–137; and Gulati, R., D. Lavie, and H. Singh (2009), "The nature of partnering experience and the gain from alliances," *Strategic Management Journal* 30: 1213–1233.

32. Ramanarayanan, S. (2008), "Does practice make perfect: An empirical analysis of learning-by-doing in cardiac surgery." Available at SSRN: http://ssrn.com/abstract=1129350.

33. Technically speaking, learning effects occur over time as output is accumulated, while economies of scale are captured at one point in time when output is increased. Although learning peters out at some point (as shown in Exhibit 6.10 as learning curves flatten out), there are no diseconomies to learning (as shown in Exhibit 6.8 past output Q_2).

34. Boston Consulting Group (1972), *Perspectives on Experience* (Boston, MA: Boston Consulting Group).

35. This discussion is based on: Porter, M. E. (1979), "How competitive forces shape strategy," *Harvard Business Review,* March–April: 137–145; Porter, M. E. (1980), *Competitive Strategy. Techniques for Analyzing Industries and Competitors;* and Porter, M. E. (2008), "The five competitive forces that shape strategy."

36. This discussion is based on: Hill, C.W.L. (1988), "Differentiation versus low cost or differentiation and low cost: A contingency framework," *Academy of Management Review* 13: 401–412; and Miller, A., and G. G. Dess (1993), "Assessing Porter's model in terms of its generalizability, accuracy, and simplicity," *Journal of Management Studies* 30: 553–585.

37. "Would you spend $14,000 for this bike? Techies drive demand for custom models," *The Boston Globe,* April 23, 2006.

38. www.leopardcycles.com/about.php.

39. "Avon to spruce up its R&D budget with $100 million and new facility," *The Wall Street Journal,* May 23, 2002.

40. "Avon plans to realign European manufacturing to meet accelerating demand and reduce costs," *Associated Press,* April 12, 2002.

41. This discussion is based on: Afuah, A. (2009), *Strategic Innovation. New Game Strategies for Competitive Advantage* (New York: Routledge); Hill, C.W.L., and F. T. Rothaermel (2003), "The performance of incumbent firms in the face of radical technological innovation," *Academy of Management Review* 28: 257–274; Rothaermel, F. T., and A. Hess, "Finding an innovation strategy that works," *The Wall Street Journal,* August 17, 2009; and Rothaermel, F. T., and A. Hess (2010), "Innovation strategies combined," *MIT Sloan Management Review,* Spring: 12–15.

42. "IKEA: How the Swedish retailer became a global cult brand," *BusinessWeek,* November 14, 2005.

43. This discussion is based on: O'Reilly, C. A., III, and M. L. Tushman (2007), "Ambidexterity as dynamic capability: Resolving the innovator's dilemma," *Research in Organizational Behavior* 28: 1–60; Raisch, S., and J. Birkinshaw (2008), "Organizational ambidexterity: Antecedents, outcomes, and moderators," *Journal of Management* 34: 375–409; and Rothaermel, F. T., and M. T. Alexandre (2009), "Ambidexterity in technology sourcing: The moderating role of absorptive capacity," *Organization Science* 20: 759–780.

44. Hamel, G. (2006), "The why, what, and how of management innovation," *Harvard Business Review,* February.

45. March, J. G. (1991), "Exploration and exploitation in organizational learning," *Organization Science* 2: 319–340; and Levinthal, D. A., and J. G. March (1993), "The myopia of learning," *Strategic Management Journal* 14: 95–112.

46. Author's interviews with Intel managers and engineers.

47. Brown, S. L., and K. M. Eisenhardt (1997), "The art of continuous change: Linking complexity theory and time-paced evolution in relentlessly shifting organizations," *Administrative Science Quarterly* 42: 1–34; and O'Reilly, C. A., B. Harreld, and M. Tushman (2009), "Organizational ambidexterity: IBM and emerging business opportunities," *California Management Review* 51: 75–99.

48. This discussion is based on: Porter, M. E. (1980), *Competitive Strategy*; and Porter, M. E. (1996), "What is strategy?"

49. This example is based on: "No small achievement," *The Economist,* March

26, 2009; "The new people's car," *The Economist,* March 26, 2009; and "Tata takes charge," *The Economist,* August 20, 2009.

50. Christensen, C. M., and M. E. Raynor (2003), *The Innovator's Solution: Creating and Sustaining Successful Growth* (Boston, MA: Harvard Business School Press).

51. Tushman, M., W. K. Smith, R. C. Wood, G. Westerman, and C. O. O'Reilly (2010), "Organizational designs and innovation streams," *Industrial and Corporate Change* 19: 1331–1366.

52. "eBay retreats in web retailing," *The Wall Street Journal,* March 12, 2009.

53. "eBay sells Skype to investor group," *The Wall Street Journal,* September 1, 2009.

54. Porter, M. E. (1996), "What is strategy?"

55. The shape of the productivity frontier is concave to indicate the trade-offs between low cost and differentiation.

56. "Taking the dull out of Dell," *BusinessWeek,* November 3, 2008.

57. "Dell to buy Perot in catch-up deal," *The Wall Street Journal,* September 22, 2009.

58. Material for this case discussion is from: "More than 500 schools awarded grants for salad bars," Whole Foods Market Press Release, February 1, 2011, www.wholefoodsmarket.com/backtoschool/; and "ECO:nomics: Whole Foods CEO says eating healthy costs less," WSJ Video, March 3, 2011.

59. "ECO:nomics: Whole Foods CEO says eating healthy costs less."

60. This section is based on: https://basss-hoes.harborghb.com/bass-shoes-history; Jennifer Irwin, "The lowly alpargata steps forward," *The New York Times,* January 17, 2007; and www.tomsshoes.com.

CHAPTER 7

Business Strategy: Innovation and Strategic Entrepreneurship

LEARNING OBJECTIVES

After studying this chapter, you will be able to:

LO 7-1 Define innovation and describe its role in the competitive process.

LO 7-2 Describe the competitive implications of different stages in the industry life cycle.

LO 7-3 Apply strategic management concepts to entrepreneurship and innovation.

LO 7-4 Evaluate different types of innovation and derive their strategic implications.

LO 7-5 Describe the long-tail concept and derive strategic implications.

LO 7-6 Evaluate discontinuities and describe the dynamics of paradigm changes.

LO 7-7 Identify the process leading to hypercompetition, and explain why competitive advantage can often be sustained through continuous innovation.

From Encyclopedia Britannica to Encarta to Wikipedia

HAILING BACK TO the 18th-century Scottish Enlightenment, the *Encyclopedia Britannica* was once the gold standard for authoritative reference works, delving into more than 65,000 topics with articles by some 4,000 scholarly contributors, including many by Nobel Laureates. The beautiful leather-bound, multivolume set made a nice decorative item in many literate homes.

In the early 1990s, when total sales for encyclopedias were over $1.2 billion annually, *Encyclopedia Britannica* was the undisputed market leader, holding more than 50 percent market share and earning some $650 million in revenues. Not surprisingly, its superior differentiated appeal was highly correlated with cost, reflected in its steep sticker price of up to $2,000.

Innovation changed all that. Banking on the widespread diffusion of the personal computer, Microsoft launched its electronic encyclopedia Encarta in 1993 at a price of $99. Although some viewed it as merely a CD-version of the lower-cost and lower-quality *Funk & Wagnall's Encyclopedia,* sold in supermarkets, Encarta still took a big bite out of Britannica's market.

Within only three years, the market for printed encyclopedias had shrunk by half, and Britannica's revenues along with it, while Microsoft sold over $100 million worth of Encarta CDs.

In 2001, Internet entrepreneur Jimmy Wales launched Wikipedia, the free online multilanguage encyclopedia. In Hawaiian, *wiki* means quick, referring to the instant do-it-yourself editing capabilities of the site. Wikipedia now has 18 million articles in 281 languages, including over 3.6 million items in English.

Since it is open source, any person, expert or novice, can contribute content and edit pages using the handy "edit this page" button. Thousands of Wikipedians across the world have done so.

Although Wikipedia's volume of English entries is almost 40 times greater than that of Britannica, the site is not as error-prone as you might think. Wikipedia relies on the "wisdom of the crowds," which assumes "the many" often know more than the expert. A peer-reviewed study by *Nature* of 42 science topics found four errors in Wikipedia and three in Britannica. Such errors can be corrected more or less in real time on Wikipedia, whereas Britannica must wait until its next printing.

Because Wikipedia was able to significantly increase value creation and drive costs to zero, there is little future for printed or CD-based encyclopedias. Today, Wikipedia is one of the most-visited websites in the world.[1]

After reading the chapter, you will find more about this case, with related questions, on page 193.

▲ **INNOVATION IS** a powerful driver in the competitive process. With introduction of its CD-based Encarta, Microsoft destroyed about half the value created by Britannica. In turn, Wikipedia used the Internet to destroy Encarta's business, which Microsoft shut down in 2009. At the same time, Wikipedia created substantial value for consumers because it shifted value creation and capture away from Britannica's and Microsoft's proprietary business models for encyclopedias to an open-source model powered by user-generated content. Innovation enables firms to redefine the marketplace in their favor and achieve growth.[2] As a key aspect of business strategy formulation, innovation and the related topic of strategic entrepreneurship are the focus of this chapter.

COMPETITION DRIVEN BY INNOVATION

Invention describes the discovery of any new product, process, or idea, or the modification and recombination of existing ones; innovation concerns the *commercialization* thereof.[3] For example, the Wright brothers invented the airplane, which was commercialized by Boeing and others. As shown in Exhibit 7.1, an innovation needs to be novel, useful, and successfully implemented in order to help firms gain and sustain a competitive advantage.

The successful commercialization of a new product or service allows a firm to extract temporary monopoly profits. Initially, for example, Apple faced no direct competition to its iPhone. Its smartphone innovation reshaped the mobile phone industry structure in its favor, resulting in a competitive advantage. To sustain a competitive advantage, however, a firm must continuously innovate—that is, it must produce a string of successful new products or services over time. In this spirit, not only has Apple introduced the improved iPhone 4, it also has launched the iPad, a multimedia tablet computer, in early 2010 with the intent to drive convergence in computing, telecommunications, and media content. The iPad is also positioned to challenge Amazon's Kindle, the market leader in e-book readers. Continuous innovation is the engine behind many other successful companies, such as 3M, GE, Google, HP, Intel, P&G, and Sony.

innovation The commercialization of any new product, process, or idea, or the modification and recombination of existing ones. To drive growth, innovation also needs to be useful and successfully implemented.

Competition is a process driven by the "perennial gale of creative destruction," in the words of economist Joseph Schumpeter.[4] The continuous waves of leadership changes in the encyclopedia business, detailed in the ChapterCase, demonstrate the potency of innovation as a competitive weapon: It can simultaneously create and destroy value. Firms must be able to innovate while also fending off competitors' innovations. A successful strategy requires both an effective offense and a hard-to-crack defense.

Many firms have dominated an early wave of innovation only to be destroyed by the next wave. Examples include:

- *The move from typewriters to computers:* Wang Laboratories, a computer company that led the market for word-processing machines, destroyed typewriter companies like Smith Corona and Underwood. It then was undone by computer makers like IBM and Compaq. Today, IBM has exited the personal computer market, selling its PC division to the Chinese technology company Lenovo, and Compaq has been acquired by HP.

- *The explosion of television-viewing options:* The traditional television networks (ABC, CBS, and NBC) have been struggling to maintain viewers and advertising

EXHIBIT 7.1

Innovation: A Novel and Useful Idea that Is Successfully Implemented

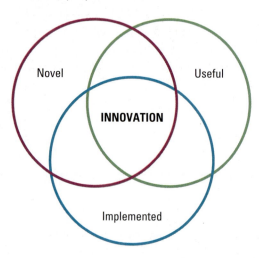

revenues as cable and satellite providers have offered innovative programming. Those same cable and satellite providers are trying hard to hold on to viewers as more and more people gravitate toward customized content online. To exploit such opportunities, Google acquired YouTube in 2006 for $1.65 billion, and Comcast, the largest cable operator in the U.S., purchased a majority stake in NBC Universal in 2009 valued at close to $14 billion.[5] Comcast's acquisition helps it integrate delivery services and content, with the goal of establishing itself as a new player in the media industry.

■ *The trend toward drugs designed for individual patients:* Established pharmaceutical companies like Merck and Pfizer brought major new drugs to market within the past decade, using a chemical-based drug discovery and development paradigm. These same companies are struggling to maintain their dominance as relative newcomers like Amgen and Genentech are leveraging advances in genomics, genetic engineering, and biotechnology to produce drugs that are better targeted to treat diseases and that eventually can be designed for individual patients.

We now turn to a discussion of how the role of innovation in driving competitive behavior changes throughout the evolution of an industry.

INNOVATION AND THE INDUSTRY LIFE CYCLE

Innovations frequently lead to the birth of new industries. Innovative advances in IT and logistics facilitated the creation of the overnight express delivery industry by FedEx and big-box retailing by Walmart. The Internet set online retailing in motion, with new companies such as Amazon and eBay taking the lead, and revolutionized the advertising industry through Yahoo and Google. Currently, advances in nanotechnology promise to revolutionize many different industries, ranging from medical diagnostics and surgery to lighter and stronger airplane components.[6]

Industries tend to follow a predictable **industry life cycle:** As an industry evolves over time, we can identify four distinct stages: *introduction, growth, maturity,* and *decline.* Exhibit 7.2 depicts a typical industry life cycle, with corresponding consumer-adoption categories.[7]

>> **LO 7-2**
Describe the competitive implications of different stages in the industry life cycle.

industry life cycle
The four different stages—introduction, growth, maturity, and decline—that occur in the evolution of an industry over time.

EXHIBIT 7.2

The Industry Life Cycle and Consumer-Adoption Categories

The number and size of competitors change as the industry life cycle unfolds. Likewise, different types of consumers enter the market at each stage. Thus, both the supply and demand sides of the market change as the industry ages. Each stage of the industry life cycle requires different competencies in order for the firm to perform well and satisfy that stage's unique customer group. In this chapter, we illustrate how the type of innovation changes at each stage of the life cycle as well as how innovation can initiate and drive a new life cycle. Be aware, too, that other factors such as fads in fashion, changes in demographics, or de-regulation, can affect the dynamics behind industry life cycles.

Introduction Stage

When an individual or company launches a successful innovation, a new industry may emerge. In this introductory stage, the innovator's core competency is R&D, necessary to creating a new product category that will attract customers. This is a capital-intensive process, in which the innovator is investing in designing a unique product, trying new ideas to attract customers, and producing small quantities—all of which contribute to a high price when the product is launched. Initial market growth is slow: Only *early adopters* are willing to pay a premium price to have the latest gadget. They frequently tolerate technological imperfections and like to tinker with the products. For example, the GRiD Compass was introduced as a laptop for early adopters in the early 1980s. By today's standards, it was not only heavy (almost three times the weight of today's laptops), but also expensive, costing about $18,000 in today's dollars. The performance of a new product also tends to be inferior in some respects. For example, not only were early laptops almost too heavy to carry around, their computing power and display capabilities were only a fraction of those available in a desktop computer.

In this introductory stage, when barriers to entry tend to be high, generally only a few innovators are active in the market. They emphasize unique product features and performance rather than price. When introduced in the spring of 2010, for example, Apple's iPad was priced at $499 for 16GB of storage space and $829 for 64GB with a 3G Wi-Fi connection.[8] Despite those hefty prices, early adopters eagerly lined up.

While there are some benefits to being early in the market, such as building a reputation for innovation, innovators also encounter some first-mover disadvantages. They must educate potential customers about the product's intended benefits, find distribution channels and complementary assets, and continue to perfect the fledgling product. While a core competency in R&D is necessary to create or enter an industry in the introductory stage, some competency in marketing also is helpful in achieving market acceptance. Competition can be intense, and early winners are well-positioned to stake out a strong position for the future. For example, though they have attracted challengers, the innovators in the personal computer industry, such as Intel and Microsoft, are still holding on to their lead some 30 years later.

The strategic objective during the introductory stage is to achieve market acceptance and seed future growth. One way to accomplish these objectives is to leverage network effects,[9] the positive effect that one user of a product or service has on the value of that product for other users. Network effects occur when the value of a product or service increases, often exponentially, with the number of users. If successful, network effects propel the industry to the next stage of the life cycle, the growth stage (which we discuss next). In the early days of the Internet, for instance, only a small network of scientists had access to e-mail. Today, e-mail is a ubiquitous communications tool with more than a billion users, and thus is much more valuable to users. Strategy Highlight 7.1 describes how Apple leveraged the network effects generated by countless complementary software applications (apps) to achieve dominance in the smartphone market.

network effects
The positive effect (externality) that one user of a product or service has on the value of that product for other users.

Apple Leverages Network Effects to Propel Growth

Apple launched its enormously successful iPhone in the summer of 2007. A year later, it followed up with the Apple App Store, which boasts that, for almost anything you might need, "there's an app for that." *Apps* are software programs developed to provide mobile users with small and inexpensive business and personal services wherever they may be. They allow iPhone (and now iPad) users to access their business contacts via LinkedIn, check their packages via FedEx, get the latest news on CNN, or engage in customer relations management using Salesforce. You can access Facebook to check on your friends and play social games such as FarmVille, where some 85 million players earn virtual currency by plowing fields and raising and trading livestock. Although the software programs are tiny, the industry is quite large. It is estimated to grow to over $4 billion by 2012, producing successful startups like Zynga (the maker of FarmVille) along the way.

Even more important is the effect apps have on the value of an iPhone. Arguably, the explosive growth of the iPhone is due to the fact that the Apple App Store offers a huge selection of apps to its users. (An estimated 300,000 apps were downloaded more than 10 billion times as of spring 2011.) In contrast, RIM (the maker of the BlackBerry), Nokia, and Microsoft are all playing

catch-up. The availability of apps, in turn, leads to network effects that increase the value of the iPhone for its users. Exhibit 7.3 shows how. Increased value creation, as we know from Chapter 6, is positively related to demand, which in turn increases the installed base of Apple iPhones. This in turn incentivizes software developers to write more apps, positively reinforcing the virtuous cycle. Making apps widely available helped Apple stake out a strong position in the smartphone industry. Moreover, all the apps, as well as purchases from the iTunes library and the newly created iBook store, are transferable from the iPhone to the iPad. Taken together, positive network efforts are likely to increase demand for the iPad as well.[10]

EXHIBIT 7.3

Leveraging Network Economics: Apple's iPhone

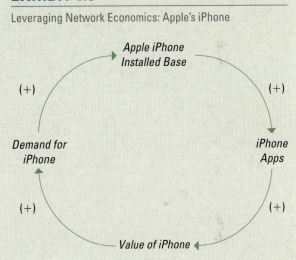

Growth Stage

Market growth accelerates in the second (the growth) stage of the industry life cycle. After the initial innovation has gained market acceptance, demand increases rapidly as first-time buyers rush to enter the market, convinced by the proof-of-concept demonstrated by early adopters in the introductory stage. The new group of buyers, called the *early majority,* is at the leading edge of a large customer wave. The early majority also sees the benefit that can be gained from adopting a new product or service.

As the size of the early majority expands, a **standard** (or *dominant design*) signals the market's agreement on a common set of engineering features and design choices.[11] An agreed-upon standard, such as the IBM PC, ensures that all components of the system work well together, regardless of who developed them. It also helps legitimize the new technology by reducing uncertainty and confusion. Thus, a standard or dominant design tends to capture a larger market share and can persist for a long time. The Wintel standard marked the beginning of exponential growth in the personal computer industry; it now holds about 90 percent of market share.

standard An agreed-upon solution about a common set of engineering features and design choices; also known as *dominant design.*

A more recent example is the high-definition format war to supersede standard DVDs and CDs. Blu-ray, backed by an association of electronics companies including Sony, Panasonic, Philips, LG, Hitachi, and Samsung, bested the HD-DVD format backed by Toshiba. Some argue that Sony's PlayStation 3 acted as a catalyst for adopting the Blu-ray format. A tipping point in favor of the Blu-ray format was reached when Warner Bros. decided to release discs only in Blu-ray format beginning in the summer of 2008. Within weeks, leading retailers such as Walmart, Best Buy, and the now-defunct Circuit City began carrying DVDs in Blu-ray format, and did not stock as large a selection in the HD-DVD format; Netflix and Blockbuster began renting Blu-ray DVDs predominantly. As a consequence, thousands of titles are now available on high-definition Blu-ray discs. The competitive implications are tremendous: Industry agreement on the format has opened a new market for both Blu-ray disc players and titles. Barriers to entry fell as technological uncertainties were overcome, and many new and established firms rushed to participate in the growth opportunity.

The high-def format war was fought in the marketplace. However, government bodies or industry associations can also set standards by making top-down decisions. The European Union determined in the 1980s that GSM (Global System for Mobile Communications) should be the standard for cell phones in Europe. The United States relied instead on a market-based approach, and CDMA (code division multiple access), a proprietary standard developed by Qualcomm, emerged as an early leader. While North American manufacturers and service providers such as AT&T, Verizon, Motorola, and others were fighting a format war, Scandinavian companies such as Nokia and Ericsson faced no such uncertainty, and they leveraged their early lead into market dominance. Today, about 80 percent of the global mobile market uses the GSM standard.

Since demand is strong during the growth phase, both efficient and inefficient firms thrive; the rising tide lifts all boats. Moreover, prices begin to fall as standard business processes are put in place and firms begin to reap economies of scale and learning. Distribution channels are thus expanded, and complementary assets become widely available.[12]

Though the emergence of a dominant design fosters the development of complementary assets, Strategy Highlight 7.2 shows that firms sometimes choose *not to support* certain new standards or applications.

After a standard or dominant design is established in an industry, the basis of competition tends to move away from product innovations toward process innovations.[13] **Product innovations,** as the name suggests, are embodied in new products—the jet airplane, electric vehicle, MP3 player, and netbook. On the other hand, **process innovations** are new ways to produce existing products or to deliver existing services. Process innovations are made possible through advances such as the Internet, lean manufacturing, Six Sigma, biotechnology, nanotechnology, and so on. The biotech startup Genentech, for example, was the first firm to use genetic engineering to discover and develop new medicines such as human insulin and human growth hormones.

As captured in Exhibit 7.4 (page 178), *product* innovation is the most important competitive weapon when initiating a new industry life cycle; at that point (typically, at the introduction stage), the level of process innovation at first is low. This pecking order, however, reverses over time. Eventually (usually in the growth stage), an industry standard emerges (indicated by the blue dashed line in the figure). At that point, most of the technological and commercial uncertainties about the new product are gone. After the market accepts a radical product innovation, and a standard for the new technology has emerged, *process* innovation rapidly becomes more important than product innovation. As market demand increases, economies of scale kick in: Firms establish and optimize standard business processes through applications of lean manufacturing, Six Sigma, and so on. As a consequence, product improvements become incremental, while the level of process innovation rises.

product innovations
New products, such as the jet airplane, electric vehicle, MP3 player, and netbook.

process innovations
New ways to produce existing products or deliver existing services.

Some Standards Die Hard: QWERTY vs. DSK

The QWERTY keyboard, named for the sequence of the first six letters on the upper-left row, was introduced in the 1870s as a way to *slow* typists in order to avoid jamming the type bars in mechanical typewriters. While generally considered an inefficient arrangement of the most frequently used letters, the QWERTY keyboard remains the standard today, but not for lack of alternatives.

In the 1930s, August Dvorak, a professor of education at the University of Washington, designed and patented an alternative keyboard intended to *speed up* typing. Professor Dvorak placed the most frequently used letters, such as vowels, in the center row where the typist's fingers rest, and he moved less commonly used letters to the first and third keyboard rows. This design, the Dvorak Simplified Keyboard or DSK, minimizes the typist's finger reach and thus increases typing speed and accuracy. But given the sunk cost people had invested in learning the QWERTY keyboard, the DSK did not catch on.

Today, however, every personal computer comes with an optional DSK setting that requires only a minor software modification. Even though most people have never heard about it, the DSK has a passionate core of devotees. They were quite surprised to learn that when smartphones with virtual keyboards, like the iPhone and the BlackBerry Storm, and the media tablet iPad were introduced, they came only with the traditional QWERTY keyboard layout. A software developer created an iPhone app to allow users to add the Dvorak layout. But since it is not an "approved Apple App," users must hack into their systems to install the unofficial program. (Caution: Such "jail breaking" voids the iPhone's warranty.) This example shows how hard it can be to overthrow entrenched standards, even when they are inferior and the cost of alternative options is quite low.[14]

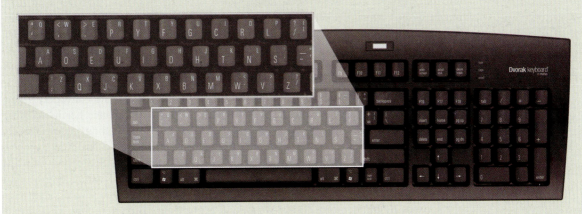

The Dvorak keyboard locates the most frequently used letters in the center row, to increase typing speed.

At the end of a life cycle (in the decline stage), the level of process innovation reaches its maximum, while the level of incremental product innovation reaches its minimum, as Exhibit 7.4 shows. This dynamic interplay between product and process innovation starts anew with the emergence of the next radical innovation that opens up a new industry.

The core competencies for competitive advantage in the growth stage tend to shift toward manufacturing and marketing capabilities, with an R&D emphasis on process innovation in order to improve efficiency. Since market demand is robust in this stage and more competitors have entered the market, there tends to be more strategic variety: Some competitors will continue to follow a *differentiation* strategy, emphasizing unique features, product functionality, and reliability. Other firms may conclude that lower prices are a potent competitive weapon and thus employ a *cost-leadership strategy*. Many firms in the

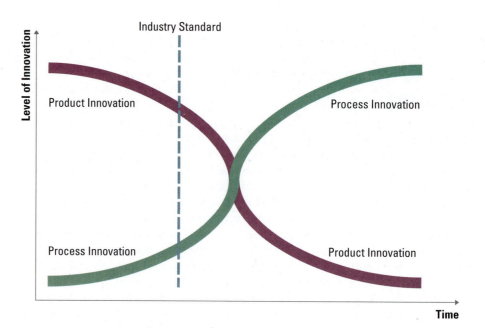

growth stage conclude that lower price is a key success factor; to bring more consumers into the market, prices have to come down. When Apple released the iPad 2 in spring 2011, prices for the original iPad dropped significantly. Access to efficient and large-scale manufacturing (such as those offered by Foxconn in China) and effective supply-chain capabilities are key success factors when market demand increases rapidly.

The key objective for firms during the growth phase is to stake out a strong strategic position not easily imitated by rivals. In the fast-growing shapewear industry, startup company Spanx has staked out a strong position. In 1998, Florida State University graduate Sara Blakely decided to cut the feet off her pantyhose to enhance her looks when wearing pants.[15] Soon after she obtained a patent for her bodyshaping undergarments, and Spanx began production and retailing of its shapewear in 2000. Sales grew exponentially after Blakely appeared on the *Oprah Winfrey Show.* By 2008, Spanx had grown to 75 employees and sold an estimated 5.4 million Spanx "power panties," with sales exceeding $750 million. The shapewear industry's explosive growth has attracted several other players: Flexees by Maidenform, Body Wrap, and Miraclesuit, to name a few. They are all attempting to carve out positions in the new industry.

Maturity Stage

As an industry moves into the mature stage, growth comes from buyers called the *late majority* entering the market. The purchasing power of the early majority subsides. Their demand was satisfied in the growth stage, and they are now making only replacement or repeat purchases. Given the large market size achieved from the growth stage, any additional market demand in the maturity stage is limited. This limited market demand in turn increases competitive intensity within the industry. Firms begin to compete directly against one another for market share, rather than trying to capture a share of an increasing pie.

The winners in this increasingly competitive environment are generally firms that stake a strong position as cost leaders. Key success factors are the manufacturing and process engineering capabilities to drive costs down. Assuming an acceptable value proposition, price is the dominant competitive weapon in the mature stage; product features and performance requirements are now well established. A few firms may be able to implement an integration strategy, combining differentiation and low cost, but given the intensity of competition, many weaker firms are forced to exit. Generally, the larger firms with economies of scale are the ones that survive as the industry consolidates and excess capacity is removed. The industry structure morphs into an oligopoly, in which only a few large firms remain. In the airline industry, for example, the large number of bankruptcies, as well as recent mega-mergers such as those of Delta and Northwest and of United and Continental, are a consequence of low growth in a mature market characterized by significant excess capacity.

Decline Stage

Changes in the external environment often take industries from maturity to decline. In this final stage of the industry life cycle, the size of the market contracts as demand falls. *Laggards*—customers who adopt a new product only if it is absolutely necessary, such as first-time cell phone adopters today—are the last consumer segment to come into the market. Their demand is far too small to compensate for reduced demand from the early and late majority, who are moving on to different products and services. Excess industry capacity in the declining stage puts strong pressure on prices and can increase competitive intensity, especially if the industry has high exit barriers. At this stage, managers generally have four strategic options: *exit, harvest, maintain,* or *consolidate.*[16]

In pursuing a *harvest strategy,* the firm reduces investments in product support and allocates only a minimum of human and other resources. While several companies such as IBM, Brother, Olivetti, and Nakajima still offer typewriters, they don't invest much in future innovation. Instead, they are maximizing cash flow from their existing typewriter product line. Philip Morris, on the other hand, is following a *maintain strategy* with its Marlboro brand, continuing to support marketing efforts at a given level despite the fact that U.S. cigarette consumption has been declining.

Although market size shrinks in a declining industry, some firms may choose to *consolidate* the industry by buying rivals (those who choose to exit). This allows the consolidating firm to stake out a strong position—possibly approaching monopolistic market power, although in a declining industry.[17] For example, although the computing industry has moved to distributed computing, where the Internet is powered by thousands of server farms made up of computers, routers, and switches, IBM still holds a dominant position in mainframe computers, on which banks and insurance companies rely because they are reliable and secure. As of 2009, IBM was selling about $3.5 billion worth of mainframes a year. The surprising fact is that although mainframe revenues make up only about 3.5 percent of IBM's overall revenues, each dollar spent on mainframes works like a multiplier because it pulls in additional dollars from lucrative service and maintenance contracts. One research firm estimates that even today 40 percent of IBM's profits are directly or indirectly related to mainframes.[18]

Exhibit 7.5 (next page) summarizes the features of the industry life cycle at each stage. A word of caution is in order, however: Although the industry life cycle is a useful framework to guide strategic choice, industries do not *have to evolve* through these stages. Motorola initiated an ill-fated satellite-based telephone system, Iridium, which was soon displaced by cell phones that rely on earth-based networks of radio towers. Thus the global satellite telephone industry never moved beyond the introductory stage of the industry life cycle.

Moreover, innovations can emerge at any stage of the industry life cycle, which in turn can initiate a new cycle. Industries can also be rejuvenated, often in the declining stage.

EXHIBIT 7.5

Features of the Industry Life Cycle

	Life Cycle Stages			
	Introduction	**Growth**	**Maturity**	**Decline**
Core Competency	R&D, some marketing	R&D, some manufacturing, marketing	Manufacturing, process engineering, marketing	Manufacturing, process engineering, marketing, service
Type of Buyers	Early adopters	Early majority	Late majority	Laggards
Market Growth	Slow	High	None to moderate	Negative
Price	High	Falling	Low	Low to high
Market Size	Small	Larger	Largest	Small to moderate
Number of Competitors	Few, if any	Many	Moderate, but large	Few, if any
Mode of Competition	Non-price Competition	Non-price competition	Price	Price or non-price competition
Business-level Strategy	Differentiation	Differentiation	Cost-leadership, or integration strategy	Cost-leadership, differentiation, or integration strategy
Strategic Objective	Achieving market acceptance	Staking out a strong strategic position	Maintaining strong strategic position	Exit, harvest, maintain, or consolidate

Although the old-line steel industry relying on fully integrated mills has been in decline for a long time, mini steel mills started a new industry life cycle by using the electric-arc furnace, a process innovation that enabled the newcomers to produce high-quality steel in small batches at low prices. Although the industry life cycle is a useful tool, it does not explain everything about changes in industries. Some industries may never go through the entire life cycle, while others are continually renewed through innovation. Entrepreneurs are the agents that introduce change into the system.

STRATEGIC ENTREPRENEURSHIP

>> **LO 7-3**
Apply strategic management concepts to entrepreneurship and innovation.

entrepreneurship
The process by which people undertake economic risk to innovate—to create new products, processes, and sometimes new organizations.

Entrepreneurship describes the process by which people undertake economic risk to innovate—to create new products, processes, and sometimes new organizations.[19] If successful, entrepreneurship not only drives the competitive process, it also creates value for the individual entrepreneurs and society at large. *Entrepreneurs* innovate by commercializing ideas and inventions. Joseph Schumpeter argued that innovating is at least as difficult and demanding as inventing.[20] Entrepreneurs are, therefore, the change agents who make the process of creative destruction happen. They seek out or create new business opportunities and then assemble the resources necessary to exploit them.[21] These new businesses create employment opportunities and value for society.

Although many new ventures fail, many achieve success, and some achieve spectacular success. Examples of the latter are:

- Jeff Bezos is the founder of Amazon.com, today the world's largest online retailer. The stepson of a Cuban immigrant, Bezos graduated from Princeton and then worked as a financial analyst on Wall Street. In 1994, after reading that the Internet was growing by

2,000 percent a month, he set out to leverage the Internet as a new distribution channel. Listing products that could be sold online, he finally settled on books, because that retail market was fairly fragmented, with huge inefficiencies in its distribution system. Perhaps even more important, books represent a perfect commodity, because they are identical regardless of where a consumer buys them.

■ Oprah Winfrey, best-known for her self-titled TV talk show, is also founder and CEO of Harpo Productions, a multimedia company. Some of Harpo's well-known products include *The Oprah Winfrey Show, Dr. Phil, The Rachael Ray Show, The Dr. Oz Show, Oprah.com, O, The Oprah Magazine,* and *O at Home.* In January 2011, she launched a new cable-TV channel jointly with Discovery Communications: *OWN, The Oprah Winfrey Network.*[22] A graduate of Tennessee State University, Oprah used her entrepreneurial talents to rise from poverty and an abusive childhood to become one of the most successful entrepreneurs in the multimedia business, with a net worth of over $2 billion.[23] In 2011, Oprah Winfrey ended her all-time record-setting talk show to devote her entrepreneurial talents to *OWN.*

■ Jeff Hawkins, a serial entrepreneur, was one of the first to understand that external opportunities were pointing toward mobile computing. In the early 1990s, despite the high-profile failure of Apple's Newton, Hawkins clearly envisioned a future in which everyone would own a "personal computer that fits in their pocket."[24] This device would be the person's primary computer and would be accessed much more frequently than a laptop or desktop. His analysis of the external environment told Hawkins this was inevitable, and he believed mobile computing would happen faster if better devices were available. He went on to invent the PalmPilot, a handheld computer, and founded Palm Computing in 1992. Later, Hawkins continued to innovate by introducing the Treo, one of the first smartphones (a mobile phone offering PC-like capabilities), and founded Handspring in 1998.

Note that beyond starting new businesses, entrepreneurs are *change agents* who transform innovation into reality. Apple Inc. is known as one of the world's most innovative companies, and its co-founder Steve Jobs is credited with Apple's most important breakthrough innovations. Steve Jobs also founded Pixar, one of the most successful film studios of all time. Leveraging 3D computer animation, Pixar has created blockbuster hits such as *Toy Story 1, 2,* and *3, A Bug's Life, Monsters Inc., Finding Nemo,* and *The Incredibles,* among others. Steve Jobs is clearly an entrepreneur extraordinaire, and has effected continuous innovation in his quest to create value through new products or services.

Strategic entrepreneurship describes the pursuit of innovation using tools and concepts from strategic management.[25] We can leverage innovation for competitive advantage by applying a strategic management lens to entrepreneurship. The fundamental question of strategic entrepreneurship, therefore, is how to combine entrepreneurial actions that create new opportunities or exploit existing ones with strategic actions we take in the pursuit of competitive advantage.[26] Procter & Gamble's continued innovation in detergents is an example of strategic entrepreneurship, because P&G managers leverage strategic analysis, formulation, and implementation when deciding which new type of detergent to research, when to launch it, and how to implement the necessary organizational changes. Each new release is an innovation, and thus an act of entrepreneurship planned and executed using strategic management concepts.

To further explore strategic entrepreneurship, we now turn to a discussion of the different types of innovation that may be pursued, as well as the strategic implications of each type.

strategic entrepreneurship
The pursuit of innovation using the tools and concepts available in strategic management.

EXHIBIT 7.6

Types of Innovation: Combining Markets and Technologies

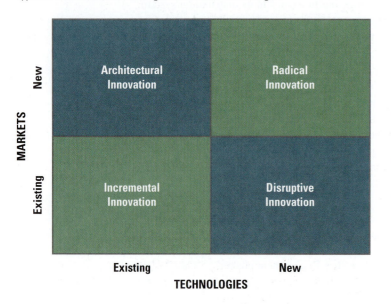

>> **LO 7-4**
Evaluate different types of innovation and derive their strategic implications.

incremental innovation An innovation that squarely builds on the firm's established knowledge base, steadily improves the product or service it offers, and targets existing markets by using existing technology.

radical innovation An innovation that draws on novel methods or materials, is derived from either an entirely different knowledge base or from the recombination of the firm's existing knowledge base with a new stream of knowledge, or targets new markets by using new technologies.

TYPES OF INNOVATION

The better we understand different types of innovation, the more accurately we can assess their strategic implications. We need to know, in particular, along which dimensions we should assess innovations.

One insightful way to categorize innovations is to measure their degree of newness in terms of *technology* and *markets*.[27] Here, *technology* refers to the methods and materials used to achieve a commercial objective.[28] For example, Apple integrates different types of technologies (hardware, software, microprocessors, the Internet, and so on) to produce and deliver an array of mobile devices and services (e.g., iBookstore). We also want to understand the *market* for an innovation—e.g., whether an innovation is introduced into a new or an existing market—because an idea or invention turns into an innovation only when it is successfully commercialized.[29] Measuring an innovation along the technology and market dimensions gives us the framework depicted in Exhibit 7.6. Along the horizontal axis, we ask whether the innovation builds on existing technologies or creates a new one. On the vertical axis, we ask whether the innovation is targeted toward existing or new markets. Four types of innovations emerge: incremental, radical, architectural, and disruptive innovations.

Incremental and Radical Innovations

Although radical breakthroughs such as MP3 players and magnetic resonance imaging (MRI) radiology capture most of our attention, the vast majority of innovations are actually incremental ones. An **incremental innovation** squarely builds on the firm's established knowledge base and steadily improves the product or service it offers.[30] It targets existing markets using existing technology. Strategy Highlight 7.3 describes how Gillette leverages incremental innovation to gain and sustain a competitive advantage.

The Gillette example shows how radical innovation created a competitive advantage that the company sustained by follow-up incremental innovation. Such an outcome is not a foregone conclusion, though. In some instances, the innovator is outcompeted by second movers that quickly introduce a very similar incremental innovation to continuously improve their own offering. For example, although CNN was the pioneer in 24-hour cable news, today it is only the third most popular choice in this category, having been surpassed by Fox News and MSNBC.[31]

On the other hand, **radical innovation** draws on novel methods or materials, is derived either from an entirely different knowledge base or from recombination of the firm's existing knowledge base with a new stream of knowledge, or targets new markets by using new technologies.[32] Well-known examples of radical innovations include the introduction of the mass-produced automobile (the Ford Model T), the X-ray, the airplane, and more recently biotechnology breakthroughs such as genetic engineering and the decoding of the human genome.

Many firms get their start by successfully commercializing radical innovations, some of which, like the airplane, even give birth to new industries. Although the British firm de Havilland first commercialized the jet-powered passenger airplane, Boeing was the company that rode this radical innovation to industry dominance. More recently, Boeing's leadership has been challenged by Airbus, and today each company has approximately half the market. This stalemate is now being contested by aircraft manufacturers such as Bombardier of Canada and Embraer of Brazil who are moving up-market by building larger luxury jets that are competing with some of the smaller airplane models offered by Boeing and Airbus.[33]

Once firms have achieved market acceptance of a breakthrough innovation, they tend to follow up with incremental rather than radical innovations. Over time, these companies morph into industry incumbents. Future radical innovations are generally introduced by new entrepreneurial ventures. Why is this so? Let's look at the reasons, which are economic, organizational, and strategic.[34]

ECONOMIC REASONS FOR INCREMENTAL INNOVATION. Economists highlight the role of *incentives* in strategic choice. Once an innovator has become an established incumbent firm (such as Google has today), it has strong incentives to defend its strategic position and market power. An emphasis on incremental innovations strengthens the incumbent firm's position and thus maintains high entry barriers. As a result, the incumbent firm uses incremental innovation to extend the time it can extract profits based on a favorable industry structure (see the discussion in Chapter 3). Any potential radical innovation threatens the incumbent firm's dominant position.

The incentives for entrepreneurial ventures, however, are just the opposite. Successfully commercializing a radical innovation is frequently the only option to enter an industry protected by high entry barriers. One of the first biotech firms, Amgen, used newly discovered drugs based on genetic engineering to overcome entry barriers to the pharmaceutical industry, in which incumbents had enjoyed notoriously high profits for several decades. Because of differential economic incentives, incumbents push forward with incremental innovations, while new entrants focus on radical innovations.

ORGANIZATIONAL REASONS FOR INCREMENTAL INNOVATION. From an organizational perspective, as firms become established and grow, they rely more heavily on formalized business processes and structures. In some cases, the firm may experience inertia, so that changes to the status quo may be resisted. Incumbent firms, therefore, tend to favor incremental innovations that reinforce the existing organizational structure and power distribution while avoiding radical innovation that could disturb the existing power distribution (e.g., between different functional areas, such as R&D and marketing). New entrants, however, do not have formal organizational structures and processes, giving them more freedom to launch an initial breakthrough.

STRATEGY HIGHLIGHT 7.3

From King Gillette to King of Incremental Innovation

In 1903, entrepreneur Mr. King C. Gillette invented and began selling the safety razor with a disposable blade. This radical innovation launched the Gillette company (now a brand of Procter & Gamble). To sustain its competitive advantage, Gillette not only made sure that its razors were inexpensive and widely available (thus introducing the "razor and razor blade" business model),[35] but also continually improved its razor blades. In a classic example of incremental innovation, Gillette kept adding an additional blade with each new version of its razor until the number had gone from one to six![36] Though this innovation strategy seems predictable, it worked: Gillette's top-selling razor today, the Fusion, holds about 45 percent market share and brings in annual revenues of more than $1 billion. Moreover, with each new razor introduction, Gillette is able to push up its per-unit cartridge price. A four-pack of razors for the new Fusion Proglide retailed for $17.99 when introduced in 2010.[37]

STRATEGIC REASONS FOR INCREMENTAL INNOVATION. A final reason incumbent firms tend to be a source of incremental rather than radical innovations is that they become embedded in a network of suppliers, buyers, complementors, and so on.[38] They no longer make independent decisions but must consider the ramifications on other parties in their value network. Continuous incremental innovations reinforce this network and keep all its members happy, while radical innovations disrupt it. Again, new entrants don't have to worry about preexisting value networks, since they will be building theirs around the radical innovation they are bringing to a new market.

Architectural and Disruptive Innovations

FedEx's architectural innovation built upon the hub-and-spoke system (first introduced by Delta in its Atlanta hub) to create the express-delivery industry.

Firms can also innovate by leveraging *existing technologies* into *new markets*. Doing so generally requires them to reconfigure the components of a technology, meaning they alter the overall "architecture" of the product.[39] An **architectural innovation,** therefore, is a new product in which known components, based on existing technologies, are reconfigured in a novel way to create new markets.

For example, in the 1980s Xerox was the most dominant copier company worldwide.[40] It produced high-volume, high-quality copying machines that it leased to its customers through a service agreement. While these machines were ideal for the high end of the market, Xerox ignored small and medium-sized businesses. By applying an architectural innovation, the Japanese entry Canon was able to redesign the copier so that it didn't need professional service—reliability was built directly into the machine, and the user could replace parts such as the cartridge. This allowed Canon to apply the "razor and razor blade" business model, charging relatively low prices for its copiers but higher prices for cartridges. What Xerox had not envisioned was the possibility that the components of the copying machine could be put together in a different way that was more user-friendly.

Finally, a **disruptive innovation** leverages *new technologies* to attack *existing markets*. It invades an existing market from the bottom up, as shown in Exhibit 7.7.[41] The dashed blue lines represent different market segments, from segment 1 at the low end to segment 4 at the high end. As first demonstrated by Professor Clayton Christensen of the Harvard Business School, the dynamic process of disruptive innovation begins when a startup firm introduces a new product based on a new technology to meet existing customer needs. To be a disruptive force, however, this new product or technology has to have additional characteristics: It begins as a low-cost solution to an existing problem. Initially, its performance is inferior to the existing technology, but its rate of technological improvement over time is faster than the rate of performance increases required by different market segments. In Exhibit 7.7, the purple path captures the new technology's trajectory, or rate of improvement over time.

The following examples illustrate disruptive innovations:

- Japanese carmakers successfully followed a strategy of disruptive innovation by first introducing small fuel-efficient cars, and then leveraging their low-cost and high-quality advantages into high-end luxury segments, captured by brands such as Lexus, Infiniti, and Acura.

- Digital photography improved enough over time to provide higher-definition pictures. As a result, it has been able to replace film photography, even in most professional applications.

architectural innovation A new product in which known components, based on existing technologies, are reconfigured in a novel way to attack new markets.

disruptive innovation An innovation that leverages new technologies to attack existing markets from the bottom up.

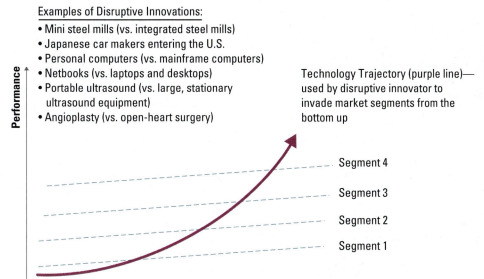

EXHIBIT 7.7

Disruptive Innovation Invading Different Market Segments from the Bottom Up

- Data storage products advanced from the floppy disk to the hard disk to the CD, then to the ZIP drive, and now to flash drives. Each new memory device invaded the market from the bottom up and performance improved over time.
- Mini computers disrupted mainframe computers; desktop computers disrupted mini computers; laptops disrupted desktop computers; now netbooks under $200 are disrupting laptops.
- Throughout the 1990s, Swatch's low-cost, fun watches disrupted watches that were like expensive jewelry. Today, timekeeping functions of smartphones are replacing wristwatches altogether.

One factor favoring the success of disruptive innovation is that it relies on stealth attack: It invades the market from the bottom up, by first capturing the low end. Many times, incumbent firms fail to defend (and sometimes are even happy to cede) the low end of the market, because it is frequently a low-margin business. The emergence of electric arc furnaces, for example, was a disruptive innovation that allowed so-called mini-mills like Nucor and Chaparral to produce steel in small batches and at lower cost compared with fully integrated steel mills such as U.S. Steel or Bethlehem Steel. Initially, though, the quality of steel produced by mini-mills was poor and could compete only in the lowest tier of the market: steel used to reinforce construction concrete (rebar steel). Once the mini-mills entered segment 1 of the steel market, the integrated mills could no longer be cost-competitive given their high fixed cost; the incumbents happily ceded segment 1 of the market to the new entrants because it was a low-margin business to begin with. However, invading segment 1 of a market creates a beachhead for a new technology, which the new entrant uses to gain more market expertise, build economies of scale, lower cost, and further improve quality. The new entrant is then able to leverage its disruptive technology to continue to invade the existing firm's territory from the bottom up, following the purple trajectory in Exhibit 7.7, one market segment at a time.

Google, for example, is using its new operating system, Chrome OS, as a beachhead to invade Microsoft's stronghold.[42] Chrome OS is optimized to run on netbooks, the

GE's Reverse Innovation: Disrupt Yourself!

GE Healthcare is a leader in diagnostic devices. Realizing that the likelihood of disruptive innovation increases over time, GE now uses reverse innovation to disrupt itself. A high-end ultrasound machine found in cutting-edge research hospitals in the United States or Europe costs $230,000. There is no market for these high-end, high-price products in developing countries. Given their large populations, however, there *is* a strong medical need for ultrasound devices.

In 2002, a local GE team in China, through a bottom-up strategic initiative, developed an inexpensive, portable ultrasound device, combining laptop technology with a probe and sophisticated imaging software. This lightweight device (11 pounds) was first used in rural China. In the spring of 2009, GE unveiled the new medical device under the name Venue 40 in the United States, at a price of less than $30,000. There was high demand from many American general practitioners, who could not otherwise afford the quarter of a million dollars needed to procure a high-end machine (that weighed about 400 pounds). In the fall of 2009, GE's chairman and CEO Jeff Immelt unveiled the Vscan, an even smaller device that looks like a cross between an early iPod and a flip phone. The Vscan is expected to cost only about $12,000. GE views it as the "stethoscope of the 21st century," which a primary care doctor can hang around her neck when visiting patients.[45]

fastest-growing segment in computing. To appeal to users who spend most of their time on the web accessing e-mail and other online applications, for instance, it is designed to start up in a few seconds. Moreover, Google provides Chrome OS free of charge.[43] In contrast to Microsoft's proprietary Windows operating system, Chrome OS is open-source software, freely accessible to anyone for further development and refinement. In this sense, Google is leveraging crowdsourcing in its new product development, just as Threadless uses crowdsourcing to design and market T-shirts and Wikipedia uses the wisdom of the crowds to collectively edit encyclopedia entries.

Another factor favoring the success of disruptive innovation is that incumbent firms often are slow to change. Incumbent firms that listen closely to their current customers will respond by continuing to invest in the existing technology and in incremental changes to the existing products. When a newer technology matures and proves to be a better solution, those same customers will switch over. At that time, however, the incumbent firm does not yet have a competitive product ready that is based on the disruptive technology. Although customer-oriented mission statements are more likely to guard against firm obsolescence than product-oriented ones (see Chapter 2), they are no guarantee that a firm can hold out in the face of disruptive innovation. One of the counterintuitive findings that Clayton Christensen unearthed in his studies is that it can hurt incumbents to listen only to their existing customers.

Although these examples show that disruptive innovations are a serious threat for incumbent firms, some have devised strategic initiatives to counter them. A first option is to invest in staying ahead of the competition. Apple continuously innovates—Steve Jobs has always believed that he knows what customers need even before they realize it. Apple is famous for not soliciting customer feedback or studying markets. A second approach is to guard against disruptive innovation by protecting the low end of the market (segment 1 in Exhibit 7.7) by introducing low-cost innovations to preempt stealth competitors. Intel introduced the Celeron chip, a stripped-down, budget version of its Pentium chip, in 1998. More recently, Intel followed up with the Atom chip, a new processor that is inexpensive and consumes little battery power, to power low-cost netbooks.[44]

A third way to guard against disruptive innovations is to use reverse innovation, rather than wait for others to do it to you. In *reverse innovation* a firm develops products specifically for emerging markets such as China and India, and then introduces these innovations into developed markets such as the United States or the European Union. Strategy Highlight 7.4 describes how GE Healthcare invented and commercialized a disruptive innovation in China that is now making a big splash in the United States.

The Internet as Disruptive Force: The Long Tail

The Internet enables digitization and, as a consequence, acts as an especially disruptive force.[46] Everything that can go digital will—creating some losers and some winners. We are all familiar with the impact that the digitization of music, books, and movies has had on brick-and-mortar sellers. Web applications like TurboTax and LegalZoom are replacing professional tax accountants and attorneys. Online gaming is the fastest-growing segment in the $55 billion video game industry.[47] Online digitization is thus both a threat and an opportunity.

>> **LO 7-5**
Describe the long-tail concept and derive strategic implications.

These observations and their strategic implications have been explained by Chris Anderson, editor-in-chief of *Wired.* The "long tail" phenomenon[48] is that 80 percent of offerings in a category are *not* big hits (see Exhibit 7.8). It turns out that 80 percent of sales in a given product category (such as movies, books, and songs) come from "blockbusters" in the "short head" of the distribution curve, which represents only 20 percent of the offerings in a category. This phenomenon is captured by the *Pareto principle,* also known as the *80-20 rule,* which says that roughly 80 percent of effects come from 20 percent of the causes.

The *short head* represents the mainstream, where all the blockbusters, bestsellers, and hits are to be found. These products tend to appeal to the largest segment of the market with homogenous tastes. In the physical world of brick-and-mortar retail stores, these product selections are often the only choice on display, because there are significant costs to carrying broader inventory to meet a wider variety of consumer needs.

The disruptive force of the Internet provides an opportunity to online retailers to benefit from marketing the long tail, which is the remaining 80 percent. Online retailers can "sell less of more" by taking advantage of low-cost virtual shelf space, which is basically unlimited. The Internet, combined with sophisticated search engines and inventory-management software, allows firms to drive down transaction costs to match individual consumer demand with supply. As shown by the dotted line in Exhibit 7.8, the combined effects of these advances in technology make it possible to increase the number of units

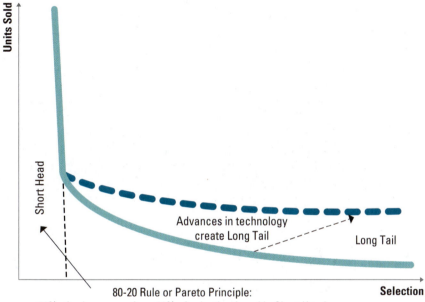

EXHIBIT 7.8

The Short Head and the Long Tail

Source: Adapted from C. Anderson (2006), *The Long Tail: Why the Future of Business Is Selling Less of More* (New York: Hyperion).

sold—that is, create the long tail. The **long tail** business model is one in which companies can obtain a large part of their revenues by selling a small number of units from among almost unlimited choices.

The long tail allows online retailers to overcome the problem of **thin markets,** in which transactions are likely not to take place because there are only a few buyers and a few sellers and they have difficulty finding each other. We can look at eBay as an example of an online retailer with an innovative approach to retailing, enabling buyers and sellers to meet online to exchange any good, no matter how exotic, at no cost to the buyer. Google also benefits from the long tail, because it is able to match even small advertisers with their target demographics.

The long tail captures the bottom of the iceberg, the non-obvious choices. By leveraging sophisticated IT systems, online retailers like Rhapsody, Netflix, and Amazon are now able to aggregate these choices (see Exhibit 7.9). Even Walmart, the world's largest retailer,

EXHIBIT 7.9

The Long-Tail Consequences: Selling Less of More

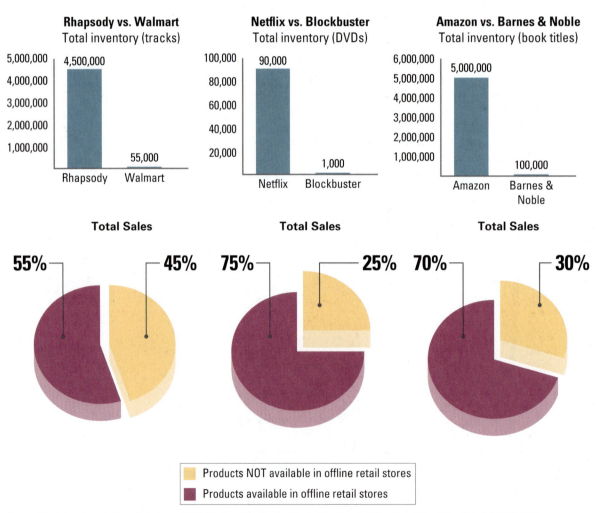

Source: Adapted and updated from C. Anderson (2006), *The Long Tail: Why the Future of Business Is Selling Less of More* (New York: Hyperion), p. 23.

carries only about 55,000 music tracks. In contrast, Rhapsody's inventory contains 4.5 million tracks. The average Blockbuster store carries about 1,000 DVD titles; Netflix carries about 90,000. The typical Barnes & Noble superstore holds some 100,000 book titles; on Amazon you can find 5 million. All in all, the leading online retailers carry an inventory 50 to 90 times larger than those of their largest brick-and-mortar competitors. Between 25 and 45 percent of all revenues for Rhapsody, Netflix, and Amazon come from the long tail, or products not available in offline retail stores.

The Internet as a disruptive innovation enables companies to solve important strategic trade-offs. It lowers the costs of shelf space, inventory, and distribution to near zero and enables firms to aggregate non-hits and match unique consumer preferences to supply. While the early experiences of media and entertainment industries illustrate the long-tail business model, it is expected that the model can be used to build a business in any product or service that can be digitized.

DISCONTINUITIES: PERIODS OF PARADIGM CHANGE

Innovation is a powerful force with potentially lethal consequences for incumbent firms. Startups like Skype are riding the wave of new technology—voice over Internet Protocol or VoIP—to offer *free* long-distance phone calls to anyone in the world. Just a decade ago, you would have paid several dollars *a minute* if you wanted to call overseas from the United States. Today, all you need is a computer or mobile phone with an Internet connection. Although this new technology is clearly an opportunity for Skype, it is a threat for traditional telephone companies the world over, and indeed it is creating major industry upheaval. Yet, Skype is still struggling to reach broader demographics and to identify a business model that allows it to earn revenue from this innovation. In 2011, Microsoft acquired Skype for $8.5 billion, providing Microsoft with a globally used Internet service of high brand recognition.[49]

Discontinuities are periods of time in which the underlying technological standard changes. As we have seen, VoIP is challenging the traditional landline technology. Earlier discontinuities include, among others, the move from:

- Propeller airplanes to supersonic jets
- Film-based to digital cameras
- Branch-based brick-and-motor banking to online banking (and the same for stock brokerage)
- Large (tube-based) computer and TV screens to high-definition flat-panel displays
- The vinyl record player to the cassette tape to the CD, and then to digital MP3 players like the iPod

Discontinuities can lead to a paradigm shift, a situation in which a new technology revolutionizes an existing industry and eventually establishes itself as the new standard.

>> **LO 7-6**
Evaluate discontinuities and describe the dynamics of paradigm changes.

---

long tail Business model in which companies can obtain a large part of their revenues by selling a small number of units from among almost unlimited choices.

thin markets A situation in which transactions are likely not to take place because there are only a few buyers and sellers, who have difficulty finding each other.

discontinuities Periods of time in which the underlying technological standard changes.

paradigm shift A situation in which a new technology revolutionizes an existing industry and eventually establishes itself as the new standard.

EXHIBIT 7.10

Likelihood of Discontinuity
Increases as Technology
Approaches Physical
Limit

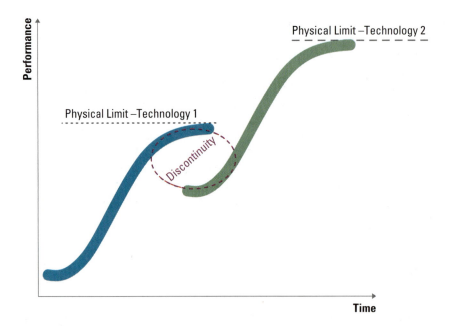

Exhibit 7.10, which plots the performance of a given technology against time, shows this transition. Each technology S-curve represents a different technology. Here, the blue one is the older incumbent technology, and the green one is the newer technology.

Given the potentially devastating effects of innovation on incumbent firms, one of the key questions managers need to answer is, "Can you predict *when* innovation leads to a discontinuity in an industry?" Although the future is unknowable, Richard Foster, formerly Senior Partner at McKinsey & Company, developed a predictive framework to address this important question. By studying the rate of improvement of many different types of technologies over time, ranging from heart replacement surgery to sailing ships, pocket watches, and chemicals, Foster found that technologies follow a predictable technology S-curve, improving in performance over time as a consequence of continued R&D effort. The take-off is slow because each new technology faces major science, engineering, and business challenges. Once these have been solved, exponential improvements set in. One key factor Foster discovered, however, is that each technology eventually reaches a physical limit due to laws of nature. For example, silicon-based computing is reaching a physical limit because we cannot place an infinite number of transistors on a tiny silicon chip. The dashed line in Exhibit 7.10 indicates the physical limit of technology 1.

The probability of a discontinuity increases as technology 1 approaches its physical limit. After 100 years of using internal combustion engines for cars and trucks, we can see the internal-combustion paradigm reaching a physical limit for several reasons, including the fact that fossil fuels are finite and there is an environmental need to lower the level of CO_2 emissions. Not surprisingly, as the rate of improvement in a given technology slows down, R&D investments in alternative solutions increase. At the onset of a discontinuity, however, the next dominant technology is far from clear, because a swarm of new technologies enters the fray.

The emergence of a number of new options requires that incumbent firms place some strategic bets on emerging technologies. Former Intel CEO Andy Grove compared a discontinuity to a situation in which a firm must pay a large entry fee to enter a casino. This fee represents the continued R&D expenditure the firm needs to create

absorptive capacity
A firm's ability to understand, evaluate, and integrate external technology developments.

hypercompetition
A situation in which competitive intensity has increased and periods of competitive advantage have shortened, especially in newer, technology-based industries, making any competitive advantage a string of short-lived advantages.

absorptive capacity—its ability to understand external technology developments, evaluate them, and integrate them into current products or create new ones.[50] By keeping many options open, the firm also avoids technological lock-out.[51] Inside the casino, so to speak, games of chance are being played at many different tables, each representing a new technology. Companies must pick which tables to play and how much to gamble.

Currently, in the car industry, different technologies are being put forth as potential alternatives to gasoline, including electric, hybrid (a cross between gasoline and electric), hydrogen, biofuels, solar, steam, and even exotic alternatives like algae. One technology will eventually emerge as the new paradigm, but during the discontinuity, the winner is far from clear. (MiniCase 7, page 375, describes the current battle for the next dominant technology in the car industry.)

When new technologies emerge, however, old ones do not simply disappear.[52] Rather, performance of the old technologies may improve, even significantly, in the face of apparently superior competition. When angioplasty was first introduced to open blocked arteries with minimal invasive heart surgery, we might have expected that the performance outcomes for patients still needing open-heart (coronary artery bypass) surgery would decline because the patients who were not eligible for angioplasty and thus still needed open-heart bypass surgery would be the sicker ones. With the overall patient pool receiving open-heart surgery now being much sicker, one would have expected a higher mortality rate. The empirical data, however, showed a *lower* mortality rate for open-heart patients. Why? Cardiothoracic surgeons were now focusing on just one specific patient group, which in turn enhanced their learning effects (see Chapter 6). Operating on more of the same type of cases allowed them to move down the learning curve more quickly and thus achieve better outcomes than before the introduction of angioplasty.

Taken together, most industries experience discontinuities over time. Discontinuities have significant implications for the competitive dynamics in an industry, creating opportunities as well as threats. Generally, discontinuities favor new entrants; they enjoy the "attacker's advantage" as Richard Foster put it.[53] In contrast, incumbent firms are often—but not always—impaired in their response. As a consequence, discontinuities frequently lead to changes in industry leadership, and thus affect which firms enjoy a competitive advantage.

HYPERCOMPETITION

The accelerated pace of innovation has had a significant impact on the nature of competitive advantage. Coining the term **hypercompetition,** Professor Rich D'Aveni of Dartmouth College argues that competitive intensity has increased and that periods of competitive advantage have shortened, especially in newer, technology-based industries.[54] As a consequence, no single strategy can sustain competitive advantage over time. Rather, any competitive advantage must be a string of short-lived advantages, achieved through a constant escalation of competition in price, quality, timing and know-how, capital commitments, and supply chain management.[55]

The phenomenon of hypercompetition is depicted in Exhibit 7.11 (next page). Here, the innovator launches a radical innovation and is able to exploit its competitive advantage over a given time period (Competitive Advantage 1). To further sustain its competitive advantage and keep new entrants out of the market, however, the innovator must follow up on its initial radical innovation before its advantage expires fully. The firm must cannibalize its own competitive advantage with a follow-up incremental innovation (Competitive Advantage 2) to preempt any potential rivals. The process continues with several subsequent incremental innovations. Each of these incremental innovations is shown as smaller

GAINING & SUSTAINING COMPETITIVE ADVANTAGE

>> **LO 7-7**
Identify the process leading to hypercompetition, and explain why competitive advantage can often be sustained through continuous innovation.

EXHIBIT 7.11

Hypercompetition Driven by Continuous Innovation

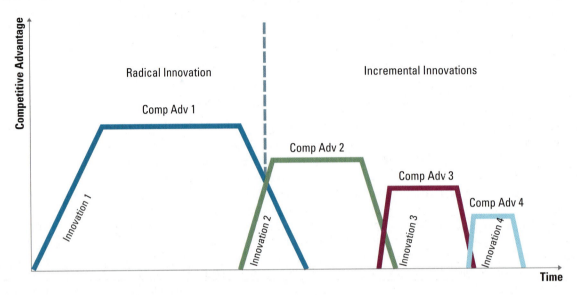

and of shorter duration than the previous one, illustrating the increased speed with which competitive advantage is lost.

As an example, Intel was successful in extending its superior performance when introducing the microprocessor embedded in the IBM PC by using continued innovation to drive the x86 chip architecture relentlessly forward: 286, 386, Pentium, Pentium II, Pentium III, Pentium 4, Pentium D, Pentium Dual Core, and so on. This process cannot go on forever, however (as shown in Exhibit 7.10), since technologies will approach their physical limits. Currently, the line widths on Intel's advanced processors is 45 nm.[56] As the number of transistors on a single chip increases, the generated heat cannot be managed satisfactorily. As silicon-based computing is reaching diminishing returns, new computing technologies will emerge.

As Exhibit 7.11 illustrates, the duration and magnitude of each subsequent competitive advantage are both smaller than for the preceding advantage. This reduction implies that a firm cannot indefinitely sustain a competitive advantage based on continuous incremental innovation. Nor can other firms gain advantages based on incremental innovation. At some point, a radical innovation is needed to start this process anew.

Professor Michael Porter, however, argues that hypercompetition is not inevitable. Rather, he says, it is a self-inflicted wound caused by a lack of distinct strategic positioning, as discussed in the last chapter.[57] Porter argues that hypercompetition is the result of firms *imitating* one another rather than attempting to be *different from* one another. Thus, firms begin to copy successful strategic initiatives of the industry leaders. This might allow these firms to excel at operational effectiveness (i.e., best in-class practices) but they will fail at strategic positioning. As a result, firms become much more competitive, but also more similar—leading to hypercompetition, where no advantage can be sustained (similar to the perfect competitive industry structure discussed in Chapter 3). 🔍

In this and the previous chapter, we discussed how firms can use business-level strategy— differentiation, cost leadership, integration, and innovation—to gain and sustain competitive advantage. We now turn our attention to corporate-level strategy to help us understand how executives make decisions about where to compete (in terms of industries, value chains, and geography) and how to create synergies among different business units. A thorough understanding of business and corporate strategy is necessary to formulate and sustain a winning strategy.

CHAPTERCASE 7 | *Consider This . . .*

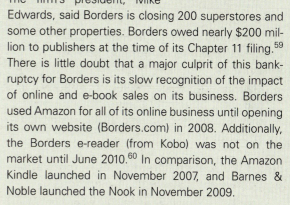

WIKIPEDIA, AS DISCUSSED in ChapterCase 7, leverages specific capabilities enabled by innovations of the Internet. Beyond the technical challenges of web interfaces, servers, and bandwidth for delivery is a sometimes-overlooked capability: the Wikipedians themselves. Over 14 million people have registered accounts to contribute edits to Wikipedia. More than 300,000 users provide edits to the website at least once a month. These volunteers build the content for the site, using a creative commons license that ensures free access to any of the more than 80 million unique visitors each *month* (as of January 2011).[58] This crowdsourcing and its legal underpinnings are successful only as long as individuals are willing to spend their own time contributing to the site for no pay or other extrinsic benefits. The ability to attract and utilize legions of interested individuals is vital to the success of Wikipedia both today and into the future.

While the death of Encarta was not a major blow for Microsoft as a whole, the same cannot be said for the effect that online shopping and e-books had for Borders Group Inc. Borders filed for bankruptcy protection in February 2011. The firm's president, Mike Edwards, said Borders is closing 200 superstores and some other properties. Borders owed nearly $200 million to publishers at the time of its Chapter 11 filing.[59] There is little doubt that a major culprit of this bankruptcy for Borders is its slow recognition of the impact of online and e-book sales on its business. Borders used Amazon for all of its online business until opening its own website (Borders.com) in 2008. Additionally, the Borders e-reader (from Kobo) was not on the market until June 2010.[60] In comparison, the Amazon Kindle launched in November 2007, and Barnes & Noble launched the Nook in November 2009.

1. How can Wikipedia maintain and grow its ability to harness the crowdsourcing of its "Wikipedians" to maintain high-quality (and quickly updated) content?

2. How has the "long tail" affected both Wikipedia and Borders Group?

3. What type of innovations should each of these two companies use to gain or sustain a competitive advantage?

Take-Away Concepts

This chapter discussed various aspects of innovation and strategic entrepreneurship as a business-level strategy, as summarized by the following learning objectives and related take-away concepts.

LO 7-1 Define innovation and describe its role in the competitive process.

>> Continuous innovation is the engine behind successful companies.

>> Innovation is a potent competitive weapon; it enables firms to redefine the marketplace in their favor and achieve much-needed growth.

>> The successful commercialization of a new product or service allows a firm to extract temporary monopoly profits.

LO 7-2 Describe the competitive implications of different stages in the industry life cycle.

>> Innovations frequently lead to the birth of new industries.

>> Industries generally follow a predictable industry life cycle, with four distinct stages: introduction, growth, maturity, and decline.

>> Different life-cycle stages have different consumer adoption rates and different competitive implications (see Exhibit 7.4).

LO 7-3 Apply strategic management concepts to entrepreneurship and innovation.

>> Strategic entrepreneurship focuses on generating integrated insights pertaining to innovation and change using the concepts available in strategic management.

LO 7-4 Evaluate different types of innovation and derive their strategic implications.

>> Four types of innovation emerge when applying the existing versus new dimensions of technology and markets: incremental, radical, architectural, and disruptive innovations.

LO 7-5 Describe the long-tail concept and derive strategic implications.

>> The Internet is a strongly disruptive force that digitizes any industry that can be digitized.

>> The long tail describes a business model in which companies can obtain a significant part of their revenues by selling a small number of units from among almost unlimited choices.

LO 7-6 Evaluate discontinuities and describe the dynamics of paradigm changes.

>> Discontinuities can lead to a paradigm shift, in which a new technology revolutionizes an existing industry and eventually establishes itself as the new standard.

>> Technologies follow a predictable technology S-curve, improving in performance over time as a consequence of continued R&D effort.

>> The probability of a discontinuity increases when a given technology approaches its physical limit.

LO 7-7 Identify the process leading to hypercompetition and explain why competitive advantage can be sustained through continuous innovation.

>> Competitive intensity has increased and periods of competitive advantage have shortened, especially in newer, technology-based industries.

>> No single strategy can sustain competitive advantage over time.

>> Any competitive advantage must be a string of short-lived advantages. This is achieved through a constant escalation of competition in the areas of price, quality, timing and know-how, capital commitments, and supply-chain management.

>> Hypercompetition can result from a lack of strategic positioning.

Key Terms

Absorptive capacity *(p. 191)*
Architectural innovation *(p. 184)*
Discontinuities *(p. 189)*
Disruptive innovation *(p. 184)*
Entrepreneurship *(p. 180)*
Hypercompetition *(p. 191)*

Incremental innovation *(p. 182)*
Innovation *(p. 172)*
Industry life cycle *(p. 173)*
Long tail *(p. 188)*
Network effects *(p. 174)*
Paradigm shift *(p. 189)*

Process innovations *(p. 176)*
Product innovations *(p. 176)*
Radical innovation *(p. 182)*
Standard *(p. 175)*
Strategic entrepreneurship *(p. 181)*
Thin markets *(p. 188)*

Discussion Questions

1. Assume you work for a small firm that developed a better and faster operating system for netbooks than Microsoft Windows. What strategy might the firm use to unseat Windows in this market?

2. How does the industry life cycle affect business strategy? Detail your answer based on each stage: introduction, growth, maturity, and decline.

3. Describe a firm you think has been highly innovative. Which of the four types of innovation—radical, incremental, disruptive, or architectural—did it use? Did the firm use different types over time?

4. Why are standards important in many industries? As standards get adapted and become dominant, how does this process influence the competitive nature of the industry?

Ethical/Social Issues

1. You are a co-founder of a startup firm making electronic sensors. After a year of sales your business is not growing rapidly, but you have some steady customers keeping the business afloat. A major supplier has informed you it can no longer supply your firm because it is moving to serve large customers only, and your volume does not qualify. Though you have no current orders to support an increased commitment to this supplier, you do have a new version of your sensor coming out that you hope will increase the purchase volume by over 75 percent and qualify you for continued supply. This supplier is important to your plans. What do you do?

2. Making innovations successful often relies on being the first to commercialize a technology. What are some practices a firm could use to enhance its first-mover advantage? Does the stage of the industry life cycle affect the available practices? Are there long-term consequences for the firm from these practices?

Small Group Exercises

SMALL GROUP EXERCISE 1

Your group works for Warner Music Group (www.wmg.com), a large music record label whose sales are declining largely due to piracy. Your supervisor assigns you the task of developing a strategy for improving this situation.

1. What are the key issues you must grapple with to improve the position of Warner Music Group (WMG)?

2. In what phase of the life cycle is the record-label industry?

3. How does this life-cycle phase affect the types of innovation that should be considered to help WMG be successful?

SMALL GROUP EXERCISE 2

Strategy Highlight 7.4 outlines GE's development of the Vscan, which will likely cannibalize the sales of its existing ultrasound machines. Part of the difficult decision to reverse-innovate is the prospect of losing not just sales revenue but also jobs. In 2010, GE Healthcare employed over 45,000 people. Assume 10,000 jobs strongly connected to supporting GE's high-end imaging systems are in imminent jeopardy if sales of the systems drop off. Put yourself in the role of GE Healthcare managers.

1. Pull together a memo of talking points for the managers of the new Vscan that may put many other men and women at GE out of work.

2. How do you explain the societal benefits of lower-cost medical scanning equipment yet address real job security concerns among the employees?

Strategy Term Project

MODULE 7: INNOVATION STRATEGY

In this section, you will study the environment of the firm you have selected for the strategy term project and the firm's susceptibility to technological disruptions from new entrants.

1. Where is your firm's industry on the life cycle as shown in Exhibit 7.2?

2. What is the dominant technological design of the industry in which your firm is primarily located?

3. Did this dominant technology develop quickly or more slowly? Can you identify what influenced the speed of diffusion?

4. Where is the dominant technology on the S-curve in your focal industry? What alternative technologies could present a paradigm shift as shown in Exhibit 7.10?

5. What is the role of standards in the focal industry?

6. From a marketing perspective, what attributes describe the current major customer segment for your firm?

7. Are intellectual property rights important for your firm? Can you find what strategies the firm is implementing to protect its proprietary position?

*my*Strategy

DO YOU WANT TO BE AN ENTREPRENEUR?

About 75 percent of Stanford MBAs plan to start their own business upon graduation. Moreover, economic downturns appear to be the best time to start a company. Many of today's *Fortune-100* and high-tech success stories were launched in economic downturns. The global depression of 1873–1895 witnessed the founding of today's industry giants like AT&T, GE, Hershey's, Gillette, Johnson & Johnson, Abbott, Lilly, Merck, and Bristol-Myers. Similarly, Hewlett-Packard (HP), Texas Instruments, and United Technologies got their starts during the Great Depression of 1929–1939 in the United States.

The success story of Silicon Valley began with the founding of HP in Palo Alto, California. This cluster of high-tech innovators, venture capitalists, and entrepreneurs took off during a time when the stock market had crashed by some 90 percent and almost one in three U.S. workers were unemployed. Apple, Microsoft, LexisNexis, FedEx, and Genentech began their corporate lives during the oil price shocks and subsequent recession in the mid-1970s. During the early 1980s, inflation raged and mortgage rates were over 20 percent. Still, during this period entrepreneurs founded Amgen, CNN, MTV, E*Trade, AOL, Adobe, and Autodesk.[61]

1. Why do you think recessions are a good time to start a business? Wouldn't that seem counterintuitive?

2. Thinking about today's business climate, would you say that now is a good time to start a business? Why or why not?

3. If you were to start a business, what type of business would you want to start, and why? What idea would you be commercializing?

4. Does it matter *where* (in terms of geography) you start your business? Why or why not?

5. Explain how your startup could gain and sustain a competitive advantage.

Endnotes

1. This ChapterCase is based on: Surowiecki, J. (2004), *The Wisdom of Crowds* (New York: Bantam Dell); "Internet encyclopedias go head-to-head," *Nature,* December 15, 2005; Anderson, C. (2006), *The Long Tail. Why the Future of Business Is Selling Less of More* (New York: Hyperion); Anderson, C. (2009), *Free. The Future of a Radical Price* (New York: Hyperion); "Wikipedia's old-fashioned revolution," *The Wall Street Journal,* April 6, 2009; www.encyclopediacenter.com; www.alexa.com/topsites; and http://en.wikipedia.org/wiki/Jimmy_Wales; http://en.wikipedia.org/wiki/Wikipedia.

2. Rothaermel, F. T., and A. Hess (2010), "Innovation strategies combined," *MIT Sloan Management Review,* Spring: 12–15.

3. Schumpeter, J. A. (1942), *Capitalism, Socialism, and Democracy* (New York: Harper & Row). For an updated and insightful discussion, see Foster, R., and S. Kaplan (2001), *Creative Destruction: Why Companies that Are Built to Last Underperform the Market—and How to Successfully Transform Them* (New York: Currency/Doubleday).

4. Schumpeter, J. A. (1942), *Capitalism, Socialism, and Democracy*; Foster, R., and S. Kaplan (2001), *Creative Destruction: Why Companies that Are Built to Last Underperform the Market—and How to Successfully Transform Them.*

5. "Comcast, GE strike deal; Vivendi to sell NBC stake," *The Wall Street Journal,* December 4, 2009.

6. This discussion is based on: Rothaermel, F. T., and M. Thursby (2007), "The nanotech vs. the biotech revolution: Sources of incumbent productivity in research," *Research Policy* 36: 832–849; and Woolley, J. (2010), "Technology Emergence through Entrepreneurship across Multiple Industries," *Strategic Entrepreneurship Journal* 4: 1–21.

7. Moore, G. A. (2002), *Crossing the Chasm* (New York: HarperCollins).

8. www.apple.com/ipad/pricing/.

9. This discussion is based on: Arthur, W. B. (1989), "Competing technologies, increasing returns, and lock-in by historical events," *Economics Journal* 99: 116–131; Hill, C. W. L. (1997), Establishing a standard: Competitive strategy and winner take all industries, *Academy of Management Executive* 11: 7–25; and Shapiro, C., and H. R. Varian (1998), *Information Rules. A Strategic Guide the Network Economy* (Boston, MA: Harvard Business School Press).

10. This Strategy Highlight is based on: "Inside the app economy," *BusinessWeek,* October 22, 2009, www.apple.com/iphone/apps-for-iphone/.

11. This discussion is based on: Utterback, J. M. (1994), *Mastering the Dynamics of Innovation* (Boston, MA: Harvard Business School Press); Anderson, P., and M. Tushman (1990), "Technological discontinuities and dominant designs: A cyclical model of technological change," *Administrative Science Quarterly* 35: 604–634; and Schilling, M. A. (1998), "Technological lockout: An integrative model of the economic and strategic factors driving technology success and failure," *Academy of Management Review* 23: 267–284.

12. This discussion is based on: Teece, D. J. (1986), "Profiting from technological innovation: Implications for integration, collaboration, licensing and public policy," *Research Policy* 15: 285–305; and Ceccagnoli, M., and F. T. Rothaermel (2008), "Appropriating the returns to innovation," *Advances in Study of Entrepreneurship, Innovation, and Economic Growth* 18: 11–34.

13. Abernathy, W. J., and J. M. Utterback (1978), "Patterns of innovation in technology," *Technology Review* 80: 40–47; Benner, M., and M. A. Tushman (2003), "Exploitation, exploration, and process management: The productivity dilemma revisited," *Academy of Management Review* 28: 238–256.

14. This Strategy Highlight is based on: Cassingham, R. R. (1986), *Dvorak Keyboard: The Ergonomically Designed Keyboard, Now an American Standard* (Calgary, Alberta: Freelance Communications); Arthur, W. B. (1989), "Competing technologies, increasing returns, and lock-in by historical events," *Economics Journal* 99: 116–131; and "Smart keyboard seem dumb to people of their type," *The Wall Street Journal,* September 28, 2009.

15. The history of Spanx is documented at www.spanx.com.

16. Harrigan, K. R. (1980), *Strategies for Declining Businesses* (Lexington, MA: Heath).

17. Ibid.

18. "Back in fashion," *The Economist,* January 14, 2010.

19. Schramm, C. J. (2006), *The Entrepreneurial Imperative,* (New York: HarperCollins). Dr. Carl Schramm is president of the Kauffman Foundation, the world's leading foundation for entrepreneurship.

20. Schumpeter, J. A. (1942), *Capitalism, Socialism, and Democracy*; Foster, R., and S. Kaplan (2001), *Creative Destruction: Why Companies that Are Built to Last Underperform the Market—and How to Successfully Transform Them.*

21. Shane, S., and S. Venkataraman (2000), "The promise of entrepreneurship as a field of research," *Academy of Management Review* 25: 217–226; Alvarez, S., and J. B. Barney (2007), "Discovery and creation: Alternative theories of entrepreneurial action," *Strategic Entrepreneurship Journal* 1: 11–26.

22. "Oprah Winfrey to end her program in 2011," *The Wall Street Journal,* November 19, 2009.

23. *Forbes Special Edition: "Billionaires,"* March 29, 2010.

24. Hawkins, J. (2009), "Inside the mind of a reluctant entrepreneur," *Presentation at the Stanford's Entrepreneurial Thought Leader Series,* May 13, 2009.

25. Hitt, M. A., R. D. Ireland, S. M. Camp, and D. L. Sexton (2002), "Strategic entrepreneurship: Integrating entrepreneurial and strategic management perspectives," in Hitt, M. A., R. D. Ireland, S. M. Camp, and D. L. Sexton (eds.), *Strategic Entrepreneurship: Creating a New Mindset* (Oxford, UK: Blackwell Publishing); Rothaermel, F. T. (2008), "Strategic management and strategic entrepreneurship," *Presentation at the Strategic Management Society Annual International Conference,* Cologne, Germany, October 12.

26. Ibid; Bingham, C. B., K. M. Eisenhardt, and N. R., Furr (2007), "What makes a process a capability? Heuristics, strategy, and effective capture of opportunities," *Strategic Entrepreneurship Journal* 1: 27–47.

27. Shuen, A. (2008), *Web 2.0: A Strategy Guide* (Sebastopol, CA: O'Reilly Media); Thursby, J., and M. Thursby (2006), *Here or There? A Survey in Factors of Multinational R&D Location* (Washington, DC: National Academies Press).

28. Byers, T. H., R. C. Dorf, and A. J. Nelson (2011), *Technology Entrepreneurship: From Idea to Enterprise* (Burr Ridge, IL: McGraw-Hill).

29. This discussion is based on: Schumpeter, J. A. (1942), *Capitalism, Socialism, and Democracy;* Freeman, C., and L. Soete (1997), *The Economics of Industrial Innovation* (Cambridge, MA: MIT Press); and Foster, R., and S. Kaplan (2001), *Creative Destruction: Why Companies that Are Built to Last Underperform the Market—and How to Successful Transform Them.*

30. The discussion of incremental and radical innovations is based on Hill, C. W. L., and F. T. Rothaermel (2003), "The performance of incumbent firms in the face of radical technological innovation," *Academy of Management Review* 28: 257–274.

31. "Pioneering CNN rates behind Fox News, MSNBC," *NBC Washington,* March 30, 2009.

32. Hill, C. W. L., and F. T. Rothaermel (2003), "The performance of incumbent firms in the face of radical technological innovation," *Academy of Management Review* 28: 257–274.

33. "The challengers. A new breed of multinational company has emerged," *The Economist,* January 10, 2008.

34. This discussion is based on Hill, C. W. L., and F. T. Rothaermel (2003), "The performance of incumbent firms in the face of radical technological innovation."

35. Gillette took off when it decided to "give away" its razors (sell them at or below cost, or give them away outright) and make money on selling expensive razors. This business model is now found in many situations: "give away" the printer, and make money on

cartridges; "give away" the video game console to make money off the games; "give away" the cell phone to make money with a two-year service plan; "give away" the coffeemakers to make money from expensive coffee sachets. For a more in-depth discussion, see Anderson, C. (2009), *Free: The Future of a Radical Price.*

36. The razor model chronology includes Trac II, Atra, Sensor, Sensor Excel, Sensor 3, Mach 3, Mach 3 Venus, Mach 3 Turbo, Mach 3 Turbo Venus Divine, Fusion, and others.

37. This Strategy Highlight is based on: Anderson, C. (2009), *Free: The Future of a Radical Price;* and "P&G razor launches in recession's shadow," *The Wall Street Journal,* February 12, 2010.

38. Brandenburger, A. M., and B. J. Nalebuff (1996), *Co-opetition* (New York: Currency Doubleday); and Christensen, C. M., and J. L. Bower (1996), "Customer power, strategic investment, and the failure of leading firms," *Strategic Management Journal* 17: 197–218.

39. Henderson, R., and K. B. Clark (1990), "Architectural innovation: The reconfiguration of existing technologies and the failure of established firms," *Administrative Science Quarterly* 35: 9–30.

40. This example is drawn from: Chesbrough, H. (2003), *Open Innovation. The New Imperative for Creating and Profiting from Technology,* (Boston, MA: Harvard Business School Press).

41. The discussion of disruptive innovation is based on: Christensen, C. M. (1997), *The Innovator's Dilemma: When New Technologies Cause Great Firms to Fail* (Boston, MA: Harvard Business School Press); and Christensen, C. M., and M. E. Raynor (2003), *The Innovator's Solution: Creating and Sustaining Successful Growth* (Boston, MA: Harvard Business School Press).

42. "Introducing the Google Chrome OS," *The Official Google Blog,* July 7, 2009, http://googleblog.blogspot.com/2009/07/introducing-google-chrome-os.html.

43. See discussion on Business Models in Chapter 1. See also: Anderson, C. (2009), *Free: The Future of a Radical Price.*

44. The new processor is not only inexpensive but also consumes little battery power. Moreover, it marks a departure from the Wintel (Windows and Intel) alliance, because Microsoft did not have a suitable operating system ready for the low-end netbook market. Many of these computers are using free software such as Google's Android operating system and Google Docs for applications.

45. This Strategy Highlight is based on: Immelt, J. R., V. Govindarajan, and C. Timble (2009), "How GE is disrupting itself," *Harvard Business Review,* October; Author's interviews with Michael Poteran of GE Healthcare (10/30/09 and 11/04/09); and "Vscan handheld ultrasound: GE unveils 'stethoscope of the 21st century,'" *Huffington Post,* October 20, 2009.

46. This section is based on: Anderson, C. (2006), *The Long Tail. Why the Future of Business Is Selling Less of More;* and Anderson, C. (2009), *Free. The Future of a Radical Price.*

47. "A giant sucking sound," *The Economist,* November 5, 2009.

48. Anderson, C. (2006), *The Long Tail. Why the Future of Business Is Selling Less of More.*

49. "Microsoft near deal to acquire Skype," *The Wall Street Journal*, May 10, 2011.

50. This discussion is based on: Cohen, W. M., and D. A. Levinthal (1990), "Absorptive capacity: A new perspective on learning and innovation," *Administrative Science Quarterly* 35: 128–152; and Rothaermel, F. T., and M. T. Alexandre (2009), "Ambidexterity in technology sourcing: The moderating role of absorptive capacity," *Organization Science* 20: 759–780.

51. Schilling, M. A. (1998), "Technological lockout: An integrative model of the economic and strategic factors driving technology success and failure," *Academy of Management Review* 23: 267–284.

52. This discussion is based on: Snow, D. (2008), "Beware of old technologies' last gasps," *Harvard Business Review,* January. See also "The Henry Ford of Heart Surgery," *The Wall Street Journal,* November 25, 2009.

53. Foster, R. N. (1986), *Innovation: The Attacker's Advantage* (New York: Summit Books).

54. This discussion is based on: D'Aveni, R. A. (1994), *Hypercompetition. Managing the Dynamics of Strategic Maneuvering* (New York: Free Press).

55. Although the notion of hypercompetition is intuitively appealing, there is an ongoing debate in the literature whether the empirical data indeed confirms it. For recent contributions, see: Gimeno, J., and C. Y. Woo (1996), "Hypercompetition in a multimarket environment: The role of strategic similarity and multimarket contact in competitive de-escalation," *Organization Science* 7: 322–341; Makadok, R. (1998), "Can first-mover and early-mover advantages be sustained in an industry with low barriers to entry/ imitation?" *Strategic Management Journal* 19: 683–696; McNamara, G., P. M. Vaaler, and C. Devers (2003), "Same as it ever was: The search for evidence of increasing hypercompetition, *Strategic Management Journal* 24: 261–278; Thomas, L. G. (1996), "The two faces of competition: Dynamic resourcefulness and the hypercompetitive shift," *Organization Science* 7: 221–242; Vaaler, P., and G. McNamara (2009), "Are technology-intensive industries more dynamically competitive? No and yes," *Organization Science* 20: in press; Thomas, L. G., and R. A. D'Aveni (2009), "The changing nature of competition in the US manufacturing sector, 1950 to 2002," *Strategic Organization* 7: 387–431; Wiggins, R.W., and T. W. Ruefli (2002), "Sustained competitive advantage: Temporal dynamics and the incidence and persistence of superior economic performance," *Organization Science* 13: 82–105; and Wiggins, R. W., and T. W. Ruefli (2005), "Schumpeter's ghost: Is hypercompetition making the best of times shorter?" *Strategic Management Journal* 26: 887–911.

56. nm = nanometer = 1 billionth of a meter.

57. Porter, M. E. (1996), "What is strategy?" *Harvard Business Review,* November–December.

58. Data from Wikipedia, www. wikipedia.org/wiki/wikipedia:about.

59. "For Borders, a scramble to be lean," *The Wall Street Journal,* March 14, 2011.

60. "Borders and the 20-20 hindsight phenomenon," *Forbes,* March 12, 2011.

61. This *my*Strategy example is based on: "14 big businesses that started in a recession," www.insidecrm.com, November 11, 2008; "Full-time MBA Programs: Stanford University," *BusinessWeek,* November 13, 2008; "Start-ups that thrive in a recession," *The Wall Street Journal,* February 4, 2009; and "Why great companies get started in the downturns," www.vcconfidential .com, February 24, 2009.

CHAPTER **8**

Corporate Strategy: Vertical Integration and Diversification

LEARNING OBJECTIVES
After studying this chapter, you should be able to:

LO 8-1 Define corporate-level strategy, and describe the three dimensions along which it is assessed.

LO 8-2 Describe and evaluate different options firms have to organize economic activity.

LO 8-3 Describe the two types of vertical integration along the industry value chain: backward and forward vertical integration.

LO 8-4 Identify and evaluate benefits and risks of vertical integration.

LO 8-5 Describe and examine alternatives to vertical integration.

LO 8-6 Describe and evaluate different types of corporate diversification.

LO 8-7 Apply the core competence–market matrix to derive different diversification strategies.

LO 8-8 Explain when a diversification strategy creates a competitive advantage, and when it does not.

CHAPTERCASE 8

Refocusing GE: A Future of Clean-Tech and Health Care?

JEFFREY IMMELT WAS appointed chairman and CEO of General Electric (GE) on September 7, 2001. Since then, the external environment has experienced continuous and dramatic change: first, the social and economic effects of the 9/11 terrorist attacks, followed later by the 2008–2009 financial meltdown. Although GE is a diversified conglomerate that spans many industries and markets, the recession in 2001 and the even deeper recession of 2008–2009 hit the company especially hard. One reason is the financial hit that GE Capital took, since more than half of GE's profits came from that unit. In a critical 17 months, GE's share price fell 84 percent, from $42.12 (on October 2, 2007) to $6.66 (on March 5, 2009), equating to a loss in shareholder value of $378 billion. Between 2008 and 2010, GE significantly underperformed the Dow Jones Industrial Index. To compound matters, GE also lost its AAA credit rating, and the company had to ask for a $15 billion liquidity injection from famed investor Warren Buffett.

The need for change was clear to Immelt. In 2009, GE's five business units (Technology Infrastructure, Energy Infrastructure, Capital Finance, Consumer and Industrial, and NBC Universal) brought in $157 billion in annual revenues. More than 50 percent of those revenues came from outside the United States, and GE employed more than 300,000 people in over 100 countries. Immelt decided to refocus GE's portfolio of businesses to reduce its exposure to capital markets and to achieve reliable and sustainable future growth by leveraging its core competencies in industrial engineering. GE sold a majority stake in NBC Universal to Comcast, the largest U.S. cable operator, and also put its century-old appliance unit up for sale. GE had identified the green economy and, more recently, health care as major future-growth industries. To capitalize on these opportunities, GE launched two strategic initiatives: *ecomagination* and *healthymagination*.

Ecomagination is GE's clean-tech strategic initiative, launched in 2005 and renewed in 2010 by adding another $10 billion in investments. As Immelt explains, its strategic intent is "to focus our unique energy, technology, manufacturing, and infrastructure capabilities to develop tomorrow's solutions such as solar energy, hybrid locomotives, fuel cells, lower-emission aircraft engines, lighter and stronger materials, efficient lighting, and water purification technology."[1] GE's stated goal is, by 2012, to reduce global greenhouse gas emissions by 1 percent and GE's total water consumption by 20 percent (from a 2006 baseline). Since 2005, GE has invested billions in clean-tech R&D. The ecomagination initiative generates roughly $25 billion in annual revenues for GE.

Healthymagination, launched in 2009, is GE's newest strategic initiative. Its goal is to increase the quality of and access to health care while lowering its cost. Investing $6 billion by 2015, GE's strategic intent is to reduce the cost of health care by 15 percent, increase access to essential health care services worldwide by 15 percent, reach a minimum of 100 million people a year, and improve health care quality by 15 percent by streamlining health care procedures, processes, and standards.[2]

After reading the chapter, you will find more about this case, with related questions, on page 226.

▲ **AS A MULTIBUSINESS** enterprise, GE has been changing its corporate strategy by moving away from slow-growing businesses (appliances and entertainment) and turning to future-growth industries such as clean-tech and health care. More importantly, Jeffrey Immelt reduced GE's exposure to the financial markets by trimming the GE Capital unit. Although GE Capital produced roughly half of GE's profits (based on one-third of its revenues), it made GE more vulnerable to changes in the macro environment, as became painfully apparent in the 2008–2009 financial crisis. These changes in GE's strategy demonstrate that firms must decide in which industries and global markets to compete, and that these choices are likely to change over time. Answers to these important questions are captured in a firm's *corporate-level strategy,* which we cover in the next three chapters.

In this chapter, we define corporate-level strategy and then look at two fundamental corporate-level strategy topics: vertical integration and diversification. We address horizontal integration by studying acquisitions, strategic alliances, and networks in Chapter 9, before turning our attention to global strategy in Chapter 10.

WHAT IS CORPORATE-LEVEL STRATEGY?

In Chapters 6 and 7, we saw that *business-level strategy* concerns the quest for gaining and sustaining competitive advantage in a *single product market* (how to compete). **Corporate-level strategy** involves the decisions that senior management makes and the actions it takes in the quest for competitive advantage in several industries and markets simultaneously (where to compete). When formulating corporate strategy, managers must clarify the firm's focus on specific product and geographic markets. Although many managers have input in this important decision-making process, the responsibility for corporate strategy ultimately rests with the CEO. We noted in ChapterCase 8, for example, Jeffrey Immelt's attempt to refocus GE on future-growth industries through the *ecomagination* and *healthymagination* strategic initiatives. In his 2010 letter to shareholders, Mr. Immelt confirmed GE's back-to-its-roots corporate strategy: "As we grew, financial services became too big and added too much volatility. GE must be an industrial company first. We have increased our investment in industrial growth."[3]

As discussed in Chapter 6, the two generic business strategies that firms can pursue in their quest for competitive advantage are to: increase differentiation (while containing cost) *or* lower costs (while maintaining differentiation). If trade-offs can be reconciled, some firms might be able to pursue an integration strategy by increasing differentiation *and* lowering costs. To gain and sustain competitive advantage, therefore, any corporate strategy must align with and strengthen a firm's business strategy, whether it is differentiation, cost leadership, or an integration strategy.

Corporate strategy concerns the **scope of the firm,**[4] which determines the boundaries of the firm along three dimensions: industry value chain, products and services, and geography (regional, national, or global markets). To determine these boundaries, executives must decide:

■ In what stages of the *industry value chain* (the transformation of raw materials into finished goods and services along distinct vertical stages) to participate. This decision determines the firm's *vertical integration.*

- What *range of products and services* the firm should offer. This decision determines the firm's *horizontal integration,* or *diversification.*

- Where in the world to compete. This decision determines the firm's *global strat*egy.

These are the fundamental corporate-level strategic decisions. Exhibit 8.1 depicts the horizontal, vertical, and geographic dimensions along which corporate strategy is assessed. The three dimensions create a space in which corporate executives most position the company for competitive advantage.

The underlying strategic management concepts that will guide our discussion of the vertical, horizontal, and geographic scope of the firm are *economies of scale and scope,* and *transaction costs.*

As discussed in Chapter 6, *economies of scale* occur when a firm's average cost per unit decreases as its output increases. Anheuser-Busch InBev, the largest global brewer (producer of brands such as Budweiser, Bud Light, Stella Artois, and Beck's), reaps significant economies of scale. Given its size, it is able to spread its fixed costs over the millions of gallons of beer it brews each year, in addition to the significant buyer power its large market share affords. Larger market share, therefore, often leads to lower costs. *Economies of scope,* in turn, are the savings that come from producing two (or more) outputs or providing different services at less cost than producing each individually, though using the same resources and technology. Leveraging its online retailing expertise, for example, Amazon benefits from economies of scope: By leveraging its core competency in superior IT systems, it can offer a large range of different product and service categories at a lower cost than it would take to offer each product line individually. This leveraging explains why Amazon offers not only a wide array of goods online but also cloud computing services. (By spreading its fixed cost over many different product and service lines, Amazon also benefits from economies of scale.)

The second underlying strategic management concept that will guide our discussion is *transaction costs,* which are all costs associated with an economic exchange. We begin our study of corporate strategy by drawing on transaction cost economics to explain the choices firms make concerning their scope. This strategic management framework enables managers to answer the question of whether it is cost-effective for their firm to grow its scope by taking on greater ownership of the *production* of needed inputs or of the *channels* by which it distributes its outputs (vertical integration). Later, we will explore managerial decisions relating to diversification, which directly affect the horizontal dimension (the firm's scope of products and services) in multi-industry competition. We take up horizontal integration in more detail in the next chapter. Although we touch upon a firm's geographic scope in this chapter, we study it in more depth in Chapter 10, which is devoted to global strategy.

EXHIBIT 8.1

The Three Dimensions of Corporate-Level Strategy: Vertical Integration, Horizontal Integration, and Geographic Scope

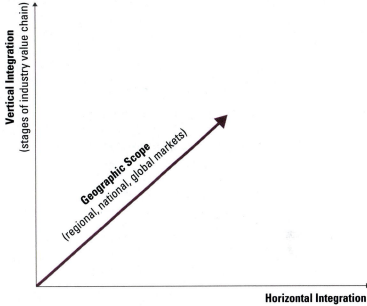

corporate-level strategy The decisions that senior management makes and the actions it takes in the quest for competitive advantage in several industries and markets simultaneously; addresses *where to compete.*

scope of the firm The boundaries of the firm along three dimensions: industry value chain, products and services, and geography (regional, national, or global markets).

TRANSACTION COST ECONOMICS AND THE SCOPE OF THE FIRM

>> **LO 8-2**
Describe and evaluate different options firms have to organize economic activity.

Determining the scope of the firm so that it is more likely to gain and sustain a competitive advantage is the critical challenge in corporate-level strategy.[5] A theoretical framework in strategic management called **transaction cost economics** explains and predicts the scope of the firm, which is central to formulating a corporate-level strategy. Insights gained from transaction cost economics help managers decide what activities to do in-house versus what services and products to obtain from the external market. The key insight of transaction cost economics is that different *institutional arrangements*—markets versus firms—have different costs attached.

To start, we need to identify **transaction costs:** these are all costs associated with an economic exchange, whether it takes place within the boundaries of a firm or in markets.[6] When companies transact in the open market, they incur the costs of searching for an economic agent (a firm or an individual) with whom to contract, negotiating, monitoring, and enforcing the contract.

Transaction costs can occur within the firm as well. Considered **administrative costs,** they include costs pertaining to organizing an economic exchange within a hierarchy—for example, the costs of recruiting and retaining employees, paying salaries and benefits, setting up a shop floor, providing office space and computers, and organizing, monitoring, and supervising work. Administrative costs also include costs associated with coordinating economic activity between different business units of the same corporation (such as transfer pricing for input factors) and between business units and corporate headquarters (including important decisions pertaining to resource allocation, among others). Administrative costs tend to increase with organizational size and complexity.

Firms vs. Markets: Make or Buy?

Transaction cost economics allows us to explain which activities a firm should pursue in-house ("make") versus which goods and services to obtain externally ("buy"). These decisions help determine the scope of the firm. In some cases, costs of using the market (such as search costs, negotiating and drafting contracts, monitoring work, and enforcing contracts when necessary) may be higher than integrating the activity within a single firm and coordinating it through an organizational hierarchy. When the costs of pursuing an activity in-house are less than the costs of transacting for that activity in the market ($C_{in\text{-}house} < C_{market}$), then the firm should *vertically integrate* by owning production of the needed inputs or the channels for the distribution of outputs. In other words, when *firms* are more efficient in organizing economic activity than are *markets,* which rely on contracts among (many) independent actors, firms should vertically integrate.[7]

For example, rather than contracting in the open market for individual pieces of software code, Microsoft hires programmers to write code in-house. Owning these software-development capabilities is valuable to the firm because its costs (salaries and benefits to in-house computer programmers) are less than what they would be in the open market. More importantly, Microsoft benefits from economies of scope in software development resources and capabilities, since skills acquired in writing software code for its Windows operating system are transferable to other Microsoft applications like Word or Excel. Indeed, Microsoft's programmers have a considerable advantage over outside developers. Due to their familiarity with the proprietary source code for Windows 7, Microsoft's newest operating system (which contains millions of lines of software code), they are able to produce applications that run seamlessly and reliably on computers that use Windows 7. Since many leading software firms rely on proprietary software code and algorithms, using

the open market to transact for individual pieces of software would be prohibitively expensive. Also the software
firms would need to disclose to outside
developers a source of their competitive
advantage, thus negating their value-
creation potential.

Firms and markets, as different institutional arrangements for organizing
economic activity, have their own distinct
advantages and disadvantages, summarized in Exhibit 8.2. Advantages of firms
include making command-and-control
decisions, by fiat along hierarchical
lines of authority; coordinating highly
complex tasks to allow for specialized
division of labor; and creating a community of knowledge. Disadvantages
of organizing economic activity within
firms include administrative costs and
low-powered incentives, such as hourly
wages and salaries (which often are less
attractive motivators than the entrepreneurial opportunities and rewards that
can be obtained in the open market), and
the principal–agent problem.

EXHIBIT 8.2

Organizing Economic Activity: Firm vs. Markets

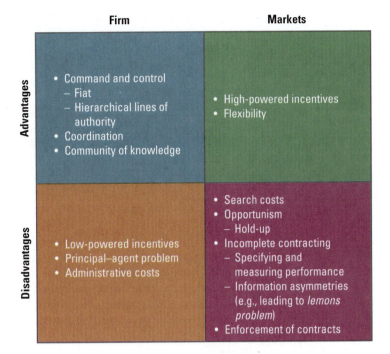

Another disadvantage of organizing economic activity within firms, as opposed to
within markets, is the **principal–agent problem** that can arise when an agent (such as a
manager), performing activities on behalf of the principal (the owner) of the firm, pursues
his or her own interests.[8] Indeed, the separation of ownership and control is one of the hall-
marks of a publicly traded company, and so some degree of the principal–agent problem is
almost inevitable.[9] The problem arises when the agents, acting on behalf of the principals,
pursue their own interests such as job security and managerial perks (e.g., corporate jets
and golf outings). These interests conflict with the principals' goals—in particular, creating
shareholder value. One potential way to overcome the principal–agent problem is to make
managers owners through stock options. We will revisit the principal–agent problem, with
related ideas, in Chapters 11 and 12.

Compared to firms, markets provide high-powered incentives. Rather than work as a
salaried engineer for an existing firm, for example, an individual can start a new venture
offering specialized software. One of the most high-powered incentives of the open market
is to take a new venture through an initial public offering (IPO), or be acquired by an existing firm. In these so-called *liquidity events,* a successful entrepreneur can make potentially
enough money to provide financial security for life.[10] Moreover, transacting in markets

transaction cost economics
A theoretical framework in strategic
management to explain and predict the
scope of the firm, which is central to
formulating a corporate-level strategy
that is more likely to lead to competitive
advantage.

transaction costs All costs associated
with an economic exchange, whether
within a firm or in markets.

administrative costs All costs pertaining
to organizing an economic exchange
within a hierarchy, including recruiting and

retaining employees, paying salaries and
benefits, and setting up a business.

principal–agent problem
Situation in which an agent performing
activities on behalf of a principal pursues
his or her own interests.

enables those who wish to purchase goods to compare prices and services among many different providers, and thus increases transparency and flexibility.

On a very fundamental level, perhaps the biggest disadvantage of transacting in markets, rather than owning the various production and distribution activities within the firm itself, entails non-trivial *search costs*. In particular, firms face search costs when they must scour the market to find suppliers from among the many firms competing to offer similar products and services. Even more difficult can be the search to find suppliers when the specific products and services needed are not offered at all by firms currently in the market.

Transacting in the market has several other notable disadvantages. First, it runs the risk of opportunism by other parties. *Opportunism* is behavior characterized by seeking self-interest with guile (which we'll discuss in more detail later). In addition, there is the problem of *incomplete contracting*. Although market transactions are based on implicit and explicit contracts, all contracts are incomplete to some extent, since not all future contingencies can be anticipated at the time of contracting. It is also difficult to specify expectations (e.g., What stipulates "acceptable quality" in a graphic design project?) or to measure performance and outcomes (e.g., What does "excess wear and tear" mean when returning a leased car?).

Frequently, sellers have better information about products and services than buyers, which in turn creates **information asymmetries,** situations in which one party is more informed than another, mostly due to the possession of private information. When firms transact in the market, such unequal information can lead to a *lemons problem.* Information asymmetries can result in the crowding out of desirable goods and services by inferior ones. Nobel Laureate George Akerlof first described this situation using the market for used cars as an example.[11] Assume only two types of cars are sold: good cars and bad cars (lemons). Good cars are worth $8,000 and bad ones are worth $4,000. Moreover, only the seller knows whether a car is good or is a lemon. Assuming the market supply is split equally between good and bad cars, the probability of buying a lemon is 50 percent. Buyers are aware of the general possibility of buying a lemon and thus would like to hedge against it. Therefore, they split the difference and offer $6,000 for a used car. This discounting strategy has the perverse effect of crowding out all the good cars because the sellers perceive their value to be above $6,000. Assuming that to be the case, all used cars offered for sale will be lemons.

As illustrated by the lemons example, information asymmetries in markets can lead to perverse effects. Applying this insight to the market for collaborative R&D projects in biotechnology, empirical research supports the lemons hypothesis.[12] In particular, the researchers suggest that biotechnology startups have a tendency to develop the most-promising R&D projects internally, while, at the same, they offer inferior R&D projects ("lemons") to large pharmaceutical companies for joint development through strategic alliances.

Finally, it often is difficult, costly, and time-consuming to *enforce legal contracts.*[13] Not only does litigation absorb a significant amount of managerial resources and attention, it can easily amount to several million dollars in legal fees. Legal exposure, therefore, is one of the major hazards in using markets rather than integrating an activity within a firm's hierarchy.

Also, note that the *resource-based view of the firm* (introduced in Chapter 4) provides an alternative perspective on the make-or-buy decision. Rather than being determined by transaction costs, a firm's boundaries are delineated by its knowledge bases and competencies.[14] Activities that draw on what the firm knows how to do well (e.g., Honda's core competency in small, highly reliable engines, or Google's core competency in developing proprietary search algorithms) should be done in-house, while non-core activities can be outsourced. In this perspective, the internally held knowledge determines a firm's boundaries.

information asymmetries
Situations in which one party is more informed than another, mostly due to the possession of private information.

Alternatives on the Make-or-Buy Continuum

The "make" and "buy" choices *anchor each end of a continuum* from markets to firms, as depicted in Exhibit 8.3. Several alternative hybrid arrangements are in fact available between these two extremes.[15] Moving from transacting in the market ("buy") to full integration ("make"), alternatives include short-term contracts as well as various forms of strategic alliances (long-term contracts, equity alliances, and joint ventures) and parent–subsidiary relationships.

SHORT-TERM CONTRACTS. When engaging in *short-term contracting,* a firm sends out *requests for proposals* (*RFPs*) to several companies, which initiates competitive bidding for contracts to be awarded with a short duration, generally less than one year. The benefit to this approach lies in the fact that it allows a somewhat longer planning period than individual market transactions. Moreover, the buying firm can often demand lower prices due to the competitive bidding process. The drawback, however, is that firms responding to the RFP have no incentive to make any transaction-specific investments (e.g., new machinery to improve product quality) due to the short duration of the contract. Since short-term contracts are unlikely to be of strategic significance, they are not subsumed under the term *strategic alliances,* but rather are considered to be *mere contractual arrangements.*

STRATEGIC ALLIANCES. As we move toward greater integration on the make-or-buy continuum, the next organizational forms are strategic alliances. In a broad sense, *strategic alliances* are voluntary arrangements between firms that involve the sharing of knowledge, resources, and capabilities with the intent of developing processes, products, or services together.[16] Alliances have become a ubiquitous phenomenon, especially in high-tech industries. Moreover, strategic alliances can facilitate investments in transaction-specific assets without encountering the administrative costs involved in owning firms in various stages of the industry value chain.

Strategic alliances is an umbrella term that denotes different hybrid organizational forms—among them, long-term contracts, equity alliances, and joint ventures. Given their prevalence in today's competitive landscape, as a key vehicle to execute a firm's corporate strategy, we take a quick look at strategic alliances here and then study them in more depth in Chapter 9.

Long-Term Contracts. We noted that firms in short-term contracts have no incentive to make transaction-specific investments. *Long-term contracts,* which work much like short-term

EXHIBIT 8.3

Alternatives along the Make-or-Buy Continuum

Toyota Locks Up Lithium for Car Batteries

Global demand for lithium-ion batteries to propel cars is estimated to grow almost a hundred-fold, to $25 billion in 2014, up from a mere $278 million in 2009. However, this type of battery requires large amounts of high-quality lithium, which is difficult and costly to extract. Given the specific geological conditions, the company mining the lithium must deploy specialized equipment.

Toyota Motor Corporation was interested in securing a long-term supply of lithium to power its growing fleet of hybrid vehicles. It approached Orocobre, which holds the exploration rights to a large salt-lake area in northwestern Argentina. Although lithium is found in several rock formations across the globe, large quantities can be extracted in a cost-effective manner only below the surfaces of salt flats. However, initial investments in specialized equipment worth several hundred million dollars are required even to understand the *quality* of the deposits. If the findings are positive, more investments would be needed to exploit them commercially.

Should Orocobre make the investment in the specialized equipment? What if the lithium is not of the quality expected, or a new technology emerges that is superior to lithium-ion batteries? Toyota would then have an incentive to walk away from the deal. To negate this concern, Toyota took an equity stake worth an estimated $100 to $120 million in this project.[17]

contracts but with a duration generally greater than one year, help overcome this drawback. Long-term contracts help facilitate transaction-specific investments. Licensing, for example, is a form of long-term contracting in the manufacturing sector that enables firms to commercialize intellectual property (such as a patent). The first biotechnology drug to reach the market, Humulin (human insulin), was developed by Genentech and commercialized by Eli Lilly based on a licensing agreement.

In service industries, franchising is an example of long-term contracting. In these arrangements, a franchisor (such as McDonald's, Burger King, 7-Eleven, H&R Block, or Subway) grants a franchisee (usually an entrepreneur owning no more than a few outlets) the right to use the franchisor's trademark and business processes to offer goods and services that carry the franchisor's brand name. Besides providing the capital to finance the expansion of the chain, the franchisee generally pays an up-front (buy-in) lump sum to the franchisor plus a percentage of revenues.

Long-term contracting, however, also has drawbacks. As mentioned earlier, all contracts are incomplete to some extent. Incomplete contracts open the door for opportunism by one of the contractual parties due to diverging motivations and incentives.

Equity Alliances. Yet another form of strategic alliance is an *equity alliance*—a partnership in which at least one partner takes partial ownership in the other partner. A partner purchases an ownership share by buying stock (making an equity investment). The taking of equity tends to signal greater commitment to the partnership.

Strategy Highlight 8.1 describes an equity alliance between Toyota and Orocobre Ltd., an Australian mineral-resource company, to make specialized investments for the exploration and mining of lithium, a critical input for lithium-ion batteries used in hybrid and electric vehicles.

In the Strategy Highlight, if Toyota were merely to transact for the lithium in the market—by simply signing a contract with Orocobre that it would purchase any lithium it mined—Toyota could walk away from the exploratory project undertaken by Orocobre if the results were not what it had expected, or if the forecasted demand for lithium-ion batteries did not materialize. In a contractual arrangement, one transaction partner could attempt to *hold up* the other, by demanding lower prices or threatening to walk away from the agreement altogether (with whatever financial penalties might be included in the contract). To assuage Orocobre's concerns, Toyota made a credible commitment—a long-term strategic decision that is both difficult and costly to reverse. Alternatively, Toyota could have bought Orocobre outright. This would have been, however, a much more costly and riskier strategic move.

Joint Ventures. In a joint venture, which is another special form of strategic alliance, two or more partners create and jointly own a new organization. Since the partners contribute equity to a joint venture, they make a long-term commitment, which in turn facilitates transaction-specific investments. Dow Corning, owned jointly by Dow Chemical and Corning, is an example of a joint venture. Dow Corning, which focuses on silicone-based technology, employs roughly 10,000 people and has $5 billion in annual revenues.[18] This example shows that some joint ventures can be Fortune 500 companies in their own right. Hulu, which offers web-based streaming video of TV shows and movies, is also a joint venture. It is owned by NBC Universal, Fox Entertainment Group, and ABC Inc. We will further discuss joint ventures in Chapter 9.

PARENT–SUBSIDIARY RELATIONSHIP. The *parent–subsidiary relationship* describes the most-integrated alternative to performing an activity within one's own corporate family. The corporate parent owns the subsidiary and can direct it via command and control. Transaction costs that arise are frequently due to political turf battles, which may include (among other areas) the capital budgeting process and transfer prices. For example, although GM owns its European carmakers Opel and Vauxhall, it had problems bringing some of their know-how and design of small fuel-efficient cars back into the U.S. This particular parent–subsidiary relationship was burdened by political problems because managers in Detroit did not respect the engineering behind the small, fuel-efficient cars that Opel and Vauxhall made. They thus were not interested in using European know-how for the U.S. market (and didn't want to pay much or anything for it). Moreover, Detroit was tired of subsidizing the losses of Opel and Vauxhall, and felt that its European subsidiaries were manipulating the capital budgeting process.[19] In turn, the Opel and Vauxhall subsidiaries felt resentment toward their parent company: GM had initially planned to sell them as part of its bankruptcy restructuring whereas they, instead, hoped to be spun out as independent companies.[20]

Having fully considered transactions cost economics and the scope of the firm to lay a strong theoretical foundation, we now turn our attention to the firm's scope along the vertical industry value chain.

VERTICAL INTEGRATION ALONG THE INDUSTRY VALUE CHAIN

The first key question when formulating corporate-level strategy is: In what stages of the industry value chain should the firm participate? Deciding whether to make (within the firm) or buy (in the market from other firms) the various activities in the industry value chain involves the concept of vertical integration. Vertical integration is the firm's ownership of its production of needed inputs or of the channels by which it distributes its outputs. In particular, vertical integration can be measured by a firm's value added: What percentage of a firm's sales is generated within the firm's boundaries?[21] The degree of vertical integration tends to correspond to the number of industry value-chain stages in which it directly participates.

---

licensing A form of long-term contracting in the manufacturing sector that enables firms to commercialize intellectual property.

franchising A long-term contract in which a franchisor grants a franchisee the right to use the franchisor's trademark and business processes to offer goods and services that carry the franchisor's brand name; the franchisee in turn pays an up-front buy-in lump sum and a percentage of revenues.

credible commitment A long-term strategic decision that is both difficult and costly to reverse.

joint venture Organizational form in which two or more partners create and jointly own a new organization.

vertical integration The firm's ownership of its production of needed inputs or of the channels by which it distributes its outputs.

EXHIBIT 8.4

Backward and Forward Vertical Integration along an Industry Value Chain

UPSTREAM INDUSTRIES

BACKWARD VERTICAL INTEGRATION

Stage 1
- Raw Materials

Stage 2
- Components
- Intermediate Goods

Stage 3
- Final Assembly
- Manufacturing

Stage 4
- Marketing
- Sales

Stage 5
- After-Sales Service and Support

DOWNSTREAM INDUSTRIES

FORWARD VERTICAL INTEGRATION

Exhibit 8.4 depicts a generic **industry value chain.** Industry value chains are also called *vertical value chains,* because they depict the transformation of raw materials into finished goods and services along distinct vertical stages. Each stage of the vertical value chain typically represents a distinct *industry* in which a number of different firms are competing.

In Chapter 4, we introduced the concept of the firm-level internal value chain. That internal value chain depicts the activities the firm engages in to transform inputs into outputs, with activities ranging from basic R&D to customer service. Internal, firm-level value chains are also called *horizontal value chains.* Thus, there are two intersecting value chains: the *industry value chain* running *vertically* from upstream to downstream, and the *firm-level value chain* running *horizontally.*[22] In this chapter on corporate-level strategy, the one of interest is the vertical, industry value chain.

To understand the concept of vertical integration along the different stages of the industry value chain more fully, let's take your cell phone as an example. This ubiquitous device is the result of a globally coordinated industry value chain of different products and services. The raw materials to make your cell phone, such as chemicals, ceramics, metals, oil (for plastic), and so on, are commodities. In each of these commodity businesses are different companies, such as DuPont (U.S.), BASF (Germany), Kyocera (Japan), and ExxonMobil (U.S.). Intermediate goods and components such as integrated circuits, displays, touch screens, cameras, and batteries are provided by firms such as Jabil Circuit (U.S.), Intel (U.S.), LG Display (Korea), Altek (Taiwan), and BYD (China). Original equipment manufacturing firms (OEMs) such as Flextronics (Singapore) or Foxconn (China) typically assemble cell phones under contract for consumer electronics and telecommunications companies like Ericsson (Sweden), Motorola (U.S.), Nokia (Finland), RIM (Canada), and so on. If you look closely at an iPhone, for example, you'll notice that it says "Designed by Apple in California. Assembled in China." Finally, to get wireless data and voice service, you pick a service provider such as AT&T, Sprint, or Verizon. All of these companies— from the raw-materials suppliers to the service providers—comprise the global industry value chain that, as a whole, delivers you a working cell phone. Determined by their corporate strategy, each firm decides where in the industry value chain to participate, and thus the vertical scope of the firm.

industry value chain Depiction of the transformation of raw materials into finished goods and services along distinct vertical stages, each of which typically represents a distinct *industry* in which a number of different firms are competing.

>> LO 8-3
Describe the two types of vertical integration along the industry value chain: backward and forward vertical integration.

Types of Vertical Integration

Along the industry value chain, there are varying degrees of vertical integration. Weyerhaeuser, one of the world's largest paper and pulp companies, is *fully vertically integrated:* all activities are conducted within the boundaries of the firm. As an example, Weyerhaeuser owns forests, grows and cuts its timber, mills it, manufactures a variety of different paper and construction products, and distributes them to retail outlets and other large customers. Weyerhaeuser's value added is 100 percent. Weyerhaeuser, therefore, competes in a number of different industries and faces different competitors in each.

On the other end of the spectrum are firms that are more or less *vertically disintegrated.* These are firms that focus on only one or a limited few stages of the industry value chain. For instance, Zara, a Spanish clothing and accessory designer, is vertically disintegrated to a large extent in the upstream industry stages. Zara runs a hyper-efficient global logistics operation that allows it to produce fashion trends faster than any competitor.[23] Zara designs new fashion trends and then outsources most of its manufacturing to Asia and the Middle East, even though some of the more high-end fashions are produced in Spain closer to its headquarters. While other international competitors take months to bring new designs to market, Zara designs, manufactures, and gets products to market in about four weeks. Zara captures significant value from orchestrating its network of suppliers, buyers, and other business partners. Designing fashionable clothing and accessories in fast cycles is a competency that obeys the VRIO principles (discussed in Chapter 4), and thus can lay the foundation for competitive advantage. (Zara does own some retail outlets, so it is not fully vertically disintegrated along the entire industry value chain.)

Be aware that *not all industry value-chain stages are equally profitable.* Zara, for instance, designs fashions but has others produce and ship the products. Similarly, Apple captures significant value by designing mobile devices through integration of hardware and software in novel ways, but it outsources the manufacturing of its device to generic OEMs. The logic behind these decisions can be explained by applying the structure-conduct-performance (SCP) model (introduced in Chapter 3) and the VRIO model. In the cell phone manufacturing industry structure, the many small OEMs are almost completely interchangeable and are thus exposed to the perils of perfect competition. On the other hand, Apple's competencies in innovation, system integration, and marketing, are valuable, rare, and unique (nonimitable) resources, and Apple is organized to capture most of the value it creates. In terms of industry structure, Apple's continued innovation through new introductions of products and services provides it with temporary competitive advantage. Even so, competitors are not sitting idle.

To compete with Apple's iPhone, Google launched the Nexus One (in 2010), a smartphone that used Google's Android open-source operating system. Google, at its heart a software company, chose to have HTC of Taiwan manufacture the product's hardware.[24] Exhibit 8.5 displays part of the value chain for smartphones. In this figure, note HTC's transformation from a no-name manufacturer (for example, of Google's Nexus One) to a significant player in the design, manufacture, and sales of smartphones. It now offers a lineup of

EXHIBIT 8.5

HTC's Backward and Forward Integration along the Industry Value Chain in the Smartphone Industry

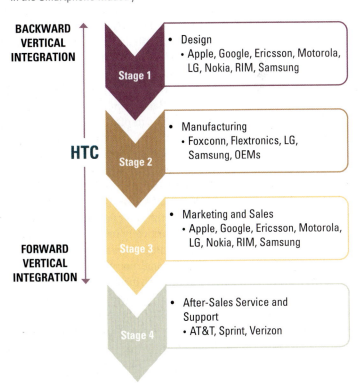

BACKWARD VERTICAL INTEGRATION

Stage 1
- Design
  - Apple, Google, Ericsson, Motorola, LG, Nokia, RIM, Samsung

HTC

Stage 2
- Manufacturing
  - Foxconn, Flextronics, LG, Samsung, OEMs

FORWARD VERTICAL INTEGRATION

Stage 3
- Marketing and Sales
  - Apple, Google, Ericsson, Motorola, LG, Nokia, RIM, Samsung

Stage 4
- After-Sales Service and Support
  - AT&T, Sprint, Verizon

smartphones under the HTC label.[25] Over time, HTC was able to upgrade its capabilities from merely manufacturing smartphones to also designing products.[26] In doing so, HTC engaged in **backward vertical integration**—moving ownership of activities upstream to the originating (inputs) point of the value chain. Moreover, by moving downstream into sales and increasing its branding activities, HTC has also engaged in **forward vertical integration**—moving ownership of activities closer to the end (customer) point of the value chain. HTC is benefitting from economies of scope through participating in different stages of the industry value chain. For instance, it now is able to share competencies in product design, manufacturing, and sales, while at the same time attempting to reduce transaction costs.

Benefits and Risks of Vertical Integration

>> LO 8-4
Identify and evaluate benefits and risks of vertical integration.

To decide the degree and type of vertical integration to pursue, managers need to understand the possible benefits and risks of vertical integration.

BENEFITS OF VERTICAL INTEGRATION. Vertical integration, either backward or forward, can have a number of benefits, including:[27]

- Securing critical supplies
- Lowering costs
- Improving quality
- Facilitating scheduling and planning
- Facilitating investments in specialized assets

As noted earlier, HTC started as an OEM for brand-name mobile device companies such as Motorola, Nokia, and others. It backwardly integrated into smartphone design by acquiring One & Co., a San Francisco–based design firm.[28] The acquisition allowed HTC to secure scarce design talent and capabilities that it leveraged into the design of smartphones with superior quality and features built in, thus enhancing the differentiated appeal of its products. Moreover, HTC can now design phones that leverage its low-cost manufacturing capabilities.

Likewise, forward integration into distribution and sales allows companies to more effectively plan for and respond to changes in demand. HTC's forward integration into sales enables it to offer its products directly to wireless providers such as AT&T, Sprint, and Verizon. HTC even offers unlocked phones directly to the end consumer via its website. Thus, HTC is now in a much better position to respond if, for example, demand for its latest phone should suddenly pick up.

There appear to be cyclical trends to vertical integration over time. A decade ago, vertical integration seemed to fall out of favor as firms focused on their core activities while outsourcing the non-core ones. More recently, however, some companies seem to be more inclined to vertically integrate, as shown in Strategy Highlight 8.2.[29]

Vertical integration allows firms to increase operational efficiencies through improved coordination and fine-tuning of adjacent value chain activities. Keeping the downstream value-chain activities independent worked well for PepsiCo and Coca-Cola during the 1980s and 1990s, when consumption of soda beverages was on the rise. However, independent bottlers are cost-effective only when doing large-volume business of a few, limited product offerings. With Pepsi's and Coke's more diversified portfolio of noncarbonated and healthier drinks, the costs of outsourcing bottling and distribution to independent bottlers increased significantly. (Some of the independent bottlers even lack the equipment to produce the niche drinks now in demand.) In addition, the independent bottlers' direct store-delivery system adds significant costs. To overcome this problem, the soft drink giants had begun to deliver some of their niche products (such as Pepsi's Gatorade and SoBe Lifewater and Coke's Powerade and Glacéau) directly to warehouse retailers like Sam's Club and Costco.

Given the increase of costs using the market, the forward integration of Pepsi and Coca-Cola is in line with predictions derived from transaction cost economics. Controlling the delivery part of the value chain also enhances the soft drink giants' bargaining power when negotiating product price, placement, and promotion. Looking at Porter's five forces model, Pepsi and Coke are reducing the bargaining power of buyers and thus shifting the industry structure in their favor. End consumers are likely to benefit from Coke's and Pepsi's forward integration in the form of lower prices and a wider variety of niche drinks. Taken together, vertical integration can increase differentiation and reduce costs, thus strengthening a firm's strategic position as the gap between value creation and costs widens.

Vertical integration along the industry value chain can also facilitate *investments in specialized assets.* What does this mean? Specialized assets have significantly more value in their intended use than in their next-best use (i.e., they have high opportunity cost).[31] They can come in several forms:[32]

- *Site specificity.* Assets are required to be co-located, such as the equipment necessary for mining bauxite and aluminum smelting.
- *Physical-asset specificity.* Assets whose physical and engineering properties are designed to satisfy a particular customer, such as bottling machinery for Coca-Cola and PepsiCo. Since the bottles have different (even trademarked) shapes, they require unique molds.

- *Human-asset specificity.* Investments made in human capital to acquire unique knowledge and skills, such as mastering the routines and procedures of a specific organization, which are not transferable to a different employer.

Why do investments in specialized assets tend to incur high opportunity costs? Making the specialized investment opens up the threat of *opportunism* by one of the partners. Opportunism is defined as self-interest seeking with guile.[33] Backward vertical integration

STRATEGY HIGHLIGHT 8.2

Back to the Future: PepsiCo's Forward Integration

In 2009, PepsiCo forwardly integrated by buying its bottlers in order to obtain more control over its quality, pricing, distribution, and in-store display. This $7.8 billion purchase reversed a 1999 decision in which PepsiCo spun out its bottlers to focus on marketing. According to CEO Indra Nooyi, Pepsi's plans (stated in 2009) were to broaden its menu of offerings to include a slew of new noncarbonated beverages like flavored water enhanced with vitamins and fruit juices. With an integrated value chain, Ms. Nooyi hoped to improve decision making and enhance flexibility to bring innovative products to market faster, while reducing costs by more than $400 million.

Due to the strategic interdependence of companies in an oligopoly (as studied in Chapter 3), it came as no surprise when only a few months later, in early 2010, Pepsi's archrival Coca-Cola responded with its own forward integration move, when it purchased its bottlers for $12.2 billion. Coca-Cola also indicated that more control of manufacturing and distribution were the key drivers behind this deal. Moreover, Coca-Cola pegged the expected cost savings at $350 million. Like PepsiCo, Coca-Cola's forward integration also represented a major departure from its decade-old business model with large independent bottlers and distributors.[30]

---

backward vertical integration
Changes in an industry value chain that involve moving ownership of activities upstream to the originating (inputs) point of the value chain.

forward vertical integration
Changes in an industry value chain that involve moving ownership of activities closer to the end (customer) point of the value chain.

specialized assets Assets that have significantly more value in their intended use than in their next-best use (high opportunity cost); they come in three types: site specificity, physical asset specificity, and human asset specificity.

is often undertaken to overcome the threat of opportunism and in securing key raw materials. For example, steelmaker Nucor recently bought SHV North America, providing Nucor with global sourcing of scrap materials for its innovative technology using electric-arc furnaces.[34]

RISKS OF VERTICAL INTEGRATION. Depending on the situation, vertical integration has several risks, including:[35]

- Increasing costs
- Reducing quality
- Reducing flexibility
- Increasing the potential for legal repercussions

A higher degree of vertical integration can lead to increasing costs for a number of reasons. In-house suppliers tend to have higher cost structures because they are not exposed to market competition. Knowing there will always be a buyer for their products reduces their incentives to lower costs. In contrast, suppliers in the open market, because they serve a much larger market, can achieve economies of scale that elude in-house suppliers. Organizational complexity increases with higher levels of vertical integration, thereby increasing administrative costs such as determining the appropriate transfer prices between an in-house supplier and buyer. Administrative costs arise from the coordination of multiple divisions, political maneuvering for resources, consumption of company perks, or simply from employees slacking off.

The knowledge that there will always be a buyer for their products not only reduces the incentives of in-house suppliers to lower costs; it also can reduce the incentive to increase quality or come up with innovative new products. Moreover, given their larger scale and exposure to more customers, external suppliers often can reap higher learning and experience effects and so develop unique capabilities or quality improvements.

A higher degree of vertical integration can also reduce a firm's strategic flexibility, especially when faced with changes in the external environment such as fluctuations in demand and technological change.[36] For instance, when technological process innovations enabled significant improvements in steel-making, mills like U.S. Steel and Bethlehem Steel were tied to their fully integrated business models and unable to switch technologies, leading to the bankruptcy of many integrated steel mills. Non-vertically integrated mini-mills such as Nucor and Chaparral, on the other hand, invested in the new steel-making process and grew their business by taking market share away from the less flexible integrated producers.[37]

U.S. regulators like the Federal Trade Commission (FTC) and the Justice Department (DOJ) tend to allow vertical integration, arguing that it generally makes firms more efficient and lowers costs, which in turn can benefit customers. However, due to monopoly concerns, vertical integration has not gone unchallenged.[38] The FTC, for example, carefully reviewed PepsiCo's plan to reintegrate its two largest bottlers, which gives the firm full control of about 80 percent of its North American distribution. Before engaging in vertical integration, therefore, managers need to be aware that this corporate strategy can increase the potential for legal repercussions.

>> **LO 8-5**
Describe and examine alternatives to vertical integration.

Alternatives to Vertical Integration

Ideally, one would like to find alternatives to vertical integration that provide similar benefits without the accompanying risks. Are there such alternatives?

TAPER INTEGRATION. One alternative to vertical integration is taper integration. It is a way of orchestrating value activities in which a firm is backwardly integrated but it also relies on outside-market firms for some of its supplies, and/or is forwardly integrated but also relies on outside-market firms for some if its distribution.[39] Exhibit 8.6 illustrates the concept of taper integration along the vertical industry value chain. Here, the firm sources intermediate goods and components from in-house suppliers as well as from outside suppliers. In a similar fashion, a firm sells its products through company-owned retail outlets and through independent retailers. Both Apple and Nike, for example, use taper integration: They own retail outlets but also use other retailers, both brick-and-mortar and online.

Taper integration has several benefits.[40] It exposes in-house suppliers and distributors to market competition, so that performance comparisons are possible. Rather than hollowing out its competencies by relying too much on outsourcing, taper integration allows a firm to retain its competencies in manufacturing and retailing.[41] Moreover, taper integration also enhances a firm's flexibility. For example, when adjusting to fluctuations in demand, a firm could cut back on the finished goods it delivers to external retailers while continuing to stock its own stores. Finally, when using taper integration, firms can combine internal and external knowledge, possibly paving the path for innovation. Based on a study of 3,500 product introductions in the computer industry, researchers have provided empirical evidence that taper integration can be beneficial.[42] Firms that pursued taper integration achieved superior performance in both innovation and financial performance when compared with firms that focused more on vertical integration or strategic outsourcing.

STRATEGIC OUTSOURCING. Another alternative to vertical integration is strategic outsourcing, which involves moving one or more internal value chain activities outside the firm's boundaries to other firms in the industry value chain. A firm that engages in strategic outsourcing reduces its level of vertical integration. Rather than developing their own human resource management systems, for instance, most firms outsource these non-core activities to companies like PeopleSoft (owned by Oracle), EDS (owned by HP), or Perot Systems (owned by Dell), who can leverage their deep competencies and produce scale effects.

In the popular media and everyday conversation, you may hear the term "outsourcing" used to mean sending jobs out of the country. Actually, when outsourced activities take place outside the home country, the correct term is *off-shoring* (or *off-shore outsourcing*). By whatever name, it is a *huge* phenomenon. For example, Infosys, one of the world's largest technology companies and provider of IT services to many Fortune 100 companies, is located in Bangalore, India. The global off-shoring market is estimated to be $1.4 trillion, and is expected to grow at a compound annual growth rate of 15 percent. Banking and financial services, IT, and health care are the most active sectors in such off-shore outsourcing.[43] More recently, U.S. law firms began to send low-end legal work, such as drafting standard contracts and background research, off-shore to India.[44]

EXHIBIT 8.6

Taper Integration along the Industry Value Chain

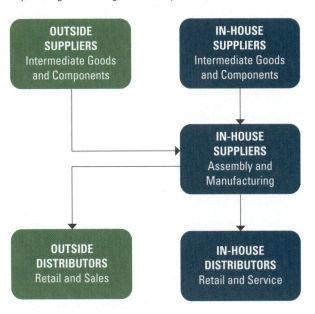

taper integration
A way of orchestrating value activities in which a firm is backwardly integrated but also relies on outside market firms for some of its supplies, and/or is forwardly integrated but also relies on outside-market firms for some of its distribution.

strategic outsourcing
Moving one or more internal value chain activities outside the firm's boundaries to other firms in the industry value chain.

CORPORATE DIVERSIFICATION: EXPANDING BEYOND A SINGLE MARKET

Early in the chapter, we listed three questions related to corporate-level strategy and, in particular, the scope of the firm. The second of those questions relates to the firm's *degree of diversification:* What range of products and services should the firm offer? In particular, why do some companies compete in a single product market, while others compete in several different product markets? Coca-Cola, for example, focuses on soft drinks and thus on a *single* product market. Its archrival PepsiCo competes directly with Coca-Cola by selling a wide variety of soft drinks and other beverages, and also offering chips (Lay's, Doritos, and Cheetos) as well as Quaker Oats products (oatmeal and granola bars).

Similarly, why do some companies compete beyond their national borders, while others prefer to focus on the domestic market? Kentucky Fried Chicken (KFC), the world's largest quick-service chicken restaurant chain, operates more than 5,200 outlets in the U.S., and more than 15,000 outlets internationally in 109 countries.[45] It is particularly popular in China. In 2010, KFC had annual revenues of $12 billion. On the other hand, Chick-fil-A with $3.5 billion in revenues (in 2010) and more than 1,500 outlets competes only domestically at this time.

Answers to questions about the number of markets to compete in and where to compete relate to the broad topic of diversification—increasing the variety of products or markets in which to compete. A *non-diversified company* focuses on a single market, whereas a *diversified company* competes in several different markets simultaneously.[46]

There are various general diversification strategies:

- A firm that is active in several different product markets is pursuing a product diversification strategy.

- A firm that is active in several different countries is pursuing a geographic diversification strategy.

- A company that pursues *both* a product *and* a geographic diversification strategy simultaneously follows a product–market diversification strategy.

Because shareholders expect continuous growth from public companies, managers frequently turn to product and geographic diversification to achieve it. It is therefore not surprising that the vast majority of the Fortune 500 companies are diversified to some degree. However, achieving performance gains through diversification is not guaranteed. Some forms of diversification are more likely to lead to performance improvements than others. We now discuss which diversification types are more likely to increase value creation, and why.

Types of Corporate Diversification

>> LO 8-6
Describe and evaluate different types of corporate diversification.

To understand the types and degrees of corporate diversification, Richard Rumelt of UCLA developed a helpful classification scheme, depicted in Exhibit 8.7. A *single-business firm* derives 95 percent or more of its revenues from one business. Although Google is active in many different businesses, it obtains more than 95 percent of its revenues ($24 billion in 2009) from online advertising.[47] A *dominant-business firm* derives between 70–95 percent of its revenues from a single business, but it pursues at least one other business activity. Although Microsoft is primarily a software company, it also offers computer hardware products such as the Xbox 360 game console, which contributed close to 8 percent of Microsoft's $59 billion revenues in 2009.[48]

A firm follows a related diversification strategy when it derives less than 70 percent of its revenues from a single business activity but obtains revenues from other lines of

Type of Diversification	Revenues from Primary Activity	Sample Firms	
Single Business	> 95%	Coca-Cola, DeBeers, Google	A
Dominant Business	70–90%	Harley-Davidson, Microsoft, Nestlé	A — B
Related Diversification			
1) Related-Constrained	< 70%	ExxonMobil, Johnson & Johnson	A / B — C
2) Related-Linked	< 70%	Amazon, Disney	A / B — C
Unrelated Diversification	< 70%	Berkshire Hathaway, GE, Tata Group	A B C

EXHIBIT 8.7

Different Types of Diversification

Source: Adapted from R. P. Rumelt (1974), *Strategy, Structure, and Economic Performance* (Boston, MA: Harvard Business School Press).

business linked to the primary business activity. The rationale behind related diversification is to benefit from economies of scale and scope: These multibusiness firms can pool and share resources as well as leverage competencies across different business lines. Strategy Highlight 8.3 (next page) describes Exxon's strategic move toward related diversification.

We can further identify two types of related diversification strategy: related-constrained and related-linked. When executives consider business opportunities only where they can leverage their existing competencies and resources, the firm is using *related-constrained diversification*. The choices of alternative business activities are limited—constrained—by the fact that they need to be related through common resources, capabilities, and activities. ExxonMobil's diversification move into natural gas is an example of related-constrained diversification.

If executives consider new business activities that share only a limited number of linkages, the firm is using *related-linked diversification*. For example, Disney follows a related-linked diversification strategy. It is active in a wide array of business activities, from cable and

diversification An increase in the variety of products or markets in which to compete.

product diversification strategy Corporate strategy in which a firm is active in several different product markets.

geographic diversification strategy Corporate strategy in which a firm is active in several different countries.

product–market diversification strategy Corporate strategy in which a firm is active in several different product markets and several different countries.

related diversification strategy Corporate strategy in which a firm derives less than 70 percent of its revenues from a single business activity but obtains revenues from other lines of business that are linked to the primary business activity.

ExxonMobil Diversifies into Natural Gas

In 2008, ExxonMobil reported the highest profits ever recorded by any company, with a net income of over $45 billion on revenues of about $475 billion. To illustrate the magnitude of ExxonMobil's profitability, it earned more than $1,426 in profit for every second of 2008!

Although ExxonMobil's financial performance is impressive, within its portfolio of current operations, the overwhelming majority of its profits come from petroleum-based products. Given the current political and regulatory sentiments and the global movement toward cleaner energy sources, if ExxonMobil fails to supplement its core business (based on petroleum-based energy sources) with greener energy sources, the company will likely not be able to sustain its superior performance over time.

To avoid this fate, ExxonMobil initiated a major strategic thrust into clean energy by focusing on natural gas, a low-carbon alternative to petroleum. This strategic move is an example of horizontal integration. In 2009, ExxonMobil bought XTO Energy, a natural gas company, for $31 billion. XTO Energy is known for its ability to extract natural gas from unconventional places such as shale rock, where huge deposits have been found recently in the United States. ExxonMobil hopes to leverage its core competency in the exploration and commercialization of petroleum energy sources into natural gas. Roughly 85 percent of the world's energy demand today is met by fossil fuels, including petroleum, coal, and natural gas. ExxonMobil is taking the lead among the energy giants by producing nearly equal numbers of barrels of crude oil and natural gas, making it the world's largest producer of natural gas. The company believes that roughly 50 percent of the world's energy for the next 50 years will continue to come from fossil fuels, but that its diversification into natural gas, the cleanest of the fossil fuels in terms of greenhouse gas emissions, will pay off.[49]

network television stations and movies to amusement parks, cruises, and retailing, which share some common resources, capabilities, and activities. Similarly, Amazon.com began business by selling only one product: books. Over time it expanded into CDs, and over time leveraged its online retailing capabilities into a wide array of product offerings. Today, as the world's largest online retailer, and given the need to build huge data centers to service its peak holiday demand, Amazon decided to leverage spare capacity into cloud computing, offering Internet-based computing services, again benefiting from economies of scope (and scale).[50]

Finally, a firm follows an unrelated diversification strategy when less than 70 percent of its revenues come from a single business and there are few, if any, linkages among its businesses. GE, for example, is following an unrelated diversification strategy. Linkages between household appliances, TV shows, jet engines, ultrasound machines, and wind turbines are not readily apparent. It should come as no surprise that each of GE's divisions has its own CEO and is managed as a standalone business with profit-and-loss responsibility. The Indian Tata Group is even more diversified.[51] Its product offering includes cars (Jaguar, Land Rover, and Nano), chemicals, steel, consulting, software, coffee, tea, and luxury hotel resorts. Some of its strategic business units are giants in their own right. The Tata group includes Asia's largest software company (TCS) and India's largest steelmaker. It also owns the renowned Taj Hotels & Resorts.

Some research evidence suggests that an unrelated diversification strategy can be advantageous.[52] This arrangement helps firms gain and sustain competitive advantage because it allows the conglomerate to overcome institutional weaknesses in emerging economies, such as lack of capital markets and well-defined legal systems and property rights. Companies like GE, Berkshire Hathaway, the South Korean LG chaebol, and the Tata group are all considered *conglomerates* due to their unrelated diversification strategy.

Leveraging Core Competencies for Corporate Diversification

In Chapter 4, when looking inside the firm, we introduced the idea that competitive advantage can be based on core competencies. Core competencies are unique skills and strengths that allow firms to increase the perceived value of their product and service offerings and/or lower the cost to produce them.[53] Examples of core competencies are:

- Walmart's ability to effectively orchestrate a globally distributed supply chain at low cost
- Apple's ability to integrate hardware and software into products that provide a superior user experience
- Infosys's ability to provide high-quality information technology services at low cost through leveraging its global delivery model (i.e., taking work to the location where it makes the best economic sense based on the available talent and the least amount of acceptable risk)

>> **LO 8-7**
Apply the core competence–market matrix to derive different diversification strategies.

To survive and prosper, companies need to grow. This mantra holds especially true for publicly owned companies, because they create shareholder value through profitable growth. Managers respond to this relentless growth imperative by leveraging their existing core competencies to find future growth opportunities. Strategy consultants Gary Hamel and C. K. Prahalad advanced the *core competence–market matrix,* depicted in Exhibit 8.8, as a way to guide managerial decisions in regards to diversification strategies. The first task for managers is to identify their existing core competencies and understand the firm's current market situation. When applying an existing or new dimension to core competencies and markets, four quadrants emerge, each with distinct strategic implications.

The lower-left quadrant combines existing core competencies with existing markets. Here, managers must come up with ideas of how to leverage existing core competencies to improve the firm's current market position. In 2010, Bank of America was the largest bank in the United States (measured by deposits) and had at least one customer in 50 percent of U.S. households.[54] Just 20 years earlier Bank of America had been North Carolina National Bank (NCNB), a regional bank in North Carolina. One of NCNB's unique core competencies was acquisitions. It bought smaller banks to supplement its organic growth throughout the 1970s and 80s, and from 1989 to 1992, NCNB purchased over 200 regional community and thrift banks, to further improve its market position. It then turned its core competency to national banks, with a goal of becoming the first nationwide bank. Known as NationsBank in the 1990s, it purchased Barnett Bank, BankSouth, FleetBank, LaSalle, CountryWide Mortgages, and its namesake Bank of America. This example illustrates how

unrelated diversification strategy Corporate strategy in which a firm derives less than 70 percent of its revenues from a single business activity and there are few, if any, linkages among its businesses.

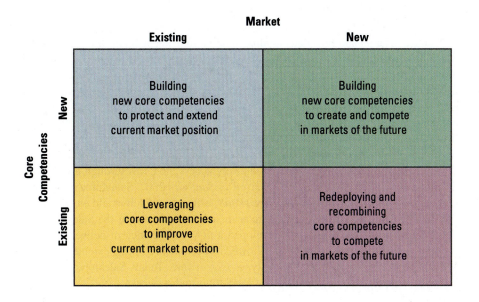

Market

	Existing	New
New	Building new core competencies to protect and extend current market position	Building new core competencies to create and compete in markets of the future
Existing	Leveraging core competencies to improve current market position	Redeploying and recombining core competencies to compete in markets of the future

Core Competencies

EXHIBIT 8.8

The Core Competence–Market Matrix

Source: Adapted from G. Hamel and C. K. Prahalad (1994), *Competing for the Future* (Boston, MA: Harvard Business School Press).

NationsBank, rebranded as Bank of America since 1998, honed and deployed its core competency of acquiring and integrating other commercial banks and dramatically grew its scope to emerge as one of the leading banks in the United States. (By the way, we will study the topic of acquisitions in more detail in Chapter 9.)

The lower-right quadrant of Figure 8.8 combines existing core competencies with new market opportunities. Here, managers must strategize about how to redeploy and recombine existing core competencies to compete in future markets. At the height of the financial crisis in the fall of 2008, Bank of America bought the investment bank Merrill Lynch for $50 billion.[55] Although many problems ensued for Bank of America following the Merrill Lynch acquisition, it is now the bank's investment and wealth management division. Bank of America's corporate managers leveraged an existing competency (acquiring and integrating) into a new market (investment and wealth management). The combined entity is now leveraging economies of scope through cross-selling when, for example, consumer banking makes customer referrals for investment bankers to follow up.[56]

The upper-left quadrant combines new core competencies with existing market opportunities. Here, managers must come up with strategic initiatives to build new core competencies to protect and extend the company's current market position. For example, in the early 1990s, Gatorade dominated the market for sports drinks, a segment in which it had been the original innovator. (Some 25 years earlier, medical researchers at the University of Florida had created the drink to enhance the performance of the Gators, the university's football team. Stokley-Van Camp commercialized and marketed the drink, and eventually sold it to Quaker Oats.) PepsiCo brought Gatorade into its lineup of soft drinks when it acquired Quaker Oats in 2001. By comparison, Coca-Cola had existing core competencies in marketing, bottling, and distributing soft drinks, but had never attempted to compete in the sports-drink market. Over a 10-year R&D effort, Coca-Cola developed competencies in the development and marketing of their own sports drink, Powerade, which launched in 1990. As of 2009, Powerade held about 20 percent of the sports drink market, making it a viable competitor to Gatorade, which still holds about 75 percent of the market.[57]

Finally, the upper-right quadrant combines new core competencies with new market opportunities. Hamel and Prahalad call this combination "mega opportunities"—those that hold significant future-growth opportunities. At the same time, it is likely the most challenging diversification strategy because it requires building new core competencies to create and compete in future markets. Salesforce.com is a company that employs this strategy well.[58] In recent years, Salesforce experienced tremendous growth, the bulk of it coming from the firm's existing core competency in delivering customer relationship management (CRM) software to its clients. Salesforce's product distinguished itself from the competition by providing software as a service via cloud computing: Clients did not need to install software or manage any servers, but could easily access the CRM through a web browser (a business model called *software as a service*, or *SaaS*). In 2007, Salesforce recognized an emerging market for *platform as a service* (*PaaS*) offerings, which would enable clients to build their own software solutions that are accessed the same way as the Salesforce CRM. Seizing the opportunity, Salesforce developed a new competency in delivering software development and deployment tools that allowed its customers to either extend their existing CRM offering or build completely new types of software. Today, Salesforce's Force.com offering is one of the leading providers of PaaS tools and services.

diversification discount Situation in which the stock price of highly diversified firms is valued at less than the sum of their individual business units.

diversification premium Situation in which the stock price of related-diversification firms is valued at greater than the sum of their individual business units.

Taken together, the core competence–market matrix provides guidance to executives on how to diversify in order to achieve continued growth. Once managers have a clear understanding of their firm's core competencies, they have four options to formulate corporate strategy: (1) leverage existing core competencies to improve current market position; (2) build new core competencies to protect and extend current market position; (3) redeploy and recombine existing core competencies to compete in markets of the future; and (4) build new core competencies to create and compete in markets of the future.

Corporate Diversification

GAINING & SUSTAINING COMPETITIVE ADVANTAGE

Corporate managers pursue diversification to gain and sustain competitive advantage. But does corporate diversification indeed lead to superior performance? To answer this question, we can evaluate the performance of diversified companies. The critical question to ask when doing so is whether the individual businesses are worth more under the company's management than if each were managed individually.

Research shows that the diversification-performance relationship is a function of the underlying type of diversification. A cumulative body of research indicates an inverted U-shaped relationship between the type of diversification and overall firm performance, as depicted in Exhibit 8.9.[59] High and low levels of diversification are generally associated with lower overall performance, while moderate levels of diversification are associated with higher firm performance. This implies that companies that focus on a single business, as well as companies that pursue unrelated diversification, often fail to achieve additional value creation. Firms that compete in single markets could potentially benefit from economies of scope by leveraging their core competencies into adjacent markets.

Firms that pursue unrelated diversification are often unable to create additional value, and thus experience a **diversification discount** in the stock market: the stock price of such highly diversified firms is valued at less than the sum of their individual business units.[60] In contrast, companies that pursue related diversification are more likely to improve their performance, and thus create a **diversification premium:** the stock price of related-diversification firms is valued at greater than the sum of their individual business units.[61]

Why is this so? At the most basic level, a corporate diversification strategy enhances firm performance when its value creation is greater than the costs it incurs. Exhibit 8.10 (next page) lists the sources of value creation and costs for different corporate strategies, for vertical integration as well as related and unrelated diversification. For diversification to enhance firm performance, it must do at least one of the following:

- Provide economies of scale, and thus reduce costs.

- Exploit economies of scope, and thus increase value.

- Reduce costs *and* increase value.

> **>> LO 8-8**
> Explain when a diversification strategy creates a competitive advantage, and when it does not.

EXHIBIT 8.9

The Diversification-Performance Relationship

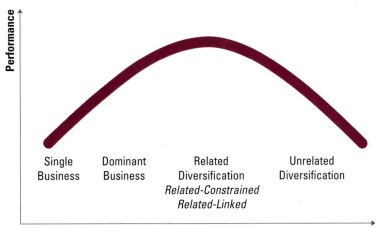

Source: Adapted from L. E. Palich, L. B. Cardinal, and C. C. Miller (2000), "Curvilinearity in the diversification-performance linkage: An examination of over three decades of research," *Strategic Management Journal* 21: 155–174.

EXHIBIT 8.10

Vertical Integration and Diversification: Sources of Value Creation and Costs

Corporate Strategy	Sources of Value Creation (V)	Sources of Costs (C)
Vertical Integration	• Securing critical supplies • Lowering costs • Improving quality • Facilitating scheduling and planning • Facilitating investments in specialized assets	• Increasing costs • Reducing quality • Reducing flexibility • Increasing potential for legal repercussions
Related Diversification	• Economies of scope • Economies of scale • Restructuring • Internal capital markets	• Coordination costs • Influence costs
Unrelated Diversification	• Restructuring • Internal capital markets	• Influence costs

We discussed these drivers of competitive advantage—economies of scale, economies of scope, and increase in value and reduction of costs—in depth in Chapter 6 in relation to business strategy. In addition to these criteria, executives can enhance performance using a diversification strategy by:

- Restructuring
- Using internal capital markets

RESTRUCTURING. *Restructuring* describes the process of reorganizing and divesting business units and activities to refocus a company in order to leverage its core competencies more fully. ChapterCase 8 highlighted the restructuring that has taken place at GE to leverage its core competency in management processes and industrial engineering. The Belgium-based Anheuser-Busch InBev recently sold Busch Entertainment, its theme park unit that owns SeaWorld and Busch Gardens, to a group of private investors for roughly $3 billion. This strategic move allows InBev to focus more fully on its core business and to pay for its 2008 acquisition of Anheuser-Busch, which cost $52 billion.[62]

Corporate-level executives can restructure the portfolio of their firm's businesses, much like an investor can change a portfolio of stocks. One helpful tool to guide corporate portfolio planning is the **Boston Consulting Group (BCG) growth-share matrix**, shown in Exhibit 8.11.[63] This matrix locates the firm's individual SBUs in two dimensions: relative market share (horizontal axis) and speed of market growth (vertical axis). The firm plots its SBUs into one of four categories in the matrix (dog, cash cow, star, and question mark), and each category warrants a different investment strategy.

SBUs identified as *dogs* are relatively easy to identify: They are the low-performing businesses. Dogs hold a small market share in a low-growth market; they have low and unstable earnings, combined with neutral or negative cash flows. The strategic recommendations are either to divest (sell) the business or to *harvest* it (stop investing in the business and squeeze out as much cash flow as possible before shutting it down or selling it).

Cash cows, in contrast, are SBUs that compete in a low-growth market but hold considerable market share. Their earnings and cash flows are high and stable. The strategic recommendation is to invest enough into cash cows to hold their current position, and to avoid having them turn into dogs (as indicated by the arrow).

Boston Consulting Group (BCG) growth-share matrix A corporate planning tool in which the corporation is viewed as a portfolio of business units, which are represented graphically along relative market share (horizontal axis) and speed of market growth (vertical axis). SBUs are plotted into four categories (dog, cash cow, star, and question mark), each of which warrants a different investment strategy.

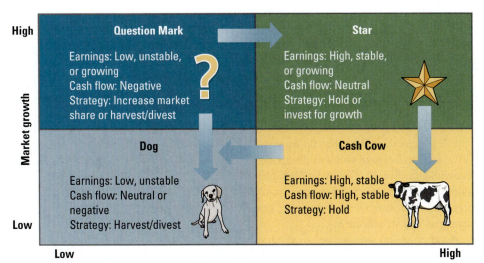

EXHIBIT 8.11

Restructuring the
Corporate Portfolio:
The Boston Consulting
Group Growth-Share
Matrix

A corporation's *star* SBUs hold a high market share in a fast-growing market. Their earnings are high and either stable or growing. The recommendation for the corporate strategist is to invest sufficient resources to hold the star's position or even increase investments for future growth. As indicated by the arrow, stars may turn into cash cows as the market in which the SBU is situated slows down due to reaching maturity.

Finally, some SBUs are *question marks:* It is not clear whether they will turn into dogs or stars. Their earnings are low and unstable, but they might be growing. The cash flow, however, is negative. Ideally, corporate executives want to invest in question marks to increase their relative market share so they turn into stars. If market conditions change, however, or the overall market growth slows down, then a question-mark SBU is likely to turn into a dog. In this case, executives would want to harvest the cash flow or divest the SBU.

INTERNAL CAPITAL MARKETS. *Internal capital markets* can be a source of value creation in a diversification strategy if the conglomerate's headquarters does a more efficient job of allocating capital through its budgeting process than what could be achieved in external capital markets. Based on private information, corporate-level managers are in a position to discover which of their strategic business units will provide the highest return to invested capital. In addition, internal capital markets may allow the company to access capital at a lower cost. Until recently, GE Capital brought in close to $70 billion in annual revenues, and generated more than half of GE's profits.[64] In combination with GE's triple-A debt rating, having access to such a large finance arm allowed GE to benefit from a lower cost of capital, which in turn was a source of value creation in itself. In 2009, GE lost its AAA debt rating and is now in the process of downsizing its finance unit. The lower debt rating and the smaller finance unit are likely to result in a higher cost of capital, and thus a potential loss in value creation through internal capital markets.

The strategy of related diversification (either related-constrained or related-linked) is more likely to enhance corporate performance than either a single or dominant level of diversification or an unrelated level of diversification. The reason is that the sources of value creation include not only restructuring, but more fundamentally, the potential benefits of economies of scope and scale. To create additional value, however, the benefits from these sources of incremental value creation must outweigh their costs. A related-diversification strategy entails two additional types of costs: coordination and influence costs. *Coordination costs* are a function of the number, size, and types of businesses that are linked to one another. *Influence costs* occur due to political maneuvering by managers to influence capital and resource allocation and the resulting inefficiencies stemming from suboptimal allocation of scarce resources.[65] In summary, related diversification is more likely to generate incremental value than unrelated diversification. 🔍

Although diversification can create shareholder value in theory, it is often difficult to realize in practice.[66] Why then do we see so much diversification taking place? One answer is the principal–agent problem discussed earlier, in which the interests of managers and shareholders diverge. Diversification generally leads to larger entities and thus bestows more power, prestige, and pay on corporate executives.[67] In Chapters 11 and 12, we study organizational structure and corporate governance to understand how to align interests of managers and shareholders.

Another reason why we see so much diversification is that interdependent competitors in oligopolistic industry structures are forced to engage in diversification in response to moves by direct rivals. Based on research conducted on competitive dynamics,[68] following ExxonMobil's acquisition of XTO Energy to move into the natural-gas sector, other oil majors also acquired natural-gas companies in response. In January 2010, the French energy company Total acquired an equity stake in Chesapeake Energy, the second largest producer of natural gas in the U.S.[69]

Some researchers suggest that *bandwagon effects* occur—firms copying moves of industry rivals.[70] A bandwagon effect can be observed, for example, in the recent related-diversification moves in the computer industry, in which hardware companies have moved into the software and services sector and vice versa:[71]

- IBM transformed itself from a hardware company into a global-services company (see Strategy Highlight 4.2). To further strengthen its strategic position in IT services, IBM acquired PricewaterhouseCoopers Consulting in 2002 for $3.5 billion and divested its low-margin PC business to the Chinese technology company Lenovo in 2005.

- In 2008, computer maker HP bought EDS, an IT services company, for more than $13 billion.

- In 2009, Oracle, a leader in enterprise software, acquired Sun Microsystems, a hardware company, for $7.4 billion.

- So as not to miss out on the apparent business opportunities available by combining computer hardware and software and services, Dell purchased Perot Systems for close to $4 billion in the fall of 2009.

- At about the same time, document-technology company Xerox bought ACS, an IT services company for $6.4 billion.

Such integration between hardware and software leads to industry convergence and brings with it a new set of competitors.

Taken together, the relationship between diversification strategy and competitive advantage depends on the *type of diversification.* There exists an inverted U-shaped relationship between the level of diversification and performance improvements. On average, related diversification (either related-constrained or related-linked) is most likely to lead to superior performance because it taps into multiple sources of value creation (economies of scale and scope, restructuring). To achieve a net positive effect on firm performance, however, related diversification must overcome additional sources of costs such as coordination and influence costs.

CORPORATE STRATEGY: COMBINING VERTICAL INTEGRATION AND DIVERSIFICATION

We are now in a position to combine vertical integration and diversification to understand a firm's corporate strategy in a more holistic fashion. A firm's overall corporate strategy concerns both its level of integration along the vertical value chain and its level of diversification.

As an example, take the computer-technology company Oracle, which earned $23 billion in revenues in 2009. Exhibit 8.12 depicts Oracle's corporate strategy along the vertical value chain and levels of diversification. Oracle's core competency lies in enterprise software (see center of figure). Oracle engaged in related diversification through backward vertical integration into computer hardware by acquiring Sun Microsystems, and forward vertical integration into human resource management systems (HRMS) and customer relations management (CRM) software by acquiring PeopleSoft. In its corporate strategy, moreover, Oracle pursues related as well as unrelated diversification. It leveraged its core competency into intellectual property (IP) management for media and entertainment businesses by its acquisition of Sophoi. Finally, Oracle pursued unrelated diversification into online identity theft and fraud protection through its acquisition of Bharosa. It is also noteworthy that through organic growth, Oracle executed its corporate strategy along the vertical value chain and on diversification through acquisitions. It now has over 40 subsidiaries, some of them quite large, such as BEA Systems.

In summary, executives determine the scope of the firm in such a fashion as to enhance the firm's ability to gain and sustain a competitive advantage. To delineate the boundaries of the firm, executives must formulate corporate-level strategy along three important dimensions (look back at Exhibit 8.1): vertical integration, horizontal integration, and global scope. As the examples in this chapter have indicated, executives implement corporate strategy through a variety of vehicles—acquisitions, alliances, and networks. Given their importance, we study these vehicles of corporate strategy in detail in the next chapter.

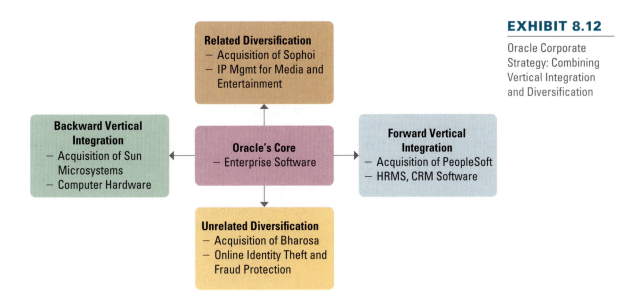

EXHIBIT 8.12

Oracle Corporate Strategy: Combining Vertical Integration and Diversification

CHAPTERCASE 8 | *Consider This . . .*

AS DISCUSSED IN the ChapterCase, General Electric has been refocusing its businesses through aggressive corporate divestitures (i.e., NBC Universal) and restructuring (GE Capital). Yet it is also making new investments: In 2010, GE produced $20 billion in revenue from businesses the firm was not in only a decade earlier. GE has also been increasing its global footprint. International sales have soared from 19 percent of sales in 1980, to 34 percent in 2000, to nearly 55 percent in 2010.[72]

Chairman and CEO Jeffrey Immelt believes that tackling big problems on a global scale is a strength of conglomerates such as GE. An example of a large-scale problem is the fact that according to the United Nations, in 2010 nearly one-fourth of the world's population lived without access to reliable power. In one of the fastest-growing economies in the world, India, the electrical coverage rate in 2008 was 65 percent. India has set a goal to provide electricity to all its citizens using a combination of national-scale power systems for the major cities and smaller "micro grids" for rural areas. India and other rapidly developing nations are seeking to replicate a "leap frog" approach in energy similar to that used in telecommunications. Instead of investing in vast quantities of landline communications wires, India built extensive mobile capabilities for communication needs. In energy, this means using software enabled "smart grid" electrical systems and smaller-scale but numerous renewable generation (such as wind, solar, and biomass) locations across the country. The Indian government is also encouraging smaller investments in order to improve the efficiency of existing fossil-fuel–based generators.[73] When completed, this energy infrastructure is likely to be more economical and robust than most systems in the "more developed" Western economies.

1. Where do *ecomagination and healthymagination* fit on the core competence–market matrix for GE? (See Exhibit 8.8.)

2. Take either the energy or health care industry and draw the industry value chain. What areas of potential vertical integration should GE consider?

3. What related diversification would you suggest for GE in reference to its focus for the future?

4. How do GE's corporate-level strategic initiatives of energy, health care, and globalization reinforce each other? How might they generate conflicts in the company?

Take-Away Concepts

This chapter defined corporate-level strategy and then looked at two fundamental corporate-level strategy topics, vertical integration and diversification, as summarized by the following learning objectives and related take-away concepts.

LO 8-1 Define corporate-level strategy, and describe the three dimensions along which it is assessed.

>> While business strategy addresses "how to compete," corporate strategy addresses "where to compete."

>> Corporate strategy concerns the scope of the firm along three dimensions: (1) vertical integration (along the industry value chain); (2) horizontal integration (diversification); and (3) geographic scope (global strategy).

>> To gain and sustain competitive advantage, any corporate strategy must support and strengthen a firm's strategic position regardless of whether it is a differentiation, cost leadership, or integration strategy.

LO 8-2 Describe and evaluate different options firms have to organize economic activity.

>> Transaction cost economics help managers decide what activities to do in-house ("make") versus what services and products to obtain from the external market ("buy").

>> When the costs to pursue an activity in-house are less than the costs of transacting in the market ($C_{in\text{-}house} < C_{market}$), then the firm should vertically integrate.

>> In the resource-based view of the firm, a firm's boundaries are delineated by its knowledge bases and competencies.

>> Moving from less integrated to more fully integrated forms of transacting, alternatives include: short-term contracts, strategic alliances (including long-term contracts, equity alliances, and joint ventures), and parent–subsidiary relationships.

LO 8-3 Describe the two types of vertical integration along the industry value chain: backward and forward vertical integration.

>> Vertical integration denotes a firm's value added—what percentage of a firm's sales is generated by the firm within its boundaries.

>> Industry value chains (vertical value chains) depict the transformation of raw materials into finished goods and services. Each stage typically represents a distinct industry in which a number of different firms are competing.

>> Backward vertical integration involves moving ownership of activities upstream nearer to the originating (inputs) point of the industry value chain.

>> Forward vertical integration involves moving ownership of activities closer to the end (customer) point of the value chain.

LO 8-4 Identify and evaluate benefits and risks of vertical integration.

>> Benefits of vertical integration include: securing critical supplies, lowering costs, improving quality, facilitating scheduling and planning, and facilitating investments in specialized assets.

>> Risks of vertical integration include: increasing costs, reducing quality, reducing flexibility, and increasing the potential for legal repercussions.

>> Vertical integration contributes to competitive advantage if the incremental value created is greater than the incremental costs of the specific corporate-level strategy.

LO 8-5 Describe and examine alternatives to vertical integration.

>> Taper integration is a strategy in which a firm is backwardly integrated but also relies on outside-market firms for some of its supplies, and/or is forwardly integrated but also relies on outside-market firms for some if its distribution.

>> Strategic outsourcing involves moving one or more value chain activities outside the firm's boundaries to other firms in the industry value chain. Off-shoring is the outsourcing of activities outside the home country.

LO 8-6 Describe and evaluate different types of corporate diversification.

>> A single-business firm derives 95 percent or more of its revenues from one business.

>> A dominant-business firm derives between 70 and 95 percent of its revenues from a single business, but pursues at least one other business activity.

>> A firm follows a related diversification strategy when it derives less than 70 percent of its revenues from a single business activity, but obtains revenues from other lines of business that are linked to the primary business activity. Choices within a related diversification strategy can be related-constrained or related-linked.

>> A firm follows an unrelated diversification strategy when less than 70 percent of its revenues come from a single business, and there are few, if any, linkages among its businesses.

LO 8-7 Apply the core competence–market matrix to derive different diversification strategies.

>> When applying an existing/new dimension to core competencies and markets, four quadrants emerge, as depicted in Exhibit 8.8.

>> The lower-left quadrant combines existing core competencies with existing markets. Here, managers need to come up with ideas of how to leverage existing core competencies to improve their current market position.

>> The lower-right quadrant combines existing core competencies with new market opportunities. Here, managers need to think about

how to redeploy and recombine existing core competencies to compete in future markets.

>> The upper-left quadrant combines new core competencies with existing market opportunities. Here, managers must come up with strategic initiatives of how to build new core competencies to protect and extend the firm's current market position.

>> The upper-right quadrant combines new core competencies with new market opportunities. This is likely the most challenging diversification strategy because it requires building new core competencies to create and compete in future markets.

LO 8-8 Explain when a diversification strategy creates a competitive advantage, and when it does not.

>> The diversification-performance relationship is a function of the underlying type of diversification.

>> The relationship between the type of diversification and overall firm performance takes on the shape of an inverted U (see Exhibit 8.9.).

>> In the BCG matrix, the corporation is viewed as a portfolio of businesses, much like a portfolio of stocks in finance (see Exhibit 8.11). The individual SBUs are evaluated according to relative market share and speed of market growth, and plotted into one of four categories (dog, cash cow, star, and question mark. Each category warrants a different investment strategy.

>> Both low levels and high levels of diversification are generally associated with lower overall performance, while moderate levels of diversification are associated with higher firm performance.

Key Terms

Administrative costs *(p. 204)*

Backward vertical integration *(p. 212)*

Boston Consulting Group (BCG) growth-share matrix *(p. 222)*

Corporate-level strategy (corporate strategy) *(p. 202)*

Credible commitment *(p. 208)*

Diversification *(p. 216)*

Diversification discount *(p. 221)*

Diversification premium *(p. 221)*

Forward vertical integration *(p. 212)*

Franchising *(p. 208)*

Geographic diversification strategy *(p. 216)*

Industry value chain *(p. 210)*

Information asymmetries *(p. 206)*

Joint venture *(p. 209)*

Licensing *(p. 208)*

Principal–agent problem *(p. 205)*

Product diversification strategy *(p. 216)*

Product–market diversification strategy *(p. 216)*

Related diversification strategy *(p. 216)*

Scope of the firm *(p. 202)*

Specialized assets *(p. 213)*

Strategic outsourcing *(p. 215)*

Taper integration *(p. 215)*

Transaction cost economics *(p. 204)*

Transaction costs *(p. 204)*

Unrelated diversification strategy *(p. 218)*

Vertical integration *(p. 209)*

Discussion Questions

1. When Walmart decided to incorporate grocery stores into some locations and created "supercenters," was this a business-level strategy of differentiation or a corporate-level strategy of diversification? Why? Explain your answer.

2. How can related diversification create a competitive advantage for the firm?

3. Franchising is widely used in the casual dining and fast-food industry, yet Starbucks is quite successful with a large number of company-owned stores. How do you explain this difference? Is Starbucks bucking the bandwagon effect, or is something else going on?

Ethical/Social Issues

1. The chapter notes that many firms choose to outsource their human resource management systems. If a firm has a core value of respecting its employees and rewarding top performance with training, raises, and promotions, does outsourcing HR management show a lack of commitment by the firm?

2. Nike is a large and successful firm in the design of athletic shoes. It could easily decide to forward-integrate to manufacture the shoes it designs. Therefore, the firm has a credible threat over its current manufacturers. If Nike has no intention of actually entering the manufacturing arena, is its supply chain management team being ethical with the current manufacturers if the team mentions this credible threat numerous times in annual pricing negotiations? Why or why not?

Small Group Exercises

SMALL GROUP EXERCISE 1

Agriculture is one of the largest and oldest industries in the world. In the U.S. and many other countries, farmers often struggle to turn a profit given the variances of weather and commodity prices. Some working farms are turning to tourism as an additional and complementary revenue source. A study from the U.S. Census of Agriculture in 2007 found nearly 25,000 farms providing some level of agri-tourism and recreation services. (There were 2.2 million farms in the census, almost triple the number from 2002.) In 2010, the Department of Agriculture announced a new grant program aimed at providing public access to private farms for such purposes. Small farms worldwide are participating in this trend by offering "pick your own" crops in season as well as small bed-and-breakfast experiences.

Perhaps one of the most successful large companies leading this marriage of industries is a dairy farm in Indiana: Fair Oaks Farms. Fair Oaks Farms is home to 30,000 cows and produces enough milk to feed 8 million people. It also hosts nearly 500,000 tourists each year, who come to see the hands-on adventure center and the working milking operations. (A video of the operation is available at www.youtube.com/watch?v=JJRy82i8e5Q.) Such ingenious business diversification can have many benefits to the agricultural industry.[74]

1. What other industrial or commercial industries could benefit from such potential tourist or recreational revenues?

2. In your group, list other industry combinations that you have seen to be successful.

SMALL GROUP EXERCISE 2

Target and Walmart are significant rivals in the retailing industry. Though Walmart is the world's largest company (2010 sales of $420 billion), Target had been growing faster than Walmart until the 2008 recession. From 2003 to 2007, same-store sales at Target grew an average of 4.6 percent, while Walmart's comparable growth was 2.9 percent.

However, in 2008 Target's same-store sales fell 2.6 percent, while Walmart's rose 3.3 percent. What drove this difference? Product mix seems to be a large factor. Target devotes less than 20 percent of its space to consumables such as health and beauty products and food. Walmart, by contrast, has 45 percent of its shelf space for consumables, with groceries being a major component. Though an obvious answer for Target is to continue following Walmart into groceries, consider that the average net profit of the grocery industry was less than 1.4 percent from 2002 to 2008. As a team, assume you've been called in to consult with Target on the problem.[75]

1. What should Target do to get back on a growth track?

2. Is Target's problem strategy or execution?

3. What action plan would you recommend?

Strategy Term Project

MODULE 8: VERTICAL INTEGRATION

In this section, you will study the boundaries of the firm you have selected for your strategy project in reference to the vertical value chain activities of its industry.

1. Draw out the vertical value chain for your firm's industry. List the major firms in each important activity along the chain (see Exhibits 8.4 and 8.5 as examples). Note that a firm's name may appear multiple times in the value chain. This indicates some level of vertical integration by the firm. If your firm is in many different industries (e.g., GE), then choose the dominant industry or the one that intrigues you the most and use only that one for this analysis.

2. Is your firm highly vertically integrated? If yes, does it also employ taper integration?

3. Are any of the vertical value chain operations off-shored? If so, list some of the pros and cons of having this part of the value chain outside the home country.

4. Use the preceding vertical value chain to identify the corporate strategy of the firm. In other words, where within the industry has the firm chosen to compete? Based on where it competes, describe what you now see as its corporate strategy.

5. In Module 2, you were asked to identify the mission and major goals for your selected company. Go back to that information now and compare the mission and goals to what you have found as the corporate strategy. Are the mission, goal, and corporate strategy in alignment? Do you see any holes or conflicts among these three elements? Can you relate the performance of the firm to this finding in any way? (If all three are consistent, is this a well-performing unit?) If there is a conflict between the corporate strategy and the mission, does this lack of alignment contribute to performance problems? Why or why not?

*my*Strategy

HOW DIVERSIFIED ARE YOU?

When someone asks a manager about diversification, quite often the questioner is referring to the manager's overall portfolio or savings and retirement investments. While that is an important financial consideration, here we are asking you to think about diversification a bit differently.

Corporations diversify by investing time and resources into new areas of business. As individuals, each of us makes choices about how to spend our time and energies. Typically, we could divide our time between school, work, family, sleep, and play. During high-stress work projects, we likely devote more of our time to work; when studying for final exams or a professional board exam (like the CPA exam), we probably spend more time and effort in the "student learning" mode. This manner of dividing our time can be thought of as "personal diversification." Just as companies can invest in related or unrelated activities, we make similar choices. While we attend college, we may choose to engage in social and leisure activities with campus colleagues, or we may focus on classwork at school and spend our "play time" with an entirely separate set of people.

Using Exhibit 8.7 as a guide, list each of your major activity areas. Think of each of these as a business. (If you are literally "all work and no play," you are a single-business type of personal diversification.) Instead of revenues, estimate the percentage of *time* you spend per week in each activity. (Most people will be diversified, though some may be dominant perhaps in school or work.) To assess your degree of *relatedness* and *unrelatedness,* consider the subject matter and community involved with each activity. For example, if you are studying ballet and working as an accountant, those would be largely unrelated activities (unless you are an accountant for a ballet company!).

1. What conclusions do you derive based on your personal diversification strategy?

2. Do you need to make adjustments to your portfolio of activities? Explain the reasons for your answer.

Endnotes

1. Jeffrey Immelt, quoted in "Ecomagination: Inside GE's Power Play," by J. Makower, May 8, 2005, www.worldchanging.com/archives/002669.html.

2. This ChapterCase is based on: "A slipping crown," *The Economist,* March 13, 2009; "Comcast, GE strike deal; Vivendi to sell NBC stake," *The Wall Street Journal,* December 4, 2009; "Ecomagination: Inside GE's power play," *Worldchanging,* May 8, 2005; "GE: How clean (and not-so-clean) tech drives Ecomagination," *The Wall Street Journal,* May 27, 2009; "GE launches 'Healthymagination'; will commit $6 billion to enable better health focusing on cost, access and quality," GE press release, May 7, 2009; "GE may shed storied appliance unit," *The Wall Street Journal,* May 15, 2008; "GE's chief declines $12 million bonus amid crisis," *The Wall Street Journal,* February 19, 2009; GE Annual Reports (various years); www.ge.com; and www.wolframalpha.com.

3. 2010 Letter to Shareholders in 2009 GE Annual Report.

4. Collis, D. J. (1995), "The scope of the corporation," *Harvard Business School Note,* 9-795-139.

5. The literature on transaction cost economics is rich and expanding. For important theoretical and empirical contributions, see: Folta, T. B. (1998), "Governance and uncertainty: The trade-off between administrative control and commitment," *Strategic Management Journal* 19: 1007–1028; Klein, B., R. Crawford, and A. Alchian (1978), "Vertical integration, appropriable rents, and the competitive contracting process," *Journal of Law and Economics* 21: 297–326; Leiblein, M. J., and D. J. Miller (2003), "An empirical examination of transformation-and firm-level influences on the vertical boundaries of the firm," *Strategic Management Journal* 24: 839–859; Leiblein, M. J., J. J. Reuer, and F. Dalsace (2002), "Do make or buy decisions matter? The influence of organizational governance on technological performance," *Strategic Management Journal* 23: 817–833; Mahoney, J. (1992), "The choice of organizational form: Vertical financial ownership versus other methods of vertical integration," *Strategic Management Journal* 13: 559–584; Mahoney, J. T. (2005), *Economic Foundations of Strategy* (Thousand Oaks, CA: Sage); Williamson, O. E. (1975), *Markets and Hierarchies,* (New York: Free Press); Williamson, O. E. (1981), "The economics of organization: The transaction cost approach," *American Journal of Sociology* 87: 548–577; and Williamson, O. E. (1985), *The Economic Institutions of Capitalism* (New York: Free Press).

6. This draws on: Mahoney, J. T. (2005), *Economic Foundations of Strategy* (Thousand Oaks, CA: Sage); Williamson, O. E. (1975), *Markets and Hierarchies* (New York: Free Press); Williamson, O. E. (1981), "The economics of organization: The transaction cost approach," *American Journal of Sociology* 87: 548–577; Williamson, O. E. (1985), *The Economic Institutions of Capitalism* (New York: Free Press); and Hart, O., and O. Moore (1990), "Property rights and the nature of the firm," *Journal of Political Economy* 98: 1119–1158.

7. Highlighting the relevance of research on transaction costs, both Ronald Coase (1991) and Oliver Williamson (2009), who further developed and refined Coase's initial insight, were each awarded a Nobel Prize in economics.

8. This is based on: Berle, A., and G. Means (1932), *The Modern Corporation & Private Property* (New York: Macmillan); Jensen, M., and W. Meckling (1976), "Theory of the firm: Managerial behavior, agency costs and ownership structure," *Journal of Financial Economics* 3: 305–360; and Fama, E. (1980), "Agency problems and the theory of the firm," *Journal of Political Economy* 88: 375–390.

9. Berle, A., and G. Means (1932), *The Modern Corporation & Private Property.*

10. This discussion draws on: Zenger, T. R., and W. S. Hesterly (1997), "The disaggregation of corporations: Selective intervention, high-powered incentives, and molecular units," *Organization Science* 8: 209–222; and Zenger, T. R., and S. G. Lazzarini (2004), "Compensating for innovation: Do small firms offer high-powered incentives that lure talent and motivate effort," *Managerial and Decision Economics* 25: 329–345.

11. This discussion draws on: Akerlof, G. A. (1970), "The market for lemons: Quality uncertainty and the market mechanism," *Quarterly Journal of Economics* 94: 488–500.

12. Pisano, G. P. (1997), "R&D performance, collaborative arrangements, and the market-for-know-how: A test of the 'lemons' hypothesis in biotechnology," *Working Paper No. 97-105,* Harvard Business School; Lerner J., Merges, R. P. (1998), "The control of technology alliances: An empirical analysis of the biotechnology industry," *Journal of Industrial Economics* 46: 125–156; Rothaermel, F. T., and D. L. Deeds (2004), "Exploration and exploitation alliances in biotechnology: A system of new product development," *Strategic Management Journal* 25: 201–221.

13. Somaya, D. (2003), "Strategic determinants of decisions not to settle patent litigation" *Strategic Management Journal* 24: 17–38.

14. Kogut, B., and U. Zander (1992), "Knowledge of the firm, combinative capabilities, and the replication of technology," *Organization Science* 3: 383–397; O'Connor, G. C., and M. Rice (2001), "Opportunity recognition and breakthrough innovation in large firms," *California Management Review* 43: 95–116; O'Connor, G.C, and R. W. Veryzer (2001), "The nature of market visioning for technology-based radical innovation," *Journal of Product Innovation Management* 18: 231–24.

15. This discussion draws on: Williamson, O. E. (1991), "Comparative economic organization: The analysis of discrete structural alternatives," *Administrative Science Quarterly* 36: 269–296.

16. This is based on: Gulati, R. (1998), "Alliances and networks," *Strategic Management Journal* 19: 293–317; Ireland, R. D., M. A. Hitt, and D. Vaidyanath (2002), "Alliance management as a source of competitive advantage," *Journal of Management* 28: 413–446; Hoang, H., and F. T. Rothaermel (2005), "The effect of general and partner-specific alliance experience on joint R&D project performance," *Academy of Management Journal* 48: 332–345; and Lavie, D. (2006), "The competitive advantage of interconnected firms: An extension of the resource-based view," *Academy of Management Review* 31: 638–658.

17. This strategy highlight is based on "Toyota sets pact on lithium," *The Wall Street Journal,* January 20, 2010.

18. www.dowcorning.com.

19. "Rising from the ashes in Detroit," *The Economist,* August 19, 2010.

20. "Small cars, big question," *The Economist,* January 21, 2010.

21. Tucker, I., and R. P. Wilder (1977), "Trends in vertical integration in the U.S. manufacturing sector," *Journal of Industrial Economics,* 26: 81–97; Harrigan, K. R. (1984), "Formulating vertical integration strategies," *Academy of Management Review* 9: 638–652; Harrigan, K. R. (1986), "Matching vertical integration strategies to competitive conditions," *Strategic Management Journal* 7: 535–555; Rothaermel, F. T., M. A. Hitt, and L. A. Jobe (2006), "Balancing vertical integration and strategic outsourcing: Effects on product portfolios, new product success, and firm performance," *Strategic Management Journal* 27: 1033–1056.

22. Besanko, D., D. Dranove, M. Shanley, and S. Schaefer (2010), *Economics of Strategy,* 5th ed. (Hoboken, NJ: John Wiley & Sons).

23. "Global stretch: When will Zara hit its limits?" *The Economist,* March 10, 2011.

24. "The lowdown on teardowns," *The Economist,* January 21, 2010.

25. "HTC clones Nexus One, launches 3 new phones," *Wired.com,* February 16, 2010.

26. www.htc.com.

27. Harrigan, K. R. (1984), "Formulating vertical integration strategies," *Academy of Management Review* 9: 638–652; Harrigan, K. R. (1986), "Matching vertical integration strategies to competitive conditions," *Strategic Management Journal* 7: 535–555.

28. "HTC clones Nexus One, launches 3 new phones," *Wired.com,* February 16, 2010.

29. "Companies more prone to go vertical," *The Wall Street Journal,* December 1, 2009.

30. This Strategy Highlight is based on: "Pepsi bids $6 billion for largest bottlers, posts flat profit," *The Wall Street Journal,* April 20, 2009; "PepsiCo buys bottlers for $7.8 billion," The Wall Street Journal, August 5, 2009; "Companies more prone to go vertical," *The Wall Street Journal,* December 1, 2009; and "Coca-Cola strikes deal with bottler," *The Wall Street Journal,* February 25, 2010.

31. Williamson, O. E. (1975), *Markets and Hierarchies* (New York: Free Press); Williamson, O. E. (1981), "The economics of organization: The transaction cost approach," American Journal of Sociology 87: 548–577; Williamson, O. E. (1985), *The Economic Institutions of Capitalism* (New York: Free Press); Poppo, L., and T. Zenger (1998), "Testing alternative theories of the firm: Transaction cost, knowledge based, and measurement explanations for make or buy decisions in information services," *Strategic Management Journal* 19: 853–878.

32. Williamson, O. E. (1975), *Markets and Hierarchies* (New York: Free Press); Williamson, O. E. (1981), "The economics of organization: The transaction cost approach," *American Journal of Sociology* 87: 548–577; Williamson, O. E. (1985), *The Economic Institutions of Capitalism* (New York: Free Press).

33. Williamson, O. E. (1975), *Markets and Hierarchies* (New York: Free Press).

34. "Companies more prone to go vertical," *The Wall Street Journal,* December 1, 2009.

35. Harrigan, K. R. (1984), "Formulating vertical integration strategies," *Academy of Management Review* 9: 638–652; Harrigan, K. R. (1986), "Matching vertical integration strategies to competitive conditions," *Strategic Management Journal* 7: 535–555; Afuah, A. (2001), "Dynamic boundaries of the firm: Are firms better off being vertically integrated in the face of a technological change?" *Academy of Management Journal* 44: 1211–1228; Rothaermel, F. T., M. A. Hitt, and L. A. Jobe (2006), "Balancing vertical integration and strategic outsourcing: Effects on product portfolios, new product success, and firm

performance," *Strategic Management Journal* 27: 1033–1056.

36. Afuah A. (2001), "Dynamic boundaries of the firm: are firms better off being vertically integrated in the face of a technological change?"

37. Ghemawat, P. (1993), "Commitment to a process innovation: Nucor, USX, and thin slab casting," *Journal of Economics and Management Strategy* 2: 133–161; Christensen, C. M., and M. E. Raynor (2003), *The Innovator's Solution: Creating and Sustaining Successful Growth* (Boston, MA: Harvard Business School Press).

38. "Companies more prone to go vertical," *The Wall Street Journal,* December 1, 2009.

39. Harrigan, K. R. (1984), "Formulating vertical integration strategies," *Academy of Management Review* 9: 638–652.

40. This is based on: Harrigan, K. R. (1984), "Formulating vertical integration strategies"; and Harrigan, K. R. (1986), "Matching vertical integration strategies to competitive conditions," *Strategic Management Journal* 7: 535–555.

41. This is based on the following: Prahalad and Hamel argued that a firm that outsources too many activities risks hollowing out ("unlearning") their core competencies because the firm no longer participates in key adjacent value chain activities. A similar argument has been made by Teece (1986); Prahalad, C. K., and G. Hamel (1990), "The core competence of the corporation," *Harvard Business Review,* May–June; and Teece, D. J. (1986), "Profiting from technological innovation: Implications for integration, collaboration, licensing and public policy," *Research Policy* 15: 285–305.

42. Rothaermel, F. T., M. A. Hitt, and L. A. Jobe (2006), "Balancing vertical integration and strategic outsourcing: Effects on product portfolios, new product success, and firm performance," *Strategic Management Journal* 27: 1033–1056.

43. "Global outsourcing market to be worth $1,430bn by 2009," *Computer Business Review,* August 2007.

44. "Passage to India," *The Economist,* June 26, 2010.

45. www.kfc.com/about/.

46. This section is based on: Rumelt, R. P. (1974), *Strategy, Structure, and*

Economic Performance (Boston, MA: Harvard Business School Press); Montgomery, C. A. (1985), "Product-market diversification and market power," *Academy of Management Review* 28: 789–798.

47. This is based on: Google Annual Reports; "Radio tunes out Google in rare miss for Web titan," *The Wall Street Journal,* May 12, 2009.

48. Microsoft 2009 Annual Report.

49. This strategy highlight is based on: ExxonMobil, Annual Reports; "Oil's decline slow Exxon, Chevron Profit Growth," *The Wall Street Journal,* January 30, 2009; "The greening of ExxonMobil," *Forbes,* August 24, 2009; Friedman, T. L. (2008), *Hot, Flat, and Crowded. Why We Need a Green Revolution—And How It Can Renew America* (New York: Farrar, Straus and Giroux); "Exxon to acquire XTO Energy in $31 billion stock deal," *The Wall Street Journal,* December 14, 2009; and "ExxonMobil buys XTO Energy," *The Economist,* December 17, 2009.

50. "Rebooting their systems," *The Economist,* March 10, 2011.

51. "The Tata group," *The Economist,* March 3, 2011.

52. This is based on: Peng, M. W., and P. S. Heath (1996), "The growth of the firm in planned economies in transitions: Institutions, organizations, and strategic choice," *Academy of Management Review* 21: 492–528; Peng, M. W. (2000), *Business Strategies in Transition Economies* (Thousand Oaks, CA: Sage); and Peng, M. W. (2005), "What determines the scope of the firm over time? A focus on institutional relatedness," *Academy of Management Review,* 30: 622–633.

53. Prahalad, C. K., and G. Hamel (1990), "The core competence of the corporation."

54. This discussion is based on: Burt, C., and F. T. Rothaermel (2013), "Bank of America and the New Financial Landscape," case study, in Rothaermel, F.T., *Strategic Management* (Burr Ridge IL: McGraw-Hill).

55. Bank of America had long coveted Merrill Lynch, a premier investment bank. Severely weakened by the global financial crisis, Merrill Lynch became a takeover target, and Bank of America made a bid. In the process, Bank of America learned that Merrill Lynch's exposure to subprime mortgages and other exotic financial instruments was much larger than previously disclosed. Other problems included Merrill Lynch's payments of multimillion-dollar bonuses to many employees, despite the investment bank's having lost billions of dollars (in 2008). After learning this new information, Bank of America (under its then-CEO Ken Lewis) attempted to withdraw from the Merrill Lynch takeover. The Federal Reserve Bank, under the leadership of its chairman, Ben Bernanke, insisted that Bank of America fulfill the agreement, noting that the takeover was part of a grand strategy to save the financial system from collapse. Once Bank of America shareholders learned that CEO Ken Lewis had not disclosed the problems at Merrill Lynch, they first stripped him of his chairmanship of the board of directors, and later fired him as CEO. For a detailed and insightful discussion on the Merrill Lynch takeover by Bank of America, see Lowenstein, R. (2010), *The End of Wall Street* (New York: Penguin Press).

56. "Bank of America and Merrill Lynch," *The Economist,* April 14, 2010.

57. "PepsiCo says Gatorade makeover on track," *The Wall Street Journal,* July 23, 2009.

58. This is based on: "Oracle vs. salesforce.com," Harvard Business School case study, 9-705-440; and "How to innovate in a downturn," *The Wall Street Journal,* March 18, 2009.

59. Palich, L. E., L. B. Cardinal, and C. C., Miller (2000), "Curvilinearity in the diversification-performance linkage: An examination of over three decades of research," *Strategic Management Journal* 21: 155–174.

60. This is based on: Lang, L.H.P., and R. M. Stulz (1994), "Tobin's q, corporate diversification, and firm performance," *Journal of Political Economy* 102: 1248–1280; Martin, J. D., and A. Sayrak (2003), "Corporate diversification and shareholder value: A survey of recent literature," *Journal of Corporate Finance* 9: 37–57; and Rajan, R., H. Servaes, and L. Zingales (2000), "The cost of diversity: The diversification discount and inefficient investment," *Journal of Finance* 55: 35–80.

61. Villalonga, B. (2004), "Diversification discount or premium? New evidence from the business information tracking series," *Journal of Finance* 59: 479–506.

62. This section is based on: "U.S. clears InBev to buy Anheuser," *The Wall Street Journal,* November 15, 2008; and "Blackstone nears deal," *The Wall Street Journal,* October 5, 2009.

63. This section is based on: Boston Consulting Group (1970), *The Product Portfolio* (Boston, MA); and Shay, J. P., and F. T. Rothaermel (1999), "Dynamic competitive strategy: Towards a multi-perspective conceptual framework," *Long Range Planning* 32: 559–572.

64. GE Annual Reports.

65. Milgrom, P., and J. Roberts (1990), "Bargaining costs, influence costs, and the organization of economic activity," in Alt, J., and K. Shepsle (eds.), *Perspectives on Positive Political Economy* (Cambridge, UK: Cambridge University Press).

66. Porter, M. E. (1987), "From competitive advantage to corporate strategy," *Harvard Business Review,* May–June: 43–59.

67. This discussion is based on: Finkelstein, S., and D. C. Hambrick (1989), "Chief executive compensation: A study of the intersection of markets and political processes," *Strategic Management Journal* 10: 121–134; and Lambert, R. A., D. F. Larcker, and K. Weigelt (1991), "How sensitive is executive compensation to organizational size?" *Strategic Management Journal* 12: 395–402.

68. This discussion is based on: Chen, M. J. (1996), "Competitor analysis and interfirm rivalry: Toward a theoretical integration," *Academy of Management Review* 21: 100–134; Ferrier, W. J., K. G. Smith, and C. M. Grimm (1999), "The role of competitive action in market share erosion and industry dethronement: A study of industry leaders and challengers," *Academy of Management Journal* 42: 372–388; and Ferrier, W. J. (2001), "Navigating the competitive landscape: The drivers and consequences of competitive aggressiveness," *Academy of Management Journal* 44: 858–877.

69. "Chesapeake Energy corporation provides quarterly operational update," *The Wall Street Journal,* May 3, 2010.

70. This discussion is based on: Bikchandani, S., D. Hirshleifer, and I. Welch (1999), "Theory of fads, fashion, custom, and cultural change as informational cascades," *Journal of Political Economy* 100: 992–1026; Abrahamson, E. (1996), "Management fashion," *Academy of Management Review* 21: 254–285; and Surowiecki, J. (2004), *The Wisdom of Crowds. Why the Many Are Smarter than the Few and How Collective Wisdom Shapes Business,* *Economies, Societies, and Nations* (New York: Doubleday).

71. This discussion is based on: "Dell to buy Perot Systems for $3.9 billion," *The Wall Street Journal,* September 21, 2009; "Dell to buy Perot Systems in catch-up deal," *The Wall Street Journal,* September 22, 2009; and "Xerox buys ACS," *The Economist,* October 1, 2009.

72. 2010 General Electric Annual Report: shareholder letter dated February 25, 2011.

73. Heintzelman, D. (2010), "India's path to renewable power," *Bloomberg* *Businessweek,* Viewpoint Column, May 27. (Mr. Heintzelman is president & CEO of GE Energy Services.)

74. This Small Group Exercise is based on: The Rural Community Building website produced by the American Farm Bureau Federation; *America's Heartland* "Episode 311"; and Fair Oaks Farms Dairy (www.fofarms.com).

75. This Small Group Exercise is based on: Gregory, S. (2009), "Walmart vs. Target: No contest in the recession," *Time,* March 14; and Food Marketing Institute Annual Financial Report, December 2008.

CHAPTER 9

Corporate Strategy: Acquisitions, Alliances, and Networks

LEARNING OBJECTIVES

After studying this chapter, you should be able to:

LO 9-1   Differentiate between mergers and acquisitions, and explain why firms would use either as a vehicle for corporate strategy.

LO 9-2   Define horizontal integration and evaluate the advantages and disadvantages of this corporate-level strategy.

LO 9-3   Evaluate whether mergers and acquisitions lead to competitive advantage.

LO 9-4   Define strategic alliances, and explain why they are important corporate strategy vehicles and why firms enter into them.

LO 9-5   Describe three alliance governance mechanisms and evaluate their pros and cons.

LO 9-6   Describe the three phases of alliance management, and explain how an alliance management capability can lead to a competitive advantage.

LO 9-7   Define strategic networks and evaluate the advantages and disadvantages of different network positions.

Facebook: From Dorm Room to Dominant Social Network

FACEBOOK WAS FOUNDED in a dorm room at Harvard in 2004 by 19-year-old Mark Zuckerberg and three college pals. What began as a hobby to let Ivy leaguers socialize online is now the world's largest social networking site, with more than 500 million users and estimated revenues of $2 billion in 2010. After Google, Facebook is the second most popular website worldwide. Zuckerberg sees online social networking as the "most powerful and transformative social change" in recent history.[1] Indeed, it's made him the world's youngest billionaire.

Before Facebook became a global phenomenon, it had to overcome the first-mover advantage held by MySpace. Launched in 2003, MySpace was an early leader in social networking. Its success attracted the attention of News Corp. and other media outlets. News Corp. acquired MySpace for $580 million in 2005. As a subsidiary of a publicly owned company, MySpace's revenues and profitability became more pressing issues after the acquisition. MySpace's business model shifted from accumulating more users to growing revenues and profits, by focusing on a few ad-heavy markets such as the U.S., UK, Germany, France, and Japan. MySpace was hit hard by the global economic downturn that began in 2008. A year later, it had laid off 45 percent of its staff.

Facebook, on the other hand, remained a private company. Among its other investors, Microsoft purchased a $240 million equity stake in 2007, and a Russian investment group added $200 million in 2009. Facebook's managers thus had less pressure to produce bottom-line results than did MySpace. This allowed the company to pursue a different business model: more users first, profits later. While MySpace concentrated on a few developed markets, Facebook pursued a truly global strategy. Facebook encouraged 300,000 users worldwide to help translate the website into more than 70 languages. Today, more than 70 percent of its users are outside the United States. In 2008, Facebook displaced MySpace as the most popular social networking site (see Exhibit 9.1, next page).

As a way to increase its online influence, Facebook also introduced features to draw wider-ranging social graphs (pictures of networks) of its user base. For example, other websites can install a "Like" or "Recommend" button which Facebook users can click to signal their activity on a specific website. Facebook users can announce to their social network when they buy a pair of shoes on Zappos.com, trade stocks on Zecco.com, or review a restaurant on Zagat.com. Mark Zuckerberg describes this innovation as "the most transformative thing we have ever done for the Web."[2]

However, it is not all smooth sailing for Facebook. The company has repeatedly come under attack for allegedly insufficient protection of users' privacy. Moreover, to maintain its elaborate technology platform and to fund future growth, the company will need to figure out a sustainable business model.[3]

After reading the chapter, you will find more about this case, with related questions, on page 257.

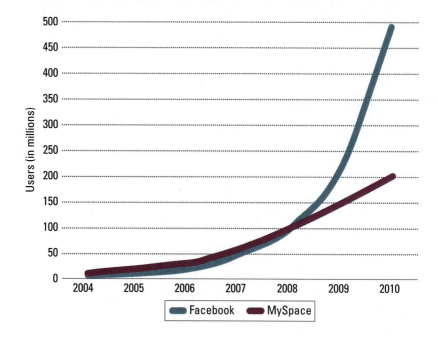

▲ **A NETWORK'S VALUE** rises exponentially with the number of its members. With more than 500 million users, Facebook benefits from network effects (a concept introduced in Chapter 7): It attracts the world's top software developers to create apps (such as FarmVille), an important complementary service. These apps in turn make Facebook more attractive for new users, further increasing its membership. The more people are on Facebook, the more valuable it is to be a member of its online community. As its users share more freely and take their networks of friends with them wherever else they may go on the web, the better Facebook is able to learn about the likes and dislikes of its users and thus serve up more customized online advertising.[4] With revenues approaching $30 billion (in 2010), Google has already proved that online advertising is a highly profitable business. Online social networking may turn out to be a winner-take-all market, and Facebook is clearly playing to win.

Firms, like individuals, often form ties such as alliances to share information and pursue common interests. Organizations also join networks, such as the innovation system orchestrated by InnoCentive, in order to get access to a diverse pool of knowledge and resources to advance strategic objectives that they couldn't pursue in isolation. In addition to internal organic growth, firms have several critical strategic options to pursue common interests, enhance competitiveness, and increase revenues: acquisitions, alliances, and networks. We devote this chapter to the study of these fundamental vehicles through which to implement corporate strategy.

INTEGRATING COMPANIES: MERGERS AND ACQUISITIONS

>> LO 9-1

Differentiate between mergers and acquisitions, and explain why firms would use either as a vehicle for corporate strategy.

A traditional and popular vehicle for executing corporate strategy is mergers and acquisitions (M&A). Thousands of mergers and acquisitions occur each year, with a cumulative value in the trillions of dollars.[5] Although people sometimes use the terms as synonymous, and usually in tandem, mergers and acquisitions are, by definition, distinct from each other. A **merger** describes the joining of two independent companies to form *a combined entity*. An **acquisition** describes the purchase or takeover of one company by another. Mergers tend to be friendly; in mergers the target firm would like to be acquired. Disney's acquisition of Pixar, for example, was a friendly one, in which both management teams believed that joining the two companies was a good idea. Acquisitions can be friendly or unfriendly. When a target firm does not want to be acquired, the acquisition is considered a **hostile takeover.** British telecom company Vodafone's acquisition of Germany-based Mannesmann, a diversified conglomerate with holdings in telephony and Internet services, at an estimated value of $150 billion, was a hostile one.

In defining mergers and acquisitions, size can matter as well. The combining of two firms of comparable size is often described as a merger (even though it might in fact be an acquisition). For example, the integration of Daimler and Chrysler was pitched as a merger, though in reality Daimler acquired Chrysler (and later sold it). In contrast, when large, incumbent firms such as the Tata Group, Cisco Systems, or GE buy up startup companies, the transaction is generally described as an acquisition. An example is HP's relatively inexpensive $1.2 billion acquisition of Palm, a pioneer in personal digital assistants (PDAs),[6] which HP hopes will provide a stronger position in the fast-growing smartphone and tablet-computer markets. The distinction between mergers and acquisitions, however, is a bit blurry, and many observers simply use the umbrella term M&A.

Horizontal Integration: Merging with Competitors

In contrast with vertical integration, which concerns the number of activities a firm participates in up and down the industry value chain (as discussed in Chapter 8), **horizontal integration** is the process of acquiring and merging with competitors. Horizontal integration is a type of corporate strategy that can improve a firm's strategic position in a single industry. An industry-wide trend toward horizontal integration leads to industry consolidation. In the computer industry, for example, HP acquired Compaq in 2002. The pharmaceutical industry has also seen considerable consolidation, with Pfizer merging with Wyeth, and Merck and Schering-Plough merging in 2009. In the event-promotion business, the only remaining segment in the music industry in which revenues are increasing, Live Nation acquired Ticketmaster in 2010. In March 2011, AT&T agreed to buy T-Mobile USA from Deutsche Telekom AG for $39 billion in cash and stock. This deal—if approved by regulators—would consolidate the industry by combining the No. 2 and No. 4 U.S. wireless phone carriers.

There are four main benefits to a horizontal integration strategy:

- Reduction in competitive intensity
- Lower costs
- Increased differentiation
- Access to new markets and distribution channels

---

merger The joining of two independent companies to form a combined entity.

acquisition The purchase or takeover of one company by another; can be friendly or unfriendly.

hostile takeover Acquisition in which the target company does not wish to be acquired.

horizontal integration The process of acquiring and merging with competitors, leading to industry consolidation.

EXHIBIT 9.2

Sources of Value
Creation and Costs in
Horizontal Integration

Corporate Strategy	Sources of Value Creation (V)	Sources of Costs (C)
Horizontal Integration	• Reduction in competitive intensity • Lower costs • Increased differentiation • Access to new markets and distribution channels	• Integration failure • Reduced flexibility • Increased potential for legal repercussions

Exhibit 9.2 previews the sources of value creation and costs in horizontal integration, which we discuss next.

>> LO 9-2
Define horizontal
integration and evaluate
the advantages and
disadvantages of this
corporate-level strategy.

REDUCTION IN COMPETITIVE INTENSITY. Looking through the lens of the structure-conduct-performance (SCP) model (introduced in Chapter 3), horizontal integration changes the underlying industry structure in favor of the surviving firms. Excess capacity is taken out of the market, and competition decreases as a consequence of horizontal integration (assuming no new entrants). As a whole, the industry structure becomes more consolidated and thus potentially more profitable. If the surviving firms find themselves in an oligopolistic industry structure and their focus is on non-price competition (e.g., R&D spending, customer service, or advertising) the industry can indeed be quite profitable, and rivalry decreases among existing firms. Recent horizontal integration in the U.S. airline industry, for example, provided several benefits to the surviving carriers. By reducing excess capacity, the mergers between Delta and Northwest Airlines (in 2008), United Airlines and Continental (in 2010), and Southwest and AirTran (in 2010) lowered competitive intensity in the industry overall.

Horizontal integration, therefore, can favorably affect several of Porter's five forces for the surviving firms: strengthening bargaining power vis-à-vis suppliers and buyers, reducing the threat of entry, and reducing rivalry among existing firms. Because of the potential to reduce competitive intensity in an industry, government authorities such as the FTC and/or the European Commission usually must approve any large horizontal integration activity. For example, the FTC did not approve the proposed merger between Staples and Office Depot, arguing that the remaining industry would have only two competitors (the other one being Office Max). Staples and Office Depot argued that the market for office supplies needed to be defined more broadly to include large retailers such as Walmart and Target. The U.S. courts sided with the FTC, which argued that the prices for end consumers would be significantly higher if the market had only two category killers.[7]

LOWER COSTS. Research provides empirical evidence that firms use horizontal integration to lower costs through economies of scale, and thus enhance their economic value creation and in turn their performance.[8] In industries that have high fixed costs, achieving economies of scale through large output is critical in lowering costs. The dominant pharmaceutical companies like Pfizer, Roche, and Novartis, for example, maintain large sales forces ("detail people") who call on doctors and hospitals to promote their products. These specialized sales forces often number 10,000 or more, and thus are a significant fixed cost to the firms, even though part of their compensation is based on commissions.

Food Fight: Kraft's Hostile Takeover of Cadbury

In 2010, Kraft Foods bought its UK-based competitor Cadbury PLC for close to $20 billion in a hostile takeover. The combined Kraft–Cadbury entity is projected to have annual sales of over $50 billion and a 15 percent worldwide market share. Unlike the more diversified food-products company Kraft, Cadbury is focused solely on candy and gum. Hailing back to 1824, Cadbury established itself in markets across the globe, in concert with the British Empire.

Kraft was strongly attracted to Cadbury due to its advantageous position in countries such as India, Egypt, and Thailand and in fast-growing markets in Latin America. Cadbury holds 70 percent of the market share for chocolate in India, with more than 1 billion people. Children there specifically ask for "Cadbury chocolate" instead of just plain "chocolate." It is difficult for outsiders like Kraft to break into emerging economies because Cadbury has perfected its distribution system to meet the needs of millions of small, independent vendors. To secure a strong strategic position in these fast-growing emerging markets, therefore, Kraft felt that horizontal integration with Cadbury was critical. Still, Kraft faces formidable competitors in global markets, including Nestlé and Mars (which is especially strong in China where its famous Snickers bar was the official chocolate of the 2008 Olympic Games in Beijing).

In the U.S. market, the Cadbury acquisition will allow Kraft to access convenience stores, a new distribution channel for the company, and one that is growing fast and tends to have high profit margins. To achieve a stronger strategic position in the domestic market, however, Kraft will have to compete with The Hershey Company, the largest U.S. chocolate manufacturer. This battle will likely be intense because Hershey's main strategic focus is on the domestic market, with less than 10 percent of its revenues coming from international operations. With the U.S. population growing slowly and becoming more health conscious,[10] Hershey will need to re-evaluate its corporate strategy soon.

Maintaining such a large and sophisticated sales force (many with MBAs) is costly if the firm has only a few drugs it can show the doctor. As a rule of thumb, if a pharma company does not possess a blockbuster drug that brings in more than $1 billion in annual revenues, it cannot maintain its own sales force.[9] When existing firms like Pfizer and Wyeth merge, they join their drug pipelines and portfolios of existing drugs. Moreover, they are able to reduce their sales forces and lower the overall cost of distribution.

INCREASED DIFFERENTIATION. Horizontal integration through M&A can help firms strengthen their competitive positions by increasing the differentiation of their product and service offerings. In particular, horizontal integration can do this by filling gaps in a firm's product offering, allowing the combined entity to offer a complete suite of products and services. To enhance its differentiated appeal, Oracle acquired PeopleSoft for $10 billion in 2005. This horizontal integration joined the world's leading enterprise software company (Oracle), whose core competency is in database management systems, with a market leader in human resource management systems (PeopleSoft). This move allowed Oracle to offer its customers a complete suite of enterprise software systems to optimize their entire vertical and horizontal value chains.

ACCESS TO NEW MARKETS AND DISTRIBUTION CHANNELS. Horizontal integration can also help firms gain access to new markets and distribution channels. Strategy Highlight 9.1 discusses Kraft's acquisition of Cadbury to tap into new distribution channels in both the U.S. and fast-growing international markets.

Mergers and Acquisitions

Do mergers and acquisitions create competitive advantage? Despite their popularity, the answer, surprisingly, is that in most cases they do not. In fact, the M&A performance track

GAINING &
SUSTAINING
COMPETITIVE
ADVANTAGE

>> **LO 9-3**
Evaluate whether mergers and acquisitions lead to competitive advantage.

record is rather abysmal. Most mergers destroy shareholder value because the anticipated synergies never materialize.[11] If there is any value creation, it generally accrues to the shareholders of the firm that was taken over (the acquiree), because acquirers often pay a premium when buying the target company.[12]

Exhibit 9.3 depicts recent M&As with record shareholder value destruction. The green bar shows how much the acquirer paid for the target firm; the beige line shows the amount of shareholder value that was destroyed after the merger. Take as an example the ill-fated AOL Time Warner merger in 2000. AOL acquired Time Warner for $164 billion, merging an Internet-access service provider with an old-line content company, and creating the first new media company of the 21st century. Since the hoped-for synergies never materialized, and due to the culture clash between a traditional media company and an Internet venture, the merger destroyed an estimated $91 billion in shareholder value, putting the total bill for this corporate-level move at over $255 billion. Similarly, Vodafone's hostile takeover of Mannesmann destroyed even more shareholder value (an estimated total of $287 billion).

Given that M&As, on average, destroy rather than create shareholder value, why do we see so many mergers? Reasons include:

- The desire to overcome competitive disadvantage
- Superior acquisition and integration capability
- Principal–agent problems

DESIRE TO OVERCOME COMPETITIVE DISADVANTAGE. In some instances, mergers are not motivated by gaining competitive advantage, but by overcoming a competitive disadvantage. For example, to compete more successfully with Nike, the worldwide leader in sport shoes and apparel, Adidas (#2) acquired Reebok (#3) for $3.8 billion in 2006. This acquisition allowed the now-larger Adidas group to benefit from economies of scale and scope that were unachievable when Adidas and Reebok operated independently. Overcoming its competitive disadvantage against Nike in turn strengthened Adidas's competitive position. Indeed, overcoming a competitive disadvantage may put an organization on the road to gaining a competitive advantage.

EXHIBIT 9.3

Value Destruction in M&A: The Worst Offenders

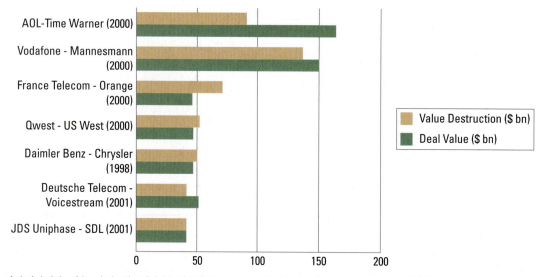

Source: Author's depiction of data obtained from C. S. Tullett (2006), "The world's worst M&A deals," *Here is the City News,* April 16, 2006. Calculation of value destruction based on the total equity value of the acquiring company, in excess of what would have occurred had it just performed in line with the market (up to three years post-merger).

SUPERIOR ACQUISITION AND INTEGRATION CAPABILITY. Acquisition and integration capabilities are not equally distributed across firms. Although there is strong evidence that M&As, *on average,* destroy rather than create shareholder value, it does not exclude the possibility that *some* firms are consistently able to identify, acquire, and integrate target companies to strengthen their competitive positions. Since it is valuable, rare, and difficult to imitate, a superior acquisition and integration capability, together with past experience, can lead to competitive advantage.

Cisco Systems, a networking and telecommunications company, is one such firm with an exemplary acquisitions record.[13] To position itself more strongly coming out of the 2001 stock market crash, Cisco embarked on an acquisitions-led growth strategy in which it acquired more than 130 technology companies.[14] Through this process, it diversified from computer networking routers to local area networking switching, Voice over IP (Internet telephony), and home networks. While Cisco acquired mainly smaller technology companies, it also acquired several larger firms including Linksys, Scientific Atlanta, and WebEx, now each multibillion-dollar businesses in their own right. Cisco buys successful companies, provides them with important complementary assets, and then lets them continue to be successful more or less on their own. Because of this superior integration template, which was refined by moving down the experience curve, Cisco kept the management of the larger firms it acquired and managed the relationships more like strategic alliances (discussed later in the chapter) than acquisitions.[15]

PRINCIPAL–AGENT PROBLEMS. When discussing diversification in the last chapter, we noted that some firms diversify through acquisitions due to principal–agent problems.[16] Managers, as agents, are supposed to act in the best interest of the principals, the shareholders. However, managers may have incentives to grow their firms through acquisitions—not for anticipated shareholder value appreciation, but to build a larger empire, which is positively correlated with prestige, power, and pay. Besides providing higher compensation and more corporate perks, a larger organization may also provide more job security, especially if the company pursues unrelated diversification.

A related problem is **managerial hubris,** a form of self-delusion in which managers convince themselves of their superior skills in the face of clear evidence to the contrary.[17] Managerial hubris comes in two forms. First, managers of the acquiring company convince themselves that they can manage the business of the target company more effectively, and thus can create additional shareholder value. This justification is often used for an unrelated diversification strategy. Second, although most top-level managers are aware that the vast majority of acquisitions destroys rather than creates shareholder value, they see themselves as the exceptions to the rule. Managerial hubris has led to many ill-fated deals, destroying billions of dollars. For example, Quaker Oats Company acquired Snapple because its managers thought that Snapple was another Gatorade, which was a standalone company that could be easily integrated.[18] In contrast, Snapple relied on a decentralized network of independent distributors and retailers who did not want Snapple to be taken over and who made it difficult and costly for Quaker Oats Company to integrate Snapple. The acquisition failed—and Quaker Oats was eventually taken over itself, by PepsiCo. Similarly, when Sony bought Columbia Pictures, its managers attempted to secure complementary products such as a movie library for its hardware, but failed to create synergies from the profoundly different types of businesses. 🔍

> **managerial hubris**
> A form of self-delusion, in which managers convince themselves of their superior skills in the face of clear evidence to the contrary.

Because mergers and acquisitions do not necessarily lead to the growth that firms expect, what other corporate strategies are there that might do so? We'll look next at strategic alliances.

STRATEGIC ALLIANCES: CAUSES AND CONSEQUENCES OF PARTNERING

>> **LO 9-4**
Define strategic alliances, and explain why they are important corporate strategy vehicles and why firms enter into them.

strategic alliance
A voluntary arrangement between firms that involves the sharing of knowledge, resources, and capabilities with the intent of developing processes, products, or services to lead to competitive advantage.

relational view of competitive advantage Strategic management framework that proposes that critical resources and capabilities frequently are embedded in strategic alliances that span firm boundaries.

Strategic alliances are voluntary arrangements between firms that involve the sharing of knowledge, resources, and capabilities with the intent of developing processes, products, or services.[19] Firms enter many types of alliances, from small contracts that have no bearing on a firm's competitiveness to multibillion-dollar joint ventures that can make or break the company. An alliance, therefore, qualifies as *strategic* only if it has the potential to affect a firm's competitive advantage. A strategic alliance has the potential to help a firm gain and sustain a competitive advantage when it joins together resources and knowledge in a combination that obeys the VRIO principles (introduced in Chapter 4).[20]

Some researchers suggest that the locus of competitive advantage is often not found within the individual firm but within strategic partnerships. According to this **relational view of competitive advantage,** critical resources and capabilities frequently are embedded in strategic alliances that span firm boundaries. Applying the VRIO framework introduced in Chapter 4, we know that the basis for competitive advantage is formed when strategic alliances create resource combinations that are valuable, rare, and difficult to imitate, and the alliances are organized appropriately to allow for value capture. In support of this perspective, over 80 percent of Fortune 1000 CEOs indicated in a recent survey that more than one quarter of their firm's revenues were derived from strategic alliances.[21]

Through a strategic alliance with DreamWorks Animation SKG, HP created the Halo Collaboration Studio, which makes virtual communication possible around the globe.[22] Halo's conferencing technology gives participants the vivid sense that they are in the same room. The conference rooms match, down to the last detail, giving participants the impression that they are sitting together at the same table. DreamWorks produced the computer-animated movie *Shrek 2* using this new technology for its meetings. People with different creative skills—script writers, computer animators, directors—though dispersed geographically, were able to participate as if in the same room, even seeing the work on each other's laptops. Use of the technology enabled faster decision making, enhanced productivity, reduced (or even eliminated) travel time and expense, and increased job satisfaction. Neither HP nor DreamWorks would have been able to produce this technology breakthrough alone,

EXHIBIT 9.4

Number of R&D Alliances

Source: Data drawn from the MERIT-CATI database; courtesy of Professor John Hagedoorn. For a detailed description of the MERIT-CATI database, see: J. Hagedoorn (2002), "Inter-firm R&D partnerships: An overview of major trends and patterns since 1960," *Research Policy* 31: 477–492.

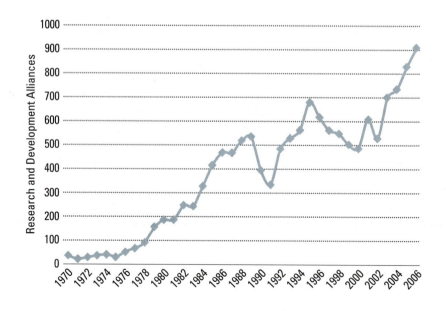

but moving into the videoconferencing arena together via a strategic alliance allowed both partners to pursue related diversification. Moreover, HP's alliance with DreamWorks Animation SKG enabled HP to compete head on with Cisco's high-end videoconferencing solution, TelePresence.[23]

The use of strategic alliances as a vehicle for corporate strategy has exploded since the 1980s, with thousands forming each year. Exhibit 9.4 depicts the number of alliances formed for R&D purposes since 1970. Such strategic alliances are attractive because they enable firms to achieve goals faster and at lower costs than going it alone. Globalization has also contributed to an increase in cross-border strategic alliances.

Why Do Firms Enter Strategic Alliances?

To affect a firm's competitive advantage, an alliance must promise a positive effect on the firm's economic value creation through increasing value and/or lowering costs (see discussion in Chapter 5). This logic is reflected in the common reasons why firms enter alliances:[24] They do so to:

- Strengthen competitive position
- Enter new markets
- Hedge against uncertainty
- Access critical complementary assets
- Learn new capabilities

STRENGTHEN COMPETITIVE POSITION. Firms can use strategic alliances to change the industry structure in their favor.[25] Firms frequently use strategic alliances when competing in so-called battles for industry standards (see discussion in Chapter 7). Or they may also initiate these alliances by themselves to challenge market leaders and thus change the underlying market structure. Strategy Highlight 9.2 shows how Apple orchestrated a web of strategic alliances with publishing houses to challenge Amazon's early lead in the delivery of e-content.

ENTER NEW MARKETS. Firms may use strategic alliances to enter new markets, either in terms of geography or products and services.[26] In some instances, governments (such as Saudi Arabia or China) require that foreign firms have a local joint venture partner before doing business in their countries. These

Strategic Alliances to Challenge Amazon

In 2007, Amazon established its Kindle device as the dominant e-reader by offering content (e-books, newspapers, and magazines) for instant download at heavily discounted prices. Kindle users paid $9.99 for e-books, including new releases and *The New York Times*'s best sellers. Amazon lost money on each e-book sold, because it had to pay publishers between $12.99 and $14.99 per e-book. Still, it was able to leverage this pricing strategy to establish Kindle as the dominant e-reader in the market.

Selling below cost is the same pricing strategy Amazon had used successfully when it first established itself as the leading e-tailer in sales of printed books. Amazon's e-book pricing strategy, however, did not sit well with content providers. They did not want to set an expectation in consumers' minds that all e-books should be priced at $9.99. Also, anchoring the e-book prices clearly would have negative repercussions for the sale of printed books, which are priced higher.

Apple crafted a different e-book business model. To attack Amazon's stronghold, Apple orchestrated a web of strategic alliances with major publishing houses such as HarperCollins, Macmillan, McGraw-Hill, and Simon & Schuster prior to launching its iPad product. To incentivize the publishers, Apple offered to let the content providers set the sales prices directly for the end consumers. These alliances aided Apple in populating its iBookstore with much needed content.

The publishers liked this deal. They retained pricing power over e-books, which allowed them to break the customer expectation that e-books should be priced at $9.99. Their alliances with Apple gave the publishers much needed leverage in negotiations with Amazon. Applying industry structural analysis, the bargaining power of suppliers—in this case, the content providers—increased from Amazon's perspective. In fact, book publishers even threatened to withhold or delay book titles if Amazon would not change its pricing structure. As a result, Amazon reluctantly changed its e-book pricing strategy and now charges between $12.99 and $14.99 for some new releases.

cross-border strategic alliances have both benefits and risks. While the foreign firm can benefit from local expertise and contacts, it is exposed to the risk that some of its proprietary know-how may be appropriated by the foreign partner. We will address such issues in the next chapter when studying global strategy.

In ChapterCase 1, we saw that Microsoft, though the leader in PC-based software, has been struggling for years to gain a foothold in the online search and advertising market. As personal computing moves more and more into the cloud, and PC-based software can be replaced by free online offerings such as Google Docs, it is critical for Microsoft to establish future revenue streams. The new cloud computing market, in which money is made from the accompanying online advertising, is expected to reach over $30 billion by 2014.[27]

Although Yahoo's co-founder and then-CEO Jerry Yang rebuffed Microsoft's $48 billion acquisition bid for Yahoo in the summer of 2008, Microsoft was able to get a much better deal through a subsequent strategic alliance. In early 2009, Yahoo appointed Carol Bartz as its new CEO, and she almost immediately rekindled negotiations with Microsoft's CEO Steve Ballmer, who suggested a strategic alliance between the two companies. Yahoo and Microsoft formed a partnership through which Yahoo's searches are powered by Microsoft's search engine, Bing. In return, Yahoo gets a portion of the revenues from the search ads sold on its sites. With its technology now powering some 30 percent of all online searches, Microsoft is able to fine-tune Bing. Thus, Microsoft can strengthen its competitive position against Google's dominance in online search and advertisement.[28] In the end, this strategic alliance was a low-cost alternative to an acquisition for Microsoft. But why did Yahoo agree to the deal? It entered this alliance because it had not generated the cash flow necessary to continuously update its own search technology.

HEDGE AGAINST UNCERTAINTY. In dynamic markets, strategic alliances allow firms to limit their exposure to uncertainty in the market.[29] For instance, in the wake of the biotechnology revolution, incumbent pharmaceutical firms such as Pfizer, Novartis, and Roche entered into hundreds of strategic alliances with biotech startups.[30] These alliances allowed the big pharma firms to make small-scale investments in many of the new biotechnology ventures that were poised to disrupt existing market economics. In some sense, the pharma companies were taking real options in these biotechnology experiments, providing them with the right but not the obligation to make further investments when new drugs were introduced from the biotech companies. Once the new drugs were a known quantity, the uncertainty was removed, and the incumbent firms could react accordingly.

For example, in 1990 the Swiss pharma company Roche initially invested $2.1 billion in an equity alliance to purchase a controlling interest (>50 percent) in the biotech startup Genentech. In 2009, after witnessing the success of Genentech's drug discovery and development projects in subsequent years, Roche spent $47 billion to purchase the remaining minority interest in Genentech, making it a wholly owned subsidiary.[31] Taking a wait-and-see approach by entering strategic alliances allows incumbent firms to buy time and wait for the uncertainty surrounding the market and technology to fade. Many firms in fast-moving markets appear to subscribe to this rationale. Besides biotechnology, it has also been documented in nanotechnology, semiconductors, and other dynamic markets.[32]

ACCESS CRITICAL COMPLEMENTARY ASSETS. The successful commercialization of a new product or service often requires complementary assets such as marketing, manufacturing, and after-sale service.[33] In particular, new firms are in need of complementary assets to complete the value chain from upstream innovation to downstream commercialization. Building downstream complementary assets such as marketing and regulatory expertise or a sales force is often prohibitively expensive and time-consuming, and thus frequently

Pixar and Disney: From Alliance to Acquisition

Pixar started out as a computer hardware company producing high-end graphic display systems. One of its customers was Disney. To demonstrate the graphic display systems' capabilities and thus increase sales, Pixar produced short, computer-animated movies. In the beginning, though, despite being sophisticated, Pixar's computer hardware was not selling well, and the new venture was hemorrhaging money. In rode Steve Jobs to the rescue. Shortly after being ousted from Apple in 1986, Jobs bought the struggling hardware company for $5 million and founded Pixar Animation Studies, investing another $5 million into the company.

To finance and distribute its newly created computer-animated movies, Pixar entered a strategic alliance with Disney. Disney's distribution network and its stellar reputation in animated movies were critical complementary assets that Pixar needed to commercialize its new type of films. In turn, Disney was able to rejuvenate its floundering product lineup, retaining the rights to the newly created Pixar characters and to any sequels.

Pixar became successful beyond imagination as it rolled out one blockbuster after another: *Toy Story* (*1, 2,* and *3*), *A Bug's Life, Monsters, Inc., Finding Nemo,* and *The Incredibles,* grossing several billion dollars. Given Pixar's huge success and Disney's abysmal performance with its own releases during this time, the bargaining power in the alliance shifted dramatically. Renegotiations of the Pixar–Disney alliance broke down altogether in 2004, reportedly because of personality conflicts between Steve Jobs and Disney Chairman/CEO Michael Eisner. After Eisner left Disney in the fall of 2005, Disney acquired Pixar for $7.4 billion, a deal that made Steve Jobs the largest shareholder of Disney.

The early Pixar–Disney alliance not only served as a vehicle to match the two entities' complementary assets, but also led eventually to the acquisition of Pixar by Disney. The alliance gave Disney an inside perspective on Pixar's valuable core competencies in the creation of computer-animated features. In 2009, driven by poor performance in its internal movie creation efforts,[34] Disney also added *Spiderman, Iron Man, The Incredible Hulk,* and *Captain America* to its lineup of characters by acquiring Marvel Entertainment for $4 billion.

---

not an option for new ventures. Strategic alliances allow firms to match complementary skills and resources to complete the value chain. Moreover, licensing agreements of this sort allow the partners to benefit from a division of labor, allowing each to efficiently focus on its core expertise. Strategy Highlight 9.3 shows how fledgling startup Pixar found itself in dire straits in the early 1990s, and how an alliance with Disney rescued the computer-animated movie studio.

LEARN NEW CAPABILITIES. Firms enter strategic alliances because they are motivated by the desire to learn new capabilities from their partners.[35] When the collaborating firms are also competitors, *co-opetition* ensues (introduced in Chapter 1).[36] Such co-opetition can lead to **learning races** in strategic alliances,[37] a situation in which both partners are motivated to form an alliance for learning, but the rate at which the firms learn may vary. The firm that learns faster and thus accomplishes its goal more quickly has an incentive to exit the alliance or, at a minimum, to reduce its knowledge sharing. Since the cooperating firms are also competitors, learning races can have a positive effect on the winning firm's competitive position vis-à-vis its alliance partner.

NUMMI (New United Motor Manufacturing, Inc.) was the first joint venture in the U.S. automobile industry, formed between GM and Toyota in 1984. Recall from Chapter 8 that joint ventures are a special type of a strategic alliance in which two partner firms create a third, jointly owned entity. In the NUMMI joint venture, each partner was motivated to learn new capabilities: GM entered the strategic alliance to learn the lean manufacturing

learning races
Situations in which both partners in a strategic alliance are motivated to form an alliance for learning, but the rate at which the firms learn may vary; the firm that accomplishes its goal more quickly has an incentive to exit the alliance or reduce its knowledge sharing.

system pioneered by Toyota in order to produce high-quality, fuel-efficient cars at a profit. Toyota entered the alliance to learn how to implement its lean manufacturing program with an American work force. NUMMI was a test-run for Toyota before building fully owned *greenfield plants* (new manufacturing facilities) in Alabama, Indiana, Kentucky, Texas, and West Virginia. In this 25-year history, GM and Toyota built some 7 million high-quality cars at the NUMMI plant. In fact, NUMMI was transformed from worst performer (under GM ownership prior to the joint venture) to GM's highest-quality plant in the U.S. In the end, as part of GM's bankruptcy reorganization during 2009–2010, it pulled out of the NUMMI joint venture.

The joint venture between GM and Toyota can be seen as a learning race. Who won? Researchers argue that Toyota was faster in accomplishing its alliance goal—learning how to manage U.S. labor—because of its limited scope.[38] Toyota had already perfected lean manufacturing; all it needed to do was to train U.S. workers in the method and transfer this knowledge to its subsidiary plants in the U.S. On the other hand, GM had to learn a completely new production system. GM was successful in transferring lean manufacturing to its newly created Saturn brand (which was discontinued in 2010 as part of GM's reorganization), but it had a hard time implementing lean manufacturing in its *existing* plants. These factors suggest that Toyota won the learning race with GM, which in turn helped Toyota gain and sustain a competitive advantage over GM in the U.S. market.

Also, note that different motivations for forming alliances are not necessarily independent and can be intertwined. For example, firms that collaborate to access critical complementary assets may also want to learn from one another to subsequently pursue vertical integration. In sum, alliance formation is frequently motivated by leveraging economies of scale, scope, specialization, and learning.

Governing Strategic Alliances

>> LO 9-5
Describe three alliance governance mechanisms and evaluate their pros and cons.

In Chapter 8, we showed that strategic alliances lie in the middle of the buy-vs.-make continuum (see Exhibit 8.3). Alliances can be governed by the following mechanisms: (1) contractual agreements for *non-equity alliances,* (2) *equity alliances,* and (3) *joint ventures.*[39] Exhibit 9.5 provides an overview of the key characteristics of the three alliance types, including their advantages and disadvantages.

NON-EQUITY ALLIANCES. The most common type of alliance is a **non-equity alliance,** which is based on contracts between firms. The most frequent forms of non-equity alliances are *supply agreements, distribution agreements,* and *licensing agreements.* As suggested by their names, these contractual agreements are vertical strategic alliances, connecting different parts of the industry value chain. In a non-equity alliance, firms tend to share **explicit knowledge**—knowledge that can be codified. Patents, user manuals, fact sheets, and scientific publications are all ways to capture explicit knowledge, which concerns the notion of *knowing about* a certain process or product.

Licensing agreements are contractual alliances in which the participants regularly exchange codified knowledge. In 1978, biotech firm Genentech licensed its newly developed drug Humulin (human insulin) to the pharmaceutical firm Eli Lilly for manufacturing, facilitating approval by the Food and Drug Administration (FDA), and distribution. This partnership was an example of a vertical strategic alliance: one partner (Genentech) was positioned upstream in the industry value chain (focusing on R&D), while the other partner (Eli Lilly) was positioned downstream (focusing on manufacturing and distribution). This type of vertical arrangement is often described as a "hand-off" from the upstream partner to the downstream partner, and is possible because the underlying knowledge is largely

non-equity alliance
Partnership based on contracts between firms. The most frequent forms are *supply agreements, distribution agreements,* and *licensing agreements.*

explicit knowledge
Knowledge that can be codified (e.g., information, facts, instructions, recipes); concerns *knowing about* a process or product.

EXHIBIT 9.5

Key Characteristics of Different Alliance Types

Alliance Type	Governance Mechanism	Frequency	Type of Knowledge Exchanged	Pros	Cons	Examples
Non-equity (supply, licensing, and distribution agreements)	Contract	Most common	Explicit	• Flexible • Fast • Easy to initiate and terminate	• Weak tie • Lack of trust and commitment	• Genentech–Lilly (exclusive) licensing agreement for Humulin • Microsoft–IBM (non-exclusive) licensing agreement for MS-DOS
Equity (purchase of an equity stake or corporate venture capital, CVC investment)	Equity investment	Less common than non-equity alliances, but more common than joint ventures	Explicit; exchange of tacit knowledge possible	• Stronger tie • Trust and commitment can emerge • Window into new technology (option value)	• Less flexible • Slower • Can entail significant investments	• Renault–Nissan alliance based on cross equity holdings, with Renault owning 44.4% in Nissan; and Nissan owning 15% in Renault • Roche's equity investment in Genentech (prior to full integration)
Joint venture (JV)	Creation of new entity by two or more parent firms	Least common	Both tacit and explicit knowledge exchanged	• Strongest tie • Trust and commitment likely to emerge • May be required by institutional setting	• Can entail long negotiations and significant investments • Long-term solution • JV managers have double reporting lines (2 bosses)	• Hulu, JV owned by NBC, Fox, and ABC • Dow Corning, JV owned by Dow Chemical and Corning

explicit and can be easily codified. When Humulin reached the market in 1982, it was the first approved genetically engineered human therapeutic worldwide.[40] Subsequently, Humulin became a billion-dollar blockbuster drug.

Because of their contractual nature, non-equity alliances are flexible and easy to initiate (and terminate). However, because they can be temporary in nature, they also sometimes produce weak ties between the alliance partners, which can result in a lack of trust and commitment.

EQUITY ALLIANCES. In an equity alliance, at least one partner takes partial ownership in the other partner. Equity alliances are less common than contractual, non-equity alliances because they often require larger investments. Because they are based on partial ownership rather than contracts, equity alliances are used to signal stronger commitments. Moreover, equity alliances allow for the sharing of tacit knowledge—knowledge that cannot be codified.[41] Tacit knowledge concerns the *knowing how* to do a certain task. It can be acquired only through actively participating in the process. In an equity alliance, therefore, the partners frequently exchange personnel to make the acquisition of tacit knowledge possible.

Toyota is using an equity alliance with Tesla Motors, a designer and developer of electric cars, to learn new knowledge and gain a window into new technology. In spring 2010, Toyota made a $50 million equity investment in the California startup company. Tesla has two cars in its lineup: a $109K roadster and a $50K family sedan. It has manufactured and sold about 1,500 roadsters and plans to build 20,000 of its sedans in 2012, to be manufactured at the New United Motor Manufacturing (NUMMI) auto plant in Fremont, California, which Tesla Motors bought from Toyota. Tesla's CEO Elon Musk stated, "the Tesla factory effectively leverages an ideal combination of hardcore Silicon Valley engineering talent, traditional automotive engineering talent and the proven Toyota production system."[42] Toyota, which plans to sell all-electric cars in the U.S. by 2012, hopes to infuse its company with Tesla's entrepreneurial spirit. Toyota President Akio Toyoda commented that "by partnering with Tesla, my hope is that all Toyota employees will recall that 'venture business spirit' and take on the challenges of the future."[43] Mr. Toyoda hopes that a transfer of tacit knowledge will take place, in which Tesla's entrepreneurial spirit reinvigorates Toyota.[44]

Another governance mechanism that falls under the broad rubric of equity alliances is corporate venture capital (CVC) investments, which are equity investments by established firms in entrepreneurial ventures.[45] The value of CVC investments is estimated to be in the double-digit billion-dollar range each year. Larger firms frequently have dedicated CVC units, such as Dow Venture Capital, Siemens Venture Capital, Kaiser Permanente Ventures, and Johnson & Johnson Development Corporation. Rather than hoping primarily for financial gains, as do traditional venture capitalists, CVC investments create real options in terms of gaining access to new, and potentially disruptive, technologies.[46] Research indicates that CVC investments have a positive impact on value creation for the investing firm, especially in high-tech industries such as semiconductors, computing, and the medical-device sector.[47]

Equity alliances tend to produce stronger ties and greater trust between partners than non-equity alliances do. They also offer a window into new technology that, like a real option, can be exercised if successful, or abandoned if not promising. The downside of equity alliances is the amount of investment that can be involved, as well as a possible lack of flexibility and speed in putting together the partnership.

JOINT VENTURES. A joint venture (JV) is a standalone organization created and jointly owned by two or more parent companies (as discussed in Chapter 8). For example, Hulu (a video-on-demand service) is jointly owned by NBC, ABC, and Fox. Since partners contribute equity to a joint venture, they are making a long-term commitment. Exchange of

equity alliance
Partnership in which at least one partner takes partial ownership in the other partner.

tacit knowledge
Knowledge that cannot be codified; concerns *knowing how* to do a certain task and can be acquired only through active participation in that task.

corporate venture capital (CVC)
Equity investments by established firms in entrepreneurial ventures; CVC falls under the broader rubric of equity alliances.

joint venture A standalone organization created and jointly owned by two or more parent companies.

both explicit and tacit knowledge through interaction of personnel is typical. Equity alliances and joint ventures are frequently stepping stones toward full integration of the partner firms either through a merger or an acquisition. Essentially, they are often used as a "try before you buy" strategic option.[48] Joint ventures are also frequently used to enter foreign markets where the host country requires such a partnership to gain access to the market in exchange for advanced technology and know-how. In terms of frequency, joint ventures are the least common of the three types of strategic alliances.

The advantages of joint ventures are the strong ties, trust, and commitment that can result between the partners. However, they can entail long negotiations and significant investments. If the alliance doesn't work out as expected, undoing the JV can take some time and involve considerable cost. A further risk is that knowledge shared with the new partner could be misappropriated by opportunistic behavior. Finally, any rewards from the collaboration must be shared between the partners.

Alliance Management Capability

Strategic alliances create a paradox for managers. Although alliances appear to be necessary to compete in many industries, between 30 and 70 percent of all strategic alliances do not deliver the expected benefits, and thus are considered failures by at least one alliance partner.[49] Given the high failure (or at least, disappointment) rate, effective alliance management is critical to gaining and sustaining a competitive advantage, especially in high-technology industries.[50]

Alliance management capability is a firm's ability to effectively manage three alliance-related tasks concurrently, often across a portfolio of many different alliances (see Exhibit 9.6):[51]

■ Partner selection and alliance formation
■ Alliance design and governance
■ Post-formation alliance management

PARTNER SELECTION AND ALLIANCE FORMATION. When making the business case for an alliance, the expected benefits of the alliance must exceed its costs. When one or more of the five reasons for alliance formation are present—to strengthen competitive position, enter new markets, hedge against uncertainty, access critical complementary resources, or learn new capabilities—the firm must select the best possible alliance partner. Research has identified partner compatibility and partner commitment as necessary conditions for successful alliance formation.[52] *Partner compatibility* captures aspects of cultural fit between different firms. *Partner commitment* concerns the willingness to make available necessary resources and to accept short-term sacrifices to ensure long-term rewards.

ALLIANCE DESIGN AND GOVERNANCE. Once two or more firms agree to pursue an alliance, managers must then design the alliance and choose an appropriate governance

>> **LO 9-6**
Describe the three phases of alliance management, and explain how an alliance management capability can lead to a competitive advantage.

alliance management capability A firm's ability to effectively manage three alliance-related tasks concurrently: (1) partner selection and alliance formation, (2) alliance design and governance, and (3) post-formation alliance management.

EXHIBIT 9.6

Alliance Management Capability

Alliance Management Capability

Partner Selection and Alliance Formation → Alliance Design and Governance → Post-Formation Alliance Management

mechanism from among the three options: non-equity contractual agreement, equity alliances, or joint venture. For example, in a study of over 640 alliances, researchers found that the joining of specialized complementary assets increases the likelihood that the alliance is governed hierarchically. This effect is stronger in the presence of uncertainties concerning the alliance partner as well as the envisioned tasks.[53]

In addition to the formal governance mechanisms, *inter-organizational trust* is a critical dimension of alliance success.[54] Because all contracts are necessarily incomplete, trust between the alliance partners plays an important role for effective post-formation alliance management. Effective governance, therefore, can be accomplished only by skillfully combining formal and informal mechanisms.

POST-FORMATION ALLIANCE MANAGEMENT. The third phase in a firm's alliance management capability concerns the ongoing management of the alliance. To be a source of competitive advantage, the partnership needs to create resource combinations that obey the VRIO criteria. As shown in Exhibit 9.7, this can be most likely accomplished if the alliance partners make relation-specific investments, establish knowledge-sharing routines, and build interfirm trust.[55]

Hewlett-Packard, for example, is known as having made relation-specific investments to create long-term partnerships with several smaller technology firms co-located in Silicon Valley.[56] HP's strategy of forming a dense network of alliances with smaller firms contrasts sharply with Digital Equipment Corporation's (DEC) strategy of "going it alone." HP's network of alliances provided a competitive advantage over DEC, which was characterized as having a "more insular organizational structure and corporate mindset."[57] Not surprisingly, DEC went defunct in 1998 and HP acquired some of its assets. Finally, firms that are able to establish effective knowledge-sharing routines with its suppliers and buyers, as does 3M, tend to be more innovative.[58]

Trust is a critical aspect of any alliance. Interfirm trust entails the expectation that each alliance partner will behave in good faith and develop norms of reciprocity and fairness.[59] Such trust helps to ensure that the relationship survives and thereby increases the

EXHIBIT 9.7

How to Make Alliances Work

Source: Adapted from J. H. Dyer and H. Singh (1998), "The relational view: Cooperative strategy and the sources of interorganizational advantage," *Academy of Management Review* 23: 660–679.

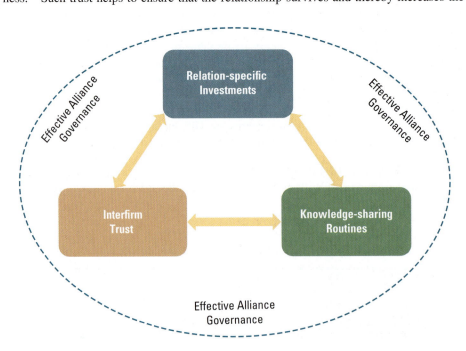

possibility of meeting the intended goals of the alliance. Interfirm trust is also important for fast decision making.[60] Indeed, several firms such as Eli Lilly, HP, Procter & Gamble, and IBM compete to obtain trustworthy reputations in order to become the alliance "partner of choice" for small technology ventures, universities, and individual inventors.

Indeed, the systematic differences in firms' alliance-management capability can be a source of competitive advantage.[61] But how do firms go about building alliance-management capability? The answer is to build capability through repeated experiences over time. In support, several empirical studies have shown that firms move down the learning curve and become better at managing alliances through repeated alliance exposure.[62]

The "learning-by-doing" approach has value for small ventures in which a few key people coordinate most of the firms' activities.[63] However, there are clearly limitations for larger companies. Firms such as ABB, GE, Philips, or Siemens are engaged in hundreds of alliances simultaneously. In fact, if alliances are not managed from a portfolio perspective at the corporate level, serious negative repercussions can emerge.[64] Groupe Danone, a large French food conglomerate, lost its leading position in the highly lucrative and fast-growing Chinese market because its local alliance partner, Hangzhou Wahaha Group, terminated their long-standing alliance.[65] Wahaha accused different Danone business units of subsequently setting up partnerships with other Chinese firms that were a direct competitive threat to Wahaha. This example makes it clear that although alliances are important vehicles by which to pursue business-level strategy, they are best managed at the corporate level.

To accomplish effective alliance management, researchers suggest that firms create a *dedicated alliance function,*[66] led by a vice president or director of alliance management and endowed with its own resources and support staff. The dedicated alliance function should be given the tasks of coordinating all alliance-related activity in the entire organization, taking a corporate-level perspective. It should serve as a repository of prior experience and be responsible for creating processes and structures to teach and leverage that experience and related knowledge throughout the rest of the organization across all levels. Empirical research shows that firms with a dedicated alliance function are able to create value from their alliances above and beyond what could be expected based on experience alone.[67]

Pharmaceutical company Eli Lilly is an acknowledged leader in alliance management.[68] Lilly's Office of Alliance Management, led by a director and endowed with several managers, manages its far-flung alliance activity across all hierarchical levels and around the globe. Lilly's process prescribes that each alliance is managed by a three-person team: an alliance champion, alliance leader, and alliance manager. The *alliance champion* is a senior, corporate-level executive responsible for high-level support and oversight. This senior manager is also responsible for making sure that the alliance fits within the firm's existing alliance porfolio and corporate-level strategy. The *alliance leader* has the technical expertise and knowledge needed for the specific technical area and is responsible for the day-to-day management of the alliance. The *alliance manager,* positioned within the Office of Alliance Management, serves as an alliance process resource and business integrator between the two alliance partners, and provides alliance training and development, as well as diagnostic tools.

Some companies are also able to leverage the relational capabilities obtained through managing alliance portfolios into a successful acquisition strategy.[69] As detailed earlier, Eli Lilly has an entire department at the corporate level devoted to managing its alliance portfolio. Following up on an earlier 50/50 joint venture formed with Icos (maker of the $1 billion-plus erectile-dysfunction drug Cialis), Lilly acquired Icos in 2007. More recently (in 2008), Eli Lilly outmaneuvered Bristol-Myers Squibb to acquire biotech venture ImClone for $6.5 billion. ImClone discovered and developed the cancer-fighting drug

Erbitux, also a $1 billion blockbuster in terms of annual sales. The acquisition of these two smaller biotech ventures allowed Lilly to fill its empty drug pipeline.[70]

Strategy researchers, therefore, have suggested that corporate-level managers should not only coordinate the firm's portfolio of alliances, but also leverage their relationships to successfully engage in mergers and acquisitions.[71] That is, rather than focusing on developing an alliance-management capability in isolation, firms should develop a *relational capability* that allows for the successful management of both strategic alliances *and* mergers and acquisitions.

STRATEGIC NETWORKS

>> LO 9-7
Define strategic networks and evaluate the advantages and disadvantages of different network positions.

When several firms form alliances to pursue a common purpose, they build a strategic network. A strategic network is a social structure composed of multiple organizations (called *network nodes*) and the links among the nodes (called *network ties*). Strategic networks emerge as companies add more and more partners over time to an existing alliance.[72] Pursuing a *network strategy*—that is, forming strategic networks—enables firms to achieve goals they cannot or would not want to accomplish alone or with more traditional two-company alliances.

Consider the Star Alliance, the first global airline network. It includes such well-known carriers as Air Canada, Air China, Continental Airlines, Lufthansa, Singapore Airlines, and United Airlines, and provides customers worldwide access to more than 21,000 daily flights to 1,100 destinations in 181 countries.[73] Through code sharing, the Star Alliance allows for seamless travel among more than 25 international airlines—a goal that the individual airlines could not accomplish on their own. Indeed, some scholars argue that in many industries it is not single firms that compete against one another but rather entire networks.[74] In the airline industry, the Star Alliance contends with two other prominent strategic networks: SkyTeam (composed of Air France, Delta, KLM, and Korean Air, among others) and Oneworld (formed by American Airlines, British Airways, Cathay Pacific, Japan Airlines, and others).

Strategic networks provide advantages but also can constrain individual members. Once a firm becomes part of a network, managers need to think about how their company's strategy affects, and is affected by, the network. Strategy Highlight 9.4 shows how membership in the European telecommunications network Unisource had negative consequences for some of its smaller member firms.

Analyzing Strategic Networks

Analysis of strategic networks enables us to understand the benefits and costs accrued by individual firms embedded in a network.[75] Not all network relationships are equally beneficial, and not all network positions provide the same advantages. One important distinction concerns the quality of the tie, in particular, the distinction between strong and weak ties.[76] *Strong ties* are characterized by trusting relationships established through frequent, face-to-face interactions between managers over time, and may even include friendships across different firms. They may contain an equity-sharing element such as an R&D joint venture. Strong ties are beneficial to the transfer of tacit knowledge and for rapid decision making. In contrast, *weak ties* are characterized by infrequent and shallower interactions. They tend

strategic network
A social structure composed of multiple organizations (*network nodes*) and the links among the nodes (*network ties*).

STRATEGY HIGHLIGHT 9.4

When Strategic Networks Become Dysfunctional

Prior to deregulation of the European telecommunications market in the 1990s, telecom providers were nationally owned, and telecom service offerings were more or less limited to their respective home countries. Despite their monopoly positions, many telecom providers lost money and needed taxpayer subsidies. The EU's deregulation of the telecom market put tremendous pressure on telecom firms in smaller countries.

To compete more effectively with larger rivals like Deutsche Telekom and France Télécom and to offer a larger service area, Swedish telecom firm Telia and Dutch telecom firm KPN formed a joint venture, Unisource. As business customers demanded global coverage and more sophisticated data and voice services, other telecom providers joined the alliance. In this period (the 1990s), breakthroughs such as the rise of the Internet and wireless telephony provided huge opportunities but also posed significant threats in terms of regulatory and technology changes in the external environment.

From the original two-partner joint venture, the Unisource alliance morphed into a global strategic network in less than a decade, encompassing about 25 telecom companies (including AT&T) in 11 countries on 4 continents. Many of the managers, especially the ones who led smaller firms, quickly learned that they were no longer able to influence the network. Instead, they were dominated by it and severely restricted in their firms' strategic flexibility. Problems arose for a number of reasons. Some network members made significant investments early on that would reap benefits only much later. Other network members behaved opportunistically, adopting a free-rider approach. When AT&T joined the network to enhance its European presence and allow Unisource members to provide services in the U.S., it became clear that AT&T, with its enormous size, would dominate the network.

In the end, for some firms, the costs of being part of Unisource outweighed the benefits. Some of the smaller firms decided to exit the network. Unisource hastily invited new telecom providers to join out of fear of losing telecommunications coverage in certain key geographic areas, but these newcomers were less committed to the overall network strategy and preferred to pursue their own strategic advantages. As a result, the once-flourishing telecom network turned dysfunctional. Unisource collapsed within a few short months of the membership shuffle.[77]

to be governed by contractual arrangements. Weak ties usually allow for the transfer of explicit knowledge only. Given the different resource requirements in terms of managerial time and attention, firms typically maintain a larger number of weak ties than strong ties.

To understand the different positions of individual firms in strategic networks, it is helpful to graph all the nodes in the network and their ties. Exhibit 9.8 (see next page) depicts a hypothetical strategic network; the purple nodes are firms and the blue connections are the ties between them. When we look at it this way, a couple of observations jump out. Firm A is centrally located in a cluster of six firms (indicated by the dotted oval); it has the highest **degree centrality** of all the firms in the network—the number of direct ties a firm has in a network, out of the possible direct ties (in this case, $n = 7$); the more direct ties, the more centrally located the firm is. Firm A not only is highly visible and prominent in this cluster, but also has access to many channels of information. Moreover, the cluster of firms around firm A exhibits a high degree of *closure*, meaning that most of the firms are connected to one another. Interfirm networks in Silicon Valley, for example, are characterized by a high degree of closure.[78] A high degree of closure implies that most firms know each other, which facilitates trust,[79] and which in turn lowers transaction costs and improves efficiency and firm performance. Since research has shown that high degree centrality improves firm performance, firm A is well positioned within this cluster.[80]

degree centrality
The number of direct ties a firm has in a network, out of the possible direct ties; the more direct ties, the more centrally located the firm is.

EXHIBIT 9.8

Firms Embedded in
Strategic Networks

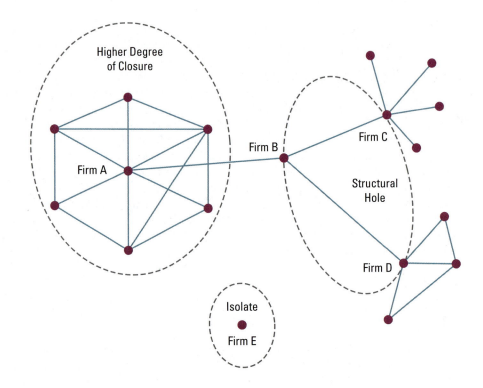

Firm B occupies a powerful position in this network because it acts as a *knowledge broker* between three subnetworks formed around firm A, firm C, and firm D. In this role, firm B bridges and connects the three clusters making up the network. In particular, firm B spans several **structural holes**—spaces where two organizations are connected to the same organization, but are not connected to each other. In Exhibit 9.8, one of the structural holes is highlighted in the dotted oval. Here, firms C and D are connected to firm B, but not to one another. Generally, firms that bridge structural holes gain information and control benefits over the nonconnected firms.[81] Firm B has access to a diverse set of information emanating from the subnetworks of firms A, C, and D, allowing it to gain access to timely information and to obtain referrals. Moreover, occupying a structural hole gives firm B power because it can play firm C off against firm D, and vice versa.

A knowledge broker is a powerful position to occupy within a network. Researchers have shown that continuous innovation is based on a firm's ability to broker, connect, and recombine different strands of knowledge.[82] A position as a knowledge broker allows a firm to find novel solutions to thorny problems because it often has access to diverse knowledge, and can link that information to implement solutions in the form of new products or processes. The design consultancy IDEO, famous for creating Apple's first computer mouse and Whole Foods's shopping cart, strategically positions itself as a knowledge broker in different design, technology, and market-domain networks to achieve continuous innovation.[83]

In contrast to knowledge brokers, some firms are considered *isolates,* meaning they are not connected to any other firm in the network. In Exhibit 9.8, for example, firm E is an isolate. Because it cannot benefit from any advantages from the resources within the network, its position is weak. Indeed, firm E is likely to have a competitive disadvantage, given the strong empirical evidence that interfirm cooperation and openness have a positive effect on continued innovation and superior firm performance.[84, 85]

structural holes
Spaces where two organizations are connected to the same organization, but are not connected to one another. Firms that bridge structural holes (*brokers*) gain information and control benefits over the nonconnected firms.

The network in Exhibit 9.8 as a whole is characterized by the small-world phenomenon.[86] The **small-world phenomenon** occurs when a network exhibits local clusters, each with high degree centrality. Here, there are local clusters around firm A, firm C, and firm D, connected by bridging ties A–B, B–C, and B–D. In a small-world network, the path length between any two nodes in the network is short, meaning any firm can reach any other firm in the network through a small number of connections. Many small-world networks have been observed. When plotting the thousands of technology alliances worldwide, for example, a small-world network emerges, with two main components (electronics-based industries, and chemical- and medical-based industries) that are connected by few brokers.[87] The Internet is also a small-world network, because clusters of local network servers are connected by a few bridging ties, increasing the speed of global communication and data transfer. Small-world networks further enhance the value of broker positions like the one held by firm B.

Strategic networks are powerful vehicles to execute business and corporate-level strategy. Managers need to be aware of the potential benefits to be had from networks, but also of potential downsides. In addition, not all network positions are created equal. Thus, in addition to managing a firm's alliance portfolio, strategists also need to understand that its alliances embed the firm in different networks. They must manage network participation in such a way as to carve out an advantageous position that will provide benefits that could not be had otherwise.

We now have concluded our discussion of corporate strategy. Acquisitions, alliances, and networks are key vehicles to execute corporate strategy, each with its distinct advantages and disadvantages. It is also clear from this chapter that mergers and acquisitions, strategic alliances, and networks are a global phenomenon. In fact, the strategic networks in the airline and telecommunications industries discussed in this chapter were formed with the intent of providing global reach, which of course provides additional challenges as well as opportunities. In the next chapter, we discuss strategy in a global world.

small-world phenomenon Situation in which a network exhibits local clusters, each with high degree centrality.

CHAPTERCASE 9 | *Consider This . . .*

I N CHAPTERCASE 9, we explored Facebook's growth into a dominant social network, and the chapter also noted the importance to the success of Facebook of complements such as software apps like FarmVille. These apps help drive users to return frequently to Facebook for updates on these social games. Zynga, founded in July 2007, is the world's largest provider of social games (including FarmVille). As of March 2011, Zynga had over 250 million active users playing its games at least monthly. In May 2010, Facebook and Zynga signed a five-year "strategic relationship" agreement that, among other things, increased the use of Facebook credits on Zynga's games.

Zynga, however, has broader ambitions than being the biggest app-provider to Facebook. By early 2011, Zynga games were available on eight different game portals including iPhone, Android, and MSN Games. Zynga purchased six firms in 2010 to fulfill the expected demand of such large and growing marketplace relationships. These acquisitions brought new content material to the Zynga platform (e.g., "Words with Friends" and "Rock Legends"). Additionally, Zynga used acquisitions to expand globally (purchasing Unoh Inc. in Tokyo and XPD in Beijing) and to build its internal growth, as it launched its first international office in Bangalore,

India, in February 2010. Finally, Zynga struck a deal in 2010 for its first retail promotion: The world's largest convenience store retail chain, 7-Eleven, branded items such as Slurpees with designs from the FarmVille, Mafia Wars, and YoVille games, offering redemption codes for in-game rewards. For Zynga, 2010 was quite a year—filled with acquisitions, alliances, and network building![88]

1. Based on ChapterCase 9 (p. 237), what do you see as some of the main differences between MySpace and Facebook? How did their business models differ? What were the strategic implications of these differences?

2. App-developers like Zynga have been credited with much of the reason for the rapid growth of both Facebook and various brands of smartphones. Yet managing eight or more delivery outlets can be difficult for new (and often small) firms, like Zynga, to coordinate. What suggestions do you have for how these young firms might handle these relationships successfully?

3. Go to www.zynga.com/about/news.php and look at the most recent press announcements from Zynga. Is the firm using more acquisitions or alliances in building its business? What seems to be the primary reason for this activity?

4. Given Zynga's recent activities in network building, what do you see as advantages and disadvantages of Zynga's network strategy?

Take-Away Concepts

This chapter discussed three mechanisms of corporate-level strategy (acquisitions, alliances, and networks), as summarized by the following learning objectives and related take-away concepts.

LO 9-1 Differentiate between mergers and acquisitions and explain why firms would use either as a vehicle for corporate strategy.

>> A merger describes the joining of two independent companies to form a combined entity.

>> An acquisition describes the purchase or (hostile) takeover of one company by another.

>> The distinction between mergers and acquisitions (M&A) can be blurry. Many observers simply use the umbrella term M&A to describe horizontal integration.

>> Firms can use M&A activity for competitive advantage when they possess a superior relational capability, which is often built on superior alliance management capability.

LO 9-2 Define horizontal integration and evaluate the advantages and disadvantages of this corporate-level strategy.

>> Horizontal integration is the process of acquiring and merging with competitors, leading to industry consolidation.

>> As a corporate strategy, firms use horizontal integration to: (1) reduce competitive intensity, (2) lower costs, (3) increase differentiation, and (4) access new markets and distribution channels.

LO 9-3 Evaluate whether mergers and acquisitions lead to competitive advantage.

>> Most mergers and acquisitions destroy shareholder value because anticipated synergies never materialize.

>> If there is any value creation in M&As, it generally accrues to the shareholders of the firm that is taken over (the acquiree), because acquirers often pay a premium when buying the target company.

>> M&As are a popular corporate-level strategy for three reasons: (1) the desire to overcome competitive disadvantage, (2) the quest for superior acquisition and integration capability, and (3) because of principal–agent problems.

LO 9-4 Define strategic alliances and explain why they are important corporate strategy vehicles, and why firms enter into them.

>> Strategic alliances have the goal of sharing knowledge, resources, and capabilities in order to develop processes, products, or services.

>> An alliance qualifies as strategic if it has the potential to affect a firm's competitive advantage by increasing value and/or lowering costs.

>> The most common reasons why firms enter alliances are to: (1) strengthen competitive position, (2) enter new markets, (3) hedge against uncertainty, (4) access critical complementary resources, and (5) learn new capabilities.

LO 9-5 Describe three alliance governance mechanisms and evaluate their pros and cons.

>> Alliances can be governed by the following mechanisms: contractual agreements for non-equity alliances, equity alliances, and joint ventures.

>> Exhibit 9.5 presents the pros and cons of each alliance governance mechanism.

LO 9-6 Describe the three phases of alliance management, and explain how an alliance management capability can lead to a competitive advantage.

>> Alliance management capability can be a source of competitive advantage.

>> Alliance management capability consists of a firm's ability to effectively manage three alliance-related tasks concurrently: (1) partner selection and alliance formation, (2) alliance design and governance, and (3) post-formation alliance management.

>> Firms build a superior alliance management capability through "learning-by-doing" and by establishing a dedicated alliance function.

LO 9-7 Define strategic networks and evaluate the advantages and disadvantages of different network positions.

>> A strategic network is an alliance of several firms to pursue a common purpose. It is a social structure of multiple organizations (network nodes) and the links among the nodes (network ties).

>> A firm with a high degree centrality in a strategic network is connected to many other firms, provides social capital to the central firm, and is trusted in the closely connected network cluster (firm A in Exhibit 9.8).

>> A network broker firm connects different network clusters (firm B in Exhibit 9.8). The broker often spans structural holes, which strengthens its position, especially in a small-world network.

>> A firm not connected to any other firm in a network is an isolate (firm E in Exhibit 9.8). Given its lack of connections, an isolate frequently is at a competitive disadvantage.

Key Terms

Acquisition *(p. 238)*

Alliance management capability *(p. 251)*

Corporate venture capital (CVC) *(p. 250)*

Degree centrality *(p. 255)*

Equity alliance *(p. 250)*

Explicit knowledge *(p. 248)*

Horizontal integration *(p. 239)*

Hostile takeover *(p. 239)*

Joint venture *(p. 250)*

Learning races *(p. 247)*

Managerial hubris *(p. 243)*

Merger *(p. 238)*

Non-equity alliance *(p. 248)*

Relational view of competitive advantage *(p. 244)*

Small-world phenomenon *(p. 257)*

Strategic alliance *(p. 244)*

Strategic network *(p. 254)*

Structural hole *(p. 256)*

Tacit knowledge *(p. 250)*

Discussion Questions

1. Horizontal integration has benefits to the firms involved. Consider the consolidation in the event-promotion business when Live Nation bought Ticketmaster in 2010. List some specific advantages of this acquisition for Live Nation. Do you see any downside to the merger?

2. The chapter identifies three governing mechanisms for strategic alliances (non-equity, equity, and joint venture). Provide the benefits for each of these mechanisms.

3. The alliance purpose can affect which governance structure is optimal. Compare a pharmaceutical R&D alliance with a prescription-drug marketing agreement, and recommend a governing mechanism for each. Provide reasons for your selections.

4. Alliances are often used to pursue business-level goals but they may be managed at the corporate

level. Explain why this portfolio approach to alliance management would make sense.

5. Describe the difference between a strong tie and a weak tie in a network. How are weak ties sometimes more useful to the firm/individual?

Ethical/Social Issues

1. If mergers and acquisitions quite often end up providing a competitive disadvantage, why do so many of them take place? Given the poor track record, is the continuing M&A activity a result of principal–agent problems and managerial hubris? Are there other reasons?

2. Alliances and acquisitions can sometimes lead to less access or higher prices for consumers. Comcast is buying NBC Universal (from GE). When one content provider and the Internet access provider are the same, will this lead to some content being favored over others on the Internet? For example, will Comcast want to send

Universal movies (which it owns) with faster download capabilities than it sends a Harry Potter movie from Warner Brothers (which it doesn't own)? (If so, this would violate a "net-neutrality" policy that has generally been honored—that all information on the Internet is treated equally as far as speed and cost per size of content.)[89]

2. When a firm builds a strategic network of alliances, there is often concern about the fair treatment of all the firms in the network. What are some ways an alliance management organization could mitigate concerns about equitable treatment within the network of firms?

Small Group Exercises

SMALL GROUP EXERCISE 1

In this chapter, we studied the idea of horizontal integration. One industry currently going through a wave of consolidation of competitors is the commercial airline industry. Assume Southwest Airlines has just changed CEOs. The new CEO vows to make Southwest the largest airline company in the United States and plans to buy another airline to increase Southwest's scale. Southwest reported cash reserves in excess of $3 billion dollars at the end of 2009, so it is in a healthy financial position for an acquisition. The chart at the top of the next page shows some relevant comparisons of major U.S. airlines ($ in millions).

Consider overall size and existing complementary airline routes as major factors in selecting an

appropriate partner for Southwest. You can find route maps on the websites of all major airlines, or go to a site such as www.airlineroutemaps.com/USA/index.shtml to compare several airlines on one web page. You may also want to refer back to Exhibit 3.7 for the strategic groups map of the U.S. airline industry. As a team, review this financial and routing data and make a recommendation to the new leadership of Southwest for its best potential partner.

SMALL GROUP EXERCISE 2

The global public relations and communications firm Burson-Marsteller studied the 100 largest companies in the 2009 *Fortune* list and found that 79 percent of them use Twitter, Facebook, YouTube, or corporate blogs to communicate with customers and other

Category	Alaska	JetBlue	US Airways	Southwest
Operating revenues	$2,718	$3,286	$8,106	$10,350
Operating expenses	$2,460	$3,007	$7,804	$10,088
Operating income	$258	$279	$302	$262
Net income	$122	$58	($205)	$99
Employees	8,912	10,583	31,340	34,874
Airplanes	115	151	349	537
Total passenger miles	18,362	25,955	57,889	74,457
Load factor	79.30%	79.7%	81.9%	76.0%

Source: 2009 data compiled by Robert Herbst at www.airlinefinancials.com.

stakeholders. Two-thirds of the Fortune 100 have at least one Twitter account (the most popular platform); 54 percent have at least one Facebook fan page; 50 percent have at least one YouTube channel; and 33 percent have at least one corporate blog. A fifth (20 percent) of the companies use all four social media platforms.

The firm also broke its findings down by region (North America, Europe, Asia-Pacific and Latin America) and network. Geographically, social networks like Twitter and Facebook are mostly West-oriented. Asia-Pacific companies don't use them as much, instead preferring corporate blogs. When Asia-Pacific companies do use Twitter or Facebook, it's usually to engage consumers in Europe and North America.[90]

In your group, select three firms and research their social media web presence.

1. Do the firms seem to do a good job of managing their web identity?

3. What differences do you find among the three firms?

Strategy Term Project

MODULE 9: STRATEGIC ALLIANCE AND M&A STRATEGY

In this section, you will study your selected firm's use of acquisitions and alliances to grow or change its business.

1. Has your firm participated in any mergers or acquisitions in the past three years? What was the nature of these actions? Did they result in a consolidation of competitors?

2. Research what strategic alliances your firm has entered in the past three years. If there are several of these, choose the three you identify as the most important for further analysis. Based on company press releases and business journal reports for each alliance, what do you find to be the main reason the firm entered these alliances?

3. Do you think each of the three alliances achieves the original intent, and therefore is successful? Why or why not?

4. Does your firm have an identifiable alliance-management organization? Can you find any evidence that this organization improves the likelihood of success for these alliances? What responsibilities does this alliance-management organization have in your firm?

5. Go to LinkedIn (www.linkedin.com) and see what executive officers or groups your firm may have set up on the professional networking site. Next, look to see if the firm has a "fan page" on Facebook. Is there also a "detractors page" for your firm? How would you assess your firm's use of web networks and social media for its business?

*my*Strategy

WHAT IS YOUR NETWORK STRATEGY?

Most of us participate in one or more popular social networks online such as Facebook, MySpace, or LinkedIn. While many of us spend countless hours in these social networks, you may not have given a lot of thought to your network strategy.

Social networks describe the relationships or ties between individuals linked to one another. An important element of social networks is the *different strengths of ties* between individuals. Some ties between two people in a network may be very strong (e.g., "soul mates" or "best friends"), while others are weak (mere acquaintances—"I talk to her briefly in my yoga class"). As a member of a social network, you have access to social capital, which is derived from the connections within and between social networks. It is a function of whom you know, and what advantages you can create through those connections. *Social capital* is an important concept in business.

Some Facebook users claim to have 2,000 or more "friends." With larger networks, one expects to have greater social capital, right? Though this seems obvious, academic research suggests that humans have the brain capacity to maintain a functional network of only about 150 people. This so-called *Dunbar number* was derived by extrapolating from the brain sizes and social networks of primates.

Far fetched? Not necessarily. You may have a lot more than 150 friends on Facebook, but researchers call that number the *social core* of any network. Why is this the case? Even though it takes only a split second to accept a new friend request on Facebook, friendships still need to be "groomed." To develop a meaningful relationship, you need to spend some time with this new friend, even in cyberspace. Recent data from Facebook provides support for the concept of a social core, as the average number of a user's friends is 120, with women having more friends than men. However, the number of friends a Facebook user frequently interacts with is a lot smaller, and tends to be stable over time. The more frequent the exchanges among friends, the smaller the inner core. For example, on average, men leave comments for 17 friends and communicate with 10, while women leave comments for 26 friends and communicate with 16.

Social networking sites allow users to broadcast their lives and to passively keep track of more people, and thus to enlarge their social networks, even though many of those ties tend to be weak. It may come as a surprise, however, to learn that research shows new opportunities such as job offers tend to come from weak ties, because it is these weak ties that allow you to access non-redundant and novel information. This phenomenon is called *strength of weak ties.* So, in thinking about how to leverage your social capital more fully as part of your network strategy, rather than always communicating with the same people, it may pay off for you to invest a bit more time grooming your weak ties.[91]

1. Draw up a list of up to 12 people at your university with whom you regularly communicate (in person, electronically, or both). Draw your network (place names or initials next to each node), and connect every node where people you communicate with also talk to one another (i.e., indicate friends of friends). Can you identify strong and weak ties in your network?

2. What is the *degree of closure* in your network? The density of your network reflects the degree of closure. Network density can be calculated in three simple steps.

   Step 1: Create a simple matrix in which you list the names of the people in your network on both the horizontal and vertical axis. (This can be easily done in an Excel spreadsheet.) Then put an X in each box, indicating who knows whom in your network. Each X corresponds to a social tie in your network. Count the total number of X's in your matrix. Let's assume X = 8.

   Step 2: If your network contains 12 people (including yourself), N = 12. The maximum network density is calculated by the following formula: $[N \times (N-1)] / 2$. If your network size is 12, then your maximum network density is $[12 \times (12-1)] / 2 = 66$. This is the maximum number of ties in your network when everybody knows everybody.

   Step 3: To calculate your actual network density, divide X by N: Network density = (X/N). In the example with 8 ties in a network of 12 people, the network density is 0.67. The closer this number is to 1, the denser the network.

3. Network density is bound by 0 and 1. Is a network density that approaches 1 the most beneficial? Why or why not? Think about weak ties, which can also be indirect connections.

4. Compare your network to that of your group members (2–4 people in your class). Do you find any commonalities in your networks? Who has the greatest social capital, and why? What can you do to "optimize" your network structure?

5. Can you draw the joint network of your study group?

6. In this joint (study group) network, can you identify different network positions such as those discussed in the chapter: centrally located person(s) and broker(s), or a person who connects different

clusters? Can you identify people with high and low social capital? Are there any dense clusters in this network? Would that indicate the existence of cliques? Is it a small-world network? What other implications can you draw?

Endnotes

1. "Facebook CEO in no rush to 'friend' Wall Street," *The Wall Street Journal,* March 3, 2010.

2. "Facebook wants to know more than just who your friends are," *The Wall Street Journal,* April 22, 2010.

3. This ChapterCase is based on: "Facebook's land grab in the face of a downturn," *Bloomberg Businessweek,* November 20, 2008; "A special report on social networking," *The Economist,* January 30, 2010; "Facebook CEO in no rush to 'friend' Wall Street," *The Wall Street Journal*; "The world's billionaires," *Forbes,* March 10, 2010; "Facebook wants to know more than just who your friends are," *The Wall Street Journal*; "Facebook's Washington problem," *Bloomberg Businessweek,* May 13, 2010; "Lives of others," *The Economist,* May 20, 2010; www.comscore.com; www.facebook.com; and www.myspace.com.

4. "Lives of others," *The Economist,* May 20, 2010.

5. Hitt, M. A., R. D. Ireland, and J. S. Harrison (2001), "Mergers and acquisitions: A value creating or value destroying strategy?" in, Hitt, M. A. R. E. Freeman, and J. S. Harrison, *Handbook of Strategic Management* (Oxford, UK: Blackwell-Wiley): 384–408.

6. "HP gambles on ailing Palm," *The Wall Street Journal,* April 29, 2010.

7. Allen, W. B., N. A. Doherty, K. Weigelt, and E. Mansfield (2005), *Managerial Economics,* 6th ed. (New York: Norton); and Breshnahan, T., and P. Reiss (1991), "Entry and competition in concentrated markets," *Journal of Political Economy* 99: 997–1009.

8. Brush, T. H. (1996), "Predicted change in operational synergy and post-acquisition performance of acquired

businesses," *Strategic Management Journal* 17: 1–24.

9. Tebbutt, T. (2010), "An insider's perspective of the pharmaceutical industry," presentation in "Competing in the Health Sciences," Georgia Institute of Technology, January 29. Mr. Tebbutt is former President of UCB Pharma.

10. This Strategy Highlight is based on: "Cadbury rejects Kraft's $16.73 billion bid," *The Wall Street Journal,* September 7, 2009; "Food fight," *The Economist,* November 5, 2009; "Cadbury accepts fresh Kraft offer," *The Wall Street Journal,* January 19, 2010; "Kraft wins a reluctant Cadbury with help of clock, hedge funds," *The Wall Street Journal,* January 20, 2010; the author's personal communication with Dr. Narayanan Jayaraman, Georgia Institute of Technology; and The Hershey Company, 2008 Annual Report.

11. Capron, L. (1999), "The long-term performance of horizontal acquisitions," *Strategic Management Journal* 20: 987–1018; Capron, L., and J. C. Shen (2007), "Acquisitions of private vs. public firms: Private information, target selection, and acquirer returns," *Strategic Management Journal* 28: 891–911.

12. Jensen, M. C., and R. S. Ruback (1983), "The market for corporate control: The scientific evidence," *Journal of Financial Economics* 11: 5–50.

13. Dyer, J. H., P. Kale, and H. Singh (2004), "When to ally and when to acquire," *Harvard Business Review,* July–August; Mayer, D., and M. Kenney (2004), "Ecosystems and acquisition management: Understanding Cisco's strategy," *Industry and Innovation* 11: 299–326.

14. "Silicon Valley survivor," *The Wall Street Journal,* July 28, 2009.

15. Kale, P., H. Singh, and A. P. Raman (2009), "Don't integrate your acquisitions, partner with them," *Harvard Business Review,* December.

16. This discussion is based on: Finkelstein, S., and D. C. Hambrick (1989), "Chief executive compensation: A study of the intersection of markets and political processes, *Strategic Management Journal* 10: 121–134; Lambert, R. A., D. F. Larcker, and K. Weigelt (1991), "How sensitive is executive compensation to organizational size?" *Strategic Management Journal* 12: 395–402; and Finkelstein, S. (2003), *Why Smart Executives Fail, and What You Can Learn from Their Mistakes* (New York: Portfolio).

17. This discussion is based on: Finkelstein, S. (2003), *Why Smart Executives Fail, and What You Can Learn from Their Mistakes*; and Finkelstein, S., J. Whitehead, and A. Campbell (2009), *Think Again: Why Good Leaders Make Bad Decisions and How to Keep It from Happening to You* (Boston, MA: Harvard Business School Press).

18. The examples are drawn from: Finkelstein, S. (2003), *Why Smart Executives Fail, And What You Can Learn from Their Mistakes;* and Finkelstein, S., J. Whitehead, and A. Campbell (2009), *Think Again: Why Good Leaders Make Bad Decisions and How to Keep It from Happening to You.*

19. Gulati, R. (1998), "Alliances and networks," *Strategic Management Journal* 19: 293–317.

20. This discussion draws on: Dyer, J. H., and H. Singh (1998), "The relational view: Cooperative strategy and the sources of interorganizational advantage," *Academy of Management Review* 23: 660–679.

21. Kale, P., and H. Singh (2009), "Managing strategic alliances: What do we know now, and where do we go from here?" *Academy of Management Perspectives* 23: 45–62.

22. The author participated in the HP demo; and "HP unveils Halo collaboration studio: Life-like communication leaps across geographic boundaries," HP Press Release, December 12, 2005.

23. "Bank of America taps Cisco for TelePresence," *InformationWeek,* March 30, 2010.

24. For a review of the alliance literature, see: Gulati, R. (1998), "Alliances and networks," *Strategic Management Journal* 19: 293–317; Dyer, J. H., and H. Singh (1998), "The relational view: Cooperative strategy and the sources of interorganizational advantage," *Academy of Management Review* 23: 660–679; Inkpen, A. (2001), "Strategic alliances," in Hitt, M. A., R. E. Freeman, and J. S. Harrison, *Handbook of Strategic Management;* Ireland, R. D., M. A. Hitt, and D. Vaidyanath (2002), "Alliance management as a source of competitive advantage," *Journal of Management* 28: 413–446; Lavie, D. (2006), "The competitive advantage of interconnected firms: An extension of the resource-based view," *Academy of Management Review* 31: 638–658; Kale, P., and H. Singh (2009), "Managing strategic alliances: What do we know now, and where do we go from here?" *Academy of Management Perspectives* 23: 45–62.

25. Kogut, B. (1991), "Joint ventures and the option to expand and acquire," *Management Science* 37: 19–34.

26. Markides, C. C., and P. J. Williamsen (1994), "Related diversification, core competences, and performance," *Strategic Management Journal* 15: 149–165 (Summer Special Issue); Kale, P., and H. Singh (2009), "Managing strategic alliances: What do we know now, and where do we go from here?" *Academy of Management Perspectives* 23: 45–62.

27. "Microsoft, Yahoo tout ad alliance," *The Wall Street Journal,* July 30, 2009.

28. Ibid.

29. Tripsas, M. (1997), "Unraveling the process of creative destruction: Complementary assets and incumbent survival in the typesetter industry,"

Strategic Management Journal 18: 119–142.

30. Rothaermel, F. T. (2001), "Incumbent's advantage through exploiting complementary assets via interfirm cooperation," *Strategic Management Journal* 22: 687–699. Rothaermel, F. T. (2001), "Complementary assets, strategic alliances, and the incumbent's advantage: An empirical study of industry and firm effects in the biopharmaceutical industry," *Research Policy* 30: 1235–1251; Hill, C. W. L., and F. T. Rothaermel (2003), "The performance of incumbent firms in the face of radical technological innovation," *Academy of Management Review* 28: 257–274; Rothaermel, F. T., and C. W. L. Hill (2005), "Technological discontinuities and complementary assets: A longitudinal study of industry and firm performance," *Organization Science* 16: 52–70.

31. Arthaud-Day, M. L., F. T. Rothaermel, and W. Zhang (2013), "Genentech: After the Acquisition by Roche," case study, in, Rothaermel, F. T. *Strategic Management* (Burr Ridge, IL: McGraw-Hill).

32. Jiang, L., J. Tan, and M. Thursby (2011), "Incumbent firm invention in emerging fields: Evidence from the semiconductor industry," *Strategic Management Journal,*; Rothaermel, F. T., and M. Thursby (2007), "The nanotech vs. the biotech revolution: Sources of incumbent productivity in research," *Research Policy* 36: 832–849.

33. This discussion is based on: Teece, D. J. (1986), "Profiting from technological innovation: Implications for integration, collaboration, licensing and public policy," *Research Policy* 15: 285–305; Tripsas, M. (1997), "Unraveling the process of creative destruction: Complementary assets and incumbent survival in the typesetter industry"; Rothaermel, F. T. (2001), "Incumbent's advantage through exploiting complementary assets via interfirm cooperation," *Strategic Management Journal* 22 (6–7): 687–699; Ceccagnoli, M., and F. T. Rothaermel (2008), "Appropriating the returns to innovation," *Advances in Study of Entrepreneurship, Innovation, and Economic Growth* 18: 11–34; Rothaermel, F. T., and W. Boeker (2008), "Old technology meets new

technology: Complementarities, similarities, and alliance formation," *Strategic Management Journal* 29 (1): 47–77; and Hess, A. M., and F. T. Rothaermel (2011), "When are assets complementary? Star scientists, strategic alliances and innovation in the pharmaceutical industry," *Strategic Management Journal* 32: 895–909.

34. This Strategy Highlight is based on: Paik, K. (2007), *To Infinity and Beyond!: The Story of Pixar Animation Studies* (New York: Chronicle Books); and "Marvel superheroes join the Disney family," *The Wall Street Journal,* August 31, 2009.

35. Mowery, D. C., J. E. Oxley, and B. S. Silverman (1996), "Strategic alliances and interfirm knowledge transfer," *Strategic Management Journal* 17: 77–91 (Winter Special Issue).

36. Brandenburger, A. M., and B. J. Nalebuff (1996), *Co-opetition* (New York: Currency Doubleday); Gnyawali, D., and B. Park (2011), "Co-opetition between Giants: Collaboration with competitors for technological innovation," *Research Policy,*; Gnyawali, D., J. He, and R. Madhaven (2008), "Co-opetition: Promises and challenges," in Wankel, C. (ed.), *21st Century Management: A Reference Handbook* (Thousand Oaks, CA: Sage): 386–398.

37. This discussion is based on: Hamel, G., Y. Doz, and C. K. Prahalad (1989), "Collaborate with your competitors—and win," *Harvard Business Review* (January–February): 190–196; Hamel, G. (1991), "Competition for competence and interpartner learning within international alliances," *Strategic Management Journal* 12: 83–103 (Summer Special Issue); Khanna, T., R. Gulati, and N. Nohria (1998), "The dynamics of learning alliances: Competition, cooperation, and relative scope," *Strategic Management Journal* 19: 193–210; Larsson, R., L. Bengtsson, K. Henriksson, and J. Sparks (1998), "The interorganizational learning dilemma: Collective knowledge development in strategic alliances," *Organization Science* 9: 285–305; and Kale, P., and H. Perlmutter (2000), "Learning and protection of proprietary assets in strategic alliances: Building relational capital," *Strategic Management Journal* 21: 217–237.

38. Nti, K. O., and R. Kumar (2000), "Differential learning in alliances," in, Faulkner, D., and M. de Rond (eds.), *Cooperative Strategy. Economic, Business, and Organizational Issues* (Oxford, UK: University Press): 119–134. For an opposing viewpoint, see: Inkpen, A. C. (2008), "Knowledge transfer and international joint ventures: The case of NUMMI and General Motors," *Strategic Management Journal* 29: 447–453.

39. This discussion is based on: Gulati, R. (1998), "Alliances and networks," *Strategic Management Journal* 19: 293–317; Ireland, R. D., Hitt, M. A. and Vaidyanath D. (2002), "Alliance management as a source of competitive advantage," *Journal of Management* 28: 413–446; Hoang, H., and F. T. Rothaermel (2005), "The effect of general and partner-specific alliance experience on joint R&D project performance," *Academy of Management Journal* 48: 332–345; and Lavie, D. (2006), "The competitive advantage of interconnected firms: An extension of the resource-based view," *Academy of Management Review* 31: 638–658.

40. This is based on: Pisano, G. P., and Mang P. (1993), "Collaborative product development and the market for know-how: Strategies and structures in the biotechnology industry," in Rosenbloom, R. and R. Burgelman (eds.), *Research on Technological Innovation, Management, and Policy* (Greenwich, CT: J.A.I. Press) 109–136; and Hoang, H., and F. T. Rothaermel (2010), "Leveraging internal and external experience: Exploration, exploitation, and R&D project performance," *Strategic Management Journal* 31 (7): 734–758.

41. The distinction of explicit and tacit knowledge goes back to the seminal work by Polanyi, M. (1966), *The Tacit Dimension* (Chicago, IL: University of Chicago Press). For more recent treatments, see: Spender, J.-C. (1996), "Managing knowledge as the basis of a dynamic theory of the firm," *Strategic Management Journal* 17: 45–62 (Winter Special Issue); Spender, J.-C., and R. M. Grant (1996), "Knowledge and the firm," *Strategic Management Journal* 17: 5–9 (Winter Special Issue); and Crossan, M. M., H. W. Lane, R. E. White (1999), "An organizational learning framework: From intuition to

institution," *Academy of Management Review* 24: 522–537.

42. "Toyota and Tesla partnering to make electric cars," *The Wall Street Journal,* May 21, 2010.

43. Ibid.

44. Ibid.

45. For an insightful treatment of CVC investments see: Dushnitsky, G., and M. J. Lenox (2005a), "When do incumbent firms learn from entrepreneurial ventures? Corporate venture capital and investing firm innovation rates," *Research Policy* 34: 615–639; Dushnitsky, G., and M. J. Lenox (2005b), "When do firms undertake R&D by investing in new ventures?" *Strategic Management Journal* 26: 947–965; Dushnitsky, G., and M. J. Lenox (2006), "When does corporate venture capital investment create value?" *Journal of Business Venturing* 21: 753–772; and Wadhwa, A., and S. Kotha (2006), "Knowledge creation through external venturing: Evidence from the telecommunications equipment manufacturing industry," *Academy of Management Journal* 49: 1–17.

46. Benson, D., and R. H. Ziedonis (2009), "Corporate venture capital as a window on new technology for the performance of corporate investors when acquiring startups," *Organization Science* 20: 329–351.

47. Dushnitsky, G., and M. J. Lenox (2006), "When does corporate venture capital investment create value?" *Journal of Business Venturing* 21: 753–772.

48. Higgins, M. J., and D. Rodriguez (2006), "The outsourcing of R&D through acquisition in the pharmaceutical industry," *Journal of Financial Economics* 80: 351–383; Benson, D., and R. H. Ziedonis (2009), "Corporate venture capital as a window on new technology for the performance of corporate investors when acquiring start-ups," *Organization Science* 20: 329–351.

49. Reuer, J. J., M. Zollo, and H. Singh (2002), "Post-formation dynamics in strategic alliances," *Strategic Management Journal* 23: 135–151.

50. This discussion is based on: Dyer, J. H., and H. Singh (1998), "The relational view: Cooperative strategy and the sources of interorganizational advantage," *Academy of Management Review* 23: 660–679; Ireland, R. D., M. A. Hitt,

and D. Vaidyanath (2002), "Alliance management as a source of competitive advantage," *Journal of Management* 28: 413–446; and Lavie, D. (2006), "The competitive advantage of interconnected firms: An extension of the resource-based view," *Academy of Management Review* 31: 638–658.

51. For an insightful discussion of alliance management capability and alliance portfolios, see: Rothaermel, F. T., and D. L. Deeds (2006), "Alliance type, alliance experience, and alliance management capability in high-technology ventures," *Journal of Business Venturing* 21: 429–460; Hoffmann, W. (2007), "Strategies for managing a portfolio of alliances," *Strategic Management Journal* 28: 827–856; Schreiner, M., P. Kale, and D. Corsten (2009), "What really is alliance management capability and how does it impact alliance outcomes and success?" *Strategic Management Journal* 30: 1395–1419; Ozcan, P., and K. M. Eisenhardt (2009), "Origin of alliance portfolios: Entrepreneurs, network strategies, and firm performance," *Academy of Management Journal* 52: 246–279; and Schilke, O., and A. Goerzten (2010), "Alliance management capability: An investigation of the construct and its measurement," *Journal of Management* 36: 1192–1219.

52. Kale, P., and H. Singh (2009), "Managing strategic alliances: What do we know now, and where do we go from here?" *Academy of Management Perspectives* 23: 45–62.

53. Santoro, M. D., and J. P. McGill (2005), "The effect of uncertainty and asset co-specialization on governance in biotechnology alliances," *Strategic Management Journal* 26: 1261–1269.

54. This is based on: Gulati, R. (1995), "Does familiarity breed trust? The implications of repeated ties for contractual choice in alliances," *Academy of Management Journal* 38: 85–112; and Poppo, L., and T. Zenger (2002), "Do formal contracts and relational governance function as substitutes or complements?" *Strategic Management Journal* 23: 707–725.

55. Dyer, J. H., and H. Singh (1998), "The relational view: Cooperative strategy and the sources of interorganizational advantage," *Academy of Management Review* 23: 660–679.

56. Saxenian, A. (1994), *Regional Advantage* (Cambridge, MA: Harvard University Press).

57. Ibid., 134.

58. von Hippel, E. (1988), *The Sources of Innovation* (Oxford, UK: Oxford University Press).

59. Zaheer, A., B. McEvily, and V. Perrone (1998), "Does trust matter? Exploring the effects of interorganizational and interpersonal trust on performance," *Organization Science* 8: 141–159.

60. Covey, S. M. R. (2008), *The Speed of Trust: The One Thing That Changes Everything* (New York: Free Press).

61. Dyer, J.H., and H. Singh (1998), "The relational view: Cooperative strategy and the sources of interorganizational advantage," *Academy of Management Review* 23: 660–679; Ireland, R. D., M. A. Hitt, and D. Vaidyanath (2002), "Alliance management as a source of competitive advantage," *Journal of Management* 28: 413–446; Lavie, D. (2006), "The competitive advantage of interconnected firms: An extension of the resource-based view," *Academy of Management Review* 31: 638–658.

62. This is based on: Anand, B., and T. Khanna (2000), "Do firms learn to create value?" *Strategic Management Journal* 21: 295–315; Sampson, R. (2005), "Experience effects and collaborative returns in R&D alliances," *Strategic Management Journal* 26: 1009–1031; Hoang, H., and F. T. Rothaermel (2005), "The effect of general and partner-specific alliance experience on joint R&D project performance," *Academy of Management Journal* 48: 332–345; and Rothaermel, F. T., and D. L. Deeds (2006), "Alliance type, alliance experience, and alliance management capability in high-technology ventures," *Journal of Business Venturing* 21: 429–460.

63. Rothaermel, F. T., and D. L. Deeds (2006), "Alliance type, alliance experience, and alliance management capability in high-technology ventures," *Journal of Business Venturing* 21: 429–460.

64. Hoffmann, W. (2007), "Strategies for managing a portfolio of alliances," *Strategic Management Journal* 28: 827–856.

65. Wassmer, U., P. Dussage, and M. Planellas (2010), "How to manage alliances better than one at a time," *MIT Sloan Management Review,* Spring: 77–84.

66. Dyer, J. H., P. Kale, and H. Singh (2001), "How to make strategic alliances work," *MIT Sloan Management Review,* Summer: 37–43.

67. Kale, P., J. H. Dyer, and H. Singh (2002), "Alliance capability, stock market response, and long-term alliance success: The role of the alliance function," *Strategic Management Journal* 23: 747–767.

68. Gueth A., N. Sims, and R. Harrison (2001), "Managing alliances at Lilly," *In Vivo: The Business & Medicine Report* (June): 1–9; Rothaermel, F. T., and D. L. Deeds (2006), "Alliance type, alliance experience, and alliance management capability in high-technology ventures," *Journal of Business Venturing* 21: 429–46.

69. Dyer, J.H., Kale, P., Singh, H. (2004), "When to ally and when to acquire," *Harvard Business Review,* July-August.

70. Rothaermel, F. T., and A. Hess (2010), "Innovation strategies combined," *MIT Sloan Management Review,* Spring: 12–15.

71. Dyer, J. H., Kale, P., Singh, H. (2004), "When to ally and when to acquire," *Harvard Business Review,* July–August.

72. Gulati, R., and M. Gargiulo (1999), "Where do interorganizational networks come from?" *American Journal of Sociology* 104: 1439–1493.

73. www.staralliance.com/en/about/.

74. This is based on: Gomes-Casseres, B. (1994), "Group versus group: How alliance networks compete," *Harvard Business Review,* July–August; and Nohria, N., and C. Garcia-Pont (1991), "Global strategic linkages and industry structure," *Strategic Management Journal* 12: 105–124.

75. This discussion is based on: Burt, R. S. (1992), *Structural Holes* (Cambridge, MA: Harvard University Press); Coleman, J. S. (1990), *Foundations of Social Theory* (Cambridge, MA: Harvard University Press); Granovetter, M. (1973), "The strength of weak ties," *American Journal of Sociology* 78: 1360–1380; Gulati, R. (1998), "Alliances and networks," *Strategic Management Journal*

19: 293–317; Wasserman, S., and K. Faust (1994), *Social Network Analysis: Methods and Applications* (Cambridge, UK: Cambridge University Press); Zaheer, A., R. Gözübüyük, and H. Milanov (2010), "It's in the connections: The network perspective in interorganizational research," *Academy of Management Perspectives* 24: 62–77.

76. Granovetter, M. (1973), "The strength of weak ties," *American Journal of Sociology* 78: 1360–1380.

77. This Strategy Highlight is based on: Lechner, C., F. T. Rothaermel, and S. Agung (2007), "The emergence, evolution, and dissolution of a network system: A complexity perspective," *Academy of Management Annual Meeting,* Philadelphia, PA, August 6.

78. Saxenian, A. (1994), *Regional Advantage* (Cambridge, MA: Harvard University Press).

79. Coleman, J. S. (1990), *Foundations of Social Theory* (Cambridge, MA: Harvard University Press).

80. This is based on: Baum, J.A.C., T. Calabrese, and B. S. Silverman (2000), "Don't go it alone: Alliance network composition and startups' performance in Canadian biotechnology," *Strategic Management Journal* 21: 267–294; Rothaermel, F. T. (2001), "Incumbent's advantage through exploiting complementary assets via interfirm cooperation," *Strategic Management Journal* 22: 687–699; Shan, W., G. Walker, and B. Kogut (1994), "Interfirm cooperation and startup innovation in the biotechnology industry," *Strategic Management Journal* 15: 387–394; Tsai, W. (2001), "Knowledge transfer in intraorganizational networks: Effects of network position and absorptive capacity on business unit innovation and performance," *Academy of Management Journal* 44: 996–1004; Tsai, W. (2002), "Social structure of 'coopetition' within a multi-unit organization: Coordination, competition, and intraorganizational knowledge sharing," *Organization Science* 13: 179–190;

81. Burt, R. S. (1992), *Structural Holes* (Cambridge, MA: Harvard University Press).

82. Hargadorn, A. B. (1998), "Firms as knowledge brokers: Lessons in pursuing continuous innovation," *California Management Review* 40: 209–227.

83. Ibid.

84. This is based on: Chesbrough, H. W. (2003), *Open Innovation: The New Imperative for Creating and Profiting from Technology* (Boston, MA: Harvard Business School Press); Chesbrough, H. W., and M. M. Appleyard (2007), "Open innovation and strategy," *California Management Review* 50: 57–76.

85. Although the cluster around firm A shows a high degree of closure, in the overall network depicted in Exhibit 9.8 there aren't that many connections among all the purple dots representing individual firms. We can calculate the network's degree of closure. A network's maximum density is calculated by the formula: $[N \times (N - 1)] / 2$, where N is the number of firms. With 17 firms in the network, the maximum network density here is 136 possible ties. However, since there are only 25 ties in the network, its actual network density or degree of closure is $(25 / 136) = 0.18$. Since network density is bound by 0 (no connections) and 1 (all firms are connected to one another), we conclude that this network is quite sparse.

86. This is based on: Watts, D. J. (1999), *Small Worlds: The Dynamics of Networks between Order and Randomness* (Princeton, NJ: Princeton University Press); Watts, D. J. (2003), *Six Degrees: The Science of a Connected Age* (New York: Norton).

87. Schilling, M. A. (2009), "The global technology collaboration network: Structure, trends, and implications," Working Paper, New York University.

88. The ChapterCase 9 extension is based on: Zynga.com Press Room, various press releases (www.zynga.com/about/news.php); "Zach Gottlieb, Zynga: Redefining the 'Game of Life,'" *Wired,* June 14, 2010; "7-Eleven to celebrate store-opening milestone," *PRNewswire,* February 25, 2011; and David Dorf, "5 ways to grab customers on Facebook," *Harvard Business Review,* March 2, 2011.

89. Data sourced from "The FCC's crusade to keep the Internet free," *Bloomberg Businessweek,* August 16, 2010.

90. Data from "Global Social Media Check Up" by Burson-Marsteller PR firm, 2010.

91. This *my*Strategy section is based on: Granovetter, M. (1973), "The strength of weak ties," *American Journal of Sociology* 78: 1360–1380; and "Primates on Facebook," *The Economist,* February 26, 2009.

CHAPTER 10

Global Strategy: Competing Around the World

LEARNING OBJECTIVES

After studying this chapter, you should be able to:

LO 10-1   Define globalization, multinational enterprise (MNE), foreign direct investment (FDI), and global strategy.

LO 10-2   Explain why companies compete abroad and evaluate advantages and disadvantages.

LO 10-3   Explain which countries MNEs target for FDI, and how they enter foreign markets.

LO 10-4   Describe the characteristics of and critically evaluate the four different strategies MNEs can pursue when competing globally.

LO 10-5   Explain why certain industries are more competitive in specific nations than in others.

LO 10-6   Evaluate the relationship between location in a regional cluster and firm-level competitive advantage.

CHAPTERCASE 10

Hollywood Goes Global

HOLLYWOOD MOVIES HAVE always been a quintessentially American product. Globalization, however, has changed the economics of the movie industry. Foreign ticket sales for Hollywood blockbusters made up 50 percent of worldwide totals in 2000; by 2010, they had jumped to nearly 70 percent. Of the total $32 billion that Hollywood movies grossed in 2010, a whopping $22 billion came from outside the United States! Today, largely due to the collapse of DVD sales, Hollywood would be unable to continue producing high-budget movies without foreign revenues, and foreign sales can make or break the success of newly released big budget movies.

Look at Exhibit 10.1 (next page), which depicts the lifetime revenues (domestic and foreign) of recent Hollywood blockbuster movies. *Avatar* is the highest-grossing movie to date, with over $2.7 billion since its release in 2009. It may surprise you to learn that non-U.S. box office sales account for almost 75 percent of that number. *Avatar* was hugely popular in Asia, especially in China, where the government gave permission to increase the number of movie theaters showing the film from 5,000 to 35,000. Another of James Cameron's

popular films, *Titanic,* grossed almost 70 percent of its $1.8 billion in overseas markets.

Given the increasing importance of non-U.S. box-office sales, especially in the BRIC countries, Hollywood studios are changing their business models. Rob Moore, Vice Chairman of Paramount Pictures, explains: "We need to make movies that have the ability to break out internationally. That's the only way to make the economic puzzle of film production work today."[1] As a result, studios are adapting scripts to appeal to global audiences, casting foreign actors in leading roles, and pulling the plug on projects that seem too U.S.-centric. For example, the film *G.I. Joe: The Rise of Cobra* prominently featured South Korean movie star Byung-hun Lee and South African actor Arnold Vosloo. On the other hand, Disney's *Wedding Banned*, a romantic comedy about a divorced couple trying to prevent their daughter from getting married, was axed in the advanced production stage despite several marquee stars (Robin Williams, Anna Faris, and Diane Keaton) because of perceptions that it would not succeed outside of the American market. Globalization also puts pressure on the pay of Hollywood stars. Given the importance of international audiences and the availability of foreign stars and movies, the days are over when stars like Tom Hanks, Eddie Murphy, and Julia Roberts can demand 20 percent royalties on total tickets sales.[2]

After reading the chapter, you will find more about this case, with related questions, on page 291.

EXHIBIT 10.1

Lifetime Revenues of Hollywood Blockbuster Movies, in $ million (release year in parentheses)

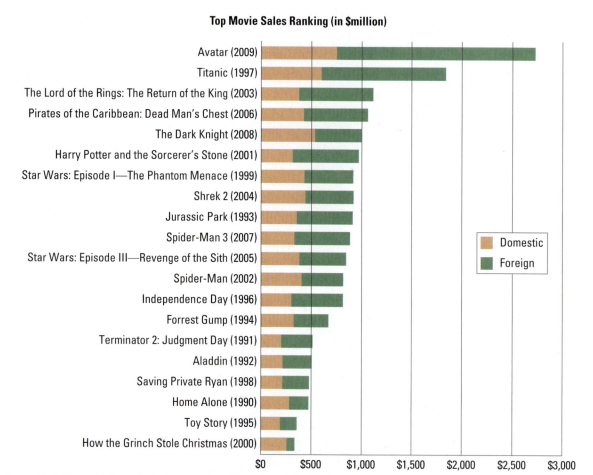

Top Movie Sales Ranking (in $million)

Legend: Domestic, Foreign

Source: Adapted from "Plot change: Foreign forces transform Hollywood films," *The Wall Street Journal,* August 2, 2010.

▲ **HOLLYWOOD HAS** always obtained some of its revenues from international sales, but it is now a truly global enterprise, with the vast majority of revenues coming from outside the United States. Moreover, the huge opportunities in the global movie market have also attracted new entrants. Besides wanting to cater to international audiences, Hollywood film studios are also feeling squeezed by low-cost foreign competition. For example, Bollywood, the Indian movie industry, creates its own productions and brings in low-cost but high-impact actors such as Freida Pinto and Dev Patel, who played the lead roles in the mega-success *Slumdog Millionaire. Slumdog*'s budget was merely $14 million, but the movie grossed almost $400 million and won eight Oscars. By comparison, Hollywood's budget for *Home Alone,* a similar success in terms of revenues, was nearly five times as large.

The shift in revenue sources away from the U.S. market and opportunities for future growth in emerging economies are changing the global strategy of many U.S. firms, not just Hollywood moviemakers. We noted in earlier chapters that GE and IBM are now truly global enterprises, obtaining the majority of their revenues from outside their home market. Once-unassailable U.S. firms now encounter formidable foreign competitors such as Brazil's Embraer (aerospace), China's Haier (home appliances) and Lenovo (PCs), India's

ArcelorMittal (steel), Infosys (IT services) and Reliance Group (conglomerate), Mexico's Cemex (cement), Russia's Gazprom (energy), South Korea's LG and Samsung (both in electronics and appliances), and Sweden's IKEA (home furnishings), to name just a few. This chapter is about how firms gain and sustain competitive advantage in a global world.

The competitive playing field is becoming increasingly global, as the ChapterCase about the movie industry indicates. This globalization provides significant opportunities for individuals, companies, and countries. Indeed, you can probably see the increase in globalization on your own campus. The number of students enrolled at universities outside their native countries tripled between 1980 (about one million students) to 2010 (three million students).[3] The country of choice for foreign students remains the United States, with some 600,000 enrolled per year, followed by the UK with some 360,000 foreign university students. The $40 billion higher-education industry is only one example of a global market. Taken together, the world's marketplace—made up of some 200 countries—is a staggering $60 trillion in gross domestic product (GDP), of which the U.S. market is $14 trillion, or about 23 percent.[4]

Chapter 8 looked at two dimensions of the corporate-strategy space (see Exhibit 8.1, page 203): managing the degree of vertical integration, and deciding which products and services to offer (horizontal integration and diversification). The question of how to compete effectively around the world is the third dimension of corporate strategy. We begin our study of global strategy by defining globalization before we discuss its strategic implications for competitive advantage.

WHAT IS GLOBALIZATION?

Globalization is a process of closer integration and exchange between different countries and peoples worldwide, made possible by falling trade and investment barriers, tremendous advances in telecommunications, and drastic reductions in transportation costs.[5] Combined, these factors reduce the costs of doing business around the world, opening the doors to a much larger market than any one home country. Consequently, the world's market economies are becoming more integrated and interdependent.

Globalization has led to significant increases in living standards in many economies around the world. Germany and Japan, countries that were basically destroyed after World War II, turned into industrial powerhouses, fueled by export-led growth. More recently, the Asian Tigers—Hong Kong, Singapore, South Korea, and Taiwan—turned themselves from underdeveloped countries into advanced economies, enjoying some of the world's highest standards of living. Today, the BRIC countries (Brazil, Russia, India, and China), with more than 40 percent of the world's population and producing roughly half of the world's economic growth over the last decade, are growing at a much faster clip than the developed industrial economies, and thus offer significant business opportunities.[6]

The engine behind globalization is the multinational enterprise (MNE)—a company that deploys resources and capabilities in the procurement, production, and distribution of goods and services in at least two countries. By making investments in value-chain activities abroad, MNEs thus engage in foreign direct investment (FDI).[7] For example, in order to avoid voluntary import restrictions, to take advantage of business-friendly conditions

> **>> LO 10-1**
> Define globalization, multinational enterprise (MNE), foreign direct investment (FDI), and global strategy.

---

globalization Process of closer integration and exchange between different countries and peoples worldwide, made possible by falling trade and investment barriers, advances in telecommunications, and reductions in transportation costs.

multinational enterprise (MNE) A company that deploys resources and capabilities in the procurement, production, and distribution of goods and services in at least two countries.

foreign direct investment (FDI) A firm's investments in value-chain activities abroad.

(low taxes, low labor cost, lower cost of living, and other incentives provided by host states) in the southern United States, and to be closer to customers in North America, the German carmaker Volkswagen recently invested $1 billion in its Chattanooga, Tennessee, plant.[8] MNEs need an effective **global strategy** that enables them to gain and sustain a competitive advantage when competing against other foreign and domestic companies around the world.[9]

global strategy
A firm's strategy to gain and sustain a competitive advantage when competing against other foreign and domestic companies around the world.

Well-known U.S. multinational enterprises include Boeing, Caterpillar, CNN, Coca-Cola, GE, John Deere, Exxon Mobil, IBM, P&G, and Walmart. According to a 2010 research report,[10] U.S. MNEs have a disproportionally positive impact on the U.S. economy. They make up less than 1 percent of the number of total U.S. companies, but they:

- Account for 11 percent of private-sector employment growth since 1990.
- Employ 19 percent of the work force.
- Pay 25 percent of the wages.
- Account for 31 percent of the U.S. gross domestic product (GDP).
- Make up 74 percent of private-sector R&D spending.

As they attempt to take advantage of opportunities in the global economy, U.S. MNEs seem to decouple more and more from their home country. Their headquarters may still be in the United States, and they are listed on U.S. stock exchanges (e.g., NYSE or NASDAQ), but their future growth is expected to come more and more from emerging economies. In preparation, companies like GM, HP, IBM, and Microsoft are adding employees overseas while reducing domestic employment.[11]

This trend indeed raises the interesting question, "What defines a U.S. company?" If it's the address of the headquarters, then IBM, GE, and others are U.S. companies—despite the fact that a majority of their employees work outside the United States. On the other hand, non-U.S. companies such as carmakers from Japan (Toyota, Honda, and Nissan) and South Korea (Hyundai and Kia) and several engineering companies (Siemens from Germany, and ABB, a Swiss-Swedish MNE) all have made significant investments in the United States and created a large number of well-paying jobs.

As a business student, you have several reasons to be interested in MNEs. Not only can these companies provide interesting work assignments in different locations throughout the world, but they also frequently offer the highest-paying jobs for college graduates. Even if you don't want to work for an MNE, chances are that the organization you will be working for will do business with one, so it's important to understand how they compete around the globe.

Strategy Highlight 10.1 provides a brief overview of three distinct stages of globalization, each stage of which reflects a different global strategy pursued by MNEs headquartered in the United States.

GOING GLOBAL: WHY?

>> **LO 10-2**
Explain why companies compete abroad and evaluate advantages and disadvantages.

Clearly, the decision to pursue a global strategy comes from the firm's assessment that doing so will enhance its competitive advantage and that the benefits of globalization will exceed the costs. Here we consider both the advantages and disadvantages of "going global."

Advantages of Expanding Internationally

Why do firms expand internationally? The main reasons firms expand abroad are to:

- Gain access to a larger market
- Gain access to low-cost input factors
- Develop new competencies

STRATEGY HIGHLIGHT 10.1

Stages of Globalization

Since the beginning of the twentieth century, globalization has proceeded through three notable stages.

GLOBALIZATION 1.0: 1900–1941. Globalization 1.0 took place from about 1900 through the early years of World War II. In that period, basically all the important business functions were located in the home country. Typically, only sales and distribution operations took place overseas—essentially exporting goods to other markets. In some instances, firms procured raw materials from overseas. Strategy formulation and implementation as well as knowledge flows followed a one-way path—from domestic headquarters to international outposts. This time period saw the blossoming of the idea of MNEs, but ended with the U.S. entry into World War II.

GLOBALIZATION 2.0: 1945–2000. With the end of World War II came a new focus on growing business—not only to meet the needs that went unfulfilled during the war years but also to reconstruct the damage from the war. From 1945 to the end of the 20th century, in the Globalization 2.0 stage, MNEs began to create smaller, self-contained copies of themselves, with all business functions intact, in a few key countries (notably, Western European countries, Japan, and Australia).

This strategy required significant amounts of foreign direct investment. Although it was costly to duplicate business functions in overseas outposts, doing so allowed for greater local responsiveness to country-specific circumstances. While the corporate headquarters back in the U.S. set overarching strategic goals and allocated resources through the capital budgeting process, local mini-MNE replicas had considerable leeway in day-to-day operations. Knowledge flow back to U.S. headquarters, however, remained limited in most instances.

GLOBALIZATION 3.0: 21ST CENTURY. We are now in the Globalization 3.0 stage. MNEs that had been at the vanguard of globalization have now become global-collaboration networks (see Exhibit 10.2). Such companies now freely locate business functions anywhere in the world based on an optimal mix of costs, capabilities, and PESTEL factors. Huge investments in fiber-optic cable networks around the world have effectively reduced communication distances, enabling companies to operate 24/7, 365 days a year. When an engineer in Minneapolis, Minnesota, leaves for the evening, an engineer in Mumbai, India, begins her workday. In the Globalization 3.0 stage, the MNE's strategic objective changes. The MNE reorganizes from a multinational company with self-contained operations in a few selected countries to a more seamless global enterprise with centers of expertise. Each of these centers of expertise is a hub within a global network for delivering products and services. Consulting companies, for example, can now tap into a worldwide network of experts in real time, rather than relying on the limited number of employees in their local offices.[12]

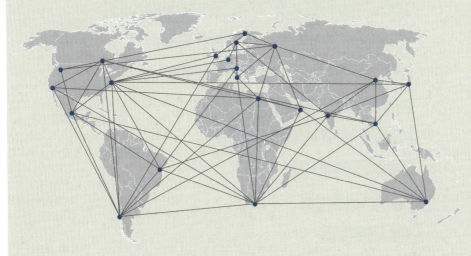

EXHIBIT 10.2

Globalization 3.0: 21st Century

Based on an optimal mix of costs, skills, and PESTEL factors, MNEs are global-collaboration networks that perform business functions throughout the world.

Source: Adapted from IBM (2009), *A Decade of Generating Higher Value at IBM,* IBM report, www.ibm.com.

GAIN ACCESS TO A LARGER MARKET. Becoming an MNE provides significant opportunities for U.S. companies, given the huge economies of scale and scope that can be reaped by participating in a much larger and more diverse market. At the same time, some countries with relatively weak domestic demand, such as China, Germany, and Japan, focus on export-led economic growth, which in turn drives many of their domestic businesses to become MNEs.

Even though the United States (with approximately 310 million people and a GDP of $14 trillion) is still the single largest economy in the world, many U.S. companies earn a significant amount of their revenues internationally. Exhibit 10.3 shows international sales as a percentage of total sales in 2010 for selected U.S. MNEs. Leading the pack, Intel obtained 80 percent of its total revenues ($44 billion) from international sales, followed by Caterpillar (67 percent, $43 billion), IBM (63 percent, $100 billion), Apple (57 percent, $87 billion), GE (53 percent, $150 billion), Boeing (42 percent, $65 billion), and Starbucks (30 percent, $11 billion). In 2010, Walmart earned about a quarter of its total sales outside the U.S. and is growing its global business at a double-digit rate. With annual sales at over $400 billion, this equates to more than $100 billion a year in global sales—a spot that would put Walmart's global unit, if it were a standalone enterprise, in the Fortune 20. Despite these impressive numbers, though, Walmart has been struggling in some major foreign markets, such as South Korea and Japan, and even exited Germany altogether (as we discuss later in the chapter).

GM once held more than 50 percent of the U.S. auto market and was the undisputed leader in global car sales between 1931 and 2008. In its heyday, GM employed 350,000 U.S. workers and was an American icon. Today, with a dismal domestic performance, GM's future will likely depend on its performance in China and other emerging economies, as Strategy Highlight 10.2 discusses.

For companies based in smaller economies, becoming an MNE may be necessary to achieve growth or to gain and sustain competitive advantage. Examples include Acer (Taiwan), Casella Wines (Australia), Nestlé (Switzerland), Nokia (Finland), Philips (Netherlands), Samsung (South Korea), and Zara (Spain). Unless companies in smaller economies "go global," their domestic markets are often too small for them to reach significant economies of scale to compete effectively against other MNEs.

EXHIBIT 10.3

International Sales as a Percentage of Total Sales in 2010 for Selected U.S. MNEs

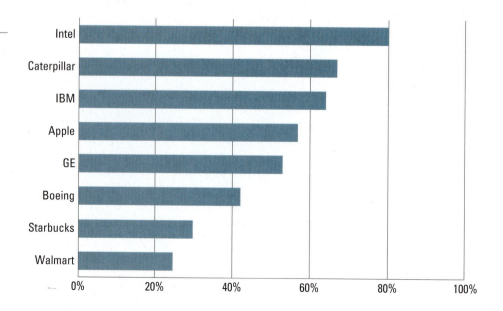

In the digital age, some MNEs are even *born global*—their founders start them with the intent of running global operations. Internet-based companies such as Amazon, eBay, Google, and LinkedIn by nature have a global presence. Indeed, Facebook, with over 600 million members around the globe, would—if it were a country—be the third most populous country worldwide after China (1.4 billion) and India (1.2 billion).[14] To better customize their websites to suit local preferences and cultures, these companies still tend to establish offices and maintain computer servers in different countries.[15] (See, for example, www.amazon.cn for China, www.amazon.de for Germany, and www.amazon.fr for France.)

Brick-and-mortar firms also can be born global. Logitech, the maker of personal peripherals such as computer mice, presentation "clickers," and video game controllers, started in Switzerland but established offices right away in Silicon Valley, California.[16] (Its two founders, one Swiss and the other Italian, each held master's degrees from Stanford University.) Pursuing a global strategy right from the start allowed Logitech to tap into the innovation expertise contained in Silicon Valley.[17] In 2010, Logitech had sales of $2 billion, with offices throughout the Americas, Asia, and Europe. Underlying Logitech's innovation competence is a network of best-in-class skills around the globe. Moreover, Logitech can organize work continuously as its teams in different locations around the globe can work 24/7.

GAIN ACCESS TO LOW-COST INPUT FACTORS.

Access to cheap raw materials such as lumber, iron ore, oil, and coal was a key driver behind Globalization 1.0 and 2.0. During Globalization 3.0, firms have expanded globally to benefit from lower labor costs in manufacturing and services. India reigns supreme in business process outsourcing (BPO), due not only to low-cost labor but also to an abundance of well-educated, English-speaking young people. Infosys and Wipro are the two most famous Indian IT service companies. Taken together, these companies employ close to 250,000 people and provide services to many of the Global Fortune 500. Many MNEs have close business ties with Indian IT firms. Some, like IBM, are engaged in foreign direct investment through equity alliances or building their own IT and customer-service centers in India. More than a quarter of Accenture's work force, a consultancy specializing in technology and outsourcing, is now in Bangalore, India.[18]

STRATEGY HIGHLIGHT 10.2

Does GM's Future Lie in China?

With a population of 1.4 billion and currently only one vehicle per 100 people—compared with a vehicle density of 94 per 100 in the U.S.—China offers tremendous growth opportunities for the automotive industry. Since China joined the World Trade Organization (WTO) in 2001, its domestic auto market has been growing at double digits annually and has now overtaken the U.S. as the largest in the world.

GM entered China in 1997 through a joint venture with Shanghai Automotive Industrial Corp (SAIC). Today, the Chinese market already accounts for 25 percent of GM's total revenues. Moreover, GM's China operation has been cost-competitive from day one. The company operates about the same number of assembly plants in China as in the U.S., but sells more vehicles while employing about half the number of employees. Chinese workers cost the firm only a fraction of what U.S. workers cost, and GM is not weighed down by additional health care and pension obligations.

GM's Buick brand is considered a luxury vehicle in China. However, GM's future may lie in the Wuling Sunshine, a small, boxy, purely functional vehicle that is currently the best-selling model in China. Priced between $5,000 and $10,000 (depending on what options the customer chooses), GM sold about 600,000 in 2009. The Wuling Sunshine may help GM further penetrate the Chinese market; it also may be an introductory car for other emerging markets, such as India. GM's low-cost strategy with this vehicle has been so successful that the firm is planning to expand the Wuling product line and offer the Wuling entry-level vehicle globally. GM already sells the Wuling Sunshine in Brazil under the Buick nameplate.

GM is betting its future on China and other emerging economies in Asia, Latin America, and the Middle East as it reinvents itself to become a lean and low-cost manufacturer of profitable small cars. To back up its strategic intent, GM has quadrupled its engineering and design personnel in China and is investing a quarter-billion dollars to build a cutting-edge R&D center on its Shanghai campus, home of its international headquarters. With car markets in the U.S. and Europe plagued by declining demand and over-capacity, GM's future may not be decided in Detroit, but in Shanghai.[13]

Likewise, China has emerged as a manufacturing powerhouse due to low labor costs and an efficient infrastructure. An American manufacturing worker costs about 20 times more in wages alone than a similarly skilled worker in China.[19] A significant cost differential exists not only for low-skilled labor, but for high-skilled labor as well. A Chinese engineer trained at Purdue University, for example, works for only a quarter of the salary in his native country compared with an engineer working in the U.S.[20] Of course, this wage disparity also reflects the difference in the two countries' cost of living.

DEVELOP NEW COMPETENCIES. Some MNEs now also pursue a global strategy in order to develop new competencies.[21] These companies are making foreign direct investments to be part of *communities of learning,* which are often contained in regional clusters.[22] AstraZeneca, a Swiss-based pharmaceutical company, relocated its research facility to Cambridge, Massachusetts, to be part of the Boston biotech cluster, in hopes of developing new R&D competencies in biotechnology.[23] Cisco is investing more than $1 billion to create an Asian headquarters in Bangalore, in order to be right in the middle of India's top IT location.[24] Unilever's new-concept center is located in downtown Shanghai, China, attracting hundreds of eager volunteers to test the firm's latest product innovations onsite, while Unilever researchers monitor consumer reactions. In these examples, AstraZeneca, Cisco, and Unilever all reap **location economies**—benefits from locating value-chain activities in optimal geographies for a specific activity, wherever that may be.[25]

Many MNEs now are replacing the one-way innovation flow from Western economies to developing markets with a *polycentric innovation strategy*—a strategy in which MNEs now draw on multiple, equally important innovation hubs throughout the world (characteristic of Globalization 3.0; see Exhibit 10.2). GE Global Research, for example, orchestrates a "network of excellence" with facilities in Niskayuna, NY (USA), Bangalore (India), Shanghai (China), and Munich (Germany). Indeed, emerging economies are becoming hotbeds for low-cost innovations that find their way back to developed markets. In Bangalore, GE researchers developed the Mac 400, a handheld electrocardiogram (ECG).[26] The device is small, portable, and runs on batteries. While a conventional ECG costs $2,000, this handheld version costs $800 and enables doctors to do an ECG test at a cost of only $1 per patient. The Mac 400 is now making its entry as a disruptive innovation into the U.S. and other Western markets, with anticipated widespread use in the offices of general practitioners and emergency ambulances.

> **location economies**
> Benefits from locating value-chain activities in the world's optimal geographies for a specific activity, wherever that may be.

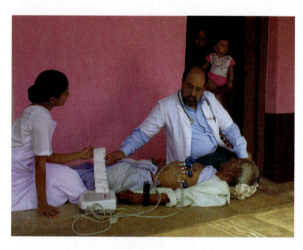

The GE Mac 400 device is small, portable, and enables doctors to do an ECG test in non-hospital settings and at low cost. It is now making its entry as a disruptive innovation in Western markets.

Disadvantages of Expanding Internationally

> **liability of foreignness**
> Additional costs of doing business in an unfamiliar cultural and economic environment, and of coordinating across geographic distances.

In international expansion, firms also face some risks. In addition to the marginal costs of adding new operations, MNEs doing business abroad also must overcome the **liability of foreignness.** This liability consists of the additional costs of doing business in an unfamiliar cultural and economic environment, and of coordinating across geographic distances.[27] Despite such costs, many firms find that the benefits of doing business abroad outweigh the costs.

There have also been some unfortunate side-effects of the MNEs' search for low-cost labor. Low wages, long hours, and poor working and living conditions contributed to a spate of suicides at Foxconn, in China.[28] The Taiwanese company, which employs more than 800,000 people, manufactures electronics, computers, and game consoles for Apple, Dell, HP, LG, Microsoft, Nintendo, Nokia, Sony, and other well-known clients. Similarly, the Japanese carmaker Honda faced labor unrest at some of its plants in China over wage issues and working conditions.[29]

China's labor costs are steadily rising in tandem with an improved standard of living, especially in the coastal regions, where wages have risen 50 percent since 2005.[30] Some MNEs have boosted wages an extra 30 percent following the recent unrest. Many now offer bonuses to blue-collar workers and are taking other measures to avoid sweatshop allegations that have plagued companies like Nike and Levi Strauss in the past. Rising wages, fewer workers due to the effects of China's one-child-per-family policy, and appreciation of the Chinese currency now combine to lessen the country's advantage in low-cost manufacturing.[31]

Economic development has two consequences for MNEs. First, rising wages (and other costs) are likely to negate any benefits of access to low-cost input factors. Second, as the standard of living rises in emerging economies, MNEs are hoping that increased purchasing power will enable workers to purchase the products they used to make for export only.[32] This shift is in alignment with the Chinese government's economic policy, which wants to see a move from "Made in China" to "Designed in China," to capture more of the value added.[33] Also, constantly on the lookout for lower-cost alternatives in a "race-to-the-bottom," MNEs are now looking to invest in countries like Vietnam and Cambodia.

Finally, the issue of protecting intellectual property in foreign markets also looms large. The software, movie, and music industries have long lamented large-scale copyright infringements in many foreign markets. In addition, when required to partner with a foreign host firm, companies may find their intellectual property being siphoned off. Japanese and European engineering companies entered China, for example, to participate in building the world's largest network of high-speed trains worth billions of dollars.[34] Companies such as Kawasaki Heavy Industries (Japan), Siemens (Germany), and Alstom (France) were joint-venture partners with domestic Chinese companies. These firms now allege that the Chinese partners built on the Japanese and European partners' advanced technology to create their own, next-generation high-speed trains. To make matters worse, they also claim that the Chinese companies now compete *against them* in other lucrative foreign markets, such as Saudi Arabia and Brazil, with trains of equal or better capabilities but at much lower prices. This example highlights the *intellectual property exposure* that firms can face when expanding overseas.

GOING GLOBAL: WHERE AND HOW?

After discussing why companies expand internationally, we now turn our attention to the question of which countries firms choose to enter, and how they do so.

>> **LO 10-3**
Explain which countries MNEs target for FDI, and how they enter foreign markets.

Which Countries Do MNEs Enter?

As we have seen, the primary drivers behind firms engaging in FDI are to gain access to larger markets and low-cost input factors and to develop new competencies. Often, several countries and locations will work. Ireland and Portugal, for example, have similar cost structures, and both provide access to the 500 million customers in the European Union. In such cases, how does an MNE decide? When more than one country makes an attractive investment target (in terms of market size, cost of input factors, or the ability to develop competencies), *additional* factors influence the decision of *where* to invest. Two country-level factors play an important role:

- National institutions
- National culture

NATIONAL INSTITUTIONS. First, MNEs consider whether countries in which they may invest have strong legal and ethical pillars as well as well-functioning economic institutions such as capital markets and an independent central bank. Such institutions, both formal and informal, reduce uncertainty, and thus reduce transaction costs.[35] *Formal institutions* are the political and legal factors that can be analyzed according to the PESTEL framework (introduced in Chapter 3). Many European countries, for example, have more stringent environmental and data-privacy regulations than the U.S. or Asian countries. *Informal institutions* comprise the social factors of the PESTEL framework such as norms, customs, culture, and ethics. For example, although managers in many Latin countries expect their administrative assistants to serve coffee during business meetings or even run personal errands such as picking up dry cleaning, these activities are generally not part of an admin's job description in the United States (due to a different understanding about what would be considered discrimination or use of company resources for personal business).[36] Informal rules and norms are closely intertwined with a country's national culture. Institutions set the formal and informal rules of the game by which managers must play in their pursuit of competitive advantage.[37]

NATIONAL CULTURE. Dutch researcher Geert Hofstede studied what he termed national culture, the collective mental and emotional "programming of the mind" that differentiates human groups.[38] Although there is no one-size-fits-all culture that accurately describes any nation, Hofstede's work provides a useful tool to guide FDI decisions. Based on data analysis from more than 100,000 individuals from many different countries, four dimensions of culture emerged: power distance, individualism, masculinity–femininity, and uncertainty avoidance.[39] Hofstede's data analysis yielded scores for the different countries, for each dimension, on a range of zero to 100, with 100 as the high end. (More recently, Hofstede added a fifth cultural dimension: *long-term orientation*. The available data on that fifth dimension is not, at this point, as comprehensive as for the four original dimensions.)

Power-Distance. The power-distance dimension of national culture focuses on how a society deals with inequality among people in terms of physical and intellectual capabilities and how those methods translate into power distributions within organizations. High power-distance cultures, like the Philippines (94/100, with 100 = high), tend to allow inequalities among people to translate into inequalities in opportunity, power, status, and wealth. Low power-distance cultures, like Austria (11/100), on the other hand, tend to intervene to create a more equal distribution among people within organizations and society at large.

Individualism. The individualism dimension of national culture focuses on the relationship between individuals in a society, particularly in regard to the relationship between individual and collective pursuits. In highly individualistic cultures, like the U.S. (91/100), individual freedom and achievements are highly valued. As a result, individuals are only tied loosely to one another within society. In less-individualistic cultures, like Venezuela (12/100), the collective good is emphasized over the individual, and members of society are strongly tied to one another throughout their lifetimes by virtue of birth into groups like extended families.

Masculinity–Femininity. The masculinity–femininity dimension of national culture focuses on the relationship between genders and its relation to an individual's role at work and in society. In more "masculine" cultures, like Japan (95/100), gender roles tend to be clearly defined and sharply differentiated. In "masculine" cultures, values like competitiveness, assertiveness, and exercise of power are considered cultural ideals, and men are expected to behave accordingly. In more "feminine" cultures, like Sweden (5/100), values like cooperation, humility, and harmony are guiding cultural principles. The masculinity–femininity dimension uncovered in Hofstede's research is undoubtedly evolving over time, and values and behaviors are converging to some extent.

Uncertainty-Avoidance. The uncertainty-avoidance dimension of national culture focuses on societal differences in tolerance toward ambiguity and uncertainty. In particular, it highlights the extent to which members of a certain culture feel anxious when faced with uncertain or unknown situations. Members of high uncertainty-avoidance cultures, like Russia (95/100), value clear rules and regulations as well as clearly structured career patterns, lifetime employment, and retirement benefits. Members of low uncertainty-avoidance cultures, like Singapore (8/100), have greater tolerance toward ambiguity and thus exhibit less emotional resistance to change and a greater willingness to take risks.

Hofstede's national-culture research becomes even more useful for managers by combining the four distinct dimensions of culture into an aggregate measure for each country. MNEs then can compare the national-culture measures for any two country pairings to inform their entry decisions.[40] The difference between scores indicates cultural distance, the cultural disparity between the internationally expanding firm's home country and its targeted host country. A firm's decision to enter certain international markets is influenced by cultural differences, and a greater cultural distance can increase the cost and uncertainty of conducting business abroad. In short, greater cultural distance increases the liability of foreignness. If we calculate the cultural distance from the U.S. to various countries, for example, we find that some countries are culturally very close to the U.S. (e.g., Australia with an overall cultural distance score of 0.02), while others are culturally quite distant (e.g., Russia with an overall cultural distance score of 4.42). As can be expected, English-speaking countries such as Canada (0.12), Ireland (0.35), New Zealand (0.26), and the UK (0.09) all exhibit a low cultural distance to the United States. Since culture is embedded in language, it comes as no surprise that cultural and linguistic differences are highly correlated. This implies that companies from Spanish-speaking countries often conduct FDI in other Spanish-speaking countries, and so on.

When Starbucks entered the Chinese market in 2000, it sought to decrease the liability of foreignness by handing out keychains, to help new customers learn how to order. Layered cylinders on the mini coffee cup represent drink options—caffeinated or not, number of espresso shots, type of syrup, and so on. The customer spins the choices into the desired position and hands the keychain to the barista.

Although Hofstede's work made a significant contribution to the understanding of national cultures, it is not without drawbacks. One shortcoming of Hofstede's work is that

---

national culture The collective mental and emotional "programming of the mind" that differentiates human groups.

power-distance dimension Dimension of culture that focuses on how a society deals with inequality among people in terms of physical and intellectual capabilities, and how those methods translate into power distributions within organizations.

individualism dimension Dimension of culture that focuses on the relationship between individuals in a society, particularly the relationship between individual and collective pursuits.

masculinity–femininity dimension Dimension of culture that focuses on the relationship between genders and its relation to an individual's role at work and in society.

uncertainty-avoidance dimension Dimension of culture that focuses on societal differences in tolerance toward ambiguity and uncertainty.

cultural distance Cultural disparity between an internationally expanding firm's home country and its targeted host country.

although the sample was large, all individuals worked for IBM, a U.S. MNE. This can introduce a selection bias because IBM does not recruit randomly among the population. Another caveat is that Hofstede's data is a few decades old, and national cultures may have changed over time. Some argue that with the widespread use of modern telecommunications (e.g., Internet and mobile phones), cultures and values have converged to some extent.[41]

COMBINING NATIONAL INSTITUTIONS AND NATIONAL CULTURE. Taken together, both national institutions and national culture are important factors for MNEs to consider when deciding which countries to enter. As an example, beginning in the 1980s, several U.S. high-tech companies were eager to make investments in the European Union to access its large and affluent consumer market. Ireland was the preferred choice for many U.S. MNEs for the country's low cultural distance from the U.S., as well as for institutional reasons.[42] In particular, many MNEs chose Ireland as the premier location for FDI into Europe because it has one of the world's lowest corporate tax rates. Exhibit 10.4 shows that Ireland's corporate tax rate is a mere 12.5 percent compared with 33.3 percent in France. Incidentally, at 40 percent, the United States has one of the highest corporate tax rates in the world.

Because of its attractive institutional framework and low cultural distance, Ireland received roughly one-quarter of all U.S. FDI into the EU.[43] The chipmaker Intel invested some $5 billion just west of Dublin to build the largest and most advanced chipmaking facility in the world. HP is one of the biggest employers in the western part of Ireland. Apple located its European software development and support center in Ireland. Likewise, Dell has made significant investments in Ireland. More recently, the consulting firm Accenture moved its location of incorporation to Ireland, citing Ireland's economic, political, and legal strengths.[44] A significant amount of the $1.2 trillion in 2009 FDI focused on BRIC countries, with China and Brazil leading the pack.[45]

How Do MNEs Enter Foreign Markets?

Assuming an MNE has decided why and where to enter a foreign market, the remaining decision is *how* to do so. Exhibit 10.5 displays the different options managers have when

EXHIBIT 10.4

Corporate Tax Rates in Different European Countries and U.S.

Source: Author's depiction of data from "Switzerland's states compete on tax cuts," *The Wall Street Journal*, February 2, 2010. Switzerland is not part of the EU, but due to bilateral agreements with many EU members, FDI into Switzerland also provides preferred access to the EU market.

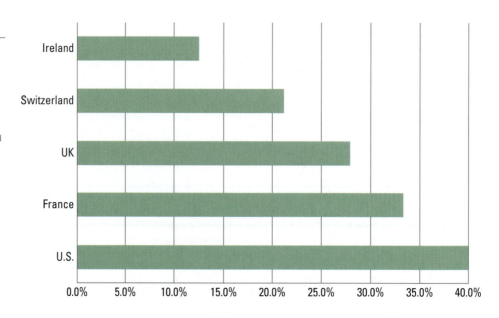

EXHIBIT 10.5

Modes of Foreign-Market Entry along the Investment and Control Continuum

entering foreign markets, along with the required investments necessary and the control they can exert.

Exporting—producing goods in one country to sell in another—is one of the oldest forms of internationalization (part of Globalization 1.0). It is often used to test whether a foreign market is ready for a firm's products. When studying vertical integration and diversification (in Chapter 8), we discussed in detail different forms along the make-or-buy continuum. As discussed in Chapter 9, acquisitions and strategic alliances (including licensing, franchising, and joint ventures) are popular vehicles for entry into foreign markets. Since we discussed these organizational arrangements in detail in previous chapters, we therefore keep this section on foreign-entry modes brief.

The framework illustrated in Exhibit 10.5, moving from left to right, has been suggested as a *stage model* of sequential commitment to a foreign market over time.[46] Though it does not apply to globally born Internet companies, it is relevant for manufacturing companies that are just now expanding into global operations. In some instances, companies are required by the host country to form joint ventures in order to conduct business there, while some MNEs prefer *greenfield operations* (building new plants and facilities from scratch), as did Motorola when it entered China in the 1990s.[47]

STRATEGY AROUND THE WORLD: COST REDUCTIONS VS. LOCAL RESPONSIVENESS

When discussing business strategy (in Chapter 6), we noted that an effective integration strategy must resolve the inherent trade-offs between cost and differentiation. In much the same fashion, MNEs face two opposing forces when competing around the globe: *cost reductions* versus *local responsiveness.*

One of the core drivers for globalization is to expand firms' total market, in order to achieve economies of scale and drive down costs. For many business executives, the move toward globalization was based on the **globalization hypothesis,** advanced by Professor Theodore Levitt, which states that consumer needs and preferences throughout the world are converging and thus becoming increasingly homogenous.[48] Levitt wrote (in 1983): "Nothing confirms [the globalization hypothesis] as much as the success of McDonald's from Champs-Élysées to Ginza, of Coca-Cola in Bahrain and Pepsi-Cola in Moscow, and of rock music, Greek salad, Hollywood movies, Revlon cosmetics, Sony televisions, and Levi jeans everywhere."[49] In support of the globalization hypothesis, Toyota is selling its hybrid Prius vehicle successfully in more than 70 countries. Most vehicles today are built on global platforms and modified (sometimes only cosmetically) to meet local tastes and standards.

The strategic foundations of the globalization hypothesis are based primarily on cost reduction. One key competitive weapon is lower price, and MNEs attempt to reap significant

>> **LO 10-4**
Describe the characteristics of and critically evaluate the four different strategies that MNEs can pursue when competing globally.

globalization hypothesis
Assumption that consumer needs and preferences throughout the world are converging and thus becoming increasingly homogenous.

EXHIBIT 10.6

The Integration-Responsiveness Framework: Global Strategy Positions and Representative MNEs

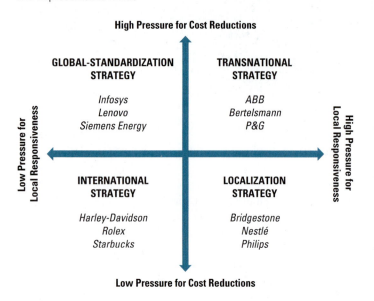

cost reductions by leveraging economies of scale and by managing global supply chains to access the lowest-cost input factors.

While there seems to be some convergence of consumer preferences across the globe, national differences remain, due to distinct institutions and cultures. For example, in the 1990s, Ford Motor Company followed this one-size-fits-all strategy by offering a more or less identical car throughout the world (the Ford Mondeo, sold as Ford Contour and Mercury Mystique in North America). Ford learned the hard way (lack of sales) that consumer preferences were not converging sufficiently to allow it to ignore regional differences.[50] In some instances, MNEs therefore experience pressure for local responsiveness—the need to tailor product and service offerings to fit local consumer preferences and host-country requirements. McDonald's, for example, uses mutton instead of beef in India and offers a teriyaki burger in Japan—though its basic business model of offering fast food remains the same the world over. Local responsiveness generally entails higher cost, and sometimes even outweighs cost advantages from economies of scale and lower-cost input factors.

Given the two opposing pressures of cost reductions versus local responsiveness, scholars have advanced the integration-responsiveness framework, shown in Exhibit 10.6.[51] This framework juxtaposes the opposing pressures for cost reductions and local responsiveness, to derive four different strategies to gain and sustain competitive advantage when competing globally. The four strategies are international strategy, localization strategy, global-standardization strategy, and transnational strategy, which we will discuss in the following sections.[52] At the end of that discussion (on page 286), Exhibit 10.7 summarizes each global strategy.

International Strategy

An international strategy is essentially a strategy in which a company sells the same products or services in both domestic and foreign markets. It enables MNEs to leverage their home-based core competencies in foreign markets. An international strategy is one of the oldest types of global strategies (Globalization 1.0) and is frequently the first step companies take when beginning to conduct business abroad. As shown in the integration-responsiveness framework, it is advantageous when the MNE faces low pressures for both local responsiveness and cost reductions.

An international strategy is often used successfully by MNEs with relatively large domestic markets and strong reputations and brand names. These MNEs, capitalizing on the fact that foreign customers want to buy the original product, tend to use differentiation as their preferred business strategy. For example, bikers in Poland like their Harley-Davidson motorcycles to roar just like the ones ridden by the Hells Angels in the United States. Similarly, a Brazilian entrepreneur importing machine tools from Germany expects superior engineering and quality. An international strategy tends to rely on exporting or the licensing of products and franchising of services to reap economies of scale.

A strength of the international strategy—its limited local responsiveness—is also a weakness in many industries. For example, when an MNE sells its products in foreign markets with little or no change, it leaves itself open to expropriation of intellectual property (IP). Looking at the MNE's products and services, pirates can reverse-engineer the products to discover the intellectual property embedded in them. In Thailand, for example, a flourishing market for knockoff luxury sports cars (e.g., Ferraris, Lamborghinis, and Porsches) has recently sprung up.[53] Besides the risk of exposing IP, MNEs following an international strategy are highly affected by exchange rate fluctuations. Given increasing globalization, however, fewer and fewer markets correspond to this situation—low pressures for local responsiveness and cost reductions—that gives rise to the international strategy.

Localization Strategy

MNEs pursuing a localization strategy attempt to maximize local responsiveness, hoping that local consumers will perceive them to be domestic companies. (For this reason, the localization strategy is sometimes called a *multi-domestic strategy*.) This strategy arises out of the combination of high pressure for local responsiveness and low pressure for cost reductions. MNEs frequently use a localization strategy when entering host countries with large and/or idiosyncratic domestic markets, such as Japan or Saudi Arabia. This is one of the main strategies MNEs pursued in the Globalization 2.0 stage.

A localization strategy is common in the consumer products and food industries. For example, Swiss-based Nestlé, the largest food company in the world (with revenues of $100 billion in 2010) is well known for customizing its product offerings to suit local preferences, tastes, and requirements. Given the strong brand names and core competencies in R&D and quality in the consumer products and food industries, it is not surprising that these MNEs generally pursue a differentiation strategy at the business level. An MNE following a localization strategy, in contrast with an international strategy, faces reduced exchange-rate exposure because the majority of the value creation takes place in the host country business units, which tend to span all functions.

On the downside, a localization strategy is costly and inefficient, because it requires the duplication of key business functions across multiple countries. Each country unit tends to be highly autonomous, and the MNE is unable to reap economies of scale or learning across regions. The risk of IP appropriation increases when companies follow a localization strategy. Besides exposing codified knowledge embedded in products, as is the case

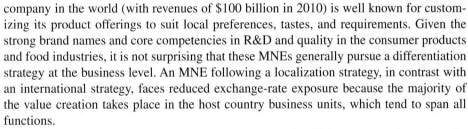

local responsiveness The need to tailor product and service offerings to fit local consumer preferences and host-country requirements; generally entails higher cost.

integration-responsiveness framework Strategy framework that juxtaposes the pressures an MNE faces for cost reductions and local responsiveness to derive four different strategies to gain and sustain competitive advantage when

competing globally: international strategy, localization strategy, global-standardization strategy, and transnational strategy.

international strategy Strategy that involves leveraging home-based core competencies by selling the same products or services in both domestic and foreign markets; advantageous when the MNE faces low pressures for both local responsiveness and cost reductions.

localization strategy Strategy pursued by MNEs that attempts to maximize local responsiveness, with the intent that local consumers will perceive them to be domestic companies; strategy arises out of the combination of high pressure for local responsiveness and low pressure for cost reductions; also called a *multi-domestic strategy*.

with an international strategy, a localization strategy also requires exposing tacit knowledge because products are manufactured locally. Tacit knowledge that is at risk of appropriation may include, for example, the process of how to create consumer products of higher perceived quality.

Global-Standardization Strategy

MNEs following a global-standardization strategy attempt to reap significant economies of scale and location economies by pursuing a global division of labor based on wherever best-of-class capabilities reside at the lowest cost. The global-standardization strategy arises out of the combination of high pressure for cost reductions and low pressure for local responsiveness. MNEs who use this strategy are often organized as networks (Globalization 3.0). This allows them to strive for the lowest cost position possible. Their business-level strategy tends to be cost leadership. Because there is little or no differentiation or local responsiveness, price becomes the main competitive weapon.

MNEs that manufacture commodity products (such as computer hardware) or offer services (such as business process outsourcing) generally pursue a global-standardization strategy. Lenovo, the Chinese computer manufacturer, is now the maker of the ThinkPad line of laptops which it acquired from IBM in 2005. To keep track of the latest developments in computing, Lenovo's research centers are located in Beijing and Shanghai in China, in Raleigh, North Carolina (in the Research Triangle Park), and in Japan.[54] To benefit from low-cost labor and to be close to its main markets in order to reduce shipping costs, Lenovo's manufacturing facilities are in Mexico, India, and China. The company describes the benefits of its global-standardization strategy insightfully: "Lenovo organizes its worldwide operations with the view that a truly global company must be able to quickly capitalize on new ideas and opportunities from anywhere. By forgoing a traditional headquarters model and focusing on centers of excellence around the world, Lenovo makes the maximum use of its resources to create the best products in the most efficient and effective way possible."[55]

One of the advantages of the global-standardization strategy—obtaining the lowest cost point possible by minimizing local adaptations—is also one of its key weaknesses. Strategy Highlight 10.3 describes how pursuing a global-standardization strategy spelled trouble for Walmart's efforts in Germany.

Transnational Strategy

MNEs pursuing a transnational strategy attempt to combine the benefits of a localization strategy (high local-responsiveness) with those of a global-standardization strategy (lowest cost position attainable). (The transnational strategy is also sometimes called *glocalization*.)[56] This strategy arises out of the combination of high pressure for local responsiveness and high pressure for cost reductions. A transnational strategy is generally used by MNEs that pursue an integration strategy at the business level by attempting to reconcile product and/or service differentiations at low cost.

Besides harnessing economies of scale and location, a transnational strategy also aims to benefit from global learning. MNEs typically implement a transnational strategy through a global matrix structure. That structure combines economies of scale along specific product divisions with economies of learning attainable in specific geographic regions. The idea is that best practices, ideas, and innovations will be diffused throughout the world, regardless of their origination. The managers' mantra is to think globally, but act locally.

global-standardization strategy Strategy attempting to reap significant economies of scale and location economies by pursuing a global division of labor based on wherever best-of-class capabilities reside at the lowest cost.

transnational strategy Strategy that attempts to combine the benefits of a localization strategy (high local-responsiveness) with those of a global-standardization strategy (lowest cost position attainable); sometimes called *glocalization*.

Walmart Retreats from Germany

In late 1997, facing a saturated U.S. market, Walmart entered Germany, then the third-largest economy in the world (behind the U.S. and Japan). At that time, the retailer was already active in six foreign countries, with some 500 stores outside the United States. Given the high pressure for cost reductions in the retail industry and Walmart's superior strategic position as the dominant cost leader in the U.S., executives decided to pursue a global-standardization strategy in Germany. In 2006, however, Walmart exited Germany, after losing billions of dollars. This massive failure came as a shock to a company that was used to success. What went wrong?

To enter Germany, Walmart acquired the 21-store Wertkauf chain and 74 hypermarkets from German retailer Spar Handels AG. Next, Walmart attempted to implement its U.S. personnel policies and procedures: the Walmart cheer, a door greeter, every associate within 10 feet of a customer smiling and offering help, bagging groceries at the checkout, video surveillance, a prohibition against dating co-workers, and so on. German employees, however, simply refused to accept these policies. There were no door greeters in the German Walmart stores. The front-line employees behaved as gruffly and rudely as they do in other retail outlets in Germany. It also didn't help that the first Walmart boss in Germany didn't speak German, and decreed that English would be the official in-house language.

Significant cultural differences aside, one of the biggest problems Walmart faced in Germany was that, lacking its usual economies of scale and efficient distribution centers, it couldn't get its costs down far enough to successfully implement its trademark cost-leadership strategy. Higher required wages and restrictive labor laws further drove up costs. As a result, the prices at Walmart in Germany weren't "always low" as the company slogan suggested, but fell in the medium range. Germany was already home to retail discount powerhouses such as Aldi and Lidl, with thousands of outlets offering higher convenience combined with lower prices. Walmart was unable to be cost-competitive against such tough domestic competition. It also faced Metro, a dominant large-box retailer, who upon entering Germany immediately initiated a price war against Walmart. In the end, a defeated Walmart sold its stores to—guess who?—Metro![57]

Although a transnational strategy is quite appealing, it is rather difficult to implement due to the organizational complexities involved. The matrix organization also is costly, because high local-responsiveness typically requires that key business functions are frequently duplicated in each host country, leading to higher costs. (We'll discuss organizational structure in more depth in the next chapter.) Further compounding the organizational complexities is the challenge of finding managers who can dexterously work across cultures in the ways required by a transnational strategy.

The German multimedia conglomerate Bertelsmann attempts to follow a transnational strategy. In 2010, Bertelsmann's revenues were 16 billion euros; it employed 104,000 people, with two-thirds of that force outside its home country. In particular, Bertelsmann operates in 63 countries throughout the world, and owns many regional leaders in their specific product categories, including Random House Publishing in the U.S. and RTL Group, Europe's second largest TV, radio, and production company (after the BBC). Bertelsmann operates its over 500 regional media divisions as more or less autonomous profit and loss centers; global learning and human resource strategies for executives are coordinated at the network level.[58]

As a summary, Exhibit 10.7 (next page) provides a detailed description of each of the four global strategies in the integration-responsiveness framework.

EXHIBIT 10.7

International, Localization, Global-Standardization, and Transnational Strategies: Characteristics, Benefits, and Risks

	Characteristics	Benefits	Risks

International Strategy	• Often the first step in internationalizing.
	
	• Used by MNEs with relatively large domestic markets (e.g., MNEs from U.S., Germany, Japan).
	
	• Well-suited for high-end products (such as machine tools) and luxury goods that can be shipped across the globe.
	
	• Products and services tend to have strong brands.
	
	• Main competitive strategy tends to be *differentiation* since exporting, licensing, and franchising add additional costs.
		• Leveraging core competence.
		
		• Economies of scale.
		
		• Low-cost implementation through:
		  • Exporting or licensing (for products)
		  • Franchising (for services)
		  • Licensing (for trademarks)
			• No or limited local responsiveness.
			
			• Highly affected by exchange rate fluctuations.
			
			• IP embedded in product or service could be expropriated.

Localization (Multi-Domestic) Strategy	• Used by MNEs to compete in host countries with large and/or lucrative but idiosyncratic domestic markets (e.g., Germany, Japan, Saudi Arabia). • Often used in consumer products and food industries. • Main competitive strategy is *differentiation*. • MNE wants to be perceived as local company.	• Highest-possible local responsiveness. • Reduced exchange-rate exposure.	• Duplication of key business functions in multiple countries leads to high cost of implementation. • Little or no economies of scale. • Little or no learning across different regions. • Higher risk of IP expropriation
Global-Standardization Strategy	• Used by MNEs that are offering standardized products and services (e.g., computer hardware or business process outsourcing). • Main competitive strategy is *price*.	• Location economies: global division of labor based on wherever best-of-class capabilities reside at lowest cost. • Economies of scale.	• No local responsiveness. • Little or no product differentiation. • Some exchange-rate exposure. • "Race to the bottom" as wages increase. • Some risk of IP expropriation.
Transnational (Glocalization) Strategy	• Used by MNEs that pursue an *integration* strategy at the business level by simultaneously focusing on product differentiation and low cost. • Mantra: Think globally, act locally.	• Attempts to combine benefits of localization and standardization strategies simultaneously by creating a global matrix structure. • Economies of scale, location, and learning.	• Global matrix structure is costly and difficult to implement, leading to high failure rate. • Some exchange-rate exposure. • Higher risk of IP expropriation.

NATIONAL COMPETITIVE ADVANTAGE: WORLD LEADERSHIP IN SPECIFIC INDUSTRIES

>> **LO 10-5**
Explain why certain industries are more competitive in specific nations than in others.

Globalization, the prevalence of the Internet and other advances in communications technology, and transportation logistics can lead us to believe that firm location is becoming increasingly less important.[59] Because firms can now, more than ever, source inputs globally, many believe that location must be diminishing in importance as an explanation of firm-level competitive advantage. This popular idea is called the death-of-distance hypothesis.[60] In his bestseller *The World Is Flat,* Thomas Friedman expressed a similar idea.[61]

Despite an increasingly globalized world, however, it turns out that high-performing firms in certain industries *are* concentrated in specific countries.[62] For example, the leading biotechnology, software, and Internet companies are headquartered in the United States. Some of the world's best computer manufacturers are in China and Taiwan. Many of the leading consumer electronics companies are in South Korea and Japan. The top mining companies are in Australia. The leading business process outsourcing (BPO) companies are in India. Some of the best engineering and car companies are in Germany. The world's top fashion designers are in Italy. The best wineries are in France. The list goes on. While globalization lowers the barriers to trade and investments and increases human capital mobility, one key question remains: *Why are certain industries more competitive in some countries than in others?* This question goes to the heart of the issue of national competitive advantage, a consideration of world leadership in specific industries. That issue, in turn, has a direct effect on firm-level competitive advantage.

death-of-distance hypothesis
Assumption that geographic location alone should not lead to firm-level competitive advantage because firms are now, more than ever, able to source inputs globally.

national competitive advantage World leadership in specific industries.

Porter's National Competitive Advantage Framework

Michael Porter advanced a framework (see Exhibit 10.8) consisting of four interrelated factors to explain national competitive advantage:

- Factor conditions
- Demand conditions
- Competitive intensity in a focal industry
- Related and supporting industries/complementors

FACTOR CONDITIONS. *Factor conditions* describe a country's endowments in terms of natural, human, and other resources. Interestingly, natural resources are often not needed to generate world-leading companies, since competitive advantage is often based on human capital and know-how. Several of the world's most resource-rich countries (such as Afghanistan,[63] Iran, Iraq, Russia, Saudi Arabia, and Venezuela) are

EXHIBIT 10.8

Porter's Diamond of National Competitive Advantage

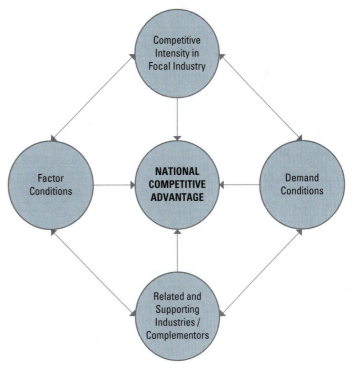

Source: Adapted from M. E. Porter (1990), "The competitive advantage of nations," *Harvard Business Review,* March–April: 78.

not home to any of the world's leading companies, even though some (though not all) do have in place institutional frameworks allowing them to be a productive member of world commerce. In contrast, countries that lack natural resources (e.g., Denmark, Finland, Israel, Japan, Singapore, South Korea, Switzerland, Taiwan, and the Netherlands) often develop world-class human capital to compensate.[64] Other important factor conditions include capital markets, a supportive institutional framework, research universities, and public infrastructure (airports, roads, schools, health care system), among others.

DEMAND CONDITIONS. *Demand conditions* are the specific characteristics of demand in a firm's domestic market. A home market made up of sophisticated customers who hold companies to a high standard of value creation and cost containment contributes to national competitive advantage. Moreover, demanding customers may also clue firms in to the latest developments in specific fields and may push firms to move research from basic findings to commercial applications for the marketplace.

For example, due to dense urban living conditions, hot and humid summers, and high energy costs, it is not surprising that Japanese customers demand small, quiet, and energy-efficient air conditioners. In contrast to the Japanese, Finns have a sparse population living in a more remote countryside. A lack of land lines for telephone service has resulted in Finnish demand for high-quality wireless services, combined with reliable handsets and long battery life that can be operated in remote areas with often hostile environments. Cell phones have long been a necessity for survival in rural areas of Finland. This situation enabled Nokia to become an early leader in cell phones.[65]

COMPETITIVE INTENSITY IN A FOCAL INDUSTRY. Companies that face a highly competitive environment at home tend to outperform global competitors that lack such intense domestic competition. Fierce domestic competition in Germany, for example, combined with demanding customers and the no-speed-limit Autobahn make a tough environment for any car company. Success requires top-notch engineering of chassis and engines as well as keeping costs and fuel consumption ($9-per-gallon gas prices) in check. This extremely tough home environment amply prepared German car companies such as Volkswagen (which also owns Audi and now Porsche), BMW, and Daimler for global competition.

RELATED AND SUPPORTING INDUSTRIES/COMPLEMENTORS. Leadership in related and supporting industries can also foster world-class competitors in downstream industries. The availability of top-notch complementors (firms that provide a good or service that leads customers to value the focal firm's offering more when the two are combined) further strengthens national competitive advantage. Switzerland, for example, leveraged its early lead in industrial chemicals into pharmaceuticals. A sophisticated health care service industry sprang up alongside as an important complementor, to provide further stimulus for growth and continuous improvement and innovation.

The effects of sophisticated customers and highly competitive industries ripple through the industry value chain to create top-notch suppliers and complementors. Toyota's global success in the 1990s and early 2000s was based to a large extent on a network of world-class suppliers in Japan.[66] This tightly knit network allowed for fast two-way knowledge sharing—this in turn improved Toyota's quality and lowered its cost, which it leveraged into a successful integration strategy at the business level.

It is also interesting to note that by 2010, Toyota's supplier advantage had disappeared.[67] It was unable to solve the trade-off between drastically increasing its volume while maintaining superior quality. Toyota's rapid growth to becoming the world's leader in volume required quickly bringing on new suppliers outside of Japan, and quality standards couldn't be maintained. Part of the problem lies in path dependence (discussed in Chapter 4), as Chinese and other suppliers could not be found quickly enough, nor could most foreign suppliers build at the required quality levels fast enough. The cultural distance between Japan and China exacerbated these problems. Combined, these factors explain the quality problems Toyota experienced recently, and serve to highlight the importance of related and supporting industries to national competitive advantage.

REGIONAL CLUSTERS

Although the death-of-distance hypothesis seems intuitive, a closer look at the economic geography at the beginning of the 21st century raises some doubts. Not only are the leading firms in specific industries located in a small number of specific countries, they also tend to be co-located in regional clusters. A regional cluster is a group of interconnected companies and institutions in a specific industry, located near each other geographically and otherwise linked by common characteristics.[68]

If globalization and drastic advancements in technology indeed reduce the importance of firm location, what accounts for the thriving clusters of computer technology firms in Silicon Valley, medical device firms in the Chicago area, and biotechnology firms in Boston? This is not only a U.S. phenomenon, it holds worldwide. Known for their engineering prowess, car companies such as Daimler, BMW, Audi, and Porsche are clustered in southern Germany. High-performance Formula One racecars are designed and crafted in England's Motor Sport Valley, near London. Many fashion-related companies (clothing, shoes, and accessories) are located in northern Italy. Singapore is a well-known cluster for semiconductor materials. India's leading BPO firms are in Bangalore. Critical masses of world-class firms are clearly apparent in these regional clusters. Here, we put under the strategy microscope the question of whether regional clusters contribute to firm-level competitive advantage.

The academic literature provides evidence for a positive link between firm location in a regional cluster and competitive advantage.[69] In fact, it is surprising to learn that in light of globalization and the emergence of the Internet, firm location has actually become *more* important. Porter captures this phenomenon succinctly: "Paradoxically, the enduring competitive advantages in a global economy lie increasingly in local things—knowledge, relationships, and motivation that distant rivals cannot match."[70]

Let's look at one regional cluster in more depth: the Research Triangle Park (RTP) in North Carolina (depicted in Exhibit 10.9, next page), bounded by the cities of Chapel Hill, Durham, and Raleigh.[71] Several important cluster ingredients are readily apparent: top-notch research universities (The University of North Carolina at Chapel Hill, Duke University, and North Carolina State University); well-known MNEs (BASF, Bayer, Cisco Systems, Ericsson, and IBM, among others); good interstate highway connections; and an international airport. The RTP has one of the highest concentrations of PhDs worldwide, and it continues to attract the brightest students, researchers, and knowledge workers from around the world.

The Research Triangle contains two distinct clusters, a biopharma cluster and a communications-technology cluster. These two clusters are anchored by both U.S. and foreign MNEs. Indeed, MNEs have operations in roughly 80 percent of all research clusters around the world. The RTP alone provides some 40,000 well-paying jobs, with about 80 percent of them working for MNEs. Researchers estimate that each job in the RTP creates an additional 2.5 jobs in North Carolina, for a total of 140,000 jobs. The RTP's resident firms gain and sustain a competitive advantage based on innovation: they have generated more than 5,000 patents and well-known service and product breakthroughs such as UPC bar code, Astroturf, and 3-D ultrasound.

GAINING & SUSTAINING COMPETITIVE ADVANTAGE

>> **LO 10-6**
Evaluate the relationship between location in a regional cluster and firm-level competitive advantage.

regional cluster A group of interconnected companies and institutions in a specific industry, located near each other geographically and also linked by common characteristics.

EXHIBIT 10.9

Mapping a Regional
Cluster: Research
Triangle Park, North
Carolina

Source: Adapted from
McKinsey Global Institute
(2010), *Growth and
Competitiveness in the
United States: The Role of
Its Multinational Companies*
(London), p. 13.

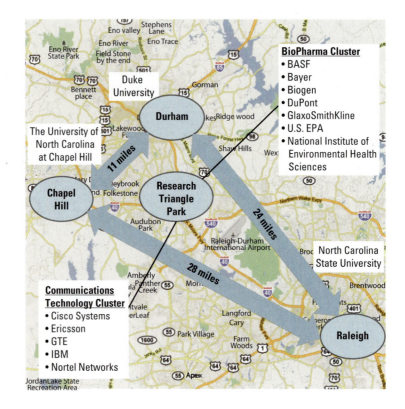

As this peek at the RTP indicates, being located in a cluster has many associated benefits: Firms located in clusters frequently benefit from knowledge spillovers provided by research universities and other firms in the vicinity. **Knowledge spillovers** are positive externalities that are regionally constrained.[72] A university or firm engaging in basic and applied research generates knowledge spillovers when employees, for example, share research ideas and their latest findings through informal social interactions (e.g., at a bar or their children's soccer games).

Moreover, regional clusters provide high labor mobility, because people can change jobs without moving. A software engineer can easily spend his/her entire life in the Silicon Valley and work for many different companies over the course of a career. Geographic proximity and close interactions among cluster firms, over time, contribute to the development of trust and enhance interorganizational exchange. Clusters provide more flexibility than vertical integrated hierarchies or networks of formalized alliances because firms within clusters are generally linked through informal ties.[73]

Finally, firms in a cluster often have privileged access to venture capital (VC) firms, which tend to co-locate near premier research universities in order to evaluate and fund commercially viable research.[74] This benefit is particularly critical for new-venture creation because VCs provide not only capital but also strategic and technical assistance. That assistance often takes the form of a monitoring role on the new venture's board of directors. Leading venture capital firms such as Kleiner Perkins Caufield & Byers (KPCB) in Silicon

knowledge spillover
A type of positive
externality that is
regionally constrained.

Valley tend to actively recruit managers, lawyers, suppliers, and customers for its portfolio companies. Because relationships between venture capitalists and their portfolio companies tend to be deep and extensive, venture capitalists generally prefer to fund ventures that are located nearby, mostly within the regional cluster. KPCB, for example, provided early-stage funding for Electronic Arts, Google, Genentech, Genomic Health, Intuit, Sun Microsystems, and VeriSign—all located in Silicon Valley.

In sum, there is strong empirical evidence that being located in a regional cluster can have a positive effect on firm competitive advantage, not only domestically, but also globally. The RTP example provides support for the paradox that, in a globalized world, the basis for firm-level competitive advantage is often local. 🔍

This concludes our discussion of global strategy. Moreover, we have now completed our study of the first two pillars of the AFI framework—Strategy Analysis (Chapters 1–5) and Strategy Formulation (Chapters 6–10). Next, we turn to the third pillar of the AFI framework— Strategy Implementation. In Chapter 11, we'll study what managers can do to implement their carefully crafted strategies successfully and how to avoid failure. In Chapter 12, we study corporate governance, business ethics, and strategic leadership.

CHAPTERCASE 10 | *Consider This . . .*

THE CHAPTERCASE discussed the surprisingly large percentage of foreign revenues garnered by the Hollywood film industry (nearly 70 percent). This number is especially large given several constraints that U.S. films have when selling internationally. First, there are numerous piracy concerns. Even in the European Union (EU), where countries like Britain and France fine consumers of pirated content, other countries such as Spain have long been havens for distribution of illegal movies and music. In February 2011, Spain passed a new law to provide better protection of copyrighted material, but enforcement may be difficult in a country where nearly 50 percent of all Internet users admit to illegally downloading copyrighted content (twice the EU average rate).[75]

China is infamous for its rampant business in illegal materials. In 2010, a Chinese government report found that the market for pirated DVDs was $6 billion. As a comparison, the *total* box-office revenues in China in 2010 were $1.5 billion.[76] One reason is that ticket prices for movies in China are steep, and are considered luxury entertainment that few can afford. Another reason that "black-market" sales in China are so high is that legitimate sales often are not allowed. China allows only about 20 new non-Chinese movies into its theaters each year. Additionally, it has strict licensing rules on the sale of home-entertainment goods. Chinese censors are not likely to approve the sale of official DVDs for movies such as *Black Swan* and *The Social Network*. As a result there is often no legitimate product competing with the bootlegged offerings available via DVD and the Internet in China.[77]

Movie studios are moving to simultaneous worldwide releases of expected blockbusters in part to try to cut down on the revenues lost to piracy. International growth is expected to continue and take increasing shares of Hollywood film revenues, especially in the face of falling U.S. DVD sales. China is reportedly building new cinema screens at a rate of three per *day* in 2011. Yet growth in China (and elsewhere) is not as profitable as traditional releases in the United States. For example, film distributors typically earn 50 to 55 percent of box-office revenues in America. The average in many other countries is closer to 40 percent (the rest goes to the cinema owner). But in China, a typical Hollywood film distributor gets only 15 percent of the box office ticket revenue.[78]

1. Given the forces on the Hollywood movie industry, is it likely we will see a decrease in the production of regional- and U.S.-centered movies, or will small independent movie producers pick up a higher share of the domestic U.S. market? Please explain.

2. What alternatives could movie producers develop to help combat the piracy of first-run movies and follow-on DVD and Internet releases?

3. How would you prioritize which nations to expand distribution into if you were working for a major Hollywood movie studio?

Take-Away Concepts

This chapter discussed the roles of MNEs for economic growth; the stages of globalization; why, where, and how companies go global; four strategies MNEs use to navigate between cost reductions and local responsiveness; national competitive advantage; and whether regional clusters can lead to competitive advantage, as summarized by the following learning objectives and related take-away concepts.

LO 10-1 Define globalization, multinational enterprise (MNE), foreign direct investment (FDI), and global strategy.

>> Globalization involves closer integration and exchange between different countries and peoples worldwide, made possible by factors such as falling trade and investment barriers, advances in telecommunications, and reductions in transportation costs.

>> A multinational enterprise (MNE) deploys resources and capabilities to procure, produce, and distribute goods and services in at least two countries.

>> Foreign direct investment (FDI) denotes a firm's investments in value-chain activities abroad.

LO 10-2 Explain why companies compete abroad and evaluate advantages and disadvantages.

>> Firms compete internationally to gain access to a larger market, gain access to low-cost input factors, and develop new competencies.

>> To compete successfully abroad, firms must overcome the liability of foreignness.

>> As local wages and costs of living increase, a low-cost location advantage evaporates. (On the upside, this can turn producers into consumers.)

>> Constant pressures to reduce cost lead to a "race-to-the-bottom" where MNEs chase the lowest cost locations.

LO 10-3 Explain which countries MNEs target for FDI, and how they enter foreign markets.

>> When an MNE has to decide between countries in which to invest, two additional country-level factors come into play: national institutions and national culture.

>> Managers have the following strategy vehicles for entering foreign markets (on a continuum from low to high investment needs and control): exporting, strategic alliances (licensing for products, franchising for services), joint venture, and subsidiary (acquisition or greenfield).

LO 10-4 Describe the characteristics of and critically evaluate the four different strategies that MNEs can pursue when competing globally.

>> To navigate between the competing pressures of cost reductions and local responsiveness, MNEs have four strategies: international, localization, global-standardization, and transnational.

>> An international strategy leverages home-based core competencies into foreign markets, primarily through exports. It is useful when the MNE faces low pressures for both local responsiveness and cost reductions.

>> A localization strategy attempts to maximize local responsiveness in the face of low pressure for cost reductions. It is costly and inefficient because it requires the duplication of key business functions in multiple countries.

>> A global-standardization strategy seeks to reap economies of scale and location by pursuing a global division of labor based on wherever best-of-class capabilities reside at the lowest cost. It involves little or no local responsiveness.

>> A transnational strategy attempts to combine the high local responsiveness of a localization strategy with the lowest-cost position attainable from a global-standardization strategy. It also aims to benefit from global learning. Although appealing, it is difficult to implement due to the organizational complexities involved.

>> Exhibit 10.7 summarizes the characteristics, benefits, and risks of the four global competition strategies.

LO 10-5 Explain why certain industries are more competitive in specific nations than in others.

>> National competitive advantage, or world leadership in specific industries, is created rather than inherited.

>> Four interrelated factors explain national competitive advantage: (1) factor conditions, (2) demand conditions, (3) competitive intensity in a focal industry, and (4) related and supporting industries/complementors.

LO 10-6 Evaluate the relationship between location in a regional cluster and firm-level competitive advantage.

>> Even in a globalized world, the basis for competitive advantage is often local.

>> Strong empirical evidence suggests that being located in a regional cluster can have a positive effect on firm-level competitive advantage, both domestically and globally.

Key Terms

Cultural distance *(p. 279)*

Death-of-distance hypothesis *(p. 287)*

Foreign direct investment (FDI) *(p. 271)*

Global-standardization strategy *(p. 284)*

Global strategy *(p. 272)*

Globalization *(p. 271)*

Globalization hypothesis *(p. 281)*

Individualism *(p. 278)*

Integration-responsiveness framework *(p. 282)*

International strategy *(p. 282)*

Knowledge spillover *(p. 290)*

Liability of foreignness *(p. 276)*

Local responsiveness *(p. 282)*

Localization strategy *(p. 283)*

Location economies *(p. 276)*

Masculinity–femininity dimension *(p. 279)*

Multinational enterprise (MNE) *(p. 271)*

National competitive advantage *(p. 287)*

National culture *(p. 278)*

Power-distance dimension *(p. 278)*

Regional cluster *(p. 289)*

Transnational strategy *(p. 284)*

Uncertainty-avoidance dimension *(p. 279)*

Discussion Questions

1. Multinational enterprises (MNEs) have an impact far beyond their firm boundaries. Assume you are working for a small firm that supplies a product or service to an MNE. How might your relationship change as the MNE moves from Globalization 2.0 to Globalization 3.0 operations?

2. Think about the last movie you saw in a movie theater. What aspects of the movie had international components in it (e.g., the plot line, locations, cast, and so on)? Are there more international elements included than compared to your favorite movie from a decade ago?

3. "Licensing patented technology to a foreign competitor is likely to reduce or eliminate the firm's competitive advantage." True or false? Write a paragraph discussing this statement.

4. Consider the city/region in which your university is located. Given the discussions in the chapter about location economies, what characteristics are unusual about your location? Do you have nearby industrial regional clusters? Access to abundant (or cheap) raw materials of some sort? University research of interest to local firms?

Ethical/Social Issues

1. The chapter notes a "race-to-the-bottom" approach that MNEs may use as they search for lower cost options. Discuss the trade-offs between the positive effects of raising the standard of living in some of the world's poorest countries with the drawbacks of moving jobs established in one country to another country.

2. The chapter notes that some firms are started in countries with relatively small populations (and thus small domestic markets), such as Taiwan, Australia, and Finland. In these cases, the firms often rapidly expand internationally to reach a large enough market for economies of scale. However, some large countries (such as Brazil, China, and Japan) have economic incentives (and sometimes mandates) for firms to export their products. There are cases where such mandates result in products available internationally but not to the local population (except perhaps through a "black-market" or unofficial distribution channel). Is this closed domestic market an ethical issue for the firm? Is it an ethical issue for the government? Why or why not?

Small Group Exercises

SMALL GROUP EXERCISE 1

The text mentions that Accenture is one firm (among many others) that has shifted its location of incorporation to Ireland. The corporate officers are still based in the United States, and the stock is traded on the NYSE. The firm stated the move was largely beneficial for corporate taxes.[79] Given the chapter discussion of "what defines a U.S. company," answer the following questions.

1. Does it matter where the firm is incorporated?

2. Are there any social or ethical arguments that the firm should be incorporated where its "home base" is located?

3. Is incorporation based on cost/quality trade-offs required to maximize shareholder wealth (thus by inference, firms that do *not* move incorporation are *reducing* the returns to their shareholders)? Please discuss.

SMALL GROUP EXERCISE 2

In this exercise, we want to apply the four types of global strategy. Imagine your group works for Clif Bar (www.clifbar.com). The firm makes nutritious, all-natural food and drinks for sport and healthy snacking. In 2010, Clif Bar was a privately held company with over 200 employees and a large majority of its sales in the United States. As of 2010, even its online sales were restricted to U.S. customers only. The firm has some distribution set up in Canada (since 1996) and the United Kingdom (since 2007). Review its website for more information about the firm and its products. Referring to the material on pages 281–286 of this chapter (including Exhibit 10.6), answer the following questions.

1. Where does this firm fall on the integration-responsiveness framework?

2. What entrance strategy should the firm employ in expanding the business to new countries?

3. Does your answer change if you find out Clif Bar is planning to expand into (a) Mexico, (b) India, or (c) Germany?

Strategy Term Project

MODULE 10: GLOBAL STRATEGY

In this section, you will study your firm's global strategy or a strategy it should pursue globally.

If your firm is already engaged in international activities, answer the following questions:

1. Is your company varying its product or service to adapt to differences in countries? Is the marketing approach different among the nations involved? Should it be?

2. Is your firm working internationally to access larger markets? To gain low-cost input factors? To develop new competencies? Is its approach in all three areas appropriate?

3. Which of the four global strategies is the firm using? Is this the best strategy for it to use? Why or why not? (Exhibit 10.7 provides a summary of the four global strategies.)

If your firm is not now engaged internationally, answer the following questions:

1. Would your firm's product or service need to be modified or marketed differently if it expanded beyond the home country?

2. Does your firm have the potential to access larger markets by expanding internationally? Does it have the possibility of lowering input factors with such expansion? Please explain why or why not.

3. If your firm decided to expand internationally, where does the firm reside on the integration-responsiveness framework? (Refer to Exhibit 10.6 if needed.) What does this result say about the best global strategy for your firm to use for international expansion?

*my*Strategy

SHOULD THERE BE MORE H1-B VISAS?

As the U.S. unemployment rate soared to 10 percent in 2010, H1-B visas (temporary work permits for skilled human capital) emerged as a political hot-button issue. Since 1990, Congress has allowed 65,000 H1-B visas each year, plus 20,000 for foreign students with a graduate degree from U.S. universities. This regulation was implemented partly in response to lobbying from computer technology companies like Microsoft, IBM, and Intel. H1-B visas are generally granted to foreign nationals who often have advanced degrees that are difficult to find among U.S. workers (e.g., in engineering or computer science).

The demand for H1-B visas, however, far outstrips supply by almost 10 to 1, with approximately 600,000 applications annually. In 2008, Infosys received 4,559 H1-B visas, followed by Wipro (2,678), and Satyam (1,197). Given their world-class excellence in business process outsourcing, it is not surprising that all of these are Indian IT companies. The consulting firm Accenture is also among the largest contingent for H1-B visas, with 731. Half of the engineers working for Google in its Mountain View, California, headquarters were born overseas.

Industry titans like Bill Gates (co-founder of Microsoft), Craig Barrett (former chairman of Intel), and John Lechleiter (CEO of Eli Lilly) are adamant about the need for more H1-B visas to stay competitive. (Said Mr. Barrett, "We should staple a green card to every U.S. diploma given to foreign students.")[80]

Those who have an opposing view see H1-B visas as reducing American jobs. U.S. Senator Charles Grassley (R-Iowa), for example, has suggested that when jobs are cut, foreigners should be laid off first, regardless of merit.

Senator Grassley's request contrasts with research showing that U.S. tech companies add five workers for each H1-B visa they receive. Another research study coming out of Duke and Harvard found that a majority of the high-tech companies started in Silicon Valley had founders born overseas. Some of the more famous foreign-born founders include Andy Grove (Hungarian-born former CEO of Intel and one of its earliest employees), Jerry Yang (Taiwanese-born co-founder of Yahoo), Sergey Brin (Russian-born co-founder of Google), and Tony Tsieh (founder of LinkExchange and CEO at Zappos.com, born to Taiwanese immigrants).[81]

1. Is the U.S. chasing away foreigners who may start their own companies that create jobs and wealth? Or are H1-B visa holders taking away jobs from U.S. citizens?

2. What skills and capabilities do you need to acquire and hone so that you can take advantage of opportunities afforded in a more global labor market?

Endnotes

1. "Plot change: Foreign forces transform Hollywood films," *The Wall Street Journal,* August 2, 2010.

2. This ChapterCase is based on: "Plot change: Foreign forces transform Hollywood films," *The Wall Street Journal;* "Hollywood squeezes stars' pay in slump," *The Wall Street Journal,* April 2, 2009; "News Corporation," *The Economist,* February 26, 2009; and "Slumdog Millionaire wins eight Oscars," *The Wall Street Journal,* February 23, 2009.

3. "Foreign university students," *The Economist,* August 7, 2010.

4. World Bank (2010), *World Development Indicators,* July 1.

5. Stiglitz, J. (2002), *Globalization and Its Discontents* (New York: Norton).

6. "BRICs, emerging markets and the world economy," *The Economist,* June 18, 2009.

7. Caves, R. (1996), *Multinational Enterprise and Economic Analysis* (New York: Cambridge University Press); and Dunning, J. (1993), *Multinational Enterprises and the Global Economy* (Reading, MA: Addison-Wesley).

8. "GM's latest nemesis: VW," *The Wall Street Journal,* August 4, 2010.

9. Following Peng (2010: 18), we define global strategy as a "strategy of firms around the globe—essentially various firms' theories about how to compete successfully." This stands in contrast to a narrower alternative use of the term "global strategy," which implies a global cost leadership strategy in standardized products. We follow Peng to denote this type of strategy as *standardization strategy* (Peng, 2010: 20); Peng, M. W. (2010), *Global Strategy,* 2nd ed. (Mason, OH: Cengage).

10. McKinsey Global Institute (2010), *Growth and Competitiveness in the United States: The Role of Its Multinational Companies* (London).

11. "IBM to cut U.S. jobs, expand in India," *The Wall Street Journal,* March 26, 2009.

12. This Strategy Highlight draws on: Friedman, T. L. (2005), *The World Is Flat: A Brief History of the Twenty-first Century* (New York: Farrar, Straus, and Giroux). Although we follow Friedman (2005) in using the terminology Globalization 1.0, Globalization 2.0, and Globalization 3.0, the time frame of the three different stages and the description thereof differs from Friedman (2005); and IBM (2009), *A Decade of Generating Higher Value at IBM,* IBM report, www.ibm.com.

13. This Strategy Highlight is based on: "Can China save GM?" *Forbes,* May 10, 2010; and Tao, Q. (2009), "Competition in the Chinese automobile industry," in M. Peng, *Global Strategy,* 2nd ed. (Mason, OH: South-Western Cengage), pp. 419–425.

14. "Social networks and statehood," *The Economist,* July 22, 2010.

15. Kotha, S., V. Rindova, and F. T. Rothaermel (2001), "Assets and actions: Firm-specific factors in the internationalization of U.S. Internet firms," *Journal of International Business Studies* 32: 769–791.

16. www.logitech.com.

17. Saxenian, A. (1994), *Regional Advantage* (Cambridge, MA: Harvard University Press); and Rothaermel, F. T., and D. Ku (2008), "Intercluster innovation differentials: The role of research universities," *IEEE Transactions on Engineering Management* 55: 9–22.

18. "A special report on innovation in emerging markets," *The Economist,* April 15, 2010.

19. "The rising power of the Chinese worker," *The Economist,* July 29, 2010.

20. Friedman, T. L. (2005), *The World Is Flat: A Brief History of the Twenty-first Century.*

21. Chang, S. J. (1995), "International expansion strategy of Japanese firms: Capability building through sequential entry," *Academy of Management Journal* 38: 383–407; Vermeulen, F., and H. G. Barkema (1998), "International expansion through start-up or acquisition: A learning perspective," *Academy of Management Journal* 41: 7–26; Vermeulen, F., and H. G. Barkema (2002), "Pace, rhythm, and scope: Process dependence in building a profitable multinational corporation," *Strategic Management Journal* 23: 637–653.

22. Brown, J. S., and P. Duguid (1991), "Organizational learning and communities-of-practice: Toward a unified view of working, learning, and innovation," *Organization Science* 2: 40–57.

23. Owen-Smith, J., and W. W. Powell (2004), "Knowledge networks as channels and conduits: The effects of spillovers in the Boston biotech community," *Organization Science* 15: 5–21.

24. Examples drawn from: "A special report on innovation in emerging markets," *The Economist,* April 15, 2010.

25. Dunning, J. H., and S. M. Lundan (2008), *Multinational Enterprises and the Global Economy,* 2nd ed. (Northampton, MA: Edward Elgar).

26. "A special report on innovation in emerging markets," *The Economist,* April 15, 2010.

27. Zaheer, S. (1995), "Overcoming the liability of foreignness," *Academy of Management Journal* 38: 341–363.

28. "The Foxconn suicides," *The Wall Street Journal,* May 27, 2010.

29. "Firms boost pay for Chinese," *The Wall Street Journal,* June 13, 2010.

30. "Supply chain for iPhone highlights costs in China," *The New York Times,* July 5, 2010.

31. Ibid.

32. "The rising power of the Chinese worker," *The Economist,* July 29, 2010.

33. This is based on: Friedman, T. L. (2005), *The World Is Flat: A Brief History of the Twenty-first Century;* "Supply chain for iPhone highlights costs in China," *The New York Times,* July 5, 2010; and "The rising power of the Chinese worker," *The Economist,* July 29, 2010.

34. This example is drawn from: "Train makers rail against China's high-speed designs," *The Wall Street Journal,* November 17, 2010.

35. This is based on: Williamson, O. E. (1975), *Markets and Hierarchies* (New York: Free Press); Williamson, O. E. (1981), "The economics of organization: The transaction cost approach," *American Journal of Sociology* 87: 548–577; and Williamson, O. E. (1985), *The Economic Institutions of Capitalism* (New York: Free Press).

36. Author's interview with a VP of Citibank in a Latin American country.

37. This is based on: North, D. (1990), *Institutions, Institutional Change, and Economic Performance* (New York: Norton); and Peng, M. W. (2003), "Institutional transitions and strategic choices," *Academy of Management Review* 28: 275–296.

38. Hofstede, G. H. (1984), *Culture's Consequences: International Differences in Work-Related Values* (Beverly Hills, CA: Sage), p. 21.

39. The description of Hofstede's four cultural dimensions is drawn from: Rothaermel, F. T., S. Kotha, and H. K. Steensma (2006), "International market entry by U.S. Internet firms: An empirical analysis of country risk, national culture, and market size," *Journal of Management* 32: 56–82.

40. This is based on: Kogut, B., and H. Singh (1988), "The effect of national culture on the choice of entry mode," *Journal of International Business Studies* 19: 411–432; Rothaermel, F. T., S. Kotha, and H. K. Steensma (2006), "International market entry by U.S. Internet firms: An empirical analysis of country risk, national culture, and market size"; Cultural distance from the United States, for example, is calculated as follows: $CD_j = \sum_{i=1}^{4} \{(I_{ij} - I_{iu})^2 / V_i\} / 4$, where I_{ij} stands for the index for the ith cultural dimension and jth country, V_i is the variance of the index of ith dimension, u indicates the United States, and CD_j is the cultural distance difference of the jth country from the United States.

41. Cairncross, F. (1997), *The Death of Distance: How the Communications Revolution Will Change Our Lives* (Boston, MA: Harvard Business School Press).

42. This is based on: O Riain, S. (2000), "The flexible developmental state: Globalization, information technology and the 'Celtic Tiger,'" *Politics and Society* 28: 157–193; and "A survey of Ireland," *The Economist,* October 14, 2004.

43. Examples drawn from: "A survey of Ireland," *The Economist.*

44. Today, some argue that Ireland's low corporate tax rate contributed to its financial difficulties in the wake of the global financial crisis; see "Tax torment," *The Economist,* March 17, 2011.

45. UNCTAD (2010), "Global FDI flows will exceed $1.2 trillion in 2010," *United Nations Conference on Trade and Development Report,* www.unctad.org.

46. Johanson, J., and J. Vahlne (1977), "The internationalization process of the firm," *Journal of International Business Studies* 4: 20–29.

47. Fuller, A. W., and F. T. Rothaermel (2008), "The Interplay between capability development and strategy formation: Motorola's entry into China," Working Paper, Georgia Institute of Technology.

48. Levitt, T. (1983), "The globalization of markets," *Harvard Business Review,* May–June: 92–102.

49. Ibid., 93.

50. Mol, M. (2002). Ford Mondeo: A Model T world car? In: Tan, F. B. (Ed.), Cases on Global IT Applications and Management: Successes and Pitfalls, pp. 69-89.

51. Prahalad, C. K., and Y. L. Doz (1987), *The Multinational Mission* (New York: Free Press); and Roth, K., and A. J. Morrison (1990), "An empirical analysis of the integration-responsiveness framework in global industries," *Journal of International Business Studies* 21: 541–564.

52. Bartlett, C. A., S. Ghoshal, and P. W. Beamish (2007), *Transnational Management: Text, Cases and Readings in Cross-border Management,* 5th ed. (Burr Ridge, IL: McGraw-Hill).

53. "Ditch the knock-off watch, get the knock-off car," *The Wall Street Journal Video,* August 8, 2010.

54. www.lenovo.com/lenovo/US/en/locations.html.

55. Ibid.

56. This is based on: Bartlett, C. A., S. Ghoshal, and P. W. Beamish (2007), *Transnational Management: Text, Cases and Readings in Cross-border Management;* and Friedman, T. L. (2005), *The World Is Flat: A Brief History of the Twenty-first Century.*

57. This strategy highlight is based on: Knorr, A., and A. Arndt (2003), "Why did Wal-Mart fail in Germany?" in A. Knorr, A. Lemper, A. Sell, and K. Wohlmuth (eds.), *Materialien des Wissenschaftsschwerpunktes "Globalisierung der Weltwirtschaft,"* Vol. 24 (IWIM—Institute for

World Economics and International Management, Universität Bremen, Germany); the author's onsite observations at Walmart stores in Germany; and "Hair-shirt economics: Getting Germans to open their wallets is hard," *The Economist,* July 8, 2010. For a recent discussion of Walmart's global efforts, see: "After early errors, Wal-Mart thinks locally to act globally," *The Wall Street Journal,* August 14, 2009.

58. Mueller, H.-E. (2001), "Developing global human resource strategies," Paper presented at the European International Business Academy, Paris, December 13–15; Mueller, H.-E. (2001), "Wie Global Player den Kampf um Talente führen," *Harvard Business Manager* 6: 16–25.

59. This section draws on: Rothaermel, F. T., and D. Ku (2008), "Intercluster innovation differentials: The role of research universities," *IEEE Transactions on Engineering Management* 55: 9–22.

60. This is based on: Buckley, P. J., and P. N. Ghauri (2004), "Globalisation, economic geography and the strategy of multinational enterprises," *Journal of International Business Studies* 35: 81–98; and Cairncross, F. (1997), *The Death of Distance: How The Communications Revolution Will Change Our Lives* (Boston, MA: Harvard Business School Press). For a counterpoint, see: Ghemawat, P. (2007), *Redefining Global Strategy: Crossing Borders in a World Where Differences Still Matter* (Boston, MA: Harvard Business School Press).

61. Friedman, T. L. (2005), *The World Is Flat: A Brief History of the Twenty-first Century.*

62. This section is based on: Porter, M. E. (1990), "The competitive advantage of nations," *Harvard Business Review,* March–April: 73–91; and Porter, M. E. (1990), *The Competitive Advantage of Nations* (New York: Free Press).

63. "U.S. identifies vast mineral riches in Afghanistan," *The New York Times,* June 13, 2010.

64. For an insightful recent discussion, see: Breznitz, D. (2007), *Innovation and the State: Political Choice and Strategies for Growth in Israel, Taiwan, and Ireland* (New Haven, CT: Yale University Press).

65. More recently, however, Nokia has lost some of its leadership to Apple, RIM of Canada, and Samsung of South Korea.

66. Dyer, J. H., and K. Nobeoka (2000), "Creating and managing a high-performance knowledge-sharing network: The Toyota case," *Strategic Management Journal* 21: 345–367.

67. This discussion is based on: "Toyota slips up," *The Economist,* December 10, 2009; "Toyota: Losing its shine," *The Economist,* December 10, 2009; "Toyota heir faces crises at the wheel," *The Wall Street Journal,* January 27, 2010; "Toyota's troubles deepen," *The Economist,* February 4, 2010; "The humbling of Toyota," *Bloomberg Businessweek,* March 11, 2010; and "Inside Toyota, executives trade blame over debacle," *The Wall Street Journal,* April 13, 2010.

68. Porter, M. E. (1998), "Clusters and the new economics of competition," *Harvard Business Review,* November–December: 77–90.

69. For a review, see: Jenkins, M., and S. Tallman (2010), "The shifting geography of competitive advantage: Clusters, networks and firms," *Journal of Economic Geography* 10: 599–618; Porter, M. E. (1988), "Clusters and competition: New agendas for companies, governments, and institutions," in Porter, M. E. (ed.), *On Competition* (Boston: Harvard Business School Press); Porter, M. E. (1990), *The Competitive Advantage of Nations* (New York: Free Press); Porter, M. E. (1998), "Clusters and the new economics of competition," *Harvard Business Review,* November–December: 77–90; Rothaermel, F. T., and D. Ku (2008), "Intercluster innovation differentials: The role of research universities," *IEEE Transactions on Engineering Management* 55: 9–22; and Tallman, S., M. Jenkins, N. Henry, and S. Pinch (2004), "Knowledge, clusters and competitive advantage," *Academy of Management Review* 29: 258–271.

70. Porter, M. E. (1990), *The Competitive Advantage of Nations* (New York: Free Press), p. 77.

71. McKinsey Global Institute (2010), *Growth and Competitiveness in the United States: The Role of its Multinational Companies.*

72. For a review, see: Agarwal, R., D. B. Audretsch, and M. B. Sarkar (2007), "The process of creative construction: Knowledge spillovers, entrepreneurship, and economic growth," *Strategic Entrepreneurship Journal* 1: 263–286; Audretsch, D. B., and M. P. Feldman (1996), "R&D spillovers and the geography of innovation and production," *American Economic Review* 86: 630–640; Audretsch, D. B., and E. E. Lehmann (2005), "Mansfield's missing link: The impact of knowledge spillovers on firm growth," *Journal of Technology Transfer* 30: 207–210; Audretsch, D. B., E. E. Lehmann, and S. Warning (2005), "University spillovers and new firm location," *Research Policy* 34: 1113–1122; Audretsch, D. B., and P. E. Stephan (1996), "Company–scientist locational links: The case of biotechnology," *American Economic Review* 86: 641–652; Rothaermel, F. T., and M. Thursby (2005), "University-incubator firm knowledge flows: Assessing their impact on incubator firm performance," *Research Policy* 34: 305–320; and Rothaermel, F. T., and M. Thursby (2005), "Incubator firm failure or graduation? The role of university linkages," *Research Policy* 34: 1076–1090.

73. Saxenian, A. (1994), *Regional Advantage* (Cambridge, MA: Harvard University Press).

74. Gompers, P. A., and J. Lerner (2001), *The Money of Invention: How Venture Capital Creates New Wealth* (Boston, MA: Harvard Business School Press).

75. "Ending the open season on artists," *The Economist,* February 17, 2011.

76. Levin, D., and J. Horn (2011), "DVD pirates running rampant in China," *Los Angeles Times,* March, 22.

77. Ibid.

78. "Bigger abroad," *The Economist,* February 17, 2011.

79. "Accenture Is Seeking to Change Tax Locales," *The Wall Street Journal,* May 27, 2009.

80. Barrett, C. (2009), "We need an immigration stimulus," *The Wall Street Journal,* April 27.

81. This *my*Strategy is based on: "U.S. tech companies add five workers for each H-1B visa they seek," *InformationWeek,* March 10, 2008; "Still coming to America," *The Wall Street Journal,* March 27, 2009; "Work-visa numbers get squishy—and get played," *The Wall Street Journal,* March 31, 2009; "Tech recruiting clashes with immigration rules," *The New York Times,* April 11, 2009; "We need an immigration stimulus," *The Wall Street Journal,* April 27, 2009; and a collection of many articles pertaining to this topic found at http://wadhwa.com/.

Analysis: Getting Started

1. What Is Strategy and Why Is It Important?
2. The Strategic Management Process

External and Internal Analysis

3. External Analysis: Industry Structure, Competitive Forces, and Strategic Groups
4. Internal Analysis: Resources, Capabilities, and Activities
5. Competitive Advantage and Firm Performance

Implementation

11. Organizational Design: Structure, Culture, and Control
12. Corporate Governance, Business Ethics, and Strategic Leadership

PART 3

GAINING & SUSTAINING COMPETITIVE ADVANTAGE

Formulation: Corporate Strategy

8. Corporate Strategy: Vertical Integration and Diversification
9. Corporate Strategy: Acquisitions, Alliances, and Networks
10. Global Strategy: Competing Around the World

Formulation: Business Strategy

6. Business Strategy: Differentiation, Cost Leadership, and Integration
7. Business Strategy: Innovation and Strategic Entrepreneurship

PART 3
Strategy Implementation

CHAPTER 11

Organizational Design: Structure, Culture, and Control

LEARNING OBJECTIVES
After studying this chapter, you should be able to:

LO 11-1 Define organizational design and list its three components.

LO 11-2 Explain how organizational inertia can lead established firms to failure.

LO 11-3 Define organizational structure and describe its four elements.

LO 11-4 Compare and contrast mechanistic versus organic organizations.

LO 11-5 Describe different organizational structures and match them with appropriate strategies.

LO 11-6 Describe the elements of organizational culture, and explain where organizational cultures can come from and how they can be changed.

LO 11-7 Compare and contrast different strategic control and reward systems.

Zappos: An Organization Designed to Deliver Happiness

DELIVERING HAPPINESS is the title of *The New York Times* bestseller by Tony Hsieh, CEO of Zappos, the online shoe and clothing store (www.zappos.com). Delivering happiness is also Zappos's mission. To make its customers, employees, and shareholders happy, Tony Hsieh (pronounced "shay") and other Zappos leaders designed a unique organization.

To live up to its mission, Zappos decided that exceptional customer service should be its core competency. They put several policies and procedures in place to "deliver WOW through service"—the first of its 10 core values (see Exhibit 11.1 on the next page). For example, shipments to and from customers within the U.S. are free of charge, allowing customers to order several pairs of shoes and send back (within a liberal 365 days) those that don't fit or are no longer wanted. Repeat customers are automatically upgraded to complimentary express shipping. One of the most important lessons Hsieh learned is, "never outsource your core competency!"[1] Customer service, therefore, is done exclusively in-house. Perhaps even more importantly, Zappos does not provide a script or measure customer-service reps' call times. Rather, the company leaves it up to the individual "Customer Loyalty Team" member to deliver exceptional customer service: "We want our reps to let their true

personalities shine during each phone call so that they can develop a personal emotional connection with the customer."[2] (In fact, one customer-service phone call lasted almost six hours!) The same trust in the customer-service reps applies to e-mail communication. Zappos's official communication policy is to "be real and use your best judgment."[3]

As Zappos grew, its managers realized that it was critical to explicitly define a set of core values from which to develop the company's culture, brand, and strategy. It wanted to make sure that, in a time of fast growth, all employees understood the same set of values and expected behaviors. Zappos's list of 10 core values was crafted through a bottom-up initiative, in which all employees were invited to participate. Zappos also restructured its performance-evaluation system, to give these values "teeth": The firm rewards employees who apply the values well in their day-to-day decision making. In this way, Zappos's managers directly connected the informal cultural control system to the formal reward system. CEO Tony Hsieh states, "Ideally, we want all 10 core values to be reflected in everything we do, including how we interact with each other, how we interact with our customers, and how we interact with our vendors and business partners. . . . Our core values should always be the framework from which we make all of our decisions."[4]

When establishing customer service as a core competency, one of the hardest decisions Tony Hsieh made was to pull the plug on drop-shipment orders (orders for which Zappos would be the intermediary, relaying orders to particular shoe vendors who then ship directly to the customer). Such orders were very profitable (Zappos would not have to stock all the shoes) and were appealing because the fledgling startup was still losing money. The problem was two-fold. The vendors were slower than Zappos in filling orders. In addition, they did not accomplish the reliability metric that Zappos wanted for exceptional service: 95 percent accuracy was simply not good enough! Instead, Zappos decided to forgo drop shipments and instead built a larger warehouse to stock a full inventory. This move enabled the firm to achieve close to 100 percent accuracy in its shipments, many of which were overnight.

In addition to making customers happy, Zappos also works to keep its own employees happy. Although it now employs over 1,500 people, Zappos's organizational structure is extremely flat. Once an employee has mastered a job, he or she is rotated to a different job, often horizontally. This system allows Zappos to create a large pool of trained talent, and makes it easier to promote from within. In keeping with another of its core values, "create fun and a little weirdness," the Las Vegas–based startup offers employees "free" lunches, employer-paid health care benefits, a designated nap room, concierge service, an onsite life coach who is also a chiropractor, a library of books on happiness (along with other bestsellers), onsite seminars on personal growth, and fun events such as pajama parties at work. In 2011, Zappos was ranked #6 in *Fortune*'s "100 Best Companies to Work For" list (the highest ranking for a relatively young firm).

Finally, Zappos has also made its shareholders happy. In 2009, Amazon acquired the startup in a deal valued at $1.2 billion. Although now a subsidiary of Amazon, Zappos continues to operate as an independent brand.[5]

After reading the chapter, you will find more about this case, with related questions, on page 324.

▲ **ZAPPOS'S CEO** Tony Hsieh and other managers thought long and hard about what type of structure, culture, and processes to put in place that would support the firm's strategic goals. They proactively designed an organization that enabled them to implement its differentiation strategy effectively. Zappos's managers further refined their organizational design through trial-and-error, being transparent, and soliciting bottom-up feedback, while making the tough strategic decisions of what not to do.

ChapterCase 11 brings us to the final piece of the AFI framework: strategy implementation. **Strategy implementation** concerns the organization, coordination, and integration of how work gets done. It is key to gaining and sustaining competitive advantage. Although the discussion of strategy formulation (what to do) is distinct from strategy implementation (how to do it), formulation and implementation must be part of an interdependent, reciprocal process in order to ensure continued success. That need for interdependence is why the AFI

strategy implementation
The part of the strategic management process that concerns the organization, coordination, and integration of how work gets done. It is key to gaining and sustaining competitive advantage.

EXHIBIT 11.1

Zappos's 10 Core Values

Source: Hsieh, T. (2010), *Delivering Happiness: A Path to Profits, Passion, and Purpose* (New York: Business Plus), pp. 157–160.

1. Deliver WOW through service.
2. Embrace and drive change.
3. Create fun and a little weirdness.
4. Be adventurous, creative, and open-minded.
5. Pursue growth and learning.
6. Build open and honest relationships with communication.
7. Build a positive team and family spirit.
8. Do more with less.
9. Be passionate and determined.
10. Be humble.

framework is illustrated as a circle, rather than a linear diagram. The design of an organization, the matching of strategy and structure, and its control and reward systems determine whether an organization that has chosen an effective strategy will thrive or wither away.

In this chapter, we study the three key levers that managers have at their disposal when *designing their organizations for competitive advantage:* structure, culture, and control. We begin our discussion with organizational structure. We discuss not only different types of organizational structures, but also why and how they need to change over time as successful firms grow in size and complexity. We highlight the critical need to match strategy and structure, and then dive into corporate culture. An organization's culture can either support or hinder its quest for competitive advantage.[6] Finally, we study strategic control systems, which allow managers to receive feedback on how well a firm's strategy is being implemented.

Managers employ these three levers—structure, culture, and control—to coordinate work and motivate employees across different levels, functions, and geographies. How successful they are in this endeavor determines whether they are able to translate their chosen business, corporate, and global strategies into strategic actions and business models, and ultimately whether the firm is able to gain and sustain a competitive advantage.

HOW TO ORGANIZE FOR COMPETITIVE ADVANTAGE

Organizational design is the process of creating, implementing, monitoring, and modifying the structure, processes, and procedures of an organization. The key components of organizational design are structure, culture, and control. The goal is to design an organization that allows managers to effectively translate their chosen strategy into a realized one. Simply formulating an effective strategy, however, is a necessary but not sufficient condition for gaining and sustaining competitive advantage. Some might argue that strategy execution is more important.[7] Often, managers do a good job of analyzing the firm's internal and external environments to formulate a promising business, corporate, and global strategy, but then fail to implement the chosen strategy successfully. That is why some scholars refer to implementation as the "graveyard of strategy."[8]

Not surprisingly, the inability to implement strategy effectively is the number-one reason boards of directors fire CEOs.[9] Strategy Highlight 11.1 (next page) shows the result of Yahoo's co-founder and CEO Jerry Yang's failure to make the necessary changes to the Internet firm's organizational structure.

Since strategy implementation transforms theory into strategic actions and business models, it often requires changes within the organization. However, strategy implementation often fails because managers are unable to make the necessary changes due to its effects on resource allocation and power distribution within an organization.[10]

As demonstrated by business historian Alfred Chandler in his seminal book *Strategy and Structure,* organizational structure must follow strategy in order for firms to achieve superior performance: "Structure can be defined as the design of organization through which the enterprise is administered... the thesis deduced [from studying the administrative history of DuPont, GM, Sears Roebuck, and Standard Oil from the early to mid-1900s] is that *structure follows strategy*."[11] This tenet implies that to implement a strategy successfully, organizational design must be flexible enough to accommodate the formulated strategy and future growth and expansion.

Organizational Inertia and the Failure of Established Firms

In reality, however, a firm's strategy often follows its structure.[12] This reversal implies that some managers consider only strategies that do not change existing organizational

>> **LO 11-1**
Define organizational design and list its three components.

organizational design
The process of creating, implementing, monitoring, and modifying the structure, processes, and procedures of an organization.

>> **LO 11-2**
Explain how organizational inertia can lead established firms to failure.

Draw Me Yahoo's Org Chart

In the fall of 2008, Yahoo's co-founder and CEO Jerry Yang was ousted precisely because he failed to implement necessary strategic changes after Yahoo lost its competitive advantage.[13] In the two years leading up to his exit, Yahoo had lost more than 75 percent of its market value. Mr. Yang was described as someone who preferred consensus among his managers to making tough strategic decisions needed to change Yahoo's structure. That preference, though, led to bickering and infighting.

Carol Bartz, who replaced Jerry Yang as CEO, recalls saying, "Well, Jerry, why don't you draw me an org chart. . . . Why don't you show me who on this org would make the big decision—the big search decision. So he started drawing arrows. And it was like a Dilbert cartoon. It was very odd. I said, you need management here. I couldn't figure out who was in charge of anything, and he didn't explain that part very well."[14] One of the first things Ms. Bartz did, therefore, was to change Yahoo's organizational structure both to decentralize decision making and to increase the accountability of individual employees. In addition, she clarified the lines of authority. With its new organizational design in place, Ms. Bartz hopes Yahoo's rate of innovation will increase to improve its competitiveness.[15]

structures; they do not want to confront the inertia that often exists in established organizations.[16] *Inertia,* a firm's resistance to change in the status quo, can set the stage for the firm's subsequent failure. Successful firms often plant the seed of subsequent failure: They optimize their organizational structure to the current situation. That tightly coupled system can break apart when internal or external pressures occur.

Exhibit 11.2 shows how success in the current environment can lead to a firm's downfall in the future, when the tightly coupled system of strategy and structure experiences internal or external shifts.[17] First, the managers achieve a mastery of, and fit with, the firm's current environment. Second, the firm often defines and measures success by financial metrics, with a focus on short-term performance. (See the discussion of metrics in Chapter 5.) Third, the firm puts in place metrics and systems to accommodate and manage increasing firm size due to continued success. Finally, as a result of a tightly coupled (albeit successful) system, organizational inertia sets in—and with it, resistance to change.

Such a tightly coupled system is prone to break apart when external and internal shifts put pressure on the system.[18] In Exhibit 11.2, the blue arrows show the firm's tightly coupled organizational design. The gray arrows indicate pressures emanating from internal shifts (such as accelerated growth, a change in business model, entry into new markets, a change in the top management team, or mergers and acquisitions). The purple arrows indicate external pressures, which can stem from any of the PESTEL forces (political, economic, sociocultural, technological, ecological, and legal, as discussed in Chapter 3). Strong external or internal pressure can break apart the current system, which may lead to firm failure.

The Key Elements of Organizational Structure

>> **LO 11-3**
Define organizational structure and describe its four elements.

Some of the key decisions managers must make when designing effective organizations pertain to the firm's **organizational structure.** That structure determines how the work efforts of individuals and teams are orchestrated and how resources are distributed. In particular, an organizational structure defines how jobs and tasks are divided and integrated, delineates the reporting relationships up and down the hierarchy, defines formal communication channels, and prescribes how individuals and teams coordinate their work efforts. The key building blocks of an organizational structure are *specialization, formalization, centralization,* and *hierarchy.*

Specialization describes the degree to which a task is divided into separate jobs—that is, the *division of labor.* Larger firms, such as Fortune 100 companies, tend to have a high

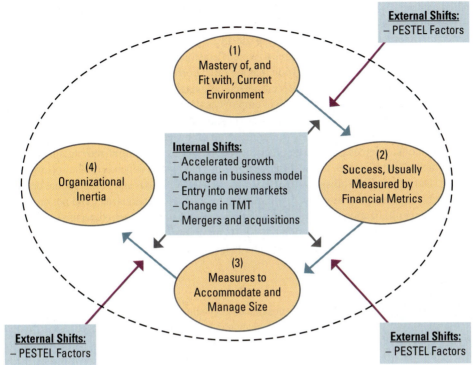

EXHIBIT 11.2

Organizational Inertia and the Failure of Established Firms When External or Internal Environments Shift

degree of specialization; smaller entrepreneurial ventures tend to have a low degree of specialization. For example, an accountant for a large firm may specialize in only one area (e.g., internal audit), whereas an accountant in a small firm needs to be more of a generalist and take on many different things (e.g., not only internal auditing, but also payroll, accounts receivable, financial planning, and taxes). Specialization requires a trade-off between breadth versus depth of knowledge. While a high degree of the division of labor increases productivity, it can also have unintended side-effects such as reduced employee job satisfaction due to repetition of tasks.

Formalization captures the extent to which employee behavior is controlled by explicit and codified rules and procedures. Formalized structures are characterized by detailed written rules and policies of what to do in specific situations. These are often codified in employee handbooks. McDonald's, for example, uses detailed standard operating procedures throughout the world to ensure consistent quality and service. Airlines also rely on a high degree of formalization to instruct pilots on how to fly their airplanes. Formalization, therefore, should not necessarily be considered bad; often it is necessary to achieve consistent and predictable results. Yet a high degree of formalization *can* slow decision making, reduce creativity and innovation, and hinder customer service.[19] Most customer service reps in call centers, for example, follow a detailed script. This is especially true when call centers are outsourced to overseas locations. (As you recall, Zappos deliberately avoided

---

organizational structure A key building block of organizational design that determines how the work efforts of individuals and teams are orchestrated and how resources are distributed.

specialization An element of organizational structure that describes the degree to which a task is divided into separate jobs (i.e., the division of labor).

formalization An element of organizational structure that captures the extent to which employee behavior is controlled by explicit and codified rules and procedures.

this approach when it made customer service its core competency.) W. L. Gore uses an extremely *informal* organizational structure to foster employee satisfaction, retention, and creativity, as discussed in Strategy Highlight 11.2.

Centralization refers to the degree to which decision making is concentrated at the top of the organization. Centralized decision making often correlates with slow response time and reduced customer satisfaction. In decentralized organizations, decisions are made and problems solved by empowered lower-level employees who are closer to the sources of issues. Different strategic management processes (discussed in Chapter 2) match with different degrees of centralization. Top-down strategic planning takes place in highly centralized organizations, whereas planned emergence is found in more decentralized organizations.

Whether centralization or decentralization is more effective depends on the specific situation. During the Gulf oil spill in 2010, BP's response was slow and cumbersome because all of the important decisions were initially made in its UK headquarters and not onsite. In this case, centralization reduced response time and led to a prolonged crisis. In contrast, the FBI and the CIA were faulted in the 9/11 Commission Report for *not being centralized enough.*[22] The report concluded that although each agency had different types of evidence

centralization
An element of organizational structure that refers to the degree to which decision making is concentrated at the top of the organization.

STRATEGY HIGHLIGHT 11.2

W. L. Gore & Associates: Informality and Innovation

W. L. Gore & Associates is the inventor of path-breaking new products such as breathable Gore-Tex fabrics, Glide dental floss, and Elixir guitar strings. Bill Gore, a former long-time employee of chemical giant DuPont, founded the company with the vision to create an organization "devoted to innovation, a company where imagination and initiative would flourish, where chronically curious engineers would be free to invent, invest, and succeed."[20] When founding the company in 1958, Bill Gore articulated four core values that still guide the company and its associates to this day:

1. Fairness to each other and everyone with whom the firm does business
2. Freedom to encourage, help, and allow other associates to grow in knowledge skill, and scope of responsibility
3. The ability to make one's own commitments and keep them
4. Consultation with other associates before undertaking actions that could cause serious damage to the reputation of the company ("blowing a hole below the waterline")

W. L. Gore & Associates is organized in an informal and decentralized manner: It has no formal job titles, job descriptions, chains of command, formal communication channels, written rules or standard operating procedures. Face-to-face communication is preferred over e-mail. There is no organizational chart. In what is called a *lattice* or *boundaryless* organizational form, everyone is empowered and encouraged to speak to anyone else in the organization. People who work at Gore are called "associates," rather than employees, indicating professional expertise and status. Gore associates organize themselves in project-based teams that are led by sponsors, not bosses. Associates invite other team members based on their expertise and interests in a more or less ad hoc fashion. Peer control in these multidisciplinary teams further enhances associate productivity. Group members evaluate each other's performance annually, and these evaluations determine each associate's level of compensation. Moreover, all associates at W. L. Gore are also shareholders of the company, and thus are part owners sharing in profits and losses.

Gore's freewheeling and informal culture has been linked to greater employee satisfaction and retention, higher personal initiative and creativity, and innovation at the firm level. Although W. L. Gore's organizational structure may look like something you might find in a small, high-tech startup company, in 2010 the firm had 9,000 employees and $2.5 billion in revenues, making Gore one of the largest privately held companies in the United States. In the same year, Gore was #13 in *Fortune's* "100 Best Companies to Work For" list, and has been included in every edition of that prestigious ranking.[21]

that a terrorist strike in the U.S. was imminent, their decentralization made them unable to put together the pieces to prevent the 9/11 attacks.

Hierarchy determines the formal, position-based reporting lines and thus stipulates *who reports to whom.* Let's assume two firms of roughly equal size: Firm A and Firm B. If many levels of hierarchy exist between the front-line employee and the CEO in Firm A, it has a *tall structure.* In contrast, if there are few levels of hierarchy in Firm B, it has a *flat structure.*

The number of levels of hierarchy, in turn, determines the managers' **span of control**— how many employees directly report to a manager. In tall organizational structures (Firm A), the span of control is narrow. In flat structures (Firm B), the span of control is wide, meaning one manager supervises many employees. In recent years, firms have de-layered by reducing the headcount (often middle managers), making themselves flatter and thus more nimble. This in turn, however, puts more pressure on the remaining managers who have to supervise and monitor more direct reports due to an increased span of control.[23] Recent research suggests that managers are most effective at an intermediate point where the span of control is not too narrow or too wide.[24]

Assembling the Pieces: Mechanistic vs. Organic Organizations

Several of the building blocks of organizational structure frequently show up together, creating distinct organizational forms—organic and mechanistic organizations.[25]

Zappos and W. L. Gore are both examples of **organic organizations.** Such organizations have a low degree of specialization and formalization, a flat organizational structure, and decentralized decision making.[26] Organic structures tend to be correlated with the following: a fluid and flexible information flow among employees in both horizontal and vertical directions; faster decision making; and higher employee motivation, retention, satisfaction, and creativity. Organic organizations also typically exhibit a higher rate of entrepreneurial behaviors and innovation. Organic structures allow firms to foster R&D and/or marketing, for example, as a core competency. Thus, firms that pursue a differentiation strategy at the business level frequently employ an organic structure. Exhibit 11.3 (next page) highlights the key features of organic organizations.

Due to significant advances in information technology, organic organizations frequently use *virtual teams.* In these teams, geographically dispersed team members are able to collaborate through electronic communications such as e-mail, instant messaging, intranets, and teleconferencing.[27] Given time differences, virtual teams often organize work flow so that projects can be pushed forward 24 hours a day, seven days a week. Use of virtual work and collaboration technologies has enabled companies to be more nimble and to employ flatter and more decentralized organizational structures. Research data show that the largest 30 companies by market capitalization utilized networked digital technologies to double their employee productivity within a decade, despite more than doubling their number of employees. In the decades prior to the widespread use of computer-mediated work, employee productivity remained more or less flat.[28]

> **>> LO 11-4**
> Compare and contrast mechanistic versus organic organizations.

---

hierarchy An element of organizational structure that determines the formal, position-based reporting lines and thus stipulates who reports to whom.

span of control The number of employees who directly report to a manager.

organic organization Organizational form characterized by a low degree of specialization and formalization, a flat organizational structure, and decentralized decision making.

EXHIBIT 11.3

Mechanistic vs. Organic Organizations: The Building Blocks of Organizational Structure

	Mechanistic Organizations	**Organic Organizations**
Specialization	• High degree of specialization • Rigid division of labor • Employees focus on narrowly defined tasks	• Low degree of specialization • Flexible division of labor • Employees focus on "bigger picture"
Formalization	• Intimate familiarity with rules, policies, and processes necessary • Deep expertise in narrowly defined domain required • Task-specific knowledge valued	• Clear understanding of organization's core competencies and strategic intent • Domain expertise in different areas • Generalized knowledge of how to accomplish strategic goals valued
Centralization	• Decision power centralized at top • Vertical (top-down) communication	• Distributed decision making • Vertical (top-down and bottom-up) as well as horizontal communication
Hierarchy	• Tall structures • Low span of control • Clear lines of authority • Command and control	• Flat structures • High span of control • Horizontal as well as two-way vertical communication • Mutual adjustment
Business Strategy	• Cost-leadership strategy • Example: McDonald's	• Differentiation strategy • Examples: W. L. Gore, Zappos

Mechanistic organizations are characterized by a high degree of specialization and formalization, and a tall hierarchy that relies on centralized decision making. The fast food chain McDonald's fits this description quite well. Each step of every job (such as deep-frying fries) is documented in minute detail (e.g., what kind of vat, the quantity of oil, how many fries, what temperature, how long, and so on). Decision power is centralized at the top of the organization: McDonald's headquarters provides detailed instructions to each of its franchisees so that they provide comparable quality and service across the board (although with some local menu variations). Communication and authority lines are top-down and well defined. To ensure standardized operating procedures and consistent food quality throughout the world, McDonald's operates Hamburger University, a state-of-the-art teaching facility in a Chicago suburb, where 50 full-time instructors teach courses in chemistry, food preparation, and marketing. In 2010, McDonald's opened a second Hamburger University campus in Shanghai, China. Mechanistic structures allow for standardization and economies of scale, and thus often are used when the firm pursues a cost-leadership strategy at the business level (again, see Exhibit 11.3).

mechanistic organization
Organizational form characterized by a high degree of specialization and formalization, and a tall hierarchy that relies on centralized decision making.

simple structure
Organizational structure in which the founders tend to make all the important strategic decisions as well as run the day-to-day operations.

functional structure
Organizational structure that groups employees into distinct functional areas based on domain expertise.

Although at first glance organic organizations may appear to be more attractive than mechanistic ones, their relative effectiveness depends on context. McDonald's, with its over 31,000 restaurants across the globe, would not be successful with an organic structure. By the same token, a mechanistic structure would not allow Zappos or W. L. Gore to develop and hone their respective core competencies in customer service and product innovation.

The key point is this: *To gain and sustain competitive advantage, not only must structure follow strategy, but also the chosen organizational form must match the firm's business strategy.* We will expand further on the required strategy-structure relationship in the next section.

MATCHING STRATEGY AND STRUCTURE

The important and interdependent relationship between strategy and structure directly impacts a firm's performance. Moreover, the relationship is dynamic—changing over time in a predictable pattern as firms grow in size and complexity. Successful new ventures generally grow first by increasing sales, then by obtaining larger geographic reach, and finally by diversifying through vertical integration and entering into related and unrelated businesses.[29] Different stages in a firm's growth require different organizational structures. This important evolutionary pattern is depicted in Exhibit 11.4. As we will discuss next, organizational structures range from simple to functional to multidivisional to matrix.

>> LO 11-5
Describe different organizational structures and match them with appropriate strategies.

Simple Structure

A simple structure generally is used by small firms with low organizational complexity. In such firms, the founders tend to make all the important strategic decisions and run the day-to-day operations. Examples include entrepreneurial ventures (such as W. L. Gore in 1958, when the company operated out of Bill Gore's basement) and professional service firms (such as smaller advertising, consulting, accounting, and law firms, as well as family-owned businesses). Simple structures are flat hierarchies operated in a decentralized fashion. They exhibit a low degree of formalization and specialization. Typically, no professional management structures nor sophisticated systems are in place, often leading to an overload for the founder and/or CEO when the firms experience growth.

Functional Structure

As sales increase, firms generally adopt a functional structure, which groups employees into distinct functional areas based on domain expertise. These functional areas often correspond to distinct stages in the company value chain such as R&D, engineering and manufacturing, and marketing and sales, as well as supporting areas such as human resources, finance, and accounting. Exhibit 11.5 (next page) shows a functional structure, with the lines indicating reporting and authority relationships. The department head of each functional area reports to the CEO, who coordinates and integrates

EXHIBIT 11.4

Changing Organizational Structures and Increasing Complexity as Firms Grow

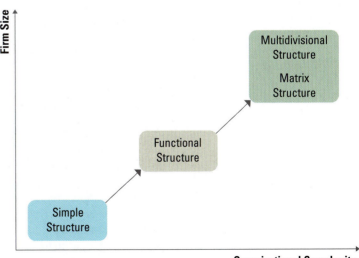

EXHIBIT 11.5

Typical Functional
Structure

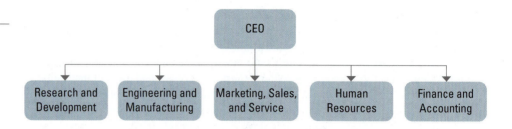

the work of each function. A business school student generally majors in one of these functional areas such as finance, accounting, IT, marketing, operations, or human resources, and is then recruited into a corresponding functional group.

Looking back to the W. L. Gore example, two years after its founding the company received a large manufacturing order for high-tech cable that it could not meet with its ad hoc basement operation. At that point, W. L. Gore reorganized itself into a functional structure. A simple structure does not provide the effective division, coordination, and integration of work required to accommodate future growth.

A functional structure allows for a higher degree of specialization and thus deeper domain expertise than a simple structure. Higher specialization also allows for a greater division of labor, which is linked to higher productivity.[30] While work in a functional structure tends to be specialized, it is centrally coordinated by the CEO (see Exhibit 11.5). A functional structure allows for an efficient top-down and bottom-up communication chain between the CEO and the functional departments, and thus relies on a relatively flat structure.

USE WITH VARIOUS BUSINESS STRATEGIES. A functional structure is recommended when a firm has a fairly narrow focus in terms of product/service offerings (i.e., low level of diversification) combined with a small geographic footprint. It matches well, therefore, with the different *business-level* strategies discussed in Chapter 6: cost-leadership, differentiation, and integration. Although a functional structure is the preferred method for implementing business strategy, *different variations and contexts require careful modifications in each case.* Exhibit 11.6 presents a detailed match between different business strategies and their corresponding functional structures.

The goal of a *cost-leadership strategy* is to create a competitive advantage by reducing the firm's cost below that of competitors while offering acceptable value. The cost leader sells a no-frills, standardized product or service to the mainstream customer. To effectively implement a cost-leadership strategy, therefore, managers must create a functional structure that contains the organizational elements of a *mechanistic structure*—one that is centralized, with well-defined lines of authority up and down the hierarchy. Using a functional structure allows the cost leader to focus on and constantly upgrade necessary core competencies in manufacturing and logistics. Moreover, the cost leader needs to create incentives to foster process innovation in order to drive down cost. Finally, since the firm services the average customer, and thus targets the largest market segment possible, it should focus on leveraging economies of scale to further drive down costs.

The goal of a *differentiation strategy* is to create a competitive advantage by offering products or services at a higher perceived value, while controlling costs. The differentiator, therefore, sells a non-standardized product or service to specific market segments in which customers are willing to pay a higher price. To effectively implement a differentiation strategy, managers rely on a functional structure that resembles an *organic organization*. In

Business-Level Strategy	Structure
Cost leadership	Functional • Mechanistic organization • Centralized • Command and control • Core competencies in efficient manufacturing and logistics • Process innovation to drive down cost • Focus on economies of scale
Differentiation	Functional • Organic organization • Decentralized • Flexibility and mutual adjustment • Core competencies in R&D, innovation, and marketing • Product innovation • Focus on economies of scope
Integration	Functional • Ambidextrous organization • Balancing centralization with decentralization • Multiple core competencies along the value chain required: R&D, manufacturing, logistics, marketing, etc. • Process and product innovations • Focus on economies of scale and scope

EXHIBIT 11.6

Matching Business-Level Strategy and Structure

particular, decision making tends to be decentralized to foster and incentivize continuous innovation and creativity as well as flexibility and mutual adjustment across areas. Using a functional structure with an organic organization allows the differentiator to focus on and constantly upgrade necessary core competencies in R&D, innovation, and marketing. Finally, the functional structure should be set up to allow the firm to reap economies of scope from its core competencies, such as by leveraging its brand name across different products or its technology across different devices.

A successful *integration strategy* requires reconciliation of the trade-offs between differentiation and low cost. To effectively implement an integration strategy, the firm must be both efficient and flexible. For example, the integrator must balance centralization (to control costs) with decentralization (to foster creativity and innovation). Managers must, therefore, attempt to combine the advantages of the functional-structure variations used for cost leadership and differentiation while mitigating their disadvantages. Moreover, the integrator needs to develop several distinct core competencies to both drive up perceived value and lower cost. It must further focus on both product and process innovations in an attempt to reap economies of scale and scope. All of these challenges make it clear that although an integration strategy is attractive at first glance, it is quite difficult to implement given the range of important trade-offs that must be addressed.

As mentioned in Chapter 6, managers can implement an integration strategy by building an *ambidextrous* organization, which attempts to balance and harness different activities in trade-off situations.[31] One example is the attempt to balance *exploitation* (applying current knowledge to enhance firm performance in the short term) with *exploration* (searching for new knowledge that may enhance future performance).[32] To transform a functional structure into an ambidextrous organization, the CEO (or a team of top executives) must personally take responsibility for the integration and coordination across different functional areas. In a recent study of 13 business units that produced 22 innovations over time, researchers found that ambidextrous organizations were most effective in executing continuous innovation.[33] Strategy Highlight 11.3 shows how *USA Today* used an ambidextrous organizational design to successfully reintegrate its independent online unit.

DRAWBACKS. While certainly attractive, the functional strategy is not without significant drawbacks. One is that, although the functional strategy facilitates rich and extensive communication between members of the *same* department, it frequently lacks effective communication channels *across* departments. (Notice in Exhibit 11.5 the lack of links between different functions.) The lack of linkage between functions is the reason, for example, why R&D managers often do not communicate directly with marketing managers. In an

---

USA Today: Leveraging Ambidextrous Organizational Design

The newspaper *USA Today*, published by Gannett Company, has one of the widest print circulations in the United States (close to 2 million). Though highly profitable, in the mid-1990s the newspaper faced the emerging threat of online news media, which is mostly free for the end user. Gannett decided to create a competing online offering—*USA Today.com*. It set up the new unit more or less independently from the namesake newspaper. The online news unit hired staff from the outside, and its first general manager put in place an organizational structure with fundamentally different roles and incentives, and a different culture. Physically separated from the print newspaper, *USA Today.com* resembled an online startup company in the media business more than a traditional newspaper outlet. *USA Today.com*'s culture was that of a new high-tech venture, whereas the print media *USA Today* had a more conservative corporate culture. Roughly 80 percent of the online news originated from sources other than the print version.

Although *USA Today.com* successfully attracted readers and advertising dollars, Gannett starved the fledgling startup by draining resources. As a result, *USA Today.com* lost some key editorial talent because it could not provide competitive compensation packages. To solve this problem, *USA Today.com*'s general manager pushed for even greater independence and for profit-and-loss responsibility. That decision further isolated the startup from the print-news unit.

By 2000, Gannett decided it was time to integrate *USA Today.com* with the newspaper, to create synergies between the two news outfits. It no longer made sense to duplicate all editorial functions and to create content separately. Given the strained relationship and large cultural differences between the print newspaper and the online business, however, this seemed a daunting task.

The newly appointed general manager of *USA Today.com* decided to put in place an ambidextrous organizational structure: the online unit remained somewhat independent but important functions were integrated at the top through joint editorial meetings and senior management teams. To support this integration, the president of *USA Today* shifted compensation incentives for both senior teams to accomplish *joint* goals rather than to focus solely on their business unit performance. General managers of each unit implemented further integration through weekly meetings of lower-level editorial staff. The general managers of each unit, therefore, were the key integrating linchpins between formerly independent business units, allowing for synergies to emerge.[34]

ambidextrous organization, a top-level manager such as the CEO must take on the necessary coordination and integration work.

To overcome the lack of cross-departmental collaboration in a functional structure, a firm can set up *cross-functional teams.* In these temporary teams, members come from different functional areas to work together on a specific project or product, usually from start to completion. Each team member has two supervisors to report to: the team leader and the respective functional department head. As we saw in Strategy Highlight 11.2, W. L. Gore employs cross-functional teams successfully.

A second critical drawback of the functional structure is that it cannot effectively address a higher level of diversification, which often stems from further growth.[35] This is the stage at which firms find it effective to evolve and adopt a multidivisional or matrix structure, both of which we will discuss next.

Multidivisional Structure

Over time, as a firm diversifies into different product lines and geographies, it implements a multidivisional or a matrix structure (as shown in Exhibit 11.4). The multidivisional structure (or M-form) consists of several distinct strategic business units (SBUs), each with its own profit-and-loss (P&L) responsibility. Each SBU is operated more or less independently from one another, and each is led by a CEO (or equivalent general manager) who is responsible for the unit's business strategy and its day-to-day operations. The CEOs of each division in turn report to the corporate office, which is led by the company's highest-ranking executive (titles vary and include president or CEO for the entire corporation). Since most large firms are diversified to some extent across different product lines and geographies, the M-form is a widely adopted organizational structure.

For example, Zappos is an SBU under Amazon, which employs a multidivisional structure. Also, W. L. Gore uses a multidivisional structure to administer its differentiation and related diversification strategies. It has four product divisions (electronic products, industrial products, medical products, and fabrics division) with manufacturing facilities in the U.S., China, Germany, Japan, Scotland, and business activities in 30 countries across the globe.[36]

A typical M-form is shown in Exhibit 11.7 (next page). In this example, the company has four SBUs, each led by a CEO. Corporations may use SBUs to organize around different businesses and product lines or around different geographic regions. Each SBU represents a self-contained business with its *own* hierarchy and organizational structure. In Exhibit 11.7, SBU 2 is organized using a functional structure, while SBU 4 is organized using a matrix structure. The CEO of each SBU must determine which organizational structure is most appropriate to implement the SBU's business strategy.

A firm's corporate office is supported by company-wide staff functions such as human resources, finance, and corporate R&D. These staff functions support all of the company's SBUs, but are centralized at corporate headquarters to benefit from economies of scale and to avoid duplication within each SBU. Since most of the larger enterprises are publicly held stock companies, the president reports to a board of directors who represents the interests of the shareholders (indicated by the dotted line in Exhibit 11.7).

The president, with help from corporate headquarters staff, monitors the performance of each SBU and determines how to allocate resources across units.[37] Corporate headquarters adds value by functioning as an internal capital market. The goal is to be more efficient at allocating capital through its budgeting process than what could be achieved in external capital markets. This can be especially effective if the corporation overall can access capital at a lower cost than competitors due to a favorable (AAA) debt rating. Corporate

multidivisional structure (M-form) Organizational structure that consists of several distinct strategic business units (SBUs), each with its own profit-and-loss (P&L) responsibility.

EXHIBIT 11.7

Typical Multidivisional (M-Form) Structure (Note SBU 2 uses a functional structure and SBU 4 uses a matrix structure)

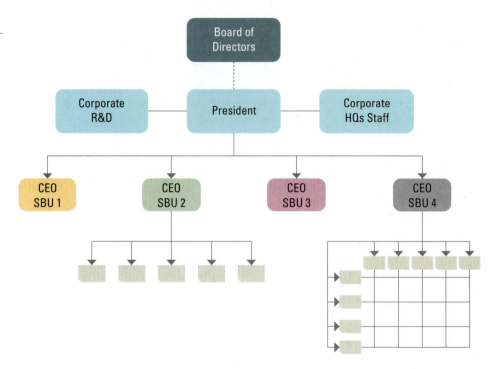

headquarters can also add value through restructuring the company's portfolio of SBUs by selling low-performing businesses and adding promising businesses through acquisitions.

General Electric (GE), featured in ChapterCase 8, has five divisions organized around different businesses. Given that GE follows an unrelated diversification strategy, it makes sense to separate its different business activities; light bulbs, *NBC Dateline,* jet engines, electrocardiograms, and nuclear reactors have little in common. Moreover, GE has sold several low-performing businesses in mature industries and acquired new businesses in promising industries such as health care and energy.

USE WITH VARIOUS CORPORATE STRATEGIES. To achieve an optimal match between strategy and structure, different *corporate-level* strategies require different organizational structures. In Chapter 8, we identified four types of corporate diversification (see Exhibit 8.7): single business, dominant business, related diversification, and unrelated diversification. Each is defined by the percentage of revenues obtained from the firm's primary activity. Firms that follow a single-business or dominant-business strategy at the corporate level gain at least 70 percent of their revenues from their primary activity; they generally employ a functional structure. For firms that pursue either related or unrelated diversification, the M-form is the preferred organizational structure. Exhibit 11.8 matches different corporate-level strategies and their corresponding organizational structures.

Managers using the M-form organizational structure to support a *related-diversification* strategy should ideally concentrate decision making at the top of the organization. Doing so allows a high level of integration. It also enables corporate headquarters to help leverage and transfer across different SBUs core competencies that form the basis for a related diversification. *Co-opetition* among the SBUs is both inevitable and necessary. They compete with one another for resources such as capital and managerial talent, but they also need to cooperate to share competencies.

Corporate-Level Strategy	Structure
Single business	Functional structure
Dominant business	Functional structure
Related diversification	Cooperative multidivisional (M-form)
	• Centralized decision making
	• High level of integration at corporate headquarters
	• Co-opetition among SBUs
	○ Competition for resources
	○ Cooperation in competency sharing
Unrelated diversification	Competitive multidivisional (M-form)
	• Decentralized decision making
	• Low level of integration at corporate headquarters
	• Competition among SBUs for resources

EXHIBIT 11.8

Matching Corporate-Level Strategy and Structure

In contrast, managers using the M-form structures to support an *unrelated-diversification* strategy should decentralize decision making. Doing so allows general managers to respond to specific circumstances, and leads to a low level of integration at corporate headquarters. Since each SBU is evaluated as a standalone profit-and-loss center, SBUs end up in *competition* with each other. A high-performing SBU might be rewarded with greater capital budgets and strategic freedoms; low-performing businesses might be spun off. As explained in Chapter 8, the BCG growth-share matrix helps corporate executives when making these types of decisions.

Matrix Structure

To reap the benefits of both the M-form and the functional structure, many firms employ a mix of these two organizational forms, called a **matrix structure.** Exhibit 11.9 (next page) shows an example. In it, the firm is organized according to SBUs (along a horizontal axis, like in the M-form), but also has a second dimension of organizational structure (along a vertical axis). In this case, the second dimension consists of different geographic areas, each of which generally would house a full set of functional activities. The idea behind the matrix structure is to combine the benefits of the M-form (domain expertise, economies of scale, and the efficient processing of information), with those of the functional structure (responsiveness and decentralized focus).

The horizontal and vertical reporting lines between SBUs and geographic areas intersect, creating nodes in the matrix. Exhibit 11.9 highlights one employee, represented by the purple node. This employee works (in a group with other employees) in SBU 2 (the company's health care unit) for the Europe division in France. Therefore, this employee has two bosses—the CEO of the health care SBU and the general manager (GM) for the Europe division. Both supervisors in turn report to corporate headquarters, which is led by the president of the corporation (indicated in Exhibit 11.9 by the reporting lines from the SBUs and geographic units to the president).

The specific organizational configuration depicted in Exhibit 11.9 is a *global matrix structure.* Firms tend to use it to pursue a *transnational strategy,* in which the firm combines the benefits of a localization strategy (high local responsiveness) with those of a global standardization strategy (lowest cost position attainable). In a global matrix structure, the

matrix structure
Organizational structure that combines the functional structure with the M-form.

EXHIBIT 11.9

Typical Matrix
Structure with
Geographic and SBU
Divisions

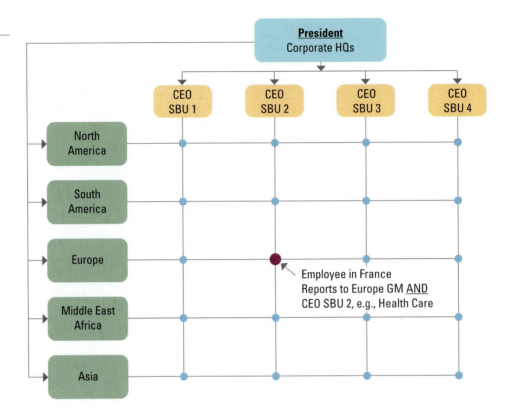

geographic divisions are charged with local responsiveness and learning. At the same time, each SBU is charged with driving down costs through economies of scale and other efficiencies. A global matrix structure also allows the firm to feed local learning back to different SBUs and thus to diffuse it throughout the organization.

The matrix structure is quite versatile, because managers can assign different groupings along the vertical and horizontal axes. A common form of the matrix structure uses different projects or products on the vertical axis, and different functional areas on the horizontal axis. In that traditional matrix structure, *cross-functional* teams work together on different projects. In contrast to the cross-functional teams discussed earlier in the W. L. Gore example, the teams in a matrix structure tend to be more permanent rather than project-based.

Though it is appealing in theory, the matrix structure does have shortcomings. It is usually difficult to implement: Implementing two layers of organizational structure creates significant organizational complexity and increases administrative costs. Also, reporting structures in a matrix are often not clear. In particular, employees can have trouble reconciling goals presented by their two (or more) supervisors. Less-clear reporting structures can undermine accountability (by creating multiple principal–agent relationships) and can thus make performance appraisals more difficult. Adding a layer of hierarchy can also slow decision making and increase bureaucratic costs.

Given the advances in computer-mediated collaboration tools, some firms have replaced the more rigid matrix structure with a *network structure*. A network structure allows the firm to connect centers of excellence whatever their global location (similar to Exhibit 10.2).[38] The firm thus benefits from *communities of practice,* which store important organizational learning and expertise. To avoid undue complexity, however, these network

Global Strategy	Structure
International	Functional
Localization (Multidomestic)	Multidivisional • Geographic areas • Decentralized decision making
Global standardization	Multidivisional • Product divisions • Centralized decision making

Transnational	Global matrix
	• Balance of centralized and decentralized decision making
	• Additional layer of hierarchy to coordinate both:
	   ◦ Geographic areas
	   ◦ Product divisions

EXHIBIT 11.10

Matching Global Strategy and Structure

structures need to be supported by corporate-wide procedures and policies to streamline communication, collaboration, and allocation of resources.[39]

USE WITH VARIOUS GLOBAL STRATEGIES. We already noted that a global matrix structure fits well with a transnational strategy. To complete the strategy-structure relationships in the global context, we also need to consider the international, localization, and standardization strategies discussed in Chapter 10. Exhibit 11.10 shows how different global strategies best match with different organizational structures.

In an *international strategy,* the company leverages its home-based core competency by moving into foreign markets. An international strategy is advantageous when the company faces low pressure for both local responsiveness and cost reductions. Companies pursue an international strategy through a differentiation strategy at the business level. The best match for an international strategy is a *functional* organizational structure, which allows the company to leverage its core competency most effectively. This approach is similar to matching a business-level differentiation strategy with a functional structure (discussed in detail earlier).

When a multinational enterprise (MNE) pursues a *localization strategy,* it attempts to maximize local responsiveness, in the face of low pressures for cost reductions. An appropriate match for this type of global strategy is the *multidivisional* organizational structure. That structure would enable the MNE to set up different divisions based on geographic regions (e.g., by continent). The different geographic divisions operate more or less as standalone SBUs to maximize local responsiveness. Decision making is decentralized.

When following a *global-standardization strategy,* the MNE attempts to reap significant economies of scale as well as location economies by pursuing a global division of labor based on wherever best-of-class capabilities reside at the lowest cost. Since the product offered is more or less an undifferentiated commodity, the MNE pursues a cost-leadership strategy. The optimal organizational structure match is, again, a *multidivisional* structure. Rather than focusing on geographic differences (as in the localization strategy), the focus is on driving down costs due to consolidation of activities across different geographic areas.

ORGANIZATIONAL CULTURE: VALUES, NORMS, AND ARTIFACTS

>> LO 11-6
Describe the elements of organizational culture, and explain where organizational cultures can come from and how they can be changed.

Organizational culture is the second key building block when designing organizations for competitive advantage. Just as people have distinct personalities, so too do organizations have unique cultures that capture "how things get done around here." **Organizational culture** describes the collectively shared values and norms of an organization's members.[40] *Values* define what is considered important. (See Zappos's 10 core values in Exhibit 11.1 as an example.) *Norms* define appropriate employee attitudes and behaviors. [41]

Employees learn about an organization's culture through *socialization,* a process whereby employees internalize an organization's values and norms through immersion in its day-to-day operations.[42] Successful socialization, in turn, allows employees to function productively and to take on specific roles within the organization. *Strong cultures* emerge when the company's core values are widely shared among the firm's employees and when the norms have been internalized.

Think back to the Zappos ChapterCase. The company's strong culture is a strategically relevant asset that allows it to gain and sustain a competitive advantage. In contrast, although GM also had a strong culture, it was a highly bureaucratic one in which people who showed "too much" initiative were not promoted. That strong culture at GM was a strategic *liability* because it increased organizational inertia.[43]

Although more or less invisible, corporate culture finds its expression in *artifacts.* Artifacts include elements like the design and layout of physical space (e.g., cubicles or private offices); symbols (e.g., the type of clothing worn by employees); vocabulary; what stories are told (see the Zappos example that follows); what events are celebrated and highlighted; and how they are celebrated (e.g., a formal dinner versus a company BBQ when the firm reaches its sales target).

Exhibit 11.11 depicts the elements of organizational culture—values, norms, and artifacts—in concentric circles. The most important, and least visible, one—values—is in the center. As we move outward in the figure, from values to norms to artifacts, culture becomes more observable. Understanding what organizational culture is, and how it is created, maintained, and changed, can help you be a more effective manager. A unique culture that is strategically relevant can also be the basis of a firm's competitive advantage (as discussed in the *Gaining & Sustaining Competitive Advantage* section that follows).

EXHIBIT 11.11

The Elements of Organizational Culture: Values, Norms, and Artifacts

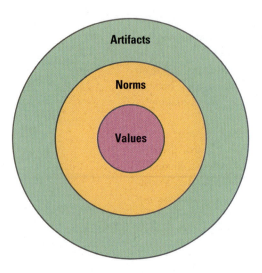

Where Do Organizational Cultures Come From?

Often, company founders define and shape an organization's culture, which can persist for many decades after their departure. This phenomenon is called **founder imprinting.**[44] Firm founders set the initial strategy, structure, and culture of an organization by transforming their vision into reality. Famous founders who have left strong imprints on their organizations include Steve Jobs (Apple), Walt Disney (Disney), Michael Dell (Dell), Sergei Brin and Larry Page (Google), Oprah Winfrey (Harpo Productions and *OWN,* the Oprah Winfrey Network), Bill Gates (Microsoft), Larry Ellison (Oracle), Ralph Lauren (Polo Ralph Lauren), Martha Stewart (Martha Stewart Living Omnimedia), and Herb Kelleher (Southwest Airlines).

Walmart's founder Sam Walton personified the retailer's cost-leadership strategy. At one time the richest man in America, Sam Walton drove a beat-up Ford pickup truck, got $5 haircuts, went camping for vacations, and lived in a modest ranch home in Bentonville, Arkansas.[45] Home to one of the largest companies on the planet, the company's Arkansas headquarters in Bentonville was described by Thomas Friedman in his book *The World Is Flat* as follows: "[Walmart's corporate headquarters] are crammed into a reconfigured warehouse . . . a large building made of corrugated metal, I figured it was the maintenance shed."[46]

The culture that founders initially imprint is reinforced by their strong preference to recruit, retain, and promote employees who subscribe to the same values. In turn, more people with similar values are attracted to that organization.[47] As the values and norms held by the employees become more similar, the firm's corporate culture becomes stronger and more distinct.

Besides founder imprinting, however, a firm's culture can also flow from its values, especially if they are linked to the company's reward system. For example, Zappos established its unique organizational culture through explicitly stated values that are connected to its reward system (see Exhibit 11.1). To recruit people that fit with the company's values, Tony Hsieh has all new-hires go through a four-week training program. It covers such topics as company history, culture, and vision, as well as customer service.[48] New-hires also spend two weeks on the phone as customer-service reps. What's novel about Zappos's approach is that at the end of the first week, the company offers any new hire $2,000 to quit (plus pay for the time already worked). This offer stands until the end of the fourth week, when the training program is completed. Individuals who choose to stay on despite the enticing offer tend to fit well with and strengthen Zappos's distinct culture.[49]

How Does Organizational Culture Change?

An organization's culture can be one of its strongest assets, but also its greatest liability. An organization's culture can turn from a core competency into a *core rigidity* if it no longer has a good fit with the external environment.[50] For example, GM's bureaucratic culture, combined with its innovative M-form structure, was once hailed as the key to superior efficiency and management.[51] However, that culture became a liability when the external environment changed following the oil-price shocks in the 1970s and the entry of Japanese carmakers into the U.S.[52] As mentioned earlier, GM's strong culture led to organizational inertia. This resulted in a failure to adapt to changing customer preferences for more fuel-efficient cars, and prevented higher quality and more innovative designs. GM lost customers to foreign competitors, who offered these things. In such times, corporate culture may need to be changed to address a breakdown in the culture-environment relationship.

The primary avenues of culture change (often combined with changes in strategy and structure) include *bringing in new leadership* and *mergers and acquisitions* (*M&As*). Leaders and top executives shape corporate culture in the way they set up an organization's structure, resource-allocation process, and reward system. As discussed in Strategy Highlight 11.1, Carol Bartz was brought in as the new Yahoo CEO to implement cultural and structural changes, in order to make the Internet services company competitive again. Strategy Highlight 11.4 (next page) describes former-CEO Carly Fiorina's attempt to change HP's organizational culture through M&A.

Organizational Culture and Competitive Advantage

Can organizational culture be the basis of a firm's (sustainable) competitive advantage? For this to occur, according to the resource-based view of the firm, the resource—in this case, organizational culture—must be valuable, rare, difficult to imitate, and the firm must

organizational culture
The collectively shared values and norms of an organization's members; a key building block of organizational design.

founder imprinting
A process by which the founder defines and shapes an organization's culture, which can persist for decades after his or her departure.

GAINING & SUSTAINING COMPETITIVE ADVANTAGE

Carly Fiorina at HP: Cultural Change via Shock Therapy

In 1999, Carly Fiorina was appointed CEO of Hewlett-Packard (HP), one of the leading U.S. technology companies. Ms. Fiorina was the first outsider to become CEO of the venerable technology company, and the first woman to lead a Fortune 20 company. The board hoped Ms. Fiorina would change HP's culture to make it more competitive, particularly in the booming Internet economy in which competitors like Cisco, Sun Microsystems, and IBM were riding high.[53]

In 2002, Ms. Fiorina engineered HP's acquisition of Compaq, for $25 billion, to pursue "high-tech at low-cost" (as discussed in Chapter 4). However, this was not the only motivation for the mega merger. An equally important but unstated reason was that Ms. Fiorina needed a shock to HP's system: She was convinced that HP had grown complacent and needed to "root out the rot that insiders tolerate or fail even to see."[54] The merger with Compaq gave Ms. Fiorina the opportunity to make some tough but necessary structural changes, including laying off some 25 percent of the work force at a place where employees were accustomed to lifetime employment. She also redesigned the organizational structure to make HP more nimble and put in a more merit-based rather than seniority-based reward system.[55]

While many believe that Carly Fiorina failed in creating the change that HP needed (the board let her go in 2005), others believe that her successor—Mark Hurd—benefited from the tough changes that Ms. Fiorina implemented.[56] (In 2010, Leo Apotheker replaced Mark Hurd in the wake of an ethics scandal, which we will discuss in the next chapter.)

be organized to capture the value created. That is, the VRIO principles must hold (see Chapter 4).[57]

Let's look at two examples of how culture affects employee behavior and ultimately firm performance:

- If you have flown with Southwest Airlines (SWA), you may have noticed that things are done a little differently there. Some argue that SWA's business strategy—being a cost leader in point-to-point air travel—is fairly simple, and that SWA's competitive advantage actually comes from its unique culture.[58] Friendly and highly energized employees work across functional and hierarchical levels. Even Southwest's pilots pitch in when needed. As a result, SWA's turn time between flights is only 15 minutes, whereas competitors frequently take two to three times as long.

- Zappos's number-one core value is to "deliver WOW through service." CEO Tony Hsieh shares the following story to illustrate this core value in action: "I was in Santa Monica, California, a few years ago at a Skechers sales conference. . . . [In the early hours of the morning], a small group of us headed up to someone's hotel room to order some food. My friend from Skechers tried to order a pepperoni pizza from the room-service menu, but was disappointed to learn that the hotel we were staying at did not deliver hot food after 11:00 p.m. We had missed the deadline by several hours. . . . A few of us cajoled her into calling Zappos to try to order a pizza. She took us up on our dare, turned on the speakerphone, and explained to the (very) patient Zappos rep that she was staying in a Santa Monica hotel and really craving a pepperoni pizza, that room service was no longer delivering hot food, and that she wanted to know if there was anything Zappos could do to help. The Zappos rep was initially a bit confused by the request, but she quickly recovered and put us on hold. She returned two minutes later, listing the five closest places in the Santo Monica area that were still open and delivering pizzas at that time."[59]

In the SWA example, the company's unique culture helps it keep costs low by turning around its planes faster, thus keeping them flying longer hours (among many other activities that lower SWA's cost structure).[60] In the Zappos example, providing a "wow" customer experience by "going the extra mile" didn't save Zappos money, but in the long run superior experience does increase the company's perceived value, and thereby its economic value creation. Indeed, Tony Hsieh makes it a point to conclude the story with the following statement: "As for my friend from Skechers? After that phone call, she's now a customer for life."[61]

Let's consider how an organization's culture can have a strong influence on employee behavior.[62] First, a positive culture motivates and energizes employees by appealing to their higher ideals. Internalizing the firm's values and norms, employees feel that they are part of a larger, meaningful community attempting to accomplish important things. When employees are intrinsically motivated this way, the firm can rely on fewer levels of hierarchy; thus close monitoring and supervision are less needed. Moreover, motivating through inspiring values allows the firms to tap employees' emotions so that they use both their heads and their hearts when making business decisions. Strong organizational cultures that are strategically relevant, therefore, align employees' behavior more fully with the organization's strategic goals. In doing so, they better coordinate work efforts, and they make cooperation more effective. They also strengthen employee commitment, engagement, and effort. Effective alignment in turn allows the organization to develop and refine its core competencies, which can form the basis for competitive advantage.

Applying the VRIO principles to the SWA and Zappos examples, we see that both cultures are valuable (lowering costs for SWA and increasing perceived value created for Zappos), rare (not many other firms, if any, have an identical culture), non-imitable (despite attempts by competitors), and organized to capture some part of the incremental economic value they create due to their unique cultures. It appears that at both SWA and Zappos, a unique organizational culture can in fact provide the basis for a (sustained) competitive advantage. These cultures, of course, need to be in sync with and in support of the respective business strategies pursued (cost leadership for SWA and differentiation for Zappos). Moreover, as the firms grow and external economic environments change, these cultures must be flexible enough to adapt.

Once it becomes clear that a firm's culture is a source of competitive advantage, some competitors will attempt to imitate that culture. Therefore, only a culture that cannot be easily copied can provide a competitive advantage. However, it can be difficult, at best, to imitate the cultures of successful firms, for two reasons: *causal ambiguity* and *social complexity*. While one can observe that a firm has a unique culture, the causal relationships among values, norms, artifacts, and the firm's performance may be hard to establish, even for people who work within the organization. For example, employees may become aware of the effect culture has on performance only after significant organizational changes occur. Moreover, organizational culture is socially complex. It encompasses not only interactions among employees across layers of hierarchy, but also the firm's outside relationships with its customers and suppliers.[63] Such a wide range of factors is difficult for any competing firm to imitate.

It is best to develop a strong and strategically relevant culture in the first few years of a firm's existence. It has been documented that the initial structure, culture, and control mechanisms set up in a new firm can be a significant predictor of later success.[64] In other empirical research, founder CEOs had a stronger positive imprinting effect than non-founder CEOs.[65] This stronger imprinting effect, in turn, resulted in higher performance of firms led by founder CEOs. In addition, consider that the vehicles of cultural change—changing leadership and growing through M&As—do not have a stellar record of success.[66] Indeed, researchers estimate that only about 20 percent of organizational change attempts are successful.[67] Thus, it is even more important to get the culture right from the beginning and then adapt it as the business evolves.

Combining theory and empirical evidence, we can see that organizational culture can help a firm gain and sustain competitive advantage *if* the culture makes a positive contribution to the firm's economic value creation and obeys the other VRIO principles. Organizational culture is an especially effective lever for new ventures due to its malleability. Firm founders, early-stage CEOs, and venture capitalists, therefore, should be proactive in attempting to create a culture that leads to or at least supports a firm's competitive advantage. 🔍

STRATEGIC CONTROL AND REWARD SYSTEMS

>> LO 11-7
Compare and contrast different strategic control and reward systems.

Strategic control and reward systems are the third and final key building block when designing organizations for competitive advantage. Strategic control and reward systems are internal-governance mechanisms put in place to align the incentives of principals (shareholders) and agents (employees). These systems allow managers to specify goals, measure progress, and provide performance feedback. In Chapter 5, we discussed how firms can use the balanced-scorecard framework as a strategic control system. Here we discuss additional control and reward systems: organizational culture, input controls, and output controls.

As discussed earlier, *organizational culture* can be a powerful motivator. It also can be an effective control system. Norms, informal and tacit in nature, act as a social control mechanism. Steelmaker Nucor, for example, achieves organizational control through an employee's peer group: Each group member's compensation, including the foreman's, depends on the group's *overall productivity.* Peer control, therefore, exerts a powerful force on employee conformity and performance.[68] Besides soliciting expected behavior, social norms also apply *sanctions* such as sarcasm, ostracism, and ridicule (and sometimes even physical force) in the face of undesirable behavior.[69] Values and norms also provide control by helping employees address unpredictable and irregular situations and problems (common in service businesses). In contrast, rules and procedures (e.g., codified in an employee handbook) can address only circumstances that can be predicted.

Input Controls

Input controls seek to define and direct employee behavior through a set of explicit and codified rules and standard operating procedures. Firms use input controls when the goal is to define the ways and means to reach a strategic goal and to ensure a predictable outcome. They are called input controls because management designs these mechanisms so they are considered *before* employees make any business decisions; thus, they are an input into the value-creation activities.

The use of *budgets* is key to input controls. Managers set budgets before employees define and undertake the actual business activities. For example, managers decide how much money to allocate to a certain R&D project before the project begins. In diversified companies using the M-form, corporate headquarters determines the budgets for each division. Public institutions, like some universities, also operate on budgets that must be balanced each year. Their funding often depends to a large extent on state appropriations and thus fluctuates depending on the economic cycle. During recessions, budgets tend to be cut, and they expand during boom periods.

Standard operating procedures, or policies and rules, are also a frequently used mechanism when relying on input controls. In our discussion on formalization, we described how McDonald's relies on detailed operating procedures to ensure consistent quality and service worldwide. The goal is to specify the conversion process from beginning to end in great detail to guarantee standardization and minimize deviation. This is important when a company operates in different geographies and with different human capital throughout the globe but needs to deliver a standardized product or service.

Output Controls

Output controls seek to guide employee behavior by defining expected results (outputs), but leave the means to those results open to individual employees, groups, or SBUs. Firms frequently tie employee compensation and rewards to predetermined goals, such as a specific sales target or return on invested capital. When factors internal to the firm determine the relationship between effort and expected performance, outcome controls are especially effective. At the corporate level, outcome controls discourage collaboration among different strategic business units. They are therefore best applied when a firm focuses on a single line of business or pursues unrelated diversification.

These days, more and more work requires creativity and innovation, especially in highly developed economies.[70] As a consequence, so-called *results-only-work-environments* (*ROWEs*) have attracted significant attention. ROWEs are output controls that attempt to tap intrinsic (rather than extrinsic) employee motivation, which is driven by the employee's interest in and the meaning of the work itself. In contrast, extrinsic motivation is driven by external factors such as awards and higher compensation or punishments such as demotion and lay-off (the *carrot-and-stick approach*). According to a recent synthesis of the strategic human resources literature, intrinsic motivation in a task is highest when an employee has autonomy (about what to do), mastery (how to do it), and purpose (why to do it).[71]

Daniel Pink's book on motivation (*Drive: The Surprising Truth About What Motivates Us*) discusses the limits of the carrot-and-stick approach versus the motivational impact of autonomy.

Today, 3M is best known for its adhesives and other consumer and industrial products.[72] But its full name reflects its origins: 3M stands for Minnesota Mining and Manufacturing Company. Over time, 3M has relied on the ROWE framework and has morphed into a highly science-driven innovation company. At 3M, employees are encouraged to spend 15 percent of their time on projects of their *own choosing*. If any of these projects look promising, 3M provides financing through an internal venture-capital fund and other resources to further develop their commercial potential. In fact, several of 3M's flagship products, including Post-It Notes and Scotch Tape, were the results of serendipity (see Chapter 2). To foster continued innovation, moreover, 3M requires each of its divisions to derive at least 30 percent of their revenues from products introduced in the past four years.

This concludes our discussion of organizational design. As we have seen, formulating an effective strategy is a necessary but not sufficient condition for gaining and sustaining competitive advantage; strategy *execution* is at least as important for success. Successful strategy implementation requires managers to design and shape structure, culture, and control mechanisms. In doing so, they execute a firm's strategy as they put its accompanying business model into action. Strategy formulation and strategy implementation, therefore, are iterative and interdependent activities. In existing firms, strategy implementation necessitates organizational change. Managing effective organizational change requires strategic leadership that is ethical and effectively governed. We now move on to our concluding chapter, where we study corporate governance, business ethics, and strategic leadership.

---

strategic control and reward systems
A key building block of organizational design; internal-governance mechanisms put in place to align the incentives of principals (shareholders) and agents (employees).

input controls Mechanisms in a strategic control and reward system that seek to define and direct employee behavior through a set of explicit and codified rules and standard operating procedures, considered prior to the value-creating activities.

output controls Mechanisms in a strategic control and reward system that seek to guide employee behavior by defining expected results (outputs), but leave the means to those results open to individual employees, groups, or SBUs.

CHAPTERCASE 11 | *Consider This . . .*

ZAPPOS WANTS TO "deliver WOW through service." We saw an example of this culture in the story of the Zappos customer service rep who provided contacts for local pizza delivery to an out-of-town guest. Though it is a memorable story, providing the pizza 411-service did not involve significant cost to the employee or the firm for delivering "WOW through service." However, at midnight on Friday, May 21, 2010, Zappos created a problem that required a significant financial cost to deliver that "WOW." Due to a programming error in its pricing engine, Zappos accidentally capped the sales price at $49.95 for all products sold on its sister site (www.6pm.com). The mistake was not discovered until 6 a.m. Zappos pulled down the site to correct the pricing problem. Once fixed, there remained a question of what to do about the products sold with the erroneous prices.

Zappos's terms and conditions clearly state that the firm is under no obligation to fulfill orders placed due to pricing mistakes. However, Zappos decided to honor every sale made in the time frame between midnight and 6 a.m.—resulting in a loss of over $1.6 million.

That's putting your money where your "WOW" is![73]

Amazon, which owns Zappos, had its own pricing mistake just two months prior to the Zappos incident. Best Buy and Dell have also both had online pricing errors.[74] None of these firms handled the situation as smoothly as Zappos.

1. What elements of an organic organization are apparent from the chapter material on Zappos? (Refer to Exhibit 11.3.)

2. How does the Zappos business strategy match its organizational structure?

3. Which strategic control and reward system discussed in the chapter would be most appropriate for Zappos?

4. Do you think Zappos's decision to honor every sale, despite its explicit business terms and conditions that would allow it not to do so, was a sound one? Why or why not?

Take-Away Concepts

In this chapter, we studied the three key levers that managers have at their disposal when designing their firms for competitive advantage—structure, culture, and control—as summarized by the following learning objectives and related take-away concepts.

LO 11-1 Define organizational design and list its three components.

>> Organizational design is the process of creating, implementing, monitoring, and modifying the structure, processes, and procedures of an organization.

>> The key components of organizational design are structure, culture, and control.

>> The goal is to design an organization that allows managers to effectively translate their chosen strategy into a realized one.

LO 11-2 Explain how organizational inertia can lead established firms to failure.

>> Organizational inertia can lead to the failure of established firms when a tightly coupled system of strategy and structure experiences internal or external shifts.

>> Firm failure happens through a dynamic, four-step process (see Exhibit 11.2).

LO 11-3 Define organizational structure and describe its four elements.

>> An organizational structure determines how firms orchestrate employees' work efforts and distribute resources. It defines how firms divide and integrate tasks, delineates the reporting relationships up and down the hierarchy, defines formal communication channels, and prescribes how employees coordinate work efforts.

>> The four building blocks of an organizational structure are specialization, formalization, centralization, and hierarchy (see Exhibit 11.3).

LO 11-4 Compare and contrast mechanistic versus organic organizations.

>> Organic organizations are characterized by a low degree of specialization and formalization, a flat organizational structure, and decentralized decision making.

>> Mechanistic organizations are described by a high degree of specialization and formalization, and a tall hierarchy that relies on centralized decision making.

>> The comparative effectiveness of mechanistic versus organic organizational forms depends on the context.

LO 11-5 Describe different organizational structures and match them with appropriate strategies.

>> To gain and sustain competitive advantage, not only must structure follow strategy, but also the chosen organizational form must match the firm's business strategy.

>> The strategy-structure relationship is dynamic, changing in a predictable pattern—from simple to functional structure, then to multidivisional (M-form) and matrix structure—as firms grow in size and complexity.

>> In a simple structure, the founder tends to make all the important strategic decisions as well as run the day-to-day operations.

>> A functional structure groups employees into distinct functional areas based on domain expertise. Its different variations are matched with different business strategies: cost-leadership, differentiation, and integration (see Exhibit 11.6).

>> The multidivisional (M-form) structure consists of several distinct SBUs, each with its own profit-and-loss responsibility. Each SBU operates more or less independently from one another, led by a CEO responsible for the business strategy of the unit and its day-to-day operations (see Exhibit 11.7).

>> The matrix structure is a mixture of two organizational forms: the M-form and the functional structure (see Exhibit 11.9).

>> Exhibits 11.8 and 11.10 show how best to match different corporate and global strategies with respective organizational structures.

LO 11-6 Describe the elements of organizational culture, and explain where organizational cultures can come from and how they can be changed.

>> Organizational culture describes the collectively shared values and norms of its members.

>> Values define what is considered important, and norms define appropriate employee attitudes and behaviors.

>> Corporate culture finds its expression in artifacts, which are observable expressions of an organization's culture.

LO 11-7 Compare and contrast different strategic control and reward systems.

>> Strategic control and reward systems are internal governance mechanisms put in place to align the incentives of principals (shareholders) and agents (employees).

>> Strategic control and reward systems allow managers to specify goals, measure progress, and provide performance feedback.

>> Besides the balanced-scorecard framework, managers can use organizational culture, input controls, and output controls as part of the firm's strategic control and reward systems.

>> Input controls define and direct employee behavior through explicit and codified rules and standard operating procedures.

>> Output controls guide employee behavior by defining expected results, but leave the means to those results open to individual employees, groups, or SBUs.

Key Terms

Centralization *(p. 306)*

Formalization *(p. 305)*

Founder imprinting *(p. 318)*

Functional structure *(p. 309)*

Hierarchy *(p. 307)*

Input controls *(p. 322)*

Matrix structure *(p. 315)*

Mechanistic organization *(p. 308)*

Multidivisional structure (M-form) *(p. 313)*

Organic organization *(p. 307)*

Organizational culture *(p. 318)*

Organizational design *(p. 303)*

Organizational structure *(p. 304)*

Output controls *(p. 322)*

Simple structure *(p. 309)*

Span of control *(p. 307)*

Specialization *(p. 304)*

Strategic control and reward
systems *(p. 322)*

Strategy implementation
(p. 302)

Discussion Questions

1. Why is it important for an organization to have alignment between its strategy and organizational structure?

2. The chapter notes that changing organizational culture is daunting and provides examples of Yahoo, GM, and HP. What other firms have attempted to change their culture in recent years? What techniques did they use for the transition? Was it successful?

3. Strategy Highlight 11.2 discusses the informal organizational structure of W. L. Gore & Associates. Go to the firm's website (www.gore .com) and review the product scope of the firm.

   a. What commonalities across the products would likely be enhanced by flexible cross-functional teams?

   b. What would be your expectations of the type of norms found at W. L. Gore?

Ethical/Social Issues

1. As noted in Chapter 5, many public firms are under intense pressure for short-term (such as quarterly) financial improvements. How might such pressure, in combination with output controls, lead to possible unethical behaviors?

2. Strong company cultures can have many benefits, such as those described in the Zappos example.

However, sometimes a strong organizational culture is less positive. Name some examples of organizational culture leading to business failure, criminal behavior, or civil legal actions.

3. What makes some strong cultures helpful to gaining and sustaining a competitive advantage, while other strong cultures are a liability to achieving that goal?

Small Group Exercises

SMALL GROUP EXERCISE 1

Your classmates are a group of friends who have decided to open a small retail shop. The team is torn between two storefront ideas. The first idea is to open a high-end antique store selling household items used for decorations in upscale homes. Members of the team have found a location in a heavily pedestrian area near a local coffee shop. The store would have many items authenticated by a team member's uncle, who is a certified appraiser.

In discussing the plan, however, two group members suggest shifting to a drop-off store for online auctions such as eBay. In this business model, customers drop off items they want to sell, and the retail store

does all the logistics involved—listing and selling the items on eBay, and then shipping them to buyers—for a percentage of the sales price. They suggest that a quick way to get started is to become a franchisee for a group such as "I Sold It" (www.877isoldit.com).

1. What is the business strategy for each store concept?

2. How would the organizational structure be different for the concepts?

3. What would likely be cultural differences in the two store concepts?

4. How would the control and reward systems be different?

SMALL GROUP EXERCISE 2 (ETHICAL/SOCIAL ISSUES)

Employee morale can directly affect productivity in the workplace. A poll taken in January 2010 found that 50 percent of respondents (in small- and medium-sized firms) indicated employee morale was down.[75] Assume your group is brought in to a business unit, and your analysis shows a significant excess headcount in the accounting and purchasing departments. Your team is now responsible for developing a plan to lay off 25 percent of the employees in those departments. You have six months to identify whom to lay off to reduce the headcount. (If you have no personal experience with work-force reductions, use an Internet search engine and look up "successful layoffs" for some guidance.)

1. How can you downsize the departments without hurting the morale of the remaining workers?

2. What steps do you take to treat with dignity the employees forced to leave?

Strategy Term Project

MODULE 11: ORGANIZATIONAL IMPLEMENTATION PROCESSES[76]

In this module, you will study the organizational implementation processes of your selected firm. You will again rely on annual reports, news articles, and press releases for information to analyze and formulate your answers. You will identify a major strategic change the firm should seriously consider implementing and then follow a six-step process to study the implementation impacts.

Implementation is a critical step in putting a planned action into effect. It often introduces change into the organization and can be met with strong resistance. The six stages outlined in Exhibit 11.12 can help

EXHIBIT 11.12

Implementation Framework

Implementation Stage	Key Questions to Ask in This Stage
Stage 1 People, skills, and organizational structure	• When must the strategy/strategic initiative be implemented? (How flexible is that date?) • Who is going to do it? What human skills are needed? • Do affected employees understand their roles? • Will the organization need to hire or lay off people? If so, how should we go about it? • How should the firm be organized? What structure should be implemented? Why and how?
Stage 2 Organizational culture	• What culture in the organization is required for the implementation to be successful? • If the current culture differs from the culture needed for the success of the strategy implementation, how should the firm go about changing its culture?
Stage 3 Reward system	• Is a reward structure in place to accomplish the task? • If not, what type of reward structure needs to be introduced to ensure successful strategy implementation?
Stage 4 Resource requirements	• What resources (financial and otherwise) are needed? • Are they in place? • If not, how can the firm obtain the required resources?
Stage 5 Supporting activities	• How is the implementation to be supported? • What policies, procedures, and IT support are needed? • Does the firm need external help (e.g., consulting services)? If so, what kind of services would the firm need, and why?
Stage 6 Strategic leadership	• What types of strategic leaders are required to make the change happen? • Does the firm have them in-house? • Should the firm hire some strategic leaders from outside? • How should the firm train its managers to create a pipeline of strategic leaders?

leaders and organizations determine *how* to implement a particular plan. These questions provide a framework for the strategic change. You may be able to find a prior successful strategic change the firm undertook and use this prior implementation as a guide for your suggested change.

As you progress through the six stages, reflect on what you have learned about your firm in the prior modules. In some cases, you will need to make educated guesses for the answer since you are looking at implementation from outside the organization. However, over the ten modules you have completed, you have already learned much about the firm.

Answer the following questions for your selected organization.

1. From your knowledge of the firm, identify a major strategic change the firm should seriously consider. Briefly describe what the goal of the initiative is for the organization.

2. Work your way through the six stages in Exhibit 11.12, answering as many of the questions as you can for the proposed strategic change. As you develop the project plans with specifics for each of the stages, the plan should provide flexibility, allowing for unexpected contingencies to emerge.

*my*Strategy

FOR WHAT TYPE OF ORGANIZATION ARE *YOU* BEST-SUITED?

A s noted in the chapter, firms can have very distinctive cultures. Recall that Zappos has a standing offer to pay any new hire $2,000 to quit the company during the first month. Zappos makes this offer to help ensure that those who stay with the company are comfortable in its "create fun and a little weirdness" environment.

You may have taken a personality test such as Myers-Briggs or The Big Five. These tests may be useful in gauging compatibility of career and personality types. They are often available for both graduate and undergraduate students at university career-placement centers. In considering the following questions, think about your next job and your longer-term career plans.

1. Review Exhibit 11.3 and circle the organizational characteristics you find appealing. Cross out those factors you think you would not like. Do you find a trend toward either the mechanistic or organic organization?

2. Have you been in school or work situations in which your values did not align with those of your peers or colleagues? How did you handle the situation? Are there certain values or norms important enough for you to consider as you look for a new job?

3. As you consider your career after graduation, which control and rewards system discussed in the concluding section of the chapter would you find most motivating? Is this different from the controls used at some jobs you have had in the past?

Endnotes

1. Hsieh, T. (2010), *Delivering Happiness: A Path to Profits, Passion, and Purpose* (New York: Business Plus), p. 130.

2. Ibid., p. 145.

3. Ibid., p. 177.

4. Ibid., pp. 157–160.

5. This ChapterCase is based on: Hsieh, T. (2010), *Delivering Happiness: A Path to Profits, Passion, and Purpose*.

6. Barney, J. B. (1986), "Organizational culture: Can it be a source of sustained competitive advantage?" *Academy of Management Review* 11: 656–665.

7. Bossidy, L., R. Charan, and C. Burck (2002), *Execution: The Discipline of Getting Things Done* (New York: Crown Business); and Hrebiniak, L. G. (2005), *Making Strategy Work: Leading Effective Execution and Change* (Philadelphia: Wharton School Publishing).

8. Grundy, T. (1998), "Strategy implementation and project management," *International Journal of Project Management* 16: 43–50.

9. Bossidy, L., R. Charan, and C. Burck (2002), *Execution: The Discipline of Getting Things Done;* and Herold, D. M., and D. B. Fedor (2008), *Change the Way You Lead Change: Leadership Strategies that Really Work* (Palo Alto, CA: Stanford University Press).

10. Herold, D. M., and D. B. Fedor (2008), *Change the Way You Lead Change.*

11. Chandler, A. D. (1962), *Strategy and Structure: Chapters in the History of American Industrial Enterprise* (Cambridge, MA: MIT Press), p. 14 (italics added).

12. Hall, D. J., and M. A. Saias (1980), "Strategy follows structure!" *Strategic Management Journal* 1: 149–163.

13. "Yang's exit doesn't fix Yahoo," *The Wall Street Journal,* November 19, 2008.

14. "A question of management: Carol Bartz on how Yahoo's organizational structure got in the way of innovation," *The Wall Street Journal,* June 2, 2009.

15. Ibid.

16. Hill, C.W.L., and F. T. Rothaermel (2003), "The performance of incumbent firms in the face of radical technological innovation," *Academy of Management Review* 28: 257–274.

17. I gratefully acknowledge Professor Luis Martins's input on this exhibit.

18. In his insightful book, Finkelstein (2003) identifies several key transition points that put pressure on an organization and thus increase the likelihood of subsequent failure. See Finkelstein, S. (2003), *Why Smart Executives Fail: And What You Can Learn from Their Mistakes* (New York: Portfolio).

19. Fredrickson, J. W. (1986), "The strategic decision process and organizational structure," *Academy of Management Review* 11: 280–297; Eisenhardt, K. M. (1989), "Making fast strategic decisions in high-velocity environments," *Academy of Management Journal* 32: 543–576; and Wally, S., and R. J. Baum (1994), "Strategic decision speed and firm performance," *Strategic Management Journal* 24, 1107–1129.

20. Hamel, G. (2007), *The Future of Management* (Boston, MA: Harvard Business School Press), p. 84.

21. This Strategy Highlight is based on: Hamel, G. (2007), *The Future of Management;* Collins, J. (2009), *How the Mighty Fall: And Why Some Companies Never Give In* (New York: HarperCollins); and www.gore.com.

22. *The 9/11 Report. The National Commission on Terrorist Attacks Upon the United States* (2004), http://govinfo .library.unt.edu/911/report/index.htm.

23. Child, J., and R. G. McGrath (2001), "Organization unfettered: Organizational forms in the information-intensive economy," *Academy of Management Journal* 44: 1135–1148; and Huy, Q. N. (2002), "Emotional balancing of organizational continuity and radical change: The contribution of middle managers," *Administrative Science Quarterly* 47: 31–69.

24. Theobald, N. A., and S. Nicholson-Crotty (2005), "The many faces of span of control: Organizational structure across multiple goals," *Administration and Society* 36: 648–660.

25. This section draws on: Burns, T., and G. M. Stalker (1961), *The Management of Innovation* (London: Tavistock).

26. This section draws on: Burns, T., and G. M. Stalker (1961), *The Management of Innovation;* Perry-Smith, J. E., and C. E. Shalley (2003), "The social side of creativity: A static and dynamic social network perspective," *Academy of Management Review* 28: 89–106; and Shalley, C. E., and J. E. Perry-Smith (2008), "The emergence of team creative cognition: The role of diverse outside ties, sociocognitive network centrality, and team evolution," *Strategic Entrepreneurship Journal* 2: 23–41.

27. Hagel III, J., J. S. Brown, and L. Davison (2010), *The Power of Pull: How Small Moves, Smartly Made, Can Set Big Things in Motion* (Philadelphia: Basic Books); Majchrzak, A., A. Malhotra, J. Stamps, and J. Lipnack (2004), "Can absence make a team grow stronger?" *Harvard Business Review,* May: 137–144; and Malhotra, A., A. Majchrzak, A, and B. Rosen, (2007), "Leading far-flung teams," *Academy of Management Perspectives* 21: 60–70.

28. Bryan, L. L., and C. I. Joyce (2007), "Better strategy through organizational design," *The McKinsey Quarterly* 2: 21–29.

29. Chandler, A. D. (1962), *Strategy and Structure: Chapters in the History of American Industrial Enterprise.*

30. Ibid. Also, for a more recent treatise across different levels of analysis, see Ridley, M. (2010), *The Rational Optimist: How Prosperity Evolves* (New York: HarperCollins).

31. Rothaermel, F. T., and M. T. Alexandre (2009), "Ambidexterity in technology sourcing: The moderating role of absorptive capacity," *Organization Science* 20: 759–780.

32. Levinthal, D. A., and J. G. March (1993), "The myopia of learning," *Strategic Management Journal* 14: 95–112; and March, J. G. (1991), "Exploration and exploitation in organizational learning," *Organization Science* 2: 319–340.

33. Tushman, M., W. K. Smith, R. C. Wood, and G. Westerman (2010), "Organizational designs and innovation streams," *Industrial and Corporate Change* 19: 1331–1366.

34. Ibid.

35. Chandler, A. D. (1962), *Strategy and Structure: Chapters in the History of American Industrial Enterprise.*

36. www.gore.com.

37. Williamson, O. E. (1975), *Markets and Hierarchies* (Free Press: New York); and Williamson, O. E. (1985), *The Economic Institutions of Capitalism* (Free Press: New York).

38. Bryan, L. L., and C. I. Joyce (2007), "Better strategy through organizational design"; Hagel III, J., J. S. Brown, and L. Davison (2010), *The Power of Pull: How Small Moves, Smartly Made, Can Set Big Things in Motion*; Majchrzak, A., A. Malhotra, J. Stamps, and J. Lipnack (2004), "Can absence make a team grow stronger?"; Malhotra, A., A. Majchrzak, and B. Rosen (2007), "Leading far-flung teams."

39. Brown, J. S., and P. Duguid (1991), "Organizational learning and communities-of-practice: Toward a unified view of working, learning, and innovation," *Organization Science* 2: 40–57.

40. This section draws on: Barney, J. B. (1986), "Organizational culture: Can it be a source of sustained competitive advantage?"; Chatman, J. A., and S. Eunyoung Cha (2003), "Leading by leveraging culture," *California Management Review* 45: 19–34; Kerr, J., and J. W. Slocum (2005), "Managing corporate culture through reward systems," *Academy of Management Executive* 19: 130–138; O'Reilly, C.A., J. Chatman, and D. L. Caldwell (1991), "People and organizational culture: A profile comparison approach to assessing person-organization fit," *Academy of Management Journal* 34: 487–516; and Schein, E. H. (1992), *Organizational Culture and Leadership* (San Francisco: Jossey-Bass).

41. Chatman, J. A., and S. Eunyoung Cha (2003), "Leading by leveraging culture," pp. 19–34

42. Chao, G. T., A. M. O'Leary-Kelly, S. Wolf, H. J. Klein, and P. D. Gardner (1994), "Organizational socialization: Its content and consequences," *Journal of Applied Psychology* 79: 730–743.

43. Hill, C.W.L., and F. T. Rothaermel (2003), "The performance of incumbent firms in the face of radical technological innovation," *Academy of Management Review* 28: 257–274.

44. Nelson, T. (2003), "The persistence of founder influence: Management, ownership, and performance effects at initial public offering," *Strategic Management Journal* 24: 707–724.

45. A&E Biography Video (1997), *Sam Walton: Bargain Billionaire.*

46. Friedman, T. L. (2005), *The World Is Flat. A Brief History of the 21st Century* (New York: Farrar, Straus and Giroux), pp. 130–131.

47. Schneider, B., H. W. Goldstein, and D. B. Smith (1995), "The ASA framework: An update," *Personnel Psychology* 48: 747–773.

48. Hsieh, T. (2010), *Delivering Happiness. A Path to Profits, Passion, and Purpose,* p. 145.

49. Less than 1 percent of new hires take Zappos up on the $2,000 offer to quit during the training program.

50. Leonard-Barton, D. (1995), *Wellsprings of Knowledge: Building and Sustaining the Sources of Innovation* (Boston, MA: Harvard Business School Press Press).

51. Chandler, A. D. (1962), *Strategy and Structure: Chapters in the History of American Industrial Enterprise.*

52. Birkinshaw, J. (2010), *Reinventing Management. Smarter Choices for Getting Work Done* (Chichester, West Sussex, UK: Jossey-Bass).

53. Collins, J. (2009), *How the Mighty Fall: And Why Some Companies Never Give In.*

54. "All Carly, all the time," *Forbes,* December 13, 1999.

55. Author's interview with a Distinguished Technologist at HP.

56. "HP says goodbye to drama," *BusinessWeek,* September 12, 2005.

57. This section is based on: Barney, J. B. (1986), "Organizational culture: Can it be a source of sustained competitive advantage?"; Barney, J. (1991), "Firm resources and sustained competitive advantage," *Journal of Management* 17: 99–120; and Chatman, J. A., and S. Eunyoung Cha (2003), "Leading by leveraging culture," pp. 19–34.

58. Hoffer Gittel, J. (2003), *The Southwest Airlines Way* (Burr Ridge, IL: McGraw-Hill); and O'Reilly, C., and J. Pfeffer, J. (1995), "Southwest Airlines: Using human resources for competitive advantage," case study, Graduate School of Business, Stanford University.

59. Hsieh, T. (2010), *Delivering Happiness. A Path to Profits, Passion, and Purpose,* p. 146.

60. See discussion in Chapter 4 on SWA's activities supporting its cost leadership strategy. Recently, SWA has experienced problems with the fuselage of their 737 cracking prematurely. See: "Southwest's solo flight in crises," *The Wall Street Journal,* April 8, 2011.

61. Hsieh, T. (2010), *Delivering Happiness. A Path to Profits, Passion, and Purpose,* p. 146.

62. Chatman, J. A., and S. Eunyoung Cha (2003), "Leading by leveraging culture," pp. 19–34.

63. Hoffer Gittel, J. (2003), *The Southwest Airlines Way* (Burr Ridge, IL: McGraw-Hill).

64. Baron, J. N., M. T. Hannan, and M. D. Burton (2001), "Labor pains: Change in organizational models and employee turnover in young, high-tech

firms," *American Journal of Sociology* 106: 960–1012; and Hannan, M. T., M. D. Burton, and J. N. Baron (1996), "Inertia and change in the early years: Employment relationships in young, high technology firms," *Industrial and Corporate Change* 5: 503–537.

65. Nelson, T. (2003), "The persistence of founder influence: Management, ownership, and performance effects at initial public offering," *Strategic Management Journal* 24: 707–724.

66. See the section "*Gaining & Sustaining Competitive Advantage*: Mergers and Acquisitions" in Chapter 9.

67. Herold, D. M., and D. B. Fedor (2008), *Change the Way You Lead Change: Leadership Strategies that Really Work.*

68. Barnes, F. C., and B. B. Tyler (2010), "Nucor in 2010," case study.

69. Roethlisberger, F. J., and W. J. Dickson (1939), *Management and the Worker* (Cambridge, MA: Harvard University Press).

70. Pink, D. H. (2009), *Drive: The Surprising Truth about What Motivates Us* (New York: Riverhead Books).

71. Ibid.

72. 3M Company (2002), *A Century of Innovation: The 3M Story* (Maplewood, MN: The 3M Company).

73. The ChapterCase 11 information is based on "Zappos screws up pricing and sells products at $1.6M below costs . . . Then honors the sales!" *Business Insider,* May 23, 2010; and "6pm.com pricing mistake," *The Zappos Family Blog,* May 21, 2010.

74. "Zappos will honor $1.6 million pricing mistake," *MSN MoneyCentral,* May 25, 2010; and "Amazon wields $25 gift certificates to pacify frustrated comic book fans," *TechCrunch.com,* March 9, 2010.

75. "Employee Morale & Engagement Survey," press release, *CheckPoint HR,* February 23, 2010.

76. Input for this module is used with the permission of Blaine Lawlor, strategic management professor, University of West Florida.

Corporate Governance, Business Ethics, and Strategic Leadership

LEARNING OBJECTIVES

After studying this chapter, you should be able to:

LO 12-1   Describe and evaluate the relationship between strategic management and the role of business in society.

LO 12-2   Conduct a stakeholder impact analysis.

LO 12-3   Critically evaluate the relationship between corporate social responsibility (CSR) and competitive advantage.

LO 12-4   Describe the role of corporate governance and evaluate different governance mechanisms.

LO 12-5   Describe and evaluate the relationship between business strategy and ethics.

LO 12-6   Describe the different roles that strategic leaders play and how to become a strategic leader.

HP's CEO Mark Hurd Resigns amid Ethics Scandal

MARK HURD WAS appointed Hewlett-Packard's CEO in the spring of 2005, following Carly Fiorina's tumultuous tenure. He had begun his business career 25 years earlier as an entry-level salesperson with NCR, a U.S. technology company best known for its bar code scanners in retail outlets and automatic teller machines (ATMs). By the time he had ascended to the role of CEO at NCR, he had earned a reputation as a low-profile, no-nonsense manager focused on flawless strategy execution. When he was appointed HP's CEO, industry analysts praised its board of directors. Moreover, investors hoped that Mr. Hurd would run an efficient and lean operation at HP, to return the company to former greatness and, above all, profitability.

Mr. Hurd did not disappoint. By all indications, he was highly successful at the helm of HP. The company became number one in desktop computer sales and increased its lead in inkjet and laser printers to more than 50 percent market share. Through significant cost-cutting and streamlining measures, Mr. Hurd turned HP into a lean operation. For example, he oversaw large-scale layoffs and a pay cut for all remaining employees as he reorganized the company. Wall Street rewarded HP shareholders with a 110 percent stock price appreciation during Mr. Hurd's tenure, outperforming the NASDAQ composite index by a wide margin.

Yet, in the summer of 2010, the HP board found itself caught "between a rock and a hard place," with no easy options in sight. Jodie Fisher, a former adult-movie actress, filed a lawsuit against Mr. Hurd, alleging sexual harassment. As an independent contractor, she worked as a hostess at HP-sponsored events. In this function, she screened attending HP customers and personally ensured that Mr. Hurd would spend time with the most important ones. With an ethics scandal looming, and despite Mr. Hurd's stellar financial results for the company, HP's board of directors forced Mr. Hurd to resign.

The HP board of directors found that Mr. Hurd had not expressly violated the company's sexual harassment policy. However, it *did* find inaccurate expense reports that he allegedly filed to conceal a "close personal relationship" with Ms. Fisher. The investigation also revealed that HP made payments to Ms. Fisher in instances where there was no legitimate business purpose. Finally, the board alleged that Mr. Hurd leaked private information to Ms. Fisher about the company's intention to acquire EDS, a large information-technology company, months prior to the actual transaction. Following his resignation, Mr. Hurd, who departed with a severance package estimated at $45 million, stated: "I realized there were instances in which I did not live up to the standards and principles of trust, respect and integrity that I have espoused at HP and which have guided me throughout my career."[1]

Reactions were mixed. Some corporate-governance scholars argued that Mr. Hurd should have been fired for cause. Others were not so sure. The most outspoken critic of the board's decision was Larry Ellison, co-founder and CEO of Oracle, who argued, "The HP board just made the worst personnel decision since the idiots on the Apple board fired Steve Jobs many years ago. That decision nearly destroyed Apple and would have if Steve hadn't come back and saved them."[2]

Investors seemed to agree with Mr. Ellison's assessment: HP's market value dropped by roughly $10 billion on the first trading day after Mr. Hurd resigned. (As you'll see in the *Consider This . . .* section at the end of the chapter, Mr. Ellison plays a key role in the unfolding story.)

After reading the chapter, you will find more about this case, with related questions, on page 357.

▲ **MARK HURD'S PROBLEMS** at HP illustrate how intricate and intertwined corporate governance, business ethics, and strategic leadership issues can be. The incident demonstrates the difficult decisions that a board of directors must make when governing a public company: Should the board force a highly successful CEO to resign when ethical shortcomings are discovered but before an investigation proves or disproves illegal behavior? Would the board (and the company, and the stockholders) have been better served by just reprimanding the CEO? On the other hand, would a mere reprimand communicate to the employees and other stakeholders that performance trumps ethics? The ChapterCase also highlights how ethical shortcomings by executives can dramatically affect firm performance. Finally, it illustrates implications for strategic leadership: CEOs of Fortune 500 companies are under constant public scrutiny and must adhere to the highest ethical standards; if they do not, they cannot expect their employees to do the same. Unethical behavior can quickly destroy the reputation of a CEO, one of the most important assets he or she possesses.

In this chapter, we wrap up our discussion of strategy implementation, and close the circle in the AFI framework, by studying three remaining areas: corporate governance, business ethics, and strategic leadership. To ensure pursuit of its intended goals, a firm must put in place effective *corporate-governance* mechanisms to direct and control the enterprise. Studying *business ethics* enables managers to reason about the role of business in society and to think through complex decisions in an increasingly dynamic, interdependent, and global marketplace. Finally, *strategic leadership* pertains to individuals' use of power and influence to direct the activities of others when pursuing an organization's goals.[3]

To integrate our discussion on corporate governance, business ethics, and strategic leadership, we begin by taking a closer look at the intersection between strategic management and the role of business in society. Strategic management provides a powerful toolkit for helping firms to gain and sustain competitive advantage. The modern business organization is one of the most powerful institutions on the planet. To be effective as a strategic manager and leader, you must understand and appreciate the role of business in society.

STRATEGIC MANAGEMENT AND THE ROLE OF BUSINESS IN SOCIETY

>> **LO 12-1**
Describe and evaluate the relationship between strategic management and the role of business in society.

The public stock company is the institutional backbone of any modern, free-market economy. Exhibit 12.1 shows the levels of hierarchy in a public stock company. The state (society) grants shareholders a charter of incorporation. In turn, shareholders appoint a board of directors to govern and oversee the firm's management. The managers in turn hire and supervise employees to perform the actual work (producing products or providing services). The public stock company enjoys four characteristics that make it an attractive corporate form: limited liability for investors, transferability of investor interests (i.e., the trading of stocks), legal personality, and separation of ownership and control.[4]

In the first decade of the 21st century, however, two major events eroded the public's trust in business as an institution and free-market capitalism as an economic system.[5] The erosion began with the accounting scandals at Enron, WorldCom, Tyco, Adelphia, Global Crossing, and Arthur Andersen, which lead to bankruptcies, large-scale employment loss, and billions of dollars of shareholder value destruction. A *BusinessWeek* reporter commented wryly: "Watching executives climb the courthouse steps became a spectator sport."[6]

Then, in the fall of 2008, the global financial crisis (GFC) struck, shaking the entire free-market system to its core. Although the reasons for the GFC are quite complex and still being debated,[7] we know a few key factors. A real estate bubble had emerged, fueled by cheap credit, especially the availability of subprime mortgages. When that bubble burst, those who had unsustainable mortgages, investors holding derivative securities based on those mortgages, and the financial institutions that had sold the securities, all faced financial stress or bankruptcy. Some went under and others were sold off at fire-sale prices. Home foreclosures skyrocketed as a large number of lenders defaulted on their mortgages. House prices in the U.S. plummeted by roughly 30 percent. By November 2008, the Dow Jones Industrial Average (DJIA) had lost about half its market value. The government bailed out struggling financial institutions and businesses with a $700 billion package. As the financial tsunami moved from Wall Street to Main Street, the result was a 10 percent unemployment rate and a deep recession in the United States (and most of the world).

Although the two crises differ in their specifics, two common features emerge that are pertinent to our study of strategic management.[8] First, both crises demonstrate that managerial actions can affect the economic well-being of large numbers of people around the

EXHIBIT 12.1

The Public Stock Company: Hierarchy of Authority

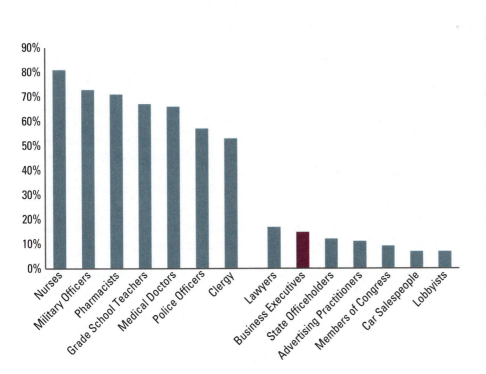

EXHIBIT 12.2

Honesty and Ethics Ranking of Different Professions

The bar chart indicates the percentage of Americans who responded to the question, "How would you rate the honesty and ethical standards of people in different fields?" with the answer "very high/high." The poll ranked 22 professions. The left part of the exhibit shows the top seven ranked professions. The right part of the exhibit shows the bottom seven professions, with business executives at 15 percent.

Source: Author's depiction of data from Gallup's 2010 "Honesty and Ethics Survey," www.gallup.com/poll/1654/honesty-ethics-professions.aspx.

globe. Effective and ethical business practices can produce significant wealth, and unethical behavior can destroy it. Respondents in a recent Gallup poll, asked to assess the honesty and ethics of different professions, ranked business executives near the bottom—just ahead of members of Congress, car salespeople, and lobbyists (see Exhibit 12.2, previous page).

The second pertinent feature is stakeholders—the large and diverse number of organizations, groups, and individuals who can affect or be affected by the actions of a firm. Managers must consider numerous stakeholders in their decisions. Doing so can be a form of corporate social responsibility (discussed more fully later in the chapter). Doing so also is important because *failure* to consider stakeholders can boomerang, and undermine corporate objectives if stakeholders' needs are not met. Borrowers, for example, who bought subprime mortgages are customers of financial institutions. When they default in large numbers, they can threaten the survival of the financial institutions (indeed, of the entire financial system). Effective stakeholder management, therefore, is necessary to ensure continued survival of the firm and to sustain any competitive advantage.[9]

Stakeholder Strategy

Stakeholder strategy has emerged as an integrative approach to connect corporate governance, business ethics, and strategic leadership, and thus to help managers think through these issues in a holistic fashion.[10] In Chapter 1, we defined *stakeholders* as individuals or groups that can affect or are affected by a firm's actions. They have a claim or interest in the firm's performance and continued survival because they make specific contributions for which they expect rewards in return. The firm has a multifaceted exchange relationship with a number of diverse internal and external stakeholders (see Exhibit 1.8, p. 19).

Stakeholder theory is a theoretical framework that is concerned with how various stakeholders create and trade value. According to this theory, the unit of analysis is the web of exchange relationships a firm has with the groups and individuals that can affect the firm or are affected by it.[11] Stakeholder theory describes "how customers, suppliers, employees, financiers (stockholders, bondholders, banks, etc.), communities and managers interact to jointly create and trade value."[12] The main thesis of stakeholder theory is that effective management of these different groups and individuals can help the firm achieve its goals and also improve its chances of gaining and sustaining competitive advantage. Indeed, a core tenet of stakeholder theory is that a single-minded focus on shareholders alone exposes a firm to undue risks that can undermine economic performance and can even threaten the very survival of the enterprise. The strategist's job, therefore, is to understand and appreciate the complex web of relationships among different stakeholders—to "manage and shape these relationships to create as much value as possible for *stakeholders* and to manage the distribution of that value."[13]

Scholars have provided several arguments as to why effective stakeholder management can benefit firm performance:[14]

■ Satisfied stakeholders are more cooperative and thus more likely to reveal information that can further increase the firm's value creation or lower its costs.

---

stakeholder strategy An integrative approach to connect corporate governance, business ethics, and strategic leadership.

stakeholder theory A theoretical framework concerned with how various

stakeholders create and trade value; its main thesis is that effective management of the web of exchange relationships among stakeholders can help the firm achieve its goals and improve its chances of gaining and sustaining competitive advantage.

stakeholder impact analysis A decision tool with which managers can recognize, assess, and address the needs of different stakeholders, to allow the firm to perform optimally and act as a good corporate citizen.

- Increased trust lowers transaction costs.

- Effective management of the complex web of stakeholders can lead to greater organizational adaptability and flexibility.

- Negative outcomes can be avoided and risk exposure can be reduced, creating more predictable and stable returns.

- Firms can build strong reputations that are rewarded in the marketplace by business partners, employees, and customers. Most managers do care about public perception of the firm, as evidenced by high-profile rankings such as the "World's Most Admired Companies" published annually by *Fortune*.[15]

Stakeholder Impact Analysis

The key challenge of stakeholder management is to ensure that a firm's primary stakeholders such as shareholders and other investors achieve their objectives, while other stakeholders' needs are recognized and addressed in an ethical manner, so that they too can be satisfied. This all sounds good in theory, but how should managers go about this in practice?

>> **LO 12-2**
Conduct a stakeholder impact analysis.

Stakeholder impact analysis provides such a tool for managers. With it, they can recognize, assess, prioritize, and address the needs of different stakeholders, to allow the firm to perform optimally while at the same time acting as a good corporate citizen. In particular, managers must go through a five-step process when recognizing and addressing stakeholders' claims. In each step, managers need to pay particular attention to three important stakeholder attributes: *power, legitimacy,* and *urgency*.[16]

- A stakeholder has *power* over a company when it can get the company to do something that it would not otherwise do.

- A stakeholder has a *legitimate claim* when it is perceived to be (legally) valid or otherwise appropriate.

- A stakeholder has an *urgent claim* when it requires a company's immediate attention and response.

Exhibit 12.3 depicts the five steps in stakeholder impact analysis and the key questions to be asked. We now discuss each step in detail.

EXHIBIT 12.3

Stakeholder Impact Analysis

Step 1 — *Who are our stakeholders?*

Step 2 — *What are our stakeholders' interests and claims?*

Step 3 — *What opportunities and threats do our stakeholders present?*

Step 4 — *What economic, legal, ethical, and philanthropic responsibilities do we have to our stakeholders?*

Step 5 — *What should we do to effectively address the stakeholder concerns?*

STEP 1. In step 1, the firm asks, "Who are our stakeholders?" In Chapter 1, we identified both key internal and external stakeholders. Internal stakeholders are stockholders, employees, and board members. External stakeholders include customers, suppliers, alliance partners, creditors, unions, communities, and governments.

In the stakeholder-identification step, the firm focuses on stakeholders that currently have, or potentially can have, a material effect on a company. This prioritization identifies the most powerful stakeholders and their needs. For public-stock companies, key stakeholders are, first and foremost, the shareholders, as well as other suppliers of capital. If shareholders are not satisfied with their returns to investment, for example, they will sell the company's stock, leading to depreciation in the firm's market value. A second group of stakeholders includes customers, suppliers, and unions. Any of these groups, if their needs are not met, can materially affect the company's operations. Labor disputes, for example, can lead to strikes and thus loss of revenues and an increase in costs. Suppliers and local communities are also powerful groups of stakeholders that can materially affect the smooth operation of the firm.

STEP 2. In step 2, the firm asks, "What are our stakeholders' interests and claims?" That is, managers need to specify and assess the interests and claims of the pertinent stakeholders using the power, legitimacy, and urgency criteria introduced earlier. As the legal owners, for example, shareholders have the most legitimate claim on a company's profits. However, the separation between ownership and control has been blurring. Many companies incentivize top executives through stock options. They also turn employees into shareholders through *employee stock ownership plans* (*ESOPs*) that allow them to purchase stock at a discounted rate or use company stock as an investment vehicle for retirement savings. For example, Coca-Cola, Google, Microsoft, Southwest Airlines, Starbucks, Walmart, and Whole Foods offer ESOPs.

Even within stakeholder groups there can be significant variation in the power a stakeholder may exert on the firm. For example, managers pay much more attention to large institutional investors than to the millions of smaller, individual investors. Institutional investors have considerable sway because of the size of their assets under management (AUM): TIAA-CREF[17] has $400 billion in AUM, CalPERS[18] has $200 billion in AUM, and The Vanguard Group has $1.4 trillion AUM. Although both individual and institutional investors can claim the same legitimacy as stockholders, institutional investors have much more power over a firm: They can buy and sell a large number of shares at once, or exercise block voting rights in the corporate-governance process. These abilities make institutional investors a much more potent stakeholder. In recent years, institutional investors have become more active participants in corporate governance.

STEP 3. In step 3, the firm asks, "What opportunities and threats do our stakeholders present?" Since stakeholders have a claim on the company, opportunities and threats are two sides of the same coin. Consumer boycotts, for example, can be a credible threat to a company's behavior. For example, some consumers boycotted Nestlé products due to the firm's promotion of infant formula over breast milk in developing countries. PETA[19] called for a boycott of McDonald's due to alleged animal-rights abuses.

In the best-case scenario, managers transform such threats into opportunities. In 2001, the Dutch government blocked Sony Corp.'s entire holiday season shipment of PlayStation game systems (valued at roughly $500 million) into the European Union[20] due to a small but legally unacceptable amount of toxic cadmium discovered in one of the system's cables. This incident led to an 18-month investigation in which Sony inspected over 6,000 supplier factories around the world to track down the source of the problem. The findings allowed

Sony to redesign and develop a cutting-edge supplier management system that adheres to a stringent extended value chain responsibility.

STEP 4. In step 4, the firm asks, "What economic, legal, ethical, and philanthropic responsibilities do we have to our stakeholders?" To identify these responsibilities more effectively, scholars have advanced the notion of corporate social responsibility (CSR). This framework helps firms recognize and address the economic, legal, ethical, and philanthropic expectations that society has of the business enterprise at a given point in time.[21] CSR goes beyond the notion of encouraging businesses to "just be nice." Instead, managers need to realize that *society* grants shareholders the right and privilege to create a publicly traded stock company, and therefore the firm owes something to society.[22] Moreover, CSR provides managers with a conceptual model that more completely describes a society's expectations and thus can guide strategic decision making more effectively. In particular, CSR has four components: economic, legal, ethical, and philanthropic responsibilities.

Economic Responsibilities. The business enterprise is first and foremost an economic institution. Investors expect an adequate return for their risk capital. Consumers expect safe products and services at appropriate prices and quality. Suppliers expect to be paid in full and on time. Governments expect the firm to pay taxes and to manage natural resources such as air and water under a decent stewardship. To accomplish all this, firms must obey the law and act ethically in their quest to gain and sustain competitive advantage.

Legal Responsibilities. Laws and regulations are a society's codified ethics, as they embody notions of right and wrong. They also establish the rules of the game. For example, business as an institution can function because property rights exist and contracts can be enforced in courts of law. Managers must ensure that their firms obey all the laws and regulations, including but not limited to labor, consumer, and environmental laws.

One far-reaching piece of U.S. legislation, for example, is the Accounting Reform and Investor Protection Act of 2002 (commonly known as the Sarbanes-Oxley Act or SOX), passed in response to the accounting scandals mentioned earlier. Among different stipulations, Sarbanes-Oxley increases a CEO's and CFO's personal responsibilities for the accuracy of reported accounting data. It also strengthens the independence of accounting firms (they are no longer allowed to provide consulting services to the firms they audit) and affords stronger protection for whistleblowers.

Due to a firm's significant legal responsibilities, many companies appoint compliance officers, and some even have an office of corporate citizenship. At GE, for example, a vice president leads the office of corporate citizenship. Its compliance group "includes more than 1,000 experienced lawyers located at GE businesses throughout the world whose job is to help the company achieve its goals with unyielding integrity and compliance with the law."[23]

Ethical Responsibilities. Legal responsibilities, however, often define only the minimum acceptable standards of firm behavior. Frequently managers are called upon to go beyond what is required by law. This is because the letter of the law cannot address or anticipate all possible business situations and newly emerging concerns (such as Internet privacy or advances in genetic engineering and stem cell research).

A firm's ethical responsibilities, therefore, go beyond its legal responsibilities; they embody the full scope of expectations, norms, and values of its stakeholders. Managers are called upon to do what society deems just and fair. Starbucks, for example, developed an ethical sourcing policy to help source coffee of the highest quality, while adhering to fair trade and responsible growing practices.

corporate social responsibility
A framework that helps firms recognize and address the economic, legal, social, and philanthropic expectations that society has of the business enterprise at a given point in time.

Philanthropic Responsibilities. Philanthropic responsibilities are often subsumed under the idea of *corporate citizenship,* reflecting the notion of voluntarily giving back to society. The top three corporate donors in 2009 among the Fortune 100 companies were:

- Walmart: $288 million for education, environmental protection, and conservation, health, and hunger
- AT&T: $240 million for arts and culture, community and economic development, education, health, and the United Way
- Bank of America: $209 million for the arts and culture, community and economic development, education, and human services[24]

The pyramid in Exhibit 12.4 summarizes our discussion of corporate social responsibility.[25] It shows the four components of CSR, beginning with economic responsibilities as the foundational building block, followed by legal, ethical, and philanthropic responsibilities. Note that economic and legal responsibilities are required of companies by society and shareholders, while ethical and philanthropic responsibilities result from a society's expectations toward business. Moreover, there will always be a tension between the different CSR dimensions discussed—e.g., not everything that is legal is also ethical, and not everything that is ethical is also legal. (We'll discuss this last point in more detail when we discuss the relationship between strategy and ethics.) Rather than recommending that a corporation fulfill its responsibilities in a sequential fashion, however, the pyramid symbolizes the need for these responsibilities to be carefully balanced and pursued simultaneously. Doing so ensures not only effective strategy implementation, but also long-term competitiveness.

STEP 5. Finally, in step 5, the firm asks, "What should we do to effectively address the stakeholder concerns?" In the last step in stakeholder management, managers need to decide the appropriate course of action, given all the preceding factors. Going back to the attributes of power, legitimacy, and urgency helps to prioritize the legitimate claims and to address them based on the company's responsibilities.

For example, in the aftermath of the Gulf oil spill, BP faced thousands of claims by many small business owners in the tourism and fishing industries along the Gulf coast. These business owners were not powerful individually, nor did they have valid legal claims

EXHIBIT 12.4

The Pyramid of Corporate Social Responsibility

Source: Adapted from A. B. Carroll (1991), "The pyramid of corporate social responsibility: Toward the moral management of organizational stakeholders," *Business Horizons,* July–August: 42.

PHILANTHROPIC RESPONSIBILITIES — Corporate citizenship

ETHICAL RESPONSIBILITIES — Do what is right, just, and fair.

LEGAL RESPONSIBILITIES — Laws and regulations are society's codified ethics; define minimum acceptable standard.

ECONOMIC RESPONSIBILITIES — Gain and sustain competitive advantage.

without facing protracted and expensive court proceedings. They were nonetheless very powerful as a collective organized in a potential class-action lawsuit. Moreover, their claims were legitimized by the political will of the U.S. government, which has the power to withdraw BP's business license altogether or cancel current permits and withhold future ones. Thus, the small business owners along the Gulf coast were powerful BP stakeholders with a legitimate claim that needed to be addressed quickly. In response, BP agreed to set apart $20 billion in a fund to be dispersed by a third-party mediator.

Corporate Social Responsibility

Following the two shocks to the free-market capitalist system discussed earlier, the notion of corporate social responsibility is rapidly gaining ground. Today, a firm's responsibilities must be expanded beyond an earlier perspective advocated by Nobel laureate Milton Friedman, who (in 1962) stated, "there is one and only one social responsibility of business—to use its resources and engage in activities designed to increase its profits so long as it stays within the rules of the game, which is to say, engages in open and free competition without deception or fraud."[26] However, Friedman's statement provides a useful foundation: Shareholders not only provide the necessary risk capital but are also the legal owners of public companies and thus have the most legitimate claim. Today, though, many firms seek to do more in terms of social responsibility. The question we investigate here is whether corporate social responsibility helps firms gain and sustain competitive advantage.

A recent survey measured attitudes toward business responsibility in various countries.[27] The survey asked the top 25 percent of income earners holding a university degree in various countries whether they agree with Milton Friedman's philosophy that "the *social responsibility* of business is to increase its profits." The results, displayed in Exhibit 12.5, revealed some intriguing national differences. When asked, the United Arab Emirates (UAE), a small and business-friendly country, came out on top, with 84 percent of respondents agreeing. The top five countries also included two of the four Asian Tigers[28] (South Korea and Singapore, where roughly two-thirds agree) as well as Japan and India, a rising economic power.

GAINING & SUSTAINING COMPETITIVE ADVANTAGE

>> LO 12-3
Critically evaluate the relationship between corporate social responsibility (CSR) and competitive advantage.

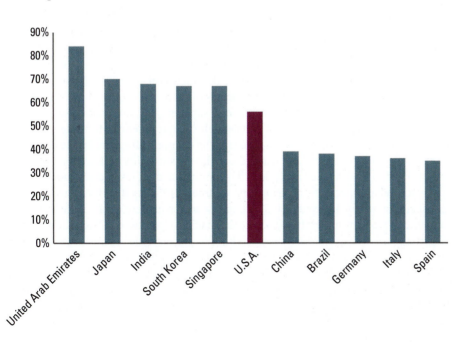

EXHIBIT 12.5

Global Survey of Attitudes Toward Business

The bar chart indicates the percentage of members of the "informed public" (defined as people who hold university degrees and are in the top 25 percent in their particular income and age groups in their respective countries) who "strongly agree/somewhat agree" with Milton Friedman's philosophy, "*The social responsibility of business is to increase its profits.*"

Source: Author's depiction of data from Edelman's (2011) Trust Barometer as included in "Milton Friedman goes on tour," *The Economist,* January 27, 2011.

Interestingly, the countries where the fewest people agreed with Friedman were China, Brazil, Germany, Italy, and Spain, where less than 40 percent of the respondents were supportive of an exclusive focus on shareholder capitalism. China and Brazil are also part of the rising BRIC powerhouses, but are found—in contrast to India—at the bottom of the ranking. Although they have achieved a high standard of living, European countries such as Germany, Italy, and Spain have always tempered the free-market system with a strong social element, leading to so-called *social market economies*. The respondents from these countries seem to be more supportive of a stakeholder-management approach to business.

The United States, often held up as the bastion of free-market capitalism, came in ninth out of 23 countries surveyed, placing roughly in the middle of the continuum. In particular, a bit more than half (56 percent) of U.S. respondents subscribed to Friedman's philosophy.

A reconciliation between the perspectives of shareholder value creation (Friedman's philosophy) and corporate social responsibility has been under way in the past few decades. Neglecting to take important stakeholders into consideration can destroy shareholder value and thus threaten the very survival of a firm.[29] Porter and Kramer suggest that managers should focus not on short-term financial performance but on *shared value*, which includes both shareholder value creation and value creation for society.[30] They argue that managers need to reestablish the important relationship between superior firm performance and social progress. They recommend that firms should focus on three things within the shared-value-creation framework:

1. Expand their customer base to bring in nonconsumers such as those at the bottom of the pyramid (discussed in Chapter 1).
2. Expand their traditional internal firm value chains to include more nontraditional partners such as *nongovernmental organizations* (NGOs). NGOs are not-for-profit organizations that pursue a particular cause in the public interest, and are independent of any governments. Habitat for Humanity and Greenpeace, for example, are NGOs.
3. Focus on creating new regional clusters (discussed in Chapter 10).

Porter and Kramer argue that these strategic actions will in turn lead to a larger pie of revenues and profits that can be distributed among a company's stakeholders.

General Electric, for example, recognizes a convergence between shareholders and stakeholders to create shared value. It states in its Governance Principles: "Both the board of directors and management recognize that the long-term interests of shareowners are advanced by responsibly addressing the concerns of other stakeholders and interested parties, including employees, recruits, customers, suppliers, GE communities, government officials and the public at large."[31] Enlightened self-interest requires a firm's leaders to consider all important stakeholders when managing an enterprise for competitive advantage.

The empirical evidence linking corporate social responsibility and firm performance is somewhat mixed. In a detailed analysis of 52 empirical studies, researchers found that CSR is likely to lead to superior firm performance in terms of financial performance and higher reputation scores.[32] In a separate study, other researchers undertook a detailed analysis of 95 empirical research studies that looked at the relationship between CSR and firms' financial performance.[33] In 80 out of the 95 studies (84 percent), the assumed *causal relationship* ("What causes what?") was that CSR would *lead to* improved financial performance, and thus potentially to competitive advantage. A little more than half of these 80 studies (53 percent) found a statistically significant positive relationship between CSR and financial performance. These studies support the notion that *firms can do well (financially) by doing good (through CSR)*.

On the other hand, in a smaller set of studies, researchers assumed that firm financial performance would *predict* CSR, meaning that firms engage in CSR when they have the financial means to do so. Roughly 68 percent of these 19 studies found that superior financial performance leads to CSR. These companies *do good* when they themselves *do well*.

Taken together, although there seems to be a positive relationship between CSR and firm financial performance in the majority of the studied cases, it is not entirely clear what causes what. 🔍

CORPORATE GOVERNANCE

Corporate governance concerns the mechanisms to direct and control an enterprise in order to ensure that it pursues its strategic goals successfully and legally.[34] Corporate governance is about checks and balances; it's about asking the tough questions at the right time. The accounting scandals and the GFC were able to get so out of hand because the enterprises involved did not properly implement or effectively use corporate governance mechanisms. Similarly, a lack of regular oversight by federal agencies such as the U.S. Security and Exchange Commission (SEC) made Bernard Madoff's $65 billion Ponzi scheme possible. A whistleblower had informed the SEC that Madoff's alleged returns were mathematically impossible, but the SEC failed to follow up. Several years later, Madoff's sons reported his fraud to the authorities.[35]

Corporate governance addresses the *principal–agent problem* (introduced in Chapter 8), which can occur any time an agent performs activities on behalf of a principal.[36] In publicly traded companies, the stockholders (the principals) are the legal owners of the company, and they give the professional managers (the agents) the authority to make decisions on their behalf. The conflict arises if the agents also pursue their own personal interests, which can be at odds with the principals' goals. For their part, agents are interested in maximizing their total compensation, including benefits, job security, status, and power. Principals desire maximization of total returns to shareholders.

The risk of opportunism on behalf of agents is exacerbated by *information asymmetry:* the agents are generally better informed than the principals. Indeed, managers tend to have access to private information that outsiders, especially investors, are not privy to. Insider trading cases provide an example of egregious exploitation of information asymmetry. In the case of ImClone, a biotech company, information asymmetry led to prison terms for its CEO Samuel Waksal and business celebrity Martha Stewart, who sold ImClone stock based on insider information provided by Mr. Waksal. In another case, the hedge fund Galleon Group was engulfed in an insider trading scandal involving several publicly traded technology companies such as Google, Intel, and IBM.

Information asymmetry also can breed on-the-job consumption, perquisites, and excessive compensation. Dennis Kozlowski, former CEO of Tyco, a diversified conglomerate, used company funds for his $30 million New York City apartment (the shower curtain alone was $6,000) and for a $2 million birthday party for his second wife.[37] John Thain, former CEO of Merrill Lynch (now part of Bank of America), spent $1.2 million of company funds on redecorating his office, while he demanded cost cutting and frugality from his employees.[38] Such uses of company funds, in effect, mean that shareholders pay for those items and activities. Mr. Thain also allegedly requested a bonus in the range of $10 to $30 million in 2009 despite Merrill Lynch having lost billions of dollars and being unable to continue independently.

The principal–agent problem is a core part of agency theory, which views the firm as a *nexus of legal contracts*. Besides dealing with the relationship between shareholders and managers, its concerns also cascade down the organizational hierarchy. Employees who perform the actual operational labor are agents who work on behalf of the managers. Such

>> **LO 12-4**
Describe the role of corporate governance and evaluate different governance mechanisms.

corporate governance
A system of mechanisms to direct and control an enterprise in order to ensure that it pursues its strategic goals successfully and legally.

agency theory
A theory that views the firm as a nexus of legal contracts.

front-line employees often enjoy an informational advantage over management. They may tell their supervisor that it took longer to complete a project or serve a customer than it actually did, for example. Some employees may be tempted to use informational advantage for their own self-interest (e.g., shirking on the job by spending time on Facebook during work hours, using the company's computer and Internet connection).

The managerial implication of agency theory relates to the management functions of organization and control: The firm needs to design work tasks, incentives, and employment contracts and other control mechanisms in ways that minimize opportunism on behalf of the agents. At the same time, the activities of the agents should maximize shareholder value creation for the principals.[39] Governance mechanisms are used to reduce information asymmetry and to align incentives between principals and agents. These governance mechanisms need to be designed in such a fashion as to overcome two specific agency problems: adverse selection and moral hazard.

In principal–agent relationships, *adverse selection* describes a situation in which an agent misrepresents his or her ability to do the job. (Such misrepresentation is especially rampant during the recruiting process.) Once hired, the principal often cannot accurately assess whether the agent can do the work for which he is being paid. The problem is especially pronounced in team production, when the principal often cannot ascertain the contributions of individual team members. This in turn creates an incentive for opportunistic employees to free-ride on the efforts of others.

Moral hazard describes the difficulty of the principal to ascertain whether the agent has really put forth a best effort. In this situation, the agent is *able* to do the work, but may decide not to do so. For example, a company scientist at a biotechnology company may decide to work on his own research project (hoping to eventually start his own firm), rather than on the project that he was assigned. While working on his own research on company time, he might also use the company's laboratory and technicians. Given the complexities of basic research, it is often hard, especially for nonscientist principals, to ascertain which problem a scientist is working on.[40]

To overcome these principal–agent problems, firms put several governance mechanisms in place. We shall discuss several of them next, beginning with the board of directors.

The Board of Directors

The day-to-day business operations of a publicly traded stock company are conducted by its managers and employees, under the direction of the chief executive officer (CEO) and the oversight of the board of directors. The board of directors, the centerpiece of corporate governance, is composed of inside and outside directors.[41] The board is elected by the shareholders to represent their interests (see Exhibit 12.1). Prior to the annual shareholders' meeting, the board proposes a slate of nominees, although shareholders can also directly nominate director candidates. In general, large institutional investors support their favored candidates through their accumulated proxy votes. The board members meet several times a year to review and evaluate the company's performance and to assess its future strategic plans as well as opportunities and threats.

In addition to general strategic oversight and guidance, the board of directors has other, more specific functions, including:

- Selecting, evaluating, and compensating the CEO. The CEO reports to the board. Should the CEO lose the board's confidence, the board may fire him or her.
- Overseeing the company's CEO succession plan. Both HP and Apple have been criticized for poor succession planning. HP's board was apparently unprepared to deal

with the unexpected departure of Mark Hurd.[42] Likewise, institutional shareholders criticized Apple for not (publicly) addressing CEO succession in light of Steve Jobs's repeated medical leaves.[43]

■ Providing guidance to the CEO in the selection, evaluation, and compensation of other senior executives.

■ Reviewing, monitoring, evaluating, and approving any significant strategic initiatives and corporate actions.

■ Conducting a thorough risk assessment and proposing options to mitigate risk. The boards of directors of the financial firms at the center of the GFC were faulted for not noticing or not appreciating the risks the firms were exposed to.

■ Ensuring that the firm's audited financial statements represent a true and accurate picture of the firm.

■ Ensuring the firm's compliance with laws and regulations. The boards of directors of firms caught up in the accounting scandals early this century were faulted for being negligent in their company oversight and not adequately performing several of the functions listed here.

The board of directors is composed of inside and outside directors. **Inside directors** are generally part of the company's senior management team, such as the chief financial officer (CFO) and the chief operating officer (COO). They are appointed by shareholders to provide the board with necessary information pertaining to the company's internal workings and performance. Without this valuable inside information, the board would not be able to effectively monitor the firm. As senior executives, however, inside board members' interests tend to align with management and the CEO rather than the shareholders. **Outside directors,** on the other hand, are not employees of the firm. They are frequently senior executives from other firms or full-time professionals appointed to serve on several boards simultaneously. Given their independence, they are more likely to watch out for the interests of shareholders.

Board independence is critical to effectively fulfilling a board's governance responsibilities. Given that board members are directly responsible to shareholders, they have an incentive to ensure that the shareholders' interests are pursued. If not, they can experience a loss in reputation or can be removed outright. The HP board of directors experienced a significant shake-up following the Mark Hurd ethics scandal (see the *Consider This* follow-up to the ChapterCase on page 357).[44]

Strategy Highlight 12.1 (next page) takes a closer look at the composition and workings of General Electric's board of directors.

In recent years, members of boards of directors have been held more and more legally responsible for the firm's strategic actions. Shareholders may sue the board, for example, for selling the company at too low a price and for other material decisions affecting the firm's market valuations. HP's shareholders sued the board of directors claiming that disclosing details pertaining to Mark Hurd's resignation led to a significant loss in the

---

board of directors The centerpiece of corporate governance, composed of inside and outside directors, who are elected by the shareholders to represent their interests.

inside directors Board members who are generally part of the company's senior management team; appointed by shareholders to provide the board with necessary information pertaining to the company's internal workings and performance.

outside directors Board members who are not employees of the firm, but who are frequently senior executives from other firms or full-time professionals. Given their independence, they are more likely to watch out for shareholder interests.

GE's Board of Directors

In 2011, the GE board is composed of individuals from the business world (chairpersons and CEOs of Fortune 500 companies spanning a range of industries), academia (university presidents, business school professors, and deans), and politics. (For the latest listing, see www.ge.com/company/leadership/directors.html.) Including the board's chairman, there are 17 members on the board. This is considered an appropriate number of directors for a company of GE's size (roughly $230 billion in market capitalization as of spring 2011). In contrast, Apple's board of directors has only six members, while its market capitalization is about $325 billion. Indeed, Apple's board of directors has been criticized for having become too insular in recent years.[45]

At GE, 15 of the 17 board members are independent outside directors. (Mr. Penske has a material relationship with GE through his business, Penske Corporation.) GE's board has only one inside director, Jeffrey Immelt, GE's CEO, who also acts as chairman of the board. In roughly two-thirds of U.S. public firms, the CEO of the company typically also serves as chair of the board of the directors. This practice has been declining somewhat in recent years. Arguments can be made both for and against splitting the roles of CEO and chairman of the board. On the one hand, the CEO has invaluable inside information that can help in chairing the board effectively. On the other hand, the chairman may influence the board unduly through setting the meeting agendas or suggesting board appointees who are friendly toward the CEO. Given the recent crises discussed earlier, the trend toward *separation of CEO/chair duality* is likely to continue. Because one of the key roles of the board is to monitor and evaluate the CEO's performance, there is clearly a conflict of interest when the CEO actually chairs the board. In Germany, the law requires this separation, while companies in other European countries also tend to separate the two roles.

Of GE's 17 directors, 4 are women (24 percent) and 2 are ethnic minorities (12 percent). In general, women and minorities remain underrepresented on boards of directors across the U.S. (and throughout most of the world). GE's board is actually fairly diverse when compared with other Fortune 500 companies, which in 2010 averaged less than 16 percent women on their boards. Diversity in the boardroom is an asset: more diverse boards are less likely to fall victim to groupthink, a situation in which opinions coalesce around a leader without individuals critically challenging and evaluating that leader's opinions and assumptions. Cohesive, non-diverse groups are highly susceptible to groupthink, which in turn can lead to flawed decision making with potentially disastrous consequences.

To accomplish their responsibilities, boards of directors are usually organized into different committees. GE's board has four committees, each with its own chair: the audit committee, the nominating and corporate governance committee, the management development and compensation committee, and the public responsibilities committee.

GE's board of directors meets a dozen or more times annually. With increasing board accountability in recent years, boards now tend to meet more often. Moreover, many firms limit the number and type of directorships a board member may hold concurrently.[46]

---

company's credibility and thus a substantial drop in the firm's shareholder value.[47] To perform their strategic oversight tasks, board members apply the strategic management theories and concepts presented in this textbook, among other more specialized tools such as those originating in finance and accounting.

Other Governance Mechanisms

While the board of directors is the central governance piece for a public stock company, several other corporate mechanisms are worth noting—*executive compensation, the market for corporate control,* and *financial statement auditors and government regulators.*

groupthink
A situation in which opinions coalesce around a leader without individuals critically challenging and evaluating that leader's opinions and assumptions.

EXECUTIVE COMPENSATION. The board of directors determines executive compensation packages. To align incentives between shareholders and management, boards use equity compensation by granting stock options. These give the recipient the right to buy a company's stock at a predetermined price sometime in the future. If the company's share price rises above the negotiated strike price (which is often the "as is" price on the day when compensation is negotiated), the executive stands to reap (significant) gains.

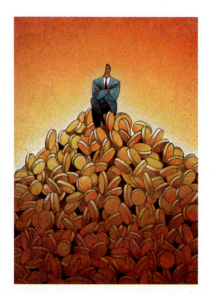

CEO pay, in particular, has attracted significant attention in recent years. Two issues are at the forefront: (1) the absolute size of the CEO pay package compared with the pay of the average employee, and (2) the relationship between firm performance and CEO pay. The ratio of CEO to average employee pay in the U.S. is about 300 to 1, up from roughly 40 to 1 in 1980.[48] In 2010, the highest paid CEO was Gregory Maffei of Liberty Media, who took home about $87 million in direct compensation. Next on the list were Larry Ellison of Oracle ($69m), Ray Irani of Occidental Petroleum ($52m), Carol Bartz of Yahoo ($45m), and Leslie Moonves of CBS ($38m).[49]

In some instances, the pay–firm performance relationship is strong, while in others it is nonexistent or even negative.[50] When we discussed competitive advantage in Chapter 5, we noted that Liberty Media was the number-one performer in return on revenue, achieving over 60 percent (see Exhibit 5.4) and a total shareholder return of 247 percent.[51] In this case, Gregory Maffei's compensation package was closely tied to performance. In other cases, the relationship between performance and pay is less clear. Yahoo, for example, underperformed the NASDAQ 100 index by a wide margin, but CEO Carol Bartz still obtained one of the largest compensation packages. As CEO of The Home Depot, Robert Nardelli earned annual compensation packages of over $200 million, but under Nardelli's tenure (2000–2007), the company's stock remained flat, while the share price of its main competitor, Lowe's, nearly doubled.

Responding to shareholder criticism, the GE board recently revised the compensation package for Jeffrey Immelt, GE's CEO and chairman of the board.[52] The compensation package was changed to include a stronger performance-related equity component. In particular, GE's board attached strings on stock options already granted to Mr. Immelt. The revised compensation package now stipulates conditions: The stock options will vest only if GE's stock and dividend performance in its industrial businesses (energy, health care, and technology infrastructure) is equal to or better than the performance of the Standard & Poor 500 stock index. In addition, half of the options will vest only if GE achieves at least $55 billion in cash flow from operating activities between 2011 and 2014. This unusual move by GE's board of directors underscores the increasing clout of vocal shareholders, who have expressed dissatisfaction with GE's performance over the last decade. They expect that linking compensation to specific performance measures tied to GE's core competency in industrial engineering will result in improved stock performance.

Some recent experiments in behavioral economics caution that incentives that are too high-powered (e.g., outsized bonuses) may have a negative effect on job performance. That is, when the incentive level is very high, an individual may get distracted because too much attention is devoted to the outsized bonus to be enjoyed in the near future. This in turn can further increase job stress and negatively impact job performance.[53]

THE MARKET FOR CORPORATE CONTROL. The board of directors and executive compensation are *internal* corporate-governance mechanisms. The *market for corporate control* is an important *external* corporate-governance mechanism. It consists of investors who

stock options An incentive mechanism to align the interests of shareholders and managers, by giving the recipient the right to buy a company's stock at a predetermined price sometime in the future.

seek to gain control of an underperforming corporation by buying shares of its stock in the open market. To avoid such attempts, corporate managers strive to maximize shareholder value by delivering strong share-price performance or putting in place poison pills (discussed later).

Here's how the market for corporate control works: If a company is poorly managed, its performance suffers and its stock price falls as more and more investors sell their shares. Once shares fall to a low enough level, the firm may become the target of a *hostile takeover* (as discussed in Chapter 9). Besides competitors, so-called *corporate raiders* (e.g., Carl Icahn and T. Boone Pickens) or *hedge funds* (e.g., The Blackstone Group and Soros Fund Management) will buy enough shares to exert control over a company. The new owner will either replace the old management (in order to manage the company in a way so as to create more value for its shareholders) or break up the company and sell off its pieces. In either case, since a firm's existing management faces the threat of losing their jobs and their reputations as effective executives if their firms sustain a competitive disadvantage, the market for corporate control is a credible governance mechanism.

To avoid being taken over against their consent, some firms put in place *poison pills.* These are defensive provisions that kick in should a buyer reach a certain level of share ownership without top management approval. For example, a poison pill could allow existing shareholders to buy additional shares at a steep discount. Those additional shares would in turn make any takeover attempt much more expensive, and thus function as a deterrent. With the rise of the institutional investors, poison pills have become rare because they retard an effective function of equity markets.

Although poison pills are becoming rarer, the market for corporate control is alive and well, as shown in the recent hostile takeover of Cadbury by Kraft (see Strategy Highlight 9.1) or the $20 billion hostile takeover of U.S. biotech firm Genzyme by Sanofi-Aventis, a French pharmaceutical company.[54] However, the market for corporate control is a last resort because it comes with significant transaction costs. To succeed in its hostile takeover bid, for example, Sanofi-Aventis had to pay a nearly 40 percent premium above Genzyme's share price. Thus, this tactic is generally activated only when internal corporate-governance mechanisms have not functioned effectively.

AUDITORS, GOVERNMENT REGULATORS, AND INDUSTRY ANALYSTS. Auditors, government regulators, and industry analysts serve as additional external-governance mechanisms. All public companies listed on the U.S. stock exchanges must file a number of financial statements with the Security and Exchange Commission (SEC). To avoid misrepresentation of financial results, all public statements must follow generally accepted accounting principles (GAAP)[55] and are audited by certified public accountants.

The SEC is the federal agency primarily responsible for enforcing the laws and regulations pertaining to publicly traded companies in the United States. As part of its disclosure policy, the SEC makes all financial reports filed by public companies available electronically via the EDGAR database (www.secfilings.com). This database contains more than 7 million financial statements, going back several years. Industry analysts scrutinize these reports in great detail, trying to identify any financial irregularities and to assess firm performance. Given recent high-profile oversights such as the accounting scandals and fraud cases mentioned earlier, the SEC has come under pressure to step up its monitoring and enforcement.

Industry analysts often base their buy, hold, or sell recommendations on financial statements filed with the SEC and other business news published in *The Wall Street Journal, Bloomberg Businessweek, Fortune, Forbes,* and other business media such as CNBC. Researchers, however, have questioned the independence of industry analysts and credit-rating agencies that evaluate companies (such as Fitch, Moody's, and Standard & Poor's).[56]

This is because the investment banks and rating agencies frequently have lucrative business relationships with the companies they are supposed to evaluate, creating conflicts of interest. A study of over 8,000 analysts' ratings of corporate equity securities, for example, revealed that investment bankers rated their own clients more favorably.[57]

In addition, an industry has sprung up around assessing the effectiveness of corporate governance in individual firms. Research outfits such as GovernanceMetrics (http://www2.gmiratings.com/) provide independent and sophisticated corporate governance ratings. The ratings from these external watchdog organizations inform a wide range of stakeholders, including investors, insurers, auditors, regulators, and others.

Corporate-governance mechanisms play an important part in aligning the interests of principals and agents. Equally important are the "most internal of control mechanisms": *business ethics*—a topic we discuss below. First, though, we'll look at different corporate governance systems around the world.

Corporate Governance Around the World

As discussed earlier, attitudes toward business vary around the world. Due to differences in national institutions and cultures, variations of free-market economic systems have emerged.[58] State-planned (communist and socialist) systems are on the retreat worldwide (with Cuba and North Korea the primary remaining examples); most economies today have some form of free markets. The extent to which markets are "free" varies, however, from country to country: *State-directed capitalism,* practiced by China, is on one end of a continuum, and *free-market capitalism* on the other end.

The United States has historically had one of the most free-market–oriented economies. In response to the global financial crisis, though, the federal government has become a bigger player in the U.S. economy, creating new monetary and fiscal policies: large stimulus packages; low or zero interest rates; increased regulation and direct government ownership of companies such as GM and AIG; and government receivership for mortgage institutions Fannie Mae and Freddie Mac.[59] Although the capitalist system remains the dominant economic system globally, governments are important players in most free-market economies.

GERMANY. Given national differences, corporate governance also differs around the world. The EU's largest economy, Germany, has, since World War II, developed *stakeholder capitalism.* In this model of governance, workers' representatives typically occupy half the seats on a company's board of directors.[60] Companies are required to act on behalf of *all* stakeholders, and not just those owning shares in the firm. Shareholder activism is quite restrained in Germany compared with the United States or Britain, and German investors have more-limited power. As a result, the tensions between shareholder value creation and employee concerns are lower in German firms.

Another reason for less tension between shareholders and management is that the largest German firms are often debt-financed rather than equity-financed. This difference puts banks, rather than shareholders, at the center of German corporate governance. Relying on debt-financing allows German managers and employees to take a longer-term perspective. In the recent Great Recession (2008–2009), German firms generally focused more on maintaining a high level of employment

than on cutting costs by laying off workers. Many German firms instituted *Kurzarbeit*—voluntary reduction of work hours by employees, to keep them on the payroll—subsidized by the federal government.[61] This contrast can be seen in the results of a survey that asked corporate managers which is more important—saving jobs or paying dividends. In Germany, 60 percent said jobs. In the United States and Britain, 90 percent said dividends.[62]

FRANCE. France, Europe's second-largest economy in the EU, also uses a stakeholder-capitalist system. France has perhaps even more direct government involvement in company ownership and in determining strategic directions of state-owned companies. For example, the French government threatened both carmaker Renault and nuclear-energy company Areva with a loss of subsidies if they shifted manufacturing jobs and operations outside France. The French government is directly involved in important strategic decisions at the company level.

In Strategy Highlight 12.1, we mentioned that less than 16 percent of the board seats of large U.S. companies are held by women. Female participation in board membership is even lower in France, at 11 percent. To overcome underrepresentation of women on corporate boards, the French government passed a law requiring large companies to reserve at least 40 percent of the board seats for women. France thus became the second country, after Norway, to set a compulsory quota for women in the boardroom.[63] However, some of the subsequent board appointments, made to be compliant with the new law, have raised eyebrows. Dassault Aviation, a manufacturer of fighter planes and corporate jets, appointed Nicole Dassault to its board of directors.[64] Ms. Dassault is the 80-year-old wife of Serge Dassault, the company's controlling shareholder. The world's largest luxury goods company, Louis Vuitton (LVMH), appointed Bernadette Chirac, the 77-year-old wife of the former French president Jacques Chirac.[65] Some executives plan to appoint their girlfriends or their 18-year-old daughters to fill the quotas.

One thing that the appointments to fill quotas demonstrates is that many companies, both French and other multinationals, have failed to create a pipeline of female executives with the potential to become board members. It often takes decades of industry and executive experience to become an effective board member. Companies that have been more progressive in training women and providing career paths into managerial and executive ranks are more likely to gain and sustain competitive advantage. This is because their boards of directors are less likely to fall victim to groupthink.

CHINA. China, now the second-largest economy worldwide in nominal GDP (behind the United States and before Japan), uses state-directed capitalism to organize economic activity. China began implementing economic reforms in the 1980s.[66] Its move toward a more market-oriented system has accelerated since 2001, when it joined the World Trade Organization (WTO), an international body that aims to liberalize and supervise global trade.

In China, the most significant businesses are *state-owned enterprises* (*SOEs*), in which the state is the majority or sole owner. Given this ownership structure, social goals such as high levels of employment and provision of benefits (e.g., housing, health care, and so on) are seen as equally important or more important than profitability. On the downside, principal–agent problems are rampant in SOEs: Managers have no incentive to run the enterprises effectively. Nonetheless, China is putting the institutional entities in place to foster a free-market capitalist system. Examples include the Shanghai stock exchange, which lists roughly 900 publicly traded companies and has (as of spring 2011) a $2.7 trillion market capitalization.

When competing around the world, managers need to be mindful of the differences in corporate governance in the countries in which they do business. Many international companies have stumbled by not managing corporate-governance relationships appropriately within the given institutional context. China sentenced employees of Australian mining giant Rio Tinto to long prison terms on alleged bribery and industrial espionage charges.[67] In Russia, BP did not consult its existing Russian joint-venture partner TNK-BP before striking a new deal in Russia with the government-owned Rosneft, an energy company.[68] TNK-BP is an equity partnership between BP and a group of Russian investors. By failing to seek approval from TNK-BP for the deal with Rosneft, BP did not follow standard communication requirements embedded in its governance structure. In this case, the principal (BP), and not the agent (TNK-BP), acted opportunistically by taking advantage of information asymmetry. The Russian owners of TNK-BP filed a successful injunction to stop the Rosneft deal with a court in the UK. Both cases point toward the intersection of corporate governance and business ethics, which we will discuss next.

STRATEGY AND BUSINESS ETHICS

The accounting scandals and GFC have placed business ethics center stage in the public eye. **Business ethics** is an agreed-upon code of conduct in business, based on societal norms. Business ethics lay the foundation and provide training for "behavior that is consistent with the principles, norms, and standards of business practice that have been agreed upon by society."[69] These principles, norms, and standards of business practice differ to some degree in different cultures around the globe. But a large number of research studies have found that some notions—such as fairness, honesty, and reciprocity—are universal norms.[70] As such, many of these values have been codified into law.

> **>> LO 12-5**
> Describe and evaluate the relationship between business strategy and ethics.

However, law and ethics are not synonymous. This distinction is important. Many managers throughout the world subscribe to Milton Friedman's dictum that the sole responsibility of business is to make as much profit as possible while staying within the law. (Again, see Exhibit 12.5.) A note of caution is in order, though: *A manager's actions can be completely legal, but ethically questionable.* For example, consider the actions of mortgage-loan officers who—being incentivized by commissions—persuaded unsuspecting consumers to sign up for exotic mortgages, such as "option ARMs." These mortgages offer borrowers the choice to pay less than the required interest, which is then added on to the principal while the interest rate can adjust upward. Such actions may be legal, but they are unethical, especially if there are indications that the borrower might be unable to repay the mortgage once the interest rate moves up.[71]

Staying within the law, therefore, is a *minimum acceptable standard.* For this reason, many organizations have explicit *codes of conduct.* These codes go above and beyond the law in detailing how the organization expects an employee to behave and to represent the company in business dealings. Since business decisions are not made in a vacuum but are embedded within a societal context that expects ethical behavior, managers can use a number of questions to improve their decision making. When facing an ethical dilemma, a manager can ask whether the intended course of action falls within the *acceptable norms of professional behavior* as outlined in the organization's code of conduct. Moreover, the manager should imagine whether he or she would feel *comfortable explaining and defending the decision in public.* How would the media report the business decision if it were to become public? How would the company's stakeholders feel about it?

While other leading professions have accepted codes of conduct (e.g., the bar association in the practice of law and the Hippocratic oath in medicine), management has not achieved the same level of professionalism and status.[72] To regain (or gain) society's trust, some argue that management needs an accepted code of conduct,[73] which holds members to a high professional standard and imposes consequences for misconduct. An attorney, for example, can be disbarred and thus lose the right to practice law. Likewise, medical

business ethics
An agreed-upon code of conduct in business, based on societal norms.

EXHIBIT 12.6

The MBA Oath

Source: www.mbaoath.org.

As a business leader I recognize my role in society.

>> *My purpose is to lead people and manage resources to create value that no single individual can create alone.*

>> *My decisions affect the well-being of individuals inside and outside my enterprise, today and tomorrow.*

Therefore, I promise that:

>> *I will manage my enterprise with loyalty and care, and will not advance my personal interests at the expense of my enterprise or society.*

>> *I will understand and uphold, in letter and spirit, the laws and contracts governing my conduct and that of my enterprise.*

>> *I will refrain from corruption, unfair competition, or business practices harmful to society.*

>> *I will protect the human rights and dignity of all people affected by my enterprise, and I will oppose discrimination and exploitation.*

>> *I will protect the right of future generations to advance their standard of living and enjoy a healthy planet.*

>> *I will report the performance and risks of my enterprise accurately and honestly.*

>> *I will invest in developing myself and others, helping the management profession continue to advance and create sustainable and inclusive prosperity.*

In exercising my professional duties according to these principles, I recognize that my behavior must set an example of integrity, eliciting trust and esteem from those I serve. I will remain accountable to my peers and to society for my actions and for upholding these standards.

This oath I make freely, and upon my honor.

---

doctors can lose their professional accreditations if they engage in misconduct. To anchor future managers in professional values, and thus to move management closer to a truly professional status, a group of Harvard Business School students developed an MBA oath (see Exhibit 12.6). Since 2009, over 2,000 MBA students from over 500 business schools around the world have taken this voluntary pledge. The oath explicitly recognizes the role of business in society, and its responsibilities beyond shareholders. It also holds managers to a high ethical standard based on more or less universally accepted principles in order to "create value responsibly and ethically."[74] Having the highest personal integrity is of utmost importance to one's career. It takes decades to build a career, but sometimes just a few moments to destroy one.

Some people believe that unethical behavior is limited to a few "bad apples" such as Bernard Madoff and Jeffrey Skilling (of Enron).[75] The assumption here is that the vast majority of the population—and by extension, organizations—are good, and that we need only to safeguard against abuses by such bad actors. According to agency theory, it's the "bad agents" who act opportunistically and whose principals we need to be on guard against. However, research indicates otherwise.[76] While there clearly are some people with unethical or even criminal inclinations, in general one's ethical decision-making capacity depends very much on the organizational context. Research shows that if people work in organizations that expect and value ethical behavior, they are more likely to act ethically.[77] The opposite is also true. Enron's *stated* key values included respect and integrity, and its mission statement proclaimed that all business dealings should be open and fair.[78] Yet, the ethos at Enron was all about creating an inflated share price at any cost, and its employees observed and followed the behavior set by their leaders. Sometimes, it's the bad barrel that can spoil the apples!

As we can see, employees take cues from their environment on how to act. Therefore, ethical leadership is critical, and strategic leaders set the tone for the ethical climate within an organization. This is one of the reasons the HP board removed Mark Hurd, even without proof of illegal behavior or violation of the company's sexual-harassment policy. In order to foster ethical behavior in employees, top management must create an organizational structure, culture, and control system that values and encourages desired behavior. Furthermore, a company's formal and informal cultures must be aligned, and executive behavior must be in sync with the formally stated vision and values. Employees will quickly see through any duplicity. As they say, actions (by executives) speak louder than words (in vision statements). This point leads us to the important role of strategic leadership in gaining and sustaining competitive advantage in an ethical manner.

STRATEGIC LEADERSHIP

Throughout this book, we've included anecdotes of executives whose vision and actions have enabled their organizations to achieve competitive advantage. Their abilities demonstrate **strategic leadership**—the behaviors and styles of executives that influence others to achieve organizational goals. Strategic leadership typically resides in "executives who have overall responsibility for an organization—their characteristics, what they do, how they do it, and particularly, how they affect organizational outcomes."[79] These executives can be individuals, generally CEOs, but also can be top-management teams. The key point is that they have responsibility for the performance of the entire company or for an important strategic business unit.

Although *managerial discretion* varies across industries and time, strategic leaders do matter to firm performance.[80] Think of great business founders and their impact on the organizations they built: Steve Jobs at Apple, Michael Dell at Dell Computer, Mark Zuckerberg at Facebook, Sergei Brin and Larry Page at Google, Bill Hewlett and David Packard at HP, Bill Gates at Microsoft, Ingvar Kamprad at IKEA, Herb Kelleher at Southwest Airlines, Richard Branson at Virgin Group, and John Mackey at Whole Foods, among many others. There are also strategic leaders who have shaped and revitalized existing businesses: Steve Jobs at Pixar, Allan Mulally at Ford, Indra Nooyi at PepsiCo, Jack Welch at GE, Louis Gerstner at IBM, and Carlos Ghosn at Nissan.

At the other end of the spectrum, unfortunately, are CEOs whose decisions have led to a massive destruction of shareholder value: Charles Prince at Citigroup, Franklin Raines at Fannie Mae, Richard Wagoner at GM, Robert Nardelli at The Home Depot (and later Chrysler), Richard Fuld at Lehman Brothers, Stanley O'Neal at Merrill Lynch, Ed Zander at Motorola, Gerald Levin at Time Warner, Kerry Killinger at Washington Mutual, and so on.

Why do some leaders create great companies or manage them to greatness, while others destroy them? To answer that question, let's first consider what strategic leaders really do.

What Do Strategic Leaders Do?

To understand why some strategic leaders are more effective than others, let's take a close look of what strategic leaders actually do. In his seminal research on this subject, Henry Mintzberg shadowed CEOs minute-by-minute. He found that they do *not* remove themselves from day-to-day operations in order to devote substantial time to strategic reflection and decision making. Rather, their schedules are filled with a flurry of intense activities,

>> **LO 12-6**
Describe the different roles that strategic leaders play and how to become a strategic leader.

strategic leadership
The behaviors and styles of executives that influence others to achieve organizational goals.

EXHIBIT 12.7

Roles that Strategic Leaders Play

Interpersonal
- *Figurehead*
- *Liaison*
- *Leader*

Informational
- *Monitor*
- *Disseminator*
- *Spokesperson*

Decisional
- *Entrepreneur*
- *Disturbance Handler*
- *Resource Allocator*
- *Negotiator*

Source: Adapted from S. Finkelstein, D. C. Hambrick, and A. A. Cannella (2008), *Strategic leadership: Theory and Research on Executives, Top Management Teams, and Boards* (Oxford, UK: Oxford University Press), p. 18. The executive roles are based on research originally conducted by H. Mintzberg (1973), *The Nature of Managerial Work* (New York: Harper & Row).

at an unrelenting pace and with constant interruptions.[81] Other studies have found that most managers prefer oral communication: They spend most of their time "interacting—talking, cajoling, soothing, selling, listening, and nodding—with a wide array of parties inside and outside the organization."[82]

Based on his observations, Mintzberg derived a model (depicted in Exhibit 12.7) that identifies three distinct roles executives play when leading an organization: interpersonal, informational, and decisional.[83]

INTERPERSONAL ROLE. In the *interpersonal role,* the executive acts as figurehead, liaison, and leader.

- As *figurehead,* the executive appears at social functions that are often symbolic in nature such as meeting with domestic and international investors and government officials, giving interviews to CNBC, breaking ground at a new overseas facility, hosting star-performer functions for valued employees, and speaking at conferences and industry meetings.

- As *liaison,* the executive spends time building, maintaining, and developing a social network with external stakeholders to obtain valuable information and provide or call in favors.

- As *leader,* the executive fulfills more internal duties by making decisions such as selecting, training, and motivating key employees and future leaders, or reviewing and deciding upon strategic initiatives that require significant resources.

  In all these roles, executives rely on interpersonal, often face-to-face, contacts.

INFORMATIONAL ROLE. In the *informational role,* the executive acts as monitor, disseminator, and spokesperson.

- As *monitor,* the executive seeks out and receives a diverse stream of often real-time information from a wide range of internal and external sources, which he or she constantly digests and evaluates. By accumulating such information about many different firm and industry aspects, the CEO serves as a kind of nerve center of the organization.

- The executive acts as *disseminator* when he or she distributes some of the stream of information *internally* to the organization. Much of the information shared is factual, based on financial data and other analysis, while some of it is based on the CEO's interpretation of events and facts.

- The *spokesperson* role occurs when the CEO distributes information *externally* to business news reporters or other stakeholders. In this case, the executive is attempting to shape and influence public opinion.

  Given the ever-increasing information overload an executive experiences, much of the work in the informational role is to act as a kind of information traffic controller.

DECISIONAL ROLE. In the *decisional role*, the executive acts as entrepreneur, disturbance handler, resource allocator, and negotiator. As the name suggests, the executive's primary task here is strategic decision making.

- As *entrepreneur*, the executive scans the internal and external environments to discover new strategic initiatives. In this role, the executive also incubates and supervises current strategic initiatives.

- As *disturbance handler*, the executive acts much like an umpire in a sporting event— trying to reconcile internal and external sources of conflict, and if needed, take corrective action.

- As *resource allocator*, the executive decides what projects receive organizational resources and support. This role is directly linked to our discussion in Chapter 2 about the resource allocation process (RAP). According to one school of thought, by setting the RAP, the executive in effect formulates and implements strategy.[84]

- Finally, as *negotiator*, the executive represents the company in any major negotiation with internal and external stakeholders. The range of negotiations runs the gamut from labor contract talks with unions, to hostile-takeover discussions with competitors, to plans for entry into foreign markets with politicians.

How Do You Become an Effective and Ethical Strategic Leader?

Every board of directors and the shareholders they represent want effective strategic leadership for their company. According to the **upper-echelons theory,**[85] it's the top management team (at the upper echelons of an organization) that primarily determines the success or failure of an organization through the strategies they pursue. This leads us to consider the source of strategic leadership: How do you become an ethical and effective strategic leader? Is it innate? Can it be learned? The upper-echelons theory favors the idea that strong leadership is the result of both innate abilities and learning. It states that executives interpret situations through a lens of their unique perspectives, shaped by personal circumstances, values, and experiences.[86] Their leadership actions reflect characteristics of age, education, and career experiences, filtered through their personalized interpretations of the situations they face.

Given the prestige, power, and compensation of top-level executives, many aspire to be effective strategic leaders. In his bestseller *Good to Great,* strategy researcher and consultant Jim Collins identified *great companies* as those that transitioned from an average performer to achieving a sustained competitive advantage. He measured that transition as "cumulative stock returns of 6.9 times the general market in the fifteen years following their transition points."[87] Collins found patterns of leadership among the companies he studied, as pictured in the **Level-5 leadership pyramid** in Exhibit 12.8 (next page).[88] The pyramid is a conceptual framework that shows leadership progression through five distinct, sequential levels. Interestingly, Collins found that all companies he identified as *great* were led by Level-5 executives.

According to the Level-5 leadership pyramid, effective executives go through a natural progression of five different levels. Each level builds upon the prior one, meaning the executive can move on to the next level of leadership only when the current level has been mastered. Characteristics of the five levels are:

- The *Level-1* manager is a highly capable individual who makes productive contributions through motivation, talent, knowledge, and skills.

- The *Level-2* manager masters the skills required at Level 1, but is also a contributing team member who works effectively with others in order to achieve synergies and team objectives.

upper-echelons theory A conceptual framework that states that it's the top management team that primarily determines the success or failure of an organization through the strategies they pursue.

Level-5 leadership pyramid A conceptual framework of leadership progression with five distinct, sequential levels.

EXHIBIT 12.8

Strategic Leaders: The
Level-5 Pyramid

Source: Adapted from J.
Collins (2001), *Good to Great:
Why Some Companies Make
the Leap ... And Others Don't*
(New York: HarperCollins),
p. 20.

Builds enduring greatness through a combination of will power and humility.
Level 5: Executive

Presents compelling vision and mission to guide groups toward superior performance. Does the right things.
Level 4: Effective Leader

Is efficient and effective in organizing resources to accomplish stated goals and objectives. Does things right.
Level 3: Competent Manager

Uses high level of individual capability to work effectively with others in order to achieve team objectives.
Level 2: Contributing Team Member

Makes productive contributions through motivation, talent, knowledge, and skills.
Level 1: Highly Capable Individual

- The *Level-3* manager is a well-rounded and competent manager, a highly capable individual who is an effective team player and organizes resources effectively to achieve predetermined goals. He or she "does things right."

- At *Level 4,* the effective manager from Level 3 turns into a leader who determines what the right decisions are. The *Level-4* leader presents and effectively communicates a compelling vision and mission to guide the firm toward superior performance. He or she "does the right things."

- Finally, at *Level 5,* the manager reaches a leadership pinnacle, turning into a strategic leader. An effective strategic leader is an executive who builds enduring greatness into the organizations he or she leads.

A strategic leader who has mastered Level 5 simultaneously combines and reconciles tremendous will power and personal modesty. Such leaders, says Collins, "channel their ego needs away from themselves and into the larger goal of building a great company. It's not that Level 5 leaders have no ego or self-interest. Indeed, they are incredibly ambitious—*but their ambition is first and foremost for the institution, not themselves.*" Indeed, Jim Collins goes so far as to argue that the greatness of a strategic leader can truly be judged only if their organizations are able to sustain a competitive advantage in the years *after* the successful executive has departed from the organization.[89]

Taken together, you become an effective and ethical leader by sequentially mastering each of the five steps in the strategic leadership pyramid. Your training in college allows you to become a highly capable individual who can make productive contributions. If you take a first job immediately after your undergraduate degree, you will likely begin your corporate career in a functional area that was your focus or major in college (e.g., accounting, operations management, marketing, finance). As you move down the learning curve through group work in college and on-the-job training, you develop the ability to work effectively with others to achieve team objectives. With these skills, you move to Level-2 leadership. As responsibilities come to you, you will be able to develop and demonstrate the ability to organize resources efficiently and effectively to achieve strategic objectives. At Level 3, you have become an effective manager—someone who produces results.

Levels 4 and 5 require a stronger element of strategic leadership than the prior levels. When given the chance to work as a general manager (someone who has profit-and-loss responsibility for a unit or group), you will need Level-4 strategic leadership qualities.

At Levels 4 and 5, you will have increasingly dramatic opportunities to put to use the AFI framework you've learned from this book: You will need to be able to present a compelling vision and mission to inspire others to achieve superior performance. Doing so requires an intimate understanding not only of the inner workings of your company (Chapters 1 and 2), but also of the external environment. The internal and external analysis concepts (Chapters 3 and 4) will help you lay the foundation to formulate strategies that can improve firm performance (Chapters 5 through 7).

Having produced results at the business level, you might be tapped as the CEO of the company. At Level-5 strategic leadership, you need to reconcile a strong will and work ethic (which got you to the top) with the humility to lead a company by example. To do this effectively, you need a deep understanding of corporate-level strategy (Chapters 8 through 10) and organizational design (Chapter 11). You also will need to exhibit unfailing personal integrity (Chapter 12).

Thus, the concepts introduced in this textbook are valid for you far beyond this semester. They will become increasingly valuable as your career progresses, and you may find the need to refresh your knowledge of strategic management over time, as new opportunities come your way. The concepts and frameworks presented herein create a foundation that you can use to climb into leadership positions in whatever organization you choose to become a part of—whether it be a local nonprofit community organization or a Fortune 100 company!

CHAPTERCASE 12 | *Consider This . . .*

LARRY ELLISON, co-founder and CEO of Oracle, was one of the chief critics of Mark Hurd's ouster as HP CEO, as ChapterCase 12 noted. Mr. Ellison and Mr. Hurd are reported to be close personal friends who play tennis together frequently. Just a few weeks after Mark Hurd's resignation from HP, Oracle hired him as co-president and appointed him to the company's board of directors. Oracle's stock market value rose by roughly $10 billion after this announcement. The entire "Hurd saga" led to a stock movement of roughly $20 billion dollars (HP lost $10 billion after Mr. Hurd's ouster and Oracle gained $10 billion after hiring him) plus an undisclosed out-of-court settlement with Ms. Fisher.[90]

In November 2010, HP announced Leo Apotheker as its new CEO. The HP boardroom drama continued, however. Leo Apotheker was let go after only 11 months on the job. Mr. Apotheker, who came to HP from the German enterprise software company SAP, proposed a new corporate strategy for HP. He suggested that HP should focus on enterprise software solutions, and thus spin out its low-margin consumer hardware business. HP's consumer hardware business resulted from the legacy acquisition of Compaq and had now grown to 40 percent of HP's total revenues of $100 billion. Under Mr. Apotheker, HP also discontinued competing in the mobile device industry, most notably tablet computers—which many viewed as HP capitulating to Apple's dominance with the iPad. Moreover, as part of his new corporate strategy, Mr. Apotheker decided to buy the British software company Autonomy for more than $10 billion, which analysts saw as grossly overvalued. Mr. Apotheker was not able to convince investors of the value of this new corporate strategy; under his 11 months as CEO, HP's stock price dropped by roughly 40 percent. In September 2011, the HP board appointed Meg Whitman to be HP's new CEO. Ms. Whitman was formerly the CEO at eBay and had been appointed early in 2011 to HP's board of directors.

1. Why do you think HP lost 40 percent of its share-holder value since the summer of 2010?

2. Given HP's poor performance described in ChapterCase 12, who is to blame? The CEO or the board of directors? What recourse do sharehold-ers have, if any?

3. Put yourself in Ms. Whitman's situation just after HP appointed her the new CEO in the fall of 2011.

What would be your strategic priorities? How would you identify them, and how would you implemented needed changes?

4. What lessons in terms of business ethics, corpo-rate governance, and strategic leadership can be drawn from ChapterCase 12?

Take-Away Concepts

In this final chapter, we looked at stakeholder strategy, corporate governance, business ethics, and strategic leadership, as summarized by the following learning objectives and related take-away concepts.

LO 12-1 Describe and critically evaluate the relationship between strategic management and the role of business in society.

>> The public stock company is the institutional backbone of any modern free-market economy.

>> Four characteristics of the public stock company make it an attractive corporate form: limited liability for investors, transferability of investor interests (the trading of stocks), legal personality, and separation of ownership and control.

>> In the first decade of the 21st century, accounting scandals and the global financial crises eroded the public's trust in business as an institution and free-market capitalism as an economic system.

>> Effective stakeholder management is necessary to ensure the continued survival of the firm and to sustain any competitive advantage.

LO 12-2 Conduct a stakeholder impact analysis.

>> Stakeholder impact analysis considers the needs of different stakeholders, which enables the firm to perform optimally and to live up to good citizenship.

>> In a stakeholder impact analysis, managers pay particular attention to three important stakeholder attributes: power, legitimacy, and urgency.

>> Stakeholder impact analysis is a five-step process that answers the following questions:

1. Who are our stakeholders?
2. What are our stakeholders' interests and claims?
3. What opportunities and threats do our stake-holders present?
4. What economic, legal, and ethical responsi-bilities do we have to our stakeholders?
5. What should we do to effectively address the stakeholder concerns?

LO 12-3 Critically evaluate the relationship between corporate social responsibility (CSR) and competitive advantage.

>> A majority of empirical research studies support the notion that firms can do well (financially) by doing good (through CSR).

>> Some studies, however, found that the relation-ship is reversed: Superior financial performance allows firms to engage in CSR (to buy good will).

>> Although there seems to be a positive relationship between CSR and firm financial performance, it is not entirely clear what causes what.

LO 12-4 Describe the role of corporate governance and evaluate different governance mechanisms.

>> Corporate governance is about checks and bal-ances, about asking the tough questions at the right time.

>> Corporate governance attempts to address the principal–agent problem, which describes any situation in which an agent performs activities on behalf of a principal.

>> The principal–agent problem is a core tenet in agency theory, which views the firm as a nexus of legal contracts.

>> The principal–agent problem concerns not only the relationship between owners (shareholders) and managers, but also cascades down the organizational hierarchy.

>> The risk of opportunism on behalf of agents is exacerbated by information asymmetry: Agents are generally better informed than the principals.

>> The board of directors is the centerpiece of corporate governance.

>> Other important corporate mechanisms are: executive compensation, the market for corporate control, and financial statement auditors, government regulators, and industry analysts.

LO 12-5 Describe and evaluate the relationship between business strategy and ethics.

>> The ethical pursuit of competitive advantage lays the foundation for long-term superior performance.

>> Law and ethics are not synonymous; obeying the law is the minimum that society expects of a corporation and its managers.

>> A manager's actions can be completely legal, but ethically questionable.

>> The following questions can help managers make sound ethical decisions.

1. Does the intended course of action fall within the acceptable norms of professional behavior?

2. Would the manager feel comfortable explaining and defending the decision in public?

3. How would the media report the particular business decision if it became public?

4. How would the company's stakeholders feel about it?

LO 12-6 Describe the different roles that strategic leaders play and how to become a strategic leader.

>> Strategic leaders play three different roles: interpersonal, informational, and decisional.

>> To become an effective strategic leader, a manager needs to develop a set of skills to move sequentially through five different leadership levels.

>> At Level 5, the executive is able to build enduring greatness for the company through a combination of will power and humility. At that level, ambition is primarily for the organization, rather than for the self.

Key Terms

Agency theory *(p. 343)*

Board of directors *(p. 344)*

Business ethics *(p. 351)*

Corporate governance *(p. 343)*

Corporate social responsibility (CSR) *(p. 339)*

Groupthink *(p. 346)*

Inside directors *(p. 345)*

Level-5 leadership pyramid *(p. 355)*

Outside directors *(p. 345)*

Stakeholder impact analysis *(p. 337)*

Stakeholder strategy *(p. 336)*

Stakeholder theory *(p. 336)*

Stock options *(p. 347)*

Strategic leadership *(p. 353)*

Upper-echelons theory *(p. 355)*

Discussion Questions

1. How can a firm lower the chances that key managers will pursue their own self-interest at the expense of the stockholders? At the expense of the employees?

2. The chapter notes that in 2010, in roughly two-thirds of U.S. firms, the CEO is also the chair of the board of directors. More broadly this can be viewed as an intermingling of management and ownership. Why are these two roles typically separated? Is it a positive development for so many firms to have a combined CEO and board chair?

3. In Chapter 6 (Strategy Highlight 6.1), we discussed how Toyota went from a "perfect recall" in the early days of its Lexus brand in 1989 to a "recall nightmare" of more than 8 million vehicles for accelerator problems in 2010. Some

analysts have questioned the role of Japanese corporate governance in the mishandling of the accelerator issues at Toyota.[91] These sources note Japan's governance system is geared around the company rather than the stockholders. Thus, boards are often all company insiders who bring a deep knowledge of company operations to the table. However, in Japan's rigid corporate hierarchy and emphasis on harmony, this can result in keeping bad news out of the boardroom. In 2010, Toyota's board of directors consisted of 29 men, *none* of whom were outsiders to the company.

a. How might Toyota's response to the initial accelerator concerns in 2009 have been different if the board had on it a former politician, the president of a communications firm, and the CEO of a major consumer-products company (as were on the board at Ford Motor Company in 2010)?

b. Does the *groupthink* discussion raised in Strategy Highlight 12.1 seem relevant here? Why or why not?

Ethical/Social Issues

1. Assume you work in the accounting department of a large software company. Toward the end of December, your supervisor tells you to change the dates on several executive stock option grants from March 15 to July 30. Why would she ask for this change? What should you do?

2. As noted in the chapter, CEO pay in 2010 was an incredible 300 times the average worker pay. This contrasts with historic values of between 25 and 40 times the average pay.

   a. What are the potentially negative effects of this increasing disparity in CEO pay?

   b. Do you believe that current executive pay packages are justified? Why or why not?

3. The MBA Oath (shown in Exhibit 12.6) says in part, "My decisions affect the well-being of individuals inside and outside my enterprise, today and tomorrow." This echoes what John Mackey of Whole Foods has in recent years called *conscious capitalism.*[92]

4. One example of a large firm reorienting toward this approach is PepsiCo. In the last few years, PepsiCo has been contracting directly with small farmers in impoverished areas (for example,

in Mexico). What started as a pilot project in PepsiCo's Sabritas snack food division has now spread to over 1,000 farmers providing potatoes, corn, and sunflower oil to the firm. Pepsi provides a price guarantee for farmers' crops that is higher and much more consistent than the previous system of using intermediaries. The farmers report that since they have a firm market, they are planting more crops. Output is up about 160 percent, and the farm incomes have tripled in the last three years.[93] The program has benefits for Pepsi as well. A shift to sunflower oil for its Mexican products will replace the 80,000 tons of palm oil it currently imports to Mexico from Asia and Africa, thus slashing transportation and storage costs.

   a. What are the benefits of this program for PepsiCo? What are its drawbacks?

   b. What other societal benefits could such a program have in Mexico?

   c. If you were a PepsiCo shareholder, would you support this program? Why or why not?

   d. Can you find other examples of firms employing "conscious capitalism"?

Small Group Exercises

SMALL GROUP EXERCISE 1

The section "Corporate Governance Around the World" makes clear that different countries have different systems of corporate governance, which in turn affect how firms compete for competitive advantage.

1. Discuss in your group the contrasting perspectives of "shareholder versus stakeholder" governance. What benefits and drawbacks can you find in each view?

2. Next, go online to find two sets of examples: (a) firms in the U.S. or Britain saving jobs by offering reduced hours to workers rather than having layoffs, and (b) large firms in Germany laying off employees or closing plants. What do the results of your search say about the impact of governance structure on corporate decisions?

3. Developments after the global financial crisis moved the U.S. away from being one of the most free-market economies in the world toward an economy with much more active and stronger government involvement. What implications does this shift in the political and economic environment in the United States have for large firms (such as GE or IBM) versus small firms (mom-and-pop entrepreneurs and technology startups)? How does this change the competitive landscape and the firms' strategies?

SMALL GROUP EXERCISE 2 (ETHICAL/SOCIAL ISSUES)

In the earlier Toyota discussion question, you may have noticed that all 29 board members were male.

Indeed, there is a greater percentage of women on corporate boards in Kuwait than in Japan.[94]

It is not unusual for even large corporate boards to have no women or minorities on them. In the U.S., women held 16 percent of board seats at Fortune 500 companies in 2010. In Europe, of the total number of board members in Britain, only 12 percent were women; Spain, France, and Germany all had less than 10 percent.[95] In Norway, by contrast, female members comprised 40 percent of the boards.

So how did Norway do it? In 2005, the government of Norway gave public firms two years to leap from 9 percent to 40 percent women on their boards. Is this a good idea? Spain, Italy, France, and the Netherlands must think so: Each country is considering implementing a similar quota (though generally with more than two years to implement it).

1. Discuss in your group to what extent it is a problem that women are proportionally underrepresented on corporate boards. Provide the rationale for your responses.

2. Would a regulatory quota be a good solution? Why or why not?

3. What other methods could be used to increase female and minority participation on corporate boards?

Strategy Term Project

MODULE 12: CORPORATE GOVERNANCE AND STRATEGIC LEADERSHIP

In this section, you will study the governance structure and leadership of your selected firm. This is also our concluding module, so we will have final questions for you to consider about your firm overall.

1. Find a list of the members of the board of directors for your firm. How large is the board? How many independent (non-employee) members are on the board? Are any women or minorities on the board? Is the CEO also the chair of the board?

2. Who are the largest stockholders of your firm? Is there a high degree of employee ownership of the stock?

3. In reviewing press releases and news articles about your firm over the past year, can you find examples of any actions the firm has taken that, though legal, may be ethically questionable?

4. Does the CEO of your firm show characteristics consistent with Level-5 leadership?

5. You have now completed 12 modular assignments about your selected firm. You know a lot about its mission, strategies, competitive advantage, and organization. Is this a company you would like to work for? If you had $1,000 to invest in a firm, would you invest it in the stock of this firm? Why or why not?

*my*Strategy

ARE YOU PART OF GEN-Y, OR WILL YOU MANAGE GEN-Y WORKERS?

Generation Y (born between 1980 and 2001) is entering the work force and advancing their careers now, as the Baby Boomers of their parents' generation begin to retire in large numbers. Given the smaller size of Gen Y compared to the Baby Boomers, this generation received much more individual attention from their immediate and extended families. Classes in school were much smaller than in previous generations. The parents of Gen Y members placed a premium on achievement, both academically and socially. Gen Y grew up during a time of unprecedented economic growth and prosperity, combined with an explosion in technology (including laptop computers, cell phones, the Internet, e-mail, instant messaging, and online social networks). Gen Yers are connected 24/7, and thus able to work anywhere, frequently multitasking. Due to the unique circumstances of their upbringing, they are said to be tech-savvy, family- and friends-centric, team players, achievement-oriented, but also attention-craving.[96]

Some have called Generation Y the "trophy kids," due in part to the practice of giving all Gen-Y children trophies in competitive activities, not wanting to single out winners and losers. When coaching a group of Gen-Y students for job interviews, a consultant asked them how they believe future employers view them. She gave them a clue to the answer: the letter E. Quickly, the students answered confidently: *excellent, enthusiastic,* and *energetic.* The answer the consultant was looking for was "entitled." Baby Boomers believe that Gen Y has an overblown sense of entitlement.

When they bring so many positive characteristics to the workplace, why do Baby Boomers view Gen-Y employees as entitled? Many managers are concerned that these young workers have outlandish expectations when compared with other employees: They often expect higher pay, flexible work schedules, promotions and significant raises every year, and generous vacation and personal time.[97] Managers also often find that for Gen-Y employees, the traditional annual or semi-annual performance evaluations are not considered sufficient. Instead, Gen-Y employees seek more immediate feedback, ideally daily or at least weekly. For many, feedback needs to come in the form of positive reinforcement rather than as a critique.

The generational tension seems a bit ironic, since the dissatisfied Baby Boomer managers are the same indulgent parents who raised Gen Yers. Some companies, like Google, RIM, and Sun Microsystems (Sun), have leveraged this tension into an opportunity. Google, for example, allows each employee to spend one day a week on any project of his or her own choosing, thus meeting the Gen-Y need for creativity and self-determination. Executives at RIM, the maker of the BlackBerry, have learned to motivate Gen-Y employees by sincerely respecting their contributions as colleagues rather than relying on hierarchical or position power.[98] The network-computing company Sun accommodates Gen-Yers' need for flexibility through drastically increasing work-from-home and telecommunicating arrangements, so that basically all employees now have a "floating office."

1. As you and your cohort enter the work force, do you expect to see a different set of business ethics take hold?

2. Are efforts such as the MBA Oath (discussed in this chapter) reflections of a different approach that Gen Y will take to the business environment, compared with prior generations?

3. Will you aspire to become a Level-5 strategic leader as you rise through your professional career? How would you go about moving from Level 1 to Level 5? What plan will you put in place?

Endnotes

1. "Mark Hurd neglected to follow H-P code," *The Wall Street Journal,* August 8, 2010.

2. "Oracle chief faults H.P. board for forcing Hurd out," *The New York Times,* August 9, 2010.

3. Finkelstein, S., D. C. Hambrick, and A. A. Cannella (2008), *Strategic Leadership: Theory and Research on Executives, Top Management Teams, and Boards* (Oxford, UK: Oxford University Press); and Yulk, G. (1998), *Leadership in Organizations,* 4th ed. (Englewood Cliff, NJ: Prentice-Hall).

4. Berle, A., Means, G. (1932), *The Modern Corporation & Private Property* (New York: Macmillan); and Monks, R.A.G., and N. Minow (2008),

Corporate Governance, 4th ed. (West Sussex, UK: Wiley).

5. This discussion draws on: Porter, M. E., and M. R. Kramer (2006), "Strategy and society: The link between competitive advantage and corporate social responsibility," *Harvard Business Review,* December: 80–92; Porter, M. E., and M. R. Kramer (2011), "Creating shared value: How to reinvent capitalism—and unleash innovation and growth," *Harvard Business Review,* January–February; Carroll, A. B., and A. K. Buchholtz (2012), *Business & Society. Ethics, Sustainability, and Stakeholder Management* (Mason, OH: South-Western Cengage); and Parmar, B. L., and R. E. Freeman, J. S. Harrison, A. C. Wicks, L. Purnell, and S. De Colle (2010), "Stakeholder theory: The state of the art," *Academy of Management Annals* 4: 403–445.

6. "The perp walk," *BusinessWeek,* January 13, 2003.

7. See the discussion by: Lowenstein, R. (2010), *The End of Wall Street* (New York: Penguin Press); Paulson, H. M. (2010), *On the Brink: Inside the Race to Stop the Collapse of the Global Financial System* (New York: Business Plus); and Wessel, D. (2010), *In FED We Trust: Ben Bernanke's War on the Great Panic* (New York: Crown Business).

8. Parmar, B. L., R. E. Freeman, J. S. Harrison, A. C. Wicks, L. Purnell, and S. De Colle (2010), "Stakeholder theory: The state of the art," *Academy of Management Annals* 4: 403–445.

9. Ibid.

10. To acknowledge the increasing importance of *stakeholder strategy,* the Strategic Management Society (SMS)—the leading association for academics, business executives, and consultants interested in strategic management—has recently created a *stakeholder strategy* division; see http://strategicmanagement.net/. Also see: Anderson, R. C. (2009), *Confessions of a Radical Industrialist: Profits, People, Purpose—Doing Business by Respecting the Earth* (New York: St. Martin's Press); Sisodia, R. S., D. B. Wolfe, and J. N. Sheth (2007), *Firms of Endearment: How World-Class Companies Profit from Passion and Purpose* (Upper Saddle River, NJ: Prentice-Hall Pearson); and Svendsen,

A. (1998), *The Stakeholder Strategy: Profiting from Collaborative Business Relationships* (San Francisco, CA: Berrett-Koehler).

11. This discussion is based on: Freeman, R. E. (1984), *Strategic Management: A Stakeholder Approach* (Boston, MA: Pitman); Jones, T. M. (1995), "Instrumental stakeholder theory: A synthesis of ethics and economics," *Academy of Management Review* 20: 404–437; Jones, T. M, and A. C. Wicks (1999), "Convergent stakeholder theory," *Academy of Management Review* 20: 404–437; and Parmar, B. L., R. E. Freeman, J. S. Harrison, A. C. Wicks, L. Purnell, and S. De Colle (2010), "Stakeholder theory: The state of the art," *Academy of Management Annals* 4: 403–445.

12. Parmar, B. L., R. E. Freeman, J. S. Harrison, A. C. Wicks, L. Purnell, and S. De Colle (2010), "Stakeholder theory," p. 406.

13. Ibid. Emphasis (*italics*) added.

14. Ibid., p. 416.

15. *Fortune 2010 The World Most Admired Companies,* http://money.cnn.com/magazines/fortune/mostadmired/2010/full_list/.

16. Mitchell, R. K., B. R. Agle, and D. J. Wood (1997), "Toward a theory of stakeholder identification and salience," *Academy of Management Review* 22: 853–886; and Eesley, C., and M. J. Lenox (2006), "Firm responses to secondary stakeholder action," *Strategic Management Journal* 27: 765–781.

17. TIAA-CREF is an acronym for Teachers Insurance and Annuity Association–College Retirement Equities Fund.

18. CalPERS is an acronym for California Public Employees' Retirement System.

19. People for the Ethical Treatment of Animals (PETA) is an animal rights organization.

20. This example is drawn from: Esty, D. C., and A. S. Winston (2006), *Green to Gold: How Smart Companies Use Environmental Strategy to Innovate, Create Value, and Build Competitive Advantage* (Hoboken, NJ: Wiley).

21. This discussion draws on: Carroll, A. B., and A. K. Buchholtz

(2012), *Business & Society. Ethics, Sustainability, and Stakeholder Management* (Mason, OH: South-Western Cengage); Carroll, A. B. (1991), "The pyramid of corporate social responsibility: Toward the moral management of organizational stakeholders," *Business Horizons,* July–August: 39–48; and Carroll, A. B. (1979), "A three-dimensional, conceptual model of corporate social performance," *Academy of Management Review* 4: 497–505.

22. For an insightful but critical treatment of this topic, see the 2003 Canadian documentary film *The Corporation.*

23. www.ge.com.

24. "Wal-Mart tops list of charitable cash contributors, AT&T No. 2," *USAToday.com,* August 9, 2010, www.usatoday.com/money/companies/2010-08-08-corporate-philanthropy-interactive-graphic_N.htm.

25. Carroll, A. B. (1991), "The pyramid of corporate social responsibility," pp. 39–48.

26. Friedman, M. (1962), *Capitalism and Freedom* (Chicago, IL: University of Chicago Press). Quoted in Friedman, M. (1970), "The social responsibility of business is to increase its profits," *The New York Times Magazine,* September 13.

27. "Milton Friedman goes on tour," *The Economist,* January 27, 2011.

28. The Four Asian Tigers denotes four highly developed economies in Southeast Asia (Hong Kong, Singapore, South Korea, and Taiwan).

29. Porter, M. E., and M. R. Kramer (2006), "Strategy and society: The link between competitive advantage and corporate social responsibility," *Harvard Business Review,* December: 80–92.

30. Porter, M. E., and M. R. Kramer (2011), "Creating shared value: How to reinvent capitalism—and unleash innovation and growth," *Harvard Business Review,* January–February.

31. *GE Governance Principles,* p. 1, www.ge.com.

32. Orlitzky, M., F. L. Schmidt, and S. L. Rynes (2003), "Corporate social and financial performance: A meta-analysis," *Organization Studies,* 24: 403–441.

33. Margolis, J. D., and J. P. Walsh (2001), *People and Profits? The Search for a Link between a Company's Social and Financial Performance* (Mahwah, NJ: Erlbaum).

34. Monks, R.A.G., and N. Minow (2008), *Corporate Governance,* 4th ed. (West Sussex, UK: Wiley).

35. Markopolos, H. (2010), *No One Would Listen: A True Financial Thriller* (Hoboken, NJ: Wiley).

36. Berle, A., and G. Means (1932), *The Modern Corporation & Private Property* (New York, Macmillan); Jensen, M., and W. Meckling (1976), "Theory of the firm: Managerial behavior, agency costs and ownership structure," *Journal of Financial Economics* 3: 305–360; and Fama, E. (1980), "Agency problems and the theory of the firm," *Journal of Political Economy* 88: 375–390.

37. "Top 10 crooked CEOs," *Time,* June 9, 2009.

38. "Thain ousted in clash at Bank of America," *The Wall Street Journal,* January 23, 2009.

39. Agency theory originated in finance; see Jensen, M., and W. Meckling (1976), "Theory of the firm: Managerial behavior, agency costs and ownership structure," *Journal of Financial Economics* 3: 305–360; and Fama, E. (1980), "Agency problems and the theory of the firm," *Journal of Political Economy* 88: 375–390. For an application to strategic management, see Eisenhardt, K. M. (1989), "Agency theory: An assessment and review," *Academy of Management Review* 14: 57–74; and Mahoney, J. T. (2005), *Economic Foundations of Strategy* (Thousand Oaks, CA: Sage).

40. Eisenhardt, K. M. (1989), "Agency theory: An assessment and review," *Academy of Management Review* 14: 57–74.

41. This section draws on: Monks, R.A.G., and N. Minow (2008), *Corporate Governance,* 4th ed. (West Sussex, UK: Wiley); Williamson, O. E. (1984), "Corporate governance," *Yale Law Journal* 93: 1197–1230; and Williamson, O. E. (1985), *The Economic Institutions of Capitalism* (New York: Free Press).

42. "HP looks beyond its ranks," *The Wall Street Journal,* August 9, 2010.

43. "Apple chief to take leave," *The Wall Street Journal,* January 18, 2010.

44. "HP shakes up board in scandal's wake," *The Wall Street Journal,* January 21, 2011.

45. "On Apple's board, fewer independent voices," *The Wall Street Journal,* March 24, 2010.

46. This Strategy Highlight is based on: "2010 Catalyst census: Fortune 500 women board directors," www.catalyst.org; Baliga, B. R., R. C. Moyer, and R. S. Rao (1996), "CEO duality and firm performance: What's the fuss," *Strategic Management Journal* 17: 41–53; Brickley, J. A., J. L. Coles, and G. Jarrell (1997), "Leadership structure: Separating the CEO and chairman of the board," *Journal of Corporate Finance* 3: 189–220; Daily, C. M., and D. R. Dalton (1997), "CEO and board chair roles held jointly or separately," *Academy of Management Executive* 3: 11–20; "GE governance principles," www.ge.com; Irving, J. (1972), *Victims of Groupthink. A Psychological Study of Foreign-Policy Decisions and Fiascoes,* (Boston, MA: Houghton Mifflin); Jensen, M. C. (1993), "The modern industrial revolution, exit, and the failure of internal control systems," *Journal of Corporate Finance* 48: 831–880; "On Apple's board, fewer independent voices," *The Wall Street Journal,* March 24, 2010; "Strings attached to options grant for GE's Immelt," *The Wall Street Journal,* April 20, 2011; Westphal, J. D., and E. J. Zajac (1995), "Who shall govern? CEO board power, demographic similarity and new director selection," *Administrative Science Quarterly* 40: 60–83; and Westphal, J. D., and I. Stern (2007), "Flattery will get you everywhere (especially if you are male Caucasian): How ingratiation, boardroom behavior, and demographic minority status affect additional board appointments at U.S. companies," *Academy of Management Journals* 50: 267–288.

47. "HP shareholders sue Hurd, Board over resignation," *Bloomberg Businessweek,* August 12, 2010.

48. www.faireconomy.org.

49. "Paychecks for CEOs climb," *The Wall Street Journal,* November 15, 2010.

50. Heineman, B. W. (2008), "The fatal flaw in pay for performance," *Harvard Business Review,* June; and Kaplan, S.

N. (2008), "Are U.S. CEOs overpaid?" *Academy of Management Perspectives* 22: 5–20.

51. "Paychecks for CEOs climb," *The Wall Street Journal,* November 15, 2010.

52. "Strings attached to options grant for GE's Immelt," *The Wall Street Journal,* April 20, 2011.

53. Ariely, D. (2010), *The Upside of Irrationality: The Unexpected Benefits of Defying Logic at Work and at Home* (New York: HarperCollins).

54. "Sanofi wins long-sought biotech deal," *The Wall Street Journal,* February 17, 2011.

55. www.fasb.gov: "The term 'generally accepted accounting principles' has a specific meaning for accountants and auditors. The AICPA Code of Professional Conduct prohibits members from expressing an opinion or stating affirmatively that financial statements or other financial data 'present fairly . . . in conformity with generally accepted accounting principles,' if such information contains any departures from accounting principles promulgated by a body designated by the AICPA Council to establish such principles. The AICPA Council designated FASAB as the body that establishes generally accepted accounting principles (GAAP) for federal reporting entities."

56. Lowenstein, R. (2010), *The End of Wall Street* (New York: Penguin Press).

57. Hayward, M.L.A., and W. Boeker (1998), "Power and conflicts of interest in professional firms: Evidence from investment banking," *Administrative Science Quarterly* 43: 1–22.

58. Gedajlovic, E. R., and D. M. Shapiro (1998), "Management and ownership effects: Evidence from five countries," *Strategic Management Journal* 19: 533–553.

59. Lowenstein, R. (2010), *The End of Wall Street* (New York: Penguin Press).

60. Tuschke, A., and G. W. Sanders (2003), "Antecedents and consequences of corporate governance reform: The case of Germany," *Strategic Management Journal* 24: 631–649.

61. "Hoard instinct," *The Economist,* July 8, 2010.

62. "Boards behaving badly," *The Economist,* August 6, 2009.

63. "La vie en rose. French companies get serious about putting women in the boardroom," *The Economist,* May 6, 2010.

64. "Preliminary Notification To The General Meeting Of The Shareholders," Dassault Systems, May 26, 2011, www.3ds.com.

65. "Bernadette Chirac, Director, LVMH Moet Hennessy Louis Vuitton," *Bloomberg Businessweek,* http://investing.businessweek.com.

66. White, G., J. Howell, and H. Shang (1996), *In Search of Civil Society: Market Reform and Social Change in Contemporary China* (Oxford, UK: Clarendon Press); and Peng, M. W. (2003), "Outside directors and firm performance during institutional transitions," *Strategic Management Journal* 25: 453–472.

67. "China sentences Rio Tinto employees in bribe Case," *The New York Times,* March 29, 2010.

68. "BP's Russian troubles: Dudley do-wrong," *The Economist,* March 31, 2011.

69. This section draws on and the definition is from: Treviño, L. K., and K. A. Nelson (2011), *Managing Business Ethics: Straight Talk About How to Do It Right,* 5th ed. (Hoboken, NJ: Wiley).

70. Several such studies, like the "ultimatum game," are described in: Ariely, D. (2008), *Predictably Irrational: The Hidden Forces That Shape Our Decisions* (New York: HarperCollins); and Ariely, D. (2010), *The Upside of Irrationality: The Unexpected Benefits of Defying Logic at Work and at Home* (New York: HarperCollins).

71. Lowenstein, R. (2010), *The End of Wall Street* (New York: Penguin Press).

72. Khurana, R. (2007), *From Higher Aims to Hired Hands: The Social Transformation of American Business Schools and the Unfulfilled Promise of Management as a Profession* (Princeton, NJ: Princeton University Press).

73. Khurana, R., and N. Nohria (2008), "It's time to make management a true profession," *Harvard Business Review,* October: 70–77.

74. www.mbaoath.org.

75. This section draws on: Treviño, L. K., and K. A. Nelson (2011), *Managing Business Ethics.*

76. Treviño, L., and A. Youngblood (1990), "Bad apples in bad barrels: A causal analysis of ethical-decision behavior," *Journal of Applied Psychology* 75: 378–385.

77. Ibid. Also, for a superb review and discussion of this issue, see Treviño, L. K., and K. A. Nelson (2011), *Managing Business Ethics.*

78. McLean, B., and P. Elkind (2004), *The Smartest Guys in the Room: The Amazing Rise and Scandalous Fall of Enron* (New York: Portfolio).

79. Finkelstein, S., D. C. Hambrick, and A. A. Cannella (2008), *Strategic Leadership,* p. 4.

80. Hambrick, D. C., and E. Abrahamson (1995), "Assessing managerial discretion across industries: A multimethod approach," *Academy of Management Journal* 38: 1427–1441.

81. Mintzberg, H. (1973), *The Nature of Managerial Work* (New York: Harper & Row).

82. Finkelstein, S., D. C. Hambrick, and A. A. Cannella (2008), *Strategic Leadership,* p. 17.

83. This section draws on: Mintzberg, H. (1973), *The Nature of Managerial Work;* and Finkelstein, S., D. C. Hambrick, and A. A. Cannella (2008), *Strategic Leadership,* p. 17–18.

84. Bower, J. L., and C. G. Gilbert (2005), *From Resource Allocation to Strategy* (Oxford, UK: Oxford University Press).

85. Hambrick, D. C. (2007), "Upper echelons theory: An update," *Academy of Management Review* 32: 334–343; and Hambrick, D. C., and P. A. Mason (1984), "Upper echelons: The organization as a reflection of its top managers," *Academy of Management Review* 9: 193–206.

86. Ibid.

87. Collins, J. (2001), *Good to Great: Why Some Companies Make the Leap . . . And Others Don't* (New York: HarperCollins), p. 3.

88. Ibid.

89. Ibid.

90. This ChapterCase discussion is based on: "Mark Hurd neglected to follow H-P code," *The Wall Street Journal,* August 8, 2010; "Oracle chief faults HP board for forcing Hurd out," *The New York Times,* August 9, 2010; "HP shakes up board in scandal's wake," *The Wall Street Journal,* January 21, 2011; "Hewlett-Packard: Worst board ever?" *The Wall Street Journal,* September 21, 2011; "Crisis unfolds at HP over CEO," *The Wall Street Journal,* September 22, 2011; "Whitman takes charge," *The Wall Street Journal,* September 24, 2011; Collins, J. (2009), *How the Mighty Fall: And Why Some Companies Never Give In* (New York: HarperCollins); and Packard, D. (1995), *The HP Way: How Bill Hewlett And I Built Our Company* (New York: HarperCollins).

91. "Accelerating into trouble," *The Economist,* February 11, 2010; and "A recall for Toyota's corporate governance?" *Pensions & Investments,* April 5, 2010.

92. "The conscience of a capitalist," *The Wall Street Journal,* October 3, 2009.

93. "For Pepsi, a business decision with social benefit," *The New York Times,* February 21, 2011.

94. "Accelerating into trouble," *The Economist,* February 11, 2010.

95. "Skirting the issue," *The Economist,* March 11, 2010.

96. This *my*Strategy module is based on: "The 'trophy kids' go to work," *The Wall Street Journal,* October 21, 2008; and Alsop, R. (2008), *The Trophy Kids Grow Up: How the Millennial Generation Is Shaking Up the Workplace* (Hoboken, NJ: Jossey-Bass).

97. Survey by CareerBuilder.com.

98. Presentation by Robin Bienfait, CIO, RIM, March 9, 2009, Georgia Institute of Technology.

PART 4
MINICASES

MICHAEL PHELPS, nicknamed MP, won an unprecedented eight gold medals at the Beijing Summer Olympics, and while doing so set seven new world records. Eight short days in August 2008 changed Olympic history and Michael Phelps's life forever, making MP one of the greatest athletes of all time. Immediately after the event, *The Wall Street Journal* reported that Phelps would be likely to turn the eight gold medals into a cash-flow stream of more than $100 million through a variety of business activities.[1] The more obvious ones were product and service endorsements: His official sponsors included AT&T Wireless, Kellogg's, Omega, PowerBar, Rosetta Stone, Speedo, Visa, and PureSport. Other offers included the exotic and the mundane: books and movies, sculptures eternalizing his muscled

torso, acrylic paintings, dog food (given Michael's love for his British bulldog, Herman), commemorative coins, tuxedos, car rims, and even bobblehead dolls.

In his youth, MP was diagnosed with attention deficit hyperactivity disorder (ADHD). Doctors prescribed swimming to help him release his energy. It worked! Between 2004 and 2008, Michael Phelps attended the University of Michigan, studying marketing and management. He had already competed quite successfully in the 2004 Athens Summer Olympics, where he won eight medals: six gold and two bronze. Right after the Athens Games, the then-19-year-old sat down with his manager, Peter Carlisle, and his long-time swim coach, Bob Bowman, to map out a detailed strategy for the next four years. The explicit goal was to win nothing less than a gold medal in each of the events in which he would compete in Beijing, thus preparing the launch pad for his superstardom.[2]

Bob Bowman was responsible for getting MP into the necessary physical shape he needed for Beijing and nurturing the mental toughness required to break Mark Spitz's 36-year record of seven gold medals won in the 1972 Munich Olympic Games. Peter Carlisle, meanwhile, conceived of a detailed strategy to launch MP

as a world superstar during the Beijing Games. While MP spent six hours a day in the pool, Carlisle focused on exposing MP to the Asian market, the largest consumer market in the world, with a special emphasis on the Chinese consumer. The earliest tie-in was with a Hong Kong–based manufacturer of MP3 players and other consumer electronics, Matsunichi, with whom MP became affiliated right after the 2004 Athens Games. MP made several other visits to China during the 2005–2007 period, among them the "Visa Friendship Lanes Tour" to promote the Special Olympics.

MP's wide-ranging presence in the real world was combined with a huge exposure in the virtual world. Phelps posts and maintains his own Facebook page, with millions of "phans" whose click-through rivaled the site of President Barack Obama in popularity. MP is also a favorite of YouTube and other online blogs (e.g., Swimroom.com), garnering worldwide exposure to an extent never before achieved by an Olympian.[3] The gradual buildup of Phelps over a number of years enabled manager Peter Carlisle to launch MP as a superstar right after he won his eighth gold medal at the Beijing Games. By then, MP had become a worldwide brand.

Clearly, a successful strategy rests on leveraging unique resources and capabilities. Accordingly, some suggest that MP's success can be explained by his unique physical endowments: his long thin torso, which reduces drag; his arm span of 6 feet 7 inches (204 cm), which is disproportionate to his 6-foot-4-inch (193 cm) height; his relatively short legs for a person of his height; and his size-14 feet which work like flippers due to hypermobile ankles.[4] While MP's physical attributes are a *necessary* condition for winning, they are *not sufficient*. Many other swimmers, like the Australian Ian Thorpe (who has size-17 feet) or the German "albatross" Michael Gross (with an arm span of 7 feet or 213 cm), also brought extraordinary resource endowments to the swim meet. Yet neither of them won eight gold medals in a single Olympics.

DISCUSSION QUESTIONS

Review Chapter 1: What Is Strategy and Why Is It Important?

1. How did Michael Phelps turn into a "global brand"?

2. What does the story of Michael Phelps have to do with strategic management?

3. Following the Beijing Olympics, a photo published by a British tabloid showed Michael Phelps using a "bong," a device for smoking marijuana, at a party in South Carolina. Kellogg's withdrew Phelps's endorsement contract. What does this incident tell you about maintaining and increasing brand value over time?

4. According to a study by two economics professors at the University of California, Davis,[5] another recent example of an athlete who lost significant "brand value" is Tiger Woods, who destroyed an estimated $12 billion in stock market value of the firms sponsoring him—Accenture, Gillette, Nike, PepsiCo (Gatorade), and Electronic Arts (EA). As a manager, what lessons about celebrity endorsements can you draw from the examples of Phelps and Woods? What are some general take-aways that a strategist should keep in mind?

5. *After reading Chapter 2:* Did Michael Phelps or his team follow one of the approaches to strategy making discussed in Chapter 2? Explain your response.

Endnotes

1. "Now, Phelps chases gold on land," *The Wall Street Journal,* August 18, 2008.

2. Ibid.

3. "Michael Phelps' agent has been crafting the swimmer's image for years," *Associated Press,* September 14, 2008.

4. "Profile: Michael Phelps – A normal guy from another planet," *Telegraph,* August 15, 2008.

5. Knittel, C. R., and V. Stango (2008), "Celebrity endorsements, firm value and reputation risk: Evidence from the Tiger Woods scandal," working paper, University of California, Davis, http://faculty.gsm.ucdavis.edu/~vstango/tiger007.pdf.

ABOUT 20 MILLION U.S. MEN experience some form of male erectile dysfunction (MED), and treating the disorder with prescription drugs is a business worth more than $3 billion a year. Was this great pharmaceutical success the result of smart strategic planning? Far from it. Without serendipity, sometimes there would be no success story. Here is how two modern blockbuster drugs were discovered.

In the 1990s, researchers at Pfizer developed the compound UK-95,480 as a potential drug to treat heart disease. In their research, they focused on two things: preventing blood clots and enhancing blood flow. The drug did not achieve the desired effects in human trials, but some men in the test group reported an unexpected side-effect: prolonged erections. Pfizer's managers were quick to turn this unintended result into the blockbuster drug Viagra.

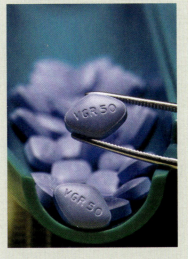

Although the old adage says lightning never strikes the same place twice, it did so in the area of MED drugs. In the mid-1990s, the biotech firm Icos was developing a new treatment for hypertension. Code named IC-351, the drug moved quickly to clinical trials because of encouraging lab results. Then unexpected things happened. First was the unusually high compliance rate of patients who took the medication required by the trial, especially males in their fifties, despite the fact that IC-351 turned out to be ineffective in treating hypertension. The second surprise was that many male patients refused to return their surplus pills. The reason: their improved sex life. Icos's IC-351 had failed to treat hypertension but succeeded at treating MED. Marketed as Cialis, it is a major competitor to Viagra, and its success led Lilly to acquire Icos for $2.3 billion in 2007.[1]

DISCUSSION QUESTIONS

Review Chapter 1: What Is Strategy and Why Is It Important?

Review Chapter 2: The Strategic Management Process.

1. Do you think "serendipity is random," as some say? Why or why not?

2. What does the "discovery" of Viagra and Cialis tell us about the strategic management process? About the role of strategic initiatives?

3. Which model of strategy process best explains the Viagra/Cialis story? Why?

4. Does the Viagra/Cialis story influence how you would design a strategic management process? Why or why not? If yes, what process would you design?

Endnotes

1. This MiniCase is based on: Mestel, R. (1999), "Sexual chemistry," *Discover*, January: 32; "Eli Lilly says Icos acquisition complete," *Reuters*, January 29, 2007; and Deeds, D. L., and F. T. Rothaermel (2003), "Honeymoons and liabilities: The relationship between alliance age and performance in R&D alliances," *Journal of Product Innovation Management* 20, no. 6: 468–484.

ACCORDING TO A STUDY by Stanford University, one-third of all U.S. consumers believe global warming is the most serious ecological issue facing the world today. More than half the respondents view this issue as extremely or very important, almost double the number just a decade ago.

The Home Depot responded to consumers' demands for more green products. On Earth Day 2007, it launched a new product label called Eco Options, using strict criteria to designate products as ecologically friendly in five ways: Sustainable Forestry, Clean Air, Water Conservation, Energy Efficient, and Healthy Home. The desire to earn an Eco Options label from The Home Depot has spurred its suppliers to innovate by offering even more ecologically friendly products, such as super low-flow toilets and energy-efficient appliances and lighting. The over 4,000 stock-keeping units (SKUs) that carry the Eco Options label brought in about $2.2 billion in sales and the brand is growing fast. The average customer's purchase basket that contains an Eco Options product was $107, compared with an overall average of $58; implying that the Eco Options label garnered an 85 percent price premium.

Competitor Lowe's was also quick to catch the green wave. Early in 2007, it began introducing organic gardening supplies, including fertilizer, soil, and insecticides that are not only ecologically friendly but also harmless for children and pets. Lowe's claims that more than 100 million people in the United States use some kind of organic lawn and garden product. It even opened new stores dedicated to ecologically friendly products such as bamboo flooring and blinds.[1]

DISCUSSION QUESTIONS

Review Chapter 3: External Analysis: Industry Structure, Competitive Forces, and Strategic Groups.

1. Apply a PESTEL analysis to the The Home Depot and Ford Motor Company. Which are the most important external forces impinging upon the companies? Are the forces the same, or are they different? Why?

2. Do you believe that The Home Depot is "catching the green wave" or merely engaging in "greenwashing" (expressing environmentalist concerns as a cover for products, policies, or activities that may not be all that green)?[2] Support your arguments.

3. Is it ethical to charge a price premium for "green-label products" even though some of them were already offered and the only change is that they now carry a "green label"? Why or why not?

4. *After reading Chapter 4:* What conclusions do you draw by applying a SWOT analysis to The Home Depot and Ford Motor Company? For which company is a stronger ecological awareness by consumers a threat, and for which one do you think it is an opportunity? Can some companies turn threats into opportunities, and if so, how?

5. *After reading Chapter 5:* Can The Home Depot's Eco Options be a significant positive contributor to firm performance as measured by:

   a. Economic value created, accounting profitability, and shareholder value?

   b. The triple bottom line?

   c. The balanced scorecard?

Endnotes

1. Author's interviews with John R. Tovar, former Regional VP, The Home Depot; "Growing number of Americans see warming as leading threat," *The Washington Post,* April 20, 2007; "More retailers go for green–The eco kind; Home Depot tags friendly products," *USA Today,* April 18, 2007; and Esty, D. C., and A. S. Winston (2009), *Green to Gold: How Smart Companies Use Environmental Strategy to Innovate, Create Value, and Build Competitive Advantage* (Hoboken, NJ: Wiley).

2. www.merriam-webster.com/dictionary/greenwashing.

INSPIRED BY ITALIAN coffee bars, Starbucks's CEO Howard Schultz set out to provide a completely new consumer experience. The trademark of any Starbucks coffeehouse is its ambience—where music and comfortable chairs and sofas encourage customers to sit and enjoy their coffee beverages. While hanging out at Starbucks, they can use the complimentary wireless hotspot or just visit with friends. The barista seems to speak a foreign language as she rattles off the offerings: Caffé Misto, Caramel Macchiato, Cinnamon Dolce Latte, Espresso Con Panna, or a Mint Mocha Chip Frappuccino, among some 30 different coffee blends. Dazzled and enchanted, customers pay $4 or more for a Venti-sized drink. Starbucks has been so successful in creating its ambience that customers keep coming back for more.

Starbucks's core competency was to create a unique consumer experience the world over. That is what customers are paying for, not for the cup of coffee or tea. The consumer experience that Starbucks created was a valuable, rare, and costly-to-imitate intangible resource. This allowed Starbucks to gain a competitive advantage.

While intangible resources are often built through learning from experience, intangible resources can atrophy through forgetting. This is what happened to Starbucks. Recently, Starbucks expanded operations by opening over 16,000 stores in some 50 countries. It also branched out into desserts, sandwiches, books, music, and other retail merchandise, straying from its core business. Trying to keep up with its explosive growth in both the number of stores and product offerings, Starbucks began to forget what made it unique. It lost the appeal that made it special, and its unique culture got diluted. For example, baristas used to grind beans throughout the day whenever a new pot of coffee had to be brewed (which was at least every eight minutes). The grinding sounds and fresh coffee aroma were trademarks of Starbucks stores. Instead, to accommodate its fast growth, many baristas began to grind all of the day's coffee beans in the morning and store them for the rest of the day.

Coming out of an eight-year retirement, Howard Schultz again took the reins as CEO and president in January 2008, attempting to re-create what had made Starbucks special. In late 2009, Starbucks introduced Via, its new instant coffee, a move that some worried might further dilute the brand. In the fall of 2010, Schultz rolled out a new guideline: Baristas would no longer multitask, making multiple drinks at the same time, but would instead focus on no more than two drinks at a time, starting a second one while finishing the first. The goal was to bring back the customer experience that built the Starbucks brand.[1]

DISCUSSION QUESTIONS

Review Chapter 4: Internal Analysis: Resources, Capabilities, and Activities.

1. How did Starbucks create its uniqueness in the first place?

2. Was Starbucks's uniqueness a VRIO resource? Did it help Starbucks gain and sustain a competitive advantage? Why or why not?

3. Why and how did Starbucks lose its uniqueness?

4. How is Starbucks attempting to re-create its uniqueness? Do you think it will be successful? Why or why not?

5. Explain Starbucks's ups and downs using (a) strategic activity systems and (b) the dynamic capabilities perspective. What implications can you draw?

6. What recommendations would you give Howard Schultz? Support your arguments.

Endnotes

1. This MiniCase is based on: Schultz, H., and D. J. Yang (1999), *Pour Your Heart Into It: How Starbucks Built a Company One Cup at a Time* (New York: Hyperion); Behar, H. (2007), *It's Not About the Coffee: Leadership Principles from a Life at Starbucks* (New York: Portfolio); "Latest Starbucks buzzword: 'Lean' Japanese techniques," *The Wall Street Journal,* August 4, 2009; and "At Starbucks, baristas told no more than two drinks," *The Wall Street Journal,* October 13, 2010, http://investor.starbucks.com.

AN INVESTMENT OF $100 in General Electric (GE) on April 22, 1981, when Jack Welch took over as chairman and CEO would have been worth $6,320 by 2000.[1] Including stock price appreciation plus dividends, GE's total shareholder return was thus 6,220 percent during this period, equating to an annual compounded growth rate of about 23 percent.

Although the sheer magnitude of GE's total returns to shareholders is impressive, to assess whether GE had a competitive advantage that produced that return, we need a benchmark. Because GE is a widely diversified conglomerate spanning financial, industrial, and media operations, one common metric for comparison is a broad stock market index like the Dow Jones Industrial Index (DJIA). The DJIA (or Dow 30) represents an average stock return, based on the stock prices of the 30 most widely held public companies in the U.S. The DJIA was established in 1896, and GE is the only company remaining from its original members.

Although the DJIA had a return of slightly over 1,000 percent between 1981 and the end of 2000, this return is dwarfed when compared with GE's more than 3,000 percent return for the same period. (See Exhibit MC5.1.) This comparison implies that GE outperformed the DJIA by a magnitude of about 3.5 during this 20-year time period.

When we apply total return to shareholders as a performance metric, GE's total return of 6,220 percent is astonishing. GE clearly enjoyed a *sustained competitive advantage* during the Jack Welch area. This feat is even more impressive for two reasons. First, the calculation was set in a way that both started at 0 percent in 1981. Second, GE is one of the 30 companies included in the DJIA, and thus it is one big reason why the DJIA performed quite well during the 1981–2000 time frame.

Jeffrey Immelt was appointed GE's CEO and chairman on September 7, 2001. The performance of GE's stock versus the DJIA during Immelt's tenure is depicted in Exhibit MC5.2.

EXHIBIT MC5.1

GE under Jack Welch: GE Stock Performance vs. DJIA, 4/1/1981–9/6/2001
Source: MSN Money.

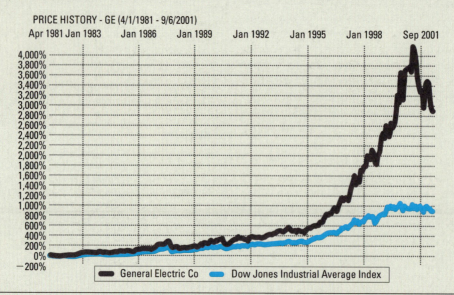

EXHIBIT MC5.2

GE under Jeffrey Immelt: GE Stock Performance vs. DJIA, 9/7/2001–1/24/2011
Source: MSN Money.

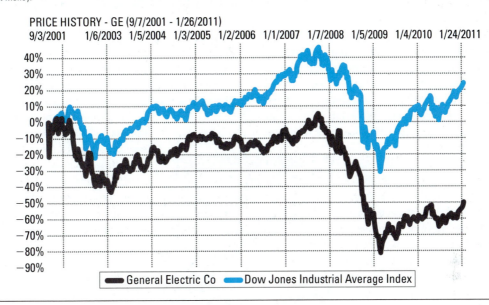

PRICE HISTORY - GE (9/7/2001 - 1/26/2011)

DISCUSSION QUESTIONS

Review Chapter 5: Competitive Advantage and Firm Performance.

1. Do you agree with the claim that "GE experienced a *sustained competitive advantage* under Jack Welch, while it experienced a *sustained competitive disadvantage* under Jeffrey Immelt"? Why or why not?

2. Shareholder value creation is one of the metrics discussed in Chapter 5 to assess firm performance. Do you consider this metric to be the most important one? Why or why not?

3. As discussed in Chapter 5, in what other ways could you assess firm performance and competitive advantage? Would that answer change your assessment of the two different time periods presented?

4. How much of the performance difference in the Welch versus Immelt time periods do you believe can be directly attributed to the respective CEO? What other factors might have played an important role in determining firm performance? (Hint: Consider especially the time period since 2001.)

Endnotes

1. "GE's Welch will be a tough act to follow; Math shows stock unlikely to repeat its rise," *The New York Times,* November 28, 2000.

JETBLUE AIRWAYS was founded by former Southwest Airlines (SWA) employee David Neeleman in 1998. Mr. Neeleman became part of SWA in 1992, when SWA acquired Morris Air, an airline he founded in 1984 at the age of 25. Morris Air was a low-fare airline that pioneered many of the activities, such as e-ticketing, that later became standard in the industry.

When Neeleman designed JetBlue, he improved upon the SWA business model to enable his new company to provide tickets at even lower costs than SWA. JetBlue reproduces many of SWA's cost-reducing activities such as flying point-to-point to directly connect city pairs. It also predominantly uses one type of airplane, the Airbus A320, to lower its maintenance costs. In addition, JetBlue flies longer distances and transports more passengers per flight than SWA, further driving down its costs. Initially, JetBlue enjoyed the lowest cost per available seat-mile in the United States.

JetBlue also attempts to enhance its differential appeal, thus driving up its perceived value. JetBlue founder Neeleman argues that the airline combines high-tech to drive down costs with "high-touch" to enhance the customer experience. Some of JetBlue's value-enhancing features include high-end 100-seat Embraer regional jets with leather seats, individual TV screens (with 20th Century Fox movies, LiveTV, Fox TV, and DirectTV programming), 100 channels of XM Satellite Radio, and free in-flight Wi-Fi capabilities (offered in partnership with BlackBerry and Yahoo), along with friendly and attentive on-board service and other amenities. (JetBlue ads invite customers to hit the in-cabin "call button.") While JetBlue offers a highly functional website for reservations and other travel-related services, some customers (about 30 percent) prefer speaking to a live agent. Rather than outsourcing its reservation system to India, JetBlue employs stay-at-home parents in the Rocky Mountain states. The company suggests this "home sourcing" is

at least 30 percent more productive than outsourcing. More importantly, customers value their reservation experience much more, which the carrier believes more than makes up for the wage differential between the U.S. and India.

In early 2007, however, JetBlue's reputation for outstanding customer service ("we bring humanity back to air travel") took a major hit when several flights were delayed due to a snowstorm in which the airline kept passengers on board the aircraft, some sitting on the tarmac for up to nine hours. Many wondered whether JetBlue was losing its magic touch. In May 2007, David Neeleman left JetBlue. He founded Azul (which means "blue" in Portuguese), a Brazilian airline in 2008.[1]

DISCUSSION QUESTIONS

Review Chapter 6: Business Strategy: Differentiation, Cost Leadership, and Integration.

1. What type of generic business strategy is JetBlue pursuing: cost leadership, differentiation, or integration?

2. What challenges is JetBlue facing with its chosen business strategy? What is the cause of these challenges? How should they be addressed?

3. What do you recommend JetBlue's top management should do to improve the airline's competitiveness?

Endnotes

1. This MiniCase is based on: Neeleman, D. (2003), *Entrepreneurial Thought Leaders Lecture,* Stanford Technology Ventures Program, April 30; Friedman, T. (2005), *The World Is Flat: A Brief History of the Twenty-First Century* (New York: Farrar, Straus and Giroux); Bryce, D. J., and J. H. Dyer (2007), "Strategies to crack well-guarded markets," *Harvard Business Review,* May; "Held hostage on the tarmac: Time for a passenger bill of rights?" *The New York Times,* February 16, 2007; and "Can JetBlue weather the storm?" *Time,* February 21, 2007.

IN THE FUTURE TRANSITION away from gasoline-powered cars, Nissan's CEO Carlos Ghosn firmly believes the next technological paradigm will be electric motors. Ghosn calls hybrids a "halfway technology" and suggests they will be a temporary phenomenon at best. A number of startup companies, including Tesla Motors in the United States and BYD in China, share Ghosn's belief in this particular future scenario.

One of the biggest impediments to large-scale adoption of electric vehicles, however, is the lack of appropriate infrastructure: There are few stations on the roads where drivers can recharge their car's battery when necessary. With the mileage range of electric vehicles currently limited to 100–200 miles, a lack of recharging stations is a serious problem.

To overcome this lack of complementary assets, the California startup Better Place is building an extensive network of stations (at present, in Hawaii, Israel, Denmark, and Australia) where drivers of electric vehicles can swap their batteries. The idea is that car manufacturers will sell electric cars without the battery (dramatically lowering their price), and drivers will rent battery power by the mile from Better Place, just as they subscribe to a mobile phone service plan. If you sign up for enough miles, Better Place will even throw in the car for free, just as you get a complimentary cell phone when you sign up for a two-year service plan with your wireless provider. Moreover, drivers will not be locked into old battery technology but can take advantage of the rapid improvements battery technology is expected to make over time.

Nissan's Ghosn believes electric cars will account for 10 percent of global auto sales over the next decade. In contrast, Toyota is convinced gasoline-electric hybrids will become the next dominant technology. These different predictions have significant influence on how much money Nissan and Toyota invest in technology, and

where. Nissan plans to build one of its fully electric vehicles, the Leaf, at a plant in Smyrna, Tennessee. Toyota is expanding its R&D investments in hybrid technology. It has sold more than 2 million of its popular Prius cars since they were first introduced in 1997 and just launched a larger hybrid sedan. By 2020, Toyota plans to offer hybrid technology in all its vehicles. Eventually, the investments made by Nissan and Toyota will yield different returns, depending on which predictions (or theories of how to compete) prove more accurate.

An alternative outcome is that neither hybrids nor electric cars will become the next paradigm. To add even more uncertainty to the mix, Honda and BMW are betting on cars powered by hydrogen fuel cells. Tesla Motors is offering its roadster equipped with solar panels to provide additional power. In sum, many alternative technologies are competing to become the winner in setting a new standard for propelling cars. This situation is depicted in Exhibit MC7.1, where the new technologies represent a swarm of new entries vying for dominance. Only time will tell which technology will win this battle.[1]

EXHIBIT MC 7.1

Several Technologies Competing for Dominance

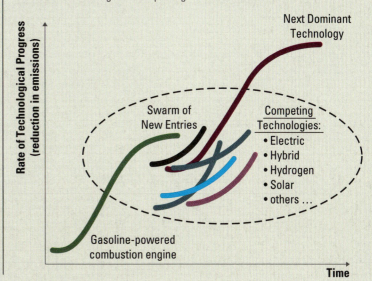

DISCUSSION QUESTIONS

Review Chapter 7: Business Strategy: Innovation and Strategic Entrepreneurship.

1. Do you believe that the internal combustion engine will lose its dominant position in the future? Why or why not? What time horizon are you looking at?

2. Which factors do you think will be most critical in setting the next industry standard for technology in car propulsion?

3. Which companies do you think are currently best positioned to influence the next industry standard in car-propulsion technology?

4. What would you recommend different competitors (e.g., Ford, GM, Toyota, Honda, and Nissan) do to influence the emerging industry standard?

Endnotes

1. This MiniCase is based on: "Bright sparks," *The Economist,* January 15, 2009; "The electric-fuel-trade acid test," *The Economist,* September 3, 2009; "At Tokyo auto show, hybrids and electrics dominate," *The New York Times,* October 21, 2009; and "Risky business at Nissan," *BusinessWeek,* November 2, 2009.

AT THE TIME OF ITS BANKRUPTCY in 2009, Circuit City was the second-largest electronics retailer in the United States, trailing only Best Buy (see ChapterCase 4). Today, however, Circuit City's core competencies—logistics and inventory management that drove down cost and allowed a focus on customer preferences in more or less real time—live on in the incarnation of CarMax, the largest used-car retailer in the U.S.[1] What's the connection here?

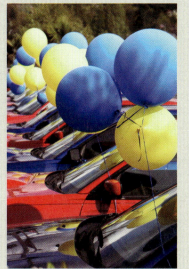

In the early 1990s, Circuit City executives began thinking about their core competencies more strategically. Then-CEO Richard Sharp and Senior VP Austin Ligon began brainstorming about how to leverage Circuit City's core competencies in other markets. They looked for businesses that were highly fragmented, which would allow them to leverage their retail core competency into nationwide standardization and cost savings. Both also wanted a business in which they could improve the customer's buying experience.

Sharp and Ligon zoomed in on the market for used cars. They launched CarMax in 1993, using the superstore format developed at Circuit City. Austin Ligon, CarMax's first CEO, knew they could exceed customer expectations in the used-car market because people likened the experience of buying a used car to that of having a root canal procedure. CarMax's first store opened in Richmond, Virginia, less than two miles from Circuit City's headquarters, easing the transfer of core competencies from Circuit City to CarMax.

CarMax has some unique features that many mom-and-pop used-car dealers lack. It buys any trade-in car for its Blue Book value, even if you only sell your car to CarMax but don't buy a car from CarMax. Each vehicle CarMax sells goes thorough a 125-point inspection and detailing, typically having some 12 hours of work done, prior to being displayed for sale.

CarMax also has a no-haggle pricing policy. Further, each car sold comes with a five-day no-questions-asked return policy and a 30-day warranty. All of these features make the buying experience much more predictable and pleasant.

Through centralized inventory management nationwide, a potential customer can choose from thousands of vehicles via CarMax's website at any given time. The company has been included in *Fortune*'s "100 Best Companies to Work For" every year since 2005. In 2010, CarMax was a Fortune 500 company and the largest used-car dealer in the U.S. with over 100 locations, employing 13,500 people, selling 350,000 cars, and earning revenue of more than $8 billion. Although Circuit City is now extinct, its core competencies continue to shape the retail industry—this time in the sale of used cars.[2]

DISCUSSION QUESTIONS

Review Chapter 4: Internal Analysis: Resources, Capabilities, and Activities.

Review Chapter 8: Corporate Strategy: Vertical Integration and Diversification.

1. Do you judge CarMax to be successful? Why or why not?

2. What type of diversification strategy is Circuit City's CarMax business venture?

3. Looking at the core competence–market matrix depicted in Exhibit 8.8, does Circuit City's CarMax diversification fall neatly into one of the four quadrants? Why or why not?

4. Was CarMax a good strategic move for Circuit City? Why or why not?

5. In 2002, Circuit City sold off CarMax, which trades on the NYSE under KMX. Was this a good decision by Circuit City's top management team? Why or why not?

Endnotes

1. For an in-depth treatment of how resources of extinct firms can live on and provide advantages in existing firms, see Hoetker, G., and R. Agarwal (2007), "Death hurts, but it isn't fatal: The post exit diffusion of knowledge created by innovative companies," *Academy of Management Journal* 50: 446–467.

2. This MiniCase is based on a presentation given by CarMax's first CEO, Austin Ligon, at the 2005 Strategic Management Society Conference in Orlando, Florida, October 26, 2005; and Collins, J. (2009), *How the Mighty Fall: And Why Some Companies Never Give In* (New York: HarperCollins). See also Prahalad, C. K., and G. Hamel (1990), "The core competence of the corporation," *Harvard Business Review,* May–June.

DURING MOST OF the 20th century, the closed-innovation approach was the dominant research and development (R&D) strategy for most leading industrial corporations: They tended to discover, develop, and commercialize new products internally. Although this approach was costly, it allowed firms to capture the returns to innovation.

Several factors led to a shift in the knowledge landscape from closed innovation to open innovation. They include:

- The increasing supply and mobility of skilled workers
- The exponential growth of venture capital
- The increasing availability of external options (such as spinning out new ventures) to commercialize ideas that were previously shelved
- The increasing capability of external suppliers

Together, these factors now force even the largest companies, such as AT&T, IBM, GE, and Sony, to shift their innovation strategy toward a model that blends internal with external knowledge-sourcing via licensing agreements, strategic alliances, joint ventures, and acquisitions.

In the open-innovation model, a company attempts to commercialize both its own ideas and research from other firms. It also finds external alternatives such as spin-out ventures or strategic alliances to commercialize its internally developed R&D. As Exhibit MC9.1 shows, the boundary of the firm has become porous (as represented by the dashed line in the right panel), allowing the firm to spin out some R&D projects while "sourcing in" (developing in-house) other promising projects. Exhibit MC9.2 (next page) compares and contrasts open-innovation and closed-innovation principles.

EXHIBIT MC9.1

Closed Innovation vs. Open Innovation

Source: Adapted from: H. Chesbrough (2003), "The area of open innovation," *MIT Sloan Management Review,* Spring: 35–41.

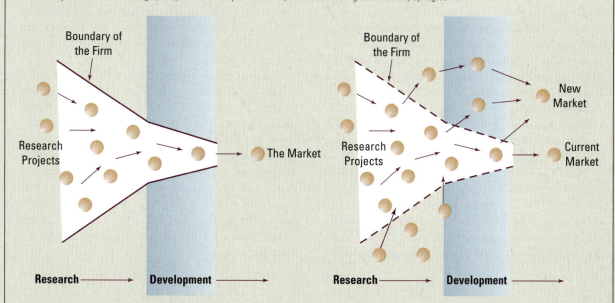

EXHIBIT MC9.2

Contrasting Principles of Closed and Open Innovation

Closed-Innovation Principles	Open-Innovation Principles
The smart people in our field work for us.	Not all the smart people work for us. We need to work with smart people inside *and* outside our company.
To profit from R&D, we must discover it, develop it, and ship it ourselves.	External R&D can create significant value; internal R&D is needed to claim (absorb) some portion of that value.
If we discover it ourselves, we will get it to market first.	We don't have to originate the research to profit from it; we can still be first if we successfully commercialize new research.
The company that gets an innovation to market first will win.	Building a better business model is often more important than getting to market first.
If we create the most and best ideas in the industry, we will win.	If we make the best use of internal and external ideas, we will win.
We should control our intellectual property (IP), so that our competitors don't profit from it.	We should profit from others' use of our IP, and we should buy others' IP whenever it advances our own business model.

Source: Adapted from H. W. Chesbrough (2003), *Open Innovation: The New Imperative for Creating and Profiting from Technology* (Boston: Harvard Business School Press).

An example of open innovation is Procter & Gamble's "Connect+Develop," or C+D (a play on research and development, or R&D). Due to the maturing of its products and markets, P&G was forced to look outside for new ideas. P&G is an $80 billion company whose investors expect it to grow 4–6 percent a year; which implies generating between $3 and $5 billion in incremental revenue annually. P&G was no longer able to generate this amount of growth through closed innovation. By 2000, P&G's closed-innovation machine had stalled, and the company lost half its market value. It needed a change in innovation strategy to drive organic growth.

P&G's Connect+Develop is a web-based interface that connects the company's internal-innovation capability with the distributed knowledge in the global community. From that external community, researchers, entrepreneurs, and consumers can submit ideas that might solve some of P&G's toughest innovation challenges. The C+D model is based on the realization that innovation was increasingly coming from small entrepreneurial ventures and even from individuals. Universities also became much more proactive in commercializing their inventions. The Internet now enables access to widely distributed knowledge from around the globe.

External collaborations fostered through the worldwide Connect+Develop network now play a role in roughly 50 percent of P&G's new products, up from about 15 percent in 2000. P&G's innovation productivity has increased, and its innovation costs have fallen. The economic benefits to an open-innovation strategy are captured in Exhibit MC9.3. Successful product innovations that resulted from P&G's open-innovation model include "Pringles meets Print" (sold for $1.5bn to Diamond Foods in 2011), Mr. Clean Magic Eraser, Swiffer Dusters, Crest SpinBrush, and Olay Regenerist.[1]

EXHIBIT MC9.3

Economic Benefits of an Open-Innovation Model

Source: Adapted from H. Chesbrough (2007), "Why companies should have open business models," *MIT Sloan Management Review,* Winter: 22–28.

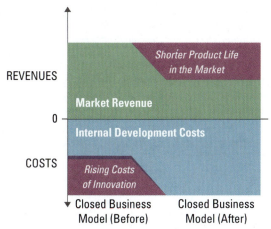

The Economic Pressure on Closed Innovation

As product life cycles become shorter and as development costs rise, the net result is that innovative companies are finding it harder to justify their investment in new products.

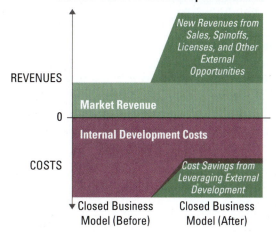

The New Business Model of Open Innovation

To offset rising development costs and shorter product life cycles, companies are experimenting with creative ways to open their business models, use external ideas and technologies in internal product development, and allow internal intellectual property to be commercialized extenally.

DISCUSSION QUESTIONS

Review Chapter 4: Internal Analysis: Resources, Capabilities, and Activities.

Review Chapter 7: Business Strategy: Innovation and Strategic Entrepreneurship.

Review Chapter 9: Corporate Strategy: Acquisitions, Alliances, and Networks.

1. Weigh the benefits and costs of closed innovation versus open innovation. What conclusions do you draw?

2. What are some of the risks of an open-innovation strategy that a company should consider before embarking on it?

3. Apply the resource-based view of the firm (discussed in Chapter 4). Do you believe P&G's Connect+Develop (C+D) open-innovation system has the potential to create a competitive advantage

for the firm? If you believe that C+D does have the potential to create a competitive advantage, do you believe it is sustainable? Why or why not?

4. Do you agree with the statement by Larry Huston and Nabil Sakkab, executives at P&G, that "Connect+Develop will become the dominant innovation model in the 21st century"?[2] Why or why not? What would its dominance do to C+D's potential to create a competitive edge for a firm?

5. *After reading Chapter 11:* Introducing the C+D innovation model requires tremendous organizational change. As Huston and Sakkab noted: "We needed to move the company's attitude from resistance to innovations 'not invented here' to enthusiasm for those 'proudly found elsewhere.' And we needed to change how we defined, and perceived, our R&D organization—from 7,500 people inside to 7,500 plus 1.5 million outside, with a permeable boundary between them."[3] Identify some of the major obstacles a manager would encounter attempting this kind of organizational change. What recommendations would you make on how to accomplish such large-scale organizational change successfully?

Endnotes

1. This MiniCase is based on: Chesbrough, H. W. (2003), *Open Innovation: The New Imperative for Creating and Profiting from Technology* (Boston: Harvard Business School Press); Chesbrough, H. (2003), "The area of open innovation," *MIT Sloan Management Review,* Spring: 35–41; Chesbrough, H. (2007), "Why companies should have open business models," *MIT Sloan Management Review,* Winter: 22–28; Chesbrough, H. W., and M. M. Appleyard (2007), "Open innovation and strategy," *California Management Review,* Fall 50: 57–76; Huston, L., and N. Sakkab (2006), "Connect & Develop: Inside Procter & Gamble's new model for innovation," *Harvard Business Review,* March: 58–66; Rothaermel, F. T., and M. T. Alexandre (2009), "Ambidexterity in technology sourcing: The moderating role of absorptive capacity," *Organization Science,* 20: 759–780; Rothaermel, F. T., and A. M. Hess (2010), "Innovation strategies combined," *MIT Sloan Management Review,* Spring 51: 13–15; and "Diamond buys P&G's Pringles," *The Wall Street Journal,* April 6, 2011.

2. Huston, L., and N. Sakkab (2006), "Connect & Develop: Inside Procter & Gamble's new model for innovation."

3. Ibid.

THE WORLD'S MOST SUCCESSFUL global retailer, in terms of profitability, is not Walmart or the French grocery chain Carrefour, but IKEA—a home-furnishings company from Sweden. In 2010, IKEA had more than 310 stores worldwide in 38 countries, employed some 127,000 people, and earned revenues of 32 billion euros. More than 80 percent of IKEA's revenues come from Europe, with the rest from North America (16 percent) and Asia and Australia (3 percent). Although IKEA's largest market is in Germany (15 percent of total sales), its fastest-growing international markets are the United States, China, and Russia. Exhibit MC10.1 shows IKEA's growth in the number of stores and revenues worldwide since 1974. Started as a small retail outlet in 1943 by then-17-year-old Ingvar Kamprad, IKEA has become a global phenomenon.

IKEA was slow to internationalize: It took 20 years before the company expanded beyond Sweden to the neighboring country of Norway. After honing and refining its core competency of designing modern functional home furnishings at low prices, offered in a unique retail experience in its home market, IKEA followed an *international strategy,* expanding first to Europe and then beyond. Using an international strategy allowed IKEA to sell the same types of home furnishings across the globe with little adaptation (although it does make some allowances for country preferences). Because IKEA focuses on both value creation *and* low cost, it shifted more recently from an international strategy to a global-standardization strategy, in which it attempts to achieve economies of scale through managing a global supply chain. For example, since wood remains one of IKEA's main input factors, it now focuses on timber-rich Russia as a key source of supply.

Yet, IKEA faces significant challenges going forward. Finding new sources of supply to support more store openings is a challenge. Currently, IKEA can open only about 20 new stores each year because the supply chain becomes a bottleneck. Related to this issue is the fact that wood remains one of IKEA's main input factors, but the world's consumers are becoming more sensitive to the issue of deforestation

EXHIBIT MC10.1

IKEA Stores and Revenues (in billions of euros) Worldwide, 1974–2010

Source: Author's depiction of data from "The secret of IKEA's success," *The Economist,* February 24, 2011.

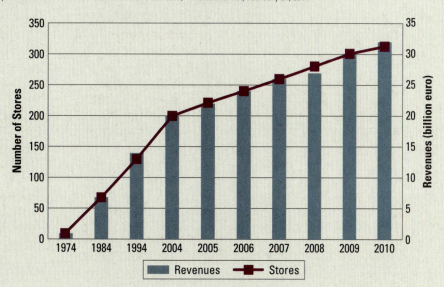

and its possible link to global warming. Thus, in the near future IKEA must find low-cost replacement materials for wood. In addition, powerful competitors have taken notice of IKEA's success. Although IKEA is growing in North America, it holds only about 5 percent of the home-furnishings market. To keep IKEA at bay, Target has recently recruited top designers and launched a wide range of low-priced furnishings. Kmart, likewise, has enrolled Martha Stewart to help with the design of its offerings of home furnishings.

Besides these external challenges, IKEA also faces significant internal ones. Although its founder Ingvar Kamprad (now in his mid-80s) no longer runs IKEA's day-to-day operations, he chairs the foundation that owns IKEA. No strategic decision is made without Mr. Kamprad's approval. Many observers compare Mr. Kamprad's influence on IKEA's culture and organization to that of the legendary Sam Walton at Walmart. Moreover, IKEA is privately held (through a complicated network of foundations and holding companies in the Netherlands, Lichtenstein, and Luxembourg); this arrangement provides benefits in terms of reducing tax exposure, but also creates constraints in accessing large sums of capital needed for rapid global expansion.[1]

DISCUSSION QUESTIONS

Review Chapter 3: External Analysis: Industry Structure, Competitive Forces, and Strategic Groups.

Review Chapter 10: Global Strategy: Competing Around the World.

1. Looking at IKEA's challenges, which ones do you think pose the greatest threat? Why?

2. How would you address the challenges you identified in Question 1?

3. Did it surprise you to learn that both a developed country (the United States) and also emerging economies (i.e., China and Russia) are the fastest-growing international markets for IKEA? Does this fact pose any challenges in the way that IKEA ought to compete across the globe? Why or why not?

4. What can IKEA do to continue to drive growth globally?

5. *After reading Chapter 12:* Assume you are hired to consult with IKEA on the topic of *business ethics* and *corporate social responsibility.* Which areas would you recommend the company be most sensitive to, and how should these be addressed?

Endnotes

1. This MiniCase is based on: "IKEA: How the Swedish retailer became a global cult brand," *BusinessWeek,* November 14, 2005; "Flat-pack accounting," *The Economist,* May 11, 2006; "Shocking tell-all book takes aim at Ikea," *Bloomberg Businessweek,* November 12, 2009; Peng, M. (2009), *Global Strategy,* 2nd ed. (Mason, OH: South-Western Cengage); and "The secret of IKEA's success," *The Economist,* February 24, 2011.

APPLE'S MARKET CAPITALIZATION in 2001 was $7 billion, while Sony's was $55 billion. Apple introduced the iPod, a portable digital music player, in October 2001 and the iTunes music store 18 months later. Through these two strategic moves Apple redefined the music industry, reinventing itself as a content-delivery mobile-device company. Signaling its renaissance, Apple changed its name from Apple Computer, Inc., to simply Apple, Inc. Many observers, however, wondered what happened to Sony—the company that created the portable-music industry by introducing the first Walkman in 1979.

Sony's strategy was to differentiate itself through the vertical integration of content and hardware, driven by its 1988 acquisition of CBS Records (later Sony Music Entertainment). This strategy contrasted sharply with Sony Music division's desire to protect its lucrative revenue-generating, copyrighted compact discs (CDs). Sony Music's engineers were aggressively combating music piracy by inhibiting the Microsoft Windows media player's ability to rip CDs and by serializing discs (assigning unique ID numbers to discs). Meanwhile Apple's engineers were developing a Digital Rights Management (DRM) system to control and restrict the transfer of copyrighted digital music. Apple's DRM succeeded, protecting the music studio's interests while creating value that enabled consumers to enjoy portable digital music.

Sony had a long history of creating electronics devices of superior quality and design. It had all the right competencies to launch a successful counterattack to compete with Apple: electronics, software, music, and computer divisions. (Sony's Electronics Division even was the battery supplier for Apple's iPod.) Cooperation among strategic business units had served Sony well in the past, leading to breakthrough innovations such as the Walkman, PlayStation, the CD, and the VAIO computer line. In this case, however, the hardware and content divisions each seemed to have its own idea of what needed to be done. Cooperation

among the Sony divisions was also hindered by the fact that their centers of operations were spread across the globe: Music operations were located in New York City and Electronics design was in Japan, inhibiting face-to-face communications and making real-time interactions more difficult.

Sony's CEO Nobuyuki Idei learned the hard way that the Music Division managers were focused on the immediate needs of their recordings competing against the consumer-driven market forces. In 2002, Idei shared his frustrations with the cultural differences between the hardware and content divisions:

> The opposite of soft alliances is hard alliances, which include mergers and acquisitions. Since purchasing the Music and Pictures businesses, more than ten years have passed, and we have experienced many cultural differences between hardware manufacturing and content businesses. . . . This experience has taught us that in certain areas where hard alliances would have taken ten years to succeed, soft alliances can be created more easily. Another advantage of soft alliances is the ability to form partnerships with many different companies. We aim to provide an open and easy-to-access environment where anybody can participate and we are willing to cooperate with companies that share our vision. Soft alliances offer many possibilities.[1]

In contrast, Apple organized a small, empowered, cross-functional team to produce the iPod in just a few months. Apple successfully outsourced and integrated many of its components and collaborated across business units. The phenomenal speed and success of the iPod and iTunes's development and seamless integration became a structural approach that Apple now applies to its successful development and launches of new products like the iPhone and iPad. By early 2011, Apple's market capitalization had increased by a factor of 44 times, to $310 billion (making it the most valuable technology company on the planet), while Sony's market value had declined by almost 40 percent, to $35 billion.[2]

DISCUSSION QUESTIONS

Review Chapter 9: Corporate Strategy: Acquisitions, Alliances, and Networks.

Review Chapter 10: Global Strategy: Competing Around the World.

Review Chapter 11: Organizational Design: Structure, Culture, and Control.

1. Why had Sony been successful in the past (e.g., with the introduction of the Walkman, PlayStation, the CD, and the VAIO computer line)?

2. What was Mr. Idei's assessment of strategic alliances vs. M&As? Do you agree or disagree? Support your assessment.

3. Why do you think Apple succeeded in the digital portable music industry, while Sony failed?

4. What could Sony have done differently to avoid failure? What lessons need to be learned?

5. What recommendations would you give Sony's CEO to help them compete against Apple?

Endnotes

1. Sony Annual Report 2002, year ended March 31, 2002, Sony Corporation, p. 9.

2. This MiniCase was prepared by Frank T. Rothaermel and Robert Redrow (of Sony Corp.). It draws on the following sources: Hansen, M. T. (2009), *Collaboration: How Leaders Avoid the Traps, Create Unity, and Reap Big Results* (Cambridge, MA: Harvard Business School Press); Sony Annual Report 2002, year ended March 31, 2002, Sony Corporation, p. 9; Sony Corporation Info, www.sony.net/SonyInfo/CorporateInfo/History/sonyhistory-e.html; and Wolframalpha, www.wolframalpha.com.

WHEN APPOINTED CEO of PepsiCo in 2006, Ms. Indra Nooyi was only the 11th woman to run a Fortune 500 company. Since then, Ms. Nooyi has been ranked in the top ten of *Forbes* magazine's list of the world's 100 most powerful women. In 2010, she topped *Fortune*'s ranking of the most powerful women in business. Today, leading a company that employs some 300,000 people worldwide, Ms. Nooyi is considered one of the most powerful business leaders globally.

A native of Chennai, India, Ms. Nooyi obtained a bachelor's degree in physics, chemistry, and mathematics from Madras Christian College, an MBA from the Indian Institute of Management, and a master's degree from Yale University. Prior to joining PepsiCo in 1994, Ms. Nooyi worked for Johnson & Johnson, Boston Consulting Group (BCG), Motorola, and ABB. For her BCG interview, right out of Yale, Ms. Nooyi wore a traditional sari. Ms. Nooyi is not the typical Fortune 500 CEO: She is well known for walking around the office barefoot and singing—a remnant from her lead role in an all-girls rock band in high school.

It should come as no surprise, therefore, that Ms. Nooyi—an executive who spends more than 50 percent of her time outside the U.S.—has been shaking up things at PepsiCo. She took the lead role in spinning off Taco Bell, Pizza Hut, and KFC in 1997. Later, she masterminded the acquisitions of Tropicana in 1998 and Quaker Oats (including Gatorade) in 2001. As CEO, Ms. Nooyi declared PepsiCo's vision as *performance with a purpose,* defined by three dimensions:

1. *Human sustainability,* which concerns the strategic intent to make PepsiCo's product portfolio healthier, to combat obesity. PepsiCo wants to make "fun foods" such as Frito-Lay and Doritos healthier (less salty and fatty), and to include healthy choices in its product portfolio (such as Quaker Oats products and Tropicana fruit juices). Ms. Nooyi is convinced that if food and beverage companies do not make their product lineups healthier to combat obesity, these companies will face the same repercussions that tobacco companies did.

2. *Environmental sustainability,* to ensure that PepsiCo's operations don't harm the natural environment. The company has initiatives such as water and energy reduction, stepping up recycling, and promoting sustainable agriculture. The goal is to transform PepsiCo into a company with a net-zero impact on the environment. Ms. Nooyi believes that young people today will not patronize a company that does not have a sustainable strategy.

3. *The whole person at work,* which attempts to create a corporate culture in which employees "not just make a living, but also have a life."[1] Ms. Nooyi argues that this allows for the unleashing of both the mental and emotional energy of every employee.

PepsiCo's vision of *performance with a purpose* acknowledges the importance of corporate social responsibility and stakeholder strategy. Ms. Nooyi is convinced that companies have a duty to society to "do better by doing better."[2] She subscribes to a triple-bottom-line approach to competitive advantage, declaring that the true profits of enterprise are not just "revenues–costs" but "revenues–costs–costs to society." Costs to society are *externalities*—such as pollution or the cost of health care to combat obesity—that companies do not bear. Ms. Nooyi argues that the time when corporations can just pass on their externalities to society is over.

Critics note, however, that although the rhetoric of *performance with a purpose* appears to be powerful, PepsiCo's financial performance so far has been disappointing. Exhibit MC12.1 (next page) shows PepsiCo's stock performance versus its archrival Coca-Cola. Since Ms. Nooyi took the helm at PepsiCo, Coca-Cola's stock has appreciated by roughly 50 percent, while PepsiCo's stock has remained flat and is merely tracking the DJIA.[3]

EXHIBIT MC12.1

Stock Performance of Pepsi vs. Coca Cola and DJIA (10/01/06–03/29/11)
Source: MSN Money.

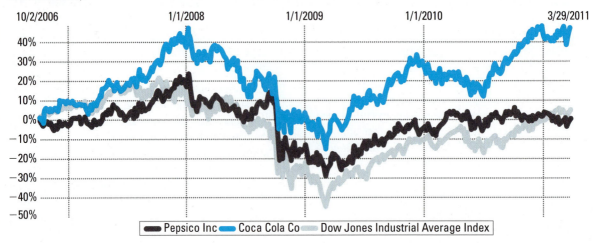

DISCUSSION QUESTIONS

Review Chapter 3: External Analysis: Industry Structure, Competitive Forces, and Strategic Groups.

Review Chapter 5: Competitive Advantage and Firm Performance.

Review Chapter 8: Corporate Strategy: Vertical Integration and Diversification.

Review Chapter 12: Corporate Governance, Business Ethics, and Strategic Leadership.

1. Apply a PESTEL framework to analyze PepsiCo's external environment. Then, conduct a SWOT analysis to see how PepsiCo is addressing the opportunities and threats present in the external environment.

2. One of the measures to assess competitive advantage (discussed in Chapter 5) is shareholder value creation. When comparing Coca-Cola and PepsiCo along this dimension, one would come to the conclusion that PepsiCo, under Ms. Nooyi's leadership, has sustained a competitive disadvantage when compared with Coca-Cola.

   a. Do you agree with this assessment? Why or why not?

   b. If you were to apply a triple-bottom-line approach to assessing competitive advantage, would you come to a different conclusion? Why or why not?

   c. If you were a board member at PepsiCo, would you be concerned? Why or why not? If you *were* concerned, what actions would you recommend?

3. As a senior executive at PepsiCo, Ms. Nooyi was the driving force behind selling PepsiCo's restaurant businesses (Taco Bell, Pizza Hut, and KFC) and acquiring Quaker Oats and Tropicana. What type of corporate-level strategic initiatives were these moves? What do you think was the rationale behind them? Using the BCG matrix, how do you assess their effectiveness?

4. What "grade" would you give Ms. Nooyi for her job performance as a strategic leader? What are her strengths and weaknesses? Where would you place Ms. Nooyi on the level-5 pyramid of strategic leadership (see Exhibit 12.8, page 356), and why? What recommendations would you give her? Support your answers.

Endnotes

1. "Conversation with Indra Nooyi Yale SOM '80," Yale University, March 3, 2010, www.youtube.com/watch?v=-msw7mJPF6A.

2. "The responsible company," *The Economist, The World in 2008.*

3. This MiniCase is based on: "PepsiCo shakes it up," *BusinessWeek,* August 14, 2006; "The Pepsi challenge," *The Economist,* August 17, 2006; "Keeping cool in hot water," *BusinessWeek,* June 11, 2007; "Pepsi gets a makeover," *The Economist,* March 25, 2010; "Indra Nooyi on Performance with Purpose 2009," PepsiCo Video, www.youtube.com/watch?v=AM-TduYdJas; "Conversation with Indra Nooyi Yale SOM '80"; and www.wolfram.alpha (use ticker symbol KO for Coca-Cola Company and PEP for PepsiCo).

PART 5
CASES

The case study is a fundamental learning tool in strategic management. We carefully wrote and chose the cases in this book to expose you to a wide variety of key concepts, industries, protagonists, and strategic problems.

In simple terms, cases tell the story of a company facing a strategic dilemma. The firms may be real or fictional in nature, and the problem may be current or one that the firm faced in the past. Although the details of the cases vary, in general they start with a description of the challenge(s) to be addressed, followed by the history of the firm up until the decision point, and then additional information to help you with your analysis. The strategic dilemma is often faced by a specific manager, who wonders what they should do. To address the strategic dilemma, you will use the AFI framework to conduct a case analysis using the tools and concepts provided in this textbook. After careful analysis, you will be able to formulate a strategic response and make recommendations about how to implement it.

Why Do We Use Cases?

Strategy is something that people learn by doing; it cannot be learned simply by reading a book or listening carefully in class. While those activities will help you become more familiar with the concepts and models used in strategic management, the only way to improve your skills in analyzing, formulating, and implementing strategy is to *practice*.

We encourage you to take advantage of the cases in this text as a "laboratory" in which to experiment with the strategic management tools you have been given, so that you can learn more about how, when, and where they might work in the "real world." Cases are valuable because they expose you to a number and variety of situations in which you can refine your strategic management skills without worrying about making mistakes. The companies in these cases will not lose profits or fire you if you miscalculate a financial ratio, misinterpret someone's intentions, or make an incorrect prediction about environmental trends.

Cases also invite you to "walk in" and explore many more kinds of companies in a wider array of industries than you will ever be able to work at in your lifetime. In this textbook alone, you will find cases about companies involved in energy infrastructure development (Siemens), medical products and services (General Electric), electronic equipment (Apple), computer networking (IBM), sustainability consulting (InterfaceRAISE), electric cars (Tesla Motors), book retailing (BetterWorld Books), and consumer products (Cola Wars), to name just a few. Your personal organizational experiences are usually much more limited, defined by the jobs held by your family members or by your own forays into the working world. Learning about companies involved in so many different types of products and services may open up new employment possibilities for you. Diversity also forces us to think about the ways in which industries (as well as people) are both similar and yet distinct, and to critically examine the degree to which lessons learned in one forum transfer to other settings (i.e., to what degree are they "generalizable"). In short, cases are a great training tool, and they are fun to study.

You will find that many of our cases are written from the perspective of the CEO or general manager responsible for strategic decision making in the organization. While you do not need to be a member of a top management team to utilize the strategic-management process, these senior leaders are usually responsible for determining strategy in most of the organizations we study. Importantly, cases allow us to put ourselves "in the shoes" of strategic leaders and invite us to view the issues from their perspective. Having responsibility for the performance of an entire organization is quite different from managing a single project team, department, or functional area. Cases can help you see the *big picture* in a way that most of us are not accustomed to in our daily, organizational lives. We recognize that most undergraduate students and even MBAs do not land immediately in the corporate boardroom. Yet having a basic understanding of the types of conversations going on in the boardroom not only increases your current value as an employee, but improves your chances of getting there someday, should you so desire.

Finally, cases help give us a *long-term* view of the firms they depict. Corporate history is immensely helpful in understanding how a firm got to its present position and why people within that organization think the way they do. Our case authors (both the author of this book and authors of cases from respected third-party sources) have spent many hours poring over historical documents and news reports in order to re-create each company's heritage for you, a luxury that most of us do not have when we are bombarded on a daily basis with homework, tests, and papers or project team meetings, deadlines, and reports. We invite you not just to learn from, but also to savor, reading each company's story.

STRATEGIC CASE ANALYSIS. The first step in analyzing a case is to *skim it for the basic facts.* As you read, jot down your notes regarding the following basic questions:

- What company or companies is the case about?
- Who are the principal actors?
- What are the key events? When and where do they happen (in other words, what is the timeline)?

Second, go back and reread the case in greater detail, this time with a focus on *defining the problem.* Which facts are relevant and why? Just as a doctor begins by interviewing the patient ("What hurts?"), you likewise gather information and then piece the clues together in order to figure out what is wrong. Your goal at this stage is to identify the "symptoms" in order to figure out which "tests" to run in order to make a definitive "diagnosis" of the main "disease." Only then can you prescribe a "treatment" with confidence that it will actually help the situation. Rushing too quickly through this stage often results in "malpractice" (that is, giving a patient with an upset stomach an antacid when she really has the flu), with effects that range from unhelpful to downright dangerous. The best way to ensure that you "do no harm" is to analyze the facts carefully, fighting the temptation to jump right to proposing a solution.

The third step, continuing the medical analogy, is to determine which analytical tools will help you to most accurately diagnose the problem(s). Doctors may choose to run blood tests or take an x-ray. In doing case analysis, we follow the steps of the *strategic-management process.* You have any and all of the following models and frameworks at your disposal:

1. Perform an **external environmental analysis** of the:
   - Macrolevel environment (PESTEL analysis)
   - Industry environment (e.g., Porter's five forces)
   - Competitive environment

2. Perform an **internal analysis** of the firm using the resource-based view:
   - What are the firm's resources, capabilities, and competencies?
   - Does the firm possess valuable, rare, costly to imitate resources, and is it organized to capture value from those resources (VRIO analysis)?
   - What is the firm's value chain?

3. Analyze the firm's current **business-level** and **corporate-level** strategies:
   - Business-level strategy (product market positioning)
   - Corporate-level strategy (diversification)
   - International strategy (geographic scope and mode of entry)
   - How are these strategies being implemented?

4. Analyze the firm's **performance:**
   - Use both financial and market-based measures.
   - How does the firm compare to its competitors as well as the industry average?
   - What trends are evident over the past three to five years?
   - Consider the perspectives of multiple stakeholders (internal and external).
   - Does the firm possess a competitive advantage? If so, can it be sustained?

CALCULATING FINANCIAL RATIOS. Financial ratio analysis is an important tool for assessing the outcomes of a firm's strategy. Although financial performance is not the only relevant outcome measure, long-term profitability is a necessary precondition for firms to remain in business and to be able to serve the needs of all of their stakeholders. Accordingly, at the end of this introductory module, we have provided a table of financial measures that can be used to assess firm performance (see Table 1, pages 396–400).

All of the following aspects of performance should be considered, because each provides a different type of information about the financial health of the firm:

- Profit ratios—how efficiently a company utilizes its resources.
- Activity ratios—how effectively a firm manages its assets.
- Leverage ratios—the degree to which a firm relies on debt versus equity (capital structure).

- Liquidity ratios—a firm's ability to pay off its short-term obligations.
- Market ratios—returns earned by shareholders who hold company stock.

MAKING THE DIAGNOSIS. With all of this information in hand, you are finally ready to *make a "diagnosis."* Describe the problem(s) or opportunity(ies) facing the firm at this point in time and/or in the near future. How are they interrelated? (For example, a runny nose, fever, stomach upset, and body aches are all indicative of the flu.) Support your conclusions with data generated from your analyses.

The following general themes may be helpful to consider as you try to pull all the pieces together into a cohesive summary:

- Are the firm's value chain (primary and support) activities mutually reinforcing?
- Do the firm's resources and capabilities fit with the demands of the external environment?
- Does the firm have a clearly defined strategy that will create a competitive advantage?
- Is the firm making good use of its strengths and taking full advantage of its opportunities?
- Does the firm have serious weaknesses or face significant threats that need to be mitigated?

Keep in mind that "problems" can be positive (how to manage increased demand) as well as negative (declining stock price) in nature. Even firms that are currently performing well need to figure out how to maintain their success in an ever-changing and highly competitive global business environment.

Formulation: Proposing Feasible Solutions

When you have the problem figured out (your diagnosis), the next step is to *propose a "treatment plan"* or solution. There are two parts to the treatment plan: the *what* and the *why.* Using our medical analogy: The *what* for a patient with the flu might be antiviral medication, rest, and lots of fluids. The *why*: antivirals attack the virus directly, shortening the duration of illness; rest enables the body to recuperate naturally; and fluids are necessary to help the body fight fever and dehydration. *The ultimate goal is to restore the patient to wellness.* Similarly, when you are doing case analysis, your task is to figure out *what* the leaders of

the company should do and *why* this is an appropriate course of action. Each part of your proposal should be justifiable based on your analyses.

One word of caution about the formulation stage: By nature, humans are predisposed to engage in "local" and "simplistic" searches for solutions to the problems they face.[1] On the one hand, this can be an efficient approach to problem solving, because relying on past experiences (what worked before) does not "waste time reinventing the wheel." The purpose of doing case analysis, however, is to *look past* the easy answers and to help us figure out not just "what works" (satisficing) but what might be the *best* answer (optimizing). In other words, do not just take the first idea that comes to your mind and run with it. Instead, write down that idea for subsequent consideration but then think about what other solutions might achieve the same (or even better) results. Some of the most successful companies engage in scenario planning, in which they develop several possible outcomes and estimate the likelihood that each will happen. If their first prediction turns out to be incorrect, then they have a "Plan B" ready and waiting to be executed.

Plan for Implementation

The final step in the AFI framework is to develop a plan for implementation. Under formulation, you came up with a proposal, tested it against alternatives, and used your research to support why it provides the best solution to the problem at hand. To demonstrate its feasibility, however, you must be able to explain *how to put it into action.* Consider the following questions:

1. *What activities need to be performed?* The value chain is a very useful tool when you need to figure out how different parts of the company are likely to be affected. What are the implications of your plan with respect to both primary activities (e.g., operations and sales/marketing/service) and support activities (e.g., human resources and infrastructure)?

2. *What is the timeline?* What steps must be taken first and why? Which ones are most critical? Which activities can proceed simultaneously, and which ones are sequential in nature? How long is your plan going to take?

3. *How are you going to finance your proposal?* Does the company have adequate cash on hand, or does it need to consider debt and/or equity financing?

How long until your proposal breaks even and pays for itself?

4. *What outcomes is your plan likely to achieve?* Provide goals that are "SMART": specific, measurable, achievable, realistic, and timely in nature. Make a case for how your plan will help the firm to achieve a strategic competitive advantage.

In-Class Discussion

Discussing your ideas in class is often the most valuable part of a case study. Your professor will moderate the class discussion, guiding the AFI process and asking probing questions when necessary. Case discussion classes are most effective and interesting when everybody comes prepared and participates in the exchange.

Actively listen to your fellow students; mutual respect is necessary in order to create an open and inviting environment in which people feel comfortable sharing their thoughts with one another. This does not mean you need to agree with what everyone else is saying, however. Everyone has unique perspectives and biases based on differences in life experiences, education and training, values, and goals. As a result, no two people will interpret the same information in exactly the same way. Be prepared to be challenged, as well as to challenge others, to consider the case from another vantage point. Conflict is natural and even beneficial as long as it is managed in constructive ways.

Throughout the discussion, you should be prepared to support your ideas based on the analyses you conducted. Even students who agree with you on the general steps to be taken may disagree on the order of importance. Alternatively, they may like your plan in principle but argue that it is not feasible for the company to accomplish. You should not be surprised if others come up with an altogether different diagnosis and prescription. For better or worse, a good idea does not stand on its own merit—you must be able to convince your peers of its value by backing it up with sound logic and support.

Things to Keep in Mind While Doing Case Analysis

While some solutions are clearly better than others, it is important to remember that there is no single, correct answer to any case. Unlike an optimization equation or accounting spreadsheet, cases cannot be reduced to a mathematical formula. Formulating and implementing strategy involves people, and working with people is inherently messy. Thus, the best way to get the maximum value from the case-analysis process is to maintain an open mind and carefully consider the strengths and weaknesses of all of the options. Strategy is an iterative process, and it is important not to rush to a premature conclusion.

For some cases, your instructor may be able to share with you what the company actually did, but that does not necessarily mean it was the best course of action. Too often students find out what happened in the "real world" and their creative juices stop flowing. Whether due to lack of information, experience, or time, companies quite often make the most expedient decision. With your access to additional data and time to conduct more detailed analyses, you may very well arrive at a different (and better) conclusion. Stand by your findings as long as you can support them with solid research data. Even Fortune 500 companies make mistakes.

Unfortunately, to their own detriment, students sometimes discount the value of cases based on fictional scenarios or set some time in the past. One significant advantage of fictional cases is that everybody has access to the same information. Not only does this "level the playing field," but it prevents you from being unduly biased by actual events, thus cutting short your own learning process. Similarly, just because a case occurred in the past does not mean it is no longer relevant. The players and technology may change over time, but many questions that businesses face are timeless in nature: how to adapt to a changing environment, the best way to compete against other firms, and whether and how to expand.

Case Limitations

As powerful a learning tool as case analysis can be, it does come with some limitations. One of the most important for you to be aware of is that case analysis relies on a process known as *inductive reasoning*, in which you study specific business cases in order to derive general principles of management. Intuitively, we rely on inductive reasoning across almost every aspect of our lives. We know that we need oxygen to survive, so we assume that all living organisms need oxygen. Similarly, if all the swans we have ever seen are white, we extrapolate this to mean that all swans are white. While such relationships are often built upon a high degree of probability, it is important to remember that they are not empirically proven. We have in fact discovered life forms (microorganisms) that rely on sulfur instead of oxygen. Likewise, just because all the swans you have seen have been white, black swans do exist.

What does this caution mean with respect to case analysis? First and foremost, do not assume that just because one company utilized a joint venture to commercialize a new innovation, another company will be successful employing the same strategy. The first company's success may not be due to the particular organizational form it selected; it might instead be a function of its competencies in managing interfirm relationships or the particularities of the external environment. Practically speaking, this is why the analysis step is so fundamental to good strategic management. Careful research helps us to figure out all of the potential contributing factors and to formulate hypotheses about which ones are most likely critical to success. Put another way, what happens at one firm does not necessarily generalize to others. However, solid analytical skills go a long way toward enabling you to make informed, educated guesses about when and where insights gained from one company have broader applications.

In addition, we have a business culture that tends to put on a pedestal high-performance firms and their leaders. Critical analysis is absolutely essential in order to discern the reasons for such firms' success. Upon closer inspection, we have sometimes found that their image is more a mirage than a direct reflection of sound business practices. Many business analysts have been taken in by the likes of Enron, WorldCom, and Bernie Madoff, only to humbly retract their praise when the company's shaky foundation crumbles. We selected many of the firms in these cases because of their unique stories and positive performance, but we would be remiss if we let students interpret their presence in this book as a whole-hearted endorsement of all of their business activities.

Finally, our business culture also places a high premium on benchmarking and best practices. Although we present you with a sample of firms that we believe are worthy of in-depth study, we would again caution you against uncritical adoption of their activities in the hope of emulating their achievements. Even when a management practice has broad applications, strategy involves far more than merely copying the industry leader. The company that invents a best practice is already far ahead of its competitors on the learning curve, and even if other firms do catch up, the best they can usually hope for is to match (but not exceed) the original firm's success. By all means, learn as much as you can from whomever you can, but use that information to strengthen your organization's *own* strategic identity.

Frequently Asked Questions about Case Analysis

1. *Is it okay to utilize outside materials?*

   Ask your professor. Some instructors utilize cases as a springboard for analysis and will want you to look up more recent financial and other data. Others may want you to base your analysis on the information from the case only, so that you are not influenced by the actions actually taken by the company.

2. *Is it okay to talk about the case with other students?*

   Again, you should check with your professor, but many will strongly encourage you to meet and talk about the case with other students as part of your preparation process. The goal is not to come to a group consensus, but to test your ideas in a small group setting and revise them based on the feedback you receive.

3. *Is it okay to contact the company for more information?*

   If your professor permits you to gather outside information, you may want to consider contacting the company directly. If you do so, it is imperative that you represent yourself and your school in the most professional and ethical manner possible. Explain to them that you are a student studying the firm and that you are seeking additional information, with your instructor's permission. Our experience is that some companies are quite receptive to student inquiries; others are not. You cannot know how a particular company will respond unless you try.

4. *What should I include in my case analysis report?*

   Instructors generally provide their own guidelines regarding content and format, but a general outline for a case analysis report is as follows: (1) analysis of the problem; (2) proposal of one or more alternative solutions; and (3) justification for which solution you believe is best and why. The most important thing to remember is not to waste precious space repeating facts from the case. You can assume that your professor has read the case carefully. What he or she is most interested in is your analysis of the situation and your rationale for choosing a particular solution.

Endnotes

1. Cyert, R. M., and March, J. G. (2001), *A Behavioral Theory of the Firm,* 2nd ed. (Malden, MA: Blackwell Publishers Inc.).

TABLE 1

When and How to Use Financial Measures to Assess Firm Performance

Overview: We have grouped the financial performance measures into five main categories:

Table 1a: Profitability: How profitable is the company?

Table 1b: Activity: How efficient are the operations of the company?

Table 1c: Leverage: How effectively is the company financed in terms of debt and equity?

Table 1d: Liquidity: How capable is the business of meeting its short-term obligations as they fall due?

Table 1e: Market: How does the company's performance compare to other companies in the market?

Table 1a: Profitability Ratios	Formula	Characteristics
Gross margin (or EBITDA, EBIT, etc.)	(Sales − COGS) / Sales	Measures the relationship between sales and the costs to support those sales (e.g., manufacturing, procurement, advertising, payroll, etc.)
Return on assets (ROA)	Net income / Total assets	Measures the firm's efficiency in using assets to generate earnings
Return on equity (ROE)	Net income / Total stockholders' equity	Measures earnings to owners as measured by net assets
Return on invested capital (ROIC)	Net operating profit after taxes / (Total stockholders' equity + Total debt − Value of preferred stock)	Measures how effectively a company uses the capital (owned or borrowed) invested in its operations
Return on revenue (ROR)	Net income / Revenue	Measures the profit earned per dollar of revenue
Dividend payout	Common dividends / Net income	Measures the percent of earnings paid out to common stockholders
Limitations	1. Static snapshot of balance sheet. 2. Many important intangibles not accounted for. 3. Affected by accounting rules on accruals and timing. One-time non-operating income/expense. 4. Does not take into account cost of capital. 5. Affected by timing and accounting treatment of operating results.	

TABLE 1 (continued)

When and How to Use Financial Measures to Assess Firm Performance

Table 1b: Activity Ratios	Formula	Characteristics
Inventory turnover	COGS / Average inventory	Measures inventory management
Receivables turnover	Sales / Average accounts receivable	Measures the effectiveness of credit policies and the needed level of receivables investment for sales
Payables turnover	Sales / Average accounts payable	Measures the rate at which a firm pays its suppliers
Working capital turnover	Sales / Average working capital	Measures how much working (operating) capital is needed for sales
Fixed asset turnover	Sales / Average fixed assets	Measures the efficiency of investments in net fixed assets (property, plant, and equipment after accumulated depreciation)
Total asset turnover	Sales / Average total assets	Represents the overall (comprehensive) efficiency of assets to sales
Cash turnover	Sales / Average cash (which usually includes marketable securities)	Measures a firm's efficiency in its use of cash to generate sales
Limitations	Good measures of cash flow efficiency, but with the following limitations: 1. Limited by accounting treatment and timing (e.g., monthly/quarterly close) 2. Limitations of accrual vs. cash accounting	

TABLE 1 (continued)

When and How to Use Financial Measures to Assess Firm Performance

Table 1c: Leverage Ratios	Formula	Characteristics
Debt to equity	Total liabilities / Total stockholders' equity	Direct comparison of debt to equity stakeholders and the most common measure of capital structure
Debt to assets	Total liabilities / Total assets	Debt as a percent of assets
Interest coverage (times interest earned)	(Net income + Interest expense + Tax expense) / Interest expense	Direct measure of the firm's ability to meet interest payments, indicating the protection provided from current operations
Long-term debt to equity	Long-term liabilities / Total stockholders' equity	A long-term perspective of debt and equity positions of stakeholders
Debt to market equity	Total liabilities at book value / Total equity at market value	Market valuation may represent a better measure of equity than book value. Most firms have a market premium relative to book value.
Bonded debt to equity	Bonded debt / Stockholders' equity	Measures a firm's leverage in terms of stockholders' equity
Debt to tangible net worth	Total liabilities / (Common equity − Intangible assets)	Measures a firm's leverage in terms of tangible (hard) assets captured in book value
Financial leverage index	Return on equity / Return on assets	Measures how well a company is using its debt
Limitations	Overall good measures of a firm's financing strategy; needs to be looked at in concert with operating results because	
	1. These measures can be misleading if looked at in isolation.	
	2. They can also be misleading if using book values as opposed to market values of debt and equity.	

TABLE 1 *(continued)*

When and How to Use Financial Measures to Assess Firm Performance

Table 1d: Liquidity Ratios	Formula	Characteristics
Current	Current assets / Current liabilities	Measures short-term liquidity. Current assets are all assets that a firm can readily convert to cash to pay outstanding debts and cover liabilities without having to sell hard assets. Current liabilities are a firm's debt and other obligations that are due within a year.
Quick (acid-test)	(Cash + Marketable securities + Net receivables) / Current liabilities	Eliminates inventory from the numerator, focusing on cash, marketable securities, and receivables.
Cash	(Cash + Marketable securities) / Current liabilities	Considers only cash and marketable securities for payment of current liabilities.
Operating cash flow	Cash flow from operations / Current liabilities	Evaluates cash-related performance (as measured from the statement of cash flows) relative to current liabilities
Cash to current assets	(Cash + Marketable securities) / Current assets	Indicates the part of current assets that are among the most fungible (i.e., cash and marketable securities).
Cash position	(Cash + Marketable securities) / Total assets	Indicates the percent of total assets that are most fungible (i.e., cash).
Current liability position	Current liabilities / Total assets	Indicates what percent of total assets the firm's current liabilities represent.
Limitations	Liquidity measures are important, especially in times of economic instability, but they also need to be looked at holistically along with financing and operating measures of a firm's performance.	

1. Accounting processes (e.g., monthly close) limit efficacy of these measures when you want to understand daily cash position.

2. No account taken of risk and exposure on the liability side.

TABLE 1 *(continued)*
When and How to Use Financial Measures to Assess Firm Performance

Table 1e: Market Ratios	Formula	Characteristics
Book value per share	Total stockholders' equity / Number of shares outstanding	Equity or net assets, as measured on the balance sheet
Earnings-based growth models	$P = kE / (r - g)$, where E = earnings, k = dividend payout rate, r = discount rate, and g = earnings growth rate	Valuation models that discount earnings and dividends by a discount rate adjusted for future earnings growth
Market-to-book	(Stock price × Number of shares outstanding) / Total stockholders' equity	Measures accounting-based equity
Price-earnings (PE) ratio	Stock price / EPS	Measures market premium paid for earnings and future expectations
Price-earnings growth (PEG) ratio	PE / Earnings growth rate	PE compared to earnings growth rates, a measure of PE "reasonableness"
Sales-to-market value	Sales / (Stock price × Number of shares outstanding)	A sales activity ratio based on market price
Dividend yield	Dividends per share / Stock price	Direct cash return on stock investment
Total return to shareholders	Stock price appreciation plus dividends	
Limitations	Market measures tend to be more volatile than accounting measures but also provide a good perspective on the overall health of a company when used holistically with the other measures of financial performance.	
	1. Market volatility/noise is the biggest challenge with these measures.	
	2. Understanding what is a result of a firm strategy/decision vs. the broader market is challenging.	

Joseph Lampel
New York University

It was in the spring of the second year of his insurrection against the High Sheriff of Nottingham that Robin Hood took a walk in Sherwood forest. As he walked, he pondered the progress of the campaign, the disposition of his forces, the Sheriff's recent moves, and the options that confronted him.

The revolt against the Sheriff had begun as a personal crusade. It had erupted out of Robin's conflict with the Sheriff and his administration. However, alone Robin Hood could do little. He therefore sought allies, men with grievances and a deep sense of justice. Later he welcomed all who came, asking few questions, and only demanding a willingness to serve. Strength, he believed, lay in numbers.

He spent the first year forging the group into a disciplined band, united in enmity against the Sheriff, and willing to live outside the law. The band's organization was simple. Robin ruled supreme, making all important decisions. He delegated specific tasks to his lieutenants. Will Scarlett was in charge of intelligence and scouting. His main job was to shadow the Sheriff and his men, always alert to their next move. He also collected information on the travel plans of rich merchants and tax collectors. Little John kept discipline among the men, and saw to it that their archery was at the high peak that their profession demanded. Scarlett took care of the finances, converting loot to cash, paying shares of the take, and finding suitable hiding places for the surplus. Finally, Much the Miller's son had the difficult task of provisioning the ever increasing band of Merry Men.

The increasing size of the band was a source of satisfaction for Robin, but also a source of concern. The fame of his Merry Men was spreading, and new recruits poured in from every corner of England. As the band grew larger, their small bivouac became a major encampment. Between raids the men milled about, talking and playing games. Vigilance was in decline, and discipline was becoming harder to enforce. "Why?" Robin reflected.

The growing band was also beginning to exceed the food capacity of the forest. Game was becoming scarce, and supplies had to be obtained from outlying villages. The cost of buying food was beginning to drain the band's financial reserves at the very moment when revenues were in decline. Travelers, especially those with the most to lose, were now giving the forest a wide berth. This was costly and inconvenient to them, but it was preferable to having all their goods confiscated.

Robin believed that the time had come for the Merry Men to change their policy of outright confiscation of goods to one of a fixed transit tax. His lieutenants strongly resisted this idea. They were proud of the Merry Men's famous motto: "Rob the rich and give to the poor." "The farmers and the townspeople," they argued, "are our most important allies." "How can we tax them, and still hope for their help in our fight against the Sheriff?"

Robin wondered how long the Merry Men could keep to the ways and methods of their early days. The Sheriff was growing stronger and better organized. He now had the money and the men, and was beginning to harass the band, probing for its weaknesses.

The tide of events was beginning to turn against the Merry Men. Robin felt that the campaign must be decisively concluded before the Sheriff had a chance to deliver a mortal blow. "But how?" he wondered.

Robin had often entertained the possibility of killing the Sheriff, but the chances for this seemed increasingly remote. Besides, killing the Sheriff might satisfy his personal thirst for revenge, but it would not improve the situation. Robin had hoped that the perpetual state of unrest, and the Sheriff's failure to collect taxes, would lead to his removal from office. Instead, the Sheriff used his political connections to obtain reinforcement. He had powerful friends at court, and was well regarded by the regent, Prince John.

Prince John was vicious and volatile. He was consumed by his unpopularity among the people, who wanted the imprisoned King Richard back. He also lived in constant fear of the barons, who had first given him the regency, but were now beginning to dispute his claim to the throne. Several of these barons had

Prepared by Joseph Lampel, Cass Business School. Copyright © 1985. Revised © 2011.

set out to collect the ransom that would release King Richard the Lionheart from his jail in Austria. Robin was invited to join the conspiracy in return for future amnesty. It was a dangerous proposition. Provincial banditry was one thing, court intrigue another. Prince John's spies were everywhere. If the plan failed, the pursuit would be relentless and the retribution swift.

The sound of the supper horn startled Robin from his thoughts. There was the smell of roasting venison in the air. Nothing was resolved or settled. Robin headed for camp promising himself that he would give these problems his utmost attention after tomorrow's raid.

Steve Gove
Virginia Tech
Brett P. Matherne
Loyola University of New Orleans

If the motion picture industry's performance was a feature film, the marquee for 2007 would have read "Massive Box Office: Smashing Records—The Sequel!" At $9.63 billion, box-office revenues set another record, a full 5 percent above the record set the prior year.[1] Theaters sold an astonishing 1.4 billion tickets (see Exhibit 1). But beyond the headlines, in 2008 the industry was a study in contradictions.

- The number of theaters is declining, but the number of screens is at an all time high.

- Revenues are up, but attendance is largely flat. That 1.4 billion tickets is little improved from 1997 when the industry sold 1.35 billion tickets, which was a fraction of the 4 billion sold in 1946. In the late 1940s, the average person attended 28 films a year; today it is 6.[2]

- The U.S. population is increasing, but the size of the market in the core demographic group is growing more slowly (see Exhibit 2, next page).

- Americans spend more time than ever on entertainment—3,500 hours annually—but only 12 of those hours at the movies.[3] The average person spends as much time watching TV every three days.

Movies remain as popular as ever, but opportunities for viewing outside the theater have greatly increased. While motion picture studios increased revenues through product licensing, DVD sales, and international expansion, the exhibitors—movie theaters—have seen their business decline. Movie content is more available than ever, but fewer are venturing to the theater to see it. Many theaters have ceased operation, driven from the market by consolidation and declining numbers of patrons.

Will the marquee at the local theater exhibitor soon change to: "A Horror Show for the Cinemaplex?"

---

*This case is developed for the purpose of class discussion. It is not intended to be used for any kind of endorsement, source of data, or depiction of efficient or inefficient management.

EXHIBIT 1

Domestic Tickets Sold and Box-Office Gross

Source: Boxofficemojo.com; and the U.S. Federal Reserve.

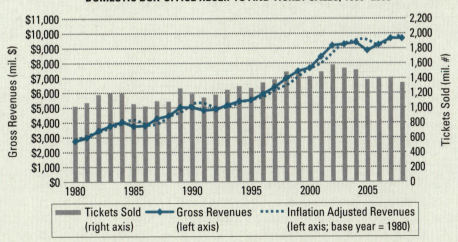

DOMESTIC BOX-OFFICE RECEIPTS AND TICKET SALES, 1980–2008

Legend:
- Tickets Sold (right axis)
- Gross Revenues (left axis)
- Inflation Adjusted Revenues (left axis; base year = 1980)

EXHIBIT 2

Population Trend among 14–17 and 18–24 Age Groups (millions)

Source: U.S. Census.

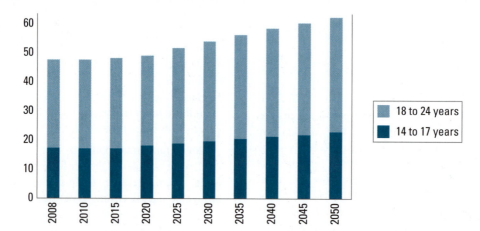

How has this come to be? And what can exhibitors do to respond?

The Motion Picture Industry Value Chain

The motion picture industry value chain consists of three stages: studio production, distribution, and exhibition (the theaters that show the films). All stages of the value chain are undergoing consolidation.

STUDIO PRODUCTION. The studios produce the lifeblood of the industry. They create content. Films from the top 10 studios produce over 90 percent of domestic box-office receipts (Exhibit 3). Studios are increasingly part of larger corporations, managed as any other profit center. Management is a challenge as investments are large and a success formula elusive. Profitability swings wildly. The cost of bringing a typical feature to market exceeds $100 million, up 25 percent in five years.[4] Typically, a third of costs are marketing expenses.

EXHIBIT 3

Market Share of Film Production (2007)

Studio Parent and Label	2007 Combined Share (%)
Time Warner (Warner Brothers and New Line)	19.8
Sony (Sony and MGM)	16.7
Viacom (Viacom and Paramount)	15.5
Disney (Disney, Buena Vista Pictures, and Miramax)	15.4
Universal Studios	11.4
News Corp (20th Century Fox)	10.5
Lion's Gate	3.6
DreamWorks SKG*	0.0
	92.9

* The DreamWorks share in 2005 was 5.7 percent.

Source: Adapted from the Mintel report: "Movie theaters - U.S. - February 2008."

Studios know their core audience: 12- to 24-year-olds. This group purchases nearly 40 percent of theater tickets. Half are "frequent moviegoers" attending at least one movie per month. Profits are driven by the studios' ability to satisfy this finicky audience. In 2008, films based on two successful comic-book characters met with widely different fates.[5] Paramount's successful *Iron Man* was produced for $140 million and grossed $318 million at the domestic box office. Warner Bros.' *Speed Racer,* produced for $20 million less and released the following weekend was a flop, grossing just $44 million.

Demographic trends are unfavorable for the studios and exhibitors. The U.S. population will increase 17 percent in 2025, an increase of 54 million people. But the number of 12- to 24-year-olds is expected to increase only 9 percent, adding just 4 million more potential viewers. Based on current theaters and screens, this is an increase of under 700 additional viewers per theater, roughly 100 per screen.

DISTRIBUTION. Distributors are the broker intermediaries between the studios and exhibitors. Distribution entails all steps following a film's artistic completion, including marketing, logistics, and administration. Exhibitors negotiate a percentage of gross by the studio or purchase rights to films and profit from the box-office receipts. Distributors select and market films to exhibitors, seeking to maximize potential attendees. Distributors also coordinate the manufacture and distribution of films to exhibitors. In addition, they handle collections, audits of attendees, and other administrative tasks. There are over 300 active distributors, but much of the distribution is done by a few major firms, including divisions of studios. Pixar, for example, co-produced *Finding Nemo* with Disney, and Disney's Buena Vista handled the distribution.

EXHIBITION. Studios have historically sought full vertical integration through theater ownership, allowing greater control over audiences and the capturing of exhibition profits. A common practice was for the studio to use its ownership to reduce competition by not showing pictures produced by rivals. This ended in 1948 with the Supreme Court's ruling against the studios in *United States v. Paramount Pictures.* Theaters were soon divested, leaving the two parties—studios and exhibitors—to negotiate film access and rental.

Theaters are classified according to the number of screens at one location (Exhibit 4). Single-screen theaters were the standard from the introduction of film through the 1980s. They have since rapidly declined in number, replaced by theater complexes. These include miniplexes (2–7 screens), multiplexes (8–15 screens), and megaplexes (16 or more screens). The number of theaters decreased more than 15 percent between 2000 and 2007, but the number of screens increased due to growth in megaplexes. Nearly 10 percent of the theaters are now megaplexes, and the number of screens is at a historical high of 40,077.[6] Many analysts argue the industry has overbuilt and too many theaters and screens exist to make the business profitable.

The economy affects attendance, historically increasing as the economy declines. During the Depression of the 1930s, movie theaters were described as "an acre of seats in a garden of dreams."[7] When 2008 saw rapid increases in gas prices, the stock market decline, and significant layoffs, one summer-movie patron commented, "There's not a whole lot you can do for $10 anymore."[8] Movies do remain a bargain in

EXHIBIT 4

Number of Theaters by Complex Size

	2000	2007	% Change
Single Screens	2,368	1,748	−26.18%
Miniplexes (2−7 Screens)	3,170	2,296	−27.57%
Multiplexes (8−15 Screens)	1,478	1,617	9.40%
Megaplexes (16+ Screens)	405	616	52.10%
Total	7,421	6,277	−15.42%

Sources: Developed by the author from Entertainment Industry, 2007 Report Motion Picture Association of America; and the Mintel report: "Movie theaters - U.S. - February 2008."

the entertainment business. The purchase of four tickets to a movie costs under $27 compared with $141 for an amusement park or $261 for a pro football game[9] (Exhibit 5). For many, watching the latest Hollywood release in the air conditioned comfort of a dark theater offers a break not just from the summer heat but from reality: "It's escapism, absolutely. It's probably a subconscious thing, and people don't realize it. But there's just so much going on, with people trying to pay their mortgages and get by. It's an escape for a couple of hours."[10]

Declining ticket sales and the increased costs associated with developing megaplexes began a wave of consolidation among exhibitors. Four companies now dominate: Regal, AMC, Cinemark, and Carmike (see Exhibit 6). Operating 1,405 theaters in the country (just 19 percent) in 2008, these companies controlled 42 percent of screens. This market share provides these exhibitors with negotiating power for access to films, prices for films and concessions, and greater access to revenues from national advertisers.

There is little differentiation in the offerings of the major theater exhibitors—prices within markets differ little, the same movies are shown on the same schedule (both in terms of the week of release and approximate daily schedule), and the food and services are

EXHIBIT 5

Average Movie Ticket Price

Source: Boxofficemojo.com; and the U.S. Federal Reserve.

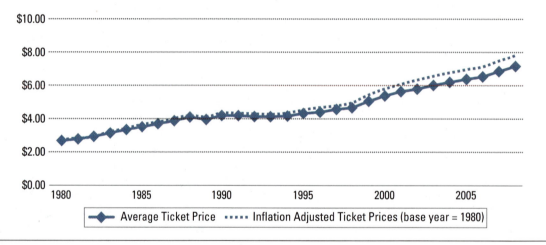

EXHIBIT 6

Exhibition Market Leaders

Company	Theater Brands	# U.S. Theater Locations	# U.S. Screens	Avg. Screens per Theater
Regal	Regal, United Artists, Edwards	526	6,355	12
AMC	AMC, Loews	315	4,585	14
Cinemark	Cinemark, Century	284	3,606	12
Carmike	Carmike	280	2,412	8
	Total for leading four	1,405	16,958	
	Industry total	7,421	40,077	

Sources: The Mintel report "Movie theaters - U.S. - February 2008;" SEC filings; and author estimates.

nearly identical. Competition between theaters often comes down to distance from home, convenience of parking, and proximity to restaurants. Innovations by one theater chain are quickly adopted by others.

The chains do serve different geographic markets and do so in different ways.[11] Regal focuses on midsized markets using multiplexes and megaplexes. Regal's average ticket price in 2007 of $7.43 was the highest among the leaders. AMC concentrates on urban areas with megaplexes and focuses on large population centers such as those in California, Florida, and Texas. Cinemark serves smaller markets, operating as the sole theater chain in over 80 percent of its markets. Cinemark's average ticket price in 2007 of $5.11 was the lowest of the majors. Carmike concentrates on small to midsized markets, targeting populations of less than 100,000 that have few other entertainment options. Carmike's average ticket price in 2007 was $5.89, but its average concession revenue of $3.05 per patron is the highest among the majors.

The different approaches of the companies are reflected in the cost of fixed assets per screens. These costs result from decisions made on how to serve customers, such as the level of technology and finish of the theater: Digital projection and marble floors cost more than traditional projectors and a carpeted lobby.[12] Despite multi- and megaplex facilities, Regal's cost per screen, $430,000, in 2008 was the highest. Rural operator Carmike's was the lowest of the four, at just $206,000. Cinemark is in the middle, at $367,000. Costs for AMC are expected to be near or to exceed Regal's.

The Business of Exhibition

Exhibitors have three primary sources of revenue: box-office receipts, concessions, and advertising. Managers have low discretion; their ability to influence revenues and expenses is limited. Operating margins among exhibitors average a slim 10 percent, and this is before significant expenses such as facility and labor costs. The result is marginal, or even negative, net income. Overall, the business of exhibitors is best described as loss leadership on movies: The firms make money selling concessions and showing ads to patrons who are drawn by the movie.

BOX-OFFICE REVENUES. Ticket sales constitute two-thirds of exhibition business revenues. The return on these receipts, however, is quite small. Historically,

the power imbalance between studios and exhibitors yielded rental contracts returning as much as 90 percent of box-office revenue to the studios during the initial weeks of a film's release. Today, the split is typically closer to 55/45 for large chains. Still, it is not uncommon for ticket revenues not to cover the full costs of film rental, advertising, and facilities. The record-setting revenues at the box office have been the result of increases in ticket prices that have flowed back to the studios and that are used to cover facilities and debt load.

CONCESSIONS. Moviegoers frequently lament the high prices for concessions. Concessions average 25 to 30 percent of revenues. Direct costs are less than 15 percent of the selling price, making concessions the largest source of exhibitor profit. These are influenced by the three factors: attendance, pricing, and material costs. The most important is attendance: more attendees equals more concession sales. Per patron sales are influenced by prices—a common moviegoer complaint is high concession prices. The $3.75 price-point for the large soda is not by accident and is the result of market research and profit-maximization calculation. Costs are influenced by purchase volume, with larger chains able to negotiate better prices on everything from popcorn and soda pop to cups and napkins.

ADVERTISING. Exhibitors also generate revenue through pre-show advertising. Though this constitutes just 5 percent of revenues, it is highly profitable. Marketing research firm Mintel reports that advertising revenues among exhibitors are expected to increase at a rate of approximately 10 percent over the coming decade.[13] Audiences signal consistent dislike for advertising at the theater, however. Balancing the revenues from ads with audience tolerance is an ongoing struggle for exhibitors, though not a new one. In the early 1970s, one industry executive argued: "It is not a policy of our corporation to use commercial advertising for income on our screen. We are selling the public one item—a particular motion picture—and to use the screen for other purposes detracts from this item."[14]

Overall, the exhibitor has limited control over both revenues and profits. Box-office receipts are the bulk of revenues, but yield few profits. Attendance allows for profitable sales of concessions and advertisements, but there are significant caps on the volume of concession sales per person, and selling prices seem to have reached maximum. Advertising remains an attractive avenue for revenues and profits, though audiences loathe it.

The Process of Exhibition

The fundamentals of film exhibition have changed little since the early 1940s. To show a picture, each theater receives a shipment of physical canisters containing a "release print" from the distributor. Making these prints requires $20,000 to $30,000 in up-front costs and $1,000 to $1,500 for each print. Thus a modern major motion picture opening on 2,500 screens simultaneously requires $2.50 to $3.75 million in print costs. The studios bear this cost, but exhibitors and, ultimately, attendees pay for it.

Each release print is actually several reels of 35 mm film which are manually loaded onto projector reels, sequenced, and queued for display by a projector operator. The film passes through the projector which shines intense light through the film, projecting the image through a lens that focuses the image on the screen. A typical projection system costs $50,000, with one needed for each screen.

Digital cinema is becoming economically viable and involves a high-resolution (4,096 × 2,160) digitized image projected onto the screen. Basic digital systems cost $150,000 to $250,000 per screen. Conversion of an existing eight-screen theater to digital thus means an investment of $1.2 to $2.0 million. The costs for digital "release prints" are far lower than for traditional film, but these costs savings most directly benefit the studio, whereas costs to convert theaters are the exhibitors'. The number of digital theaters is expanding rapidly. In 2004, less than 100 existed. In 2008, there were approximately 4,600, translating to 12 percent of the screens. Due to the costs, most theaters use a mixture of technologies, with a minority of screens in any one facility using digital projection.

The Theater Experience

For a significant number of moviegoers, the draw of the theater is far more than simply the film that is showing. Moviegoers describe attending the theater as an experience, with the appeal based on:[15]

- The giant theater screen
- The opportunity to be out of the house

- Not having to wait to see a particular movie on home video
- The experience of watching the movie with a theatrical sound system
- The theater as a location option for a date

The ability of theaters to provide these benefits, beyond what audiences can achieve at home, appears to be diminishing. Of the reasons why people go to the movies, only the "place" aspects—the theater as a place to be out of house and as a place for dating—seem immune from substitution. Few teenagers want movie and popcorn with their date at home with mom and dad.

The overall "experience" that theaters currently offer falls short for many. Marketing research firm Mintel reports the reasons for not attending the theater more frequently are largely the result of the declining experience. Specific factors include: the overall cost, at-home viewing options, interruptions such as cell phones in the theater, rude patrons, the overall hassle, and ads prior to the show.[16] Patrons report general dismay with the theater experience. A *Wall Street Journal* article reported on interruptions ranging from the intrusion of soundtracks in adjacent theaters to cell phones: "The interruptions capped a night of movie going already marred by out-of-order ticketing kiosks and a parade of preshow ads so long that, upon seeing the Coca-Cola polar bears on screen, one customer grumbled: 'This is obscene.'"[17] Recounting bad experiences is a lively topic for bloggers. A typical comment: "I say it has gotten worse. I hate paying $9 for a ticket and the movie is 90–100 minutes long, people talking on the cell phone, the people who work at the theaters look like they are bored, and when you ask them a question, the answer is very rude. I worked as a [sic] usher in the late '60s and we had to wear uniforms and white gloves on Friday and Saturday nights; those days are long gone."[18]

A trip to the local cinemaplex can be eye-opening even for industry insiders. In 2005, Toby Emmerich, New Line Cinema's head of production, faced a not-so-common choice: attending *War of the Worlds* in a theater or in a screening room at actor Jim Carrey's house. Said Emmerich in a *Los Angeles Times* article, "I love seeing a movie with a big crowd, but I had no idea how many obnoxious ads I'd have to endure—it really drove me crazy. After sitting through about 15 minutes of ads, I turned to my wife and said, 'Maybe we should've gone to Jim Carrey's house after all.'"[19]

The unique value proposition offered by movie theaters—large screens, the long wait for DVD release, and advantages of theatrical sound systems—also appear to be fading. Increasingly larger television sets, DVD content, and the adoption of high-definition technology for home use are all eroding the advantages offered by movie theaters. One blogger posts, "Whereas the electronics industry has been innovating to create immersive experiences from the comfort of our own home, the U.S. theater industry has been dragging their feet."[20]

HOME-VIEWING TECHNOLOGY. Home television sets are increasingly large high-definition sets, coupled with inexpensive yet impressive audio systems. In 1997, the screen size of the average television was just 23 inches. Currently, almost all LCD televisions sold have screens 36 inches or larger.[21] Because set size is measured as the diagonal screen size, increases in viewable area are greater than the measurement suggests. The viewing area of sets doubled from 250 inches to 550 inches.

The FCC requirement that all broadcasters convert to digital broadcasts by 2009 is widely credited with starting a consumer movement to upgrade televisions. Since the 1950s, television transmissions were formatted as 480 interlaced vertical lines (480i) of resolution. The new digital format is high-definition (HD), providing up to 1,080 vertical lines of resolution (1,080p).[22] At least three-quarters of all televisions sold since 2006 are HD-capable.

As LCD technology became the standard for both computer and television screens, manufacturing costs declined. Wholesale prices for televisions fell 65 percent from the late 1990s to 2007.[23] In 2006, the average television retailed for $29 per diagonal inch of set size. This is expected to decrease to $22 within five years.[24] Consumers, however, are actually spending more on every television, consistently electing to purchase larger sets to achieve a better viewing experience. Sharp, a leading TV-set manufacturer, predicts that by 2015 the average screen will reach 60 inches.[25]

Large-screen televisions, DVD players, and audio and speaker components are commonly packaged as low-cost home theaters. The average DVD player now costs just $72[26] and high-definition DVD players are beginning to penetrate the market. Retail price wars during the 2008 holiday season led to HD Blu-ray players dropping below $200. These home-theater systems offer a movie experience that rivals many theaters, all for between $1,000 and $2,000. Says Mike Gabriel, Sharp's head of marketing and communications, "People can now expect a home cinema experience from their TV. Technology that was once associated with the rich and famous is now accessible to homes across the country."[27]

CONTENT AVAILABILITY AND TIMING. Even the best hardware offers little value without content for display. Rental firm Netflix advertises a selection of 100,000+ titles, extending well beyond new and classic films to include television shows, sports, and music performances. HD content is increasingly available to maximize the experience offered by those HD televisions. Satellite and cable television providers have engaged in a game of one-upmanship to provide the greatest percentage of HD content available to subscribers. By 2010, over 3,000 movies were already available on Blu-ray DVD in some countries.[28]

Movie fans no longer have to wait long for the summer's blockbusters to appear on DVD. The time period between theatrical and DVD release has declined 40 percent since 2000. The top five films in 2000 were released on DVD an average of 37 weeks after their box-office opening. In 2007, the lag was just 23 weeks. Studios have experimented with simultaneous release to theaters, pay-per-view, and DVD.

Overall, the visual and audio experience available in the home is rapidly converging with that available at the movie theater. As a blogger on the movie fan site Big Picture posted:

> I used to go to the movies all the time—even my blog is called the Big Picture. Then I started going less—and then less still and now—hardly at all. My screen at home is better, the sound system is better, the picture is in focus, the floors aren't sticky and the movies start on time. My seat is clean. And there's no idiot chattering away 2 rows behind me, and (this is my favorite) THERE'S NO CELL PHONES RINGING. EVER.[29]

The industry may have reached an inflection point in 2008. For just the fifth time in nearly three decades, total box-office receipts declined, falling nearly half a percent below 2007's record. Admissions too have fallen, nearly 5 percent for the year. Will the future be only horror shows for the cinemaplex? What can exhibitors do to improve their industry? What can they do to improve the profitability of their own firm?

Endnotes

1. Motion Picture Association of America (MPAA) 2007 Entertainment Industry Market Statistics.

2. Serwer, A. (2006), "Extreme makeover: With big screens and high-def in more and more living rooms, movie theaters are taking radical new measures to woo filmgoers," *Fortune* 153: 108–116

3. Mintel report, "Movie theaters - U.S. - February 2008."

4. MPAA 2007 Entertainment Industry Market Statistics.

5. All data on these two films are from www.BoxOfficeMojo.com.

6. Developed by the author from: Entertainment Industry, 2007 Report Motion Picture Association of America.

7. Fuller, K. H. (2002), "'You can have the strand in your own town': The struggle between urban and small-town exhibition in the picture palace era," in Waller, G. A. (ed.), *Moviegoing in America: A Sourcebook in the History of Film Exhibition* (Malden, MA: Blackwell Publishers Ltd.), pp. 88–98.

8. Woestendiek, J. and C. Kaltenbach (2008), "$10 is small price for a big escape: Movie box office figures are flourishing despite, or because of, economic worries," *The Baltimore Sun,* July 8; accessed on Factival, December 5, 2008.

9. MPAA 2007 Entertainment Industry Market Statistics.

10. Woestendiek, J. and C. Kaltenbach (2008), "$10 is small price for a big escape."

11. Data on the firms, screen sizes, and locations from websites and SEC filings.

12. All data is from SEC filings, based on net property, plant, and equipment reported in the 2007 balance sheet and the number of screens.

13. Mintel report, "Movie theaters - U.S. - February 2008 - Segment Performance - Cinema Advertising."

14. Durwood, S. H. (2002), "The exhibitors (1972," in Waller, G. A. (ed.), *Moviegoing in America: A Sourcebook in the History of Film Exhibition* (Malden, MA: Blackwell Publishers Ltd.), pp. 279–281.

15. Mintel report, "Movie theaters - U.S. - February 2008 - Reasons to go to movies over watching a DVD."

16. Mintel report, "Movie theaters - U.S. - February 2008 - Reasons why attendance is not higher."

17. Kelly, K., B. Orwall, and P. Sanders (2005), "The multiplex under siege," *The Wall Street Journal,* December 24.

18. Blog comment on *Cinema Treasures:* "Over the past ten years, the movie theater experience has . . . ," http://cinematreasures.org/polls/22/.

19. Goldstein, P. (2005), "Now playing: A glut of ads," *Los Angeles Times,* July 12, http://articles.latimes.com/2005/jul/12/entertainment/et-goldstein12.

20. "Designs of the week: The movie theater experience," November 23, 2008, www.sramanamitra.com/2008/11/23/designs-of-the-week-the-movie-theater-experience/.

21. DuBravac, 2007.

22. Ibid.

23. Ibid.

24. Keefe, B. (2008), "Prices on flat-screen TVs expected to keep falling," *The Atlanta Journal-Constitution,* March 15.

25. "Average TV size up to 60-inch by 2015 says Sharp," *TechDigest,* www.techdigest.tv/2008/01/average_tv_size.html.

26. MPAA 2007 Entertainment Industry Market Statistics.

27. "Average TV size up to 60-inch by 2015 says Sharp."

28. http://en.wikipedia.org/wiki/Blu-ray.

29. Blog comment on *The Big Picture:* "Why is movie theatre revenue attendance declining?" http://bigpicture.typepad.com/comments/2005/07/declining_movie.htm.

Steve Gove
Virginia Tech
Brett P. Matherne
Loyola University of New Orleans

As Hollywood exalts 2011's blockbuster season, the movie-exhibition industry remains a study in contrasts. According to the industry, going to the movies remains an affordable escape as an economic recession turns into a slow recovery. Yet, industry revenues declined 0.3 percent in 2010 to $10.6 billion on an admission decline of 5 percent (Exhibit 1). The 3D format made a triumphant return to the box office, netting 21 percent of all revenues, but 3D led to unprecedented price increases during a recession. Exhibitors fear disintermediation as studios seek to combat declining DVD sales through shortened release windows and a shift toward international markets. Fitch Ratings, an independent credit-rating agency, cautions that "revenues and profitability of movie theatres could be increasingly challenged by factors that are largely out of managements' control."[1]

Has the picture changed for exhibitors? Who is writing the script—the exhibitors or the studios? How did exhibitors respond to the technology dilemma in 2008? What happened in 2009 and 2010 during the economic recession? Is exhibition poised for growth and profitability going forward in 2011 and beyond? What can exhibitors do to improve the situation?

Industry Technological Transformation

The "most transformative revolution since talkies"[2]—transitioning from physical film to digital distribution and projection—is fully under way in 2011. The change began years ago with two enabling actions: a digital content standard and financing alternatives.

Early digital systems utilized different formats, limiting adoption (because equipment could become obsolete once a dominant design emerged) and limiting cost savings from distribution. AMC, Cinemark, and Regal formed Digital Cinema Implementation Partners (DCIP) to facilitate the transition. Each invested $8 million in the partnership. DCIP established

---

*This case is developed for the purpose of class discussion. It is not intended to be used for any kind of endorsement, source of data, or depiction of efficient or inefficient management.

EXHIBIT 1

Domestic Box-Office Receipts and Ticket Sales, 1980–2010

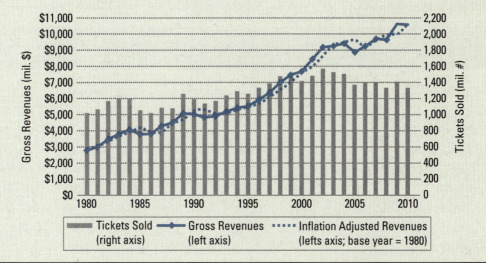

a technological standard for quality and security.[3] Agreement was reached with five of the major studios to ensure digital-content availability. This ensured a supply of content and created a de facto standard, encouraging investments in technology.

Conversion is prohibited by the high-capital investments needed. The cost of a digital-projection system is considerable, averaging $75,000 per screen, and 3D capability adds an additional $25,000. Financing these investments was the second significant issue for exhibitors due to the total costs and their weak balance sheets. The major theater chains used two financing avenues. Forming an agreement with Christie Digital Systems, Carmike went solo with a lease-service approach. Under this 10-year agreement, digital and digital 3-D systems are installed with an up-front cost of $800 per screen. Christie provides equipment service, and maintenance is $2,340 per screen annually. This arrangement effectively puts both the risk and upside with Carmike as fixed costs are increased. Revenues beyond these fixed costs benefit Carmike. Alternatively, AMC, Cinemark, and Regal financed the transition through the DCIP partnership, securing $660 million in financing to convert nearly 14,000 (over 90 percent) of their screens. Each pays a $5,000 to $10,000 per screen conversion charge and subsequent royalty fees of approximately $0.50 per admission.

With the financing in place, conversion to digital is proceeding rapidly at the industry level (Exhibit 2).

At the end of 2007, just 2,650 digital screens were installed in the United States. At the end of 2010, there were 16,522—an increase of more than 600 percent. Carmike had converted over 90 percent of its screens to digital. The DCIP firms had, on average, converted approximately 27 percent of their screens. Plans are in place for near-complete conversion to digital among the leading four exhibitors.

To the audience, the most visible aspect of the digital transition is 3D, which went mainstream in 2010. In 2005, just 192 digital-3D–capable screens were installed. By 2010, that number climbed to 8,459. Carmike has converted 27 percent of its screens to digital-3D–capable. For the DCIP partners, the number averages 22 percent, with plans to achieve approximately 45 percent. In 2010, these 3D screens were responsible for one-fifth of total box-office receipts. A study by the International 3D Society reports 3D is responsible for the majority of opening-weekend revenues.[4] Of *Avatar*'s $77 million opening weekend, 82 percent was from 3D; for *Alice in Wonderland*, it was 70 percent.

Still, some argue that 3D may be a novelty. The appeal of 3D varies by film, with action and animated movies the leaders in the industry. "Because the pricing of 3-D tickets is now so high, people are becoming more selective about what they see in 3-D," said Rich Greenfield, media analyst for BTIG.[5] A focus on 3D may result in more action movies and fewer comedies and dramas, further alienating the non-core audience

EXHIBIT 2

Exhibition Market Leaders Entering 2011

Company	Theater Brands	# U.S. Theater Locations	# U.S. Screens	Avg. Screens per Theater	Digital Screens		3D-Capable Screens	
					#	% of Screens	#	% of Screens
Regal	Regal, United Artists, Edwards	539	6,698	12.4	2,202	33%	1,710	26%
AMC*	AMC, Loews	297	4,513	15.2	568	13%	475	11%
Cinemark	Cinemark, Century	293	3,832	13.1	1,363	36%	1,136	30%
Carmike	Carmike	239	2,236	9.4	2,103	94%	596	27%
	Total for leading four	1,368	17,279	12.6	6,236	36%	3,917	23%
	Industry total	6,039	39,547	6.5	16,522	42%	8,459	21%

* Excludes AMC's 81 IMAX screens.

for movies.[6] The long term popularity of 3-D appears to be downward, though the threshold is unknown (Exhibit 3).

The Home-Option Threat

While 3D is the big draw at theaters, changes in home-viewing habits are increasingly threatening the revenues of both exhibitors and studios. The consumer value chain for watching movies is to increasingly skip the theater in favor of home viewing—and renting, not purchasing—the DVD. Sales of DVDs have been a primary source of studio profits for more than a decade, but have fallen precipitously, down over 40 percent in three years.[7] At $8.2 billion, 2010's U.S. DVD sales were just 77 percent of box-office receipts, continuing a downward trend that in 2009 saw DVD revenues drop below box-office receipts for the first time since 2000.[8]

This decline in DVD sales is due in part to the expanded availability of rentals and pay-per-view, and at least partially attributable to the studios. For rentals, Netflix revenues grew 300 percent from 2005 to 2010, with online streaming being its highest area of growth. Coinstar's Redbox has over 32,000 rental kiosks offering $1-a-night rentals through partnerships with McDonald's (which is also an investor in the company), Walmart, Walgreen's, and other retailers.

Studios are responding by trying to spur DVD and pay-per-view fees through shorter release windows, actions seemingly incompatible and inconsistent with the drive to increase theater attendance. In 2000, the average window between theatrical release and DVD sales was five months, 16 days. In 2010, it was four months, 12 days—a decline of five weeks, or 20 percent, over 10 years.[9] Studios are eager to accelerate DVD revenue streams and capitalize on initial marketing expenditures. Arguing in favor of a reduced window, Bob Iger, CEO of Disney said, "The problem with waiting these days is that we're dealing with a much more competitive marketplace than ever before—there are more choices that people have."[10] Theaters may fear complete disintermediation.

The accelerated DVD release of *Alice in Wonderland* in the United States (just 88 days after opening and while the film remained in theaters) created great concern among film exhibitors. Exhibitors fear that shorter windows deter attendance (Exhibit 4). U.S. theater owners and major Hollywood studios reached an agreement wherein the studios will be able to release one or two movies each year on an accelerated schedule, cutting a month off the traditional four-month DVD release window.[11] *The Wall Street Journal* reported, "Theaters have benefited recently from a boom in box-office receipts, even as studios have suffered from a steep decline in DVD sales. Adjusting the

EXHIBIT 3

Percent of Opening Weekend Sales from 3D

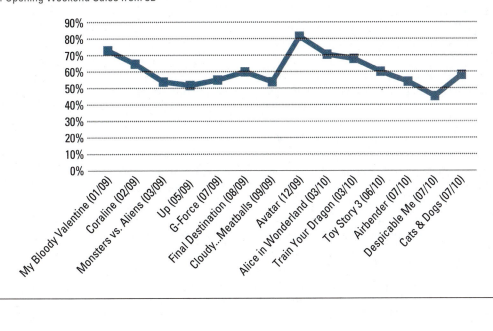

EXHIBIT 4

Alice in Wonderland: Weekly Domestic Box-Office Gross

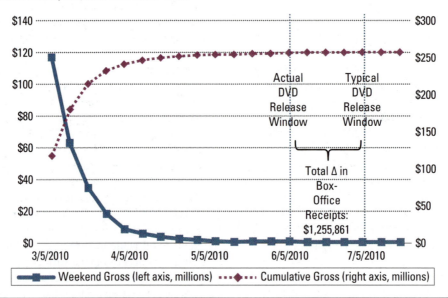

windows is an attempt to maintain the health of both camps, which depend on one another."[12]

Hollywood is also seeking to expand direct-to-viewer delivery. Studios won regulatory approval to temporarily block analog outputs on viewers' electronics during pay-per-view movies. While controls for digital outputs are features that are built into modern electronics, viewers with analog equipment could record pay-per-view movies if the regulatory block failed. Studios considered this loophole a security issue. Allowing temporary blockage paves the way for studios to pursue short release windows, offering "premium" pay-per-view opportunities prior to DVD release.

Declining DVD sales have studios looking for new profit sources. While pursuing direct pay-per-view and other options, studios increasingly focus their attention on the international market where growth is highest. While U.S. revenues grew 20 percent from 2005 to 2010, international revenues grew more than 50 percent, from $14 billion to $21 billion.[13] Internationally both attendance and receipts are expanding.[14] Studios' proportional revenues are also further shifting toward international. In 2005, international box-office receipts totaled $23 billion with $14 billion (60 percent) from international. By 2010, that increased to two-thirds on $32 billion total.[15] There appear opportunities to increase revenues from increased attendance

and ticket price increases. In India, for example, last year's 3.3 billion attendees paid an average of just $0.50.[16] In just that market at current growth rates, the annual volume increase in attendance equals total current U.S. annual theater admissions.[17] Among leading U.S. exhibitors, Cinemark has the largest international presence with 130 theaters (1,066 screens) in Mexico and seven Central and South American countries.

Industry Revenue Streams

As 2008 ended, exhibitors and studios were fixated on the public's reaction to an economic recession. Would attendance increase, as it had during five of the last seven recessions?[18] After a slow start in summer 2008, same-period attendance grew 10–15 percent, with final attendance essentially equal to the prior year, increasing an additional 5 percent in 2009 before declining 4 percent as the recession ended in 2010. The pattern of the movies serving as escapism thus appears to have changed little from 1911, when one observer described movies as a "door of escape, for a few cents, from the realities of life."[19] Attendance at matinees, commonly half the price of evening tickets, grew most rapidly during the recession.[20]

However, many industry observers are cautious about a long-term change in the attendance trend. Some attributed 2008's recovery to unexpectedly high admissions to just a few blockbusters, including *The Dark Night* and *Iron Man,* and 2009's performance to the sleeper hits *The Blindside* and *The Hangover.* Critics cautioned that while ticket sales did increase for the year, admissions remain below 2006 levels. The idea of movies being a bargain during a recession was also being tested. After offering bargain movie nights and other inducements during the start of the recession, exhibitors changed approaches. Prior to the March 2010 opening of *How to Train Your Dragon,* theaters increased base ticket prices another $2 to $3, the largest increases in recent memory. From 2005 to 2010, ticket price increases averaged 4.1 percent per year, double the rate of inflation.

Much of the price increase is due to 3D. While these increases set records, an even greater opportunity materialized for 3D. A $1 to $2 "3D surcharge" has traditionally been charged to cover the cost of glasses, license fees paid to 3D equipment providers, and higher rental rates to studios. Following the success of *Avatar,* exhibitors saw an opportunity to use the surcharge as an alternative to ticket-price increases. The 3D premium now reaches $3 to $5; for IMAX it is $4 to $7. Price increases in March 2010 by AMC, Regal, and Cinemark averaged 8.3 percent nationally on 3D movies, rising from $13.60 to $14.73.[21] In some markets, 3D prices jumped 20 percent.[22]

Overall, recent-year revenue increases for exhibitors can be attributed almost entirely to 3D. In 2005, the box office for 3D was just $40 million. In 2010, it was $2.2 billion, 21 percent of all revenues. From 2005 to 2010, 3D box-office receipts grew 5,400 percent, while revenues for non-3D *declined* 4 percent.[23] These data may actually underrepresent the actual demand for 3D as rapid expansion in the number of 3D films in production created a bottleneck for the 3D screen space.[24] Longer runs on 3D screens will likely increase the proportion of revenues from 3D. However, Paul Dergarabedian of Hollywood.com cautions that the ticket-price increases are not sustainable: "It's what we call a recession-resistant business. Times get tough and people go to the movies because it's the one thing they see as a relative bargain. The minute they cease to see it that way, it's not good for the industry."[25]

AMC may have, intentionally or not, stumbled onto a price cap when several of its New York theaters hit $20 per ticket for *Shrek 4* in IMAX 3D. Amidst a public outcry and unwanted media attention, the chain apologized, citing a pricing error, and reduced

prices to $17 and $19. This situation suggests there is indeed a cap on the willingness to pay for even the most extreme viewing experience. The backlash may make it difficult to raise prices in the near future. Any cap on ticket prices is a serious cause for concern for exhibitors, as increasing prices has been the primary way to increase revenues.

The evidence is mixed that 3D is having a positive impact on the bottom line for exhibitors. This suggests either that the cost benefits are yet to accrue to exhibitors or are being appropriated by studios. The National Association of Theater Owners (NATO) estimates the savings of digital over film as $1 billion annually[26] from lower production costs, master reels and prints, the elimination of shipping, and so on. They argue these cost savings will largely accrue to distributors.

By all accounts, revenues per admission have increased, but this revenue is split with studios. At Regal, for example, film rental and advertising costs as a percent of revenues dropped slightly, to 53.3 percent from 54.2 percent for the second quarter of 2010 compared to the same period 2009. Similarly, Carmike's exhibition costs declined slightly as a percent of revenue, from 57.6 percent to 56.8 percent, but other theater operating costs grew from 59.6 percent to 62.9 percent of admissions revenue. In each of these cases, the data reflect substantial increases in ticket prices and the 3D surcharges imposed during spring 2010. This suggests studios are appropriating a large portion of the revenue increases.

At Regal, this holds true for operating profits, as a percent of revenues, decreased from 12.2 percent in the second quarter of 2009 to 9.0 percent in 2010. For Carmike, the net effect was operating income declining significantly, from 8.8 percent of total revenue to 4.1 percent. The overall picture appears similar for Cinemark. Operating income as a percentage of revenues for the second-quarter of 2010 declined from same-period 2009 levels, dropping from 14.6 percent to 14.4 percent. While limited to just the first comparative quarter in which most price increases and surcharges went into effect, this suggests that, despite substantial investments in digital and 3D, exhibitors may not be able to capitalize on them.

Alternative Revenue Streams

The investments in digital distribution and projection increase quality and flexibility and serve as a classic "enabling technology," opening the door for alternative content. New York Metropolitan Opera's *Live in HD* is an alternative content leader, now entering its fifth season. The series offers opera to audiences where it may not be available locally. Featuring 12 performances on Saturday afternoons, the series is broadcast to more than 500 HD-equipped theaters, around the world. Exhibitors continue to experiment with alternative content, mostly for individual sporting events where exhibitors must compete directly with home viewing. Says Jeremy Devine, marketing VP for a Dallas-based theater chain showing the NBA All-Star game: "I don't care how good your buddy's system is, this is a 52-foot screen. And it's in 3D."[27]

Despite the potential for alternative content, virtually all admissions continue to be for studio movies. The evidence suggests continued problems with profitability under this studio-dominated model. The surge in revenues from 3D does not appear to be increasing profitability. Under the standard theater model, unchanged since the 1930s, just two other revenue streams exist: concessions and advertising.

While ticket prices have increased fourfold since the 1970s, per capita spending on concessions has only slightly more than doubled.[28] Theater chains have expanded food offerings, some to the point of rivaling mall food courts. NATO estimates that over 400 theaters have onsite restaurant or bar service. Some also offer valet parking and child care to attract customers.[29] These theaters appear at odds with the primary demographic market for movies. While the average moviegoer is the teen to 20-something, these theaters seek 35- to 50-year-olds. AMC is experimenting with an in-theater food model to serve this market. Gold Class Cinemas adds a service approach with 40-seat theaters more akin to club lounges than auditoriums, and offers full food and wine service. Tickets, $20 to $25 per person, are purchased not from a ticket booth but from a concierge. Food sales average near $20 per person. Rob Goldberg, Gold Classes COO, explains this is part of the appeal: "We don't get the teenage crowd," he said.[30]

Advertising is usually fit to the target market's tolerance, and the ability to increase revenues and profits is questionable. While an Arbitron survey indicates 63 percent of those 12 and older report they "do not mind the ads they put on before the movie begins,"[31] other viewers loathe them. Bob Pisano, President of

the MPAA, calls increased advertising or higher concession prices "mutually assured destruction" for both exhibitors and the studios. "They try moviegoers' patience," he argues, "leading them to stay home and rent or, worse, illegally download a film."[32]

Is the Curtain Opening or Closing in 2011?

Despite a continuing recession, the start of the 2011 season saw an alarming statistic: revenues declined 22 percent from 2010 levels. The increased costs of going to the theater may be causing audiences to be more selective in the movies they see at the theater. Perhaps the escapism of movies is bumping into the reality of empty wallets. Higher prices are "a very dangerous situation for the movie industry," says Paul Dergarabedian, box-office analyst for Hollywood.com. "When is too much too much? The demand has been huge, but theater owners should not just think that they can charge whatever they want, because there is a point when people will literally just stop coming because they can't afford it."[33] Others explain the decline as a lack of content. Even with expectedly high revenues from big budget movies, no sleeper hits emerged.

The industry, not surprisingly, has already turned attention to upcoming fall debuts. For studios and exhibitors, the financial performance for 2011 rests largely on sequels, including live-action features *Pirates of the Caribbean, The Hangover,* and the final chapter of the *Harry Potter* franchise and animated sequels to *Cars* and *Kung Fu Panda.*

As referenced earlier, Fitch Ratings summarized the long-term situation: "[R]evenues and profitability of movie theatres could be increasingly challenged by factors that are largely out of managements' control. . . . [T]he significant degree of operating leverage means that cashflow can be meaningfully affected by moderate top-line declines. These factors and financial policy decisions will remain the main drivers of credit quality over the longer term."[34]

Beyond 2011, what can exhibitors do to improve their performance? To reverse the downward trend in attendance? To improve their profitability at a time when the studios, relying on the box office more than ever, are increasingly looking internationally?

Endnotes

1. "Fitch: High debt levels reduce flexibility for U.S. movie exhibitors in 2009," *Business Wire,* January 27, 2009; retrieved from Factiva.

2. National Association of Theater Owners (2010), *Reflections on the Kind of Exhibition Industry that Best Serves Movie Patrons, Makers, and Exhibitors in the Digital Era* (Cinema Buyers Group of the National Association of Theater Owners).

3. "Digital Cinema Implementation Partners announces agreement with five studios for digital cinema upgrade," press release, Digital Cinema Implementation Partners, 2008.

4. International 3D Society (2010), *3D Movie Fans Expand Box Office Says International 3D Society Study.*

5. Schuker, L.A.E. (2010), "A 2-D 'Eclipse' stakes its claim in 3-D world," *The Wall Street Journal,* July 6.

6. "The box office strikes back," *The Economist,* May 6, 2010; accessed from Factiva.

7. National Association of Theater Owners (2009), "ShoWest 2010 talking points," www.natoonline.org.

8. Kung, M. (2011), "The force of unity at CinemaCon," *The Wall Street Journal,* March 28.

9. "CinemaCon 2011 talking points & fact sheet," National Association of Theater Owners, 2011.

10. Smith, E., and L.A.E. Schuker (2010), "Studios unlock DVD release dates," *The Wall Street Journal,* February 12; accessed from Factiva.

11. Ibid.

12. Ibid.

13. *Theatrical Market Statistics: 2009,* Motion Picture Association of America, 2009.

14. "The box office strikes back."

15. *Theatrical Market Statistics: 2010,* Motion Picture Association of America, 2010.

16. Thakur, A. (2009), "India dominates world of films," *The Times of India,* July 29; retrieved from Factiva.

17. Ibid.

18. "ShoWest 2008 talking points & fact sheet," National Association of Theater Owners, 2008, www.natoonline.org.

19. Vorse, M. H. (2002), "Some picture show audiences (1911)," in G. A. Waller (ed.), *Moviegoing in America: A Sourcebook in the History of Film Exhibition* (Malden, MA: Blackwell Publishers Ltd.), pp. 50–53.

20. Joyner, T. (2009), "Movies are popular in recession," *The Atlanta Journal—Constitution,* June 28.

21. "U.S. movie ticket sales strong despite price hike," *Reuters News,* April 6; retrieved from Factiva.

22. Schuker, L.A.E., and Smith, E. (2010), "Higher prices make box-office debut," *The Wall Street Journal,* March 25.

23. *Theatrical Market Statistics: 2009.*

24. Ibid.

25. Muther, C. (2010), "Prices for 3-D movies flyaway with 'Dragon,'" *Boston Globe,* March 27.

26. "Talking points: Digital cinema," National Association of Theater Owners, 2010, www.natoonline.org.

27. Moore, M. T. (2009), "Moving beyond movies," *USA Today,* February 9.

28. Brodesser-Akner, C. (2008), "What popcorn prices mean for movies; Ethanol and rising costs of paper eat into sales that subsidize tickets," *Advertising Age,* May 19; retrieved from Factiva.

29. Russell, J. (2009), "Winning ticket? Cinemas hope high-end services pack 'em in," *Los Angeles Business Journal,* November 2; retrieved from Factiva.

30. Ruggless, R. (2009), "Dinner and a movie: One hot ticket for operators," *Nation's Restaurant News* 43: 41.

31. Brodesser-Akner, C. (2008), "What popcorn prices mean for movies."

32. Ibid.

33. Wood, D. B., and G. Goodale (2010), "Want to see a 3D movie? Ticket prices go up 20 percent," *The Christian Science Monitor,* March 26; retrieved from Factiva.

34. "Fitch: High debt levels reduce flexibility for U.S. movie exhibitors in 2009."

Better World Books: Social Entrepreneurship and the Triple Bottom Line

Better World Books collects and sells books online to fund literacy initiatives worldwide. We're a self-sustaining, triple-bottom-line company that creates social, economic, and environmental value for all our stakeholders.

—WWW.BETTERWORLDBOOKS.COM

Frank T. Rothaermel
Georgia Institute of Technology
Marne L. Arthaud-Day
Kansas State University
Konstantinos Grigoriou
Georgia Institute of Technology

IT IS ALMOST MIDNIGHT. David Murphy, President and CEO of Better World Books (BWB), sits at his desk, buried beneath market research and financial reports. BWB was founded as a "B corporation," one that is committed in its incorporation documents to meeting a triple bottom line of financial, social, and environmental performance. While traditional firms focus primarily on satisfying their shareholders, BWB recognizes that it has a responsibility to all stakeholders, including its employees, literacy partners, and "Mother Earth." Over the past few years, BWB has grown significantly, from a small, niche player frequenting college campuses to one of the most widely recognized social-entrepreneurship firms in the United States. As testament to its success, the company generated an estimated $45 million in revenues for 2010.[1,2] It has also raised close to $9 million for charities, saved countless books from landfills, and advanced literacy around the globe.

Although BWB's investors are happy with the venture's initial performance, they are demanding to know how Mr. Murphy plans to scale up BWB to ensure future growth and continued triple-bottom-line results. Glancing at the lights outside his office window, Mr. Murphy wonders how much more growth BWB's social-entrepreneurship model can sustain. Competition in the online book market has grown intense in recent years, both from companies like Amazon and eBay and from individual booksellers who now populate such online marketplaces. Because of its social emphasis, BWB also competes with other socially minded enterprises like Books4Cause, which follows a strikingly similar business model. Meanwhile, the supply of used, printed books is likely to shrink due to the increasing popularity of e-book readers like the Kindle. Mr. Murphy wonders if BWB will need to expand to other products or foreign markets to ensure its survival. With challenges arising from all sides, he is not quite sure how to address these issues when meeting with BWB's investors the next morning.

BWB's History, 2003–2010

INCEPTION. As students attending Notre Dame University, Xavier Helgesen and Christopher "Kreece" Fuchs dreamed of jumping on the Internet bandwagon. In 1999, they developed a user-generated content application in which students could post teacher evaluations. The application quickly spread to other universities. Unfortunately, the dot-com bust halted their plans, and the pair was forced to sell the company at only a small profit.

Once again searching for a way to make some money, Fuchs and Helgesen went to sell their old textbooks to the campus bookstore. They left disappointed when the bookstore offered no more than a few dollars to buy back books that had cost them over $150. Believing that the books were worth significantly more, they decided to reach out to a wider audience and listed their books for sale on the Internet. Much to their delight, the pair found that Internet customers were willing to pay much higher prices: Books for which the bookstore was not offering even a dollar were selling for $50 online![3] Eager to take advantage of this business opportunity, they asked their friends for their old textbooks and sold those as well.

Realizing that they could use the Internet to create a market connecting sellers and buyers of used books, Fuchs and Helgesen began to search for more inventory. Their first project was a book drive to benefit afterschool reading programs at a local community learning center. Their motive was twofold: They genuinely wanted to give back to their college community, and they recognized that people were usually more willing to contribute when a charitable cause was involved. They collected 2,000 books in just a few months and raised $20,000, splitting the funds evenly with the community center.[4]

Encouraged by their initial success, Fuchs and Helgesen decided to take their idea to the next level. With the help of classmate Jeff Krutzman, who had experience in investment banking and finance, they drafted a business plan. The venture they envisioned had built-in social and environmental components. By sourcing used books through book drives and selling them online, they could not only generate profits but also raise funding for literacy and education programs. At the same time, they would be keeping old books out of landfills and thereby helping the environment. Building on their community-center experience, they sought to form partnerships with worthy and appealing causes that people would be willing to support through book donations. Xavier boasted, "Social and environmental responsibility is the core of the initiative—it's in our DNA."[5] Their idea won as "Best Social Venture" at a Notre Dame University business-plan competition, netting the young entrepreneurs $7,000 in startup capital.[6] David Murphy, one of the competition's judges, saw great potential in the idea which they had named Better World Books, and offered to advise the trio as they continued to build their business. His expert guidance led to his eventual nomination as CEO and president of the young company.

EARLY GROWTH. The eager entrepreneurs expanded their book drives to university campuses nationwide, partnering with student groups who received a small royalty payment for each book collected. The incentive for student groups was threefold: get students involved in a good cause, raise money for their student organization, and help fight global illiteracy. BWB benefitted through access to increased inventory.

Soon, other opportunities emerged. After discovering that libraries had millions of excess books, BWB decided to make them an attractive offer:[7] They could donate used books to BWB, which in turn would use

the proceeds to support both the donating libraries and world literacy programs. Libraries already had a system in place to deal with unwanted books—by holding book sales ("yard sales") and community giveaways, and then hauling the leftovers to landfills. CEO David Murphy explained how they managed to convince libraries to send their books to BWB instead: "We don't want to compete with your yard sale, but you are missing a huge opportunity to create revenue by not selling online." The company now gets more than half of its revenues from ex-library books. One important advantage to libraries as an inventory source is that the supply is much less seasonal in nature. By 2007, BWB had received books from 1,800 college campuses and 2,000 libraries in the United States.[8]

The company also cultivated strategic partnerships with bookstores in order to increase its product offerings and access to consumers. For example, in 2009 BWB partnered with Alibris, the largest independently owned and operated marketplace for sellers of new, out-of-print, rare, hard-to-find, and used books. Alibris's website featured over 100 million items, while BWB carried around 3 million. The partnership made Alibris's vast inventory available through the BWB website, giving BWB's customers access to a much wider selection of both new and used books. At the same time, Alibris listed BWB's inventory on its own website, increasing BWB's customer base. The alliance has been very successful: Within the first six months, Alibris's independent sellers netted $1.5 million in sales on BetterWorldBooks.com.[9] Similarly, BWB reached an agreement with Powell's, an independent bookstore carrying both new and used books, to sell books that Powell's could not keep due to space constraints. BWB helped Powell's create shelf and inventory space by taking over the shipping costs and providing a generous percentage of revenues. The deal was attractive to both companies, as they have different but complementary customer bases and sales channels. Books sold through BWB but sourced from one of its more than 20 online partner companies follow the same revenue distribution model as the books in BWB's internal inventory.[10]

As a result of the company's efforts to increase in scale, inventory multiplied over 30 times, from 92,000 books in 2003 to 2.7 million in 2009.[11] Revenues doubled every other year with a total revenue growth of 80 times the starting value in just six years (Exhibits 1 and 2).[12] BWB now adds more than 5,000 books an hour to inventory, sells more than 10,000 books a day

EXHIBIT 1

Better World Books (BWB) Revenues, 2005–2010

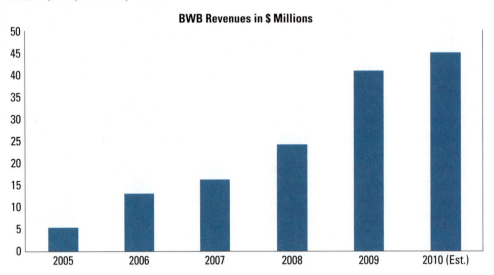

BWB Revenues in $ Millions

Source: Murphy D. (2009), "For profit social enterprise: Building to scale and delivering triple bottom line results," IMPACT Speaker Series, Georgia Institute of Technology, August 26.

EXHIBIT 2

BWB's Growth from Its Inception (2003) to August 2009

	As of October 2003	As of August 2009
Full-time employees	5	187 (282 total with part-time)
Campus book drives	52	1,800+
Library clients	0	1,900+
Inventory	92,000 books	2.7 million books (process 300k+ books/week)
Marketplaces	2	21
Footprint	3,000 sq. ft. in two separate locations	■ Corporate headquarters in Alpharetta, GA ■ 250,000 sq. ft. distribution center in Mishawaka, IN ■ 15,000 sq. ft. in Edinburgh, Scotland (launched BWB UK in 2008)
Revenue	$500,000 annual	$40m + current run rate (80x in six years)

Source: Murphy, D. (2009), "For profit social enterprise: Building to scale and delivering triple bottom line results," IMPACT Speaker Series, Georgia Institute of Technology, August 26. Note: Some of the numbers cited in the text come directly from the company website, and represent more current data.

(up to 20,000 during rush periods, such as beginnings of academic semesters), and ships more than 300,000 books a week![13] Roughly 25 percent of BWB's book sales take place through its proprietary website, which the company launched in 2008.[14] Based on sales volume, BWB ranks among the top five sellers on Amazon.com and as the sixteenth seller with the most feedback on eBay.

Social Entrepreneurship as a Business Model

Entrepreneurship describes the process by which people undertake economic risk to innovate—to create new products, processes, and sometimes new organizations. Entrepreneurs innovate by creating new business opportunities and then assembling the necessary resources to exploit them.[15] BWB represents a form of *social entrepreneurship,*[16] which involves generating value to society and thereby enhancing social wealth.[17] BWB's social emphasis is evident in its mission statement, which describes the company as "a global bookstore that harnesses the power of capitalism to bring literacy and opportunity to people around the world" (see Exhibit 3).[18]

As is common for many social entrepreneurship firms, BWB evaluates its performance based on a *triple bottom line.* The first pillar of a triple-bottom-line company is the traditional *economic* value created, which is measured using standard financial and accounting tools. The second pillar is a *social* commitment to business practices that promote the interests of the firm's full array of stakeholders. In BWB's case, the stakeholders include employees, readers across the world, and local communities. The third pillar is an

---

EXHIBIT 3

Mission and Core Values of Better World Books

Mission

Better World Books is a global bookstore that harnesses the power of capitalism to bring literacy and opportunity to people around the world.

Core Values

WE ♥ BOOKS
Respect the book: read often and help others to do the same.

FLABBERGAST OUR CUSTOMERS
Seek out opportunities to make a difference with value, service & selection.

INVEST WELL. WASTE NOT.
Choose wisely; consider the return on your efforts & the impact in your actions. Reuse, reuse, reuse....then reduce & recycle.

LEAD THE MOVEMENT
Take a stand; share your enthusiasm and build momentum through human connections.

SPEAK THROUGH ACTION
Put your ideas to work; play to win but never fear failure.

BE PASSIONATE
Wear your heart on your sleeve; stand up for what you believe.

PURSUE GROWTH & LEARNING
Challenge yourself; make a point to try new things.

BE GENUINE
Keep it real; be honest with others and true to your quirktastic self.

EMBRACE CHANGE
Adapt to circumstances; help others find ways to succeed in our evolving world.

RESPECT OUR TEAM
Be humble; welcome diversity and recognize that shared success is the only kind that matters.

Source: www.betterworldbooks.com.

environmental commitment to sustainable business practices.

BWB was incorporated as a "B corporation" (Benefit Corporation) to signal the company's commitment to economic, social, and environmental objectives. The B corporation is a new form of business that voluntarily submits to external audits to ensure that the company's business practices promote the interests of all relevant stakeholders.[19] The B Impact Rating System is a management tool to help companies assess their impact on each stakeholder and improve their social and environmental performance.[20] While the more traditional S and C corporations confer official IRS tax status, B corporations do not (yet). However, supporters of the B corporation concept are working hard to provide tax benefits to its members, with the first official tax break signed into law in Philadelphia in 2009.[21] In 2010, Maryland became the first state to officially recognize B corporations. Vermont quickly followed suit, and similar efforts are in the works in both New York and Pennsylvania.[22]

ECONOMIC PROFITABILITY. BWB is a for-profit company; this was an intentional choice by its founders, who believed that a business model provided greater assurance of long-term survival than did pure charity.[23] Money raised through book sales is split three ways:

1. A fixed percentage of the net revenue is paid to the donor, based on the specific books sold. (Libraries typically receive 15 percent of the net sale price.)

2. Another 5 percent of net sales goes to one of BWB's major nonprofit literacy partners, selected by the donor (Books For Africa, Invisible Children, The National Center for Family Literacy, Room to Read, and Worldfund). (See BetterWorldBooks.com for detailed descriptions of BWB's major NGO partners.)[24,25] Importantly, the literacy partners receive their designated share of net revenues regardless of whether the company earns an economic profit in that time period or not. This arrangement provides them with a reliable source of income.

3. BWB receives a "social profit" margin of 7 to 8 percent from each used textbook it sells, all of which is reinvested in the company.

BWB has never paid economic distributions to company owners or employees.[26] Mr. Murphy estimates that BWB had a positive EBITA by the end of 2010.[27]

A recent posting stated that the company is poised to move from $45+ million to $100+ million in annual revenues in the near future.[28]

The company's other major economic impact has been through the creation of more than 350 jobs, 200 of which are full-time with health care and other benefits. The account management team is based in Alpharetta, Georgia, with a technology and operations team in Mishawaka, Indiana, and warehouses in Mishawaka and Edinburgh, Scotland. The Mishawaka warehouse was previously an abandoned packaging plant in an industrial center that was hit hard by the decline of the U.S. automotive industry.[29]

In 2009, BWB took an innovative step to make sure that its nonprofit partners share directly in its economic success. Books for Africa, Room to Read, Worldfund, the Robinson Community Learning Center (the site of BWB's very first book drive), and the National Center for Family Literacy each received stock option grants, making them partial owners of BWB. Orchestrated through Good Capital, a social equity investor, BWB has set aside a 5 percent (combined) ownership stake for these five and other potential future literacy partners. Subsequent grants will be in the form of performance-based options based on two metrics: (1) the ability of the nonprofits to achieve their own internal objectives for literacy and educational improvements, and (2) their effectiveness in promoting the collection and sale of books through book drives for BWB.[30]

SOCIAL COMMITMENT. BWB's second objective is to confer social power by promoting literacy and education through their network of partners (nonprofits and libraries). On the company's web page, a money meter counts the amount raised for global literacy. As of November 2010, the meter stood at nearly $9 million, of which roughly $5 million had gone to 80+ literacy and education nonprofits and $4 million to thousands of libraries nationwide. The company anticipates reaching a cumulative $25 million in direct funding to its literacy partners in the next few years.[31]

In addition, BWB has donated almost $2 million to college organizations that run book drives. These organizations have collected a total of 45 million books, of which 3+ million have been sent at no charge to organizations such as Books for Africa, the National Center for Family Literacy, and Feed the Children.[32]

BWB provides detailed data to make the case for literacy as a legitimate social cause. Globally,

781 million adults, 64 percent of whom are women, are illiterate. In the United States, 30 million adults have literacy-skill deficiencies. Of the world's illiterate population, 73 percent lives in Asia. In Africa, 42 million children do not attend school; in Latin America, most children go to school for an average of only 5.4 years.[33] There is a clear correlation between poverty and illiteracy. The consequences of illiteracy are tremendous: literacy is the foundation for respect, opportunity, and personal development.

BWB has received numerous accolades in recognition of its social efforts. The company took first place in *BusinessWeek*'s 2009 survey ranking the "Most Promising Social Entrepreneurs," receiving 36 percent of the vote and outscoring the second place honoree by a wide margin.[34] *Fast Company* magazine called BWB a "social entrepreneur who is changing the world," and *Time* magazine in September 2009 listed the firm as one of the "Top 25 Responsibility Pioneers."[35]

ENVIRONMENTAL COMMITMENT. As a B corporation, BWB is also committed to protecting the environment through sustainable business practices. The company's core operation is collecting and reselling used books, thereby prolonging their circulation life. By focusing on reuse of an existing product, BWB eliminates the need for additional raw materials and production waste. Books that cannot be sold are channeled through the literacy partners to build libraries or equip schools in developing nations. Any books unsuitable for donation are recycled. BWB estimates that it has reused or recycled over 53 million pounds of books and kept over 8,000 tons of books out of landfills. In addition, BWB builds the shelves in its warehouses using old metal shelving from libraries across the nation. It has already reclaimed more than 700,000 pounds of metal shelving that would otherwise have ended up in landfills.[36, 37]

BWB believes in maintaining a neutral carbon footprint for all of its business activities. A few cents from every customer transaction goes to support wind-energy projects. Because the U.S. Postal Service uses less energy per package than any other carrier, BWB also offers an eco-shipping option that utilizes local post offices whenever possible. The company has worked closely with Sustainable Business Consulting to determine its carbon inventory, and partnered with 3Degrees to determine the appropriate amount of carbon offsets to balance its shipping and all other operations. CarbonFund uses these donations to fund third-party projects (planting trees, developing clean energy sources, and so on) and then retires the carbon credits created by the projects.[38] BWB estimates that it has offset 11,200 tons of carbon on BetterWorldBooks.com sales, and 17,000 tons on all BetterWorldBooks.com shipping.[39, 40, 41]

The company's environmental efforts have not gone unnoticed. BWB received the EPA's WasteWise Gold Award for Paper Reduction in 2009, and the WasteWise Gold Award for Climate Change in 2010.[42] To ensure that its efforts to protect the environment continue well into the future, BWB has created a full-time management position dedicated solely to sustainability.

The Online Used-Books Industry

The foundation of the online used-book industry dates back to 1995, when Amazon.com chose books as the first products to be sold on its e-commerce website.[43] Amazon concentrated its operations on selling new copies of books, which it kept stocked in vast inventory warehouses, which totaled 11.8 million square feet in North America alone.[44] Since its early days, Amazon has added a wide variety of other products (music, toys, clothing, jewelry, videogames, and so on) and services (customer ratings, recommendations, Prime shipping, and others) to its online offerings. Maintaining such a wide variety of books and other media in stock proved to be a costly strategy, so in 2001, Amazon opened its online marketplace to third-party vendors, vastly increasing its available inventory. In return for a referral fee and either a per-item or flat monthly access fee, outside vendors can list their products for sale through Amazon, and elect whether or not to have Amazon pack and ship their orders for them. This created an unprecedented opportunity for used booksellers, who previously were limited to customers in their store's local geographic area.

Half Price Books was actually the first company to develop the idea of an online used-books market. It began in 1999 by offering a fixed-price platform for selling used media including books, recorded music, movies, and games online. Sellers could list both used and new items for free on the website but were required to pass on 15 percent of the proceeds to Half.com once the sale was completed.[45] Users could search the website's contents using several methods, including an item's title, author, keywords, and International Standard Book Number (ISBN). Search results listed the current inventory available for sale, organized both by condition (New, Like New, Good, and Acceptable) and by best price in each condition category. When listing an item, sellers had access to statistics such as the price of the last such book sold and the average list price based on condition. Within a year of its launch, Half.com was acquired by eBay for approximately $350 million.[46] In 2007, Half.ebay.com had 9.50 percent of visits to bookseller websites, second only to Amazon.com, which had a 62 percent share.[47]

Alibris started in 1998 as a marketplace portal for independent sellers of new and used books, music, and movies. Sellers pay a fee to join, an annual membership fee, and various other sales-based charges in order to have access to the Alibris marketplace, library sales channels, and a host of other partner sites, including Amazon.com, Half.com, eBay, and Better World Books (see Exhibit 4 for other outlets). Other services that Alibris provides include market-intelligence data to assist with item pricing, online inventory management, and a sales notification system.[48] Now owned by Monsoon Commerce, Alibris offers more than 100 million books for sale to its customers through its network of thousands of independent sellers.[49]

Yet another form of used-book distribution includes book rental websites such as Chegg.com, which specializes in textbooks due to their high, predictable turnover rate. Chegg offers students the option of renting textbooks at a discounted price for a specified time (e.g., semester, quarters, 60 days, and so on), rather than buying them. In a search, rental prices were one-fifth of the sale price of a new finance book, and about one-third of the price for a new strategic management text. For students who need a textbook for a single course, renting is an attractive option as it can save the student hundreds of dollars each semester. Book rental services also address environmental concerns, as a textbook may be utilized by several students before the end of its circulation life. Chegg partners with American Forest and pledges to plant a tree for every textbook rented.[50] Chegg has also begun to extend its services to universities through an in-store textbook rental solution. They place an electronic kiosk inside the school's bookstore that enables students to search for a given textbook on Chegg's database, and then deliver it to the bookstore for student pick-up.[51]

With dozens upon dozens of websites listing the same book for sale or rent, competition in the used-book industry has become fierce. Search tools (such as directtextbook.com and dealoz.com) and aggregate marketplaces (like Amazon and Alibris) provide price comparisons at the touch of a mouse, pitting vendors against each other and forcing prices downward. A search for a textbook on Amazon.com, for example, returned 43 hits with copies of varying conditions. BWB's listing placed tenth overall in terms of price, and fourth among vendors with books in good condition. A company called "goodwillbooks" had the same exact textbook selling for $40 less, while other companies were selling better-quality copies for less than the $153 that BWB was asking.

In addition, the traditional printed book industry is facing challenges from technological advances, which threaten to disrupt existing business models for new and used books alike. Amazon, Apple, HP, RIM, and Sony, among others, have recently developed electronic book (or e-book) readers, and their popularity is mounting quickly. Ongoing price wars among the different e-book sellers have placed downward pressure on prices, which in turn has led to increased demand. Kindle sales tripled in 2010 and are expected to continue to rise.[52] E-book readers gained even more traction with Apple's release of its iPad,[53] of which some 6 million units had sold by the fall of 2010.[54] Amazon reported that e-book sales for its Kindle outstripped printed books for new releases for the first time ever in 2010. As e-books gain in popularity, they not only put increasing pressure on print book margins (e-books typically sell for $9.99, significantly less than the price of a new hardback) but also decrease the eventual supply available to used-book merchants.

Future Growth for BWB

Future growth for BWB will depend on supply chain issues, operations management, and brand management.

SUPPLY CHAIN. BWB has an advantage over its competitors because it builds its inventory through donations. However, in order to grow the business, Mr. Murphy knows that BWB must continuously expand its donation sources. To date, the company's two main sources of donated books have been campus book drives and libraries:

■ Through BWB's campus collection program, called "Book Drives for Better Lives," local organizations have put together book drives on more than 1,800 colleges and universities. These activities remain an important source of inventory. BWB

	Books from US sellers	Books from Canadian sellers	Books from EU sellers	Books from all other sellers	Music and movies from US sellers	Music and movies from Canadian sellers	Music and movies from EU sellers	Music and movies from all other sellers	Videogames from all sellers
Alibris Web Sites	▪	▪	▪	▪	▪	▪	▪	▪	
Alibris for Libraries	▪	▪	▪	▪	▪	▪	▪	▪	
Amazon.com*	▪	▪	▪	▪	▪	▪	▪	▪	
Barnes & Noble.com**	▪	▪	▪	▪	▪	▪			
Better World Books	▪	▪	▪	▪					
Blackwell UK	▪	▪	▪	▪					
BookByte	▪								▪
Bookrenter	▪								
Books-a-Million	▪	▪	▪	▪	▪	▪	▪	▪	
Borders Australia	▪	▪	▪	▪	▪	▪	▪	▪	
Borders Marketplace	▪	▪	▪	▪	▪	▪	▪	▪	▪
Buy.com	▪	▪	▪	▪			▪		
Campus Book Rentals	▪								
Chapters/Indigo	▪	▪	▪	▪	▪	▪	▪		
Chegg	▪								
eBay	▪				▪				
Half.com	▪				▪				▪
Infibeam	▪	▪	▪			▪	▪		
Ingram	▪	▪	▪	▪					
Nebraska Book Company	▪								
Textbooks.com	▪	▪							
TextbookX.com	▪								
Waterstone's Marketplace	▪	▪	▪	▪	▪	▪	▪	▪	

* Items will be listed on Amazon.com if you have an Amazon Pro-Merchant Account and you opt in to the Amazon.com Seller Program.

** Items will be listed on Barnes and Noble if you opt into the program.

Source: www.alibris.com/sellers/help#qualify.

provides free advertising supplies and book collection bins (see Exhibits 5 and 6) to the sponsoring student organizations, which collect and pack up the books for shipping to BWB. BWB covers all costs including shipping; students receive a flat fee for each accepted book and also get to pick which nonprofit receives the associated donation. Competition for student textbooks has tightened significantly in the years since BWB first started its campus program, however, and remains seasonal (based on the academic calendar) in nature.[55]

■ BWB instituted its Library Discards and Donations Program in 2004, through which over 2,000 U.S. libraries have donated books they can no longer keep or shelve.[56] Again, BWB covers all costs including shipping, while the libraries and a non-profit literacy program of their choice each earn a percentage of net sales. BWB makes payments on a quarterly basis, or holds them until a minimum of $50 accrues as payable commission.[57]

To supplement its inventory, BWB has also started to develop other supply channels, described more fully below. Still, with the increasing competition for existing used books and the likelihood of a decline in supply as e-books become more popular, Mr. Murphy wonders if the firm has cast a broad enough net to support its present and future inventory needs.

■ Through its Reuse First for Booksellers Program, independent booksellers send their surplus inventory to BWB at no cost or obligation. BWB provides all necessary materials and shipping free of charge, plus it gives the vendor (and the designated nonprofit) a percentage of the commission.[58]

■ BWB pays for college, corporate, and municipal recyclers to package and ship books by the ton to their warehouse for sorting.[59]

■ BWB has reached out to community and business groups with an initiative called the Great American Book Drive, to assist them with conducting book drives to benefit literacy programs.[60] Unlike BWB's regular sources (college campuses, libraries, and booksellers), the community and business groups do not get a share of the proceeds. A recent effort organized by Open Books in Chicago netted over 25,000 books.[61]

■ Individuals are also invited to donate books, either via postal service, or in Atlanta and "Michiana" (an area around the city of South Bend, Indiana, that covers both northern Indiana and southwestern Michigan) only, by dropping them in a bin. BWB pays for shipping if three or more books are donated at one time.[62]

■ BWB has created a portal for selling textbooks on its website, where individuals can type in the ISBNs for their books and get an instant quote for the amount that BWB is willing to pay, as well as the amount to be donated to the person's choice of nonprofit.[63]

OPERATIONS MANAGEMENT. Another key to sustainable and profitable future growth for the company is continued investment in its operations management systems. BWB has already invested

---

EXHIBIT 5

BWB Process for Campus Book Drives

Source: www.betterworldbooks.com/Info-Tell-Me-More-m-26.aspx.

So, you wanna run a book drive? Here's what you need to know:

 First, **sign up with us** and we'll send you everything that you need to run your drive

 Next, advertise your book drive. We'll send you materials but it's up to you how to use them. Get creative!

 Then, strategically place the book drive collection bins around your campus

 Now watch the bins fill up with books

 Then (after admiring the bins) sort the books and pack them. You can schedule a pickup wherever the boxes are located

 Last, we pay you and your nonprofit partner for the accepted books!

You can now go to the next level [but unfortunately, the Princess is in another castle]

EXHIBIT 6

Better World Books Collection Bin

Source: Famlit.org.

$3 million to develop customized software to manage its inventory and track market data. The in-house proprietary algorithm determines whether a book still has market value and can be sold, if it is a suitable donation for a nonprofit partner, or if it needs to go to recycling. If the book has market value, the algorithm assigns a sale price based on real-time market data, and BWB simultaneously posts the books for sale on BetterWorldBooks.com and all of its market network websites. The software considers each website's inventory and commission structure and optimally prices the book compared to other vendors.[64] Taking the process one step closer to the source, BWB also provides scanners to libraries and other donors to help them determine which books BWB can accept. This initiative has helped significantly to lower the amount of time BWB spends sorting and then recycling unusable inventory.

BWB pays all inbound and outbound expenses worldwide,[65] so the company is continuously looking for ways to reduce its shipping costs. It tries to ship in bulk using railcars or truckloads, for both cost and environmental reasons, and has created 20 consolidation points around the country to make that possible.[66] Once

BWB obtains books through donations, it sends them to the main warehouse in Indiana via UPS. UPS recognized the potential of BWB's business model early on. It offered convenient service at low cost for shipping the books, and it provided BWB's founders with credit and logistics expertise at the company's beginning, when they needed it most.[67] All outbound shipping within the United States is handled by the USPS because of its low-carbon footprint. BWB sorts all of its outbound mail before passing it off to the postal service, which helps to keep down outbound shipping costs. Still, Mr. Murphy wonders if BWB's "no shipping costs" policy—one of the ways in which BWB tries to differentiate itself from its competitors—will be sustainable as the company grows over the upcoming years.

To address its ongoing operational needs, BWB hired Jamie Bardin as its first Chief Operating Officer in August 2010. As COO, Mr. Bardin is expected to help develop the company's vision as well as execute it at both the strategic and tactical levels. His anticipated job responsibilities include:[68]

- Driving BWB's entire book-collection efforts and ensuring that its supply chain of used books continues to grow and diversify.
- Driving excellence across the enterprise. Responsibilities will be to help lower costs, increase customer satisfaction, drive outstanding employee recruitment, and implement top-notch training and development programs.
- All aspects of BWB's third-party marketplace relationships, including new third-party marketplace opportunities both in the U.S. and around the world.
- Helping senior leadership implement a deep understanding of NPS (Net Promoter Score)[69] across the enterprise.
- Working with technology, pricing, operations, analytics, and finance to expand gross and operating margins.

Jamie Barden clearly has his work cut out for him, and will play an integral role in the firm's future success or failure. As part of its triple-bottom-line philosophy, BWB operates on very narrow margins, and therefore needs to carry out all of its business activities in as lean and efficient a manner as possible.

BRAND MANAGEMENT. In addition to inventory sourcing and operations management, Mr. Murphy believes brand management will be central to BWB's future livelihood. One of the first steps is to increase brand awareness and build brand loyalty from a broader array of customers. The company's initial focus had been on consumers who "vote with their dollars"—conscientious customers who want to support a good cause and make a meaningful impact with their purchases. They found that one of the customer groups most receptive to social and environmental causes was educated women, over 35 years old, childless, and with higher-than-average disposable income.[70] Women in this target segment tend to be brand-loyal, prefer independent bookstores, and frequently buy dozens of books. Unfortunately, they are not a particularly large demographic in terms of numbers.

Most customers are not going to make purchases just to do something good for the world. To attract these people to BWB's online bookstore, the company has to offer great customer service and competitive prices to provide them with an attractive value proposition. With the influx of new competitors into the used-book market, BWB does not always have the lowest prices, so it tries to stand out by interacting with customers as personally as possible. Employees respond to customers with a personal note following the sale of each book, giving them some background on the book's journey while also expressing the company's passion and authenticity. Xavier Helgesen notes, "It's a simple way to communicate what we're about, which is being real people and not a faceless website."[71] One of the key questions facing BWB is just how much of a price premium various customer groups are willing to pay for a "personal touch" and the satisfaction of knowing that a portion of the purchase price goes to help fight illiteracy.

BWB also faces the challenge of increasing brand awareness on a shoestring budget. Many are surprised to learn that BWB has been able to organize big book drives, team up with global nonprofits, and collaborate with libraries without a large marketing department or organized marketing campaigns. Helgesen admits: "We have grown on a very scrappy budget," and continues, "we are not going to out-market Amazon or Barnes & Noble. So we differentiate ourselves by our interaction with customers."[72] Instead of spending large amounts of money on advertising, BWB relies extensively on word of mouth and viral networks. Online channels such as Facebook have been quite helpful in spreading the word (as of July 2011, BWB's Facebook profile had nearly 54,000 fans).[73] The effectiveness of BWB's viral networks, however, depends on its ability to maintain its relationships with partners

and customers, online and off—which is a time- and people-intensive process.

Challenges Ahead

As David Murphy begins working on his slide deck for the next morning's presentation, it becomes clear to him that BWB's future is full of uncertainty. Social entrepreneurship is a new business model. A triple bottom line may prove too difficult to uphold as the market becomes more competitive. Donating a portion of sales to charity and shipping books to Africa comes at a price, and if the company finds itself in a difficult financial situation, will it be able to afford its social endeavors? Can it stay focused and keep a triple bottom line at the heart of its organization? To do so, the company must continue to grow.

How should the company achieve its growth objectives? One possibility is to expand globally. BWB already has a warehouse and website in the United Kingdom (see Exhibit 2), but where should BWB go next, and how? If the company is not able to expand the breadth of its territory, then it will be imperative to deepen its penetration of existing markets, but that places the firm in head-to-head competition with the likes of Amazon and eBay. Mr. Murphy is not sure BWB can attract a mass market while continuing to rely primarily on word-of-mouth advertising and viral networks.[74]

And what should the company do about the predicted decline in overall supply of used books thanks to the meteoric rise of e-book readers? Perhaps even more threatening, Google recently came to an agreement with authors and publishers to create online libraries holding digital copies of books, including out-of-print books, orphan works, and copyright protected books, without having to explicitly ask for permission from the copyright holders (an opt-out, rather than opt-in, system). In return, Google promises to share with authors and publishers a percentage of the revenues it gets from book selling, digital library subscriptions, and online advertising. Will Google's offering simply replace BWB and its entire network of suppliers?

In addition, BWB has to compete with multiple new market entrants for "conceptual space" in people's minds as "the" socially and environmentally responsible used-book company. Mr. Murphy fears this could be increasingly difficult to do as competitors learn from BWB's success and adopt social causes of their own. Will customers understand and appreciate the difference between BWB as a company that has social and environmental responsibility embedded in its DNA, compared to its for-profit competitors who simply offer such things as an "add-on 'cause' component"?[75] BWB also is starting to face challenges from "copycat" competitors such as Books4Cause (www.books4cause.com), which likewise runs book-donation campaigns and sells or donates the most usable books to support nonprofit literacy programs such as "Good Books for Africa" (all nonusable items are recycled). Like BWB, Books4Cause actively solicits donations from college campuses and takes care of all pick-up and transportation costs.[76] Given the choice between a for-profit and a nonprofit company that promise the "same" results, Mr. Murphy wonders how to convince donors that BWB is the better option.

Lastly, although BWB was initially embraced with enthusiasm, critics have become more vocal about its for-profit status. Some argue that BWB misuses the word "donation," leading people to believe that all profits will go directly to charity.[77] In actuality, donated books are treated as any other method of acquired inventory, and charitable contributions come out of net revenues, after the costs of doing business are covered. Critics charge that the company cloaks itself as a charitable organization, when in fact it contributes to charity "only" 7 to 10 percent of revenue from donated books. They are starting to demand more transparency and full disclosure from BWB with respect to its donation policy.

Murphy knows that investors want thorough answers about how he plans to address these issues. The decisions he makes tonight will ultimately affect BWB's future. At this thought, and armed with a large cup of coffee to combat the long night ahead of him, Murphy turns once more to his research and wonders where BWB will be in five years. . . .

Endnotes

1. "Better World Books," *INC.com*, accessed December 6, 2010, www.inc.com/inc5000/profile/better-world-books.

2. "What will you change: A better book store," Duke University's Fuqua School of Business, accessed December 6, 2010, www.fuqua.duke.edu/news_events/feature_stories/book_store.

3. Elam, S., (2010), "Building Better World a book at a time," *CNN.com*, July 1, 2009, http://articles.cnn.com/2009-07-01/living/mainstreet.books_1_world-books-american-library-association-conference-small-business?_s=PM:LIVING.

4. "How it all began," *BetterWorldBooks.com*, accessed December 6, 2010, www.betterworldbooks.com/info.aspx?f=beginning.

5. "Buying from Better World Books," *MaplewoodMuse.com*, December 2, 2009, http://maplewoodmuse.com/buying-from-better-world-books-funds-literacy.

6. "What will you change: A better book store."

7. Elam, S., (2010), "Building Better World a book at a time," *CNN.com*, July 1, 2009, http://articles.cnn.com/2009-07-01/living/mainstreet.books_1_world-books-american-library-association-conference-small-business?_s=PM:LIVING.

8. http://www.ajc.com/search/content/business/stories/2008/05/18/upclosc.html.; Norton, M., F. Wilson, J. Avery, and T. Steenburgh (2010), *Better World Books* (9-511-057) (Boston, MA: Harvard Business School Publishing).

9. *Better World Books and Alibris Report Wildly Successful Partnership Out of the Gate, Alibris*, January 26, 2010.

10. Lieberman, M. (2010), "Better or not? Better World Books adds donation boxes, a book drive for Haiti and a partnership with Powell's to the mix," Interview, blog post, *Book Patrol*, April 28, www.bookpatrol.net/2010/04/better-or-not-better-world-books-adds.html.

11. Murphy, D. (2009), "For profit social enterprise: Building to scale and delivering triple bottom line results," IMPACT Speaker Series, Georgia Institute of Technology, Atlanta, August 26, lecture.

12. Ibid.

13. Leiber, N. (2009), "The most promising social entrepreneurs," *BusinessWeek.com*, May 1, www.businessweek.com/smallbiz/content/may2009/sb2009051_730988.htm.

14. Murphy, D. (2009), "For profit social enterprise: Building to scale and delivering triple bottom line results."

15. Shane, S., and S. Venkataraman (2000), "The promise of entrepreneurship as a field of research," *Academy of Management Review* 25.1: 217–226; and Alvarez, S., and J. B. Barney (2007), "Discovery and creation: Alternative theories of entrepreneurial action," *Strategic Entrepreneurship Journal* 1: 11–26.

16. Dacin, P. A., M. T. Dacin, and M. Matear (2010), "Social entrepreneurship: Why we don't need a new theory and how we move from here," *Academy of Management Perspectives*, August: 37–57; and Short, J. C., T. W. Moss, and G. T. Lumpkin (2009), "Research in social entrepreneurship: Past contributions and future opportunities," *Strategic Entrepreneurship Journal* 3: 161–194.

17. Zahra, S. A., E. Gedajlovic, D. O. Neubaum, and J. M. Shulman (2009), "A typology of social entrepreneurs: Motives, search processes and ethical challenges," *Journal of Business Venturing* 24: 519–532.

18. www.betterworldbooks.com/info.aspx?f=corevalues.

19. *About Certified B Corps*, accessed December 6, 2010, www.bcorporation.net/about.

20. "B Corporation - Become a B Corp - B Impact Rating System," *B Corporation – Home*, accessed December 6, 2010, www.bcorporation.net/become/BRS.

21. "Become a B corporation: The business case," *Bcorportation.net*, accessed December 6, 2010, www.bcorporation.net/resources/bcorp/documents/The%20Business%20Case_Become%20a%20B%20Corporation1.pdf.

22. Wallace, N. (2010), "A nonprofit's push to certify socially conscious businesses," *Chronicle of Philanthropy* 25.1: 15.

23. Lieberman, M. (2010), "Better or not? Better World Books adds donation boxes, a book drive for Haiti and a partnership with Powell's to the mix," interview, web log post, *Book Patrol,* April 28, 2010; accessed December 6, 2010, www.bookpatrol. net/2010/04/better-or-not-better-world-books-adds.html.

24. "Our literacy partners," *BetterWorldBooks.com,* accessed December 6, 2010, www.betterworldbooks.com/info. aspx?f=partners.

25. www.betterworldbooks.com/info.aspx?f=iaq.

26. Ibid.

27. EBITA = Earnings before the deduction of interest, tax, and amortization expenses. Also, see Murphy, D. (2009), "For profit social enterprise: Building to scale and delivering triple bottom line results."

28. www.bcorporation.net/index.cfm/nodeID/6D3E6C99-8CFA-47A1-8E96-29C74CA5A931/fuseaction/content.page.

29. Ibid.

30. www.betterworldbooks.com/custom.aspx?f=equity.

31. www.bcorporation.net/index.cfm/nodeID/6D3E6C99-8CFA-47A1-8E96-29C74CA5A931/fuseaction/content.page.

32. www.betterworldbooks.com/info.aspx?f=our_impact.

33. Ibid.

34. Leiber, N. (2009), "The most promising social entrepreneurs," *Bloomberg Businessweek,* May 1, www.businessweek. com/smallbiz/content/may2009/sb2009051_730988.htm.

35. www.bcorporation.net/index.cfm/nodeID/6D3E6C99-8CFA-47A1-8E96-29C74CA5A931/fuseaction/content.page.

36. Ibid.

37. www.betterworldbooks.com/info.aspx?f=bottomlines.

38. *Carbonfund.org,* accessed December 6, 2010, www. carbonfund.org.

39. www.bcorporation.net/index.cfm/nodeID/6D3E6C99-8CFA-47A1-8E96-29C74CA5A931/fuseaction/content.page.

40. www.betterworldbooks.com/info.aspx?f=our_impact.

41. www.betterworldbooks.com/info.aspx?f=bottomlines.

42. Ibid.

43. "FAQs," *Amazon.com,* accessed December 6, 2010, http:// phx.corporate-ir.net/phoenix.zhtml?c=97664&p=irol-faq#6986.

44. Norton, M., F. Wilson, J. Avery, and T. Steenburgh, (2010), *Better World Books.*

45. eBay's 10-K Financial Report, December 31, 2000, http:// sec.gov/Archives/edgar/data/1065088/000109581101001836/ f70837e10-k.txt.

46. Regan, K. (2001), "eBay moves to absorb Half.com," *E-Commerce Times,* October 11, www.ecommercetimes.com/ story/14078.html.

47. "Top book web sites, 2007," *Investor's Business Daily,* January 2, 2007, p. A4, from Hitwise, Market Share Reporter 2008, Thomson Gale, 2008. Reproduced in Business and Company Resource Center (Farmington Hills, MI: Gale Group), June 2002, http://galenet.galegroup.com/servlet/BCRC.

48. www.alibris.com/sellers/help#price.

49. www.alibris.com/about/aboutus.

50. "Saving green by being green," accessed December 6, 2010, www.chegg.com/ecofriendly.

51. "In-store textbook rental solution," accessed December 6, 2010, www.chegg.com/bookstores.

52. Albanesius, C. (2010), "Borders fights e-reader war with Kobo, gift cards," *PCMag.com,* June 22, accessed December 6, 2010, www.pcmag.com/article2/0,2817,2365488,00.asp.

53. Trachtenberg, J. (2010), "Textbooks up their game," *WSJ. com,* August 19, accessed December 6, 2010, http://online.wsj. com/article/SB10001424052748703791804575439522126865 254.html.

54. Elmer-DeWitt, P. (2010), "How many iPads has Apple really sold?" *Fortune Tech: Technology Blogs, News and Analysis from Fortune Magazine,* October 5, accessed December 6, 2010, http://tech.fortune.cnn.com/2010/10/05/ how-many-ipads-has-apple-really-sold.

55. www.betterworldbooks.com/Info-Book-Drives-for-Better-Lives-m-2.aspx.

56. "Library discards & donations," *BetterWorldBooks.com,* accessed December 6, 2010, www.betterworldbooks.com/Info-Discards-Donations-Program-m-4.aspx.

57. www.betterworldbooks.com/content/reusefirst/files/ LibraryDiscardsDonationsInformationPacketMay52009.pdf.

58. www.betterworldbooks.com/Info-Booksellers-m-3.aspx.

59. www.betterworldbooks.com/Info-Recyclers-m-58.aspx.

60. www.betterworldbooks.com/Info-Great-American-Book-Drive-m-5.aspx.

61. www.betterworldbooks.com/Info-Tell-Me-More-m-47. aspx.

62. www.betterworldbooks.com/Info-Donate-Books-m-7.aspx.

63. www.betterworldbooks.com/buyback.aspx.

64. Mills, E. (2008), "Eco-alternative to Amazon funds literacy programs," web log post, *Technology News - CNET News,* January 9, accessed December 6, 2010, http://news.cnet. com/8301-10784_3-9846876-7.html?tag=contentMain;content Body;1n.

65. www.betterworldbooks.com/custom.aspx?f=pr-free-shipping-worldwide.xml.

66. Vaccaro, A. (2009), "Better World Books creates better world through triple bottom line," *Triple Pundit,* February 18, accessed December 6, 2010, www.triplepundit.com/2009/02/ better-world-books-creates-better-world-through-triple-bottom-line.

67. Hosni, N. (2010), "Getting paid with purpose: Better World Books," *Tonic.com,* May 13, accessed December 6, 2010, www. tonic.com/article/getting-paid-with-purpose-better-world-books.

68. www.bcorporation.net/index.cfm/nodeID/6D3E6C99-8CFA-47A1-8E96-29C74CA5A931/fuseaction/content.page.

69. Reichheld, F. F. (2003), *"One Number You Need to Grow." Harvard Business Review,* December.

70. "Betterworldbooks.com," *Alexa.com,* accessed December 6, 2010, www.alexa.com/siteinfo/betterworldbooks.com#.

71. Ifeanyi, K. C. (2009), "Better World's books talk back," *CNNMoney.com,* March 2, 2009, accessed December 6, 2010, http://money.cnn.com/2009/02/27/smallbusiness/books_that_talk_back.fsb/index.htm?postversion=2009030311.

72. Ibid.

73. "Better World Books," *Facebook.com,* accessed July 19, 2011, www.facebook.com/betterworldbooks.

74. Root, J. (2009), "Meet Xavier Helgesen, co-founder of Better World Books," *PlanetGreen.com,* July 2, accessed December 6, 2010, http://planetgreen.discovery.com/work-connect/change-maker-xavier-helgesen.html.

75. Norton, M., F. Wilson, J. Avery, and T. Steenburgh, (2010), *Better World Books.*

76. www.books4cause.com/.

77. Lieberman, M. (2008), "Better World Books: Are they better for the book world?" *Seattlepi.com,* April 13, accessed December 6, 2010, http://blog.seattlepi.com/bookpatrol/archives/136400.asp.

Frank T. Rothaermel
Georgia Institute of Technology

NEW YEAR'S EVE, 2009: It's a pleasant sunny 78 degrees with a slight breeze. Elon Musk, the 38-year-old serial entrepreneur and multimillionaire, is sitting on his yacht, anchored in Hawaii, and enjoying a premium cup of coffee. He needs a break, because he has been working day and night for the past several weeks chasing his dream: to leave a legacy.

In 1989, Elon Musk left his native South Africa at age 17 to avoid being conscripted in the army. Says Musk, "I don't have an issue with serving in the military per se, but serving in the South African army suppressing black people just didn't seem like a really good way to spend time."[1] He went to Canada and subsequently enrolled in Queen's University in 1990. After receiving a scholarship, Elon Musk transferred to the University of Pennsylvania. He graduated in 1995 with bachelor's degrees in both economics and physics and then moved to California to pursue a PhD at Stanford University in applied physics and material sciences.[2]

After only two days, Mr. Musk left graduate school to found Zip2, an online provider of content publishing software for news organizations, with his brother, Kimbal Musk. Four years later, in 1999, computer maker Compaq acquired Zip2 for $341 million (and was in turn acquired by HP in 2002).

Not one to stand still, Elon Musk moved on to co-found PayPal, an online payment processor. eBay acquired PayPal for $1.5 billion in 2002, netting Mr. Musk $175.5 million for his 11.7 percent share of the company. Although it was financially lucrative, Elon Musk still harbors resentment about this deal. He feels that letting eBay acquire PayPal sold short the company's potential, dooming it to a future as a niche tool rather than a launch pad for a full-fledged, online financial institution.

Mr. Musk is now leading Silicon Valley on three different fronts: electric cars, renewable energy, and space exploration. Two of his three ventures—SolarCity and Space Exploration Technologies (SpaceX)—seem to be doing well. SolarCity's goal is to become the Walmart of solar-panel installations. With 500 employees, it is the number one provider of residential solar power in California, and growing fast. SpaceX aims to send satellites into orbit at a quarter of the current cost. Since Elon Musk took over engineering responsibilities, he has managed to launch rockets that reach outer space successfully. With 900 employees and a big government contract from NASA, SpaceX's short-term future likewise seems secure.

Although crowned "2007 Entrepreneur of the Year" by *Inc.* magazine, Mr. Musk feels that his personal ambitions have not yet been fulfilled. Many in California's venture-capital and high-tech community view Elon Musk as someone who has good ideas and is able to breathe life into risky ventures, but then fizzles out on them. He aims to prove them wrong. As a result, Musk's dreams for Tesla Motors, the California-based designer and manufacturer of electric vehicles, are big; he wants to leave a legacy through this car. Musk has been described as "Henry Ford and Robert Oppenheimer in one person,"[3] and he believes Tesla just might be the company that seals his fate in the history books. Thus, after firing three CEOs in the last four years, Musk has decided to lead the company himself.

Although he has tried to keep his BlackBerry switched off to enjoy some rest and relaxation on New Year's Eve, the problems at Tesla have Mr. Musk worried. The company launched its Tesla Roadster in 2008 and later announced plans for the Model S family sedan, but it has been under tremendous pressure from investors. Due to a poor initial pricing strategy and weaker than anticipated demand, Tesla Motors has been burning cash like crazy. Musk needs capital, and he needs it fast.

Professor Frank T. Rothaermel prepared this case from public sources. This case is developed for the purpose of class discussion. It is not intended to be used for any kind of endorsement, source of data, or depiction of efficient or inefficient management. All opinions expressed and all errors and omissions are entirely the author's. The author thanks Matt Hoepfer (GT MBA '10 and GT PhD candidate in Engineering), Mike Janovec (GT MBA '11), and Vipul Singh (GT MBA '10) for research assistance and Professor Marne L. Arthaud-Day for editorial assistance. © Rothaermel, 2013.

Given his past reputation of starting a business and then selling it to move on to the next big thing, Mr. Musk has received a lot of calls and e-mails with unsolicited overtures. Several venture capitalists and large automobile companies have expressed an interest in acquiring Tesla Motors. Elon Musk is facing a serious dilemma: Should he sell Tesla? And if so, to whom? GM, Ford, and Chrysler all would like to get their hands on Tesla's product line and technology. Ford is the only one likely to be able to muster the necessary capital. What about the Japanese carmakers? Toyota is facing some challenges due to major recalls, alleged quality problems, and accusations of inadequate safety disclosures. Honda has been hedging its bets by focusing on multiple alternative technologies. Nissan already has its own fleet of electric vehicles. On the other hand, both Daimler and BMW are currently doing quite well. Daimler already owns a minority stake (less than 10 percent) in Tesla Motors, purchased in spring 2009 for $50 million.[4]

Or, wonders Musk, can he continue to go it alone and turn Tesla into a viable company? If so, he would need to take Tesla through an initial public offering to obtain the necessary funds for expansion. Would that be wise at a time when the demand for cars (at least in the United States) is slumping (Exhibit 1) and the Dow Jones Industrial Average (DJIA) is hovering around 10,000 points?[5] Thinking about all this gives Elon Musk a headache . . .

A Brief History of Tesla Motors

In 2003, in San Carlos, California, Martin Eberhard and Mark Tarpenning founded Tesla Motors, an automobile company dedicated to developing electric vehicles. Elon Musk was one of the first investors, putting up $7 million and later an additional $30 million.

Tesla Motors held a design contest for the styling of its first product: the Roadster, code-named "Dark Star." Lotus Cars, a British manufacturer, won the contest and jointly engineered and manufactured the new vehicle (Exhibit 2, next page). Lotus was a natural partner for this project because of its experience and expertise in building its own line of sports and racing cars. In fact, the Tesla Roadster was modeled using the Lotus Elise as a template. The partners designed the Roadster's chassis using Lotus software tools and had it manufactured by the same Norwegian company that built the Elise.

In December 2006, *Time* magazine hailed the Tesla Roadster as the best invention of the year in the transportation category.[6] In 2007, however, it became clear that sales were not enough to sustain business; the company was bleeding money. Looking in more depth at the financial situation, Musk found that Tesla Motors was losing $50,000 on each car sold. As CEO, Martin Eberhard had led investors to believe that the manufacturing of the Roadster cost only $65,000 per car, which appeared to justify the $92,000 sticker price. In reality, Musk found that it cost Tesla $140,000 just for the parts, subassemblies, and supplies to make each vehicle, and that the Roadster could not even be built with Tesla's current tools. He also discovered major safety issues with the existing design. Completely taken aback by the messy state of affairs, Musk commented,

EXHIBIT 1

U.S. Vehicle Sales by Car Manufacturer, 2000–2009

Source: http://wardsauto.com/keydata/historical/UsaSa28summary.xls.

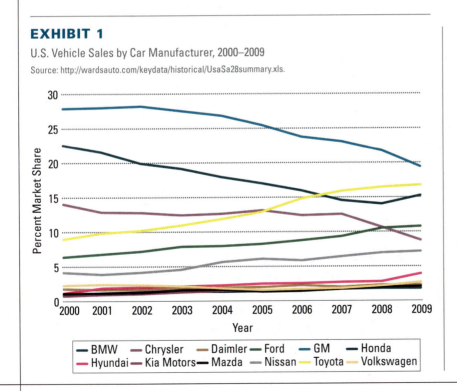

EXHIBIT 2

Tesla Roadster

Source: http://teslamotors.com.

EXHIBIT 3

Tesla Model S

Source: http://teslamotors.com.

"We should have just sent a $50,000 check to each customer and not bothered making the car."[7]

As a consequence, Elon Musk fired Martin Eberhard and took over the engineering himself. Almost every important system on the car, including the body, motor, power electronics, transmission, battery pack, and HVAC, had to be redesigned, retooled, or switched to a new supplier. Such dramatic changes were necessary to get the Roadster on the road at something close to the published performance and safety specifications, as well as to cut costs to make the Roadster profitable.[8]

By December 31, 2009, Tesla had 514 employees and had sold 937 Roadster models in 18 countries around the world. More than 1,200 additional people had put in deposits to reserve a Roadster, giving the company $70 million in interest-free loans. The base price of the Tesla Roadster is currently $101,000 (after a $7,500 tax deduction).[9] Tesla also introduced a new model, the Tesla Roadster 2, with improved electric power-train performance and lower production costs. The Roadster Sport, which accelerates from zero to 60 miles per hour in 3.7 seconds (faster than a Porsche 911 GT), was the next vehicle added to the pipeline.

In addition, in March 2009 Tesla introduced to the public an early prototype of the Model S family sedan (Exhibit 3). By year-end, Tesla had received approximately 2,000 customer reservations for the car, with a minimum down payment of $5,000 each. The company hopes to begin volume production of 20,000 Model S vehicles by 2012. The anticipated base price is $49,900 (after a $7,500 tax deduction).[10]

The U.S. Automotive Industry

The Big Three automakers—GM, Ford, and Chrysler—have dominated the U.S. automotive industry for decades (Exhibits 4, 5A–B, and 6A–B). GM was once the leading U.S. carmaker, with a market share of over 50 percent in 1962. By 2009, GM's market share had eroded to less than 20 percent, while the market share of the Big Three *combined* dropped below 50 percent for the first time ever.[11] GM and Chrysler filed for bankruptcy while Ford was fighting hard to become profitable again. What had caused their decline?

In the 1990s, the Big Three shifted resources away from midsize and compact cars to lead the "SUV craze." They built their business models around the assumptions that gas prices would remain low for the foreseeable future, and that Americans would continue to prefer big trucks and sport utility vehicles (SUVs). For as long as these assumptions held true, the strategy was quite profitable; pick-up trucks and SUVS provided the highest margins of any vehicle class. In fact, the Ford F-150 pickup truck remains the most-sold vehicle in the United States *of all time.* For a while, the Hummer 1 (with gas mileage of 7 mpg) was one of GM's most profitable vehicles.

However, when SUV sales peaked in 2004 and started to decline (Exhibit 7, page C39), the Big Three were slow to detect and adapt to the shift in customer purchase patterns. Then, in the wake of the 2008 financial crisis, U.S. car sales hit a historic low of some 11 million vehicles, down from 18 million in 2000 (Exhibit 8, page C39). Meanwhile, the price for a gallon

EXHIBIT 4

U.S. Market Share: The Big Three vs. "Others," 2000–2009

Source: http://wardsauto.com/keydata/historical/UsaSa28summary.xls.

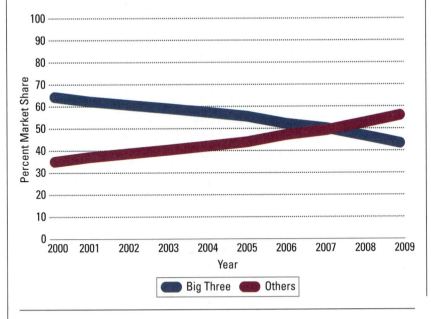

GM. The Big Three found it particularly difficult to compete in this leaner financial environment due to their higher cost structure. Unlike their foreign counterparts, U.S. companies had to cover long-term legacy costs for employee health care and pensions. GM was particularly vulnerable in this regard. At one point, GM paid the *full cost* of health insurance premiums for all of its employees and their dependents, as well as GM retirees and survivors. When U.S. health care costs rose precipitously in the latter part of the 20th century, most of these legacy plans ended up chronically underfunded. Taking steps like providing retirement packages to older workers and negotiating agreements with unions to transfer pension dues to an independent trust helped, but fell far short of solving GM's financial woes.

of gas rose to over $4 in the summer of 2008, up from about $2 in 2005 (Exhibit 9, page C40). While all car segments experienced a dramatic reduction in demand, trucks and SUVs were hit particularly hard.

EXHIBIT 5A

GM Financial Data, 2005–2008 ($ in millions)

Selected Income Statement Data				
Year Fiscal	2008	2007	2006	2005
Total Revenue	$148,979	$179,984	$204,467	$193,050
Cost of Sales	149,311	165,573	163,214	158,254
Gross Profit	(332)	14,411	41,253	34,796
SG&A	14,253	14,412	13,650	13,003
Interest Expense	–	–	–	–
Other Expenses	5,407	2,099	4,238	7,024
Financial Services and Insurance	1,292	2,209	29,188	30,813
Total Costs and Expenses	170,263	184,293	210,290	209,094
Operating Income Loss	(21,284)	(4,309)	(5,823)	(16,044)
Net Income	(30,860)	(38,732)	(1,978)	(10,417)

Source: GM Annual Reports 2005–2008.

EXHIBIT 5B ($ in millions)

Selected Balance Sheet Data (Consolidated)				
Year Fiscal	2008	2007	2006	2005
Assets				
Cash and Equivalents	$13,953	$24,549	$35,283	$15,187
Marketable Securities	13	2,139	138	1,416
Receivables	7,711	9,659	8,216	5,917
Inventory	13,042	14,939	13,921	13,862
Equipment on Operating Leases, Net	3,363	5,283	6,125	6,993
Financing and Insurance Operations Assets	4,507	16,989	22,123	311,944
PP&E	39,656	43,017	41,934	38,543
Deferred Income Taxes	98	2,116	32,967	23,761
Goodwill	265	1,066	1,118	1,869
Prepaid Pension	109	20,175	17,366	37,576
Equity in Net Assets of Nonconsolidated Affiliates	1,655	1,919	1,969	3,242
Other Assets	3,533	3,466	4,584	4,864
Total Assets	91,047	148,883	186,192	474,156
Liabilities				
Payables	22,236	29,439	26,931	26,402
Accrued Liabilities	35,921	34,024	35,225	42,697
ST Debt	1,192	4,908	9,438	253,508
Deferred Income Taxes	607	875	925	26,325
LT Debt	29,594	33,384	33,067	32,580
Post-Retirement Benefits & Pensions	54,097	58,756	62,020	40,215
Total Liabilities	176,387	184,363	190,443	458,456
Equity				
Common Stock	1,017	943	1,190	1,047
Capital in Excess of Par	15,755	15,319	15,336	15,285
Accumulated Other Comprehensive Income	(32,316)	(13,964)	(22,126)	(4,535)
Accumulated Deficit	(70,610)	(39,392)		
Treasury Stock				
Retained Earnings			406	2,960
Total Equity	(86,154)	(37,094)	(5,441)	14,653
Total Liabilities and Equity	91,047	148,883	186,196	474,156

Source: GM Annual Reports 2005–2008.

Compounding the company's financial situation further, GM had also made large concessions to the United Auto Workers (UAW) union, driving up hourly wages and benefits. For example, laid-off auto workers could await re-employment while enjoying almost full wages at so-called *job banks*. GM was caught in a classic catch-22. Given the costs of unionized labor, GM was unable to make money on small, fuel-efficient cars without heavy government subsidies through tax incentives.[12] Yet because the UAW had a monopoly

EXHIBIT 6A

Ford Financial Data, 2005–2009 ($ in millions)

	Selected Income Statement Data				
Year Fiscal	2009	2008	2007	2006	2005
Total Revenue	$118,308	$145,114	$170,572	$160,065	$176,835
Cost of Sales	100,016	127,102	142,587	148,866	144,920
Gross Profit	18,292	18,012	27,985	11,199	31,915
SG&A	13,258	21,430	21,169	19,148	24,588
Goodwill Impairment	–	–	2,400	–	–
Interest Expense	6,828	9,805	11,038	8,783	8,417
Financial Services and Insurance	1,030	1,874	688	241	483
Total Costs and Expenses	121,132	160,211	177,862	177,038	178,408
Operating Income	(2,824)	(15,097)	(7,290)	(16,973)	(1,573)
Net Income	2,717	(14,766)	(2,795)	(12,613)	1,440

Source: Ford Annual Reports 2005–2009.

over GM's labor force, GM could not take appropriate actions to reduce its labor expenses, either by laying off workers or by negotiating more competitive wages. Bankruptcy was inevitable. The GM that reemerged 60 days after the bankruptcy filing had a significantly restructured balance sheet and four fewer brands (Hummer, Pontiac, Saab, and Saturn). In order to "bail out" the firm, the U.S. government provided close to $58 billion under the Troubled Asset Relief Program (TARP), making it the de facto owner of the company.

CHRYSLER. In 1998, German car manufacturer Daimler paid $36 billion to acquire a troubled Chrysler Corporation. Touted by some as a "merger of equals," the true nature of the deal became apparent when several senior U.S. managers either left or were fired and then replaced by Germans. Daimler's decision to retire the Plymouth brand fueled the brewing mistrust even more.[13] Theoretically, the acquisition gave Chrysler entry into European markets, created a larger, complementary product line (Chrysler sold SUVs, minivans, and mass-market cars while Daimler specialized in luxury sedans and sports cars), and provided both companies with increased market power.

However, the management cultures of the two companies clashed, and DaimlerChrysler never achieved the anticipated synergies.[14] Ultimately deciding it was better off on its own, Daimler sold 80.1 percent of Chrysler to Cerberus Capital for $7.4 billion

in August 2007. Cerberus took Chrysler private in a leveraged buyout, hoping to restructure the company away from the pressure of public financial reporting. Unfortunately, Chrysler's problems were too big for even Cerberus to fix, and the company declared Chapter 11 bankruptcy on April 30, 2009. At this point, the federal government intervened, paying $6.6 billion to finance the company's restructuring into the "New Chrysler." Of that amount, 55 percent was owned by a pension fund and 25 percent by the Italian car maker Fiat, with minority stakes for the U.S. and Canadian governments.[15, 16] Fiat provided Chrysler with a platform for smaller, more fuel-efficient cars and access to Fiat's global distribution network. Chrysler hoped to realize cost savings in design, engineering, manufacturing, purchasing, and marketing, while Fiat gained significant access to the U.S. auto market.

FORD. Ford, on the other hand, had raised $24.5 billion in capital by mortgaging almost all of its assets during the height of the financial bubble, giving it access to a large line of credit.[17] While supporting GM's and Chrysler's requests for a government bail-out, Ford did not request, nor did it receive, any government funding.

FOREIGN COMPETITION. Since the first oil price shock in 1973–1974, foreign car manufacturers have made steady inroads into the U.S. market. Investing more in research and development, compared with

EXHIBIT 6B ($ in millions)

Ford Balance Sheet (consolidated)					
Year Fiscal	2009	2008	2007	2006	2005
Assets					
Cash and Equivalents	$21,441	$22,049	$35,283	$28,896	$28,406
Marketable Securities	21,387	17,411	5,248	21,472	10,672
Receivables	84,583	99,158	127,530	119,186	117,972
Net Investment in Operating Leases	17,270	25,250	33,255	29,787	27,099
Inventory	5,450	6,988	10,121	10,017	10,271
Equity in Net Assets of Affiliated Companies	1,550	1,599	2,853	2,790	2,579
PP&E	24,778	24,143	36,239	36,055	40,676
Deferred Income Taxes	3,440	3,108	3,500	4,922	5,880
Goodwill	209	246	2,069	3,611	5,945
Held for Sale Assets	7,923	8,612	7,537	8,215	5
Other Assets	6,819	9,734	14,976	13,255	18,534
Total Assets	**194,850**	**218,298**	**279,264**	**279,196**	**269,459**
Liabilities					
Payables	14,594	13,145	20,832	21,214	22,910
Accrued Liabilities	46,599	59,526	74,738	80,058	73,047
Debt	132,441	152,577	168,530	171,832	153,278
Deferred Income Taxes	2,375	2,035	3,034	2,744	5,660
Held for Sale Liabilities	5,356	5,542	5,081	5,654	–
Total Liabilities	201,365	232,825	272,215	281,502	254,895
Equity					
Common Stock	34	24	22	19	19
Capital in Excess of Par	16,786	10,875	7,834	4,562	4,872
Accumulated Other Comprehensive Income	(10,864)	(10,124)	(558)	(7,846)	(3,680)
Treasury Stock	(177)	(181)	(185)	(183)	(833)
Retained Earnings	(13,599)	(16,316)	(1,485)	(17)	13,064
Equity Attributable to Noncontrolling Interests	1,305	1,195	1,421	1,159	1,122
Total Equity	(6,515)	(14,527)	7,049	(2,306)	14,564
Total Liabilities and Equity	**194,850**	**218,298**	**279,264**	**279,196**	**269,459**

Source: Ford Annual Reports 2005–2009.

the Big Three, German, Japanese, and Korean carmakers were perceived to offer vehicles of higher quality, more advanced engineering, and better fuel efficiency. Because they were not burdened with extraordinarily high health care and pension costs, the foreign companies could also make and sell their vehicles at lower prices (leading to increased sales and/or higher margins). By 2009, Japanese automakers Toyota and Honda were number two and four in sales volume in the United States, respectively. Nissan (Japan), Hyundai (Korea), and Kia (Korea) also became strong competitors in the U.S. market.

Japanese carmakers Toyota and Honda have long been considered the leaders in producing small, fuel-efficient

EXHIBIT 7

Distribution of Different Vehicle Segments in United States, 1975–2009

Source: U.S. Environmental Protection Agency (EPA). Data available at www.epa.gov/otaq/cert/mpg/fetrends/fullreport-tables-nov2009.xls.

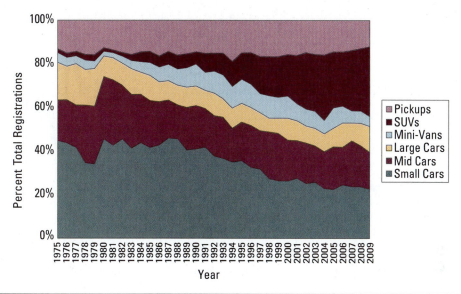

EXHIBIT 8

U.S. Vehicle Sales, 2000–2009

Source: http://wardsauto.com/keydata/historical/UsaSa01summary.xls.

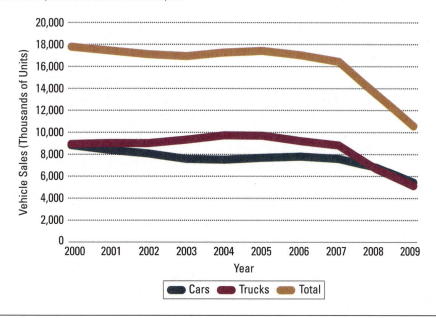

cars. Toyota has always been Japan's largest automaker, and in early 2009, it overtook perennial world leader GM in both production and sales. Honda is Japan's second largest automaker and ranks fifth in the world, behind Toyota, GM, Volkswagen, and Ford. Due to Voluntary Export Restraints (VERs) enacted by the Reagan administration in 1981, Japanese companies have invested heavily in U.S. production facilities. Japanese plants are

EXHIBIT 9

U.S. Gasoline Prices, 1993–2009

Source: Data adapted from www.eia.gov/oog/ftparea/wogirs/xls/pswrgvwag.xls.

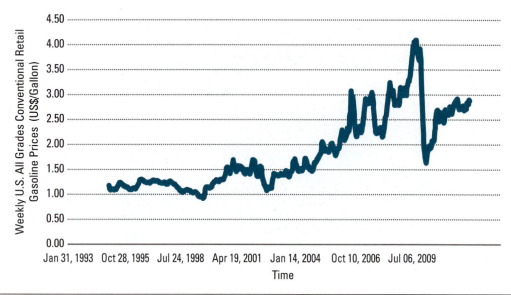

Alternative Propulsion for Cars

The oil embargos of the 1970s first highlighted the need for smaller, more fuel-efficient vehicles. Concerned about U.S. reliance on foreign oil, Congress voted to append Title V, "Improving Automotive Efficiency," to the Motor Vehicle Information and Cost Savings Act. This legislation established CAFE (Corporate Average Fuel Economy) standards for passenger cars and light trucks, and set a goal of doubling new-car fuel economy by model year 1985.[18]

In 1990, the California Air Resource Board (CARB) passed a mandate for the introduction of zero emission vehicles (ZEVs). The act specified that 2 percent of the vehicles produced for sale in California had to have zero emissions by 1998, increasing to 5 percent in 2001 and 10 percent in 2003. Subsequent amendments dropped the 1998 and 2001 requirements, but left the 10 percent value for 2003 in place while also allowing credits for partial-ZEV cars.[19]

Importantly, the ZEV mandate is credited with stimulating increased research and development of the electric-car prototype. The first electric production car EV-1 (made by GM) came to market in 1996 in California and Arizona as a lease-only vehicle. Competitors Toyota and Honda quickly followed suit with their own EV cars. However, most of these early

typically non-unionized and are located in the southern United States, away from their "northern" domestic competitors and where the costs of living are lower. Along with philanthropy, lobbying efforts, and sharing technology, establishing U.S. production facilities was a significant step in improving public relations and decreasing their liability of foreignness.

Developmentally, Korean car manufacturers today occupy a position in the U.S. automobile market similar to that of the Japanese companies in the 1980s. Viewed as the cheaper, fuel-efficient alternatives to American, Japanese, and European cars, they are gaining more widespread recognition and acceptance among American car buyers. Some experts argue that Hyundai is already on par in quality with Toyota and Honda (Exhibit 10).

The three largest German carmakers—Daimler, BMW, and Volkswagen—each hold between 2 and 3 percent of the U.S. market. Porsche is a strong niche player in the luxury sports vehicle segment, while Audi, a wholly owned subsidiary of Volkswagen since 1966, has gained a strong reputation for its mid-size luxury sedans and SUVs. Like their Japanese counterparts, German car manufacturers have gained market share steadily over the last several years through aggressive marketing campaigns. As fuel prices have increased, demand for German vehicles has also risen, since they offer sportiness and luxury with good fuel efficiency.

EXHIBIT 10

J.D. Power Quality Rankings, 2010

Source: Data adapted from www.jdpower.com/autos/ratings/quality-ratings-by-brand/sortcolumn-0/ascending/page-1/#page-anchor, and www.jdpower.com/autos/ratings/dependability-ratings-by-brand/.

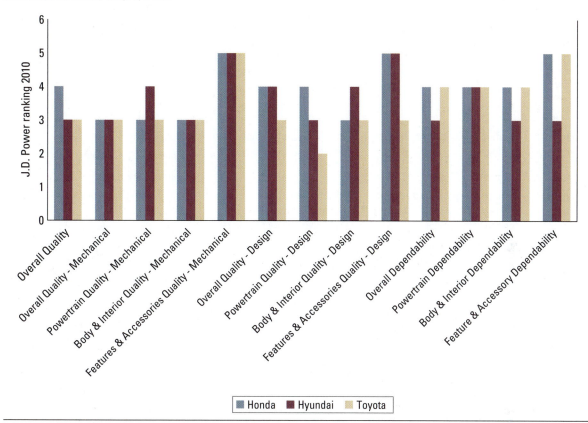

models were discontinued after automakers successfully challenged the mandate in Federal District Court in 2002, winning significant concessions and delays from the CARB. In hindsight, former GM Chairman and CEO Rick Wagoner said that the worst decision of his tenure at GM was "axing the EV1 electric-car program and not putting the right resources into hybrids. It didn't affect profitability, but it did affect image."[20] GM R&D chief Larry Burns now wishes GM had not killed the EV1 prototype his engineers had on the road over a decade ago: "If we could turn back the hands of time," says Burns, "we could have had the Chevy Volt 10 years earlier."[21]

The next major development occurred in 2003, when the U.S. government supported investments of $1.3 billion in hydrogen-powered–vehicle research. Ironically, around this same time Congress also passed accelerated depreciation tax breaks of up to $100,000 for buyers of gas-guzzling SUVs, compared with

$4,000 for buyers of electric cars, with major unintended consequences. Although the $100,000 tax break was intended for commercial trucks, as written, it included all trucks. This allowed GM to push sales of the original Hummer 1, with a sticker price of $125,000 and a 7-mile-per-gallon fuel consumption.

Recently, alternative energy sources have been thrust into the limelight again due to growing environmental concerns, an upsurge in crude-oil prices, and the U.S.'s continued dependence on unstable Middle Eastern countries for oil. This time, car manufacturers have responded by making significant investments in the research and development of various competing energy technologies. A classic standards battle seems to be emerging, with the winner likely to create a new paradigm for personal transportation. Electricity, hydrogen, biodiesel, compressed natural gas, and ethanol are the most common alternatives being considered as replacements for fossil fuels (Exhibit 11).

EXHIBIT 11

Comparison of Alternative Car Technologies

	Pros	Cons	Vehicles, Availability, and Starting Prices
Hybrids	Increases fuel economy significantly, especially in stop and go driving.	Price premium of $2.5k over standard models and $8k for hybrid SUVs. Mileage improvements modest in larger vehicles.	Toyota Prius—$23k. Toyota Lexus RX400h—$43k. Ford Escape Hybrid, GMC Yukon Hybrid—$50k. Chrysler Aspen Hybrid, Dodge Durango Hybrid—$45k.
Mild Hybrids	Generally less expensive than full hybrids.	Only modest improvements in fuel economy.	Honda Civic Hybrid—$22k. Chevy Malibu—$24k. Saturn Aura Hybrid—$24k.
Plug-in Hybrids	Dramatic boost in fuel economy. Can go up to around 120 miles on the battery alone.	Advanced batteries not yet available. Currently very expensive and can overheat.	GM working on Chevy Volt—$40k. Volt due by 2011. Fisker Karma—$85k.
Flexible Fuel Vehicles	No price premium; reduced greenhouse emissions.	Ethanol not widely available and has less density of energy than gas. High demand may drive up food prices. Ethanol is subsidized in U.S.	Almost all GM, Ford, and Chrysler models.
Fuel Cell Vehicles	Use no fossil fuel, hydrogen is widely available, and the only tailpipe emission is water vapor.	Still in experimental stage, hydrogen not widely available as fuel technology, and still too expensive for commercial use.	Models now in testing include Honda FCX Clarity and Chevrolet Equinox, among others. Small number available for lease through test programs.
Electric Cars	Practically no emissions or engine noise. Can be recharged from AC outlet.	Technology still unproven. Standard, high-performance batteries not available.	Tesla Roadster—over $100k.
Clean Diesel Cars	20–40 percent more miles per gallon and more torque than gas engines; reduced greenhouse gas emissions.	More expensive than models with gas engines. Diesel fuel more expensive than gasoline.	VW Jetta diesel—$22k. Jeep Grand Cherokee—$31k. BMW and Mercedes-Benz are also offering clean diesel models.

Source: Adapted from exhibit "The Road Ahead" in "Why the gasoline engine isn't going away any time soon," *The Wall Street Journal*, September 15, 2008.

Meanwhile, others predict that the internal combustion engine will be around for another 50 to 100 years, at least in hybrid vehicles.

BATTERY ELECTRIC VEHICLES. There are two basic types of electric vehicles. One is the *"pure" electric* vehicle (sometimes referred to as the battery electric vehicle or BEV), which uses only batteries to supply the electric energy needed for propulsion. Leveraging the fact that electric motors can also act as generators, electric vehicles utilize regenerative braking to save a significant portion of the energy expended during acceleration, thus increasing the energy efficiency of the vehicle. In addition, pure electric vehicles have a high torque over a larger range of speeds during acceleration compared with internal-combustion engines. For example, the Tesla Roadster is rated at 288 horsepower (hp) and accelerates faster than a 911 Porsche Carrera. Running and servicing costs of the electric car are also much lower than its gasoline-based counterparts; Tesla Motors estimates that the cost per mile driven with the Roadster is just $0.02.

This is because electric motors and gearboxes have relatively few moving pieces, compared with the hundreds of precision-engineered parts necessary for an internal combustion engine. BEVs are usually very quiet, and do not emit any exhaust gases.

The major disadvantage of BEVs is the battery. It is the most expensive part of the car, is subject to deterioration over its lifetime, is heavy, requires long charging times, and offers a very limited energy-to-weight ratio. This low ratio significantly restricts the driving range of electric vehicles. Finding an economic balance of range versus performance, battery capacity versus weight, and battery type versus cost therefore challenges every EV manufacturer. A nickel-metal hydride (NiMH) battery typically lasts the life of the vehicle, but the range tends to be less than 200 miles, and it takes hours to recharge the battery. Newer EVs equipped with lithium-ion batteries provide 250 to 300 miles of range per charge. Many experts believe that battery-production problems could be the limiting factor for the electric-car industry. "Batteries are absolutely the No. 1 constraint for electric cars," says Mark Duvall, a researcher at the Electric Power Research Institute in Palo Alto, California, a utility-funded research organization. "It's also the single-most expensive component right now."[22]

To address this technological gap, a number of small U.S. firms are focusing their R&D on lithium-ion batteries with the hope of supplying automakers. Both Boston Power Co., which supplies batteries for Hewlett-Packard laptops, and Valence Technology Corp., which makes batteries for the Segway scooter, are planning to expand into making automotive batteries. At the same time, Chinese and Japanese firms, such as BYD Motors, Panasonic, Sony, and Sanyo Electric, who already have expertise making lithium-ion batteries, are jockeying for a share of this emerging industry. Former chairman Andy Grove is even pushing Intel to manufacture advanced batteries for plug-in electric cars.[23] According to Mr. Grove, unless U.S. firms get serious about developing a cutting-edge battery soon, the nation may achieve a Pyrrhic victory, breaking an addiction to imported oil through the use of electric cars but replacing it with dependence on imported batteries.

Despite battery constraints, car manufacturers are racing to introduce their first electric-only vehicles to the market. Chrysler founded its ENVI division in 2007 to create electric-drive vehicles and introduced its first "production intent" prototype one year later: an electric-only Dodge EV sports car. However, after

Fiat took over Chrysler, the company disbanded the ENVI electric car division and dropped its models from future product plans.[24] In January 2009, Ford announced its plans to introduce several all-electric cars to the U.S. market in 2010 and 2011, including an all-electric version of the Ford Focus and a commercial vehicle based on the Ford Transit small van.[25] The van will be produced in Europe and imported to the United States, with an estimated sales price in the range of $50,000 to $70,000.[26, 27]

Among Japanese carmakers, Nissan introduced its Nuvu concept for an all-electric city car with $2 + 1$ seating at the Paris Auto Salon in 2008, and is anticipating a limited worldwide release of its Leaf model in 2010. The Nissan Leaf is a compact five-door, five-passenger hatchback, with an all-electric range of 100 miles (160 km) in city driving, and an estimated fuel economy of at least 90 miles per gallon gasoline equivalent. It is listed at an estimated sticker price of roughly $32,000 without any subsidies or tax credits applied.[28] Mitsubishi sells its i-MiEV (Mitsubishi innovative Electric Vehicle) to the Japanese market, but the U.S. launch is not expected until November 2011. In addition, several smaller European companies have introduced future concept cars. Monaco-based Venturi has one high-end electric sports car in production, the Fétish, which sells for about $400,000 but is not intended for mass markets.[29]

PLUG-IN HYBRID ELECTRIC VEHICLES. The other type of electric vehicle relies on *hybrid propulsion,* which combines an electric motor with an internal-combustion engine. Hybrid electric vehicles (HEVs) have all the advantages of pure electric vehicles, but avoid the range-restriction problem through the use of a gasoline-powered internal-combustion engine. Plug-in hybrid electric vehicles (PHEV) contain a battery that stores electricity for the electric motor and can be recharged. Since the battery shares the propulsion load, hybrid engines are significantly smaller than their traditional gasoline counterparts, reducing vehicle weight and cost share. PHEVs can reduce air pollution, dependence on petroleum, and greenhouse-gas emissions that contribute to global warming. Other benefits include improved national energy security, fewer fill-ups at gas stations, the convenience of home recharging, opportunities to provide emergency backup power in the home, and vehicle-to-grid applications.

Elon Musk is a strong opponent of hybrid vehicles. His argument is that HEVs combine the disadvantages of both electric and gasoline-powered vehicles, negating the advantages that each type offers. He argues that hybrids are "bad electric cars" because they must carry around an additional engine and drive train,[30] adding weight, cost, and additional parts to maintain and repair. He criticizes the combustion engines as too small, "anemic," and inherently less efficient than full-size engines. Moreover, the combination of these technologies in a single vehicle adds to the technological complexity, which increases cost, error rates, and maintenance efforts. Hybrid supporters, on the other hand, are optimistic that these disadvantages can be mitigated through continued research and development.

Despite their shortcomings, sales of hybrid vehicles in the United States increased steadily from 1999 through 2007, and then started to decline slightly. Toyota sold the majority of these early hybrids, introducing the Prius in 2000, only one year after the first commercial HEV, the Honda Insight, entered the market. As of the 2009 financial year, Toyota had sold more than 814,000 units, making the Prius the most widely sold HEV by a wide margin (Exhibit 12). In July 2006, Toyota announced plans to develop a new hybrid vehicle that will run locally on batteries charged by a household electrical outlet before switching over to a gasoline engine for longer hauls.

American manufacturers have been relatively slow to follow Toyota's lead in hybrid technologies. At the 2009 North American International Auto Show in Detroit, Chrysler unveiled the 200C EV Concept minivan ("Electric Town and Country") and the Jeep Patriot EV, both range-extended (electric and gas engine) vehicles. As with Chrysler's pure electric sports car prototype, however, these models were discontinued when Fiat shut down Chrysler's ENVI division. Ford also introduced the latest edition of its Escape Hybrid in 2009, priced at roughly $30,000.[31] The Escape was initially sold as a pure hybrid, but Ford converted it to a plug-in after finding out that customers were having their vehicles altered by other service companies after purchasing them from Ford. The new Escape has intelligent vehicle-to-grid (V2G) communications and control system technology, allowing the vehicle operator to program when to recharge the vehicle, for how long, and at what utility rate.

More than 10 years after the Toyota Prius first debuted, GM is seeking to challenge the Prius's market dominance with its Chevrolet Volt, first introduced in 2007. The Volt is a PHEV-40 that features a plug-in–capable, battery-dominant series hybrid architecture called E-Flex. The combustion engine starts when 40 percent of the battery charge remains, enabling the

EXHIBIT 12

Toyota Prius Sales, 2000–2009 (Units)

Source: Data adapted from www.afdc.energy.gov/afdc/data/docs/hev_sales.xls.

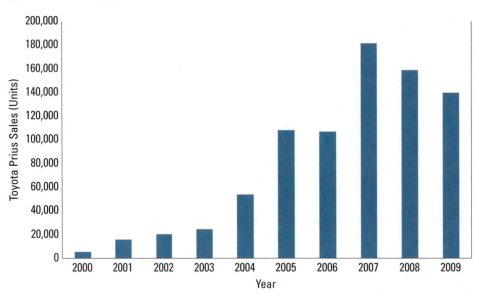

Volt to achieve a fuel economy of 50 miles per U.S. gallon. The Volt has a long way to go before it can become a serious contender for the mass hybrid market, however. Not only does it come with a sticker price of about $40,000, compared with $23,000 for the Prius, but the Volt has some serious technical problems. It needs to be charged for six hours to gain the necessary battery power for a single 40-mile drive. The Volt's gas engine extends its range beyond the 40-mile battery limit, but this introduces another issue: The gas tank must be drained periodically in order to keep the gasoline from going bad. Even worse, GM is unlikely to recoup its R&D expenses, causing some analysts to charge that the Volt is nothing more than a "show car" to demonstrate that GM understands the trends in the market and is investing in next-generation vehicle technologies.[32]

A more potent threat is BYD Motors, a Chinese startup, which is already selling plug-in electric hybrids in China and is planning to introduce its vehicles in the United States in 2011. As the first Chinese car manufacturer poised to break into Western markets, BYD has attracted the attention of Warren Buffett, who invested some $230 million for a 10 percent equity stake in the company. BYD has an advantage in that it started as a battery company and has developed lithium iron phosphate batteries which permit cars to run 250 miles on a single three-hour charge.[33,34] The sticker price of BYD cars is anticipated to be about one-half that of the price for the Chevy Volt.

In the luxury segment, Quantum Technologies and Fisker Coachbuild, LLC, announced the launch of a joint venture (Fisker Automotive) in September 2007. Fisker intends to build an $80,000 luxury PHEV-50, the Fisker Karma, as a plug-in hybrid sports car to be pitted against the Tesla Roadster (a pure electric vehicle). The Karma goes from 0 to 60 mph in 6 seconds with top speeds capped at 125 mph due to safety reasons. The driver has an option to select between two modes of driving. The first mode is "stealth drive," which is the quiet economy mode for optimal relaxed and efficient driving. By flipping a second paddle behind the steering wheel, the driver can switch the car to "sport drive," which accesses the full power of the vehicle. For fun, the Karma features an option to let the engine "roar," because otherwise electric vehicles are completely silent. The Karma's proprietary design allows consumers to drive the car on zero emissions for up to 50 miles a day, provided the car is charged every evening. If consumers follow this daily routine

faithfully, it is conceivable that they will need to fuel the car only once a year.

BIOFUELS AND NATURAL GAS. In addition to electricity, researchers are exploring *ethanol* and *natural gas* as alternative fuels for automobile propulsion systems. Ethanol is a biofuel easily derived from natural sugars (starch) in crops like sugar cane and corn. With a small amount of redesign, gasoline-powered vehicles can run on ethanol concentrations as high as 85 percent (E85). While biofuels do not contribute to CO_2 emissions, they are still not free of criticism. Some believe that the use of ethanol as a source of fuel is responsible for an increase in food prices.[35] Not only must huge swaths of land be devoted to specific crops, but the crops that are grown must go to make fuel instead of feeding people or farm animals. Critics also argue that growing the crops requires more energy than the fuel they produce, making the process inherently inefficient. Further, the use of crops for fuels is highly politicized. In the United States, ethanol derived from corn or sugar cane can be competitive in price only because of government subsidies. Other countries, such as Brazil, can produce biofuels much more cost effectively due to their ready availability of an unskilled labor force, but the U.S. government has barred these cheaper Brazilian imports from entering the U.S. market in order to protect domestic producers. Factoring in these subsidies and trade barriers makes biofuels a net-loss-incurring business.[36]

Biodiesel, produced from oilseed, has been a more popular substitute in European countries, where gasoline is four times more expensive than in the United States. Although biodiesel is commercially available in most oilseed-producing states, it is somewhat more expensive than fossil diesel. In addition, biodiesel has lower energy density than either fossil diesel or gasoline, resulting in decreased fuel economy. Nevertheless, biodiesel engines are considered to be more environmentally friendly than gasoline engines because they do not emit carbon dioxide.

High-pressure compressed natural gas, composed mainly of methane, can also be utilized in place of gasoline to fuel normal combustion engines. The combustion of methane produces the lowest amount of CO_2 of all fossil fuels. Cars can be retrofitted to run on compressed natural gas as well as gasoline, allowing the driver to alternate between fuel sources during operation.

HYDROGEN AND FUEL CELLS. Finally, hydrogen may serve as an alternative fuel through one of two methods: combustion or fuel-cell conversion. In combustion, the hydrogen is "burned" in engines in fundamentally the same way as gasoline. In fuel-cell conversion, the hydrogen is turned into electricity through fuel cells which then power electric motors. German carmakers Volkswagen and Audi have started their own research departments on fuel cells, while Mercedes plans to start a limited 200-car series of its B-class model based on fuel-cell technology.

One primary area of ongoing research is to increase the range of hydrogen vehicles while reducing the weight, energy consumption, and complexity of the storage systems. The major disadvantage for both the combustion and fuel-cell methods is that there is no infrastructure to supply and store hydrogen in mass quantities. Building such infrastructure will require not only the automakers, but also governments, to make commitments to hydrogen technology. As a result, some experts believe it will be a long time before hydrogen cars are economically viable.[37]

QUEST FOR A STANDARD. Although many alternative fuel sources are currently in production and development, no overall industry standard has yet emerged. Companies that have invested considerable sums of money in R&D continue to push their technology as the best. Wary of betting on the wrong technology, many car manufacturers have opted to sit on the sidelines until a clear winner emerges, which slows the pace of progress.

Meanwhile, determining a new standard for fuel and propulsion systems is only the first step toward reducing our reliance on fossil fuels. Just as we have multiple oil companies, nationwide systems of gas stations, and pipelines to ship gasoline from the refineries to the pump, any alternative energy will require its own unique infrastructure. At the same time, standardized supporting technologies and peripheral devices must be developed so that the new vehicles can be "refueled," repaired, and serviced anywhere they travel. We take for granted that the same gas pump nozzle fits into the tank of a Honda minivan and a Mini Cooper, and that the same grade of gasoline is available no matter where we stop to refuel. Similarly, windshield wiper fluid, engine oil, and antifreeze can be purchased without regard for make or model. These supporting "details" are perhaps the biggest obstacle that has kept any of the new alternative propulsion technologies from being fully embraced.

Electric Car Infrastructure

At least three major types of infrastructures are being developed to extend the range and decrease the charging times of pure electric vehicles. First, the U.S. National Institute of Standards and Technology and the Federal Energy Regulatory Commission are heavily involved in the definition of future smart-grid standards.[38] The U.S. government currently offers economic incentives to encourage electric-vehicle ownership, and realizes that an electric infrastructure must be in place to meet the needs of on-the-go Americans. Smart grids are electricity networks that utilize two-way digital metering, sensing, monitoring, and control technologies to improve electricity production, transmission, distribution, and consumption. By providing information about grid conditions to system users, operators, and automated devices, the smart grid enables dynamic responses to energy needs, which in turn saves energy, reduces costs, and increases reliability. Once installed nationwide, the smart grid could also provide a means of recharging batteries for electric-powered vehicles.

Better Place is a California-based electric-vehicle services provider that is actively working to create its own (for-profit) version of an electric recharge-grid infrastructure. Shai Agassi, the Israeli-American founder of Better Place, has likened the firm's model to that of a telecom provider, from whom users buy charged-battery minutes. If the service contract is large enough, Better Place might even provide a "free" or highly subsidized car, much like telecom providers provide discounted cell phones when customers sign two-year service agreements. To service the vehicles, Better Place plans to create a chain of electric-battery exchange and charge stations. Instead of charging the battery in-car, the customer can exchange the empty battery for a new, fully charged battery, in about the same amount of time it takes to fill a tank with gas. Agassi is investing heavily in R&D to complete Better Place's infrastructure in Israel and Denmark, with future expansions intended for the United States, Australia, and the remainder of Europe.[39] In March 2008, Deutsche Bank analysts stated that the company's approach could mark a "paradigm shift" that causes a "massive disruption" to the auto industry, and that Better Place has "the potential to eliminate the gasoline engine altogether."[40] However, major German carmakers (who wield considerable market power) are skeptical of Agassi's model. They claim that Better Place's business plan stifles creative design freedom by introducing too many constraints on the car's body. Further, there are unresolved legal issues with battery ownership between the station operator, Better Place, and car owners.

A group of scientists at the Fraunhofer Institute for Chemical Technology in Pfinztal, Germany, is currently investigating yet another proposal. This technology involves a flushable, liquid electrolyte for electric-car batteries;[41] batteries would be recharged by draining the used electrolyte and refilling the battery with charged electrolyte. The time for such a recharge would be in line with current times for filling a car with gasoline. The electrolyte could be recharged locally, possibly using wind or solar energy, in contrast to the costs of transporting other types of fuel sources cross-country. As a result, the German approach would allow for an improved CO_2 footprint for electric cars.

Tesla Motors: Where to Go or Where to Stop?

Tesla is facing a serious laundry list of problems. Consumers are still reluctant to invest in all-electric cars, especially with so many other alternative technologies vying for market dominance. The infrastructure is not yet ready to support widespread use of electric vehicles, so buying one comes with significant inconvenience. No all-electric car has proven to be even a quasi-standard, with the result that any investment in an electric vehicle could backfire in the long term. Also, not enough models are available to enable consumers to make an educated selection, especially compared to the number of hybrid vehicles available.

Meanwhile, the gasoline-powered car industry keeps chugging along. The 2009 Car Allowance Rebate System (CARS) program (commonly referred to as "Cash for Clunkers") announced by the U.S. government in 2009 did not exactly help reduce sales of traditional gas-powered vehicles. According to the U.S. Department of Transportation, about 700,000 cars were exchanged for newer, more fuel-efficient models, which will remain on the roads for the next 10 to 15 years.[42]

Tesla also has legal problems. It sued Fisker Automotive, alleging that Fisker stole design ideas and confidential information regarding the design of hybrid and electric cars. In turn, Tesla was sued by Magna International, which claimed Tesla never paid it for services rendered in designing the two-speed transmission that Musk insisted the Roadster must have.

Then there is the issue of Tesla's cash flow. Although the company received a $465 million loan from the U.S. Department of Energy in June 2009 (Tesla initially asked for $450 million),[43, 44] it was burning through a lot of money. By year-end 2008, Tesla's losses totaled almost $205 million, and it added another $31.5 million in losses by September 30, 2009.[45] It may take another couple of years before Tesla can actually sustain a profit.

Another difficulty for the Tesla Roadster is its hefty price tag of more than $100,000, which significantly limits the number of potential buyers. In the past, established companies with high-end automotive niche products could not sustain their businesses and were bought up by the major car companies. For example, Fiat acquired Ferrari and Maserati; Volkswagen purchased Lamborghini, Bugatti, and Porsche; and Ford bought Aston Martin and later spun it out to an investment company. Potential buyers for electric cars may also want to go beyond the limited usability for a roadster, and look for more family-friendly means of transportation. While Tesla is expanding its product line to include the Model S Sedan, more and more companies are entering the electric-vehicle market. The race is on, and it is not a foregone conclusion that Tesla will be the winner.

Strategic Choices

Elon Musk has been sunbathing on the yacht for hours. To Musk, the current crisis at Tesla Motors feels like a déjà vu of the PayPal scenario. The Tesla Roadster is the first successful battery-only–powered, mass-produced car, which created and legitimized the EV market in the United States. It shattered previously negative stereotypes of electric vehicles by solving the trade-off between electric-car performance and acceptable range. The Roadster's performance is on par with high-end gasoline-powered sports cars, especially in terms of acceleration and top speed, and its range is suitable for most day-to-day applications. Now everyone in Silicon Valley is watching and waiting to see what Elon Musk will do next, and most are betting that he'll sell the company, just like he did before. After all, they reason, he cannot continue to run three companies at once and manage to give them all his full attention.

While sipping his coffee, Elon Musk ponders several possible options. Daimler already owns a 10 percent stake in Tesla (40 percent of Daimler's stakes are in the hands of Aabar Investments of Abu Dhabi). In 2009, both companies agreed to work together on the Model S, which stands for an electric "smart" car.[46] Is this the way to go, trying to get a major carmaker to partner with the company? Or perhaps he should sell out completely? While Mr. Musk would like for Tesla to remain independent, he wonders whether going it alone is sustainable in the long run.

Another option is to go public. An IPO would provide a potentially large source of capital, but at the cost of reduced independence. Although Tesla prides itself on its uniqueness,[47] a legitimate concern remains as to whether investors are likely to put money into such a high-risk company. Investors may also be more interested in the announced GM IPO, which could draw available capital away from Tesla. In any case, Tesla's IPO may not supply enough of a capital infusion to continue operations, especially considering the upcoming expenses for the S model. This is especially worrisome because of the high-cost and high-risk activities leading up to an IPO, such as finding and paying an investment bank, determining the right price, wide information disclosure, and so on. Moreover, Mr. Musk worries about leading a publicly traded stock company and the disclosure requirements and 90-day reporting time horizons that come with it.

The "Electric Avenue" at the latest Detroit Motor Show provided a sneak peak at the future of the electric-car industry. All the major automotive companies have electric vehicles in the pipeline, with models ranging from affordable economy cars to expensive luxury models. Larger automakers have a significant competitive advantage: They have the financial and technological resources to invest heavily in research and development. For example, French automaker Peugeot has a brand-new prototype, the BB1.[48] Nissan is planning to launch its LEAF (*L*eading, *E*nvironmentally friendly, *A*ffordable, *F*amily car) in late 2010. Audi presented its E-Tron, based on cutting-edge technologies and priced comparable to or lower than the Tesla Roadster. Another company, Trexa, unveiled the world's first fully electric-vehicle development platform, allowing even small niche companies to start designing and building electric vehicles.[49]

Should Tesla stay in its niche and focus on one product (the high-end roadster), or should it pursue the Model S even more aggressively? And where would Tesla produce the car? It doesn't even own a factory. Perhaps Tesla has aimed too high with both models, and should redirect its efforts at a lower-end, mass-producible vehicle that would generate higher sales volumes. Or is it already too late to enter the mass market? Will electric cars turn out to be the new standard, or are Tesla and its competitors chasing an expensive but passing fad? Are electric cars in general—and Tesla's models in particular—even a viable business at all? What will the other market players do? Thinking about all this gives Elon Musk a headache. Perhaps he should just sell Tesla, and focus on his other two ventures, SolarCity and SpaceX, which cause fewer problems. As his BlackBerry keeps buzzing, he wonders what to do . . .

Endnotes

1. Belfiore, M. (2007), "Chapter 7: Orbit on a Shoestring," *Rocketeers* (New York: HarperCollins), pp. 166–195.

2. This case draws on: Davis, J. (2010), "How Elon Musk turned Tesla into the car company of the future," *Wired Magazine*, September 27, www.wired.com/magazine/2010/09/ff_tesla/all/1; and Malone, M. (2009), "Uber entrepreneur: An evening with Elon Musk," April 7, http://fora.tv/2009/04/07/Uber_Entrepreneur_An_Evening_with_Elon_Musk.

3. Malone, M. (2009), "Uber entrepreneur: An evening with Elon Musk."

4. "Tesla worth more than half a billion dollars after Daimler investment," *TechCrunch*, May 19, 2009.

5. On December 31, 2009, the DJIA stood at 10,428 points.

6. www.time.com/time/2006/techguide/bestinventions/inventions/transportation2.html.

7. Malone, M. (2009), "Uber Entrepreneur: An evening with Elon Musk"; and Davis, J. (2010), "How Elon Musk turned Tesla into the car company of the future."

8. www.theregister.co.uk/2009/06/23/musk_broadside_eberhard/.

9. www.sec.gov/Archives/edgar/data/1318605/000119312510068933/ds1a.htm.

10. Ibid.

11. Wardsauto.com key automotive data, retrieved October 29, 2010.

12. "Obama's car puzzle," *The Wall Street Journal*, November 12, 2008.

13. Keegan, M. C. (2005), "DaimlerChrysler: Merger or acquisition?" October 31, www.thearticlewriter.com/daimler-chrysler-merger-oracquisition.htm.

14. Surowiecki, J., "The Daimler-Chrysler collision," *Slate*, www.slate.com/id/2654/; accessed March 3, 2011.

15. Merced, M. J. (2009), "Judge clears way for sale of Chrysler to Fiat," *The New York Times,* June 1, www.nytimes.com/2009/06/01/business/01chrysler.html?_r=1.

16. http://documents.nytimes.com/chrysler-bankruptcy-filing#p=1

17. "Big Three seek $34 billion aid," *The Wall Street Journal,* December 3, 2008.

18. www.nhtsa.dot.gov.

19. www.arb.ca.gov/msprog/zevprog/background.htm.

20. *Motor Trend,* June, 2008.

21. "Comin' through!" *Newsweek,* March 13, 2007.

22. "Ex-chief says Intel should power cars," *The Wall Street Journal,* December 12, 2008.

23. Ibid.

24. "Chrysler dismantles electric car plans under Fiat," *Reuters,* November 6, 2009.

25. http://blogs.cars.com/kickingtires/2009/01/ford-electric-car.html.

26. www.foxnews.com/story/0,2933,512423,00.html.

27. www.fordvehicles.com/transitconnect/.

28. www.nissanusa.com/leaf-electric-car/index?dcp=ppn.39666654.&dcc=0.216878497#/leaf-electric-car/.

29. www.hybridcars.com/electric-cars/venturi-fetish.html.

30. http://fora.tv/2009/04/07/Uber_Entrepreneur_An_Evening_with_Elon_Musk.

31. www.fordvehicles.com/suvs/escapehybrid/.

32. "The great IPO race: Tesla vs. GM," *The Wall Street Journal,* January 29, 2010.

33. "Bright sparks. Electric propulsion provides some excitement amid the gloom," *The Economist,* January 15, 2009.

34. "BYD zooms past Toyota, GM in electric car race," *China Daily,* December 16, 2008.

35. Mitchell, D. (2008), "A note on rising food prices," *World Bank – Development Economics Group (DEC),* July 1, 2008, World Bank Policy Research Working Paper No. 4682.

36. Ridley, M. (2010), "The rational optimist: How prosperity evolves," *Harper.*

37. "Hydrogen vehicles won't be viable soon, study says," *MIT Tech Talk,* March 3, 2003.

38. Friedman, T. L. (2008), *Hot, Flat, and Crowded: Why We Need a Green Revolution—And How It Can Renew America,* 1st ed. (New York: Farrar, Straus and Giroux).

39. www.nytimes.com/2010/01/25/business/energy-environment/25electric.html.

40. "Deutsche Bank: Project Better Place has 'the potential to eliminate the gasoline engine,'" *Cleantech Investing in Israel,* April 15, 2008, http://westernlithium.com/_resources/electric_cars.pdf.

41. "All pumped up," *The Economist online,* December 16, 2009, www.economist.com/sciencetechnology/tm/displaystory.cfm?story_id=15125038.

42. www.dot.gov/affairs/2009/dot13309.htm.

43. "Ford, Nissan among first to tap loans for retooling," *The Wall Street Journal,* June 23, 2009.

44. "Ford, Nissan and Tesla win green loans," *Financial Times,* June 24, 2010.

45. www.sec.gov/Archives/edgar/data/1318605/000119312510017054/ds1.htm#toc51863_11.

46. www.wired.com/autopia/2009/01/tesla-motors-jo/.

47. "Tesla charges up for $100m listing," *Financial Times,* January 30, 2010.

48. www.bb1-peugeot.com/.

49. www.trexa.com.

Michael Janovec
Georgia Institute of Technology

Frank T. Rothaermel
Georgia Institute of Technology

ELON MUSK, CEO of Tesla Motors, sped past the security guard in his brand new Tesla Roadster without waving. Despite his reputation as a brash leader, Mr. Musk normally took the time to exchange pleasantries in the morning. Today, however, Mr. Musk's mind was traveling a mile a minute. The company had just filed its first annual 10-K with the U.S. Securities and Exchange Commission (SEC), and Musk had an important meeting with Tesla's board of directors at the end of the week to discuss the company's future.

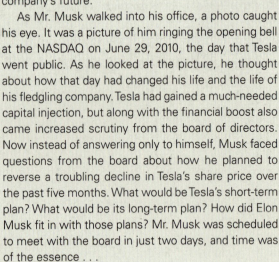

As Mr. Musk walked into his office, a photo caught his eye. It was a picture of him ringing the opening bell at the NASDAQ on June 29, 2010, the day that Tesla went public. As he looked at the picture, he thought about how that day had changed his life and the life of his fledgling company. Tesla had gained a much-needed capital injection, but along with the financial boost also came increased scrutiny from the board of directors. Now instead of answering only to himself, Musk faced questions from the board about how he planned to reverse a troubling decline in Tesla's share price over the past five months. What would be Tesla's short-term plan? What would be its long-term plan? How did Elon Musk fit in with those plans? Mr. Musk was scheduled to meet with the board in just two days, and time was of the essence . . .

Going Public

On January 29, 2010, Tesla Motors filed an S-1 form (a preliminary prospectus) with the SEC, indicating its intention to file an initial public offering (IPO).[1] The S-1 was underwritten by Goldman Sachs, Morgan Stanley, J.P. Morgan, and Deutsche Bank Securities.[2] Many analysts and investors perceived the IPO filing as a sign that Tesla's financial troubles were deeper than anticipated.[3] Despite these concerns, the underwriters' road show went extremely well, resulting in an initial offering price of $17 per share, up from the target range of $14 to $16. The number of initial shares also increased, from 2.2 million to 13.3 million. Tesla's NASDAQ debut on June 29, 2010, marked the first IPO by an American automaker since Ford in 1956. On the first day of trading, Tesla's shares closed up 40 percent at $23.89—on a day when the NASDAQ dropped 3.85 percent and the Dow fell by 2.65 percent.[4] The IPO raised $226.1 million, money that Tesla urgently needed.

Despite an initial drop in share price post-IPO, Tesla's stock quickly rebounded and rose as high as $35.42 by November 2010. By April 2011, shares had corrected back down to $25 a share (Exhibit 1). Investors' initial positive outlook regarding the future of the electric car seemed to have given way to a more realistic estimation of recent market developments. Insufficient infrastructure, slow public acceptance, and a lack of cheap batteries with adequate capacity had kept electric vehicles in their niche and prevented them from becoming much more than a technology used for company utility-truck fleets. This, together with the fact that the Tesla Roadster (still the only Tesla model available) cost more than $100,000, had kept Tesla from turning a profit. In its first annual report, Tesla reported an operating loss of $146.8 million.[5] As of June 2010, Tesla had lost a total of more than $400 million (Exhibits 2 and 3, pages C52 and C53).[6]

Strategic Partnerships

Despite financial setbacks, Tesla continued to improve its current model, the Roadster, and announced the Roadster 2.5, a spiced-up version of the original with several improvements. As of June 2010, Tesla had sold more than 1,200 vehicles.[7]

Research Associate Michael Janovec (GT MBA '11) and Professor Frank T. Rothaermel prepared this case from public sources. It is developed for the purpose of class discussion. It is not intended to be used for any kind of endorsement, source of data, or depiction of efficient or inefficient management. All opinions expressed, and all errors and omissions are entirely the authors'. © Janovec and Rothaermel, 2013.

EXHIBIT 1

Tesla Stock Price, Compared to the DJIA, NASDAQ, and S&P 500 Indices

Source: Yahoo Finance.

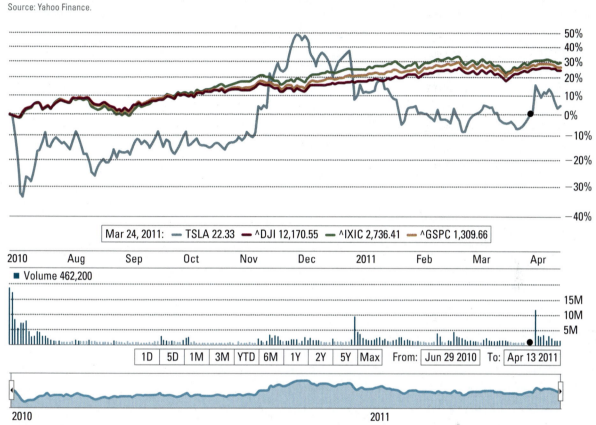

Mar 24, 2011: — TSLA 22.33 — ^DJI 12,170.55 — ^IXIC 2,736.41 — ^GSPC 1,309.66

Volume 462,200

1D | 5D | 1M | 3M | YTD | 6M | 1Y | 2Y | 5Y | Max   From: Jun 29 2010   To: Apr 13 2011

Tesla also managed to strike some remarkable deals with big players in the automotive industry. In 2009, German automotive engineering powerhouse Daimler purchased a nearly 10 percent stake in Tesla, worth an estimated $50 million.[8] Musk and his team wowed the skeptical Daimler executives by modifying an off-the-shelf Daimler Smart car into an all-electric vehicle in only six weeks.[9] The partnership with Daimler provides Tesla with access to Daimler's engineering expertise and global supply chain, and could also improve Tesla's ability to raise capital. Daimler, meanwhile, could profit significantly from its investment in the nimble startup that lies on the forefront of technological development. In addition, Daimler has reportedly experimented with Tesla's battery technology,[10] but has since stated that it will use its own in-house-developed products for its Smart electric vehicle (EV) program.[11]

Another breakthrough came in May 2010, when Toyota announced that it would buy $50 million (roughly 3 percent) of Tesla's stock in the upcoming IPO.[12] With this deal, Tesla got ownership of the NUMMI automotive factory plant in Fremont, California.[13] For Toyota, this deal served as advertising for the company's commitment to alternative-vehicle technologies, while Tesla's benefits were similar to those received from the Daimler venture. The first fruits of collaboration between the two companies were evident when Tesla announced that it would deliver two EV prototypes based on existing Toyota models in July 2010.[14] Both companies have also signed a joint vehicle-development agreement. Toyota has since announced that it plans to develop an electric SUV based on its RAV4 model, using Tesla battery technology.[15, 16]

In addition, Tesla managed to bring Panasonic, one of the world's electronic giants, on board. Panasonic's aim is to combine its experience in battery technology with Tesla's capabilities in electric power-train development. The goal for Panasonic is to become the

EXHIBIT 2

Tesla Motors, Inc., Statement of Income (in thousands, except share and per share data)					
	2010	2009	2008	2007	2006
Revenues					
Automotive sales	$ 97,078	$111,943	$ 14,742	$ 73	—
Development services	19,666	—	—	—	—
Total revenues	**116,744**	**111,943**	**14,742**	**73**	**—**
Cost of revenues					
Automotive sales	79,982	102,408	15,883	9	—
Development services	6,031	—	—	—	—
Total cost of revenues	86,013	102,408	15,883	9	—
Gross profit (loss)	**30,731**	**9,535**	**(1,141)**	**64**	**—**
Operating expenses					
Research and development	92,996	19,282	53,714	62,753	$ 24,995
Selling, general and administrative	84,573	42,150	23,649	17,244	5,436
Total operating expenses	**177,569**	**61,432**	**77,363**	**79,997**	**30,431**
Loss from operations	(146,838)	(51,897)	(78,504)	(79,933)	(30,431)
Interest income	258	159	529	1,749	938
Interest expense	(992)	(2,531)	(3,747)	—	(423)
Other income (expense), net	(6,583)	(1,445)	(963)	137	59
Loss before income taxes	(154,155)	(55,714)	(82,685)	(78,047)	(29,857)
Provision for income taxes	173	26	97	110	100
Net loss	$(154,328)	$ (55,740)	$(82,782)	$(78,157)	$(29,957)
Net loss per share of common stock	$(3.04)	$(7.94)	$(12.46)	$(22.69)	$(10.18)
Weighted average shares used in computing net loss per share of common stock	50,718,302	7,021,963	6,646,387	3,443,806	2,941,411

Source: Tesla Annual Reports (www.sec.gov).

number one Green Innovation Company in the electronics industry by 2018, the 100th anniversary of its founding.[17]

International Expansion

At the same time that Tesla was pursuing strategic relationships with leading electronic and automotive companies, it started to expand its network of company-owned stores. Previously, all sales had been conducted either via the phone or Internet or in person at corporate events or company headquarters. By February 2011, Tesla had opened 17 new sales locations, spanning North America, Europe, and Asia. The company targeted major metropolitan areas including Chicago, New York, Los Angeles, London, Munich, Madrid, Tokyo, Hong Kong, and Sydney (Australia). In conjunction with the 2012 rollout of the Model S, Tesla anticipates establishing nearly 50 stores worldwide over the next several years, at a cost of $5 to $10 million annually.

To differentiate itself from its competitors and provide superior customer experience, Tesla has opted not to create franchised dealers, but instead maintains all sales and service operations in-house. The company also created a wholly owned subsidiary, Tesla Motors Leasing Inc., to provide a leasing alternative to its customers starting in 2010.[18]

EXHIBIT 3

Tesla Motors, Inc., Selected Consolidated Balance Sheet Data (in Thousands)					
	2010	**2009**	**2008**	**2007**	**2006**
Cash and cash equivalents	$ 99,558	$ 9,627	$ 9,277	$ 17,211	$ 35,401
Restricted cash—current	73,597	—	—	—	—
Property, plant and equipment, net	114,636	23,535	18,793	11,998	7,512
Working capital (deficit)	150,321	43,070	(56,508)	(28,988)	8,458
Total assets	**386,082**	**130,424**	**51,699**	**34,837**	**44,466**
Convertible preferred stock warrant liability	—	1,734	2,074	191	27
Common stock warrant liability	6,088	—	—	—	—
Capital lease obligations, less current portion	496	800	888	18	—
Long-term debt	71,828	—	—	—	—
Convertible preferred stock	—	319,225	101,178	101,178	60,173
Total liabilities and stockholders' equity (deficit)	**207,048**	**(253,523)**	**(199,714)**	**(117,846)**	**(43,923)**

Source: Tesla Annual Reports (www.sec.gov).

Price Pressure

Importantly, a study conducted by Nielsen found that in the United States, 72 percent of people polled have considered buying or would buy an electric vehicle. However, 65 percent of Americans would not pay more for an electric vehicle than for traditional car models. Of those who said they would be ready to pay more, most were willing to pay no more than an additional $1,000 to $5,000.[19] Thus, electric vehicles will need to compete heavily on price, and not on technology alone.

The contents of the Nielsen report may spell trouble for Musk's second generation of electric vehicles, the Model S. Tesla plans to deliver approximately 5,000 Model S sedans in mid-2012 and an additional 20,000 in 2013. Buyers will have the option to purchase a model with either a 160-mile or 230-mile battery life. The 160-mile edition's sticker price will be $57,400 ($49,900 after a $7,500 federal tax credit); the 230-mile edition will sell for $67,400 ($59,900 after tax credit). In addition, Tesla is developing a 300-mile model slated for production in 2013. While cheaper than the Roadster, the Model S will still retail at a premium to current electric vehicles such as the Nissan Leaf, which sells for $25,280 after the tax credit.[20] Critics are skeptical that Tesla can get its prices down

to a competitive level[21] and still produce the Model S on time and have it be able to perform as promised.[22]

Negative Press

Adding to potential troubles, Tesla Motors and Elon Musk have received some negative press. In December 2008, the BBC show *Top Gear* featured a race between a Tesla Roadster and the Lotus Elise. During the episode, the Tesla Roadster ran out of charge after just 55 miles, far below its advertised 200-mile range. In response, Elon Musk filed a libel suit against the show in March 2011 claiming that the scene was faked. The filing stated that *Top Gear*'s claim "grossly misled potential purchasers of the Roadster."[23, 24]

In addition to the *Top Gear* disaster, a CNBC show entitled *Divorce Wars* featured Justine Musk, Elon Musk's ex-wife, in an episode that aired in April 2011.[25] The episode discussed the couple's split and bitter court battle, during which time Mr. Musk claimed that his bank account was empty and that he was living off loans from his rich friends. His financial situation was further complicated by the fact that a loan from the U.S. Energy Department requires Mr. Musk to retain at least a 65 percent stake in Tesla, limiting his access to cash. As the largest shareholder of Tesla stock, Mr. Musk's purported financial position raised eyebrows among investors about the future of the company. Continued negative press of this kind could potentially weigh down the share price and erode the board of directors' confidence in Elon Musk as CEO.[26]

On the Positive Side

Despite Mr. Musk's personal and business troubles, not all is doom and gloom at Tesla. On March 31, 2011, Tesla shares received a boost after President Obama stated that he would direct federal agencies to purchase alternative-fuel vehicles by 2015. In his address, the President remarked, "There are few breakthroughs as promising for increasing fuel efficiency and reducing our dependence on oil as electric vehicles."[27]

Along with Obama's statements, Morgan Stanley analyst Adam Jones upgraded Tesla's stock, saying that Tesla could become "America's fourth automaker."[28] Morgan Stanley further projects that plug-in hybrids and pure electric vehicles will account for 7 percent of U.S. car sales and 5.5 percent of global sales by 2020, increasing to 15 percent of global sales by 2025.[29] In line with his growth predictions, Jones projected that Tesla shares may rise to $70 over the next year. In order to achieve these goals, however, Jones believes that Tesla will need to mass-produce a vehicle with a sticker price around $30,000.[30] Analysts from J.P. Morgan are likewise bullish on Tesla, setting a target share price of $40 to $50 over the next three years provided Tesla can realize a lower cost structure.[31]

Takeover Target?

Despite bullish forecasts, analysts warn that liquidity could remain a challenge for Tesla. Morgan Stanley estimates that Tesla could spend 75 percent of its current liquidity by 2013.[32] In fact, Tesla's liquidity crisis has led some analysts to suggest that the company may become a takeover target. As a leader in electric-vehicle technology, Tesla could provide a larger, more traditional automaker an entry into the alternative-fuel market as oil prices rise.

Alternatively, Tesla's elite brand image may appeal to luxury automakers. Analysts cite Tesla's partnership with Daimler as evidence that Daimler may be considering Tesla as a potential takeover target. Under their existing deal, Musk is barred from voting for a sale to any car manufacturer other than Daimler, without Blackstar's (an affiliate of Daimler) consent.[33]

Nevertheless, Musk has fervently insisted that Tesla will remain independent. Musk told *Bloomberg*, "Their analysis of Tesla is incredibly bad. Tesla is of course a potential takeover target, like almost all public companies. However, I'm also highly confident that we can succeed as an independent company."[34]

Decision Time—Again

As Elon Musk stared at the photo on the wall, he wondered, What should I recommend? Could the firm produce a car priced to compete with manufacturers such as Nissan? And if so, by when? Could Tesla remain independent? If so, how will Tesla address liquidity concerns? Given the distractions in his personal life and the negative publicity from the *Top Gear* suit, would the board remain confident in his leadership? More importantly, how would Tesla reach long-term profitability?

Endnotes

1. "Tesla Motors files for an IPO, by the numbers," *The Wall Street Journal,* January 29, 2010.

2. www.sec.gov/Archives/edgar/data/1318605/000119312510017054/ds1.htm.

3. "Tesla Motors files for IPO – So much for the profits," *The Wall Street Journal,* January 29, 2010.

4. www.businessweek.com/news/2010-06-29/tesla-posts-second-biggest-rally-for-2010-u-s-ipo.html.

5. Tesla 10-K filing, March 3, 2010, www.sec.gov/Archives/edgar/data/1318605/000119312511054847/d10k.htm#tx151489_8.

6. Compiled from Tesla's 10-K filing, March 3, 2010, www.sec.gov/Archives/edgar/data/1318605/000119312511054847/d10k.htm#tx151489_8.

7. www.teslamotors.com/about/press/releases/tesla-unveils-roadster-25-newest-stores-europe-and-north-america.

8. www.wired.com/autopia/2009/05/daimler_tesla/.

9. www.wired.com/magazine/2010/09/ff_tesla/all/1.

10. www.wired.com/autopia/2009/01/tesla-motors-jo/.

11. www.wired.com/autopia/2009/01/tesla-deal-help/.

12. www.ft.com/cms/s/0/433ddb64-653a-11df-b648-00144feab49a.html.

13. NUMMI was a joint venture by Toyota and GM. GM withdrew from the JV as part of its bankruptcy reorganization in 2009.

14. "Tesla to deliver prototypes to Toyota this month," *The Wall Street Journal* (online), July 12, 2010.

15. "Toyota plans electric SUV with Tesla," *The Wall Street Journal* (online), July 16, 2010.

16. "Toyota plans 2 electric autos in the U.S. and 6 hybrids by 2012," *The New York Times,* September 14, 2010.

17. "Tesla Motors; Panasonic invests $30 million in Tesla: Companies strengthen collaborative relationship," *Energy Weekly News,* November 19, 2010.

18. *Tesla Motors 2010 Annual Report* (Form 10-K), http://ir.teslamotors.com/secfiling.cfm?filingID=1193125-11-54847&CIK=1318605.

19. "Buyers loath to pay more for electric cars," *The Financial Times,* September 20, 2010.

20. "Tesla to release a Model S with 300-mile range," *The Oakland Tribune,* March 7, 2011.

21. www.wired.com/autopia/2009/05/daimler_tesla.

22. www.nytimes.com/2010/07/25/business/25elon.html?_r=1&adxnnl=1&adxnnlx=1281139208-CSLYpDV6HTnlBaA/DbnqUg.

23. "Top Gear, hot water," *The Daily Telegraph,* March 31, 2011.

24. "Tesla (TSLA) sues BBC's Top Gear for libel, falsehood in Roadster review," *StreetInsider.com,* March 30, 2011.

25. "Is divorce different for the rich?" *SmartMoney,* March 29, 2011.

26. "Elon Musk, of PayPal and Tesla fame, is broke," *DealBook, The New York Times,* June 22, 2010, http://dealbook.nytimes.com/2010/06/22/sorkin-elon-musk-of-paypal-and-tesla-fame-is-broke/.

27. "Tesla shares cruise after Obama backs clean-fuel cars," *Dow Jones News Service,* March 31, 2011.

28. "Morgan Stanley says Tesla Motors could become 'America's fourth automaker'; Shares jump," *Associated Press Newswires,* March 31, 2011.

29. "Tesla shares cruise after Obama backs clean-fuel cars."

30. "Morgan Stanley says Tesla Motors could become 'America's fourth automaker'; Shares jump."

31. "Tesla shares could reach $50 in 3 years – Analyst," *Reuters,* January 24, 2011.

32. "2nd update: Tesla shares rise after Obama backs clean-fuel cars," *Dow Jones News Service,* March 31, 2011.

33. "Tesla's future: Will another company be in the driver's seat?" *StreetInsider.com,* March 28, 2011.

34. "Tesla Motors CEO: 'We can succeed as an independent company,' Bloomberg says," *Theflyonthewall.com,* March 29, 2011.

Charlene Zietsma
The University of Western Ontario

Steve Parkhill was thinking about his options for growing Rogers' Chocolates (Rogers'). It was March 2007, and he had just started his new job as president of the company, after training with the former president for two months. The board of directors had asked him to double or triple the size of the company within 10 years. Each board member of the privately held company, and each member of the management team (most of whom also held shares), had a different idea about what Rogers' needed to do to achieve that growth. Parkhill needed to devise a strategy that would fit the company's culture, and then gain the support of the board, the management team and the employees.

The Premium Chocolate Market

The Canadian market size for chocolates was US$ 167 million in 2006 and it was projected to grow at 2 per cent annually.[1] The growth rate in the chocolate industry as a whole had been falling, however, so traditional manufacturers such as Hershey's and Cadburys were moving into the premium chocolate market through acquisitions or upmarket launches. The premium chocolate market was growing at 20 per cent annually,[2] as aging baby boomers purchased more chocolate and emphasized quality and brand in their purchases.

About one quarter of chocolate sales typically occur in the eight weeks prior to Christmas. Twenty per cent of "heavy users" accounted for 54 per cent of these pre-Christmas sales in 2006. These heavy users tended to be established families, middle aged childless couples and empty nesters with high incomes, and they tended to purchase more high quality boxed chocolate than bars or lower quality chocolate.[3] The margins in premium chocolate were much better than those in lower quality segments.

Purchasers were also demanding more from chocolate than taste. In line with a broad social trend for healthier diets, the demand for organic products, including organic chocolates was growing. Consumers looked for products with no trans fats.[4] Demand for dark chocolate, traditionally less popular than milk chocolate in North America, was growing in part because of its heart-healthy anti-oxidant properties. At the same time, however, larger chocolate manufacturers were seeking a redefinition of the term "chocolate" under USFDA guidelines, so that they could produce cheaper versions of the product and still call it chocolate.

Consumers and employees were also demanding that chocolate companies (like other companies) followed good corporate social responsibility practices. Environmental concerns, which were very strong in Victoria, influenced packaging, procurement and operational decisions. Human rights concerns were also high on the list for consumer expectations of chocolate companies, as forced labour and child labour were still used in some of the production of cocoa beans in West Africa. One customer email received by Rogers' read as follows:

> I am drawing the conclusion that Rogers' buys their raw product from West Africa. Rogers' is uninterested in making a real effort to eradicate this crisis. Furthermore, Rogers' is making contributions to the unethical side of the conflict and in so doing is endorsing the vile acts that continue to occur in West Africa. If any of my conclusions are incorrect, please let me know. I would appreciate it if you kept my email address on file and notified me if Rogers' begins to value the lives of people even though they are not potential consumers.

Competitors

Chocolate competitors in the premium chocolate segment in Canada featured strong regional brands plus a few larger players. Godiva, backed by Nestlé, had taken the business by storm with glitzy packaging, high price points, and widespread distribution among retailers of

 Ivey
Richard Ivey School of Business
The University of Western Ontario

Charlene Zietsma wrote this case solely to provide material for class discussion. The author does not intend to illustrate either effective or ineffective handling of a managerial situation. The author may have disguised certain names and other identifying information to protect confidentiality.

gift items. Godiva's quality was not as high as Rogers' but it was able to obtain about 15 per cent higher price points for standard products on the strength of its packaging, advertising and distribution. For truffle only collections and seasonal collections, the price points were often two to three times the price of Rogers' chocolates, though these featured exceptionally sleek and modern packaging, significant variations in chocolate molding, and chocolates of various colours.

Bernard Callebaut[5] was a premium chocolate producer out of Calgary that had begun to grow in similar locations to Rogers' (tourist and downtown retail), though it also had mall locations. There were 32 stores, mostly across the West, but with four in the United States and two in Ontario. The company's quality was good and it excelled in new flavour introductions, with an often seasonal influence. Callebaut's packaging was also superior with copper and gold boxes that could be customized for the consumer at the store, and great seasonal displays. Bernard Callebaut attracted similar price points to Godiva, but emphasized a retail strategy instead of a wholesale strategy, though bars for immediate consumption could be found in grocery outlets and other retailers.

Lindt was a large and well established Swiss chocolate producer that offered a large variety of chocolates and distributed them broadly in mass merchandisers, drug and grocery retailers. The product quality and packaging was mid-range and their pricing was about 90 per cent of Rogers' pricing. They emphasized bars and small bags of truffles for immediate consumption though they also produced gift boxes. They also produced the Ghirardelli brand, which was of higher quality but focused on pure chocolate squares.

Purdy's was a Vancouver based company that was 120 years old, and had been very successful with a variety of products, particularly its hedgehogs. Purdy's had over 50 locations, nearly all of which were based in malls. While they had stores nationally, their biggest and most successful presence was in British Columbia. Purdy's had tried to launch its products in Seattle, but had not done well there. Purdy's price point was significantly lower than Rogers' (about 35 per cent lower), and product quality level was also lower than Rogers', though still high. Their packaging and store displays were very good. Purdy's did a strong business in corporate gifts and group purchases, offering 20 per cent to 25 per cent discounts for high volume orders.

Other premium chocolate companies ranged from the extremely high end custom chocolatiers that carried a very small line of chocolates in exclusive packaging, and often produced custom orders, to Belgian producers that sold in Canada through established retailers or online, to niche players in single varietal bean chocolates or organic chocolates carried only at high end grocery or retail stores.

There were also companies that commanded price premiums over their quality level because of their distribution and/or store concept. For example, Laura Secord, which emphasized mall stores, and Rocky Mountain Chocolate Company, which sold more candy than chocolate and used a franchise model, had higher price points than Purdy's but lesser quality. Laura Secord had had several ownership changes over the last decade.

Rogers' Company History

Founded by Charles "Candy" Rogers in 1885, Rogers' Chocolates, based in Victoria, British Columbia (BC), was Canada's oldest chocolate company and British Columbia's second oldest company. After Charles's death, his wife ran the company until the late 1920s, when she sold the firm to a customer. Since then the company has changed hands three times. For the last two decades (during which time the company had grown sales by more than 900 per cent), the company had been owned by a private group comprised principally of two financial executives and partners with Connor, Clark & Lunn, a Vancouver-based investment firm; an art dealer and private investor; and a former owner of Pacific Coach Lines, a Victoria based bus company. These four plus a past president of Rogers' comprised the board of directors.

Current Operations

Rogers' head office was located above its flagship store in the Inner Harbour area of Victoria, near the world famous Empress Hotel. The head office consisted of a board room and offices for the management team. Those involved in production worked out of the factory about eight kilometres away, and the national wholesale sales manager worked in Kitchener, Ontario.

Rogers' main products were high-quality, hand-wrapped chocolates including its premiere line, the Victoria Creams, along with truffles, nuts and chews, almond bark, nutcorn and various assortments. In addition to pure milk chocolate, dark chocolate and white chocolate bars, and baking/fondue chocolate blocks, Rogers' also produced specialty items, such as chocolate-covered ginger, truffles, caramels, brittles and orange peel. Rogers' also produced no-sugar-added chocolates. Select Rogers' products are shown in Exhibit 1. The company also produced and sold a line of premium ice cream novelty items through its retail stores. Rogers' chocolates were of the highest quality, and the company had many loyal customers around the world. In 2006, the company won a prestigious 2006 Superior Taste Award from the International Taste & Quality Institute (ITQI), an independent organization of leading sommeliers, beverage experts and gourmet chefs, based in Brussels, Belgium. A company press release stated:

> "Classy, refined and elegant," were just a few of the words used to describe the 120-year-old company's chocolate line. The discerning panel of European chefs also identified the Rogers' assortment as a "top-of-the-range-product," filled with "abundant and rich chocolate aromas."[6]

PRODUCTION. Rogers' chocolates were produced in a 24,000-square-foot manufacturing facility on the outskirts of Victoria. There were about 110 non-unionized retail and production employees, with about 35 in production and the remainder in retail. Twenty employees worked seasonally in the two departments for the Christmas season. An additional 20 employees worked in management, administration and sales, as shown in the organization chart in Exhibit 2. Production, which took place on a one-shift operation (day shift), was labor-intensive, since most chocolates were handmade then hand-packed. Since there were so many different product offerings, most production consisted of batch processing, utilizing technology that had been used in the chocolate business for decades. Set-up times and equipment cleaning times were a significant component of costs, especially since they were required at the beginning and end of each eight-hour shift. To date, there had

EXHIBIT 1

Rogers' Products

Empress Squares

Dark Chocolate Almond Brittle

Marquis Assortment

Collectible Gift Tins

Fruit & Nut Collection

Ice Cream and Ice Cream Bars

EXHIBIT 2

Organization Chart

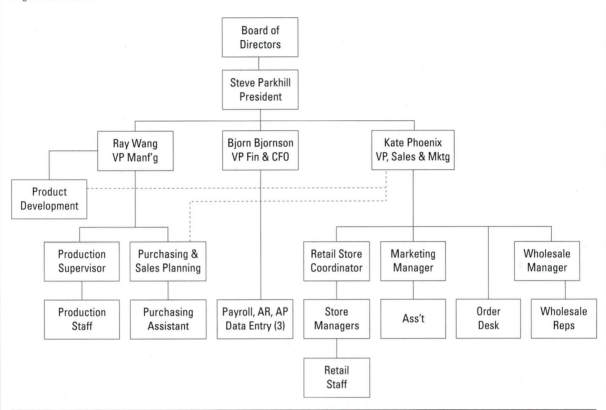

been no meaningful measures of productivity or efficiency in the plant, and thus no way of telling on a day to day basis if the plant was doing a good job.

Demand forecasting was difficult due to the seasonality of sales, but a long product shelf life (approximately six months) and a monthly sales forecast allowed Rogers' to deal with the ups and downs of sales patterns through healthy inventories kept on site. Nevertheless, the complicated nature of seasonal production created problems with out-of-stocks: souvenir items and ice cream were required in the spring and summer, then core Rogers' products and seasonal items were required for the fall and Christmas. The Christmas season was particularly chaotic, with 24 per cent of annual sales occurring in the eight-week run up to Christmas. Valentines and spring items were required for early January, which overlapped with the end of Christmas production. The wholesale business

required early production for seasonal needs, whereas the online and retail business required late production. Art tins used for chocolate assortments came from China, and some were season-specific. The Chinese supplier was sometimes unable to produce tins in a timely way due to lack of electricity. As soon as there were out-of-stocks for one product, the back order production of that product would throw the schedule off for the next product.

Production planning was made even more complicated by the impact of out-of-stocks on the historical information that was used to plan the following year's sales. For example, when an item was out of stock for a month, and the back orders were filled in a short period of time, the sales graph would be distorted with unnatural spikes; yet these spikes would be used for production planning for the following year. When there were over-stock problems on an item, the retail stores would push the items, sometimes discounting them, again creating distortions in the sales data, which would be replicated over time since that data would be used for production planning. Because the same process recurred for hundreds of items, these issues created significant havoc for production planning and inventory management. Ice cream presented a problem in that it was a new item (two years old), and it was difficult to predict sales volume accurately.

The out-of-stock issue was a major one for the company. Each week, numerous products were shorted. Because out-of-stocks in the wholesale channel created problems with customers, and because the previous president had favoured the wholesale channel, short supplies were diverted from the company's own stores and delivered to wholesalers. Furthermore, when a special order arrived in wholesale, it was not uncommon for the president to tell the plant to put production plans on hold to focus on the special order.

The plant was non-union, which was a direct reflection of the company's long history and strong family values. Some production workers were third-generation Rogers' employees. Employees were quite proud of the Rogers' heritage and commitment to quality and were quite passionate about the company. This passion sometimes created resistance to change: anything new caused concern that the company was compromising its values and its heritage. Employees learned multiple job functions and enjoyed a variety of work and tasks. Employees took great care in hand wrapping chocolates, folding the traditional gingham packaging "just so," and hand ribboning boxes, tins and bags. Several disabled people were employed in the plant, and Rogers' supported a local social service agency by allowing a group of brain-damaged individuals in every Friday to help with production. Turnover was low, and wages were competitive. Permanent employees were on a first-name basis with all of the senior leaders, including the president.

Markets

Rogers' currently earned revenues in four major areas: retailing chocolate products through company-owned stores, wholesaling chocolate products, online/mail order sales of chocolate products and sales from Sam's Deli, a well-known eatery in Victoria, which Rogers' had purchased in 2004.

RETAIL. Approximately 50 per cent of the company's sales came from Rogers' 11 retail stores. The stores featured Rogers' many products displayed attractively in glass cases, merchandised to suit the season, with an overall Victorian theme. Rogers' flagship store on Government Street had been designated a Heritage Site by Parks Canada. Uniformed sales staff offered chocolate samples to customers, and the aromas and images in the store contributed to an excellent retail experience. In 2000, Rogers' had won the Retail Council of Canada's Innovative Retailer of the Year award in the small business category, for demonstrating "outstanding market leadership and innovative approaches to customer and employee relations. Through creative ideas and strong delivery, the winning retailer has taken their brand to the top of their class."[7] Each of Rogers' retail stores, other than the factory store itself, was located in a tourist area, such as Whistler, Granville Island and Gastown, or at BC Ferry locations.[8]

Each store was wholly owned by Rogers'. Most were leased, with a minimum of a 10-year lease. The factory store and the downtown Victoria store were owned. The stores were typically about 500 square feet in size, with the exception of the ferry terminal locations, which were booths or catering wagons open on a seasonal basis and selling primarily ice cream. The ferry terminal locations were leased on an annual agreement basis, and rents were fixed as a percentage of sales. Although other retailers sold Rogers' Chocolates, they purchased the products wholesale through direct sales from Rogers'. Exhibit 3 shows the store locations and their approximate annual sales.

The Victoria stores could sell almost anything because of Rogers' positive brand image on the Island. They were often used to clear inventory problems. The two newest stores, Gastown and Granville Island in Vancouver, were showing steady sales growth in their first two years of operations, but were significantly shy of expectations. The Granville Island store was located next to the popular Arts Club Theatre, but it was, unfortunately, also behind several large metal refuse bins. Rogers' had waited a number of years for a location to open up on Granville Island, so although the present location wasn't perfect, it was the best that could be obtained. The Gastown store was in a good location, likely to attract considerable cruise ship business.

WHOLESALE. Approximately 30 per cent of sales came from wholesale accounts in five categories: 1) independent gift/souvenir shops, 2) large retail chains,

EXHIBIT 3

Retail Stores Sales in Fiscal 2007 (rounded to nearest thousand)

Store	Date Acquired	Approximate Annual Sales		Contribution Margin
Downtown Victoria	1885	$2,775,000		45.3%
Sam's Deli	2004	$1,598,000		8.9%*
Factory	1985	$726,000		36.7%
Granville Island	Dec. 2005	$686,000		(11.5%)
Whistler	1995	$639,000		8.2%
Tudor Sweet Shoppe	1983	$517,000		22.86%
Sidney	2003	$401,000		29.1%
Gastown	April 2006	$138,000		(22.3%)
Swartz Bay – BC Ferries	2000	$60,000	(Mostly ice cream)	15.5%
Departure Bay – BC Ferries	2006	$42,000	(All ice cream; summer only)	18.2%
Duke Point – BC Ferries	2005	$35,000	(All ice cream; summer only)	21.1%

*Reflects full cost of expenses to refurbish the store.

3) tourist retailers, such as duty-free stores, airport or train station stores and hotel gift shops, 4) corporate accounts that purchased Rogers' products for gifts for customers or employees and 5) a new segment, specialty high-end food retailers, such as Thrifty Foods on Vancouver Island, Sobeys in Western Canada, Sunterra in Alberta and Whole Foods in Toronto, Oakville and Vancouver. Some large accounts, such as the Bay, Crabtree & Evelyn and Second Cup, had been significant Rogers' customers, but had recently changed their purchasing to focus either on their own products or on less expensive lines. As a result, Rogers' wholesale sales had dropped over the last two years. Sales were strongest in BC, followed by Ontario. Sales in Alberta, Manitoba and Saskatchewan had increased very recently due to the Sobeys roll-out, but sales were weak in Quebec and the Maritimes.

The wholesale business was supported by a sales structure that included a salaried national sales manager based in Ontario, who had been with the company for eight years, and nine sales reps across Canada, of which eight were sales agents. The one salaried rep, who had been with the company for 10 years, was located on Vancouver Island. Currently, sales agents were in place in the following territories: Vancouver/Lower Mainland; Interior BC and Alberta; Saskatchewan and Manitoba; Northern Ontario; Niagara Falls and Metro Toronto; east of Toronto to Ottawa area; Quebec and the Maritimes.

Sales agents maintained independent businesses but made agreements with Rogers' to have exclusive rights to sell Rogers' products within a certain geographical territory. These agreements were not contracted, and thus they were open to review at any time. Generally, terminations were given 90 days' notice by either party. Many had been with the company as long as the previous president, who had established the wholesale division nearly two decades earlier. Rogers' sales agents typically carried several non-competing lines, such as maple syrup, gourmet condiments, plush toys, smoked salmon and kitchenware. A couple of sales agents were also customers as they also operated independent retail outlets that carried Rogers' Chocolates. Marketing Vice-President Kate Phoenix had the following to say about sales agents and the sales rep on Vancouver Island:

> Some perform very well. They cite many challenges with our brand—niche market, high prices, inadequate shelf life, old fashioned ("not glitzy or fashionable enough") packaging, and an unknown brand in many areas of Canada. We intend to introduce a "Tastes of Canada" product this year that we hope will play well to our wholesale and souvenir buyers.
>
> Some reps have other much stronger lines and just carry Rogers' as an add-on to their existing accounts,

which can be effective as their existing relationships with buyers gives us an "in" that a new salesperson would not have. The salaried rep on Vancouver Island receives a constant series of requests for our products, as it is our "home turf" and we do extensive advertising in our local market for our own stores. The brand is very well established and seen as a desirable product. In the Victoria area, some accounts will say they are honored to carry Rogers'. In other parts of Canada they have not heard of us and are dismissive of the products and their price points as they do not understand the brand and the value of the product. If the remote reps are not well trained, they just cannot present the brand adequately and sell it.

Similar to most gift products, retailers typically marked items up by about 100 per cent. Rogers' earned about half the gross margins on wholesale sales as it did on retail and online sales and the company paid its sales agents approximately 10 per cent commission. The salaried sales rep on the island earned a 1 per cent commission on sales above her salary, but benefited significantly from Rogers' high profile in Victoria, and the extensive advertising the company did there.

There were 585 active wholesale customers in 2006. Of those, 346 purchased less than $2000 per year. Of the 346, 221 purchased less than $1000 per year. Rogers' provided these smaller customers with the same level of service as other retailers, sometimes crediting them for stale stock, and paying the shipping expenses on orders of more than $350. There had been problems in the past with smaller accounts selling stock past its expiration date.

Some of the wholesale accounts ordered custom products, such as logo bars for special events. Rogers' would custom-produce molds, then chocolate bars for the customers featuring their logos. In the past, some regular customers had created problems by ordering with too little lead time, so the plant typically kept some logo bars in inventory for customers in anticipation of their orders.

ONLINE, PHONE AND MAIL ORDERS. A further 10 per cent of sales came from the company's online (approximately 4 per cent) and mail order (approximately 6 per cent) business. Sixty per cent of all orders were from regular customers. The average sale per phone or mail order was $138, while the average sale per website order was $91. Parkhill felt that online orders could be increased, since 30 per cent of men, and 18 per cent of women in Canada were shopping

online in 2006—these tended to be people in the 18–34 age group (44 per cent), while only 20 per cent of online purchasers were in the 35–54 age group.

Orders received by phone, mail or online were generally processed within three to four days, wrapped in attractive packaging, then shipped via FedEx in a sturdy outer box. In addition to the order, a separate thank you and confirmation letter from Rogers' was sent with a catalogue. In the summer, orders were shipped in insulated containers and packed with frozen ice packs. Shipping charges ranged from $10 for three- to five-day delivery within Canada and $15 to the United States for five-day shipping, to $42 for international air shipping, on products up to a $27 value. As the value of the product increased, shipping charges also increased: with product approaching $500, the costs were $18.50 within Canada for three- to five-day shipping, $37.50 to the United States and $122 internationally. For orders over $500, Rogers' paid the shipping charges.

Approximately 60 per cent of phone, mail and online sales were shipped to Canadian destinations, while 35 per cent went to the United States and 5 per cent shipped to 50 countries internationally. Many of the mail-order sales came from rural locations in Canada, where the mail-order tradition was strong. Rogers' chocolates were delivered to the far North, sometimes via dogsled, and were shipped to lighthouses on both coasts. Many of the rural mail-order customers placed very large orders.

Products ordered through the online and mail-order business were given priority for inventory allocation, and thus could usually be shipped within one or two working days. If there was a shortage of a particular product, its stock would be transferred back to the factory from the retail stores to meet mail-order commitments. The next priority for shipping was wholesale accounts, since wholesale back orders had to be shipped at Rogers' expense, and many accounts would not accept back orders. Yet, given that Rogers' margins on wholesale sales were much lower than in the retail business, this policy meant that sometimes a high-margin retail sale would be foregone for the much lower margins at wholesale.

SAM'S DELI. The remaining sales were generated from Sam's Deli, a cafeteria-style restaurant on the Inner Harbour in Victoria, between the Rogers' head office store and the Empress Hotel. Sam's Deli featured made-to-order sandwiches, soups and salads, desserts (many featuring Rogers' chocolate) baked on the premises or at the Rogers' chocolate factory, and wine and beer. Sam's had strong sales of ice cream as well. At lunchtime in the summer, the lineup regularly extended out the door.

Sam's Deli had been a Victoria institution for many years. Since Rogers' purchased it, most of the long-term staff had turned over, and recruiting new employees was difficult in Victoria's tight labour market. Sam's had had to curtail its evening hours of operations due to staff recruiting problems. Although Sam's had a liquor license, the volume of alcohol sold was very small. Parkhill felt that Sam's wasn't living up to its potential.

Marketing

TARGET MARKET. Since Rogers' chocolates were fairly expensive relative to others in the market (due to their quality ingredients and their hand packaging processes), the company targeted affluent customers looking for a luxury experience with a superior taste, or an elegant, prestigious and uncommon gift item. Many were cruise ship visitors and general tourists, though many locals were frequent visitors to the store and loyal to the brand. Some were huge spenders. Many local businesses also saw Rogers' as their corporate gift of choice. According to Phoenix:

> Our best and most loyal client base comes from customers (in all three sales channels) that have an emotional connection to Rogers'. For example, they were in the Victoria store on a holiday or a honeymoon, etc., or it was a traditional gift in their family. By tending this market carefully, it has grown. Many of those people then give Rogers' as a corporate gift or a personal gift to a substantial list and some of those recipients then become loyal customers. It's classic viral marketing.
>
> Other customers are affluent people who want to give something unique. They've found us on the Internet or in their travels and see us as an obscure but classic gift. What do rich people give each other as a present in this society of indulgence and privilege? Unique wines, flowers, a handmade cake or cookies from a remote little shop, or Rogers'!
>
> But how do you reach these people to promote to them? Advertising to this target is so expensive and they are scattered across Canada and USA predominantly and of course they are courted by every advertiser around so are ceasing to respond to advertising. The best way in our experience to sell to

them is not to make mistakes or disappoint them in any way. If you do, apologize and replace the product immediately—good old-fashioned service. This segment continues to grow for us.

Tourists often became mail-order or online customers—especially American tourists, since there were no American resellers. Happy customers from resellers often became mail-order or online customers as well since information about Web and mail-order sales was available in all packaging. Rogers' also had an easy-to-navigate website and a superior search engine ranking that attracted Web shoppers.

BRAND. The Rogers' brand had both significant strengths and some weaknesses. The brand was established around Rogers' long history, with traditional packaging, including pink or brown gingham-wrapped Victoria Creams, Chocolate Almond Brittle and Empress Squares. Chocolates were packed in Rogers' traditional burgundy box, a new gold box, or tins. Some tins featured old-fashioned scenes such as English roses, cornucopias or floral arrangements, while others featured Canadian art, particularly from the west coast. Chocolate and candy bars were also available, with a mixed variety of packaging. In the retail stores, individual chocolates could be purchased for immediate consumption or custom-packed into gift boxes to suit the buyers' tastes. Rogers' was a classic premium brand, Canadian and of high perceived value. Ingredients were mostly natural.

The brand had a very loyal following, particularly in the Victoria area. Parkhill described the brand perception:

> When I first began investigating Rogers', I asked everyone I knew what they thought of the brand. I received one of two reactions. People either said, "I've never heard of it," or they said "Oooooh, Rogers'. That is the best chocolate I've ever tasted," People would tell me stories about what Rogers' meant to them.
>
> It's become clear to me that the retail experience is key in creating the memories that lead to repeat sales. Through our store décor, sampling, aromas, taste and service, I think we are delivering "chocolate orgasms" to our customers.

If the company wanted to grow, it needed to become known more broadly. The challenge would be to increase awareness without diluting the brand with weak messaging or presentation to wholesale accounts, or without cheapening the product. The premium price scared some consumers and wholesale accounts away. Although those who knew the brand were willing to pay for the product, those who didn't know the brand were often unwilling to try it. Discounting the product, or developing cheaper products to piggyback on the brand, would risk destroying brand integrity.

An additional problem was associated with the traditional image of the brand. As Rogers' loyal customers aged, who would take their place? Younger buyers were less likely to be attracted by the traditional image of Rogers' brand. Developing an organic or fair trade product might be a possibility, but Rogers' chocolate supplier did not yet have organic or fair trade capabilities, and Rogers' was not large enough to pressure its supplier to change. Rogers' would also have to source organic versions of all the other ingredients. Phoenix identified with brands such as Chanel and Lancome, which had developed classic images and refused to compromise the brand, and brands such as Jaguar, Cadillac, BMW and Volvo, which had developed a younger, sexier image while maintaining core design elements to keep the integrity of the brand.

ADVERTISING. Rogers' used several types of advertising. To reach tourists, the company advertised in guide magazines, such as *WHERE;* in flyers available on the ferry boat brochure rack; in hotel magazines and in the *Enroute* magazine available on Air Canada flights. Seasonal print advertising, radio spots and a small amount of TV advertising (in Victoria only) were also used. Rogers' also donated product extensively to charitable events in its markets, and participated in promotional events; for example, Rogers' was the headline sponsor for the Arts Club Theatre, next door to the Granville Island store. Rogers' had also purchased a delivery truck for Victoria last year and covered it with advertising. Rogers' preferred to use advertising that served each of the three major channels; for example, the *Enroute* magazine advertisements promoted Rogers' stores, its wholesale accounts and its website to Air Canada flyers, a demographic with a large number of online shoppers. Direct mail and solid search engine rankings promoted the online business.

WEBSITE. Rogers' website was the key point of contact for the online business. It featured beauty shots of the different chocolate assortments, an easy ordering facility, a reminder service that emailed customers when a special occasion they had entered was upcoming, frequently updated online links and optimized search engine placement. The website also had links to resellers, which provided added value to those retailers and helped customers find the nearest location that carried Rogers' chocolates. However, the sales agents had not been prompt about responding to requests to provide links for their top accounts, as they did not seem to understand the value provided by such links.

Financials[9]

Rogers' was in a strong financial position. As a privately held firm, Rogers' was under less pressure than a public firm to manage shareholders' expectations. Therefore, many of its financial strategies were designed to minimize taxable earnings. Assets were depreciated as quickly as possible under the Canada Revenue Agency's guidelines.

Although Rogers' had gone through a period of significant growth just after the current shareholders acquired the company, growth had slowed considerably in the past few years. In part, this decline had resulted from the slowdown in tourism from the United States since September 11, 2001, and the subsequent decline in the U.S. dollar. In fact, chocolate sales had declined since 2004, though the company's revenues had grown slightly, due to the contributions of Sam's Deli. Margins remained strong, however, at about 50 per cent of sales on average. Financial statements are shown in Exhibits 4 to 7.

Leadership

Jim Ralph had been president and general manager of Rogers' from 1989 until 2007. It was his impending retirement that had launched the search for a new president. Ralph had been a well-networked sales manager in the gift business prior to his appointment as president, and as a result, he had grown Rogers' wholesale business during his tenure. Ralph arrived every morning at 5 a.m. and oversaw Rogers' operations closely.

When Ralph announced his intention to retire in 2005, the controlling shareholders (and board of directors) considered selling Rogers'. It was a healthy company with significant assets, great cash flow and good margins. Yet the board felt that Rogers' had significant potential to grow even more. They decided to hold onto the company and seek a leader who could take the company to the next level. They retained an executive recruitment firm, and the job ad shown in

EXHIBIT 4

Rogers' Chocolates Ltd. Consolidated Statement of Earnings and Retained Earnings

Year Ended March 31	2006	2005
Sales	$11,850,480	$11,991,558
Cost of sales		
Amortization of property and equipment	135,385	108,759
Direct labour	1,545,794	1,677,247
Direct materials	1,770,603	2,745,995
Overhead	1,933,306	846,186
	5,385,088	5,378,187
Gross profit	6,465,392	6,613,371
Interest income	664	1,610
	6,466,056	6,614,981
Expenses		
Interest on long term debt	91,465	86,943
Selling and administrative	5,221,520	5,007,145
	5,312,985	5,094,088
Earnings before income taxes	1,153,071	1,520,893
Income taxes	261,989	451,567
Net earnings	$891,082	$1,069,326
Retained earnings, beginning of year	$4,748,611	4,381,155
Net earnings	891,081	1,069,326
Dividends	–	(701,870)
Retained earnings, end of year	$ 5,639,692	$4,748,611

EXHIBIT 5

Rogers' Chocolates Ltd.—Schedule of Selling and Administrative Expenses

Year ended March 31		2006	2005
Selling	Advertising & promotion	$489,345	$536,886
	Bad debts	23,000	12,796
	Credit card charges	125,198	125,544
	Mail order	118,606	133,081
	Office & telephone	29,975	27,274
	Postage and freight	483,003	476,724
Stores:	Factory Store	112,885	122,897
	Sam's Deli	572,495	323,995
	Sidney	75,854	84,047
	Swartz Bay	42,709	38,592

(continued)

EXHIBIT 5 *(continued)*

Year ended March 31	2006	2005
The Bay Vancouver (closed in 2006)	3,938	4,058
The Bay Victoria (closed in 2006)	4,236	2,759
Tsawwassen	–	24,179
Tudor Sweet Shoppe	87,103	119,058
Whistler	168,157	182,939
Royalties	29,862	31,099
Salaries & benefits	812,269	715,325
Travel	68,364	46,830
Total	3,246,999	3,013,658
Less: postage and freight recoveries	343,116	369,823
	2,903,883	2,638,260
Admin Amortization	196,970	135,267
Automotive	28,658	24,404
Bank charges and interest	22,533	20,882
Consulting	102,241	107,379
Foreign exchange	−6,272	
Insurance	80,704	78,777
Management fees	191,226	183,627
Office supplies and postage	134,159	118,582
Professional fees	42,872	67,952
Rent, property taxes and utilities	61,211	56,815
Repairs and maintenance	18,378	21,105
Stores: Sam's Deli	326,901	179,834
Sidney	26,559	28,159
Swartz Bay	22,038	26,927
The Bay Vancouver	10,082	18,251
The Bay Victoria	32,123	37,939
Tsawwassen		14,647
Tudor Sweet Shoppe	49,849	45,002
Whistler	112,450	105,720
Salaries and benefits	810,049	1,030,336
Telecommunications	27,824	32,588
Travel and promotion	27,082	34,692
Total Admin Expenses	$2,317,637	$2,368,885
TOTAL S, G & A Expenses	$5,221,520	$5,007,145

EXHIBIT 6

Rogers' Chocolates Ltd.—Consolidated Balance Sheet

March 31	2006	2005
Assets		
Current		
Cash	$ 112,185	$ 750,948
Receivables	358,969	461,874
Inventories		
Packaging materials	620,452	576,287
Raw materials	169,235	179,119
Work in progress	89,146	66,467
Manufactured finished goods	643,105	692,517
Finished goods for resale	21,878	36,241
	1,543,816	1,550,631
Investments	103,136	76,822
Income taxes receivable	127,515	–
Prepaids	84,620	56,566
	2,330,241	2,896,842
Property and equipment (see Note 1)	4,364,527	3,922,183
Intangible assets		
Goodwill	916,999	916,999
Trademarks	783,596	783,596
Total intangible assets	1,700,595	1,700,595
TOTAL ASSETS	$ 8,395,363	$ 8,519,620
Liabilities		
Current		
Bank indebtedness	$ 186,929	$ 599,146
Payables and accruals	1,098,232	1,226,570
Income taxes payable	-	127,845
Current portion of long term debt	419,971	373,405
	1,705,132	2,326,966
Long term debt	1,017,679	1,411,184
TOTAL LIABILITIES	2,722,811	3,738,150
Shareholders' Equity		
Capital stock	32,860	32,860
Retained earnings	5,639,691	4,748,611
TOTAL EQUITY	5,672,551	4,781,471
TOTAL LIABILITIES & EQUITY	$ 8,395,362	$ 8,519,621

(continued)

EXHIBIT 6   *(continued)*

Note 1

Property and equipment			2006	2005
	Cost	Accumulated Amortization	Net Book Value	Net Book Value
Land	1,219,819.20	–	1,219,819.20	1,219,819.20
Buildings	2,799,181.35	1,099,926.90	1,699,254.45	1,770,056.19
Manufacturing equipment	1,693,140.69	1,375,596.00	317,544.69	231,858.99
Furniture and fixtures	749,496.78	385,684.35	363,812.43	249,376.83
Office equipment	108,352.86	90,299.22	18,053.64	24,020.76
Computer equipment	250,683.90	225,157.26	25,526.64	53,214.81
Leasehold improvements	914,332.83	193,817.19	720,515.64	373,836.12
	7,735,007.61	3,370,480.92	4,364,526.69	3,922,182.90

EXHIBIT 7

Rogers' Chocolates Ltd.—Consolidated Statements of Cash Flows

Year Ended March 31	2006	2005
Increase (decrease) in cash and cash equivalents		
Operating		
Net earnings	$891,081	$1,069,326
Amortization	332,355	244,026
	1,223,436	1,313,352
Change in non-cash oper. working capital	(328,344)	350,045
	895,092	1,663,397
Financing		
(Repayments of) advances from LT debt	(349,168)	661,806
Dividends paid	–	(701,870)
	(349,168)	(40,064)
Investing		
Purchase of assets of Sam's Deli	–	(1,198,500)
Purchase of property and equipment	(772,470)	(419,307)
	(772,470)	(1,617,807)
Net (decrease) increase in cash and cash equivalents	(226,546)	5,526
Cash and cash equivalents, beginning of year	151,802	146,276
Cash and cash equivalents, end of year	$74,744	$151,802
Comprised of:		
Cash	$112,185	$750,948
Bank indebtedness	(186,929)	(599,146)
	$74,744	$151,802

Exhibit 8 was posted on www.workopolis.com. In the two years during the search, managers were aware that Ralph was retiring, and significant decisions were put off until a new leader could be found.

A friend of Steve Parkhill saw the ad and thought it fitted Parkhill perfectly. Parkhill agreed. At the time, he was vice-president of operations for Maple Leaf Foods, in charge of six plants and approximately 2,300 employees. Previously, Parkhill had been president of a seafood company and general manager of a meat processing subsidiary. His career had involved stints in marketing and sales in addition to operations, and he had an MBA from the Richard Ivey School of Business. Parkhill was known as an exceptional leader with an empowering style and significant personal integrity. He missed the strategy involved in his general management days and was looking for a smaller company to settle into: the west coast was very appealing. After several rounds of interviews, Parkhill was offered the position, and he accepted with excitement. Both Parkhill and the board of directors agreed that the position was intended to be a long-term one—10

EXHIBIT 8

Workopolis Job Ad

A unique company........ a unique location........... a unique opportunity.

Our client, one of Canada's oldest and respected confectionery companies, is seeking a **PRESIDENT** to oversee the entire business on a day-to-day basis, and provide the vision and guidance for long-term success and profitable growth.

Reporting to the Board of Directors, the President will:

>> Deliver superior results and guide the organization to improve.

>> Develop formal planning systems and ongoing personnel development.

>> Oversee the development of business and marketing strategies to maintain market leadership.

>> Provide the necessary leadership to motivate and transform the organization to meet growth expectations.

>> Leads, protects and reinforces the positive corporate culture, and is the overseer of the ethics and values in the organization.

An executive level compensation plan commensurate with the importance of this role is offered.

An opportunity that blends an executive level position with the lifestyle only Victoria can offer.

CANDIDATE PROFILE:
Given the high levels of autonomy and accountability, the President must display considerable maturity and business experience.

From a personal perspective, the ideal candidate will be:

>> A strong non-authoritative team builder.

>> A highly motivated and results oriented self-starter.

>> Extremely, customer, quality and safety oriented.

>> People oriented with the innate ability to establish a high degree of credibility.

>> Capable of providing objective insight in a non-confrontational manner.

The successful candidate will likely be or have been in one of the following positions in a manufacturing environment:

>> President or General Manager

>> At a VP level in operations/finance/marketing looking to rise to the next level

While food manufacturing experience would be a clear asset, it is not a pre-requisite.

years or more. To that end, the offer had a provision requiring Parkhill to purchase a significant number of shares in the company each year for the first three years, with an option to increase his holdings further after that.

The senior management team included three others. Kate Phoenix, vice-president of Sales and Marketing and a Rogers' employee since 1994, managed the retail outlets, developed marketing plans and oversaw the online and wholesale businesses, as well as Sam's Deli. She was also responsible for the ice cream business. She supervised the wholesale sales manager, the retail operations manager, a communications manager and the order desk staff. The product development person and purchasing and sales planning person also reported indirectly to Phoenix, though they worked more directly with Ray Wong. Phoenix worked long hours at the office, had regularly helped out at Sam's Deli during short staff situations, and often drove product around to stores on the weekends when they ran out or were short-shipped by the factory. Before coming to Rogers', Phoenix had been an independent systems consultant, and had served as director, information systems and distribution, and assistant divisional manager, retail operations for Gidden Industries. Phoenix was a shareholder in the company.

Ray Wong, vice-president of production, oversaw production and worked at the factory. Wong completed a Bachelor of Food Science from the University of Alberta in 1978, and later took courses in material requirements planning, candy-making, ice-cream making and management. He had worked in progressively responsible operations positions in a variety of food and beverage companies prior to joining Rogers' in 1990. Wong did not own shares in the company. Wong was especially interested in computer programming, and he had developed all of Rogers' internal production planning systems himself.

Bjorn Bjornson, vice-president of Finance and chief financial officer, had retired as chief financial officer of Pacific Coach Lines in 1991, but joined Rogers' in 1997 at the urging of his former partner, who was on Rogers' board. Previously, Bjornson had worked in financial management in manufacturing and retail after articling as a chartered accountant with Price Waterhouse. Bjornson's expertise was in reorganizations, acquisitions and dispositions. He maintained Rogers' books by hand, as he had never learned accounting or spreadsheet software programs. Bjornson owned shares in the company.

Phoenix and Bjornson were a cohesive team. In the past, there had been conflict between marketing and production, as marketing sought to reduce out of stocks and launch new products, while production sought to retain control of its own scheduling and production processes. Conflict between Phoenix and Wong had escalated to the board level during the past two years of uncertainty. Furthermore, because the wholesale division was favoured by the past president, the wholesale manager in Kitchener had regularly gone over Phoenix's head to have the president overturn her decisions. Phoenix had indicated significant frustration with her job.

Growth Opportunities

During the recruitment process, and in his first few months on the job, Parkhill had been probing the managers and board members to get their perspectives on growth options. There was a dizzying array of options. One board member, who was very well connected in the tourism business in Victoria, had said Rogers' approach to cruise ship traffic needed to be reconsidered. Although for years Rogers' had counted on cruise ship passengers for business, representatives from Victoria's Butchart Gardens now boarded the cruise ships in San Francisco, and promoted bus tours from the ship north to Butchart Gardens in Victoria. Many of the passengers were thus no longer going downtown.

The idea of franchising Rogers' outlets had been discussed but not truly investigated, because the board was concerned about giving up control of the brand and pricing. Parkhill had visited a store in Banff that had a Rogers' chocolate store attached to a larger gift store. Yet the store was not owned or franchised by Rogers': the gift store had merely displayed the Rogers' chocolates in a separate area for their own purposes. Others who purchased Rogers' chocolates wholesale merely displayed Rogers' merchandise along with their regular merchandise. For example, the Kingsmill's department store in London, Ontario, carried Rogers' chocolates in its food section. Of course, it might also be possible to franchise Sam's Deli.

The online business also appeared exciting. With low costs of sales and no intermediaries, the profits on the online business were exceptional. With such a high reorder rate, the chance to build a loyal following of online customers seemed like a sure winner.

The corporate gift market also seemed promising. Offering discounts of 25 per cent to corporate purchasers enabled Rogers' to still earn stronger margins than wholesale, without the costs of retail. Furthermore, corporate gifting expanded trial of the product.

There were many other possibilities for growth. The Olympics were coming to Vancouver and Whistler in 2010, promising a huge boon for BC tourism. Although Rogers' wasn't big enough to gain official Olympic status, it needed a strategy to take advantage of the crowds. With two stores in Vancouver, and one in Whistler, Rogers' should be able to generate increased sales. Should Rogers' obtain more stores in Vancouver? Or should Rogers' extend its product line to take advantage of its strong franchise in British Columbia? Although ice cream had not been the runaway success the company had hoped, its sales were still building. Rogers' had a sugar-free chocolate line that served a small but growing market.

Another option might be for Rogers' to concentrate its efforts outside of BC. If American tourists had stopped coming to Victoria, due to the decline in the American dollar, should Rogers' go to them? Should Rogers' attempt to increase its penetration in Ontario or other parts of Canada? Should Rogers' attempt to extend its wholesale distribution outside of British Columbia? Would the current sales agency structure be appropriate for increased penetration? Should Rogers' consider an acquisition of another niche chocolate company or a joint venture with another firm to increase its geographical reach? Were there opportunities to pair Rogers' chocolates with other high end products or brands for mutual benefit?

There was also the issue of the brand image. While Rogers' traditional image was treasured by loyal customers and employees alike, it didn't seem to play as well outside of Victoria. The packaging had been described as homey or dowdy by some, yet others were adamant that it should not be changed. Parkhill had spoken to a brand image consultant that had won numerous awards in the wine industry for the spunky brands he had designed. The consultant had suggested that the only dangerous thing in today's market was to play it safe—consumers loved edgy brands. Should Rogers' throw off tradition and try to reinvent itself?

Of course, if sales were to be increased, Rogers' would need more internal capacity to produce products and fill orders. Should more capacity be added in Victoria, with its expensive real estate and significant shipping costs to get product off the island, or should it be placed somewhere with lower costs and easier access to markets?

As Parkhill pondered all these options, he also knew that he had to take into consideration the culture of the organization and the desires of the board of directors and owners. Would the current managers and employees be willing and able to grow the organization? Would the board endorse a growth strategy that would increase the risk profile of the company? And with all these options, what should Rogers' do first?

Endnotes

1. P. M. Parker, "The World Outlook for Chocolate and Chocolate Type Confectionery," INSEAD, http://www.market-research. com/, February 20, 2007.

2. S. David. Sprinkle, The U.S. Chocolate Market, Packaged Facts. New Orleans: MarketResearch.com, 2005.

3. Company insider citing a presentation by Neilson at the Confectionery Manufacturer's Association of Canada conference, 2007.

4. Rogers' was one of the first chocolate companies to announce a trans-fat free product line.

5. Note that Bernard Callebaut was not the same as the international chocolatier, Callebaut.

6. "Canadian Chocolate Legend Receives Taste Award from Top European Chefs," Press Release, May 9, 2006, available at www.rogerschocolates.com/archives, accessed December 21, 2006.

7. From www.retailcouncil.org/awards/rcc/innovative, accessed December 7, 2006.

8. The Whistler store was at the world-class Whistler ski area. Gastown and Granville Island were tourist attractions in Vancouver.

9. Since Rogers' is a privately held company, all financial figures in the case are disguised.

What then is intelligence such that brains have it but computers don't?
Why can a six-year-old hop gracefully from rock to rock in a streambed while the most advanced
robots of our time are lumbering zombies?...
Why can you tell a cat from a dog in a fraction of a second while a supercomputer cannot make
that distinction at all?

—JEFF HAWKINS, *ON INTELLIGENCE*

Frank T. Rothaermel
Georgia Institute of Technology
Wei Zhang
Georgia Institute of Technology
Marne L. Arthaud-Day
Kansas State University

A SMALL COMPUTER SITS on top of a soldier's backpack. It alerts him when it detects anything suspicious, playing the role of night-vision goggles combined with radar, and providing 360-degree long-range coverage. So far, this scenario is possible only in video games like Call of Duty or Halo 3. But with Hierarchical Temporal Memory (HTM), a cutting-edge, pattern-recognition software developed by Numenta, such equipment may soon become reality.

HTM is the culmination of Jeff Hawkins's lifelong quest to understand how the brain works. A successful serial entrepreneur, Hawkins founded Palm Computing in 1992, followed by Handspring in 1998. He is credited with bringing to market devices like the Palm Pilot, Treo smartphone, and Palm Pre. These significant technological breakthroughs paved the way for today's ubiquitous iPhones and BlackBerrys. Next, Hawkins continued his pursuit of "smart" computing by founding the Redwood Neuroscience Institute (RNI) in 2002. RNI is a nonprofit organization devoted to developing "biologically accurate and mathematically well-founded models of memory and cognition."[1]

In March 2005, Hawkins partnered with Dileep George and Donna Dubinsky to form Numenta, a startup company whose objective is to maximize the impact of Hawkins's HTM technology.[2] HTM is based on Hawkins's theory of the brain, which he published, with Sandra Blakeslee, in his 2004 book *On Intelligence*. HTM is an intelligent software platform designed to process information in the same way as the neocortex, the area of the human brain responsible for sensory perception, motor control, spatial reasoning, conscious thought, and language.[3] Hawkins believes that HTM can be used to create "thinking machines" with a wide array of applications in fields such as security and monitoring, energy management systems, digital pathology, web-based analytical tools, and the detection of financial fraud.

Given Hawkins's legendary reputation, many people in Silicon Valley speculate that HTM will be hugely successful. Many even wonder if HTM will become the standard for intelligent computing, much like how Microsoft became the industry standard for PC operating systems. But whether Jeff Hawkins will be able to successfully commercialize this new technology is an important question. How can he translate HTM into business opportunities and grow the company while keeping away competitors like IBM? Should Numenta continue to "go it alone" with its current licensing strategy? How long can Hawkins continue to fund this venture without receiving outside financing of some kind? Whether that should come in the form of venture capital, an IPO, a strategic alliance, or even an acquisition is a dilemma for Hawkins and Numenta.

Professor Frank T. Rothaermel, Wei Zhang (GT PhD in Bioengineering), and Professor Marne L. Arthaud-Day prepared this case from public sources without the collaboration of Numenta. This case is developed for the purpose of class discussion. It is not intended to be used for any kind of endorsement, source of data, or depiction of efficient or inefficient management. © Rothaermel, Zhang, and Arthaud-Day, 2013.

Hawkins's Quest to Discover How the Brain Works

Hawkins's interest in the brain started when he was a teenager. When young Jeff wanted to understand something, he would go to the library and find a book that explained it. He could almost always find at least some information on whatever topic interested him. Surprisingly, he found no theories, good or bad, on how the brain works. It bothered him that people had no idea how this master organ functioned.[4]

CHILDHOOD DREAM REKINDLED. In September 1979, three months after he graduated from Cornell University with a degree in electrical engineering, Jeff Hawkins's interest in brain theory was rekindled. Working as a junior engineer at Intel (which was then merely 11 years old), he came across a newly published issue of *Scientific American* dedicated entirely to the brain. To many aspiring neuroscientists, including Hawkins, it was "one of the best *Scientific American* issues of all time."[5] Hawkins thought the most intriguing article was the final one, "Thinking about the Brain," written by Francis Crick who, with James D. Watson, discovered the double-helix structure of DNA. Hawkins later described this eureka moment as follows:

> Crick argued that in spite of a steady accumulation of detailed knowledge about the brain, how the brain worked was still a profound mystery. Scientists usually don't write about what they don't know, but Crick didn't care. He was like the boy pointing to the emperor with no clothes. According to Crick, neuroscience was a lot of data without a theory. His exact words were, "What is conspicuously lacking is a broad framework of ideas." To me this was the British gentleman's way of saying, "We don't have a clue how this thing works." It was true then, and it is still true today.[6]

When he finished reading, Hawkins put down the magazine and thought to himself, "I have to work on this." He believed that once he understood how the brain worked, he would be able to build more-intelligent machines. Hawkins decided to pitch his idea to his current employer, the company that invented memory chips and microprocessors. He wrote a letter to Gordon Moore, Intel's co-founder, asking permission to start a research group—even if Hawkins was the only member—that would focus on understanding how the brain works.[7]

Moore referred Hawkins to Intel's chief scientist, Ted Hoff, who was an avid researcher in neural network theory and had a long history working with artificial neurons. After listening to Hawkins's proposal, Hoff responded, "No, I know all about brains, you are never going to succeed."[8] Hoff simply did not believe anyone could work out brain theory "in the foreseeable future."[9] While Hoff's assessment that brain theory was nowhere near advanced enough to be useful for commercial application was correct, the young and eager Hawkins was still disappointed.

Not one to give up easily, Hawkins decided to pursue his passion by enrolling in a doctoral program at MIT, a hotbed for artificial intelligence (AI) research. According to John McCarthy, who coined the term in 1956, artificial intelligence "is the science and engineering of making intelligent machines, especially intelligent computer programs."[10] A machine is considered intelligent when it can "successfully pretend to be human to a knowledgeable observer."[11] Hawkins was hoping to find someone who would be interested in brain theory. When he went to MIT to interview, however, he was surprised to learn that the MIT computer scientists believed brains were just messy computers and there was nothing to be learned by studying them. Hawkins's application to MIT's doctoral program in computer science was rejected.

Jeff Hawkins continued to work at Intel, where he taught courses on microprocessor design and trained field applications engineers. He finally left Intel for GRiD Systems in 1982, looking for an atmosphere that offered more room for growth and influence. GRiD, which was founded in 1979 and went public in 1981, was exactly such a place.[12] In 1982, GRiD scientists invented the first clamshell laptop computer, the GRiD Compass.[13] One of the first things Hawkins created was GRiDTask, a high-level programming language optimized for creating applications on GRiD's laptops. "GRiDTask and I became more and more important to GRiD's success,"[14] said Hawkins.

BIOPHYSICS STUDENT AT UC-BERKELEY. Although Hawkins's career was going well, his desire to pursue brain theory persisted. Thus, after seven years of working in the computing industry, Hawkins enrolled in the biophysics doctoral program at the University of California, Berkeley, in January 1986. He explained, "Well, if I cannot do it in the computer science world, I figure I will do it in the neuroscience world."[15] His creative value was so rare that GRiD offered him a leave of absence with the option to return at any time with the same salary, position, and even stock options.

Hawkins was excited to be a graduate student, immersing himself in hundreds of papers by anatomists, physiologists, philosophers, linguists, computer scientists, and psychologists. A year into his doctoral studies, he wrote his PhD thesis proposal on a theoretical mathematical approach to understanding the neocortex. However, because no one on the faculty would sponsor his research, Hawkins's thesis proposal was rejected. While at Berkeley, Hawkins also wrote a pattern-classifier program based on his theory of auto-associative memories, which he later patented and developed into a handprinted-character recognizer. This was the predecessor to the handwriting recognition software Grafitti, which runs on today's Palm operating system.

After the second failed attempt to study brain theory, Hawkins did some major soul searching. He decided to return to GRiD and do four things:

> One thing I decided to do was that I am going to mature and learn how to make institutional change . . . how to influence people, how to make people change ideas and so on. . . . I am going to work on that. The second thing was that I have to make a name for myself. If people respect me, they will listen more to me. . . . The third thing I want to do is to make some money. I need to raise my family. . . . I may need to fund my research down the road . . . The last thing, let the neuroscience mature.[16]

Back at GRiD, Hawkins continued to work on product design. Although GRiD gave him a VP title, he had no direct reports. GRiD told him just to do whatever he wanted as long as he created new ideas that were commercially viable. And so he created GRiDPAD, the first tablet laptop computer.[17]

Jeff Hawkins: Serial Entrepreneur

While working at GRiD, Hawkins realized that a handheld computer that serves the consumer market could be a huge business opportunity. Despite the failure of Apple's Newton, Hawkins strongly believed that in the future everyone was going to have a personal computer that fit into their pocket. He thought to himself, "The personal (mobile) computer will become the primary computing device for everybody. This is inevitable. But I am going to make it happen sooner!"[18]

However, his idea seemed too risky to GRiD because of the company's focus on the GRiDPAD and the vertical application of laptops. As a consequence, Hawkins left GRiD and started his first new venture, Palm Computing.

PALM COMPUTING AND PALM PILOT. Hawkins recruited Donna Dubinsky, a Harvard MBA who had previously worked for Apple, to run Palm's day-to-day business, which freed him to focus solely on new-product development. Yet despite their combined expertise, Palm Computing was not an immediate success. After several initial product failures, Hawkins went back to the drawing board and came up with a completely different design, something small and simple. After talking to customers who had bought the Newton, Hawkins realized that the initial mobile devices needed to compete with paper-based planning systems and not full-blown personal computers. He also learned that Palm Computing would have to build everything—the hardware, the handwriting recognition software, the operating system, synchronization—and integrate the pieces.

But there was a major obstacle to commercializing the new "Palm Pilot": The company had only $3 million left, which was not enough to bring the product to market. Therefore, Hawkins sold the company for $44 million to U.S. Robotics in 1995.[19] The entire Palm team stayed on because they all felt passionate about the future of mobile computing. The Palm Pilot was brought to market in early 1996 and turned out to be a huge success.

In 1997, 3Com acquired U.S. Robotics. Dissatisfied with the direction that Palm was going under 3Com's management, Jeff Hawkins and Donna Dubinsky requested that 3Com spin out Palm as an independent company. When 3Com refused to do so, Hawkins and Dubinsky left Palm in the summer of 1998. Hawkins believes that "if they [3Com] had spun us out, I'd still be there."[20] (3Com eventually did spin out Palm in the summer of 2000. In the spring of 2010, HP acquired 3Com for $2.7 billion and Palm for $1.2 billion.)

HANDSPRING AND TREO. Hawkins and Dubinsky almost immediately formed a new company, Handspring, with the intent of advancing handheld computing technology to a higher level. With venture capital from firms such as Benchmark Capital and QUALCOMM, they launched their first product, the Visor, in late 1999. The Visor's Springboard expansion slot created an open platform that radically expanded its functionality, while maintaining compatibility with the PalmOS software that Handspring leased from its primary competitor. Developers quickly came up with modules that included features such as MP3 players, wireless communications, global positioning systems, and digital photography.

Handspring held a successful IPO in 2000, and introduced its next-generation Treo in 2001.[21] The Treo was among the earliest smartphones, with an integrated cellular phone and built-in keyboard to enhance e-mail and SMS capabilities. Handspring merged with the hardware division of Palm in 2003, and was renamed palmOne, Inc.[22] As Handspring was being folded into Palm, Hawkins knew it was time for him to go back to his "brain dream."

REDWOOD NEUROSCIENCE INSTITUTE. It had been almost 25 years since the young Hawkins was inspired by *Scientific American* to study how the brain worked. After being rebuffed repeatedly from academic institutions, Hawkins realized that the only way to advance brain theory was to start his own research institute. Thus, in 2002, Jeff Hawkins founded the nonprofit Redwood Neuroscience Institute (RNI), his third new venture. Located in Menlo Park, California, RNI was a single-task scientific organization, devoted to understanding how the human neocortex processes information.[23] The institute's structure was based on a combination of corporate and scientific principles, and grew to 10 full-time employees under Hawkins's leadership.

As the inventor of the Palm Pilot and the Treo, Hawkins was elected to the National Academy of Engineering in 2003.[24] Already a legend in the computer industry, Hawkins made his mark on neuroscience when he published his book, *On Intelligence,* describing his "memory prediction framework" of how brains work. The book was highly acclaimed, selling millions of copies around the world with translations in 16 languages. In it, Hawkins proposed a single principle or algorithm underlying all cortical information processing. While there are different regions in the neocortex that are linked to different functions (e.g., visual or auditory), they are remarkably similar in their structure. The only thing that makes the visual region different is that it is connected to the eyes and not the ears.

One of the first major breakthroughs at RNI was the creation of a proof-of-concept program for Hawkins's memory prediction theory. Dileep George, then a graduate student in electrical engineering at Stanford University, turned Hawkins's neuroscience theory into a mathematical algorithm for his dissertation research. The algorithm was then transformed into computer software,[25] resulting in the development of a machine-based learning model called hierarchical temporal memory (HTM). George's research made the operationalization of Hawkins's brain theory possible.

Hawkins's Fourth Venture—Numenta

RNI made so much progress on neocortical theory that Hawkins moved RNI to the University of California–Berkeley to continue its neuroscience research,[26] and founded Numenta in 2005 to commercialize the HTM technology. Dileep George joined the Numenta managerial team as co-founder and chief technology officer, after graduating from Stanford. (In May 2010, Dileep George went on "an extended leave of absence from Numenta to explore forming a new company focused on applications.")[27]

To run Numenta, Hawkins brought in long-time business partner Donna Dubinsky as chief executive officer and board chair. Ms. Dubinsky had spent 10 years at both Apple Computer and Claris, a software subsidiary of Apple, where she gained formidable experience in operations and strategy. The Dubinsky–Hawkins business partnership is a powerful team with a proven entrepreneurial track record (i.e., Palm and Handspring). "With the combination of Donna at the helm and Jeff leading the technology—that's about all I needed to know," says Mr. Saal, investor and a member of Numenta's board of directors.[28] Numenta also has a strong technical advisory board comprised of leading scholars in developmental biology, computer science, neuroscience, and electrical engineering.

Numenta's headquarters is in Redwood City, California, at the center of Silicon Valley, one of the world's leading high-tech hubs and home to a large number of cutting-edge entrepreneurs, engineers, and venture capitalists. Numenta is also surrounded by world-class research universities (e.g., Stanford and UC-Berkeley), providing the company with access to a large pool of talented scientists. Thus, Numenta's location provides it with multiple opportunities for increasing its innovative potential.[29] (See Exhibit 1 for a map of companies located in Silicon Valley.)

EXHIBIT 1

Companies in Silicon Valley

Source: www.siliconmaps.com/Silicon_Valley_10.html.

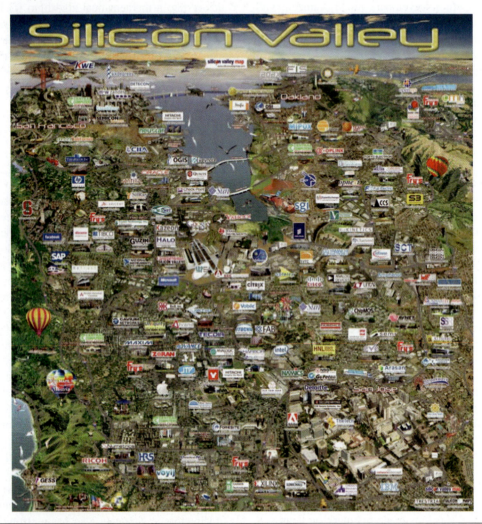

HIERARCHICAL TEMPORAL MEMORY. HTM's way of building an intelligent machine is fundamentally different from the approach taken by artificial intelligence. AI makes the assumption that intelligence is defined by behavior;[30] it can be likened to a box where inputs (data) go in and behavior comes out. According to Hawkins, however, real intelligence is defined not by behavior but by the ability to make accurate predictions about the future (see Exhibit 2):

> We experience the world as a sequence of patterns, and we store them and we recall them. When we recall them we match them up with reality and we are making predictions all the time. Assume some-

one changes your door at home and moves your door knob by two inches. When you get home you put your hand out and reach for the door knob, you will notice it at the wrong spot. The AI people approach this by building a door database which has all the door attributes. This is not how we humans do it. What the brain does is that it is making constant predictions all the time. As you put your hand down on the table you expect to feel it stop. When you walk, even if you miss by 1/8th of an inch, you will know something is changed. You are constantly making predictions about your environment all the time. It is the prediction that leads to intelligent behavior . . .[31]

EXHIBIT 2

Comparison of AI and Hawkins's Real Intelligence

Source: Adapted from Jeff Hawkins, "Brain science is about to fundamentally change computing," www.youtube.com/watch?v=G6CVj5IQkzk.

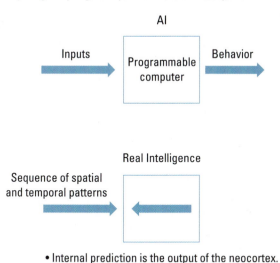

- Internal prediction is the output of the neocortex.
- Prediction leads to intelligent behavior.

In other words, AI attempts to anticipate every single data permutation, and thus requires an extremely large knowledge database. Constructing such databases is a time- and labor-intensive process, compounded by problems such as how to collect the data and organize it in useful ways. It also takes millions of lines of computer code for AI to model human intelligence. HTM solves the efficiency problem, one of the biggest obstacles faced by AI, by using data from the past to make predictions about the future.

Hawkins further explains the difference between AI and HTM by comparing reptiles to mammals: An alligator has very complex behavior including running, sensing, seeing, hearing, and touching. It has a brain, which Hawkins calls the *old brain,* but it is not considered intelligent. Through evolution, however, mammals developed the neocortex, which is a new (memory) layer on top of the old (sensory) brain. As a sensory signal feeds into the old brain, it also goes up into the neocortex where it is stored in memory. In the future when a person experiences similar things again, the neocortex plays back the stored memories, informing the person what to expect next. Hawkins provides an illustrative example: "A rat runs into a maze and learns the maze. The next time it gets into the maze it still has the same behavior but all of a sudden it is smarter because it recognizes the maze and knows which way to go."[32]

HTM accomplishes this by feeding the system with information and letting it learn by itself through observations, just as a child learns by observing the world around her (Exhibit 3). Modeled after the structure and algorithms of the neocortex, HTM consists of a collection of nodes arranged in an inverted tree-shaped hierarchy (Exhibit 4, next page). Each node in the hierarchy performs two basic operations: (1) It looks for common spatial patterns, things that happen at the same time, and (2) it observes their sequences over time. Once it recognizes a sequence from prior experience, the node passes the name of that sequence to its parent node in the level above. Meanwhile, the parent nodes are doing the same thing, passing the recognized sequences up to the next highest level. Each node also knows statistically what is likely to happen next, enabling it to make predictions. It passes these predictions down the hierarchy, telling the respective child nodes, "Here is what you should be expecting next."

Take vision as an example. Input patterns begin at the low-level retinal signals. More meaningful information, such as lines and regions, is extracted further up the hierarchy. At even higher levels, specific objects and their behaviors are identified. Once the inputs are fully processed, information about the recognized objects and prediction of their behavior over time flows back down to lower levels. Hawkins argues that this process is nature's data structure for knowledge about the world: "If we understand how

EXHIBIT 3

HTM Interfacing to the World

Source: Adapted from an HTM white paper (www.numenta.com).

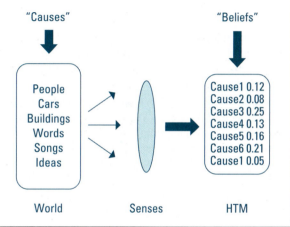

EXHIBIT 4

Tree-Shaped Hierarchy of HTM

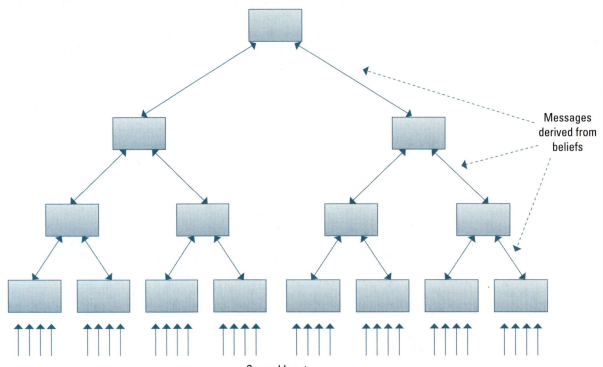

Messages
derived from
beliefs

Sensed Input

Each node:	Discovers causes (of its input).
	Passes beliefs up.
	Passes predictions down.
Each node:	Stores common sequences.
	Changing sensory data forms stable beliefs at top.
	Stable beliefs at top form changing sensory predictions.

Source: Adapted from the Numenta company website (http://numenta.com).

the structure works we can build machines that work like this."[33]

Taken together, HTM models the behavior of an intelligent being by doing four things. First, it discovers and assigns causes to events happening in the world. Second, once the causes have been discovered, it can use this previously accumulated experience to infer causes of novel inputs. Third, HTM makes predictions regarding future causes and inputs based on probabilities assigned at each level. In a final step, it generates motor behavior from its probabilistic predictions. (For more on how HTM models work, see www.numenta.com/htm-overview/htm-algorithms.php.)

As a result, HTM software applications can be trained for a specific use. Consider the task of differentiating a picture of a dog from a picture of a cat. While this is a simple job for even a three-year-old child, it is almost impossible for computers to do. Yet Dileep George demonstrated that this could be done using HTM (see Exhibit 5).[34] George first made line drawings of simple objects such as a cat, a dog, and a helicopter. He loaded up his algorithm and trained the computer to identify these objects by animating the original drawings. After the computer was trained, it could slowly put variations of drawings in the right category and even give a probability estimate of how sure it was of its answers.

EXHIBIT 5

HTM Recognizes a Dog

Source: http://spectrum.ieee.org/images/apr07/images/htmf1.pdf.

EVERYONE KNOWS YOU'RE A DOG

A Hierarchical Temporal Memory (HTM) is trained to recognize patterns by being exposed to a large number of examples of a particular kind of object–in this illustration, dogs, cups, and helicopters. (The input patterns must be presented as moving in time, some thing not shown in the diagram.) After training, the HTM correctly classified patterns to which it had not been exposed even when they were distorted, translated, or marred by noise.

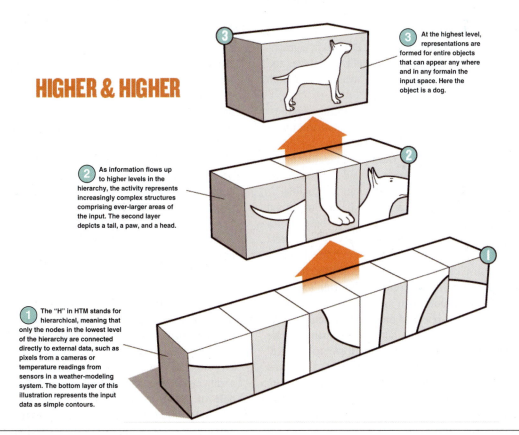

HIGHER & HIGHER

3 At the highest level, representations are formed for entire objects that can appear any where and in any formain the input space. Here the object is a dog.

2 As information flows up to higher levels in the hierarchy, the activity represents increasingly complex structures comprising ever-larger areas of the input. The second layer depicts a tail, a paw, and a head.

1 The "H" in HTM stands for hierarchical, meaning that only the nodes in the lowest level of the hierarchy are connected directly to external data, such as pixels from a cameras or temperature readings from sensors in a weather-modeling system. The bottom layer of this illustration represents the input data as simple contours.

"Numenta's objective is to maximize the impact of the HTM technology. The potential applications for this tehnology are diverse. Therefore we have structured our technology as a platform, enabling the emergence of an independent, application developer community. We will generate revenue by selling support, licensing software, and licensing intellectual property. The exact revenue mix will change over time, but we always will seek to make our developer partners successful, as well as be successful ourselves."

—NUMENTA FOUNDERS

PROGRESS AND CURRENT BUSINESS MODEL. After 25 years of starts and stops, Hawkins's vision of creating a "thinking machine" that mimics the processes of the human brain finally became reality. Numenta released the first version of NuPIC (Numenta Platform for Intelligent Computing), a technology platform for HTM implementation, in March 2007. A Windows-compatible version followed just five months later. NuPIC now runs on Windows, Linux, and Mac OS X. The Vitamin D Toolkit, a graphical user interface designed to visualize, analyze, and optimize HTM networks, is also available on both Windows and Mac OS platforms.

After considering several structural options, Numenta decided to offer NuPIC as a platform under a free research license which grants rights for broad research purposes. The goal was to facilitate the emergence of a developer community and get "as many people experimenting on the technology as possible."[35] Once a developer reaches a point where commercial value is created, Numenta provides a fee-based commercial license. Hawkins firmly believed the fastest pathway to commercial success was to offer developers the promise of financial returns down the road. To support developers in their efforts, Numenta's website features multiple tools such as a forum, wikis, and a blog written by members of the Numenta team. Users are encouraged to become active participants, share their work, report bugs, and contribute to forums. Numenta also offers a Partner Program, a fee-based support initiative in which participants receive a high level of consulting and technical support. As a result, Numenta currently has between 100 to 200 developers and eight partner companies.

Numenta plans to release its second-generation software based on newer algorithms in 2011, in anticipation of which they have already ceased active maintenance of NuPIC and its related vision applications.

Current users will have to decide whether to adopt the newer version, or continue using the legacy software without the benefit of Numenta's support.

CURRENT PARTNERS. Among Numenta's eight corporate partners using the early HTM version is Vitamin D, which debuted a beta version of its video object recognition program in November 2009. Compared with traditional software, Vitamin D's program provides state-of the-art detection of people and moving objects in video streams at a fraction of the cost.[36] Vitamin D Video may be used with generic webcams and cameras on both PCs and Macs, eliminating the need for high-tech equipment and making sophisticated video-monitoring systems for home and business security available to a wide range of customers.[37] One of the main advantages of HTM over traditional surveillance systems is that the software can be trained to recognize false alerts caused by insignificant events such as moving leaves or lighting changes. Jeff Hawkins stated, "Vitamin D Video is a compelling first step in making real the promise of intelligent computing."[38]

Another early adopter is EDSA Micro, a San Diego–based maker of software that designs and analyzes electrical power systems in a variety of industries, including data centers. Energy usage at data centers doubled between 2000 and 2006, reaching $4.5 billion, and could hit twice that amount by 2011.[39] According to EDSA, an hour of downtime at a data center can cost as much as $6 million. With the help of HTM, EDSA plans to create more sophisticated algorithms to supervise energy usage and create significant savings. EDSA believes HTM can serve as the "brains" of the system, learning the difference between "routine" and "non-routine" events, and alerting operators to anomalies before they lead to power failures.[40]

Forbes.com utilizes HTM to analyze user web clicks and to predict topics of interest to individual users. After training HTM with historical sequences of user click patterns, the software demonstrated higher levels of accuracy compared with traditional technologies. Numenta believes HTM may represent an important advance in web-based advertising and web recommendation engines.[41]

Another Numenta partner is an anonymous major automaker. It wants to use HTM to build a smart car that can understand traffic and predict dangerous situations. This will be achieved by installing the HTM-trained system with outward-looking sensors (camera, infrared, radar, ultrasound) attached to the vehicle. If a ball rolls into the street or smoke comes from the car ahead, a car equipped with HTM may know to step on the brakes or even accelerate to get out of harm's way.[42]

In other examples, Lockheed Martin Advanced Technology Laboratories wants to apply HTM to satellite image analysis. It wants to incorporate HTM into its ORBIT (Object Recognition via Brain-Inspired Technology) program for the Defense Advanced Research Projects Agency's (DARPA) Urban Reasoning and Geospatial Exploitation Technology program and the National Geospatial-Intelligence Agency.[43] An oil company likewise approached Numenta wanting to use HTM to find geologic patterns that could lead to the discovery of new oil resources. Meanwhile, Numenta continues to actively seek new partners who are able to collaborate and to commit dedicated resources, and who have access to training data, domain expertise, and go-to-market ability.[44]

INDUSTRIAL APPLICATIONS. Despite a promising start, HTM technology is still in its early development stage. If it works as Hawkins expects, though, HTM has the potential to lead to tremendous technical advances with far-ranging implications for many different industries. Hawkins describes "anything that humans can do easily, but traditional computers can't do at all, to be a good candidate"[45] for the application of HTM.

To identify potential uses, it is necessary to consider the ways in which HTM is more effective and efficient than brain power. First, as a silicon-based system, HTM is exponentially faster at processing data and running calculations. Silicon operates on the order of nanoseconds compared to the milliseconds required by human neurons. The second advantage of HTM is

its potentially unlimited capacity. HTM systems can be built much larger through a broader and deeper hierarchy in a targeted area. "What is exciting to me," Hawkins says, "is the prospect of building intelligent machines that sit comfortably in the realms of science where we have difficulty thinking. It will be like having a dedicated Einstein working around the clock on these problems."[46] A third advantage is that HTM is not confined to the human senses. A multifaceted and diverse HTM sensory system, where powerful computing is combined with infrared, radar, or sonar technologies, means that HTM can perform tasks that are beyond ordinary human capabilities. "It is in the realm of [these] exotic senses that the revolutionary uses of intelligent machines lie," Hawkins suspects.[47]

As an example, Hawkins points out that we constantly collect real-time data about the earth via space satellites and on-ground weather stations. HTM could be used not only to combine all these varied data from across the globe, but also to predict events such as hurricanes and floods more accurately. According to Hawkins, HTM could even be used to pinpoint the causes of global climate change more accurately.[48]

Prediction markets, championed in James Surowiecki's 2004 book *The Wisdom of Crowds,* represent another good candidate for HTM. Betfair and Intrade are successful online trading exchange websites focused on the making and commercialization of prediction markets. Here, HTM could be used to predict machine failures, tornados, and even stock prices. In addition, HTM technology could be used by government agencies such as the FBI and CIA to analyze e-mail records and voice data in order to predict the likelihood, date, location, and type of future terrorist attacks. For other potential applications, see Exhibit 6.

Challenges Ahead

Numenta faces some particular challenges relating to protection of its intellectual property and the potential competition it is facing in the intelligent-computing industry.

INTELLECTUAL PROPERTY PROTECTION. Numenta holds two patents related to its HTM technology, and it has several other applications pending.[49] The first, U.S. patent number 7,620,608, was issued on November 17, 2009, on "Hierarchical computing modules for performing spatial pattern and temporal sequence recognition." The second, U.S. patent number 7,624,085,

EXHIBIT 6

Potential HTM Industry Applications

Potential Industry	Applications
Automobiles	Make smarter cars
Financial markets	Predict market behavior
Government agencies (DHS, FBI, CIA, NASA)	Analyze e-mail records and voice data to predict likelihood, date, location, and type of future terrorist attacks
Home and business security	Video monitoring and image analysis
Manufacturing	Predict machine failure
Medical diagnostics	Help radiologists interpret X-ray images
Natural resources	Find geological patterns that lead to discovery of new natural resources (oil, gas, coal, uranium, lithium, etc.)
Search and data centers	Analyze data to identify abnormalities
Weather forecasting	Predict hurricanes floods, earthquakes, etc.; pinpoint causes of global warming
Web retailing	Model and predict consumer clicking and purchasing behavior; make better product recommendations

was issued on November 24, 2009, on "Hierarchical-based system for identifying objects using spatial and temporal patterns."[50]

A patent is a grant made by the U.S. government that confers the inventor or assignee the sole right to make, use, and sell that invention for a limited period of time (between 14 and 20 years).[51] Patent law is based upon the Patent Act of 1952, codified in Title 35 of the United States Code. According to the statute, one who "invents or discovers any new and useful process, machine, manufacture, or any composition of matter, or any new and useful improvement thereof, may obtain a patent therefore, subject to the conditions and requirements of this title."[52] To receive a patent, an invention must be judged to consist of patentable subject matter, possess utility, and be novel and non-obvious. It is not unusual for the U.S. Patent Trade Office (PTO) to take two to three years to approve a patent application.

The effectiveness of patents as a way to protect intellectual property rights varies widely across industries. Whereas patents are considered critical to shielding innovations in the pharmaceutical industry,[53] patent protection in the computer software industry is much weaker. Reverse-engineering of computer code is generally easier, not too time-consuming, and costs only 40 to 60 percent of the original investment. Nevertheless, if a company owns a technology that becomes an industry standard (e.g., Microsoft's and Intel's Wintel standard for the personal computer), it can become the source of a sustained competitive advantage.

Recently, there has been intense debate over whether software patents should be granted at all. Prior to the Supreme Court's *State Street Bank* decision of 1998, abstract ideas, including mathematical algorithms, were not considered patentable. The *State Street Bank* decision reversed that position, stating that an invention was eligible for patent protection if "it produces a useful, concrete and tangible result." New patent applications on computer software surged following the decision. For example, Microsoft held about 600 patents on the day the *State Street Bank* verdict was rendered,[54] but now holds more than 9,000. Ironically, the *State Street Bank* decision has proved to be both an asset and a liability to software developers. While it is now easier to protect their intellectual property, many find it nearly impossible to write new software without infringing on numerous existing patents. The resulting multimillion-dollar lawsuits consume valuable resources that would arguably be better spent hiring more engineers or investing in better infrastructure to create better products.

The *In re Bilski* case illustrates efforts to overturn the *State Street Bank* decision.[55] This case concerns a patent application by Bernie Bilski involving a method of hedging risks in commodities trading. The PTO rejected the patent as too abstract, and Bilski appealed the decision to the Federal Circuit, where the decision was reaffirmed. The case was then appealed to the Supreme Court and on June 1, 2009, received *certiorari* (an order by a higher court directing a lower court to send up a given case for review).[56] Hearing oral arguments in November 2009, the Supreme Court justices showed an apparently hostile attitude toward the Bilski patent application. In addition, it appeared that the court was trying to establish a new and stricter test of what is patent-eligible.[57]

All this creates considerable legal uncertainty for Numenta, which finds itself caught between the desire to protect its intellectual property and the need to make HTM available to developers in order to advance the technology. On January 11, 2011, the company released the following statement regarding enforcement of its patent rights:

> In order to encourage exploration and development of HTM technology, Numenta promises that it will not assert its current patent rights against development or use of independent HTM systems, as long as such development or use is for research purposes only, and not for any commercial or production use. Any commercial or production use of HTM technology that infringes on Numenta's patents will require a commercial license from Numenta. For these purposes, "commercial or production use" includes training an HTM network with the intent of later deploying the trained network or application for commercial or production purposes, and using or permitting others to use the output from HTM technology for commercial or production purposes.[58]

POTENTIAL COMPETITORS. Numenta is not the only company pursuing intelligent computing. Identifying trends in rivers of data is an important goal in a variety of sectors, ranging from scientific research to national security. A breakthrough in any industry could easily spread to other areas because of the similarity in basic pattern-finding processes. Therefore, any successes for HTM could bring tremendous opportunities for Numenta, but at the same time attract capable and powerful competitors.

IBM Stream Technology, called System S, is one direct rival. It is a major research initiative at IBM aimed at rapidly analyzing real-time data as it is being streamed from many sources. Applications include increasing the speed and accuracy of decision making in fields as diverse as homeland security and Wall Street trading.[59] Stream computing emerged in response to the need for faster data handling and analysis in business and science. It also tries to tackle the issue of the growing flood of information in digital form, including websites, blogs, e-mail, video and news clips, telephone conversations, transaction data, and electronic sensors. Traditional computer analytical and data-mining processes collect data, store them in a database, and then search the database for patterns or run queries. In contrast, stream computing uses advanced software algorithms to analyze the data as they stream in real time. It uses text, voice, and image-recognition technology to determine whether some data are more relevant to a particular problem than others. "It's a computing system that can morph and adapt to the problems it sees,"[60] says Nagui Halim, director of System S.

A slew of other companies are equally eager to enter the intelligent-computing industry. Recently, Google acquired PeakStream, a startup in stream computing, in hopes of improving its video search functions.[61] Fair Issac Corporation (FIC) acquired HNC Software (HNCS), a neural-network company and a member of the Standard & Poor's small cap 600. The merger is a way of combining expertise in analytics and credit scoring (FIC) with decision-management technology and fraud detection (HNCS) for customer acquisition and relationship management strategies.[62]

Decision Time

Numenta is the result of Hawkins's lifelong pursuit of brain theory. With HTM, Hawkins believes that the time has finally come to build intelligent computers that "think" using the same principles as human brains. In his words, this marks the true "beginning of the computer era."[63] With Numenta's promising start and the upcoming release of second-generation HTM algorithms in 2011, this 52-year-old "reluctant entrepreneur"[64] is facing yet another pivotal decision: What is the best way to keep this company going and ensure HTM's long-term success?

While Palm and Handspring made Hawkins and Donna Dubinsky independently wealthy, they cannot continue to fund Numenta indefinitely on their own. One of the primary challenges for a technology startup is to obtain funding and maintain a steady cash flow to support natural growth. New algorithms mean new applications and new business opportunities, but will also require new programmers and support staff. At some point, it will also become necessary to market HTM more aggressively and make clear to potential customers HTM's advantages over AI and competing technologies like IBM's System S. Numenta has nowhere near the financial resources of a giant like IBM, which can easily outspend and outpromote Numenta and put it out of business, even though Numenta has (what Hawkins believes to be) a superior technology.

Grabbing a Diet Mountain Dew from the cooler in Numenta's lobby, Hawkins wonders what Numenta's future might hold. He has been down this path before with Palm, when he made the decision to sell to U.S. Robotics in order to generate the cash to bring the Palm Pilot to market. While the relationship with U.S. Robotics had been fruitful, their success was part of the attraction for 3Com's acquisition, which marked the beginning of the end of his relationship with the company. As hard as it had been for him to leave Palm, Hawkins couldn't fathom abandoning his "brain theory" baby, let alone permitting someone else to decide how it should be "raised."

An IPO is another option, but comes with its own list of potential risks. Timing plays a crucial factor in determining the initial stock price, and with the ongoing financial recession, investors are not as eager to fund uncertain technologies as they have been in times past. Does Hawkins have the resources to keep Numenta going until the IPO market recovers? Will the markets recover by the time HTM is ready for full-fledged commercialization? Assuming an IPO is successful, can Hawkins live within the constraints of a publicly traded company? Or will he find a fate similar to the one faced by Steve Jobs in 1985, who was pushed out of the company he personally founded and bankrolled for so many years?

Yet another option is to keep doing what Numenta has been doing, and build its network of licensing partners. One significant downside to this approach is that it places Numenta at the mercy of its colleagues. Numenta gains royalties as applications are created and utilized, but has no control over how many resources its partners put into their HTM projects or their development timelines. Numenta also bears the risk of a dishonest partner taking advantage of the license and using Numenta's technology for its own gain. Still, it remains one of the easiest ways to put HTM into the hands of as many interested parties as possible.

A more selective approach would be to form strategic alliances or joint ventures with partners of Numenta's own choosing. This appeals to Hawkins because he could share both the risks and rewards of development with other companies. Numenta could even start to pursue its own applications, combining its knowledge of the HTM technology with another company's expertise in its applied field. Currently, Numenta advises but does not actively co-develop with the companies that license HTM; perhaps if they worked more closely together, they could be even more successful. At the same time, alliances can always be broken. The business world is full of companies that shared a novel technology with a trusted partner, only to watch the partner walk away and take full advantage of what they learned. Just like any relationship, alliances take time to form and maintain so that both parties continue to feel their needs are being met.

Although described as "reluctantly making a choice" every time, Hawkins has been incredibly successful in "making the right choice at the right time"[65] throughout his business career. Will he be able to make the right decision yet again? Hawkins knows this situation holds a tremendous amount of uncertainty: the technology itself, commercial applications, IP protection, competition, and so on. While Hawkins feels excited to see his technology making such great progress, he realizes he needs a solid plan for the future to ensure that his dream of making computing "more human" becomes a reality.

Endnotes

1. http://rni.org/mission.html.
2. www.numenta.com/about-numenta.php.
3. http://en.wikipedia.org/wiki/Neocortex.
4. This discussion is based on: Hawkins, J., and S. Blakeslee (2004), *On Intelligence. How a New Understanding of the Brain Will Lead to the Creation of Truly Intelligent Machines* (New York: Owl Books).
5. Ibid., p. 10.
6. Ibid.
7. Ibid., p. 17.
8. Stanford University's Entrepreneurship Corner, Entrepreneurial Thought Leader Lecture: "Inside the mind of a

reluctant entrepreneur," May 13, 2009. http://ecorner.stanford.edu/authorMaterialInfo.html?mid=2217.

9. Hawkins, J., and S. Blakeslee (2004), *On Intelligence. How a New Understanding of the Brain Will Lead to the Creation of Truly Intelligent Machines,"* p. 11.

10. John McCarthy, December 11, 2007, "What is artificial intelligence?" www-formal.stanford.edu/jmc/whatisai/node1.html.

11. www-formal.stanford.edu/jmc/whatisai/node1.html.

12. http://en.wikipedia.org/wiki/GRiD_Systems_Corporation.

13. http://en.wikipedia.org/wiki/Grid_Compass_1100.

14. Hawkins, J., and S. Blakeslee (2004), *On Intelligence. How a New Understanding of the Brain Will Lead to the Creation of Truly Intelligent Machines,* p. 21.

15. TED. Talks: Jeff Hawkins on How Brain Science Will Change Computing. Filmed February 2003; posted May 2007, www.ted.com/talks/jeff_hawkins_on_how_brain_science_will_change_computing.html.

16. Stanford University's Entrepreneurship Corner, "Inside the mind of a reluctant entrepreneur"; and http://ecorner.stanford.edu/authorMaterialInfo.html?mid=2217

17. http://en.wikipedia.org/wiki/Jeff_Hawkins.

18. Stanford University's Entrepreneurship Corner, "Inside the mind of a reluctant entrepreneur"; and http://ecorner.stanford.edu/authorMaterialInfo.html?mid=2217.

19. Computergram, "US Robotics Has Paid $44M in Shares for Palm Computing," CBRonline.com, September 06, 1995, www.cbronline.com/news/us_robotics_has_paid_44m_in_shares_for_palm_computing.

20. Stanford University's Entrepreneurship Corner, "Inside the mind of a reluctant entrepreneur"; and http://ecorner.stanford.edu/authorMaterialInfo.html?mid=2217.

21. www.fundinguniverse.com/company-histories/Handspring-Inc-Company-History.html.

22. http://en.wikipedia.org/wiki/PalmOne.

23. www.rni.org/mission.html.

24. http://en.wikipedia.org/wiki/Jeff_Hawkins.

25. George, D. (2008), "How the brain might work: A hierarchical and temporal model for learning and recognition," unpublished dissertation, Stanford University.

26. Stanford University's Entrepreneurship Corner, "Inside the mind of a reluctant entrepreneur"; and http://ecorner.stanford.edu/authorMaterialInfo.html?mid=2217

27. www.dileepgeorge.com/tiki/tiki-index.php?page=homepage.

28. Tam, P-W. (2005), "Next case for Palm Pilot creators: The brain," *The Wall Street Journal,* March 25.

29. Rothaermel, F., et al. (2008), "Intercluster innovation differentials: The role of research universities," *IEEE Transactions on Engineering Management,* Vol. 55, No. 1, February 2008.

30. Hawkins, J., "Brain science is about to fundamentally change computing," Filmed Feb 2003, posted May 2007, www.youtube.com/watch?v=G6CVj5IQkzk.

31. Ibid.

32. Ibid.

33. Hawkins, J., RSA Conference 2008, uploaded on June 23, 2008 "Artificial intelligence," www.youtube.com/watch?v=oozFn2d45tg.

34. Schonfeld, E. (2007), "Jeff Hawkins and the brain," *Business 2.0,* January 1.

35. www.youtube.com/watch?v=oozFn2d45tg.

36. www.numenta.com/about-numenta/customers.php.

37. "Smart video pioneer Vitamin D turns inexpensive web cameras into sophisticated security systems for homes and businesses," *BusinessWire,* November 9, 2009.

38. Ibid.; and www.businesswire.com/portal/site/home/permalink/?ndmViewId=news_view&newsId=20091109000555 1&newsLang=en.

39. Anderson, N. (2007), "EPA: Power usage in data centers could double by 2011," *ARS Technica,* August 6, http://arstechnica.com/old/content/2007/08/epa-power-usage-in-data-centers-could-double-by-2011.ars.

40. www.numenta.com/about-numenta/customers.php.

41. Ibid.

42. Schonfeld, E. (2007), "Jeff Hawkins hacks the human brain," *CNN Money.com,* March 6.

43. "Lockheed announces Cherry Hill unit contracts," *Philadelphia Business Journal,* October 12, 2007, http://albany.bizjournals.com/philadelphia/stories/2007/10/08/daily27.html.

44. www.numenta.com/numenta-partner-program.php.

45. Hawkins, J. (2005), "Can a new theory of the neocortex lead to truly intelligent machines?" lecture, September 28, MIT World, http://mitworld.mit.edu/video/316.

46. Schonfeld, E. (2007), "Jeff Hawkins hacks the human brain," *CNN Money.com,* March 6.

47. Hawkins, J., and S. Blakeslee (2004), *On Intelligence. How a New Understanding of the Brain Will Lead to the Creation of Truly Intelligent Machines*, p. 228.

48. Hawkins, J. (2005), "Can a new theory of the neocortex lead to truly intelligent machines?"

49. www.faqs.org/patents/asn/1706.

50. United States Patent Office. http://patft.uspto.gov/netacgi/nph-Parser?Sect1=PTO2&Sect2=HITOFF&p=1&u=%2Fnetahtml%2FPTO%2Fsearch-bool.html&r=0&f=S&l=50&TERM1=hierarchical&FIELD1=TI&co1=AND&TERM2=hawkins&FIELD2=INNM&d=PTXT

51. http://en.wikipedia.org/wiki/Patent.

52. 35 U.S.C. §101.

53. Cohen, W. M., R. R. Nelson, and J. P. Walsh (2000), "Protecting their intellectual assets: Appropriability conditions and why US manufacturing firms patent (or not)," *NBER working paper,* 7552, February.

54. Lee, T. B. (2008), "Analysis: Appeals court unlikely to fix software patent mess," *Ars Technica,* May 15, http://arstechnica.com/tech-policy/news/2008/05/software-patent-problems-abound.ars.

55. http://en.wikipedia.org/wiki/In_re_Bilski.

56. Ibid.

57. http://thepriorart.typepad.com/the_prior_art/2009/11/bilski-oral-arguments.html.

58. www.numenta.com/about-numenta/licensing.php.

59. Lohr, S. (2007), "IBM to show stream computing system," *The New York Times*, June 19.

60. Ibid.

61. Ibid.

62. www.tgc.com/dsstar/02/0611/104343.html.

63. Hawkins, J. (2005), "Can a new theory of the neocortex lead to truly intelligent machines?" lecture.

64. Stanford University's Entrepreneurship Corner, "Inside the mind of a reluctant entrepreneur"; and http://ecorner.stanford.edu/authorMaterialInfo.html?mid=2217.

65. Ibid.

I believe that, in the future, war will not be waged with guns, but with innovations.

—MARIO POLEGATO, FOUNDER AND CHAIRMAN OF GEOX[1]

Ali Farhoomand

On 28 July 2009, the board of directors of Geox approved the footwear and apparel company's half-year results, which showed consolidated sales of US$653 million. This was a remarkable achievement for a company that had only been around since 1995.

It was in the early 1990s that inventor, entrepreneur and erstwhile winemaker Mario Moretti Polegato, suffering from hot and sweaty feet, used a pocketknife to cut holes in the soles of his sneakers, thereby creating the first pair of "shoes that breathe." His crude adjustment worked well in dry weather, but as soon as it started to rain, water would seep through the holes. Collaborating with Italian universities, it took Polegato several years to develop and patent a breathable membrane for shoes that would allow his feet to breathe while remaining watertight. When he succeeded in producing the prototype of such a technology in the laboratory, he immediately patented it and began marketing it to existing shoe manufacturers. However, none showed any interest in his product. He thus decided to embark on his own, opening a small factory with five other young businessmen to manufacture these "breathing" shoes under the GEOX[2] brand name.

Geox's innovative product rapidly carved out a niche for itself in the global footwear market. By 2002, the company had extended its "breathability" technology to fabric and entered the apparel market. By 2009, after a mere 14 years, Geox had become a global name and was ranked the world's second-largest casual lifestyle footwear sector operator.[3] The company was conducting its business in 68 countries around the world through over 10,000 multi-brand points of sale and about 997 single-brand Geox shops.[4]

By successfully introducing a new product to the established and intensely competitive shoe industry, Geox had demonstrated the power of innovation. However, like any other innovative company, Geox had to fret about sustainability of its competitive advantage.

The History of Geox
FROM IDEA TO BUSINESS.

Italian people are very creative, but we lack the ability to go from an idea to a great business. I see Geox as a project, which is made of three main components: a good idea, constant collaboration with universities in order to see if your idea works and how to improve it, and a patent to protect it. When these three elements are present, you have a solid project, which can grow exponentially.

—MARIO POLEGATO, FOUNDER AND
CHAIRMAN OF GEOX[5]

Geox's short history was intrinsically tied to that of its founder and chairman, Mario Moretti Polegato.[6] Until the early 1990s, Polegato had little interest in the manufacture of shoes, and was instead passionate about his family's wine-producing and exporting business based in Italy. His family had been in this business for three generations and was internationally renowned for the fine wines it produced. Polegato had

Havovi Joshi prepared this case under the supervision of Professor Ali Farhoomand for class discussion. This case is not intended to show effective or ineffective handling of decision or business processes.

also studied wine production at the School of Enology in Conegliano, Italy.[7]

It was in the summer of 1992 that the genesis of Geox took place, at a wine trade fair in the arid American state of Nevada. During a break between meetings and speeches, Polegato decided to take a short walk in the Nevada desert. He decided to wear a pair of old, rubber sneakers for his walk and, to his dismay, found that they were completely inappropriate for the environment. The rubber soles of the shoes overheated, and his feet became excessively suffocated and uncomfortable. To ease the discomfort, Polegato removed his sneakers and, with his pocketknife, proceeded to make a hole in the sole of each shoe. That brought immediate relief and also got Polegato thinking—a thought process that resulted in the creation of Geox, "the shoe that breathes."

At first I was thinking only of my own feet, and only later, after I returned to Italy, did I begin to think about it as a business idea. I went looking for breathable soles in sports shops all around Italy, and I couldn't find them. I thought, is it possible that nobody has thought of this idea yet? And nobody had.

—MARIO POLEGATO, FOUNDER AND CHAIRMAN OF GEOX[8]

Polegato was convinced that his idea for a "breathing" shoe had immense potential. He returned to Italy and, using the laboratory of a small shoe manufacturing company owned by his family, he set about trying to transform his idea into a product. He realised that there were two key features that the perforated rubber sole had to possess: it should breathe, and it should be watertight. He then commenced researching his idea.

The product development research process was exhaustive, as Polegato had no prior knowledge in the field of engineering or the shoe industry.[9] After consulting several publications and encyclopaedias, his attention was drawn to the breathable membrane used in the material employed for manufacturing the overalls worn by NASA astronauts. This was a watertight breathing membrane, and Polegato recognised that it could be successfully used to develop a prototype for his shoes. He then proceeded to collaborate with several university research centres to create a new technology for the ventilated soles.

Polegato was successful in his endeavours, and the first "shoe that breathes" was created. The central feature of the new technology was a membrane in the shoe's sole that had many small channels. These channels were too narrow to allow water to enter, but wide enough to allow water vapour to exit. Hence the membrane worked well for both rubber and leather outsoles, allowing the rubber ones to breathe and keeping the leather ones waterproof. Polegato immediately patented the new technology and tried to sell the invention to leading shoe companies in Italy and other parts of the world. However, none of them showed any interest.

Undeterred, Polegato decided to manufacture the shoes himself.

I didn't have any plans to start making shoes myself at all. But I couldn't believe that no one was interested as I was convinced the technology would work. So, one day, I talked to a few friends about doing it ourselves. I come from a rich family, but I didn't want to ask them for money, so I went to the local bank—the Cassa di Risparmio di Treviso— and took out a €500,000 loan. We started by making children's shoes, selling them here in Montebelluna. The mothers liked them so much they asked us to make them for them. Then for men. That's how it started.

—MARIO POLEGATO, FOUNDER AND CHAIRMAN OF GEOX[10]

GEOX, 1995 TO 2009. Initially Geox only manufactured children's shoes. As Polegato said, "Our risk was more limited, because the life of a child's shoe is fairly short."[11] However, the company soon gained confidence, and expanded into producing adult shoes. For approximately five years the shoes were sold largely in the Italian domestic market; it was only in 2000 that the company expanded into the international market, and from 2000 to 2003, it boosted sales in the international market through both exclusive and multi-brand channels.

In 2002, Geox took its concept of patented breathable fabric one step further and entered the apparel market with a patented jacket that allowed air through at the shoulders. This move was in line with the practice of most other major footwear brands, which had capitalised on the strength of their brand names by expanding their target market segment and diversifying their product portfolios into apparel and other products.[12]

On 1 December 2004, Geox was listed on the Milan Stock Exchange. However, after going public, Polegato maintained majority ownership with a 71% stake in the company, enabling him to become one of the world's wealthiest people. In 2009, the annual *Forbes* classification of the world's wealthiest individuals ranked Polegato 469th, with a net worth of US$1.5 billion.[13] Polegato took pride in this ranking because, as he said, "I am the fourth richest man in Italy, and I am proud of that, because it came from my brain."[14] Polegato was also recognised for his entrepreneurship and leadership capabilities [see Exhibit 1].

Geox continued to be very much a family owned business, and in 2008, Polegato installed his son, Enrico Moretti, as deputy chairman of the company.[15]

Interestingly, Geox did not enter the sports shoe market until 2008, as Polegato felt this would require a very different technology. As he explained, "The shoe business is very large. It's impossible to enter every sector immediately because there's a different mindset in every sector, a different ability."[16]

We needed to introduce a different technology in the breathing shoe. With sport, you increase perspiration. We now have a new patent, we're testing the product, and we're getting ready to introduce the new sports line in the market next January (2008).

—MARIO POLEGATO, FOUNDER AND CHAIRMAN OF GEOX[17]

During 2008, the company sold over 20 million pairs of shoes and over 2 million items of clothing. As of 31 December 2008, the net sales for the year were €892.5 million,[18] with a net income of €118.2 million [see Exhibit 2 for financial results].

In April 2009, Geox added to its sporting goods products and launched its golf shoe range, which Polegato claimed was in response to customer requests.

Golf is a perfect environment for GEOX technology. You walk long hours, often on a damp surface, and in warm if not hot climates. In the third millennium, it is impossible that people still suffer from such a basic problem as sweaty, smelly feet.

—MARIO POLEGATO, FOUNDER AND CHAIRMAN OF GEOX[19]

However, the golf shoes industry was a highly competitive one. In the U.S. for example, Nike controlled 56% of the market, and analysts predicted that it would be difficult for a newcomer like Geox to make serious inroads.[20] As stated by Matt Powell, an analyst at SportsOneSource, "It's not like the industry is crying out for a new brand or a new idea. It will be a very difficult challenge for GEOX."[21] Polegato, however, believed that Geox's unique "NET System Technology," which provided an actual net inside the golfer's shoe sole to keep the foot dry, would be popular enough to boost the company's growth.

As of 30 June 2009, the company owned shops in prime locations in cities around the world and continued to turn a substantial profit [see Exhibit 3]. Geox then further expanded its reach by buying Diadora, Italy's famous but debt-laden sportswear brand [see Exhibit 4 for a timeline of key milestones].

The Global Footwear Industry

While estimates varied significantly, by all accounts the global footwear industry was a giant in the consumer world. In 2007, it was estimated that the global production of footwear reached 16 billion pairs.[22] China continued to be the towering leader, contributing over 63% of the world's production (approximately 10 billion pairs), while Vietnam came in a far second (making less than a tenth what China produced), followed by Italy, Indonesia, Belgium and Brazil[23] [see Exhibit 5].

The U.S. continued to be the leading consumer in this market, contributing about one-third of the dollar demand [see Exhibit 6]. Even in value terms, it was projected that in the coming years, Europe, which was one of the largest markets in terms of value, would probably be eclipsed by the U.S. and the fast-growing Asia region.[24]

EXHIBIT 1

Awards and Recognition Mario Moretti Polegato

Polegato spends much time teaching "Intellectual Property" in schools and universities, both in Italy and abroad. This commitment has earned him the title of "Affiliate Professor of Entrepreneurship" from ESCP-EAP in Paris, one of the leading international business schools. He has taught at the University of Florence, University of Pisa, Ca' Foscari University of Venice, Federico II University of Naples, Catholic University of Lisbon, MIT of Boston and University of Cambridge.

Listed next are some of the key distinctions that Polegato has been awarded.

1994	Italian Creativity Award from Confindustria (Italian Industrials Association).
1995	Appointed "Commendatore Nazionale" of the Italian Republic (a title conferred in recognition of the results obtained in the footwear sector).
1997	Appointed Honorary General Consul of Romania for North-Eastern Italy.
2000	Appointed Cavaliere al Merito dell'Ordine Nazionale of Romania.
2002	Appointed Member of Board of Directors of Unicredit – Romania.
2002	Appointed Entrepreneur of the year 2002. Ernst & Young, the Italian Stock Exchange and Italian financial newspaper Il Sole 24 Ore gave Mario Moretti Polegato the "Entrepreneur of the Year Award".
2002	Became member of international no profit association Aspen Institute Italia.
2003	Honoris Causa Master in Integrated Logistics and Supply Chain Integrated Management at the University of Verona, Economics department.
2003	Doctor Honoris Causa in Agricultural Studies and Veterinary Science at the University of Banatului, Timisoara–Romania.
	Elected Proboviro of Confindustria (Italian Industrials Association).
2003	Appointed "Best Italian Entrepreneur in the World" by Ernst & Young Global.
2003	Member of Board of Directors of Siparex Italia, Private Equity Italian-French fund.
	Founder and member of Board of Directors of ONLUS "Il Ponte del Sorriso", Italian no profit association established by UIL (Italian Workers Union), which helps needy Romanian minor orphans.
2004	Received the Marketing 2004 Award from the Italian Marketing Association for the remarkable diffusion, promotion and development of the marketing culture.
2004	Received the "Premio Fedeltà al Lavoro" (Loyalty to Work) from the "Consorzio dei Santi Crispino e Crispiniano" (Footwear producers Association) as best footwear entrepreneur.
2005	Elected member of Governing Council of UPA (Association of Advertising High Spenders).
	Appointed Cavaliere del Lavoro by the Italian President (honorary title conferred in recognition of the good results obtained in the footwear sector).
	He was conferred the honorary degree in Chemistry by the Cà Foscari University of Venice.
2006	He was appointed "Grand'Ufficiale al Merito della Repubblica Italiana" by the Italian President.
	He was conferred the Honorary Degree by the CUOA Foundation.
2007	Elected member of the Managing Committee of Comitato Leonardo - Italian Quality Committee.
	Received the "Premio Leone del Veneto" from the "Ufficio di Presidenza del Consiglio Regionale del Veneto".
	Confindustria appointed him Member of Council.
2008	Confindustria appointed him Member of the Executive Council for 2008–2010.
	Received the "Premio Internazionale AEREC alla Carriera" from the European Academy for Economic and Cultural Relations.

Source: Geox (30 June 2009) "Mario Moretti Polegato: Geox Chairman" Company Presentations.

EXHIBIT 2

Geox's Income Statement 2004–2008 (US$ million[83])

	2008	2007	2006	2005	2004
Sales					
Sales by Product					
Footwear	1092.4	970.8	781.6	585.4	442.9
Apparel	113.6	70.0	45.8	29.3	16.5
Total Net Sales	**1206.0**	**1040.8**	**827.4**	**614.7**	**459.4**
Y-o-Y growth	*16%*	*26%*	*35%*	*34%*	*34%*
Sales by Region					
Italy	450.0	398.0	357.7	311.5	258.5
Europe	546.4	486.9	369.6	246.2	162.8
North America	67.3	52.7	37.0	18.8	18.4
Rest of the World	142.3	103.2	63.1	38.4	19.7
Total Net Sales	**1206.0**	**1040.8**	**827.4**	**614.9**	**459.4**
Sales by Channel					
Wholesale	823.0	737.3	624.1	475.4	356.5
Franchising	193.0	167.0	117.0	88.1	63.1
DOS	190.0	136.5	86.3	51.4	39.8
Total Net Sales	**1206.0**	**1040.8**	**827.4**	**614.9**	**459.4**
EBITDA	**269.6**	**271.5**	**207.4**	**163.5**	**117.7**
EBIT	**230.4**	**242.8**	**182.3**	**139.1**	**98.4**
PBT	**224.6**	**241.1**	**180.9**	**143.4**	**92.6**
PBT%	*18.6%*	*23.2%*	*21.9%*	*23.3%*	*20.1%*
Net Income	**158.9**	**166.2**	**131.5**	**101.8**	**71.4**
Net Income %	*13.2%*	*16.0%*	*15.9%*	*16.5%*	*15.5%*

Source: Geox (2010) "Investor Relations", www.geox.com (accessed 19 February 2010).

EXHIBIT 3

Geox's Income Statement as of 30 June 2009 (US$ million[84])

	First Half 2009	First Half 2008	Full Year 2008
Net sales	652.5	627.1	1,206.0
Cost of sales	(311.2)	(287.7)	(573.6)
Gross profit #	341.3	339.5	632.5
Selling and distribution costs	(31.6)	(30.0)	(58.4)
General and administrative expenses	(152.5)	(117.3)	(253.2)
Advertising and promotion	(26.6)	(47.6)	(89.3)
EBIT *	130.4	144.5	231.5
Net interest	(3.9)	(2.6)	(5.8)
Profit before tax	126.5	141.9	225.7
Net income *	**76.5**	**106.1**	**159.7**

\# The decrease in Gross Profit was primarily due to higher promotional selling activities through the Directly Operated Sales channel, in the first quarter, and to a different regional sales mix.

* The EBIT and Net income for the first half of 2009 have been adjusted for non-cash, non-comparable costs. In particular EBIT was adjusted for US$7.8 million primarily due to asset impairment of stores.[85] Net income too was adjusted for US$10.8 million for the above mentioned asset impairment net of tax effect, and write-down of deferred tax assets.

EXHIBIT 4

Significant milestones in Geox's history

Early 1990s	The idea of a breathable shoe germinates in Polegato. He commenced research and invented a "shoe that breathes".
1995	After unsuccessfully trying to sell his invention to several established footwear manufacturers, and after having passed the market testing phase for a line of children's footwear, Polegato established the company "Geox", and begins large-scale production of shoes under the Geox brand name.
	In the same year, he improved the original patent and extended the product range to men's and women's footwear.
1999	The company continued to study the human body's perspiration mechanism, and patented its ideas for apparel, applying its technology to jackets of many kinds.
2000	Geox went international, selling in stores outside Italy.
2001	The company invented and patented its new technology for shoes using waterproof leather.
2004	Geox went public, and was listed on the Milan Stock Exchange on 1 December, 2004.
2005	On November 16th, 2005 Geox inaugurated its largest shop of 600 square metres in prime property of Madison Avenue and 57th Street, New York City.
2008	The company entered the sports shoe industry after having concentrated on the leisure and urban footwear market.
2009	Geox enters the golf shoes market. The company buys Diadora, a famous Italian sportswear brand.

Source: Geox (2010) "History", www.geox.com (accessed 19 February 2010).

EXHIBIT 5

Leading Footwear-Exporting Countries

Source: SATRA (2008) "World Footwear Markets", www.satra.co.uk/bulletin/article_view.php?id=284 (accessed 22 February 2010).

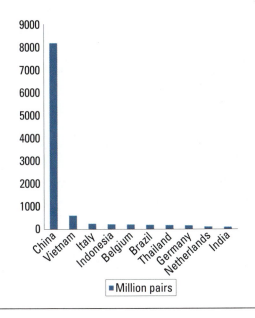

■ Million pairs

EXHIBIT 6

Leading Footwear-Consuming countries

Source: SATRA (2008) "World Footwear Markets", www.satra.co.uk/bulletin/article_view.php?id=284 (accessed 22 February 2010).

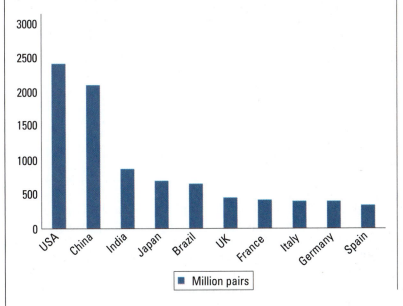

■ Million pairs

In particular, India and China, with their burgeoning populations and growing urban affluence, were being increasingly regarded as attractive new customer target groups. Major global sportswear brands, especially Nike and Adidas, had strengthened their presence in the Chinese market, particularly following the 2008 Olympics. However, unlike the U.S. where the upwardly mobile consumer was willing to pay high prices for shoes, in countries such as China and India, affordability remained a significant factor.

KEY PLAYERS IN THE CASUAL/SPORTS FOOTWEAR INDUSTRY. Footwear manufacturers typically focused on either the customer group they were targeting, such as men, women or children, or the product type, such as casual wear, formal wear or sports shoes. For instance, Timberland would focus on casual footwear to be worn outdoors, ECCO on comfortable casual-wear shoes, and Ferragamo (like most other Italian brands) on high-end formal wear.

In 2006, casual footwear (also known as the "brown shoes" market) was the largest and fastest-growing product segment, with an estimated 7 billion pairs.[25] By the end of 2009, Geox was the world's second-largest casual lifestyle sector operator, following the market leader, Clarks Shoes.[26] The other big players were ECCO, Birkenstock, Hush Puppies and Rockport [see Exhibit 7].

In the sports footwear market, the big players were Nike and Adidas, which together controlled nearly 60% of the global market [see Exhibit 8].[27] The other dominant players were Brown Shoe, Fila and Timberland.

C&J CLARK LTD. Founded in 1828 as a sheepskin tannery, the C&J Clark ("Clarks") group was the largest shoe manufacturer in the UK. By 2009, the company was also one of the country's biggest privately owned companies, with 400 high-street shops in the UK and 11,300 employees.[28] The group's most important product in the UK was children's shoes, particularly school shoes.

EXHIBIT 7

Top 10 Manufacturers in the International Lifestyle Casual Footwear Market in 2007

	Global Sales (in US$ Million)	Change over the Previous Year	Market Share
Clarks	1,646	9.7%	21.1%
Geox	**1,053**	**31.9%**	**13.5%**
ECCO	1,035	29.4%	13.3%
Birkenstock	487	13.3%	6.2%
Hush Puppies	464	2.0%	5.9%
Rockport	398	8.2%	5.1%
Mephisto	319	5.3%	4.1%
Caterpillar	294	15.7%	3.8%
Josef Seibel	223	16.8%	2.9%
Stonefly	131	10.1%	1.7%

Source: Shoe Intelligence (3 October 2008) "International Lifestyle Casual Footwear Market".

EXHIBIT 8

Top 10 Manufacturers in the International Branded Athletic Footwear Market in 2003

	Global Sales (in US$ Million)	Change over the Previous Year	Market Share
Nike	6,236	7.4	33.27
Adidas	2,993	6.8	15.97
Reebok	1,836	11.8	9.80
New Balance	1,228	(3.8)	6.55
Puma	1,114	45.1	5.94
Converse	815	40.5	4.35
ASICS	692	5.5	3.69
K-Swiss	429	52.1	2.29
Fila	335	(30.1)	1.79
Vans	312	(3.7)	1.66

Source: Sporting Goods Intelligence (25 September 2004), "International Branded Athletic Footwear Market", www.sginews.com/sginews/gifs/SGI_afwint_2003.pdf (accessed 5 March 2010).

For the year ending 31 January 2009, Clarks recorded an increase of 6.6% over the previous year in shoe sales from the sale of 49 million shoes, contributing to group sales of US$1.73 billion (£1.122 billion).[29] This was despite the company suffering a sharp reduction in sales volumes and profitability, particularly in North America. However, partly on account of favourable dollar to pound sterling exchange rates,[30] pre-tax profits rose by 16% over the previous year to US$ 133.8 million (£86.8 million).[31]

Despite functioning in a highly competitive footwear market, Clarks had succeeded in holding on to its market share, due in no small part to its strong pedigree and the associated value of its brand name.

NIKE. In the fiscal year ending 31 May 2009, Nike generated US$19.2 billion in revenue, an increase of 3% percent over the previous year. Footwear sales topped US$10 billion and apparel sales topped US$5 billion [see Exhibit 9].[32] This again placed Nike as the foremost seller of athletic footwear and athletic apparel in the world.

Sales in the U.S. made up approximately 42% of total revenues, a drop from 43% in the previous year.[33] Almost all of the company's footwear was produced outside of the U.S. and contract suppliers in China, Vietnam and Indonesia manufactured 36%, 36% and 22% of Nike brand footwear, respectively.[34] Similarly, almost all Nike brand apparel was manufactured outside the U.S. by independent contract manufacturers located in 34 countries, including China, Thailand and Indonesia.

Nike's footwear products were essentially for specific athletic use. Running, training, basketball, soccer, sport-inspired casual shoes, and kids' shoes were its top-selling footwear categories in 2009. The company also marketed footwear designed for aquatic activities, baseball, cheerleading, football, golf, lacrosse, outdoor activities, skateboarding, tennis, volleyball, walking, wrestling, and other athletic and recreational activities. Complementing its footwear products, Nike sold sports apparel and accessories, as well as sports-inspired lifestyle apparel, athletic bags and accessory items. It also sold a line of performance equipment under the Nike brand name, including products such as bags, socks, golf clubs and other equipment designed for sports activities. In addition, the company entered into licence agreements that allowed unaffiliated parties to manufacture and sell various apparel, equipment and accessory items, such as swimwear and children's apparel, under the Nike brand.

Nike had the following wholly owned subsidiaries: Cole Haan, which designed and distributed dress and casual footwear, apparel, and accessories for men and women under the brand names Cole Haan and Bragano; Converse Inc, which designed, distributed and licensed athletic and casual footwear, apparel and accessories under the Converse, Chuck Taylor, All Star, One Star, and Jack Purcell trademarks; Hurley International LLC, which designed and distributed a line of action sports apparel for surfing, skateboarding and snowboarding, youth lifestyle apparel, and accessories under the Hurley trademark; and Umbro Ltd, which designed, distributed and licensed athletic and casual footwear, apparel and equipment, primarily for the sport of soccer, under its own trademarks.

ADIDAS. The Adidas Group, which marked its 60th year in 2009, bought Reebok, the world's number-three

EXHIBIT 9

Nike Income Statement as of 31 may 2009 (US$ million)

	2009	2008	2007	2006	2005
Revenues	19,176.1	18,627.0	16,325.9	14,954.9	13,739.7
Gross margin	8,604.4	8,387.4	7,160.5	6,587.0	6,115.4
Gross margin %	44.9%	45.0%	43.9%	44.0%	44.5%
Restructuring charges *	195.0	–	–	–	–
Goodwill impairment *	199.3	–	–	–	–
Intangible and other asset impairment *	202.0	–	–	–	–
Net income	1,486.7	1,883.4#	1,491.5	1,392.0	1,211.6
Cash flow from operations	1,736.1	1,936.3	1,878.7	1,667.9	1,570.7

* The fiscal 2009 reported results contained significant non-comparable transactions, including after-tax charges of US$144.5 million for restructuring activities (also included reducing the global workforce by approximately 5%), which were completed in the fourth quarter of fiscal 2009, and US$240.7 million for the impairment of goodwill, intangible and other assets of Umbro, which was recorded in the third quarter of fiscal 2009.

\# Further, fiscal 2008 reported results which included combined gains from the sale of the company's Starter Brand and Nike Bauer Hockey businesses of US$35.4 million, net of tax, and a one-time tax benefit of $105.4 million.

Source: Nike (2009) "Annual Report".

sports footwear and apparel brand, in 2005. This placed the company second in the global market, with a 26% market share.[35] Reebok had acquired Rockport, a global casual footwear brand, in 1986, and this too became a property of the Adidas Group.

The group had five principal brands. The Adidas brand consisted of a portfolio of products focusing on activities such as football, running, basketball and training. The focus of the Reebok brand was on fitness and training, with the three key businesses of women's fitness, men's training and classics. TaylorMade was the market leader in the metal woods category of high-performance golf products, and comprised three brands: TaylorMade, Adidas Golf and Ashworth. Rockport was a U.S.-based manufacturer of leather footwear, and CCM was one of the largest manufacturers of hockey equipment.

Despite 2009 being a tough year for the industry globally, Adidas turned in record revenue of US$14 billion. Of total net sales, footwear and apparel products contributed 45% each, and the remaining 10% was from sales of hardware such as sports equipment.[36] The group manufactured 171 million pairs of footwear (down from 221 million pairs in 2008). However, a decline in gross margin of over 3% to 45.4% in 2009 resulted in a 53% decline in operating profit [see Exhibit 10]. To minimise the cost of production, Adidas had outsourced over 95% of its production to independent third-party suppliers, of which 74% were located in Asia.[37]

GEOX: The Company

GROUP STRUCTURE. As of 31 December 2008, the Geox Group was controlled by Geox S.p.A., which acted as an operating holding company, and comprised three key groups [see Exhibit 11]:

- Technical production companies: Notech Kft (Hungary) was the company that headed the group's production activities in Europe.
- EU trading companies: These companies managed the group's own shops in the EU, and also provided customer services and co-ordinated the sales network.
- Non-EU trading companies: The role of these companies was to monitor and develop the business in various non-EU markets. They operated on the basis of licensing or distribution agreements stipulated by the parent company.

THE PRODUCT. Approximately 90% of Geox's sales were from sales of shoes, with the remaining 10% from sales of apparel.[38] The company had positioned itself in the footwear industry as a one-of-a-kind brand catering to the entire family.[39] The company's three product categories were based on the target consumer (women, men and children), and the products were priced in the medium to medium-high price range of the market.

The product categories were further divided into two key areas:[40]

- Classic products, which were elegant and traditional
- Casual products, which were wearable and adaptable

The company entered the sports shoe market later and, as of the end of 2009, two lines were available: one for running and the gym, and the other for golf.

The company also extended its breathability concept to clothing. Given that heat rises, the heat emanated from the human body would move upwards to the shoulder area in shirts and jackets, and just below the belt for trousers. Based on this concept, Geox created a special chamber in this area of the apparel, where discrete perforations with membrane-lined air vents allowed the warm and humid air to escape while keeping the garment waterproof.

PRODUCTION. Geox recognised early on that producing a "breathing" shoe would not be sufficient on its own in the fashion-conscious footwear industry. It would have to ensure that the shoes looked good too, and stay on top of fashion trends, as Polegato knew that fashion and technology were equally important in the shoes market.

Geox was born in Italy, home to creativity and ideas. Each Geox product is the result of patented research which is carried out in our laboratories. Each new collection is created by the best Italian designers. Geox breathes and walks all around the world thanks to its double soul made of Italian fashion and technology.

—MARIO POLEGATO, FOUNDER AND CHAIRMAN OF GEOX[41]

EXHIBIT 10

Adidas Income Statement as of 31 December 2009 (US$ Million[86])

	2009	2008	2007	2006	2005
Net sales	14028.4	14593.2	13917.6	13627.0	8967.6
Gross profit	6367.6	7102.7	6597.3	6074.3	4320.3
Royalty and commission income	116.2	120.3	137.8	121.6	63.5
Other operating income	135.1	139.2	108.1	74.3	48.6
Other operating expenses	5932.4	5916.2	5560.8	5079.7	3477.0
EBITDA	1054.1	1729.7	1574.3	1456.8	1089.2
Operating profit	686.5	1445.9	1282.4	1190.5	955.4
Financial result	(202.7)	(224.3)	(182.4)	(213.5)	(70.3)
Income before taxes	483.8	1221.6	1101.4	977.0	885.1
Income taxes	152.7	351.4	351.4	306.8	298.6
Minority interests	0.0	(2.7)	(5.4)	(17.6)	(10.8)
Net income attributable to shareholders	331.1	867.6	744.6	652.7	517.6

Sales by Brand (in US$ million)

	2009	2008	2007	2006	2005
Adidas	10162.2	10568.9	9612.2	8954.1	7920.3
Reebok	2166.2	2320.3	2474.3	2674.3	
TaylorMade - Adidas Golf	1123.0	1097.3	1086.5	1156.8	958.1
Rockport	313.5	328.4	393.2	395.9	
Reebok-CCM Hockey	239.2	254.1	283.8	273.0	

Source: Geox (2008) "Annual Report".

Geox's production system was geared to achieve the following key objectives:[42]

- Maintaining high quality standards
- Continuously improving flexibility and time to market
- Increasing productivity and reducing costs.

Geox outsourced most of its production to factories in China, Vietnam, Indonesia and Brazil, and only produced small quantities in its own two factories in Romania and the Slovak Republic. By 2008, the output of these two plants contributed only around 5% of total production, while the other 95% was primarily in East Asia and South America.[43]

In 2003, Geox signed a co-operation agreement with China's Aokang Group, whereby the Aokang Group, as an agent of Geox, became one of its main production bases, manufacturing 8 million pairs of shoes per year for Geox. Under the agreement, Aokang was also responsible for the brand promotion, sales network construction and marketing of Geox shoes in China.[44] The Aokang Group was founded in 1988 and was one of China's top 500 private enterprises, involved in activities ranging from shoemaking to commercial property to biotech products. By 2009, the group employed about 20,000 staff, with an annual turnover of approximately US$600 million.[45] Aokang Shoes itself had a staff of over 16,000 and operated three shoe production bases and five shoe brands, including Geox and Tommy Hilfiger.[46] In April 2008, it was decided that all the leisure shoes sold by Geox globally would carry the Aokang Wenzhou mark from design to production.[47]

Geox took great care to ensure that its third-party producers had the necessary technical skills, quality standards and ability to handle their assigned production volumes by the agreed deadlines.[48] The company

EXHIBIT 11

Geox group structure

As of 31 December 2008, the Geox Group was structured as follows.

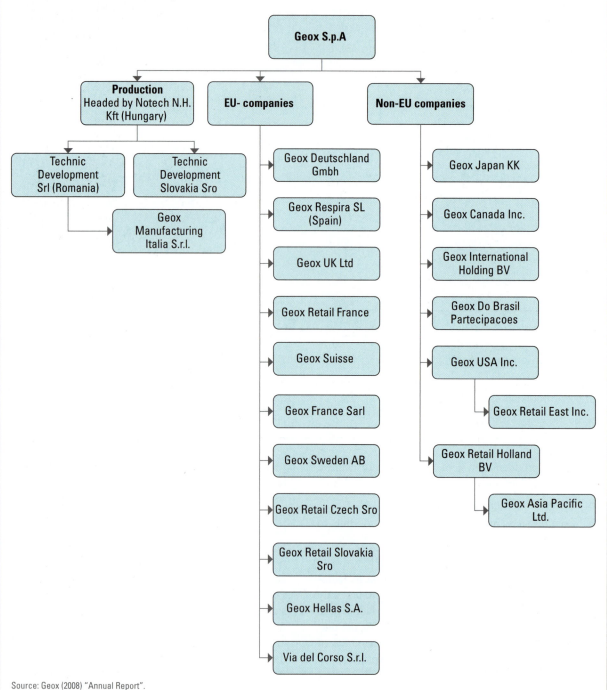

Source: Geox (2008) "Annual Report".

also maintained a close watch on all the production activities carried out by the third-party manufacturers. All of the output from these manufacturing locations would then be consolidated at the group's distribution centres in Italy for Europe, New Jersey for the U.S. and Canada, Tokyo for Japan, and Hong Kong for the rest of Asia.[49]

In the first half of 2009, Geox continued with its strategy to maintain flexibility and optimise production sources, transferring entirely to third parties the production activities that had previously been carried out in Romania by Technic Development Srl. The company also cut back on the production activities carried out in the Slovak Republic by Technic Development Slovakia Sro [see Exhibit 12].

MARKETING. Geox had defined a clear brand marketing strategy that centred on the product's ventilation features. The strategy worked quite effectively because, unlike most of Geox's competitors, the focus was not on fashion and style alone, but on a technical aspect of the product that clearly differentiated it from other products. Moreover, the same message could be used to address consumers of all target groups around the world, whereas most competitors would invariably target one or just a few customer groups or product types in a given market.

Thus, in its marketing, rather than using models or even the celebrities[50] who were known to wear Geox shoes, the company used images of the product and its breathable sole technology.[51]

> *We deliberately don't do campaigns with celebrities. Our product is based on innovative technology. That's why the technology is the core message in our marketing campaigns, illustrated by a sole from which steam is escaping. Lots of advertisers hated it at the start, but we didn't care.*
>
> —MARIO POLEGATO, FOUNDER AND CHAIRMAN OF GEOX[52]

Advertising played an important role in Geox's marketing strategy, and approximately 10% of the company's turnover was invested in promotion.[53] The communication strategy used, while simple, was effective and involved various advertising campaigns and media such as billposting and print. In line with Polegato's thinking, the company perceived that, although its pricing was such that its products targeted middle- to high-income consumers, the potential target group was substantially larger—no one wanted wet or smelly feet.

DISTRIBUTION. Geox's distribution network, which had been developed according to "each country's individual distribution structure and calibrated to the widespread network of multibrand clients," was cited by the company as one of its key success factors.[54]

By 30 June 2009, Geox products were available through approximately 10,000 multi-brand stores around the world. The company also had 997 single-brand Geox stores located on prime urban property worldwide [see Exhibit 13], of which about 77% were franchises and 23% were directly operated stores ("DOS"). The goal of both networks, was to "optimize market share and, at the same time, to promote the Geox brand to end-consumers on a consistent basis."[55]

Recognising the tremendous growth potential in markets such as China and India, the company had committed to expanding in these regions. In 2008, Geox entered into a strategic partnership with Hong Kong–listed company Belle (the largest women's shoe retailer in China in 2007, with a 22% market share),[56] whereby Belle became the exclusive distributor of Geox products in China.[57] The deal supported the penetration of Geox products in the Chinese market by opening over 200 points of sale, including shop-in-shops, over the next two years.[58]

Geox: The Innovative Company

TECHNOLOGY AND INNOVATION. "Geox first is a technology company," said Polegato, emphasising that the company invested heavily[59] in research and development ("R&D").[60]

Ever since the company's first patent in the early 1990s, Polegato had been quite emphatic about the value of patents, which he claimed was the core of Geox's success.

> *We Italians have created some of the greatest inventions in the world—the espresso machine and the pizza, for example. But the men and*

EXHIBIT 12

Geox's Human resources as of 31 December 2008

As of 31 December 2008, the Geox Group had 4043 employees located across the world.

The distribution of these employees across different levels for 2008 and 2007 was as follows.

Level	Number of Geox employees (30 June 2009)	Number of Geox employees (31 December 2008)	Number of Geox employees (31 December 2007)
Factory workers	503	1,721	1,978
Office staff	654	720	665
Shop employees	1,565	1,462	794
Middle managers	107	112	77
Managers	28	28	29
TOTAL	**2,857**	**4,043**	**3,543**

Across key geographic locations, the distribution was as follows.

	Number of Geox employees (30 June 2009)	Number of Geox employees (31 December 2008)	Number of Geox employees (31 December 2007)
Italy	1,074	1,060	898
Romania	–	1,051	1,274
Slovak Republic	470	672	712
Others	1,313	1,260	659
TOTAL	**2,857**	**4,043**	**3,543**

Source: Geox (2009) "Interim Report—First Half 2009".

EXHIBIT 13

Geox's distribution system as of 30 June 2009

As of 30 June 2009, Geox products were delivered through approximately 10,000 multi-brand stores across the world.

The company also had 997 mono-brand stores, of which 770 were franchise and 227 were DOS (Directly Operated Stores).

The distribution of these stores globally was as follows.

Country	Number of Geox shops
Italy	322
Europe *	288
North America	55
Other countries	176
Countries with licensing arrangements	156
TOTAL	**997**

*Europe included France, Benelux, Germany, Austria, UK, Iberia, Switzerland and Scandinavia.

Source: Geox (28 July 2009) "Interim Report—First Half of 2009", www.geox.biz/pdf/Relazione/%2030
_09_09_ING.PDF (accessed 20 February 2010).

women behind them have lost out to the Pizza Huts or Starbucks of this world. This is terrible . . .

I tell all my students to make sure they patent their ideas. After all, one idea is worth more than a factory.

—MARIO POLEGATO, FOUNDER AND
CHAIRMAN OF GEOX[61]

Geox made the development of "breathing technology" its mission.[62] Its work in this field resulted in a stream of patents, and by 30 September 2009, the company held over 50 patents.[63] Of these, three were related to the original key concepts:[64]

- Rubber soles patent: The rubber sole was perforated and contained a special microporous membrane that was waterproof and breathable.
- Leather soles patent: This too was a waterproof and breathable membrane fitted onto the sole, allowing the feet to breathe by passing sweat out through the leather sole, and simultaneously repelling water and humidity.
- Apparel patent: The damp air created by the evaporation of sweat would rise upwards to a special cavity and be expelled through holes in a perforated strip positioned over the shoulders.

There were also patents related to processes, equipment and machinery, and materials. By developing such patents, Geox hoped that competitors would find it difficult to copy its products, even when the original patents expired.[65]

The company invested much in its state-of-the-art R&D facility where, along with continuous experiments on new technology for footwear and apparel products, studies were conducted on temperature and humidity distribution in the human body, spanning such disciplines as physics and orthopaedics. According to Polegato, "There are 15 engineers in our laboratory: they don't work on shoe design though, they specialise in human movement, work in collaboration with people at the best universities, and their job is to constantly generate new ideas."[66]

Along with research, staff development too received much attention.

Innovation is the combination of three factors: creativity, patent and scientific research. We have a unique study program on the premises where we welcome students from around the world and train engineers in our technology.

—MARIO POLEGATO, FOUNDER AND
CHAIRMAN OF GEOX[67]

The company started the Geox School in 2001. This was a training centre which prepared new recruits, providing training on company policy, the characteristics of Geox products and the business development needs of the group.[68]

LOOKING AHEAD. Polegato envisioned the future of his company in terms of four key themes:

It must strive to change the world, it must innovate beyond the imagination of its clients, it must be globally integrated and it must demonstrate that it is not just generous but genuine. Generous is when you look after your employees. By genuine I mean that a company shouldn't have anything to hide.

—MARIO POLEGATO, FOUNDER AND
CHAIRMAN OF GEOX[69]

Polegato's goal was to become the world's biggest shoemaker.[70] By 2009, Geox already ranked second and controlled a 13% share in the lifestyle market. Polegato recognised that, if the company hoped to become the largest, it would need to boost its position from the small fractional share it held in the casual/sports shoes industry and take on giants such as Nike and Adidas. So far, the company had produced only golf shoes and basic running shoes for this market.

To be the biggest we have to take on the casual to sports market. First of all, I produce the breathable shoe for comfort. Now we are bringing top Italian style to make them high fashion as well. We are also making the clothes which we will continue to develop. But the sports shoe is our big goal.

—MARIO POLEGATO, FOUNDER AND
CHAIRMAN OF GEOX[71]

In 2009, Geox listed the following key strategy guidelines for its business development:[72]

- Product innovation: Geox planned to continue researching, patenting and implementing new solutions.
- Consolidation of the leadership position achieved in Italy: This was to be achieved by opening new (primarily franchise) shops in high-traffic city centres and key shopping malls, and increasing the market share and strengthening the loyalty of multi-brand customers through a greater use of corner shops and shop-in-shops.
- International expansion: This was hoped to be achieved by increasing the number of customers served and boosting market share and loyalty among existing customers, by opening new Geox shops in city centres and shopping malls, and by balancing the sales mix through increasing the volume of the men's and women's lines relative to the children's line.

Until 2008, Geox showed rapid two-digit growth in its annual profit. However, in 2008, the effects of the global recession started catching up with the company, and its net income began flattening out. While Geox fared better than sportswear competitors such as Adidas, this was largely due to the resilient Italian consumer and the mid-price range the company operated in.[73]

However, Italy too soon caught up with the global downturn, and on 14 May 2009, Geox shares dropped by 9% after the company announced in its first-quarter results that orders for fall/winter were down by 13% from the previous year.[74] The company decided to boost its promotional activities while at the same time halving its capital expenditure for the year. This would immediately impact the rate at which Geox stores were being opened in prime locations around the world, as this was one of the key components of the capital expenditure incurred by the company in 2008 [see Exhibit 14].

In particular, the company made a decision not to open any new stores during 2009 in the U.S. (traditionally the largest market) until the economy there showed some signs of improvement.[75] This resulted in the company's capital expenditure for the first half of 2009 being reduced to US$30 million—almost half the expenditure of the same period in the previous year—and the overall cash flow situation improving [see Exhibit 15].

Polegato remained confident about Geox's future prospects. In his opinion, Geox would continue to do well given that only 10% of the world's population used leather soles, while the remaining 90% used rubber soles, and the arrival of Geox had made all other rubber soles obsolete.[76] He felt that the unique technological edge that Geox shoes possessed set them so far apart from others in the market that the company had in fact no competitors.[77]

Polegato surmised that the company's innovative products and flexible business model focusing on outsourcing production to countries such as China, along with its cost base with less than 30% of costs being fixed, would see it through the tough times.[78]

Our high profitability, thanks to tight discipline over operating costs, and our solid cash position equal to Euro 75.9 million at the end of June (2009), which is the result of constant attention to investments and strict control over working capital, have protected us from the negative consequences of this crisis.

Despite this, we have decided to take immediate actions to tighten our already streamlined supply and distribution chain. This means that the Group can now count on an even more efficient production structure, an EBITDA margin of around 25% and a network of 1,000 monobrand stores.

—MARIO POLEGATO, FOUNDER AND
CHAIRMAN OF GEOX[79]

Polegato also hoped that Geox-branded apparel would pick up, and move from representing less than

EXHIBIT 14

Geox's cash flow and capital expenditure statement for 2008 and 2007 (US$ million[87])

As of 31 December 2008, Geox's consolidated cash flow statement was as follows.

	As of 31 December 2008	As of 31 December 2007
Net income	158.9	166.2
Depreciation and amortization	39.2	28.6
Other non-cash items	(19.5)	2.3
	178.5	197.1
Change in net working capital	(56.8)	(67.3)
Change in other current assets/liabilities	(8.7)	28.0
Cash flow from operations	112.9	157.8
Capital expenditure	**(130.2)**	**(60.1)**
Disposals	2.8	2.4
Net capital expenditure	(127.4)	(57.7)
Free cash flow	**(14.5)**	**100.0**
Dividends	(84.1)	(52.5)
Increase in share capital	2.2	
Change in net financial position	(96.3)	47.6

The free cash flow of 2008 was negative US$14.5 million (positive US$100.1 million in 2007), mainly due to the increase in capital expenditure to US$130.1 million in 2008 from US$60.1 million in 2007.

The consolidated capital expenditure for the company was as follows.

	As of 31 December 2008	As of 31 December 2007
Trademarks and patents	1.8	0.9
Opening and restructuring of Geox Shop	104.5	39.1
Industrial equipment	5.6	5.5
Industrial plants	1.7	2.5
Offices furniture, warehouse and fittings	10.2	3.3
Information technology	6.4	8.8
Total	**130.2**	**60.1**

Source: Geox (2008) "Annual Report".

10% of the company's net sales to about half.[80] This would improve overall profit margins, which at around 24% for apparel were much higher than for footwear.[81]

What Next?

At the moment, the shoes business is very difficult. I believe, however, that GEOX is in a great situation, because we can mix technology and style. . . . In this economic situation, the best thing for a company is to offer innovative products. It's the only way out of the crisis.

—MARIO POLEGATO, FOUNDER AND CHAIRMAN OF GEOX[82]

EXHIBIT 15

Geox's cash flow and capital expenditure statement for the first half of 2009 (US$ million[88])

As of 30 June 2009, Geox's consolidated cash flow statement was as follows.

	First Half 2009	First Half 2008	As of 31 December 2008
Net income	76.5	106.1	158.9
Depreciation and amortization	31.2	16.5	39.2
Other non-cash items	14.6	(25.9)	(19.5)
	122.2	96.7	178.5
Change in net working capital	(2.2)	(62.5)	(56.8)
Change in other current assets/liabilities	41.8	29.1	(8.7)
Cash flow from operations	161.8	63.4	112.9
Capital expenditure	(29.7)	(54.8)	(130.2)
Disposals	1.8	0.7	2.8
Net capital expenditure	(27.9)	(54.1)	(127.4)
Free cash flow	133.9	9.3	(14.5)
Dividends	(84.1)	(84.1)	(84.1)
Increase in share capital	0.03	2.0	2.2
Change in net financial position	49.9	(72.7)	(96.3)

The consolidated capital expenditure for the company was as follows.

	First Half 2009	First Half 2008	As of 31 December 2008
Trademarks and patents	0.7	0.6	1.8
Opening and restructuring of Geox Shop	17.5	45.8	104.5
Industrial equipment	3.2	2.6	5.6
Industrial plants	0.4	1.1	1.7
Offices furniture, warehouse and fittings	5.6	2.5	10.2
Information technology	2.4	2.1	6.4
Total	**29.7**	**54.8**	**130.2**

Source: Geox (28 July 2009) "Interim Report—First Half of 2009", www.geox.biz/pdf/Relazione/%2030_09_09_ING.PDF (accessed 20 February 2010).

Geox had used distinctive innovation to break into a mature and saturated industry flooded with brands, and had carved out a niche for itself. Now it had to decide what strategy to adopt to ensure that it could successfully renew its technology, products and processes, and maintain its long-term competitiveness.

Endnotes

1. Lo, M. (22 September 2008) "Big Bucks, No Sweat", *The Standard*, http://203.80.2.2/news_detail.asp (accessed 8 March 2010).

2. The GEOX brand name was chosen by Polegato and combined the Greek word for "earth" and the letter "x", which symbolised technology.

3. Shoe Intelligence (3 October 2008) "International Lifestyle Casual Footwear Market", Company Presentations.

4. Geox (30 June 2009) "Press Map", Company Presentations.

5. Tsouvalas, D. (29 June 2009) "Q&A: Mario Moretti Polegato", *ExecDigital, www.execdigital.co.uk/Q-A--Mario-Moretti-Polegato--GEOX-_27773.aspx* (accessed 1 March 2010).

6. Polegato was born in 1952 in the Alpine foothills of Crocetta del Montello, Italy.

7. Geox (30 June 2009) "Press Map", Company Presentations.

8. Boland, V. (22 April 2009) "Italy's Entrepreneur with Sole", *Financial Times*.

9. Polegato held degrees in wine technology and law.

10. Pagano, M. (29 November 2009) "Watch Out World: Geox Is Sticking the Boot In", *The Independent, www.independent. co.uk/news/business/analysis-and-features/watch-out-world-geox-is-sticking-the-boot-in-1830372.html* (accessed 24 February 2010).

11. Kolesnikov-Jessop, S. (7 October 2007) "A Desert Jog Leads to a Fortune", *International Herald Tribune*.

12. Driscoll, M and Wagle, Y. (4 March 2004) "Industry Surveys—Apparel & Footwear", *Standard & Poor's, www. sandp.ecnext.com › Home › S&P Industry Surveys.html* (accessed 10 March 2010).

13. Geox (30 June 2009) "Mario Moretti Polegato—Geox Chairman", Company Presentations.

14. ExecDigital (5 June 2008) "IP Protection Is the Key to Knowledge Businesses, Says Polegato", *www.execdigital. co.uk/IP-protection-the-key-to-knowledge-businesses--says-Poleagato_6112.aspx* (accessed 2 March 2010).

15. Laurent, L. (19 May 2009) "Sweating the Recession, Italian-Style", *Forbes.com, www.forbes.com/2009/05/19/ polegato-geox-fashion-face-markets-retail.html* (accessed 24 February 2010).

16. Mahpar, M. (7 November 2009) "Up Close and Personal", *The Star Online, www.biz.thestar.com.my/news/story.asp* (accessed 2 March 2010).

17. Kolesnikov-Jessop, S. (7 October 2007) "A Desert Jog Leads to a Fortune", *International Herald Tribune*.

18. US$1 = €0.74 on 22 February 2010.

19. Gregory, S. (1 April 2009) "Can a Golf Shoe Help Geox Beat the Recession", *Time CNN, www.time.com/time/business/ article/0,8599,1888616,00.html* (accessed 25 February 2010).

20. Ibid.

21. Ibid.

22. SATRA (2008) "World Footwear Markets", *www.satra. co.uk/bulletin/article_view.php?id=284* (accessed 22 February 2010).

23. Ibid.

24. AndhraNews.net (12 July 2007) "Global Footwear Market to Exceed $192 Billion by 2010, According to New Report by Global Industry Analysts, Inc", *www.andhranews.net/ intl/2007/July/12/em-Global-Footwear-Market.asp* (accessed 22 February 2010).

25. Ibid.

26. Shoe Intelligence (3 October 2008) "International Lifestyle Casual Footwear Market", Company Presentations.

27. Schenker, J. (2 April 2008) "Geox Takes On the Goliaths of Sport", *BusinessWeek, www.businessweek.com/magazine/ content/08_15* (accessed 2 March 2010).

28. Tyler, R. and Halls, J. (25 May 2009) "Clarks Makes Strides as Rivals Feel the Pinch", *Telegraph, www.telegraph. co.uk/finance/newsbysector/retailandconsumer/5383850/ clarks-makes-strides-as-rivals-feel-the-pinch.html* (accessed 7 April 2010).

29. US$1 = £0.65 on 10 April 2010.

30. Tyler, R. and Halls, J. (25 May 2009) "Clarks Makes Strides as Rivals Feel the Pinch", *Telegraph, www.telegraph. co.uk/finance/newsbysector/retailandconsumer/5383850/ clarks-makes-strides-as-rivals-feel-the-pinch.html* (accessed 7 April 2010).

31. Ibid.

32. Nike (2009) "Annual Report".

33. Ibid.

34. Ibid.

35. Landler, M. (4 August 2005) "Nike Will Be Facing a Pumped-Up Rival", *The New York Times*.

36. Adidas (2009) "Annual Report".

37. 32% of all Adidas suppliers were based in China alone.

38. As of 30 September 2009, 89% of the net sales were from footwear products.

39. For further details, see Geox's website: www.geox.com.

40. Geox (30 June 2009) "Press Map", Company Presentations.

41. Geox (2008) "Annual Report".

42. Ibid.

43. Ibid.

44. Pan, S. (1 November 2004) "Geox Launches World's Largest Shoe Making Base in Wenzhou", *HKTDC, www.hktdc. com/.../Geox-Launches-World-s-Largest-Shoe-Making-Base-in-Wenzhou.htm* (accessed 3 March 2010).

45. Pan, S. (19 June 2009) "Shoes That Strode From OEM To ODM", HKTDC, www.hktdc.com/.../Shoes-That-Strode-From-OEM-To-ODM.htm(accessed 3 March 2010).

46. Ibid.

47. Ibid.

48. Geox (2008) "Annual Report".

49. Ibid.

50. Such celebrities included Spanish royalty, Pope John Paul II, Barack Obama and actress Angelina Jolie.

51. Zemach, O. (2 March 2010) "It's in His Sole", *The Jerusalem Post, www.jpost.com/Magazine/Features/Article. aspx?id=105584* (accessed 2 March 2010).

52. Thomann, A. (3 January 2007) "All Steamed Up about Geox", *Credit Suisse Online Publications, www.emagazine. credit-suisse.com/apps/article/index.cfm* (accessed 6 March 2010).

53. Geox (2007) "Annual Report".

54. Ibid.

55. Geox (2008) "Annual Report".

56. Balfour, F. (5 September 2008) "Shoe Seller Belle Conquers China", *www.businessweek.com/globalbiz/con-tent/2008/gb2008095_430889.htm* (accessed 4 May 2010).

57. ArticlesBase (16 September 2008) "Geox Distribution Deal Confirmed", *www.articlesbase.com/free-articles/china-geox-distribution-deal-confirmed-564132.html* (accessed 4 March 2010).

58. ArticlesBase (16 September 2008) "Geox Distribution Deal Confirmed", *www.articlesbase.com/free-articles/china-geox-distribution-deal-confirmed-564132.html* (accessed 4 March 2010).

59. In 2008, the company spent US$20.6 million on R&D expenses, up from US$19.2 million in 2007.

60. Kuchment, A. (14 April 2008) "Soles with Holes", *Newsweek, www.newsweek.com/id/130289* (accessed 20 February 2010).

61. Pagano, M. (29 November 2009) "Watch Out World: Geox Is Sticking the Boot In", *The Independent, www.independent. co.uk/news/business/analysis-and-features/watch-out-world-geox-is-sticking-the-boot-in-1830372.html* (accessed 24 February 2010).

62. Geox (2008) "Annual Report".

63. Geox (30 June 2009) "Press Map", Company Presentations.

64. Pagano, M. (29 November 2009) "Watch Out World: Geox Is Sticking the Boot In", *The Independent, www.independent. co.uk/news/business/analysis-and-features/watch-out-world-geox-is-sticking-the-boot-in-1830372.html* (accessed 24 February 2010).

65. Typically, design patents expired after 10 years, and industrial or process patents after 20 years.

66. ExecDigital (5 June 2008) "IP Protection Is the Key to Knowledge Businesses, Says Polegato", *www.execdigital. co.uk/IP-protection-the-key-to-knowledge-businesses--says-Poleagato_6112.aspx* (accessed 2 March 2010).

67. Zemach, O. (2 March 2010) "It's in His Sole", *The Jerusalem Post, www.jpost.com/Magazine/Features/Article. aspx?id=105584* (accessed 2 March 2010).

68. Geox (2008) "Annual Report".

69. Boland, V. (21 April 2009) "Italy's Entrepreneur with Sole", *Financial Times*.

70. Pagano, M. (29 November 2009) "Watch Out World: Geox Is Sticking the Boot In", *The Independent, www.independent. co.uk/news/business/analysis-and-features/watch-out-world-geox-is-sticking-the-boot-in-1830372.html* (accessed 24 February 2010).

71. Ibid.

72. Geox (2008) "Annual Report".

73. Laurent, L. (19 May 2009) "Sweating the Recession, Italian-Style", *Forbes.com, www.forbes.com/2009/05/19/ polegato-geox-fashion-face-markets-retail.html* (accessed 24 February 2010).

74. Ibid.

75. Ibid.

76. Thomann, A. (3 January 2007) "All Steamed Up about Geox", *Credit Suisse Online Publications, www.emagazine. credit-suisse.com/apps/article/index.cfm* (accessed 6 March 2010).

77. Ibid.

78. Laurent, L. (19 May 2009) "Sweating the Recession, Italian-Style", *Forbes.com, www.forbes.com/2009/05/19/ polegato-geox-fashion-face-markets-retail.html* (accessed 24 February 2010).

79. Geox (28 July 2009) "Interim Report—First Half of 2009", www.geox.biz/pdf/Relazione/%2030_09_09_ING.PDF (accessed 20 February 2010).

80. For the first half of 2009, footwear sales represented 91% of consolidated sales, with a 1% increase compared to the first half of 2008. Apparel sales accounted for 9% of consolidated sales, showing a 43% increase over the same period in the previous year.

81. Laurent, L. (19 May 2009) "Sweating the Recession, Italian-Style", *Forbes.com, www.forbes.com/2009/05/19/ polegato-geox-fashion-face-markets-retail.html* (accessed 24 February 2010).

82. Gregory, S. (1 April 2009) "Can a Golf Shoe Help Geox Beat the Recession?", *Time CNN, www.time.com/time/business/article/0,8599,1888616,00.html* (accessed 25 February 2010).

83. US$1 = €0.74 on 22 February 2010.

84. US$1 = €0.74 on 22 February 2010.

85. Asset impairment referred largely to investments made for the stores' network that, given the macroeconomic scenario, were not certain to be recovered. Each shop had a current value of the forecast net cash flow (the so-called "value in use") determined, and if the value in use was lower than its book value, its assets would be written down accordingly.

86. US$1 = €0.74 on 22 February 2010.

87. US$1 = €0.74 on 22 February 2010.

88. US$1 = €0.74 on 22 February 2010.

Frank T. Rothaermel
Georgia Institute of Technology

Michael Janovec
Georgia Institute of Technology

MR. JIM HARTZFELD walked into the Interface offices at 6:25 a.m. on Monday morning. Having just purchased a coffee and bagel from the local indie coffee shop, Octane, Mr. Hartzfeld was looking forward to catching up on e-mails and perhaps even glancing at the latest *Fast Company* magazine. This type of morning was rare for the Managing Director of InterfaceRAISE, the sustainability consulting arm of Interface, Inc. In fact, "leisure" had become a foreign term to Mr. Hartzfeld over the past five years.

As Jim walked through the door into the building, he was greeted by John Wells, CEO and President of Interface Americas. "What a great chance to catch up with John," Jim thought to himself, and invited him to his office. Once the two men were seated, Mr. Wells started to speak:

Jim, as you are well aware, it appears that we've successfully weathered the downturn, and our business is gaining momentum. Dan [Hendrix, CEO of Interface, Inc., and John and Jim's boss] has been challenging all of us to come up with big ideas to double our businesses. I think InterfaceRAISE can do much more than that and can become a more powerful influence on Interface's brand, and therefore my business. At the same time, I think InterfaceRAISE can contribute significantly to our corporate goal, "becoming restorative through the power of influence." I would like for you to grow to $5 million in five years. Can you do it? I know that we're in separate businesses and we normally compete for resources, but I think we should take advantage of this strong quarter and request additional funding for RAISE from Dan. It sounds unusual, but I'd be willing to help you do it. To get his buy-in, we'll need to show Dan

a strong business plan detailing how much money you would need and how you would grow RAISE. Dan wants to look at all of our proposals on Friday, so bring me your plan no later than Thursday noon to brainstorm.

Interface and Sustainability

InterfaceRAISE's inception was closely intertwined with sustainability at Interface, Inc., a modular carpet and commercial broadloom company. In the summer of 1994, Jim Hartzfeld, a recent MBA graduate from Emory University and then a research associate at Interface, approached Ray Anderson, founder and CEO of Interface. Jim handed Mr. Anderson a handwritten letter from a sales manager in California that posed the question, "Some customers want to know what Interface is doing for the environment. How should we answer?"[1] The letter continued, "When it comes to the environment, some customers believe Interface just doesn't get it."[2]

Reading this, Ray Anderson's first reaction was, "Don't get what? Making carpet tiles demands so many petroleum-derived chemicals that we aren't just dependent on oil companies, we are like an extension of them. We haven't broken a single environmental rule. Not even bent one. We were legal, in compliance—100 percent."[3] As Anderson reflected further on this question, however, he knew he had to respond. After all, Interface had been built on responding to customer needs. He thought, "If we don't answer the question [the] sales manager had relayed, we stand to lose other sales. How many? I have no idea. But I do know that telling our customers, 'we comply with all environmental laws' isn't going to cut it."[4]

Professor Frank T. Rothaermel and Michael Janovec (GT MBA 2011) prepared this case. It is developed for the purpose of class discussion. It is not intended to be used for any kind of endorsement, source of data, or depiction of efficient or inefficient management. We thank Mr. Jim Hartzfeld and Mr. John Wells for generously sharing their time and expertise. All opinions expressed and all errors and omissions are entirely those of the authors. © Rothaermel and Janovec, 2013.

To craft a proper response, one of Ray's lieutenants suggested that Interface organize a task force to determine what Interface was doing for the environment. Ray supported the idea and chose to put Jim Hartzfeld in charge, due to his marketing and technical background. Jim had recently joined Interface with over a decade of experience with the largest oil and chemical company in the world. Jim reflected on this assignment saying:

> I got assigned to create this task force not knowing anything about the environment, so I turned it around on Ray. I said, "If you're going to do any kind of change work or any kind of big process, you've got to create a vision from the top."[5]

Mr. Anderson reluctantly agreed to kick off the first meeting of the task force on August 31, 1994. In the days leading up to the event, he struggled with writing his speech: "At the time, I hadn't given one thought about the environment; I was concerned with dollars and cents. How could I possibly speak passionately about a topic in which I was neither an expert nor cared a great deal about?" Mr. Anderson's question was answered a few days later when a book by Paul Hawken, *The Ecology of Commerce,* appeared on his desk. As Ray Anderson read through the book that afternoon and later that night, he had an epiphany:

> While reading a section on how a deer population without any natural predators over-consumed to the point of decimation, *it hit me like a spear in the chest.* Titans of industry like me had been fueling the human species' overconsumption for the past one hundred years. We needed to do something to stop this. . . .
>
> Our civilization was chewing up resources faster than the earth could renew them. I stood indicted as a plunderer, a destroyer of the earth, a thief, stealing my own grandchildren's future. And I thought, *My God, someday what I do here will be illegal. Someday they will send people like me to jail.*[6]

Yet Mr. Anderson wondered what he could do. He was in the carpet business, and carpets needed huge amounts of petroleum-based products in their resource-intensive production process. Reading further, Mr. Anderson found Hawken's encouragement for people exactly like Anderson to act. Hawken argued that business people alone could reverse the trend of environmental degradation from industrialization. Individuals did not possess the collective power to do so. Governments were typically reactive rather than proactive and thus were unequipped to provide the transformational change. Thus, said Hawken, it was up to capitalist businesses, "the only institution large enough, wealthy enough, and pervasive and powerful enough to lead humankind out of the mess we are making."[7] After finishing the final page of Hawken's book at 3:00 a.m. that morning, Anderson began to write his keynote speech.[8]

On August 31, 1994, at about 10:15 a.m., Mr. Anderson walked up to the podium, paused, and took a deep breath. He was about to change the face of Interface forever. Mr. Anderson started by telling the story that he'd read a few days earlier about the reindeer population on St. Martin's Island that had vanished because their numbers exceeded the carrying capacity on the island—a vivid example of the consequences of overconsumption.

> What happened on St. Martin's Island is a metaphor for the world. Look around and you'll see many of the same signs. World grain production has already peaked and is in decline. So is the world's fish catch. Forests are disappearing. Aquifers are dropping. Deserts are growing. Oil is getting more expensive and harder to find. Nobody can predict what the implications might be for our business or our civilization. But I do know that, like the reindeer, we are far exceeding the carrying capacity of this good earth. Unless somebody does something to arrest and reverse the tide, catastrophe *will* strike. Now what somebody am I talking about? The strongest institution in the world has to take the lead. That is not the church, it is not education, and it is not the government, either. It is business and industry. It's people just like us. Us!
>
> Every company has to face three ecological challenges honestly and head-on:

1. What we **take** from the earth;
2. What we **make,** and what collateral damage we do in the making of it (pollution of all kinds);
3. What we **waste** along the way (in all forms), from the wellhead to the landfill.[9]

Ray Anderson then posed a challenge to his stunned employees: "What if Interface became the first industrial company in the world to achieve sustainability?"[10] He proposed that by achieving sustainability, the company could boost its brand image and as a result, its bottom line. He told the silent crowd of engineers and senior managers that he wanted them to put together a proposal of how long they expected it would take for Interface to achieve sustainability and how much it would cost. Then, he asked them to consider what was beyond sustainability: What would a "restorative company" look like? Anderson then left the podium.[11]

The reaction of the crowd and the industry in general was utter shock. Bob Shaw, owner of Shaw Industries, one of the world's largest carpet manufacturers told Ray, "You're a dreamer. It's OK to be a dreamer and lose your money, but you're going to take your whole company down with you."[12] Jim Hartzfeld recalled a speech that Mr. Anderson gave at a large company meeting:

> Before the meeting, I told him [Ray] that some of the guys thought he had lost his mind. He's got this vein that popped out of his forehead; he was not happy with that message. He opened his talk by saying, "I hear some of you think I've gone around the bend. That's my job, to go around that corner and see what's on the other side."[13]

"Mount Sustainability"

What did Ray Anderson see around that corner? Mr. Anderson set the goal for Interface to be entirely independent of oil by 2020. That included not using oil in raw materials or as energy to fuel its plants.[14] At a 1997 sales meeting, Mr. Anderson described the journey to achieve Interface's newly found mission to develop the first sustainable industrial company as follows: "I have a mental image of a mountain to climb. A mountain that's taller than Everest, and infinitely more difficult to scale. The name of the mountain is Sustainability."[15]

Mr. Anderson stated that at the peak of Mount Sustainability lay Interface's ultimate goal of MissionZero. MissionZero was the company's commitment to eliminate all negative impacts that Interface had on the environment by 2020. Not only did Ray Anderson want Interface to be completely sustainable, the company had to achieve it profitably; otherwise there would be no future for the business. As others had said, "No margin, no mission." To reach this lofty goal, Mr. Anderson challenged his employees to join him in ascending the Seven Fronts of Mount Sustainability (Exhibits 1 and 2).[16] The seven faces of the summit that Anderson set forth were:

1. Moving toward zero waste.
2. Increasingly benign emissions, working up the supply chain.
3. Increasing efficiency and using more renewable energy.
4. Closed-loop recycling, copying nature's way of turning waste into food.
5. Resource-efficient transportation, from commuting to logistics to plant sitting.
6. Sensitivity hook-up, changing minds and getting [all stakeholders] on the same page, replacing confrontation with cooperation.
7. Redesigning commerce, teaching a new Economics 101 that puts it all together and assesses accurate costs, sets real prices, and maximizes resource-efficiency.[17]

EXHIBIT 1

Typical Company of the 20th Century

Source: Anderson, R. C. (2009), *Confessions of a Radical Industrialist* (New York: St. Martin's Press), Appendix C, Fig. 1.

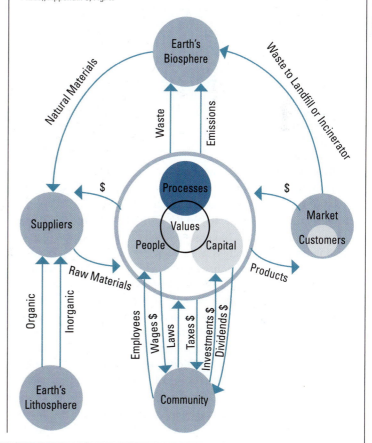

EXHIBIT 2

Prototypical Company of the 21st Century

Source: Anderson, R. C. (2009), *Confessions of a Radical Industrialist* (New York: St. Martin's Press), Appendix C, Fig. 2.

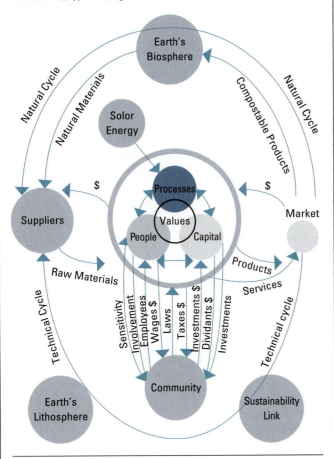

To scale Mount Sustainability, Interface focused attention across all of the seven fronts enumerated by Mr. Anderson. For example, focusing on waste (Front 1), Interface implemented the QUEST (Quality Utilizing Employees' Suggestions and Teamwork) program in 1995 to address waste reduction. Interface defined waste as any cost that does not add value to the customer. This program encouraged employees to identify, measure, and eliminate waste.[18] To reduce waste, Interface employed revolutionary manufacturing techniques, sought out new manufacturing materials, and implemented the latest waste-reducing installation techniques. In addition to traditional, tangible forms of waste, Interface added any use of nonrenewable energy to its target list of waste to be eliminated.

Through its QUEST program and other company-sponsored initiatives, Interface avoided $433 million in waste expenses between 1995 and 2009.[19] In addition, the company reduced its reliance on wet-printing by shifting manufacturing to yarns that had already been colored in the extrusion process, resulting in reduced internal waste, toxic emissions, and energy consumption.[20] Interface's Bentley Prince Street plant in California saved 28 tons of yarn in just the first two months of 2008, equating to about $168,000.[21]

Traditional carpet tile manufacturers sold tiles on the premise that companies could replace only worn tiles, rather than the entire carpet. However, an obvious problem with this approach had been matching slightly worn carpet tiles with the new replacements. When tiles did not match, most end users replaced more tiles and left worn ones only in hard-to-see areas, which negated the benefits of using tiles to reduce waste and save money. To solve this challenge, Interface's design consultant, David Oakey, applied a concept called *bio-mimicry*. He observed that in nature, no two patches of forest floor or grass are alike, yet they still blend together. Based on this premise, Mr. Oakey designed a radical new random carpet pattern and process named Entropy. In this product line, no two tiles are identical. Instead, shades and patterns vary slightly, allowing the tiles to blend with one another no matter their age or the direction in which they are installed. This innovation had the added benefit of reducing installation time since installers could place the tiles without regard to direction; at the same time, customers needed to replace only their worn tiles.[22] Entropy became the largest selling product in Interface's history. Today, the multiple variations of the Entropy design principle account for roughly 40 percent of Interface's carpet tile sales.[23]

Another innovation designed to reduce installation waste was Interface's TacTiles. These small adhesive squares rest below the carpet tiles at the corners that secure four tiles together. Using TacTiles eliminated the need for glue, which typically contained volatile organic compounds (VOCs) associated with adverse health effects.[24] Further, traditional glues often destroyed the floor underneath the carpet, resulting in thousands of dollars in damage upon removal. Using the TacTiles eliminated this cost entirely.[25]

Another step in Interface's efforts to reduce the impact of its raw material stream was aimed at recycling, through its ReEntry 2.0 program that began in 1995. Under this program, Interface agreed to take back used carpet (even from competitors). At the Interface facility, the carpet fibers were separated from the backing and either sent to yarn suppliers, where they were reprocessed to make new nylon fibers, or to other industry partners that used post-consumer nylon. The vinyl carpet backing was recycled within the Interface facility to make GlassBacRE, Interface's recycled backing material.

Progress Toward Sustainability

Through 2009, Interface had diverted over 200 million pounds of materials from landfills by recycling it through its ReEntry 2.0 program. It had reduced its own manufacturing waste sent to landfills by 80 percent. It reduced its greenhouse gas emissions by 44 percent, and when you included offsets from its landfill gas project, net greenhouse gas emissions had fallen by 94 percent. The company's water usage had decreased by 80 percent from 1996 levels. Interface engineers were working diligently toward the goal of having all the energy required to operate its plants come from renewable sources by the end of 2020.

Interface operated eight manufacturing facilities that ran on 100 percent renewable electricity.[26]

Through Mr. Anderson's vision and the efforts of countless associates, Interface became a leader in sustainability. Between 1996 and 2009, the company estimated that it had saved $433 million in waste costs due to its energy efficiency and waste elimination efforts (Exhibits 3 and 4). Moreover, Interface's business model forever changed the carpet industry. Speaking of sustainability as a business model, Mr. Anderson stated:

> Sustainability has given my company a competitive edge in more ways than one. It has proven to be the most powerful marketplace differentiator I have known in my long career. Our costs are down, our profits are up, and our products are the best they have ever been [see Exhibits 5 and 6]. Sustainable design has provided an unexpected wellspring of innovation, people are galvanized around a shared higher purpose, better people are applying, the best people are staying and working with a purpose, the goodwill in the marketplace generated by our focus on sustainability far exceeds that which any amount of advertising or marketing expenditure could have generated—this company believes it has found a better way to a bigger and more legitimate profit—a better business model.[27]

EXHIBIT 3

Cumulative Cost Avoided from Waste Elimination Activities (QUEST Program) ($ in millions)

Source: Anderson, R. C. (2009), *Confessions of a Radical Industrialist* (New York: St. Martin's Press), p. 60.

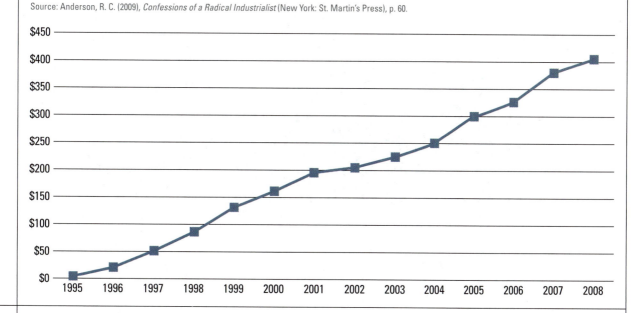

EXHIBIT 4

Energy Consumption Profile (2008)

Source: Anderson, R. C. (2009), *Confessions of a Radical Industrialist* (New York: St. Martin's Press), p. 108.

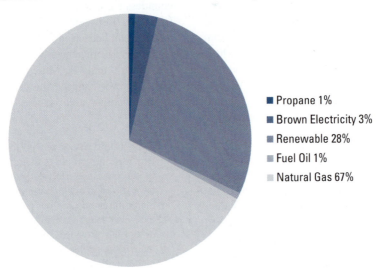

- Propane 1%
- Brown Electricity 3%
- Renewable 28%
- Fuel Oil 1%
- Natural Gas 67%

EXHIBIT 5

Interface, Inc. (Consolidated) Sales from Continuing Operations ($ in millions)

Source: Anderson, R. C. (2009), *Confessions of a Radical Industrialist* (New York: St. Martin's Press), p. 85.

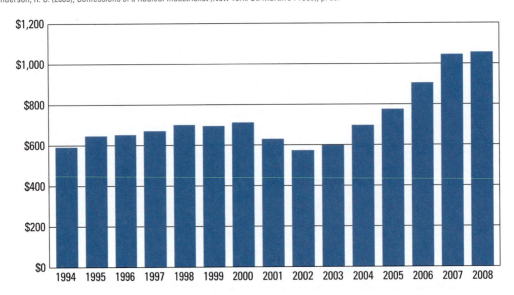

EXHIBIT 6

Interface, Inc. (Consolidated) Income from Continuing Operations ($ in millions)

Source: Anderson, R. C. (2009), *Confessions of a Radical Industrialist* (New York: St. Martin's Press), p. 108.

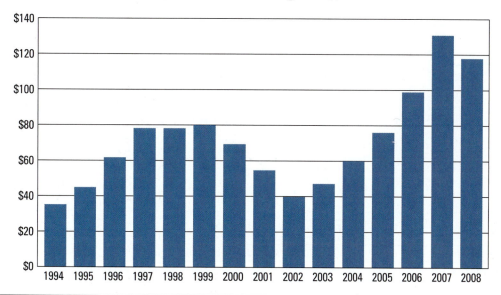

How had the changes affected the company's bottom line? Interface reported that between 1996 and 2008 it increased sales by 66 percent and more than doubled earnings. The share price of Interface stock rose from $6.75 in 1994 to $15.00 by 1997 (Exhibit 7, next page).[28] Savings thus far had arisen primarily due to reduced energy and water usage (as opposed to raw material savings).[29] In addition, Interface and Mr. Anderson had received numerous accolades (Exhibit 8, page C115).

Interface, Inc. Company History

Ray Anderson attended the Georgia Institute of Technology on a football scholarship, majoring in Industrial Engineering. One key lesson from Georgia Tech that stuck with him was the mantra of then-Dean of Industrial Engineering, Frank Groseclose, which he shared frequently with his students during his lectures: "There is always a better way."[30]

Upon graduating from Georgia Tech in 1956, Ray Anderson began his career as an engineer in the carpet and textile business. For the next 14 years, Mr. Anderson served in various positions at Callaway Mills and Milliken & Co.[31] During his tenure at Milliken, Mr. Anderson, then a research manager, was sent to England to research the technology behind carpet tiles, also known as modular carpet. Here, he met

with representatives from Carpets International (CI). Seeing the potential to apply this process to carpet tile manufacturing in the United States, Anderson returned to Milliken and presented his results. Mr. Milliken, however, balked at Anderson's proposal and tabled the project, citing fears of inflation and concern over the lack of demand for carpet tiles.

Mr. Anderson knew, though, that carpet tiles would be a hit in the burgeoning office market. Unlike broadloom carpet, tiles allowed companies the flexibility to rearrange the office layout without the need to reinvest in new carpeting, thereby reducing expenses. Unable to convince management to employ the fusion-bonding process and enter the carpet-tile market, Ray Anderson resigned his position at Milliken. He then met with executives from CI to discuss the possibility of expanding their technology into the United States through a joint venture. In 1973, CI agreed to provide Anderson with $750,000 in seed money, and they founded Carpets International of Georgia, Inc. in West Point, Georgia.

Over the next 20 years the company grew, from $800,000 in revenues in 1973 to revenues of over $582 million in 1991, via a series of mergers with companies such as Heuga Holdings B.V. and Stiehl.[32] Innovation, coupled with an office building boom in the mid-1970s, further fueled Interface's rise during the first phase of its existence.

EXHIBIT 7

Interface, Inc. (IFSIA) Stock Price vs. Dow Jones Industrial Average (DJIA) (past five years)

Source: http://finance.yahoo.com/echarts? s=IFSIA#chart2:symbol=ifsia;range=5y;compare=^dji;indicator=volume;charttype=line;crosshair=on;ohlcvalues=0;logscale=on;source=undefined.

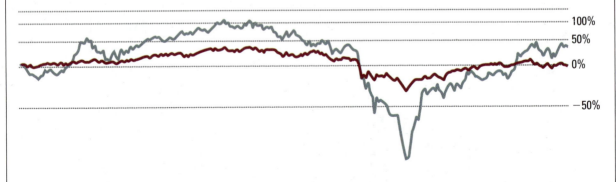

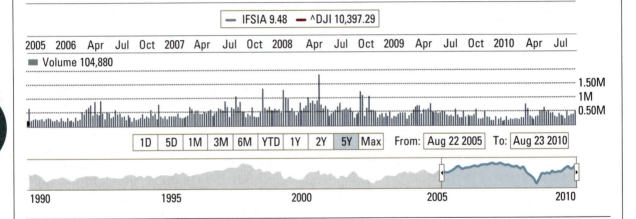

Despite the company's early success and ascension in the marketplace, Interface was not immune to economic conditions. In 1991, Interface's sales shrank for the first time in company history, from $623 million in 1990 to $582 million in 1991, with a net income of $8.9 million. To boost Interface's earnings, Mr. Anderson began exploring new possible sources of revenue. Thus in 1992, the company founded Interface Service Management, Inc. to provide carpet cleaning and maintenance services.[33] It wasn't until the summer of 1994, though, that Mr. Anderson found the change (sustainability) he was looking for.

The Birth of InterfaceRAISE

In 1994, an idea that had been brewing in Ray Anderson's mind came into focus with a single phone call. One of the top executives of the largest non-oil company in the world—Mike Duke, CEO of Walmart's U.S. store division, and future CEO of Wal-Mart Stores, Inc.—wanted to bring his management team to Interface. Ray's credibility as a corporate leader moving toward sustainability resulted in his invitation to speak at a Walmart offsite retreat in October 2004. Ray was such a hit that Mr. Duke wanted to see Interface in person.[34]

Jim Hartzfeld remembered, "When the man who was maybe third on the pecking order of the *Fortune 100* called, we thought maybe it was worth spending a little more time thinking about how we were implementing our sustainability model."[35] Until that point, Interface had seen its share of visitors inquiring about its sustainability practices; however, while there were many common themes, there was little consistency in explaining what they did. Whoever happened to be in the factory at the time would explain the model from

EXHIBIT 8

Interface, Inc. Accolades

Year	Recognition
2005	Global Mindchange Award for Business Responsibility
2005	Best 50 Corporate Citizens List (Ranked 8th), *Corporate Knights Magazine*
2006	Business Ethics Best Corporate Citizens List (Ranked 24th)
2006	Alliance for Sustainability Award
2006	Business Achievement Award for Cool Blue technology, *The Environmental Business Journal*
2006	Top 10 Green Company of 2006, *Portfolio 21 Magazine*
2007	Ray Anderson named in list of the "Heroes of the Environment," *Time Magazine*
2007	Ray Anderson named a Top 20 Hero, *Elle Magazine*
2008	Georgia 100 (Ranked 8th), *The Atlanta Journal Constitution*
2008	One of the World's Top Sustainable Stocks, *Sustainablebusiness.com*
2009	2009 Honor Roll, *The Centers for Companies that Care*

Source: www.interfaceglobal.com/Company/Awards/InterfaceFLOR-2009-Highlights.aspx.

his or her perspective. Now that Messrs. Hartzfeld, Anderson, and the plant team had to give a day-long presentation to executives from one of the world's largest companies, everything changed.

Jim Hartzfeld, Ray Anderson, and Dr. Mike Bertolucci, President of Interface Research Corporation, started reflecting about their model from its origins, asking questions such as, "What is it that we have learned? What have we learned on the human front? On the technical front? On the operations front? On the financial front? What would the case study look like, and how would we present it to Mike [Duke at Walmart]?"[36]

Mr. Duke's visit was so successful that Interface began to consider the idea of creating a formalized group to reflect more thoroughly on what Interface had learned from its sustainability efforts. The hope was to develop the skills to help other companies accelerate their sustainability journeys—not as a clever strategy to sell more carpet, but as a viable, separate business unit. That idea was built on an earlier business called, "One World Learning," an experiential learning company. The concept solidified into a real project when Doug McMillon, then CEO of Sam's Club, decided to bring another Walmart executive team to Interface a few months later for the same experience—the "Sustainability Cultural Immersion," as it was nicknamed by Walmart executive Andy Ruben.

Walmart's reaction was so enthusiastic that it drove home the realization that in order to live up to Ray Anderson's vision of truly changing how the world does business, Interface would have to get serious about sharing its sustainability business model. Thus was born InterfaceRAISE, a sustainability consultancy, and Jim Hartzfeld was appointed as Managing Director. Interface founder Ray Anderson explained, "we chose to call it 'RAISE' because its job was to help other companies:

- Reshape corporate culture and *raise* awareness;
- Measure progress toward sustainability and *raise* standards;
- Uncover new opportunities and *raise* expectations; and
- Inspire process and product innovation to *raise* profits."[37]

As of spring 2010, InterfaceRAISE had less than $1 million in annual revenues, and one part-time and three full-time employees. As a core part of its resource strategy and external positioning, it had tapped over 20 "peer experts" for its projects from other Interface businesses. Many of those peers had over a decade of practice applying the concepts of sustainability in their Interface responsibilities, be it leading manufacturing, technology, marketing, sales, or other functions within the company. InterfaceRAISE's customers ranged in size from $30 million to $400 billion in revenues, and hailed from a wide variety of industries.

SERVICES OFFERED. InterfaceRAISE provided sustainability-strategy consulting services that enabled businesses to transform the way their organizations viewed and implemented sustainability. The firm adopted a three-pronged, integrated approach, targeting sustainability from:

- *Leadership* (vision), which asks, "Who are we becoming, and how do we get there?" [38]
- *Culture* (identity), which asks, "Who are we and how do we demonstrate it?"[39]
- *Application* (action), which asks, "What do we produce and how does it affect the world?"[40]

To achieve a transformative approach to sustainability, InterfaceRAISE worked with clients to understand and then determine their needs. The firm then partnered with its clients to develop solutions catered to their individual business strategy. Some examples of education and engagement services included:

- Speeches: Clients could engage over 27 executives from the Interface Speakers Bureau to discuss how their firm could implement triple-bottom-line growth through sustainability.
- Workshops: The firm offered half-day workshops with both informational and interactive components "to provoke dialogue about emerging opportunities and risks for businesses."[41]
- Sustainability immersion: Held at Interface facilities in the United States or Europe, these 1.5- to 2-day events were designed to immerse a leadership team in "an enlightening dialogue around the facets of a successful sustainability strategy."[42]

Along with educational services, InterfaceRAISE also offered strategic services such as:

- Coaching/mentoring: An InterfaceRAISE sustainability expert worked with clients to "inspire solutions to the challenges and opportunities of adopting a sustainability strategy."
- Current-state assessment: These quick, high-level reviews included internal and external business

analysis, and featured discussion with senior leaders "to identify risks and opportunities for further consideration."

- Sustainability Strategy 1.0: This interactive strategy session with a client's senior leaders featured internal and external analysis, and resulted in a sustainability strategy that leveraged the company's current strengths.
- Sustainability Strategy 2.0: A follow-on to the Strategy 1.0 session, Strategy 2.0 identified the top priorities in a company's sustainability strategy, and culminated in a facilitated meeting with senior leaders to envision the next level of success.[43]

Interface, Inc. after the 2008 Financial Crisis

Like the rest of the industry, Interface was significantly affected by the worldwide financial crisis and the 2008 recession. The company reported a net loss of $10.8 million in 2007, down from a net income of $10 million in 2006, due to the cooling off of the construction boom.[44] In 2008, the company posted a net loss of $40.9 million on sales of $1.1 billion. (See Exhibits 9 and 10, pages C117–C119.)

Interface's international diversification, however, helped it to weather the recession. Interface operated in three U.S. locations and also had manufacturing facilities in the Netherlands, the United Kingdom (UK), Australia, and Thailand. Interface had used its worldwide manufacturing facilities to gain a foothold in emerging markets such as the BRIC countries (Brazil, Russia, India, and China). These new markets accounted for approximately 40 percent of the company's sales. Interface, like most carpet manufacturers, received its largest share of revenues domestically: U.S. carpet sales comprised 47 percent of the company's revenues ($507 million), followed by 14 percent in the UK ($147 million).

Meanwhile, the company's 2007 divestiture of its fabric business placed an even greater focus on the modular carpet business. In 2008, modular carpet tiles accounted for 87 percent ($946.8 million) of Interface's total revenue. The company's Bentley Prince Street broadloom carpet made up the remaining 13 percent of revenues ($135.5 million).[45]

Over the last two decades, the price of oil has trended upward. Interface believed that eventually the price of oil would reach a point where Interface—given its focus on dematerialization and increasing

EXHIBIT 9

Interface, Inc. 2001–2009 Income Statements (in thousands)

	2009	2008	2007	2006	2005	2004	2003	2002	2001
Net sales	$859,888	$1,082,344	$1,081,273	$1,075,842	$985,766	$881,658	$923,509	$924,084	$1,058,846
Cost of sales	576,871	710,299	703,751	736,247	681,069	616,297	670,532	659,910	746,320
Gross profit on sales	283,017	372,045	377,522	339,595	304,697	265,361	252,977	264,174	312,526
Selling, general and administrative expenses	218,322	258,198	246,258	241,538	222,696	204,619	231,306	225,569	259,039
Loss on disposal of subsidiaries	—	—	1,873	1,723	—	—	—	—	—
Impairment of goodwill	—	61,213	—	20,712	—	—	—	—	—
Restructuring charges	7,627	10,975	—	3,260	—	—	6,196	23,449	54,577
Income from litigation settlements	(5,926)	—	—	—	—	—	—	—	—
Operating income	62,994	41,659	129,391	72,362	82,001	60,742	15,475	15,156	(1,090)
Interest expense	34,297	31,480	34,110	42,204	45,541	46,023	42,820	42,022	35,887
Bond retirement expenses	6,096	—	—	—	—	1,869	—	—	—
Other expense	576	1,652	727	1,319	933	2,366	1,280	798	490
Income from continuing operations before tax	22,025	8,527	94,554	28,839	35,527	10,484	(28,625)	(27,664)	(37,467)
Income tax expense	9,352	43,040	35,582	18,816	17,561	4,044	(10,215)	(9,905)	(11,546)
Income (loss) from continuing operations	12,673	(34,513)	58,972	10,023	17,966	6,440	(18,410)	(17,759)	(25,921)
Loss from discontinued operations, net of tax	(909)	(5,154)	(68,660)	(31)	(16,726)	(61,842)	(14,847)	(14,525)	(10,366)
Cumulative effect of a change in accounting principle, net of tax	—	—	—	—	—	—	—	(55,380)	—
Net income (loss)	11,764	(39,667)	(9,688)	9,992	1,240	(55,402)	(33,257)	(87,664)	(36,287)
Net income attributable to noncontrolling interest in subsidiary	(846)	(1,206)	(1,124)	—	—	—	—	—	—
Net income (loss) attributable to Interface, Inc.	$ 10,918	$ (40,873)	$ (10,812)	$ 9,992	$ 1,240	$ (55,402)	$ (33,257)	$ (87,664)	$ (36,287)

Source: www.sec.gov/Archives/edgar/data/71587/000095014402003002/g74140e10-k405.txt.

EXHIBIT 10

Interface, Inc. 2001–2009 Balance Sheets (in thousands)

	2009	2008	2007	2006	2005	2004	2003	2002	2001
					Fiscal Year Ended				
ASSETS									
Current									
Cash and cash equivalents	$115,363	$71,757	$82,375	$109,157	$51,312	$22,164	$16,633	$34,134	$793
Accounts receivable, net	129,833	144,783	178,625	143,025	141,408	142,228	174,366	137,486	161,070
Inventories	112,249	128,923	125,789	112,293	130,209	137,618	143,885	134,656	168,249
Prepaid expenses and other current assets	30,528	30,492	29,640	186,956	26,690	65,544	24,062	60,445	48,658
Total current assets	387,973	375,955	416,429	551,431	349,619	367,554	358,946	366,721	378,770
Property and equipment, net	162,269	160,717	161,874	134,631	185,643	194,702	211,457	213,059	260,327
Deferred tax asset	44,210	42,999	60,942	65,841	69,043	67,448	62,045	27,502	
Goodwill	80,519	78,489	142,471	135,610	193,705	205,913	224,129	210,529	251,874
Other assets	52,268	47,875	53,516	40,827	40,980	34,181	37,697	45,699	63,783
TOTAL ASSETS	$727,239	$706,035	$835,232	$928,340	$838,990	$869,798	$894,274	$863,510	$954,754
LIABILITIES AND SHAREHOLDERS' EQUITY									
Current liabilities									
Accounts payable	$35,614	$52,040	$57,243	$49,542	$50,312	$46,466	$62,352	$55,836	$65,805
Accrued expenses	101,143	102,592	120,388	98,702	85,581	86,856	128,104	106,143	100,566
Current portion of long-term debt	14,586	—							1,667
Liabilities of businesses held for sale			220	22,934	4,214	5,390	—	6,933	—
Total current liabilities	151,343	154,632	177,851	171,178	140,107	138,712	190,456	168,912	168,038
Senior notes	280,184	287,588	310,000	411,365	458,000	460,000	445,000	445,000	453,327
Deferred income taxes	7,029	7,506	7,413	2,058	23,534	26,790	32,462	20,520	26,474
Other	42,502	38,872	38,852	63,839	40,864	45,987	4,165	—	—
Total liabilities	481,058	488,598	534,116	648,440	662,505	671,489	672,083	634,432	647,839

EXHIBIT 10 *(continued)*

	2009	2008	2007	2006	2005	2004	2003	2002	2001
					Fiscal Year Ended				
Commitments and contingencies									
Common stock	6,328	6,316	6,184	6,066	5,334	5,243	5,135	5,120	5,082
Additional paid-in capital	343,348	339,776	332,650	323,132	234,314	229,382	222,984	221,751	219,490
Retained earnings (deficit)	(55,332)	(65,616)	(15,159)	5,217	(1,443)	(2,683)	52,719	85,976	175,940
Accumulated other comprehensive income	(57,243)	(70,980)	(29,533)	(60,021)	(66,129)	(37,764)	(62,105)	(91,830)	(98,037)
Unrealized gain on hedges, net of tax								3,154	
Total shareholders' equity – Interface, Inc.	237,101	209,496	294,142	274,394	172,076	194,178	218,733	224,171	302,475
Noncontrolling interest in subsidiary	9,080	7,941	6,974	5,506	4,409	4,131	3,458	4,907	4,440
Total shareholders' equity	246,181	217,437	301,116	279,900	176,485	198,309	222,191	229,078	306,915
TOTAL LIABILITIES & EQUITY	**$727,239**	**$706,035**	**$835,232**	**$928,340**	**$838,990**	**$869,798**	**$894,274**	**$863,510**	**$954,754**

Source: www.sec.gov/Archives/edgar/data/715787/000009501440200300/g74140e10-k405.txt.

recycled content—would reach a break-even point, after which recycled materials would cost less than virgin materials.[46]

As a result of this and other factors, the company returned to profitability in the second quarter of 2009, with a net income of $3.8 million on $211.3 million in revenues.[47] At the end of 2009, Interface reported an annual net income of $10.9 million on sales of $859.9 million. However, sales year over year had dropped by $222.5 million (21 percent) from 2008. As of this writing, the stock stood at $12.68. (See Exhibits 7, 9, and 10.)

Interface was mindful of perceived value as well as cost savings. In a survey performed by *Floor Focus* magazine, Interface was recently rated as the "Best Overall Business Experience" for the fifth straight year. In this survey, Interface products ranked second (modular tiles) and third (Bentley Prince broadloom carpet) in terms of service and design. The two product lines (modular tiles and broadloom) were ranked first and second in quality, first and third in terms of performance, and first and fourth in terms of value.[48]

The Sustainability-Consulting Industry

As indicated earlier, InterfaceRAISE does business as a sustainability consultant. In 2008, there were 118 distinct types of consulting services spanning 98 industries in the United States. Collectively, the consulting industry generated over $330 billion in revenue during 2008. Of this, nearly half of the industry's revenue ($158 billion) was generated in North America,[49] with management consulting (the largest area) accounting for approximately $100 billion of that amount.[50] The management-consulting industry employed over 1.1 million people across 190,000 firms[51] and was projected to grow by 5.3 percent annually through 2011.[52]

The sustainability-consulting industry, a subsector of management consulting, boasted revenues of $16.8 billion in 2009, employing an estimated 122,922 people across 58,814 firms.[53] Sustainability-sector revenues grew year over year by 7.7 percent, outpacing the industry as a whole. Historically, growth in the management- and sustainability-consulting industry has been propelled by business fads and changes in philosophies that create interest for a few years and then fade away.[54] The 2008 recession led to a renewed interest in sustainability, as companies looked for ways to reduce costs via environmental initiatives. According to Forrester Research, the green-IT consulting industry (a subsector of sustainability consulting) alone could grow to $4.8 billion by 2013.[55]

Firm size within the management-consulting industry varied. At the top of the industry were large management-consulting firms, ranging from generalist consulting firms with a wide breadth of expertise to firms with a more specialized focus. These companies often charged clients from $300,000 to $1 million in monthly fees, billing consultants at $5,000 a day. This resulted in annual firm revenues in the billions of dollars.[56] Many of these larger firms, such as Accenture, Deloitte, Boston Consulting Group, McKinsey, PricewaterhouseCoopers, and A.T. Kearney, had created divisions focusing on sustainability-consulting practices. Similarly, IBM had developed a consulting practice to help companies implement green data centers, while CH2M HILL had created a green building and carbon footprint division.[57]

The next level of management consultants was comprised of middle-market firms such as InterfaceRAISE and Blu Skye. These firms employed from two or more employees to hundreds of consultants. Clients typically were located within the Fortune 1000 and had incomes of $30 million to $40 billion. Consulting engagements ranged from one-day educational seminars for corporate-level executives to full-scale sustainability-practice implementation.[58]

At the lowest level in terms of size were small consulting firms owned by a sole proprietor. Many of these firms were started by executives and environmental engineers displaced by the recession of 2008, who then started their own sustainability-consulting practices. These consultants typically worked with smaller firms on a project-by-project basis.

INTERFACERAISE'S COMPETITORS. Three of InterfaceRAISE's main competitors were large-scale consulting firms Accenture and A.T. Kearney, and mid-sized Blu Skye.

Accenture. Accenture was a publically traded global management and technology-consulting company. It employed over 181,000 people with over 4,500 senior executives, operating in more than 200 cities and 52 countries across the globe, and earning revenues of $21.58 billion in 2009. The firm's clients included 96 of the Fortune Global 100 and 75 percent of the Fortune Global 500. Client retention was high: 99 of the firm's top 100 clients had worked with Accenture for at least five years.

Accenture offered clients end-to-end sustainability consulting. The firm aimed to create:

- "An organization-wide understanding of the value of sustainability, coupled with a willingness to change;
- A mindset of sustainability consciousness that permeates the enterprise;
- A visible commitment of all employees to 'live' the organization's strategy for sustainability."[59]

Accenture offered consulting in numerous categories related to sustainability: strategy; talent; organization and learning; supply chain; intelligent cities; smart buildings; carbon data and analytics services; clean energy; climate and energy management; stakeholder management services; sustainable infrastructure; and carbon markets and financial trading.

A.T. Kearney. Tom Kearney revolutionized the consulting industry by approaching a firm's problems with "a general survey perspective, examining all aspects of the company to develop more comprehensive solutions."[60] Implementing this model from its founding in 1926 through the present, A.T. Kearney grew to more than 170 officers in 26 countries. The firm's sustainability group employed over 90 professionals in A.T. Kearney's global markets. The company offered clients three levels of service to meet their needs:

- *Corporate sustainability strategy:* This strategy provided clients with "a holistic approach—from measuring and mitigating the future forces that affect a company's strategy, portfolio, and operations, to assessing the company's impact on the environments and communities it touches."[61]
- *Product and service optimization:* This methodology helped "clients understand the sustainability impact of their offering, and helped in developing new, revised, or enhanced products and services."[62]
- *Sustainable value chain:* A.T. Kearney evaluated where and how materials were sourced, where and how products were manufactured, and where and how the company distributed. Based on these analyses, Kearney sought to reduce carbon footprints within the distribution channel and to help firms adopt environmentally friendly materials and process chemicals.

Blu Skye. Blu Skye was a middle-market firm with 44 employees that focused on sustainability strategies. The firm was founded in 2004 when Jib Ellison, co-founder of the management consulting firm Trium Group, took a one-year sabbatical. During this time, Mr. Ellison met Lee Scott, then the CEO and chairman of Walmart.[63] Walmart had a public relations nightmare on its hands. It had just received the results of a McKinsey & Company study that showed "between 2 and 8 percent of consumers had stopped shopping at Walmart because of the company's [environmental] practices."[64] Mr. Scott told Mr. Ellison that he was looking for a way to use sustainability to bring back lost customers. Ellison replied, "With all due respect, there's an entirely different way you should be thinking about this. Sustainability is an offensive strategy that is consistent with Walmart's culture and business model." After subsequent talks regarding how Walmart could implement sustainability practices, Scott hired Ellison as a consultant to the firm."[65]

To manage his relationship with Walmart, Scott formed a team of environmental consultants and created Blu Skye. The company then leveraged its environmental expertise and relationship with Walmart to gain engagements with many top firms and organizations, including: Sony Pictures, The American Dairy Association, The University of Arkansas, Hilton, Waste Management, Mars Incorporated, Microsoft, and Burt's Bees.

Blu Skye offered a three-phase approach to sustainability:

- *Education and development:* Blu Skye sought to help firms educate executives and employees on how to incorporate sustainability into daily functions. This was accomplished through activities ranging from day-long seminars to lengthy engagements aimed at gaining employee buy-in.[66]
- *Strategic development:* The firm sought to quantify "sustainability impacts and the key activities that drive them."[67] Blu Skye also assessed the client's current practices compared with the client's industry and competition. Finally, it helped firms determine "the right action at a given time . . . and how to balance short-term quick wins against longer term, more game-changing efforts."[68]
- *Strategic implementation:* Blu Skye involved itself in all aspects of implementation, from coaching and program management to working with corporate-level executives to gain stakeholder

engagement that would create "sustainable value networks."[69] The firm also helped clients implement "whole system change,"—transforming the supply chain, to reinforce a sustainable strategy while benefiting society.[70]

Walmart and Sustainability

Walmart's interest in sustainability began in an unlikely place: Rob Walton (son of Walmart founder Sam Walton), Rob's son Ben, musician Stone Gossard (member of Pearl Jam), and Peter Seligmann (CEO of Conservation International), sat on the bow of Rob's yacht. As they reflected on the manta rays and sharks they had seen while scuba-diving off the coast of Coco Island, Costa Rica, Seligmann and Walton discussed Walton's generous $21 million grant to Conservation International (CI). Seligmann then pitched an even bigger idea to Walton. He recalls saying, "Rob, we greatly appreciate your generosity towards CI, but whatever money your foundation could contribute to CI would pale in comparison to what Walmart could do. Your company could be a driver of change."[71] As they discussed the possibilities, Walton admitted to Seligmann that he was intrigued, but cautioned, "I took myself out of an operational role at Walmart years ago. I have to be really careful about mixing personal interests with the business."[72] However, he agreed to introduce Seligmann to Walmart's CEO, Lee Scott.

In June 2004, Rob Walton, Lee Scott, Peter Seligmann, Glenn Prickett (also from CI), and Seligmann's friend Jib Ellison met at Walmart headquarters in Bentonville, Arkansas, to discuss sustainability. The timing could not have been more fortuitous. Walmart had just been fined millions of dollars for violating air and water pollution laws,[73] and a recent McKinsey study had revealed that 2 to 8 percent of Walmart's customers had left because of Walmart's environmental practices.[74] The company needed to respond. It was at this meeting that Jib Ellison suggested that sustainability was consistent with Walmart's culture. After talking all day, Mr. Scott told his guests that he wanted to review the company's options with his executive team and thanked them for their time.

When Lee Scott met with his executive team to discuss sustainability at Walmart, Mike Duke, head of U.S. Stores at Walmart, mentioned that the team ought to speak with a fellow Georgia Tech alumnus, Ray Anderson. Mr. Duke described to the team Interface's transformation into a leader in corporate sustainability. The team agreed to hold a sustainability summit on October 24, 2004, and invited Ray Anderson and Jib Ellison as speakers.

At the summit, Mr. Anderson realized that Interface could best help Walmart by helping the 60,000-some companies in Walmart's supply chain reinvent themselves to meet the sustainability standards that were sure to come."[75] The executive's reaction to Anderson's speech was so enthusiastic that he invited two Walmart groups to LaGrange, Georgia, for a walkthrough of Interface's flagship manufacturing facility.[76]

After the first large-scale consulting event, the Interface team sat down to discuss what its role with Walmart would be. The team decided that they could have more impact in their relationship with Walmart as peers exploring sustainability, rather than as a paid contractor. Jim Hartzfeld stated, "We realized we didn't want to be a supplier to Walmart. If our mission was to become restorative through the power of influence, there is no billing level that we [could] achieve in the short term that ha[d] more power to fulfill our mission statement than influencing the biggest non-oil company in the world."[77]

It was at that time that Walmart officially hired Jib Ellison and Blu Skye to serve as sustainability consultants to the firm. In October 2005, Lee Scott laid out the goals of the plan that Walmart had developed with Blu Skye: (1) to be supplied 100 percent by renewable energy; (2) to create zero waste; and (3) to sell products that sustain our resources and environment."[78]

Although Walmart did not set a targeted date for these three goals, the company had made tremendous strides. Working with Blu Skye, Walmart implemented many green innovations, including one involving laundry detergent. Walmart approached detergent suppliers and asked them to remove the water from detergent to create concentrated detergents. After accepting Walmart's request, suppliers were able to shrink the packaging of detergents by 50 percent,[79] thereby saving 125 pounds of cardboard and reducing water usage by 430 million gallons.[80]

This dedication to sustainability was passed on from Lee Scott to Mike Duke, Walmart's current [2011] CEO, who described Walmart's vision of sustainability as follows: "We want to be like a camper and leave the campsite better than we found it. What we've discovered is that sustainability is good business. It's good for value creation and therefore good for shareholders."[81] Under Mr. Duke's tutelage, Walmart had pledged to "reduce greenhouse gas emissions by 20 million metric tons across its vast network of suppliers by 2015."[82] Walmart had also required suppliers to change labels to show the product's sustainability index and carbon footprint.[83]

Decision Time

When John Wells left his office, Mr. Hartzfeld sat down and took a swig of coffee as a multitude of thoughts raced through his mind: How was he going to position his consulting startup for growth over the next five years? It was certainly a question he posed to himself quite often. What was InterfaceRAISE's core competence? How should he leverage this into profitable growth? How much money would he need, and when? How would he invest it to get to his goal of $5 million in revenues in five years? Would InterfaceRAISE's growth plan be at odds with or support the strategies of the parent company? Would it be best for InterfaceRAISE to continue to operate under its parent company's umbrella? Were there other avenues, beyond fee-for-service consulting, in which InterfaceRAISE could contribute to Interface's vision, "to become restorative through the power of influence"?

Mr. Hartzfeld knew that this would be a long week—but he was excited about the possibilities. This was the moment he had been waiting for. After years of bootstrapping, finally the moment had arrived where he could position InterfaceRAISE for profitable growth. Jim went to work . . .

Endnotes

1. Anderson, R. C. (2009), *Confessions of a Radical Industrialist* (New York: St. Martin's Press), p. 9.
2. Ibid.
3. Ibid.
4. Ibid.
5. Interview with Jim Hartzfeld, March 31, 2010.
6. Anderson, R. C. (2009), *Confessions of a Radical Industrialist*, pp. 10–16.
7. Ibid., p. 14.
8. Ibid., pp. 10–16.
9. Ibid., pp. 16, 39.
10. *Ray Anderson Reflects on Interface's Journey to the Top of Mount Sustainability,* www.interfaceglobal.com/getdoc/7004276e-0f10-4c64-b08c-b7889a717b2b/Ray-Reflects.aspx.
11. Anderson, R. C. (2009), *Confessions of a Radical Industrialist*, pp. 10–34.
12. Interview with Jim Hartzfeld, March 31, 2010.

13. Ibid.
14. Anderson, R. C. (2009), *Confessions of a Radical Industrialist*, p. 18.
15. *Ray Anderson Reflects on Interface's Journey to the Top of Mount Sustainability,* www.interfaceglobal.com/getdoc/7004276e-0f10-4c64-b08c-b7889a717b2b/Ray-Reflects.aspx.
16. www.interfaceglobal.com/Sustainability/Our-Journey/7-Fronts-of-Sustainability.aspx.
17. Anderson, R. C. (2009), *Confessions of a Radical Industrialist*, p. 41.
18. www.interfaceglobal.com/Sustainability/Sustainability-in-Action/Waste.aspx.
19. http://gmj.gallup.com/content/123464/business-sustainability.aspx#1.
20. www.cdf.org/issue_journal/interfaces_chairman_ray_c._anderson_on_sustainable_design-2.html.
21. Anderson, R. C. (2009), *Confessions of a Radical Industrialist*, pp. 48–49.
22. www.forumforthefuture.org.uk/greenfutures/articles/60891.
23. www.cdf.org/issue_journal/interfaces_chairman_ray_c._anderson_on_sustainable_design-2.html.
24. www.epa.gov/iaq/voc.html#Health Effects.
25. www.cdf.org/issue_journal/interfaces_chairman_ray_c._anderson_on_sustainable_design-2.html.
26. www.interfaceglobal.com/Sustainability/Progress-to-Zero.aspx.
27. Anderson, R. C. (2009), *Confessions of a Radical Industrialist*, p. 167.
28. Ibid., p. 45.
29. http://gmj.gallup.com/content/123464/business-sustainability.aspx#1.
30. Anderson, R. C. (2009), *Confessions of a Radical Industrialist*, p. 20.
31. http://11thhouraction.com/ideasandexperts/rayanderson.
32. www.fundinguniverse.com/company-histories/Interface-Inc-Company-History.html.
33. Ibid.
34. Interview with Jim Hartzfeld, March 31, 2010.
35. Ibid.
36. Ibid.
37. Anderson, R. C. (2009), *Confessions of a Radical Industrialist*, pp. 16, 39.
38. http://interfaceraise.com/what-we-do/approach-and-methods/.
39. Ibid.
40. Ibid.
41. http://interfaceraise.com/what-we-do/services/.
42. Ibid.
43. Ibid.
44. Interface, Inc. (February 15) Hoover's Company Records, 13798; retrieved February 16, 2010, from Hoover's Company Records. (Document ID: 168173361).

45. Ibid.

46. http://gmj.gallup.com/content/123464/business-sustainability.aspx#1.

47. http://finance.yahoo.com/q/ks?s=IFSIA.

48. http://phx.corporate-ir.net/External.File?item=UGFyZW50SUQ9MjE2NjF8Q2hpbGRJRD0tMXxUeXBlPTM=&t=1.

49. "Consulting trends," *Plunkett Research, Ltd.,* 2010, www.plunkettresearch.com/Industries/Consulting/ConsultingTrends/tabid/178/Default.aspx.

50. "Management consulting services," *Encyclopedia of American Industries,* Online Edition, Gale, 2010. Reproduced in Business and Company Resource Center (Farmington Hills, MI: Gale Group) 2010, http://galenet.galegroup.com/servlet/BCRC.

51. Ibid.

52. "Consulting industry overview," *Plunkett Research Industry Almanac 2009,* www.plunkettresearch.com/Industries/Consulting/ConsultingStatistics/tabid/177/Default.aspx.

53. "Environmental consulting," *IBISWorld Industry Reports 2010,* www.ibisworld.com/industry/default.aspx?indid=1427.

54. "Management consulting services."

55. www.sustainablelifemedia.com/content/story/greenIT/green_it_consulting_to_hit_4.8_billion_by_2013.

56. "Consulting industry overview."

57. "Emerging careers: Sustainability consulting," www.triplepundit.com/2008/08/emerging-careers-sustainability-consulting/.

58. Interview with Jim Hartzfeld, March 31, 2010.

59. www.accenture.com/NR/rdonlyres/1BA9D0DA-EF2C-4C32-BE50-7E77952152D4/0/Accenture_Driving_Value_from_Integrated_Sustainability.pdf.

60. www.atkearney.com/index.php/About-us/history.html.

61. www.atkearney.com/index.php/Our-expertise/sustainability-corporate-sustainability-strategy.html.

62. www.atkearney.com/index.php/Our-expertise/sustainability-product-and-service-optimization.html.

63. "Who you gonna call to help you go green?" *Corporate Board Member,* First Quarter 2009, www.boardmember.com/MagazineArticle_Details.aspx?id=3056.

64. Plambeck, E. L., and L. Denend (2008), "The greening of Walmart," *Stanford's Social Innovation Review,* Spring, www.ssireview.org/articles/entry/the_greening_of_wal_mart/.

65. "Who you gonna call to help you go green?"

66. www.bluskye.com/methods.php.

67. Ibid.

68. Ibid.

69. Ibid.

70. Ibid.

71. "The Green Machine," *Fortune,* July 31, 2006.

72. Ibid.

73. Ibid.

74. Ibid.

75. Anderson, R. C. (2009), *Confessions of a Radical Industrialist,* p. 168.

76. Ibid.

77. Interview with Jim Hartzfeld, March 31, 2010.

78. Plambeck, E. L., and L. Denend (2008), "The greening of Walmart."

79. "Will big business save the earth?" *The New York Times,* December 6, 2009.

80. Mike Duke, CEO of Walmart, Georgia Tech speech, April 1, 2010.

81. Ibid.

82. "Walmart vows greenhouse gas emissions cut by 2015," *The Washington Post,* February 26, 2010.

83. "The greenest big companies in America," *Newsweek,* September 28, 2009.

Willy Shih

Stephen Kaufman

David Spinola

Late one afternoon in January 2007, Reed Hastings had just concluded a meeting with his senior management team in the King Kong board room at Netflix's corporate headquarters in Los Gatos, California. Hastings, the founder and CEO of the company, which pioneered online DVD rentals, was preparing to unveil Netflix's highly anticipated entrance into the online video market. Many industry observers believed that the ability of customers to order movies through their computers for instant viewing, commonly referred to as video-on-demand (VOD), would quickly impact the large user base for Netflix's core business.

Hastings looked across the third floor of the office building and the conference rooms named for some of his staff's favorite films. A love of movies clearly ran deep among Netflix employees, and he was confident that one way or another, his team would maintain the company's position as a leader in the home video market. But, as he reflected upon the years of investment and discussions surrounding the new feature that Netflix would be offering its customers, he could not help but think of the merits of the paths not chosen.

As the management team filed out of the board room around him, Hastings returned his thoughts to the present. While he believed that the DVD rental market would remain healthy for years into the future, he knew that this announcement would impact not just the market's perception of his company but its ability to sustain its position as a giant in the media industry. With new resolve, Hastings returned to his desk to review his forthcoming announcement one more time.

Company Background

Netflix, an online subscription-based DVD rental service, was first conceived by Hastings after he discovered an overdue rental copy of *Apollo* 13 in his closet. After paying the $40 late fee, Hastings, a successful entrepreneur who had already founded and sold a software business, began to consider alternative ways to provide a home movie service that would

better satisfy customers. The business that emerged from Hastings' frustration was a rental company that used the U.S. Postal Service to deliver DVDs to its subscribers. By year-end 2006, subscribers could use Netflix's website to choose from among over 70,000 different titles held on over 55 million DVDs. Through its 44 distribution centers across the country, Netflix could deliver to more than 90% of its 6.6 million subscribers within a single business day. Netflix's flagship subscription plan offered unlimited monthly rentals, allowing customers to hold up to three movies in their possession at any one time for a monthly fee of $17.99. For the year ending December 31, 2006, Netflix had achieved revenues of nearly $1 billion, generating free cash flow of $64 million. (See Exhibit 1 for Netflix financials.)

The History of Home Video Rental

When Netflix was founded in 1997, the home video market was a fragmented industry largely populated with "mom-and-pop" retail outlets. Customers rented movies, primarily on VHS cassette, from a retail location for a specified time period, usually between two days and one week, and paid a fee of $3 to $4 for each movie rented. The market leader was rental giant Blockbuster Inc. Blockbuster's success was based on the insight that movie rentals were largely impulse decisions. To customers deciding at the last minute that a given night was "movie night," the ability to quickly obtain the newest release was a priority. Statistics showed that new releases represented over 70% of total rentals.

 HARVARD|BUSINESS|SCHOOL

9-607-138

Senior Lecturers Willy Shih and Stephen Kaufman and David Spinola (MBA 2007) prepared this case. HBS cases are developed solely as the basis for class discussion. Certain details have been disguised. Cases are not intended to serve as endorsements, sources of primary data, or illustrations of effective or ineffective management.

EXHIBIT 1

Netflix Financial Statements

(Dollars in Thousands)	1998	1999	2000	2001	2002	2003	2004	2005	2006
Income Statement									
Sales Subscription	585	4,854	35,894	74,255	150,818	270,410	500,611	682,213	996,660
Cost of Revenues									
Subscription	535	4,217	24,861	49,088	77,044	147,736	273,401	393,788	532,621
Fulfillment	763	2,446	10,247	13,452	19,366	31,274	56,609	70,762	93,439
Total	**1,298**	**6,663**	**35,108**	**62,540**	**96,410**	**179,010**	**330,010**	**464,550**	**626,060**
Gross Profit	**(713)**	**(1,809)**	**786**	**11,715**	**54,408**	**91,400**	**170,601**	**217,663**	**370,600**
Operating Expenses									
Tech and Development	3,857	7,413	16,823	17,734	14,625	17,884	22,906	30,942	44,771
Marketing	4,052	14,070	25,727	21,031	35,783	49,949	98,027	141,997	223,386
G&A	1,358	1,993	6,990	4,658	6,737	9,585	16,287	29,395	30,130
Restructuring	0	0	0	671	0	0	0	0	0
Stock-based Comp	1,151	4,742	8,803	5,686	8,832	10,719	16,587	14,327	12,696
Gain on Disposal of DVDs	22	4	0	(838)	(896)	(1,209)	(2,560)	(1,987)	(4,797)
Total Operating Expenses	**10,440**	**28,218**	**58,343**	**49,780**	**65,081**	**86,928**	**151,247**	**214,674**	**306,186**
Operating Income	**(11,153)**	**(30,027)**	**(57,557)**	**(38,065)**	**(10,673)**	**4,472**	**19,354**	**2,989**	**64,414**
Interest and Other Income	72	924	1,645	461	1,697	2,457	2,592	5,753	15,904
Interest Expense	0	(738)	(1,451)	(1,852)	(11,972)	(417)	(170)	(407)	0
Pre-Tax Income	**(11,081)**	**(29,841)**	**(57,363)**	**(39,456)**	**(20,948)**	**6,512**	**21,776**	**8,335**	**80,318**
Taxes	0	0	0	0	0	0	181	(33,692)	31,236
Net Income	**(11,081)**	**(29,841)**	**(57,363)**	**(39,456)**	**(20,948)**	**6,512**	**21,595**	**42,027**	**49,082**
Cash Flow Summary									
Cash Flows from Operations	(5,408)	(16,529)	(22,706)	4,847	40,114	89,792	145,269	157,507	247,862
Acquisition Costs of DVD Library	(2,186.0)	(9,866)	(23,895)	(8,851)	(24,070)	(55,620)	(100,087)	(111,446)	(169,528)
Purchase of Property, Plant and Equipment	(103.0)	(3,295)	(6,210)	(3,233)	(2,751)	(8,872)	(15,720)	(27,653)	(27,333)
Proceeds from Sales of DVDs	0.0	0	0	0	1,988	1,833	5,617	5,781	12,886
Free Cash Flow	**(7,697)**	**(29,690)**	**(52,811)**	**(7,237)**	**15,281**	**27,133**	**35,079**	**24,189**	**63,887**

Source: Netflix 2006 10-K, March 16, 2007, Netflix S1, March 6, 2002.

Much of Blockbuster's growth strategy revolved around opening new locations, both to expand geographic coverage and to increase penetration and share in existing markets. In 2006, Blockbuster had 5,194 U.S. locations, of which 4,255 were company owned, with the balance franchised. Locations were chosen based upon a careful review of local data, including customer concentration and proximity to competition, focusing on highly visible stores in high-traffic areas. Management commonly proclaimed that "70% of the U.S. population lives within a 10 minute drive of a Blockbuster,"[1] highlighting how its retail network offered unmatched convenience to impulse movie renters. Stores were staffed primarily with part-time employees, averaging 10 staff members per store plus one manager. Occupancy and payroll represented a significant percentage of total costs.

The nationwide network of Blockbuster outlets carried a similar selection of movies, offering about 2,500 different titles per store. Shelf space in each store was mostly dedicated to hit movies, with the newest releases receiving the most prominent positioning. Locations acquired multiple copies of popular and high-profile movies, at a cost of about $18 per film or DVD, in anticipation of high customer demand at the release date. Blockbuster's financial success depended on maximizing the days that any individual movie was out for rent. Stores were reluctant to stock large numbers of lesser-known and independent films, since the demand for these titles was inconsistent. With a relatively narrow selection of mostly familiar movies, customers could generally select a title with a limited amount of advice from the sales staff. In time, each Blockbuster retail outlet would begin to sell previewed copies of its new releases at a discount, generating incremental return on its investment and clearing shelf space for the next wave of new movies.

Traditionally, any movies not returned to the same location from which they were rented by the end of the specified rental period were subject to extended viewing fees, or "late fees." In 2004, these fees represented over $600 million for Blockbuster, or about 10% of revenues. In addition to the revenue benefit, late fees served a critical asset utilization function for Blockbuster. They encouraged a timely return of each rented film, allowing it to be rented by another customer. In their absence, delayed returns could lead to increased levels of stockouts, costing Blockbuster incremental rental opportunities as well as reducing customer satisfaction.

When Netflix went public in 2002, Blockbuster was enjoying record levels of revenue and profitability amidst a period of industry expansion. According to research reports cited in Blockbuster's 2002 public filings, DVD players were present in 37% of U.S. television households, up from 24% the prior year. The increase in the popularity of the DVD format had helped to grow industry movie rental revenues from $8.5 billion to $8.7 billion. The year 2002 also represented Blockbuster's fifth consecutive year of same-store sales growth, and the Blockbuster brand achieved nearly 100% recognition with active movie renters.

Netflix History

Netflix was founded in 1997 during the emergent days of Internet retailing, when online competitors to traditional "brick-and-mortar" retail stores were gaining prominence. Rather than attempt to attract customers to a retail location, Netflix offered home delivery of DVDs through the mail.

When its original website was launched in early 1998, most available movies for rent in video stores used the VHS cassette format. In contrast, Netflix concentrated efforts on early-technology adopters who had recently purchased DVD players. Its marketing strategy was to develop crosspromotional programs with the manufacturers and sellers of DVD players, providing a source of content for customers. Hastings elaborated on Netflix's goals in its early days: "We were targeting people who just bought DVD players. At the time our goal was just to get our coupon in the box. We didn't have too much competition. The market was underserved, and stores didn't carry a wide selection of DVDs at the time."

Netflix's website included a search engine that allowed its customers to easily sort through its selections by title, actor, director, and genre. Using this search engine, customers built a list of movies, called a queue, to be received from Netflix. Netflix sent movies to its subscribers based on the order of titles on the list, with subscribers receiving a new movie from their queue upon the return of a currently outstanding film.

Rather than replicate the model of video rental chains and lease retail locations, Netflix depended on the U.S. Postal Service to deliver DVDs to its subscribers. DVDs are small and light, enabling inexpensive delivery and easy receipt by nearly every potential U.S. customer. Hastings related how he determined that the delivery performance offered by the USPS was satisfactory: "I went out, bought a whole bunch of CDs and started mailing them to myself to see how quickly they would come back and what condition they would be in. I waited for two days—and they all arrived in perfect condition. All the pieces started to fall into place after that."[2]

Netflix initially used a pricing model similar to that offered by traditional video stores. Customers chose their film using the company's website, were charged $4 per movie rented plus a $2 shipping and handling charge, and were expected to return films by a specific due date or be charged extended rental fees.

Hastings and his team used the models of the most successful Internet retailers of the time to identify characteristics they thought might appeal to customers: (1) value, (2) convenience, and (3) selection. Hastings referred to value customers as "eBay customers," those to whom Internet shopping was an opportunity to target a great deal. Convenience and selection, in contrast, attracted the "Amazon customers," those who used online shopping as an alternative to traveling to retail outlets and choosing among limited in-stock offerings.

Netflix's early strategy extended beyond DVD rentals. While marketing a 2000 IPO, management described the company as the ultimate online destination for movie enthusiasts. Along with the DVD-by-mail service, Netflix was offering its recommendation system to any user, whether they were a subscriber or not, creating a Web portal rather than simply a subscription service. Hastings described this early strategy: "Our 2000 prospectus was spun towards things that were hot . . . it reflected a tension in our strategy. We would offer price comparisons, theater tickets. That strategic tension didn't resolve itself until the bubble crashed. That summer we realized we weren't going to make it unless we did it on rentals. . . . It was a cash-induced strategic focusing."

This focus was forced in part by the rapid adoption rate of DVD players among U.S. households, which became the fastest technology adoption in history. U.S. household penetration, at 5% in 1999, leapt to 13% by 2000, a level that attracted the attention of other channels. DVDs started being sold at large retailers such as Best Buy and Walmart and began replacing VHS cassettes on the shelves of traditional video rental outlets. As this transition occurred, the convenience advantage that Netflix offered to DVD viewers suffered in comparison to the video stores. The company shelved its plans for an IPO and struggled through a large layoff as it began to adjust its business model in an effort to reach profitability. Chief among Hastings' concerns were the general customer dissatisfaction with Netflix's value proposition and the high cost of building a DVD library to support the growing subscriber base.

Feedback from early customers revealed a frustration with Netflix charging rental prices in line with competing retail locations while providing a slower delivery service. Neil Hunt, the company's chief product officer, described Netflix's motivation for shifting to its popular no-late-fee subscription model in 1999:

> Pricing had been a discussion point for a long time. Our original model didn't work—we needed to overcome the shipping delay. It just wasn't a high enough value product to overcome the delivery waiting time. We spent a lot of money to market to and attract new customers, and they wouldn't be repeat renters. We were spending $100 to $200 to bring in a customer, and they would make one $4 rental. There was no residual value.

Hastings believed that moving to a prepaid subscription service could provide better value to Netflix's customers and also turn their longer delivery times into an advantage. The first iteration of the subscription model allowed customers to have four movies in their possession at once and receive up to four new films each month. Hunt explained the effectiveness of the new pricing model: "We turned the disadvantage of delivery time into having a movie at home all the time. The value to Netflix of having our movies in the customers' homes at all times was our key insight."

Very soon afterwards, Netflix adjusted its pricing system again, offering unlimited rentals for the first time. Subscribers could now keep three movies at a time and exchange them as frequently as they liked. Hunt explained the reasons behind this quick adjustment in strategy:

> We made the observation that this change would dramatically simplify the program and make it easier to explain the service. It also allowed us to market a more compelling value proposition. The term "unlimited" is great marketing. . . . We had some vigorous debates about this, but in the end it was a leap of faith. The dot-com boom was still in full growth mode, and everyone around us was growing fast. It wasn't the time to do months of testing and analysis. We had to make some bets and not worry about getting it wrong. At that time, the ones who got it right would succeed, and the ones who got it wrong wouldn't be around.

With this change in pricing, the company added a new group of fans for whom movie rentals were a regular part of their daily entertainment. Many of these high-volume customers were turned off by the high cost of paying for each movie being rented yet still chose to rent from video stores because of limited alternatives. Others were dissatisfied with how large late fees inhibited their ability to view movies at the times most convenient to them. If "movie night" was not an event but an ordinary form of entertainment, the option to hold movies beyond a two-day rental period was important. For these frequent viewers, Netflix's "all you can eat" model was an attractive alternative to the traditional per-day fee structure.

Subscription costs, the expense of acquiring movies for rent, were still a major burden. Hunt explained the impact that customer demand had on managing the cost of building their film library:

We began struggling with a new problem. Half of the DVDs we were shipping out were brand new. We realized that we had to fix that. Top new releases received a lot of external marketing support and as a result had strong customer awareness and demand. Of course, those movies were the most expensive to acquire. . . . We couldn't just blindly promote movies that already had external demand generation. We needed to stimulate demand on the older and less known movies and things already in our catalog. By marketing from the rest of the "tail" we could drive the average price down of building our catalog.

Netflix initially relied on traditional merchandising to complement its search engine and connect subscribers to the company's library of titles. A small number of employees highlighted different films on the website's homepage each week, effectively providing the same recommendations to all subscribers. Hunt explained the consequence of this marketing technique:

We started with a system that relied heavily on editorial content, but we realized that an editor could only write so many Web pages. Five movies would be highlighted on the website, then everything that was promoted was instantly rented out. That changed to a different five movies each day of the week, and they were all still instantly rented out. We tried to improve the system to ensure that subscribers weren't referred to movies they had already rented. Eventually, we realized that the promotional value of writing the editorial blurbs was zero.

Realizing the inadequacy of the traditional merchandising system, Netflix engineers developed a proprietary recommendation system to better balance customer demand. Upon signing into a new account for the first time, customers took a short survey to identify their favorite movie genres, as well as rate specific movie titles from one to five. Netflix's proprietary algorithm then relied upon these survey results and the respective ratings of millions of similar customers to recommend films to its subscribers. The recommendations page not only included a list of titles with a ranking of how closely they matched the customer's preferences but also a synopsis of the film, a description of why the film was being recommended, and a collection of reviews from other subscribers. As customers rated each movie they saw, Netflix's software refined its understanding of that customer's preference and more accurately recommended movies that would appeal to him or her.

Key to the success of Netflix's inventory management was a filter placed between the output of the recommendation system and the results shown to the subscriber, screening for those movies that were out of stock. The intent was to avoid frustrating a customer by recommending a title that was not immediately available, but a side benefit was that new releases were rarely on recommendation lists, as they were the most likely films to be in short supply. The system increased the utilization of Netflix's library of films by satisfying customers with movies already acquired and in stock, rather than requiring the purchase of more copies of newer films. Compared to traditional video rental outlets, where new releases would make up over 70% of total rentals, new releases represented less than 30% of Netflix's total rentals in 2006. Hunt explained the power of Netflix's recommendations:

The recommendation system will pick the best movie for a customer, period. But it has to be something that can ship overnight. High-demand new releases are less visible because they are less frequently in stock. However, the customer benefits from this system. We have recognized improved customer satisfaction by eliminating the "bait and switch" perception. Most revealing about the value of the recommendations is that ratings are three-fourths of a star higher on recommended movies compared to new releases.

While the investment in software engineering was modest, this shift marked a cultural battle within the company with those who remained loyal to the traditional merchandising system. Hastings described his insistence on this change by highlighting another benefit: "A personalized experience is the benefit of the Internet. If you can otherwise do it offline, people won't pay for it online. If our Internet offering was going to be better than stores, we had to find something stores couldn't do well."

Movies are a taste-based product, for which many titles are consumed only once. As such, consumers must make a series of purchases without knowing for sure if they will like the product. Netflix's website resonated with subscribers because they so frequently enjoyed the less well-known films recommended to them that they might not otherwise have seen. This software established a relationship with customers that was not matched by part-time employees at a retail video store, nor easily replaceable upon switching to a competitor's service. Netflix's size and growth rate also generated a positive "network effect" from its large customer-generated rating system. Because it had the largest collection of movie ratings in the world, customers recognized that they were more likely to have their tastes and preferences accurately reflected in recommendations from Netflix's site than any other offered by a competitor.

Even with the increased customer awareness of lower-profile films that Netflix's recommendation system generated, building the company's movie library still represented a major use of cash. As a small player in the video rental market, Netflix had no direct relationships with the major studios. It filled its film library through relationships with a small number of movie distributors, at prices that reflected minimal discounts. Up-front costs forced Netflix to choose carefully when stocking new films and often resulted in fewer than the desired number of copies of a title being acquired. As a result, one of the major sources of customer dissatisfaction was the inability to rent new releases in a timely manner. Netflix took steps to address this by hiring Ted Sarandos as chief content officer to manage content acquisition. Sarandos, who joined Netflix in May 2000 from Video City, a major U.S. video rental chain, led Netflix's transition to revenue-sharing agreements with the major studios:

> We were handicapped with vendors when I first arrived because other Internet vendors at the time had not been successful. As a pure rental business that was 100% subscription based and 100% Internet based, we were reinventing the wheel on three dimensions for the studios. However, it is very much a relationship business working with the studios, and I had worked with those people all of my career, so I managed to bring my relationships with me from my prior company. Within a year, Netflix had negotiated direct revenue-sharing agreements with nearly all the major studios.

Rather than pay an up-front price of $20 per DVD, the studios would reduce their unit up-front price in return for a fee based on the title's total number of rentals for a given period of time. Hastings described this transition with the company's suppliers: "We spent more money, not less, with the studios but got bigger customer satisfaction. It was like paying 20% more and getting two times the number of copies."

The benefit of the new relationships with the studios extended beyond lowering the acquisition costs for high-demand releases. Hastings recognized early on the number of customers who were frustrated with the poor selection offered at many video stores, where shelf space is focused on hit movies and new releases. Customers interested in exploring a much broader range of movie titles were left unsatisfied by their options. Sarandos explained: "The thing that

Reed and I connected on before I even joined Netflix was the promise of a business model that promoted lesser-known movies. Films outside of the top 20 are not distributed widely. If you didn't see a movie within six months of when it was in the theaters, it often disappeared forever."

The use of a national inventory allowed Netflix to satisfy the diverse demands of movie watchers, serving the same number of customers as a local network of Blockbuster retail locations with far fewer copies of a given movie title. Sarandos explained the difference in economics:

> Half the equation of packaged media is allocation—getting the right amount of product in the right locations. This was more of a challenge for products that did not enjoy broad promotion. The trade radius of a single video store was so small that even a single copy of a lesser-known film had lousy economics. By using a national inventory, we avoid that issue. We never have overstocks on one side of town with understocks on the other side. Using the subscribers' queues provides a great deal of data. By looking into the demand in the near future, we can replicate near-perfect inventory. Overall, we can satisfy demand in an area with about one-third to one-fifth of the inventory needed by a retail chain.

In the summer of 2001, Netflix operated out of a single distribution center located in Sunnyvale, California. While several years of operations had allowed for improvements in this center, the majority of the country was still not able to enjoy next-day delivery of their rented movies. These extended delivery times were a barrier for Netflix in attracting and retaining customers in those regions. Hastings explained: "Post Office variability was long on cross-country mail. . . . It essentially meant one-week delivery times. So in the summer of 2001, we realized that regions with overnight delivery were being disproportionately successful. We tested the theory by upgrading Sacramento. The numbers popped quickly."

Netflix's Sunnyvale distribution center could serve the San Francisco Bay Area with overnight delivery. But while outbound mail from Sunnyvale could reach Sacramento overnight, returns often took several days. Netflix tested Sacramento by arranging with the Postal Service to intercept returns at a Sacramento mail-sort center and then truck them to Sunnyvale. This would shorten the turnaround dramatically. Added Hastings, "As we added centers in Boston, New York, and D.C., they started performing like the Bay Area."

Armed with this evidence of success, Netflix quickly opened more distribution centers across the country, and subscriber numbers continued to respond to the improved delivery service. The company promised 500,000 subscribers to its investors in its 2002 prospectus and delivered 700,000 at the time of the May 2002 IPO. These changes in Netflix's pricing and cost structure allowed the company to reach profitability for the first time in the quarter ending June 2003. After establishing the viability of this business model, Netflix continued to build its subscriber base and upgrade the customer experience by opening new centers (see Exhibit 2 for Netflix's operating statistics). The centers themselves were inexpensive investments; it cost about $60,000 to convert an existing warehouse to Netflix's needs. The company continually added centers to improve upon its nationwide coverage and reduce delivery time to its customers. With the number reaching 44 by early 2007, over 90% of subscribers could be reached within one delivery day. The improved ability for Netflix to provide next-day delivery to more regions of the country allowed it to compete more successfully with retail video stores for new customers drawn by all three of the targeted characteristics of convenience, value, and selection.

Netflix considered delivery time to be the key measure of customer satisfaction and continually sought to improve the operations within each of its existing distribution centers. Much of the process of opening return envelopes and filling outgoing mailers with DVDs was still performed manually. However, with careful hiring practices and thorough time and motion studies, Netflix's employees could open and restuff an average of 800 DVDs per hour, allowing the entire distribution center network to ship over 1.6 million DVDs per day. (See Exhibit 3 for photos of the distribution center operations.)

Netflix's relationship with the USPS grew. While the USPS was facing a general decline in first-class mail, Netflix represented its fastest-growing first-class customer. Along with receiving the standard discount for presorting of its outbound envelopes by zip code, Netflix worked with the USPS to reduce the time it took to receive a movie return. Rather than deliver returns to the distribution center of origin, the USPS brought the easily recognizable red Netflix envelopes to the closest Netflix distribution center. And recently, Netflix began using multiple "truck routes," supporting each distribution center to expedite returns. This shortened turnaround time for new movies and improved the overall customer experience.

As the company added subscribers, content acquisition continued to grow in importance for Netflix. Sarandos explained:

> For a technology company like Netflix, we are the group that is most dependent on art. What we do is probably 70% science, 30% art. Our buying staff has to have their finger on the pulse of the market to make their decisions. A high box-office performer won't necessarily be a high video performer, and vice versa. The box office is an indicator, as a proxy for awareness, but not for demand. . . . If rental demand for a title is lower than we forecast, it is a tax on the overall economics of Netflix's model. Even with the benefit of profit sharing, it is a margin eroder. If we underforecast demand, the problem is correctable, but it takes time.

As Netflix built its film library, it grew in importance as a distribution channel for many small and independent film studios. For lower-profile and independent films that did not enjoy the advertising support of major releases, generating customer awareness was a major priority. As Netflix became known as the best source for lesser-known movies, the studios began to look upon this partnership with increasing favor. Sarandos explained:

> It wasn't all about fulfilling demand for mainstream videos. We were also providing the studios large markets for their films that they were having trouble

EXHIBIT 2

Netflix Subscriber Growth

	1999	2000	2001	2002	2003	2004	2005	2006
Total Subscribers (000)	107	292	456	857	1,487	2,610	4,179	6,316

Source: Netflix 2006 10-K, March 16, 2007, Netflix S1, March 6, 2002.

EXHIBIT 3

Sunnyvale Distribution Center

Automated Sorter for Outbound Envelopes

Movie Archives

"Relabeling" Station

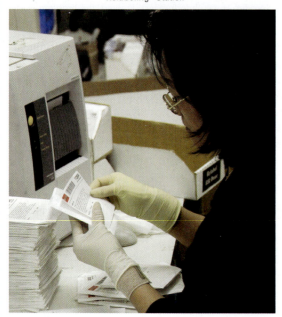

Repackaging DVDs for Resale

Source: Casewriter.

reaching. And for the independent films, Netflix can be the dominant channel, representing between 60% and 75% of the earnings for some films. At Netflix, a lesser-known film can really succeed on its merits.

Hotel Rwanda, the Don Cheadle film about the genocide in Rwanda, is an excellent example. It enjoyed some box-office sales, but generally it was a difficult topic and a difficult film to market, with a low viewership. At Netflix, however, it is our fourth-most-rented film. The rest of the top 10 are movies you would expect, but there is this wonderful independent film right there at number four. More people have seen it at Netflix than at the box office.

In 2006, Netflix evolved from its *de facto* marketing efforts and began acquiring the distribution rights to certain independent films through its Red Envelope Entertainment subsidiary. Sarandos, who led this initiative, explained the shift in strategy:

> Red Envelope Entertainment is 90% about content acquisition. While we do distribute films in other channels, including retail and other video stores, we did this to bring more excellent movies to DVD. Of the 100 films that are featured at a festival such as Sundance, only 10 will make it to DVD. We are looking through the other 90 films for top-tier content to bring to our customers.

By helping to bring high-potential films to market, Netflix hoped to enhance its reputation as the highest-quality source of independent films, a designation that contributed to its popularity.

As it was for many subscription-based services, customer churn was a critical issue for Netflix. In an average month in 2006, 3.6% of customers would cancel their subscription. In 2002, that churn rate was even higher, at 6.3%. Since customer acquisition was a major expense, retaining existing customers and reclaiming old ones who had previously unsubscribed was a key opportunity.

Originally, customers wishing to unsubscribe had to deal with a salesperson by phone, who attempted to convince the customer to retain their account. In 2002, the company changed its approach completely. Customers could unsubscribe online from Netflix as easily as they had been able to join. The only request was that they complete a brief survey explaining why they left. Hastings believed that it was more fruitful to encourage departing customers to return later on than attempt to coerce unwilling customers to stay: "We were on the AOL style of it being really hard to cancel our service. We realized, 'This is stupid. It's a false savings.' We turned it off, enabling the customer to unsubscribe on the website. We had a 30-day burst of churn, but we are convinced that it led to return visitors."

Instead of making Netflix a difficult service to leave, Hastings wanted to make it a service that former customers would return to. Customers appreciated the personalized aspect of Netflix's service, a dimension that continued to improve. The proprietary recommendation system grew more accurate in predicting a user's taste as the number of films rated by a subscriber increased. Hastings also emphasized the role of the customer's queue as a major retention tool: "Our explicit strategy is to invest in things that are strategically relevant to customer satisfaction potential. The key invention behind our subscription model is the queue. Our average queue length is 50 movies. It turned out to be an amazing invention. It's our biggest switching cost."

Just as importantly, a customer's profile was maintained if they left Netflix. If the customer were to return, everything was already in place, as if they had never left. Hastings found that growing the business in the face of a high churn rate was easier if many lost customers eventually returned.

Blockbuster Responds

Early public statements by Blockbuster dismissed the notion that its customers would benefit from an online rental business. In May 2002, a spokesperson addressed the online rental market: "Obviously, we pay attention to any way people are getting home entertainment. We always look at all those things. We have not seen a business model that's financially viable long-term in this arena. Online rental services are 'serving a niche market.'"[3]

Three months later, clarifying that Blockbuster did not intend to launch an online business to compete with Netflix, a spokesperson announced, "We don't believe there is enough of a demand for mail order—it's not a sustainable business model."[4] Furthermore, the 2002 annual report made only a cursory mention of the threat posed by online rental websites, with no mention at all in the "Risks" section. Not until 2003 did Blockbuster's management publicly discuss Netflix by name as a threat to their core business model.

Blockbuster did not formally respond to Netflix until the introduction of Blockbuster Online in 2004.

The offering first appeared in the company's disclosures in 2003, which included a tersely worded intent to launch an online subscription service during 2004. This service, closely matching Netflix's business model, offered subscribers a far greater selection of movies than was available in stores. When Blockbuster finally did enter the marketplace, it did so with what Hastings described as a "land grab" mentality, undercutting Netflix's pricing in an aggressive effort to recover lost market share. Blockbuster also tried to improve the performance of its service and distinguish itself from Netflix by integrating its online offering with its traditional store-based business. By using cross-promotions, giving in-store rental coupons to online customers, and stocking online rental requests out of its store inventory, Blockbuster attempted to find ways to productively utilize its existing resources and improve performance for its customers. While by the end of 2006 Blockbuster Online had grown to 2.2 million members, the 2006 annual report reported that Blockbuster Online still required meaningful advertising support and continued to suffer from "significant" operating losses. In the words of Hastings in 2005: "We're just thankful Blockbuster didn't enter four years ago."[5]

Blockbuster also unveiled its "no late fees" program, effective at all of its stores on January 1, 2005. Blockbuster felt that its competitors, most importantly Netflix, were differentiating their business offering from Blockbuster's due to the absence of late fees in their service offerings. This change in business strategy was not without a cost. In addition to the $60 million of marketing and implementation costs of the program, Blockbuster chose to forgo about $600 million of revenue by eliminating late fees. While early signs suggested this program resulted in increased traffic and rental volumes, it did not offset the loss of revenue as base movie rental revenue grew only 5%.

Video-on-Demand

During Netflix's rise, industry observers anointed video-on-demand (VOD) as the "next big thing" in home video. VOD was viewed as the marriage of pay-per-view programming combined with Internet downloading of entertainment, including movies and TV shows. The expectation was that viewers would search through a vast library of movies online and then watch a film on their normal TV set in a full-screen, DVD-quality format. The increasing popularity of content delivery methods such as high-definition pay-per-view and streaming Internet video, as well as the participation of some significant well-funded players in the media industry, suggested that a VOD service fully integrating personal computers and television was not a question of "if" but "when."

ONLINE VIDEO ALTERNATIVES. Netflix had been following the development of VOD since the company's inception, and Hastings sorted the available forms of Internet video into three groups. The first was advertising-supported video. Comparable to standard network television, newspapers, and magazines, this would include content that would be interrupted by regular advertising. Due to the gap between potential advertising revenue and content acquisition costs, this channel would have difficulty supporting new-release feature-length films. More common content was expected to be user-generated video, television-style programming, and older films. Online participants in this space in early 2007 included YouTube and various network websites that contained streaming video (such as ABC.com and CBS.com).

The second channel would offer digital file ownership. This approach was similar to purchasing the latest bestseller at a bookstore or a DVD from a traditional retailer and would focus on feature-length films. Sites would let customers permanently download a film to a limited number of devices, similar to the purchase of music files on popular sites such as Apple's iTunes. Revenue would not be generated through advertising but through the actual sale of content, at prices comparable to the retail price of DVDs.

The final channel was the online video rental and pay TV. This channel was characterized by limited rights and finite durations common to traditional rentals. Like digital file ownership, this channel would offer primarily feature-length films with limited advertising support. Revenue would be generated through low-priced (around $3) temporary downloads. This was the segment of the market in which Netflix expected to participate.

VOD COMPETITION. By early 2007, the VOD market had already attracted multiple competitors with approaches that spanned the three delivery channels. Stand-alone online VOD services included Vongo, launched by the Starz subscription cable channel, and CinemaNow, a venture formed by Lionsgate, Microsoft, and Cisco offering a few thousand titles from major studios. Depending on price, customers were able to rent movies for a limited time, purchase them for viewing on a limited number of devices, or even burn them directly to a DVD.

Other participants relied on a set-top box to bypass the computer and bring films directly to the user's television. MovieBeam was offered by Walt Disney and included Intel and Cisco as major investors. Customers purchased a set-top box in advance and paid per movie viewed, choosing among a limited but regularly refreshed selection of films. In early 2007, MovieBeam was acquired by Movie Gallery Inc., the second-largest video rental chain in the U.S.

Blockbuster announced in early 2007 that it was in talks to acquire MovieLink, a venture between several major studios (including MGM, Paramount, Sony, Warner Brothers, and Universal) that offered a pay-per-view downloading service, with a library of about 1,500 films.

Traditional cable and satellite providers also offered on-demand delivery at an increasing pace. They were thought to have a head start since they already had a large share of use of the television set and did not require the user to purchase new equipment. Cable and satellite providers offered an expanded and more flexible pay-per-view system, providing high-definition on-demand programming and a growing number of "free" offerings included as part of the regular monthly fee.

All of these services had two primary limitations to broader appeal: technology and content availability. VOD was perceived as limited until hardware to connect a user's computer to their television was more widely available. With the increasing adoption of big-screen, high-definition televisions, consumers were unwilling to pay equivalent prices for movies that could only be viewed on their computers.

Even more limiting was content availability. Concern about pirated downloads and a lack of urgency to supplant their profitable DVD sales made studios reluctant to offer much content to VOD websites. Hastings described the U.S. rights of physical media and the consequences they had on the studio's cooperation with online video distribution: "U.S. laws enable anyone to buy a DVD and rent it as many times as they want. We can go to Walmart, buy DVDs, and place them in our rental library. We don't need a license from the content owner to do so. Online content doesn't work like that. You have to negotiate the distribution rights with the studios. We're dealing with the same problem as everyone else."

Hunt concurred with his analysis:

> A member of the public can purchase a DVD for $20 at Walmart, but most people are not prepared to pay $20 and watch a movie only once. They want to pay $1 per hour of viewing, not $10, and the physical media rights allow us to rent for that. . . . This does not hold in an electronic media market. Without the rights for an external party to rent their content, studios believe the proper price for their content is $20 per viewing, even for a rental. Therefore, online content is limited to older or less popular films that have a limited sell-through market that we can get more cheaply.

ONLINE VIDEO AT NETFLIX. Most industry observers believed that the emergence of a viable VOD technology posed a threat to Netflix's online DVD rental business. With a fully developed VOD offering, customers would no longer have to choose between selection and impulse rentals. Those who found online DVD rentals and traditional video stores to be inconvenient would now be able to watch their selection immediately, without waiting for it to arrive via the mail or even leaving their home. While the timing of mass adoption of VOD was unclear, it appeared that the long-term success of Netflix would require some consideration of this new delivery method.

Throughout the company's history, Hastings had repeatedly stated that Netflix's purpose was not to provide DVD rentals through the Internet but rather to allow for the best home video viewing for its customers. Hastings stated in a 2003 interview, in response to a question regarding video-on-demand, "Our hope is that we'll eventually be able to download more movies. It's why we named the business Netflix and not DVD by Mail." In fact, the company publicly stated its plans to offer VOD services as early as 2001. Hastings' attitude revealed his belief that Netflix could address this growth opportunity early on. Rather than view VOD as an option that could only appeal to a niche customer set, he seemed responsive to the benefits it could provide to the mass market.

Early development of an online video feature was also a matter of preparedness. The company had been dedicating cash for investment to VOD for several years, including $10 million in 2006 and plans for an additional $40 million in 2007, even as it grew its core online rental business. Hastings recognized that the resolution of the two large impediments to widespread adoption of VOD, the connectivity between a user's computer and television and the current limitations in available content, were, to a large degree, beyond the scope of Netflix's core focus, which was movie recommendations and delivery. Given the pace of technology improvement, it was critical that Netflix have a functional VOD offering in place when those issues were resolved.

Another challenge was lack of an obvious customer base for any online viewing feature. Hastings and his team searched for a group that could serve as their "beachhead," becoming early adopters for this streaming video offering. But no niche group of viewers emerged around a particular genre to drive early demand for Netflix's online viewing offering.

Through this investment and development process, Hastings and his team had reviewed three alternatives for Netflix's online video feature. The first was a licensing arrangement through which the company would offer its proprietary recommendation system to cable providers seeking to enhance their VOD offering. Management recognized that Netflix's greatest asset was the personalized user experience created by the ratings and recommendations system. Perhaps there was an opportunity to license the strongest part of its business model and effectively outsource delivery to the cable companies, much as was done with the USPS. Cable subscribers could, for an additional fee, use the Netflix website and benefit from its familiar recommendation system, ordering movies for instant viewing on their television. This would also bypass the technology challenge of connecting a user's computer with their television, and a VOD feature that did not rely on downloading could mitigate concerns over piracy and accelerate premium-content acquisition. While this might eventually cannibalize the core business, Netflix would be replacing one stream of positive cash flows with another. Despite these benefits, Hastings was still uncomfortable partnering with a competitor. With the fast pace of technology improvements, what was the likelihood that a satisfactory connection between a user's computer and television would emerge shortly after settling on this sort of agreement?

A second option was to integrate a streaming online video feature into their core offering. The rationale here was to take advantage of Netflix's existing strengths, including its brand, its recommendation system, and its large market share of online customers. By offering the streaming feature at no additional cost to the existing online DVD rental business, Netflix could increase its penetration of the young VOD market simply by continuing to grow its existing business. Hastings believed that leveraging Netflix's existing brand and market share was the only way to differentiate his business from the stand-alone sites such as Vongo and MovieLink. Without a clear link between the streaming offering and the traditional DVD rental business, Netflix's VOD offering would have no advantage over those of its start-up competitors. Still, Hastings was concerned with what was effectively giving away this new feature for no additional revenue. While online delivery meant no shipping costs and no additional employees needed to handle extra volume in a distribution center, there were still content acquisition costs for online video, along with a material amount of programming support needed. Part of Netflix's early success had been to reach for positive cash flows before growing wildly. Hastings wondered if this was a step in the wrong direction.

Finally, he considered the merits of building a stand-alone online video business, similar to what was being offered by Vongo or MovieLink. Hastings was somewhat concerned with distracting his core team from his stated goal of growing Netflix's core business to 20 million subscribers. He was worried that asking these same employees to pursue an online video initiative would create some confusion about the future of the company. One solution would be to create a separate profit center and an entirely different service through which customers would pay exclusively for online video access. While Hastings acknowledged that the market for this service would be small in early 2007, he believed that there would eventually be resolution for the issues of content and connectivity, allowing this market to mushroom. When this happened, he was confident that the Netflix brand name and customer awareness would give it a distinct advantage over many newer entrants.

The announcement was just days away.

Endnotes

1. Pete Barlas, "Blockbuster Borrows from Netflix' Playbook, but Stays Offline Monthly DVD Rental Program Subscribers," *Investor's Business Daily*, August 12, 2002.

2. Aline Van Duyn, "DVD Rentals Pass Their Screen Test," *Financial Times*, October 4, 2005, p. 15.

3. Brian McClimans, "Frustration Leads to New Internet, Mail DVD Service," *Associated Press Newswires*, May 18, 2002.

4. Pete Barlas, "Blockbuster Borrows from Netflix' Playbook, but Stays Offline Monthly DVD Rental Program Subscribers," *Investor's Business Daily*, August 12, 2002.

5. Gary Rivlin, "Does the Kid Stay in the Picture?" *The New York Times*, February 22, 2005.

Frank T. Rothaermel
Georgia Institute of Technology
Marne L. Arthaud-Day
Kansas State University
Nicola McCarthy
Georgia Institute of Technology

WHEN BRIAN DUNN joined Best Buy as a 24-year-old entry-level sales associate in 1985, he hardly could have imagined his appointment to CEO in June 2009 or the global scale of the operation now in his charge. In the intervening years, Best Buy had grown from a dozen stores to a multinational corporation with nearly 1,400 stores in the United States and Canada and 2,600 locations in 13 other countries, including Mexico, China, and several European nations.[1] Best Buy's annual sales had likewise increased, reaching close to $50 billion in 2010. Yet despite the fact that earnings had shown a steady increase for the past five years (up from $30.8 billion in 2006), Best Buy's stock price was displaying a troubling downward trend, hovering in the low $30 range after a 2006 high of $56.66. Sales in domestic stores declined by 5.0 percent in the third quarter of 2010, driven primarily by lower demand in key product categories (TVs, mobile computing, and gaming software) and loss of market share.[2]

Unlike Circuit City, Best Buy had survived the deep 2008–2010 recession, but its struggles were far from over. Not only had the company taken a significant hit due to recent economic conditions, it was still recovering from the damage done by the flat-screen-TV price war of 2006 and 2007. Meanwhile, multiple major competitors like Amazon, Walmart, Target, and even Apple were aggressively challenging Best Buy's traditional dominance of the electronics retail market.

In fact, almost all of Best Buy's revenue growth in fiscal year 2010 (a 10.94 percent increase over 2009) was attributable to its acquisition of Best Buy Europe and a favorable impact of foreign-currency fluctuations.[3] With most of its primary growth derived from acquisitions, investors and analysts were starting to question the company's ability to grow organically. They worried that continued reliance on inorganic growth could destroy Best Buy's cash reserves and ability to assume debt.

Mr. Dunn knew the company needed to deliver some better news with the next quarterly earnings report. But he feared this might be hard to do given the disappointing nature of the latest economic and unemployment figures, the threat of a double-dip in the recession, and the possibility of even further price wars with an expanded pool of competitors. One article in *The Wall Street Journal* noted that customers were using "Best Buy as Amazon's show room."[4] Customers would have Best Buy salespeople demonstrate the latest electronics wares, and then purchase them online. To add insult to injury, some customers then would have their flat-screen TVs installed by Best Buy's Geek Squad.

To ease investors' (and his own) concerns regarding Best Buy's future viability, Mr. Dunn had announced to the Wall Street community that he would unveil a five-year growth strategy for the company at the upcoming shareholder meeting. With just two months to go until the meeting, Mr. Dunn knew time was of the essence. He gathered his closest advisors and they began discussing the issues: How would Best Buy protect itself from a waning economy and uncertainty in consumer spending? How could Best Buy avoid following Circuit City into bankruptcy? How could Best Buy protect itself from invading competitors? How long could/should Best Buy continue to grow through acquisitions without doing permanent damage to its financial security and corporate culture? What strategies should the company employ to grow over the next five years?

Professors Frank T. Rothaermel and Marne L. Arthaud-Day, and Research Associate Nicola McCarthy (PhD Candidate) prepared this case from public sources. It is developed for the purpose of class discussion. It is not intended to be used for any kind of endorsement, source of data, or depiction of efficient or inefficient management. We thank Michael Janovec (GT MBA '11) for research and editorial assistance. All opinions expressed, and all errors and omissions are entirely the authors'. © Rothaermel, Arthaud-Day, and McCarthy, 2013.

Best Buy History

After growing tired of working at his father's electronics distribution company, Dick Schulze quit.[5] Together with his new business partner, James Wheeler, in 1966 Schulze founded The Sound of Music, an audio specialty store, in Minnesota. The fledgling company ended its first fiscal year with gross sales of $173,000, and continued to grow rapidly over the next few years. By the time of its initial public offering in 1969, the home-town enterprise had acquired two of its competitors (Kencraft Hi-Fi Company and Bergo Company)[6] and had opened two new outlets near the University of Minnesota in downtown Minneapolis.

Schulze bought out Wheeler in 1971,[7] shortly after the Sound of Music hit the $1 million mark in annual revenues.[8] Subsequent years saw continued growth and expansion through additional locations, new product lines, and novel promotional techniques. For example, in 1979 the Sound of Music became the first supplier of video and laserdisk equipment from companies that included Panasonic, Magnavox, Sony, and Sharp. After a tornado hit the Roseville, Minnesota, store in June 1981, the company responded with a "Tornado Sale," which became an annual event, storm or no storm. This strategy boosted The Sound of Music's average sales per square foot to $350 in 1981, compared with an industry average of $150 to $200.[9]

ARRIVAL OF THE SUPERSTORE. With ambitions to capture even larger market share, the Sound of Music in 1983 changed its name to Best Buy Co., Inc. Shortly thereafter, it adopted its now-familiar superstore format, with an increasingly diversified product range. Boosted by an infusion of cash from a successive series of public offerings, Best Buy proceeded to grow from 8 to 24 stores and saw its revenues increase from $29 to $290 million from 1984 to 1987.[10] On July 20, 1987, Best Buy made its debut on the New York Stock Exchange (NYSE: BBY) with an initial offering of 8.3 million shares of common stock.

Best Buy changed its logo to the yellow tag in 1987, and in 1989 its stores adopted a new "grab-and-go" store format, called Concept II. Schulze's revolutionary new approach to big-box retailing combined Walmart's prices with Circuit City's assortment, in a shopping warehouse with a 35,000-square-foot footprint.[11] The new stores consisted of well-stocked showrooms with self-help information so that people could make their product selections independently and check out in a single stop. Answer Centers were still available for people who desired assistance, but salespeople no longer needed to attend to each individual customer or fetch merchandise from storage. This change reduced Best Buy's employment costs by one-third, which compensated for the corresponding de-emphasis on service contracts. One analyst called Concept II "the most innovative thing to happen in this industry—ever."[12]

Spurred by the success of its warehouse format, Best Buy hit $1 billion in sales revenues in 1992. The company landed on the Fortune 500 list (debuting at #373) for the first time in 1995. *Fortune* magazine named Best Buy one of the top 10 performing stocks from 1990 to 2000, and honored it as "Company of the Year" in 2004.[13] By 2009, Best Buy controlled 4.8 percent of the global market in consumer electronics, up from just 2 percent of the domestic market in 1994.[14]

GROWTH THROUGH ACQUISITIONS. The year 2000 marked the launch of a new phase of inorganic growth through acquisitions. Best Buy grew its revenues from $12.5 billion in 2000 to $49.7 billion in 2010 (Exhibits 1 and 2).[15] The company first purchased Magnolia, a high-end consumer electronics chain with 13 locations throughout Washington, California, and Oregon, for $88 million in 2000.[16] The next year, Best Buy purchased Musicland for $425.1 million. The acquisition of the mall-based music and entertainment retailer gave Best Buy access to an additional 1,300 stores across the United States and Puerto Rico, including 650 Sam Goody and 400 Suncoast Motion Picture outlets. In 2002, the company acquired Geek Squad, a 24-hour computer-support task force. By 2004, Best Buy had opened Geek Squad precincts within all of its stores, as well as two experimental locations in FedEx Kinko's in Indianapolis, Indiana, and Charlotte, North Carolina.[17]

In contrast to the rapid expansion of Geek Squad, Best Buy divested Musicland in 2003 due to declining mall sales after 9/11, coupled with increased competition from Walmart and Target in the CD segment. Sun Capital Partners Inc., a private equity firm, purchased the failing firm for the assumption of Musicland's debt and lease obligations. Brad Anderson, who succeeded Schulze as CEO in 2002, described the Musicland venture as, "a very expensive but powerful learning experience for Best Buy."[18]

After the Musicland debacle, Best Buy took a two-year acquisition hiatus before purchasing AudioVisions, a custom integrator of electronic products such as flat-screen TVs and security solutions, in 2005.[19] In

EXHIBIT 1

Best Buy Financial Data (in $ millions, except EPS data)

Fiscal Year	2001	2002	2003	2004	2005	2006	2007	2008	2009	2010	2011
Cash and short-term investments	747	1,855	1,914	2,600	3,506	3,910	4,175	1,438	996	1,916	1,125
Receivables total	209	247	312	343	375	506	548	549	1,868	2,020	2,348
Inventories total	1,767	2,258	2,046	2,607	2,851	3,338	4,028	4,708	4,753	5,486	5,897
PP&E total (net)	1,444	1,897	2,062	2,244	2,464	2,712	2,938	3,306	4,174	4,070	3,823
Depreciation depletion and amortization	543	823	1,027	1,330	1,728	2,124	1,966	2,302	2,766	3,383	4,082
Assets total	4,840	7,375	7,663	8,652	10,294	11,864	13,570	12,758	15,826	18,302	17,849
Accounts payable	1,773	2,449	2,195	2,535	2,824	3,234	3,934	4,297	4,997	5,276	4,894
Long-term debt total	181	813	828	482	528	178	590	627	1,126	1,104	711
Liabilities total	3,018	4,854	4,933	5,230	5,845	6,607	7,334	8,234	10,670	11,338	10,557
Stockholders' equity total	1,822	2,521	2,730	3,422	4,449	5,257	6,201	4,484	4,643	6,964	7,292
Sales (net)	15,327	19,597	20,946	24,547	27,433	30,848	35,934	40,023	45,015	49,694	50,272
COGS	12,100	14,858	15,400	17,965	20,479	22,663	26,652	29,892	33,215	37,534	37,635
SG&A	2,440	3,493	4,226	4,893	5,053	6,069	6,770	7,385	8,984	9,873	10,325
Income taxes	246	366	392	496	509	581	752	815	674	802	714
Income before extraordinary items	396	570	622	800	934	1,140	1,377	1,407	1,009	1,323	1,277
Net income	396	570	99	705	984	1,140	1,377	1,407	1,003	1,317	1,277
EPS (basic)	1.92	2.70	1.93	2.47	2.87	2.33	2.86	3.20	2.43	3.16	3.14
EPS (diluted)	1.86	2.66	1.91	2.44	2.79	2.27	2.79	3.12	2.39	3.10	3.08

Source: Compustat.

EXHIBIT 2

Best Buy Financial Charts

Source: Best Buy 2011 shareholder meeting presentation, June 21, 2011.

December of that same year, Best Buy acquired, for $410 million, Pacific Sales, a Los Angeles–headquartered company that specialized in selling premium kitchen appliances.[20] In 2007, Best Buy announced plans to purchase Seattle-based Speakeasy Inc., a broadband and VoIP services provider, for $97 million.[21] This transaction was followed by the 2008 announcement of Best Buy's acquisition of Napster for $121 million in cash, in an effort to compete with Apple's 70 percent share of the digital-music marketplace.[22]

In the meantime, Best Buy was also engaged on the international front. Its first cross-border expansion was the 2001 acquisition of Futureshop Ltd., a Canadian electronics chain, which added annual sales of $1.32 billion.[23] Maintaining Futureshop as a wholly owned subsidiary, Best Buy strengthened its Canadian presence by opening eight stores of its own in the Toronto area.[24] By 2003, Best Buy had over 600 stores outside the United States, prompting it to open its first global-sourcing office in Shanghai.[25]

Best Buy first established an active presence in the growing Asian markets with its 2006 acquisition of a majority interest in the retail chain Jiangsu Five Star Appliance Co., Ltd., China's fourth-largest appliance and consumer electronics retailer, for $180 million.[26] A year later on January 26, 2007, the first Best Buy store in China—touted as the largest Best Buy in existence—opened in Shanghai.[27] Other regions quickly followed.

In 2008, Best Buy announced the opening of its first pilot stores in Mexico and Turkey, as well as multiple branded superstores in the United Kingdom and other European countries.[28] Also in 2008, Best Buy agreed to buy a 50 percent stake in the retail division of Carphone Warehouse, a cellular phone retailer based in the United Kingdom.

A Brief History of the Consumer-Electronics Retail Industry

The consumer-electronics retail industry grew rapidly in the second half of the 20th century due to several converging trends. At the end of World War II, a significant portion of the U.S. population migrated from cities to suburbs, creating a need for suburban retail centers. At the same time, the cost of technology decreased, generating an increase in demand for televisions and other consumer electronics. Many of these new customers were price-sensitive, first-time homeowners, who were willing to accept decreased customer service in return for discounted prices, leading to a rapid growth in discount stores.[29]

As the children of the WWII generation—the baby boomers—reached adulthood in the 1970s, demand for consumer electronics soared. Retailers shifted from carrying just one or two lines of equipment toward stocking a diverse set of product lines. Strong industry growth continued through the late 1980s, until the new VCR market became saturated and a recession slowed consumer sales. By 1991, 98 percent of all homes had at least one color TV and 77 percent of those that owned TVs also owned a VCR. The United States alone had at least 10,000 radio, television, and consumer-electronics stores that had sprung up to meet the surge in demand. With market saturation, however, growth in the 1990s was limited to replacement and upgrading of existing devices.[30] As a result, competition intensified and many companies, such as Highland Superstores Inc., left the electronics market.[31]

Technology advancements and improved economic conditions in the mid- to late-1990s again led to a period of growth that supported the rise of large superstores such as Best Buy and Circuit City. In 1998, sales at Best Buy and Circuit City increased by 21 percent and 48 percent, respectively.[32] It was about this time that the industry faced yet another great shakeup—the birth of online retailing.

In 1998, Amazon.com, a previously unheard of competitor, entered the consumer-electronics market by offering music CD sales online.[33] Not willing to cede this potentially lucrative market, Circuit City, Tweeter Home Entertainment Group, and Outpost.com all opened online consumer-electronics sites of their own within the next year. Best Buy followed suit with Bestbuy.com in 2000, making it a relatively late mover in online retailing.[34]

The ability to reach new consumers online, coupled with increased interest in digital cameras and DVDs, led to yet another period of rapid expansion throughout the early 2000s. This time, however, growth occurred primarily through acquisitions and industry consolidation. From 1994 to 2007, the three largest consumer electronics retailers (Circuit City, Best Buy, and Radio Shack) increased channel share from approximately 22 percent to 45 percent. Meanwhile, the total number of firms in electronics retailing with over 100 employees declined by 4 percent per annum from 1998 to 2004.[35]

From 2005 to 2007, the industry compound annual growth rate (CAGR) was approximately 6 percent. With the onset of the global recession, growth fell to 4.4 percent in 2008 and –0.5 percent in 2009 (Exhibit 3), for a four-year mean CAGR of 4 percent (2005 to 2009). Despite the decelerating growth rates over the prior two years, the industry was forecasted to recover in 2010 and grow at a rate of 6.1 percent from 2009 to 2014. If this prediction holds true, revenues should show a corresponding increase from $553.1 billion in 2009 to $745.3 billion by the end of 2014.

Trends in the Consumer-Electronics Industry

The consumer-electronics retail industry is both cyclical and seasonal. Industry sales during the holiday season in the fourth quarter typically exceed sales

EXHIBIT 3

Global Computer and Electronics Retail Industry, 2005–2009

Global Computer & Electronic Retail Sector Value: $ billion, 2005–09			
Year	$ billion	€ billion	% Growth
2005	472.7	340.0	
2006	501.1	360.4	6.0%
2007	532.1	382.7	6.2%
2008	555.7	399.6	4.4%
2009	553.1	397.8	(0.5%)
CAGR: 2005-09			4.0%

Source: Datamonitor

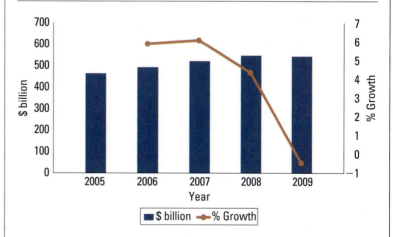

Source: "Industry profile: Global computer & electronics retail," *Datamonitor,* March 2010, www.datamonitor.com. Reference Code: 0199-2025.

from the other three quarters combined. As most consumer-electronics items are considered discretionary purchases, sales are directly correlated with macroeconomic factors such as consumer confidence, unemployment, the housing market, and the ability to obtain credit.[36]

A distinctive trend in the electronics-consumer industry is that of ever-falling prices. These falling prices place constant pressure on consumer-electronics manufacturers to improve functionality, portability, and style as a way of differentiating their products from those of competitors. As a result, the product life cycle has grown increasingly shorter as manufacturers cannibalize their own products in an effort to maintain customer interest and loyalty.

This cannibalization has led to the evolution of consumer electronics as a measure of socioeconomic status in countries such as the United States. Financial wealth buys access to the latest and greatest technology. As prices fall, the technology becomes affordable to a wider demographic, but the technological elite have already moved on to the next generation of devices. Cellular phones were once fantasy gadgets seen only in James Bond movies. In the 1980s, yuppies proudly displayed their cell phones on their belts as a status symbol. These days, nearly everyone has a cell phone whose design and functionality make those early "dinosaurs" laughable. Laptops, large-screen TVs, and smartphones have enjoyed a similar proliferation among the masses. Today's must-have is tomorrow's bargain commodity at Walmart, so retailers must strike while the product is hot. A product will, in its boom days, attract a very different clientele than in the later, less-exclusive phases of its shelf life. Consequently, understanding and predicting consumer demand is an imperative in the modern consumer-electronics industry. This is not an easy feat when operating in more than 1,800 stores worldwide.

Comparatively speaking, the consumer-electronics retail industry remains fragmented. Prior to the 2008 recession, the top three consumer electronics retainers (Circuit City, Best Buy, and Radio Shack) accounted for 42 percent of the U.S. market. In comparison, the top three firms in home improvement and office supply retail controlled 58 percent and 79 percent, respectively. Globally, the market is even more divided, with Best Buy controlling just 4.8 percent of the worldwide market in consumer electronics in 2009.[37] This fragmentation increased further with the fall of Circuit City in March of that same year.

The Rise and Fall of Circuit City

Dunn's career had fared better than that of his one-time colleague, Philip Schoonover. Immediately prior to his appointment as CEO of Circuit City in 2004, Schoonover served as Executive Vice-President for Customer Segments at Best Buy (April 2004 through September 2004). He had previously served the company in a series of executive vice-president positions, with responsibilities for business development, digital technology solutions, and merchandising. Before joining Best Buy, Schoonover served as executive vice-president at TOPS Appliance City and held senior sales and marketing positions with Sony Corporation of America.[38]

Dunn and Schoonover's careers unfolded largely within the same corporate culture that had apparently found favor with both, promoting each to senior leadership positions. Yet in 2009, the two found themselves facing vastly different outcomes. On January 5, 2008, Herb Greenberg of *The Wall Street Journal* named Philip Schoonover as the worst CEO of the year.[39] A few months later, Schoonover resigned and was replaced by James Marcum, who served as Circuit City's CEO and acting president until the firm's demise. Marcum had assumed the helm of a sinking ship, and the rest, as they say, was history. What follows is the tale of two firms, the tale of Dunn and Schoonover, and the tale of thousands of others whose livelihoods and careers either flourished or came to an early end (see Circuit City's financial statements in Exhibit 4).

EARLY HISTORY. If Best Buy was born amidst The Sound of Music, Circuit City was born against the sound of TV. It is said that Circuit City's founder, Samuel Wurtzel, decided to get a haircut while vacationing in Richmond, Virginia. In chatting with the barber, he learned that the first commercial television station in the South was soon to hit the local airwaves. Wurtzel decided that a store selling TVs sounded lucrative,[40] and he opened the first Wards Company store in Richmond in 1949. Soon thereafter, Wurtzel and his partner, Abraham L. Hecht, diversified their product offerings to include a range of home appliances as well as television sets. As profits grew over the next decade, they expanded further by opening three additional stores in the Richmond area. The total sales volume for the four Richmond stores quickly approached $1 million a year.[41] The company went public in 1961, selling 110,000 shares at a price of $5.375 through a Baltimore stockbroker.[42]

EXHIBIT 4

Circuit City Financial Data (in $ millions, except EPS data)

Fiscal Year	1999	2000	2001	2002	2003	2004	2005	2006	2007
Cash and short-term investments	634	437	1,248	885	783	1,005	838	739	297
Receivables total	464	451	553	775	580	173	226	425	489
Inventories total	1,406	1,411	1,234	1,410	1,517	1,460	1,698	1,637	1,574
PP&E total (net)	753	797	733	650	586	739	839	921	1,037
Depreciation depletion and amortization	66	748	830	951	1,021	1,104	1,179	1,300	1,448
Assets total	3,537	3,453	4,133	3,799	3,633	3,789	4,069	4,007	3,746
Accounts payable	884	820	1,020	964	830	962	1,053	1,114	1,108
Long-term debt total	128	33	14	11	23	12	52	50	57
Liabilities total	1,483	1,195	1,573	1,458	1,409	1,702	2,114	2,216	2,243
Stockholders' equity total	2,055	2,257	2,560	2,342	2,224	2,087	1,955	1,791	1,503
Sales (net)	10,599	10,458	9,590	10,016	9,778	10,478	11,598	12,430	11,744
COGS	7,844	7,810	7,117	7,446	7,320	7,749	8,603	9,320	9,131
SG&A	2,081	2,199	2,101	2,353	2,266	2,487	2,620	2,806	2,775
Income taxes	200	71	78	25	0	36	88	31	-32
Income before extraordinary items	328	149	191	42	-1	60	151	-10	-321
Net income	197	149	191	106	-89	62	140	-8	-320
EPS (basic)	0.98	0.73	0.93	0.51	-0.43	0.32	0.79	-0.05	-1.94
EPS (diluted)	1.60	0.73	0.92	0.20	0	0.31	0.84	-0.06	-1.95

Source: Compustat.

Wards expanded across the Southeast and Midwest through a series of acquisitions from 1965 to 1970. In 1970, Samuel Wurtzel retired as president of the company, though he remained as chairman of the company's board. He passed the torch to his son, Alan Wurtzel, who exhibited a keen sense of strategy in his stewardship of his father's business empire.[43] In 1974, Wards arguably suffered adverse effects due to its rapid expansion and diversification, losing $3 million on overall sales of $69 million. In response, Wurtzel junior withdrew Wards from areas outside its core competencies, such as tire sales, where the company was not turning a profit. In addition, he narrowed Wards's product line from a broad range of appliances to focus on consumer electronics.

To showcase its new strategy, the company opened a 40,000-square-foot store called "The Wards Loading Dock."[44] This "big box" format had ample room to display Wards's extensive selection of 2,000 products, giving the company an edge over its competitors. As a result of its novel store design, Wards increased its sales ten-fold to $246 million by 1983.[45] The high volume of sales enabled Wards to lower prices, which effectively put several smaller firms out of business.

RISE TO MARKET DOMINANCE. In 1984, Wards changed its name to Circuit City Stores, Inc., and listed on the New York Stock Exchange. That same year, Alan Wurtzel assumed the post of chairman of the board and was succeeded as CEO by Richard Sharp. Under Sharp, the company consolidated its operations in very large stores located mainly in clusters throughout the Southeast. These consolidated "Circuit City Superstores" encompassed up to an acre of floor space and were considered massive for their era.[46] Circuit City's approach of opening a number of very large stores at once in the same region, accompanied by heavy advertising of their arrival, represented a methodical determination to win the lion's share of sales in that market. By 1987, the company was reaping $1 billion in annual revenues and dominated the U.S. market.[47]

In 1992, Circuit City Superstores expanded their offerings to include personal computers and recorded music. In 1993, Circuit City stretched its boundaries even further and opened the first of what became the chain of used-car lots known as CarMax. Later ventures included a credit card operation (eventually sold to Bank One Corporation in May 2004). Circuit City's history is speckled with such detours outside its core electronics business. The well-being of the firm has always depended upon returning to its focus on creating competitive advantage in the cut-throat consumer-electronics retail industry.[48]

Also in 1993, Circuit City found itself in an intense price war with Best Buy that pitted the companies' sales forces against one another. Circuit City was known for its hard-sell tactics, with salespeople working for commission. In contrast, Best Buy employees enjoyed a more relaxed, self-service–oriented sales environment, in which they were paid a flat hourly rate.[49] Best Buy's "we're here if you need us" approach was so popular with customers that Circuit City was forced to adapt. By 2003, Circuit City's 600 stores were barely profitable, and the company posted a net annual loss of $89.3 million. The difficulty of implementing such a radical change in sales culture, however, was evidenced by the board's 2003 veto of a proposal to adopt a more self-service–oriented style. By the end of the year, Circuit City had nevertheless dismissed 3,900 workers and implemented a single hourly pay structure. The company continued to restructure in 2004, closing dozens of stores at less-desirable sites and opening some 70 new stores in more ideal locations.

FLAT-PANEL PRICE WAR. Circuit City's reaction to the flat-screen price war likely helped to decide its fate. The U.S. housing bubble in the early 2000s led to a boom in the consumer-electronics industry. Homes popped up as lax lending practices gave Americans access to mortgages that were unobtainable in previous generations. In turn, easy access to cheap credit led to a boost in flat-panel TV sales to furnish the newly constructed primary and secondary homes.

This dramatic increase in demand for consumer electronics created a flood of investment in new factories, resulting in excess supply and inventory for retailers. Then, in the fourth quarter of 2006, strain from the weakening housing market led to a decline in consumer spending. To move inventory, discount retailers such as Walmart began slashing prices of flat-panel TVs. Circuit City followed suit. The price of the popular Panasonic 42-inch plasma high-definition television dropped from $1,762 at Circuit City in September to $1,199 just two months later. By the end of 2006, flat-panel TV prices had declined between 40 and 50 percent. In fact, prices fell so quickly during the holiday season and in the weeks preceding the Super Bowl that Circuit City's weekly advertising circulars were outdated by the time they reached customers.[50]

Circuit City was especially vulnerable to eroding margins caused by the price war since nearly 44 percent of its revenues came from TV sales. By November 2006, Circuit City realized a net loss of $16 million, down from a quarterly profit of $10.1 million in 2005. Shares of Circuit City stock plummeted 80 percent by the end of that year.[51]

DEMISE. In an arguably misguided attempt to mollify investors in the aftermath of the flat-screen price-war, Circuit City CEO Schoonover fired some 3,400 of the firm's most experienced employees and replaced them with less-costly, less-experienced personnel. *The Washington Post* quoted Circuit City spokesman Bill Cimino as saying, "We know we needed to change. What you're seeing today is us trying to change to become more competitive within our industry."[52] MSNBC quoted another Circuit City spokesperson, Jim Babb, as saying, "The essential need we have was to bring expenses of our business in line with current marketplace realities. We acknowledge this is a painful step."[53] Circuit City's hope was to save $110 million in fiscal 2007 year and $140 million in 2008.

Circuit City's decision to sacrifice human capital in the interest of efficiency stood in sharp contrast with Best Buy's customer-centricity, which required a work force that knew both its customer base and its products thoroughly.[54] Indeed, some analysts alleged that many of the laid-off Circuit City employees took their experience and their customers to Best Buy, bolstering the company's main competitor. Analyst Holly Dolezalek predicted that the mass layoff of experienced, mainly in-store employees and their subsequent replacement with cheaper labor would lead to poor salesmanship and lower sales.[55] The prophets of doom were not to be disappointed.[56] In the wake of disappointing sales figures, Circuit City anticipated a loss of $80 to $90 million in the first quarter of fiscal 2008.

Circuit City filed for Section 11 bankruptcy in November 2008, closing 155 stores in an attempt to preserve a future for the rest.[57] After failing to find a buyer, Circuit City began liquidation of the remainder of its assets in January 2009. The firm cited reduced consumer spending and an overall economic downturn as the reasons for its demise. In May 2009, Systemax purchased the Circuit City brand and trademark for $6.5 million for use in online electronics retail.[58] Circuit City's liquidation led many industry analysts to ask what went wrong. By the time it liquidated in 2009, Circuit City was the second largest U.S.

electronics retailer with 567 stores nationwide, ranked second only to Best Buy. What had Best Buy done that enabled it to survive economic hardship while Circuit City collapsed?

Current Competitors

The power vacuum left by Circuit City led to increased competition in the consumer-electronics industry. In the year after Circuit City closed, Best Buy reported a 5.5 percent increase in market share, to approximately 22.9 percent of the $170 billion domestic market (Exhibit 5).[59, 60, 61] However, other retailers and e-tailers such as Amazon.com, Target, and Walmart rapidly entered the fray and established significant footholds. By the 2010 holiday season, Best Buy's gains from the fall of Circuit City had started to erode. A price war with Walmart and Amazon caused Best Buy to cede 1.1 percent in market share to these competitors from November through December of 2010.[62]

AMAZON.COM. Founded in 1994 by Jeffrey Bezos as an online book retailer, Amazon.com's sales grew from $20,000 in 1995 to over $24 billion in 2009 (Exhibit 6).[63] Since the company went public in 1997, it has rapidly diversified into multiple product areas, undercutting existing specialty and brick-and-mortar retailers in price.[64] In 1998, Amazon.com launched its online music and video store and began to sell toys as well as consumer electronics; it added clothing in 2002. More recently, Amazon.com has engaged in a

EXHIBIT 5

Best Buy Market Share (Basis Points)

Source: Best Buy 2010 Shareholder Meeting presentation, June 24, 2010.

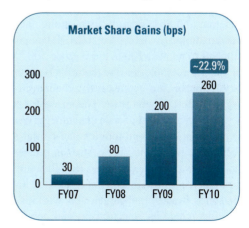

EXHIBIT 6

Amazon Financial Data (in $ millions, except EPS data)

Fiscal Year	2000	2001	2002	2003	2004	2005	2006	2007	2008	2009	2010
Cash and short-term investments	1,101	997	1,301	1,395	1,779	2,000	2,019	3,112	3,727	6,366	8,762
Receivables total	0	0	0	0	0	0	0	0	711	836	1,587
Inventories total	175	144	202	294	480	566	877	1,200	1,399	2,171	3,202
PP&E total (net)	366	272	239	224	246	348	457	543	854	1,290	2,414
Depreciation depletion and amortization	406	266	88	78	76	118	210	271	340	432	568
Assets total	2,135	1,638	1,990	2,162	3,249	3,696	4,363	6,485	8,314	13,813	18,797
Accounts payable	485	445	618	820	1,142	1,366	1,816	2,795	3,594	5,605	8,051
Long-term debt total	2,127	2,156	2,277	1,855	1,945	1,480	1,247	1,282	409	252	641
Liabilities total	3,102	3,078	3,343	3,198	3,476	3,450	3,932	5,288	5,642	8,556	11,933
Stockholders' equity total	(967)	(1,440)	(1,353)	(1,036)	(227)	246	431	1,197	2,672	5,257	6,864
Sales (net)	2,762	3,122	3,933	5,264	6,921	8,490	10,711	14,835	19,166	24,509	34,204
COGS	2,022	2,239	2,858	3,931	5,244	6,338	8,055	11,224	14,585	18,594	26,561
SG&A	998	848	881	984	1,170	1,569	2,037	2,685	3,452	4,300	4,397
Income taxes	0	0	0	0	(233)	95	187	184	247	253	352
Income before extraordinary items	(1,441)	(577)	(150)	35	588	359	190	476	645	902	1,152
Net income	(1,441)	(570)	(150)	35	588	359	190	476	645	902	1,152
EPS (basic)	(4.02)	(1.53)	(0.40)	0.09	1.45	0.81	0.46	1.15	1.52	2.08	2.58
EPS (diluted)	(4.02)	(1.53)	(0.40)	0.08	1.39	0.78	0.45	1.12	1.49	2.04	2.53

Source: Compustat.

series of acquisitions to further expand the breadth of products offered. The firm acquired the number-one online shoe retailer, Zappos, for $890 million in 2009. In 2010, Amazon.com added both Woot Inc., a social shopping e-commerce site, and Quidsi, the owner of Diapers.com and Soap.com, to its portfolio. Through these acquisitions, Amazon grew to 24,300 employees and climbed to number 100 in the Fortune 500.[65]

To gain a foothold in the consumer-electronics industry, Amazon has aggressively challenged both Walmart and Best Buy on price. The growth of smartphone usage has aided Amazon in this strategy. Whereas before customers had to go to brick-and-mortar stores and then come home and check Amazon prices, consumers can now price-shop *within* a Best Buy store and purchase directly from Amazon if its prices are lower.[66]

Amazon's strategy appears to be working. The e-tailer increased its electronics and non-media revenues by 66 percent in 2010, reaching $18 billion. From 2007 to the end of 2010, Amazon.com increased its share of LCD TV sets from 1.3 percent to 3.7 percent; its share of portable audio-device sales increased from 4.6 percent to 11 percent.[67] According to a study cited by Retrevo, Amazon has increased its mind share ("When you think about buying electronics, who comes to mind first?") by 30 percent (11 percent to 15 percent) from 2009 to 2010, and its gains appear to have been largely at Best Buy's expense (Exhibits 7 and 8).[68]

WALMART. As the world's largest retailer, Walmart employs 2.1 million associates across more than 8,986 stores in 15 countries.[69] Walmart was founded by Sam Walton in 1945 in Newport, Arkansas, where it operated for five years before Walton moved his company to its now-famous Bentonville, Arkansas, location. Walmart has expanded internationally through its

EXHIBIT 7

Top 15 Most Valuable Retail Brands

	Brand	Brand Value ($ in billions)	Brand Change Year over Year
1	Walmart	39.42	(4%)
2	Amazon	27.46	29%
3	Tesco	25.74	12%
4	Carrefour	14.98	0%
5	Target	12.15	(1%)
6	eBay	9.33	(28%)
7	Home Depot	8.97	(3%)
8	ALDI	8.75	1%
9	Auchan	7.85	(26%)
10	Lowes	7.01	10%
11	Best Buy	5.81	18%
12	IKEA	5.71	(15%)
13	Marks and Spencer	5.70	(5%)
14	Kohl's	4.37	12%
15	Lidl & Schwartz Stiftung & Co	4.10	(1%)

Source: Kantar Retail.

EXHIBIT 8

Customer Perceptions

When you think about buying electronics, who comes to mind first?

Source: www.retrevo.com/content/bestbuy-competitors-gained-ground (January 5, 2010).

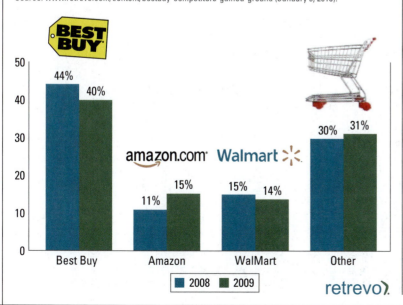

logistics management, low prices, and breadth of merchandise.[70] Walmart carries products in areas such as family apparel, health and beauty aids, toys, home furnishings, housewares, hardware, lawn and garden supplies, and automotive products, in addition to consumer electronics. In 2000, the company launched Walmart.com to compete with online retailers such as Amazon.com, and now sells more than a million products through its website. In 2009, the company recorded $408 billion in sales with a net income of $14.8 billion (Exhibit 9).

Like Amazon, Walmart moved aggressively into the consumer-electronics market in the wake of Circuit City's collapse. In May 2010, the company announced that it was significantly expanding its

EXHIBIT 9

Walmart Financial Data (in $ millions, except EPS data)

Fiscal Year	2000	2001	2002	2003	2004	2005	2006	2007	2008	2009	2010
Cash and short-term investments	2,054	2,161	2,758	5,199	5,488	6,414	7,373	5,569	7,275	7,907	7,395
Receivables total	1,768	2,000	2,108	1,254	1,715	2,662	2,840	3,654	3,905	4,144	5,089
Inventories total	21,442	22,614	24,891	26,612	29,447	32,191	33,685	35,180	34,511	33,160	36,318
PP&E total (net)	40,934	45,750	51,904	58,530	68,567	79,290	88,440	97,017	95,653	102,307	107,878
Depreciation depletion and amortization	2,387	2,700	3,100	3,500	4,300	4,717	5,459	6,317	6,739	7,157	7,641
Assets total	78,130	83,451	94,685	104,912	120,223	138,187	151,193	163,514	163,429	170,706	180,663
Accounts payable	15,092	15,617	17,140	19,332	21,671	25,373	28,090	30,370	28,849	30,451	33,557
Long-term debt total	28,949	27,282	16,597	17,102	20,087	26,429	27,222	29,799	31,349	33,231	40,692
Liabilities total	46,787	48,349	55,348	61,289	70,827	85,016	89,629	98,906	98,144	99,957	112,121
Stockholders' equity total	31,343	35,102	39,337	43,623	49,396	53,171	61,573	64,608	65,285	70,749	68,542
Sales (net)	192,003	218,529	245,308	257,157	286,103	313,335	345,977	375,376	402,298	408,214	421,849
COGS	147,868	168,862	188,738	195,247	215,493	235,674	258,693	280,295	299,419	297,500	315,287
SG&A	31,550	36,173	41,043	44,909	51,105	56,733	64,001	70,297	76,299	79,347	81,020
Income taxes	3,692	3,897	4,487	5,118	5,589	5,803	6,365	6,908	7,145	7,139	7,579
Income before extraordinary items	6,295	6,671	8,039	9,054	10,267	11,231	11,284	12,731	13,400	14,335	15,355
Net income	6,295	6,671	8,039	9,054	10,267	11,231	11,284	12,731	13,400	14,335	16,389
EPS (basic)	1.41	1.49	1.81	2.03	2.41	2.68	2.92	3.17	3.36	3.73	4.48
EPS (diluted)	1.40	1.49	1.81	2.03	2.41	2.68	2.92	3.16	3.35	3.72	4.47

Source: Compustat.

offerings of Blu-ray players, HDTVs, home theater systems, DVDs and Blu-ray movies, and wireless products for home networks. At the same time, Walmart rolled out a dedicated area for pay-as-you go mobile broadband products from well-respected vendors such as Verizon, Cricket, Virgin, and AT&T, as well as a new pay-as-you-go program with Sprint for cellular users. The company also increased its smartphone offerings by close to 60 percent compared with 2009.

Gary Severson, senior vice president for Home Entertainment, explained Walmart's strategy as follows: "Starting this month, customers will discover more high quality Internet-ready home entertainment products, new wireless technologies and new mobile devices in stores and online that offer simple, affordable solutions for creating a more connected life. . . . We also continue to design a well-defined shopping experience in Entertainment that enables customers to find what they need quickly, learn about new technology, compare prices among top brands, and every day find amazing value. Our commitment to the best price and surprising value is always a top priority."[71]

TARGET. Target is the second-largest discount retailer in the United States, behind Walmart. Target was founded in 1962, when Dayton's, a Minneapolis department store, expanded into a shopping mall in Roseville, Minnesota. The store was named Target, to distinguish the discount retailer from Dayton's higher-end stores.

From 1970 to 1990, Target grew from 24 to 420 stores through organic and inorganic growth, becoming the leading brand in the Dayton Hudson Corporation portfolio in 1977. In 1998, Dayton Hudson increased the company's Internet presence through the purchase of Rivertown Trading. In 2006, Target.com formed a partnership with Amazon.com's Enterprise Solutions to develop better e-commerce technology that would enable it to compete more effectively online. The company continues to maintain a strong online presence as well as over 1,700 Target and Target Superstore outlets across 49 states. Across all of its operating units, Target posted revenues of $65 billion in 2010, with a net income of $2.5 billion (Exhibit 10).[72]

Following Circuit City's collapse, Target also increased its consumer electronics offerings, focusing on TVs, videogames, and digital imaging "as part of its electronics makeover."[73] Changes included the installation of new TV-merchandising walls to make side-by-side comparisons easier for customers, as well as expanding store inventory to include larger and more technologically advanced TV sets. At the same time, Target enlarged its videogame section by a third and added demo stations for players to try out new releases. Target was also the first physical retailer to carry Amazon's Kindle e-book reader.[74] The company added a TV delivery and installation service in January 2010.[75]

In August 2010, Mark Schinele, senior vice president of Target, unveiled three new consumer electronics services to further enhance consumers' shopping experience: 1-877-myTGTtech, Target Mobile, and Target Electronics Trade-In. In his words, "Our goal is to create the best and easiest shopping experience for our guests. As we continue to grow and enhance our consumer electronics business, we designed 1-877-myTGTtech to assist guests with any questions and technical support on their electronics purchases. . . . Target Electronics Trade-In offers our guests an opportunity to upgrade their consumer electronics items for less. And Target Mobile ensures a convenient cell phone shopping experience."[76] All three services were expected to be rolled out nationwide sometime in 2011.

APPLE. Meanwhile, Apple has rolled out more than 300 of its own retail stores worldwide since 2001, creating direct competition for Best Buy and other firms that carry Apple products. In addition to providing consumers with hands-on access to the latest iPods, iPads, iPhones, and Macs, Apple's retail stores offer one-to-one tech support as well as a variety of training workshops and youth programs. Sales at Apple stores reached $2.8 billion by the end of 2010, placing it third behind Best Buy and Amazon in the consumer-electronics market (see Exhibits 11 and 12).[77] Morgan Stanley estimated that Apple has captured 9 percent of the U.S. electronics market, and its numbers are continuing to rise in spite of less than desirable economic conditions.[78]

In a radical new move that could boost sales even further, Apple opened its first "pop-up store" (temporary location) at the South by Southwest music festival held in Austin, Texas, in March 2011. The festival conveniently coincided with the planned release of the iPad2.[79] Temporary stores are a relatively new phenomenon, focusing on high-traffic areas during specific events. They provide access to new customers in a down economy while taking advantage of vacant retail space.

EXHIBIT 10

Target Financial Data (in $ millions, except EPS data)

Fiscal Year	2000	2001	2002	2003	2004	2005	2006	2007	2008	2009	2010
Cash and short-term investments	356	499	758	716	2,245	1,648	813	2,450	893	2,200	1,712
Receivables total	1,941	3,881	5,565	5,776	5,497	6,226	6,757	8,651	8,753	7,882	7,075
Inventories total	4,248	4,449	4,760	5,343	5,384	5,838	6,254	6,780	6,705	7,179	7,596
PP&E total (net)	11,418	13,533	15,307	16,969	16,860	19,038	21,431	24,095	25,756	25,280	25,493
Depreciation depletion and amortization	940	1079	1212	1,320	1,259	1,409	1,524	1,659	1,826	2,023	2,084
Assets total	19,490	24,154	28,603	31,392	32,293	24,995	37,349	44,560	44,106	44,533	43,705
Accounts payable	3,576	4,160	4,684	4,956	5,779	6,268	6,575	6,721	6,337	6,511	6,625
Long-term debt total	5,634	8,088	10,186	10,155	9,034	9,119	8,675	15,126	17,490	15,118	15,607
Liabilities total	12,971	16,294	19,160	20,284	19,264	20,790	21,716	29,253	30,394	29,186	28,218
Stockholders' equity total	6,519	7,860	9,443	11,065	13,029	14,205	15,633	15,307	13,712	15,347	15,487
Sales (net)	36,903	39,888	43,917	48,163	46,839	52,620	59,490	63,367	64,948	65,357	67,390
COGS	25,295	27,246	29,260	31,790	31,445	34,927	39,399	41,895	44,157	44,062	46,585
SG&A	8,190	8,816	10,181	11,534	10,534	11,988	13,526	14,541	14,563	14,599	13,469
Income taxes	789	842	1,022	1,119	1,146	1,452	1,710	1,776	1,322	1,384	1,575
Income before extraordinary items	1,264	1,368	1,654	1,841	3,198	2,408	2,787	2,849	2,214	2,488	2,920
Net income	1,264	1,368	1,654	1,841	3,198	2,408	2,787	2,849	2,214	2,488	2,920
EPS (basic)	1.40	1.52	1.82	2.02	2.09	2.73	3.23	3.37	2.87	3.31	4.03
EPS (diluted)	1.38	1.51	1.81	2.01	2.07	2.71	3.21	3.33	2.86	3.30	4.00

Source: Compustat.

EXHIBIT 11

Apple Financial Data (in $ millions, except EPS data)

Fiscal Year	2000	2001	2002	2003	2004	2005	2006	2007	2008	2009	2010
Cash and short-term investments	4,027	4,336	4,337	4,566	5,464	8,261	10,110	15,386	24,490	23,464	25,620
Receivables total	953	466	565	950	1,050	1,312	2,845	4,029	4,704	5,057	5,510
Inventories total	33	11	45	56	101	165	270	346	509	455	1,051
PP&E total (net)	700	924	1,057	1,174	1,298	1,481	2,075	2,841	3,747	4,667	4,768
Depreciation depletion and amortization	387	360	436	505	591	664	794	1,009	1,292	1,713	2,466
Assets total	6,803	6,021	6,298	6,815	8,050	11,551	17,205	25,347	39,572	47,501	75,183
Accounts payable	1,157	801	911	1,154	1,451	1,779	3,390	4,970	5,520	5,601	12,015
Long-term debt total	300	317	316	0	0	0	0	0	0	0	0
Liabilities total	2,696	2,101	2,203	2,592	2,974	4,085	7,221	10,815	18,542	15,861	27,392
Stockholders' equity total	4,107	3,920	4,095	4,223	5,076	7,466	9,984	14,532	21,030	31,640	47,791
Sales (net)	7,983	5,363	5,742	6,207	8,279	13,931	19,315	24,006	32,479	42,905	65,225
COGS	5,733	4,026	4,021	4,387	5,870	9,738	13,525	15,568	20,925	25,025	39,541
SG&A	1,546	1,568	1,557	1,683	1,910	2,393	3,145	3,745	4,870	5,482	5,517
Income taxes	306	(15)	22	24	107	480	829	1,512	2,061	3,831	4,527
Income before extraordinary items	786	(37)	65	68	276	1,335	1,989	3,496	4,834	8,235	14,013
Net income	786	(37)	65	68	276	1,335	1,989	3,496	4,834	8,235	14,013
EPS (basic)	2.42	(0.11)	0.18	0.19	0.74	1.65	2.36	4.04	5.48	9.22	15.41
EPS (diluted)	2.18	(0.11)	0.18	0.19	0.71	1.56	2.27	3.93	5.36	9.08	15.15

Source: Compustat.

EXHIBIT 12

Share Performance of Four Main Competitors

Source: Google Finance, http://www.google.com/finance.

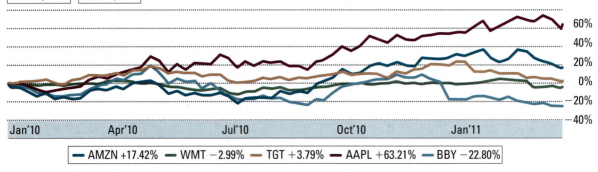

Zoom: <u>1d</u> <u>5d</u> <u>1m</u> <u>3m</u> <u>6m</u> <u>VTD</u> <u>1y</u> <u>5y</u> <u>10y</u> <u>All</u>

Dec 31, 2009 - Mar 22, 2011

— AMZN +17.42%   — WMT −2.99%   — TGT +3.79%   — AAPL +63.21%   — BBY −22.80%

Best Buy's Strategy

Best Buy is focusing its strategy in three areas: customer-centricity, employment policies, and exclusive branding.

CUSTOMER-CENTRICITY. Best Buy's strategy is characterized by a commitment to customer-centricity attained through systematic customer segmentation. The term *customer-centricity* indicates a business orientation that caters to specific customer needs and behaviors. Compared to traditional product-centered marketing, customer-centricity looks at a business from the "outside in," asking what problems its customers are facing, and then providing solutions.[80] The firm then customizes sales strategies to appeal to the more lucrative customer segments ("angels") and to discourage the "devils" who actually cost the store money (i.e., buying returned merchandise, loading up on loss leaders, insisting on price matching, and so on).[81]

Best Buy segments customers based on three types of information—demographic, attitudinal or behavior-based, and value tiers (based on profitability and lifetime value of the customer). In an age when "profiling" is greeted with suspicion at airports and traffic stops, Best Buy excels at profiling of a relatively innocuous and lucrative kind. Through market research, Best Buy identified four overarching segments that account for 90 percent of its customer base: Urban Trendsetters, Upscale Suburban, Empty Nesters, and Middle America. Each is identified with a male and a female persona that encompasses all of the associated customer characteristics.[82] For example, "Jill" is an "Upscale Suburban" mom who appreciates personal shopping assistants who can help her find the right products for her family quickly. She usually purchases items with accessories and requires help with installation. "Buzz" is a young "Urban Trendsetter" with a passion for new technology. He comes to Best Buy seeking products that are "hip" and unique. He likes to check out the newest gadgets while hanging out at the store, and he likes stores that have a wide assortment of video games.[83] The same segments also apply to small businesses, depending on their needs and relationship with Best Buy.

Stores are specifically configured to serve the needs of the predominant customer segment(s) in a given region. As of 2006, nearly 40 percent of Best Buy's 300 reconfigured stores were focused on "Barry" (Upscale Suburban, professional male), and therefore feature highly trained salespeople, mobile-technology experts, and a separate home-theater department. Stores can also target multiple segments, depending on the profile of the local population.[84] Despite renovation expenses that approach $1 million per store, former CEO and Vice Chairman Brad Anderson claimed that stores that were configured toward local demographics doubled their growth rate compared with other company stores.

Implementation of customer-centricity presented a significant challenge, however. Nearly all companies claim to be "customer oriented," but being "customer-centric" required a radical reorganization and shift in employee mindset. In addition to reformatting the physical space in the stores, related products needed to be bundled, distribution schedules adjusted, and store personnel and merchandisers had to work together on cross-departmental and cross-functional teams.[85] Thus, when the growth rate of the segmented stores slowed, Best Buy responded by overhauling employee training, providing them with the analytical tools necessary to aid in decision making and optimizing the customer experience. One internal Best Buy analyst described the 2008 fiscal year as follows: "We needed to make sure that the district, territory, and store teams have the tools that they need to actually look at things like: what kind of traffic do they have coming in their stores today, how effectively are they selling to the people that are in the stores today, what do their close rates look like, what does their customer information look like, what segments do they have coming in, what kind of market share do they have for those segments. . . . We have invested in the right tools so that the field knows what to focus on and can identify what indicators to move a little bit that will help us a lot."[86]

Another important aspect of Best Buy's customer-centricity strategy is an ongoing effort to learn systematically about its customers and squeeze actionable information from its masses of customer data. In 2005, Best Buy retained the services of Accenture to help increase customer satisfaction, sales, and profits. Best Buy's Chief Information Officer, Bob Willet, remarked, "You don't get good sales or performance if customer satisfaction is going backward. One breeds the other."[87] Best Buy and Accenture pored over millions of sales transactions and identified significant relationships between product categories and demographic groups. The success of the project lay in its translation of customer insights into merchandising action. The project, named Purchase Path Solution, won a CIO 100 award from *CIO* magazine.

EMPLOYMENT POLICIES. To achieve a legitimate localization strategy, Best Buy invests in its people. Soon after unveiling its customer-centricity program, the company realized that the same principles applied equally well to its employees. The corporate communications team therefore set up an employee-listening program that used open communication to better understand the needs of its workers. Techniques included simple tools such as annual company-wide surveys, a virtual discussion board ("The Water Cooler"), and one-on-one dialogue sessions. Best Buy

filters the data it collects from these methods, utilizing three screens—importance, ownership (is it communications related), and surprise—to discern issues that are important to employees but about which management was previously unaware.[88]

In 2007, Best Buy made headlines when it announced its plan to extend its "results-only work environment" (ROWE) to the retail setting.[89] In place at the company's headquarters near Minneapolis since 2002, ROWE permitted employees to set their own schedules as long as they completed their tasks successfully. Bosses had no role in scheduling, and could judge only whether a task was accomplished on time and in a satisfactory manner, even if none of the work occurred at the office. Best Buy estimated that employee productivity increased by 35 percent overall in departments in which the policy had been implemented. Whether "results only" worked as well in the retail setting, where floor coverage was necessary, remained to be seen, but Best Buy was optimistic that the program would help reduce staff turnover. A recent research study found that turnover in big-box retail stores such as Best Buy was close to 100 percent annually. By Best Buy's own accounts, the recruitment, training, and operational costs associated with each new-hire was $102,000 per sales associate, or 250 percent of their actual salary.[90] Any reduction of staff turnover should therefore cut recruitment and training costs.

Best Buy has also been honored for its efforts on behalf of multiple minority groups. The company received recognition from the Rehabilitation Association and Springboard Consulting for its efforts in recruiting, hiring, and accommodating persons with disabilities in both 2010 and 2011. It is engaged in an ongoing partnership with LatIN Minnesota to provide educational and leadership development programs for Latina youth, which in turn generates important insights into the needs of Best Buy's Latino customers. In 2010, the American Muslim Consumer Conference (AMCC) gave Best Buy its Multicultural Award for its acknowledgment of all gifting holidays from November to January, including Eid. According to AMCC, Best Buy was the only retail company to recognize this important Muslim festival throughout all of its U.S. locations.[91]

EXCLUSIVE BRANDS. Best Buy currently owns five private labels: Insignia, Dynex, Init, Rocketfish, and Geek Squad.[92] Insignia focuses on electronic equipment, including televisions, monitors, car stereos, home-theater systems, and portable video and audio players. Dynex produces a wide variety of economically priced computer and entertainment accessories such as storage media, data and power cables, webcams, and office supplies, with recent forays into electronics such as high-definition LCD televisions. Init offers storage solutions for many of the products made by both Insignia and Dynex, including media storage, equipment bags, totes and furniture for home theaters. Rocketfish's high-end cables are predominantly used in home-theater installation and setup as well as on computer accessories, providing another complementary product line. The Geek Squad is the most well known of all of Best Buy's private brands, and provides both computer repair and installation services as well as high-end computer accessories and cables.

Decision Time

As Mr. Dunn and his advisors sat down to discuss the upcoming shareholder meeting, they reflected on the past several years and the flat-panel TV war that contributed to Circuit City's demise. While consumer spending reports for the 2010 holiday season indicated that consumers were purchasing more electronic goods, they feared that this increase in demand had come at the cost of lower prices. Dunn wondered how he could grow Best Buy's bottom line when analysts projected another series of price cuts from aggressive competitors such as Amazon, Walmart, and Target. Dunn's worst fear was that the price cuts would focus yet again on flat-panel and 3D TVs, which accounted for 44 percent of Best Buy's revenues. How could Best Buy avoid following Circuit City into bankruptcy?

Best Buy had a long reputation as a retail innovator, starting with its Concept II "grab-and-go" stores in the 1980s. Dunn wondered if the time had come to reinvent Best Buy yet again. The company's strategic competitive advantage was being attacked on multiple fronts. In the past, Best Buy had prided itself on its broad selection of the most respected name brands in the consumer-electronics industry. Because of its sales volume, Best Buy could negotiate favorable agreements with vendors like Sony and Apple, who shunned non-specialty retailers. But Apple now operated its own retail stores, siphoning off Best Buy's profits on Apple merchandise. At the same time, Best Buy was finding it increasingly more difficult to get exclusive contracts with vendors, given the considerable market power wielded by Amazon and Walmart.

Moreover, Amazon could carry an almost-limitless inventory online, while Best Buy was constrained by the amount of available showroom space. Soon, Dunn feared, the only products that would be truly unique to Best Buy would be its private-label brands. As much as Dunn believed they were a valuable part of the company's strategy, he knew Init and Dynex were not the primary reason for customers to come to the store. They came because they wanted to see and try out the latest technologies in person—but Dunn had no way to ensure that customers who came to the store actually purchased the product from Best Buy.

More recently, the company had taken a big risk on its customer-centricity program, but it was not clear that relationship marketing alone was enough to differentiate Best Buy from its competitors. Investing in people was expensive and took significant amounts of time and energy, which Dunn was willing to provide, as long as the company's efforts translated into long-term sales. Yet he wondered whether the promise of a customized shopping experience coupled with knowledgeable and caring sales personnel was enough for customers to justify the higher prices Best Buy needed to charge to be able to train and pay its people. If forced to cut its staffing costs in order to match Amazon and Walmart on price, what would Best Buy have left to offer?[93]

Then there was the issue of the five-year growth targets. With multiple competitors paying increased attention to consumer-electronics retailing, the U.S. market was getting crowded. Should Best Buy invest in more stores? Or would product diversification offer better growth prospects? International markets held significant promise for expansion, but investors were getting concerned about Best Buy's cash position and their ability to continue growing inorganically through acquisitions.

There were no easy answers, even for a company that currently dominated the market share in its industry. Dunn and his advisors had multiple long days and nights ahead of them if they were to be ready for that shareholder meeting.

Endnotes

1. Best Buy Co., Inc. (October 1), Hoover's Company Records, 10209, retrieved October 9, 2010, from Hoover's Company Records. (Document ID: 168149891).

2. www.bby.com/2010/12/14/ best-buy-reports-fiscal-third-quarter-diluted-eps-of-0-54/.

3. "Best Buy Co, Inc.," *Datamonitor*, June 25, 2010, www. datamonitor.com.

4. Jannarone, J. (2011), "Forecast for Best Buy: Worst is yet to come," *The Wall Street Journal,* March 4.

5. Best Buy Co., Inc. (October 1), Hoover's Company Records, 10209.

6. Best Buy Timeline, www.bby.com/wp-content/uploads/2010/04/BBY_TimeLine.pdf.

7. Best Buy Co., Inc. (October 1), Hoover's Company Records, 10209.

8. Best Buy Timeline.

9. Ibid.

10. Best Buy Co., Inc. (October 1), Hoover's Company Records, 10209.

11. "Best Buy and Circuit City: The gloves come off," *Bernstein Research,* April 1994, http://web.ebscohost.com/bsi/pdf?vid=10&hid=111&sid=260056c3-7252-467f-acdf-688f3a981bfa%40sessionmgr13.

12. www.fundinguniverse.com/company-histories/Best-Buy-Co-Inc-Company-History.html.

13. www.bby.com/wp-content/uploads/2010/04/BBY_TimeLine.pdf.

14. "Industry profile global—Computer & electronics retail," *Datamonitor PLC,* March 2009.

15. Best Buy's annual 10-K filing. Filed February 27, 2010, www.sec.gov/Archives/edgar/data/764478/000104746910004349/a2197223z10-k.htm.

16. www.fundinguniverse.com/company-histories/Best-Buy-Co-Inc-Company-History.html.

17. Best Buy Timeline, www.bby.com/wp-content/uploads/2010/04/BBY_TimeLine.pdf.

18. www.fundinguniverse.com/company-histories/Best-Buy-Co-Inc-Company-History.html.

19. www.crn.com/news/channel-programs/189400424/anatomy-of-a-marriage-how-best-buy-acquired-integrator-audio-visions.htm;jsessionid=X-sfiMfEl7ZesiicnLiDSQ**.ecappj03.

20. "Pacific Sales will be acquired in deal valued at $410 million," *The Wall Street Journal,* December 23, 2005.

21. www.speakeasy.net/press/pr/pr032707.php.

22. www.reuters.com/article/idUSN1550308820080915.

23. www.fundinguniverse.com/company-histories/Best-Buy-Co-Inc-Company-History.html.

24. Ibid.

25. Best Buy Timeline, www.bby.com/wp-content/uploads/2010/04/BBY_TimeLine.pdf.

26. "Best Buy will pay $180 million for majority of China's Jiangsu," *The Wall Street Journal,* May 13, 2006.

27. www.icmrindia.org/casestudies/catalogue/Business%20strategy/BSTR299.htm.

28. "Best Buy to expand into Europe," *The StarTribune,* May 8, 2008.

29. "Radio, television, consumer electronics, and music stores," *Encyclopedia of American Industries,* Online Edition, Gale, 2009. Reproduced in Business and Company Resource Center (Farmington Hills, MI: Gale Group), http://galenet.gale-group.com/servlet/BCRC.

30. Ibid.

31. Ibid.

32. Ibid.

33. www.novelguide.com/a/discover/cps_02/cps_02_00304.html.

34. "Radio, television, consumer electronics, and music stores," *Encyclopedia of American Industries.*

35. "Rewiring Best Buy: A longer look at capital allocation and acquisition strategies," *Bernstein Weekly Note,* May 16, 2008.

36. Best Buy's third-quarter 10-Q filing. Filed August 28, 2010, www.sec.gov.

37. "Industry profile global – Computer & electronics retail," *Datamonitor PLC.*

38. Circuit City's annual 10-K filing. Filed February 29, 2008, www.sec.gov/Archives/edgar/data/104599/000119312508093063/d10k.htm#tx15038_18.

39. "MarketWatch weekend investor: 'Worst' CEOs of year – of 2008, that is," *The Wall Street Journal,* January 5, 2008.

40. Rourke, E., A. Woodward, and D. Salamie (1994), "Circuit City Stores, Inc.," *International Directory of Company Histories,* Vol. 65, 1994.

41. Ibid.

42. Ibid.

43. Ibid.

44. Ibid.

45. Ibid.

46. Ibid.

47. Ibid.

48. Ibid.

49. Ibid.

50. Lynch, D. J. (2007), "Flat-panel TVs display effects of globalization," *USA Today,* May 8, www.usatoday.com/educate/college/business/articles/20070513.htm.

51. www.mediapost.com/publications/index.cfm?fa=Articles.showArticle&art_aid=52831.

52. "Circuit City revamps its retail strategy," *Washington Post,* February 9, 2007.

53. "Circuit City plan: Bold strategy or black eye?" *MSNBC.com,* April 2, 2007, www.msnbc.msn.com/id/17857697/ns/business-going_green/.

54. "Circuit City swings to loss," *BusinessWeek,* April 4, 2007, www.businessweek.com/investor/content/apr2007/pi20070404_851371.htm.

55. www.hci.org/category/tracks/talent-communities/talent-strategy/workforce-planning?page=18.

56. "Circuit City's job cuts backfiring, analysts say," *The Washington Post,* May 2, 2007.

57. www.marketwatch.com/story/circuit-city-may-shut-stores-to-avoid-bankruptcy-report.

58. www.internetretailer.com/2009/05/29/a-tale-of-two-bankruptcies-systemax-nabs-circuitcity-com-linen

59. Best Buy 2010 Shareholder Meeting Presentation, June 24, 2010, http://phx.corporate-ir.net/External.File?item=UGFyZW50SUQ9Mzg3NDk3fENoaWxkSUQ9MzkwMDEwfFR5cGU9MQ==&t=1.

60. "Profit at Best Buy beats expectations," *The New York Times,* March 25, 2010.

61. "Best Buy Co, Inc.," *Datamonitor,* June 25, 2010, www.datamonitor.com.

62. "Best Buy's sales suffer as shoppers chase deals," *The Wall Street Journal,* December 15, 2010.

63. http://finance.yahoo.com/q/is?s=AMZN+Income+Statement&annual.

64. Jannarone, J. (2011), "Forecast for Best Buy: Worst is yet to come."

65. Amazon.com, Inc. (December 15), Hoover's Company Records, 51493. Retrieved December 22, 2010, from Hoover's Company Records. (Document ID: 168253201).

66. "Best Buy feels the pressure of rivals on the web," *The New York Times,* December 18, 2010.

67. Ibid.

68. www.retrevo.com/content/bestbuy-competitors-gained-ground.

69. http://walmartstores.com/AboutUs/.

70. Walmart.com USA, LLC (December 15), Hoover's Company Records, 125250. Retrieved December 20, 2010, from Hoover's Company Records. (Document ID: 548531731).

71. http://hothardware.com/News/Walmart-Expands-Consumer-Electronics-Offerings/.

72. Target Corporation (December 15), Hoover's Company Records, 10440. Retrieved December 20, 2010, from Hoover's Company Records. (Document ID: 168153501).

73. http://blogs.consumerreports.org/electronics/2010/05/walmart-target-home-entertainment-electronics-upgrades-tvs-smart-phones-bluray-best-buy-competition.html.

74. Ibid.

75. http://pressroom.target.com/pr/news/target-launches-new-electronics.aspx.

76. Ibid.

77. Jannarone, J. (2011), "Forecast for Best Buy: Worst is yet to come."

78. www.tuaw.com/2010/04/28/apple-retail-store-sales-climb-8/.

79. www.ifoapplestore.com/db/2011/03/10/radical-move-for-apple-retail-a-pop-up/.

80. http://blogs.hbr.org/hbsfaculty/2010/04/inside-best-buys-customer-cent.html.

81. www.scdigest.com/assets/NewsViews/04-11-18-1.cfm.

82. www.dailytech.com/article.aspx?newsid=11133.

83. http://money.cnn.com/magazines/fortune/fortune_archive/2006/04/03/8373034/index.htm.

84. Ibid.

85. http://blogs.hbr.org/hbsfaculty/2010/04/inside-best-buys-customer-cent.html.

86. Best Buy Q1 FY09 Earnings Call, June 16, 2009.

87. "100 transformers," *CIO Magazine,* August 15, 2007.

88. http://cecinsider.exbdblogs.com/2010/11/23/best-buy%E2%80%99s-employee-listening-system/.

89. Pink, D. H. (2009), *Drive: The Surprising Truth about What Motivates Us* (New York: Riverhead Books).

90. http://money.cnn.com/magazines/business2/business2_archive/2007/03/01/8401022/index.htm.

91. www.diversityatbestbuy.com/Awards.html.

92. www.bby.com/about/.

93. Jannarone, J. (2011), "Forecast for Best Buy: Worst is yet to come."

Robert S. Huckman
Gary P. Pisano

IT WAS MAY 11, 2007, and David Barger finally had a moment to take in the view from his office window at JetBlue Airways' modest corporate headquarters in Forest Hills, New York. Less than 24 hours earlier, Barger, previously president and COO of JetBlue, was named the airline's CEO. JetBlue's board promoted Barger to the CEO role in the wake of a highly publicized operational crisis in February that led to the cancellation of over 1,100 JetBlue flights and adversely affected the travel plans of thousands of passengers. Though numerous interviews and meetings during the past day allowed Barger to outline his vision for the airline, he realized that he needed to move quickly in implementing that vision to maintain the confidence of customers, employees, and shareholders.

Just a few miles outside Barger's window was John Fitzgerald Kennedy (JFK) Airport, where JetBlue began operations as a low-cost carrier (LCC) in 2000 and, by the beginning of 2007, held a 30% share of domestic departures. Looking beyond the construction site for JetBlue's new Terminal 5—an $800 million state-of-the-art facility that was scheduled to open in the fall of 2008 and would offer 26 gates and a wide range of passenger amenities—Barger noticed one JetBlue plane, a 100-seat Embraer 190 (E190), taking off. Immediately following it was another JetBlue plane, a 150-seat Airbus 320 (A320). Wrapping up some email responses, Barger was pleased to see other JetBlue planes—some E190s and some A320s—take to the air over the next fifteen minutes. He could not help but appreciate this setting as an appropriate backdrop for some critical short-term decisions that the airline needed to make.

In late 2005, JetBlue added the E190 to its fleet, which was then composed exclusively of 85 A320s. This decision was a break with the traditional practice of many LCCs of limiting their fleets to one type of aircraft to streamline operations and reduce costs. JetBlue was in the simultaneously advantageous and risky position of being the launch customer for the E190. By the end of 2006, JetBlue had 23 E190s in its fleet of 119 planes.

By late 2006 JetBlue, like other airlines, faced softening demand and higher costs due to increasing fuel prices. Barger played a large role in the airline's decision at the end of 2006 to slow its rate of growth by reducing its purchase commitments for new planes.

In light of the operational challenges faced by JetBlue in February 2007, as well as the unabated rise in fuel costs (Exhibit 1), Barger realized that the airline would need to take further steps to slow its rate of growth. Though convinced JetBlue needed to decrease plane deliveries once again, Barger was not certain as to how these reductions should be distributed across E190s and A320s. The E190 was a promising plane that presented interesting growth opportunities and challenges for JetBlue. At the same time, the A320 was a proven plane that served as the basis for JetBlue's operations over the past six years and the company had developed a high level of comfort with it. Given the current pressures facing JetBlue and the industry, Barger knew this decision would not be easy.

LCCs and the Airline Industry

The airline industry in 2006 included two groups of competitors: legacy carriers and LCCs. Most of the best-known U.S. airlines, such as United or American Airlines, were legacy carriers, so called because of their long histories reaching back, in some cases, as far as the 1920s. One part of this legacy was the "hub and spoke" system that characterized the operations of these companies. In this system, airlines created large "hubs" at specific airports where thousands of passengers were shuttled every day to connecting flights (the "spokes"). The "hub and spoke" was pioneered by

 HARVARD | BUSINESS | SCHOOL

9-609-046

Professors Robert S. Huckman and Gary P. Pisano prepared this case with the assistance of Global Research Group Research Associate Mark Rennella. HBS cases are developed solely as the basis for class discussion. Cases are not intended to serve as endorsements, sources of primary data, or illustrations of effective or ineffective management.

EXHIBIT 1

Average Fuel Prices for U.S. Domestic Commercial Air Travel, 2001 to 2007

Note: Figures for 2007 are estimated.

Source: U.S. Department of Transportation, Research and Innovative Technology Administration website (http://www.transtats.bts.gov/fuel.asp?pn=1), accessed August 9, 2008.

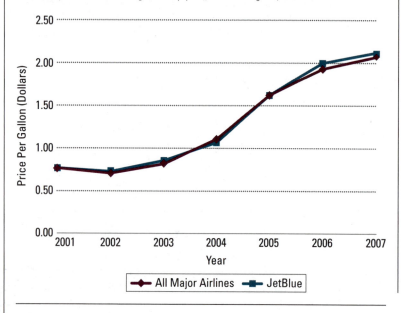

costs was its reliance on a single type of plane—the Boeing 737. Over time, Southwest's ground and flight personnel became very familiar with the 737; this decreased the airline's average turnaround time between landing a plane and putting it back into the air. This efficiency, combined with the shrewd use of fuel hedges, buoyed Southwest's profits.

Attempts by competitors to mimic Southwest's LCC model typically were unsuccessful, as demonstrated by the infamous rise and fall of no-frills People Express Airlines during the 1980s and the short-lived attempts of several major airlines—including Continental Airlines, Delta Air Lines, and United Airlines—to create LCC subsidiaries during the 1990s. By 2006, Southwest was firmly established as the only consistently profitable airline in an industry rocked by deregulation, fare wars, over-capacity, and the terrorist attacks of September 11, 2001. Specifically, Southwest was the only airline in America to show a profit for each year since 1973 up to 2005. Exhibit 2 provides a comparison of Southwest, JetBlue, and selected major carriers in 2005.

After September 11, the airline industry experienced more troubles. Domestic airline yields (computed by dividing passenger revenues by revenue passenger miles) dropped almost 20% in the aftermath of the attack and remained below pre-attack levels until 2005. As of October 2006, five major U.S. airlines, including US Airways Group, were operating under Chapter 11 bankruptcy protection.[2]

Delta Air Lines in 1955;[1] it became increasingly useful to airlines in the turbulent years after airline deregulation in 1978 as a means to keep their costs low and protect their market share. By centralizing the transfer of passengers during long journeys across the country, such structures allowed passengers to travel between numerous destinations without changing airlines. Some carriers also used hubs to dominate geographical segments of the market, as did Delta in Atlanta's Hartsfield International Airport. Despite the advantages of the hub-and-spoke model, this kind of centralization proved challenging if weather, maintenance problems, and air traffic delays interfered with flight schedules.

Emerging in Texas in the late 1960s, Southwest Airlines offered an alternative business model of air transportation. In contrast to the hub-and-spoke model, Southwest took passengers direct (i.e., "point to point") between cities that were often less than 500 miles apart and, wherever possible, used secondary airports serving major metropolitan areas. Attracting passengers who would have otherwise traveled by car or bus, Southwest was able to maintain high levels of plane utilization, thereby keeping its operating costs low enough to support its discounted fares. A key component of Southwest's ability to manage

JetBlue: A Short History

JetBlue was founded by David Neeleman in 1999 after he had already established a strong record as a leader in the airline industry. Neeleman previously was Executive Vice President of Morris Air, an airline based in his home state of Utah and modeled after Southwest Airlines. In 1993, at the age of 34, Neeleman sold Morris Air to Southwest for $129 million in stock.[3]

EXHIBIT 2

2005 Financial and Operational Results for Selected Carriers

	Continental	Delta	Southwest	JetBlue	American[a]	United[b]
Operating Revenues ($ millions)	$11,208	$ 16,191	$ 7,584	$ 1,701	$ 20,657	$ 17,304
Operating Expenses ($ millions)	11,247	18,192	6,764	1,653	21,008	17,529
Operating Profit (Loss) ($ millions)	(39)	(2,001)	820	48	(351)	(225)
Net Income (Loss) ($ millions)	(68)	(3,836)	548	(20)	(892)	(21,036)
Earnings (Loss) per share	(0.96)	(23.75)	0.70	(0.13)	(5.21)[f]	
Wages, benefits, etc (millions)	$ 2,649	$ 5,058	$ 2,702	$ 428	$ 6,173	$ 4,014
Fuel/Oil ($ millions)	2,443	4,271	$ 1,342	$ 488	5,080	4,032
Passengers (thousands)[c]	44,939	118,856	77,693	14,729		67,000
Revenue Passenger Miles (millions)[d]	71,261	119,954	60,223	20,200	138,374	114,272
Available Seat Miles (millions)	89,647	156,659	85,172	23,703	176,112	140,300
Passenger Load Factor[e]	79.5%	76.5%	70.7%	85.2%	78.6%	81.4%
Breakeven Load Factor		87.0%		86.1%		82.8%
Employment	42,200	55,700	31,729	6,797	88,400[g]	57,000
Fleet	356	649	445	92	699	460

Source: Compiled from 10-K and Annual Reports for Selected Carriers, 2005.

[a]American is a subsidiary of the AMR Corporation, which also owns regional carrier American Eagle.

[b]United is a subsidiary of UAL Corporation.

[c]Revenue passengers measured by each flight segment flown.

[d]The number of scheduled miles flown by revenue passengers.

[e]Revenue passenger miles divided by available seat miles.

[f]Loss per share for AMR Corporation.

[g]For the AMR Corporation.

JetBlue entered the market by connecting large, typically northeastern, U.S. cities (e.g., New York) with warmer cities in the southeast (e.g., Ft. Lauderdale, Florida). Starting with just 10 airplanes in 2000, the company achieved major-airline status in 2004 by exceeding $1 billion in annual revenue. As JetBlue's CEO, Neeleman planned from the beginning to make the airline a "growth company" and set ambitious annual goals that were largely met. These included consistent, quarterly profitability during each of the airline's first five years. In 2005, JetBlue became the ninth-largest passenger carrier in the United States.[4] Exhibit 3 provides information on financial performance and selected operating statistics for JetBlue from 2003 to 2006. By 2011, the company planned to have 290 planes in service.

JetBlue was often compared to Southwest Airlines—where Neeleman had spent a short tenure in the 1990s—due to its emphasis on low fares and its decision to eschew the hub-and-spoke architecture of legacy airlines. Consistent with Southwest's decision to limit its aircraft fleet to a single type of plane, JetBlue's fleet was comprised entirely of A320s. The A320 was introduced by Airbus in 1988 and had rapidly become one of the most popular planes in commercial use.[a] Its maximum capacity (162 passengers[b])

[a]Between the launch of the A320 and the end of 2006, Airbus had received orders for more than 2,932 of these aircraft; as of the end of 2006, 1,633 of these planes had been delivered. This significant and growing backlog, together with the A320s' ubiquity across airlines and regions, created a vibrant secondary market for A320s.

[b]Between 2005 and 2007, JetBlue removed two rows of seats (i.e., 12 seats) from the standard 162-seat A320 configuration to create several rows with additional legroom.

EXHIBIT 3

JetBlue Financial and Operating Summary, 2003–2006

	2006	2005	2004	2003
Selected Financial Data (in millions)				
Operating revenues	$ 2,363	$ 1,701	$ 1,265	$ 998
Salaries, wages and benefits	553	428	337	267
Aircraft fuel	752	488	255	147
Total operating expenses	2,236	1,653	1,154	831
Operating income	127	48	111	167
Net income (loss)	(1)	(20)	46	103
Cash and cash equivalents	10	6	19	103
Short-term investments	689	478	431	505
Other current assets				
Total current assets	927	635	514	746
Total other assets				
Total assets	4,843	3,892	2,797	2,186
Total current liabilities	854	676	488	370
Total long-term debt	2,626	2,103	1,396	1,012
Total other liabilities				
Total liabilities	3,891	2,981	2,043	1,515
Total shareholders' equity	952	911	754	671
Total liabilities and shareholders' equity	4,843	3,892	2,797	2,186
Selected Operating Statistics				
Average fare	$119.93	$110.03	$103.49	$107.09
Flights	159,152	112,009	90,532	66,920
Average flight length (miles)	1,186	1,358	1,339	1,272
Revenue passengers (thousands)	18,565	14,729	11,783	9,012
Revenue passenger miles (millions)	23,320	20,200	15,730	11,527
Available seat miles (ASMs) (millions)	28,594	23,703	18,911	13,639
Passenger load factor	81.6%	85.20%	83.20%	84.50%
Breakeven load factor	81.4%	86.10%	77.90%	72.60%
Operating revenue per ASM (cents)	8.26	7.18	6.69	7.32
Operating expense per ASM (cents)	7.82	6.98	6.1	6.09
Operating expense per ASM, excluding fuel (cents)	5.19	4.92	4.75	5.01
Employees (FTEs)	9,515	8,326	6,601	5,012
Pilots	1,545	1,253	897	684
Fleet (average number of operating aircraft)	106.5	77.5	60.6	44
Cities served	50	34	26	21

Source: Adapted from JetBlue Corporation Annual Reports.

and range (2,700 nautical miles, or approximately 3,100 miles) made it capable of serving a variety of medium- and long-haul routes, and it did so with relatively high fuel efficiency. By using the A320 as its sole aircraft type, JetBlue was able to standardize its training and servicing processes around the aircraft and also gained flexibility in scheduling and capacity management.

Despite some similarities, JetBlue differed from Southwest in several ways. Southwest focused on customers whose priority was low-cost, on-time performance. There were no frills, not even seat assignments. JetBlue offered fares up to 65% lower than legacy competitors but added comfort features such as assigned seating, leather upholstery and satellite TV on individual screens in every seat.[5] A key operating principle for JetBlue was that flight cancellations should be avoided at all costs. As such, JetBlue was routinely a top performing airline in terms of flight completion, though success on that dimension came at the expense of performance in terms of on-time arrivals. In contrast to Southwest, JetBlue flew significantly more long-haul flights (i.e., flights longer than 500 miles) and offered numerous overnight "red eye" flights from California to eastern cities. Exhibit 4 provides data on the routes served by JetBlue as of late 2005.

JetBlue supported its lower fares by providing customers with incentives to reserve and purchase tickets via the company's website. To support customers who wanted to make reservations over the phone, the company set up a corps of reservations agents,[c] most of whom worked part-time from their homes. Given the flexibility offered to these part-time employees, JetBlue was able to run its reservations function at significantly lower cost relative to other airlines.

Despite JetBlue's success in gaining share along its existing routes, Neeleman and his colleagues realized the need to consider new markets as a source of growth. They decided that the largest growth opportunity existed in connecting the large cities already served by JetBlue to medium-sized cities that were currently served by regional airlines affiliated with legacy carriers.[d]

Regional airlines tended to serve medium- and small-sized markets with regional jets (RJs) that had capacity of no more than 76 seats. To a large degree, these size limits were dictated by the demands of the Air Line Pilots Association (ALPA).[e] ALPA's demands concerning the size of RJs helped to shape the relationship between regional airlines and major airlines. To ensure that regional airlines would not encroach upon the routes flown by the larger legacy airlines, pilots' unions demanded the inclusion of "scope clauses" in their contracts. These clauses limited the number and seating capacity of the flights that regional airlines could fly. After 2001, the demand for smaller regional routes expanded as many airlines cut longer routes as a way to reduce costs. Since that time, regional carriers had become quite profitable.[6] One source of this profitability was financial support from their affiliated legacy airlines in the form of profit margin guarantees and coverage of key expense items (e.g., insurance, fuel and landing fees). This support helped ensure that regional airlines provided a steady flow of passengers to fill the seats on the longer-haul routes of their affiliated legacy carriers. Exhibit 5 provides data on passenger emplanements and fleet size for mainline and regional airlines.

Because its employees were not unionized and it did not have an affiliation with a legacy carrier, JetBlue did not face limitations on the size of the planes that it could use to serve routes traditionally served by RJs. Nevertheless, JetBlue—like other LCCs—had not entered these markets in any significant way due to concerns that they would not generate enough traffic to fill the larger jets (e.g., the A320 or Boeing 737) that served as the mainstay of the LCCs' fleets.

Unwilling to forego the opportunity to serve regional markets, JetBlue decided to consider whether it could profitably enter such markets using a mid-sized aircraft. After looking at seven airplanes ranging from a capacity of 68 passengers (the CRJ-700) to 117 passengers (Airbus A318), JetBlue decided that the Embraer's E190—a new airplane for which JetBlue would serve as the launch customer—represented its best option for efficiently serving medium-sized markets while offering passengers a more comfortable

---

[c] By 2007, JetBlue employed roughly 2,000 reservations agents.
[d] For example, American Eagle was the regional affiliate of American Airlines, and Northwest Airlink was the regional affiliate of Northwest Airlines.
[e] As of the summer of 2006, the maximum RJ seating capacity that ALPA agreed upon was 76, up from the limit of 50 that most airlines had abided by for years. Only US Airways had a higher limit, which was agreed upon with the ALPA as the airline was emerging from bankruptcy protection and merging with America West Airlines in September of 2006. A US Airways executive explained that its regional feeder airlines could now fly "'anything below an E-190,'" which meant a fixed number of 90-seater aircraft. See Mary Kirby, "Drawing the Line," *Flight International*, May 16, 2006, via LexisNexis, accessed January 31, 2007.

EXHIBIT 4

Routes Served by JetBlue as of November 2005

Airport	City	Airport	City	Distance (Miles)	Average Passengers/ Flight	A320 Round Trips/Day	Revenue/ Available Seat-Mile (Cents)
BOS	Boston, MA	DEN	Denver, CO	1,751	111.82	1	4.18
BOS	Boston, MA	FLL	Fort Lauderdale, FL	1,240	130.54	4	6.49
BOS	Boston, MA	LGB	Long Beach, CA	2,599	129.66	2	4.25
BOS	Boston, MA	MCO	Orlando, FL	1,124	121.91	4	5.97
BOS	Boston, MA	OAK	Oakland, CA	2,690	125.33	2	3.89
BOS	Boston, MA	RSW	Fort Myers, FL	1,252	127.19	1	7.01
BOS	Boston, MA	TPA	Tampa, FL	1,187	122.86	2	5.62
FLL	Fort Lauderdale, FL	IAD	Washington, DC	904	130.57	2	8.76
FLL	Fort Lauderdale, FL	LGA	New York, NY	1,079	132.86	7	7.55
FLL	Fort Lauderdale, FL	LGB	Long Beach, CA	2,326	131.54	1	4.51
IAD	Washington, DC	LGB	Long Beach, CA	2,275	134.43	4	5.01
IAD	Washington, DC	OAK	Oakland, CA	2,405	132.15	2	4.50
IAD	Washington, DC	SMF	Sacramento, CA	2,355	99.67	1	2.89
JFK	New York, NY	BQN	Aguadilla, PR	1,582	135.01	1	6.31
JFK	New York, NY	BTV	Burlington, VT	267	129.78	3	16.22
JFK	New York, NY	BUF	Buffalo, NY	301	126.72	7	16.91
JFK	New York, NY	DEN	Denver, CO	1,623	123.90	2	5.45
JFK	New York, NY	FLL	Fort Lauderdale, FL	1,072	136.97	10	8.12
JFK	New York, NY	LAS	Las Vegas, NV	2,246	131.39	4	5.18
JFK	New York, NY	LGB	Long Beach, CA	2,462	140.89	7	5.07
JFK	New York, NY	MCO	Orlando, FL	947	137.85	9	8.95
JFK	New York, NY	MSY	New Orleans, LA	1,183	136.59	1	7.72
JFK	New York, NY	NAS	Nassau, BS	1,100	112.98	1	8.16
JFK	New York, NY	OAK	Oakland, CA	2,572	132.21	5	4.25
JFK	New York, NY	ONT	Ontario, CA	2,427	139.27	2	4.86
JFK	New York, NY	PBI	West Palm Beach, FL	1,031	136.01	7	8.57
JFK	New York, NY	PHX	Phoenix, AZ	2,151	123.67	1	4.31
JFK	New York, NY	ROC	Rochester, NY	264	123.61	4	17.18
JFK	New York, NY	RSW	Fort Myers, FL	1,077	131.27	6	7.78
JFK	New York, NY	SAN	San Diego, CA	2,443	132.30	2	4.46
JFK	New York, NY	SDQ	Santo Domingo, DO	1,555	101.18	1	3.88
JFK	New York, NY	SEA	Seattle, WA	2,418	139.46	1	4.77
JFK	New York, NY	SJC	San Jose, CA	2,566	127.75	2	3.99
JFK	New York, NY	SJU	San Juan, PR	1,603	130.25	3	6.42
JFK	New York, NY	SLC	Salt Lake City, UT	1,986	128.61	1	4.80

EXHIBIT 4 *(continued)*

Airport	City	Airport	City	Distance (Miles)	Average Passengers/ Flight	A320 Round Trips/Day	Revenue/ Available Seat-Mile (Cents)
JFK	New York, NY	SMF	Sacramento, CA	2,518	130.93	1	4.30
JFK	New York, NY	STI	Santiago, DO	1,476	109.47	1	4.78
JFK	New York, NY	SYR	Syracuse, NY	209	133.14	3	20.65
JFK	New York, NY	TPA	Tampa, FL	1,008	137.27	7	7.94
LGB	Long Beach, CA	LAS	Las Vegas, NV	231	133.14	2	20.31
LGB	Long Beach, CA	OAK	Oakland, CA	354	126.40	6	13.75
LGB	Long Beach, CA	SLC	Salt Lake City, UT	590	129.53	1	10.48

Note: During 2005, the typical JetBlue A320 had 156 available seats.

Source: Company documents.

EXHIBIT 5

Passenger Emplanements and Aircraft for Mainline and Regional Airlines, 2000 to 2007E

Source: Federal Aviation Administration, *FAA Aerospace Forecast, 2008-2025.*

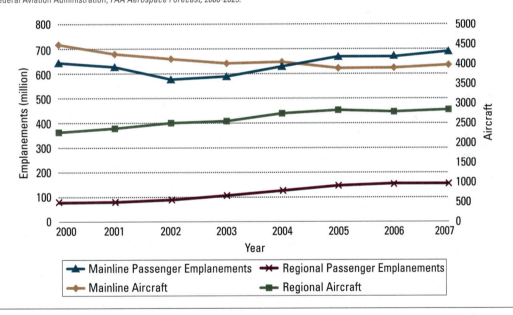

flight than they would receive on the typical RJ. In 2003, JetBlue signed a deal with Embraer for the purchase of 101 E190s (for delivery through 2011) and options to purchase up to 100 additional E190s between 2011 and 2016.

The E190

When JetBlue agreed to become the launch customer for the E190 in 2003, the airplane existed only on paper and was planned as Embraer's largest plane to date. This gave JetBlue the opportunity to play a significant role in designing the interior of the aircraft to improve passenger comfort. Exhibits 6a and 6b provide pictures of the interiors of the A320 and E190, respectively. Exhibit 7 presents a comparison of various features of the two planes.

JetBlue projected that the E190 could be operated at a cost per available seat-mile (CASM) that was 12% *greater* than that for an A320 and 34% *less* than that for a typical RJ. Because of its greater range and seating capacity relative to RJs (see Exhibit 8), the E190 could target a wider range of profitable destinations. Rob Maruster, senior vice president of customer service, claimed, "If we decided to open a focus city in Kansas City tomorrow, we could probably serve every market in the U.S. with the E190. That's an incredibly powerful corporate weapon."

The E190 increased the range of choices available to JetBlue passengers by feeding customers to connecting A320 flights at "focus cities," such as New York. For example, a customer flying on an E190 from Portland, Maine, to JFK could connect with an A320 flight to Oakland, California. Prior to the introduction of the E190, this Portland customer would not have considered JetBlue as an option. Of course, A320s could feed into E190 flights as well, resulting in higher loads and improved economics for JetBlue. Transfers at focus cities would also improve the utilization of existing airport facilities, thus increasing productivity and reducing downtime for airport crewmembers. This synergy between the E190 and A320 enabled JetBlue to run E190s at an average daily utilization of 10 to 11 hours a day, significantly more than the average of 8 hours per day for RJs. In 2004, JetBlue flew its A320s an average of 13.4 hours a day.

RAMPING UP. The initial plans for integrating the E190 were ambitious. After taking on seven E190s in the last two months of 2005, JetBlue took delivery of 16 additional E190s in 2006 and planned to take on another 18 in 2007. Maruster noted that, because the number of passengers required for a flight to meet the typical "breakeven" load of 75-to-80 percent was much lower on the E190 than the A320, the new plane made it easier for JetBlue to introduce service in new markets. In fact, a key assumption in JetBlue's planning was that it would add an average of one new city-pair market with the delivery of each E190. See Exhibit 9 for data on the routes served by JetBlue as of April 2007.

Tom Anderson, senior vice president of Fleet Programs, explained: "We wanted to get to efficient scale quickly. With any new airplane type in your fleet, in general, you need to get to 40 or 50 airplanes before you benefit from economies of scale."

Successful integration of the E190 into the fleet also provided some extra advantages over competitors. According to Barger, JetBlue was buying E190s "as fast as Embraer could make them." Neeleman added, "Embraer is somewhat limited in its production capacity—it was able to build about ten planes a month, and that was split between several models—E170s, E175s, E190s, and E195s. To go bigger than that, Embraer would have to build a whole other facility."

While taking delivery of new E190s, JetBlue also continued its purchases of A320s. The A320 had proven to be an extremely reliable plane around which JetBlue had standardized its operations. Furthermore, the wide adoption and popularity of the A320 across airlines—combined with the relatively standard formats for the plane—provided significant flexibility with respect to firm orders and options for additional planes. In comparison, the E190 was a newer plane with many aspects that were customized to the specific needs of each of the relatively small number of airlines that had already adopted it.

Though individual pilots could theoretically be trained to fly both the A320 and the E190, simultaneous dual certification was practically infeasible. Certification depended on the number of flights a pilot had flown on a given aircraft type within the prior month. As a result, it was simply not possible for a pilot to obtain enough flights as an E190 captain and enough as an A320 captain during a single month to retain dual certification in the following month. Shifting from one plane to another thus required a period of non-revenue "training" flying that was simply too expensive for the airline to subsidize. As a result, most JetBlue pilots were only trained to fly one of the two plane types.

EXHIBIT 6a

Photograph of the A320 Interior, Rear to Front

Source: http://www.airliners.net/usephotos/, accessed July 31, 2008.

EXHIBIT 6b

Photograph of the E190 Interior, Front to Rear

Source: Company document.

EXHIBIT 7

Comparison of Airbus A320 and Embraer 190

	Airbus A320	Embraer 190
Seats	150[a]	100
Seat configuration	25 rows (3-and-3 layout)	25 rows (2-and-2 layout)
Seat pitch	34-36 inches	32-33 inches
Seat width	17.8 inches	18.25 inches
Cabin height	7 feet, 1 inch	6 feet, 7 inches
Bathrooms	3	2
Length	123 feet, 3 inches	118 feet, 11 inches
Wingspan	111 feet, 10 inches	94 feet, 3 inches
Range	2,700 nautical miles (~3,100 miles)	2,100 nautical miles (~2,400 miles)
Estimated acquisition cost per plane	$50-60 million	$30-40 million

Source: Adapted from http://www.jetblue.com/about/whyyoulllike/about_whyairbusstats.html and http://www.jetblue.com/about/whyyoulllike/about_whyembraerstats.html, accessed August, 2007.

[a]Initially, JetBlue's A320s were equipped with the standard 162 seats offered by Airbus. Between 2005 and 2007, JetBlue decreased the number of seats on its A320 on two occasions. First was the reduction from 162 to 156 seats by removing one row of seats from each plane. Later, a second row of seats was removed, reducing capacity to 150 seats. Federal Aviation Administration (FAA) regulations required the staffing of one flight attendant per 50 seats on an aircraft.

EXHIBIT 8

Range and Seating Capacity of the E190 and Selected RJs

Source: Company documents.

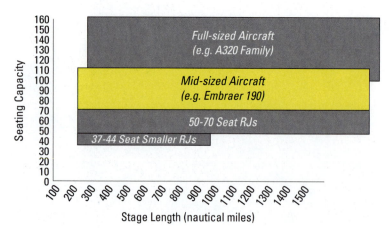

EXHIBIT 9

Routes Served by JetBlue as of April 2007

Airport	City	Airport	City	Distance (Miles)	Average Passengers/ Flight	A320 Round Trips / Day	E190 Round Trips / Day	Revenue/ Available Seat-Mile (Cents)
BOS	Boston, MA	AUS	Austin, TX	1,695	71.88		1	6.51
BOS	Boston, MA	BUF	Buffalo, NY	395	59.36		3	9.33
BOS	Boston, MA	CMH	Columbus, OH	639	59.47		1	6.53
BOS	Boston, MA	DEN	Denver, CO	1,751	101.88	1		5.11
BOS	Boston, MA	FLL	Fort Laud., FL	1,240	132.35	2		8.60
BOS	Boston, MA	IAD	Washington, DC	413	72.14		5	14.06
BOS	Boston, MA	LAS	Las Vegas, NV	2,378	114.19	1		4.36
BOS	Boston, MA	LGB	Long Beach, CA	2,599	130.21	3		5.84
BOS	Boston, MA	MCO	Orlando, FL	1,124	125.75	4		8.99
BOS	Boston, MA	OAK	Oakland, CA	2,690	128.72	2		5.75
BOS	Boston, MA	PBI	W Palm Bch, FL	1,200	126.83	1		8.85
BOS	Boston, MA	PHX	Phoenix, AZ	2,297	92.41	1		3.44
BOS	Boston, MA	PIT	Pittsburgh, PA	495	55.16		2	8.42
BOS	Boston, MA	RDU	Raleigh, NC	612	62.16		1	9.99
BOS	Boston, MA	RIC	Richmond, VA	474	61.81		2	10.79
BOS	Boston, MA	RSW	Fort Myers, FL	1,252	119.26	2		8.63
BOS	Boston, MA	SEA	Seattle, WA	2,492	116.33	1		5.15
BOS	Boston, MA	SJC	San Jose, CA	2,685	126.16	1		5.38
BOS	Boston, MA	TPA	Tampa, FL	1,187	102.66	1	1	8.47
EWR	Newark, NJ	PBI	W Palm Bch, FL	1,027	131.41	1		9.97
EWR	Newark, NJ	RSW	Fort Myers, FL	1,071	122.44	1		8.37
FLL	Fort Laud., FL	EWR	Newark, NJ	1,068	130.61	4		9.55
FLL	Fort Laud., FL	IAD	Washington, DC	904	123.54	2		8.81
FLL	Fort Laud., FL	LGA	New York, NY	1,079	134.46	5		9.78
FLL	Fort Laud., FL	LGB	Long Beach, CA	2,326	124.39	1		5.29
FLL	Fort Laud., FL	OAK	Oakland, CA	2,574	102.20	1		3.76
FLL	Fort Laud., FL	SWF	Newburgh, NY	1,122	113.94	2		7.01
IAD	Washington, DC	LAS	Las Vegas, NV	2,063	107.85	1		3.99
IAD	Washington, DC	LGB	Long Beach, CA	2,275	128.23	4		6.05
IAD	Washington, DC	OAK	Oakland, CA	2,405	125.03	3		5.80
IAD	Washington, DC	SAN	San Diego, CA	2,251	113.34	1		4.90
JFK	New York, NY	AUS	Austin, TX	1,519	78.00		3	7.63
JFK	New York, NY	BNA	Nashville, TN	765	68.37		3	8.30
JFK	New York, NY	BOS	Boston, MA	187	81.71	5	3	21.22
JFK	New York, NY	BQN	Aguadilla, PR	1,582	134.08	2		7.36

(continued)

EXHIBIT 9   (continued)

Routes Served by JetBlue as of April 2007

Airport	City	Airport	City	Distance (Miles)	Average Passengers/ Flight	A320 Round Trips / Day	E190 Round Trips / Day	Revenue/ Available Seat-Mile (Cents)
JFK	New York, NY	BTV	Burlington, VT	267	117.47	4		17.31
JFK	New York, NY	BUF	Buffalo, NY	301	119.75	8	1	19.72
JFK	New York, NY	BUR	Burbank, CA	2,462	132.48	5		6.66
JFK	New York, NY	CLT	Charlotte, NC	541	76.19	1	4	12.60
JFK	New York, NY	CMH	Columbus, OH	482	60.00		3	8.13
JFK	New York, NY	CUN	Cancun, MX	1,559	117.82	2		8.18
JFK	New York, NY	DEN	Denver, CO	1,623	120.35	2		6.58
JFK	New York, NY	FLL	Fort Laud., FL	1,072	131.96	10		9.36
JFK	New York, NY	HOU	Houston, TX	1,428	90.45		3	4.22
JFK	New York, NY	IAD	Washington, DC	228	65.54		5	14.63
JFK	New York, NY	JAX	Jacksonville, FL	831	103.59	3		8.57
JFK	New York, NY	LAS	Las Vegas, NV	2,246	129.64	6		6.59
JFK	New York, NY	LGB	Long Beach, CA	2,462	135.83	6		6.63
JFK	New York, NY	MCO	Orlando, FL	947	132.96	11		9.84
JFK	New York, NY	MSY	New Orlns, LA	1,183	124.78	2		8.81
JFK	New York, NY	NAS	Nassau, BS	1,100	123.28	2		9.35
JFK	New York, NY	OAK	Oakland, CA	2,572	132.32	4		6.12
JFK	New York, NY	ONT	Ontario, CA	2,427	133.57	1		6.28
JFK	New York, NY	ORD	Chicago, IL	739	89.63	2	3	6.10
JFK	New York, NY	PBI	W Palm Bch, FL	1,031	128.63	5	1	9.53
JFK	New York, NY	PDX	Portland, OR	2,450	120.88	1		5.35
JFK	New York, NY	PHX	Phoenix, AZ	2,151	122.27	2		5.76
JFK	New York, NY	PIT	Pittsburgh, PA	339	61.07		4	11.84
JFK	New York, NY	PSE	Ponce, PR	1,623	126.02	1		6.24
JFK	New York, NY	PWM	Portland, ME	274	93.60	3	1	16.77
JFK	New York, NY	RDU	Raleigh, NC	427	70.95		5	14.17
JFK	New York, NY	RIC	Richmond, VA	288	67.54		4	15.84
JFK	New York, NY	ROC	Rochester, NY	264	113.34	5		18.77
JFK	New York, NY	RSW	Fort Myers, FL	1,077	124.63	4		8.53
JFK	New York, NY	SAN	San Diego, CA	2,443	130.05	3		5.72
JFK	New York, NY	SEA	Seattle, WA	2,418	132.64	2		6.17
JFK	New York, NY	SJC	San Jose, CA	2,566	129.02	2		5.77
JFK	New York, NY	SJU	San Juan, PR	1,603	129.13	4		7.20
JFK	New York, NY	SLC	Salt Lake Cty, UT	1,986	128.68	1		6.25
JFK	New York, NY	SMF	Sacramento, CA	2,518	121.78	1		5.18

EXHIBIT 9 *(continued)*

Routes Served by JetBlue as of April 2007

Airport	City	Airport	City	Distance (Miles)	Average Passengers/ Flight	A320 Round Trips / Day	E190 Round Trips / Day	Revenue/ Available Seat-Mile (Cents)
JFK	New York, NY	SRQ	Sarasota, FL	1,044	130.11	1		9.66
JFK	New York, NY	STI	Santiago, DO	1,476	128.39	1		8.07
JFK	New York, NY	SYR	Syracuse, NY	209	119.50	3	1	21.55
JFK	New York, NY	TPA	Tampa, FL	1,008	131.62	6		9.09
JFK	New York, NY	TUS	Tucson, AZ	2,134	101.24	1		4.28
LGB	Long Beach, CA	LAS	Las Vegas, NV	231	113.43	6		21.39
LGB	Long Beach, CA	OAK	Oakland, CA	354	113.24	5		14.64
LGB	Long Beach, CA	ORD	Chicago, IL	1,734	126.93	2		4.74
LGB	Long Beach, CA	SLC	Salt Lake Cty, UT	590	121.94	2		11.61
LGB	Long Beach, CA	SMF	Sacramento, CA	388	89.32	2		9.20
MCO	Orlando, FL	BQN	Aguadilla, PR	1,131	114.15	1		7.37
MCO	Orlando, FL	EWR	Newark, NJ	940	123.72	4		9.67
MCO	Orlando, FL	LGA	New York, NY	953	129.42	11		9.65
MCO	Orlando, FL	SJU	San Juan, PR	1,191	126.48	2		8.01
MCO	Orlando, FL	SWF	Newburgh, NY	992	125.17	2		8.24
MCO	Orlando, FL	SYR	Syracuse, NY	1,056	129.50	1		9.09
PBI	W Palm Bch, FL	LGA	New York, NY	1,038	127.47	1		9.62

Note: As of April 2007, the typical JetBlue A320 had 156 available seats and each E190 had 100 available seats.

Source: Company documents.

In addition to training, the introduction of the E190 brought changes in pilot compensation. An E190 captain (i.e., pilot in command) received hourly pay that was lower than that for an A320 captain but higher than that for an A320 first officer (i.e., co-pilot). Anderson explained that JetBlue had to manage pilot expectations with respect to these changes. He observed:

> The way you get the pilots comfortable with this sort of quasi-regional jet being introduced into our fleet is you keep taking deliveries of A320s at the same rate and creating A320 captain jobs that are the top of the pyramid—the highest paying pilot jobs in the company. So from a career-path perspective, pilots would not feel that we slowed down A320 deliveries to make room for the E190. We'd have a lot of unhappy, highly influential employees. So we had to keep the status quo with the A320 deliveries.

LONG-HAUL VS. SHORT-HAUL ROUTES. After some debate over the best initial market for the E190, JetBlue decided to introduce the plane in November 2005 on select flights between New York and Boston. Though both cities represented major markets with busy airports, JetBlue already had well-established operations in each city. Although the short-haul routes to be served by the E190 promised an increase in JetBlue's revenues (Exhibit 10), they also brought increased costs, as more frequent flights required E190s to spend more time on the ground than A320s for taxiing, loading, and unloading between flights.

Reactions to the E190

PILOTS. An additional problem with the introduction of short-haul routes was that most E190 pilots would be at a disadvantage in accumulating flying hours (and

EXHIBIT 10

Average Number of Daily JetBlue Roundtrips by City-Pair Distance and Year

City-Pair Distance	2005	2006	2007
<500 miles	27	57	78
500-1,000 miles	12	22	50
1,000-1,500 miles	49	55	67
1,500-2,000 miles	10	17	21
2,000-2,500 miles	34	40	40
>2,500 miles	16	17	19
TOTAL	148	208	275

Source: Company documents.

increasing their seniority) vis-à-vis pilots of the long-haul A320. Pilots accumulated flying hours only for time spent in the air; any time spent on the ground because of bad weather or congested air traffic (which could be acute on routes connecting busy airports like Boston and New York) was not included in their block accumulation of hours. Seniority was important not only in terms of raising pilots' compensation per flight hour but also in terms of providing them with greater say over their number of flight hours per month.[f]

These changes were concerning to many JetBlue pilots. Scott Green, vice president of Flight Operations, described the initial reaction of many pilots to the adoption of the E190: "If it ain't broke, don't fix it. We're doing well financially with the A320, so why on earth would we put our company at risk by doing this?"

EMPLOYEES. In addition to requiring changes to JetBlue's airport infrastructure (e.g., lowering the height of its current jetways to accommodate a smaller plane), the E190 posed challenges for the airline's personnel who had grown accustomed to the A320.

Steven Predmore, vice president and chief safety officer, described how seemingly innocuous variations in the design of the two planes resulted in unexpected changes for employees. He noted innovation of using non-skid flooring on the cargo bins of the E190 (versus the bare floors found on the A320). This was adopted as a safety feature to prevent baggage handlers from slipping on the floor of the cargo bin while loading and unloading bags under rainy or snowy conditions. With respect to the non-skid flooring, Predmore noted:

From a health and safety standpoint, it seems to be a good thing. But the loading procedure established with the A320 was to slide bags along the floor of the bins. Well, now we couldn't slide bags. This not only increased loading time, but also increased the potential for strains and back sprains as handlers had to lift bags they previously would have slid.

Vicky Stennes, vice president of inflight service, added that flight attendants also had to make a significant adjustment to the E190. Though the ratio of available seats to flight attendants was the same (i.e., 50 to 1) for both the A320 and E190, the latter plane had smaller galleys from which to serve customers. Further, the shorter duration of E190 flights provided less time for each attendant to provide the high level of service to which JetBlue passengers had become accustomed.

For those employees involved with servicing and maintaining JetBlue's aircraft, the adoption of the E190 created additional operating complexity. Because the A320 and E190 were different sizes and their engines, avionics, and other major components were manufactured by different companies, there were few opportunities to standardize parts and servicing procedures across the two types of aircraft. Given the volume of E190 flights either originating or arriving at JFK, JetBlue decided to invest in maintenance capabilities (i.e., equipment and staff) for the E190 at that airport. However, investing in similar capabilities at other airports—smaller JetBlue focus cities and other destinations—was not economically justifiable. Further, the novelty of the E190 meant that there were

---

[f] In contrast, the seniority of flight attendants was not determined by hours spent in flight.

few opportunities to outsource or share with other carriers the maintenance responsibilities for E190s at airports other than JFK.

CUSTOMERS. The E190 required changes in behavior and expectations for JetBlue's existing customers. For example, overhead storage bins on the E190 were smaller than those on the A320, causing many passengers to be surprised and disappointed when they were told that they would need to check their luggage at the gate. Maruster reflected on the impact of this and related differences between the two planes, "So now we had to tell customers to do two different things. If it's the first plane, you do this. If it's the other plane, you do that. Those kind of differences were a bit concerning to me."

Beyond the airline's existing customers, the short-haul routes that JetBlue introduced with the E190 brought new customers with new expectations. JetBlue had grown as an airline geared toward personal and leisure travel, determined to overcome delays and technical problems to get passengers to their destinations. Passengers flying from New York to vacation spots in Florida, for example, were usually not following a tight schedule. This was not the case, however, for the business travelers who would fly short-haul routes on the E190. David Ramage, vice president of technical operations, described the attitude of these business travelers: "I've got to be in Boston by 8:00, and if I'm not, there are serious consequences." Ian Deason, director of alliances and partnerships, added, "With business customers, you get one chance. If they are not satisfied the first time, it's hard to get them back."

The short-haul routes attracted other passengers that tested the limits of JetBlue's "get-to-the-destination-at-all-costs" culture. One such test occurred during on New Year's Eve in 2005. A 6:00 p.m. E190 flight from Boston to New York was filled with revelers who were planning to spend the evening in New York and return the next morning. Mechanical problems combined with bad weather resulted in a long delay. As usual, JetBlue was determined to get its passengers in the air, but the flight crew did not communicate how long the delay was expected to last. After a while, flight attendants soon had to soothe angry passengers. One passenger's complaint captured the feeling of many: "If you had cancelled me I would have been happier. I would have gotten off the plane and *driven* to New York."

These were new kinds of demands that Mike Barger and others involved in training JetBlue employees now had to face. He noted:

> Our "secret sauce" historically has been that when something goes wrong, you buy a pizza and give somebody a hug, and everything's great. As for the business customers, they do not want a slice of pizza. Instead, they are thinking, "I've got a meeting in the city." The "a-ha moment" from a training perspective was that we did not prepare our customer-facing people to deal with the passenger who says, "I don't want a pizza. In fact, go get my bag off the airplane!"

COMPLEX INTANGIBLES. Drawing on his experience at one of the legacy airlines, Maruster reflected on another issue that arose from adding a new plane into JetBlue's operating system:

> When you start adding complexity, you start to lose your ability to track it and put your finger on it. When I was at another airline, we got rid of a sub-fleet of 12 airplanes that was sitting out there all by itself, requiring different processes and training. We really didn't have a strong financial case for getting rid of this fleet; everybody just knew we had to do it.

The high standards of service and reliability JetBlue had set in the past increased the frustrations of working through the integration of the E190. Neeleman noted:

> We wanted the plane to work, and we wanted to make sure that it worked every time. When you launch an airplane, there's this process of flying it and figuring out why this thing broke, particularly when the plane is so new. Does it need to be re-engineered? Does the software need to be re-written? Does this clamp need to be replaced? Moreover, why did this clamp fail? Well, it wasn't strong enough. Why wasn't it strong enough? Well, because it's a new plane.

Applying the Brakes

On a crisp autumn evening in 2006, Barger held a meeting with several members of JetBlue's management team, and others from a key banking advisor, over dinner at Il Corso in New York City. The goal of the meeting was to discuss options for financing the future growth of the airline. Mark Powers, senior vice president and treasurer, presented data on the cash flow implications of the airline's prior and planned aircraft purchases and growth over the next several years.

Though Powers presented several slides, he spent the majority of his time discussing only one of them—a picture showing the cash flows associated with acquisition of each new airplane. Powers recalled:

> That slide showed a much longer path to breaking even on a cash basis than most of us in that room ever assumed. When you took the cash flow picture for the average plane acquisition and multiplied it by the number of planes we were acquiring each year, it was clear that, if we stayed on the current course, we would grow ourselves to death.

By the end of the dinner, it was clear that the data and analysis presented by Powers—combined with rapidly increasing fuel prices—dictated that JetBlue slow its rate of growth significantly. To that end, within several months of the dinner, JetBlue announced that it would decrease the rate at which it took delivery of new airplanes and redouble efforts to sell used aircraft. With respect to new aircraft, the company reduced its planned deliveries of A320s from 17 to 12 for both 2007 and 2008. For E190s, planned deliveries decreased from 18 to 10 for both 2007 and 2008. Exhibit 11 provides JetBlue's actual and expected fleet size from 2000 to 2011 under its original and revised assumptions about annual plane deliveries. At the time JetBlue announced these reductions, the airline noted that its plan was to slow the annual rate of growth in available seat miles (ASMs) for the airline from 18–20% to 14–17%.[7]

JetBlue's pilots were arguably impacted more than any other department by the decision to slow growth. Reducing aircraft purchases, explained Scott Green, "hurts the pilot group unlike any other work group, because your whole seniority and income ability is tied to the number of airplanes that we take."

The Valentine's Day Crisis

On February 14, 2007, JetBlue faced the beginning of what then-CEO Neeleman would later refer to as "the worst operational week in JetBlue's seven-year history."[8] JetBlue's flights from JFK were heavily booked on that particular Wednesday, as many customers in northeastern states hoped to get a head

EXHIBIT 11

JetBlue Fleet by Plane Type, December 2005 Plan vs. December 2006 Plan

Note: Figures for 2006 forward are based on planned deliveries.

Source: JetBlue Annual Reports.

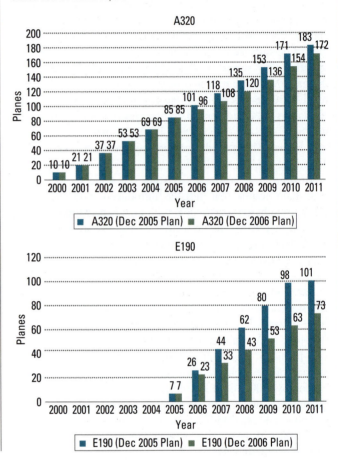

start on travel for the upcoming President's Day weekend. The weather forecast for JFK predicted early snow turning to rain. Despite the fact that the snow lingered longer than expected, JetBlue continued to board flights at JFK and have them taxi to their runways in anticipation of the expected changeover to rain.

Unfortunately, the snow turned to freezing rain, creating "ice pellet" conditions under which the FAA prohibited domestic flights from taking off. Because planes were still able to land at JFK under these conditions, the planes on the tarmac were left without gates to which they could return. The result was that several JetBlue planes were stranded on the tarmac at JFK, with nine spending at least 6 hours each waiting for gates.[9] Beyond the disgruntled passengers on these flights, the inability of JetBlue planes to leave JFK wreaked havoc on the entire JetBlue system as planes and flight crews were increasingly out of position and unable to make scheduled flights. Over the course of the six-day event over 1,100 flights were cancelled in total—approximately 40% of JetBlue's operations. In total, more than 131,000 JetBlue customers were affected by cancellations, delays, or diversions during the period.[10]

The crisis exposed the informal patchwork of operating systems that had emerged since JetBlue's founding but had not previously created significant problems for the airline. In response to the crisis, JetBlue took several steps to shore up its operations in the areas of reservations staffing, airport staffing (e.g., the credentialing of corporate staff at Forest Hills to staff selected operations positions at JFK on an emergency basis), and information systems. Most importantly, the crisis highlighted the need to reconsider JetBlue's long-standing operating principle of not canceling flights.

The crisis prompted Neeleman, on February 20, to introduce JetBlue's Customer Bill of Rights. The Bill of Rights, which was the first of its kind among U.S. airlines and was retroactively applied to those affected by the February crisis, delineated JetBlue's responsibilities to its customers in the following areas: information-sharing, cancellations, departure delays, overbookings, and onboard ground delays for arrivals and departures (Exhibit 12). Prior to the crisis, *BusinessWeek* had compiled its list of top performing companies with respect to customer service, placing JetBlue in the fourth spot. When the list appeared in the March 5 issue of the magazine, however, the cover showed JetBlue's name scratched off the list with the title "Customer Service Champs . . . and One Extraordinary Stumble."

At multiple points during February and March, the provisions of the company's Bill of Rights were tested by weather conditions in the eastern U.S. On those occasions, the airline moved proactively to cancel flights. In early March, JetBlue introduced Russ Chew, former COO of the FAA, as the airline's new COO with Barger retaining the title of president. In May, Neeleman announced his resignation as CEO, and Barger was named as his successor.

EXHIBIT 12

JetBlue Customer Bill of Rights

Source: http://www.jetblue.com/p/about/ourcompany/promise/Bill_Of_Rights.pdf, accessed April 2007.

Moving Forward

Though disappointed by the crisis itself, Barger was pleased with the manner in which the airline had moved swiftly to shore up its operating procedures in the three subsequent months. As the immediate stress of crisis recovery began to subside, however, Barger found himself facing an equally perplexing issue related to JetBlue's capacity. Despite the steps taken to slow JetBlue's rate of aircraft deliveries in late 2006, it was clear—particularly in light of rapidly increasing fuel costs—that the airline needed to curtail further its capacity growth.

While the exact magnitude of the necessary reductions in capacity growth was still being determined, Barger realized that the cuts would be significant. What was not clear was how much of the capacity reduction should come from the E190 fleet versus that of the A320. Barger saw the E190 as a unique plane that JetBlue could use as an engine for future growth. At the same, the A320 was a proven aircraft around which JetBlue had standardized its training and operating activities over the past seven years. Ultimately, Barger knew that neither Embraer nor Airbus would be pleased with any future reductions or deferrals sought by JetBlue. While the need for slower capacity growth was clear, the best path for achieving this was less certain.

Endnotes

1. Delta Air Lines, "Delta Through the Decades," Delta Air Lines Company website, http://www.delta.com/about_delta/corporate_information/delta_stats_facts_/detla_through_the_decades/in dex.jsp, accessed February 7, 2007.

2. This section draws from Jim Corridore, "Airlines," Industry Surveys, Standard & Poor's Industry Surveys, November 23, 2006, via NetAdvantage, accessed November 15, 2006.

3. Steve Huettel, "Soaring Ahead," *St. Petersburg Times,* accessed via Factiva, December 12, 2006.

4. JetBlue, December 31, 2005 10-K (Forrest Hills: JetBlue, 2005), p. 1, via Thomson Research, accessed January 2007.

5. Susan Carey, "Balancing Act: Amid JetBlue's Rapid Ascent, CEO Adopts Big Rivals' Traits," *Wall Street Journal*, August 25, 2005, accessed via Factiva, December 19, 2006.

6. Brian Nelson, "Worst Has Yet to Come for Regional Airlines," Morningstar Column, October 16, 2006, via LexisNexis, accessed January 31, 2007.

7. JetBlue Airways, "JetBlue Adjusts Fleet Delivery Plan Through 2016," company press release, December 4, 2006.

8. David Neeleman, "An Apology from David Neeleman," JetBlue Company website, http://www.jetblue.com/about/ourcompany/apology/index.html, accessed March 2007.

9. Jeff Bailey, "JetBlue Cancels More Flights, Leading to Passenger Discord," *The New York Times*, February 18, 2007, via Factiva, accessed September 2007.

10. JetBlue Airways Conference Call to Announce Details of Customer Bill of Rights Program, February 20, 2007, accessed via Thomson Financial, April 2007.

Casey Burt
Capgemini

Frank T. Rothaermel
Georgia Institute of Technology

STEPHANIE MILNER SPENT the fall and winter of 2008–2009 like many Americans, watching and reading the dire financial news as it was streamed, blogged, and reported directly from Wall Street. Milner, however, had an even more personal interest. As a manager in the Global Corporate and Investment Banking (GCIB) division of Bank of America, she worked every day in the middle of the financial storm. Now, as the dark clouds are beginning to part and the recovery gathers steam, she has been asked to join a committee of managers from throughout the organization who will analyze the strategic direction of the bank and locate opportunities for growth.

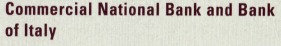

Historically, Bank of America has pursued a strategy of growth through acquisition. (See Exhibits 1, 2, and 3 for Bank of America's historical financial information.) This strategy was evident even at the height of the financial crisis, when the bank purchased mortgage lending powerhouse Countrywide Financial in the summer of 2008 and brokerage Merrill Lynch in early 2009. (See Exhibit 4 for a list of important company dates.) These latest acquisitions made Bank of America the largest bank holding company in the United States by asset value (Exhibits 5 and 6).[1] They also led to the absorption of nearly $100 billion dollars in toxic assets from Merrill and increased the bank's exposure to potentially massive losses in the mortgage industry.[2]

Like its competitors, Bank of America had significant problems in late 2008 and was on the verge of collapse. The U.S. federal government came to its rescue, providing $25 billion and then an additional $20 billion in TARP funds. The U.S. Treasury and the Federal Deposit Insurance Corporation (FDIC) also guaranteed $118 billion to "provide protection against the possibility of unusually large losses"[3] (Exhibit 7).

Without this cash injection, Bank of America could possibly have received the dubious distinction of being the largest bankruptcy in U.S. history. Instead, that "honor" went to another victim of the 2008 financial crisis, Lehman Brothers, which destroyed more than $40 billion in shareholder value when it filed for bankruptcy in September 2008.

With economists agreeing that the recession ended in mid-2009, Bank of America has some important work to do.[4] As Milner enters the conference room, she surveys the scene. The group looks weary, but optimistic. After greeting several colleagues, she takes a seat and begins to scrawl a few notes on the questions she feels the committee should address: Where is the bank heading? What can Bank of America do in the future to prevent such exposure to economic meltdowns? What will the financial landscape look like as the U.S. economy continues to recover? Where will the bank's opportunities lie in the new economy? And most importantly, how should the bank position itself strategically to compete successfully and grow in the future? These questions swirl in Stephanie Milner's head as the room quiets and the team gets to work.

Commercial National Bank and Bank of Italy

Bank of America's history is really the history of two banks on opposite coasts of the United States—one in North Carolina and the other in San Francisco.[5]

COMMERCIAL NATIONAL BANK. The foundations of the first bank were laid in 1874 in Charlotte, North Carolina, with the formation of Commercial National Bank. It grew steadily in the Charlotte area for nearly

Consultant Casey Burt (GT MBA '11) of Capgemini and Professor Frank T. Rothaermel prepared this case from public sources. It is developed for the purpose of class discussion. It is not intended to be used for any kind of endorsement, source of data or depiction of efficient or inefficient management. All opinions expressed, all errors and omissions are entirely the authors'. © Burt and Rothaermel, 2013.

EXHIBIT 1

Bank of America Corporation Historical Balance Sheets at December 31st (in millions)

	2010	2009	2008	2007	2006	2005
Assets						
Federal funds sold and securities borrowed or purchased under agreements to resell	$ 209,616	$ 189,933	$ 82,478	$ 129,552	$ 135,478	$ 149,785
Trading account assets	194,671	182,206	159,522	162,064	153,052	131,707
Debt securities	338,054	311,441	277,589	214,056	192,846	221,603
Loans and leases, net of allowance	898,555	862,928	908,375	864,756	697,474	565,746
All other assets	624,013	683,724	389,979	345,318	280,887	222,962
Total Assets	**$2,264,909**	**$2,230,232**	**$1,817,943**	**$1,715,746**	**$1,459,737**	**$1,291,803**
Liabilities						
Deposits	$1,010,430	$ 991,611	$ 882,997	$ 805,177	$ 693,497	$ 634,670
Federal funds purchased and securities loaned or sold under agreements to repurchase	245,359	255,185	206,598	221,435	217,527	240,655
Trading account liabilities	71,985	65,432	57,287	77,342	67,670	50,890
Commercial paper and other short-term borrowings	59,962	69,524	158,056	191,089	141,300	116,269
Long-term debt	448,431	438,521	268,292	197,508	146,000	100,848
All other liabilities	200,494	178,515	67,661	76,392	58,471	46,938
Total Liabilities	**2,036,661**	**1,998,788**	**1,640,891**	**1,568,943**	**1,324,465**	**1,190,270**
Shareholders' Equity	228,248	231,444	177,052	146,803	135,272	101,533
Total Liabilities and Shareholders' Equity	**$2,264,909**	**$2,230,232**	**$1,817,943**	**$1,715,746**	**$1,459,737**	**$1,291,803**

Source: Bank of America Corporation Annual Reports.

EXHIBIT 2

Bank of America Corporation Consolidated Statement of Income (in millions)

	2010	2009	2008	2007	2006	2005
Revenue						
Net interest income	$ 51,523	$ 47,109	$ 45,360	$34,441	$34,594	$30,737
Non-interest income	58,697	72,534	27,422	32,392	38,182	26,438
Total Revenue, Net of Interest Expense	110,220	119,643	72,782	66,833	72,776	57,175
Expenses						
Provision for credit losses	28,435	48,570	26,825	8,385	5,010	4,014
Noninterest expense, before merger and restructuring charges	81,288	63,992	40,594	37,114	34,988	28,269
Merger and restructuring charges	1,820	2,721	935	410	805	412
Total Expenses	111,543	115,283	68,354	45,909	40,803	32,695
Income before Income Taxes	(1,323)	4,360	4,428	20,924	31,973	24,480
Income tax expense (benefit)	915	(1,916)	420	5,942	10,840	8,015
Net Income (Loss)	$ (2,238)	$ 6,276	$ 4,008	$14,982	$21,133	$16,465

Source: Bank of America Corporation Annual Reports.

EXHIBIT 3

Other Financial Data and Ratios

	2010	2009	2008	2007	2006	2005
Performance Ratios						
Return on average assets	N/M	0.26%	0.22%	0.94%	1.44%	1.30%
Return on average common shareholders' equity	N/M	N/M	1.80%	11.08%	16.27%	16.51%
Return on average tangible common shareholders' equity	N/M	N/M	4.72%	26.19%	38.23%	31.80%
Return on average tangible shareholders' equity	N/M	4.18%	5.19%	25.13%	37.80%	31.67%
Total ending equity to total ending assets	10.08	10.38	9.74	8.56	9.27	7.86
Total average equity to total average assets	9.56	10.01	8.94	8.53	8.90	7.86
Dividend payout	N/M	N/M	N/M	$72.26	$45.66	$46.61
Per Common Share Data						
Earnings (loss)	$(0.37)	$(0.29)	$ 0.54	$ 3.32	$ 4.63	$ 4.08
Diluted earnings (loss)	$(0.37)	$(0.29)	$ 0.54	$ 3.29	$ 4.58	$ 4.02
Dividends paid	$ 0.04	$ 0.04	$ 2.24	$ 2.40	$ 2.12	$ 1.90
Book value	$20.99	$21.48	$27.77	$32.09	$29.70	$25.32
Tangible book value	$12.98	$11.94	$10.11	$12.71	$13.26	$13.51
Market Price per Share of Common Stock						
Closing	$13.34	$15.06	$14.08	$41.26	$53.39	$46.15
High closing	$19.48	$18.59	$45.03	$54.05	$54.90	$47.08
Low closing	$10.95	$ 3.14	$11.25	$41.10	$43.09	$41.57

(continued)

EXHIBIT 3 Other Financial Data and Ratios *(continued)*

	2010	2009	2008	2007	2006	2005
Market capitalization	$134,536	$130,273	$70,645	$183,107	$238,021	$184,586
Asset Quality						
Allowance for credit losses ($M)	$ 43,073	$ 38,687	$23,492	$ 12,106	$ 9,413	$ 8,440
Nonperforming loans, leases, and fore closed properties ($M)	$ 32,664	$ 35,747	$18,212	$ 5,948	$ 1,856	$ 1,603
Allowance for loan and lease losses (% of total loans)	4.47%	4.16%	2.49%	1.33%	1.28%	1.40%
Net charge-offs	$ 34,334	$ 33,688	$16,231	$6,480	$ 4,539	$ 4,562
Net charge-offs (% of total loans)	3.60%	3.58%	1.79%	0.84%	0.70%	0.85%
Nonperforming loans (% of total loans)	3.27%	3.75%	1.77%	0.64%	0.25%	0.26%
Ratio of the allowance for loan and lease losses	1.22	1.1	1.42	1.79	1.99	1.76

Source: Compiled from Bank of America Corporation Annual Reports.

EXHIBIT 4

Key Dates in the History of Bank of America

Year	Event
1874	Commercial National Bank was founded in Charlotte, North Carolina
1904	Amadeo Giannini founds the Bank of Italy in San Francisco, California
1922	Bank of Italy purchases Banca dell'Italia Meridonale and rebrands as Bank of America and Italy
1927	Bank of America and Italy merges with Liberty Bank of America to form Bank of Italy National Trust & Savings Association
1930	Bank of Italy National Trust & Savings Association merges with Bank of America Los Angelas and rebrands as Bank of America
1958	Commercial National Bank purchases Charlotte competitor American Trust Company and rebrands as American Commercial Bank
1958	Bank of America issues the first BankAmericard, ushering in the era of credit cards
1960	American Commercial Bank purchases Securities National Bank and rebrands as North Carolina National Bank (NCNB)
1967	The Bank Holding Company Act of 1967
1975	The BankAmericard association rebrands as Visa
1982	NCNB exbands beyond North Carolina by purchasing First National Bank of Lake City in Lake City, Florida
1983	Hugh McColl becomes CEO of NCNB
1983	BankAmerica Corporation purchases Seattle, Washington–based Seattle First National Bank
1986	Large BankAmerica losses due to third-world lending lead to unsuccesful takeover attempt by First Interstate Bancorp
1991	NCNB rebrands as NationsBank after the purchase of Atlanta, Georgia–based C&S/Sovran Corpoation
1992	Bank America Corporation purchases Security Pacific Corporation and gains a foothold in all major West Coast markets

EXHIBIT 4 *(continued)*

Year	Event
1994	BankAmerica purchases Continental Illinois National Bank & Trust Co. and overtakes NationsBank as the largest bank in America
1995	NationsBank purchases BankSouth for $1.6 billion
1996	NationsBank purchases St. Louis's Boatmen's Bankshares for $9.6 billion
1997	NationsBank purchases Florida-based Barnett Bank for $15.5 billion
1997	BankAmerica loans hedge fund D.E. Shaw $1.4 billion in exchange for services
1998	Russian bond defaults cripple D.E. Shaw and weaken BankAmerica
1998	NationsBank purchases BankAmerica for $64.8 billion and rebrands as the Bank of America Corporation
2001	Hugh McColl steps down as CEO of Bank of America and is succeeded by Ken Lewis
2004	Bank of America Corporation purchases FleetBoston Financial for $47 billion
2005	Bank of America Corporation purchases MBNA for $35 billion
2005	Bank of America Corporation purchases ABN AMRO North America and LaSalle Bank from ABN AMRO for $21 billion
2008	Bank of America Corporation purchases Countrywide Financial and rebrands the firm as Bank of America Home Loans
2008	Bank of America Corporation purchases Merrill Lynch for $50 billion
2008	Bank of America Corporation recieves $25 billion in federal TARP funds
2009	Bank of America Corporation receives an additional $20 billion in TARP funds, plus $118 billion in guarantees against Merrill Lynch losses from the FDIC

Source: Bank of America (www.bankofamerica.com).

EXHIBIT 5

Bank of America–Total Assets ($M)

Source: Compiled from Bank of America 10-K filings.

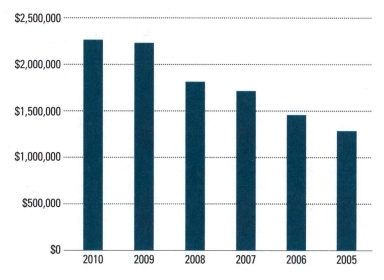

EXHIBIT 6

Total Assets of Largest U.S. Bank Holding Companies

Source: Federal Reserve Board, National Information Center, www.federalreserve.gov/releases/lbr/current/default.htm.

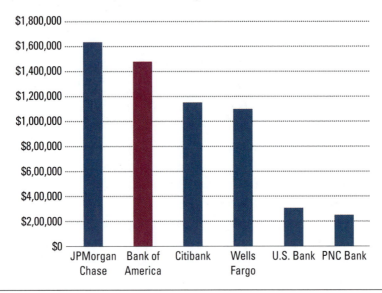

85 years. Then, in 1958, it purchased Charlotte banking competitor American Trust Company and took on the new name American Commercial Bank. Regional expansion continued in 1960 when American Commercial Bank purchased another local competitor, Securities National Bank, and again renamed itself, this time as North Carolina National Bank (NCNB).

In 1982, NCNB expanded beyond the borders of North Carolina through the acquisition of First National Bank of Lake City in Lake City, Florida. The next year began an era of rapid growth for the company with the appointment of Hugh McColl as chief executive officer. Assets swelled to $118 billion after the purchases of failed Dallas bank, First Republic Bank Corporation, from the FDIC in 1988, and Atlanta-based C&S/Sovran Corporation in 1991. Upon completion of the latter acquisition, NCNB became NationsBank.

Under McColl's leadership, the asset base of NationsBank more than doubled throughout the mid-1990s. To further strengthen its presence in the Atlanta banking market, NationsBank purchased BankSouth in an all-stock deal valued at $1.6 billion in 1995. Next came the acquisitions of St. Louis's Boatmen's Bankshares for $9.6 billion in 1996, and Florida-based Barnett Bank for $15.5 billion in 1997. These purchases made NationsBank the largest bank in the South, with $284 billion in assets and more than 2,600 branches stretching as far west as New Mexico.

BANK OF ITALY. Thirty years after the founding of Commercial National Bank in Charlotte, Italian-American Amadeo Giannini founded Bank of Italy in San Francisco. Although Giannini first established the bank to cater to immigrants, he had much larger dreams.

Like Commercial National Bank, Bank of Italy achieved much of its early growth through acquisitions. In 1922, Giannini purchased Banca dell'Italia Meridonale and renamed the combined entity the Bank of America and Italy. Five years later, he increased his holdings again in a merger with the newly formed Liberty Bank of America. The new entity, the Bank of Italy National Trust & Savings Association, served customers through a network of 276 branches in California. After the completion of yet another merger, this time with the Bank of America Los Angeles, in 1930 the Bank of Italy was renamed Bank of America.

Giannini continued throughout the 1930s and 1940s to pursue his vision of creating a national bank. Bank of America expanded into most of the states surrounding California. It also expanded its service offerings to include insurance through the formation of a holding company, Transamerica Corporation. However,

EXHIBIT 7

Largest Recipients of TARP Funds

Source: "Tracking the $700 Billion Bailout," *The New York Times*, www.nytimes.com/packages/html/national/200904_CREDITCRISIS/recipients.html.

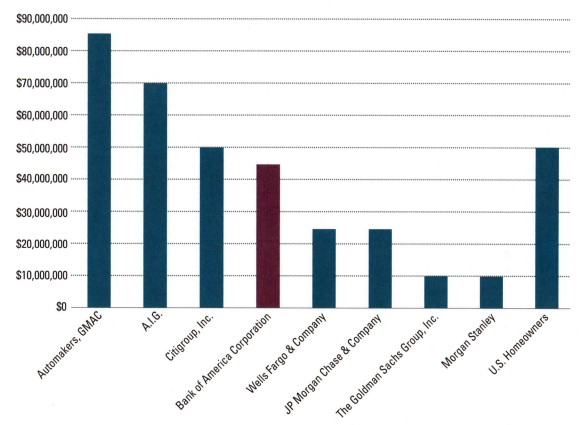

the 1956 passage of the Bank Holding Company Act prohibited banks from owning nonbank subsidiaries, forcing Giannini to spin off Transamerica Corp. Bank of America continued its traditional banking activities and retained the Transamerica name for the insurance arm. Additionally, due to new federal interstate banking regulations, Bank of America's domestic non-California banks were formed into a new corporation that would eventually become First Interstate Bancorp (which was acquired by Wells Fargo & Company in 1996).

The 1950s did not represent all bad news for Bank of America's aspirations. New technology that allowed credit cards to be directly linked to bank accounts led to the introduction of the BankAmericard in 1958. The credit card ushered in a new era for the bank as well as for American consumer spending in general. BankAmericard became Visa in 1975. In response, a

consortium of other California banks joined together to form Master Charge, the forerunner of MasterCard.

During the late 1960s, the regulatory environment changed again. The Bank Holding Company Act of 1967 allowed for the establishment of BankAmerica Corporation, to serve as parent company to Bank of America, its subsidiaries, and any future acquisitions. Growth continued slowly in the ensuing years until the bank began a new wave of expansion outside of California by acquiring the insolvent Seattle-based Seafirst Corporation and its subsidiary, Seattle-First National Bank, in 1983.

Bank of America faced a crisis in the mid-1980s due to massive losses on loans made to third-world nations, particularly those in Latin America. As a result, the company replaced then-CEO Sam Armacost with former CEO A. W. Clausen, but the damage was already done. Stock price depreciation made the bank vulnerable to hostile takeover. Ironically, one of the attempts was made by First Interstate Bancorp, its former spin-off. Bank of America rebuffed this and other takeover efforts by liquidating several subsidiaries such as FinanceAmerica (sold to Chrysler), Charles Schwab and Co. (sold back to Schwab), and Bank of America and Italy (sold to Deutsche Bank).

After the 1987 stock market crash, BankAmerica's stock rallied strongly. Major acquisitions resumed in 1992 with the purchase of Security Pacific Corporation and the banks owned by its subsidiaries in California, Arizona, Idaho, Oregon, and Washington. Despite having to liquidate Rainier Bank due to concerns of federal regulators about competition in Washington state, the Security Pacific deal was the largest bank acquisition in history at that time.

In 1994, BankAmerica acquired Continental Illinois National Bank & Trust Co. Continental had been run by the federal government for more than 10 years due to insolvency issues stemming from the same oil-industry exposure suffered by Seafirst in 1983. This transaction allowed BankAmerica to regain its position as the largest bank in America by total deposits, a title that the company had lost to NationsBank Corporation in 1997. That was also the year that BankAmerica embarked on a path that would change the face of the bank forever.

In exchange for running various business units at the bank, BankAmerica loaned $1.4 billion to hedge fund D. E. Shaw & Company. When Russian bonds defaulted in 1998, D. E. Shaw suffered massive losses, limiting its ability to repay the loans and thereby weakening BankAmerica's financial position. This led, later that same year, to the acquisition of BankAmerica by NationsBank for $64.8 billion, easily the largest bank acquisition to date. The combined bank controlled $570 billion in assets and operated more than 4,800 branches in 22 states. Although technically NationsBank purchased BankAmerica, the deal was structured as a merger and resulted in the new bank holding company being named the Bank of America Corporation and the banking subsidiary taking the name Bank of America, N.A.

Growth and Financial Meltdown in the New Millennium

The new century brought new leadership, new crises, and the growth of shadow banks.

NEW LEADERSHIP AND NEW CRISES. In 2001, Hugh McColl stepped down, and Ken Lewis succeeded him as CEO. The change in leadership did little to slow the bank's growth through strategic acquisition. (See Exhibit 8 for the level of diversification in 2003.) In 2004, Bank of America purchased FleetBoston Financial (the nation's seventh-largest bank) for $47 billion in cash and stock.[6] The next year it acquired MBNA for $35 billion in cash and stock, making Bank of America a major credit card issuer both in the United States and abroad. Shortly thereafter came the purchase of ABN AMRO North America and LaSalle Bank Corporation from Dutch giant ABN AMRO for $21 billion.[7]

Despite growing storm clouds on the mortgage horizon, 2007 and 2008 saw a repurchase agreement and then outright acquisition of Countrywide Financial, giving Bank of America a substantial position in the mortgage business. The purchase made the newly named Bank of America Home Loans the largest mortgage originator and servicer in the United States, with a service portfolio valued at $1.4 trillion at the end of 2007 (representing 20 to 25 percent of the home loan market). Bank of America must have had at least some suspicions of the developing storm, however: It structured the deal to protect itself in case Countrywide was forced to declare bankruptcy due to losses on subprime home loans.[8]

EXHIBIT 8

Bank of America's Diversification Strategy in 2003

Source: Blamely, R. S., S. Griffin, Q. Makins, B. Rule, and D. Thompson (2010), "A strategic perspective on Bank of America," Georgia Institute of Technology.

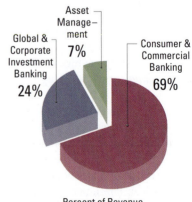

Percent of Revenue

Those potential losses were looking more and more real every day. Beginning in 2007, the U.S. economy slid into what has been described by many economists as the most serious financial crisis since the Great Depression.[9] Most economists also agree that the cause of this crisis was the housing bubble that peaked in 2005 or 2006, fueled by the availability of low interest rates on a variety of loans caused by an influx of foreign capital into the U.S. market (Exhibit 9).

During this time, the debt of the average U.S. consumer rose to unprecedented heights (Exhibit 10).[10] Strong historical home value growth (Exhibit 11), combined with easy initial loan terms, incentivized many Americans to take on mortgages they could not afford in the hope that they could refinance later at more favorable terms. A leveling off and slight decline in home values in some parts of the country in 2006 and 2007, combined with rising interest rates, caused the bubble to burst. Refinancing became difficult, adjustable-rate mortgage (ARM) interest rates reset at higher levels, and a wave of defaults and foreclosures followed.[11]

As the number of mortgage loans (as well as credit card balances and automobile loans) increased, so did the popularity of a financial instrument known as asset-backed securities, or ABS (Exhibit 12). Asset-backed securities are financial instruments securitized by the underlying assets on which they are based. The underlying assets provide a stream of capital from payments made on those assets. In the case of housing, for example, this stream is comprised of homeowners' mortgage payments.[12] Banks packaged mortgages and other debt into tranches that were given debt ratings and sold to investors around the world who wanted to invest in the U.S. real estate market.

Collateralized debt obligations, or CDOs, are a special form of asset-backed security pioneered by Drexel Burnham Lambert in 1987. Like other asset-backed securities, CDOs carry a credit rating that is based on the fundamental strength of their underlying components—in this case, investment-grade fixed-income assets. These investments appeal to investors because they offer higher returns than similarly rated corporate bonds and allow the buyer to customize their level of risk through diversification. Because of these benefits, the popularity of CDOs skyrocketed: From 2004 to 2007, the compound annual growth rate of global CDO issuance volume was 45 percent. Issuances rose from $157.4 billion to $481.6 billion in value over this same period.

When home prices began to decline and foreclosures rose, however, the value of asset-backed securities fell sharply. Mass exodus from the CDO market followed, causing the 2008 issue value to drop to $61.9 billion (Exhibit 13).[13] From the standpoint of the CDO and ABS issuers, the precipitous drop in prices, combined with the recent installation of mark-to-market accounting standards, caused massive losses for banks as they were forced to write down the value of assets on their balance sheets.

THE SHADOW BANKS. The financial crisis had a particularly large effect on the U.S. shadow banking system. *Shadow banks* are nonbank financial institutions (for example, investment banks, hedge funds, pension funds) that lend corporations the capital necessary to operate, most notably through the use of commercial paper. What differentiated members of this system from traditional banks was their inability to accept deposits, which meant they were not subject to the same regulations as traditional banking institutions. For example, investment banks were not required to maintain minimum capital levels to protect against potential losses. They also did not have the ability to draw on federally insured customer deposits

EXHIBIT 9

Historic Mortgage Rates, June 2003–January 2011

Source: www.hsh.com/mtghst.html.

Legend: 30-Year-FRM, 15-Year-FRM, 30-Year-1-ARM

EXHIBIT 10

U.S. Household Debt Outstanding 1979–2010 (in billions)

Source: www.federalreserve.gov/releases/z1/current/z1r-2.pdf.

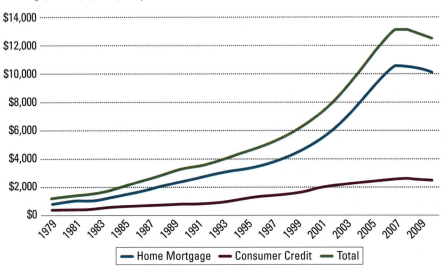

EXHIBIT 11

Historical U.S. Home Price Indices

Source: www.standardandpoors.com/servlet/BlobServer?blobheadername3=MDT-Type&blobcol=urldocumentfile&blobtable=SPComSecureDocument&blobheadervalue2=inline%3B+filename%3Ddownload.pdf&blobheadername2=Content-Disposition&blobheadervalue1=application%2Fpdf&blobkey=id&blobheadername1=content-type&blobwhere=1245301368714&blobheadervalue3=abinary%3B+charset%3DUTF-8&blobnocache=true.

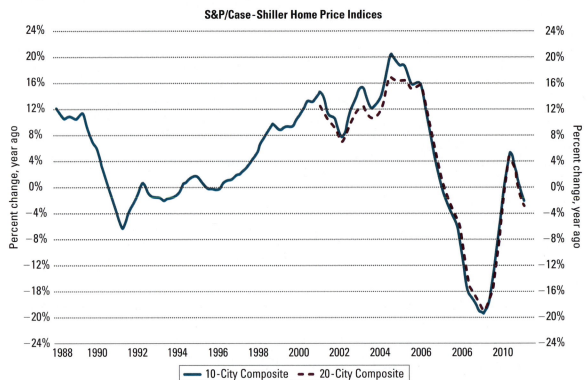

EXHIBIT 12

Total Issuance of Asset-Backed Securities

Source: The Securities Industry and Financial Markets Association, www.sifma.org/research/item.aspx?id=23319.

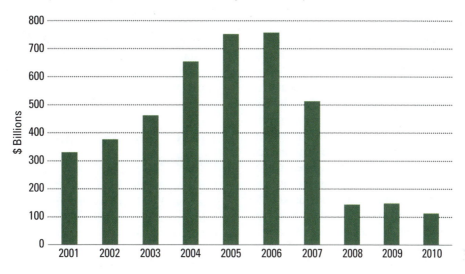

EXHIBIT 13

Global CDO Issuance (in millions)

Source: Securities Industry and Financial Markets Association, http://search.sifma.org/search?q=CDO+issuance&submit=Go&site=SIFMA&client=SIFMA&proxyst ylesheet=SIFMA&output=xml_no_dtd.

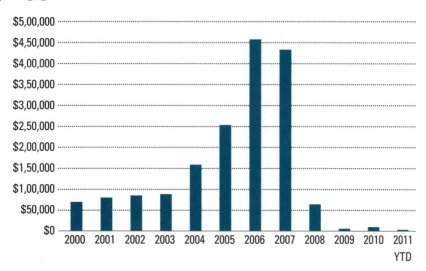

or borrow directly from the federal government in times of financial need. By early 2007, the shadow banking system had grown to roughly the same size as the traditional banking system in terms of assets—more than $10 trillion.[14]

Several investment banks and hedge funds had significantly increased their leverage in the ABS market in the years leading up to the financial crisis. They were therefore especially vulnerable to ABS devaluation.[15] These shadow institutions used funds from the sale of commercial paper to invest in asset-backed securities, either directly or through structured investment vehicles which they sponsored. As those securities lost value, concerns mounted about the investment banks' ability to repay their debt obligations. The result was a virtual freezing of the commercial paper markets. To encourage lending, central banks around the world felt they had to inject capital into their respective markets. According to Timothy Geithner, then president of the New York Federal Reserve Bank, the size and importance of the shadow banking system, combined with the lack of strict regulation, "made the crisis more difficult to manage."[16]

Ironically, the first major U.S. casualty was the venerable investment bank and securitization pioneer Bear Stearns. In March 2008, the Federal Reserve Bank of New York furnished Bear Stearns with an emergency loan to prevent its sudden collapse, but the writing was on the wall. Later that same month, JPMorgan Chase purchased the firm for a fraction of its previous market value.[17]

Meanwhile, the clock was ticking at Lehman Brothers. In September 2007, Lehman Brothers Holding Inc. had closed BNC Mortgage, its subprime mortgage lender, amid deteriorating market conditions. However, the bank was left in an exposed position due to billions of dollars worth of mortgage-backed securities that remained on its books. On September 15, 2008, Lehman Brothers Holdings Inc. filed for Chapter 11 bankruptcy protection after revealing it had become insolvent. It had bank debt of $613 billion and bond debt of $155 billion while assets totaled only $639 billion.[18]

Like its peers, brokerage house Merrill Lynch also suffered substantial losses due to unhedged subprime mortgage exposure. Despite the removal of CEO E. Stanley O'Neal for approaching Wachovia Bank about a merger without board approval,[19] Merrill Lynch lost $19.2 billion between July 2007 and July 2008 (an astounding $52 million per day).[20] New CEO John

Thain attempted to bail out the company by selling its commercial finance division to General Electric and selling stock and select hedge funds to Singapore investment group, Temasek Holdings, but the bank remained near collapse.[21] On September 15, the same day that Lehman Brothers filed for bankruptcy, Bank of America announced its intent to purchase Merrill Lynch for $50 billion, a 38 percent premium over current book value. (See Exhibit 14 for the level of diversification in 2009 after the Merrill Lynch acquisition.)[22]

The U.S. Financial Industry after the Meltdown

In the midst of the financial meltdown, Federal Reserve Chairman Ben Bernanke and Treasury Secretary Hank Paulson were essentially left with two choices, and neither was a good option. On the one hand, they could allow several more of the largest financial institutions in the world to fail, risking a global market collapse. Thousands of working Americans would lose their jobs, pensions, and investments, leading to a dramatic increase in unemployment as the failures rippled through the broader economy. Riots would have been likely in some of the larger U.S. cities, necessitating activation of the National Guard. If Wall Street tanked, repercussions on Main Street would be severe; this clearly was not an attractive choice.

EXHIBIT 14

Bank of America's Diversification Strategy in 2009

Source: Blamely, R. S., S. Griffin, Q. Makins, B. Rule, and D. Thompson (2010), "A strategic perspective on Bank of America," Georgia Institute of Technology.

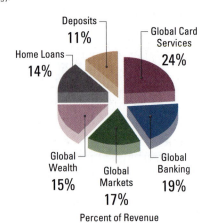

Deposits 11%
Global Card Services 24%
Home Loans 14%
Global Wealth 15%
Global Markets 17%
Global Banking 19%

Percent of Revenue

Or, the U.S. government could bail out the banks and work toward tighter regulatory controls in the future. This was more in line with Chairman Bernanke's promise to himself that he would not preside over a second Great Depression.

GOVERNMENT OWNERSHIP. While Main Street strongly opposed a "Wall Street bailout," it did support tighter bank regulations. Thus, during a seven-day period in early September 2008, the federal government took mortgage lenders Fannie Mae and Freddie Mac into conservatorship, which equates to national securitization. The financial markets viewed the move negatively, and financial stocks dropped 31 percent. Stocks fell further in October when President George W. Bush signed the $700 billion Troubled Asset Relief Program (TARP) into law. TARP was designed to stabilize the balance sheets of large financial institutions and to increase liquidity in short-term funding markets. The government's first action under TARP's capital purchase program was to buy $81 billion of preferred shares in seven banks (including Bank of America). Over the next five weeks, financial stocks collapsed, shedding 46 percent of their market value.[23] Many have since asked whether the bailout was necessary. By socializing losses while privatizing profits, was the government creating a moral hazard that promoted or even incentivized risk?

The U.S. government did not see itself as a long-term investor in bank equities, which helped to ease criticism of government ownership of financial institutions.[24] Thus in April 2010, the U.S. Treasury announced plans for the sale of 7.7 billion shares of common stock in Citigroup. (It had previously exchanged its $25 billion in preferred stock for common stock at a price of $3.25 per share.)[25] Many similar announcements followed throughout the rest of the year. In March 2011, after three more financial institutions repaid a total of $7.4 billion in borrowed funds, the Treasury announced that the TARP program had turned a profit.[26]

"NO MORE SHADOWS." In order to receive assistance under TARP, several of the remaining large investment banks, including Goldman Sachs and Morgan Stanley, as well as other shadow institutions like American Express, CIT Group, and General Motors Acceptance Corporation (GMAC), were forced to reorganize as bank holding companies.[27] As a result, TARP fundamentally altered the shadow banking system that had contributed so forcefully to the financial crisis. These firms now fall under the regulation of the Federal Reserve and therefore have a more limited exposure to risk. They are also now permitted to take consumer deposits.

THE END OF THE RECESSION. The National Bureau of Economic Research (NBER) defines a recession as "a significant decline in economic activity spread across the economy, lasting more than a few months, normally visible in real GDP, real income, employment, industrial production, and wholesale-retail sales. A recession begins just after the economy reaches a peak of activity and ends as the economy reaches its trough. Between trough and peak, the economy is in an expansion."[28] According to the NBER's business-cycle dating committee, the peak of the most recent recession occurred in December 2007 and concluded with a trough in June 2009, lasting for a total of 18 months. It was the longest recession experienced by the United States since World War II.[29]

NBER based its assessment on several statistics, including higher productivity, lower production costs, and increasing factor orders.[23] After bottoming out in June 2009, U.S. GDP grew 2.2 percent in the third quarter and increased at an annualized rate of 5.7 percent in the fourth quarter of 2009. GDP growth during the fourth quarter reflected an acceleration in private inventory investment, a deceleration in imports, and increased nonresidential investment. However, it was partially offset by decelerations in federal government spending and in personal consumption expenditures. In addition, the third quarter of 2009 saw worker productivity (amount of output per hour worked) increase at its highest rate (annualized 8.1 percent) in six years, beating Labor Department estimates, while labor costs shrunk by an annualized 2.5 percent. Meanwhile, the Commerce Department reported that factory orders for July 2009 increased for the fifth time in six months, gaining 1.3 percent. This gain was led by the strong performance of durable goods, in particular transportation goods, which surged 18.5 percent at least partially due to the federal government's Cash for Clunkers incentive program.[30]

Unemployment took somewhat longer to improve, reaching a high of 10.1 percent in October 2009 and hovering between 9 and 10 percent through the end of 2010 (Exhibit 15). Then, after several consecutive monthly drops, the national unemployment rate fell to a two-year low of 8.8 percent in March 2011. Most of

EXHIBIT 15

Seasonally Adjusted Unemployment Rates and Non-Farm Payroll Employment Change (Month over Month)

Source: U.S. Bureau of Labor Statistics, www.bls.gov/news.release/pdf/empsit.pdf.

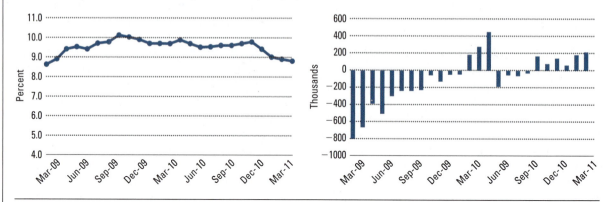

the 216,000 jobs created that month were in the private sector, offsetting job cuts by local governments, which were still experiencing financial difficulties.[31]

BANKS AS A LAGGING INDICATOR. Even as other indicators showed signs of recovery, the U.S. banking sector continued to lag. Just three banks were forced to close in 2007, compared with 25 in 2008. In 2009, an astonishing 140 banks were shuttered, leaving the FDIC's insurance fund at its lowest point in more than 15 years. Such a large number of bank failures had not occurred since the savings and loan crisis of the early 1990s.

At the time the recession technically ended (second quarter 2009), the FDIC had 416 banks on its "problem list," meaning they were undercapitalized or deficient in some way. Experts predicted another 100 to 300 banks, particularly small ones, could fail while the crisis ran its course.[24] In fact, conditions grew even worse in 2010 with 157 closures, and remained elevated through first quarter 2011, during which 26 bank failures occurred (Exhibit 16).

EXHIBIT 16

Yearly Bank Failures, 2000–2011

Source: FDIC, www2.fdic.gov/hsob/hsobRpt.asp.

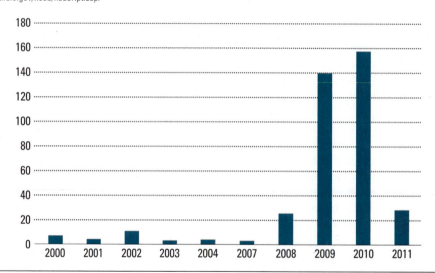

Unfortunately for many regional banks, the mantra "too big to fail" did not apply. They were too *small* to be bailed out, and thus became mass casualties of the financial meltdown. One of the most noteworthy failures was the regional commercial real-estate lending giant Colonial Bank, based in Montgomery, Alabama. With total deposits of $20 billion and assets of $22 billion as of mid-August 2009, Colonial was the sixth-largest bank failure in U.S. history. Its assets and deposits, along with its 346 branches, were sold to BB&T.[32] Overall, the dramatic rise in bank failures was attributed to defaults on commercial loans given to developers, many of whom simply walked away from projects as demand dried up. Another potent contributor was rising default rates on traditional prime mortgages, driven by the increase in unemployment.

Bank of America after the Crisis

As the financial situation regained its footing, Bank of America's senior management came under heavy fire for decisions made during the crisis. Serious questions were raised regarding the role played by the Federal Reserve in Bank of America's acquisition of Merrill Lynch.

CRISIS CLEAN-UP. An April 2009 report by New York Attorney General Andrew Cuomo alleged that federal officials, namely former Treasury Secretary Hank Paulson and Federal Reserve Chairman Ben Bernanke, pressured CEO Ken Lewis into proceeding with the merger without disclosing significant losses the brokerage was carrying on its books. Lewis's concerns proved to be valid when it was ultimately revealed that Merrill Lynch's fourth-quarter losses topped $15 billion.[33] Concerned about the viability and value of the merger, stockholders voted (narrowly) to replace Ken Lewis as chairman of the board of directors, but allowed him to remain as CEO for the time being.

Outraged Bank of America shareholders also questioned the large bonus pool paid at Merrill Lynch, despite the $27.6 billion in losses incurred by the firm in 2008. In all, the Merrill Lynch compensation committee approved $3.6 billion in bonus payments only three days after Bank of America shareholders approved the merger. Bonus payments were made just one day prior to the deal becoming effective.[34] Under questioning from federal investigators, former Merrill Lynch CEO John Thain claimed that Bank of America, and Ken Lewis in particular, were fully aware of the incentive-compensation plan in place when the bank purchased the floundering brokerage firm, effective January 1, 2009. This contradicted Lewis's testimony to the House Financial Services Committee on February 11, 2009, when he claimed to have very little involvement in the Merrill Lynch bonus plan.

The SEC also took notice and launched an investigation to determine whether Bank of America's management misled shareholders prior to the December 2008 meeting in which the merger was approved. In August 2009, the SEC filed a civil suit in U.S. District Court for the Southern District of New York, claiming that proxy documents mailed to shareholders failed to disclose Bank of America's prior agreement with Merrill Lynch authorizing the payment of billions of dollars in year-end bonuses prior to the close of the merger. Then in January 2010, the SEC filed a second charge that Bank of America failed to disclose to shareholders the extraordinary losses incurred by Merrill Lynch in the fourth quarter of 2008.

Bank of America denied any wrongdoing but agreed to a settlement that stipulated payment of $150 million to shareholders harmed by the disclosure violations. The bank also had to promise to adhere for the next three years to a series of remedial actions designed to improve its corporate governance with respect to executive compensation and financial transparency.[35]

EXECUTIVE SHAKEUP. The year following the Merrill Lynch merger saw a massive shakeup of the executive leadership at Bank of America. Starting in early August, several members of the guiding team left and were replaced by fresh faces. According to the official press release, the changes were meant to "enhance future success at the company."[36] Brian Moynihan, former head of Global Corporate and Investment Banking (GCIB) replaced Liam McGee, a 20-year Bank of America veteran, as head of Consumer Banking. Tom Montag took over responsibility for GCIB from Moynihan in addition to his role as head of Global Markets.

The largest news-grabber, however, was the addition of Sallie Krawcheck as head of Global Wealth and Investment Management. Ms. Krawcheck has a long and accomplished resume and is widely regarded as one of the most powerful women in business. Before moving to Bank of America, she rose from her position as an equity analyst to CEO of research firm Sanford C. Bernstein & Co. She subsequently served as CFO and head of strategy for Citigroup. Most recently, she served as CEO in charge of Smith Barney and the Citi Private Bank, Citigroup's wealth-management businesses. Bank of America expected big things from the addition of Ms. Krawcheck. Upon her hiring, Ken Lewis stated, "She is acknowledged to be one of the premier executives in the wealth-management industry. Her experience and perspective will lead that business to the next level."[31]

The biggest change came at the end of September 2009 when CEO Lewis announced that he would leave the company at the end of the year.[37] Those close to the decision said that Lewis had grown weary of the criticism surrounding the Merrill Lynch acquisition. Those sources said the decision was solely Lewis's and that he was under no pressure from the board of directors or government officials. "The Merrill Lynch and Countrywide integrations are on track and returning value already," said Lewis in his official statement. "Our board of directors and our senior management include more talent, and more diversity of talent, than at any time in this company's history. We are in position to begin to repay the federal government's TARP investments. For these reasons, I decided now is the time to begin to transition to the next generation of leadership at Bank of America." In January 2010, the bank's board named Brian Moynihan as Lewis's successor as CEO. Moynihan inherited a bank with 280,000 employees that was active in more than 180 countries across the globe.

TARP FUNDS. In June 2009, 10 banks repurchased a combined $68 billion worth of preferred stock that the government had purchased from the banks under TARP to inject capital into the banking system. Included among the ten were major rivals JPMorgan Chase, Morgan Stanley, and Goldman Sachs Group. The repayment was in direct response to government "stress tests" of 19 of the nation's largest financial institutions, a test that large banks like Wells Fargo, Citigroup, and Bank of America failed.[38]

Eager to restore some luster to its tarnished image, Bank of America announced the complete repayment of its own $45 million in TARP funds on December 9, 2009. Despite the fact that the bank lagged behind several of its major competitors in this regard, CEO Lewis looked positively toward the future: "We owe taxpayers our thanks for making these funds available to the nation's financial system and to our company during a very difficult time," said Lewis. "Now that we have cleared this significant hurdle, which demonstrates the strength of our company, we look forward to continuing to play a key role in the economic recovery and helping to meet the changing needs of our customers and clients."[39]

Critics were a bit less optimistic, however. An analyst cited by huffingtonpost.com argued that the timing was too soon, given the number of delinquent loans that were likely to default in the near future. Using $26 billion in extra cash to pay back TARP funds at the same time the Federal Reserve was in the process of withdrawing other subsidies for large banks was also likely to leave Bank of America in a weak cash position.[40] Others argued that the payback was a mere sleight of hand designed to allow Lewis to take a "victory lap"[41] before stepping down as CEO. Bank of America continued to take advantage of low-interest loans from the federal government that did not have any of the restrictions that TARP funds did.[42]

BUSINESS OUTLOOK. In 2008, analysts estimated that U.S. property owners lost $3.3 trillion in housing value and that one in six Americans owed more than their homes were worth.[43] Unfortunately for homeowners and the banks holding their mortgages, the real estate market continued to struggle even after the technical end of the recession in June 2009. Due to its acquisition of mortgage-lending giant Countrywide Financial, Bank of America had become the leading servicer of mortgages in the United States. This left the bank vulnerable as struggling homeowners continued to abandon their properties at unprecedented rates.

In July 2009, Bank of America reached a settlement with the Attorneys General of 40 states to start three programs aimed at relieving homeowners' financial distress. The Foreclosure Relief Program provided $150 million in assistance for certain borrowers who experienced a foreclosure, short sale, or deed-in-lieu of foreclosure on mortgages originated by Countrywide. The second initiative, the National Homeownership Retention Program, was aimed at creating affordable and sustainable mortgage payments for 400,000 homebuyers who financed their purchases with subprime or adjustable-rate mortgages serviced by Countrywide. The third component provided cash assistance for individuals subject to a foreclosure sale who vacated their property voluntarily.

In its 2010 Annual Report, Bank of America reported that it had modified nearly 775,000 mortgages since January 2008. It had also reached an agreement to pay $2.8 billion to Freddie Mac and

Fannie Mae to resolve claims related to mortgages they had purchased from Countrywide and its affiliates. Despite these positive steps, Bank of America was not yet out of the "mortgage woods": The housing market remained weak throughout 2010, with house prices showing a downward trend in the second half of the year.[44]

However, the Merrill Lynch acquisition was starting to look up. According to an April 2010 article in *The Economist* magazine, attrition at Bank of America and Merrill Lynch's combined investment banking operations had slowed considerably.[45] New management that was brought in to refresh the firm seemed to be having the desired effect. Overall the bank earned $3.2 billion in the first quarter of 2010, driven mostly by a reduction in provisions for credit losses and strength in the capital markets. Thus, while some things were improving, Bank of America still had a long way to go toward full financial recovery.

Management's Challenge

In Stephanie Milner's conference room, consensus is easy to achieve on one point: Executive management is ready to get the bank back on track to profitability. However, many obstacles stand in the way. First and foremost are the many challenges that come with the merging of any large organizations. Bank of America's case is even more complicated because it is integrating two distinct entities at the same time, both of which were failing when the bank assumed control. Each has a significant amount of "baggage" that needs to be sorted through in order to clear a path toward a better future. Bank of America's Home Retention program represents a significant effort to undo the negative aspects of Countrywide's legacy, but how much longer will the past continue to haunt the bank's financial statements? Major competitors like JPMorgan Chase and Morgan Stanley were able to pay back their TARP funds and put the financial crisis behind them much more quickly. Bank of America cannot afford to fall behind. (See Exhibit 17 for a revenue and net income comparison among major competitors.)

Then there is the question of what integration should look like—which activities should stay, which should be spun off, and what redundancies should be eliminated? The longer it takes Bank of America to sort out these issues, the more likely it is to lose star talent to other firms, especially as the financial sector perks back up. Should the bank go with a single brand and

EXHIBIT 17

Revenue and Net Income of Major U.S. Banks, 2005–2009

Source: Blamely, R. S., S. Griffin, Q. Makins, B. Rule, and D. Thompson (2010), "A strategic perspective on Bank of America," Georgia Institute of Technology.

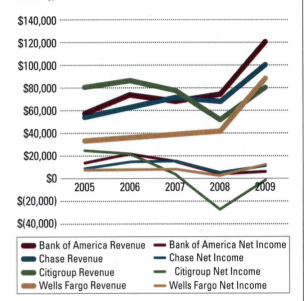

image, or take advantage of the equity that remains in the Merrill Lynch name? (Letting go of Countrywide seems to be a foregone conclusion.) One of the attractive aspects of Merrill Lynch is its international presence and the promise it holds for global expansion. Will foreign countries embrace the bank as readily if it renames Merrill Lynch's worldwide operations as Bank of America?

As the bank continues to grow in the future, what competencies should it rely on? Historically, Bank of America has been known for its willingness to innovate and push the boundaries of banking technology. The bank led the way in online banking, including advanced bill-payment options for customers, mobile-banking applications for smartphones, and ATM technology that can accept deposits without envelopes, scan and recognize checks, and count cash. Bank of America has also developed a reputation for developing class-leading, customer-oriented promotions and services, such as its "Keep the Change" and "Privacy Assist" programs (see Exhibits 18 and 19). Should innovation and service continue to be the building blocks of its future competitive advantage, or have the changes brought about by the financial crisis rendered them less effective going forward? How could these

EXHIBIT 18

Bank of America's Ranking in the Fortune 500

Source: Blamely, R. S., S. Griffin, Q. Makins, B. Rule, and D. Thompson (2010). "A strategic perspective on Bank of America," Georgia Institute of Technology.

Rank	Company	Overall Score
1	**Bank of America**	6.69
2	JPMorgan Chase	6.53
2	Credit Suisse Group	6.53
4	Wells Fargo	6.38
5	Deutsche Bank	6.03
6	ING Group	5.63
7	BNP Paribas	4.89

EXHIBIT 19

Bank of America's Fortune 500 Ranking by Attribute

Source: Blamely, R. S., S. Griffin, Q. Makins, B. Rule, and D. Thompson (2010), "A strategic perspective on Bank of America," Georgia Institute of Technology.

Nine Key Attributes of Industry Reputation	Rank
Innovation	1
Social responsibility	1
Quality of products/services	1
People management	2
Quality of management	2
Long term investment	2
Use of corporate assets	4
Financial soundness	4
Global competitiveness	10

strengths be combined with what Merrill Lynch and Countrywide have to offer?

Further, how should the company grow in the future? In the past, Bank of America has displayed a steady appetite for acquisitions, making it the mammoth financial institution it is today. But how big is too big, and how can a firm know when it has reached that threshold? With the number of annual bank failures still quite high, plenty of acquisition targets exist, but do their discounted prices merit taking on even more financial distress? How healthy does Bank of America have to be in order to consider additional purchases?

Finally, in order to avoid repeating previous mistakes, Bank of America needs to understand how Merrill Lynch and Countrywide got themselves into such precarious financial positions in the first place. What risk-management mechanisms were in place to prevent such massive losses, and why were they ineffective? Was the financial crisis created by good people making bad decisions at an inopportune time? Or were the people themselves to blame? To what extent did corporate strategy and compensation incentives promote unnecessary risk-taking? And most importantly, how can situations like the 2008 financial crisis be avoided in the future?

Stephanie Milner and the rest of the team must assess all of these issues and draft a set of recommendations to help guide future strategy development. Their recommendations need to address weaknesses in past strategy that may have contributed to the crisis at each firm (Bank of America, Countrywide, and Merrill Lynch). In addition, they need to discuss how Bank of America can harness the inherent strengths of the legacy firms and build a stronger, more financially secure organization. The group begins to work.

Endnotes

1. "Top 50 Bank Holding Companies," United States Federal Reserve System, National Information Center.

2. Dash, E., L. Story, and A. R. Sorkin (2009), "Bank of America to receive additional $20 billion," *The New York Times,* January 15.

3. Board of Governors of the Federal Reserve Board System, press release, January 16, 2009, www.federalreserve.gov/news-events/press/bcreg/20090116a.htm.

4. Robb, G. (2009), "Bernanke declares 'recession is very likely over,'" MarketWatch, *The Wall Street Journal,* September 15.

5. Bank of America Online Heritage Center; http://newsroom.bankofamerica.com/heritagecenter/.

6. "U.S. banking mega-merger unveiled," BBC World News. October 27, 2003.

7. Henderson, T. (2008), "BOA to 'paint the town red' with LaSalle name change," *Crain's Detroit Business,* April 14.

8. Bauerlein, V, and J. R. Hagerty (2008), "Behind Bank of America's big gamble," *The Wall Street Journal,* January 12, 2008.

9. "Three top economists agree 2009 worst financial crisis since Great Depression; risks increase if right steps are not taken," Reuters, February 27, 2009.

10. Krugman, P. (2009), "Revenge of the glut," *The New York Times,* March 1.

11. Steverman, B, and D. Bogoslaw (2008), "The financial crisis blame game," *BusinessWeek.com,* October 18.

12. Asset-Backed Security, www.investopedia.com.

13. Mongoose, D., "Collateralized debt obligations: from boon to burden," *Investopedia.com.*

14. Barr, A. (2008), "Brokers threatened by run on shadow bank system," MarketWatch, *The Wall Street Journal,* June 20.

15. Greenspan, A. (2009), "We need a better cushion against risk," *Financial Times,* March 26.

16. Barr, A. (2008), "Brokers threatened by run on shadow bank system."

17. Onaran, Y. (2008), "Fed aided Bear Stearns as firm faced Chapter 11, Bernanke says," *Bloomberg.com.* April 2.

18. Mamudi, S. (2008), "Lehman folds with record $613 billion debt," MarketWatch, *The Wall Street Journal,* September 15.

19. Anderson, J., and L. Thomas Jr. (2007), "NYSE chief is chosen to lead Merrill Lynch," *The New York Times,* November 15.

20. Story, L. (2008), "Chief struggles to revive Merrill Lynch," *The New York Times,* July 18.

21. Dash, E. (2007), "Merrill Lynch sells stake to Singapore firm," *The New York Times,* December 25.

22. Moyer, L. (2008), "They all fall down," *Newsweek,* September 15.

23. Reynolds, A. (2009), "The government's influence on the stock market," Forbes.com, March 25.

24. Crutsinger, M. (2010), "Treasury plans first Citigroup stock sale," *Washingtontimes.com,* April 26.

25. www.treasury.gov/press-center/press-releases/Pages/tg660.aspx.

26. www.treasury.gov/press-center/press-releases/Pages/tg1121.aspx.

27. "Fed approves GMAC bank request in boost for GM," AFP, December 24, 2008.

28. Business Cycle Dating Committee, NBER, www.nber.org/cycles/recessions.html.

29. www.nber.org/cycles/sept2010.html.

30. "Who needs more workers?" *The Economist,* September 3, 2009.

31. www.bbc.co.uk/news/business-12935003.

32. Pepitone, J. "Bank failures stack up: now 106 for 2009," *CNNMoney.com,* October 23, 2009.

33. Wingfield, B. (2009), "Did Bernanke bully B of A?" *Forbes.com*, April 23.

34. Fitzpatrick, D. and K. Scannell (2009), "B of A denies misleading its investors on bonuses," *The Wall Street Journal,* August 25.

35. www.sec.gov/litigation/litreleases/2010/lr21407.htm.

36. Bank of America Online Newsroom,August 3, 2009. http://newsroom.bankofamerica.com.

37. "Ken Lewis announces his retirement," *Nasdaq.com*, PRNewswire September 30, 2009.

38. "Ten banks allowed to repay $68 billion to the TARP fund," CNBC, June 9, 2009.

39. http://mediaroom.bankofamerica.com/phoenix.zhtml?c=234503&p=irol-newsArticle&ID=1390319&highlight=.

40. www.huffingtonpost.com/2009/12/04/bank-of-america-tarp-repa_n_380776.html.

41. Ibid.

42. http://consumerist.com/2009/12/why-bank-of-americas-tarp-payback-is-bad-news.html.

43. Levy, D. (2009), "U.S. property owners lost $3.3 trillion in home value," *Bloomberg.com,* February 3.

44. 2010 Annual Report, http://media.corporate-ir.net/media_files/irol/71/71595/reports/2010_AR.pdf.

45. "Might the most controversial deal of the financial crisis pay off after all?" *The Economist,* April 14, 2010.

The mystique of natural diamonds has been built by the industry. One hundred fifty million carats of mined diamonds are produced every year, so they are really not that special if you look at those terms.[1]

—CEO OF GEMESIS CORPORATION

We don't see synthetic diamonds as a threat, but you cannot ignore it completely.[2]

—STUART BROWN, FINANCE DIRECTOR, DE BEERS

David McAdams
Cate Reavis

T WAS EARLY summer 2007 and Lee Mandell decided that the time was right to propose to Diane, his girlfriend of four years. Being the romantic he was, Lee wanted to pop the question over a candlelight dinner that included an exceptional bottle of Bordeaux. Logistical details of where to buy the special ring and what type of diamond, however, were less certain in his mind.

Lee and Diane had recently rented the movie *Blood Diamond*, set in Sierra Leone in the 1990s when a civil war was raging and the rebel group, the Revolutionary United Front, relied on proceeds from smuggled diamonds to finance its military operation. The 11-year war, which ended in 2002, resulted in the deaths of tens of thousands and the displacement of more than 2 million people, nearly one-third of the country's population. Both Diane and Lee had been disturbed by the story the movie told, the hardship and violence, the children who were forcibly recruited to fight, and the lives that were destroyed all over gems that were worn by hundreds of millions of people, men and women alike, throughout the world.

As he thought about his options, Lee recalled a magazine article he had recently read about the growing market for synthetic diamonds. The article described the process by which diamonds could be grown in a laboratory environment, far from the war-torn lands of Africa. Chemically, lab-grown diamonds were identical to diamonds that were extracted from the ground. Instead of taking millions or billions of years to form, hundreds of miles underground,

however, a laboratory environment could produce a flawless diamond within days.

Lee was starting to think that a synthetic diamond was a great alternative. But how would Diane react upon learning he had bought her a diamond that was made in a laboratory just outside of Boston? Would she be relieved and touched by his humanitarian and eco-friendly purchase or would she wonder if the 20% to 40% he would save by buying a synthetic diamond was an indication of the depth of his love?

For producers of synthetic diamonds, it was consumers like Lee Mandell that proved there was a market demand for an alternative to the natural diamond. But for South Africa-based De Beers, which up until the late 1990s single-handedly controlled the world's supply of diamonds, Lee's rationale was misguided and he was giving his girlfriend nothing more than costume jewelry. Nevertheless, the fact of the matter was that people were buying lab-produced diamonds and the number doing so was growing at a faster rate than those buying those extracted from the ground.

The dilemma that De Beers faced came down to whether it should enter the market with its own synthetic diamonds or whether it should have faith that synthetics would be a passing fad and that, at the end of the day, consumers would always prefer buying what,

This case was prepared by Cate Reavis under the supervision of Professor David McAdams. Professor McAdams is the Cecil and Ida Green Career Development Professor. The case was developed at the MIT Sloan School of Management.

in De Beers's mind, was the real thing. Complicating the company's dilemma, however, was the fact that it was in the midst of trying to remake its image, tarnished from decades of anti-competitive business practices, to one that was demand driven and focused on brand development. While De Beers at one time produced 45% of the world's rough diamonds and sold 80% of the total supply, by 2007 it was producing 40% and selling just 45%.[3]

Did synthetic diamonds in fact pose a threat to the diamond industry and if so, what should De Beers's response be if any?

The Diamond Industry

Natural diamonds, the hardest, most transparent material in existence, were made of carbon atoms that over the course of millions of years and with tremendous heat and pressure deep under the earth's surface bonded into a cubic structure.[4] Due to their heterogeneity, unlike gold or silver, diamonds were not considered a commodity. As one diamond trader explained, "When you talk about commodities, you know that a ton of copper is worth this much, and an ounce of gold is worth this much because they are homogenous. But diamonds are not homogenous."[5]

SUPPLY. The global diamond industry produced an estimated $13 billion of rough stones and $62 billion in jewelry annually. Between 2000 and 2005, world production of diamond rough grew 31% by volume and 70% by value, highlighting the upward trend of diamond prices (Figures 1 and 2).

Seven countries—Angola, Australia, Botswana, Canada, the Democratic Republic of the Congo, Russia, and South Africa—represented 88% of the value of diamond production and 96% of global production volume.[6] As depicted in Figure 3, for some producers, there was great disparity in the relationship between the volume and value of production. While the Congo and Australia were significant producers on a volume basis, the value of their production was quite low. Angola presented the reverse scenario.

CHANGE IN INDUSTRY STRUCTURE. The $19 billion processing industry (which involved the cutting and polishing of diamonds) was dominated by India. The 1 million people employed by India's processing industry processed more than half of the world's diamonds in value terms, at costs significantly lower than other processing countries—$10 per carat as opposed to $17/carat in China, $40/carat in South Africa and Israel and $70/carat in Belgium. Israel and China were the second and third largest processors with 15% and 10% of the market, respectively.[7] But this part of the value chain, at one time dominated almost exclusively by Belgium and Israel, was undergoing significant changes.[8]

Since the late 1990s, empowered by De Beers's shrinking market position, the voices from Southern African countries to keep more of the value added activities such as cutting and polishing in country had become noticeably louder and a number of countries were amending their diamond laws to support and build local diamond-related industries. In 1999, Namibia inserted a clause in a new law permitting the government to force miners to sell a percentage of their diamonds to local polishers,[9] and in 2004, Lev Leviev, an Israeli of Uzbek decent who was one of Israel's largest manufacturers of polished stones, opened the country's first cutting and polishing factory. At the opening of the new factory, Namibia's president was quoted as saying, "To our brothers and sisters of neighboring states, Angola, Botswana, South Africa, I hope that this gives you inspiration to try to imitate what we have here."[10] In 2005, South Africa passed the Diamonds Amendment Act establishing a State Diamond Trader

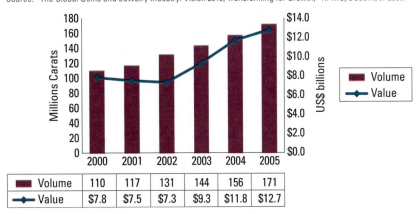

FIGURE 1

Diamond Rough Production by Volume and Value (2000–2005)

Source: "The Global Gems and Jewelry Industry: Vision 2015; Transforming for Growth," KPMG, December 2006.

	2000	2001	2002	2003	2004	2005
Volume	110	117	131	144	156	171
Value	$7.8	$7.5	$7.3	$9.3	$11.8	$12.7

FIGURE 2

Diamond Rough Prices, 1996–2005

Source: "The Global Gems and Jewelry Industry: Vision 2015; Transforming for Growth," KPMG, December 2006.

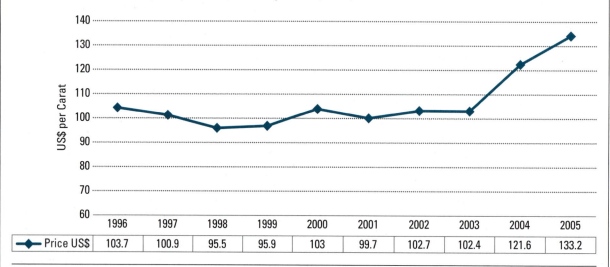

	1996	1997	1998	1999	2000	2001	2002	2003	2004	2005
Price US$	103.7	100.9	95.5	95.9	103	99.7	102.7	102.4	121.6	133.2

FIGURE 3

Top Diamond Producers by Volume and Value

Source: "The Global Gems and Jewelry Industry: Vision 2015; Transforming for Growth," KPMG, December 2006.

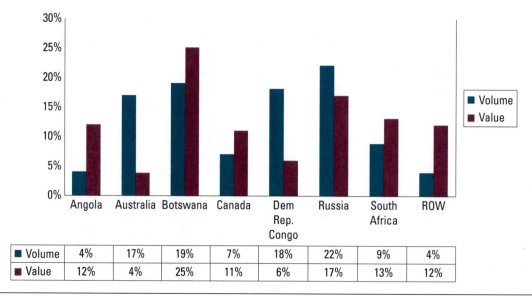

	Angola	Australia	Botswana	Canada	Dem Rep. Congo	Russia	South Africa	ROW
Volume	4%	17%	19%	7%	18%	22%	9%	4%
Value	12%	4%	25%	11%	6%	17%	13%	12%

as well as a Diamonds and Precious Metals Regulator. Under the new legislation, scheduled to take effect in 2007, producers would be hit with duties on exported rough diamonds.[11] In response to Southern Africa's attempts to enter into more downstream activities, one industry expert remarked, "There's a political and an emotional point. [Africa] is saying, 'We have these resources as Africans, why are we not able to capitalize on the beneficiation on these resources in our possession? Why are Indians cutting African diamonds?'"[12]

Alongside shifts in the value chain, the industry was experiencing an increasing level of forward and backward integration: mines were integrating forward into retail and retail outlets were integrating backward by investing in mines. In 1999, high-end jeweler Tiffany & Co. announced that it was buying a stake in a Canadian mining concern for $104 million and would no longer source its diamonds through De Beers. In 2003, Aber Diamond, a Canadian mining group, purchased U.S. luxury jewelry retailer Harry Winston giving it storefronts in the United States, Japan and Switzerland.[13] In 2005, Russia's mining giant Alrosa opened up a diamond retail store in a shopping complex off Red Square.[14] As De Beers's CEO remarked, "The verticalization of the industry is clearly its long-term trend; it's absolutely the way to grow a business and build a brand. Retail clearly adds value. But there are several different kinds of know-how involved in the different levels of the chain and you have to respect, and learn, all of them."[15]

DEMAND. The United States was far and away the world's biggest purchaser of diamonds accounting for 46% of total demand followed by the Middle East with 12% and Japan with 9% (Figure 4). However, demand, particularly for diamonds over 2 carats (worth $15,000 or more), was soaring in India and China[16] in concert with increasing disposable incomes and a growing middle class. India was the fastest growing diamond jewelry market with a growth rate of 19% in 2005.

While at one time the diamond industry was supply-side driven, with little attention given to the end consumer, by the late 1990s the industry began focusing more on the demand side. The main catalyst for this shift was De Beers's decision to conduct business in a whole new way.

De Beers under Attack

In the early 1990s De Beers ruled the diamond industry. While it only produced 45% of the world's rough diamonds, it sold 80% of the total supply from its marketing unit in London. Its market dominance enabled its Central Selling Organization to choose whom to sell

FIGURE 4

World Sales of Diamonds, 2005 (polished wholesale price)

Source: "The Global Gems and Jewelry Industry: Vision 2015; Transforming for Growth," KPMG, December 2006.

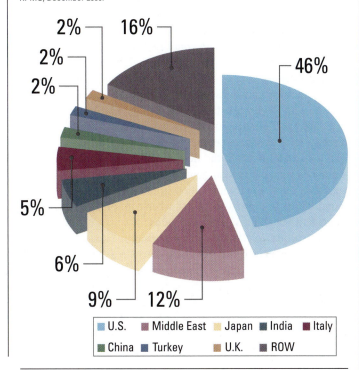

to, how much to sell, and at what price. Buyers who turned down an offer to purchase a parcel of diamonds might not be invited to purchase from De Beers again. Meanwhile, buyers who strayed from De Beers's selling arm and purchased directly from a mine would be dropped by the company or financially punished.[17] In 1981, after Zaire decided to stop selling its industrial-grade diamonds to the syndicate, De Beers dipped into its stockpile and flooded the market bringing down the price of Zairian diamonds by 40%.[18]

De Beers's monopoly was shaken in the 1990s by the emergence of three producers that fell outside of its grasp, making its strategy of controlling supply costly both financially and legally. The first big hit came shortly after the collapse of the Soviet Union in 1991. Through a marketing agreement that dated back to the late 1950s when diamond deposits were first discovered in Siberia, the Soviets had sold their entire diamond production to De Beers's Central Selling Organization. Once the Soviet system disintegrated, however, De Beers was unable to enforce contracts and Russian diamonds were soon being smuggled onto the international market causing prices to fall.

But De Beers' challenges in Russia could not be blamed solely on the country's economic and political upheaval. Lev Leviev, one of Israel's largest manufacturers of polished stones, was making his move in Russia where he was well connected politically. In 1989, two years after Leviev became a sightholder for De Beers, Russia's state-run diamond mining and trading group, now known as Alrosa, entered into a joint venture with Leviev to establish the country's first cutting factory, the stones of which would be supplied directly by Russian mines, not through De Beers.[19] The partnership marked the first time in which rough diamonds were cut in their country of origin. Over the next five years, Leviev's position in the Russian diamond industry grew to the point where, in 1995, De Beers terminated his sightholder status.[20]

The second jolt to De Beers's position came in 1996 with the decision by Australia's Argyle diamond mine, which produced low quality diamonds suitable for inexpensive jewelry, to terminate its contract with De Beers and begin marketing its own diamonds. It sold 42 million carats directly to polishers in Antwerp that year.[21]

Finally, the emergence of Canada in the early 1990s as a diamond producer served as a further threat to De Beers's position. While the company was successful in acquiring stakes in a couple of Canadian mines, the majority of the country's production fell outside of its control.

In order to keep prices high, and therefore safeguard its market dominance, De Beers was forced to both hold back a large portion of its diamonds from the market and purchase much of the excess supply from these producing countries often at inflated prices. By the end of the 1990s, De Beers's market share had fallen from 85% to 65% while its diamond stockpile had grown from $2.5 billion to $5 billion. Between December 1989 and 1998 De Beers's share price fell from $17 to $12, a nearly 30% drop.[22]

In addition to the financial sting De Beers was feeling resulting from its supply-side strategy, antitrust regulators in the United States and the European Union were becoming increasingly aggressive in their attempts to formally end the company's price control practices. In a 1994 indictment, the United States accused De Beers of violating the Sherman Antitrust Act by fixing the price of industrial diamonds. The government contended that a subsidiary of De Beers conspired with General Electric, another producer of industrial diamond products, to fix the world prices of industrial diamonds in 1991 and 1992. While the United States Justice Department was unable to prosecute De Beers because its operations were overseas and it refused to subject itself to the jurisdiction of an American court, the company was prohibited from conducting business in the United States.

On a completely different front, De Beers faced yet another threat, which was quickly turning into a public relations nightmare for the entire diamond industry. In the mid-1990s, Angola, the world's third largest producer of rough diamonds, was overrun by rebel forces opposed to President Dos Santos. Gaining control of the country's diamond supplies, the rebels flooded the market with up to $1.2 billion worth of rough diamonds. To maintain control over supply, and therefore prices, De Beers had little choice but to buy what were becoming known as "blood diamonds," the proceeds of which went toward financing the armed conflict. Angola was not a lone participant in the blood diamond trade. Rebel forces in Sierra Leone, Liberia, and the Democratic Republic of the Congo were also using the illicit diamond trade to finance their respective armed conflicts.

De Beers's involvement in the "blood diamond" trade was exposed in a 1998 report by Global Witness which accused the company of "operat[ing] with an extraordinary lack of accountability."[23] As Martin Rapaport, publisher of the diamond industry pricing guide, asked rhetorically, "How can it be that tens of millions of dollars are exported from diamond areas and yet there is no electricity, no plumbing, no wells, no improvement in the lives of the people?" Rapaport went on to ask the more complicated question, "Do we owe anything to the people of Africa just because we buy their diamonds? Are we responsible for what we buy?"[24]

For De Beers, these challenges and threats in aggregate were creating a "perfect storm" of sorts. Significant changes to the company's strategy that had served it well for decades had to be made.

A NEW DIRECTION. In 1998, on the advice of U.S. consulting firm Bain and Company, De Beers decided to "ditch its role of buyer of last resort" and develop a strategy that was demand-driven and brand-focused whereby profits were more important than market share.[25] When explaining its strategic shift, De Beers's Managing Director stated, "We don't have to go rushing about the world trying to buy every diamond. What is the point of us buying diamonds close to or over our selling prices? It's silly. I'm perfectly happy to market 60%. What I want to do is differentiate the portion that does come to us and create value on those goods . . . in order to sell them first, more advantageously, and at better prices."[26]

As a part of its strategy, De Beers ended its practice of stockpiling diamonds, stopped buying diamonds on the open market, and began only selling diamonds from its own operations which enabled it to guarantee that its supply was "conflict free." The company promised the European Union it would stop buying diamonds from Alrosa, the state-owned Russian firm that accounted for 20% of global production by 2009 to promote competition.[27] The promise was formalized in a 2006 agreement with Russia.

A new demand-centered strategy required that De Beers build new relationships with its suppliers. This came about in what was dubbed the "Supplier of Choice" program, the goal of which was to make De Beers the supplier of choice in the eyes of its customers, in lieu of the buyer of last resort. De Beers scaled down the number of its sightholders from 120 to 80 and formalized business relationships with those that were chosen with a written contract.[28] Sightholders were no longer expected to purchase whatever stones De Beers offered to them. Rather, they requested a specific package of stones based on sales and marketing strategies they had created.[29] The criteria to being a sightholder were no longer based on financial strength and manufacturing capabilities but rather marketing savvy.

Under the new arrangement, sightholders were entitled to use De Beers's Forevermark, a tiny logo that was etched into natural diamonds which guaranteed the polished diamonds were natural, ethically traded and non-treated. (The Forevermark diamond was sold in Hong Kong, China, Japan, and India.) Sightholders also benefited from De Beers's marketing data including consumer buying habits and patterns and the number of engagements worldwide. Those sightholders that successfully built strong brands were partially reimbursed for the money they spent on advertising and marketing efforts. As Nicky Oppenheimer, De Beers's Chairman, explained, "We want people to say, 'While I can get diamonds from people other than De Beers, the package De Beers gives me is so valuable, I get a better return from them.'"[30] Accompanying De Beers' efforts at building a new identity, the company's Central Selling Organization was renamed the Diamond Trading Company (DTC).

In step with the Supplier of Choice Program, De Beers developed a marketing and retail strategy to position its diamonds as a branded luxury item. Unlike other luxury brand producers, diamond producers had suffered from poor financial performance over the years due to the lack of branding. In fact, many in the industry lamented that although not traded as one, diamonds had become a commodity of sorts. Lev Leviev implied that De Beers was largely responsible: "There are two main reasons why diamond retailers fail. Lack of innovation—they have the same stones in the same settings in the window year after year—and dependence on one supplier for their stones. You can never plan your sales even one year ahead, because you can only work with what they give you, and they decide."[31]

A Boston-based diamond wholesaler, however, had proven that branding diamonds could work, especially since the market was shifting to a demand-driven model. In 1997, the wholesaler, who sourced his raw stones from De Beers sightholders and others, began selling a branded diamond called Hearts on Fire which was differentiated by its cut. Marketed as "the world's most perfectly cut diamond," the diamonds were cut by hand in Antwerp, Belgium in a pattern known as "hearts and arrows." When viewed under magnification, each diamond revealed a symmetrical ring of hearts and eight pointed arrows.[32] The brand produced $40 million in sales each year. In 1999, De Beers entered into the brand world by marketing a limited-edition (20,000 stones) Millennium diamond, engraved with the company's logo and the year 2000. The Millennuim diamond's campaign came with a tag line of, "Show her you'll love her for the next thousand years."

De Beers's brand positioning was accompanied by attempts to widen its customer base. A number of non-wedding advertisement campaigns were launched including the "Celebrate Her" campaign which urged men to show their love for their significant other by buying her a three-stone diamond ring. The campaigns' advertisement pictured a middle-aged man on bended knee asking, "Will you marry me again?" There was the "Women of the World Raise Your Right Hand" campaign which encouraged women to indulge in a diamond ring to be worn on their right hand as an expression of personal style.[33] In addition to new messages enticing consumers to buy diamonds for purposes other than engagements, in 2001, De Beers entered into a joint venture with LVMH to open up a series of retail stores. Diamond jewelry was sold under the De Beers name. By early 2007, De Beers had 22 stores spanning the United States (3), Europe (4), the Middle East (1), and Asia (14).

From Public to Private

At the same time the new strategy was being rolled out, De Beers delisted from the Johannesburg Stock Exchange where it had traded since 1893. Purchased by a consortium that included the Oppenheimer family, Anglo American plc, and Debswana Diamond Co. (Pty) Ltd, De Beers became the world's largest private diamond mining company. The privatization, which cost $17.6 billion (a 31% premium)[34] left De Beers heavily in debt. Ironically, the terrorist attacks in the United States on September 11, 2001 helped alleviate the company's debt. As De Beers's Chairman Nicky Oppenheimer explained, "Sentiment changed dramatically after September 11, though we did not realize it at the time. There was a swing back to traditional values such as family and all the sorts of things that diamond jewelry plays into."[35]

One of De Beers's first major media grabbing acts as a private company came in 2004 when it pleaded guilty to charges of price-fixing of industrial diamonds and agreed to pay a $10 million fine. Settling the 10-year-old charges meant that De Beers executives could visit and conduct business in the United States. In 2005, the company agreed to pay $250 million to settle a class action suit by diamond consumers who accused the company of monopolizing the international diamond business through its control of mines and agreements with diamond suppliers around the world.

In 2006, De Beers made another surprising move when it signed an agreement with the Botswana government to establish the Diamond Trading Company Botswana. The 50:50 joint venture would start sorting and valuing all of the diamond production of Debswana (50:50 partnership between De Beers and the Botswana government) likely at the end of 2007 or early 2008 upon completion of a $83 million complex near the capital's airport. From 2009, the partnership would take over aggregation duties (mixing of diamonds from different countries into similar assortments) of De Beers's entire aggregation operation, currently carried out by De Beers's DTC in London. As a result of the deal, Botswana had moved up the value chain from mining and sorting to sales and

marketing.[36] As of 2006, four international diamond businesses had cutting factories and 11 new licenses had been issued. By some estimates, 3,500 new jobs would be created. Costs of cutting and polishing, however, would likely be significantly higher than they were in India and China.[37]

In early 2007, De Beers signed a similar agreement with the Namibian government. All diamonds produced by their joint venture, Namdeb, would be sorted in Namibia and just under 50% of output, worth $300 million, would be sold locally.[38]

While De Beers was reorganizing its traditional operations and making various amends, a new potential competitor to the natural diamond quietly began to emerge: laboratory-grown or, as De Beers would call them, "synthetic" diamonds.

Enter Synthetic Diamonds

Unlike a cubic zirconium which was altogether a different chemical substance, synthetic diamonds were chemically identical to the mined variety.[39] Nearly $50 million worth of synthetic diamonds were sold each year and analysts predicted the market would grow at a CAGR of 45% until 2015, by which time sales would exceed $2 billion.[40] In 2006, 400,000 synthetic diamond carats were produced in the United States and prices rose 20%. "We are selling all that we can produce," admitted one synthetic producer[41]

There were a handful of synthetic diamond producers in the United States including Adia Diamonds (Michigan/Ontario), Gemesis (Sarasota, Florida), Apollo (Boston, Massachusetts), Chatham Created Gems (San Francisco, California), and an outfit called Life Gem (Chicago, Illinois) that created lab-grown diamonds with the carbon from a person's ashes. The company's slogan was "Love knows no boundaries; love knows no end." A 1-carat diamond from Gem Life sold for $13,000.[42] Producers typically retailed their collections through a wide variety of jewelers spread mainly throughout the United States. Apollo was scheduled to begin selling its diamonds via its website sometime in 2007.

While there was no disagreement over the fact that, chemically speaking, synthetic diamonds were equal to their natural counterparts, there was disagreement within the industry over what to call them. Preferring the term "cultured," synthetic manufacturers objected to the term synthetic, used by various industry groups including the European Gemological Laboratories, as consumers could very well associate it with imitation stones. The Gemological Institute of America, the organization responsible for developing the color, cut, clarity and carat standards for diamonds back in the late 1950s, used the terms *synthetic, man-made* and *laboratory grown* interchangeably.

The diamond industry was appealing to the U.S. Federal Trade Commission to prohibit laboratory diamond producers from calling their products "cultured," suggesting that *synthetic* be the formal descriptor. Their fear was that the natural diamond industry could suffer the same fate as natural pearls did as a result of the introduction of cultured pearls in the early 1900s. According to Gem World International, cultured pearls accounted for more than 95% of all pearls sold globally.[43] "It's essential that synthetics are readily detectable from diamonds and that clear, unequivocal language is used to describe these man-made products," noted a De Beers spokeswoman.[44]

PROCESS. The technology used to make lab-grown diamonds had been around since 1955 when General Electric began making industrial diamonds used to cut hard substances such as stones, ceramics, metals, and concrete.[45] De Beers followed suit and also began making industrial diamonds and in the late 1950s, De Beers's Chairman Harry Oppenheimer let it be known that the company would not produce synthetic stones unless it became economically necessary.

There were two types of processes for producing synthetic diamonds. The first process, called high pressure high temperature (HPHT), involved mixing a microscopic diamond grain with graphite and metal and placing the mixture into a 4,000-pound machine the size of a kitchen oven. The grain, put under pressure equal to 58,000 atmospheres and exposed to 2,300 degrees Fahrenheit (close to the melting point of steel), would then grow one atom at a time.[46] It typically took four days to grow a 2.5 carat diamond and approximately 20 kilowatts of energy was used per carat.[47] HPHT was the process General Electric used starting in the 1950s to manufacture industrial diamonds.

The second process was known as chemical vapor deposition (CVD). A more modern and delicate process than HPHT, CVD used a combination of carbon gases, temperature and pressure that replicated conditions present at the beginning of the universe. Atoms from the vapor landed on a tiny diamond chip placed in the chamber. Then the vapor particles took on the structure of that diamond—growing the diamond, atom by atom, into a much bigger diamond. The process could be tweaked to produce diamonds other than those used for jewelry. For instance, by adding enough boron to allow the diamond to conduct a current, the CVD process could turn a diamond into a semiconductor.[48] In 1996, Robert Linares, founder of Apollo Diamond Inc., received a patent for the CVD process he had developed for producing flawless diamonds. As one diamond scientist exclaimed upon putting a CVD diamond under a microscope, "It's too perfect to be natural. Things in nature have flaws. The growth and structure of this diamond is flawless."[49]

Unlike their natural counterparts, the majority of synthetic diamonds came in colors—yellow, green, pink, orange, and blue—filling a market niche. Colored natural diamonds, formed by impurities in the earth (e.g., nitrogen-yellow, boron-blue, natural radiation-green[50]) were rare and therefore prohibitively expensive for most consumers. "The market wants more fancy [colored] diamonds, so this is what we've decided to concentrate on," explained the CEO of Gemesis.[51] Although possible, manufacturing colorless diamonds (a process that entailed removing the nitrogen from yellow stones) was an expensive process.

One challenge the industry faced was that none of the synthetic manufacturers had found a way to produce a synthetic diamond bigger than 1 carat for the jewelry market.

WHY BUY SYNTHETIC? Laboratory diamond producers focused on the financial, environmental and political advantages that their product had over natural diamonds. Synthetic diamonds cost anywhere from 15% to 40% less than naturally mined diamonds and sometimes considerably less for colored stones. As Table 1 shows, a one-carat natural pink diamond could cost upwards of $100,000, while its synthetic counterpart would retail for around $4,000.

Environmentally, compared to a natural diamond which required several hundred tons of earth be extracted for each carat[52] often at the expense of both human and animal habitats, lab-grown diamonds were considerably more eco-friendly. According to the Canadian Arctic Resources Committee, as far as 200 kilometers downstream from the lake where Canada's Ekati diamond mine sat, environmental destruction, particularly of fish habitats, was seen in numerous lakes and streams. Diamond mining had also taken a toll on land-based wildlife habitats.

TABLE 1

Natural vs. Lab-Made Diamond Price Comparisons

	Natural	Lab-Made	Cubic Zirconia
Colorless Stones	1 carat = $6,800–$9,100	½ carat = $900–$2,500	1 carat = $5–$15
Colored Stones	1 carat = $9,000 (yellows)–$100,000 (pinks)	1 carat = $2,000–$7,000	1 carat = $10–$15

Source: Vanessa O'Connell, "Gem War," *The Wall Street Journal*, January 13, 2007.

Scientists had observed that caribou and grizzly bears were spending far less time feeding in areas around the mines. Meanwhile diamond mines required the use of diesel fuel to operate, adding to the production of greenhouse gases.[53]

More than their financial and environmental advantages, lab-grown diamond producers emphasized the political advantages of buying a synthetic diamond, namely that consumers would in no way be at risk of acquiring a "blood diamond." A growing number of customers wanted to know where their diamonds came from and wanted a guarantee that they were clean. Once cut and polished, however, it was impossible for consumers to tell which diamonds were blood diamonds. All distinguishing characteristics which identified a diamond's country of origin were washed away with the polishing process.[54]

Measures had been taken by the diamond industry and various governments to assuage agitated consumers and curtail the number of blood diamonds that circulated on the open market and by 2006 blood diamonds made up a mere 1% of the overall diamond trade.[55] Much of this success was attributed to the Kimberley Process Certification Scheme, introduced in 2002, as an attempt by the industry to monitor its own abuses, and as a way to avoid a widespread consumer boycott. The 70 countries that participated in the Kimberley process could only trade with other participants who met the minimum standards. Each participant pledged to prevent the trade of conflict diamonds by implementing stricter monitoring practices which included shipping all diamonds in tamper-proof containers with certificates verifying they came from a legitimate source. (Exhibit 1 provides more details on requirements.) Everyone who handled a diamond was responsible for maintaining an identity tag affixed to the stone from the time it was extracted from the ground.[56] Non-compliers were punished. The Democratic Republic of the Congo was ousted in 2004 and Venezuela was threatened with suspension in 2006 after reporting that it had no diamond exports for 2005. The process, however, was far from perfect and enforcement was proving to be next to impossible. As one example, Sierra Leone, which accounted for up to 33% of the world's smuggled diamonds, had a mere 200 monitors for the entire country sharing 10 USAID-donated motorcycles.[57]

However, some in the industry felt the Kimberley process was working and that the human rights argument could in fact hurt those it intended to help. As one industry observer stated, "When you're buying mined diamonds, you're helping communities in Africa. When you're buying them made from a machine, you're helping 20 guys in Florida."[58] One international diamond trader took issue with this sentiment stating that working conditions for many Africans involved in the mining business remained appalling, opining, "Conflict-free diamonds should not be confused with ethical diamonds."[59]

A new selling point for the synthetic diamond industry came in early 2007 when the Gemological Institute of America's Synthetic Diamond Report began grading the quality of lab-grown diamonds using the same 4-Cs (cut, carat, color, clarity) rating system used for natural diamonds. Certification papers would now accompany synthetic diamonds just as they did natural stones and would include a note stating, "This is a man-made diamond and has been produced in a laboratory."[60] GIA's public benefit mission required it to "describe and report on synthetics so that consumers can rely on full and proper disclosure" upon entering the marketplace.[61]

BEYOND JEWELRY. Whether or not synthetic diamonds would make a significant dent in the natural diamond market was still unclear. But many in the industry believed that due to the chemical composition of the diamond and its ability to be used in a wide array of industries, synthetics would inevitably have a bright future beyond the jewelry industry. As microprocessors became hotter, faster, and smaller in accordance

EXHIBIT 1

The Kimberley Process Certificate

Each Participant should ensure that:

(a) a Kimberley Process Certificate (hereafter referred to as the Certificate) accompanies each shipment of rough diamonds on export;

(b) its processes for issuing Certificates meet the minimum standards of the Kimberley Process as set out in Section IV;

(c) Certificates meet the minimum requirements set out in Annex I. As long as these requirements are met, Participants may at their discretion establish additional characteristics for their own Certificates, for example their form, additional data or security elements;

(d) it notifies all other Participants through the Chair of the features of its Certificate as specified in Annex I, for purposes of validation.

Undertakings in respect of the international trade in rough diamonds

Each Participant should:

(a) with regard to shipments of rough diamonds exported to a Participant, require that each such shipment is accompanied by a duly validated Certificate;

(b) with regard to shipments of rough diamonds imported from a Participant:
require a duly validated Certificate;
ensure that confirmation of receipt is sent expeditiously to the relevant Exporting Authority. The confirmation should as a minimum refer to the Certificate number, the number of parcels, the carat weight and the details of the importer and exporter;
require that the original of the Certificate be readily accessible for a period of no less than three years;

(c) ensure that no shipment of rough diamonds is imported from or exported to a non-Participant;

(d) recognise that Participants through whose territory shipments transit are not required to meet the requirement of paragraphs (a) and (b) above, and of Section II (a) provided that the designated authorities of the Participant through whose territory a shipment passes, ensure that the shipment leaves its territory in an identical state as it entered its territory (i.e. unopened and not tampered with).

Minimum requirements for Certificates

A Certificate is to meet the following minimum requirements:

›› Each Certificate should bear the title "Kimberley Process Certificate" and the following statement: "The rough diamonds in this shipment have been handled in accordance with the provisions of the Kimberley Process Certification Scheme for rough diamonds"

›› Country of origin for shipment of parcels of unmixed (i.e. from the same) origin

›› Certificates may be issued in any language, provided that an English translation is incorporated

›› Unique numbering with the Alpha 2 country code, according to ISO 3166-1

›› Tamper and forgery resistant

›› Date of issuance

›› Date of expiry

›› Issuing authority

›› Identification of exporter and importer

›› Carat weight/mass

›› Value in US$

›› Number of parcels in shipment

›› Relevant Harmonised Commodity Description and Coding System

›› Validation of Certificate by the Exporting Authority

with Moore's law, diamonds could be used as a substitute to heat sensitive silicon. Diamond microchips could handle extreme temperatures allowing them to run at speeds that would liquefy ordinary silicon. As a professor of materials science from MIT explained, "If Moore's law is going to be maintained, processors are going to get hotter and hotter. Eventually silicon is just going to turn into a puddle. Diamond is the solution to that problem."[62]

Up until the recent improvements in laboratory technology, there had been three main barriers to using diamonds as an input to semiconductors. First, diamonds had always been viewed as too expensive to use in such a scaled-up way. Synthetic diamonds helped address that problem. Second, there had never been a steady and consistent supply of large pure diamonds. One mined diamond did not necessarily have the same electrical properties as the next. CVD-produced diamonds solved that problem. Finally, prior to the new processes used for lab created diamonds, no company or individual had been able to manufacture a negative charged diamond with sufficient conductivity needed to form microchip circuits.[63]

Alongside their use in the semiconductor industry, the thermal conductivity, hardness and transparency of diamonds made them an attractive component for next-generation optics, digital data storage,[64] as well as for biological purposes including skin implanted electrodes due to their ability to resist corrosion from acids and other organic compounds.[65]

The market for industrial diamonds was growing at 10% to 15% a year.[66] Synthetic diamonds accounted for 90% of the industrial market.[67] As the CEO of synthetic diamond manufacturer Apollo remarked, "Man-made diamonds will be with us in many different ways that we can only begin to imagine right now that will materially affect everybody on the planet."[68]

De Beers Responds

Although De Beers maintained a fairly nonchalant attitude about the emergence of jewelry-grade synthetic diamonds, there were two ways in which the company was attempting to protect the future of the natural diamond. One way was through its Gem Defensive Programme. In the early years, De Beers warned jewelers about the arrival of synthetic stones and in 2000, the company began supplying gem labs, at no charge, with machinery designed to distinguish man-made from natural stones. Many synthetic manufacturers,

however, were proactively supporting De Beers's detection efforts by lasering the words "lab-created" on their diamonds. De Beers had spent $17 million on research to differentiate natural and synthetic diamonds.[69]

A second defensive strategy focused on consumer education. In anticipation of the movie *Blood Diamond*, De Beers launched a completely different kind of diamond advertisement campaign than those of the past. In lieu of the glitzy pictures of model-esque women donning the perfect sparkler, the ads focused on how the industry provided mining communities with access to employment opportunities, schools for its children, and access to anti-HIV drugs for its mine workers, giving off the general sentiment that buying a diamond from Southern Africa was "an act of altruism."[70]

For the most part, however, De Beers was fairly quiet about the potential threat posed by synthetic diamonds. As a De Beers spokesperson put it, "Synthetics and diamonds are very different products. Diamonds are unique, ancient, natural treasures—the youngest diamond is 900 million years old."[71] Believing that the "real thing" would trump synthetics, the company was actively searching out new supplies of natural diamonds. In 2004, the company discovered 39 new diamond deposits and signed marketing agreements with producers in Canada, Botswana, India, the Democratic Republic of the Congo, the Central African Republic, Russia, Australia, Brazil, and Madagascar.[72]

Conclusion

Lee Mandell walked up to the counter in one of the more reputable jewelry stores in Boston. The salesman asked if he would like some help. Lee responded that he was shopping for an engagement ring but was uncertain as to whether he was in the market for a natural or a synthetic diamond. With a look of utter horror on his face, the salesman said, "You simply can not give your girlfriend a synthetic. I won't let you. The appeal of a diamond is its age and where and how it was created. Where is the romance in something created in a lab by a cold, metallic machine? Besides, the synthetics don't come in sizes larger than 1 carat and I can tell that you want something grander for your loved one."

The jeweler's response was not totally convincing to Lee. His mind kept drifting back to that article he had read about the emerging synthetic diamond industry and the rationale one distributor gave for buying a lab-made diamond: "If you go into a florist and buy a beautiful orchid, it's not grown in some steamy hot jungle in Central America. It's grown in a hothouse somewhere in California. But that doesn't change the fact that it's a beautiful orchid."[73]

Endnotes

1. Karen Goldberg Goff, "Cultivated Carats," *The Washington Times*, February 4, 2007.

2. Danielle Rossingh, "De Beers Says it Can't Ignore Synthetic Diamonds," *Bloomberg*, May 17, 2007.

3. "Diamonds: Changing Facets," *Economist Intelligence Unit*, February 26, 2007.

4. Karen Goldberg Goff, "Cultivated Carats," *The Washington Times*, February 4, 2007.

5. James Dunn, "Glittering Prizes," *The Australian*, October 4, 2006.

6. "The Global Gems and Jewelry Industry: Vision 2015; Transforming for Growth," *KPMG*, December 2006.

7. Ibid.

8. Ibid.

9. Nicole Itano, "Looking to Africa to Polish Its Diamonds," *The New York Times*, September 17, 2004.

10. "The Cartel Isn't For Ever," *The Economist*, July 17, 2004.

11. John Reed and David White, "Beneficiation: A Chance to Spread Southern African wealth," *Financial Times*, July 14, 2006.

12. Nicole Itano, "Looking to Africa to Polish Its Diamonds," *The New York Times*, September 17, 2004.

13. Danielle Cadieux, "De Beers and the Global Diamond Industry," *Ivey Case Study No. 9B05M040*, 2005.

14. Ben Aris, "A Diamond in the Rough," *The Moscow Times*, September 11, 2001.

15. Vanessa Friedman, "The New Rocks on the Block," *Financial Times*, May 10, 2006.

16. James Dunn, "Glittering Prizes," *The Australian*, October 4, 2006.

17. Danielle Cadieux, "De Beers and the Global Diamond Industry," *Ivey Case Study No. 9B05M040*, 2005.

18. Debora L. Spar, "Continuity and Change in the International Diamond Market," *Journal of Economic Perspectives*, Volume 20, Number 3, Summer 2006.

19. "The Cartel Isn't For ever," *The Economist*, July 17, 2004.

20. Phyllis Berman and Lea Goldman, "Cracked De Beers," *Forbes.com*, September 15, 2003.

21. Ibid.

22. Nicholas Stein, "The De Beers Story: A New Cut On An Old Monopoly," *Fortune*, February 19, 2001.

23. Phyllis Berman and Lea Goldman, "Cracked De Beers," *Forbes.com*, Spetember 15, 2003.

24. Kate Reardon, "Guilt Free Diamonds Sparkle Brighter for Ethical Shoppers," *The Times*, June 17, 2006.

25. "The Cartel Isn't For Ever," *The Economist*, July 17, 2004.

26. Nicholas Stein, "The De Beers Story: A New Cut on an Old Monopoly," *Fortune*, February 19, 2001.

27. "Diamonds Get Their Sparkle Back," *New Zealand Herald*, February 26, 2007.

28. Danielle Cadieux, "De Beers and the Global Diamond Industry," *Ivey Case Study No. 9B05M040*, 2005.

29. Debora L. Spar, "Continuity and Change in the International Diamond Market," *Journal of Economic Perspectives*, Volume 20, Number 3, Summer 2006.

30. Nicholas Stein, "The De Beers Story: A New Cut on an Old Monopoly," *Fortune*, February 19, 2001.

31. Vanessa Friedman, "The New Rocks on the Block," *Financial Times*, May 10, 2006.

32. Greg Gatlin, "Branding Becomes Gem of an Idea," *Boston Herald*, February 11, 2001.

33. Danielle Cadieux, "De Beers and the Global Diamond Industry," *Ivey Case Study No. 9B05M040*, 2005.

34. David McKay, "A Private Life: Oppenheimer at 60," *miningmx.com*, July 4, 2005.

35. Brendan Ryan, "Nicky Oppenheimer, Private Treasure," *Financial Mail*, August 30, 2002.

36. John Reed and David White, "Beneficiation: A Chance to Spread Southern African wealth," *Financial Times*, July 14, 2006.

37. David White, "A Question of Profile Image and Status," *Financial Times*, June 20, 2006.

38. "Diamonds Get Their Sparkle Back," *New Zealand Herald*, February 26, 2007.

39. Elsa Wenzel, "Synthetic Diamonds Are Still a Rough Cut," *CNET News.com*, February 14, 2007.

40. Melvyn Thomas, "Lab Tag for Synthetic Diamonds," *The Economic Times*, May 19, 2007.

41. Karen Goldberg Goff, "Cultivated Carats," *The Washington Times*, February 4, 2007.

42. Ibid.

43. Vanessa O'Connell, "Gem War," *The Wall Street Journal*, January 13, 2007.

44. Ibid.

45. Ibid.

46. Danielle Rossingh, "Diamonds by Linares," *Bloomberg.com*, July 5, 2007.

47. Elsa Wenzel, "Synthetic Diamonds Are Still a Rough Cut," *CNET News.com*, February 14, 2007.

48. Kevin Maney, "Man Made Diamonds Sparkle with Potential," *USA Today*, October 6, 2005.

49. Joshua Davis, "The New Diamond Age," *Wired*, September 2003.

50. "Diamonddaze," *South China Morning Post*, November 19, 2004.

51. Victoria Finaly, "Diamonds Are No Longer a Girl's Best Friend," *The Daily Telegraph*, December 22, 2006.

52. Elsa Wenzel, "Synthetic Diamonds Are Still a Rough Cut," *CNET News.com*, February 14, 2007.

53. http://www.carc.org/mining_sustain/diamonds_arent.php.

54. Sharon Barker, "Diamonds in the Rough," *The Jerusalem Post*, April 6, 2001.

55. Vivienne Walt, "Diamonds Aren't Forever," *Fortune*, December 11, 2006.

56. Debora L. Spar, "Continuity and Change in the International Diamond Market," *Journal of Economic Perspectives*, Volume 20, Number 3, Summer 2006.

57. Vivienne Walt, "Diamonds Aren't Forever," *Fortune*, December 11, 2006.

58. Elsa Wenzel, "Synthetic Diamonds Are Still a Rough Cut," *CNET News.com*, February 14, 2007.

59. "Diamonds: Changing Facets," *Economist Intelligence Unit*, February 26, 2007.

60. "GIA Launches Synthetic Grading Report," *Modern Jeweler*, January 1, 2007.

61. Ibid.

62. Joshua Davis, "The New Diamond Age," *Wired*, September 2003.

63. Ibid.

64. Elsa Wenzel, "Synthetic Diamonds Are Still a Rough Cut," *CNET News.com*, February 14, 2007.

65. Alice Park, "Diamonds De Novo," *Time*, February 12, 2007.

66. Ibid.

67. "Diamonds: Changing Facets," *Economist Intelligence Unit*, February 26, 2007.

68. Elsa Wenzel, "Synthetic Diamonds Are Still a Rough Cut," *CNET News.com*, February 14, 2007.

69. Danielle Rossingh, "De Beers Says it Can't Ignore Synthetic Diamonds," *Bloomberg*, May 17, 2007.

70. Victoria Finlay, "Diamonds Are No Longer a Girl's Best Friend," *The Daily Telegraph*, December 22, 2006.

71. Amy Keller, "Carat Factory," *Florida Trend*, August 1, 2007.

72. Debora L. Spar, "Continuity and Change in the International Diamond Market," *Journal of Economic Perspectives*, Volume 20, Number 3, Summer 2006.

73. Joshua Davis, "The New Diamond Age," *Wired*, September 2003.

Konstantinos Grigoriou
Georgia Institute of Technology

German Retana
Georgia Institute of Technology

Frank T. Rothaermel
Georgia Institute of Technology

THE TEAM SAT SILENTLY in the conference room. Sam Palmisano, IBM's Chairman, President, and CEO, had just finished a presentation to Bruce Harreld, Senior Vice President of Strategy, and his team, comprised of several VPs, directors, mid-level managers, and some summer interns. Mr. Palmisano's words still rang in their ears: "Cloud computing is coming on strong, and is here to stay. The economics and the structure of the IT industry will change forever. We have to leverage it. I don't want a repeat of the PC disaster. Understood?"

The weather was changing; clouds were emerging on IBM's horizon and the company had no time to lose. Pressing questions needed urgent but effective strategic answers. IBM had been through many ups and downs following previous platform, technological, market, and strategic shifts in the IT industry. It remained to be seen if IBM had learned anything from the lessons of the past that would help it survive the coming cloud-computing storm.

The question facing Harreld and his team was what kind of reference point it should use with respect to cloud computing. IBM had numerous strategic options to consider, the first being how far to venture into this new uncharted "cloud" territory. With mainframes, IBM excelled at vertically integrating all related activities in-house: hardware, software, sales, and service were all part of the "Big Iron" (a term referring to business involving large mainframes or supercomputers). While that business model had not proven successful in the PC market, it could provide a means of establishing a dominant position in cloud computing if executed in a smart and timely manner. Alternatively, the company could choose to focus on specific value chain activities—for example, supply the hardware needed by cloud service providers, develop and sell the systems-management software needed to grow the distributed and scalable infrastructures, or become a cloud service provider (to firms that did not want to implement cloud services by themselves). Yet another option was to pursue two or more of these activities in combination.

Then there was the question of whether to work with a partner, acquire existing businesses, or go it alone. Partnerships could ease the burden of doing everything in-house and secure a critical mass of famous players (like Amazon or Google) that could potentially dominate the cloud market. However, IBM would have to share some (or perhaps even most) of the value created. The attraction of acquiring smaller players that were already active in the cloud market was that it could infuse IBM with relevant and essential talent. Between 2000 and 2009, IBM consummated over 100 such technology acquisitions to strengthen its portfolio of businesses.[1] Yet, acquisitions could also delay IBM's response because of the time needed for integration and coordination procedures. Going it alone would keep the bulk of value created in-house, but it would not be easy to *do* everything in-house in such a competitive multilayer industry, nor could things be done very quickly. Going it alone would also be the most resource-intensive of all the options.

Another issue was market segmentation. Should IBM target individual consumers, or should they focus on small and medium-sized companies, or large enterprises, or even whole nations? Would it be better off serving public, private, or hybrid clouds? Traditionally, IBM's strength had been at the enterprise level, which would seem to indicate a focus on private clouds.[2] However, the real question was: What would be the most profitable market segment(s) in the cloud-computing business?

PhD candidates Konstantinos Grigoriou, German Retana, and Professor Frank T. Rothaermel prepared this case from public sources. This case is developed for the purpose of class discussion. It is not intended to be used for any kind of endorsement, source of data, or depiction of efficient or inefficient management. © Grigoriou, Retana, and Rothaermel, 2013.

Mr. Palmisano had tasked the group with formulating a strategy for responding to the challenges posed by cloud computing. He also wanted step-by-step recommendations for how to implement their ideas. Bruce Harreld and his team began to discuss how to tackle the problem . . .

Background on Cloud Computing and the IT Industry

Cloud computing is an emerging, web-based form of information technology (IT), defined as "a model for enabling convenient, on-demand network access to a shared pool of configurable computing resources (e.g., networks, servers, storage, applications, and services) that [could] be rapidly provisioned and released with minimal management effort or service provider interaction."[3] (See Exhibit 1 for a full definition and further explanation of cloud computing.) It was made possible by cheap and powerful processors combined with high-bandwidth availability across networks.[4] The cloud was radically changing the distribution of value across the entire IT industry. Traditional "big fish" in the IT industry sold hardware (e.g., Intel, Dell, IBM), operating systems (e.g., Microsoft), database engines (e.g., Oracle, IBM), office applications (e.g., Microsoft), or business applications such as enterprise resource planning (e.g., SAP, Oracle) or customer relationship management tools (e.g., SAP, Oracle, Microsoft). But through the cloud, these components could all be accessed as an online service by users whenever needed. The IT industry was undergoing a platform shift from product- to service-oriented strategies, and companies that did not adapt to this new reality might not survive.

The industry's first big platform shift in the early 1990s—the move from mainframes to smaller machines, first so-called minicomputers, and then personal computers (PCs)—had nearly done in IBM. After first dismissing the PC as a toy, IBM made a belated effort to shape its development by introducing the IBM PC in 1981. Although it set the (open) standard for the industry, IBM made multiple strategic blunders that nearly bankrupted the company. In order to accelerate time-to-market, IBM chose not to build the operating system and microprocessor internally; instead, it sourced these vital components from Microsoft and Intel, respectively. This decision effectively passed IBM's historic source of monopolistic power (operating system and processor architecture) to Microsoft

and Intel, exporting hundreds of billions of dollars of value to its major competitors. At the same time, the PC completely disrupted IBM's business model. PC users had no need for IBM's expertise in mainframe computing systems, data processing centers, or sales and service support, but IBM persisted in these activities long after their decline in value. On January 19, 1993, IBM announced the largest single-year corporate loss in U.S. history. Since then, IBM had chosen to actively engage in everything new in the IT sector (see Exhibit 2 for a history of the IT industry), in order to maintain its reputation as a "reference point" in the industry.

The Rise of a Giant

IBM's ("Big Blue's") history dated back to long before electronic computers. It originated as the Tabulating Machine Company in 1896 and specialized in the development of punch-card data-processing equipment. Thomas J. Watson, Sr. became General Manager of the company in 1914 and in 1924 changed its name to International Business Machines Corporation, or IBM. During the next 20 years, IBM grew rapidly. Despite the Great Depression of the 1930s, IBM continued to manufacture new products, and after passage of the Social Security Act of 1935, IBM secured a major government contract to maintain employment data for 26 million people. This was described as "the biggest accounting operation of all time,"[5] and it opened the door for a variety of other government contracts. After the United States entered World War II, all IBM facilities were placed at the disposal of the federal government and IBM's product line expanded to include bombsights, rifles, and engine parts.[6]

In the 1950s, IBM became a chief contractor for developing computers for the U.S. Air Force's automated defense systems, a product that generated tremendous profits. More importantly, the company gained access to cutting-edge research on digital computers being done under military auspices. However, IBM failed to dominate the emerging industry by letting RAND Corporation take over the job of programming the new computers. According to one project participant, Robert P. Crago, "we couldn't imagine where we could absorb two thousand programmers at IBM when this job would be over some day, which shows how well we were understanding the future at that time."[7]

IBM was the largest of the eight major computer companies through most of the 1960s. (Others were UNIVAC, Burroughs, NCR, Control Data Corporation,

EXHIBIT 1

Working Definition of Cloud Computing

Note 1: Cloud computing is still an evolving paradigm. Its definitions, use cases, underlying technologies, issues, risks, and benefits will be refined in a spirited debate by the public and private sectors. These definitions, attributes, and characteristics will evolve and change over time.

Note 2: The cloud-computing industry represents a large ecosystem of many models, vendors, and market niches. This definition attempts to encompass all of the various cloud approaches.

Definition of Cloud Computing:

Cloud computing is a model for enabling convenient, on-demand network access to a shared pool of configurable computing resources (e.g., networks, servers, storage, applications, and services) that can be rapidly provisioned and released with minimal management effort or service provider interaction. This cloud model promotes availability and is composed of five **essential characteristics,** three **service models,** and four **deployment models.**

Essential Characteristics:

On-demand self-service. A consumer can unilaterally provision computing capabilities, such as server time and network storage, as needed automatically without requiring human interaction with each service's provider.

Broad network access. Capabilities are available over the network and accessed through standard mechanisms that promote use by heterogeneous thin or thick client platforms (e.g., mobile phones, laptops, and PDAs).

Resource pooling. The provider's computing resources are pooled to serve multiple consumers using a multitenant model, with different physical and virtual resources dynamically assigned and reassigned according to consumer demand. There is a sense of location independence in that the customer generally has no control or knowledge over the exact location of the provided resources but may be able to specify location at a higher level of abstraction (e.g., country, state, or datacenter). Examples of resources include storage, processing, memory, network bandwidth, and virtual machines.

Rapid elasticity. Capabilities can be rapidly and elastically provisioned, in some cases automatically, to quickly scale out and can be rapidly released to quickly scale in. To the consumer, the capabilities available for provisioning often appear to be unlimited and can be purchased in any quantity at any time.

Measured service. Cloud systems automatically control and optimize resource use by leveraging a metering capability at some level of abstraction appropriate to the type of service (e.g., storage, processing, bandwidth, and active user accounts). Resource usage can be monitored, controlled, and reported, providing transparency for both the provider and consumer of the utilized service.

Service Models:

Cloud Software-as-a-Service (SaaS). The capability provided to the consumer is to use the provider's applications running on a cloud infrastructure. The applications are accessible from various client devices through a thin client interface such as a web browser (e.g., web-based e-mail). The consumer does not manage or control the underlying cloud infrastructure, including the network, servers, operating systems, storage, or even individual application capabilities, with the possible exception of limited user-specific application configuration settings.

Cloud Platform-as-a-Service (PaaS). The capability provided to the consumer is to deploy onto the cloud infrastructure consumer-created or acquired applications created using programming languages and tools supported by the provider. The consumer does not manage or control the underlying cloud infrastructure, including the network, servers, operating systems, or storage, but has control over the deployed applications and possibly application hosting environment configurations.

Cloud Infrastructure-as-a-Service (IaaS). The capability provided to the consumer is to provision processing, storage, networks, and other fundamental computing resources where the consumer is able to deploy and run arbitrary software, which can include operating systems and applications. The consumer does not manage or control the underlying cloud infrastructure but has control over operating systems, storage, and deployed applications, and possibly limited control of select networking components (e.g., host firewalls).

(continued)

EXHIBIT 1 Working Definition of Cloud Computing *(continued)*

Deployment Models:

Private cloud. The cloud infrastructure is operated solely for an organization. It may be managed by the organization or a third party and may exist on-premises or off-premises.

Community cloud. The cloud infrastructure is shared by several organizations and supports a specific community that has shared concerns (e.g., mission, security requirements, policy, and compliance considerations). It may be managed by the organizations or a third party and may exist on-premises or off-premises.

Public cloud. The cloud infrastructure is made available to the general public or a large industry group and is owned by an organization selling cloud services

Hybrid cloud. The cloud infrastructure is a composition of two or more clouds (private, community, or public) that remain unique entities but are bound together by standardized or proprietary technology that enables data and application portability (e.g., cloud bursting for load-balancing between clouds).

Note: Cloud software takes full advantage of the cloud paradigm by being service-oriented with a focus on statelessness, low coupling, modularity, and semantic interoperability.

Source: National Institute of Standards and Technology, Information Technology (NIST), Laboratory Authors: Peter Mell and Tim Grance, Version 15, October 7, 2009, http://csrc.nist.gov/groups/SNS/cloud-computing/.

EXHIBIT 2

Technological Discontinuities in the Computing Industry, 1890–2000

Source: IBM Prospectus (2004), "Understanding our company." Vertical axis shows total industry revenues.

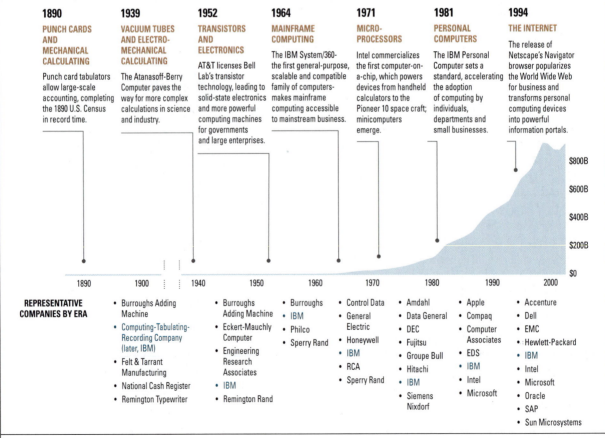

1890
PUNCH CARDS AND MECHANICAL CALCULATING
Punch card tabulators allow large-scale accounting, completing the 1890 U.S. Census in record time.

1939
VACUUM TUBES AND ELECTRO-MECHANICAL CALCULATING
The Atanasoff-Berry Computer paves the way for more complex calculations in science and industry.

1952
TRANSISTORS AND ELECTRONICS
AT&T licenses Bell Lab's transistor technology, leading to solid-state electronics and more powerful computing machines for governments and large enterprises.

1964
MAINFRAME COMPUTING
The IBM System/360- the first general-purpose, scalable and compatible family of computers-makes mainframe computing accessible to mainstream business.

1971
MICRO-PROCESSORS
Intel commercializes the first computer-on-a-chip, which powers devices from handheld calculators to the Pioneer 10 space craft; minicomputers emerge.

1981
PERSONAL COMPUTERS
The IBM Personal Computer sets a standard, accelerating the adoption of computing by individuals, departments and small businesses.

1994
THE INTERNET
The release of Netscape's Navigator browser popularizes the World Wide Web for business and transforms personal computing devices into powerful information portals.

	$800B
	$600B
	$400B
	$200B
	$0

1890   1900   1940   1950   1960   1970   1980   1990   2000

REPRESENTATIVE COMPANIES BY ERA

- Burroughs Adding Machine
- Computing-Tabulating-Recording Company (later, IBM)
- Felt & Tarrant Manufacturing
- National Cash Register
- Remington Typewriter

- Burroughs Adding Machine
- Eckert-Mauchly Computer
- Engineering Research Associates
- IBM
- Remington Rand

- Burroughs
- IBM
- Philco
- Sperry Rand

- Control Data
- General Electric
- Honeywell
- IBM
- RCA
- Sperry Rand

- Amdahl
- Data General
- DEC
- Fujitsu
- Groupe Bull
- Hitachi
- IBM
- Siemens Nixdorf

- Apple
- Compaq
- Computer Associates
- EDS
- IBM
- Intel
- Microsoft

- Accenture
- Dell
- EMC
- Hewlett-Packard
- IBM
- Intel
- Microsoft
- Oracle
- SAP
- Sun Microsystems

General Electric, RCA, and Honeywell.) People in the industry talked about "IBM and the seven dwarfs," as IBM dominated its competitors with a 70 percent market share. In the 1970s, a number of mergers and acquisitions resulted in an increasingly concentrated market, with IBM still firmly in the lead. Many companies chose to focus on niche areas, in order to avoid competing directly with IBM. The IBM mainframe that earned the company its dominant position during this period was actually still part of IBM's product line. Originally dubbed the IBM System/360, it was now known as the IBM System z10.

The Decline of Mainframe Computing

Up through the 1970s, IBM relied on a vertically integrated strategy, building most key components of its systems itself, including processors, operating systems, peripherals, and databases. IBM preferred to do things in-house, and the prevailing attitude was that no one could do things better anyway. The company was able to capture high margins capitalizing on its reputation for technical prowess, reliability, and outstanding service, even when the technology was not cutting-edge. IBM's strategy was virtually flawless, routinely out-competing its rivals. In 1976, however, IBM faced a life-threatening discontinuity that was not the result of a traditional competitor's action. It started in a California garage far from IBM's New York headquarters, when college dropouts Steve Jobs and Steve Wozniak put together the Apple I personal computer kit. On April Fools' Day of the same year, they founded Apple Computer, Inc.

Once among its greatest assets, IBM's size and industry dominance caused it to underestimate the power and speed of the computer revolution that was taking place. Instead, IBM's disdain toward Apple and other emerging competitors gave the new companies five unchallenged years during which to perfect their new technology. IBM did not introduce its own version of the PC until 1981, and though it set the (open) standard for the industry, IBM's delayed response meant that it had already forfeited the opportunity to dominate this new market. To add insult to injury, IBM then chose to outsource the operating system and microprocessors for its new machines from Microsoft and Intel, respectively, creating the Wintel standard in the PC industry. In yet another misjudgment, IBM sold its 20 percent equity stake in Intel in the mid-1980s.

Meanwhile, IBM held on tight to other activities in the computing value chain, only to find that its vertically integrated business model had no advantage in the evolving computer industry. PCs could be sold in a variety of retail outlets, eliminating the need for a highly trained sales force. Data-processing centers were no longer essential, as PCs had their own memory and processing systems inside. Nor was there a need for IBM to maintain these machines, as businesses increasingly internalized the service function and hired their own computer technicians.

As the computer value chain disintegrated, different companies took the lead in specific segments. Intel was the leader in microprocessors, Microsoft in operational systems, Novell in networking, HP in printers, Seagate in disk drives, and Oracle in databases. Even in personal computers, cost-efficient competitors like Compaq and Dell easily outpaced IBM. Many dedicated software developers and vendors also popped up. Thus, in 1992, IBM's CEO John Akers began to split IBM into business units (e.g., for processors, storage, software, services, printers, and so on) to compete more effectively with the focused niche players.

The growth of local area networking capabilities and the subsequent decline of mainframe sales led to the inevitable outcome: On January 19, 1993, IBM announced the largest single-year corporate loss in U.S. history ($8.1 bn). The "Big Iron" business divisions had not recognized the need for the company to adapt in time. As a result, 250,000 workers departed, and a decade of radical transformation followed. Louis Gerstner was the first non-IBMer to take over, inheriting the daunting task of saving Big Blue.

The Louis Gerstner Era

When Louis V. Gerstner, Jr., became chairman and chief executive in 1993, the question was whether IBM would survive. Mr. Gerstner was not a lifetime IBMer. Even worse, he had no particular understanding of the computer-technology industry. He came with a background in consumer products, financial services, and consulting. The IBM board had decided that IBM needed a leader, a strategist, and a manager—and Mr. Gerstner's portfolio of skills fit the bill.

Mr. Gerstner received a bachelor's degree in engineering from Dartmouth College in 1963 and an MBA from Harvard Business School in 1965. He worked as a McKinsey consultant and later became president of American Express and then CEO of NJR Nabisco.

He was not the obvious choice for the fallen icon of American technology. Nevertheless, he brought to the table a strong vision and a passion for change. As soon as he took the reins at IBM, he began traveling to meet customers to get a sense of the market. His verdict was bold: "We were going to build this company from the customer back, not from the company out."[8]

One major decision Mr. Gerstner made was to reverse Akers's plan to split IBM into 13 "Baby Blues." In theory, dividing the company into multiple strategic business units addressed IBM's fundamental trouble—that as an integrated company, IBM was not flexible. Mr. Gerstner, however, liked the concept of "integrated solutions," recalling his days as an IBM customer. IBM could provide one-stop shopping and service to tackle tough business problems without forcing its customers to deal with different vendors. He heard similar sentiments from customers. Within three months, Gerstner decided to keep the company together. "I knew it was a big risk, but I never doubted that it was the right thing to do at IBM," he said.[9]

Mr. Gerstner developed three strategic pillars that were "the fundamental underpinnings of building an integrated company," as he later wrote in his best-selling book, *Who Says Elephants Can't Dance?,* describing IBM's legendary comeback.[10] First, he initiated a broad computer services unit that sold bundles of hardware, software, consulting, and maintenance to manage business processes. His decision to move into services set off "an incredible bomb in the company," Mr. Gerstner recalled, adding, "here was a part of IBM that was going to work closely with Oracle, Sun Microsystems and, god forbid, Microsoft." Ultimately, IBM Global Services became the company's biggest business, because it was able to "look at technology through the eyes of the customer."[11]

The second pillar of Gerstner's turnaround strategy targeted another IBM tradition: that of relying exclusively on its own homegrown technology (see Exhibits 3a and 3b for IBM's patent history). Earlier when the company had gone outside—giving programming to RAND, processors to Intel, and software to Microsoft—the move had been regarded as a grave mistake. But now, there was a conscious decision to move to "open systems." Mr. Gerstner wanted all of IBM's software to run on competitors' hardware, and all of IBM's hardware to support competitors' software. For many IBMers, this was tough medicine to swallow.

Gerstner's third pillar was to fully embrace the Internet and the "networked world" model of computing. The move to open systems facilitated this transition. The networked model of computing suited IBM's strengths—as the Internet shift made big data-serving computers essential again and took the interest away from PCs. Along with big computers, the Internet brought with it a host of complexity and compatibility issues, since heterogeneous software and hardware had to be connected and work together. IBM's breadth and its services were big advantages in this environment. "Here was a chance for IBM to lead again," Mr. Gerstner declared. "We were able to articulate a role for IBM in the networked world that spoke of the value of all we did."[12] Needless to say, Gerstner's Internet strategy was quite visionary in 1993.

IBM's new strategy evolved quite rapidly. In late 1995, the firm formed an Internet division to make sure the entire company was focused on the Internet. Then, beginning in 1997, IBM started a massive advertising and marketing campaign to push "e-business," a term coined by IBM. Many observed that the notion of e-business served as a wake-up call to Wall Street about the upcoming shift in business models.[13] While experts and competitors were slow to comprehend the full value of e-business, IBM's corporate customers loved the new focus. The dot-com boom in 1999 was an opportunity for Gerstner to say that he regarded the hot Internet startups as "fireflies before the storm," suggesting that there was much more to come. At the time, that was hardly conventional wisdom.

At the conclusion of Gerstner's tenure, his three strategic pillars had come together in a sound strategic vision. This fundamental strategic shift guaranteed real change in IBM's stiff corporate culture. In addition, the buildup of the services business led to increased hiring, bringing in a new sea of faces and fresh ideas. In 2008, IBM Global Services employed 150,000 people, up from 7,600 in 1992. More than half of these employees had worked for the company five years or less, in stark contrast to the company's heritage of long-term staff retention. Gerstner's success as CEO clearly demonstrated the dynamism of the IT industry, and the fact that even if one misses a turn of the innovation cycle, there is still hope to survive and get back in the game.

The Sam Palmisano Era

On January 1, 2003, Sam J. Palmisano took the helm at IBM. "Sam," as the IBMers knew him, pushed the e-business strategy even farther. However, Mr. Palmisano

EXHIBIT 3a

IBM's Patenting over Time, 1993–2009

Source: Data obtained from U.S. PTO.

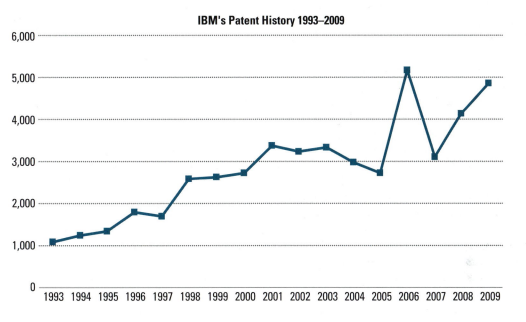

EXHIBIT 3b

Total Number of Patents, IBM vs. Selected Competitors, 1993–2009

Source: Data obtained from U.S. PTO.

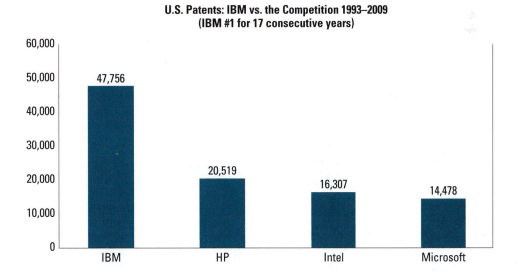

had a very different leadership style when compared with Gerstner, differences that ranged from body language to conversation style. He was tall, beefy, and relaxed, looking every inch the former college football lineman he was, and he spoke to people with trademark informality.[14]

Palmisano was a life-long IBMer, having joined the company as a 22-year-old salesman in 1973. Since then, Sam had held a series of leadership positions, including Senior Vice President for the Enterprise Systems and Personal Systems groups. He had played an instrumental role in creating and leading IBM's Global Services (rising to Senior Vice President) and building the largest IT services organization in the industry. He also served as Senior Managing Director of Operations for IBM Japan. Palmisano was appointed IBM's President and Chief Operating Officer in 2000.

The strategic moves Palmisano had made since becoming CEO were bold, some would even argue risky. His strategy promised to redefine what it meant to be a computer company—making IBM a valuable complement to all business value chain activities and supporting functions, thus expanding its role well beyond that of equipment supplier. Consulting and software were the cornerstones of his strategy,

so Palmisano invested in solution-driven consulting, services, and software, keeping only the high-margin components of hardware. (See Exhibit 4 for IBM's offerings and market segments.) In 2002, he acquired PricewaterhouseCoopers Consulting for $3.5 billion and Rational Software for $2.1 billion. Also in that same year, IBM announced a $10 billion program to develop infrastructure technology to provide supercomputer-level resources "on demand" to all businesses.[15]

When the market appeared to flatten in 2005 (see Exhibits 5 through 7 for IBM financial data), Palmisano pushed the shift to services even faster, selling IBM's PC division to China's largest computer maker, Lenovo. "Software had to play a bigger role," Palmisano explained. "Then we could offset the transition in services." In software, IBM built expertise mainly with acquisitions of small companies in fields like security, data management, and web commerce. From 2003 until 2007, IBM spent $11.8 billion on 54 acquisitions—36 software and 18 services companies—in order to facilitate the transformation process.[16] In addition, IBM encouraged universities and other technology companies to promote education for an emerging field that within IBM was called "service science."[17]

Palmisano's strategy represented an aggressive effort to increase profit margins in response to intense

EXHIBIT 4

IBM's Offerings and Market Segments

Source: IBM 2007 Annual Report.

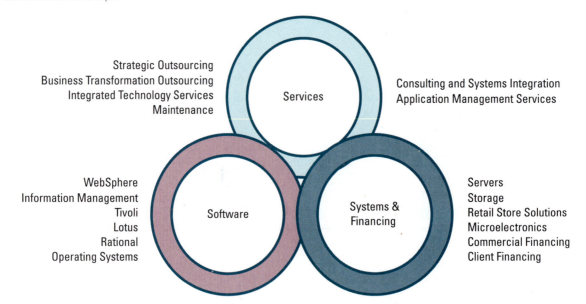

Strategic Outsourcing
Business Transformation Outsourcing
Integrated Technology Services
Maintenance

Services

Consulting and Systems Integration
Application Management Services

WebSphere
Information Management
Tivoli
Lotus
Rational
Operating Systems

Software

Systems & Financing

Servers
Storage
Retail Store Solutions
Microelectronics
Commercial Financing
Client Financing

EXHIBIT 5

IBM Revenue by Geographic Region, 2009

Source: IBM 2009 Annual Report.

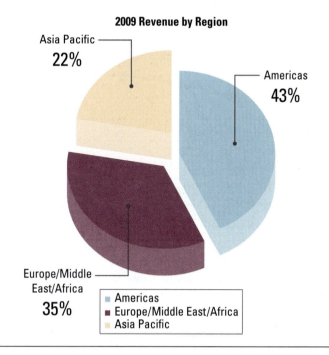

2009 Revenue by Region

Asia Pacific
22%

Americas
43%

Europe/Middle
East/Africa
35%

- Americas
- Europe/Middle East/Africa
- Asia Pacific

EXHIBIT 6

IBM Financial Information by Segment, 2007–2009 (in $ millions)

	2009	2008	2007
Global Technology Services	37,347	39,264	36,103
Gross Margin	35.00%	32.60%	29.90%
Global Business Services	17,653	19,628	18,041
Gross Margin	28.20%	26.70%	23.50%
Software	21,396	22,089	19,982
Gross Margin	86.00%	85.40%	85.20%
Systems and Technology	16,190	19,287	21,317
Gross Margin	37.80%	38.10%	39.70%
Global Financing	2,302	2,559	2,502
Gross Margin	47.50%	51.30%	46.70%
Other	869	803	842
Gross Margin	11.60%	13.40%	4.40%
Total Revenue	95,758	103,630	98,786

Source: IBM Annual Reports.

EXHIBIT 7

IBM Margins, 2002–2009

Source: IBM Annual Reports.

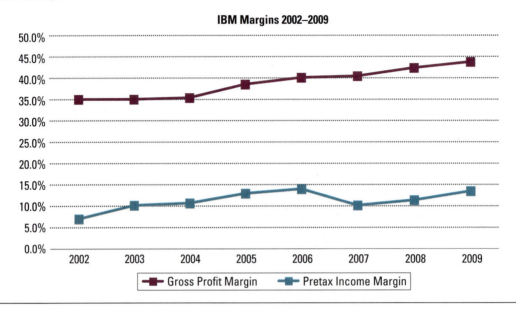

IBM Margins 2002–2009

Legend: Gross Profit Margin — Pretax Income Margin

price competition in hardware and software. Under his leadership, IBM transformed itself from a multinational company with worldwide operations to a more seamless global enterprise with centers of expertise, each of which was a hub in a global service network. The corresponding change in IBM's corporate mindset was illustrated by employees' responses to a 2003 survey regarding the company's future values. Three strategic thrusts emerged: "Dedication to every client's success," "Innovation that matters—for our company and for the world," and "Trust and personal responsibility in all relationships." It was a case of a company successfully responding to the challenges of globalization and rapid technological change. (See IBM's stock-performance chart in Exhibit 8.) IBM now had 400,000 employees worldwide and an annual R&D budget of $5 billion. In 2009, some 284,000 employees (71 percent) were from outside the United States, up from about 65 percent in 2006.[18]

IBM still faced daunting long-term challenges—particularly in services, which contributed 57 percent of the company's 2009 revenues (Exhibit 9). New entrants from India enjoyed a significant cost advantage in the technology-services business, given their access to a cheap educated workforce. Companies like Infosys, Tata Consulting Services, and Wipro had average operating profit margins of more than 20 percent, twice as much as IBM's margins.[19] In response, IBM announced the cut of 5,000 jobs from its U.S. global services unit in March 2009, transferring them to India to take advantage of cheaper Asian engineering work.[20] At the same time, IBM continued to climb the economic ladder and take on more complicated work, competing on the basis of specialized expertise (Exhibit 10). Although Palmisano had yet to declare victory, he thought the future looked quite promising (Exhibits 11 and 12). "The encouraging thing is that we've made progress," he said, " . . . but there's still a lot to be done."[21] The challenge of cloud computing loomed large on the horizon.

Cloud Computing as a Harbinger of Change

"The cloud" was a significant threat to the IT industry because it had the potential to change all the layers of the IT stack (Exhibit 13).

CHANGING THE IT STACK. At the infrastructure level, cloud computing allowed data centers to achieve higher utilization rates by providing services to a larger and more dispersed client base, resulting in enormous

EXHIBIT 8

IBM Stock Performance vs. S&P 500 and S&P IT Index, 1999–2009

Source: IBM 2009 Annual Report.

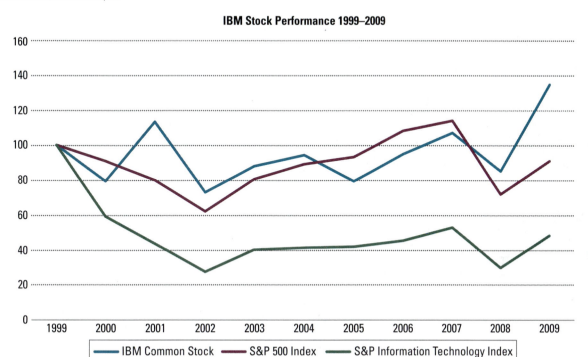

economies of scale. Servers depreciated whether they were powered on or off.[22] The cloud provided a means by which a data center could use as much of its installed capacity as possible, rather than shutting down servers to save power. Organizations, and particularly system administrators, were starting to adopt public clouds from *Infrastructure-as-a-Service* (*IaaS*) providers or building their own private clouds to capture a share of these benefits. The call for greater business efficiency was likely to speed up this trend.[23]

At a higher level in the IT stack, developers were looking at *Platform-as-a-Service* (*PaaS*) offerings. These services allowed developers to launch applications online, without knowledge of, or interest in, the underlying hardware. This was particularly useful for software development teams in organizations, as they no longer needed to deploy full infrastructures to test, show, and perhaps later deploy their prototypes, proof of concepts, or applications.

At the highest level of the stack, *Software-as-a-Service* (*SaaS*) offerings were radically changing the way end-users perceived and used software applications.

Through the cloud, software was provided as a combination of digital services and did not have to be installed on local servers or computers. Users would no longer need standalone software packages. Google Docs was an early example of distributed computing for popular applications like word processing, spreadsheets, and presentations. Microsoft's Office 2010 was also meant to be run off a web browser. Yet another example of this shift toward Software-as-a-Service was Salesforce.com, a firm founded in 1999 by former Oracle executive Marc Benioff. Salesforce.com offered an online CRM (customer relationship management) system that users accessed over the web, instead of through the traditional boxed license. By 2008, Salesforce.com was already third in terms of revenue market share, and SaaS offerings comprised 20 percent of the CRM market.[24]

CHANGING COMPUTING DEVICES. Since applications were increasingly run off web servers, the requirements of end-users' devices were also changing. The cloud could be accessed through a greater variety of

EXHIBIT 9

IBM Financial Data, 1999–2009 (numbers in $ millions except per-share amounts)

Year Fiscal	1999	2000	2001	2002	2003	2004	2005	2006	2007	2008	2009
Revenue	83,334	85,089	83,067	81,186	89,131	96,293	91,134	91,424	98,786	103,630	95,758
Net Income	7,712	8,093	6,484	2,376	6,558	7,479	7,934	9,492	10,418	12,334	13,425
EPS (Basic)	4.25	4.58	3.74	1.4	3.81	4.47	4.96	6.18	7.27	9.02	10.12
EPS (Diluted)	4.12	4.44	3.69	1.39	3.74	4.38	4.86	6.11	7.15	8.89	10.01
Cash Dividends Paid on Common Stock	859	909	956	1,005	1,085	1,174	1,250	1,683	2,147	2,585	2,860
Per Share of Common Stock	0.47	0.51	0.55	0.59	0.63	0.7	0.78	1.1	1.5	1.9	2.15
Investments in Plants, Rental Machines, and Other Property	5,959	5,616	5,660	5,022	4,398	4,368	3,842	4,362	4,630	4,171	3,447
Return on Stockholders' Equity	39.10%	40.00%	28.50%	9.80%	24.50%	25.60%	25.80%	29.30%	42.60%	48.70%	80.40%
Total Assets	89,571	90,412	91,207	97,814	106,021	111,003	105,748	103,234	120,431	109,524	109,022
Net Investments	17,590	16,714	16,504	14,440	14,689	15,175	13,756	14,440	15,081	14,305	14,165
Working Capital	3,577	7,474	7,483	6,927	7,205	7,357	10,509	4,569	8,867	6,568	12,933
Total Debt	28,354	28,576	27,151	26,017	23,632	22,927	22,641	22,682	35,274	33,926	26,099
Stockholders' Equity	20,426	20,550	24,352	24,112	29,531	31,688	33,209	28,635	28,615	13,584	22,755

Source: IBM Annual Reports, 1999–2009.

EXHIBIT 10

IBM Pretax Income Mix, 2000 and 2009

Source: IBM 2009 Annual Report.

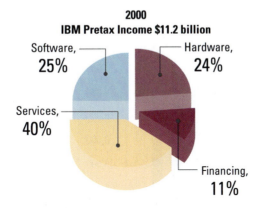

2000
IBM Pretax Income $11.2 billion

Software, 25%
Hardware, 24%
Services, 40%
Financing, 11%

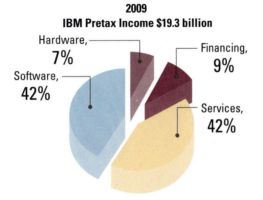

2009
IBM Pretax Income $19.3 billion

Hardware, 7%
Financing, 9%
Software, 42%
Services, 42%

user interfaces, such as low-priced netbooks, tablets, or smart mobile phones with web access. Freed from the need to house applications that required large amounts of internal memory, these devices were smaller, more portable, and provided a more interactive computing experience.

CHANGING THE IT INDUSTRY. As the cloud increased in prevalence, hardware-makers would have to choose between supplying servers to cloud service providers and becoming service providers themselves. Doing both would not be easy, because the hardware suppliers would be competing with their biggest customers. Software-makers faced a greater challenge in that they would have to develop a means of metering application usage, either by charging a computing utility rate (much as is currently done for electricity) or a periodic subscription fee.[25] The cloud was also a hospitable environment for open-source programming, which would increase the competition and decrease overall prices for proprietary software.

At the same time, cloud computing was already blurring such traditional distinctions among industry participants,[26] placing giant companies that used to be partners on a direct collision course. Cisco was moving into servers, which had previously been HP and IBM's domain. Dell had introduced data-center software and was likewise starting to compete with HP and IBM. Sun, before being acquired by Oracle, took on Oracle's database dominance by introducing its own database offerings. HP purchased EDS and thus initiated an intense rivalry with IBM on IT services. Similarly, Dell bought Perot Systems to move upstream into value-added IT services.

Consequently, boundaries between competitors were far from clear in the cloud. Winners and losers

EXHIBIT 11

IBM Revenue and Income, 1999–2009

Source: IBM 2009 Annual Report.

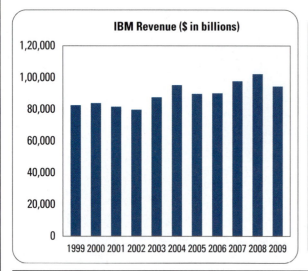

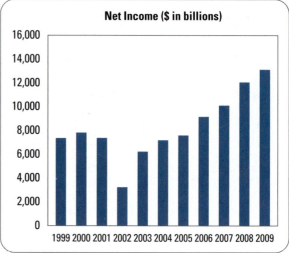

EXHIBIT 12

IBM Earnings per Share and Net Cash, 2003–2009

Source: IBM 2009 Annual Report.

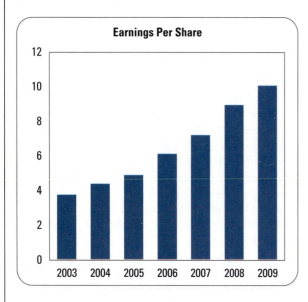

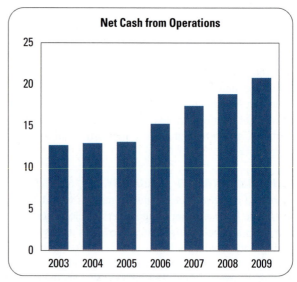

EXHIBIT 13

Examples of Providers of Different Cloud Service Models

Service Model	Intended Users	Level of IT Stack	Examples of Providers
Infrastructure-as-a-Service (IaaS)	System administrators	Lowest. Closest to hardware.	Public Cloud: Amazon, Rackspace, GoGrid, Joyent Private Clouds: VMware, Enomaly
Platform-as-a-Service (PaaS)	Developers	Moderate. Developers care only about application code.	Google App Engine, Force.com, Engine Yard, Heroku
Software-as-a-Service (SaaS)	End-users	Highest. Users only access application.	Google Docs & Gmail (office apps), Microsoft Software Plus Services (office apps), Salesforce.com (CRM), NetSuite (ERP)

in this game would be determined by their respective capabilities to understand where value was created and how to capture it along the newly emerging industry value chain. Intense competition, along with *Moore's law* (which states that the number of transistors placed on an integrated circuit doubles roughly every 18 months), was likely to drive down prices and margins for all cloud providers.

CHANGING THE WAY PEOPLE DO BUSINESS. Just as with the emergence of the personal computer, the cloud was changing how people worked and companies operated. The cloud was expected to make businesses more adaptable, interconnected, and specialized—and often smaller. Its main advantage was that it turned capital expenditures into operational expenditures, making it attractive in a period of cutting IT budgets. Instead of each company building and maintaining its own IT infrastructure, it could procure those services from a third party. This was particularly significant for firms with uncertain demand for computing resources, as the cloud would allow them to scale upward or downward and consume exactly what they needed. Currently, companies had to buy the equipment necessary to cope with peak demand, which then sat unutilized in off-peak periods. Software applications could also be maintained at a centralized location, meaning that technicians no longer had to update individual PCs each time an upgrade or patch was issued.

Not surprisingly, cloud services were hugely successful with startups, which could now enjoy an infrastructure of the same quality as larger companies. As a Microsoft executive commented, "Even if the entrepreneurs were smarter, large firms [had] a competitive advantage because they [had] the hardware. Now that the hardware is available to all, entrepreneurs can win because they can ask more interesting questions—being smart now matters more."[27] In other words, cloud computing negated any scale advantages. At the same time, large companies stood to benefit as the cloud's service-oriented IT architecture freed their business processes from more restrictive ERP (enterprise resource planning) systems. Companies of all sizes were likely to find it easier to adapt through combinatorial innovation (innovating by combining one or more existing technologies), given that the cloud was basically a huge collection of digital services.

A possible side-effect of the migration toward cloud computing was that businesses might engage in even further specialization and expansion of outsourcing, keeping only their core strengths in-house. This would mean increased dependence on services provided by others, leading to the development of "process networks" and higher levels of virtual integration. Ultimately, the cloud could change not just computing, but business and economic reality as organizations became increasingly interdependent. The cloud was not constrained by physical, geographic, or political boundaries.

An Emerging Ecosystem of Cloud Competitors

Thomas Watson allegedly once said that there was a world market for maybe only five computers. Despite the fact that he was probably referring to mainframes, this statement had been widely used to illustrate IBM's failure to see the future and understand the upcoming dominance of personal computers. Ironically, it could prove to be most true in the cloud world. Technically, all that was needed was a cloud for consumer applications, a cloud for enterprise applications, two clouds to provide the necessary infrastructure, and one to act as a content provider to make the four other clouds work together.[28]

Thinking this way, a clearer picture of the industry emerged. (See Exhibits 14 and 15 for lists of current and potential industry contenders, respectively.) With respect to consumer applications, Google's App Engine and Force.com (provided by Salesforce.com) were the footholds of the platform as a service market. Salesforce.com was also active in the Software-as-a-Service segment, though the market was still quite dispersed without any dominant players. At the same time, there was an increasingly wide variety of enterprise applications (including ERPs and office suites) offered as cloud-based services. Estimates of the cloud-services market size in 2012 ranged all the way from $42 billion (IDC) on the low end to $160 billion (Merrill Lynch) on the high end.[29]

The public cloud–infrastructure segment was largely dominated by Amazon, with Rackspace a distant second. Companies that offered complementary technologies were also starting to emerge. Early examples included RightScale, CloudKick, and enStratus, which offered tools to manage public cloud infrastructures. Meanwhile, traditional web-hosting companies were using tools like Enomaly's ECP to utilize their existing infrastructures to provide cloud services. Even content-delivery networks like Limelight were partnering with infrastructure providers to further expand their services. Players outside of the traditional IT industry (e.g., telecommunications, big retailers) could also enter the market, capitalizing on their infrastructures, brand names, and scale and cost capabilities. For example, telecom companies like AT&T controlled bandwidth, which was a key cost driver in cloud technologies.

The private cloud–infrastructure segment was still largely a no-man's land. One possible reason for this was that private clouds required firms to make significant investments in and reconfigure their own data centers. Any firm with a preinstalled base would therefore be cautious in implementing changes, and private cloud providers had thus far been unable to accelerate the adoption process.

Finally, the integration of cloud-based services was still in its infancy. An early first-mover, Grand Central, had tried to serve as a "bus in the cloud" and connect SaaS providers, but it went under in 2005. OpSource had recently introduced its Services Bus (based on technology from a company named Boomi), while Workday acquired the enterprise service bus, CapeClear. An article published in *InfoWorld* commented that such little integration was present that perhaps the cloud was best termed "sky computing," where IT customers plugged into multiple isolated clouds floating on the horizon.[30]

IBM's Cloud Strategy

Cloud computing fit with the notion of rapid business innovation, which was the driving force behind IBM's cloud strategy.

EARLY INITIATIVES. IBM made its first foray into the cloud in 2007. The "Blue Cloud" was a combination of software and hardware components through which IBM sought to provide customized, cloud-based services for each of its client organizations, a so-called "private cloud." Some analysts viewed IBM's efforts critically, claiming that Blue Cloud was just "Web computing by another name."[31] IBM responded that Blue Cloud was never intended as a full-fledged cloud service; rather, it was an initiative crafted by IBM to experiment with the emerging technology.

In 2008, IBM started offering integrated Cloud Computing Centers. Their purpose was to enable IBM's clients to transition to virtualized data centers and to provide them the freedom to innovate in a controlled and secure computing environment. According to IBM, the Cloud Centers could deliver standardized services through IT automation, resulting in reduced system and application management costs. They were targeted at clients in emerging markets, to facilitate growth as well as to acquaint them with the benefits of the new delivery model. The first Cloud Center opened in February 2008 in Wuxi, China. After that, IBM built centers in Vietnam, Japan, Brazil, India, Korea, Ireland, Poland, and South Africa, and was continuing to expand this program.[32]

Later that same year (2008), IBM started to extend its consulting and technology services to the cloud, building on knowledge gained from its earlier Blue Cloud project. IBM envisioned helping its customers in three main ways. First, IBM would communicate the

EXHIBIT 14

Current Cloud Providers

Amazon. A retailing company founded in 1994, Amazon initially launched its Web Services in 2002 as an integration tool for its marketplace, only to relaunch it in 2006 as a suite of cloud services. Amazon is by far the leader in the public infrastructure cloud segment, offering a wide variety of tools that complement their own infrastructure service. Amazon has a vast ecosystem of firms that offer services based on its infrastructure platform. The ecosystem includes traditional software vendors such as IBM and Oracle, who make their software available on Amazon's infrastructure through Amazon Machine Images (AMIs), which are preconfigured server images that can be launched by users. Amazon leverages its knowledge on how to manage distributed and scalable systems, and is recognized as the company that made the cloud model as known as it is today.

Rackspace. Founded in 1998 and traditionally focused on enterprise-level web hosting services, Rackspace launched its cloud in March 2009. It attained the capability to use its data centers to offer cloud services by acquiring smaller players (Slicehost and Jungledisk) and by developing its own private ventures (Mosso). Rackspace's enterprise-level personalized technical support distinguishes it from Amazon, where support is limited to a community forum. The firm's reported consumer base grew from 43,000 users in the first quarter of 2009 to 80,000 in the first quarter of 2010.

Google. Google is a point of reference in the PaaS segment with its Google App Engine, and in the SaaS segment with its suite of online applications, particularly Google Docs and Gmail. The App Engine has attracted a vast amount of Java and Python developers. Free versions of Google Docs and Gmail have been widely adopted by individual end users as well as academic institutions. The enterprise version of these applications has been adopted by governments (including parts of the federal government in Washington, D.C.) and small firms, but not so much by businesses.

Salesforce.com. This CRM vendor was founded in 1999 by former Oracle executive Marc Benioff. Its SaaS offering has disrupted the traditional CRM market. Managers in marketing departments of firms of all sizes have preferred to opt for Salesforce.com's online offerings instead of going through traditional software-procurement processes with their IT departments. In addition to its CRM application, Salesforce.com offers Force.com, a Java-based PaaS that integrates with its SaaS offering.

Enomaly. This startup, founded in 2004, deployed its Elastic Compute Platform (ECP) to thousands of web-hosting firms, who have used it to adapt their preexisting infrastructures to offer cloud services. The firm's sales have been particularly important in countries like China and Japan. Enomaly has already established important alliances with Intel and HP to provide cloud solutions in China.

message of the cloud to help its customers understand its full potential. Second, it would help them assess the cost of their own cloud initiative and plan accordingly. Finally, IBM would be in a position to provide expertise in the installation, configuration, and usage of a "private" cloud in its customers' data centers.

At the same time, IBM moved even further into the cloud revolution by developing a certification program covering the resiliency of cloud-based applications or services delivered by its partners. Companies hoping to gain IBM's seal of approval had to work with IBM's cloud consulting practice, making IBM a "reference point" in the cloud market.[33] The idea behind the certification program was to help create some standards around security and interoperability in the rapidly emerging world of cloud computing. Generally, the program seemed to have attained its goal, as smaller companies were utilizing it as a signal of expertise in the cloud arena.

ALLIANCE WITH GOOGLE. Apart from these independent moves, IBM formed an important alliance with Google. Though the companies initially stated that the purpose of their relationship was to facilitate university research by providing Internet-scale computing to academic institutions, many suspected this was not just an educational initiative. Sure enough, the CEOs of Google (Eric Schmidt) and IBM (Sam Palmisano) appeared onstage together at a conference in Los Angeles just a few months later, in May 2008, declaring their joint intention to promote commercial cloud-based services.[34] "Cloud computing is the story of our lifetime," stated Eric Schmidt (Google). "Eventually all devices will be on the network."

EXHIBIT 15

Firms Likely to Become Strong Cloud Players

Microsoft. The IT-industry giant has been slow in moving into the cloud but is coming on strong. Microsoft is starting to address the PaaS segment with its Windows Azure offering, which is particularly appealing to .NET developers. It has also started offering the MS cash cow, Microsoft Office, as a web service in its 2010 version. Microsoft's Software Plus Services suite is a set of web applications that include mail (based on Exchange) and collaboration tools (founded on Share Point) targeted for enterprise consumers. It also offers Live@Edu as a free e-mail and collaboration platform for academic institutions.

AT&T. Even though its initial on-demand server offering called Synaptic Hosting was not picked up by consumers, AT&T's control and understanding of the telecommunication networks puts it in a favorable position. The consumption of bandwidth is a key cost driver in cloud services.

Savvis and Terremark. These two firms are primarily enterprise-level web-hosting firms. Both have engaged in alliances with other enterprise-level firms such as VMware to start offering cloud services from their existing data centers. The fact that they use VMware, which is among the most popular virtualization tools used by enterprises, may make it easier for enterprise consumers to adopt them over other public cloud providers.

VMware. VMware has been pushing its vSphere solution into its established enterprise market. It has struggled in distinguishing its traditional virtualization solutions from its new cloud, scalable solutions. VMware has a strong presence in standards-setting organizations and has established alliances with a wide variety of cloud players. Its most recent move involved an alliance with Salesforce.com, in which they jointly launched VMforce. VMforce is an enterprise-oriented Java-based PaaS offering that runs on top of VMware's virtualization software.[43]

The two companies hoped to capitalize on each other's strengths to help get the job done. IBM's reputation could help drive sales of Google Apps (Google's cloud offering), while IBM would provide the infrastructure and services to offer an integrated solution for customers around the globe. Sam Palmisano declared: "This project combines IBM's historic strengths in scientific, business, and secure-transaction computing with Google's complementary expertise in Web computing and massively scaled clusters."[35] Less-tangible benefits of this partnership included the development of a "dominant design"—a cloud-like platform backed by the brand values of both the Google and IBM names.

Microsoft and other competitors were watching this relationship very closely, fearing that Google would try to monopolize key parts of the cloud with the advertising market. According to Nicholas Carr, a technology writer and blogger, there was some basis for this concern. What Google did—building huge data centers, fighting copyright restrictions, digitizing the world's libraries, and launching its new web browser (Chrome)—was aimed at increasing the use of the Internet. "Google wants information to be free," Carr recently wrote in his blog, "because as the cost of information falls it makes more money."[36]

RECENT EFFORTS. In March 2009, IBM initiated negotiations to buy Sun, which would have been the largest acquisition in IBM's history.[37] Analysts saw this purchase as a questionable strategic move, arguing that it made sense only as a financial opportunity since Sun could be bought at a sharp discount.[38] Sun was later bought by Oracle, whose CEO, Larry Ellison, believed the cloud was not distinct from what enterprise-IT had already been doing[39] and promptly shut down Sun's weak cloud-oriented steps. The question remains: What would IBM have done with Sun's cloud infrastructure initiatives?

Undaunted by its failure to capture Sun, IBM went on to introduce new offerings at every level of the cloud infrastructure later that same year. For Software-as-a-Service, IBM promoted Lotus Live as the "Facebook for enterprises." For Platform-as-a-Service, IBM made some bold moves: All product groups within IBM learned that they should align their offerings to work in the cloud, including some of IBM's most successful product lines (Rational, Tivoli, Websphere, and others). A couple of Tivoli-branded offerings showed great promise as easy-to-use automation tools to help managers set up private and hybrid clouds. Another sign of IBM's increasing commitment to the cloud was its focus on developing middleware, defined as "in-the-cloud integration services between as-a-service offerings."[40] In terms of infrastructure, IBM publicized several success stories on building private or hybrid clouds for its clients, showing signs of something big to come. Finally, to combine this surge with IBM's overall strategy of expanding services, IBM's consulting arm announced that it would start helping clients determine the right cloud formation for them.

Industry analysts expected 2010 to be a breakout year for IBM's cloud agenda, with accelerated efforts to increase cloud computing offerings and to compete directly with its major competitors (Google, Microsoft, and others). IBM Fellows and other distinguished IBM-affiliated individuals had spent nearly three years experimenting with the cloud and brainstorming on a wide range of cloud-related issues: early signs of cloud adoption; security in the cloud; the potential of the cloud; business strategy and models for cloud providers; benefits of cloud computing for clients; and so on. This commitment to the development of the cloud started to pay off in January 2010 when IBM announced the largest enterprise cloud deployment yet, as Panasonic moved from Microsoft Exchange to IBM's LotusLive cloud service.[41] In February, IBM announced that it had started a 10-month project to develop a cloud network infrastructure for the U.S. Air Force—representing a major vote of confidence in IBM's cloud security.

Meanwhile, IBM continued to offer highly successful private clouds for its clients to run behind their firewalls. It planned to keep growing its cloud-integration capabilities through acquisitions of smaller companies offering the necessary middleware. At the same time, IBM invited application vendors to address specific business processes that would align with IBM's offerings. The final objective was an ecosystem of partners in which every vendor addressed a specific business need and all were working in unison to provide integrated business solutions that IBM could offer to its clients.

IBM had its sights on the public sphere as well, announcing its plans for a public cloud facility in Raleigh, North Carolina, to go live in summer 2010. IBM insisted that the company's ultimate goal was a hybrid model, where clients could integrate their private clouds with public infrastructure. This new effort fit well with the "green revolution." Initial evidence suggested that the new data center was so efficient it saved 15 percent in annual energy costs.

Globally, IBM's recent efforts were no less impressive. The company continued to build cloud-computing centers in emerging markets, entering through alliances with local, leading small enterprises. It also recently announced an agreement with the European Union to collaborate with universities to develop new cloud-related computer science models.

A SMARTER PLANET. Finally, IBM initiated a massive advertising campaign—much as it did with "e-business"—to promote the idea of building a "smarter" planet. Many believed this push was directly related to the company's cloud strategy. According to IBM, the world was already "instrumented" (transistors, mobile phones, RFID tags, and sensors were the dominant building blocks of the digital age) and interconnected (2 billion people on the Internet, immense information exchanges, and smart interacting devices). The next step was to make our planet "intelligent." What IBM meant with the slogan "smarter planet" was that we could use integrated technology to tackle most of today's pressing environmental and social issues—in other words, make the world smart enough to be sustainable.

IBM cited a number of examples that illustrated the urgent need for a smarter planet: inefficiencies in energy supply systems; over- and undersupply of water in different geographic regions; congested highways and their impact on air quality; the waste of money in inefficient supply chains; the climbing costs of inefficient health care systems; and the 2008–2010 financial crisis. All of these incidents were evidence of a trajectory that needed to be stopped—by investing in intelligent infrastructure.[42]

IBM also cited a number of applications that had proved successful. Coincidentally, many of them were already part of the company's expanding portfolio in smart infrastructures. Stockholm's traffic had been reduced by 20 percent using a smart traffic system; oil extraction technologies could exploit more than the current 20 percent of the available reserves; smart food systems could trace everything back to the farm level; and smart health care networks were envisioned to lower the cost of therapy by 90 percent.

Outsiders characterized IBM's proposal as a "technology-fueled economic recovery plan," noting that its reach extended well beyond the company's own capabilities. IBM's message was far too comprehensive and holistic to be taken as a mere advertising campaign. Palmisano even gave a speech to the Council on Foreign Relations in which he called for increased public and private investment in efficient system infrastructures to fuel future growth. In IBM's vision, the move to a smarter planet would involve cities, regions, and even nations. It was a period of radical discontinuity in the systems we used, and therefore provided an opportunity for visionary leaders and companies to make a profound contribution to societies all around the world. Of course, the cloud, and IBM's investment in cloud computing, would be a key resource in achieving that reality.

Decision Time

Bruce Harreld's strategy team had a lot of data to review and little time to complete its report. The IT industry had always been full of turmoil and frequent technological changes, but cloud computing represented a radical paradigm shift that paralleled the introduction of the PC and the Internet. IBM was adamant (if not paranoid) about not being left behind. It had staged a successful comeback once before, but there was no guarantee it could rise from the ashes a second time if it made similar mistakes again.

Indeed, in its efforts to maintain its reputation as a "reference point" in the industry, IBM had staked some kind of initial claim on almost every emerging cloud front: Software-as-a-Service, Platform-as-a-Service, Infrastructure-as-a-Service, and middleware. It had established private, hybrid, and public clouds for a variety of clients, both in the United States and abroad. Through its certification program, the company was building a network of interconnected providers, and it had just announced a key strategic alliance with Google. IBM's client base currently included national governments, business enterprises, and end-use consumers. Perhaps the real question facing Harreld's team was whether and how long IBM could continue to do it all.

Harreld believed that IBM had been smart to hedge its bets in the early days of the cloud, but that tough choices loomed ahead as the cloud grew increasingly more complex. IBM would have to become more selective regarding which segments to specialize in, which companies to acquire, which ones to partner with, and when it made more strategic sense to go it alone. Trying to do all things for all types of clients was not an efficient business strategy for the long term, and would ultimately spread IBM's resources too thin. Those were the difficult decisions that Palmisano wanted his team to make. Harreld sighed, knowing they had better get to work. . . .

Endnotes

1. IBM Annual Report, 2009.

2. IBM Smart Business Thought Leadership White Paper (2010), "Dispelling the vapor around cloud computing: Drivers, barriers and considerations for public and private cloud adoption," January.

3. Mell, P., and T. Grance, Version 15, October 7, 2009, http://csrc.nist.gov/groups/SNS/cloud-computing/.

4. Adapted from Sam Johnston's definition on Wikipedia.org, "Cloud computing."

5. IBM Archives: 1930s.

6. IBM Archives: 1940s.

7. Wikipedia.org, "History of IBM."

8. Lohr, S. (2002), "He loves to win; At IBM, he did," *The New York Times,* March 10.

9. Gerstner, L. (2002), *Who Says Elephants Can't Dance? Inside IBM's Historic Turnaround* (New York: Collins).

10. Ibid.

11. Ibid.

12. Ibid.

13. IBM Archives: 1997.

14. Lohr, S. (2004), "Big blue's big bet: Less tech, more touch," *The New York Times,* January 25.

15. Spooner J., and S. Junnarkar (2002), "IBM talks up 'computing on demand,'" *CNET News,* October 30.

16. Bulkeley, W. M. (2009), "IBM set to cut more U.S. jobs," *The Wall Street Journal,* March, 25.

17. Lohr, S. (2007), "New effort to tap technology to aid the service economy," *The New York Times,* March 28.

18. Bulkeley, W. M. (2009), "IBM set to cut more U.S. jobs."

19. Lohr, S. (2007), "IBM showing that giants can be nimble," *The New York Times,* July 18.

20. Bulkeley, W. M. (2009), "IBM set to cut more U.S. jobs."

21. Ibid.

22. Hamilton, J. (2010), "Cloud computing economies of scale," Mix 10 Conference, March 10.

23. Interview with Irving Wladawsky-Berger accessible at www.ibm.com/ibm/cloud/why_ibm/.

24. Gartner Newsroom (2009), "Gartner says worldwide CRM market grew 12.5 percent in 2008," July 15.

25. http://en.wikipedia.org/wiki/Cloud_computing.

26. Worthen, B., and J. Scheck (2009), "As growth slows, ex-allies square off in a tech turf war," *The Wall Street Journal,* March 16.

27. Talk by Dan Reed, Scalable and Multicore Computing Strategist, Microsoft, at CERCS Cloud Computing Workshop, Georgia Tech, April 23, 2009.

28. Karadogan, B. (2007), "Five computer clouds are all we need," *GigaOM,* November 22.

29. "The Internet industry is on a cloud–Whatever that may mean," *The Wall Street Journal,* March 26, 2009.

30. www.infoworld.com/d/cloud-computing/what-cloud-computing-really-means-031?page=0,2.

31. Schonfeld, E. (2007), "IBM's blue cloud is just web computing by another name," *Techcrunch,* November 15.

32. "IBM opens four Cloud Computing Centers to meet growing demand in emerging markets," IBM Press Center, September 24, 2008, Armonk, NY.

33. Higginbotham S. (2008), "IBM gives cloud computing a seal of approval," *GigaOM,* November 23.

34. Thibodeau P. (2008), "Google and IBM are bonding in a serious way–PC era fading, cloud computing rising–watch out, Microsoft?" *ComputerWorld,* May 2.

35. "Google and IBM announce university initiative to address Internet-scale computing challenges," Google Press Center, October 8, 2007.

36. Rough Type—Nicholas Carr's Blog: "The Omnigoogle," September 7, 2008.

37. Karnitschnig M., W. M. Bulkeley, and J. Scheck (2009), "IBM in talks to buy Sun in bid to add to web heft," *The Wall Street Journal,* March 18.

38. Hechinger, J., W. M. Bulkeley, and B. Worthen (2009), "IBM signals strategy shift with talks to buy Sun," *The Wall Street Journal,* March 19.

39. "The Internet industry is on a cloud–Whatever that may mean."

40. http://cloudmiddleware.com/.

41. Rosenberg, D. (2010), "IBM grabs largest enterprise cloud deployment," *CNET News,* January 13.

42. Palmisano, S. J. (2008), "A smarter planet: Instrumented, interconnected, intelligent," *IBM.com,* November 2008.

43. "Salesforce.com and VMware form strategic alliance to launch VMforce, the world's first enterprise Java cloud," VMware news release, April 27, 2010.

More innovative. More customer-focused. Leaner and more agile. These are the defining characteristics of the new Merck we are continuing to build . . .

—2008 MERCK ANNUAL REPORT TO SHAREHOLDERS

Alicia Horbaczewski
Merck & Co., Inc.

Frank T. Rothaermel
Georgia Institute of Technology

DR. MERVYN TURNER, Merck's newly appointed Chief Strategy Officer, had never faced a more challenging time in his 23 years with the company. He worried about the expiration of eminent patents on existing drugs, an empty drug pipeline, an adverse regulatory environment, an increasingly competitive marketplace, and a harsh economic climate. With all these challenges to overcome, Merck was more reliant on the development of blockbuster drugs than ever before. In the past, Merck's significant investment in internal research and development (R&D) was a strategic advantage with which few companies could compete. However, Merck's pipeline of potential new drugs seemed to be drying up. With the U.S. and international laws favoring generic drug-makers and offering shorter exclusivity periods for patents, drug companies had less time to make up for significant R&D investments. In order for Merck to stay competitive, Dr. Turner felt strongly that change was necessary. Merck needed to innovate.

Dr. Turner remembered what Dr. Roy Vagelos, former Merck CEO and Chairman, had repeatedly told him: "Organizations that don't change don't last unless they are in some very isolated, unchallenging environment. Organizations . . . need to be revitalized periodically if only because people tend to settle into routines and drop out of touch with their changing environments. One role of a leader is to convince people, before the fact, that they should change."[1]

The position of Chief Strategy Officer at Merck was a new one, and Dr. Turner knew it was his job to envision a game-changing strategy that would restore Merck's long-term leadership in the pharmaceutical industry. He also knew he would need the insights and support of his strategy team to get this monumental task accomplished. That is why he called this meeting—to ask the company's strategic leadership to come up with a detailed analysis and set of recommendations to move Merck toward a more innovative future.

He looked around at the faces of his new strategy team, comprised of executives, directors, mid-level managers, and several eager MBA interns, took a deep breath, and determinedly spoke: "There is no doubt that innovation is the way forward."[2] The expectant eyes continued to stare at Dr. Turner while he patiently explained what he knew they had to do. "Merck accounts for about 1 percent of the biomedical research in the world. To tap into the remaining 99 percent, we must actively reach out to universities, research institutions, and companies worldwide to bring the best of technology and potential products into Merck. The cascade of knowledge flowing from biotechnology and the unraveling of the human genome—to name only two recent developments—is far too complex for any one company to handle alone."[3]

Dr. Turner knew that what he was talking about would have been considered heresy just a few years before. Merck's identity as a science-led company was deeply rooted in its history of having a strong competence in internal research and systems that churned out blockbuster drug after blockbuster drug. Yet Merck's former model, focused on internal R&D, would no longer suffice in an industry where thousands of innovative ideas were generated daily, both inside and outside the company. Importantly, Merck's

Alicia Horbaczewski of Merck (GT MBA '10) and Professor Frank T. Rothaermel prepared this case from public sources. This case is developed for the purpose of class discussion. It not intended to be used for any kind of endorsement, source of data, or depiction of efficient or inefficient management. © Horbaczewski and Rothaermel, 2013.

recent $41 billion "reverse-merger" with Schering-Plough represented a significant step away from a closed R&D model toward a more open innovation strategy. Following the industry trend of consolidation from major to mega-drug companies, Merck was starting to move past its tradition of relying solely on its own internally grown research. However, the company's ability to capitalize fully on this investment depended heavily on whether—and how—Merck's strategy team would embrace any ideas that originated from outside the walls of Merck's hallowed laboratories.

Merck & Co. History

Merck is a global research-driven company that discovers, develops, manufactures, and markets a broad range of innovative products to improve human and animal health. Merck was founded in 1668, when pharmacist Friedrich Merck acquired an apothecary in Darmstadt, Germany. Some 200 years later, Emanuel Merck built a pharmaceutical and chemical company that led to steadily increasing sales and international expansion. In 1891, Merck & Co. was established in Germany and emerged as one of the largest producers of prescription drugs in the world. After World War I, the Merck family, along with their shareholders, incorporated as a U.S. firm with no ties to the original German parent company.

Over the next few decades, Merck developed prominence as a research powerhouse, attracting the most highly respected scientists from around the world. By 1950, five Merck researchers had won Nobel prizes for their contributions to medicine. Head scientists were successful in the recruitment and retention of superior research personnel because Merck maintained an academic, university-like atmosphere in which scientists were given freedom to explore their personal research interests. The hallways in the research sites in Rahway, New Jersey, and Boston had academic disciplines written on them, such as "Biology" and "Chemistry." With a campus-like setting, world-renowned scientists, and cutting-edge research, Merck became known as "The Harvard of Pharma."

By 1989, Merck had expanded to six divisions, 70 business units, 13,000 products, 21,000 employees, and production facilities in 27 countries. Merck's internally focused, research-driven culture received accolades for excellence in the industry, landing it on *BusinessWeek*'s list of Top 10 Most Valuable Companies from 1987 to 1990.[4] *Fortune* magazine

anointed Merck as the most-admired company in America from 1987 to 1993.[5] Even people who knew nothing about the pharmaceutical industry had heard of Merck.

Yet Merck has been unable to replicate its past successes for almost two decades. For the second time in recent years, Merck's 2008 revenues fell by 1 percent from $24.2 billion in 2007. (Exhibits 1 and 2 contain Merck's 2009 income statement and balance sheet.) This decline was largely due to lower sales of Fosamax, which lost its patent for the treatment and prevention of osteoporosis. Also contributing to the loss of revenue were the still lower sales of the cholesterol-lowering drug Zocor, which lost market exclusivity for all formulations in the United States in 2006. Merck has three more key product patents due to expire in upcoming years: in 2010, Cozaar/Hyzaar (to treat hypertension); in 2012, Singulair (to treat asthma and allergic rhinitis); and in 2012, Maxalt (to treat migraine headaches).

Adding tremendous pressure on Dr. Turner to devise a winning strategy for the future was the largest drug recall in history. Merck invested almost $1 billion in the R&D of the arthritis and acute-pain medicine Vioxx, which had been brought to market in a record time of just six years. Upon the launch of Vioxx in May 1999, Merck's revenues increased by over 10 percent. However, increasing controversy in the medical community over the allegation that Vioxx caused heart attacks and strokes tarnished Merck's otherwise spotless reputation. On September 30, 2004, Merck announced the voluntary withdrawal of Vioxx from the market. The recall had a terrible impact on Merck's stock price and adversely affected the sales of Merck's other drugs. Shares fell 27 percent to $33, eradicating $27 billion in market value almost overnight. Merck has been burdened by lawsuits ever since, and it is estimated that legal liabilities have cost Merck up to $30 billion thus far.[6]

"Reverse-Merger" with Schering-Plough

In 2008, Merck had 59,000 employees, sales revenues of $23.9 billion, and a market value of $44.4 billion. Schering-Plough (SP) with 51,000 employees had sales revenues of $18.5 billion and a market value of $32.6 billion.[7] The joining of these two former rivals in March 2009 was seen as a necessary step toward diversification and increased economies of scale,

EXHIBIT 1

Selected Financial Data for Merck & Co., Inc. and Subsidiaries (U.S. $ in millions)

	2009	2008	2007	2006	2005	2004	2003
Sales	$27,428.30	$23,850.30	$24,197.70	$22,636.00	$22,011.90	$22,938.60	$22,485.90
Net income	$12,899.20	$7,808.40	$3,275.40	$4,433.80	$4,631.30	$5,813.40	$6,830.90
Earnings per common share assuming dilution	$5.65	$3.64	$1.49	$2.03	$2.10	$2.61	$3.03
Cash dividends paid per common share	$1.52	$1.52	$1.52	$1.52	$1.52	$1.49	$1.45
Average common shares outstanding assuming dilution (millions)	2,273.20	2,145.30	2,192.90	2,187.70	2,200.40	2,226.40	2,253.10
Total assets	$112,089.70	$47,195.70	$48,350.70	$44,569.80	$44,845.80	$42,572.80	$40,587.50
Net cash flows provided by operating activities	$3,392.00	$6,571.70	$6,999.20	$6,765.20	$7,608.50	$8,799.10	$8,426.50
Capital expenditures	$1,460.60	$1,298.30	$1,011.00	$980.20	$1,402.70	$1,726.10	$1,915.90
Net income as % of average total assets	16.2%	16.3%	7.0%	9.9%	10.6%	14.0%	15.5%
Number of stockholders of record	175,600	165,700	173,000	184,200	172,077	216,100	233,000
Number of employees	100,000	55,200	59,800	60,000	61,500	62,600	63,200

Source: Merck & Co. Annual Reports.

EXHIBIT 2

Consolidated Balance Sheet

Merck & Co., Inc. and Subsidiaries (U.S. $ in millions)

Merck & Co., Inc. and Subsidiaries, December 31, 2009 ($ in millions)

	2009	2008	2007	2006	2005	2004	2003
Assets							
Current Assets							
Cash and cash equivalents	$ 9,311.4	$ 4,368.3	$ 5,336.1	$ 5,914.7	$ 9,585.3	$ 2,878.8	$ 1,201.0
Short-term investments	293.1	1,118.1	2,894.7	2,798.3	6,052.3	4,211.1	2,972.0
Accounts receivables	6,602.9	3,778.9	3,636.2	3,314.8	2,927.3	3,627.7	4,023.6
Inventories (excludes inventories of $345.2 in 2007 and $416.1 in 2006 classified in Other assets)	8,055.3	2,283.3	1,881.0	1,769.4	1,658.1	1,898.7	2,554.7
Prepaid expenses and tax	4,165.9	7,756.3	1,297.4	1,433.0	826.3	858.9	775.9
Total current assets	28,428.6	19,304.9	15,045.4	15,230.2	21,049.3	13,475.2	11,527.2
Investments	432.3	6,491.3	7,159.2	7,788.2	1,107.9	6,727.1	7,941.2
Property, Plant and Equipment (at cost)							
Land	666.7	386.1	405.8	408.9	433.0	366.6	356.7
Buildings	12,210.3	9,767.4	10,048.0	9,745.9	9,479.6	8,874.3	8,016.9
Machinery, equipment and office furnishings	16,173.6	13,103.7	13,553.7	13,172.4	12,785.2	11,926.1	11,018.2
Construction in progress	1,817.5	871.0	795.6	882.3	1,015.5	1,641.6	1,901.9
Less allowance for depreciation	12,594.6	12,128.6	12,457.1	11,015.4	9,315.1	8,094.9	7,124.7
Property, Plant and Equipment, Net	18,273.5	11,999.6	12,346.0	13,194.1	14,398.2	14,713.7	14,169.0
Goodwill	11,923.1	1,438.7	1,454.8	1,431.6	1,085.7	1,085.7	1,085.4
Other Intangibles, Net	47,655.8	525.4	713.2	943.9	518.7	679.2	864.0
Other Assets	5,376.4	7,435.8	11,632.1	5,981.8	6,686.0	5,891.9	5,000.7
Total Assets	**$112,089.7**	**$47,195.7**	**$48,350.7**	**$44,569.8**	**$44,845.8**	**$42,572.8**	**$40,587.5**

EXHIBIT 2 *(Continued)*

	2009	2008	2007	2006	2005	2004	2003
Liabilities and Stockholders' Equity							
Current Liabilities							
Loans payable and current portion of long-term debt	$1,379.2	$2,297.1	$1,823.6	$1,285.1	$2,972.0	$2,181.2	$1,700.0
Trade account payable	2,236.9	617.6	624.5	496.6	471.1	421.4	735.2
Accrued and other current liabilities	9,453.8	9,174.1	8,534.9	6,653.3	5,381.2	5,288.1	3,772.8
Income tax payable	1,285.2	1,426.4	444.1	3,460.8	3,649.2	3,012.3	2,538.9
Dividends payable	1,189.0	803.5	831.1	826.9	830.0	841.1	822.7
6% Mandatory convertible preferred stock	206.6	—	—	—	—	—	—
Total Current Liabilities	15,750.7	14,318.7	12,258.2	12,722.7	13,303.5	11,744.1	9,569.6
Long-Term Debt	16,074.9	3,943.3	3,915.8	5,551.0	5,125.6	4,691.5	5,096.0
Deferred Income Taxes and Noncurrent Liabilities	18,771.5	7,766.6	11,585.3	6,330.3	6,092.9	6,442.1	6,430.3
Stockholders' Equity							
Common stock, one cent par value							
Authorized - 6,500,000,000 shares	1,781.3	29.8	29.8	29.8	29.8	29.8	29.8
Other paid-in capital	39,682.6	8,319.1	8,014.9	7,166.5	6,900.0	6,869.8	6,956.6
Retained earnings	41,404.9	43,698.8	39,140.8	39,095.1	37,918.9	36,626.3	34,142.0
Accumulated other comprehensive loss	(2,766.5)	(2,553.9)	(826.1)	(1,164.3)	52.3	(45.9)	65.5
Stockholders' equity before deduction for treasury stock	80,102.3	49,493.8	46,359.4	45,127.1	44,901.0	43,480.0	41,193.9
Less treasury stock, at cost:	21,044.3	30,735.5	28,174.7	27,567.4	26,984.4	26,191.8	25,617.5
Total Merck & Co., Inc. Stockholders' Equity	59,058.0	18,758.3	18,184.7	17,559.7	17,916.6	17,288.2	15,576.4
Noncontrolling Interests	2,434.6	2,408.8	2,406.7	2,406.1	2,407.2	2,406.9	3,915.2
Total Equity	61,492.6	21,167.1	20,591.4	19,965.8	20,323.8	19,695.1	19,491.6
Total Liabilities and Stockholders' Equity	$112,089.7	$47,195.7	$48,350.7	$44,569.8	$44,845.8	$42,572.8	$40,587.5

Source: Merck & Co. Annual Reports

propelled by imminent patent expirations and increasing pressure from shareholders, government, and customers to control costs. Under the proposed agreement, the newly combined Merck would rank second in market share (5.5 percent) and fifth in market capitalization ($77 billion) worldwide. (See Exhibits 3–5 for comparative rankings and financial data for the global leaders in the pharmaceutical industry. Exhibit 6 shows Merck's and SP's blockbuster drugs, with sales over $1 billion annually.)

Merck Chairman and CEO Dick Clark justified the deal as follows: "The combined company will benefit from a formidable R&D pipeline, a significantly broader portfolio of medicines, and an expanded presence in key international markets, particularly in high-growth emerging markets."[8,9] As a result of acquiring SP, Merck would gain over 20 new compounds in stage 2 or stage 3 of the FDA approval process. Merck would also benefit from SP's globally diverse portfolio, increasing Merck's international sales from $10.5 billion to $25 billion (Exhibit 7 shows the sales structure of the new company), with operations in over 140 countries. For the first time in its history, Merck expected that more than 50 percent of its revenues would come from outside of the United States.[10] In addition, Merck's yearly savings resulting from this merger were forecast to be as large as $3.5 billion after 2011.

On November 4, 2009, Merck completed its merger with SP. The new company used the name "Merck" in the United States and Canada and went by "MSD" elsewhere in the world. The deal was structured as a "reverse-merger" to permit SP to bypass a change-of-control clause in a drug partnership it had with Johnson & Johnson (J&J). SP and J&J shared the rights to the blockbuster drugs Remicade and Simponi, which have generated a combined net present value of $6.9 billion.[11] Under the "change-of-control" clause, J&J would acquire the full rights to the drugs if SP were to be taken over. Under the "reverse-merger" agreement, SP technically survived the merger with respect to accounting practices, although it renamed itself as Merck, was run by Merck's CEO, and was headquartered at Merck's base in Whitehouse Station, New Jersey. Merck's original shareholders controlled 68 percent of the combined company, while the new board was comprised of 14 members from Merck and just 3 directors from SP.[12] Additionally, only about 40 percent of SP's senior leaders joined the new Merck.[13]

EXHIBIT 3

The New Landscape: The Largest Pharmaceutical Players by Market Capitalization if Pending Deals Are Completed (U.S. $ in billions)

Source: Adapted from "Merck to buy rival for $41 billion," *The Wall Street Journal*, March 10, 2009.

Company	Market Cap
Eli Lily	$31.7
Bristol Myers Squibb	$37.4
AstraZeneca	$43.8
Sanofi-Aventis	$65.7
Abbot	$71.8
GlaxoSmithkline	$74.7
Merck & Schering-Plough	$77.0
Novartis	$91.6
Roche Holding	$114.1
Johnson & Johnson	$130.2
Pfizer and Wyeth	$139.5

EXHIBIT 4

Global Rankings of Pharmaceutical Firms by Market Share: The Combined Merck (including SP) Will Rank #2 Globally with 5.5 Percent Market Share vs. Pfizer-Wyeth's 8.2 Percent

Source: Adapted from *IMS Health MIDAS MAT*, December 2008.

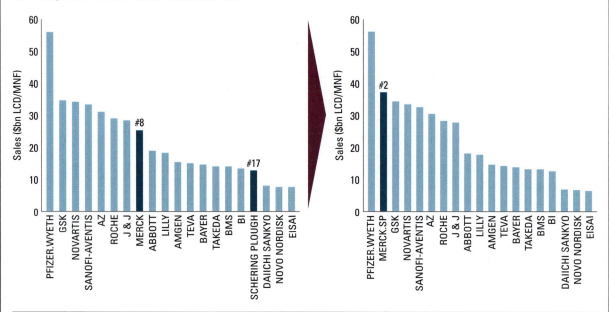

EXHIBIT 5

Financial Data for the Global Leaders in the Pharmaceutical Industry

Company	Merck	Pfizer / Wyeth	Glaxo Smith Kline	Novartis	Astra Zeneca	Johnson & Johnson
Market capitalization	$114.4	$143.6	$109.7	$122.2	$63.6	$173.1
Revenue	$19.57	$45.82	$42.62	n/a	32.05	$60.53
Employees	55,200	81,800	99,003	99,834	66,100	118,700
Revenue / employee	$354,600	$560,100	$430,559	n/a	$484,900	$509,900
Net income	$3.6 B	$8.134 B	$7.752 B	n/a	7.225	$12.77
Shares outstanding	3.099 B	8.07 B	2.831 B	2.274	1.448	2.759
Annual earnings /share	$1.93	$1.22	$2.41	n/a	$4.12	$4.62
P/E ratio	19.13	14.59	25.2	n/a	10.67	13.58
Annual dividends / share	$1.52	$0.66	$1.93	$1.00	$3.80	$1.96
Dividend yield	4.12%	3.71%	4.99%	3.70%	8.65%	3.12%
Trade price	$37.58	$17.68	$39.25	$54.27	$43.95	$63.54

Source: Adapted from WolframAlpha, February 16, 2010.

EXHIBIT 6

Merck's and Schering-Plough's Blockbuster Drug Lineup

	Drug	Indication	2008 Sales
Merck	Singular	Asthma	$4.3 bn
	Cozaar/Hyzaar	Hypertension	$3.6 bn
	Gardasil	HPV vaccine	$1.4 bn
	Januvia	Diabetes	$1.4 bn
Schering-Plough	Remicade	Inflammatory diseases	$2.1 bn
	Nasonex	Allergies	$1.2 bn
	Temodar	Brain tumors	$1.0 bn
Merck-SP Joint Venture	Zetia/Vytorin	Cholesterol	$4.6 bn

Source: "Merck to buy rival for $41 billion," *The Wall Street Journal*, March 10, 2009.

EXHIBIT 7

Merck's Sales Structure (before and after the SP reverse-merger)

Merck had $23.9 billion in 2008; $10.5 billion were in international sales.

Merck, combined with Schering-Plough, had $46.9 billion in 2008; $25 billion were in international sales.

Source: Adapted from Merck's Announcement to Investors, 2009.

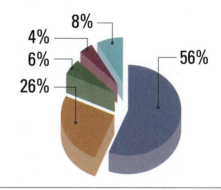

- United States - Europe & Canada - Asia Pacific
- Latin America - Japan

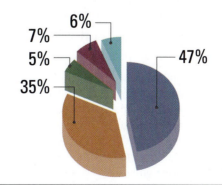

- United States - Europe & Canada - Asia Pacific
- Latin America - Japan

Despite the new company's elaborate legal structure, J&J claimed that the practical reality was that Merck had in effect acquired SP, and filed suit in court.[14] The companies resolved their dispute through arbitration in April 2011. Merck (SP) agreed to relinquish marketing rights in all territories outside the United States, except Europe, Russia, and Turkey. In addition, profits in the "retained" territories would be split equally between the two companies, and Merck would make a one-time payment of $500 million to J&J. Despite the financial loss, investors viewed the resolution of the dispute positively. Merck's shares rose 2.7 percent on the day of the announcement.[15]

This "reverse-merger" was the first major external venture Merck had participated in since 2006, when Dr. Turner led Merck's acquisitions of biotechnology firms GlycoFi and Abmaxis for a combined total of $480 million. In December of that same year, Dr. Turner also led the much larger acquisition of Sirna Therapeutics for $1.1 billion. Such strategic purchases helped to strengthen Merck's drug pipeline, and its stock price immediately rose more than 1 percent to a total of $34.84.[16] After Merck's announcement of the merger with SP, however, SP's stock rose by 14 percent to end the day at $20.13 a share, while Merck's stock price fell 7.7 percent to close at $20.99 a share.[17]

Dr. Turner knew that the upcoming year would be tough and thought about what his boss, CEO Dick Clark, told the media on the day the SP merger was announced: "This is a uniquely complementary match. . . . The combined company will be well-positioned for sustainable growth through scientific innovation."[18] Dr. Turner felt intense pressure as Merck's first Chief Strategy Officer to deliver on that promise of a more innovative, more customer-focused, leaner, and more agile Merck for customers, employees, and the scientific community, as well as for Merck itself.[19]

Consolidation of the Pharmaceutical Industry

The pharmaceutical industry is one of the largest and most profitable in the world. In 2006, biotechnology and pharmaceutical companies combined created approximately 700,000 direct jobs and 3.2 million total indirect and induced jobs in the United States alone.[20] In 2009, the U.S. pharmaceutical market grew by 1 to 2 percent to approximately $300 billion, while global sales increased at 3 to 5 percent to surpass $775 billion, reflecting sustained growth in key emerging countries tempered by a slower pace in more established markets.[21] However, the rate of annual growth in the pharmaceutical market has been decreasing steadily since its peak in 2001 (see Exhibit 8), because the industry has been facing a slew of ongoing problems.

Perhaps most importantly, companies are anticipating severe declines in sales in upcoming years as several blockbuster products lose their patents. The pharmaceutical industry in total is expected to lose as much as $65 billion through 2012 (see Exhibit 9). As a result, many drug companies—like Merck—have recently acquired or merged with others to keep their pipelines full of potential drug candidates. Novartis bought Chiron for $5.4 billion in 2006; AstraZeneca bought MedImmune for $15.6 billion in 2007. In the same year that Merck spent $41 billion to take on SP, Pfizer announced its takeover of Wyeth for $68 billion, and the Swiss firm Roche bought the remaining 44 percent of shares of biotech wunderkind Genentech for $47 billion. In March 2009, the CEO of Eli Lilly declared that the company, even after it had acquired ImClone for $6.5 billion, was still looking for additional acquisitions worth as much as $15 billion.[22]

This wave of mega-mergers was seen as necessary to mitigate the risk of developing new commercially successful products and to replenish the diminishing drug pipelines faced by major pharmaceutical companies. Horizontal consolidation, however, may not address the lack of innovation in the industry as a whole. Many analysts fear that consolidation, while facilitating cost containment, will hinder breakthrough R&D needed to procure long-term, life-saving drugs. The concern is that "making R&D bigger does not make it more efficient,"[23] and that the large, bureaucratic organizations created through such mega-deals stifle the innovation needed to create new knowledge and products.

Drug Discovery, Development, and the FDA Approval Process

In the United States, drugs are developed by pharmaceutical companies without any significant help from the government.[24] The science-driven process for drug development takes an average of 12 years and may exceed $1 billion. (See Exhibit 10 for details on the stages of the drug-development process.) It is estimated that out of every 5,000 to 10,000 compounds screened in the discovery phase, only 250 enter preclinical testing. Only five of those molecules enter the three phases of clinical testing, which is where most of

EXHIBIT 8

Global Pharmaceutical Sales, 2001–2008

	2001	2002	2003	2004	2005	2006	2007	2008
Total world market (current U.S, $ in billions)	393	429	499	560	605	648	715	773
Growth over previous year (growth rate in constant U.S. $)	11.8%	9.2%	10.2%	7.9%	7.2%	6.8%	6.6%	4.8%

Global Pharmaceutical Sales vs. Growth, 2004–2010

Source: Adapted from IMS Health Market Prognosis (includes IMS Audited and Unaudited markets). All information current as of March 2009. www.imshealth.com/deployedfiles/imshealth/Global/Content/StaticFile/Top_Line_Data/Global_Pharma_Sales_2001-2008_Version_2.pdf.

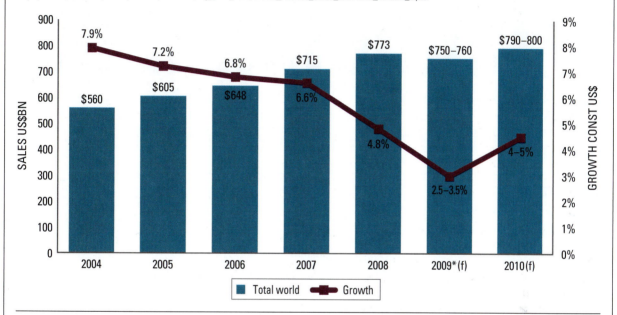

the drug development costs are incurred. Companies must conduct large-scale clinical trials, in hundreds of patients, to demonstrate that a drug has adequate safety and efficacy before filing a new drug application (NDA) with the Food and Drug Administration (FDA). An FDA advisory council then reviews the data provided by the company and holds a public hearing to determine if approval will be granted.

Drug development has always been a costly and risky process, but expenses have risen sharply in recent years. R&D expenditures among Pharmaceutical Research and Manufacturers of America (PhRMA) members grew from $8.4 billion in 1990, to $26 billion in 2000, to $50.3 billion in 2008.[25] As a whole, the pharmaceutical sector invested a record $65.2 billion in R&D in 2008.[26] At the same time, average sales per patented product fell from $457 million in 1990 to $337 million in 2001

(in inflation-adjusted 1999 U.S. dollars).[27] These figures suggest the declining productivity of research and development in the pharmaceutical industry.

Despite increasingly expensive R&D efforts, fewer molecules are being approved by the FDA than ever before (see Exhibit 11). Moreover, only one of every five drugs that hit the market actually achieves enough financial success to recoup its investment.[28] However, when a new drug provides a breakthrough for the health of a large patient population, it may reach sales levels of a blockbuster. A blockbuster drug in the 1980s and 1990s was one whose annual sales topped $500 million. Since 2000, a blockbuster drug must have annual sales of at least $1 billion.

Despite predictions that the business model based on patent-protected blockbuster drugs is slowly dying, the number of blockbuster drugs has actually tripled in

EXHIBIT 9

Top 20 Global Corporations: Exposure to Loss of Exclusivity

Source: Adapted from IMS Health, MIDAS, Market Segmentation, Rx only, December 2008, 27 market segmentation countries.

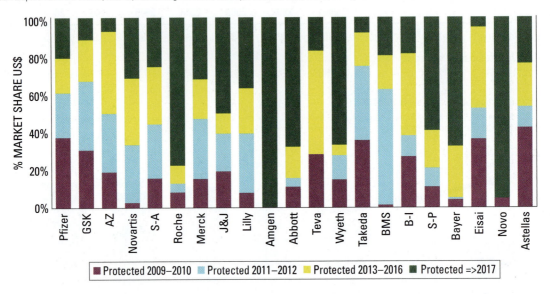

EXHIBIT 10

Stages in Drug-Discovery Process

Compound Success Rates by Stages

Preclinical Trials:
Laboratory and animal testing

Clinical Testing:
Phase 1: 20–100 healthy volunteers used to determine safety and dosing range
Phase 2: 100–500 patient volunteers used to determine safety and efficacy
Phase 3: 1,000–5,000 patient volunteers used to generate statistically significant data about safety and efficacy over a longer time period

Source: Adapted from Drug Discovery and Development: Understanding the R&D Process, www.innovation.org;

CBO, Research and Development in the Pharmaceutical Industry, 2006.

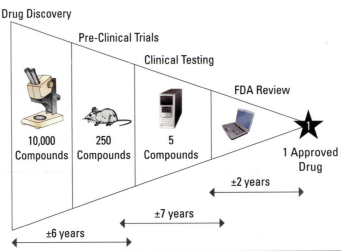

EXHIBIT 11

R&D Investment and New Drug Approvals

Note: Includes biological products.

Source: Adapted from Datamonitor, PhRMA. *Acumen Journal of Sciences*, Vol. 1, Issue II.

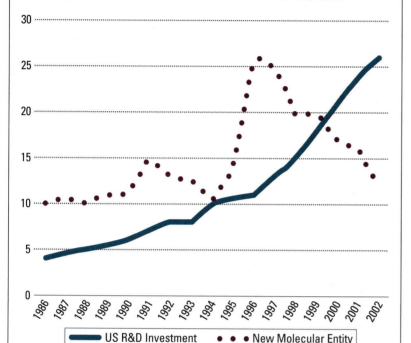

US R&D Investment (in billions of USD) — New Molecular Entity Approvals

new drug launched by a major company, at $1.3 billion in 2004.[34] This has caused the profits of biotechnology firms to remain close to zero, even while revenues have grown dramatically. Instead of accelerating FDA approval at decreased costs, the short-term alliances biotech companies once formed with pharmaceutical giants were now thought to hinder innovation instead of spread scientific knowledge. This fueled industry consolidation even further, as major pharmaceutical companies sought to merge with or acquire biotechnology firms in an effort to become more diversified and build joint long-term capabilities.

Merck found this new industry terrain especially challenging. The company had long relied on its ability to pump out blockbuster after blockbuster drug from its internal research pipeline. It would charge a premium under patent protection for the duration of the legally set exclusivity periods for existing drugs to help cushion the company's R&D costs for the next blockbuster. Former CEO Henry Gadsden had once said, "We'd cut back in every part of the company. We'd cut back in sales and promotion. We'd tighten up our production. We'd do everything we could to hold down costs. But we'd try very hard not to cut back on research because that's our future."[35] Even in today's troubling times, Merck saw a 57 percent drop in profit in the first quarter of 2009, but Merck increased its investment in R&D by 14 percent to $1.2 billion.[36] Based on current industry trends, Mr. Turner was not sure this money was well spent.

U.S. Health Care Reform and the Generic Challenge

Pharmaceutical companies are facing additional price pressures driven by changes in U.S. and worldwide regulatory restrictions on the industry. In March 2010, Congress approved and President Obama signed the Affordable Care Act into law, creating significant uncertainties for the health care industry. Under the new law, patients have increased access to health

the last decade.[29] In 2006, 101 drugs each sold more than $1 billion worldwide.[30] Of these, 18 were biotechnology innovations, compared to only 3 biotech products in 2000 (see Exhibit 12).[31] The rapid rise of the biotechnology industry seemed to promise a solution to the R&D drought in pharmaceutical companies' pipelines, attracting more than $40 billion of venture capital to date.[32] Major pharmaceutical firms rushed to partner with biotech companies, hoping to discover the next great medical breakthrough and then apply their competencies in development, distribution, and marketing to maximize its profit potential. In fact, between 25 and 40 percent of current sales by major pharmaceutical companies are from products that originated in the biotechnology sector.[33]

However, biotechnology has hardly been the hoped-for panacea for the pharmaceutical companies' R&D problems. Instead of providing cheaper and more lucrative alternatives to traditional pharmaceuticals, the average cost of R&D of a new biotechnology drug was $1.2 billion, quite similar to the average cost per

EXHIBIT 12

Top Biotechnology Drugs by Sales

There are at least 23 protein therapeutics with sales of $1 billion or more. Below are aggregate sales figures recorded by the companies listed. Average annual exchange rates were used to convert to U.S. dollars in certain cases.

Product	Company	2005 Sales (in US$)	2006 Sales (in US$)	Change (in %)
Enbrel	Amgen, Wyeth, Takeda	3.70	4.40	20
Aranesp	Amgen	3.30	4.10	26
Rituxan/MabThera	Biogen Idec, Genentech, Roche	3.30	3.90	16
Remicade	J&J, Schering-Plough, Tanabe	3.00	3.60	20
Epogen/Procrit/Eprex	Amgen, Kirin, Johnson & Johnson	3.30	3.20	−4
Herceptin	Genentech, Roche	1.70	3.10	82
Epogen	Amgen, Kirin	2.80	2.90	0
Neulasta	Amgen	2.30	2.70	18
Human insulins (A)	NovoNordisk	2.50	2.50	1
Avastin	Genentech, Roche	1.30	2.40	77
Lantis/Lantus	Sanofi-Aventis	1.40	2.20	53
Humira	Abbott	1.40	2.00	46
Insulin analogs	NovoNordisk	1.20	1.80	50
Neorecormon	Roche	1.80	1.80	−2
Avonex	Biogen Idec	1.50	1.70	11
Rebif	Merck Serono	1.30	1.50	14
Neupogen	Amgen, Kirin	1.40	1.30	−1
Humalog	Eli Lilly	1.20	1.30	8
Pegasys	Roche	1.10	1.20	4
Betaseron/Betaferon (B)	Bayer Schering	1.00	1.20	20
Erbitux	ImClone, Bristol-Myers, Merck KGaA	0.70	1.10	57
Synagis	MedImmune	1.10	1.10	0
Cerezyme	Genzyme	0.90	1.00	7

Note: (A) Sales includes related insulin products; (B) 2006 estimated from 1Q-3Q06 sales; $B.

Source: Lawrence, S. (2007), "Billion dollar babies—Biotech drugs as blockbusters," *Nature Biotechnology* 25: 380–382.

care, whether through Medicaid, subsidized employer plans, or state-run medical exchanges. Insurance companies are no longer able to impose lifetime limits, and coverage can no longer be denied for preexisting conditions. Nearly everyone is required to get insurance or pay a penalty.[37] One change likely to benefit both pharmaceutical firms and patients is that insurers may no longer drop or limit coverage on individuals who participate in clinical trials for cancer or other life-threatening diseases.[38]

Pharmaceutical firms rank second only to the tobacco industry in the corporations-hated-most department[39] and have frequently been blamed by politicians for the nation's health care woes. In an attempt to place pharmaceutical companies in a positive public relations light, PhRMA made an unexpected $80 billion pledge over the next 10 years to help pay for health care reform. Its hope was to position pharmaceutical companies to take advantage of the enormous new customer base that would be created by expanding health care coverage. PhRMA's investment could potentially backfire, though, if the government uses its increased purchasing power to squeeze margins on prescription drugs and accelerate the shift to generics.

However, the generic drug manufacturers also have a strong political lobby, the Generic Pharmaceutical Association (GphA). GphA is perceived as the voice of the American public, demanding ever-lower prices for drugs and pushing for importation of lower-priced drugs from foreign companies such as Israeli-based Teva Pharmaceuticals, the largest supplier of generic prescription medicines in the United States.[40] In 2003, generic drugs comprised 54 percent of the market. That figure leaped to 72 percent of total pharmaceutical sales in 2008.[41] In 2006, eight of the top 10 drugs launched in the United States were generic products, while 61 percent of senior prescriptions were generic.[42] Generic companies incur no expense for the discovery or the development of the new drugs they copy; such R&D expenses fall solely on the innovator.

The legal basis for generic drugs dates back to the Hatch-Waxman Act of 1984, otherwise known as the Drug Price Competition and Patent Term Restoration Act of 1984. Under the Hatch-Waxman Act (which does not apply to biologics), the FDA may approve a generic drug in the form of an Abbreviated New Drug Application (ANDA) if the generic company can establish that its product is "pharmaceutically equivalent" to the drug it wishes to copy.[43] No clinical trials are required, which confers an important advantage on the generic manufacturers over the brand-name companies that developed the original compound. This law was the foundation for cheap generics copying the work of large pharmaceuticals without the up-front risk or cost, and selling at a discount.

When a generic company files an ANDA, it also makes a patent certification claim, the most disruptive of which is Paragraph IV, alleging that the listed patent is invalid and will not be infringed upon. This provides generic companies with the right to copy an innovator's drug as soon as its exclusivity period elapses. The standard exclusivity period is five years for a new chemical entity, but there are additional provisions: seven years for "orphan drugs" (indications with a prevalence of less than 200,000 cases per year), three years for a new use or formulation, and six months for a pediatric drug.[44]

The generic industry continued to grow with the 2003 Medicare Act Amendments, which implemented several new rights for generics and limitations for the pharmaceutical industry. First, it increased regulation regarding agreements between generic companies and innovators. Next, it considered not one company, but all generic companies that file on the same day to be "first-filers," each with legal claims against the original patent. As a result, 2003 became the year that many more generic companies than ever before began to embrace Paragraph IV challenges as a viable strategy. As a result, by 2007 over 160 generic companies had active Paragraph IV filings, compared with fewer than 40 in 2001 (Exhibit 13).[45] A multitude of new players

EXHIBIT 13

ANDAs with a Paragraph IV Challenge

Source: *The Paragraph Four Report: Annual Trends,* from Parry Ashford Inc., 2008.

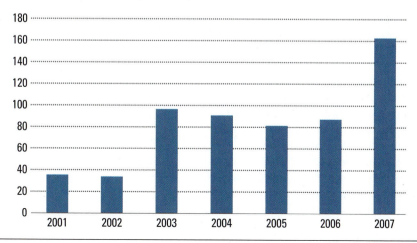

entered the generic industry, with the result that pharmaceutical companies like Merck now find virtually all of their commercially viable products under attack as soon as their patent protection expires. There is a delicate balance between providing accessible, reasonably priced drugs for today and investing in the development of new innovative drugs for the future. If the generic industry continues to gain strength, cheap but old drugs will likely persist while the introduction of new and innovative drugs will decline.

After 10 years of resistance, biotech companies have recently started to lobby Congress to allow the FDA to approve generic biotechnology products. Biotechnology firms have never faced the generic competition that makers of chemical-based drugs have when their patents expire. The FDA currently lacks authority to approve generic biotechnology products, but as the political clout of the generic drug industry increases, this may soon change. "With nowhere else to turn, BIO (the Biotechnology Industry Organization) and PhRMA now want to come to the table to cut a deal. They want unprecedented and excessive market exclusivity and patent protections to ensure their monopolies," said Kathleen Jaeger, President of the Generic Pharmaceutical Association.[46] With such increasing pressures from the political sphere, regulatory environment, and generic competition, the strategic mantra for the pharmaceutical CEO or Chief Strategy Officer is simple: innovate or die.

Open Innovation[47]

According to the closed-innovation philosophy adopted by most pharmaceutical giants in the 20th century, successful innovation requires complete control. A company would generate its own ideas and develop, manufacture, market, and distribute the resulting products alone. This closed approach has worked especially well for Merck in the past, forming a virtual circle in which fundamental scientific breakthroughs led to new drugs and increased sales, which were in turn poured back into more R&D investment to create more new discoveries.[48] However, with the rise of the Internet and the increased mobility of knowledge workers (individuals, such as scientists, engineers, physicians, and consultants, valued for their ability to work with complex information and data), companies heavily dependent on human capital are increasingly unable to protect their intellectual property, causing the closed-innovation system to break down. This

effect is further compounded by the ready availability of venture capital to fund risky startups. Dr. Turner knew that the closed-innovation paradigm and self-reliance Merck had grown accustomed to would not work in this age of open innovation.

In contrast, open innovation involves companies opening up their business models by actively searching for and exploiting outside ideas, as well as allowing unused internal technologies to flow to the outside where other firms can unlock their latent economic potential (see Exhibit 14). Firms actively seek external R&D by bringing in new human capital, engaging in strategic alliances, or acquiring technology ventures, while continuing to innovate internally. At the same time, any internal inventions that the firm decides not to pursue should be considered for commercialization

EXHIBIT 14

The Closed-Innovation Model

Source: Adapted from Chesbrough, H. (2003), "The era of open innovation," *MIT Sloan Management Review*, Spring: 35–41.

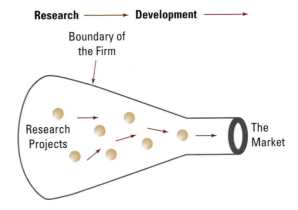

The Open-Innovation Model

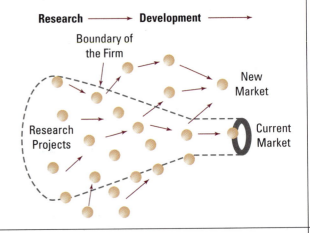

through licenses, spin-offs, or joint ventures. Research indicates that fewer than half of companies actually use their patented technologies because the innovation either costs too much to develop, its potential value is uncertain, or it does not fit the company's business strategy. As a consequence, patented technology too often remains on the shelf.[49] Such inefficiencies in the innovation market are overcome when companies open up and share ideas and technology, permitting them to flow freely to where they can be most efficiently developed. See Exhibit 15 for a comparison of closed- and open-innovation principles.

Open innovation comes with incredible risks with which many scientists, fiercely protective of their research and intellectual property, do not feel comfortable. It may be difficult for a company to capture the value that open innovation creates. While open innovation systematically increases the availability of knowledge by finding highly capable partners for scientists to collaborate with, it also inevitably leads to the loss of individual control over potentially invaluable technology. As a result, a company may end up giving away a billion-dollar patent to its direct competitor because it does not understand the value of a discovery. This loss of control coupled with uncertain monetary outcomes led many scientists to wonder whether open innovation was worth all the hype. Was it really necessary to change?

Yet Dr. Turner had seen a number of smaller upstarts, such as Amgen, Genentech, and Genzyme, successfully parlay their research discoveries to become major players in the biotechnology industry through open innovation.[50] Moreover, some of Merck's smaller and more formidable competitors were already well on their way to leveraging external research capabilities. For example, InnoCentive, a formerly wholly owned subsidiary of Eli Lilly, offers firms a mechanism to facilitate the development and commercialization of new technology. Using a global network of independent researchers, InnoCentive acts as a knowledge broker and facilitates the exchange of technological know-how, primarily associated with chemistry and biotechnology. Through this system of open innovation, InnoCentive has realized a success rate that is higher than the traditional internal R&D approach, at approximately one-sixth the cost.[51]

EXHIBIT 15

Contrasting Principles of Closed and Open Innovation

Closed Innovation	Open Innovation
The best and brightest people in our industry work for us.	We need to work with smart people inside and outside our company because not all the smart people work for us.
We must discover the best molecules, develop them, manufacture them, and distribute them internally in order to profit from our investment R&D.	While internal R&D is needed to claim competitive value, external research can also create significant value for the company.
If we are the first to discover a molecule, we will be the first to get it to market and thus profit from its development.	Our company does not have to originate the molecule to actually profit from it in the market.
The company that succeeds in first getting an innovative drug to the market will win.	Creating a more open business model will be more successful in the long run than getting an innovative drug to the market first.
If we discover, develop, and create the most and the best molecules in the industry, we will win.	If we tap into the plethora of internal and external ideas in the industry, we will win.
We must control our intellectual property, so that our competitors don't profit from our ideas.	We should share our intellectual property with others and profit from others' use of our intellectual property, whenever it advances our business model.

Source: Adapted from Chesbrough, H. (2003), *Open Innovation: The New Imperative for Creating and Profiting from Technology* (Boston, MA: Harvard Business School Press).

Meanwhile, as a consequence of its historically closed R&D system, Merck had the lowest percent of new approved drugs based on externally derived technology at only 13 percent (see Exhibit 16), whereas Bristol-Myers, Sanofi-Aventis, and Roche had approximately 80 percent of their new drugs coming from external sources. Dr. Turner passionately believed that Merck also needed to become more open, but knew that implementing this change would not be easy.

Open Innovation at Merck

Merck suffered from the "not invented here" syndrome, meaning that if a product was not created and developed at Merck, it could not be good enough. Merck's culture and organizational systems perpetuated this logic, which assumed that since they hired the best people, the smartest people in the industry must work for Merck, and so the best discoveries must be invented at Merck. Merck led the industry in terms of R&D spending, because Merck believed that if it was the first to discover and develop a new drug, it would be the first to market. In 2009, Merck was ranked as the fourth most successful company by total number of active R&D projects (see Exhibit 17), a considerable point of pride for Merck's personnel. Changing from a closed-innovation system to operating within an open-innovation network would require a fundamental shift in Merck's culture and mindset. Merck's researchers were simply not accustomed to listening to "outsiders."[52] To begin changing the behavior of Merck's top scientists, Dr. Turner had sent them to a "charm school" where they could learn courtesy and manners to use when corresponding with non-Merck people.

Dr. Turner knew that innovation attempts often fail in large and historically successful companies. But he was optimistic that Merck could change based on its past successful experiences with several open-innovation initiatives, including the hepatitis B vaccine in the 1980s, the Merck Gene Index Project in the 1990s, and Merck Bioventures in the 2000s. Additionally, Merck was already tapping into external knowledge held in the scientific community through informal networks, conference attendance, publications, and creative business arrangements with other scientific organizations. In fact, Merck actively encouraged its researchers to publish their findings in medical and scientific journals. Dr. Turner himself was the author of more than 80 articles in peer-reviewed journals and had served on the editorial board of a number of scientific journals.[53] He firmly believed that the need to foster connectivity with the external environment outweighed the potential losses associated with publication of once-proprietary intellectual knowledge.[54]

Overall, the number of publications by dedicated pharmaceutical companies doubled to 40,000 from 1990 to 2003, illustrating the increasing participation in open science across the industry (see Exhibit 18). Based on this trend, Dr. Turner knew it was more important than ever to be connected to the wider scientific community by collaborating across institutional boundaries with other companies and universities. Research has shown that "the extent of this collaboration is positively related to private sector research productivity,"[55] and the more collaboration a company has in co-authorships, the greater its chance of discovering a new drug. Having a large number of such collaborations is also positively associated with the number of important patents a firm acquires.[56]

Dr. Turner was also hopeful because research has shown that past productivity is the most important predictor of a research program's future success. A company's past success in attaining FDA approval for any therapeutic class is significantly and

---

EXHIBIT 16

Percent of New Approved Drugs, Based on Externally Driven Technology, 1989–2004

Source: FDA Orange Book and U.S. Patent and Trademark Office.

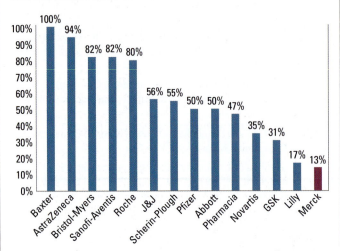

EXHIBIT 17

Top 10 Companies by R&D Projects League Table

The table below summarizes the top 50 companies in PharmaProjects, a database tracking pharmaceutical development from early preclinical study through to launch or discontinuation. It lists companies in descending order by total number of active research and development (R&D) projects (excluding suspended products). Each company's total R&D products are separated into the number of drugs originating from its own research and the number of drugs it has licensed-in. The table also shows subtotals at 10 place intervals. The percentage values represent the number of drugs in R&D as a proportion of the total number of R&D projects listed in PharmaProjects in March 2009.

Position February 2009	No. of R&D Drugs	No. of Own Drugs	No. Under License
1 GlaxoSmithKline *	228	141	87
2 Pfizer *	199	150	49
3 Sanofi-Aventis *	176	125	51
4 Merck & Co *	**165**	**109**	**56**
5 AstraZeneca *	157	113	44
6 Novartis *	156	94	62
7 Hoffmann-La Roche *	133	83	50
8 Johnson & Johnson	128	73	55
9 Eli Lilly *	117	88	29
10 Wyeth	101	75	26
Subtotal: top 10	**1560 (16.6%)**	**1051 (11.2%)**	**509 (19.4%)**

*Pharma-Documentation-Ring member company

Source: www.p-d-r.com/ranking/Top50_Mar09.pdf. For further information, see www.pharmaprojects.com. Copyright Informa UK Ltd 2009. All rights reserved.

EXHIBIT 18

Publications by Pharmaceutical Firms in Scientific Journals

Source: Hess, A. M., and F. T. Rothaermel (2010), "Sensing, seizing, and strategic renewal: A micro-foundation model of dynamic capability formation," working paper, Georgia Institute of Technology.

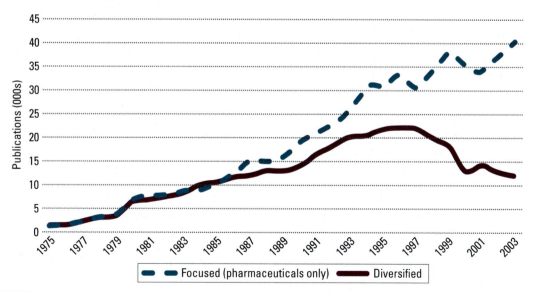

positively associated with the probability of a new project's successful outcome.[57] "The keys to this determinant are the 'knowledge capital' accumulated by the program as an organizational unit as well as the skills and experience of individual scientists," allowing for the ability to exploit internal spillovers of knowledge.[58] Merck's historical success in bringing new drugs to market should make it an attractive candidate for partnerships with other organizations, if Merck can learn to embrace such relationships.

Ultimately, Dr. Turner knew that Merck people took their founder's mission seriously, and they truly wanted to help improve lives. The words of George W. Merck form the basis of Merck's corporate philosophy: "We try to never forget that medicine is for the people. It is not for profits. The profits follow, and if we have remembered that, they have never failed to appear. The better we have remembered it, the larger they have been." It would be his job as Chief Strategy Officer to convince them that the best way to put patients first would be to open Merck up to external innovation. In short, he needed his own people to believe what he so ardently stressed to potential licensing partners. "Most of the world's biomedical research takes place outside of our laboratories, so we charge our scientists with building a 'virtual lab'—the blending of the best scientific programs from internal research and external collaborations. We want to help you to take your great science and turn it into great medicine. We want to help you make a difference in the lives of patients all around the world. That's why we are all in this together."[59]

Show Time: Should Merck Implement an Open-Innovation Strategy, and if So, How?

Merck's management used to believe strongly that a merger would jeopardize the company's scientific culture. The team had decided that "Merck would not consider large-scale mergers which might provide short-term benefits, but would not add to long-term growth prospects of the company."[60] In light of the recent "reverse-merger" with SP, Dr. Turner could not help but reflect on how drastic times called for new measures. With 55 percent of SP's new drugs originating from external sources, this merger represented a significant step toward opening up Merck's boundaries and promoting open innovation.

The merger with SP was nevertheless a very risky strategy. Research has shown that between 1993 and 1998, no correlation between the size of the R&D budget and productivity was found in 40 pharmaceutical firms. Another study showed that as companies merged, the number of development projects declined by 34 percent as merged companies trimmed their product pipelines.[61] Consequently, most mergers in the pharmaceutical industry created neither synergies nor shareholder value. Two equally large and unique organizations such as Merck and SP would be incredibly difficult to integrate, especially considering the differences in their corporate cultures. Dr. Turner wondered what dangerous side-effects the merger might inflict on Merck's vaunted scientific capabilities. The merger was also adding increased complexity to Merck's structure, businesses, and geography of operations. Many implementation issues remained to be managed.

And yet, Dr. Peter Kim, current President of Merck Research Laboratories, had recently reflected on the integration with SP as follows: "The talent and dedication of Schering-Plough scientists [have] helped to build an outstanding clinical development pipeline. . . . The Schering-Plough and Merck pipelines are remarkably complementary and will greatly increase our ability to deliver important new medicines to patients. I believe the combined pipeline will be the best in the industry, by far."[62] Combined with Merck's expertise in early-stage collaborations, the new company was poised to dramatically improve the diversity of platform technologies and hence the number of new compounds they develop. In many ways, this merger could provide the impetus to bring the words of former CEO Ray Gilmartin to fruition. At an offsite meeting with the management committee in July 2000, Mr. Gilmartin had confidently stated that it was time to "break away" from the rest of the pharmaceutical industry: "We have more chemical entities moving through early development than ever before in our history. This is the most productive time ever for Merck research."

Open Innovation at Merck?

Looking out at his strategy team, Dr. Turner could see that not all were convinced that open innovation was the way to go. Still, Dr. Turner persisted. "Pharmaceutical companies will have to grow more outward-facing to source innovation wherever it can be found. . . . Ideas know no boundaries and science is an international language. We really have to embrace that and think about the world as our oyster of opportunity!"[63] But in the back of his mind, even Dr. Turner had his doubts. Can open innovation really help Merck meet the needs of its customers in creative and cost-effective ways that also bring value to its shareholders? If so, how can Merck change from its current legacy R&D structure to one that promotes more open innovation without jeopardizing the strong, scientific-led culture that made Merck famous? How was he to lead his team to execute his vision of open innovation as its winning, long-term strategy? And how does the SP merger fit into an open innovation strategy? The team went to work . . .

Endnotes

1. Vagelos, R. (2004), *Medicine, Science, and Merck* (Cambridge, UK: Cambridge University Press) p. 90.

2. Nair, P. (2009), "Straight talk with . . . Mervyn Turner," *Nature Medicine* 15: 8–9.

3. Merck Annual Report, 2000.

4. "The *BusinessWeek* top 1000: America's most valuable companies," *BusinessWeek,* April 17, 1987, April 15, 1988, April 14, 1989, and April 13, 1990.

5. "Merck at risk," *The Chief Executive,* June 2003.

6. "Jury finds Merck liable in Vioxx death and awards $253 million," *The New York Times,* August 19, 2005.

7. "Merck to buy rival for $41 billion," *The Wall Street Journal,* March 10, 2009.

8. Ibid.

9. "Schering-Plough, Merck set $41.1B merger," *Ind. U.S. Business Journal Online,* April 7, 2009.

10. "New Merck begins operations," Merck press release, November 4, 2009.

11. "Johnson and Johnson: The elephant in the Merck-Schering living room," www.seekingalpha.com, November 4, 2009.

12. Ibid.

13. "New Merck begins operations."

14. "Johnson and Johnson: The elephant in the Merck-Schering living room."

15. http://www.nj.com/business/index.ssf/2011/04/njs_merck_signs_away_revenues.html, accessed August 2011.

16. "Merck to buy two biotech firms for $480M," *CNNMoney.com,* May 9, 2006.

17. "Merck to buy rival for $41 billion," *The Wall Street Journal,* March 10, 2009.

18. "Merck, Schering-Plough in $41B merger," *NPR Online,* March 9, 2009.

19. Merck Annual Report, 2008.

20. "The biopharmaceutical sector's impact on the U.S. economy: Analysis at the national, state, and local levels," Archstone Consulting LLC, March 2009.

21. "IMS Health lowers 2009 global pharmaceutical market forecast to 2.5–3.5 percent growth," *IMS Health Intelligence,* April 22, 2009.

22. "Eli Lilly is on hunt for acquisitions," *The Wall Street Journal,* March 31, 2009.

23. Arnst, C. (2009), "The drug mergers' harsh side effects," *BusinessWeek,* March 23: 26.

24. Voet, M. A. (2008), *The Generic Challenge: Understanding Patents, FDA & Pharmaceutical Life-Cycle Management* (Boca Raton, FL: Brown Walker Press).

25. Pharmaceutical Research and Manufacturers of America (PhRMA) Annual Member Survey, 1980–2009.

26. Pharmaceutical Industry Profile, PhRMA, 2009.

27. DiMasi, J. A. (2001), "New drug development in U.S. 1963–1999," *Clinical Pharmacology and Therapeutics* 69: 286–296.

28. Vernon J., J. Golec, and J. A. Dimasi (2008), "Drug development costs when financial risk is measured using the Fama-French three factor model," unpublished working paper, January.

29. Lawrence, S. (2007), "Billion dollar babies—biotech drugs as blockbusters," *Nature Biotechnology* 25: 380–382.

30. Ibid.

31. Ibid.

32. Pisano, G. (2006), "Can science be a business? Lessons from biotech," *Harvard Business Review,* October: 114–125.

33. Comanor, W. (2007), "The economics of research and development in the pharmaceutical industry." In F. Sloan and C. R. Hsieh (eds.), *Pharmaceutical Innovation: Incentives, Competition, and Cost-Benefit Analysis in International Perspective* (Cambridge, UK: Cambridge University Press), pp. 54–72.

34. Ibid.

35. Vagelos, R. (2004), *Medicine, Science, and Merck,* p. 110.

36. "Merck sees 57 percent drop in first-quarter profit," *Yahoo! Finance,* April 29, 2009.

37. "Healthcare reform," *The New York Times,* January 20, 2010.

38. www.healthcare.gov/, accessed September 26, 2010.

39. Voet, M. A. (2008), *The Generic Challenge: Understanding Patents, FDA & Pharmaceutical Life-Cycle Management.*

40. Ibid.

41. IMS Health, National Sales Perspectives, National Prescription Audit, March 2009.

42. Voet, M. A. (2008), *The Generic Challenge: Understanding Patents, FDA & Pharmaceutical Life-Cycle Management.*

43. Ibid.

44. Graham, S. J. H., and M. J. Higgins (2008), "Timing new drug introductions: The roles of regulatory rules and firms complementary assets," *SSRN Working Paper* 1312784.

45. *The Paragraph Four Report: Annual Trends,* Parry Ashford Inc., 2008.

46. "Biotech industry pushes for generics deal before November," *The News & Observer,* February 15, 2008.

47. The discussion of closed and open innovation in this section is based on: Chesbrough, H. (2003), *Open Innovation. The New Imperative for Creating and Profiting from Technology* (Boston, MA: Harvard Business School Press).

48. Ibid.

49. Chesbrough, H. (2007), "Why companies should have open business models," *MIT Sloan Management Review,* Winter: 22–28.

50. Chesbrough, H. (2003), "The era of open innovation," *MIT Sloan Management Review,* Spring: 35–41.

51. Raynor, M. E., and J. A. Panetta (2005), *A Better Way to R&D?* (Boston, MA: Harvard Business School Publishing).

52. Vagelos, R. (2004), *Medicine, Science, and Merck,* p. 103.

53. "Mervyn J. Turner biography; About MRL Research Management Committee," Merck & Co. intranet, August 2009.

54. Henderson, R., and I. Cockburn (1994), "Measuring competence? Exploring firm effects in pharmaceutical research," *Strategic Management Journal* 15: 63–84.

55. Comanor, W. (2007), "The economics of research and development in the pharmaceutical industry."

56. Ibid.

57. Ibid.

58. Ibid.

59. www.merck.com/licensing/.

60. "Merck: Conflict and change," *Harvard Business School Case Study #805079.*

61. "Discovering the future: R&D strategy at Merck," *Harvard Business School Case Study #601-086.*

62. "Merck and Schering-Plough to merge," Merck press release, March 9, 2009.

63. Nair, P. (2009), "Straight talk with . . . Mervyn Turner."

**Marcus Møller Larsen, Torben Pedersen,
and Dmitrij Slepniov**
The University of Western Ontario

Prologue

The last five years' rather adventurous journey from 2004 to 2009 had taught the fifth-largest toy-maker in the world—the LEGO Group—the importance of managing the global supply chain effectively. In order to survive the largest internal financial crisis in the company's roughly 70 years of existence, resulting in a deficit of DKK1.8 billion in 2004, the management had, among many initiatives, decided to offshore and outsource a major chunk of LEGO's production to Flextronics, a large Singaporean electronics manufacturing services (EMS) provider. In this pursuit of rapid cost-cutting sourcing advantages, the LEGO Group planned to license out as much as 80 per cent of its production, besides closing down major parts of the production in high-cost countries. Confident with the prospects of the new partnership, the company signed a long-term contract with Flextronics. "It has been important for us to find the right partner," argued Niels Duedahl, a LEGO vice-president, when announcing the outsourcing collaboration, "and Flextronics is a very professional player in the market with industry-leading plastics capabilities, the right capacity and resources in terms of molding, assembly, packaging and distribution. We know this from looking at the work Flextronics does for other global companies."[1]

This decision would eventually prove to have been too hasty, however. Merely three years after the contracts were signed, LEGO management announced that it would phase out the entire sourcing collaboration with Flextronics. In July 2008, the executive vice-president for the global supply chain, Iqbal Padda, proclaimed in an official press release, "We have had an intensive and very valuable cooperation with Flextronics on the relocation of major parts of our production. As expected, this transition has been complicated, but throughout the process we have maintained our high quality level. Jointly we have now come to the conclusion that it is more optimal for the LEGO Group to manage the global manufacturing setup ourselves. With this decision the LEGO supply chain will be developed faster through going for the best, leanest and highest quality solution at all times."[2]

This sudden change in its sourcing strategy posed LEGO management with a number of caveats. Despite the bright forecasts, the collaboration did not fulfill the initial expectations, and the company needed to understand why this had happened. Secondly, what could LEGO management have done differently? Arguably, with little prior experience in outsourcing this large amount of production, the LEGO Group had had a limited knowledge base to draw on to manage a collaboration like this. Yet, with Flextronics' size and experience with original equipment manufacturers (OEMs), this, in theory, should not have been a problem. Lastly, one could ponder whether the unsuccessful collaboration with Flextronics had been a necessary evil for the LEGO Group. LEGO management's ability to handle its global production network after the Flextronics collaboration had surely changed, and aspects like standardization and documentation had to a much larger extent become valued.

Introducing the LEGO Group: Only the Best Is Good Enough

The LEGO Group's vision was to "inspire children to explore and challenge their own creative potential." Its motto, "Only the Best Is Good Enough," had stuck with the company since 1932 when Ole Kirk Christiansen, a Danish carpenter, established the company in the small town of Billund in Jutland, Denmark, to manufacture his wooden toy designs. As the company itself said, "It is LEGO philosophy that 'good play' enriches a child's life—and its subsequent adulthood. With this in

PhD Fellow Marcus Møller Larsen, Professor Torben Pedersen and Assistant Professor Dmitrij Slepniov wrote this case solely to provide material for class discussion. The authors do not intend to illustrate either effective or ineffective handling of a managerial situation. The authors may have disguised certain names and other identifying information to protect confidentiality.

Richard Ivey School of Business
The University of Western Ontario

mind, the LEGO Group has developed and marketed a wide range of products, all founded on the same basic philosophy of learning and developing—through play."[3] With this simple idea, the company, through its history, had grown into a major multinational corporation, and, by 2009, was the world's fifth-largest manufacturer of toys in terms of sales. The same year, the LEGO Group earned DKK11.7 billion in revenues and DKK2.2 billion in profits, and had a workforce of approximately 7,000 employees around the world (see Exhibit 1). Its corporate management consisted, besides the chief executive officer and the chief financial officer, of four executive vice-presidents with respective business areas (markets and products; community, education and direct; corporate centre; and global supply chain) (see Exhibit 2).

EXHIBIT 1

The Lego Group Financial Figures

mDKK	2009	2008	2007	2006	2005
HIGHLIGHTS					
Income statement					
Revenue	11,661	9,526	8,027	7,798	7,027
Expenses	(8,659)	(7,522)	(6,556)	(6,393)	(6,605)
Operating profit	3,002	2,002	1,471	1,405	423
Financial income and expenses	(15)	(248)	(35)	(44)	(51)
Profit before tax	2,887	1,852	1,414	1,281	329
Net profit for the year	2,204	1,352	1,028	1,290	214
Balance sheet					
Total assets	7,788	6,496	6,009	6,907	7,058
Equity	3,291	2,066	1,679	1,191	563
Liabilities	4,497	4,430	4,330	5,716	6,495
Cash flow statement					
Cash flow from operating activities	2,655	1,954	1,033	1,157	587
Investment in activities, plans and equipment	1,042	368	399	316	237
Investment in intangible assets	216	75	34	–	–
Cash flow from financing activities	(906)	(1,682)	(467)	597	(656)
Total cash flow	501	128	592	1,925	1,570
Employees					
Average number of employees	7,058	5,388	4,199	4,908	5,302
RATIO					
Financial ratios (in %)					
Gross margin	70.3	66.8	65.0	64.9	58.0
Operating margin (ROS)	24.9	22.0	18.1	17.0	5.4
Net profit margin	18.9	14.2	12.8	16.5	3.0
Return on equity (ROE)	82.3	72.2	71.6	147.1	44.2
Equity rate	42.3	31.8	27.9	17.2	8.0

Source: The LEGO Group Annual Report, 2009.

EXHIBIT 2

The Lego Group Structure

Source: The LEGO Group Annual Report, 2009.

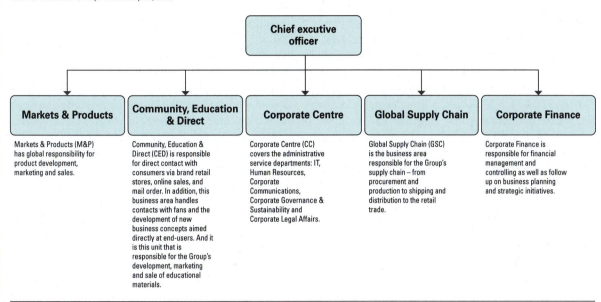

```
                        ┌─────────────────┐
                        │  Chief excutive │
                        │     officer     │
                        └─────────────────┘
```

Markets & Products	Community, Education & Direct	Corporate Centre	Global Supply Chain	Corporate Finance
Markets & Products (M&P) has global responsibility for product development, marketing and sales.	Community, Education & Direct (CED) is responsible for direct contact with consumers via brand retail stores, online sales, and mail order. In addition, this business area handles contacts with fans and the development of new business concepts aimed directly at end-users. And it is this unit that is responsible for the Group's development, marketing and sale of educational materials.	Corporate Centre (CC) covers the administrative service departments: IT, Human Resources, Corporate Communications, Corporate Governance & Sustainability and Corporate Legal Affairs.	Global Supply Chain (GSC) is the business area responsible for the Group's supply chain – from procurement and production to shipping and distribution to the retail trade.	Corporate Finance is responsible for financial management and controlling as well as follow up on business planning and strategic initiatives.

PRODUCTS AND MARKETS. The LEGO brick was the company's main product (see Exhibit 3). The iconic brick with the unique principle of interlocking tubes offering unlimited building possibilities was first introduced in 1958 and had basically remained unchanged ever since. The underlying philosophy of the brick was that it would stimulate creative and structured problem-solving, curiosity and imagination. In the company's own words: "In the hands of children, the products inspire the unique form of LEGO play that is fun, creative, engaging, challenging—all at the same time. . . . We strive to accomplish this by offering a range of high quality and fun products centred around our building systems."[4] The simple yet multifunctional and combinational structure of the brick (there were as many as 915 million possible combinations to choose from with six eight-stud LEGO bricks of the same color) had therefore been core to the company's history and success. In fact, the LEGO brick had been rewarded the "Toy of the Century" designation by both *Fortune* magazine and the British Association of Toy Retailers.

To segment the products, however, a number of categories had been created: First, "pre-school products" comprised products for the youngest children, who had yet to start school. The LEGO DUPLO products were

EXHIBIT 3

The Lego Brick

Source: www.lego.com.

examples of this category. Second, the "creative building" category targeted sets or buckets of traditional LEGO bricks without building instructions. Third, "play themes" products were the products that had a particular story as their basis. This could be themes such as airports, hospitals and racing tracks. The classic LEGO City line and futuristic BIONICLE theme products were examples of this category. Fourth, and related to the play themes, were the "licensed products," which were built up around movies or books that the LEGO Group had acquired the rights for, such as *Harry Potter, Star Wars* and *Indiana Jones.* Fifth, "MINDSTORM NXT" was a programmable robot kit, where consumers could construct and program robots to perform different tasks and operations. Sixth, "LEGO Education" comprised products that had been specifically developed for educational purposes. Last, in 2009 the LEGO Group made its first move into the board game category with the launch of the "LEGO Games" product line. The underlying logic of the entire product portfolio was to reflect the fact that children grow older and develop, and thus demand more challenging stimulation.

LEGO products were sold in more than 130 countries. The largest single market was the United States, which in 2007 accounted for 30 per cent of the revenue in combination with Australia, New Zealand and the United Kingdom. Central and Southern Europe represented 27 per cent, while Scandinavia, Benelux, Eastern Europe and Asia represented 26.5 per cent.

DEALING WITH A CRISIS. In 2004, radical changes took place within the LEGO organization as a consequence of a major internal crisis that drew the company near bankruptcy. The crisis, which could be traced back to the end of the 1990s, had accumulated with net losses worth DKK888 million and DKK1.8 billion in 2003 and 2004, respectively. Sales had fallen by 30 per cent in 2003 and 40 per cent in 2004. These results had been the most disappointing in the history of the company. On average, the toy-maker had made economic losses equivalent to DKK2.2 million per day in the period from 1998 to 2004.

The reasons for the crisis had been many. The immediate explanation was the company's general loss of confidence in its core product—the LEGO brick. With an initiative to create new engines of growth and to address a decline in the traditional toy market, LEGO had sought over the last decade to broaden its portfolio into new, rather discrete areas, including computer games, television and clothing. This act of diversification had resulted in vast complexity and inefficiencies, as well as highly confused customers and employees.

For instance, with the surge of licensed products like Harry Potter and Star Wars, the LEGO Group produced a range of unique bricks for each single new product. The LEGO Group had at the time roughly 11,000 suppliers—a number almost twice what Boeing used for its planes. Unfavorable developments in the global toy market as well as in the exchange rates of key currencies of important markets had not made matters easier. As former chief executive officer Kjeld Kirk Kristiansen argued, "We have been pursuing a strategy which was based on growth, increase in market shares and growth by focusing on totally new products. This strategy did not give the expected results."[5] Moreover, he noted that "we shifted the focus from our actual core product, which at the same time faced difficulties in a more competitive and dynamic market."[6]

In October 2004, Jørgen Vig Knudstorp was appointed as Kristiansen's successor. Kristiansen, who was the grandson of the founder, Ole Kirk Christiansen, had been the president and CEO of the LEGO Group since 1979. Knudstorp was only the second person outside the founding family who held the position of CEO, and his primary task was to steer the company back on track. "I don't have any miracle cure," he explained as to how he would put an end to the financial turmoil. "LEGO shall first and foremost drop its arrogance. We have been too sacred with our own virtues, not open enough, and not willing to listen to what other people say. We shall now listen to customers and consumers; simply drop the sacredness. We must be aggressive in the market; work closely with retailers; and manage LEGO very tightly, also financially."[7] Accordingly, a strategy titled "Shared Vision" was soon implemented, and was defined around three core principles:

- "Be the best at creating value for our customers and sales channels."
- "Refocus on the value we offer our customers."
- "Increase operational excellence."

After divesting its theme parks and receiving an extraordinary loan from the founding family of 800 million DKK, the LEGO Group embarked on the comprehensive strategy of right-sizing its activities, its cost base and its many assets. In particular, careful scrutiny of the organization made the LEGO Group aware of the fact that its ineffective and inflexible supply chain was a key problem for the creation of a sound business platform. The degree of organizational complexity on multiple levels had basically undermined an otherwise sound business platform. According to Knudstorp: "From my perspective, the supply chain is a company's circulation system. You have to fix it to keep the blood flowing."[8]

Learning From Offshore Outsourcing: A Story in Three Parts

1. PREPARING FOR OUTSOURCING. A key revelation of the comprehensive analysis that was initiated in 2004 was that urgent transformations in all major areas of the supply chain were needed. In the development function, the main focus was to simplify the LEGO sets, which over the years had grown highly elaborate. One LEGO senior director noted, "This excessive complexity of shapes and colors of LEGO elements that was coming from the development was badly hitting the supply chain."[9] A major challenge was to ensure that the right components were constantly in stock. Significant forecast errors and seasonal demand fluctuations coupled with customers' expectations of short delivery times resulted in large stocks of many different components. The high numbers of components also required heavy investment in molds. The decision was therefore made to limit the growth in the number of product components and then to gradually reduce it. This was not only supposed to drive costs out of the supply chain, but was also to prepare the company for the new scenarios of the outsourced production set-up.

In the area of distribution, the analysis uncovered the need for major changes in how the company approached its retailers. Describing the situation, a senior director was quoted as saying, "It was impossible to be efficient and manage the supply chain with the level of flexibility we had towards all retailers, including the smallest outlets. We clearly needed to put certain rules here."[10] To manage this, clearly defined service policies were established. The new policies distinguished explicitly between different approaches to the retailers and helped the company to focus more on the large retail chains that were increasingly gaining dominance in the toy market. This immediately helped to drive down the cost of distribution, provided a more reliable overview of demand and, along with reducing complexity, took some pressure away from the supply chain. Moreover, the company's five European distribution facilities (Flensburg and Hohenwestedt

in Germany, Billund in Denmark, and Lyon and Dunkerque in France) were all centralized in Jirny, 10 kilometres east of Prague, Czech Republic. Occupying 51,000 square metres, the new European distribution centre was in full operation at the beginning of 2007 and handled customers in Europe and distribution centres throughout the world (except North America). The operation was outsourced to DHL Solutions. In addition, the distribution of LEGO products in the United States and Canada was outsourced to Exel Inc., a contract logistics provider operating in Alliance, Texas.

However, no matter how significant the problems were in product development and distribution, suboptimizing only those areas without improving various aspects of the actual production could hardly bring the company back on track. The LEGO Group's production value chain was divided into the following steps: the development of the molding machine, molding, assembling, pre-packing and post-packing (see Exhibit 4). Assembling and post-packing were the most cost-intensive parts of the value chain. Prior to the crisis, the company owned and operated production plants in Denmark, the United States, Switzerland, the Czech Republic and South Korea. Allocation of roles and responsibilities to most of these factories followed a branding strategy in which one of the Swiss factories only produced DUPLO toys and another produced Technic products. Furthermore, the Danish factory only manufactured LEGO System products, while the U.S. facility predominately served American demands. The vast majority of the production took place in the Danish and U.S. sites, while roughly 5 to 10 per cent of the LEGO Group's total production was outsourced to Chinese contract manufacturers.

With the new strategic direction of achieving a lighter production portfolio, however, the company started to look for external partners to carry out a larger bulk of its production. There were two main strategic rationales for this. First of all, there was the cost-saving rationale. With the majority of the production in high-cost countries, the management saw major potential for cutting costs by relocating production to lowcost countries. "We were basically turning the 50-year-old idea that Denmark and Switzerland were good countries for automatic production upside down," recalled Duedahl, a LEGO vice-president. "The new mantra was: aggressive outsourcing to low-cost countries."[11]

In spite of the fact that up to 95 per cent of global toy production was located in China, the LEGO Group decided to avoid relocating production facilities to

EX]HIBIT 4

Production Value Chain

Source: Authors' own creation.

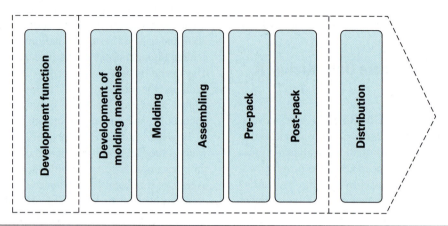

Asia and instead emphasized proximity to its main markets in Europe and the United States. Based on the fact that the European market accounted for approximately 60 per cent of the company's sales, the Czech Republic and Hungary, two low-cost Eastern European countries, fulfilled both the market proximity and cost-saving criteria. These countries were supposed to accommodate most of the capacity transferred from Denmark and Switzerland. In addition, the decision was made to move the company's U.S. plant in Enfield to Mexico in order to supply the North American market, which constituted approximately 30 per cent of the LEGO Group's sales.

Secondly, with a production of approximately 24 billion bricks per year, the LEGO Group rationalized sourcing through potential economies of scale as well as the opportunity to drastically reduce production complexity by targeting large subcontractors. Thus, besides scaling down production in Denmark and closing sites in Switzerland and Korea, it was decided that production should be outsourced to a number of partners. These included Sonoco (a global manufacturer of consumer and industrial packaging products and provider of packaging services); Greiner (a global manufacturer of consumer and industrial packaging products); Weldenhammer (packaging products and services); 2B Pack (packaging products and services); and Flextronics (an electronics manufacturing services company). While the Technic and Bionicle product lines, to a large extent, were to be retained in-house, the Duplo and System lines (characterized by their high-volume production) were predominantly outsourced to Flextronics.

Flextronics, a leading multinational electronics manufacturing services (EMS) provider based in Singapore, had a long history of offering services to original equipment manufacturers (OEMs), and was going to be the LEGO Group's largest partner in terms of production undertaken. Flextronics was actually founded in 1969 in Silicon Valley, California, and became in 1981 the first U.S. manufacturer to formally start offshoring production by establishing a manufacturing facility in Singapore. In 1990, however, the company moved its headquarters to Singapore, and had since succeeded in building a network of manufacturing facilities in 30 countries on four different continents. By 2009, Flextronics' net sales were US$31 billion, and it had a workforce of approximately 160,000 employees (see Exhibit 5). Flextronics' major clients included large multinational companies like Cisco Systems (consumer electronics products), Hewlett-Packard Company (inkjet printers and storage devices), Microsoft Corporation (computer peripherals and consumer electronics gaming products) and Sony-Ericsson (cellular phones). The company had focused its segments into six core areas—automotive, computing, industrial, infrastructure, medical, and mobile and consumer—and it operated with five business units that consisted of "strategic technologies and augmented services that are leveraged across all segments and customer product categories to create scalability and to add flexibility and speed to our

EXHIBIT 5

Flextronics in Brief

- $31 billion in annual sales
- 160,000+ employees worldwide
- 120,000 employees in Asia (90,000 in China)
- Operating in 30 countries
- 27 million square feet of capacity (nine industrial parks)
- Large customers: Casio, Cisco Systems, Dell, Eastman Kodak, Ericsson, Hewlett-Packard, Microsoft, Motorola, Research in Motion, Sony, Sony-Ericsson, Sun Microsystems, and Xerox

Flextronics' Market Segment Portfolio, 2007

Source: www.flextronics.com.

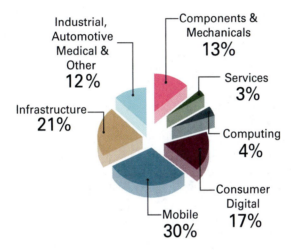

segments."[12] The five business units were Multek (multi-layer printed and flexible circuit boards, interconnected technologies and complex display technologies); Vista Point Technologies (unique product solutions for camera modules); Global Services (logistics, reverse logistics and repair operations); FlexPower (design and manufacturing of semicustom and custom power supplies and battery chargers); and Retail Technological Services (competitive and flexible field services for customer operations) (see Exhibit 6 for Flextronics' service model).

2. A TROUBLED MARRIAGE. Following the decision to outsource major parts of production to Flextronics, a contract with Flextronics was finalized in June 2006. This was, according to the Danish company, a "brilliant idea," as it locked the prices over a long period and thus eliminated the risk of production price fluctuations. In the period from 2004 to 2006, the following were outsourced to Flextronics: parts of the production facilities' capacity in Denmark and Switzerland were relocated to Flextronics' plants in Nyíregyháza and Sarvar, Hungary; the operating control of the LEGO Group's Kladno site in the Czech Republic was handed over to Flextronics; and the Enfield plant in the United States was closed in favour of using Flextronics' newly opened site in Juárez, Mexico. Throughout the transition phase, the LEGO Group was working intensely towards reducing its in-house production capacity from 90 to 95 per cent to the set target of approximately 20 per cent. Actually, the 20 per cent target had never been a strategic goal in itself. "It is very difficult to give such an estimate," a LEGO vice-president explained. "Right from the beginning, the 80/20 per cent [outsourcing/in-house] ratio was more a communication way. What we have decided is that there are two competences that we need to keep in-house in Billund; that is, molding and packing

EXHIBIT 6

Flextronics' Service Model

Design

■ Flextronics employs over 4,000 design engineers.

■ Flextronics owns 364 patents.

Capabilities

■ Industrial design

■ Systemic architecture

■ Mechanical design

■ Embedded systems design

■ Software systems

■ Product launch/NPI

■ DFx Services

Build

■ Flextronics runs nine industrial parks around the world focused on building the world's leading technology products.

Capabilities

■ PCB/Flex circuits

■ Optomechatronics

■ LCD displays

■ Cables

■ Machining

■ Plastics

■ Metal fabrications

■ SMT assembling System integration and final test

Ship

■ Flextronics is involved in doing BTO and CTO for many of the most complex technology products in the world from industry leading companies such as Cisco, HP, Huawei, and Lenovo.

Capabilities

■ Build-to-order (BTO)

■ Configure-to-order (CTO)

■ Distribution and direct fulfilment

■ Outbound logistics and hubbing

Service

■ Flextronics Global Services is the global repair leader for electronic products servicing 3 million (M) cell phones, 2M laptops, 9M PCBAs, and 2M game consoles every year.

■ RTS Technicians handle 600,000+ customer transactions per month.

■ Global Services' sites dedicated to Service Parts Logistics process and ship over 12M spare parts for customers every year.

Capabilities

■ Repair/refurbishment and warranty support

■ Service parts logistics

■ Remarketing

■ Retail technical services

■ Asset recovery

■ Reverse logistics

Source: www.flextronics.com.

competences. Whether it is 20 or 10 per cent of production it doesn't matter; what matters is that in the future we will still be able to do what we are doing from the production point of view."[13]

Flextronics had indeed been the LEGO Group's preferred partner to undertake this task. Because of Flextronics' long history and vast experience in standardizing and documenting work routines and processes to move business activities from site to site, LEGO management was convinced that Flextronics would excel in reducing the complexity of the LEGO production and organization in general. Knudtrup commented after ramping up the collaboration: "We have come to know Flextronics as a very professional partner in connection with the outsourcing of our DUPLO products, which has taken place over the past year. They understand and appreciate the unique values that LEGO products represent, not least the importance of quality and safety which are fundamental to the good play experience."[14] In an equal manner, Matt Ryan, executive vice-president of Flextronics' worldwide operations, stated that the relationship "is characterized by intense supply chain collaboration that provides strategic and efficient cost-savings to help improve the company's competitive market positioning. We are excited to expand our partnership with the LEGO Group as this allows Flextronics further market diversification and enhanced plastic molding capabilities in low-cost regions."[15] A large part of Flextronics' motivation for getting into business with the LEGO Group had thus been its interest in getting more competencies and knowledge about plastics, which constituted an important part of its electronics manufacturing activities.

However, the collaboration did not last for long. Despite LEGO's goal of optimizing its global supply chain, the outsourcing collaboration was cancelled after merely three years. As became evident, the result of attempting to manage and overcome the complexity of the production network by outsourcing it to external providers was actually only a more complex global manufacturing footprint. In particular, the collaboration with Flextronics presented the LEGO Group with some rather daunting and unexpected challenges. Considering the extreme pace of the transition, it eventually turned out problematic for LEGO to coordinate and control the increasingly global and complex network of production facilities as well as to ensure a reliable and seamless transfer of production knowledge between the two. For example, there was the challenge

of aligning the LEGO products' seasonal fluctuations and unpredictable demand with Flextronics' business model. About 60 per cent of the LEGO production was made in the second half of the year, the product had an average lifespan of 16 to 18 months, and the demand uncertainty fluctuated with plus or minus 30 per cent. The LEGO Group's need for flexible and market-responsive business solutions presented a strategic misfit with Flextronics' more stable and predictable operations in which economies of scale was a key phrase. Divergence and misalignments between the two had therefore become the outcome.

3. A BOUNDED NEW START. In 2008, as the LEGO Group announced that it would phase out the cooperation with Flextronics, the process of sourcing back the production was initiated. This was embarked on by the LEGO Group taking over the control of the Kladno factory in the Czech Republic in February 2008. Flextronics was still in charge of molding LEGO products at two sites in Hungary (Sarvar and Nyíregyháza) and one site in Mexico (Juárez) until July 2008, when LEGO management affirmed that these would follow suit with the site in the Czech Republic. In Hungary, LEGO concentrated its activities at the Nyíregyháza facility by taking over the plant and its workforce. During the first quarter of 2009, the Juárez production moved to a new site fully owned by the LEGO Group in Monterrey in northeast Mexico, and the site was up and running in the second quarter of 2009.

"We are not satisfied with the effectiveness in the outsourced facilities," commented Knudstorp briefly after the decision to end the cooperation was made. "It takes more time to educate people than we had expected, and that means that we are still more effective in Billund."[16] Duedahl, however, argued that it might just as well have been the LEGO Group that had not been correct for Flextronics as the other way around: "All in all, we had to realize that our contract also made it difficult for Flextronics to carry out the responsibilities of the collaboration with LEGO in a sound manner. The supplier, like us, has the same need for a profitable business model."[17]

Looking back, the attempt to cut costs and reduce complexity quickly had, in fact, complicated matters for the worse, and thus hindered a conducive foundation for creating profitable synergies. At a glance, the Flextronics adventure therefore looked like a failure. "We have learned that even though everything points at outsourcing, it might still not be the best solution," said Duedahl.[18] Still, however, the collaboration had brought along a number of positive externalities. The engagement had first of all helped LEGO to expand its global operations footprint despite its difficult financial situation. Prior to Flextronics, it was hardly possible to establish the new and needed operating bases in Mexico and Hungary. Flextronics had thus provided the Danish company with the necessary impetus for altering its global production network to serve important markets while saving costs.

Perhaps more importantly, the collaboration had given the LEGO Group an indispensable lesson in understanding its own processes and structures. As Duedahl explained, "We have learned that we are more special than we expected to be."[19] In addition, Flextronics possessed valuable experience and knowledge in relation to the documentation and standardization of the production. Previously, the LEGO Group, to a large extent, had carried out its production processes without paying too much attention to the documentation of it. "We had had the pleasure of being in Billund for 40 years with many loyal colleagues," said Thomas Nielsen, a LEGO manufacturing vice-president. "The downside to this, however, is that you become rather lazy on the documentation side as everybody with many years of experience knows exactly what to do."[20]

As the LEGO Group went from producing the absolute majority in-house to becoming highly dependent on external partners, changes were unavoidable. With the Flextronics collaboration, LEGO management came to realize not only the need, but also the value, of documenting work processes, communication lines and interfaces between activities and tasks in the production. "Production in another country—even within the same company—requires ten times more documentation than in the company that it is moved from," rationalized Michael Vaag, a LEGO supply chain manager.[21] The increased employment of process documentation had given the LEGO Group transparency and control, and thus ample room to manage challenges of complexity and to identify the stronger and weaker parts and links of the production network. In this respect, LEGO management had introduced in 2005 a deliberate sales and operations planning (S&OP) process to monitor and coordinate the different production facilities' roles, capacities and responsibilities in relation to the supply. This approach had stuck with the company also after the break-up with Flextronics and was considered "a strong fundament for the process." Before being

introduced in 2005 as a global process covering all LEGO in-house and outsourced sites, S&OP ran for a year at the company's site in Enfield, Connecticut, resulting in significant operations performance improvements. Michael Kehlet, a LEGO flow planning director, described S&OP as "a process gluing all operations' work flows together."[22] The global S&OP process at LEGO was organized around three key areas: sales, production and product development. Monitoring and coordinating these areas took place through a multistage cycle, which started with data consolidation at the site level and concluded at a global executive S&OP meeting. The S&OP cycle took place every month, providing LEGO with a reliable and constantly updated overview of global operations for the following 12 months. Gradually, the S&OP process evolved into a rather critical tool for creating transparency and supporting management efforts in a relatively fragmented and globally distributed operations set-up, which involved numerous capacity groups and outsourcing partners.

Along with its surge in documenting business processes, the LEGO Group, through Flextronics, had also recognized the strength of standardizing its processes. Actually, standardizing the business processes had always been an integral part of the LEGO Group's approach to production. With the production of around 24 billion bricks per year, a high degree of standardization was obviously imperative for the extreme accuracy required. The collaboration with Flextronics, however, had illuminated LEGO management's perception of how standardization could be used more strategically in the firm. Chresten Bruun, a senior production director, explained how the virtues of standardization had been taken to new frontiers within the company. "We are standardizing on three levels," he said, "the upper level: that is our way of thinking, our mindset, values, attitudes; on the mid level: how we operate our planning processes, follow-up processes, etc.; and the lower level: that is more the hardware part, the machines, lines and the layout in the production."[23] The total number of component portfolios had accordingly decreased from approximately 12,000 in 2004 to roughly half that number in 2008 (reaching levels that existed before 1996), with the final target being 5,500 for the year 2011. The LEGO mini figure policeman, for instance, was reduced from 16 different versions to only four. The standardization had implications throughout the whole value chain starting with the design of new products—as every new product should contain at least 70 percent "evergreen" bricks—i.e., bricks that could be used in more products. Reducing the more unique and product-specific bricks to only 30 percent of all bricks allowed for a more flexible and smooth supply chain.

Its international network of production facilities had also changed from mainly branding factories, where each facility had been responsible for one single product, to facilities that were more standardized, with their main purpose being to serve their respective markets. This gave the company considerable room to benchmark the factories, and thus optimize the total cost advantage of the production facilities in which the reaction time to market was a decisive parameter. In the aftermath of Flextronics, Michael Vaag, supply chain manager, summarized his success criteria for global production in four ways: "(1) It is easy to move technology—it takes more time to build competences; (2) a clear plan for training and education shall be present; (3) there shall be local leaders who know the working culture in the country; and (4) there shall be a clear key figure structure which ensures actual benchmarks/KPI between the factories."[24]

In sum, the LEGO Group read the collaboration with Flextronics in three different stages—before, during and after—each stage with different challenges and opportunities (see Exhibit 7). What seemed to be the recurring theme throughout the entire process, however, was how LEGO management continuously increased its stock of knowledge concerning how to optimize its processes and organization to overcome and manage the multitude of complex issues deriving from having a global network of production.

Epilogue

The LEGO Group's recent financial record showed that Knudstorp and his executive management had indeed been successful with the turnaround strategy: the profits

---

EXHIBIT 7

The Three Stages of the Lego Group's Offshore Outsourcing

Pre-Flextronics			Flextronics			Post-Flextronics	
2003	2004	2005	2006		2007	2008	2009
■ Tight control of all elements of the value chain			■ Plan to outsource up to 80% of production capacity to external partners			■ Backsourcing of the plants operated by the strategic external partner Flextronics	
Challenges:			**Challenges:**			■ LEGO maintains relationships with a number of smaller external suppliers	
■ Cost of production located in predominantly high-cost countries			■ Fast pace of transition			**Challenges:**	
■ Overdiversified and complex products portfolio			■ Production know-how transfer to external partners			■ Stabilizing and optimizing the operations after another stage of transition	
■ Underperforming in-house supply chain			■ Brand vulnerability and dependency on partners			■ Balancing predominately internal supply capacity with market demands	
■ Negative financial results			■ Supply uncertainty				
■ High capital investment requirements			■ Developing new capabilities				
■ High fixed costs			■ Maintaining knowledge about production				
			■ Management of new relationships				
			■ Increasing complexity of production footprint				

Source: Authors' own assessment.

for 2008 and 2009 of DKK1.85 billion and DKK2.2 billion, respectively, were the largest in the Group's history. Commenting on this, Knudstorp said, "Our results for 2008 have been extraordinarily good. And this applies not only to the financial results. During 2008, we also took over two factories in the Czech Republic and Hungary, and we began the construction of a factory in Mexico. The successful change to [more in-house] production, combined with strong sales increases, is attributable to the impressive performance by all our employees."[25] The backsourcing from Flextronics had played an inevitable part in achieving this. The new dominantly in-house production network consisting of factories in Denmark, Hungary, the Czech Republic and Mexico seemingly gave the LEGO Group enough controllable flexibility to balance market demands with its network of offshoring activities. However, the LEGO executive management knew not to rest on its laurels. Although looking promising, the new production network was, in fact, a mere result of avoiding the emerging unexpected costs from having outsourced the production. A central question was therefore: What had the LEGO Group learned from the Flextronics collaboration and how could it use this knowledge constructively in the future?

Endnotes

1. LEGO press release, December 21, 2005.
2. LEGO press release, June 1, 2008.
3. LEGO Annual Report, 2009.
4. Ibid.
5. LEGO press release, January 8, 2004.
6. LEGO Life, September 2007.
7. *Politiken*, October 23, 2004.
8. s+b, Autumn 2007.
9. Interview with LEGO manager, August 27, 2007.
10. Ibid.
11. *Ingenøren*, October 24, 2008.
12. Flextronics Annual Report, 2009.
13. Interview with LEGO manager, August 27, 2004.
14. LEGO press release, June 20, 2006.
15. Ibid.
16. *JydskeVestkysten*, July 1, 2008
17. *Ingenøren*, October 24, 2008.
18. Ibid.
19. Ibid.
20. Interview with Thomas Nielsen, October 7, 2009.
21. *Ingenøren*, March 14, 2008.
22. Interview with Michael Kehlet, September 13, 2008.
23. Interview with Chresten Bruun, January 8, 2010.
24. *Ingenøren*, March 14, 2008.
25. LEGO press release, February 23, 2009.

Time magazine called this era "The Decade From Hell," and "when you are going through hell,"
Winston Churchill advised, "keep going."

—OPENING STATEMENT OF THE GE 2009 ANNUAL REPORT

Marne L. Arthaud-Day
Kansas State University
Alicia Horbaczewski
Merck & Co., Inc.
Frank T. Rothaermel
Georgia Institute of Technology

IT HAD BEEN a heck of a decade for Jeffrey Immelt, Chairman and CEO of General Electric (GE), the quintessential American blue-chip company. Mr. Immelt's new role as chief executive started on September 7, 2001, just four days before the 9/11 terrorist attacks. Since that tragedy, Mr. Immelt had spent his time putting out fire after fire. Because of 9/11, the U.S. economy was pushed into a recession, and a global economic slowdown began. Several of GE's key industrial sectors such as aviation and energy were especially hard hit, and even GE's insurance business lost $600 million. The company that had repeatedly promised and delivered annual profit growth rates of 16 to 18 percent in the 1990s struggled to grow at half that pace in the new millennium.[1]

Beginning his tenure as CEO in 2001, Immelt continued GE's transition from a low-margin, mainly commodities manufacturer to a more lucrative services company.[2] At the same time, he took several steps to unify the GE brand around a stronger focus on innovation, including changing the GE motto to "Imagination at Work." Immelt remembered keenly what GE's former CEO Jack Welch had preached: "If the rate of change inside an organization is less than the rate outside, the end is in sight. . . . Leaders must develop a sixth sense, an ability to see around the corner."[3] Immelt's ability to "see around the corner" was precisely the star talent that had gotten him to his job as CEO.

The global financial crisis beginning in 2008 compounded the company's troubles even further. Because the conglomerate relied on its financial services unit,

GE Capital, for more than 50 percent of its profits, the company found itself in grave danger. In 2009, GE announced that it had missed its quarterly earnings forecast just weeks after Immelt had reassured investors the company was on track, sending shockwaves throughout the financial industry.[4] GE's stock price fell by 13 percent by the end of that day, resulting in a $47 billion loss.[5] One month later, Standard & Poor's downgraded GE's AAA credit rating, further underscoring the market's lost confidence in GE's financial health.[6] Immelt quickly undertook a series of drastic actions to restabilize the company, including cutting the company's dividend by 68 percent,[7] downsizing the work force by 10 percent, and giving up his own bonus in both 2009 and 2010. He even asked Warren Buffett for a $15 billion liquidity injection. On March 5, 2009, GE's share price hit an all-time low of $6.66, a figure symbolizing the culmination of GE's "Decade from Hell." From his assumption of the company leadership in 2001, Immelt had seen GE's market capitalization cut in half, to about $200 billion by 2010. (See Exhibits 1a through 1d for financial performance data.)

As the financial crisis persisted, it became clear to both Immelt and GE's investors that the company needed to rethink its corporate strategy. Once a key resource utilized to finance acquisitions and smooth quarterly earnings for the other divisions, GE Capital's losses were now a drain on the overall health of the firm. Increasingly, Immelt saw the financial crisis as an opportunity to move the company away from dependence on GE Capital and toward a new identity for the 21st century. He believed the key to future success was to figure out how to refocus GE away from

Professor Marne L. Arthaud-Day, Research Associate Alicia Horbaczewski (GT MBA '10) and Professor Frank T. Rothaermel prepared this case from public sources. This case is developed for the purpose of class discussion. It not intended to be used for any kind of endorsement, source of data, or depiction of efficient or inefficient management. © Arthaud-Day, Horbaczewski, & Rothaermel, 2013.

EXHIBIT 1a

GE Share Price, 2001–2010

Source: www.WolframAlpha.com.

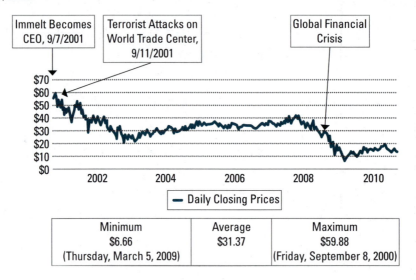

Minimum	Average	Maximum
$6.66	$31.37	$59.88
(Thursday, March 5, 2009)		(Friday, September 8, 2000)

EXHIBIT 1b

GE Performance Relative to the Dow Jones Industrial Average, 2000–2010

Source: MSN money (http://money.msn.com/).

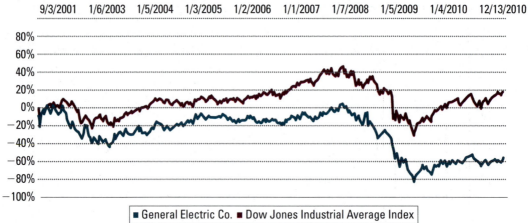

EXHIBIT 1c

Consolidated Income Statement, 2005–2010 ($ in millions, except per-share amounts)

Revenues	2010	2009	2008	2007	2006	2005
Sales of goods	$60,812	$65,068	$69,100	$60,670	$64,297	$59,837
Sales of services	39,625	38,709	43,669	38,856	36,403	32,752
Other income	1,151	1,006	1,586	3,019	2,537	1,683
General Electric Capital Services, Inc. (GECS) revenues from services	48,623	50,495	68,160	69,943	60,154	55,970
Total revenues	150,211	155,278	182,515	172,488	163,391	150,242
Costs & Expenses						
Cost of goods sold	46,005	50,580	54,602	47,309	50,588	46,169
Cost of services sold	25,708	25,341	29,170	25,816	23,522	20,645
Interest & other financial charges	15,983	18,309	26,209	23,762	19,286	15,138
Investment contracts, insurance losses & insurance annuity benefits	3,012	3,017	3,213	3,469	3,214	5,474
Provision for losses on financing receivables	7,191	10,627	7,518	4,431	3,839	3,841
Other costs & expenses	38,104	37,409	42,662	41,089	38,322	36,257
Total costs & expenses	136,003	145,283	163,374	145,876	138,771	127,524
Earnings (loss) from continuing ops before income taxes	14,208	9,995	19,141	26,612	24,620	22,718
Benefit (provision) for income taxes	(1,050)	1,148	(1,052)	(4,155)	(3,954)	(4,085)
Earnings from continuing operations	13,158	11,143	18,089	22,457	20,666	18,633
Earnings (loss) from discontinued operations	(979)	82	(679)	(249)	163	(1,922)
Net earnings (loss)	12,179	11,225	17,410	22,208	20,829	16,711
Less net earnings attributable to noncontrolling interests	(535)	(200)	—	—	—	—
Less effect of accounting changes	—	—	—	—	—	—
Net earnings attributable to the company	11,644	11,025	17,410	22,208	20,829	16,711
Preferred stock dividends declared	(300)	(300)	(75)	—	—	—
Net earnings attributable to common shareowners	$11,344	$10,725	$17,335	$22,208	$20,829	$16,711
Per Share Amounts						
Earnings (loss) per share-continuing operations-basic	1.15	1.03	1.79	2.21	1.99	1.73
Earnings (loss) per share-discontinued operations-basic	(0.09)	(0.02)	(0.07)	(0.03)	0.02	(0.18)
Earnings (loss) per share-continuing operations-diluted	1.15	1.03	1.78	2.20	1.99	1.72
Earnings (loss) per share-discontinued operations-diluted	(0.09)	(0.02)	(0.07)	(0.03)	0.02	(0.18)
Net earnings (loss) per share-basic	1.06	1.01	1.72	2.18	2.01	1.55
Net earnings (loss) per share-diluted	1.06	1.01	1.72	2.17	2.00	1.54
Dividends declared per share	0.46	0.61	1.24	1.15	1.03	0.91
Weighted average shares outstanding-basic	10,661	10,614	10,080	10,182	10,359	10,570
Weighted average shares outstanding-diluted	10,678	10,615	10,098	10,218	10,394	10,611
Year end shares outstanding	10,615	10,663	10,537	9,988	10,277	10,484
Total number of employees	287,000	304,900	323,000	327,000	319,000	316,000
Number of common stockholders	578,000	598,000	605,000	607,000	626,000	646,000

Source: GE Annual Reports.

EXHIBIT 1d

Consolidated Balance Sheets, 2005–2010

CONSOLIDATED BALANCE SHEET

(in millions except per share amounts)	2010	2009	2008	2007	2006	2005
Assets						
Current Assets						
Cash and cash equivalents	$ 78,958	$ 70,488	$ 48,187	$ 15,731	$ 14,275	$ 9,011
Investment Securities	43,938	51,343	41,446	45,276	47,826	53,144
Current receivables Net	18,621	16,458	21,411	22,259	13,954	14,851
Inventories Net	11,526	11,987	13,674	12,897	11,401	10,474
Total Current Assets	153,043	150,276	124,718	96,163	87,456	87,480
Financing receivables Net	310,055	319,247	365,168	376,123	334,205	287,639
Other GECS receivables	8,951	14,056	13,439	16,514	17,067	14,767
Property, Plant and Equipment						
Property, Plant and Equipment (GE)	30,860	12,253	35,242	31,348	39,633	39,378
Property, Plant and Equipment (GECS)	79,185	56,717	90,429	88,255	80,801	72,355
Less Allowance for depreciation	(43,831)	—	(47,141)	(41,715)	(45,468)	(44,205)
Property, Plant and Equipment Net	66,214	68,970	78,530	77,888	74,966	67,528
Goodwill	64,473	65,076	81,759	81,116	—	—
Other Intangibles, Net	9,973	11,751	14,977	16,142	86,433	81,726
Asset from discontinued operations						46,756
All Other Assets	138,507	152,525	119,178	131,737	97,112	87,425
Total Assets	$751,216	$781,901	$797,769	$795,683	$697,239	$673,321
Liabilities and Stockholders' Equity						
Current Liabilities						
Short term borrowings	$117,959	$129,869	$193,695	$195,100	$172,153	$158,156
Trade account payable	14,657	19,527	20,819	21,338	21,697	21,273
Accrued and other current liabilities	11,142	12,192	12,536	9,885	5,248	4,456
Dividends payable	1,563	1,141	3,340	3,100	2,878	2,623
All other current liabilities	11,396	13,386	18,220	15,816	18,538	18,419
Total Current Liabilities	156,717	176,115	248,610	245,239	220,514	204,927

EXHIBIT 1d *(Continued)*

CONSOLIDATED BALANCE SHEET

(in millions except per share amounts)

	2010	2009	2008	2007	2006	2005
Long-Term Borrowings	293,323	336,172	330,067	319,013	260,804	212,281
Bank Deposits & Non-recourse borrowings	67,358	37,402	—	—	—	—
Deferred Income Taxes	2,840	2,081	4,584	12,490	14,171	16,330
Investment contracts, insurance liabilities & insurance annuity benefits	29,582	31,641	34,032	34,068	34,499	45,432
All other liabilities	77,198	73,354	66,864	61,310	47,359	76,964
Total Liabilities	627,018	656,765	684,157	672,120	577,347	555,934
Stockholders' Equity						
Minority Interest in equity of consolidated affiliates	—	—	8,947	8,004	7,578	8,054
Preferred Stock (30,000 shares outstanding)	—	—	—	—	—	—
Common stock (10,615,376,000 and 10,663,075,000 shares outstanding at year-end 2010 and 2009, respectively)	702	702	702	669	669	669
Other paid-in capital	36,890	37,729	40,390	26,100	25,486	25,227
Retained earnings	131,137	126,363	122,123	117,362	107,798	98,117
Accumulated gains (losses) net	(17,855)	(15,265)	(21,853)	8,324	3,254	2,667
Stockholders' equity subtotal	150,874	149,529	150,309	160,459	144,785	134,734
Less treasury stock (at cost)	31,938	32,238	36,697	36,896	24,893	17,326
Stockholders' equity total	118,936	117,291	113,612	123,563	119,892	117,408
Noncontrolling interests	5,262	7,845	0	0	0	0
Total Equity	124,198	125,136	113,612	123,563	119,892	117,408
Total Stockholders' Equity and Liabilities	**$751,216**	**$781,901**	**$797,769**	**$795,683**	**$697,239**	**$673,342**

Source: GE Annual Reports.

declining businesses toward the rapidly growing industries of the future. The time was ripe for GE to return to its roots and become an industrial company again.

The first step in Immelt's plan involved a series of corporate restructurings. Earlier in his tenure, Immelt had divested business units representing 40 percent of revenues and consolidated GE's multiple business divisions into just five: *GE Capital, GE Technology Infrastructure, GE Energy, NBC Universal,* and *GE Home & Business Solutions.* In 2008, he extended that process, selling portions of GE Capital and spinning off the famed GE Consumer and Industrial division, allowing GE to focus on an even narrower group of businesses. (See Exhibits 2a and 2b for changing product and geographic scope.) In 2009, Immelt announced his intent to shrink GE Capital to no more than 30 percent of the total corporate profits, and he sold a majority stake in NBC Universal to Comcast Corp.[8] (See Exhibit 3 for an organizational chart.) The funds generated from the sale of NBC were used to offset loan losses from GE Capital and to fund investments in aviation, health care, and energy.[9]

These efforts were met with mixed reactions. While some analysts wondered whether the company was becoming too narrowly focused and losing the ability to hedge its bets, others recommended even further divestment. They pointed out that the company's simplified organizational structure belied the fact that GE had engaged in 307 acquisitions and purchased stakes in another 105 firms from 2001–2010, while selling only 266 business units.[10] In fact, acquisitions exceeded divestitures in all but 3 of the past 10 years (see Exhibit 4). Moreover, some of the purchases (e.g., homeland security, commercial real estate, and subprime mortgages) were at best tangentially related to GE's stated focus on global technology, infrastructure, and industrial businesses.[11] GE remained a sprawling conglomerate with a presence in a vast array of industries including electrical distribution, oil and gas, water and process technologies, aviation, health care, transportation, appliances, consumer electronics, lighting, and media.

Without the financial economies once supplied by GE Capital, Mr. Immelt needed to persuade investors that his acquisitions were justified and that there was still a strategic reason for keeping these companies together under the GE corporate umbrella. Otherwise, investors would be better off investing in growth markets on their own, instead of subsidizing GE's administrative costs. In the words of one analyst, "Reshaping GE [was] vital if the stock and Mr. Immelt [were] to regain their former luster."[12]

EXHIBIT 2a

GE's Changing Product Scope

Source: GE Annual Reports, 2001 and 2010 (annual revenues in parentheses).

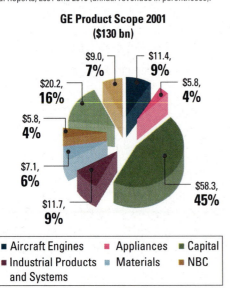

GE Product Scope 2001
($130 bn)

- $11.4, **9%**
- $5.8, **4%**
- $58.3, **45%**
- $11.7, **9%**
- $7.1, **6%**
- $5.8, **4%**
- $20.2, **16%**
- $9.0, **7%**

Legend:
- ■ Aircraft Engines ■ Appliances ■ Capital
- ■ Industrial Products and Systems ■ Materials ■ NBC

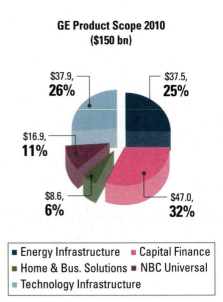

GE Product Scope 2010
($150 bn)

- $37.5, **25%**
- $47.0, **32%**
- $8.6, **6%**
- $16.9, **11%**
- $37.9, **26%**

Legend:
- ■ Energy Infrastructure ■ Capital Finance
- ■ Home & Bus. Solutions ■ NBC Universal
- ■ Technology Infrastructure

EXHIBIT 2b

GE's Changing Geographic Scope

Source: GE Annual Reports, 2001 and 2010 (annual revenues in parentheses).

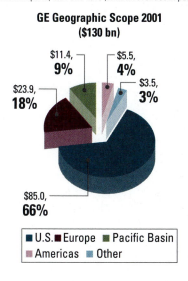

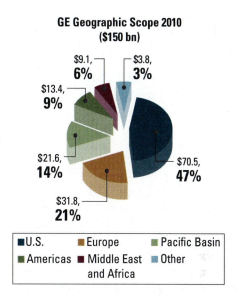

GE Geographic Scope 2001 ($130 bn)

- $85.0, **66%** U.S.
- $23.9, **18%** Europe
- $11.4, **9%** Pacific Basin
- $5.5, **4%** Americas
- $3.5, **3%** Other

Legend: ■ U.S. ■ Europe ■ Pacific Basin ■ Americas ■ Other

GE Geographic Scope 2010 ($150 bn)

- $70.5, **47%** U.S.
- $31.8, **21%** Europe
- $21.6, **14%** Pacific Basin
- $13.4, **9%** Americas
- $9.1, **6%** Middle East and Africa
- $3.8, **3%** Other

Legend: ■ U.S. ■ Europe ■ Pacific Basin ■ Americas ■ Middle East and Africa ■ Other

EXHIBIT 3

GE Organizational Chart, April 2010

Source: GE website for Investor Relations (www.ge.com).

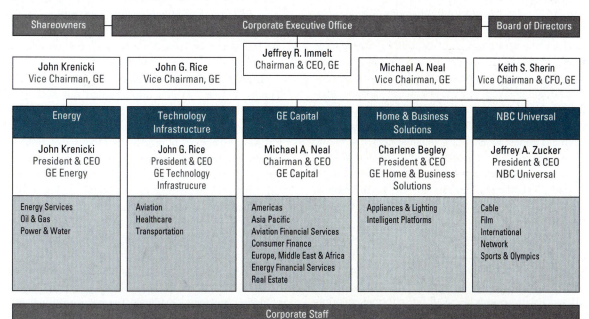

Shareowners	Corporate Executive Office	Board of Directors

Jeffrey R. Immelt — Chairman & CEO, GE

John Krenicki Vice Chairman, GE	John G. Rice Vice Chairman, GE	Michael A. Neal Vice Chairman, GE	Keith S. Sherin Vice Chairman & CFO, GE

Energy	Technology Infrastructure	GE Capital	Home & Business Solutions	NBC Universal
John Krenicki President & CEO GE Energy	John G. Rice President & CEO GE Technology Infrastrucure	Michael A. Neal Chairman & CEO GE Capital	Charlene Begley President & CEO GE Home & Business Solutions	Jeffrey A. Zucker President & CEO NBC Universal
Energy Services Oil & Gas Power & Water	Aviation Healthcare Transportation	Americas Asia Pacific Aviation Financial Services Consumer Finance Europe, Middle East & Africa Energy Financial Services Real Estate	Appliances & Lighting Intelligent Platforms	Cable Film International Network Sports & Olympics

Corporate Staff

Business Development	Marketing & Communications	Information Technology	Finance	Global Research	Human Resources	International	Legal
Pamela Daley	Elizabeth J. Comstock	Charlene Begley	Keith S. Sherin	Mark M. Little	John F. Lynch	Ferdinando Beccalli-Falco	Brackett B. Denniston III

EXHIBIT 4

GE's Acquisitions, Stake Purchases, and Divestitures, 2001–2010

Year	Acquisitions	Stakes	Divestitures
2010	14	3	23
2009	8	8	22
2008	31	16	26
2007	32	17	23
2006	40	13	29
2005	22	10	33
2004	34	6	19
2003	33	10	31
2002	48	6	32
2001	45	16	28

Source: www.alacrastore.com/mergers-acquisitions/General_Electric_Company-1006912.

History of Strategic Leadership at GE

The decline of GE's value under Jeffrey Immelt's leadership was striking when compared to the widely acknowledged successes of his predecessors. When Reginald Jones became the seventh CEO in 1972, he shifted GE away from its traditional focus on electrical equipment and appliances and concentrated instead on services, transportation, and natural resources. Even more important, he is credited with implementing the notion of strategic planning at GE, having created 43 strategic business units to oversee its groups, divisions, and departments as well as manage the information generated by 43 strategic plans. Over time, Reginald Jones added more management layers and finally grouped the businesses into three divisions: consumer products, power systems, and technical products.[13] Under his leadership, GE's sales almost tripled to $27 billion, and he was named "CEO of the Decade" in 1979.[14]

Jack Welch began working at GE in 1961 and was well known for his disdain for bureaucracy. Upon becoming CEO in 1981, Mr. Welch immediately instituted a massive downsizing effort. The restructuring did away with several layers of GE's formal reporting structure, increasing the number of direct reports per manager from 5 to 15. The number of employees at GE dropped from 404,000 in 1980 to 292,000 by 1989.[15] Mr. Welch's strategy was not just to cut employees and costs, however. He envisioned a GE in which each of the businesses would be first or second in its industry in terms of market share, or else would be fixed, sold, or closed. From 1981 to 1987, he sold 200 businesses and acquired 370 businesses, for a net cost of $10 billion,[16] earning Welch the title of "The Toughest Boss in America."[17] While Welch reigned over GE, market capitalization increased from $18 billion to over $500 billion.[18] With GE's performance outshining all other companies during his tenure, he gained not only admiration but also converts and devotees to the "Welch Way."

The GE motto under Welch was "We Bring Good Things to Life." Welch implemented this successful slogan by introducing GE to Six Sigma (6σ), which was invented by Motorola in 1981. *Six Sigma* is a business-management process that focuses on improving the quality of outputs by removing the causes of potential defects and minimizing variability. The name Six Sigma comes from the statistical modeling of a manufacturing process in which the percentage of a process is 99.99966 percent free of defects. Under Welch's leadership, every GE employee underwent extensive training to learn how to improve quality, lower costs, and increase productivity. GE now had decades of experience as a best-practice Six Sigma company and was renowned for its operational efficiency and mature management processes. Analysts estimated that the resulting performance tools that GE developed in technology, process, information, and culture brought in an additional $40 billion in revenue per year.[19]

A former football player for Dartmouth College and an MBA graduate from Harvard Business School, Jeff Immelt joined GE in 1982. He was only 45 years old when Jack Welch handpicked him as his successor above two other, more-experienced candidates—Robert Nardelli, who went on to become CEO of Home Depot and then Chrysler amidst considerable controversy, and Jim McNerney, who went on to head 3M and currently serves as CEO of Boeing.

Ecomagination

Immelt saw GE as a company known for solving problems. He believed energy and health care to be two of the most pressing problems in the world today, and he placed his bets accordingly. With GE's long-standing expertise in industrial engineering, Immelt believed that GE was uniquely positioned to develop technological solutions for the world's future energy needs. In 2004, GE spent $700 million on clean technology. With the launch of a new *ecomagination* initiative in 2005, Immelt pledged to triple that amount over the next five years.[20]

The *ecomagination* initiative was intended to "develop tomorrow's solutions such as solar energy, hybrid locomotives, fuel cells, lower-emission aircraft engines, lighter and stronger durable materials, efficient lighting, and water purification technology."[21] Immelt saw it as a way to deliver more energy-efficient products and services to GE's customers while generating reliable growth for the company. The program's goals included increasing GE's investment in green technology R&D, increasing the revenues raised from *ecomagination* products, reducing GE's own greenhouse-gas emissions and improving energy intensity, reducing water use and improving water reuse, and increasing communication with the public.[22] In rolling out this initiative, Mr. Immelt also called upon the Bush administration to formulate a clear policy on environmental values and global warming.[23]

Despite GE's strong track record in industrial engineering and program management, some observers received the news of the new eco-initiative with considerable skepticism. They questioned how serious GE was in its commitment to a green economy, given its past reputation for large-scale air and water pollution. As of 2000, GE was the fourth-largest producer of air pollution in the United States and the fifth-largest creator of toxic waste, after companies like Honeywell and Chevron. Critics argued that "Mr. Immelt's credibility as a spokesman on national environmental policy is fatally flawed because of his company's own intransigence in cleaning up its own toxic legacy."[24]

Yet over the next few years, Mr. Immelt succeeded in turning both the company and public opinion around with *ecomagination*. In 2009, *BusinessWeek* ranked GE as the #17 Most Innovative Company in the world, mostly because of its environmental initiatives. GE personnel created nearly 100 new green products spanning across company segments ranging from appliances to aviation, energy, lighting, transportation, and water. Indeed, there was such positive market response to *ecomagination* products that revenues from the program grew 260 percent, to $18 billion by 2009. That same year, Immelt committed $1.5 billion annually in clean-technology R&D, with pledges to increase that value to $10 billion by 2015.[25]

The *ecomagination* initiative proved to be a success for GE (see Exhibit 5 for the results) in both real dollars and intangible goodwill. GE became one of the largest players in the wind-power industry, and was continuing to develop innovative new products such as the Evolution Series locomotive and GEnx aircraft engine, which burned significantly less fuel than their

EXHIBIT 5

Results of *ecomagination*

2005 Goals	2009 Status
Double R&D to $1.5B on "green products"	$1.5B on R&D for 75 "eco" products
Work with customers to increase revenues from $5B in 2005 to $20B in sales by 2010	$18B of revenue in 2009; 17% growth rate Global engagement
Reduce GE carbon footprint by 1%	Reduction of 8%; save $100 MM/year
Be transparent and involved	Founding member of USCAP

predecessors. By 2009, GE had successfully lowered its greenhouse gas emissions by 22 percent and reduced its water use by 30 percent, with even further reductions planned for the future. In an *ecomagination* advertising campaign, Immelt was quoted as saying, "It's no longer a zero-sum game—things that are good for the environment are also good for business."[26] Mr. Immelt learned through the *ecomagination* experience that with innovation, all stakeholders— customers, employees, investors and the public—can win.[27]

Healthymagination

"It's the most valuable thing on earth.

All the money in the world can't buy it.

Those who have it don't always appreciate it.

Those who have lost it will do anything to get it back.

What is it?

It's Health.

At GE, we believe what's needed, right now,

is a new mindset that embraces that health is everything.

We call it healthymagination.*"* [28]

Inspired by the success of *ecomagination*, Mr. Immelt launched GE's $6 billion *healthymagination* initiative in May 2009, hoping to leverage the company's technical knowledge, global position, and financial strength to transform the health care industry.[29] He needed a repeat performance to rebuild the company's value, as well as to demonstrate that he could formulate and implement innovative strategies for GE on an ongoing basis. While *ecomagination* grew naturally from GE's strengths in industrial engineering, however, *healthymagination* would be a bit more of a stretch for GE's employees on multiple fronts.

ESTABLISHED COMPETITORS. Although GE first entered the health care business in 1915, it did not aggressively expand its presence until the advent of ultrasound technology in the 1980s. By that time, several competitors had already established a formidable presence in the health care market, placing GE at a competitive disadvantage. Playing catch-up through a series of acquisitions and joint ventures, GE quickly began competing in all of the primary health care market segments, including obstetrics, cardiology, and general radiology. The company's strategy was deceptively simple: Launch premium

medical products based on cutting-edge technologies. By 2010, GE Healthcare had gained envious market positions in most developed countries in the world,[30] with $20 billion in assets and $18 billion in annual revenue.[31]

A NEW BUSINESS MODEL. The *healthymagination* initiative represented a significantly new business strategy aimed at addressing the "changing needs and emerging opportunities in healthcare."[32] No longer content with supplying medical practitioners in developed economies with high-quality (and expensive) imaging equipment, Immelt viewed *healthymagination* as a bold declaration of GE's intent to help "revolutionize health care all over the world"[33] by addressing three critical needs: lowering health care costs, increasing access to innovations, and improving the quality of health outcomes.[34] He believed all three metrics could be improved by 15 percent over the next five years. (See Exhibit 6 for the assessment process.) Though grounded in GE's Healthcare division, the initiative would require the active involvement of GE Capital, GE Global Research, GE Water, and NBC Universal, as well as an advisory board of international health care experts. Immelt pledged to invest $3 billion in health care–related R&D, $2 billion in financing, and $1 billion in technology and content by 2015:[35]

> "We will invest in innovations that measurably improve cost, access and quality," Mr. Immelt said. "That means lower-cost technology for more customers, products matched to specific local needs, and process expertise to help customers win. This reflects the new opportunities we see in health care. Our newest innovations—low-cost digital x-ray machines, portable ultrasounds, more affordable cardiac equipment—will save costs for doctors, hospitals, the government, families and businesses. This will help level the playing field in healthcare."[36]

By the end of 2009, GE had already validated 24 new products through its *healthymagination* program. (See Exhibit 7 for a progress update and Exhibit 8 for a full list of validated products.) Some, like the handheld Vscan ultrasound and Brivo CT device, promised to make previously bulky and expensive diagnostic tools available to primary-care physicians, both in the United States and in developing nations such as India and China. Information technology innovations such as Qualibria (a patient data management system) and

EXHIBIT 6

Assessment Process

Source: *GE healthymagination*, May 7, 2009 (http://www.ge.com/pdf/investors/events/05072009/ge_healthymagination_overview.pdf).

$6B Investment: $3B Healthcare Product/Service, $2B Financing, $1B GE in these Areas

 Cost Savings   Access Improvement Quality Improvement

Cost Savings	Access Improvement	Quality Improvement

1) Greater efficiency
  • Asset optimization
  • Maximize throughput
  • Reduce diagnosis & treatment variance
2) Therapy decision support
3) Managing chronic diseases
	1) Maternal & infant care
	2) Water & sanitation
	3) Screening for life-threatening conditions
	4) Technology to extend reach (remote access and portability)
		1) Reducing medical errors
		2) Improving diagnostic capability
		3) Remote medicine/monitoring
		4) Early disease detection

15% ↓	15% ↑	15% ↑

3ʳᵈ Party Validation by Oxford Analytica

 Imagination at Work

Healthymagination
May 7, 2009

Centricity EMR (an electronic medical-records system) were designed to increase the quality and accessibility of medical data, enabling doctors to make better health care decisions while simultaneously reducing costs. In yet another example, GE Performance Solutions utilized its AgileTrac software suite to help Mount Sinai Hospital in New York City optimize its processes so that existing personnel could treat up to 10,000 more patients within its current treatment facility. To deepen the innovation pipeline even further, GE created a $250 million equity investment fund to support the development of new companies and technologies consistent with its *healthymagination* goals.[37]

CHANGING MANAGERIAL MINDSETS. While GE's management center at Crotonville, New York, had a longstanding reputation for selecting and training the best managers in the world, it was not clear how readily they would embrace Immelt's new approach to doing business. GE was renowned for being lean and productive, but not necessarily agile and entrepreneurial. Changing long-established structures, processes, practices, and attitudes of the past several decades was a mammoth mission. This would be especially true at

GE, where the prevailing attitude was, "Why do we have to change if we're good?"[38]

GE's development goal was to get young professionals ready to run a big business by age 30. Training programs that rotated almost 3,000 employees annually kept GE's talent pipeline full. Senior executives spent at least 12 months in training and professional development during their first 15 years with GE.[39] Yet recently, *Bloomberg Businessweek* had run a cover story entitled, "Can GE Still Manage?"[40] while *The Wall Street Journal* reporter Evan Newmark wondered "whether GE's management still possesses superior skills and capabilities."[41] The central question seemed to be whether a formal HR system that originated in the 1950s could effectively equip leaders for the current-day decentralized business environment, in which the next breakthrough innovation was as likely to come from India or China as from the United States. Mr. Immelt had good reason to wonder whether GE's managers would be able to embrace the highly uncertain environment as the "new normal"[42] and respond in brave new ways. Yet he needed the buy-in and support of GE's legendary managers if he was to successfully embed innovation in a company long known for its performance culture.[43]

EXHIBIT 7

Validation Progress for healthymagination

Source: *GE healthymagination* (http://www.healthymagination.com/).

Work with partners to focus innovations on critical needs.

TO DATE, GE HAS:

Partnered with Intel and the Mayo Clinic for a study on home–based patient care.

Launched "Developing Health" a three–year $25 million program providing grant funding and volunteer support to nonprofit health centers in the United States.

Joined with Eli Lilly to develop technology that could enable faster, cheaper and smarter cancer therapies.

Expand employee health efforts.

TO DATE, GE HAS:

Launched Health Ahead, a global employee wellness and site certification program to build a culture of health.

Invest $3 billion in R&D, $2 billion in financing and $1 billion in technology and content by 2015.

TO DATE, GE HAS:

Invested $700 million in R&D toward healthymagination innovations.

Increased its healthymagination portfolio to 24 products, on target for 100 innovations by 2015.

Pledged $350 million through Stimulus Simplicity and the healthymagination Fund.

Increase the "value gap."

TO DATE, GE HAS:

Taken steps to lower GE's healthcare costs by focusing on key cost drivers and making our employees more aware of and responsible for cost-conscious decisions.

Engage and report on healthymagination progress.

TO DATE, GE HAS:

In addition to this report, GE is keeping the public informed through its healthymagination Web site, NBC/Universal platforms and its healthymagination Advisory Board.

GETTING PERSONAL. At the same time that he was asking his employees to embrace a new business model, Immelt also issued them a more personal challenge. As an employer, GE was faced with health care costs of $2.5 billion a year, covering the lives of 600,000 U.S. employees.[44] HealthAhead was implemented as a four-pronged approach to bringing better health to GE's people, thereby reducing the company's own health expenses. The components included health verification of company worksites, wellness programs such as Health by Numbers, and a new consumer-based health insurance program.[45] GE also issued a new policy mandating all worksites to be tobacco-free by March 2011, promising lower insurance premiums for employees who successfully quit smoking.[46]

Although promotional materials depicted workers exercising happily, praising the virtues of being smoke-free, and embracing the switch from name-brand to generic drugs, it was not yet clear that this picture accurately portrayed the sentiments of the entire work force. In the same year that GE stock prices took a dive, dividends were cut, and salaries were frozen at current levels, the new health plan (mandated for salaried employees and retirees under the age of 65) levied deductibles as high as $4,000 per year.[47] How willingly would GE's employees embrace *healthymagination* at such a personal level?

GAINING PUBLIC BUY-IN. As with *ecomagination*, Immelt also sought to engage the public in a national conversation on health care. GE conducted a national survey of consumers and doctors and found significant differences in their perceptions of healthy lifestyles.[48] The company then utilized the 2010 Winter Olympics in Vancouver, Canada, as a platform to launch a full-scale media campaign on health awareness, using athletic spokespeople like skaters Michelle Kwan and Scott Hamilton. At the same time, NBC Universal sought to increase its emphasis on health and wellness programming through shows like *Today* and *The Biggest Loser*, while its *The More You Know* spots targeted issues such as diabetes, strokes, and nutrition.[49] GE gained additional exposure through the launch of

EXHIBIT 8

List of *healthymagination* Validated Products

Diagnostic Technologies

AdreView

Brivo DR-F Digital X-Ray

Discovery NM/CT 570c

Discovery PET/CT 690 VCT

Discovery CT750 HD

Innova Interventional X-Ray

LightSpeed VCT Xte with ASiR or Snapshot Pulse

Logiq C5

MR Elastography

MRgFUS

Optima CT 660

Venue 40

Voluson Automated Technology

MAC 400

MAC 800

MAC i

Achilles

Life Support

Engstrom Carestation

Lullaby Incubator XP

Lullaby Warmer

Health Care IT

Centricity Practice Solution

Clinical Decision Support for Diagnostic Imaging (CDS-DI)

Performance Solutions

AgileTrac

Home Health

QuietCare

Source: *GE healthymagination,* May 7, 2009 (http://www.ge.com/pdf/investors/events/05072009/ge_healthymagination_overview.pdf).

a *healthymagination* homepage, as well as its presence on sites such as Facebook, Twitter, and YouTube. The initial numbers were impressive. In its 2009 *healthymagination* Annual Report, GE claimed to have made 247 million media impressions and helped facilitate the sharing of 2,225,834 healthy ideas.[50] However, it was much more difficult to measure the financial return on this investment.

GOING INTERNATIONAL. Ultimately, Mr. Immelt saw lack of access to adequate health care as not just an American problem, but a global ill. According to the *healthymagination* website, 1.1 billion people on earth do not have access to clean drinking water, while another 2 billion lack basic sanitation and health care. In Canada, there is one doctor for every 470 people; in China, one doctor for every 950 people, and in Africa, one doctor for every 50,000 people.[51] Immelt's goal was for *healthymagination* to become a worldwide movement that would help to change these numbers. He believed that GE, with its international reach and influence, was in a unique position to foster global cooperation, spur health-related innovation, and leave a lasting impact around the world.

GE already had significant experience in international markets on which *healthymagination* could build. After the financial crisis plunged the world into a deep recession, GE had started to look even more to revenues from outside of the United States. Because annual growth in emerging markets could be three times that in developed markets,[52] Mr. Immelt had strongly encouraged international sales in areas such as China, India, Turkey, Eastern Europe, Russia, and Latin America. In 1980, GE's revenues outside the United States, at $4.8 billion, constituted 19 percent of total revenues; in 2008, this number had soared to $97 billion and more than half of GE's total revenues.[53] The percentage of GE's sales from the U.S. market had declined from 66 percent to 46 percent just over the first eight years of Immelt's tenure as CEO.

When Immelt traveled around the world and "looked around the corner," he saw that success in developing countries was a prerequisite for continued vitality in developed ones.[54] Yet he also realized that emerging economies presented new and difficult challenges. For decades, GE and other industrial manufacturers had developed high-end products for primary use in industrialized nations and then adapted them for less-developed markets around the world. The world was different now. Economic growth in the United States and other wealthy countries was slowing, while information technology was increasing awareness of new technologies abroad. However, many second- and third-world nations still lacked the funds and basic infrastructure needed to support the resulting increase in technological demand.

GE had experimented—successfully—with some alternative approaches to doing business in low-income countries. In Kenya, it had established a partnership with a rural educational and clinical hospital to conduct research on the need for robust, low-maintenance, and inexpensive ICU/anesthesia products. In China, GE collaborated with the Ministry of Health to create a pilot program for stroke screening, utilizing GE's ultrasound and EKG equipment. Projects in India were focused on providing better neonatal care to both rural and urban communities.[55] Information gathered from such initiatives was resulting in a new model of "reverse-innovation," in which products were developed in and for countries in Africa, China, or India, and then distributed globally as well as back at home (see Exhibit 9).[56] Mr. Immelt believed this strategy would help prevent emerging corporate giants from developing countries from overtaking GE at home and abroad. But such a locally based approach was both time-consuming and more resource-intensive than GE's traditional way of doing business.

EXHIBIT 9

GE's New Model for Health Care Innovation

Source: *GE healthymagination*, May 7, 2009 (http://www.ge.com/pdf/investors/events/05072009/ge_healthymagination_overview.pdf).

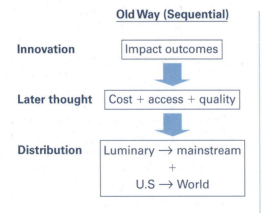
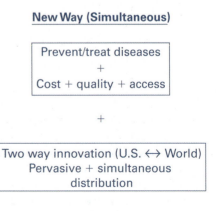

Old Way (Sequential)

Innovation → Impact outcomes

Later thought → Cost + access + quality

Distribution → Luminary → mainstream + U.S → World

New Way (Simultaneous)

Prevent/treat diseases + Cost + quality + access

+

Two way innovation (U.S. ↔ World) Pervasive + simultaneous distribution

Perfect Timing?

The U.S. health care system was in dire straits at the time GE launched its *healthymagination* initiative. Health care spending as a percentage of GDP had more than tripled in the past 50 years, from 5 percent in 1960 to 17 percent in 2010.[57] Some predicted that health care spending would reach 20 percent of the U.S. GDP within the next few years, implying that one out of every five dollars would be spent on health care of some sort. Americans had the most expensive health care system in the world, spending almost $8,000 per person annually.[58] The countries with the next highest per capita expenditures on health care were Canada, the Netherlands, France, Germany, and Sweden, all of which spent between $3,000 and $4,000 per year.[59] Sadly, comparisons with other developed countries showed that America's health care system did not provide significantly better outcomes, despite costing a lot more money. The United States fared worse than the OECD average in basic health indicators such as life expectancy, stroke survival rates, and infant mortality.[60]

The United States was also unique among industrialized countries in that it did not have 100 percent coverage for its citizens. Some countries like Britain, Canada, and Sweden had "single-payer" systems in which the public service was supported through taxes. Others, like the Netherlands and Switzerland, required every family or individual to purchase insurance. Analysts estimated that 49 million Americans were without health insurance in 2009, including not just people who truly could not afford it but also people who chose not to buy it. Instead of treating preventable diseases with early care and detection, these uninsured free-riders turned up in emergency rooms where insured people and taxpayers were forced to cross-subsidize their expensive treatments amounting to tens of billions of dollars per year.[61] Further contributing to the lack of access to health care in America were the insurance companies themselves, which had been allowed to select the safest patients and reject the sickest. This placed an unfair burden on the elderly and the ill who were unable to receive insurance coverage due to a preexisting condition. Even Americans who had health insurance coverage often found it "bankruptingly inadequate" if they became seriously ill or injured.[62]

After years of acrimonious debate over why these problems existed and what should be done to fix them, President Obama signed the Affordable Care Act into law on March 23, 2010. Its objectives were strikingly similar to those stated by GE's *healthymagination* program just one year prior: to improve quality, increase access, and lower the costs of health care in the United States. One of the primary provisions was that 32 million of the current 49 million uninsured would be mandated to purchase insurance by 2014. Government subsidies for this expense would be given for families making less than $88,000 a year. In the meantime, small businesses and non-profit organizations could receive tax credits for providing health-insurance benefits to their employees, young adults would be permitted to remain on their parents' plans until they turned 26 years old, and a new program was established to preserve employer coverage for people who retired before age 65. A second thrust of the new law was to bolster primary-care services and to place an increasing emphasis on preventive medicine. The legislation also enacted a host of new consumer protections aimed at limiting the power of the insurance companies, which would henceforth be forbidden from dropping people with preexisting conditions, placing lifetime caps on coverage allowances, or charging higher rates based on gender or health status.[63, 64]

Mr. Immelt believed that GE was in a unique position to take advantage of the business opportunities created by this new legislation. Not only did the company have a penchant for the evidence-based, data-driven, and quality-control operations so desperately needed in the health care industry, but through *healthymagination*'s advisory board, it had direct access to several high-profile health care experts. One of the most prominent was Tom Daschle, who had served four terms as a U.S. senator from South Dakota, as a member of the Democratic Party. He co-authored a recent book entitled *Critical: What We Can Do About the Healthcare Crisis,* advocating for universal health care in America. (Daschle was offered the position of the Secretary of the Department of Health and Human Services in the Obama administration, but withdrew his nomination amid controversy over his income tax filings.[65]) GE was counting on the insights and connections of Mr. Daschle and the other advisory board members to guide the development of *healthymagination*'s new products and services and to get them into the health care plans of the future.

However, GE's efforts could be in vain if Congress succeeds in its bid to repeal the Affordable Care legislation, or at a minimum de-fund the program. Critics were quick to point out the significant risk associated with building a business plan around legislation that could be repealed and subsidies that could be withdrawn due to a change in political administration.[66]

Back to Its Roots for Future Success?

Immelt knew the next few years would be especially critical for *healthymagination*—not to mention his career—for several reasons. The economy and GE's earnings were finally starting to turn around, positioning the company for further growth in the future. In July 2010, GE's profits increased by 16 percent—making this the biggest increase since the end of 2007. GE Capital's credit losses were decreasing, and health care sales were rising, especially in China and India.[67] At the same time, health care needs were as urgent as ever, both in the United States and abroad. The Affordable Care Act promised to create new opportunities for the types of technological and process innovations at which GE excelled, and GE had strong relationships with the U.S. government, at least for the time being. GE needed to make the most of these opportunities while they lasted.

As he prepared to address a cadre of several hundred GE leaders from across the globe at GE's leadership center in Crotonville, Immelt found himself wondering whether *ecomagination* and *healthymagination* would be enough to restore GE's former glory. Though up from its all-time low of $6.66, GE's share price had yet to break $20 since the 2008 financial crisis—a far cry from the $60 per share value Immelt inherited when he took office. It would take more time and a concerted effort to recover the $200 billion GE had lost in market capitalization. CEOs were supposed to create—not destroy—firm value. While the board

had been supportive of his turnaround efforts to date, Immelt had been at the helm for nearly 10 years with what some considered mediocre results. He wondered how much longer they would be willing to wait to reap the full benefits of his strategic plan.

In the meantime, the calls for further divestment continued. Once considered the "exception to the conglomerate rule,"[68] GE's financial premiums had evaporated with the downfall of GE Capital. Immelt himself saw the benefits of maintaining the company's expertise in technology, services, and finance in order to achieve his *ecomagination* and *healthymagination* visions, but he was feeling increasing pressure to justify his decisions to retain or spin off longstanding divisions as he reconfigured the corporate strategy around those far-reaching goals. He needed to show investors there would be a clear benefit to keeping at least some financial and media capabilities in-house. He also knew it would be challenging to demonstrate that *ecomagination* and *healthymagination* were broad enough to create synergy across GE's different business units (see Exhibits 10a and 10b for business-unit financials), yet not so broad that the company would find its resources stretched across too many projects in too many disparate industries. He knew that GE needed to return to its roots in industrial products and services, but sighed as he thought about the obstacles to be faced in the process of getting there. Could he persuade his managers, investors, and directors to continue on this journey with him?

EXHIBIT 10a

Revenues and Earnings by Strategic Business Unit, 2005–2010

| | Summary of Operating Segments | | | | | |
| | General Electric Company and Consolidated Affiliates | | | | | |
(In millions)	**2010**	**2009**	**2008**	**2007**	**2006**	**2005**
Revenues						
Energy Infrastructure	$ 37,514	$ 37,134	$ 38,571	$ 30,698	$ 25,221	$ 21,921
Technology Infrastructure	37,860	42,474	46,316	42,801	37,687	33,873
NBC Universal	16,901	15,436	16,969	15,416	16,188	14,689
Capital Finance	47,040	50,622	67,008	66,301	56,378	49,071
Consumer & Industrial	8,648	9,703	11,737	12,663	13,202	13,040
Total segment revenues	147,963	155,369	180,601	167,879	148,676	132,594
Corporate items and eliminations	2,248	1,414	1,914	4,609	2,892	3,668
Consolidated revenues	$150,211	$156,783	$182,515	$172,488	$151,568	$136,262

EXHIBIT 10a *(Continued)*

	Summary of Operating Segments					
	General Electric Company and Consolidated Affiliates					
(In millions)	2010	2009	2008	2007	2006	2005
Segment profit						
Energy Infrastructure	$ 7,271	$ 7,105	$ 6,080	$ 4,817	$ 3,518	$ 3,222
Technology Infrastructure	6,314	6,785	8,152	7,883	7,308	6,188
NBC Universal	2,261	2,264	3,131	3,107	2,919	3,092
Capital Finance	3,265	1,462	8,632	12,243	10,397	8,414
Consumer & Industrial	457	370	365	1,034	970	732
Total segment profit	19,568	17,986	26,360	29,084	25,112	21,648
Corporate items and eliminations	(3,321)	(2,826)	(2,691)	(1,840)	(1,548)	(372)
GE interest and other financial charges	(1,600)	(1,478)	(2,153)	(1,993)	(1,668)	(1,319)
GE provision for income taxes	(2,024)	(2,739)	(3,427)	(2,794)	(2,552)	(2,678)
Earnings from cont. operations	12,623	10,943	18,089	22,457	19,344	17,279
Earnings (loss) from discontinued operations, net of taxes	(979)	82	(679)	(249)	1,398	(559)
Consolidated net earnings	$11,644	$11,025	$17,410	$22,208	$20,742	$16,720

Source: GE 2011 Form 10-K.

EXHIBIT 10b

Additional Financial Data for Selected Business Units, 2007–2010

	Energy Infrastructure			
(in millions)	2010	2009	2008	2007
Revenues	$37,514	$37,134	$38,571	$30,698
Segment Profit	$7,271	$6,842	$6,080	$4,817
Revenues				
Energy(a)	$30,854	$30,185	$31,833	$24,788
Oil & Gas	7,561	7,743	7,417	6,849
Segment Profit				
Energy(a)	$6,235	$ 5,782	$ 5,067	$ 4,057
Oil & Gas	1,205	1,222	1,127	860

(a) Effective January 1, 2009, the Water business was combined with Energy. Prior period amounts were reclassified to conform to the current period's presentation.

(continued)

EXHIBIT 10b *(Continued)*

Technology Infrastructure				
(in millions)	2010	2009	2008	2007
Revenues	$37,860	$38,517	$41,605	$38,339
Segment Profit	$6,314	$6,758	$7,460	$7,187
Revenues				
Aviation	$30,854	$30,185	$19,239	$16,819
Health Care	16,897	16,015	17,392	16,997
Transportation	7,561	7,743	5,016	4,523
Segment Profit				
Aviation	$3,304	$3,923	$3,684	$3,222
Health Care	2,741	2,420	2,851	3,056
Transportation	315	473	962	936

GE Capital				
(in millions)	2010	2009	2008	2007
Revenues	$47,040	$49,746	$67,645	$66,301
Segment Profit	$3,625	$1,462	$8,063	$12,243
Total Assets	$575,908	$607,707	$ 572,903	
Revenues				
CLL (a)	$18,447	$20,762	$26,856	$26,982
Consumer (a)	17,822	17,634	24,177	25,054
Real Estate	3,744	4,009	6,646	7,021
Energy Financial Services	1,957	2,117	3,707	2,405
GECAS (a)	5,127	4,594	4,688	4,839
Segment Profit				
CLL (a)	$1,554	$963	$1,838	$ 3,787
Consumer (a)	2,629	1,419	3,623	4,283
Real Estate	(1,741)	(1,541)	1,144	2,285
Energy Financial Services	367	212	825	677
GECAS(a)	1,195	1,016	1,140	1,211
Total Assets				
CLL (a)	$202,650	$ 210,742	$ 228,176	
Consumer (a)	154,469	160,494	187,927	
Real Estate	72,630	81,505	85,266	
Energy Financial Services	19,549	22,616	22,079	
GECAS (a)	49,106	48,178	49,455	

(a) During the first quarter of 2009, GE transferred Banque Artesia Nederland N.V. (Artesia) from CLL to Consumer. Prior period amounts were reclassified
     to conform to the current period's presentation.

Source: GE 2011 Form 10-K.

Endnotes

1. "The hard way," *The Economist*, October 18, 2003.

2. Mark, K. (2008), "General Electric: From Jack Welch to Jeffrey Immelt," *Ivey Business School Case*.

3. "Peripheral vision: Detecting the weak signals that can make or break your company," Wharton School of Pennsylvania, 2008.

4. "Embarrassed Immelt owns up to impact of credit crisis," *Financial Times*, April 12, 2008.

5. "Immeltdown," *The Economist*, April 19, 2008.

6. Glader, P. (2009), "GE's Immelt to cite lessons learned," *The Wall Street Journal*, December 15.

7. McGregor, J. (2009), "Health care: GE gets radical," *BusinessWeek*, November 30.

8. Glader, P. (2009), "GE's Immelt to cite lessons learned."

9. Glader, P. (2009), "GE to invest in industrial businesses—Cash from NBC deal will help burnish aviation, healthcare and energy units," *The Wall Street Journal*, December 4.

10. www.alacrastore.com/mergers-acquisitions/ General_Electric_Company-1006912; accessed January 6, 2011.

11. Glader, P. (2010), "Live, from New York, GE's moment of truth," *The Wall Street Journal*, December 10.

12. Ibid.

13. Bartlett, C. A., and M. Wozny (2005), "GE's two-decade transformation: Jack Welch's leadership," *Harvard Business School Case*, May 3.

14. Ibid.

15. Welch, J. (2001), *Straight from the Gut* (New York: Warner Books), p. 121.

16. Mark, K. (2008), "General Electric: From Jack Welch to Jeffrey Immelt."

17. "Fortune's survey lists nation's toughest bosses," *The Washington Post*, July 19, 1984.

18. Mark, K. (2008), "General Electric: From Jack Welch to Jeffrey Immelt."

19. GE *healthymagination*, May 7, 2009 (http://www.ge .com/pdf/investors/events/05072009/ge_healthymagination_ overview.pdf).

20. Schiafo, R., and N. Sullivan (2005), "Talking green, acting dirty," *The New York* Times, June 12.

21. Carney, Timothy (2011), "Want to know how GE paid $0 income taxes? Think green," *Washington Examiner*, April 7.

22. GE *ecomagination* Annual Report, 2009.

23. Schiafo, R., and N. Sullivan, (2005), "Talking green, acting dirty."

24. Ibid.

25. GE *ecomagination* Annual Report, 2009.

26. Schiafo, R., and N. Sullivan (2005), "Talking green, acting dirty."

27. GE *healthymagination*, May 7, 2009 (http://www.ge .com/pdf/investors/events/05072009/ge_healthymagination_ overview.pdf).

28. http://www.ge.com/pdf/company/advertising/ healthymagination-manifesto.pdf.

29. GE *healthymagination*, May 7, 2009.

30. Immelt, J. R., V. Govindarajan, and C. Trimble (2009), "How GE is disrupting itself," *Harvard Business Review*, October.

31. GE *healthymagination*, May 7, 2009.

32. Ibid.

33. GE *healthymagination* Annual Report, 2009, p. 6.

34. GE *healthymagination*, May 7, 2009 (http://www.ge.com/pdf/ investors/events/05072009/ge_healthymagination_overview.pdf).

35. GE *healthymagination* Annual Report, 2009, p. 2.

36. Monegain, B. (2009), "GE's '*healthymagination*' tags $6 billion for IT innovation," *Healthcare IT News Online;* accessed September 07, 2009.

37. GE *healthymagination* Annual Report, 2009.

38. "Can GE still manage?" *Bloomberg Businessweek,* April 25, 2010.

39. Ibid.

40. Ibid.

41. "Newshub," *The Wall Street Journal*, April 17, 2010.

42. Immelt, J. R. (2009), "Letter to shareholders," GE 2009 Annual Report.

43. Crainer, S. (2009), "From Edison to Immelt: The GE way," *Business Strategy Review*, Autumn.

44. GE *healthymagination*, May 7, 2009.

45. GE *healthymagination* Annual Report, 2009.

46. Martin, J., (2010), "General Electric to go tobacco-free in 2011: Work sites to be tobacco-free," *McClatchy–Tribune Business News*, March 4.

47. McGregor, J. (2009), "Health care: GE gets radical," *BusinessWeek*, November 30.

48. GE *healthymagination* Annual Report, 2009.

49. "NBCU announces new company-wide initiative: 'Healthy at NBCU'; Campbell Soup company signs on as first 'Healthy at NBCU' advertiser; Multiplatform campaign promoting nutritional literacy to launch 2010; 'The More You Know' launches new season of health-themed PSAs, co-branded with GE's *healthymagination*," *PR Newswire,* October 14, 2009.

50. GE *healthymagination* Annual Report, 2009.

51. "*healthymagination*: Changing the way we approach healthcare around the world," www.healthymagination.com.

52. Immelt, J. R., V. Govindarajan, and C. Trimble (2009), "How GE is disrupting itself."

53. Ibid.

54. Ibid.

55. GE *healthymagination* Annual Report, 2009.

56. Immelt, J. R., V. Govindarajan, and C. Trimble (2009), "How GE is disrupting itself."

57. Centers for Medicare and Medicaid Service, National Health Statistics Group, 2010.

58. "Heading for the emergency room," *The Economist*, September 9, 2009.

59. Ibid.

60. "This is going to hurt," *The Economist*, September 25, 2009.

61. "Heading for the emergency room," *The Economist*, September 9, 2009.

62. "This is going to hurt," *The Economist*.

63. "Signed, sealed, delivered," *The Economist*, March 25, 2010.

64. "Provisions of the Affordable Care Act, by year," HealthCare.gov; accessed August 31, 2010.

65. "Daschle withdraws as nominee for HHS secretary," Associated Press, February 3, 2009.

66. Katz, J. (2010), "GE returns to its roots," *Industry Week*, July.

67. Glader, P., and B. Sechler (2010), "GE's earnings rise, ending a losing streak—Profit jumps 16% with assist from GE Capital Unit; Conglomerate's revenue declines as industrial businesses lag," *The Wall Street Journal*, July 17.

68. "Solving GE's big problem," *The Economist*, October 26, 2002.

Green is going from boutique to better, from a choice to a necessity, from a fad to a strategy to win, from an insoluble problem to a great opportunity.

—THOMAS FRIEDMAN, *HOT, FLAT, AND CROWDED*

Frank T. Rothaermel
Georgia Institute of Technology

Matt Hoepfer
Georgia Institute of Technology

RETURNING FROM DAVOS, Wolfgang Dehen, CEO of Siemens Energy, steps off the plane and stretches. He has just met with executives of the partner companies of the Energy Industry Partnership Programme, sponsored by the World Economic Forum. At their annual meeting in Davos, Switzerland, these partners and the energy ministers from various countries define and address the leading industry issues for the upcoming year. Siemens is proud to be recognized as a member of this esteemed group, which includes oil companies like Chevron, Exxon, Shell, and Kuwait Petroleum; alternative-energy experts such as Vestas Wind systems; and major energy suppliers like Duke Energy and Tokyo Electric Power. It is always intriguing to meet with energy leaders from across the globe, and especially so when Siemens's leading competitors (e.g., ABB and GE) are in the same room, talking about collaborative ways to improve worldwide energy efficiency.[1]

Energy efficiency has not always been a hot-button topic, least of all in corporate circles. Awareness of the need to reduce nations' economic dependence on fossil fuels first came to the forefront during the oil crisis of the 1970s. As the OPEC countries[2] reduced supply, oil prices quadrupled, effectively shutting down Western economies, at least temporarily. Then, as oil prices decreased and vast new oil fields were discovered around the world, public and industry interest in energy conservation waned. As long as oil is cheap and abundant, the public remains unwilling to pay premium prices for their energy needs, and there is no financial incentive to invest in alternative energy.

However, the price of oil has been trending upward in recent decades in a dramatic roller-coaster fashion (see Exhibit 1). When crude oil prices spiked at an all-time high of $145.15 per barrel on July 3, 2008 (up from $50 only 18 months earlier), the news sent a shockwave throughout the energy sector. Combined with a growing global awareness of the impact of greenhouse gases on climate change as well as increased concerns regarding energy security, energy issues are now receiving renewed interest from governments and corporations alike.[3]

One thing the Davos meeting participants have agreed on is that innovation will be essential to increasing energy efficiency.[4] Both continuous improvements in existing technologies and new breakthrough approaches to energy generation and distribution are necessary if major economies like the United States, China, Russia, and the European Union are to meet their respective energy targets over the next few years. For an energy company like Siemens, this presents both a challenge and an opportunity to carve out a leadership position in the new energy economy. A group of 20 CEOs captured this sentiment eloquently in their 2008 Climate Policy Recommendations to G8 Leaders:

> A paradigm shift to a low-carbon economy by 2050 has the potential to drive forward the next chapter of technological innovation. It will require a third— this time a green—industrial revolution. To realize this potential, the new framework must harness the power of the market to deliver on the environmental objective.[5]

However, a host of new, alternative-energy technologies are vying to replace carbon-based fossil fuels,

Professor Frank T. Rothaermel and PHD in engineering candidate Matt Hoepfer (GT MBA '09) prepared this case from public sources. This case is developed for the purpose of class discussion. It is not intended to be used for any kind of endorsement, source of data, or depiction of efficient or inefficient management. © Rothaermel and Hoepfer, 2013.

EXHIBIT 1

Crude Oil Price per Barrel and Trend Line, 1990–2012

(in constant, inflation-adjusted U.S. dollars)

Source: "Short-term energy outlook – Real petroleum prices," U.S. Energy Information Administration, June 10, 2010, www.eia.doe.gov/emeu/steo/pub/fsheets/real_prices.html.

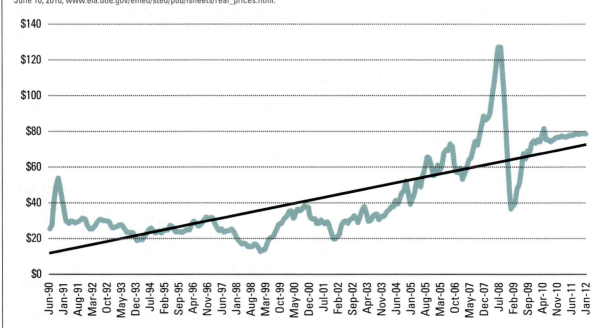

and it is hard to figure out what to do first and where to place the greatest emphasis. Wind and solar have reached high levels of technology readiness and are relatively mature compared to other renewable-energy sources. Better materials have enabled specialized companies to build ever-larger wind turbines, thus increasing efficiencies and reducing costs of wind energy. Large wind farms have been installed in several countries, and offshore wind parks have been erected to harvest the more constant and abundant winds over the oceans. Betting on wind as an alternative energy source, former oil man T. Boone Pickens announced in 2007 his plans to build the world's largest wind farm in the Texas Panhandle. (He later changed locations due to a lack of transmission-line capacity to transport the energy to either West or East Coast population centers.)[6] Meanwhile, solar panels have reached a production cost of less than $1 per kW (kilowatt) output. And these are only two options out of a portfolio of technologies that range from useful-yet-untested to plain science fiction. Some other candidates, such as geothermal energy and hydropower (water and wave exploitation), not to mention next-generation nuclear

reactors, have evolved quite rapidly in recent years and seem poised to pose a serious threat to wind and solar applications.

First thing tomorrow, Wolfgang Dehen plans to summon his strategy team and charge them with a formidable task: to formulate a strategy on how to best position Siemens in the global renewable-energy market. The stakes are high, and the recent financial turmoil and credit crunch do not make the decisions any easier. The questions racing through Dehen's mind are as diverse as they are complex:

- Should Siemens make its best guess on the future and invest deeply in a limited number of options, or cast a wider net and hedge its bets on multiple forms of alternative energy?
- If Siemens is to focus on a narrower field, how can it identify which alternative energy will become the leading technology in the future? Can a new disruptive innovation be foreseen and capitalized upon? Or can Siemens pick an alternative technology and help make it the winner?
- How should Siemens Energy compete in the new field(s)? Should it go it alone, developing proprietary

knowledge and keeping potential profits to itself, but also bearing the full risk of going too far down the wrong road? Or should it focus on acquiring smaller companies that have already made promising technological advances, and help them down the path to development? Or will alliances, which allow Siemens to share both the risks and returns with a partner, provide the optimal solution?

Siemens's History

From its humble beginnings as the Telegraphen-Bauanstalt von Siemens & Halske in 1847, Siemens has grown to become the second-largest employer in Germany (behind Deutsche Post), with 427,000 employees worldwide in 2009. The company's 150-year history is replete with ingenious inventions and trend-setting developments. After Werner von Siemens built the first wire telegraph from cigar boxes, tinplate, some iron, and insulated copper wire in 1846, he went on to improve the Wheatstone telegraph with the help of mechanical engineer and Physical Society member Johann Georg Halske.

The new Siemens & Halske Company internationalized quickly, as by nature the telegraph was used for cross-border communications. Then, as electricity became more accessible and less expensive as a source of energy, Siemens diversified its businesses to include a wide variety of electrical-engineering applications. One of the company's earliest areas of specialty was heavy-current engineering, or finding ways to meet the increased power requirements of the new industrial machinery. Other branches included telephone, electric lighting, electric cable cars and locomotives, radios, motion picture projectors, vacuum cleaners, and other electrical systems.

Based on its expertise in electrical engineering, Siemens next expanded its activities to include electrical power generation. Siemens Electrical Works was established in 1896 to engineer and build turnkey power plants to supply electricity. It operated numerous electrical power plants in Germany and across Europe. One year later, Siemens founded The Electric Light and Power Systems Company to provide financing solutions for its new power plant contracts. Collectively, these business units enabled Siemens to offer a complete package of power plant financing, construction, operation, and maintenance.

While many of Siemens's initial power plants were fueled by coal, the company also invested in the research and development (R&D) of alternative-energy sources almost from its very beginning.[7] In fact, the world's first publicly owned power plant—a small 8-kW hydroelectric plant built in the southern English town of Godalming in 1881—was connected to a Siemens alternator that provided electricity to a number of street lamps and shops.[8] From this time until the Second World War, Siemens built many more hydroelectric energy plants, both within Germany and abroad. Like the plant in Godalming, many of these represented world records or first-of-their-kind applications.

During WWII, many of Siemens's resources were diverted to the modernization of Nazi Germany's war technologies.[9] The company renewed its focus on alternative energy exploration after the war ended, and by 1955 had started theoretical preparations for the development of nuclear reactors. In 1961, Siemens received an order for a 57-MW multipurpose research reactor in Karlsruhe, Germany, which was fueled by natural uranium. Soon afterward, Siemens contracted the 1,200-MW Biblis, a nuclear power plant that had the largest single-shaft turbine generator in the world at that time.

Siemens diversified its efforts in alternative energy even further starting in the mid-1980s, expanding into wind energy. In 1987, Siemens's 3-MW wind energy converter Mod-5B began operations in Hawaii. In 1991 and 1992, two 500-kW photovoltaic systems started to supply electricity for the public grids in Mont Soleil, Switzerland, and Kerman, California, respectively. Alternative-energy generation technologies remain a major priority within Siemens, with a primary emphasis on wind and solar applications. Siemens also continues to conduct research in nuclear power, even though the German government made a controversial decision to withdraw from nuclear energy in the late 1990s. At the same time, Siemens's R&D efforts target multiple complementary technologies such as steam and gas turbines, thermal waste recycling, combined cycle technology, superconducting generators, electric power grids, high-efficiency power transmission technology, and exhaust gas catalysts and treatment.

Siemens's Corporate Structure

Siemens underwent a major reorganization in 2008, consolidating the number of sectors from more than one dozen down to just three—Industry, Energy, and Health care. These three main sectors were further divided into 15 divisions (strategic business units, SBUs [as presented in Exhibit 2]). Together, they

EXHIBIT 2

Siemens's Corporate Structure

Source: Adapted from "Siemens Energy Sector Presentation," Renewable Energy Division (ER), June 2009, Version 9.1.

Sectors	Divisions		Former Groups
Industry	• Industry Automation • Drive Technologies • Building Technologies	• Osram • Industry Solutions • Mobility	• Automation and Drives (A&D) • Industrial Solutions and Services (I&S) • Siemens Building Technologies (SBT) • Osram • Transportation Systems (TS)
Energy	• Oil & Gas • Fossil Power • Generation • Renewable Energy	• Energy Service • Power Transmission • Power Distribution	• Power Generation (PG) • Power Transmission and Distribution (PTD) • Industrial Solutions and Services (I&S OGM)
Health	• Imaging & IT • Workflow & Solutions • Diagnostics		• Medical Solution (Med)

comprise approximately 95 percent of company revenues and profits (see Exhibits 3 and 4).

In 2009, the Siemens Energy sector earned 26 billion euros in revenues, and more than 3 billion euros in profits. This amounted to roughly 33 percent of the overall company revenues, but 42 percent of the profits. Siemens Energy claimed to be "the only company worldwide that supports customers with [. . .] efficient products, solutions, and know-how along the entire chain of energy conversion from the production of oil and gas to power generation and the transmission and distribution of electrical energy."[10] Exhibit 5 shows a conceptual depiction of Siemens's energy supply chain.

The Energy sector was subdivided into five divisions, including Fossil Power Generation, Renewable Energy, Oil & Gas, Power Transmission, and Power Distribution. Exhibit 6 shows the 2009 revenues generated by the different divisions within the Energy sector, and Exhibit 7 depicts the 2009 profits. Together, Fossil Power Generation and Oil & Gas created 54 percent of the revenues, but just 39 percent of the sector's profits. In contrast, renewable energy generated just 11 percent of the revenues, but nearly 21 percent of the profits.

The Global Energy Market

The global energy market consists of traditional carbon-based fuels and newer alternative energies.

CARBON-BASED FUELS. Carbon-based fuels such as oil, coal, and natural gas make up some 84 percent of the world's energy sources. These fuels are based on the fossilized remains of living organisms that became a part of the earth millions of years ago and then were transformed under extreme pressure and heat. Of these three, oil is most easily extracted, converted, and stored in a liquid phase. Thus, it has become the primary energy source for vehicles.

EXHIBIT 3

2009 Siemens Business Sector Revenues

Source: Adapted from the Siemens 2009 Annual Report.

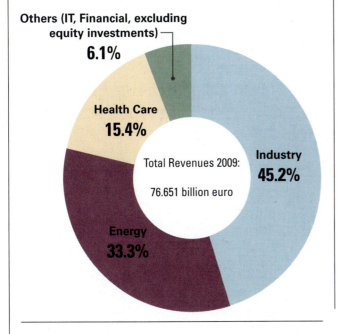

Others (IT, Financial, excluding equity investments)
6.1%

Health Care
15.4%

Industry
45.2%

Total Revenues 2009:

76.651 billion euro

Energy
33.3%

EXHIBIT 4

2009 Siemens Business Sector Profits

Source: Adapted from the Siemens 2009 Annual Report.

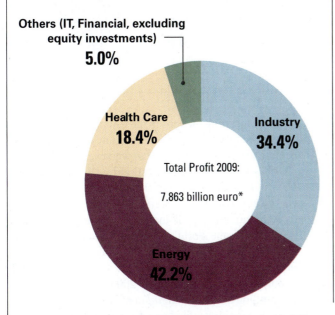

Others (IT, Financial, excluding equity investments)
5.0%

Health Care
18.4%

Industry
34.4%

Total Profit 2009:

7.863 billion euro*

Energy
42.2%

* Siemens's business sector profit of 7.863 billion euro was reduced to 6.012 billion as a result of 1.851 billion in write-offs due to losses in equity investments.

Although oil is relatively cheap, it comes with significant externalities. These are costs that are not reflected in the price of the commodity but rather are borne by the public. For example, the burning of fossil fuels releases carbon dioxide (CO_2) into the atmosphere, which has been linked to global warming. The CO_2 concentration in the earth's atmosphere remained at about 280 ppm (parts per million by volume) for the last several thousand years prior to the Industrial Revolution. In 2007, CO_2 levels in the atmosphere reached about 384 parts per million by volume, and seemed to be increasing at a rate of approximately 2 parts per million per year (see Exhibit 8).[11] In addition, many cities have become contaminated by smog, and people are suffering health problems caused by increased pollution. While experts debate the magnitude of the remaining carbon-based fuel supply, the reality is that fossil fuels are finite; supplies will eventually run out—it is just a matter of when.

Ever since humans began using fossil fuels, the amount of fuel needed has grown exponentially to accommodate ever-increasing living standards and populations. Accelerated industrialization has led to a spike in the demand for energy over the past 20 years (see global electricity consumption in Exhibit 9). Currently, rapidly developing Asian countries such as India and China are the main energy consumers, contributing almost 40 percent to global CO_2 emissions (see Exhibit 10 for CO_2 emissions by world region). Yet despite the large volume of CO_2 generated, India's and China's per capita consumption of energy is still quite low. For 2010, the U.S. Department of Energy projected per capita CO_2 emissions of 5.3 and 1.1 metric tons per person for China and India, respectively. In comparison, the projection for the continental United States was 18.6 metric tons per person.[12] Taking into account that both China and India have populations of more than one-billion each and together account for roughly one quarter of the world population, it is obvious that a per capita energy consumption rate similar to Western countries is not sustainable. Meanwhile, the continued industrialization of developing countries combined with rising populations will require more and more energy.

EXHIBIT 5

Siemens's Energy Supply Chain

Source: Adapted from Siemens Energy Sector Presentation, Renewable Energy Division (ER), June 2009, Version. 9.1.

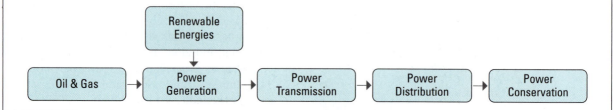

EXHIBIT 6

2009 Siemens Revenues by Division within the Energy Sector

Source: Adapted from the Siemens 2009 Annual Report.

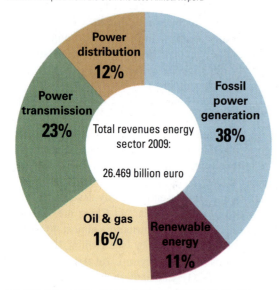

EXHIBIT 7

2009 Siemens Profits by Division within the Energy Sector

Source: Adapted from the Siemens 2009 Annual Report.

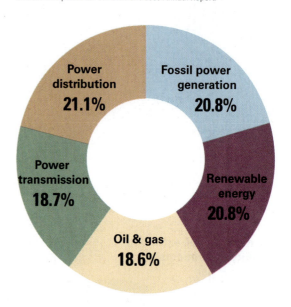

ALTERNATIVE ENERGIES. Underlying alternative energy is the principle of using natural resources such as wind, water, solar radiation, or heat to create energy instead of carbon-based fuels. Natural energy is regarded as infinite, at least as far as it can be assumed that the sun and wind will not cease to exist within a time frame significant for humanity. Also termed renewable energy, the biggest advantage of such natural energy sources is that they are carbon dioxide (CO_2) neutral. Unfortunately, most alternative-energy creation methods also have one major drawback: They can generate energy only in places where nature provides the required energy input. For example, wind does not blow steadily and strongly enough everywhere

on the planet. Fluctuations in the natural energy supply need to be taken into account, and any natural energy captured must be transported to wherever it is needed. This has spurred immense R&D efforts to find optimal ways not just to capture but also to store and distribute energy generated from natural resources.

Alternative energy is increasingly being viewed as a panacea for the world's economic as well as environmental concerns. Companies no longer see investments in green technologies as a burden, but as a business opportunity. For example, in 2005, GE launched a multibillion dollar *ecomagination* initiative to leverage its wide-ranging technological capabilities to address problems in the green-energy arena. Politicians are

EXHIBIT 8

Global CO_2 Emissions (historic and projected)

Source: Data from www.eia.doe.gov/oiaf/ieo/excel/ieoreftab_10.xls.

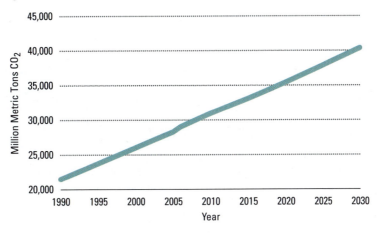

EXHIBIT 9

Global Electricity Consumption, 1980–2006

Source: Data from www.eia.doe.gov/pub/international/iealf/table62.xls.

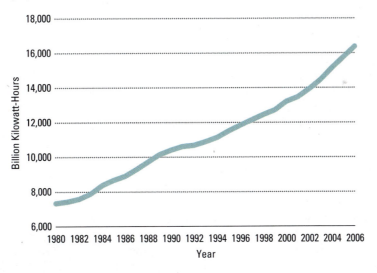

also jumping on the bandwagon, partly because they believe that millions of new green jobs may help to reduce high unemployment rates. In the United States, this could be especially true in Midwestern states that rely heavily on industrial manufacturing. In Germany, the federal government is supporting a geographic cluster in the alternative energy industry in its eastern region around Frankfurt/Oder. The race for global leadership in alternative energy is on.

Siemens and Alternative Energies

See Exhibit 11 for the current distribution of the global production of alternative energy sources.

WIND ENERGY. Modern windmills are high-tech devices capable of producing several megawatts of energy each, enough for one turbine to supply electricity to an entire small village. The technological progress of wind turbines has been noteworthy. From 1980 to 2008, the average effective power output capacity for a wind turbine generator increased by a factor of 200.[13] Wind power is deemed to have immense upward potential for at least the next two decades.

Wind turbines have their disadvantages as well. Despite advances in material engineering, the size of wind turbines is not infinitely scalable due to technological constraints. To increase capacity, multiple wind turbines therefore must be spread out over large distances from one another, so each has full exposure to the wind. Densely populated urban areas do not have adequate space to house wind parks, and rural areas have expressed annoyance with the sound made by the turbines as well as their interference with wildlife migratory patterns and agricultural productivity. In addition, wind turbines possess limited efficiency. Physical conditions determine that the maximum energy that can be extracted from the wind is around 59 percent (Betz's law), a theoretical value that so far cannot actually be achieved. Take into account the losses that occur due to the conversion of rotational to electrical energy and electronic conditioning, and the efficiency of wind turbines falls to a range of 40 to 45 percent. This is comparable to the efficiency of a good diesel engine, leading critics to argue that wind turbines are not an economical alternative.

Producing industrial-scale wind turbines requires large and highly specialized assembly facilities. The entry-level barriers are high, and up-front investments are extensive. The turbine

EXHIBIT 10

2010 Global CO_2 Emissions by World Region

Source: Data from www.eia.doe.gov/oiaf/ieo/excel/ieoreftab_10.xls.

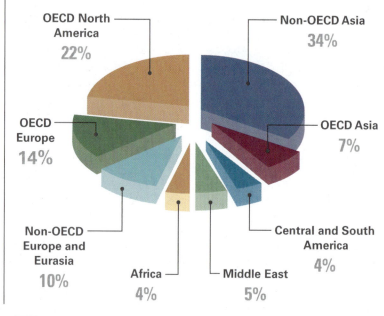

EXHIBIT 11

2008 Global Energy Production by Type (in billions of btu)

Source: Data adapted from www.eia.doe.gov/emeu/aer/txt/stb0102.xls.

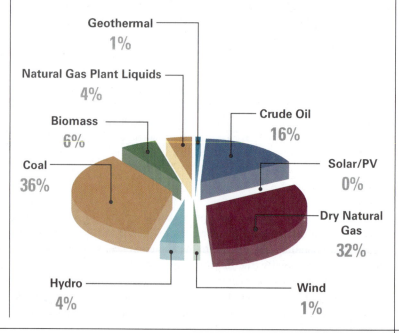

blades must be able to withstand high centrifugal forces, vibrations, varying weather conditions, radiation, and foreign-object impacts (e.g., birds), while at the same time they need to be lightweight. To achieve these requirements, blades are currently made from glass and carbon fiber–base materials, which require special labor-intensive manufacturing techniques. The towers are usually made of reinforced spun concrete, a manufacturing process that becomes quite complex for tall structures. Transportation and installation also pose challenges. Turbine blades, sometimes longer than 60 meters (180 feet), and towers, sometimes as tall as 135 meters (400 feet), need to be transported to the final site, a task that involves huge logistical efforts. In many cases, bridges must be elevated and/or reinforced, and roads straightened out to transport these large industrial components.

SIEMENS AND WIND ENERGY. Despite its disadvantages, wind energy is the fastest-growing alternative-energy sector, a trend that is predicted to continue. Siemens has therefore staked a strong presence in the wind-turbine business, winning several large contracts for installing both on- and offshore wind turbines.[14,15] Globally, Siemens claimed to be the fifth-largest installer of wind-turbine power in 2009 (with 8.8 GW installed), and aims to become number 3 by 2012.[16,17] The company's portfolio includes all stages of wind-turbine development, including component and system design, R&D, manufacturing, installation, and maintenance. These combined activities earned the company revenues of nearly 19 billion euros in fiscal year 2008, accounting for roughly a quarter of total revenues. One of the unit's most recent accomplishments was the introduction of a new 3.6-megawatt wind turbine featuring a 120-meter diameter rotor equipped with 58.5-meter-long rotor blades.

Siemens has developed a particularly strong focus on offshore wind turbines, with some large-scale projects recently acquired.[18] Together with the Norwegian energy company StatoilHydro, Siemens was instrumental in developing the first-ever floating wind turbine off the coast of Norway in late 2009.[19] This new technology is being tested to evaluate whether a wind turbine installation in deep-sea water is feasible, as the wind there blows stronger and more consistently than along the coast. The main concerns are the durability and maintenance of the equipment against aggressive environmental conditions at sea.

The majority of Siemens's wind-energy operations are centralized in Europe. Since transportation

of the increasingly large turbine blades is difficult even on land, international expansion often means the company must install production facilities overseas. (Even a C-5 cargo aircraft is not large enough, and cargo ships are not designed to transport wind turbines.) Siemens operates a wind-turbine blade factory in Fort Madison, Iowa, which was visited by President Obama in April 2010, receiving important political recognition. Siemens also recently took the first steps in building a production facility in China, taking into account that "China could soon become the largest wind-energy market in the world."[20] Some have even suggested that wind power alone might be able to cover all of China's future electricity demands.[21, 22]

Due to the technological complexity of the wind-turbine business, Siemens has relatively few competitors. Notable European players include Enercon (Germany) and Vestas (Denmark), while its major U.S. rival is General Electric (GE), which installed 15 GW of new wind-power capacity globally in 2009. However, since the market has high future potential, other players are entering the competition, most notably from China. Mitsubishi Heavy Industries (Japan) also poses a future challenge since the company possesses the industrial capabilities and finances to become a major global player, and has recently ramped up its development and installations of new wind-turbine capacities.[23] One of the attractions of wind power is that, once installed, the turbines need constant maintenance, which means lucrative long-term service contracts for the original maker and installer of the equipment.

SOLAR ENERGY. Solar is the second most-established renewable energy technology. The amount of solar radiation that reaches earth at any given moment is far more energy than humans consume during that same amount of time. This means that solar energy alone could easily meet all of the energy needs on the planet.

Sunlight can be converted into electricity in various ways. One way is direct conversion through semiconductors (i.e., photovoltaics). Alternatively, solar power may be used to heat up a medium such as water, convert it to steam, and propel a turbine that in turn generates energy. The advantage of these methods is that they require few moving parts, and therefore minimal maintenance. Solar panels are also easily installed in deserts and other remote areas exposed to high levels of solar radiation. Solar cells are used to successfully recharge batteries and propel cars. Toyota even offers the option of powering the Prius's air conditioning through photovoltaic panels on the car's roof.

The disadvantages of solar energy are nevertheless considerable. Like wind energy, solar power must be extracted where it occurs naturally. Many of the best places to harvest solar energy are actually over the oceans. To produce significant quantities of solar energy, panels must be installed over large areas, which increases their exposure to adverse weather conditions. In addition, solar panels have a low efficiency, reaching only about 25 percent under optimal laboratory conditions; mass-produced panels achieve rates of only 18 to 20 percent. Moreover, these efficiencies can only be accomplished when sunlight reaches the panels unobstructed at an optimum angle, which requires clear weather, clean air, and clean panel surfaces. The panels also must be actively adjusted to follow the sunlight throughout the day. Finally, the semiconductors upon which the materials are based require exceptional degrees of purity, and can only be manufactured in special (and costly) production facilities that are hermetically shielded from the environment.

The solar industry is segmented into several categories. On one side of the spectrum is the production and manufacturing of solar panels. In recent years, China has become the leading manufacturer and global exporter of low-cost solar panels due to a combination of cheap labor and available industrial infrastructure. *The New York Times* reported that China drove prices down by almost 50 percent from 2008 to 2009.[24] Since it is now possible to mass-produce solar panels with a cost of less than $1 per kW, this is a well-developed commodity market, with a readily available technology and minimal R&D expenses. The only up-front cost is for manufacturing equipment and plants. Rivalry within this market is strong and almost perfectly competitive.

In the center are the solar-technology installation and service industries. These businesses take hardware like solar panels and install them for the customer, making them easier and more cost-effective than traditional energy sources. While it is not necessary, installation and service providers benefit greatly from having the support of the manufacturer of the basic technology. Depending on their capabilities, many have expanded into the development of complementary products, such as switchboards and distributors for solar panels. For example, the U.S. firm SolarCity[25] offers solar system design, installations, financing, and leasing for commercial and residential customers. Co-founded in 2006 by serial entrepreneur Elon Musk (who also runs Tesla Motors and SpaceX), SolarCity had grown to be one of the biggest solar system installers in the United States by 2007.[26]

On the other side of the spectrum lies the commission of turnkey high-tech solar plants and installations. Examples of these technologies included CSP (Concentrated Solar Power) and ISCCS (Integrated Solar Combined Cycle System) plants,[27] both on the Siemens product list. In general, these plants consist of large arrays of mirrors that reflect and concentrate sunlight onto receivers. The receivers collect the solar energy and convert it to heat, which is then used to produce electricity via a steam turbine or heat engine driving a generator. One advantage of this technology is that it allows for limited storage of the heat produced in a transfer medium (often oil or molten salt).[28] Turnkey solar plants require large amounts of experience and infrastructure for building and operation, resulting in an oligopolistic market with only a few major competitors.

SIEMENS AND SOLAR ENERGY. Siemens is the market leader in turnkey CSP plants, an area where the company can effectively leverage its size, experience in power-plant development, and reliability as a long-term service provider. Part of the attractiveness of this sector is that turbines and generators require long-term (and often lucrative) service contracts, long after plant construction is completed.

In March 2009, Siemens expanded its solar presence by acquiring a 24 percent stake in the Italian solar-thermal specialist Archimede Solar Energy (ASE). Siemens's new business unit received its first photovoltaic order from Statkraft in June 2009. René Umlauft, CEO of the Renewable Energy Division at Siemens Energy, stated that this contract "proves that we are . . . on the right track with the expansion of our solar business" and that "in the coming months we are anticipating further orders for projects in the Mediterranean region."[29] Also in June 2009, Siemens took its efforts in solar and wind to the next level by leading the Desertec initiative. This transcontinental project aims to generate solar power in North Africa, where it is most abundant, and then transport it to Europe. The project fits particularly well with Siemens because it requires not only experience in the primary wind and solar technologies but also in complementary technologies such as power grids and switchboards, which have traditionally been strong business fields for the company.

NUCLEAR ENERGY. Nuclear power is an infinitely renewable energy that creates a controlled nuclear reaction of special radioactive material, usually Uranium-235 or Plutonium-239. The energy from the chain reaction is used to heat up water to produce steam, which in turn propels steam turbines and generators to produce electricity. In 2007, about 14 percent of electricity worldwide was produced using nuclear power.[30] Nuclear reactors are the strongest power plants possible and the most economically feasible.

Yet nuclear power has serious limitations. Issues include potential nuclear accidents (e.g., Chernobyl in the Ukraine and the Fukushima reactor after the 2011 tsunami in Japan) and how to store nuclear waste products. The U.S. Department of Energy claims that its Waste Isolation Pilot Plant,[31] a salt mine in the southern New Mexico desert, can safely store all of the nuclear waste humans can create in the next 10,000 years. However, disposing of nuclear waste in old caves and salt mines is not 100 percent safe, as shown by a recent incident in Asse, Germany. Nuclear waste that had been stored at a waste dump salt mine leaked out of its allegedly safe storage containers, after the salt mine flooded at a much higher rate than assumed.[32] In addition, there have been reports of increased leukemia rates in areas close to nuclear reactors, changes in the microclimate due to the vast amounts of steam released into the atmosphere, and concerns regarding nuclear terrorism. Nuclear energy is also not entirely CO_2-neutral.

In countries such as France, where nuclear reactors cover 80 percent of the national electricity produced, a more liberal stance is taken toward these questions. Germany, meanwhile, has vowed to stop all its nuclear reactors one by one. Given the need to address global warming and create sustained economic growth, however, Germany is reconsidering this decision. The German parliamentary election in September 2009 spawned new hopes that the German nuclear industry might be revitalized. The newly elected center-right government (CDU and FDP coalition) believes that the country's energy demands might not be met by renewable resources alone, and is considering building new reactors while keeping the existing nuclear power plants running. Not surprisingly, stocks of German nuclear companies jumped after the election results were announced.[33, 34]

SIEMENS AND NUCLEAR ENERGY. Siemens has been involved in nuclear research since 1955. However, these efforts were put on hold in the 1990s when the German government passed a law that would gradually withdraw the country from nuclear-power generation. During that time, Siemens's primary activity in the nuclear sector was upgrading its existing plants.[35, 36] Recently, Siemens has taken up its nuclear activities anew and is expanding to become involved in international agreements.[37] Russia alone has been deemed to be a market for dozens of new reactors in the near future, with Siemens being a potential partner for many of these projects.[38] China also looks to be very active, with plans to have 100 new reactors in operation or under construction by 2020.[39] Many other countries that have planned or built nuclear power plants, such as the United Kingdom, Finland, Japan, Taiwan, South Korea, and India, are difficult markets to enter because they possess their own technology and production capabilities. Also, due to national security issues, many countries strongly prefer or even require domestic suppliers.

In the United States, licenses for 35 new nuclear power units are in progress.[40] Some of the dominant players in the U.S. nuclear market are Westinghouse, GE Energy, Hitachi America, Bechtel Corporation, and Southern Company. The U.S. Department of Energy recently announced $40 million in funding to support design and planning work for the Next Generation Nuclear Plant (NGNP),[41] and also pledged to support basic university research in nuclear energy.[42]

HYDROPOWER. There are many different means of establishing hydropower generators, which utilize turbines to extract energy from water current flows. The most obvious are dams built along rivers. Dams provide significant amounts of energy and have the lowest CO_2 emissions of any energy source.[43] Dams are also unique in that they can store excess available energy by pumping water uphill back into a reservoir, which can then be used during peak demand times. Since energy storage is one of the main challenges in the use of alternative energies, this property makes dams especially attractive. On the negative side, dams require huge up-front investments, pose significant risks regarding potential failure, have a limited service life due to silt and sediment accumulation, and require severe modifications of the natural environment. For example, building the Three Gorges Dam in China resulted in the flooding of dozens of small villages and required the relocation of tens of thousands of people who lived in the river plain; a manmade lake of considerable size now stands in their place. Although there are more than 45,000 large dams around the world,[44] only a limited number of hydro dam projects are active worldwide, and many of these face problems due to environmental or financial issues.[45, 46]

Other methods of hydropower generation with lesser environmental impact include river and tide turbines and wave power. River turbines are small hydro turbines that are installed in rivers without a dam being required, frequently at support posts for bridges. River turbines extract a small but consistent power supply from the natural water flow, and are best suited for local energy needs. Theoretically, tide turbines can also provide a reliable power source, as tides change twice a day and can be very strong in certain areas. Due to significant engineering challenges, however, only a few mass-produced tide turbines are currently in service. For the technology to work, the seashore needs to be flat with only a slight slope, and requires long stretches of littoral waters. Also, tide turbines are restricted to uninhabited beaches, since moving parts under the water surface can create hazards for swimmers, water sports, and coastal ships. Lastly, harnessing the power of ocean waves has attracted significant attention since oceans cover some 71 percent of the earth's surface. Some drawbacks to wave power include the efficiency of current applications, necessary resistance against hostile environments (e.g., storms and salt water corrosion), cost of electricity (including transport to shore), possible impacts on marine life, and hazards to shipping. As with tidal power, several different technologies (e.g., the Pelamis Wave Energy Converter) are vying to emerge as the industry standard.

SIEMENS AND HYDROPOWER. Siemens has been a strong player in hydroelectric power dams since 1881. More recently, Siemens acquired a contract for complementary high-voltage gas-insulated transmission line technologies for China's second largest hydropower plant.[47] Otherwise, Siemens has no stake in any of the other alternative hydropower technologies described earlier.

Opportunities to expand more fully into hydropower do exist. In 2007, the U.S. Department of Energy (DOE) established the Hydropower Program, designed to "conduct research and development that [will] improve the technical, societal, and environmental benefits of hydropower and provide cost-competitive technologies that enable the development of new and incremental hydropower capacity, adding diversity to the nation's energy supply."[48, 49] A total of 5,677 sites with an undeveloped capacity of about 30,000 MW were identified across the country.[50] In 2008, only 2.4 percent of the overall energy consumption in the United States was covered by hydroelectric power generation. This is, however, still much more than that covered by either solar or wind energy alternatives.[51]

GEOTHERMAL POWER. Geothermal power is yet another form of renewable energy. The idea here is to drill two shafts deep into the earth, pumping water down one of the shafts and extracting energy from the steam that comes out the other shaft, as the water is heated under the earth's surface. This technology has the major advantage that it can be installed wherever energy is actually needed. Geothermal plants require minimal freshwater and external fuel supplies, and due to their layout are highly scalable.

Yet the effort of drilling two shafts into the earth creates significant up-front costs as well as engineering and safety issues. Drilling affects the stability of the surrounding soil, resulting in subsidence and possible local earthquakes. As a result, geothermal plants can be installed only in areas with low seismic activity. In addition, this technology is limited to lowlands, since the geothermal heat necessary to create steam is located too deep in the ground in mountainous regions. Another problem is that the fluids conveyed from the earth carry a mixture of gases, notably carbon dioxide (CO_2) and hydrogen sulfide (HS_2). While these pollutants do contribute to global warming, geothermal emissions make up only a minor fraction of those generated by conventional fossil-fuel plants. Lastly, the temperature achievable from this technology might not be enough to heat water sufficiently for use in a steam turbine. This limits the use of geothermal energy to heating and possibly air conditioning, but not power generation.

SIEMENS AND GEOTHERMAL POWER. Siemens currently has no stakes in geothermal technologies.

Distributing Alternative Energy

A major disadvantage of most renewable energy sources (i.e., wind, solar, and hydropower) is that they are stationary. They produce energy where it is supplied by nature, which is not necessarily where it is needed most. Connecting the dots requires large investments in power storage and distribution, often across national and international borders. The electrical equipment for doing so is a very low-tech power grid whose development has not kept pace with technological advances in power-generation methods. The current grid does not possess any correction mechanisms, relying instead on customers to tell if there is a power outage.

Consequently, a new, complementary industry branch has developed around the concept of a "smart grid." Smart grids include self-monitoring and possibly self-repairing capabilities, smart sensors and meters, and a communications network similar to the Internet. This will help avoid power outages, make the grid more reliable, reduce maintenance, and save energy. It will also be expandable with future technologies, such as connecting electric cars to the grid and using their batteries for storage capacity. Smart distribution will also greatly reduce the current problems with peak power demand, and can serve to integrate both traditional and alternative energies into a common power supply and distribution network. Smart-grid technology is therefore likely to have a strong impact on future pricing strategies, which can turn out to be highly beneficial to alternative energies and their future development.[52]

Having seen the importance and market potential of the smart grid, industries and politicians are eager to get their share of the business. The Obama administration set aside funding to build smart-grid technologies as part of its recent economic stimulus plan. Startups as well as established companies are investing significant resources in research and development. Two of these startups, GridPoint and Silver Spring Networks, have managed to raise $220 million and $170 million, respectively. One major part of IBM's "smarter planet" vision is smart-grid technology. Meanwhile Cisco, the world's biggest maker of networking gear, expects that the underlying communications network will be "100 or 1,000 times larger than the Internet." Google and Microsoft likewise have started to identify feasible business areas, in the hope of providing the software that will control the grid.[53, 54]

SIEMENS AND SMART GRIDS. Smart-grid technologies seem to be a natural business opportunity for Siemens, based on the company's long history with electronic technologies and products. The company recently established a partnership with Landis & Gyr (a leading provider of integrated energy-management solutions for energy companies) to develop smart meters, a technology that enables the tracking of power requirements and the ability to adapt where energy is generated and distributed.[55] The market volume for smart meters was expected to be about one billion euros in fiscal year 2009, and Siemens hopes to acquire orders worth more than six billion euros for intelligent-power networks through 2014. Wolfgang Dehen believes that the market for smart grids will have "increasingly dynamic growth fueled by climate change and economic stimulus programs" and that Siemens will "grow twice as fast as the overall market" within this sector.[56, 57]

Siemens's Competition

The global energy market is a capital-intensive business in a regulated environment. As a consequence, there are only a few major players in this industry. Financial data for the main global energy companies are shown in Exhibit 12 (Siemens), Exhibit 13 (ABB), Exhibit 14 (General Electric), and Exhibit 15 (Alstom), respectively. There are, however, numerous small and highly innovative companies that focus on R&D in specialized areas of the renewable-energy supply chain. The vast majority of these are privately owned technology startups.

Siemens's technological accomplishments have made it the world's second-largest industrial conglomerate, next to General Electric (GE), its major competitor. Exhibits 3 and 16 show 2009 sector revenues for Siemens and GE, respectively. Exhibits 4 and 17 show 2009 sector profits for Siemens and GE, respectively. Like Siemens, GE is also active worldwide. Exhibits 18 and 19 compare the major world markets for Siemens and GE, respectively. GE Energy is involved in all the major energy fields that Siemens covers, including wind, solar, and nuclear. This also includes complementary systems, components (such as gas turbines), and services and maintenance. GE has the "home advantage" in the very important U.S. market, while Siemens has a long history of service in the European Union. Both increasingly have to put up with third-party competitors,

EXHIBIT 12

Selected Financial Data, Siemens (revenue and earnings in millions of euros)

	2009	2008	2007	2006	2005	2004	2003
Revenue	76,651	77,327	72,448	66,487	55,781	61,480	61,624
Gross profit	20,710	21,043	20,876	17,379	15,683	18,710	18,089
Net income	2,497	5,886	4,038	3,345	2,576	3,405	2,445
Assets, liabilities, and equity (millions of euros):							
Current assets	43,634	43,015	47,932	50,014	45,502	45,946	43,489
Current liabilities	36,486	42,117	43,894	38,964	38,376	33,435	32,041
Debt	19,638	16,079	15,497	15,297	12,035	11,219	13,178
Long-term debt	18,940	14,260	9,860	13,122	8,040	9,785	11,433
Pension plans and similar commitments	5,938	4,361	2,780	5,083	5,460	4,392	5,843
Equity	27,287	27,380	29,627	25,895	23,791	26,454	23,404
As a percentage of total assets	29	29	32	30	29	33	30
Total assets	94,926	94,463	91,555	87,528	81,579	79,239	77,378
Key capital market data (in euros):							
Earnings per share from continuing operations	2.60	1.91	4.13	2.78	2.96	3.37	2.31
Diluted earnings per share from continuing operations	2.58	1.90	3.99	2.77	2.85	3.23	2.28
Dividend per share	1.60	1.60	1.60	1.45	1.35	1.25	1.10
Siemens stock price							
High	66.45	108.86	111.17	79.77	66.18	68.30	58.32
Low	35.52	64.91	66.91	60.08	56.20	52.02	32.05
Year-end (September 30)	63.28	65.75	96.42	68.80	64.10	59.21	51.14
Number of shares (in millions)	914	914	914	891	891	891	891
Market capitalization at period-end (millions of euros)	54,827	56,647	88,147	61,307	57,118	52,761	45,559
Credit rating of long-term debt:							
Standard & Poor's	A+	AA–	AA–	AA–	AA–	AA–	AA–
Moody's	A1	A1	A1	Aa3	Aa3	Aa3	Aa3

Source: Company financial reports. Years 2005 and forward are according to IFRS, years 2004 and earlier according to U.S. GAAP.

EXHIBIT 13

Consolidated Income Statement Data, ABB ($ in millions, except per-share data in $)

Year ended December 31	2009	2008	2007	2006	2005	2004	2003
Total revenues	31,795	34,912	29,183	23,281	20,964	18,987	17,891
Total cost of sales	(22,470)	(23,972)	(20,215)	(16,537)	(15,510)	(14,219)	(13,307)
Gross profit	9,325	10,940	8,968	6,744	5,454	4,768	4,584
SG&A	(5,528)	(5,822)	(4,975)	(4,326)	(3,780)	(3,672)	(3,781)
Other income, expense (net)	329	(566)	30	139	37	(41)	(193)
EBIT	4,126	4,552	4,023	2,557	1,711	1,055	610
Interest and dividend income	121	315	273	147	153	146	132
Interest and other finance expense	(127)	(349)	(383)	(307)	(407)	(355)	(538)
Income from continuing operations before taxes and minority interest	4,120	4,518	3,913	2,397	1,457	846	204
Provision for taxes	(1,001)	(1,119)	(595)	(686)	(464)	(258)	(99)
Income (loss) from discontinued operations, net of tax	17	(21)	586	(142)	(127)	(523)	(803)
Income before cum effect of acctg change, net of tax	3,136	3,378	3,904	1,569	866	65	(698)
Cum. effect of accounting change, net of tax	–	–	(49)	–	(5)	–	–
Net income	3,136	3,378	3,855	1,569	861	65	(698)
Net income attrib. to noncontrolling interests	(235)	(260)	(244)	(179)	(126)	(100)	(81)
Net income	2,901	3,118	3,611	1,390	735	(35)	(779)
Basic earnings (loss) per share:							
Income from continuing operations	1.26	1.37	1.37	0.72	0.43	0.24	0.02
Income (loss) from discontinued operations, net of tax	0.01	(0.01)	0.25	(0.07)	(0.07)	(0.26)	(0.66)
Cum. effect of accounting change, net of tax	–	–	(0.02)	–	–	–	–
Net income	1.27	1.36	1.60	0.65	0.36	(0.02)	(0.64)
Diluted earnings (loss) per share:							
Income from continuing operations	1.26	1.37	1.34	0.69	0.42	0.24	0.02
Income (loss) from discontinued operations, net of tax	0.01	(0.01)	0.25	(0.06)	(0.06)	(0.26)	(0.66)
Cum. effect of accounting change, net of tax	–	–	(0.02)	–	–	–	–
Net income	1.27	1.36	1.57	0.63	0.36	(0.02)	(0.64)

Source: Company financial reports. Prepared according to U.S. GAAP.

EXHIBIT 14

Income Statement Data, General Electric and Consolidated Affiliates ($ in millions, except per-share data in $)

	2009	2008	2007	2006	2005
Revenues	156,783	182,515	172,488	151,568	136,262
Earnings from continuing operations before accounting changes	11,218	18,089	22,457	19,344	17,279
Earnings (loss) from discontinued operations, net of taxes	(193)	(679)	(249)	1,398	(559)
Net earnings	11,025	17,410	22,208	20,742	16,720
Dividends declared	6,785	12,649	11,713	10,675	9,647
Return on average shareowners' equity	10.1%	15.9%	20.4%	19.8%	18.1%
Per common share:					
Earnings from continuing operations before accounting changes, diluted	1.03	1.78	2.20	1.86	1.63
Earnings (loss) from discontinued operations — diluted	(0.02)	(0.07)	(0.02)	0.13	(0.05)
Net earnings — diluted	1.01	1.72	2.17	2.00	1.57
Earnings from continuing operations before accounting changes, basic	1.03	1.79	2.21	1.87	1.63
Earnings (loss) from discontinued operations — basic	(0.02)	(0.07)	(0.02)	0.14	(0.05)
Net earnings — basic	1.01	1.72	2.18	2.00	1.58
Dividends declared	0.61	1.24	1.15	1.03	0.91
Year-end closing stock price	15.13	16.20	37.07	37.21	35.05
Total assets of continuing operations	780,298	796,046	786,794	674,966	588,821
Total assets	781,818	797,769	795,683	697,273	673,210
Long-term borrowings	338,215	322,847	318,530	260,656	212,082
Common shares outstanding — average (in millions)	10,614	10,080	10,182	10,359	10,570
Shareowner accounts — average	605,000	604,000	608,000	624,000	634,000
Employees at year end:					
United States	134,000	152,000	155,000	155,000	161,000
Other countries	154,000	171,000	172,000	164,000	155,000
BAC Credomatic GECF Inc.	16,000	-	-	-	-
Total employees	304,000	323,000	327,000	319,000	316,000

EXHIBIT 14 *(Continued)*

	2009	2008	2007	2006	2005
GE Data:					
Short-term borrowings	504	2,375	4,106	2,076	972
Long-term borrowings	11,681	9,827	11,656	9,043	8,986
Minority interest	5,797	6,678	6,503	5,544	5,308
Shareowners' equity	117,291	104,665	115,559	111,509	108,633
Total capital invested	135,273	123,545	137,824	128,172	123,899
Return on average total capital invested	9.5%	14.8%	18.9%	18.5%	16.7%
Borrowings as a percentage of total capital invested	9.0%	9.9%	11.4%	8.7%	8.0%
Working capital	(1,596)	3,904	6,433	7,527	7,853
GECS Data:					
Revenues	54,163	71,287	71,936	61,351	54,889
Earnings from continuing operations before accounting changes	1,590	7,774	12,417	10,219	8,929
Earnings (loss) from discontinued operations, net of taxes	(175)	(719)	(2116)	439	(1,352)
Net earnings	1,415	7,055	10,301	10,658	7,577
Shareowners' equity	70,833	53,279	57,676	54,097	50,812
Total borrowings and bank deposits	500,334	514,601	500,922	426,262	362,042
Ratio of debt to equity at GE Capital	6.74:1[a]	8.76:1[a]	8.10:1	7.52:1	7.09:1
Total assets	650,241	660,902	646,485	565,258	540,584

[a]Note: Ratios of 5.22:1 and 7.07:1 for 2009 and 2008, respectively, net of cash and equivalents and with classification of hybrid debt as equity.

Source: Company financial reports. Prepared according to U.S. GAAP.

EXHIBIT 15

Income Statement Data, Alstom (in millions of euros)

Year ended March 31	2009	2008	2007	2006	2005
SALES	18,739	16,908	14,208	13,413	12,920
From products	13,787	12,433	10,225	9,773	9,127
From services	4,952	4,475	3,983	3,640	3,793
Cost of sales	(15,225)	(13,761)	(11,586)	(11,080)	(10,886)
Research and development expenses	(586)	(554)	(456)	(364)	(405)
Selling expenses	(666)	(619)	(567)	(569)	(535)
Administrative expenses	(726)	(679)	(642)	(654)	(623)
INCOME FROM OPERATIONS	1,536	1,295	957	746	471
Other income	44	26	18	252	67
Other expenses	(137)	(100)	(149)	(191)	(589)
EARNINGS (LOSS) BEFORE INTEREST AND TAXES	1,443	1,221	826	807	(51)
Financial income	122	115	101		
Financial expense	(101)	(184)	(212)	(222)	(381)
PRE-TAX INCOME (LOSS)	1,464	1,152	715	585	(432)
Income tax charge	(373)	(291)	(145)	(125)	(163)
Share in net income (loss) of equity investments	27	1		(1)	
NET PROFIT (LOSS) FROM CONTINUING OPERATIONS	1,118	862	570	459	(595)
NET PROFIT (LOSS) FROM DISCONTINUED OPERATIONS	–	–	(32)	(198)	(32)
NET PROFIT	1,118	862	538	261	(627)
Attributable to equity holders of the parent	1,109	852	547	258	328
Minority interests	9	10	(9)	3	(1)
EARNINGS PER SHARE (in euros)					
From continuing and discontinued operations:					
- Basic	3.87	3.01	1.94	1.84	(5.76)
- Diluted	3.81	2.95	1.90	1.82	(5.76)
From continuing operations:					
- Basic	3.87	3.01	2.05	3.25	(5.47)
- Diluted	3.81	2.95	2.01	3.22	(5.47)
From discontinued operations:					
- Basic	–	–	(0.12)	(1.41)	(0.29)
- Diluted	–	–	(0.11)	(1.39)	(0.29)

Source: Company financial reports. Prepared according to IFRS.

EXHIBIT 16

GE 2009 Sector Revenues

Source: Adapted from the GE 2009 Annual Report.

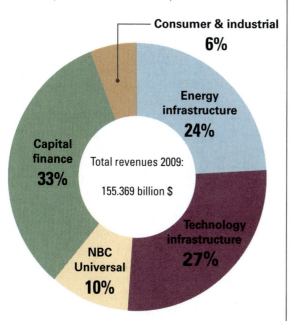

Consumer & industrial **6%**

Energy infrastructure **24%**

Capital finance **33%**

Total revenues 2009:

155.369 billion $

Technology infrastructure **27%**

NBC Universal **10%**

EXHIBIT 17

GE 2009 Sector Profits

Source: Adapted from the GE 2009 Annual Report.

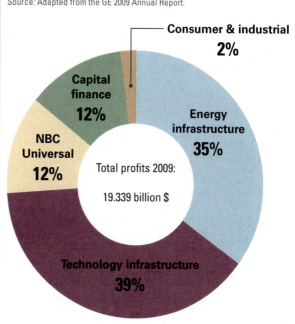

Consumer & industrial **2%**

Capital finance **12%**

Energy infrastructure **35%**

NBC Universal **12%**

Total profits 2009:

19.339 billion $

Technology infrastructure **39%**

EXHIBIT 18

Siemens 2009 Global Market Revenues

Source: Adapted from the Siemens 2009 Annual Report.

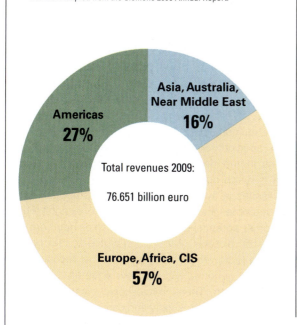

Asia, Australia, Near Middle East **16%**

Americas **27%**

Total revenues 2009:

76.651 billion euro

Europe, Africa, CIS **57%**

EXHIBIT 19

GE 2009 Global Market Revenues

Source: Adapted from the GE 2009 Annual Report.

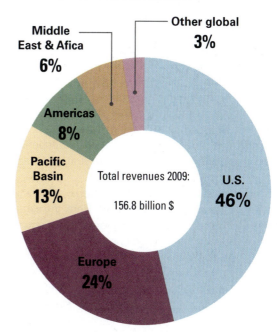

Middle East & Afica **6%**

Other global **3%**

Americas **8%**

Pacific Basin **13%**

Total revenues 2009:

156.8 billion $

U.S. **46%**

Europe **24%**

such as Chinese manufacturers of wind-technology products.

Siemens was recently plagued by a bribery scandal that reached high into the management and directorate ranks, placing it at a temporary disadvantage compared to GE. Investigators alleged that Siemens spent more than $1 billion bribing governments in at least 10 countries, including Greece, Italy, and Nigeria, in an effort to obtain lucrative contracts.[58] Although Greece and Italy have official laws against such business conduct, countries like Nigeria have lower ethics standards and tend not to provide any contracts without sufficient "grease money." In fact, bribery is commonplace in countries such as Nigeria, China, and Russia. However, because both the United States and the European Union have laws that make such business practices illegal, Siemens was sentenced to more than $1.6 billion in fines by the German and U.S. authorities in 2008, and it had to forgo bidding on any World Bank contracts for two years.[59]

Decision Time—What to Do? Where to Invest?

Wolfgang Dehen believes it is time for Siemens Energy to place some significant bets, as disruptive innovations in alternative energies are clearly coming. If Siemens bets badly, the company risks being relegated to the sidelines as newer, more innovative firms squeeze slower-moving incumbents out of the market. Investing in the right areas, though, could ensure Siemens and others a stake in the future of the energy industry, allowing them to leverage their immense assets and keep new entrants at bay. Siemens appears weakened due to the bribery scandal, but in many ways is experiencing a resurgence under its new management and structure.[60] Could Siemens harness that momentum to capture a leading role in the new energy economy? The answer to that question depends on the decisions made by Dehen's strategic planning team over the upcoming months.

Currently, Siemens's primary focus in alternative energy is wind-based technologies. Here, the company operates as a one-stop shop, providing its customers with comprehensive wind-energy solutions that do not need third-party components or outside service contracts. As the leading supplier of offshore wind turbines, Siemens's market share in the wind sector is strong and growing.[61] One option is for Siemens to utilize its size, competency, and cutting-edge technology to further increase its market share and global footprint in wind energy. Demand for wind turbines is not likely to fall in the near future. What is not so clear, however, is whether wind energy will turn out to be the leading alternative technology, and if it does, whether wind technologies alone can generate enough profit to keep Siemens aloft.

The company's other main alternative-energy emphasis is solar power, whose future is equally in question. Here, initial investments have been made, and several projects of significant magnitude have recently been acquired. These represent good first steps into the solar field, but are they enough? Or is Siemens's entry too late to allow it to establish a stronghold in this relatively mature industry? Siemens currently must rely on third-party suppliers for complete solar plants, and this dependency makes the firm vulnerable. Nevertheless, solar technology seems to have a bright future, with steadily increasing demand, suggesting there might be enough capacity to support both new and established competitors.

Then there is the question of whether—and how much—to invest in other alternative energies, such as nuclear and hydroelectric power. Is it worth reengaging in nuclear technology, not knowing how long the currently pro-nuclear German legislature will remain in charge? Can nuclear technology be improved enough to reduce concerns regarding waste byproducts, the risk of accidents, and environmental terrorism? Siemens has a rich history in hydroelectric dam projects as well, but it is not clear whether this is a strength or weakness in the current climate. Fewer and fewer dams are being commissioned as these projects grow increasingly more expensive and controversial. Dehen is not sure it is wise to stake Siemens's reputation as a green energy provider on a technology that causes so much environmental damage.

In addition, Siemens has made limited investments in the development of hydrogen-based fuel cells,[62] which hold great promise if significant logistical issues in hydrogen storage and distribution can be overcome. Siemens also has yet to explore multiple other potential technologies, such as geothermal energy or biofuels. Many high-profile researchers, including Craig Venter, a key figure in the decoding of the human genome, actually view algae as the most promising path. These microscopic plant cells are present in an infinite supply and can generate energy quickly, effectively, and in an environmentally friendly manner, if scientists can figure out how to capture it cost effectively. It is also possible that the next great breakthrough in renewable energy technology has not yet even been discovered.

After deciding how many and which alternative-energy fields to pursue, Siemens's strategic leaders still have to figure out how to compete in the chosen sectors. Historically, Siemens tends to bridge a middle ground between being a first mover and merely taking up existing technologies and capitalizing on them (as a second or later mover). Its preferred mode of operation is to monitor market trends and stay on the lookout for smaller companies with innovative technologies in promising market segments. If the new technology is determined to be a sustainable business opportunity, Siemens will acquire the target company and integrate it into its portfolio. While this means that initial gains on the technology may not be realized under the Siemens name, it does ensure that the investment pays off in the long run. It also means that Siemens does not have to invest much in basic R&D of uncertain technologies, but instead should spend its R&D budget continuing and enhancing acquired innovations.

However, history is full of examples in which a company creates a first-mover advantage by capitalizing on a new disruptive technology and setting the standard for everyone else to follow. Popular examples include Henry Ford's introduction of the conveyor belt in manufacturing, or the online auction platform at eBay.[63] By not investing more in primary R&D, Siemens risks being placed at a permanent disadvantage in the area of alternative energies. In many ways, innovation is like a muscle that grows stronger with repeated workouts, but weakens when you stop using it.

Having just returned from Davos, Mr. Dehen also finds himself wondering whether Siemens is taking full advantage of all the benefits that alliances have to offer. If major corporations could come together under the leadership of the World Economic Forum to discuss issues and obstacles in the development of sustainable energy sources, could they not collaborate under other circumstances as well? Climate change and renewable energy are, after all, problems on a global scale. Perhaps it is not even realistic to expect a single corporation, no matter how large, to discover and develop the next big energy breakthrough without support from other interested parties. Yet he suspects it would be difficult for previously fierce competitors to forget their past and build a trust-based, collaborative relationship.

Mr. Dehen's head is spinning with these thoughts as he heads to his car for the drive home. The strategic planning group will certainly have much to discuss tomorrow, not to mention in the days and months to come . . .

Endnotes

1. www.weforum.org/pdf/ip/energy/Energy_VisionUpdate2010.pdf.

2. OPEC is the acronym for Organization of the Petroleum Exporting Countries, and has 12 members: Algeria, Angola, Ecuador, Iran, Iraq, Kuwait, Libya, Nigeria, Qatar, Saudi Arabia, the United Arab Emirates, and Venezuela.

3. www.weforum.org/pdf/ip/energy/Energy_VisionUpdate2010.pdf.

4. www.weforum.org/pdf/ip/energy/Energy_VisionUpdate2010.pdf.

5. www.weforum.org/documents/initiatives/CEOStatement.pdf, p. 7.

6. "The winds blow for clean energy," *The Wall Street Journal*, July 9, 2009.

7. Siemens: "Progress is our tradition," Peter von Siemens, chronicle of Power Plant Engineering at Siemens, promotional material, Siemens publication.

8. http://en.wikipedia.org/wiki/Electrical_power_industry.

9. "150 years of Siemens, the company from 1847 to 1997," promotional material, Siemens publication.

10. www.energy.siemens.com/entry/energy/hq/en/?tab=energy-1213565-Power%20Generation#429870.

11. Friedman, T. L. (2008), *Hot, Flat, and Crowded: Why We Need a Green Revolution–And How It Can Renew America*, 1st ed. (New York: Farrar, Straus, and Giroux).

12. www.eia.doe.gov/oiaf/ieo/pdf/table17.pdf.

13. http://bc1.handelsblatt.com/ShowImage.aspx?img=2496509&l=1, with data from: Bundesverband Windenergie e.V., Germany.

14. www.reuters.com/article/rbssEnergyNews/idUSL618914420090306.

15. Siemens Power Generations press release website.

16. www.reuters.com/article/idUKLDE62B0OD20100312.

17. www.siemens.com/press/en/pressrelease/?press=/en/press-release/2009/renewable_energy/ere 200912024.htm.

18. www.powergeneration.siemens.com/press/press-releases/renewable-energy/2009/ERE200904035.htm.

19. www.powergeneration.siemens.com/press/press-releases/renewable-energy/2009/ERE200906064.htm.

20. www.powergeneration.siemens.com/press/press-releases/renewable-energy/2009/ERE200905053.htm.

21. McElroy, M. B., et al. (2009), "Potential for wind-generated electricity in China," *Science*, September: 1378–1380.

22. www.chinadaily.com.cn/bizchina/2009-09/11/content_8680007.htm.

23. www.bloomberg.com/apps/news?pid=20601101&sid=adz ZiLUAMODU.

24. "China races ahead of U.S. in drive to go solar," *The New York Times*, August 25, 2009.

25. http://solarcity.com/.

26. www.time.com/time/specials/2007/article/ 0,28804,1730759_1730843_1730983,00.html.

27. www.energy.siemens.com/hq/pool/hq/power-generation/ steam-turbines/downloads/E50001-W410-A105-V1-4A00_ solarbroschuere.pdf.

28. www1.eere.energy.gov/solar/thermal_storage.html.

29. www.powergeneration.siemens.com/press/press-releases/ renewable-energy/2009/ERE200906067.htm.

30. www.iaea.org.

31. www.miller-mccune.com/science_environment/the-salt-mine-solution-1092, Miller-McCune, June 6, 2009.

32. www.spiegel.de/international/germany/0,1518,577018,00. html.

33. http://spectrum.ieee.org/blog/energy/renewables/ energywise/german-election-a-likely-reprieve-for-nuclear.

34. http://theenergycollective.com/ TheEnergyCollective/48659.

35. www.powergeneration.siemens.com/press/press-releases/ service-rotating-equipment/2007/PG200706-047.htm.

36. www.powergeneration.siemens.com/press/press-releases/ service-rotating-equipment/2007/PG200712-011.htm.

37. http://nuclearstreet.com/blogs/nuclear_power_news/ archive/2009/03/04/rosatom-and-siemens-sign-memorandum-of-understanding-on-the-creation-of-a-nuclear-joint-venture.aspx.

38. www.businessweek.com/globalbiz/content/may2009/ gb20090522_165515.htm.

39. www.pittsburghlive.com/x/pittsburghtrib/s_575073.html.

40. www.nrc.gov/reactors/new-licensing/new-licensing-files/ expected-new-rx-applications.pdf.

41. www.ne.doe.gov/newsroom/2009PRs/nePR091809.html.

42. www.ne.doe.gov/newsroom/2009PRs/nePR081409.html.

43. "Externalities of energy: Extension of accounting framework and policy applications," European Commission, August 2005, www.externe.info/expoltec.pdf.

44. www.unep.org/dams/documents/Default. asp?DocumentID=648.

45. www.sacw.net/article1007.html.

46. www.rnw.nl/english/radioshow/ coroversial-dam-project-turkey-loses-funding-again.

47. www.powergeneration.siemens.com/press/press-releases/ power-transmission/2009/EPT200905054.htm.

48. http://hydropower.id.doe.gov/.

49. www.eia.doe.gov/cneaf/solar.renewables/ilands/chapter3. html#hydro.

50. www1.eere.energy.gov/windandhydro/hydro_potential .html.

51. www.eia.doe.gov/fuelrenewable.html.

52. "Drive to link wind, solar power to distant users," *The Wall Street Journal,* October 13, 2009.

53. "Wiser wires," *The Economist,* October 8, 2009.

54. "Clever, but unprincipled," *The Economist,* October 8, 2009.

55. www.powergeneration.siemens.com/press/press-releases/ power-distribution/2009/EPD200910007.htm.

56. http://w1.siemens.com/press/en/pressrelease/?press=/en/ pressrelease/2009/corporate_communication/ axx20090981. htm.

57. http://w1.siemens.com/press/en/pressrelease/?press=/en/ pressrelease/2009/power_distribution/epd200910008.htm.

58. "Siemens settles with World Bank on bribes," *The Wall Street Journal,* July 3, 2009.

59. Ibid.

60. "Siemens: A giant awakens," *The Economist*, September 9, 2010.

61. Ibid.

62. www.powergeneration.siemens.com/ products-solutions-services/products-packages/fuel-cells/.

63. Arthur, W. B. (1989), "Competing technologies, increasing returns, and lock-in by historical events," *Economics Journal* 99: 116–131; and Hill, C.W.L. (1997), "Establishing a standard: Competitive strategy and winner-take-all industries," *Academy of Management Executive* 11: 7–25.

Say no to Bangalore, yes to Buffalo.[1]

—PRESIDENT BARACK OBAMA

Marne L. Arthaud-Day
Kansas State University

Sukonya Gogoi
The North Highland Company

Leena Makhija
Ernst & Young

Frank T. Rothaermel
Georgia Institute of Technology

ABOARD DELTA FLIGHT 184 from Mumbai, India, to Atlanta, Georgia, Adrian Patel found herself engulfed by a swarm of worries. She was returning from STRAP, Infosys's Annual Strategy Retreat,[2] at company headquarters in Bangalore, India. Each year, Infosys leaders from across the globe gathered to discuss strategy formulation and action-planning. The STRAP meetings help the company adapt to the rapid pace of change in the information technology (IT) industry and to coordinate activities across its widely dispersed operations. This year, the Chief Operating Officer (COO) of Infosys, S. D. Shibulal, had given Adrian the daunting responsibility of developing strategic scenarios to help the U.S. Division of Infosys Consulting gain and sustain a competitive advantage that would lead to tangible bottom-line results. She had just four short weeks before she had to return to India with a proposal in hand.

This promised to be a tough assignment, given the current backlash in the United States against outsourcing. For Infosys's global delivery model, outsourcing was a key component: The company sourced technology work from wherever high-quality talent was available at a cost-competitive rate. Infosys had watched the 2008 U.S. presidential election with great concern, because President Obama had made outsourcing one of the key issues of his campaign platform, promising to leave no stone unturned in the effort to create and keep jobs "at home." His mantra, "Say no to Bangalore, yes to Buffalo,"[3] was expected to end many years of tax incentives to U.S. companies that create jobs overseas in places like Bangalore, shifting them instead to companies willing to hire people in cities like Buffalo, New York. Meanwhile, officials in Washington were engaged in heated debate about how to reform the H-1B visa program, which many companies use to bring skilled foreign technical workers to the United States. The results of that debate could have vast implications for Infosys's ability to bring Indian employees over to work on projects for its U.S. clients. Despite a promising start for Infosys's U.S. consulting subsidiary, the future was starting to look uncertain.

Having climbed the ranks to managing partner at Infosys Consulting, Adrian was used to facing challenges. She was a proud recipient of the "Electrocomponents Silver Salver" award for the best strategic consulting project during her MBA program at the Saïd Business School, Oxford University. Since then, she had spent 15 years in the IT-consulting industry, scaling the corporate ladder. Yet the task ahead of her was of a much larger scale and greater complexity than she had ever tackled—spanning at least two continents and subject to the whims of the U.S. and Indian governments. Thankfully, she had another 17 hours to figure out how she would present the issues to her colleagues in the Atlanta office, who were eagerly awaiting news from STRAP. She dreaded even thinking about the meeting four weeks later when she would have to present a final report to the members of the board back in India. She opened a can of Diet Coke and booted up her laptop. It was time to get to work. She wished that the 100,000 engineers at the Infosys campus in Bangalore could just come up with a magic algorithm to solve the problem for her.

Professor Marne L. Arthaud-Day, Research Associates Leena Makhija (GT MBA '10) and Sukonya Gogoi (GT MBA '10), and Professor Frank T. Rothaermel prepared this case from public sources. This case is developed for the purpose of class discussion. It not intended to be used for any kind of endorsement, source of data, or depiction of efficient or inefficient management. © Arthaud-Day, Gogoi, Makhija, and Rothaermel, 2013.

Infosys: Origins and Growth

Infosys is one of the world's leading IT service firms, with annual revenues approaching $5 billion. The company was founded in July 1981 by N. R. Narayana Murthy and six of his friends in Pune, the eighth-largest metropolis in India. According to his wife, the entrepreneurial Murthy was "always broke," so she provided the startup capital of 10,000 INR (approximately $US 250).[4]

Starting a business in India was challenging in the 1980s due to extensive governmental red tape. It took the company nine months to get a phone line and three years to obtain permission to import computers. Because India did not yet have an established software development market, Infosys focused its energies on the United States from the very beginning. It secured its first U.S. client, Data Basics Corporation, in 1983, and relocated its headquarters to Bangalore that same year. (Bangalore is known as the "Silicon Valley" of India due to the high number of IT companies located there.)[5] In 1987, Infosys opened its first international office in Boston, Massachusetts, and formed a joint venture with Kurt Salmon Associates (KSA)[6] to market its U.S. operations. KSA solicited projects while Infosys provided the personnel and programming expertise. The company faced its first major crisis when the joint venture collapsed in 1989, and one of Infosys's founders, Ashok Arora, left, discouraged about the company's future prospects.[7] Another founder, Senapathy ("Kris") Gopalakrishnan, later recalled, "We had nothing after eight years of trying to bring up a company. Those who studied with us had cars and houses."[8]

Murthy challenged the remaining partners, saying, "If you all want to leave, you can. But I am going to stick [with it] and make it."[9] All five elected to stay, and through their efforts, Infosys continued to grow slowly.[10, 11] Then in the early 1990s, the Indian government instituted economic reforms and lifted many of the regulations that had stagnated the country's development, enabling Infosys to grow much more rapidly.[12] The firm went public on the Indian stock exchange in 1993 with a market capitalization of $10 million.[13] Morgan Stanley salvaged the undersubscribed IPO and later reaped millions in windfall profits.[14] In 1999, Infosys joined the NASDAQ, becoming the first Indian company to be listed on a U.S. stock exchange.

After just one full year as a listed company, Infosys's market capitalization reached more than $17 billion in 2000. Meanwhile, the company's international operations grew to nine marketing offices in the United States as well as a presence in Canada, Australia, the United Kingdom, Japan, Hong Kong, Sweden, Belgium, France, and Germany. Some of its major clients included such well-known firms as General Electric, Reebok International, Nestlé S.A., and Holiday Inn.[15]

Today, Infosys is engaged in every aspect of IT services, ranging from business and technology consulting to application services, custom software development, IT infrastructure services, and business-process outsourcing.[16] It has 65 offices and 59 development centers spanning more than 30 countries; the firm employs more than 125,000 people worldwide (see Exhibits 1 and 2). Infosys's North American operations account

EXHIBIT 1

Infosys's Human Capital

Source: Adapted from Infosys, "Infosys annual report," 2009, Infosys Technologies Ltd., www.infosys.com/investors/reports-filings/annual-report/annual/Infosys-AR06.pdf.

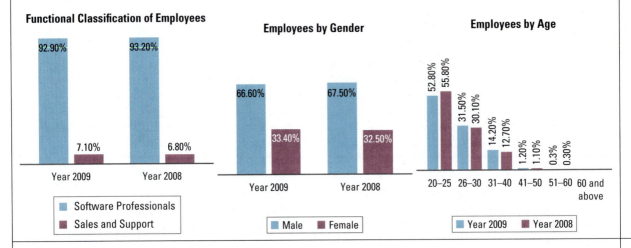

EXHIBIT 2

Intangible Assets: Human Capital

	2009	2008
Growth/ Renewal		
Total employees added during the year:	104,850	91,187
Gross	28,231	33,177
Net	13,663	18,946
Laterals added	5,796	8,523
Staff education index	272,664	251,970
Number of nationalities	76	70
Gender classification (%)		
Male	66.6	67.5
Female	33.4	32.5
Number of non-Indian national employees	4,698	3,678
Stability		
Average age of employees	26	26
Attrition—excluding subsidiaries (%)	11.1	13.4
Attrition—excluding involuntary separation (%)	9.1	12.1

Source: Adapted from Infosys, "Infosys annual report," 2009, Infosys Technologies Ltd., www.infosys.com/investors/reports-filings/annual-report/annual/Infosys-AR06.pdf.

EXHIBIT 3

Revenue Growth and Repeat Business

Source: Adapted from Intangible Assets score sheet (External structure: our clients), Infosys Annual Report 2008–2009.

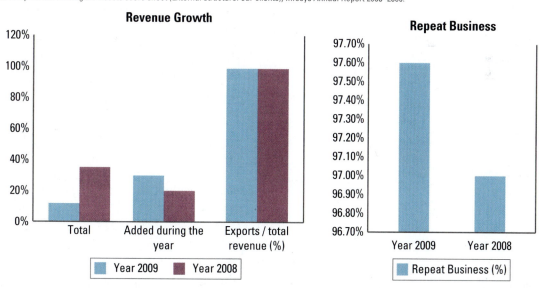

for 68 percent of sales, with another 22 percent from Europe, and 10 percent from the rest of the world.[17] Future expansion is targeted for Australia, China, Eastern Europe, and Latin America.

Concurrent with geographic growth, Infosys seeks both to increase business from existing customers and to add and retain new clients. As evidence of its emphasis on long-term client relationships, the company proudly points out that over 97 percent of its 2010 revenues came from its existing client base (Exhibit 3).[18] Infosys's ability to understand and meet the needs of its clients is an important reason it

EXHIBIT 4

Infosys Financial Performance Data (Currency in Rupees Crore)

Financial Performance	2000	2001	2002	2003	2004	2005	2006	2007	2008	2009
Income	882	1,901	2,604	3,623	4,761	6,860	9,028	13,149	15,648	20,264
Operating profit (PBIDTA)	347	765	1,038	1,272	1,584	2,325	2,989	4,225	4,963	6,906
Depreciation	53	113	161	189	231	268	409	469	546	694
Provision for taxation	40	73	135	201	227	325	303	352	630	895
Profit after tax	286	623	808	958	1,242	1,859	2,421	3,777	4,470	5,819
Dividend	30	66	132	179	196	310	412	649	758	1,345
One time / special dividend					668		830		1,144	
Margins (%)										
Operating profit margin	39.3	40.2	39.9	35.1	33.3	33.9	33.1	32.1	31.7	34.1
Net profit margin	32.4	32.8	31.0	26.4	26.1	27.1	26.8	28.7	28.6	28.7
Return on average net worth	40.6	56.1	46.6	38.8	40.7	43.8	39.9	41.9	36.3	37.2
Return on average capital employed	46.3	62.6	54.4	46.9	48.1	51.4	44.9	45.7	41.1	42.9
Per share data (Rs.)										
Basic EPS	5.41	11.78	15.27	18.09	23.43	34.63	44.34	67.82	78.24	101.65
Dividend	0.056	1.25	2.5	3.38	3.69	5.75	7.5	11.5	13.25	23.5
One time / special dividend					12.5		15		20	
Book value	15.75	26.26	39.29	53.98	61.03	96.87	125.15	195.41	235.84	310.9
Financial position										
Share capital	33	33	33	33	33	135	138	286	286	286
Reserves and surplus	800	1,357	2,047	2,828	3,220	5,107	6,759	10,876	13,204	17,523
Net worth	833	1,390	2,080	2,861	3,253	5,242	6,987	11,162	13,490	17,809
Debt	—	—	—	—	—	—	—	—	—	—
Gross block	284	631	961	1,273	1,570	2,183	2,837	3,889	4,508	5,986
Capital expenditure	160	463	323	219	430	794	1,048	1,443	1,370	1,177
Cash and cash equivalents	508	578	1,027	1,639	1,819	1,683	3,779	5,610	7,689	10,289
Investment in liquid mutual funds and CDs					930	1,168	684			
Net current assets	612	798	1,293	2,018	1,220	2,384	3,832	7,137	8,496	12,288
Total assets	833	1,390	2,080	2,861	3,253	5,242	6,897	11,162	13,490	17,846
Shareholding related										
Number of shareholders	46,314	89,643	88,650	77,010	66,945	158,725	195,956	488,869	555,562	496,907
Market capitalization (period-end)	59,338	26,926	24,654	26,847	32,909	61,073	82,154	115,307	82,362	75,837
Public shareholding (%)	67.55	67.69	68.08	68.32	65.56	70.2	66.55	64.35	64.31	64.38
Credit rating										
Standard & Poor's						BBB	BBB	BBB	BBB+	BBB+
Dun & Bradstreet						5A1	5A1	5A1	5A1	5A1
Corporate governance rating										
CRISIL - (GVC)						Level 1	Level 1	Level 1	Level 1	Level 1
ICRA						CGR 1	CGR 1	CGR 1	CGR 1	CGR 1

Source: Adapted from Infosys, "Infosys annual report," 2009, Infosys Technologies Ltd., www.infosys.com/investors/reports-filings/annual-report/annual/Infosys-AR06.pdf.

is ranked among *WIRED* magazine's top 40 companies. Similarly, *Bloomberg Businessweek* lists Infosys among its IT 100 and 50 Most Innovative companies, and *Forbes* cites it as one of the five best-performing companies in the software and services sector in the world.[19] A *FinanceAsia* poll lists Infosys as the best managed company in India.[20]

Infosys further distinguishes itself from its competitors by maintaining a distinct corporate culture. The company believes that "the softest pillow is a clear conscience" and aims "to achieve our objectives in an environment of fairness, honesty, and courtesy towards our clients, employees, vendors and society at large."[21] These values drive the firm's commitment to provide customer delight, exemplary leadership, integrity and transparency, fairness, and pursuit of excellence.[22] In keeping with its values, Infosys adheres to numerous international governance guidelines, including the UN Global Compact.[23] Its efforts have won recognition for best practices in corporate governance by *Asiamoney* and best company in corporate governance, investor relations, and corporate social responsibility by *FinanceAsia*.[24, 25]

Infosys believes that its employees are its "vital and most valuable assets,"[26] and also stands out for its human resource practices. For example, it was the first company to initiate an employee stock option plan in India. Currently, all new hires undergo an integrated on-the-job training program of 20 to 29 weeks before they are assigned to a business unit, and all employees participate in continuing education through Infosys's Education & Research unit and Leadership Institute. The Education & Research unit employs over 600 full-time faculty members, a third of whom hold at least a master's degree. These investments have enabled Infosys to attract the best talent in the industry and to keep attrition rates lower than competitors (13.4 percent in 2009–2010).[27, 28] The company also has executive-level talent with a high macro-economic literacy; almost all of its top executives have been invited to speak at the Davos World Economic Forum.

Infosys's financial performance has improved steadily over the last decade (Exhibit 4) and represents another important strength as the company faces changing market conditions. Infosys has a $2 billion cash reserve that it can use to fund future growth, through both increased investment in R&D and the acquisition of promising new technology ventures.[29] Nevertheless, the company was hit badly by the global economic crisis.[30] Between December 2008 and April

2009, Infosys laid off over 2,100 employees for poor performance and asked 50 people from executive management to work with nonprofit organizations for a year at half their salary.[31] On April 15, 2009, Infosys reported its first drop in revenues in a decade.[32]

This revenue decline prompted the company to develop a new method of pricing software maintenance projects, called *transaction-* or *ticket-based pricing*.[33] Transaction-based pricing means that customers are charged based on the units of functionality consumed.[34] For example, an Infosys client is charged a prespecified price for every bug that is fixed in the software code instead of being charged a fixed amount for a few months for maintenance of the software. "Customers are increasingly looking at adopting the transaction model as cost-cutting becomes imperative," said Gautam Thakkar, Vice-President and head of Finance and Accounting, Infosys's Business Process Operations (BPO). The company claims to have gained traction with its new pricing model as customers look to economize on operational expenditures while recovering from an economic downturn.[35]

The Birth of Infosys Consulting

Outsourcing is subcontracting a process, such as product design or manufacturing, to a third-party company. The outsourcing partner can be domestic or foreign. If the third party is located outside the home country (assuming a U.S. firm), say in China or India, this process is called *offshore outsourcing*. The global outsourcing market reached over $1.4 trillion by the end of 2009, and is growing at a compound annual growth rate of 15 percent. Firms in the banking and financial services, technology, and health care industries spend the most on outsourcing.[36]

The rise of outsourcing and offshoring in the IT industry can be traced to the global delivery model (GDM) (Exhibit 5) pioneered by Infosys in the 1990s. GDM is based on the principle of taking work to the location where it makes the best economic sense given the available talent and the least amount of acceptable risk. In practice, this means that Infosys maintains a flexible offshore-onsite ratio—the ratio of billable project employees at offshore locations (low-cost labor) to billable project employees at the client location (cost-intensive)—for all of its service contracts.[37] By employing cheaper, offshore labor, as well as providing an onsite presence, Infosys can provide better

EXHIBIT 5

Global Delivery Model

Source: Adapted from Prof Saby Mitra, "Conceptual overview of the global delivery model," The Global Delivery Model at Infosys, February 2007, Georgia Institute of Technology.

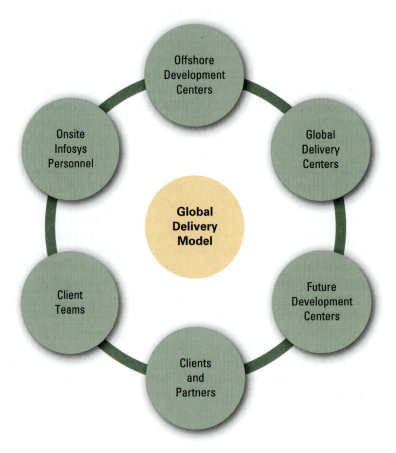

value to its clients without sacrificing quality. The industry benchmark is 80:20 (80 percent of resources offshore and 20 percent onsite), but Infosys's proportions vary from 70:30 to 90:10 depending on the type of project and resources available. Infosys Technologies has been a consistent top performer in the offshore-outsourcing market, with growth of more than 40 percent annually.

Infosys first applied GDM to its existing software development activities. Clients would define the project and requirement specifications, and then contact Infosys with specific programming requests. The company quickly realized, however, that its revenue growth was directly proportional to employee growth, and started to look for ways to expand its employee base.[38] Around the same time, Stephan Pratt and Raj Joshi of

Deloitte Touché Tohmatsu began developing a proposal to increase the offshore component in the traditional management consulting model. When Deloitte's leadership proved to be less than enthusiastic about altering their operational strategy, Pratt and Joshi approached Infosys.[39]

Having been successful at technology implementation, Infosys established Infosys Consulting, a wholly owned subsidiary, headquartered in Fremont, California, in 2004. Stephan Pratt and Raj Joshi left Deloitte to head the new division. By expanding the services it provided to existing clients, Infosys hoped to avoid the typically high entry barriers (brand equity and client base) to the IT consulting industry. Strategically, the firm believed that consulting capabilities would help Infosys deepen its client relationships at the boardroom level and to start conversations with business heads instead of IT managers. As a result, Infosys would have the opportunity to implement broader operational changes and have a greater impact on client profitability.[40] By using GDM, Infosys Consulting would be able to provide a blended offering of high-quality business consulting onsite with high-quality technology implementation offsite, distinguishing the firm from its competitors. Just as GDM disrupted the IT services industry, Infosys Consulting believed GDM had the potential to "reinvent and redefine" the IT consulting industry by seamlessly integrating IT strategy and technology implementation, while simultaneously taking advantage of opportunities for globalization.[41]

To date, Infosys's proposed consulting model has had limited success. As of March 31, 2009, Infosys had invested $45 million in the consulting subsidiary with a net loss of $18 million.[42] The breakeven point has been deferred at least two times since the company's launch in 2004.[43] Whereas competitors such as Accenture generated almost $10 billion from IT consulting in 2007, Infosys Consulting generated a little more than $47 million. In contrast to its major competitors, Infosys failed to make the Washington Technology newspapers' list of the Top 100 Federal Contractors in 2006. Infosys's inability to garner greater market share has impeded the development of a steady flow of revenue, putting the company at even further competitive disadvantage.

The Information Technology (IT) Consulting Industry

According to Plunkett Research estimates, global revenues from the consulting industry were close to $330 billion in 2008. Geographically, more than 97 percent of all consulting revenues come from North America, Europe, the Middle East, Africa, and Asia, areas where Infosys Consulting has a strong presence. The percent of total revenues by sector is as follows: technology consulting (46 percent), business advisory services (26 percent), operations management consulting (15 percent), strategy consulting (8.4 percent) and human resources consulting (4.5 percent). Hoovers similarly estimates that "computer consulting services is nearly twice that of management and scientific consulting" in terms of annual revenues.[44]

During the 1980s and 1990s, the overall consulting industry grew at a rate of 20 percent per year and

witnessed the entry of many small to medium-sized firms. However, since 2001, the industry has experienced either low growth or decline; industrywide revenue growth was –3.5 percent in 2009.[45] Today, the consulting industry is generally considered to be in the maturity stage of its life cycle. Although there are over 300,000 "enterprise firms," the market is dominated by a few key players[46] who compete for large client accounts. Jointly, Accenture, Bain, Boston Consulting Group, Booz, IBM Global Services, McKinsey, and Monitor account for around 25 percent of all industry revenues.

IT consulting falls broadly under technology consulting. Activities include the design and delivery of computer systems, producing design specifications, computer programming, and developing complex software solutions such as enterprise resource planning, customer relationship management, and sales force automation. Some IT consultants also provide onsite management of the client's computer systems and data processing facilities.[47] Because IT consulting requires minimal contact with clients, the industry tends to be globalized and is well suited for outsourcing to low-cost, high-skill destinations. India has been a particularly attractive location for IT outsourcing due to its financial attractiveness (compensation, infrastructure, and tax/regulatory costs), the availability of people and skills (labor experience, education, language, attrition), and its business environment (see Exhibits 6 and 7).

Major Competitors

Infosys Consulting's competitors include both management consulting firms with an IT division[48] and boutique firms that focus exclusively on information technology.

Accenture is the world's largest consulting firm, providing management consulting, information technology services, and business process outsourcing services to customers in more than 120 countries. It is a privately held firm, recently reincorporated in Ireland, with annual revenues of $21.6 billion in 2010. Across all of its divisions, Accenture has 215,000 employees and maintains physical offices and operations in 53 countries.[49] Future areas of geographic expansion include India, Brazil, China, Japan, and the Philippines.[50] In July 2005, Accenture launched its Information Management Services unit, which now comprises a network of more than 16,000 IT

EXHIBIT 6

The 2009 A. T. Kearney Global Services Location Index

Note: A higher number indicates more attractiveness.

Source: Adapted from "The shifting geography of outsourcing, the 2009 A. T. Kearney's Global Services Location Index (GSLI)," 2009, www.atkearney.com.mx/res/home/gsli2009.pdf.

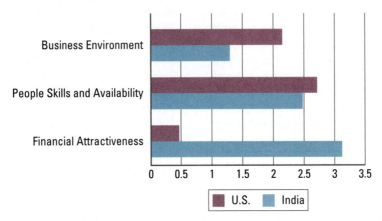

EXHIBIT 7

What Drives Outsourcing?

Source: Adapted from Josh Hyatt, "The new calculus of offshoring," *CFO Magazine,* October 1, 2009, www.cfo.com/article.cfm/14443115/1/c_14443798.

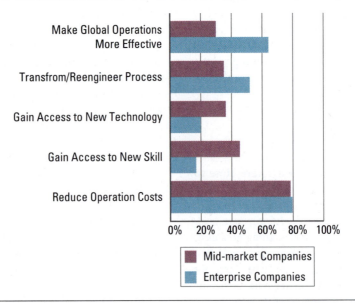

professionals and 50 delivery centers worldwide. Accenture leverages its Delivery Suite, consisting of proprietary assets, toolkits, and capabilities, to help its clients with their IT needs. It also has an Innovation Center for Information Management located in Mumbai, India, where potential customers can talk to service representatives, observe project delivery activities, and preview the latest technologies.[51] Recent growth has primarily been through acquisitions, such as the purchase of a Tokyo-based consulting firm and a freight-order management software company based in California.[52]

As the pioneer of IT outsourcing in the United States, *HP Enterprise Services* (formerly *EDS*), originated many of the industry's central practices such as systems management, systems integration, centralized transaction processing, and private digital networks. Purchased by Hewlett-Packard (HP) in May 2008 for $13.9 billion, Enterprise Services continues to boast one of the broadest service portfolios in the industry, spanning infrastructure technology, applications and business process outsourcing.[53] The acquisition of EDS bolstered HP's stance against IBM and expanded its global presence to nearly 50 countries. While the company continues to maintain a strong emphasis on government contracts, Enterprise Services has branched out further in the commercial sector under HP's leadership. Examples of recent transactions include a $1 billion deal with UK-based insurance firm Aviva in 2009. HP also owns a controlling stake in MphasiS, a Bangalore-based business process outsourcing services provider.[54]

An affiliate of global accounting powerhouse Deloitte Touché Tohmatsu, *Deloitte Consulting's* expertise lies in technology, human capital, and strategy and operations.[55] It likewise has a broad offering of technology products and services, including analytics, technology strategy, technology-enabled process transformation, systems integration, application management services, service delivery transformation, and enterprise sustainability (green IT).[56] To differentiate itself, Deloitte develops dedicated project teams around each industry (for example, automotive, insurance, life sciences, and so on) it serves, taking advantage of the specialized knowledge of recognized industry leaders.[57] At the same time, Deloitte maintains nearly 25 strategic alliances with other IT providers to deepen its expertise in key areas. For example, Deloitte has been designated a Platinum Partner by Oracle for more than 10 years.[58] In May 2009, Deloitte acquired BearingPoint's North American Public Services practice after BearingPoint declared bankruptcy. This move significantly enhanced Deloitte's presence with federal government agencies,[59] placing it more directly in competition with HP.

IBM IT Services is the IT consulting arm of IBM and provides both IT and outsourcing services. IT Services include cloud computing, end-user support, IT strategy and architecture, maintenance and technical support, security, servers, and storage and data services, while Outsourcing is comprised of applications-on-demand, global process services, and IT outsourcing and hosting.[60] Application innovation and management services fall under IBM's Global Business Services division, which also houses analytics and business consulting. In 2008, technology services provided 67 percent of sales compared to 33 percent for business services.[61] IBM claims to provide clients with access to the best service professionals in the field while delivering results more quickly and less expensively compared to its competitors.[62] The company has about 20 focal industries and maintains strategic alliances with Lenovo, Motorola, NetApp, Research in Motion, Wyse, Zebra, Oracle, and SAP.[63] In recent years, IBM has shifted positions from the United States to India and other emerging economies, in an effort to cut costs as well as increase its presence in these important markets. Laid-off U.S. employees were given the option to apply for the newly created positions, which were compensated at local rates. Many of IBM's foreign workers voluntarily chose to return to their native countries.[64]

McKinsey is a privately held consulting company with more than 15,000 employees distributed across 99 global offices in 50 countries.[65] Its eight functional areas of emphasis are strategy, business technology, corporate finance, marketing and sales, operations, organization, risk management, and sustainability practices. The company has also developed expertise in 18 focal industries. McKinsey positions itself based on its depth of functional and industry expertise, as well as geographical reach, and cultivates these strengths by investing deeply in employee development. In light of its human resource practices, McKinsey has repeatedly been recognized as one of the 100 Best Companies for working mothers. The company is also one of *Fortune*'s top 10 World's Best Companies for Leaders, while partner Eric Braverman is one of *Fortune*'s 40 Under 40 "movers and shakers" in the business world.[66] Overall revenues in 2007 were estimated at $5.3 billion,[67] roughly 5 percent of which came from strategy consulting, with a significantly larger portion from its technology consulting activities.

The 650 members of McKinsey's business technology group utilize the company's proprietary tools to help clients with their needs in application management, enterprise architecture, IT infrastructure, IT strategy and organization, lean IT, outsourcing and offshoring, tech-enabled marketing and sales, tech-enabled operations, and value assurance.[68] Examples include the Benchmarking and Performance Center, which helps clients diagnose operational and technological gaps in performance, and P360°, a comprehensive "benchmarking-to-implementation" approach to improving service centers.[69]

Tata Consultancy Services (*TCS*) is an IT services, business solutions, and outsourcing company that provides services, infrastructure, enterprise solutions, and consulting as part of its technology-based offerings. A subsidiary of the Tata group, one of India's largest conglomerates, TCS employs more than 174,000 IT specialists in 42 countries. The company's revenues exceeded $6.3 billion in fiscal year 2010.[70] Through its Global Network Delivery Model, Tata combines the advantages of having a global work force, integrated processes in quality, security, and project management, and an interconnected network of more than 50 global development centers to manage risks and provide "follow-the-sun" coverage to its clients.[71] TCS credits this model with its ability to achieve an 87 percent customer satisfaction rating for on-time delivery and 89 percent for meeting quality expectations, with an average project budget variation of 3 percent (figures that exceed industry standards).[72] Like other major competitors, TCS is a preferred alliance partner for other IT products and platforms (e.g., Oracle and SAP) and has won several industry awards, such as the 2009 SAP Pinnacle Award.[73] It has also engaged in several recent acquisitions, including the 2008 purchase of Financial Network Services in Australia and TKS Teknosoft in Switzerland, followed by Citigroup Global Services in 2009.[74]

Yet another India-based competitor is *Wipro IT Business* (a division of Wipro Ltd.), which specializes in IT services such as enterprise technology integration, enterprise applications, infrastructure management, and business technology services. Wipro also provides consulting, business process outsourcing, and product engineering services.[75] Wipro employs more than 100,000 people and has more than 70 global delivery centers in over 55 countries. In 2009–2010, the company generated revenues of U.S. $6 billion;[76] 90 percent of this came from technology services.[77] Wipro seeks to distinguish itself based on its commitment to quality and innovation. It was the first IT services company to adopt Six Sigma, the world's first PCMM Level 5 software company, and the first IT services company to achieve SEI CMM/CMMI Level 5 distinction. Its emphasis on innovation is evident through its ownership of 135 patents

and related disclosures. As the world's largest independent R&D services provider, Wipro benefits from 95 percent repeat business.[78] It is currently looking to countries in Asia, Europe, and the Middle East for continued growth.

The Changing Political-Legal Environment

Infosys is feeling the effects of recent changes in the Indian tax code. Also looming on the horizon are possible changes in the U.S. tax system that could affect firms doing business in India.

CHANGES IN THE INDIAN TAX CODE. Infosys and other Indian-based IT companies have benefited immensely from a tax holiday provided under the Software Technology Parks of India (STPI) plan set forth in 1991. Under the STPI scheme, firms engaged in software development for export were exempt from paying corporate income tax for up to 10 years, resulting in an overall tax break of 10 to 20 percent.[79] The scheme initially expired in 2009, but was extended twice for one year each, pushing the sunset date to March 31, 2011. Despite appeals from Indian IT firms, the Finance Ministry announced in September 2010 that it would not consider any further extensions.[80]

In advance of the deadline, many of the larger firms moved to special economic zones (SEZs), which offer a similar tax break for five years and then a 50 percent tax rebate for another five years. Most small-to-medium-sized companies do not meet the 7,000 square foot size requirement for the SEZs, however, and face a doubling of their overall tax rate from 15 percent to 30 percent (on average).[81] In the meantime, the Indian government has started to bill software companies for work that does not qualify under the export tax exemption (for example, purely onsite services, software work with an onsite component of more than 70 percent, and so on). Infosys was the first company to receive such an unexpected invoice.[82] As services constitute about 56 percent of India's GDP and are expected to grow further,[83] the specter of higher business costs in India raises serious questions about the long-term sustainability of the current offshore/outsourcing-based business model.[84]

As an example, Infosys received STP-related tax discounts of $282 and $325 million for fiscal 2008 and 2009, respectively.[85] For the fiscal year

2008–2009, 82 percent of Infosys's revenue came from STP operations, while 11 percent came from SEZs. As a result, only 7 percent of Infosys's 2009 revenues of over $4 billion were subject to full tax rates in India.[86] For details on Infosys's financials, see Exhibits 8, 9, 10, and 11.

Another major change on the horizon is the implementation of India's new direct tax code (DTC) scheduled for April 2012. The DTC is a comprehensive tax code designed to replace the 1961 Income Tax Act and a patchwork of other tax laws, which both Indian and foreign businesses find confusing and costly to comply

---

EXHIBIT 8

Infosys Revenue Segmentation

Source: Adapted from Infosys, "Infosys annual report," 2009, Infosys Technologies Ltd., www.infosys.com/investors/reports-filings/annual-report/annual/Infosys-AR06.pdf.

Revenue Segmentation by Geography

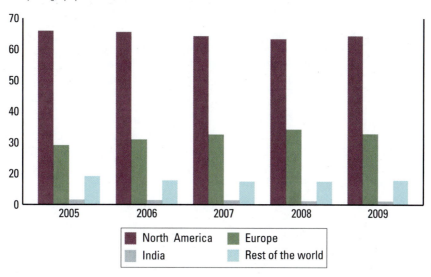

Revenue Segmentation by Industry

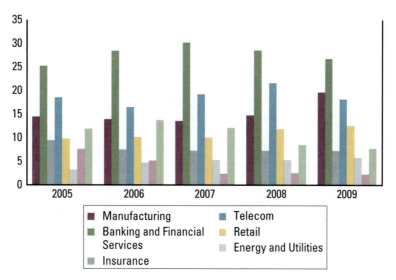

(continued)

EXHIBIT 8 *(continued)*

Revenue Segmentation by Services

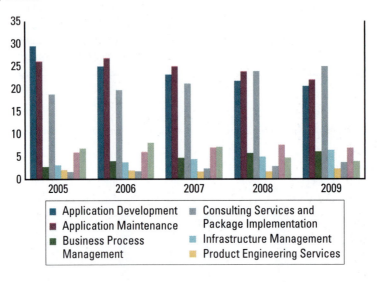

- ■ Application Development
- ■ Application Maintenance
- ■ Business Process Management
- ■ Consulting Services and Package Implementation
- ■ Infrastructure Management
- ■ Product Engineering Services

EXHIBIT 9

Infosys Selected Financial Performance

Source: Adapted from Infosys, "Infosys annual report," 2009, Infosys Technologies Ltd., www.infosys.com/investors/reports-filings/annual-report/annual/Infosys-AR06.pdf.

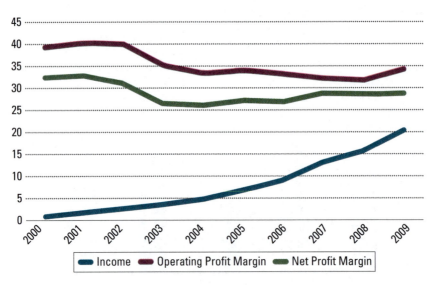

EXHIBIT 10

Infosys Employee and Income Growth

Source: Adapted from Infosys, "Infosys annual report," 2009, Infosys Technologies Ltd., www.infosys.com/investors/reports-filings/annual-report/annual/Infosys-AR06.pdf.

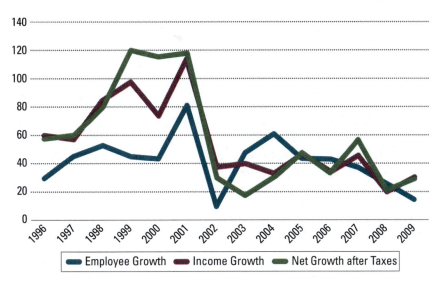

EXHIBIT 11

Offshoring Market

Source: Adapted from Kanakamedala, K., J. M. Kaplan, and G. L. Moe (2006), "Moving IT infrastructure labor offshore," *McKinsey,* May.

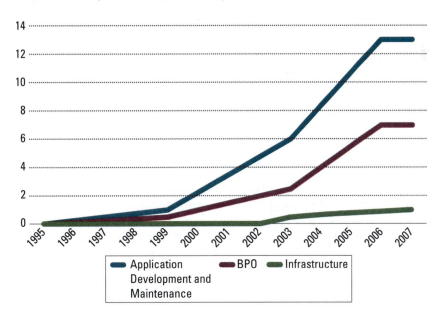

with. Many of the changes look positive for corporations on the surface: a lowering of corporate taxes from 40 percent to 30 percent for foreign firms and from 33.2 percent to 30 percent for domestic firms, a variety of changes intended to tax domestic and foreign firms more equivalently, and a simpler tax regime resulting in lower administrative expenses. Still, critics warn that the DTC is likely to create significant uncertainty and may not have the intended effects on promoting economic growth. Changes in the definition of residency status place additional burdens on foreign-owned businesses to document where decisions are made and key functions are performed. The code also introduces several "general anti-avoidance rules" (GAAR) that are aimed at ending tax evasion and extending India's legislative reach over foreign firms. Furthermore, the taxation of offshore deals is expected to increase the cost of acquisitions and therefore have a negative effect on foreign direct investment, at least in the short term.[87]

REFORMING THE U.S. TAX CODE? In a recent speech, President Barack Obama pointed out that one problem with the U.S. tax code is that it offers incentives for outsourcing. Reiterating his campaign rhetoric, the U.S. President stated: "The way we make our businesses competitive is not to reward American companies operating overseas with a roughly 2 percent tax rate on foreign profits; a rate that costs taxpayers tens of billions of dollars a year."[88] He wants the U.S. Congress to pass several measures designed to save the American taxpayers $210 billion over the next 10 years.

Ganesh Natarajan, vice-chairman and CEO of Zensar Technologies and former chairman of Nasscom, explained: "The primary intent is to address the tax rate differentials that exist across the world. If implemented, this would impact American-headquartered companies that have overseas operations. The current outsourcing tax law states that any income that is earned outside the United States is not taxed until such time as it is brought back into the United States. The Obama proposal aims to alter that to raise the revenues of the U.S government."

Infosys's co-founder, N. R. Narayana Murthy, believes that Obama's tax proposal will not impact Indian firms because they already pay taxes in the United States. Rather, American firms operating in India would have to repatriate taxes on profit earned outside their home country.[89] Azim Premji, CEO of Wipro, further warned that if passed, the new law would just cause America to suffer, by excluding it from the only growth markets left—Asia, Africa, and China.[90]

A back-of-the-envelope calculation shows that even if the tax proposals have the maximum impact on U.S. companies, it still makes sense for them to continue with their Indian operations. According to analysts, a service that costs around $48 per seat per hour in the United States is available for about $12 in India. This is for basic-level work; the difference is even higher for more sophisticated services.

The U.S. H-1B Visa Debate

In the tech world, stories of H-1B visa dilemmas abound. (Although both the H-1B and L-1 visas apply to non-immigrants, the H-1B visa is more valuable, as it is valid for a duration of three years. L-1 visas are for a much shorter duration and are used by employees who are transferred to the U.S. offices of a company.) One such story is that of Google's Sanjay Mavinkurve.[91] An Indian immigrant and Harvard graduate who helped lay the foundation of Facebook, Sanjay is a key engineer on many of Google's projects. But he works as a lone engineer in Google's sales office in Toronto. He has believed in the American dream since he was a child. He excelled in college, and finally got his work visa. Then he married another Indian and since his wife does not have a work visa, they decided to migrate to Canada where she could find employment.

Similarly, Microsoft has built a cutting-edge research center just 130 miles north of its Redmond, Washington, headquarters to overcome its current H-1B limitations. Only a two-hour car drive on I-5 from Redmond, the new facility is located in the Vancouver suburb of Richmond, British Columbia. Since it is located in Canada, U.S. immigration rules do not apply. Emphasizing this point, Microsoft stated: "The Vancouver area is a global gateway with a diverse population, is close to Microsoft's offices in Redmond, and allows the company to recruit and retain highly skilled people affected by immigration issues in the U.S."[92] Many of the big technology companies like Google and Microsoft spend millions on their immigration efforts, and maintain a full-time legal staff just to deal with immigration issues.[93]

Bill Gates, Microsoft's co-founder and chairman, is a vocal advocate of the economic benefits of foreign workers, and has testified before Congress to this effect (see Exhibit 12 for the full text of his March 12, 2008 speech). Citing a survey by Duke University and the University of California, Berkeley, he pointed out that "one-quarter of all start-up U.S. engineering and technology firms established between 1995 and 2005 had at least one foreign-born founder. By 2005, these companies produced $52 billion in sales and employed 450,000 workers." For example, Sergei Brin, Google's co-founder, is an immigrant from Russia. Proponents also argue that foreign workers bring their knowledge networks with them, linking the United States back to the best ideas across the globe. These knowledge networks allow the easy exchange of information, reduce the cost of business, leverage any innovation in the immigrant's home country, and make America's global presence stronger.[94] For instance, about 35 percent of Microsoft's patent applications in 2008 came from new inventions by visa and green card holders. In addition, there is evidence to indicate that technology companies create an average of four new U.S. jobs for every H-1B visa holder they hire.[95]

On the other side of the debate, Kim Berry, an engineer who operates a nonprofit advocacy group for American-born technologists, argues that, "There are plenty of Americans to do these jobs."[96] As of January 2009, there were 241,000 unemployed U.S. citizens in IT occupations whereas the number of H-1B IT workers far exceeded this number.[97] However, companies that use the H-1B visas argue that the market (rather than Congress) should

---

EXHIBIT 12

Text of Bill Gates's Testimony Before the Committee on Science and Technology, U.S. House of Representatives, March 12, 2008

We face a critical shortfall of skilled scientists and engineers who can develop new breakthrough technologies. Today, knowledge and expertise are the essential raw materials that companies and countries need in order to be competitive. We live in an economy that depends on the ability of innovative companies to attract and retain the very best talent, regardless of nationality or citizenship. Unfortunately, the U.S. immigration system makes attracting and retaining high-skilled immigrants exceptionally challenging for U.S. firms.

Congress's failure to pass high-skilled immigration reform has exacerbated an already grave situation. For example, the current base cap of 65,000 H-1B visas is arbitrarily set and bears no relation to the U.S. economy's demand for skilled professionals. For fiscal year 2007, the supply ran out more than four months before that fiscal year even began. For fiscal year 2008, the supply of H-1B visas ran out on April 2, 2007, the first day that petitions could be filed and six months before the visas would even be issued. Nearly half of those who sought a visa on that day did not receive one.

This situation has caused a serious disruption in the flow of talented science, technology, engineering, and math (STEM) graduates to U.S. companies. Because an H-1B petition generally can be filed only for a person who holds a degree, when May/June 2007 graduates received their degrees, the visa cap for fiscal year 2008 had already been reached. Accordingly, U.S. firms will be unable to hire those graduates on an H-1B visa until the beginning of fiscal year 2009, or October 2008.

As a result, many U.S. firms, including Microsoft, have been forced to locate staff in countries that welcome skilled foreign workers to do work that could otherwise have been done in the United States, if it were not for our counterproductive immigration policies. Last year, for example, Microsoft was unable to obtain H-1B visas for one-third of the highly qualified foreign-born job candidates that we wanted to hire.

If we increase the number of H-1B visas that are available to U.S. companies, employment of U.S. nationals would likely grow as well. For instance, Microsoft has found that for every H-1B hire we make, we add on average four additional employees to support them in various capacities. Our experience is not unique. A recent study of technology companies in the S&P 500 found that, for every H-1B visa requested, these leading U.S. technology companies increased their overall employment by five workers.

Moreover, the simple fact is that highly skilled foreign-born workers make enormous contributions to our economy. A recent survey by Duke University and the University of California, Berkeley, found that one-quarter of all startup U.S. engineering and technology firms established between 1995 and 2005 had at least one foreign-born founder. By 2005, these companies produced $52 billion in sales and employed 450,000 workers.

The United States will find it far more difficult to maintain its competitive edge over the next 50 years if it excludes those who are able and willing to help us compete. Other nations are benefiting from our misguided policies. They are revising their immigration policies to attract highly talented students and professionals who would otherwise study, live, and work in the United States for at least part of their careers.

dictate the visa cap. During the recession, it has taken 99.5 percent more time for the H-1B limit to be reached. Companies like Microsoft view this as evidence that the market can effectively temper demand for visas, and that the H-1B program can help fill gaps to grow the market when needed.

"BUFFALO, NOT BANGALORE." President Obama's proposal to provide tax incentives to companies creating jobs inside the United States has further fueled the immigration debate.[98] However, according to Ravi Aron, a senior fellow at the Mack Center for Technological Innovation at Wharton, the impact of the president's proposed tax incentives is likely to be minimal (despite their political appeal). He explains that service delivery centers in India:

> are fully owned by U.S. firms, and their employees work for U.S. corporations. Under the proposed scheme, there may be some marginal impact on these centers to the extent that the tax rate differences between India and the U.S. are quite low—unlike, say, in Ireland, where the corporate tax rate is as low as 12.5 percent. So even if the captive centers of these firms attract a slightly higher tax rate than they face in their Indian operations, given the very significant wage disparity, the incremental tax will, at best, have a marginal impact. It will be a small fraction of the wage difference between Asia and the U.S. IBM did not hire its nearly 90,000 workers in India and Accenture its 50,000 or so workers for lower taxes.

In fact, experts feel that the legislation may actually help Indian firms as they try to become more competitive, whereas the U.S.-based companies that do business in India may be negatively affected.[99] It is during times of crisis that companies come up with some of their most innovative ideas. For example, when Toyota faced Voluntary Export Restrictions under the Reagan administration, it forged an alliance with GM to create the NUMMI plant. Toyota gained a legal means of entering the U.S. market, while GM learned Toyota's lean manufacturing techniques.[100] Not only are protectionist measures likely to be challenged by the World Trade Organization (WTO), but they are also likely to motivate Indian companies to seek similar deals.

What the heated rhetoric on both sides has done is to create significantly more uncertainty for foreign-born innovators, who are increasingly returning to their home countries to start new companies.

According to Duke University's Vivek Wadhwa, "60 of the 65 foreign engineers among the 120 he helped train this year to be business executives are leaving for India, China, and Turkey."[101] Despite the global recession, most of the students of the class of 2010 at the Indian Institute of Management got placement offers one year before graduation from firms such as McKinsey & Co., Boston Consulting Group, and Bain & Co.[102] Even the big U.S. companies which have implemented hiring freezes at home are still offering jobs in India. The job profiles and opportunities are comparable and the pay is quite attractive by Indian standards.

THE H-1B AND L-1 VISA REFORM ACT OF 2009. In September 2008, the U.S. Citizenship and Immigration Services (CIS) issued a report indicating that the H-1B visa program was marred by fraud.[103] Surprise investigations into a random sample of 246 cases out of nearly 100,000 visa holders revealed a 20 percent violation rate, with problems ranging from forged documents, fake degrees, and fake companies at phony locations. A long-time advocate of visa reform, Senator Chuck Grassley (R-Iowa) seized this opportunity as a call for action and fired off a letter to the acting CIS director demanding to know what actions the agency was taking to end the "rampant fraud and abuse taking place in the program."[104]

When Microsoft announced plans to lay off 5,000 employees a few months later in January 2009, Grassley sent another pointed letter, this time to Microsoft CEO Steve Balmer (Exhibit 13), in which he asked for verification that American workers would have priority over any foreign visa workers. Microsoft's General Counsel Bradford Smith countered in a letter explaining that the company was legally bound to avoid discrimination based on nationality, and that Microsoft did not qualify as "H-1B dependent" because less than 15 percent of Microsoft's U.S. force were H-1B holders (see Exhibit 14). Though Microsoft steadfastly stood its ground, other companies were considerably more alarmed by Senator Grassley's inquiries. Bank of America actually withdrew its 2009 job offers made to MBA students graduating from U.S. business schools who were not U.S. citizens.[105]

Building on this momentum, Grassley, along with assistant Senate majority leader Dick Durbin (D-Illinois), introduced a bill to amend the H-1B and L-1 visa programs on April 24, 2009 (a prior version of the bill had been introduced in 2007 but

EXHIBIT 13

Senator Grassley's Open Letter to Steve Ballmer, CEO Microsoft

January 22, 2009
Mr. Steve Ballmer
Microsoft Corporation
One Microsoft Way
Redmond, WA 98052-6399

Dear Mr. Ballmer:

I am writing to inquire about press reports that Microsoft will be cutting approximately 5,000 jobs over the next 18 months. I understand that the layoffs will affect workers in research and development, marketing, sales, finance, legal and corporate affairs, human resources, and information technology.

I am concerned that Microsoft will be retaining foreign guest workers rather than similarly qualified American employees when it implements its layoff plan. As you know, I want to make sure employers recruit qualified American workers first before hiring foreign guest workers. For example, I cosponsored legislation to overhaul the H-1B and L-1 visa programs to give priority to American workers and to crack down on unscrupulous employers who deprive qualified Americans of high-skilled jobs. Fraud and abuse is rampant in these programs, and we need more transparency to protect the integrity of our immigration system. I also support legislation that would strengthen educational opportunities for American students and workers so that Americans can compete successfully in this global economy.

Last year, Microsoft was here on Capitol Hill advocating for more H-1B visas. The purpose of the H-1B visa program is to assist companies in their employment needs where there is not a sufficient American workforce to meet their technology expertise requirements. However, H-1B and other work visa programs were never intended to replace qualified American workers. Certainly, these work visa programs were never intended to allow a company to retain foreign guest workers rather than similarly qualified American workers, when that company cuts jobs during an economic downturn.

It is imperative that in implementing its layoff plan, Microsoft ensures that American workers have priority in keeping their jobs over foreign workers on visa programs. To that effect, I would like you to respond to the following questions:

» What is the breakdown in the jobs that are being eliminated? What kind of jobs are they? How many employees in each area will be cut?

» Are any of these jobs being cut held by H-1B or other work visa program employees? If so, how many?

» How many of the jobs being eliminated are filled by Americans? Of those positions, is Microsoft retaining similar ones filled by foreign guest workers? If so, how many?

» How many H-1B or other work visa program workers will Microsoft be retaining when the planned layoff is completed?

My point is that during a layoff, companies should not be retaining H-1B or other work visa program employees over qualified American workers. Our immigration policy is not intended to harm the American workforce. I encourage Microsoft to ensure that Americans are given priority in job retention. Microsoft has a moral obligation to protect these American workers by putting them first during these difficult economic times.

Sincerely,
Charles E. Grassley
United States Senator

Source: "Grassley works to ensure American workers are priority," January 23, 2009, http://grassley.senate.gov/news/Article.cfm?customel_dataPageID_1502=18922.

EXHIBIT 14

Microsoft's Response to Senator Grassley's Open Letter

March 3, 2009
The Honorable Charles E. Grassley
United States Senator
135 Hart Senate Office Building
Washington, D.C. 20510-1501

Dear Senator Grassley,

Thank you for your letter of January 22, 2009. Steve Ballmer asked me to respond on the company's behalf.

Your letter expressed concern about Microsoft's recently announced lay-offs and asked us to provide you with information about them. I have included that information below, but first I'd like to provide a bit of context.

Since the company's founding in 1975, Microsoft's consistent growth has enabled us to increase employment every year. In the last three fiscal years, for example, our employment in the United States increased by 40 percent. Today we have more than 90,000 employees worldwide and over half of them are in the United States. The vast majority of these U.S. jobs are filled by American citizens.

Because of our partner-based business model, our impact on employment is even larger than these numbers indicate. For every dollar that Microsoft earns in the United States, our business partners earn $6. This creates many additional jobs. One recent study found that 4.2 million people in the United States are working in jobs that are the result of Microsoft's business model. . . .

This year, in response to the economic crisis, Microsoft is reducing its employment level for the first time. . . . We announced in January that the company would eliminate up to 5,000 jobs over 18 months. It's important to note that we also expect to create 2,000 to 3,000 new jobs during this same timeframe, as we continue to invest in innovation. As a result, the total net impact on our employment will be a decline of about 2,000 to 3,000 jobs, not 5,000.

You asked about the kinds of jobs that will be eliminated and how many employees will be affected in each area.

Because the job reduction decisions will be made over 18 months, we do not yet know all of the specific jobs that will be eliminated. We do know, however, that the 5,000 positions that will be eliminated will include jobs in marketing, sales, finance, Legal and Corporate Affairs, HR, R&D, and IT. In addition to the 5,000 figure, our workforce in support, consulting, operations, billing, and manufacturing will continue to change in direct response to customer needs.

We also know that the 5,000 figure likely will include positions in a large number of countries. Given the distribution of our jobs, however, it is likely that the Puget Sound region in Washington State will see the largest number of job eliminations. . . .

As we add new positions to support key investments, we will prioritize R&D investments that promote long-term innovation. That is why we plan to invest over $9 billion in research and development this year, one of the highest such figures in the world. Over two-thirds of this total will be spent in the United States.

You also asked in your letter how we decide which jobs to eliminate, whether employees with H-1B or other work visas are affected, and how many of the jobs being eliminated are held by Americans.

Because these decisions will be made over 18 months, it's too early to know the precise answers. We do know, however, that the job reductions will impact non-Americans who hold jobs outside the United States, as well as both visa holders and U.S. workers inside the United States. . . . Workers on H-1B visas and other temporary work visas make up only a small percentage of our overall workforce, but they were also among the employees impacted by the reductions announced in January. Employees outside the United States were also impacted. . . .

Finally, you asked about Microsoft's plans for retaining H-1B or other work visa program workers after the job eliminations.

H1-B employees have always accounted for less than 15 percent of Microsoft's U.S. workforce, the level that is used in immigration law to determine whether a company is "H-1B dependent." Nonetheless, the ability to tap into the world's best minds has long been essential to our success. Although they are a small percentage of our workforce, H-1B workers have long made crucial contributions to Microsoft's innovation successes and to our ability to help create jobs in this country. We are confident this will continue to be true in the future.

We focus our recruiting for core technology jobs at U.S. universities, which continue to be among the best in the world for computer science and engineering graduates. However, as one recent study found, in 2005 temporary residents earned more than 40 percent of the engineering and computer science degrees at U.S. higher education institutions. For doctoral degrees, that number was even higher, as temporary residents accounted for 59 percent of the degrees awarded in these fields that year.

The substantial majority of H-1B petitions filed by Microsoft are for core technology positions, and technology and engineering positions account for about 90 percent of Microsoft's H-1B workforce. Many of these H-1B employees have been seeking permanent resident status for many years and would no longer be dependent on their H-1B visas but for multi-year delays in the green card process.

With these factors taken together, we do not expect to see a significant change in the proportion of H-1B employees in our workforce following the job reductions.

EXHIBIT 14 *(Continued)*

I want to underscore that we are rigorous in our compliance with the requirements of the H-1B program. We are familiar with published reports about abuse by some employers in the H-1B visa category. We believe that the H-1B fraud issue is important and needs to be addressed. We recognize that every H-1B employer has an obligation to ensure that the program's rules are followed. We support H-1B reform efforts to ensure that users of the program follow both the spirit and the letter of the law.

Finally, I want to convey our commitment to help broaden opportunities for all Americans. The country's long-term competitiveness requires that the United States produce more university graduates in science, technology, engineering, and math. . . . At Microsoft, we have a number of education-focused public initiatives. . . .

Ultimately, as a company and as a country we need to combine short-term adjustments to the economic crisis with long-term efforts to strengthen our economic competitiveness. We recognize the impact that our decisions have on employees who are affected. We strive to make thoughtful employment decisions and then assist the individuals who are impacted by them. We also strive to take a long-term approach that will enable Microsoft to remain a leader in technology innovation and an important contributor to the country's competitiveness now and in the future.

We hope that this information is helpful to you. We look forward to working with you and your staff if we can be of assistance in addressing these important issues.

Sincerely,
Bradford L. Smith
General Counsel

Source: www.businessinsider.com/microsoft-to-grassley-were-still-using-H-1Bs-no-moral-imperative-to-hire-americans-2009-3.

EXHIBIT 15

Details of U.S. H-1B Visas Filed (2008, Top 50 Companies)

Rank	Company	No. of Visas	Percentage of Top 50
1	Infosys Technologies Limited	4,559	21.11%
2	Wipro Limited	2,678	12.40%
3	Satyam Computer Services Limited	1,917	8.88%
4	Tata Consultancy Services Limited	1,539	7.13%
5	Microsoft Corp	1,037	4.80%
6	Accenture LLP	731	3.39%
7	Cognizant Tech Solutions US Corp	467	2.16%
8	Cisco Systems Inc	422	1.95%
9	Larsen & Toubro Infotech Limited	403	1.87%
10	IBM (NYSE: IBM) India Private Limited	381	1.76%
11	Intel Corp	351	1.63%
12	Ernst & Young LLP	321	1.49%
13	Patni Americas Inc	296	1.37%
14	Terra Infotech Inc	281	1.30%
15	Qualcomm Incorporated	255	1.18%
16	Mphasis Corporation	251	1.16%
17	KPMG LLP	245	1.13%
18	Prince Georges County Public Schools	239	1.11%
19	Baltimore City Public School System	229	1.06%
20	Deloitte Consulting LLP	218	1.01%
21	Goldman Sachs & Co	211	0.98%
22	Verinon Technology Solutions LTD	208	0.96%

(continued)

EXHIBIT 15 *(Continued)*

Details of U.S. H-1B Visas Filed (2008, Top 50 Companies)

23	Everest Business Solutions Inc	208	0.96%
24	Google Inc	207	0.96%
26	Deloitte & Touche LLP	195	0.90%
27	University of Maryland	191	0.88%
28	University of Pennsylvania	186	0.86%
29	University of Michigan	183	0.85%
30	Marlabs Inc	177	0.82%
31	Oracle USA Inc	168	0.78%
32	University of Illinois at Chicago	168	0.78%
33	Allied Solutions Group Inc	166	0.77%
34	Rite Aid Corporation	161	0.75%
35	V-Soft Consulting Group Inc	161	0.75%
36	Cummins Inc	159	0.74%
37	The Johns Hopkins Med Institutes OIS	157	0.73%
38	Vedicsoft Solutions Inc	156	0.72%
39	University of Wisconsin, Madison	151	0.70%
40	JPMorgan Chase & Co	150	0.69%
41	I-Flex Solutions Inc	148	0.69%
42	Clerysys Inc	147	0.68%
43	Yale University	145	0.67%
44	State University of NY at Stony Brook	143	0.66%
45	Harvard University	143	0.66%
46	DIS National Institutes Of Health	141	0.65%
47	Yahoo Inc	139	0.64%
48	Stanford University	138	0.64%
49	CDC Global Services Inc	135	0.63%
50	Global Consultants Inc	131	0.61%
	Sum of Top 50	**21,593**	

not passed).[106] The proposed legislation did not aim to reduce the number of H-1B visas (Exhibit 15)—85,000 per year[107]—but rather contained provisions to increase oversight and enforcement while discouraging outsourcing. Anti-outsourcing sentiment was at an all-time high due to large-scale job cuts and double digit unemployment in the United States. The bill proposed the following changes:

- Before an employer submits an H-1B application, the employer must first advertise the job opening for 30 days on a U.S. Department of Labor (DOL) website.

- Companies were prohibited from hiring H-1B holders if they employed more than 50 people and more than 50 percent of their employees were H-1B visa holders.

- Any company that had received government funding and sought to hire new H-1B workers would be considered an "H-1B dependent employer." All H-1B dependent employers must make additional attestations to the U.S. Department of Labor (DOL) when filing the Labor Condition Application.

- The U.S. Department of Homeland Security (DHS) agreed to share with DOL any potential fraud cases.

- Employers were to pay employees the prevailing wages to prevent undercutting American workers by paying substandard wages to foreign workers.[108]

Despite all the public attention generated by the Durbin–Grassley bill, the legislation never made it out of committee and was removed from the books when the 112th Congress came into session.[109] However,

Senators Sanders (I-Vermont) and Grassley did manage to incorporate a watered-down version of the bill as an amendment to the economic stimulus package approved in February 2009. Under the so-called "Employ American Workers Act," any company that received Troubled Asset Relief Program (TARP) funds who applied for H-1B workers had to comply with H-1B dependent rules. The rules stipulated that the company must make a good-faith effort to recruit American workers and that it could not replace American workers with H-1B visa holders.[110] One expert interviewed by *Bloomberg Businessweek* estimated that only about 1,000 jobs in the banking industry would be affected by the legislation. Meanwhile, banks could continue to use H-1B visa holders that were brought into the United States by foreign outsourcing firms such as Infosys, Wipro, and Tata (a much more significant source of foreign workers).[111] The initial version of the TARP amendment introduced by Sanders and Grassley (which was not passed) was much more stringent and would have prevented banks from hiring any workers on H-1B visas for an entire year.[112]

VISA REFORM IN 2011? Senators Durbin (in office until 2014) and Grassley (re-elected in 2010 for another six-year term) have continued to advocate for broader visa reform since the passage of the TARP amendment. In January 2011, they once again declared their intent to reintroduce legislation to overhaul the H-1B program. This announcement followed on the heels of a Government Accounting Office (GAO) report that found the H-1B program "vulnerable to fraud and abuse" due to the inability to accurately track the number of foreign workers in the program, how many stayed in the country after their visa expired, and problems with implementation of the protections provided to American workers.[113, 114, 115] The GAO also found that demand for foreign workers exceeded the visa cap and was dominated by a few large companies. In response, Durbin and Grassley wrote a letter to Homeland Security Director Janet Napolitano, asking the federal government to take action to end visa abuse, stating the GAO report "verifies what we have argued for years—that loopholes in the program have resulted in adverse effects for American and foreign workers."[116] In an interview, Grassley added, "It's time we get the program back to its original intent where employers use H-1B visas only to shore-up employment in areas where there is a lack of qualified American workers."[117]

Yet President Obama's 2011 State of the Union address seemed to signal that H-1B reform might be moving in another direction altogether. In a comment many interpreted as giving a "green light" to increase the flow of foreign workers, he stated: "Others come here from abroad to study in our colleges and universities. But as soon as they obtain advanced degrees, we send them back home to compete against us. It makes no sense."[118] Yet despite broad bipartisan and industry support for expanding the visa cap, Congressional efforts to increase the number of visas offered have likewise repeatedly failed. For example, Representative Gabrielle Giffords (D-Arizona) introduced an unsuccessful bill in 2008 that proposed implementing a market-based formula with an initial ceiling of 130,000, as well as removing any limits on foreign graduate students' ability to stay in the U.S. after they finish their degrees. The obstacles to reform are many. Senators Durbin and Grassley and their supporters want to limit visa holders to no more than 50 percent of a company's work force. Other legislators have been unwilling to pass any changes to the visa program that are not part of a more comprehensive approach to immigration reform.[119] Meanwhile, more than 60 technology CEOs travelled en masse to Washington in March 2011 to petition for increased access to the skilled foreign workers they need to continue to innovate.[120] Overall, the consensus seems to be that H-1B visa reform is coming—the question is what kind of change and when.

Decision Time

The announcement that Delta Flight 184 was beginning its descent shook Adrian awake from her slumber. Rising to consciousness, her thoughts returned to the external challenges that lay ahead for the strategy planning committee at Infosys Consulting. She wondered what should be their first priority—was it the increased competition that was bringing global competitors into Infosys's backyard? Direct competition from Tata and Wipro? Or perhaps the recent and proposed changes in the Indian and U.S. tax codes? Then there was the difficulty of predicting exactly which way U.S. H-1B visa reform would go. She wondered what the company's next steps should be in light of all these potential opportunities and threats.

Her head swimming, Adrian tried to focus her thoughts on the internal workings of Infosys Consulting instead. How could they get to the point of profitability? Where would future growth come from? She wondered if it made sense for Infosys to invest further capital in the consulting arm, or if it would be better to spin it out as a separate company? Perhaps they should partner or merge with a more established consulting firm? Or maybe they should follow Anderson's lead and relocate to Ireland to take advantage of lower corporate tax rates?

Then there was the issue of where to get the human resources to support future growth. Perhaps one of the underlying problems the company faced was that Infosys's processes and culture were not adapting well to the U.S. market. How could they train their international employees better? Should they hire more personnel locally? What if Durbin and Grassley were successful in their attempts to limit the foreign workers that Infosys depended on so heavily? If Infosys did have to hire more people locally, where would the money come from for higher salaries? Perhaps it would make sense to hire undergraduates from U.S. universities instead of MBAs, and then train them for specific projects in order to keep costs down? Amidst the welter of questions in her mind, the aircraft touched down at Hartsfield-Jackson International Airport. In a few hours, she would face her co-workers in the Atlanta office, and the real work would begin.

Endnotes

1. "Say No to Bangalore, Yes to Buffalo: Obama," *Rediff Business*, May 5, 2009, http://business.rediff.com/report/2009/may/05/bpo-say-no-to-bangalore-says-obama.htm.

2. Infosys, Infosys Annual Report, 2009, Infosys Technologies Ltd., www.infosys.com/investors/reports-filings/annual-report/annual/Infosys-AR06.pdf.

3. "Say No to Bangalore, Yes to Buffalo: Obama."

4. http://20twentytwo.blogspot.com/2008/06/inspiring-infosys-story.html.

5. "The Amazing Infosys Story," *Rediff* News, July 11, 2006, http://specials.rediff.com/money/2006/jul/11sld3.htm.

6. "Infosys Technologies Limited," Hoover's Company Records, October 15, 2009.

7. http://abhisays.com/sofware-companies/early-days-of-infosys.html.

8. http://20twentytwo.blogspot.com/2008/06/inspiring-infosys-story.html.

9. Ibid.

10. "The Amazing Infosys Story," *Rediff* News, July 11, 2006, www.rediff.com/money/2006/jul/11sld5.htm.

11. "Murthy, Narayana," *Encyclopædia Britannica*, 2009, Encyclopædia Britannica Online, October 15, 2009, www.britannica.com/EBchecked/topic/1012874/Narayama-Murthy.

12. www.fundinguniverse.com/company-histories/Infosys-Technologies-Ltd-Company-History.html.

13. Pfeiffer, E. W. (1999), "From India to America," *Forbes Asia*, August 23, pp. 21–24.

14. www.india-today.com/itoday/19991108/business.html.

15. www.fundinguniverse.com/company-histories/Infosys-Technologies-Ltd-Company-History.html.

16. www.infosys.com/about/what-we-do/Pages/index.aspx.

17. Infosys Annual Report 2009–10.

18. Ibid.

19. www.infosys.com/investors/Documents/pdfs/Global-Facts.pdf.

20. www.infosys.com/about/awards/Pages/best-managed-company.aspx.

21. "Infosys Website," 2009, www.infosys.com.

22. "Who we are," October 15, 2009, www.infosys.com/about/who-we-are/default.asp.

23. www.infosys.com/investors/corporate-governance/Pages/report.aspx.

24. www.infosys.com/about/awards/Pages/corporate-governance-awards.aspx.

25. www.infosys.com/about/awards/Pages/best-managed-company.aspx.

26. Infosys Annual Report, 2009-2010.

27. "Infosys Technologies Ltd: Company profile," *Datamonitor*, April 24, 2009.

28. Infosys Annual Report, 2009–2010.

29. Rothaermel, F. T., and A. M. Hess (2009), "Finding an innovation strategy that works," *The Wall Street Journal*, August 17.

30. "The Global 2000: Special Report," *Forbes*, August 4, 2009, www.forbes.com/lists/2009/18/global-09_The-Global-2000-Software-Services_9Rank.html.

31. "Infosys tells 50 of top brass: Work with non-profit for a year, will pay you half your salary," *ENS Economic Bureau*, March 25, 2009, www.indianexpress.com/news/infosys-tells-50-of-top-brass-work-with-non/438778/.

32. "Infosys Q4 revenue falls Qoq 1st time in decade," OnlineEquityCalls.com, April 15, 2009, www.onlineequitycalls.com/2009/04/infosys-q4-revenue-falls-qoq-1st-time-in-decade/.

33. Palanisamy, B. K. (2009), "Transaction based pricing model for outsourcing – Quality focused approach," www.sqs-conferences.com/de/vortraege/palanisamy_ab.pdf.

34. "Transaction Based Pricing (TBP) has arrived!" July 21, 2009, www.infosysblogs.com/microsoft/2009/07/transaction_based_pricing_tbp_1.html.

35. "Transaction based pricing," *Business Editor*, March 2, 2009, www.thehindubusinessline.com/2009/03/02/stories/2009030251090200.htm.

36. "Global outsourcing market to be worth $1,430bn by 2009," *Computer Business Review*, August, 2007, www.cbr.co.za/article.aspx?pklArticleId=4714&pklCategoryId=404.

37. Staples, S. (2009), "Top three outsourcing initiatives of 2009," *CIO*, January 27, www.cio.com/article/478098/Top_Three_Outsourcing_Initiatives_for_2009?page=2.

38. "IT giant Infosys group change of guard," *Dataquest*, August 4, 2007, http://dqindia.ciol.com/content/DQTop20_07/ITGaints07/2007/107080405.asp.

39. Professor Chris Trimble, Infosys Consulting: Tuck School of Business at Dartmouth, 2008.

40. Ibid.

41. "Infosys website," 2009, www.infosys.com; and Infosys Annual Report, 2009–2010.

42. "Infosys annual report," Infosys Technologies Ltd., 2009, www.infosys.com/investors/reports-filings/annual-report/annual/Infosys-AR06.pdf.

43. "Breakeven Infosys consulting deferred," April 15, 2006, www.business-standard.com/india/news/breakeveninfosys-consulting-deferred/243874/.

44. Geographic data from "Plunkett research," April 2010, www.plunkettresearch.com/Industries/Consulting/ConsultingStatistics/tabid/177/Default.aspx. Sector data from http://www.infosys.com/about/awards/Pages/best-managed-company.aspx.

45. Abhinav C., A. Courtney, B. Edwards, M. Gutierrez, M. Janovec, and K. Winkler (2010), "Infosys consulting paper," April 2010.

46. IBIS World website, www.ibisworld.com/industry/default.aspx?

47. "IT consulting U.S. industry report," October 15, 2009, www.ibisworld.com/industry/retail.aspx?indid=1415&chid=1.

48. "Industry Overview: Consulting Services," Hoover's, October 15, 2009, www.hoovers.com/consulting-services-/—ID__119—/free-ind-fr-profile-basic.xhtml.

49. www.accenture.com/us-en/company/overview/description/Pages/index.aspx.

50. "Accenture Ltd.," Hoover's Company Records, October 15, 2009.

51. www.accenture.com/us-en/Pages/service-technology-information-management-group-overview-summary.aspx.

52. "Accenture Ltd.," Hoover's Company Records.

53. http://h10134.www1.hp.com/news/features/5855/.

54. "HP Enterprise Services," Hoover's Company Records, November 15, 2009.

55. www.deloitte.com/view/en_US/us/Services/consulting/index.htm.

56. www.deloitte.com/view/en_US/us/Services/consulting/technology-consulting/technology-offerings/index.htm.

57. www.deloitte.com/view/en_US/us/Services/consulting/technology-consulting/index.htm.

58. www.deloitte.com/view/en_US/us/Services/consulting/technology-consulting/oracle-consulting/index.htm.

59. "Deloitte Consulting LLP," Hoover's Company Records, October 15, 2009.

60. www-935.ibm.com/services/us/en/it-services/gts-it-service-home-page-1.html.

61. "IBM Global Services," Hoover's Company Records, October 15, 2009.

62. www-304.ibm.com/shop/americas/content/home/store_IBMPublicUSA/en_US/IT-services-catalog.html.

63. www-935.ibm.com/services/us/en/it-services/alliances-eus.html.

64. "IBM to cut U.S. jobs, expand in India," *The Wall Street Journal*, March 26, 2009.

65. "McKinsey & Company," Hoover's Company Records, October 15, 2009.

66. www.mckinsey.com/en/About_us.aspx.

67. "McKinsey & Company," Hoover's Company Records.

68. www.mckinsey.com/en/Client_Service/Business_Technology.aspx.

69. www.mckinsey.com/en/Client_Service/Business_Technology/Tools_and_solutions.aspx.

70. www.tcs.com/about/corp_facts/Pages/default.aspx.

71. www.tcs.com/about/tcs_difference/global_delivery/Pages/default.aspx.

72. www.tcs.com/about/tcs_difference/Pages/default.aspx.

73. www.tcs.com/about/corp_facts/Pages/default.aspx.

74. "Tata Consultancy Services Limited," Hoover's Company Records, October 15, 2009.

75. www.wipro.com/services/index.htm.

76. www.wipro.com/corporate/aboutus/index.htm.

77. "Wipro Limited," Hoover's Company Records, October 15, 2009.

78. www.wipro.com/corporate/aboutus/fact-sheet.htm.

79. www.chennai.stpi.in/scheme.htm.

80. www.thehindubusinessline.in/2010/09/30/stories/2010093052610400.htm.

81. http://epaper.timesofindia.com/Repository/getFiles.asp?Style=OliveXLib:LowLevelEntityToPrint_TOI&Type=text/html&Locale=english-skin-custom&Path=TOIBG/2010/05/12&ID=Ar02102.

82. http://articles.timesofindia.indiatimes.com/2011-01-26/software-services/28361313_1_tax-sops-onsite-tax-holiday.

83. "FM must extend tax holiday," June 25, 2009, http://news.oneindia.in/columns/sivakumar/2009/fm-must-extend-tax-holiday-it-sector.html.

84. "Infosys moves to new pricing strategy," July 2008, http://economictimes.indiatimes.com/News/News_By_Company/Corporate_Trends/Infosys_moves_to_new_pricing_strategy/articleshow/3224805.cms.

85. "STPI withdrawal may hit Infosys, Wipro net profit," *The Economic Times*, May 26, 2009, http://economictimes.indiatimes.com/Infotech/Software/STPI-withdrawal-may-hit-Infosys-Wipro-net-profit/articleshow/4578115.cms.

86. "Infosys annual report," Infosys Technologies Ltd., 2009.

87. Atkins, M. (2011), "The impact of India's direct tax code," *Financierworldwide.com*, January 2011, www.financierworldwide.com/article_printable.php?id=7632.

88. "Obama: Common sense, fairness and corporate non-sense," May 5, 2009, http://taxjustice.blogspot.com/2009/05/obama-common-sense-fairness-and.html.

89. "Nasscom changes stance at US visa issue," *Business Standard*, May 8, 2009, www.business-standard.com/india/news/nasscom-changes-stanceus-visa-issue/357471/.

90. "Obama move won't impact Indian firms: N. R. Narayana Murthy," *The Economic Times*, May 8, 2009, http://economictimes.indiatimes.com/Features/OutsourcingProtectionism/Obama-tax-move-wont-impact-Indian-firms-Murthy/articleshow/4500385. cms.

91. Richtel, M. (2009), "Tech recruiting clashes with immigration rules," *The New York Times*, April 11.

92. "Microsoft expanding Canadian operations in greater Vancouver area," Microsoft press release, July 5, 2007.

93. Richtel, M., "Tech recruiting clashes with immigration rules."

94. "The hub nation," *Economist.com*, April 22, 2010.

95. Bill Gates's testimony before the Committee on Science and Technology, U.S. House of Representatives, March 12, 2008.

96. Richtel, M. "Tech recruiting clashes with immigration rules."

97. Thibodeau, P. (2009), "U.S.: H-1B workers outnumber unemployed techies," *Computerworld*, May 26.

98. "Say no to Bangalore, yes to Buffalo: Obama."

99. "Is the U.S. government's new tax proposal just political rhetoric?" October 15, 2009, http://knowledge.wharton.upenn. edu/india/article.cfm?articleid=4382.

100. "Toyota's Nummi dilemma," October 15, 2009, www. thedeal.com/corporatedealmaker/2009/06/toyotas_nummi_ dilemma.php.

101. Lawsky, D. (2009), "U.S. immigration rules blamed for tech brain drain," *Forbes,* June 23.

102. Balakrishna, S. (2009), "Good times are back: Job offers flood IIMs," *The Times of India,* July 17.

103. http://www.deloitte.com/view/en_US/us/Services/consulting/technology-consulting/index.htm.

104. http://grassley.senate.gov/news/Article. cfm?customel_dataPageID_1502=17678.

105. "Bank of America withdraws job offers to foreign MBAs," March 11, 2009, www.fiercecio.com/story/ bank-america-withdraws-job-offers-foreign-mbas/2009-03-11.

106. L1 visa is a non-immigrant visa valid for a relatively short amount of time—generally three years. This visa allows foreign workers to relocate to a corporation's U.S. office after having worked abroad for the company for at least one year.

107. A cap of 65,000 per year for foreign workers in occupations that require theoretical or technical expertise in a specialized field and a bachelor's degree or its equivalent like architects, engineers, computer programmers, accountants, doctors and college professors and an additional 20,000 for foreign workers with a Master's or higher-level degree from a U.S. academic institution.

108. "USCIS announces new requirements for hiring H-1B foreign workers," March 20, 2009, www.uscis.gov/portal/site/ uscis/menuitem.5af9bb95919f35e66f614176543f6d1a/?vgnex toid=108. 34dd9b5d82420210VgnVCM1000004718190aRCR D&vgnextchannel=e7d696cfcd6ff110VgnVCM10000047181 90aRCRD.

109. www.govtrack.us/congress/bill.xpd?bill=s111-887.

110. www.dcemploymentlawupdate.com/2009/02/articles/ immigration/stimulus-bill-amendment-restricts-tarp-recipients-from-hiring-h1b-visa-holders/.

111. www.businessweek.com/blogs/money_politics/ archives/2009/02/H-1B_visas_buy.html.

112. www.dcemploymentlawupdate.com/2009/02/articles/ immigration/stimulus-bill-amendment-restricts-tarp-recipients-from-hiring-h1b-visa-holders/.

113. http://thehill.com/blogs/on-the-money/801-economy/141357-grassley-durbin-looking-for-changes-in-visa-program.

114. www.foxnews.com/politics/2011/01/31/durbin-grassley-ask-homeland-security-prevent-abuses-legal-foreign-worker-visa/.

115. http://washingtontechnology.com/articles/2011/01/18/ congress-needs-to-reform-h1b-visa-program-watchdog-says. aspx.

116. http://thehill.com/blogs/on-the-money/801-economy/141357-grassley-durbin-looking-for-changes-in-visa-program.

117. www.foxnews.com/politics/2011/01/31/durbin-grassley-ask-homeland-security-prevent-abuses-legal-foreign-worker-visa/.

118. http://blogs.computerworld.com/17722/ obama_makes_h_1b_green_card_reform_a_priority.

119. Ibid.

120. http://apnews.com/2011/03/11/ tech-ceos-visit-washington-to-lobby-for-h1b-visa-tax-reforms/.

David Wesley
Ravi Sarathy
The University of Western Ontario

On April 4, 2000, Clarence C. Comer, president and chief executive officer (CEO) of Southdown, Inc. (Southdown), wrote a letter to the company's shareholders, expressing his disappointment with the company's share price:

> Management is pleased with the Company's accomplishments in 1999 and prior years, which have created one of the strongest and most profitable building materials companies in the U.S. . . . Unfortunately, the stock market has failed to appropriately reflect the value that has been created, or the prospects for further growth.[2] Therefore, Southdown's Board of Directors is exploring and evaluating a number of alternatives. Options include, among other things, a significant share repurchase, expansion through domestic or international acquisitions, or the merger or sale of the Company.[3]

What Comer's letter did not say was that he had already approached Lorenzo Zambrano, president and CEO of Mexico-based Cemex, with an offer to sell Southdown. In fact, Zambrano had just arrived in Houston, Texas, and was scheduled to meet with Comer at Southdown's headquarters the following day.

Cement Industry

Cement was the primary material used in the construction of commercial, industrial and residential infrastructure. Concrete producers, industrial firms and building contractors purchased cement in bulk, while homeowners, gardeners and other small-quantity consumers purchased pre-bagged quantities from commercial distributors.

Fuel was the largest cost in the production of cement, accounting for 50 percent or more of total variable costs. Therefore, production costs tended to fluctuate in tandem with energy prices. In 1998, the cement industry benefited from lower oil prices which averaged US$11 per barrel for the year. In 1999, however, there was a steady rise in energy costs, and by late summer 2000, oil prices had risen to over $30 per barrel.

Dry-process production was considerably more energy efficient than wet-process production, but required considerably more investment in plant and equipment (see Glossary). In less developed countries, subsidized fuel and insufficient investment in new plant and equipment favored wet-process production.

Cement consumption was cyclical in nature and correlated to population and economic growth (see Tables 1 and 2 for consumption and production trends, respectively; Exhibit 1 provides cement production trends and growth rates). In less developed countries, demand was driven by government infrastructure projects and by first-time homeowners who undertook construction themselves. The latter typically purchased prebagged cement in small quantities.[4] Cement was a small portion of overall construction costs and there were few available substitutes. As such, sales were more dependent on overall construction levels than price. Large-scale government infrastructure projects, such as highway construction, were even more cyclical than housing starts. The number of government projects depended more on spending policy than cement prices.

Industrialized countries, on the other hand, typically consumed cement in bulk quantities. Even residential users contracted with ready-mix suppliers to undertake building projects. Although long-term demand correlated strongly with economic indicators, day-to-day demand was unpredictable, with approximately half of all ready-mix orders being cancelled on the delivery date, due to unforeseeable circumstances, such as inclement weather.[5]

Richard Ivey School of Business
The University of Western Ontario

Northeastern UNIVERSITY

David Wesley prepared this case under the supervision of Professor Ravi Sarathy solely to provide material for class discussion. The authors do not intend to illustrate either effective or ineffective handling of a managerial situation. The authors may have disguised certain names and other identifying information to protect confidentiality.

Ivey Management Services is the exclusive representative of the copyright holder and prohibits any form of reproduction, storage or transmittal without its written permission. Reproduction of this material is not covered under authorization by any reproduction rights organization. To order copies or request permission to reproduce materials, contact Ivey Publishing, Ivey Management Services, c/o Richard Ivey School of Business, The University of Western Ontario, London, Ontario, Canada, N6A 3K7; phone (519) 661-3208; fax (519) 661-3882; e-mail cases@ivey.uwo.ca.

This case was made possible through the generous support of Darla and Frederick Brodsky through their endowment of the Darla and Frederick Brodsky Trustee Professorship in International Business and The Institute for Global Innovation Management at Northeastern University.

Copyright © 2003, Northeastern University, College of Business Administration Version: (A) 2009-10-22

TABLE 1

World Cement Consumption by Region, 2000

Region %	
East Asia	46
Southeast Asia	5
Southwest Asia	7
Middle East	4
Africa	5
Europe	19
Central America and South America	6
North America	8
Total, 2000 (billion metric tons)	1.650
Total, 1995	1.405
Total, 1990	1.138

Source: Ocean Shipping Consultants, Nov. 2001.

TABLE 2

World Cement Production and Capacity ('000 of metric tons)

Country	1996	2000
China	490,000	583,190
India	25,000	95,000
United States (includes Puerto Rico)	80,818	89,510
Japan	94,492	81,300
Korea, Republic of (South Korea)	57,334	51,255
Brazil	34,597	39,208
Germany	40,000	38,000
Italy	34,000	36,000
Turkey	32,500	35,825
Russia	27,800	32,400
Thailand	35,000	32,000
Mexico	22,829	31,677
Spain	25,157	30,000
Indonesia	34,000	27,789
France	20,000	20,000
Taiwan	21,537	18,500
Other countries (rounded)	367,280	375,000
World total	1,445,000	1,620,000

Source: U.S. Geological Survey, Mineral Commodity Summaries, 1997 and 2001.

EXHIBIT 1

Cement Production Trends and Average Annual Growth Rates for Major World Regions, 1970 to 1995 (in millions of tons)

Region	1970	1975	1980	1985	1990	1995	Average % Growth 1990-1995	Average % GDP Growth* 1991-1998
China (incl. Hong Kong)	27	47	81	148	211	477	17.7	11.4
Europe	185	194	223	178	196	181	−1.7	1.7
OECD-Pacific	69	83	113	100	126	154	4.1	6.0
Rest of Asia	20	31	49	57	89	130	8.0	5.9
Middle East	19	29	44	75	93	116	4.6	2.9
Latin America	36	52	76	71	82	97	3.4	3.6
Eastern Europe/former Soviet Union	134	177	190	190	190	96	−12.7	−4.0
North America	76	73	79	81	81	88	1.5	3.0
India	14	16	18	31	49	70	7.3	6.1
Africa	15	20	28	35	38	44	2.7	2.8
World	**594**	**722**	**901**	**965**	**1,156**	**1,453**	**4.7**	**2.5**

*Gross domestic product growth rates adapted from: "Global Economic Prospects and the Developing Countries," *International Bank for Reconstruction and Development*, 2000.

Source: Cembureau, 1998.

World cement production amounted to about 1.6 billion tons in 2000. The top 16 countries (in descending order, China, Japan, the United States, India, South Korea, Brazil, Germany, Turkey, Thailand, Italy, Spain, Mexico, Russia, Indonesia and Taiwan) accounted for more than 70 percent of the world total production.

A low value-to-weight ratio for the transportation of cement favored regionally based mining, production and distribution. The geographic reach of a given plant at an inland location was roughly circular, with the edge of the circle demarcated by the point at which the combined production and transportation costs of deliveries would break even, based on current market prices. Any deliveries outside of this "natural market" would result in a loss to the company. For plants located along railway lines and waterways, the reach was extended along these corridors, as shipments by sea and rail were more economical than truckbased transportation.

The natural market for cement was not fixed, but fluctuated with changes in market prices and conditions. During periods of high demand, the delivery range tended to shrink as producers found markets closer to production facilities, thereby increasing margins. Under such circumstances, producers charged customers "phantom freight," the difference between the cost of transporting cement and the price actually charged to customers. Since customers paid the same rates, regardless of their distance from the cement plant, customers closer to the plant tended to pay higher phantom freight. In contrast, during periods of lower demand, cement producers needed to extend their reach in order to find buyers and maximize capacity utilization, thereby offsetting the high fixed costs associated with cement kilns.[6] Under low-demand conditions, producers practiced what was termed "freight absorption," charging less to customers than actual transportation costs.

Despite the high cost of transportation, regionally diversified producers were considered more competitive, as they could shift distribution to areas of higher demand when local demand was depressed. When natural markets of company plants overlapped, production was simply transferred to customers within the higher demand market. Shifting deliveries to higher demand markets allowed geographically diverse producers to maximize plant utilization.

In most countries, the cement industry was highly fragmented with numerous regional and national players. In the 1990s, producers in most countries began to consolidate. Three companies emerged as leading multinational producers, namely Holderbank of

FIGURE 1

Top Five Cement Producers (Millions of Metric TONS-MMT)
Source: Lafarge Group.

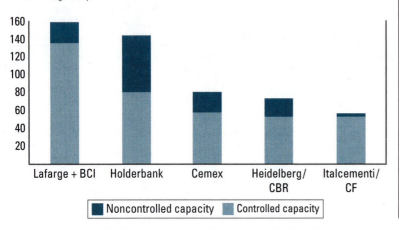

Switzerland,[7] Lafarge Group of France[8] and Cemex of Mexico (see Figure 1). All three were engaged in significant acquisitions, especially in less developed countries where industry growth was expected to outpace industrialized countries (see Table 1).

Cemex S.A. de C.V.

Cemex was founded in 1906, in the northern industrial city of Monterrey, Mexico. The company expanded rapidly in the 1970s on the back of Mexico's oil boom, and entered into numerous unrelated industries, such as hotels and chemical plants. In the early 1980s, an economic crisis forced the company to shed unrelated businesses and instead focus on its core product—cement.

In the latter half of the 1980s, Cemex acquired several large Mexican competitors to become the leading cement producer in Mexico. Residential consumers of bagged cement accounted for a large portion of sales in Mexico, where more than half of all homes were constructed by homeowners rather than professional contractors. As a result, bagged cement accounted for approximately 75 percent of private-sector demand. Unlike most industrialized countries, where cement was considered a commodity product, Cemex had established strong brand loyalty within its home market, based on differences in quality and service. Branded bags of cement were sold through 5,500 regional distributors.[9]

In 1999, Cemex operated 15 plants and 74 distribution centers in Mexico, accounting for 44 percent of Cemex's total worldwide sales. The company's Tepeaca plant, completed in 1995 at a cost of US$314 million, was the largest and most advanced in North America, with a capacity of 3.2 million tons. Cemex also operated 1,140 ready-mix delivery trucks, which served commercial and government customers. Exports, which accounted for 16 percent of Mexican revenues, were primarily destined for the United States (47 percent), the Caribbean (30 percent), and Central America and South America (23 percent).

Cemex used a variety of energy sources, including oil, natural gas and petcoke,[10] and was often able to shift from one source of fuel to another depending on fluctuations in price. The company had a 20-year energy contract with Pemex, a state-owned oil company, to supply the company with petcoke.

Cemex summarized its mission as follows:

> To serve the global building needs of its customers and build value for its stakeholders by becoming the world's most efficient and profitable multinational cement company. Cemex's strategy is to focus on and leverage its core cement and ready-mix concrete franchises in the international markets it serves, primarily concentrate on the world's most dynamic markets, where the demand for housing, roads and other needed infrastructure is greatest, and maintain high growth by applying free cash flow toward selective investments that further its geographic diversification.[11]

ANTI-DUMPING. In 1986, Cemex entered into a 20-year joint venture with Southdown, Inc. to market Cemex cement and clinker in the southern United States. The joint venture, known as Sunbelt Cement, paid management fees to Southdown and split the remaining earnings equally between the partners. On September 8, 1989, Cemex purchased Southdown's share of the joint venture and began operating Sunbelt as a subsidiary of Cemex. The properties included distribution terminals, ready-mix plants and a fleet of 360 ready-mix trucks in Texas, California and Arizona. "Southdown complained that Cemex gradually reduced the joint venture's management fees, and increased its imported cement price in order to squeeze the profits of the joint venture, and therefore of Southdown."[12]

Two and half weeks after the dissolution of the partnership, Southdown filed a dumping suit against Mexican cement producers. The retaliatory action proved successful when the U.S. International Trade Commission imposed anti-dumping duties of 58 percent on Cemex imports, beginning in 1990. The commission ruled that Mexican producers received unfair subsidies from the Mexican government in the form of lower oil prices, which had resulted in material harm to U.S. producers through the loss of market share. Cemex maintained that U.S. producers, such as Southdown, had been responsible for marketing the cement and, therefore, determined the local market price, which was often higher for Mexican cement. In fact, U.S. producers relied on imports to supplement their domestic production and actively sought out foreign producers to supply them with additional cement. As a result, when Mexican imports into Florida were all but eliminated in 1991, imports from Venezuela surged 152 percent, as suppliers sought new sources to meet increasing local demand.[13]

Cemex partially bypassed the anti-dumping action by adding domestic production capacity in 1994 when it purchased the plant in Balcones, Texas from Lafarge for $100 million.[14] At the time, it was considered to be the most advanced cement plant in the United States. By 1999, the Sunbelt Group, which accounted for 11 percent of total company sales, had one plant with an annual capacity of 910,000 tons, 530 ready-mix trucks, 48 ready-mix concrete plants and 13 cement terminals.

EUROPEAN EXPANSION. In the wake of the anti-dumping ruling in the United States, Cemex decided to look across the Atlantic for further expansion opportunities. In July 1992, Cemex acquired Spain's two largest cement companies for $1.85 billion.[15] The largest, Compañía Valenciana de Cementos, became the holding company for all of Cemex's future international acquisitions. Following the acquisition, Cemex merged its two Spanish subsidiaries, reduced staff, closed all but one of the 19 administrative offices and implemented various technological and operational improvements. By 1999, operating margins had increased to 32.5 percent, as compared with 6.85 percent in 1992. Cemex CEO, Lorenzo Zambrano, noted:

> For Spaniards, the idea of a Mexican company coming to Spain and changing top management, 500

years after the conquest of Mexico, was unthinkable. They said a Mexican company couldn't manage in Europe. But we increased our operating margin in Spain by more than three times in three years. We made that company much better than before.[16]

In 1999, Spain represented 15 percent of Cemex net sales, with more than 72 percent of company exports destined for the United States.

CEMEX LATIN AMERICA. The company's most significant expansion thrust began later in the 1990s, when Cemex acquired producers in Venezuela (1994), the Dominican Republic (1995), Colombia (1996), the Philippines (1997), Indonesia (1998), Costa Rica (1999), Chile (1999) and Egypt (1999). In almost every case, Cemex initially became a minority shareholder and within one year increased its stake to become the controlling shareholder. Cemex was the largest cement producer in most of these countries and typically owned and operated its own mines, trucks and port facilities (see Table 3). By comparison, Holderbank obtained about 36 percent of its sales from Europe, 26 percent from Latin America, 22 percent from North America, and eight percent each from Asia-Pacific and Africa-Middle East.

The company's expansion in emerging markets coincided with the Mexican peso crisis of December 1994. In the period preceding the 1994 election, the Mexican government failed to take a number of potentially unpopular fiscal decisions that were needed to maintain the stability of Mexico's economy. Despite the risk of a peso devaluation, the government continued to offer artificially low interest rates. The peso was instead supported through foreign reserves, which fell by more than $7 billion in only one month. In December 1994, the new government announced that it would maintain the previous government's fiscal policy, and investors became concerned about the government's ability to meet its debt obligations. The resulting currency flight to U.S. dollars caused a major devaluation of the peso. This was followed by stock market declines and devaluations across most of Latin America.

Cemex, like most Mexican companies, was severely affected by the peso crisis, as most of the company's dollar-denominated debt was being financed by peso-denominated domestic cash flows. With 50 percent of company revenues generated from Spanish and other foreign subsidiaries, Cemex, however, turned the crisis to its advantage. Instead of liquidating assets in order to pay off foreign debt obligations, Cemex used

TABLE 3

Cemex Global Operations (as of December 31, 1999)

	% of Sales	% of total assets	Prod. Capacity (MMT)	# of Plants
Mexico	47.3	42.2	27.2	18
United States	12.2	5.0	1.2	4
Venezuela & Dominican Republic	13.7	11.4	5.0	4
Colombia	3.7	7.2	4.8	5
Central America and the Caribbean	3.6	2.7	2.0	8
Spain	16.6	17.4	10.4	8
Egypt	0.3	5.3	4.0	1
Philippines	2.6	6.8	5.8	3
Indonesia	2.0	5.0[17]	4	
Total	100.0	100.0	65.4	55

Source: Company files.

overseas cash flows to acquire other Latin American producers at discounted prices.[18]

A few months before the peso crisis hit, Cemex launched its Latin America expansion with the purchase of a majority stake in Vencemos, Venezuela's leading cement producer, for $550 million.[19] The Venezuelan market, which had been dominated by three local producers, all but collapsed following the demise of the Venezuelan banking system, which led to a national economic crisis beginning in 1989. Over the next several years, domestic producers attempted to steal market share from competitors by engaging in predatory pricing. As a result, Vencemos posted losses of $117 million in 1994. A few months after the Cemex purchase, Lafarge and Holderbank purchased the remaining two Venezuelan producers.[20]

Cemex reorganized the company and refocused efforts on the export market. Within 18 months, Vencemos revenues increased significantly, while margins more than tripled.[21] The company's relatively low energy costs made it the lowest cost producer in the Cemex Group. In 1999, more than half of the company's revenues were derived from exports to the United States and the Caribbean, while Cemex's Venezuelan operations contributed approximately nine percent to Cemex Group revenues.

The company's next foray into the region came with the purchase of Cementos Nacionales, the leading cement producer in the Dominican Republic. As demand in that country exceeded supply, Cementos Nacionales became a net importer of Cemex cement. In 1999, Cemex was making capital investments in its Dominican operations in order to increase distribution capacity. Net sales represented four percent of Cemex Group totals. An additional three percent of net sales came from the company's operations in Panama and Costa Rica, which primarily served the Central American market.

In May 1996, after nearly a year of legal wrangling with local industry groups that wanted to keep the Mexican giant out, Cemex acquired majority stakes in Colombian producers, Cementos Diamante and Cementos Samper, for $600 million. Cemex merged the administration of the two companies and implemented a number of technological and operational upgrades. A protracted civil war, however, prevented the type of economic recovery seen in other parts of Latin America in the late 1990s. Hence, Colombia represented less than four percent of Cemex net sales in 1999, and had no significant exports.

In 1997, Cemex began to turn its attention to southeast Asia. From the 1960s through to 1997, the "Asian Miracle" produced regional economic growth that was three times greater than Latin America, and resulted in a quadrupling of average real income, while construction, and hence cement consumption, soared in tandem. "Between 1992 and 1997, Thailand alone built nearly three times Britain's total cement capacity."[22]

In 1997, however, the miracle came to an abrupt end, as local markets, beginning with Thailand, collapsed and currencies went into a steep decline against the U.S. dollar. "The crisis stemmed from excessive short-term borrowing that led to economic overheating. Problems were made worse by fixed exchange rates, inadequate financial systems, cronyism, corruption and inadequate political responses."[23] With construction at a standstill, cement consumption all but collapsed in 1997 and 1998.

As with the 1994 to 1995 peso crisis, Cemex saw the economic crisis in southeast Asia as an opportunity for further expansion. Currency devaluations produced dollar-denominated costs well below those of developed countries. Thai cement, which cost only $12 to $15 per ton to produce, could be shipped to the United States for an additional cost of $30 per ton, and sold in the U.S. market for more than $70 dollars per ton.[24] The crisis created a unique opportunity for foreign producers to acquire domestic firms at depressed prices. By 1999, multinational ownership of Asian cement companies had increased to 60 percent of total regional capacity, up from 20 percent in 1997.[25]

Cemex began its Asian acquisitions with a 30 percent interest in Philippine producer Rizal Cement for $93 million. In the wake of the Asia crisis, the Philippines found itself with an installed cement capacity that was more than double domestic consumption, while cement prices fell to an eight-year low. Rizal had two plants with a total capacity of 2.8 million tons. In January and February of 1999, Cemex increased its stake in Rizal by another 40 percent for $103 million, while acquiring another Philippine producer, APO Cement, for $400 million.[26] The combined capacity of these two producers provided Cemex with nationwide coverage, including access to that country's major cities. Competition came from Holderbank, Lafarge and Blue Circle, all of which had major operations in the Philippines. In 1999, the company's Philippine operations contributed approximately two percent to Cemex Group sales.

The next Asian acquisition was Indonesia's Semen Gresik, which represented Cemex's largest installed capacity outside of Mexico at 20.3 million tons per annum.[27] Even though Semen Gresik was an Indonesian state-owned company, the Asian economic crisis threatened its very survival. Cemex was the first foreign company to invest in the cement industry in Indonesia when, in 1998, it purchased 25 percent of the company for approximately $200 million. As a result, Indonesia's annual cement exports more than quadrupled from less than two million tons in 1997 to more than eight million tons in 1999. Meanwhile, Indonesia remained one of the two largest cement markets in southeast Asia, accounting for 24 percent of regional consumption.[28]

Cemex's most recent major acquisition came with the $319-million purchase of a 77 percent interest in Assiut Cement (Assiut), the largest cement producer in Egypt with an installed capacity of four million tons. Due to government-imposed price controls, cement prices in Egypt had not been affected by either the peso crisis or the Asia crisis. Some 95 percent of Assiut's production was sold in bags to domestic consumers. Cemex planned to increase capacity to five million tons within two years, and build a new 1.5-million-ton capacity plant in southern Egypt.

In 2000, Cemex was investigating investment opportunities in Thailand, Malaysia and India. Jose Domene, president of Cemex's international division boasted, "We can buy any cement company in the world and turn it around."[29] In order to be considered by Cemex as a possible acquisition target, a company had to fit within the following basic criteria:

- Value creation must be principally driven by factors that the company can influence, particularly the application of Cemex's management and turnaround expertise.
- Acquisition must maintain or improve Cemex's financial position.
- The investment must offer superior long-term returns.

In June 2000, Cemex employed 24,000 people worldwide and had an equity market valuation of $5.8 billion. Of the company's 39 majority-owned productions plants, 33 used the more modern dry process. More than 80 percent of the company's $4.5 billion debt was denominated in U.S. dollars.

In the 1980s, Mexico remained an underdeveloped country with poor transportation and telecommunications infrastructures. As a result, it was impossible for Cemex to provide reliable on-time delivery of cement to construction projects. Average delivery time to work sites was approximately three hours, which irked many construction companies that had to pay for hundreds of workers to sit idly by while they waited for cement trucks to arrive.[30]

EXHIBIT 2

Cemex Financial Summary (for years ending December 31) (in millions of dollars, except percentage amounts)

	1999	1998	1997	1996	1995	1994	1993
REVENUES	$4,828	$4,315	$3,788	$3,365	$2,564	$2,101	$2,897
Gross Profit	2,138	1,820	1,467	1,325	1,000	889	1,150
Net Income	973	803	761	977	759	376	522
Cash & Investments	326	407	380	409	355	484	326
Net Plant & Equipment	6,922	6,142	6,006	5,743	4,939	4,093	4,407
Short-term and Long-term Debt	4,371	4,242	4,618	4,769	3,904	3,764	3,550
Stockholders' Equity	5,182	3,887	3,515	3,337	2,878	2,832	3,225
EBITDA	1,791	1,485	1,193	1,087	815	719	914
EBITDA Margin %	37.1	34.4	31.5	32.3	31.8	34.2	31.6
Operating Margin %	29.8	27.3	23.6	23.8	23.9	26.9	24.4

Source: Cemex S.A. de C.V.

In 1985, Lorenzo Zambrano, a grandson of the company's founder, became president and CEO of Cemex. Zambrano, who held an engineer degree from Instituto Tecnologico y de Estudios Superiores de Monterrey (ITESM), Mexico's leading technical university (the Mexican equivalent to the Massachusetts Institute of Technology or MIT), and an MBA from Stanford, immediately began to implement a technology-centered restructuring of the company. He visited several foreign companies who were leaders in transportation logistics, including Exxon and Federal Express in the United States, borrowing whatever ideas he believed could be adapted to the cement industry.

In order to bypass Mexico's unreliable phone system, in the early 1990s, the company began using global positioning satellites and a digital control center to track orders and co-ordinate deliveries.

> With trucks acting less like trucks and more like fast, switchable packets within a data network, Cemex could quickly dispatch the right one to pick up and deliver a particular grade of cement, reroute trucks when chaotic traffic conditions demanded it, and redirect deliveries from one customer to another as last minute changes were made. Gradually, Cemex reduced the three-hour delivery window to 20 minutes.[31]

Cemex eventually employed its information technology systems throughout its worldwide operations, thereby significantly reducing costs and increasing reliability. By the end of the 1990s, Cemex was the most technologically advanced among its many competitors. Jose Domene explained:

> When we take over new operations, the first thing we do is install a satellite feed so we can incorporate them into our information system. I'm always surprised that our competitors have next to no computers. It means that their headquarters has only last month's operating figures. I can look at last night's at the touch of a button.[32]

In 2000, Cemex introduced an Internet-based strategy known as Cx Networks that would allow customers to place and track orders on the Internet, and which Cemex hoped would eventually save the company approximately $120 million annually.

Southdown, Inc.

Southdown, Inc. was one of the largest cement producers in the United States, and among the few that remained American-owned (see Table 4). In the early 1970s, most U.S. cement producers were relatively small independent companies. Many ran older inefficient plants that relied heavily on low oil prices to keep variable costs low. An oil crisis in the early 1970s, however, sent costs soaring, which resulted in most U.S. producers being taken over by European companies that had already implemented cost-saving upgrades in their home markets. Toward the close of the 1980s, approximately two-thirds of U.S. cement capacity was in the hands of European cement multinationals.[33]

TABLE 4

U.S. Cement Industry (1999)

Company Name	Rank	(000 TONS)	% Total
Holnam, Inc.	1	10,699	12.7
Southdown, Inc.	2	10,109	12.0
Lafarge Corporation	3	6,935	8.2
Ash Grove Cement Company	4	5,648	6.7
CBR-HCI Construction Materials	5	5,503	6.5
Blue Circle, Inc.	6	4,386	5.2
Essroc Corporation	7	4,135	4.9
Lone Star Industries, Inc.	8	3,953	4.7
Texas Industries, Inc.	9	3,399	4.0
California Portland Cement	10	3,317	3.9
Total Top Ten		58,084	68.7
Others		26,409	31.3
Total Industry		**84,493**	**100.0**

Source: Southdown, Inc.

In 1988, Clarence C. Comer became president and CEO of Southdown. The following year, he became chairman of an ad hoc committee of U.S. cement producers and labor unions that successfully petitioned the U.S. government to impose anti-dumping duties against Cemex and other importers.[34] In 1990, the U.S. International Trade Commission imposed anti-dumping duties of between 40 and 100 percent against Mexico, Venezuela and Japan. As a result, cement imports declined from 17 percent in 1989 to eight percent in 1992.

In 1999, the cement industry in the United States was commodity-driven and very competitive, with numerous national and regional players. Few ready-mix operators had more than 20 mixers or revenues in excess of $3 million, and the country's 5,845 quarries were in the hands of more than 3,800 companies.

Beginning in 1990, the United States entered a period of recession. Cement prices and demand began to decline, and Southdown posted annual losses in excess of $40 million for each of the next three years. To make matters worse, the company's environmental subsidiary, which burned hazardous waste in Southdown's cement kilns, was facing two lawsuits from the U.S. Environmental Protection Agency for exceeding certified feed rates. In 1992, the company began to liquidate its hazardous-waste disposal facilities.

In an effort to reduce costs, the company began to invest heavily in technology, retiring or upgrading inefficient wet plants with newer dry-process technology. Instead of mixing crushed limestone with water before heating, the new process recycled heat from the kiln to a preheating stage, thereby significantly reducing energy consumption. By 1998, approximately 88 percent of the company's cement clinker was processed using the dry/preheater technology, compared with only 52 percent for the U.S. industry.[35]

As the United States emerged from the recession of the early 1990s, Southdown once again became profitable. By upgrading its plants, the company was also able to achieve productivity improvements of between 50 and 100 percent. Ten years after Comer took the helm of Southdown, the company had more than doubled its capacity while maintaining employment levels at just under 4,000 people. In 1999, the company spent $161 million upgrading its main plant in California, making it the largest in the country with a capacity of 3.1 million tons per year.[36]

Southdown operated 12 cement plants with a total clinker capacity of 10 million tons[37] per year (see Table 4). The company also operated its own mines, where it produced raw material for its cement plants as well as aggregates and specialty mineral products. At the other end of the production cycle, Southdown also operated 616 ready-mix trucks, 66 batch plants and 12 concrete-block plants. Transportation was typically conducted by rail or sea.[38] In addition, the company constructed highway safety devices, such as traffic signals, and had a lawn and garden division that marketed aggregates through retail garden centers.

In recent years Southdown continued to grow revenue while decreasing costs through the implementation of newer technology. The company had also benefited from a technology-led economic boom, which was reflected in high employment levels and increased investment in construction. Additionally, as the U.S. federal government committed significant new funds to upgrade the federal highway system, U.S. demand for cement continued to exceed available supply (see Figure 2). As a result, imports rose from 18 percent in 1997 to 31 percent in 1999.

Clarence Comer could not understand why his company's recent successes were not being translated into higher valuations on the stock market. While his company had more than doubled earnings over the past year and was virtually debt-free, Southdown's shares had declined steadily from $74 per share in mid-1998 to just above $45 per share at the end of 1999

(see Exhibits 3, 4 and 5). Meanwhile, the NASDAQ Composite Index had nearly tripled in value over the same period.

The Southdown Offer[39]

Throughout the 1990s, Comer met with Lorenzo Zambrano from time to time to discuss anti-dumping litigation, for which Southdown was a plaintiff and Cemex a defendant. In 1999, the two companies discussed the formation of a joint venture to pool ready-mix resources in California, and in 2000 Southdown withdrew its support for the continuation of anti-dumping tariffs (see Exhibit 6). Comer also expressed an interest in selling Southdown to Cemex, but Zambrano did not at first appear interested.

On April 5, 2000, Zambrano met with Comer at Southdown's Houston headquarters. The purpose of the meeting was to discuss a price at which Zambrano would be interested in purchasing Southdown. Zambrano replied that "At a price of approximately $65 per share, Cemex would be interested." That brought the total cost to over $2.5 billion, which would have made it by far the largest purchase ever undertaken by Cemex.[40] Comer, however, believed that Cemex's offer was too low, given the company's performance and growth prospects. It also appeared that

FIGURE 2

U.S. Demand Forecast—Portland Cement

Source: Southdown, Inc.

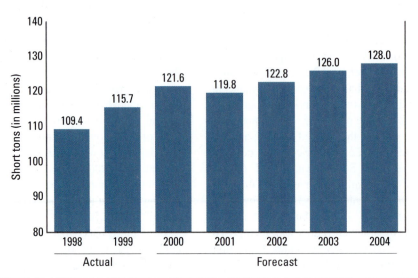

FIGURE 3

Map of Southdown Operations

Source: Southdown.

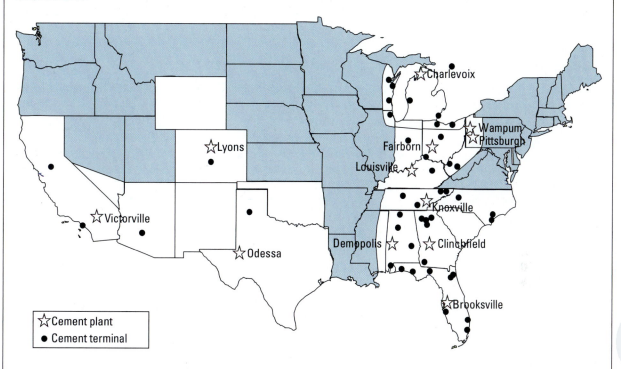

EXHIBIT 3

Southdown Consolidated Earnings (for years ending December 31) (in millions of dollars, except per share amounts not listed)

	1999	1998	1997
REVENUES	$1,271.8	$1,184.7	$1,095.2
Costs and expenses:			
Operating	774.7	717.6	698.3
Depreciation, depletion and amortization	74.6	71.1	64.1
Selling and marketing	29.4	27.8	24.7
General and administrative	65.8	71.4	65.6
Acquisition charge (credit)	(1.5)	75.2	—
Other income, net	(11.0)	(4.8)	(6.7)
	932.0	958.3	846.0
Earnings from continuing operations before interest, income taxes and minority interest	339.8	226.4	249.2
Interest income	4.1	5.9	3.3
Interest expense, net of amounts capitalized	(13.7)	(16.5)	(15.5)

(continued)

EXHIBIT 3 *(Continued)*

	1999	1998	1997
Earnings from continuing operations before income taxes and minority interest	330.2	215.8	237.0
Income tax expense	(112.0)	(86.2)	(78.3)
Earnings from continuing operations before minority interest	218.2	129.6	158.7
Minority interest, net of income taxes	(4.8)	(4.6)	(5.0)
Earnings from continuing operations	213.4	125.0	153.7
Loss from discontinued operations, net of income taxes	(1.0)	(1.6)	–
Extraordinary charge, net of income taxes	(9.2)	–	–
Net earnings	203.2	123.4	153.7
Dividends on preferred stock	–	–	(2.5)
Earnings attributable to common stock	$ 203.2	$ 123.4	$ 151.2

Source: Southdown.

EXHIBIT 4

Southdown, Inc. Consolidated Balance Sheet (for years ending December 31) (in millions of dollars)

	1999	1998
ASSETS		
Current assets:		
Cash and cash equivalents	$ 21.8	$ 143.8
Short-term investments		14.8
Accounts and notes receivable, net	129.4	120.0
Inventories	135.4	107.7
Prepaid expenses and other	20.0	18.4
Total current assets	306.6	404.7
Property, plant and equipment, less accumulated depreciation, depletion and amortization	920.3	819.9
Goodwill	134.2	105.5
Other long-term assets	69.6	70.3
	$1,430.7	$1,400.4
LIABILITIES AND SHAREHOLDERS' EQUITY		
Current liabilities:		
Current maturities of long-term debt	$ 0.4	$ 0.6
Accounts payable and accrued liabilities	146.8	139.3
Total current liabilities	147.2	139.9
Long-term debt	165.7	167.3
Deferred income taxes	131.1	139.4
Minority interest in consolidated joint venture	35.9	27.7

EXHIBIT 4 *(Continued)*

	1999	1998
Long-term portion of postretirement benefit obligation	87.7	91.5
Other long-term liabilities and deferred credits	30.0	30.4
	597.6	596.2
Commitments and contingent liabilities		
Shareholders' equity		
Common stock, $1.25 par value, 200,000,000 shares authorized, 39,987,000 and 35,904,000 shares issued and outstanding, respectively, in 1999 and 39,849,000 and 38,683,000 shares issued and outstanding, respectively, in 1998	50.0	49.8
Capital in excess of par value	376.3	370.6
Reinvested earnings	612.2	431.6
Currency translation adjustment	(1.2)	(1.5)
Treasury stock, at cost	(204.2)	(46.3)
	833.1	804.2
	$1,430.7	$1,400.4

Source: Southdown.

EXHIBIT 5

Southdown, Inc. Consolidated Cash Flow (for years ending December 31) (in millions of dollars)

	1999	1998	1997
Operating Activities:			
Earnings from continuing operations	213.4	125.0	153.7
Adjustments to reconcile earnings from continuing operations to cash provided by operating activities:			
Depreciation, depletion and amortization	74.6	71.1	64.1
Deferred income tax expense	1.9	6.2	14.5
Other non-cash charges	0.8	9.7	3.0
Changes in operating assets and liabilities:			
(Increase) decrease in accounts and notes receivable	(4.0)	(11.1)	6.1
Increase in inventories	(22.6)	(10.2)	(1.9)
(Increase) decrease in prepaid expenses and other	(2.6)	2.6	–
Increase in other long-term assets	(4.7)	(11.2)	(6.1)
Increase in accounts payable and accrued liabilities	8.6	33.4	0.5
Decrease in other liabilities and deferred credits	(4.2)	(5.1)	(0.6)
Other adjustments	(1.0)	2.6	4.7
Net cash used in discontinued operations	(1.4)	(0.4)	(1.0)
Net cash provided by operating activities	258.8	212.6	237.0
Investing Activities:			

(continued)

EXHIBIT 5 *(Continued)*

	1999	1998	1997
Additions to property, plant and equipment	(152.4)	(116.4)	(94.6)
Acquisitions, net of cash acquired	(69.4)	(6.0)	(30.2)
Purchase of short-term investments	(14.8)	(18.7)	(6.9)
Maturity of short-term investments	29.6	7.9	14.7
Proceeds from asset sales	16.2	13.9	8.6
Other investing activities	(0.2)	(0.1)	–
Net cash used in investing activities	(191.0)	(119.4)	(108.4)
Financing Activities:			
Additions to long-term debt	122.0	30.0	–
Reductions in long-term debt	(123.6)	(63.6)	(7.2)
Purchase of treasury stock	(159.0)	–	(59.9)
Dividends	(22.6)	(19.4)	(22.9)
Contributions from minority partner	10.0	–	
Distributions to minority partner	(9.3)	(7.0)	(7.8)
Premium on early extinguishment of debt	(11.5)	–	
Other financing activities	4.2	11.7	(2.3)
Net cash used in financing activities	(189.8)	(48.3)	(100.1)
Net increase (decrease) in cash and cash equivalents	(122.0)	44.9	28.5
Cash and cash equivalents at the beginning of the year	143.8	98.9	70.4
Cash and cash equivalents at the end of the year	$ 21.8	$ 143.8	$ 98.9

Source: Southdown.

EXHIBIT 6

Anti-Dumping Letter

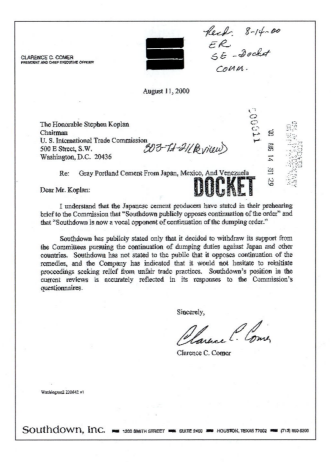

the valuation had not given proper consideration to an estimated $60 million in annual cost savings through the integration of Southdown into Cemex's existing U.S. assets.

Toward the close of the summer of 1999, it was clear that the U.S. cement industry would not meet forecasted demand. Delays in federal highways projects and unusually wet weather conditions resulted in a moderate decline in Southdown's quarterly revenues. At the same time, costs were rising as energy shortages hit the southern states, leading to an 11 percent decline in operating margins. Southdown strongly asserted that decline was only temporary. After all, the U.S. economy was still growing at a record pace, and highway infrastructure projects were expected to get back on track in 2001.

TABLE 5

Annual Cement Production Capacity ('000 tons)

Plant Location	12/31/96	12/31/99	2001*
Victorville, CA	1,666	2,050	3,100
Charlevoix, MI	1,400	1,540	1,690
Kosmosdale, KY	791	875	1,575
Brooksville, FL	1,304	1,460	1,460
Demopolis, AL	840	990	990
Wampum, PA	720	750	910
Clinchfield, GA	660	835	835
Knoxville, TN	729	830	830
Fairborn, OH	650	750	750
Odessa, TX	538	600	600
Lyons, CO	448	575	575
Pittsburgh, PA	408	408	408
Total Production	**10,154**	**11,663**	**13,723**

*Pro Forma
Source: Southdown.

Glossary of Terms

Aggregate: Inert solid bodies such as crushed rock, sand and gravel.

Batch Plant: Equipment used for introducing the ingredients for a batch of concrete materials into the mixer.

Clinker: The material that emerges from the cement kiln after burning. The dark, porous nodules are ground with a small amount of gypsum to produce cement.

Concrete: A hard compact building material formed when a mixture of cement, sand, gravel and water undergoes hydration.

Dry Process: In the manufacture of cement, the process in which the raw materials are ground, conveyed, blended and stored in a dry condition. Exhaust from the kiln is recycled into a preheater tower where raw materials are precalcinated. This eliminates the need for adding water.[1]

Kiln: High-temperature oven.

Limestone: Mineral rock of calcium carbonate.

Portland Cement: A commercial product which when mixed with water alone or in combination with sand, stone or similar materials, has the property of combining with water, slowly, to form a hard solid mass. Physically, Portland Cement is a finely pulverized clinker produced by burning mixtures containing lime, iron, alumina and silica at high temperature and indefinite proportions, and then intergrinding gypsum to give the properties desired.

Ready-Mixed Concrete: Concrete manufactured for delivery to a purchaser in a plastic and unhardened state.

Wet Process: In the manufacture of cement, the process in which the raw materials are ground, blended, mixed and pumped while mixed with water; the wet process is chosen where raw materials are extremely wet and sticky, which would make drying before crushing and grinding difficult. This process requires greater energy inputs than dry-processing, in order to evaporate water during production.

---

1 For an interactive tour and description of a dry-process cement plant, see the Portland Cement Association Web site's "Virtual Plant Tour" at www.portcement.org.

Endnotes

1. This case has been written on the basis of published sources only. Consequently, the interpretation and perspectives presented in this case are not necessarily those of Cemex or any of its employees.

2. Southdown's share price had reached a high of $74 in 1998, before declining. It had ranged between $45 and $58 in the fourth quarter of 1999, and between $48 and $60 in the first quarter of 2000. Based on 1999 earnings, this gave Southdown a price-earnings ratio of just over 10.

3. "The Year in Review," *Southdown Annual Report*, 1999.

4. Worldwide, Cemex distributed approximately 70 percent of its cement in bags, compared to five percent in the United States.

5. "Concrete Solution," *The Industry Standard*, August 28, 2000.

6. H. Dumez, and A. Jeunemaitre (2000), *Understanding and Regulating the Market at a Time of Globalization*, St. Martin's Press, New York.

7. Capacity of 90 million tons, 1999 revenues approx. $6.8 billion.

8. Capacity of 64.3 million tons, 1999 revenues approx. $10 billion.

9. Ravi Sarathy, "Cemex(A); Case 1-1: Managing the Global Corporation," in J. De la Torre et al., *Case Studies in Strategy & Management*, Irwin/McGraw-Hill, 2001.

10. Petcoke: a petroleum coke made from a solid or fixed carbon substance that remains after the distribution of hydrocarbons in petroleum. It may be used as a fuel source in the production of cement.

11. Cemex 2000 Annual Report.

12. H. Dumez, and A. Jeunemaitre (2000), *Understanding and Regulating the Market at a Time of Globalization*, St. Martin's Press, New York.

13. Ibid.

14. "Emerging Multinationals," *The Economist*, May 21, 1994.

15. Ravi Sarathy, "Cemex(A); Case 1-1: Managing the Global Corporation," in J. De la Torre et al., *Case Studies in Strategy & Management*, Irwin/McGraw-Hill, 2001.

16. "Well-Built Success," *Industry Week*, May 5, 1997.

17. Total capacity adjusted for 25 percent of the 20.3 million tons total by Semen Gresik, although Cemex had been given management control for 100 percent of production.

18. "Winners? In Mexico?" *Global Finance*, May 1995.

19. "Emerging Multinationals," *The Economist*, May 21, 1994.

20. H. Dumez, and A. Jeunemaitre (2000), *Understanding and Regulating the Market at a Time of Globalization*, St. Martin's Press, New York.

21. "Well-Built Success," *Industry Week*, May 5, 1997.

22. "Bagged Cement," *The Economist*, June 19, 1999.

23. Robert Garran, *Tigers Tamed : The End of the Asian Miracle*, University of Hawaii Press, 1998.

24. "Bagged Cement," *The Economist*, June 19, 1999.

25. Ibid.

26. APO's only plant had a capacity of three million tons.

27. The 20.3-million-ton capacity included the Indonesian government share. Cemex, however, had management responsibility for the entire operation, including trading access to Semen Gresik's full production capacity.

28. "Mixing Salsa with Islam," *Latin Trade*, June 2000.

29. "Well-Built Success," *Industry Week*, May 5, 1997.

30. "Concrete Solution," *The Industry Standard*, August 28, 2000.

31. Ibid.

32. "Well-Built Success," *Industry Week*, May 5, 1997.

33. H. Dumez, and A. Jeunemaitre (2000), *Understanding and Regulating the Market at a Time of Globalization*, St. Martin's Press, New York.

34. Ibid.

35. Plant Information Summary, *Portland Cement Association*, December 31, 1998. Updated for 1999 and 2000 expansion projects and the Victorville expansion.

36. "Southdown: Concrete Results," *Forbes*, January 10, 2000.

37. Equivalent to 11.7 million tons of cement.

38. Southdown owned two ocean freighters.

39. Adapted from Cena Acquisition Corporation's *Offer to Purchase* Southdown, Inc., October 5, 2000.

40. At the time, Southdown had a book value of $971.8 million or $27.07 per share.

David B. Yoffie

For more than a century, Coca-Cola and Pepsi-Cola vied for "throat share" of the world's beverage market. The most intense battles in the so-called cola wars were fought over the $66 billion carbonated soft drink (CSD) industry in the United States.[1] In a "carefully waged competitive struggle" that lasted from 1975 through the mid-1990s, both Coke and Pepsi achieved average annual revenue growth of around 10%, as both U.S. and worldwide CSD consumption rose steadily year after year.[2] According to Roger Enrico, former CEO of Pepsi:

> The warfare must be perceived as a continuing battle without blood. Without Coke, Pepsi would have a tough time being an original and lively competitor. The more successful they are, the sharper we have to be. If the Coca-Cola company didn't exist, we'd pray for someone to invent them. And on the other side of the fence, I'm sure the folks at Coke would say that nothing contributes as much to the present-day success of the Coca-Cola company than . . . Pepsi.[3]

That cozy relationship began to fray in the late 1990s, however, as U.S. per-capita CSD consumption declined slightly before reaching what appeared to be a plateau. In 2004, the average American drank a little more than 52 gallons of CSDs per year. At the same time, the two companies experienced their own distinct ups and downs, as Coke suffered several operational setbacks and as Pepsi charted a new, aggressive course in alternative beverages. Although their paths diverged, however, both companies began to modify their bottling, pricing, and brand strategies.

As the cola wars continued into the 21st century, Coke and Pepsi faced new challenges: Could they boost flagging domestic CSD sales? Would newly popular beverages provide them with new (and profitable) revenue streams? Was their era of sustained growth and profitability coming to a close, or was this slowdown just another blip in the course of the cola giants' long, enviable history?

Economics of the U.S. CSD Industry

Americans consumed 23 gallons of CSDs annually in 1970, and consumption grew by an average of 3%

per year over the next three decades. (See Exhibit 1—U.S. Beverage Industry Consumption Statistics.) Fueling this growth were the increasing availability of CSDs and the introduction of diet and flavored varieties. Declining real (inflation-adjusted) prices played a large role as well.[4] There were many alternatives to CSDs, including beer, milk, coffee, bottled water, juices, tea, powdered drinks, wine, sports drinks, distilled spirits, and tap water. Yet Americans drank more soda than any other beverage. Within the CSD category, the cola segment maintained its dominance, although its market share dropped from 71% in 1990 to 60% in 2004.[5] Non-cola CSDs included lemon/lime, citrus, pepper-type, orange, root beer, and other flavors. CSDs consisted of a flavor base (called "concentrate"), a sweetener, and carbonated water. The production and distribution of CSDs involved four major participants: concentrate producers, bottlers, retail channels, and suppliers.[6]

CONCENTRATE PRODUCERS. The concentrate producer blended raw material ingredients, packaged the mixture in plastic canisters, and shipped those containers to the bottler. To make concentrate for diet CSDs, concentrate makers often added artificial sweetener; with regular CSDs, bottlers added sugar or high-fructose corn syrup themselves. The concentrate manufacturing process involved little capital investment in machinery, overhead, or labor. A typical concentrate manufactur-

HARVARD|BUSINESS|SCHOOL
9-607-138

Professor David B. Yoffie and Research Associate Yusi Wang prepared the original version of this case, "Cola Wars Continue: Coke and Pepsi in the Twenty-First Century," HBS No. 702-442, which derives from earlier cases by Professor David B. Yoffie (HBS No. 702-442 and 794-055) and Professor Michael E. Porter (HBS No. 391-179). This version was prepared by Professor David B. Yoffie and Research Associate Michael Slind from published sources. HBS cases are developed solely as the basis for class discussion. Cases are not intended to serve as endorsements, sources of primary data, or illustrations of effective or ineffective management.

EXHIBIT 1

U.S. Beverage Industry Consumption Statistics

	1970	1975	1981	1985	1990	1994	1996	1998	2000	2002	2003	2004
Historical Carbonated Soft Drink Consumption												
Cases[a] (millions)	3,090	3,780	5,180	6,500	7,780	8,710	9,290	9,880	9,950	10,087	10,140	10,240
Gallons/capita	22.7	26.3	34.2	40.3	46.9	50.0	52.0	54.0	53.0	52.5	52.3	52.3
As share of total beverage consumption	12.4%	14.4%	18.7%	22.1%	25.7%	27.4%	28.5%	29.6%	29.0%	28.8%	28.7%	28.7%
U.S. Liquid Consumption Trends (gallons/capita)												
Carbonated soft drinks	22.7	26.3	34.2	40.3	46.9	50.0	52.0	54.0	53.0	52.5	52.3	52.3
Beer	22.8	21.8	20.6	24.0	24.0	22.4	21.8	21.8	21.8	21.8	21.7	21.6
Milk	18.5	21.6	24.3	25.0	24.2	23.0	22.7	22.0	21.3	20.7	20.4	20.1
Bottled water[b]	—	1.2	2.7	4.5	8.1	9.6	11.0	11.8	13.2	15.4	16.6	17.7
Coffee[c]	35.7	33	27.2	26.9	26.2	23.3	20.2	18.0	16.8	16.8	16.7	16.6
Juices	6.5	6.8	6.9	8.1	8.5	9.0	9.0	9.5	9.5	8.9	8.5	8.6
Tea[c]	5.2	7.3	7.3	7.3	7.0	7.1	6.9	6.9	7.0	7.0	7.0	7.0
Sports drinks[d]	—	—	—	—	—	1.2	1.5	1.9	2.2	2.6	3.0	3.5
Powdered drinks	—	4.8	6	6.2	5.4	4.8	4.8	3.7	3.0	2.4	2.5	2.6
Wine	1.3	1.7	2.1	2.4	2.0	1.7	1.8	1.9	1.9	2.0	2.1	2.1
Distilled spirits	1.8	2	2	1.8	1.5	1.3	1.2	1.2	1.2	1.3	1.3	1.3
Subtotal	114.5	126.5	133.3	146.5	153.8	153.3	152.2	152.7	150.9	151.4	152.1	153.4
Tap water/hybrids/all others	68	56	49.2	36.0	28.7	29.2	30.3	29.8	31.6	31.1	30.4	29.1
Total[e]	182.5	182.5	182.5	182.5	182.5	182.5	182.5	182.5	182.5	182.5	182.5	182.5

Source: Compiled from *Beverage Digest Fact Book 2001*, *The Maxwell Consumer Report*, Feb. 3, 1994; *Adams Liquor Handbook*, casewriter estimates; and *Beverage Digest*, *Beverage Digest Fact Book 2005*. Data for 1990 and afterward comes from *Beverage Digest Fact Book 2005*, which reports that some of that data has been "restated compared to previous editions of the Fact Book."

[a] One case is equivalent to 192 oz.

[b] Bottled water includes all packages, single-serve as well as bulk.

[c] For 1985 and afterward, coffee and tea data are based on a three-year moving average.

[d] For pre-1992 data, sports drinks are included in "Tap water/hybrids/all others."

[e] This analysis assumes that each person consumes, on average, one half-gallon of liquid per day.

ing plant cost about $25 million to $50 million to build, and one plant could serve the entire United States.[7]

A concentrate producer's most significant costs were for advertising, promotion, market research, and bottler support. Using innovative and sophisticated campaigns, they invested heavily in their trademarks over time. While concentrate producers implemented and financed marketing programs jointly with bottlers, they usually took the lead in developing those programs, particularly when it came to product development, market research, and advertising. They also took charge of negotiating "customer development agreements" (CDAs) with nationwide retailers such as Wal-Mart. Under a CDA, Coke or Pepsi offered funds for marketing and other purposes in exchange for shelf space. With smaller regional accounts, bottlers assumed a key role in developing such relationships, and paid an agreed-upon percentage—typically 50% or more—of promotional and advertising costs. Concentrate producers employed a large staff of people who worked with bottlers by supporting sales efforts, setting standards, and suggesting operational improvements. They also negotiated directly with their bottlers' major suppliers (especially sweetener and packaging makers) to achieve reliable supply, fast delivery, and low prices.[8]

Once a fragmented business that featured hundreds of local manufacturers, the U.S. soft drink industry had changed dramatically over time. Among national concentrate producers, Coca-Cola and Pepsi-Cola (the soft drink unit of PepsiCo) claimed a combined 74.8% of the U.S. CSD market in sales volume in 2004, followed by Cadbury Schweppes and Cott Corporation. (See Exhibit 2—U.S. Soft Drink Market Share by Case Volume. See also Exhibit 3—Financial Data for Coca-Cola, Pepsi-Cola, and Their Major Bottlers.) In addition, there were private-label manufacturers and several dozen other national and regional producers.

BOTTLERS. Bottlers purchased concentrate, added carbonated water and high-fructose corn syrup, bottled or canned the resulting CSD product, and delivered it to customer accounts. Coke and Pepsi bottlers offered "direct store door" (DSD) delivery, an arrangement whereby route delivery salespeople managed the CSD brand in stores by securing shelf space, stacking CSD products, positioning the brand's trademarked label, and setting up point-of-purchase or end-of-aisle displays. (Smaller national

brands, such as Shasta and Faygo, distributed through food store warehouses.) Cooperative merchandising agreements, in which retailers agreed to specific promotional activity and discount levels in exchange for a payment from a bottler, were another key ingredient of soft drink sales.

The bottling process was capital-intensive and involved high-speed production lines that were interchangeable only for products of similar type and packages of similar size. Bottling and canning lines cost from $4 million to $10 million each, depending on volume and package type. In 2005, Cott completed construction of a 40-million-case bottling plant in Fort Worth, Texas, at an estimated cost of $40 million.[9] But the cost of a large plant with four lines, automated warehousing, and a capacity of 40 million cases, could range as high as $75 million.[10] While a handful of such plants could theoretically provide enough capacity to serve the entire United States, Coke and Pepsi each required close to 100 plants to provide effective nationwide distribution.[11] For bottlers, packaging accounted for 40% to 45% of the cost of sales, concentrate for roughly the same amount, and sweeteners for 5% to 10%. Labor and overhead made up the remaining variable costs.[12] Bottlers also invested capital in trucks and distribution networks. Bottlers' gross profits routinely exceeded 40%, but operating margins were usually in the 7% to 9% range. (See Exhibit 4—Comparative Costs of a Typical U.S. Concentrate Producer and Bottler.)

The number of U.S. soft drink bottlers had fallen steadily, from more than 2,000 in 1970 to fewer than 300 in 2004.[13] Coke was the first concentrate producer to build a nationwide franchised bottling network, and Pepsi and Cadbury Schweppes followed suit. The typical franchised bottler owned a manufacturing and sales operation in an exclusive geographic territory, with rights granted in perpetuity by the franchiser. In the case of Coke, territorial rights did not extend to national fountain accounts, which the company handled directly. The original Coca-Cola franchise agreement, written in 1899, was a fixed-price contract that did not provide for renegotiation, even if ingredient costs changed. After considerable negotiation, often accompanied by bitter legal disputes, Coca-Cola amended the contract in 1921, 1978, and 1987. By 2003, more than 88% of Coke's U.S. volume was covered by its 1987 Master Bottler Contract, which granted Coke the right to determine concentrate price and other terms of sale.[14] Under

EXHIBIT 2

U.S. Soft Drink Market Share by Case Volume (percent)

	1966	1970	1975	1980	1985	1990	1995	2000	2004E
Coca-Cola Company									
Coke Classic	–	–	–	–	5.2	20.1	20.8	20.4	17.9
Coca-Cola	27.7	28.4	26.2	25.3	16.5	0.6	0.1	–	–
Diet Coke	–	–	–	–	6.8	9.3	8.8	8.7	9.7
Sprite and Diet Sprite	1.5	1.8	2.6	3.0	4.7	4.5	5.7	7.2	6.3
Caffeine Free Coke, Diet Coke, Tab	–	–	–	–	1.8	2.9	2.6	2.2	2.0
Fanta[a]	–	–	–	–	0.9	0.7	0.7	0.2	1.3
Barq's and Diet Barq's	–	–	–	–	–	–	0.2	1.2	1.2
Minute Maid brands	–	–	–	–	–	0.7	0.7	1.5	0.4
Tab	1.4	1.3	2.6	3.3	1.1	0.2	0.1	–	–
Others	2.8	3.2	3.9	4.3	2.5	2.1	2.6	2.6	4.3
Total	**33.4**	**34.7**	**35.3**	**35.9**	**39.5**	**41.1**	**42.3**	**44.1**	**43.1**
PepsiCo, Inc.									
Pepsi-Cola	16.1	17.0	17.4	20.4	19.3	17.6	15.0	13.6	11.5
Mountain Dew	1.4	0.9	1.3	3.3	3.1	3.9	5.7	7.2	6.3
Diet Pepsi	1.9	1.1	1.7	3.0	3.9	6.3	5.8	5.3	6.1
Sierra Mist	–		–	–	–	–	–	0.1	1.4
Diet Mountain Dew	–	–	–	–	–	0.5	0.7	0.9	1.3
Caffeine Free Pepsi, and Diet Pepsi	–	–	–	–	2.5	2.3	2.0	1.7	1.4
Mug Root Beer	–	–	–	–	–	0.3	0.3	0.8	0.7
Wild Cherry Pepsi (reg and diet)	–	–	–	–	–	–	0.2	0.5	0.6
Mountain Dew Code Red	–	–	–	–	–	–	–	–	0.4
Slice and Diet Slice	–	–	–	–	0.7	1.0	1.0	0.5	0.3
Others	1.0	0.8	0.7	1.1	0.8	0.5	0.2	0.8	1.7
Total	**20.4**	**19.8**	**21.1**	**27.8**	**30.3**	**32.4**	**30.9**	**31.4**	**31.7**
Cadbury Schweppes[b]									
Dr Pepper (all brands)	–	–	–	–	–	–	6.8	7.5	7.2
7UP (all brands)	–	–	–	–	–	–	3.3	2.8	1.8
A&W brands	–	–	–	–	–	–	1.7	1.5	1.4
Royal Crown brands	–	–	–	–	–	–	–	–	1.1
Sunkist	–	–	–	–	1.2	0.7	0.7	0.8	1.0
Canada Dry	–	–	–	–	1.5	1.2	1.0	0.9	0.8
Schweppes	–	–	–	–	0.5	0.6	0.5	0.4	0.4
Others	–	–	–	–	1.5	0.7	1.1	0.8	0.8
Total					**4.7**	**3.2**	**15.1**	**14.7**	**14.5**

(continued)

EXHIBIT 2 *(Continued)*

	1966	1970	1975	1980	1985	1990	1995	2000	2004E
Dr Pepper/Seven-Up Cos.[c]									
Dr Pepper brands	2.6	3.8	5.5	6.0	4.5	5.2	–	–	–
7UP brands	6.9	7.2	7.6	6.3	5.8	3.9	–	–	–
Others	–	–	–	–	–	0.5	–	–	–
Total						9.6	–	–	–
Cott Corporation	–	–	–	–	–	–	2.7	3.3	5.5
Royal Crown Cos.	6.9	6.0	5.4	4.7	3.1	2.6	2.0	1.1	–
Other companies	29.8	28.5	25.1	19.3	12.1	11.1	7.0	5.4	5.2
Total case volume (in millions)[d]	**2,927**	**3,670**	**4,155**	**5,180**	**6,385**	**7,780**	**8,970**	**9,950**	**10,240**

Sources: Compiled from *Beverage Digest Fact Book 2001; The Maxwell Consumer Report*, February. 3, 1994; the Beverage Marketing Corporation, cited in *Beverage World*, March 1996 and March 1999; and *Beverage Digest Fact Book 2005*.

[a] For the period before 1985, Fanta sales are included under "Others."

[b] Cadbury Schweppes acquired A&W brands in 1993, Dr Pepper/Seven-Up Cos. (DPSU) brands in 1995, and Royal Crown brands in 2000.

[c] Dr Pepper/Seven-Up Companies (DPSU) was formed in 1988. For the years preceding 1988, Dr Pepper and 7UP brand shares refer to the shares of the respective independent companies, the Dr Pepper Company and the Seven-Up Company.

[d] One case is equivalent to 192 oz.

EXHIBIT 3

Financial Data for Coca-Cola, Pepsi-Cola, and Their Largest Bottlers ($ millions)

	1975	1980	1985	1990	1995	2000	2001	2002	2003	2004
Coca-Cola Company[a]										
Beverages, North America										
Sales	–	1,486	1,865	2,461	5,513	7,870	7,526	6,264	6,344	6,643
Operating profits/sales	–	11.1%	11.6%	16.5%	15.5%	17.9%	19.7%	23.9%	18.9%	24.2%
Beverages, International										
Sales	–	2,349	2,677	6,125	12,559	12,588	12,386	13,089	14,477	15,076
Operating profit/sales	–	21.0%	22.9%	29.4%	29.1%	27.1%	37.1%	35.8%	33.3%	33.6%
Consolidated										
Sales	2,773	5,475	5,879	10,236	18,127	20,458	20,0092	19,564	21,044	21,962
Net profit/sales	9.0%	7.7%	12.3%	13.5%	16.5%	10.6%	19.8%	15.6%	20.7%	22.1%
Net profit/equity	21.0%	20.0%	24.0%	36.0%	55.4%	23.4%	34.9%	25.8%	30.9%	30.4%
Long-term debt/assets	3.0%	10.0%	23.0%	8.0%	7.6%	4.0%	5.4%	11.0%	9.2%	3.7%
PepsiCo, Inc.[b]										
Beverages, North America										
Sales	1,065	2,368	2,725	5,035	7,427	6,171	6,888	7,200	7,733	8,313
Operating profit/sales	10.4%	10.3%	10.4%	13.4%	16.7%	22.3%	21.3%	21.9%	21.9%	23.0%
Beverages, International										
Sales	–	–	–	1,489	3,040	1,981	2,012	2,036	–	–
Operating profit/sales	–	–	–	6.3%	3.9%	8.0%	10.5%	12.8%	–	–
Consolidated										

EXHIBIT 3 *(Continued)*

	1975	1980	1985	1990	1995	2000	2001	2002	2003	2004
Sales	2,709	5,975	7,585	17,515	19,067	20,438	26,935	25,112	26,971	29,261
Net profit/sales	4.6%	4.4%	5.6%	6.2%	7.5%	10.7%	9.9%	13.2%	13.2%	14.4%
Net profit/equity	18.0%	20.0%	30.0%	22.0%	19.4%	30.1%	30.8%	35.6%	30.0%	31.0%
Long-term debt/assets	35.0%	31.0%	36.0%	33.0%	35.9%	12.8%	12.2%	9.3%	6.7%	
Coca-Cola Enterprises (CCE)										
Sales	–	–	–	3,933	6,773	14,750	15,700	16,889	17,330	18,158
Operating profit/sales	–	–	–	8.3%	6.9%	7.6%	4.3%	8.0%	8.6%	7.9%
Net profit/sales	–	–	–	2.4%	1.2%	1.6%	-2.0%	2.9%	3.9%	3.3%
Net profit/equity	–	–	–	6.0%	5.7%	8.3%	-11.5%	14.9%	15.5%	11.1%
Long-term debt/assets				39.0%	46.3%	46.7%	43.7	46.1%	41.1%	39.9%
Pepsi Bottling Group (PBG)[b]										
Sales	–	–	–	–	–	7,982	8,443	9,216	10,265	10,906
Operating profit/sales	–	–	–	–	–	7.4%	8.0%	9.7%	9.3%	9.0%
Net profit/sales	–	–	–	–	–	2.9%	3.6%	4.6%	4.1%	4.2%
Net profit/equity	–	–	–	–	–	13.9%	19.1%	23.5%	22.1%	23.4%
Long-term debt/assets	–	–	–	–	–	42.3%	41.8%	45.1%	38.9%	41.6%

Source: Company annual reports.

[a] Coca-Cola's beverage sales consisted mainly of concentrate sales. Coke's stake in CCE was accounted for by the equity method of accounting, with its share of CCE's net earnings included in its consolidated net income figure. In 1994, Coke began reporting U.S. data as part of a North American category that included Canada and Mexico.

[b] PepsiCo's sales figures included sales by company-owned bottlers. In 1998, PepsiCo began reporting U.S. data as part of a North American category that included Canada. As of 2000, data for "Beverages, North America" combined sales for what had been the Pepsi-Cola and Gatorade/Tropicana divisions. In 2003, PepsiCo ceased reporting its international beverage business separately from its international food business. PBG financial data for the pre-1999 period refer to the PepsiCo bottling operations that were combined and spun off to form PBG in 1998. From 1999, PepsiCo's share of PBG's net earnings was included in PepsiCo's consolidated net income figure.

EXHIBIT 4

Comparative Costs of a Typical U.S. Concentrate Producer and Bottler, 2004

	Concentrate Producer		Bottler	
	Dollars per Case[a]	**Percent of Sales**	**Dollars per Case[a]**	**Percent of Sales**
Net sales	$0.97	100%	$4.70	100%
Cost of sales	$0.16	17%	$2.82	60%
Gross profit	$0.81	83%	$1.88	40%
Selling and delivery	$0.02	2%	$1.18	25%
Advertising and marketing	$0.42	43%	$0.09	2%
General and administration	$0.08	8%	$0.19	4%
Pretax profit	$0.29	30%	$0.42	9%

Sources: Industry analysts and casewriter estimates. Profit and loss percentage data are adapted from Andrew Conway, "Global Soft Drink Bottling Review and Outlook: Consolidating the Way to a Strong Bottling Network," Morgan Stanley Dean Witter, August 4, 1997, p. 2, and supplemented with 2004 data supplied by Corey Horsch, of Credit Suisse First Boston.

[a] One case is equivalent to 192 oz.

this contract, Coke had no legal obligation to assist bottlers with advertising or marketing. Nonetheless, to ensure quality and to match Pepsi, Coke made huge investments to support its bottling network.[15] In 2002, for example, Coke contributed $600 million in marketing support payments to its top bottler alone.[16]

The 1987 contract did not give complete pricing control to Coke, but rather used a formula that established a maximum price and adjusted prices quarterly according to changes in sweetener pricing. This contract differed from Pepsi's Master Bottling Agreement with its top bottler. That agreement granted the bottler perpetual rights to distribute Pepsi's CSD products but required it to purchase raw materials from Pepsi at prices, and on terms and conditions, determined by Pepsi. Pepsi negotiated concentrate prices with its bottling association, and normally based price increases

on the consumer price index (CPI).[17] From the 1980s to the early 2000s, concentrate makers regularly raised concentrate prices, even as inflation-adjusted retail prices for CSD products trended downward. (See Exhibit 5—U.S. CSD Industry Pricing and Volume Statistics.)

Franchise agreements with both Coke and Pepsi allowed bottlers to handle the non-cola brands of other concentrate producers. These agreements also allowed bottlers to choose whether to market new beverages introduced by a concentrate producer. Bottlers could not carry directly competing brands, however. For example, a Coke bottler could not sell Royal Crown Cola, yet it could distribute 7UP if it chose not to carry Sprite. Franchised bottlers could decide whether to participate in test marketing efforts, local advertising campaigns and promotions, and new package introductions (although they could only use packages

EXHIBIT 5

U.S. CSD Industry Pricing and Volume Statistics, 1998–2004

	1988	1990	1992	1994	1996	1998	2000	2002	2004
Retail price per case[a]	$8.78	$8.99	$8.87	$8.63	$8.70	$8.55	$9.08	$9.38	$9.68
Change in retail price[b]	–	1.2%	−0.7%	−1.4%	0.4%	−0.9%	3.1%	1.6%	1.6%
Total Change 1988–2004: 0.6%									
Concentrate price per case[a]	$0.79	$0.86	$0.97	$1.00	$1.07	$1.14	$1.29	1.35	1.45[c]
Change in concentrate price	–	4.3%	6.2%	1.5%	3.4%	3.2%	6.4%	2.3%	3.6%
Total Change 1988–2004: 3.9%									
Volume (cases, in billions)[a]	4.9	5.2	5.3	5.8	6.2	6.6	6.6	6.7	6.8
Change in volume	–	3.0%	1.0%	4.6%	3.4%	3.2%	0.0%	0.8%	0.7%
Total Change 1988–2004: 2.1%									
Consumption (gallons/capita)	40.3	46.9	47.2	50.0	52.0	54.0	53.0	52.5	52.3
Change in consumption	–	7.9%	0.3%	2.9%	2.0%	1.9%	−0.9%	−0.5%	−0.2%
Total Change 1988–2004: 1.6%									
Consumer Price Index[d]	100	110	119	125	133	138	146	152	160
Change in CPI	–	5.1%	3.6%	2.8%	2.9%	1.9%	2.8%	2.0%	2.6%
Total Change 1988–2004: 3.0%									

Source: Compiled from *Beverage Digest Fact Book 2001* and *Beverage Digest Fact Book 2005*, and using the Inflation Calculator tool, U.S. Bureau of Labor Statistics website, http://data.bls.gov/cgi-bin/cpicalc.pl, accessed November 2005.

[a] For the purposes of this exhibit only, "case" refers to a 288-oz case.

[b] All change figures are calculated using Compounded Annual Growth Rate (CAGR).

[c] Concentrate price for 2004 is based on a weighted average of concentrate prices for the top 10 CSD brands. Concentrate price data for previous years appear in aggregated form in *Beverage Digest Fact Book 2003*, p. 64.

[d] CPI data use 1988 as the index year (1988 = 100).

authorized by their franchiser). Bottlers also had the final say in decisions about retail pricing.

In 1971, the Federal Trade Commission initiated action against eight major concentrate makers, charging that the granting of exclusive territories to bottlers prevented intrabrand competition (that is, two or more bottlers competing in the same area with the same beverage). The concentrate makers argued that interbrand competition was strong enough to warrant continuation of the existing territorial agreements. In 1980, after years of litigation, Congress enacted the Soft Drink Interbrand Competition Act, which preserved the right of concentrate makers to grant exclusive territories.

RETAIL CHANNELS. In 2004, the distribution of CSDs in the United States took place through supermarkets (32.9%), fountain outlets (23.4%), vending machines (14.5%), mass merchandisers (11.8%), convenience stores and gas stations (7.9%), and other outlets (9.5%). Small grocery stores and drug chains made up most of the latter category.[18] Costs and profitability in each channel varied by delivery method and frequency, drop size, advertising, and marketing. (See Exhibit 6—U.S. Refreshment Beverages: Bottling Profitability per Channel.)

The main distribution channel for soft drinks was the supermarket, where annual CSD sales reached $12.4 billion in 2004.[19] CSDs accounted for 5.5% of "the total edible grocery universe," and were also a big traffic draw for supermarkets.[20] Bottlers fought for shelf space to ensure visibility for their products, and they looked for new ways to drive impulse purchases, such as placing coolers at checkout counters. An ever-expanding array of products and packaging types created intense competition for shelf space.

The mass merchandiser category included warehouse clubs and discount retailers, such as Wal-Mart. These companies formed an increasingly important channel. Although they sold Coke and Pepsi products, they (along with some drug chains) often had their own private-label CSD, or they sold a generic label such as President's Choice. Private-label CSDs were usually delivered to a retailer's warehouse, while branded CSDs were delivered directly to stores. With the warehouse delivery method, the retailer was responsible for storage, transportation, merchandising, and stocking the shelves, thereby incurring additional costs.

Historically, Pepsi had focused on sales through retail outlets, while Coke had dominated fountain sales. (The term "fountain," which originally referred to drug store soda fountains, covered restaurants, cafeterias, and any other outlet that served soft drinks by the glass using fountain-type dispensers.) Competition for national fountain accounts was intense, and CSD companies frequently sacrificed profitability in order to land and keep those accounts. As of 1999, for example, Burger King franchises were believed to pay about $6.20 per gallon for Coke syrup, but they received a substantial rebate on each gallon; one large Midwestern franchise owner said that his annual rebate ran $1.45 per gallon, or about 23%.[21] Local fountain

---

EXHIBIT 6

U.S. Refreshment Beverages: Bottling Profitability per Channel, 2005

	Super-markets	Convenience and Gas	Super-centers[a]	Mass Retailers[a]	Club Stores[a]	Drug Stores	Fountain and Vending	Total
Share of industry volume[b]								
	31%	15%	9%	4%	4%	3%	34%	100%
Index of bottling profitability[c]								
Net Price	1.00	1.54	0.95	1.08	1.07	1.19	1.48	NA
Variable Profit	1.00	1.86	0.90	1.17	0.81	1.31	1.80	NA

Source: Compiled from estimates provided by beverage industry source, April 2006.

[a] "Supercenters" include Wal-Mart Supercenter stories and similar outlets. "Mass Retailers" include standard Wal-Mart stores, Target stores, and the like. "Club Stores" include Sam's Club, Costco, and similar membership-based retailers.

[b] Figures here and below refer to the entire refreshment beverage industry, encompassing CSD and non-carb beverage volume.

[c] Using supermarket information as a baseline, these figures indicate variance by channel of both by-volume pricing and byvolume profit. The variable profit figures take into account cost of goods sold as well as delivery costs.

accounts, which bottlers handled in most cases, were considerably more profitable than national accounts. Overall, according to a prominent industry observer, operating margins were 10 percentage points lower in fountain sales than in bottle and can sales.[22] To support the fountain channel, Coke and Pepsi invested in the development of service dispensers and other equipment, and provided fountain customers with cups, point-of-sale advertising, and other in-store promotional material.

After Pepsi entered the fast-food restaurant business by acquiring Pizza Hut (1978), Taco Bell (1986), and Kentucky Fried Chicken (1986), Coca-Cola persuaded competing chains such as Wendy's and Burger King to switch to Coke. In 1997, PepsiCo spun off its restaurant business under the name Tricon, but fountain "pouring rights" remained split along largely pre-Tricon lines.[23] In 2005, Pepsi supplied all Taco Bell and KFC restaurants and the great majority of Pizza Hut restaurants, and Coke retained exclusivity deals with Burger King and McDonald's (the largest national account in terms of sales). Competition remained vigorous: In 2004, Coke won the Subway account away from Pepsi, while Pepsi grabbed the Quiznos account from Coke. (Subway was the largest account as measured by number of outlets.) And Coke continued to dominate the channel, with a 68% share of national pouring rights, against 22% for Pepsi and 10% for Cadbury Schweppes.[24]

Coke and Cadbury Schweppes had long retained control of national fountain accounts, negotiating pouring-rights contracts that in some cases (as with big restaurant chains) covered the entire United States or even the world. Local bottlers or the franchisors' fountain divisions serviced these accounts. (In such cases, bottlers received a fee for delivering syrup and maintaining machines.) Historically, PepsiCo had ceded fountain rights to local Pepsi bottlers. In the late 1990s, however, Pepsi began a successful campaign to gain from its bottlers the right to sell fountain syrup via restaurant commissary companies.[25]

In the vending channel, bottlers took charge of buying, installing, and servicing machines, and for negotiating contracts with property owners, who typically received a sales commission in exchange for accommodating those machines. But concentrate makers offered bottlers financial incentives to encourage investment in machines, and also played a large role in the development of vending technology. Coke and Pepsi were by far the largest suppliers of CSDs to this channel.

SUPPLIERS TO CONCENTRATE PRODUCERS AND BOTTLERS. Concentrate producers required few inputs: the concentrate for most regular colas consisted of caramel coloring, phosphoric or citric acid, natural flavors, and caffeine.[26] Bottlers purchased two major inputs: packaging (including cans, plastic bottles, and glass bottles), and sweeteners (including high-fructose corn syrup and sugar, as well as artificial sweeteners such as aspartame). The majority of U.S. CSDs were packaged in metal cans (56%), with plastic bottles (42%) and glass bottles (2%) accounting for the remainder.[27] Cans were an attractive packaging material because they were easily handled and displayed, weighed little, and were durable and recyclable. Plastic packaging, introduced in 1978, allowed for larger and more varied bottle sizes. Single-serve 20-oz PET bottles, introduced in 1993, steadily gained popularity; in 2005, they represented 36.7% of CSD volume (and 56.7% of CSD revenues) in convenience stores.[28]

The concentrate producers' strategy toward can manufacturers was typical of their supplier relationships. Coke and Pepsi negotiated on behalf of their bottling networks, and were among the metal can industry's largest customers. In the 1960s and 1970s, both companies took control of a portion of their own can production, but by 1990 they had largely exited that business. Thereafter, they sought instead to establish stable long-term relationships with suppliers. In 2005, major can producers included Ball, Rexam (through its American National Can subsidiary), and Crown Cork & Seal.[29] Metal cans were essentially a commodity, and often two or three can manufacturers competed for a single contract.

The Evolution of the U.S. Soft Drink Industry[30]

EARLY HISTORY. Coca-Cola was formulated in 1886 by John Pemberton, a pharmacist in Atlanta, Georgia, who sold it at drug store soda fountains as a "potion for mental and physical disorders." In 1891, Asa Candler acquired the formula, established a sales force, and began brand advertising of Coca-Cola. The formula for Coca-Cola syrup, known as "Merchandise 7X," remained a well-protected secret that the company kept under guard in an Atlanta bank vault. Candler granted Coca-Cola's first bottling franchise in 1899 for a nominal one dollar, believing that the future of the drink rested with soda fountains. The company's bottling network grew quickly, however, reaching 370 franchisees by 1910.

In its early years, imitations and counterfeit versions of Coke plagued the company, which aggressively fought trademark infringements in court. In 1916 alone, courts barred 153 imitations of Coca-Cola, including the brands Coca-Kola, Koca-Nola, and Cold-Cola. Coke introduced and patented a 6.5-oz bottle whose unique "skirt" design subsequently became an American icon.

Candler sold the company to a group of investors in 1919, and it went public that year. Four years later, Robert Woodruff began his long tenure as leader of the company. Woodruff pushed franchise bottlers to place the beverage "in arm's reach of desire," by any and all means. During the 1920s and 1930s, Coke pioneered open-top coolers for use in grocery stores and other channels, developed automatic fountain dispensers, and introduced vending machines. Woodruff also initiated "lifestyle" advertising for Coca-Cola, emphasizing the role that Coke played in a consumer's life.

Woodruff developed Coke's international business as well. During World War II, at the request of General Eisenhower, Woodruff promised that "every man in uniform gets a bottle of Coca-Cola for five cents wherever he is and whatever it costs the company." Beginning in 1942, Coke won exemptions from wartime sugar rationing for production of beverages that it sold to the military or to retailers that served soldiers. Coca-Cola bottling plants followed the movement of American troops, and during the war the U.S. government set up 64 such plants overseas—a development that contributed to Coke's dominant postwar market shares in most European and Asian countries.

Pepsi-Cola was invented in 1893 in New Bern, North Carolina, by pharmacist Caleb Bradham. Like Coke, Pepsi adopted a franchise bottling system, and by 1910 it had built a network of 270 bottlers. Pepsi struggled, however; it declared bankruptcy in 1923 and again in 1932. But business began to pick up when, during the Great Depression, Pepsi lowered the price of its 12-oz bottle to a nickel—the same price that Coke charged for a 6.5-oz bottle. In the years that followed, Pepsi built a marketing strategy around the theme of its famous radio jingle: "Twice as much for a nickel, too."

In 1938, Coke filed suit against Pepsi, claiming that the Pepsi-Cola brand was an infringement on the Coca-Cola trademark. A 1941 court ruling in Pepsi's favor ended a series of suits and countersuits between the two companies. During this period, as Pepsi sought to expand its bottling network, it had to rely on small local bottlers that competed with wealthy, established Coke franchisees.[31] Still, the company began to gain market share, surpassing Royal Crown and Dr Pepper in the 1940s to become the second-largest-selling CSD brand. In 1950, Coke's share of the U.S. market was 47% and Pepsi's was 10%; hundreds of regional CSD companies, which offered a wide assortment of flavors, made up the rest of the market.[32]

THE COLA WARS BEGIN. In 1950, Alfred Steele, a former Coke marketing executive, became CEO of Pepsi. Steele made "Beat Coke" his motto and encouraged bottlers to focus on take-home sales through supermarkets. To target family consumption, for example, the company introduced a 26-oz bottle. Pepsi's growth began to follow the postwar growth in the number of supermarkets and convenience stores in the United States: There were about 10,000 supermarkets in 1945; 15,000 in 1955; and 32,000 in 1962, at the peak of this growth curve.

Under the leadership of CEO Donald Kendall, Pepsi in 1963 launched its "Pepsi Generation" marketing campaign, which targeted the young and "young at heart." The campaign helped Pepsi narrow Coke's lead to a 2-to-1 margin. At the same time, Pepsi worked with its bottlers to modernize plants and to improve store delivery services. By 1970, Pepsi bottlers were generally larger than their Coke counterparts. Coke's network remained fragmented, with more than 800 independent franchised bottlers (most of which served U.S. cities of 50,000 or less).[33] Throughout this period, Pepsi sold concentrate to its bottlers at a price that was about 20% lower than what Coke charged. In the early 1970s, Pepsi increased its concentrate prices to equal those of Coke. To overcome bottler opposition, Pepsi promised to spend this extra income on advertising and promotion.

Coke and Pepsi began to experiment with new cola and non-cola flavors, and with new packaging options, in the 1960s. Previously, the two companies had sold only their flagship cola brands. Coke launched Fanta (1960), Sprite (1961), and the low-calorie cola Tab (1963). Pepsi countered with Teem (1960), Mountain Dew (1964), and Diet Pepsi (1964). Both companies introduced non-returnable glass bottles and 12-oz metal cans in various configurations. They also diversified into non-CSD industries. Coke purchased

Minute Maid (fruit juice), Duncan Foods (coffee, tea, hot chocolate), and Belmont Springs Water. In 1965, Pepsi merged with snack-food giant Frito-Lay to form PepsiCo, hoping to achieve synergies based on similar customer targets, delivery systems, and marketing orientations.

In the late 1950s, Coca-Cola began to use advertising messages that implicitly recognized the existence of competitors: "America's Preferred Taste" (1955), "No Wonder Coke Refreshes Best" (1960). In meetings with Coca-Cola bottlers, however, executives discussed only the growth of their own brand and never referred to its closest competitor by name. During the 1960s, Coke focused primarily on overseas markets, apparently basing its strategy on the assumption that domestic CSD consumption was approaching a saturation point. Pepsi, meanwhile, battled Coke aggressively in the United States, and doubled its U.S. share between 1950 and 1970.

THE PEPSI CHALLENGE. In 1974, Pepsi launched the "Pepsi Challenge" in Dallas, Texas. Coke was the dominant brand in that city, and Pepsi ran a distant third behind Dr Pepper. In blind taste tests conducted by Pepsi's small local bottler, the company tried to demonstrate that consumers actually preferred Pepsi to Coke. After its sales shot up in Dallas, Pepsi rolled out the campaign nationwide.

Coke countered with rebates, retail price cuts, and a series of advertisements that questioned the tests' validity. In particular, it employed retail price discounts in markets where a company-owned Coke bottler competed against an independent Pepsi bottler. Nonetheless, the Pepsi Challenge successfully eroded Coke's market share. In 1979, Pepsi passed Coke in food store sales for the first time, opening up a 1.4 share-point lead. In a sign of the times, Coca-Cola president Brian Dyson inadvertently uttered the name Pepsi at a 1979 bottlers' conference.

During this period, Coke renegotiated its franchise bottling contract to obtain greater flexibility in pricing concentrate and syrups. Its bottlers approved a new contract in 1978, but only after Coke agreed to link concentrate price changes to the CPI, to adjust the price to reflect any cost savings associated with ingredient changes, and to supply unsweetened concentrate to bottlers that preferred to buy their own sweetener on the open market.[34] This arrangement brought Coke in line with Pepsi, which traditionally had sold unsweetened concentrate to its bottlers. Immediately after securing approval of the new agreement, Coke announced a significant concentrate price increase. Pepsi followed with a 15% price increase of its own.

COLA WARS HEAT UP. In 1980, Roberto Goizueta was named CEO of Coca-Cola, and Don Keough became its president. That year, Coke switched from using sugar to using high-fructose corn syrup, a lower-priced alternative. Pepsi emulated that move three years later. Coke also intensified its marketing effort, more than doubling its advertising spending between 1981 and 1984. In response, Pepsi doubled its advertising expenditures over the same period. Meanwhile, Goizueta sold off most of the non-CSD businesses that he had inherited, including wine, coffee, tea, and industrial water treatment, while retaining Minute Maid.

Diet Coke, introduced in 1982, was the first extension of the "Coke" brand name. Many Coke managers, deeming the "Mother Coke" brand sacred, had opposed the move. So had company lawyers, who worried about copyright issues. Nonetheless, Diet Coke was a huge success. Praised as the "most successful consumer product launch of the Eighties," it became within a few years not only the most popular diet soft drink in the United States, but also the nation's third-largest-selling CSD.

In April 1985, Coke announced that it had changed the 99-year-old Coca-Cola formula. Explaining this radical break with tradition, Goizueta cited a sharp depreciation in the value of the Coca-Cola trademark. "The product and the brand," he said, "had a declining share in a shrinking segment of the market."[35] On the day of Coke's announcement, Pepsi declared a holiday for its employees, claiming that the new Coke mimicked Pepsi in taste. The reformulation prompted an outcry from Coke's most loyal customers, and bottlers joined the clamor. Three months later, the company brought back the original formula under the name Coca-Cola Classic, while retaining the new formula as its flagship brand under the name New Coke. Six months later, Coke announced that it would henceforth treat Coca-Cola Classic (the original formula) as its flagship brand.

New CSD brands proliferated in the 1980s. Coke introduced 11 new products, including Caffeine-Free Coke (1983) and Cherry Coke (1985). Pepsi introduced 13 products, including Lemon-Lime Slice (1984) and Caffeine-Free Pepsi-Cola (1987). The number of packaging types and sizes also increased dramatically, and the battle for shelf space in supermarkets and other stores became fierce. By the late 1980s, Coke and Pepsi each offered more than 10 major brands and 17 or more container types.[36] The struggle for market share intensified, and retail price discounting became the norm. Consumers grew accustomed to such discounts.

Throughout the 1980s, the growth of Coke and Pepsi put a squeeze on smaller concentrate producers. As their shelf space declined, small brands were shuffled from one owner to another. Over a five-year span, Dr Pepper was sold (all or in part) several times, Canada Dry twice, Sunkist once, Shasta once, and A&W Brands once. Philip Morris acquired Seven-Up in 1978 for a big premium, racked up huge losses in the early 1980s, and then left the CSD business in 1985. In the 1990s, through a series of strategic acquisitions, Cadbury Schweppes emerged as the third-largest concentrate producer—the main (albeit distant) competitor of the two CSD giants. It bought the Dr Pepper/Seven-Up Companies in 1995, and continued to add such well-known brands as Orangina (2001) and Nantucket Nectars (2002) to its portfolio. (See Appendix A—Cadbury Schweppes: Operations and Financial Performance.)

BOTTLER CONSOLIDATION AND SPIN-OFF. Relations between Coke and its franchised bottlers had been strained since the contract renegotiation of 1978. Coke struggled to persuade bottlers to cooperate in marketing and promotion programs, to upgrade plant and equipment, and to support new product launches.[37] The cola wars had particularly weakened small, independent bottlers. Pressures to spend more on advertising, product and packaging proliferation, widespread retail price discounting—together, these factors resulted in higher capital requirements and lower profit margins. Many family-owned bottlers no longer had the resources needed to remain competitive.

At a July 1980 dinner with Coke's 15 largest domestic bottlers, Goizueta announced a plan to refranchise bottling operations. Coke began buying up poorly managed bottlers, infusing them with capital, and quickly reselling them to better-performing bottlers. Refranchising allowed Coke's larger bottlers to expand outside their traditionally exclusive geographic territories. When two of its largest bottling companies came up for sale in 1985, Coke moved swiftly to buy them for $2.4 billion, preempting outside bidders. Together with other recently purchased bottlers, these acquisitions placed one-third of Coke's volume in company-owned operations. Meanwhile, Coke began to replace its 1978 franchise agreement with what became the 1987 Master Bottler Contract.

Coke's bottler acquisitions had increased its long-term debt to approximately $1 billion. In 1986, the company created an independent bottling subsidiary, Coca-Cola Enterprises (CCE), selling 51% of its shares to the public and retaining the rest. The minority equity position enabled Coke to separate its financial statements from those of CCE. As Coke's first "anchor bottler," CCE consolidated small territories into larger regions, renegotiated contracts with suppliers and retailers, merged redundant distribution and purchasing arrangements, and cut its work force by 20%. CCE also invested in building 50-million-case production lines that involved high levels of automation. Coke continued to acquire independent franchised bottlers and to sell them to CCE.[38] "We became an investment banking firm specializing in bottler deals," said Don Keough. In 1997 alone, Coke put together more than $7 billion in such deals.[39] By 2004, CCE was Coke's largest bottler. It handled about 80% of Coke's North American bottle and can volume, and logged annual sales of more than $18 billion. Some industry observers questioned Coke's accounting practice with respect to CCE, since Coke retained substantial managerial influence in the putatively independent anchor bottler.[40]

In the late 1980s, Pepsi acquired MEI Bottling for $591 million, Grand Metropolitan's bottling operations for $705 million, and General Cinema's bottling operations for $1.8 billion. After operating the bottlers for a decade, Pepsi shifted course and adopted Coke's anchor bottler model. In April 1999, the Pepsi Bottling Group (PBG) went public, with Pepsi retaining a 35% equity stake in it. By 2004, PBG produced 57% of PepsiCo beverages in North America and about 40% worldwide, while the total number of Pepsi bottlers had fallen from more than 400 in the mid-1980s to a mere 102.[41]

Bottler consolidation made smaller concentrate producers increasingly dependent on the Pepsi and Coke bottling networks for distribution of their products. In response, Cadbury Schweppes in 1998 bought and merged two large U.S. bottling companies to form its own bottler. In 2004, Coke had the most consolidated system, with its top 10 bottlers producing 94.7% of domestic volume. Pepsi's and Cadbury Schweppes' top 10 bottlers produced 87.2% and 72.9% of the domestic volume of their respective franchisors.[42]

Adapting to the Times

Starting in the late 1990s, the soft drink industry encountered new challenges that suggested a possible long-term shift in the marketplace. Most notably, demand for its core product seemed to have leveled off. Although Americans still drank more CSDs than any other beverage, U.S. sales volume grew at a rate of 1% or less in the years 1998 to 2004. Total U.S. volume topped 10 billion cases in 2001, but had risen to only 10.2 billion cases in 2004. (A case was equivalent to 24 eight-ounce containers, or 192 ounces.) That was in contrast to annual growth rates of 3% to 7% during the 1980s and early 1990s.[43] Globally, too, demand remained flat. Worldwide volume in 2003 was 31.26 billion cases, which marked only a slight increase over the 1999 total of 31 billion cases. During that period, worldwide annual per-capita consumption declined from 125 eight-ounce servings to 119 servings.[44]

In responding to changing times, Coca-Cola struggled more than PepsiCo, in part because of its own internal difficulties and execution failures, and in part because of its greater reliance on a traditional CSD-oriented model. But, in their different ways, both companies sought to retain or recapture their historically high growth and profitability within an apparently new environment. Toward that end, they focused on addressing challenges related to performance and execution, on providing alternative beverages to increasingly health-conscious consumers, on adjusting key strategic relationships, and on cultivating international markets.

REVERSAL OF FORTUNE. When Coke CEO Robert Goizueta died unexpectedly in 1997, the company that he had led was at its zenith. During Goizueta's 16-year tenure, Coke's share price rose by 3,500%, and its brand was routinely deemed the most valuable in the world.[45] Pepsi, meanwhile, lagged behind its rival in most key measures of its beverage operations, including market share and sales growth.[46] By the middle of the following decade, however, Coke appeared to stumble from one embarrassment to another, while Pepsi was flying high.

Under the brief, rocky tenure of CEO Douglas Ivester (1997–1999), Coke lost a high-profile race discrimination suit, underwent financial shocks caused by currency crises in Asia and Russia, and conducted the largest recall in its history after a contamination scare in Belgium. In the latter episode, there was no

evidence of actual contamination; nonetheless, it was a public relations disaster.[47] Troubles continued under the next CEO, Douglas Daft (1999–2004). Layoffs of 7,000 employees from 2001 to 2004 cut Coke's work force by 20%—damaging morale and seriously weakening its executive ranks, many observers believed.[48] A contamination scare in India in 2003 hindered Coke's (as well as Pepsi's) push into a promising market, and a similar crisis in 2004 led the company to abort plans to roll out its Dasani water brand in Europe.[49] A series of legal problems burdened the company as well. In 2003, Coke agreed to pay Burger King $21 million following the revelation that it had rigged a marketing test involving the restaurant chain. That same year, the U.S. Justice Department and the Securities Exchange Commission (SEC) launched wide-ranging investigations of various Coke accounting practices, focusing on allegations of "channel stuffing." Under this practice, Coke pressured bottlers to buy excess concentrate in order to meet earnings targets. Coke in 2005 settled with the SEC on charges involving the Japanese market, but a shareholder suit alleging such practices in Europe, North America, and elsewhere remained in the courts.[50]

Coke also suffered from clumsy execution (or non-execution) of several initiatives. In 2001, it bailed out on a planned joint venture with Procter & Gamble. Around the same time, after two years of negotiation, it opted against buying the South Beach Beverage Co. (SoBe), only to watch Pepsi acquire that company. Similarly, in 2000 Coke allowed Pepsi to purchase Quaker Oats. Daft had agreed to buy Quaker for $15.75 billion, but several Coke directors halted the deal, arguing that the price was too high.[51] Coke installed a new CEO, E. Neville Isdell, in April 2004.[52] A 35-year Coke veteran, Isdell focused early in his tenure on regaining the company's lost luster as a high-performing soft drink maker. "We are not talking about radical change in strategy. We are talking about a dramatic change in execution," he said in November 2004.[53] Yet, at around the same time, he noted the need for Coke to take "corrective actions with a great urgency." During his first year as CEO, he committed to spending an additional $400 million per year on marketing and innovation, and on addressing Coke's "people deficit and skills deficit."[54]

While Coke struggled, Pepsi quietly flourished. In 2001, Steve Reinemund succeeded Roger Enrico as its CEO.[55] At a broad level, both men pursued the same simple strategy, which Reinemund couched in this way: "Grow the core and add some more."[56] Along with launching new CSDs, such as Sierra Mist (2000) and Mountain Dew Code Red (2001), Pepsi expanded into other beverage categories—an effort capped by its $14 billion acquisition of Quaker Oats, maker of Gatorade, in 2000.[57] Partly as a result, the company's North American beverage volume grew by 3% in 2004, compared with virtually flat volumes for Coke.[58] As the world's fourth-largest food and beverage company, meanwhile, Pepsi also benefited from having a more diversified portfolio of products.

Financial returns for the two companies told a stark tale. Between 1996 and 2004, Coca-Cola logged an average annual growth in net income of 4.2%—a huge drop from the 18% average growth of the years 1990–1997. PepsiCo, by contrast, saw its net income rise by an average of 17.6% per year over the 1996–2004 period.[59] In 2003, Pepsi recorded a return on invested capital of 29.3%, up from 9.5% in 1996; for the first time in decades, it surpassed Coke in that measure.[60] From 1997 to 2004, Pepsi shareholders enjoyed a return of 46%, while Coke shareholders suffered a return of −26%.[61] (Coke shares, which reached a peak price of $89 in 1998, traded at half that amount in 2005.[62])

THE QUEST FOR ALTERNATIVES. Early in 2005, Pepsi announced that it would no longer set its marketing course by its regular cola brand. "We are treating Diet Pepsi as the flagship brand," said Dave Burwick, chief marketing officer for Pepsi-Cola North America. Although the marketing budget for regular Pepsi still exceeded that of the diet brand, the balance of attention and resources would now shift within the company.[63] More important, the move was a bellwether of a larger shift throughout the beverage industry. After several years of little or no growth in CSD sales—especially sales of regular, sugared sodas—companies responded aggressively to consumers' increasing demand for alternative beverages

New federal nutrition guidelines, issued in 2005, identified regular CSDs as the largest source of obesity-causing sugars in the American diet.[64] Schools in New York City, throughout California, and elsewhere banned the sale of soft drinks on their premises.[65] Late in 2005, using earlier actions against tobacco companies as a model, lawyers planned to file a suit against CSD makers for allegedly causing harm to children's health.[66] The American Beverage Association, an industry group, responded to such pressures by announcing rules to limit CSD sales in

some schools. (In another noteworthy development, the ABA had changed its name from the National Soft Drink Association in 2004.)[67] But the widespread linkage of CSDs with obesity and other health-related concerns was hard to dispel from people's minds. From 2003 to 2004, according to a Morgan Stanley survey, the proportion of Americans who said that cola was "too fattening" increased from 48% to 59%.[68]

In such a climate, diet sodas offered one path to reviving sales. In the U.S. market, their share of total CSD volume grew from 24.6% in 1997 to 29.1% in 2004, thus making up for a decline in regular soda consumption.[69] New or renamed products, such as Coca-Cola Zero (2005) and Sierra Mist Free (2004), targeted consumers—especially younger men—who shunned the "diet" label. With products like Pepsi One (2005) and Diet Coke with Splenda (2005), CSD makers sought to expand the diet market still further.[70]

But the search for alternatives centered on non-carbonated beverages, or "non-carbs"—a category that included juices and juice drinks, sports drinks, energy drinks, and tea-based drinks—and also on bottled water. In 2004, CSD volume in the United States grew by just 1%, whereas non-carb volume increased by 7.6% and single-serve bottled-water volume leaped by 18.8%. That year, CSDs accounted for 73.1% of U.S. non-alcoholic refreshment beverage volume (down from 80.8% in 2000), with the remaining volume made up of bottled water at 13.2% (up from 6.6% in 2000) and non-carbs at 13.7% (up from 12.6%).[71] In 2001, non-carbs and bottled water together contributed more than 100% of Coke's total volume growth and roughly three-fourths of Pepsi's volume growth.[72]

Pepsi was more aggressive than Coke in shifting to non-CSDs. "Politicians expect us to be on the defensive when we talk about health and wellness but we're not," said Pepsi CEO Reinemund. "It's a huge opportunity to build new brands and products."[73] His company launched a "Smart Spot" program that labeled all products (including diet sodas and non-carbs) that met certain "good for you" criteria; in 2004, such products reportedly grew at twice the rate of other Pepsi food and beverage items.[74] Declaring itself to be a "total beverage company," Pepsi developed a portfolio of non-CSD products that outsold Coke's rival product in each key category: In 2004 volume sales, Gatorade (80.4%) led PowerAde (18.1%) in the $5.4 billion sports drink segment, Lipton (35.2%) led Nestea (23.9%) in the $3.2 billion tea-based drink segment, and Tropicana (26.8%) led Minute Maid (14.8%) in the $3.8 billion refrigerated juice segment. In the U.S. non-carb market overall (excluding bottled water), Pepsi had a market share of 47.3%, compared with Coke's share of 27.0%.[75]

Missed opportunities marked Coke's U.S. non-carb operations. In 2001, Coke acquired the Planet Java coffee-drink brand and the Mad River line of juices and teas; two years later, it folded both brands.[76] KMX, the company's entry in the fast-growing, $1.9 billion energy-drink segment, also foundered. Coke hoped for better luck with Full Throttle, introduced in 2005 to compete with segment leader Red Bull.[77] Observers noted Coke's continued focus on its traditional source

of strength. "Regardless of what the skeptics think, I know carbonated soft drinks can grow," said Coke CEO Isdell.[78] In 2005, CSDs still accounted for 80% of Coke's worldwide beverage volume, while making up just two-thirds of Pepsi's volume.[79]

Coke fared better in the $11.4 billion bottled-water category. Both Pepsi (with Aquafina, 1998) and Coke (with Dasani, 1999) had introduced purified-water products that had surged to become leading beverage brands. (See Exhibit 7—Non-Alcoholic Refreshment Beverage Megabrands.) Using their distribution prowess, they had outstripped competing brands, many of which sold spring water. By 2004, Aquafina (13.6%)

EXHIBIT 7

Non-Alcoholic Refreshment Beverage Megabrands, 2004 and 2000

Brand (Owner)	Category	2004 Cases (mil)	2004 Share	2000 Cases (mil)	2000 Share	Annual Volume Change[b] 2000–04	Annual Share Change[b] 2000–04
Coke (Coke)	CSD	3,272.3	23.4%	3,192.6	25.9%	0.6%	−2.5%
Pepsi (Pepsi)	CSD	2,098.4	15.0%	2,159.9	17.5%	−0.7%	−3.8%
Mountain Dew (Pepsi)	CSD	871.1	6.2%	809.8	6.6%	1.8%	−1.5%
Dr Pepper (Cadbury)	CSD	738.3	5.3%	747.5	6.1%	−0.3%	−3.5%
Sprite (Coke)	CSD	683.2	4.9%	713.0	5.8%	−1.1%	−4.1%
Gatorade (Pepsi)	Non-Carb	546.0	3.9%	325.0	2.6%	13.9%	10.7%
Aquafina (Pepsi)	Water	251.0	1.8%	100.7	0.8%	25.7%	22.5%
Dasani (Coke)	Water	223.0	1.6%	65.1	0.5%	36.0%	33.8%
Poland Spring (Nestlé Waters)	Water	217.0	1.5%	91.8	0.7%	24.0%	21.0%
7UP (Cadbury)	CSD	186.7	1.3%	276.1	2.2%	−9.3%	−12.3%
Minute Maid (Coke)	CSD/Non-Carb	176.4	1.3%	145.0	1.2%	5.0%	2.0%
Sierra Mist (Pepsi)	CSD	166.9	1.2%	–	–	–	–
Lipton (Pepsi/Unilever)	Non-Carb	164.0	1.2%	155.2	1.3%	1.4%	−2.0%
Crystal Geyser (CG Roxanne)	Water	135.5	1.0%	50.2	0.4%	28.2%	25.7%
Arrowhead (Nestlé Waters)	Water	127.0	0.9%	46.6	0.4%	28.5%	18.9%
PowerAde (Coke)	Non-Carb	122.7	0.9%	62.6	0.5%	18.3%	15.9%
Nestlé Pure Life (Nestlé Waters)	Water	113.2	0.8%	–	–	–	–
Barq's (Coke)	CSD	112.5	0.8%	121.2	1.0%	−1.8%	−5.4%
Sunkist (Cadbury)	CSD	105.2	0.8%	80.3	0.7%	7.0%	3.4%

Source: Compiled from *Beverage Digest Fact Book 2005; Beverage Digest Fact Book 2001;* and casewriter estimates.

[a] *Beverage Digest Fact Book* defines a "megabrand" as a "brand or trademark with total volume of more than 100 million 192-oz cases." A megabrand encompasses all varieties (Coke Classic, Diet Coke, Cherry Coke, and so on) of a given trademark ("Coke"). Only single-serve products are included here.

[b] All changes calculated using Compounded Annual Growth Rate (CAGR).

led the segment in market share, with Dasani (12.1%) trailing close behind.[80] Moreover, by arrangement with Danone, Coke handled U.S. marketing and distribution of that company's water brands, including Dannon and Evian. In 2004, Coke/Danone had an overall market share of 21.9%, behind market leader Nestlé Waters (42.1%) and ahead of Pepsi (13.6%). Coke bought out Danone's share of the venture in 2005.[81]

EVOLVING STRUCTURES AND STRATEGIES. Early in the 21st century, both Coke and Pepsi worked to improve "system profitability"—the arrangement whereby concentrate makers and their bottlers created and then divided overall profits from beverage sales. Bottler consolidation continued apace, and the relationship between Coke or Pepsi (on the one hand) and bottlers like CCE or PBG (on the other) became a key element of the cola wars. In the 1990s, a price war in the supermarket channel had highlighted a divergence of interest between the two camps. To compete against bargain private-label brands, bottlers had pursued a low-price strategy. Through the decade, retail CSD prices decreased or remained flat, even as the CPI inched up and as concentrate prices rose; Coke, for instance, raised its concentrate prices by 7.6% in 2000. Bottlers, already burdened by huge debts from consolidation and infrastructure investments, saw profit margins dwindle. In 1999 and 2000, they shifted course, as CCE increased its retail pricing in the supermarket channel by 6% to 7% and as PBG followed suit. Consumers balked, sales volume dipped, and concentrate makers saw their profits drop as a result.[82]

In later years, Coke struggled to adjust its relations with CCE and other bottlers—relations that one writer in 2004 called "dysfunctional."[83] In 2001, the company made an arrangement with CCE to link concentrate prices more tightly to CCE's wholesale CSD prices.[84] Starting in 2003, the two companies began negotiating a deal that would move toward "incidence pricing," an approach that Coke often used with its overseas bottlers. Under that system, concentrate prices varied according to prices charged in different channels and for different packages. As a rule, bottlers favored such arrangements in a deflationary market (which the CSD market had become) but resisted them in an inflationary market.[85] Isdell, Coke's new CEO in 2004 and a former bottler himself, emphasized the need to improve bottler relations. Yet late that year, he tabled the CCE pricing initiative.[86] He also oversaw a proposed rise in concentrate prices that led Coca-Cola FEMSA, the Coke system's largest Mexican bottler, to threaten a cut in its marketing expenditure.[87]

Pepsi, observers noted, had less difficulty than Coke in aligning its strategy with that of its bottlers. "We believe PBG's relationship with PepsiCo is strong and has been critical to its success," one analyst's report asserted in 2003. During that period, PBG consistently posted net-revenue-percase growth that exceeded CCE's growth by several percentage points. Supported by Pepsi, PBG excelled in higher-margin channels—especially the convenience-and-gas channel, in which the bottler actually led CCE. Bottlers profited immensely in such "immediate consumption" venues, where sales of the increasingly popular 20-oz PET bottle yielded margins as high as 35%, compared with the 5% to 7% margin on cans.[88]

All CSD companies faced the challenge of achieving pricing power in the take-home, or future-consumption, channels. Supermarket retail prices did rise, modestly but steadily, in the mid-2000s.[89] Yet retailers, accustomed to using CSD sales to drive in-store traffic, still resisted price increases.[90] Rapid growth of the mass-merchandiser channel, led by Wal-Mart and various club stores, posed a new threat to profitability for Coke, Pepsi, and their bottlers. By 2004, Wal-Mart was the largest U.S. food retailer; for PepsiCo, it represented 14% of the company's total (food and beverage) net revenue.[91] Such retailers used their size not only to exert pricing pressure; they also demanded that beverage companies alter longstanding business practices. Wal-Mart, for example, insisted on negotiating chain-wide marketing and shelving arrangements directly with concentrate makers. Although bottlers continued to handle deliveries to these accounts, relations between Coke or Pepsi and their bottlers underwent a great deal of stress because of this channel shift.[92]

To counter these pressures, CSD makers focused on enticing consumers through stepped-up marketing and innovation. In 2005, Coke combined authority for all of its marketing and product development in a new position that became the company's "de facto No. 2 spot."[93] It also launched a major advertising campaign, built around a new tag line: "The Coke Side of Life."[94] (See Exhibit 8—Advertisement Spending for Selected Refreshment Beverage Brands.) Packaging innovation received special emphasis. Coke in 2001 rolled out its Fridge Pack (later imitated by Pepsi, which introduced a Fridge Mate package), a reconfiguration of the

EXHIBIT 8

Advertisement Spending for Selected Refreshment Beverage Brands ($ thousands)

	Share of Market[a]		Advertisement Spending[b]		
	2004	**2003**	**2004**	**2003**	**per 2004 share point**
Coca-Cola	23.4%	24.3%	246,243	167,675	10,523
Pepsi-Cola	15.0%	15.5%	211,654	236,396	14,110
Mountain Dew	6.2%	6.4%	57,803	60,555	9,323
Dr Pepper	5.3%	5.3%	104,762	96,387	19,766
Sprite	4.9%	5.3%	45,035	31,835	9,191
Gatorade	3.9%	3.5%	141,622	130,993	36,313
Aquafina	1.8%	1.7%	22,037	24,647	12,243
Dasani	1.6%	1.5%	17,633	18,833	11,021
7UP	1.3%	1.5%	34,608	25,071	26,206
Minute Maid	1.3%	1.5%	35,797	21,097	27,228
Sierra Mist	1.2%	1.2%	60,327	64,129	50,273
PowerAde	0.9%	0.8%	11,008	10,100	12,231

Source: Compiled from "Special Report: 100 Leading National Advertisers," *Advertising Age*, June 27, 2005, and casewriter estimates.

[a] Share of the total single-serve non-alcoholic beverage market (about 14 billion cases in 2004).

[b] Spending as measured across 17 national media channels using data compiled by TNS Media Intelligence.

---

standard 12-pack of cans that seemed to improve CSD sales.[95] In 2004, the company introduced a 1.5-liter bottle in select markets, aiming to replace the 2-liter version and thus to boost per-ounce pricing. While the launching of new products and packages brought clear benefits, it also increased costs for bottlers, which had to produce and manage an ever-rising number of stock-keeping units (SKUs).[96] (See Exhibit 9—Retailers' Assessment of Brand Performance.) That problem was most salient in the area of non-CSD beverages. The proliferation of such products, many of them sold in relatively low volume, led to an increasing use of "split pallets." By loading more than one product type on a pallet (the hard, wooden bed used to organize and transport merchandise), bottlers incurred higher labor costs.

In general, alternative beverages complicated CSD makers' traditional production and distribution practices. CSD manufacturing was a cold-fill process. Some non-CSD beverages (such as Lipton Brisk) were also cold-fill products, and bottlers could adapt their infrastructure to those products with little difficulty. But other beverage types (such as Gatorade and Lipton Iced Tea) required costly new equipment and major process changes. More often than not, Coke and Pepsi took direct charge of manufacturing such beverages, which they then sold to their bottlers. The bottlers, in turn, distributed these finished goods alongside their own bottled products at a percentage markup. In others cases, especially that of bottled water, Coke and Pepsi paid for half or more of the cost of building bottling plants that allowed for filtration and other necessary processes. Bottlers then either purchased concentrate-like additives from the concentrate maker (as with Dasani's mineral packet) or compensated Coke or Pepsi via per-unit royalty fees (as with Aquafina). In addition, Coke and Pepsi distributed some non-carbs (such as Gatorade) through food brokers and wholesalers, rather than through DSD delivery.[97]

These arrangements affected profitability in ways that were complex and evolving. With many non-carb beverages, especially energy drinks and sports drinks, high retail pricing and consumers' preference for immediate, single-serve consumption meant that margins were actually higher than they were for CSDs.

EXHIBIT 9

Retailers' Assessment of Brand Performance, 2004

	Top 6 Brands[a]					
	P&G	**Kraft**	**Gen'l Mills**	**Pepsi-Cola**	**Coca-Cola**	**Unilever**
Brands most important to retailers	57.1%	47.3%	19.8%	15.8%	13.7%	11.8%
	Kraft	**P&G**	**Gen'l Mills**	**Nestle**	**Con-Agra**	**Pepsi-Cola**
Best combination of growth, profitability	33.3%	27.6%	26.3%	13.6%	12.5%	11.2%
	Kraft	**P&G**	**Gen'l Mills**	**Pepsi-Cola**	**Nestle**	**Frito-Lay**
Best sales force/customer teams	32.7%	31.5%	26.4%	14.1%	13.9%	8.4%
	P&G	**Kraft**	**Gen'l Mills**	**Pepsi-Cola**	**Coca-Cola**	**Unilever**
Most innovative marketing programs	30.7%	29.6%	28.9%	14.7%	13.4 %	12.7%
	P&G	**Kraft**	**Gen'l Mills**	**Nestle**	**Pepsi-Cola**	**Coca-Cola**
Most helpful customer information	50.3%	27.2%	23.1%	13.1%	9.4%	9.1%
	P&G	**Kraft**	**Gen'l Mills**	**Nestle**	**Campbell's**	**Unilever**
Best supply chain management	55.0%	36.9%	25.9%	15.9%	10.2%	8.8%

Source: Cannondale Associates, PoweRanking Survey®, 2004.

[a] Each brand measured by percentage of respondents who rank the brand first, second, or third for each category.

Yet volume for such products, while growing fast, remained very small in comparison with CSD volume.[98] With bottled water, a different set of dynamics was in play. Here, sales volume soared (bottled water, one observer noted, was "the most frequent next stop for lapsed soft-drink users"),[99] and the cost, production, and distribution structures closely matched those of the traditional CSD industry. In the early 2000s, bottler margins on water were high; one research report estimated that a bottle of Pepsi's Aquafina garnered a profit of 22.4%, compared with a 19.0% profit for a bottle of Pepsi-Cola.[100] But as consumption shifted from single-serve to multi-pack options, pricing shifted accordingly. At some locations, at one point in 2002, a 24-bottle case of Dasani or Aquafina sold for $3.99, which was less than the cost of bottling it.[101] By 2006, according to one estimate, multi-serve products accounted for about 70% of the bottled water market, up from about 30% a decade earlier. Rising plastic costs also cut sharply into margins in this category.[102] In addition, compared with the CSD market, the water market appeared to involve low brand loyalty and high price sensitivity. A 2002 survey found that while 37% of respondents said that they chose a CSD because "it's my favorite brand," only 10% of respondents said so about a bottled water choice.[103]

INTERNATIONALIZING THE COLA WARS. As U.S. demand for CSDs reached an apparent plateau, Coke and Pepsi increasingly looked abroad for new growth. In 2004, the United States remained by far the largest market, accounting for about one-third of worldwide CSD volume. The next largest markets were, in order, Mexico, Brazil, Germany, China, and the United Kingdom.[104] But improved access to markets in Asia and Eastern Europe stimulated a new, intense phase of the cola wars. In many such markets, per-capita consumption levels were a small fraction of the level seen in the United States. For example, while the average American drank 837 eight-ounce cans of CSDs in 2004, the average Chinese drank just 21. Among major world regions, Coke dominated in Western Europe and much of Latin America, while Pepsi had a marked presence in the Middle East and Southeast Asia.[105] (See Exhibit 10—CSD Industry: Selected International Consumption Rates and Market Shares.) Although the growth potential of both established and emerging markets held great attraction, those markets also posed special challenges.

Coke flourished in international markets, and also relied upon them, far more than Pepsi. As far back as the end of World War II, the company had secured a position as the largest international producer of soft drinks. Coke steadily expanded its overseas operations in the following decades, and the name Coca-Cola became synonymous with American culture. By the early 1990s, Coke CEO Roberto Goizueta would note, "Coca-Cola used to be an American company with a large international business. Now we are a large international company with a sizable American business."[106] Roughly 9 million outlets, located in more than 200 countries, sold Coke products in 2004.[107] About 70% of Coke's sales and about 80% of its profits came from outside the United States; only about one-third of Pepsi's beverage sales took place overseas.[108] Coke enjoyed a world market share of 51.4%, compared with 21.8% for Pepsi and 6% for Cadbury Schweppes.[109]

Pepsi entered Europe soon after World War II. Later, benefiting from Arab and Soviet exclusion of Coke, it moved into the Middle East and Soviet bloc. During the 1970s and 1980s, however, Pepsi put relatively little emphasis on its overseas operations. By the early 1990s, the company once again attacked Coke in the latter's core international markets—though with relatively little success, since Coke struck back aggressively. In one high-profile skirmish, Pepsi's longtime bottler in Venezuela defected to Coke in 1996, temporarily reducing Pepsi's 80% share of the cola market there to nearly nothing.[110] Pepsi had moved away from bruising head-to-head competition with Coke by the early 2000s. Instead, it focused on emerging markets that were still up for grabs.[111] In 2004, its international division (which also covered food offerings) grew faster than any other division, and that division's operating profit was up by 25%. Its international beverage volume was up by 12% overall for the year, driven by a strong performance in its Asia Pacific (up 15%) and Europe, Middle East, and Africa (up 14%) divisions. For both CSDs and non-carbs, the company logged double-digit growth overseas, and double-digit growth also marked volume sales in China, India, and Russia.[112]

Both beverage giants encountered obstacles in their international operations, including antitrust regulation, price controls, advertising restrictions, foreign exchange controls, lack of infrastructure, cultural differences, political instability, and local competition. When Coke acquired most of Cadbury Schweppes's international CSD business in 1999, regulators in Europe, Mexico, and Australia barred the transaction from occurring in those markets.[113] In Germany, a 2003 bottle return law (later rescinded) led many retailers to stop carrying Coke and Pepsi products;

for Coke, that disruption resulted in a year-over-year sales drop of 11%.[114] In Colombia, Marxist rebels in 2003 killed a local Coke executive in a bombing, while union activists accused the company of collaborating with rightwing death squads.[115] In many Latin American countries, low-cost upstarts like Peru's Kola-Real dented market share or eroded pricing power for the larger companies. In 2003, for example, these "B-brands" claimed 30% of CSD share in Brazil, up from about 3% in the early 1990s.[116]

Waging the cola wars in non-U.S. markets enabled Coke and Pepsi not only to expand revenue, but also to broaden their base of innovation. To cope with immature distribution networks, for example, they created novel systems of their own, such as Coke's network of vending machines in Japan—a high-margin channel that at one point accounted for more than half of the company's Japanese sales.[117] Japan also proved to be an impressive laboratory for new products. Teas, coffees, juices, and flavored water made up the majority of that country's 200-plus Coke items, and Coke's largest-selling product there was not soda but canned coffee. "If you're looking for a total beverage business we've got one in Japan," said Coke CEO Isdell.[118] During the same period, Coke introduced 20 new products with a health or diet emphasis into the Mexico market. New approaches to packaging abounded as well.[119] In China and India, use of small returnable glass bottles allowed Coke to reach poor, rural consumers at a very low price point, while boosting revenue-per-ounce.[120]

The End of an Era?

In the early years of the 21st century, growth in soft drink sales for both Coke and Pepsi was falling short of precedent and of investors' expectations. Was the fundamental nature of the cola wars changing? Was a new form of rivalry emerging that would entail reduced profitability and stagnant growth—both inconceivable under the old form of rivalry? Or did the changes under way represent simply another step forward in the evolution of two of the world's most successful companies? In 2000, a Coke executive noted, "the cola wars are going to be played now across a lot of different battlefields."[121] What remained unclear in 2006 was whether those wars were still about "cola," and whether anyone knew for certain where those battlefields were located.

EXHIBIT 10

CSD Industry: Selected International Consumption Rates and Market Shares, 2003 and 1999

	Population	Consumption (8-oz servings per capita)		Annual Growth[a]	2003 Share			1999 Share		
	(thousands)	2003	1999	1999–2003	Coke	Pepsi	Cadb'ry	Coke	Pepsi	Cadb'ry
Europe (23.4%)										
Germany	82,476	340	344	−0.3%	51	5	1	56	8	1
United Kingdom	59,251	420	370	3.2%	47	11	0	43	12	0
Spain	41,060	425	386	2.4%	65	15	5	60	16	5
Italy	57,423	216	212	0.5%	44	6	1.5	45	8	1
France	60,144	180	158	3.3%	60	6	18.6	60	8	5
Russia	143,246	70	52	7.7%	21	18	0	26	12	0
Poland	38,587	167	155	1.9%	19	15	1	28	17	1
Netherlands	16,149	335	356	−1.5%	80	14	0	45	15	1
Hungary	9,877	279	273	0.5%	49	25	4	57	29	5
Romania	22,334	145	104	8.7%	46	8	0	44	9	0
Czech Republic	10,236	410	215	17.5%	13	7	1	36	13	2
Latin America (24.3%)										
Mexico	103,457	610	590	0.9%	73	20	5.1	70	19	3
Brazil	178,470	312	276	3.1%	46	7	0	51	7	0
Argentina	38,428	400	374	1.7%	50	19	0	59	24	0
Colombia	44,222	159	181	−3.2%	51	11	0	60	8	0
Venezuela	25,699	205	290	−8.3%	49	21	0	70	30	0
Chile	15,805	402	392	0.6%	73	5	0	81	4	0
Peru	27,167	166	108	11.4%	39	9	0	50	16	0
Asia Pacific (13.6%)										
China	1,304,196	21	22	−1.2%	51	24	0	34	16	0
Philippines	79,999	187	205	−2.3%	80	16	0	70	18	0
Japan	127,654	80	92	−3.4%	64	11	0	55	11	0
Australia	19,731	490	502	−0.6%	56	10	18.5	57	10	16
Thailand	62,833	95	114	−4.5%	56	43	0	52	45	0
India	1,065,462	8	6	7.5%	45	43	0	56	44	0
South Korea	47,700	118	108	2.2%	47	17	0	54	13	0
Indonesia	219,883	14	9	11.7%	75	5	0	94	6	0
Pakistan	153,578	24	14	14.4%	26	73	0	25	71	3
Vietnam	81,377	20	15	9.3%	39	34	0	63	36	0
Africa/Middle East (7.8%)										
South Africa	45,026	218	207	1.3%	94	0	0	97	0	0
Saudi Arabia	24,217	270	229	4.2%	15	82	0	24	76	0

(continued)

EXHIBIT 10 *(Continued)*

	Population	Consumption (8-oz servings per capita)		Annual Growth[a]	2003 Share			1999 Share		
	(thousands)	2003	1999	1999–2003	Coke	Pepsi	Cadb'ry	Coke	Pepsi	Cadb'ry
Egypt	71,931	61	50	5.1%	48	42	0	60	40	0
Israel	6,433	452	400	3.1%	55	11	0	70	14	0
Morocco	30,566	56	63	−2.9%	87	3	8	96	4	0
North America										
United States	290,809	837	874	−1.1%	44	31	14	44	31	15
Canada	31,510	463	489	−1.4%	38	37	9	39	35	9
Total Worldwide	6,305,252	119	125	−1.2%	51	22	6	53	21	6

Sources: Compiled from *Beverage Digest Fact Book 2005* and *Beverage Digest Fact Book 2001*.

[a] Change calculated using Compounded Annual Growth Rate (CAGR).

[b] Share of worldwide market by volume.

Appendix A—Cadbury Schweppes: Operations and Financial Performance

By the late 1990s, Cadbury Schweppes had emerged as the clear, albeit distant, third-largest player in the U.S. soft drink industry. Its products accounted for 14.5% of CSDs and 9.3% of non-carbs sold in 2004. Its brands include Dr Pepper, 7UP, RC Cola, Schweppes, Canada Dry, A&W, Squirt, Sundrop, Welch's, Country Time, Clamato, Hawaiian Punch, Snapple, Mistic, and Stewart's.

The U.K.-based firm was born of the 1969 merger between Jacob Schweppes' mineral water business (founded in 1783) and John Cadbury's cocoa and

TABLE A

Cadbury Schweppes Financial Data ($ millions)

	2004	2003	2002	2001	2000
Americas Beverages					
Sales	$ 3,854	$ 3,239	$3,190	$2,770	$1,950
Operating profits/sales	25.2%	29.3%	29.5%	29.7%	32.7%
Europe Beverages[a]					
Sales	$ 1,253	$ 1,236	$ 882	$ 560	$ 477
Operating profit/sales	17.9%	17.3%	19.0%	18.2%	15.4%
Consolidated[b]					
Sales	$12,927	$11,500	$8,528	$7,220	$6,161
Operating margin	13.6%	11.6%	17.4%	17.9%	18.9%
Return on assets	5.2%	3.9%	7.0%	7.6%	8.4%

Source: Company financial reports; OneSource, Global Business Browser, http://globalbb.onesource. com/web/Reports/cia.aspx?KeyID=L5018&Process=CP, accessed November 2005.

[a] Soft drink sales in Asia Pacific; Africa, India, and Middle East; and Central and Other divisions are not reported separately from confectionery sales in those regions.

[b] Consolidated figures include worldwide confectionery sales.

chocolate business (founded in 1842). In the mid-1980s, the group decided to focus on its core international confectionery and soft drink businesses. In 1989, its beverage headquarters relocated from London, England, to Stamford, Connecticut. During the 1980s and the early 1990s, its soft drink and confectionery brand portfolio was extended through the acquisition of a number of key brands, notably Mott's (1982), Canada Dry (1986), Trebor (1989), and Bassett's (1989). Its acquisition of Dr Pepper/Seven-Up Companies in 1995 boosted its U.S. CSD market share from 4.6% in 1994 to 15.1% in 1995, and its acquisition of Triarc's Mistic and Snapple brands in 2001 more than doubled its non-carb market from 6.0% in 1999. Further acquisitions included the Orangina and Yoo-Hoo brands (bought from Pernod Ricard in 2001), Squirt (a top-selling brand in Mexico, purchased in 2002), and Nantucket Nectars (bought in 2002 and folded into the Snapple brand). In 1999, Cadbury Schweppes disposed of its soft drink brands in around 160 countries, concentrating its beverages interests on North America, Europe, and Australia.

In 2004, Cadbury Schweppes operated primarily as a licensor, selling concentrate and syrup to independently owned bottling and canning operations (some of which were affiliated with competitors). It also provided marketing support and technical manufacturing oversight to these companies. In the United States, Cadbury Schweppes had a 40% interest in the Dr Pepper/Seven Up Bottling Group (DPSUBG), which accounted for 28.7% of its CSD volume. With its non-carb products and in certain markets (particularly Mexico), it manufactured and distributed its beverages directly or through third-party bottlers.

Endnotes

1. *Beverage Digest Fact Book 2005*, p. 14.

2. See Exhibit 1 and Exhibit 3 in this case.

3. Roger Enrico, *The Other Guy Blinked and Other Dispatches from the Cola Wars* (New York: Bantam Books, 1988).

4. Robert Tollison et al., *Competition and Concentration* (Lexington Books, 1991), p. 11.

5. *Beverage Digest Fact Book 2005*, p. 45.

6. Unless otherwise noted, information on industry participants and structures comes from Michael E. Porter (with research associate Rebecca Wayland), "Coca-Cola versus Pepsi-Cola and the Soft Drink Industry," HBS No. 391-179 (Boston: Harvard Business School Publishing, 1994); Andrew J. Conway et al., "Global Soft Drink Bottling Review and Outlook:

Consolidating the Way to a Stronger Bottling Network" (analysts' report), Morgan Stanley Dean Witter, August 4, 1997; and from casewriter interviews with industry executives.

7. Casewriter conversation with industry insider, April 2006.

8. Ibid.

9. "Cott Begins Shipping from New Fort Worth, Texas Plant," Cott Corporation press release, July 13, 2005; casewriter conversation with industry analyst, November 2005.

10. "Louisiana Coca-Cola Reveals Crown Jewel," *Beverage Industry*, January 1999.

11. Casewriter conversation with industry insider, April 2006.

12. Bonnie Herzog and Daniel Bloomgarden, "Coca-Cola Enterprises" (analysts' report), Salomon Smith Barney, February 19, 2003, pp. 31–32; Bonnie Herzog and Daniel Bloomgarden, "Pepsi Bottling Group" (analysts' report), Salomon Smith Barney, February 24, 2003, pp. 26–27.

13. Timothy Muris, David Scheffman, and Pablo Spiller, *Strategy, Structure, and Antitrust in the Carbonated Soft Drink Industry* (Quorum Books, 1993), p. 63; *Beverage Digest Fact Book 2005*, p. 76.

14. Coca-Cola 2003 Annual Report.

15. Bonnie Herzog, "The Coca-Cola Company" (analyst's report), Credit Suisse First Boston, September 8, 2000, p. 16.

16. Dean Foust, with Geri Smith, "Coke: The Cost of Babying Bottlers," *BusinessWeek*, December 9, 2002, p. 93.

17. Herzog, "The Coca-Cola Company," p. 16.

18. *Beverage Digest Fact Book 2005*, p. 43.

19. Ibid., p. 20.

20. Ibid.

21. Nikhil Deogun and Richard Gibson, "Coke Beats Out Pepsi for Contracts with Burger King, Domino's," *The Wall Street Journal*, April 15, 1999.

22. Casewriter conversation with industry observer, December 2005.

23. "History" section of entry for PepsiCo, Hoover's Online, http://www.hoovers.com, accessed December 2005; *Beverage Digest Fact Book 2005*, p. 62.

24. Ibid., pp. 62–63.

25. Ibid., p. 63.

26. Casewriter examination of ingredients lists for Coke Classic and Pepsi-Cola, November 2005.

27. Casewriter conversation with industry analyst, January 2006.

28. *Beverage Digest Fact Book 2005*, p. 71.

29. Ibid., p. 74.

30. Unless otherwise attributed, all historical information in this section comes from J.C. Louis and Harvey Yazijian, *The Cola Wars* (Everest House, 1980); Mark Pendergrast, *For God, Country, and Coca-Cola* (Charles Scribner's, 1993); and David Greising, *I'd Like the World to Buy a Coke* (John Wiley & Sons, 1997).

31. Louis and Yazijian, *The Cola Wars*, p. 23.

32. David B. Yoffie, *Judo Strategy* (Harvard Business School Press, 2001), Chapter 1.

33. Pendergrast, *For God, Country, and Coca-Cola*, p. 310.

34. Ibid., p. 323.

35. Timothy K. Smith and Laura Landro, "Coke's Future: Profoundly Changed, Coca-Cola Co. Strives to Keep on Bubbling," *The Wall Street Journal*, April 24, 1986.

36. Timothy Muris et al., *Strategy, Structure, and Antitrust in the Carbonated Soft Drink Industry*, p. 73.

37. Greising, *I'd Like the World to Buy a Coke*, p. 88.

38. Ibid., p. 292.

39. *Beverage Industry, January* 1999, p. 17.

40. Albert Meyer and Dwight Owsen, "Coca-Cola's Accounting," *Accounting Today,* September 28, 1998; Herzog and Bloomgarden, "Coca-Cola Enterprises," p. 22; Dean Foust, with Nanette Byrnes, "Gone Flat," *BusinessWeek,* December 20, 2004, p. 76.

41. *Beverage Digest Fact Book 2005*, p. 77.

42. Ibid., p. 77.

43. Ibid., p. 38.

44. Ibid., pp. 90, 93; *Beverage Digest Fact Book 2001*, pp. 77, 80.

45. Foust, with Byrnes, "Gone Flat." On Coca-Cola, see also Andrew Ward, "Coke Gets Real," *Financial Times,* September 25, 2005, p. 17; Michael Santoli, "A New Formula for Coke: How to Put the Fizz Back in the World's Most Famous Brand," *Barron's,* October 4, 2004, p. 21; Betsy Morris, "The Real Story: How Did Coca-Cola's Management Go from First-Rate to Farcical in Six Short Years?" *Fortune,* May 31, 2004, p. 84; Chad Terhune and Betsy McKay, "Bottled Up: Behind Coke's Travails," *The Wall Street Journal,* May 4, 2004, p. A1; Julie Creswell and Julie Schlosser, "Has Coke Lost Its Fizz?" *Fortune,* November 10, 2003, p. 215.

46. Jeremy Grant and Andrew Ward, "A Better Model? Diversified Pepsi Steals Some of Coke's Sparkle," *Financial Times,* February 28, 2005, p. 19. On PepsiCo, see also Patricia Sellers, "The Brand King's Challenge," *Fortune,* April 5, 2004, p. 192; Bethany McLean, "Guess Who's Winning the Cola Wars," *Fortune,* April 2, 2001, p. 164; John A. Byrne, "PepsiCo's New Formula," *BusinessWeek,* April 17, 2000, p. 172.

47. Luisa Dillner, "Mass Hysteria Blamed in Coke Safety Scare," *Chicago Sun-Times,* July 7, 1999, p. 42; Bert Roughton Jr., "Food Scare Put Belgium on Edge," *Atlanta Journal-Constitution,* July 17, 1999, p. D1; "Coca-Cola Recalls Bottles of Drink Sold in Belgium," *The Wall Street Journal,* May 21, 2001, p. B11.

48. Claudia H. Deutsch, "Coca-Cola Reaches into Past for New Chief," *The New York Times,* May 5, 2004, p. 1.

49. Amy Waldman, "India Tries to Contain Tempest over Soft Drink Safety," *The New York Times,* August 23, 2003, p. 3; Terhune and McKay, "Bottled Up: Behind Coke's Travails."

50. Creswell and Schlosser, "Has Coke Lost Its Fizz?"; Betsy McKay and Chad Terhune, "Coca-Cola Settles Regulatory Probe," *The Wall Street Journal,* April 19, 2005, p. A3.

51. Foust, with Byrnes, "Gone Flat"; Morris, "The Real Story."

52. Theresa Howard, "Coke CEO Takes Open Approach to Problems," *USA Today,* September 29, 2004, p. B3.

53. Foust, with Byrnes, "Gone Flat."

54. Chad Terhune, "CEO Says Things Aren't Going Better with Coke," *The Wall Street Journal,* September 16, 2004, p. A1; Renee Pas, "The Top 100 Beverage Companies," *Beverage Industry,* June 1, 2005, p. 38.

55. Barbara Murray, "PepsiCo, Inc.," Hoover's Online, http://www.hoovers.com, accessed November 2005; Nanette Byrnes, "The Power of Two at Pepsi," *BusinessWeek,* January 29, 2001, p. 102.

56. Theresa Howard, "Deal Puts Reinemund on the Fast Track," *USA Today*, December 5, 2000, p. B3.

57. Betsy McKay, "Pucker Up! Pepsi's Latest Weapon Is Lemon-Lime," *The Wall Street Journal,* October 2000, p. B1; Greg Winter, "PepsiCo Looks to a New Drink to Jolt Soda Sales," *The New York Times,* May 1, 2001, p. C1; McLean, "Guess Who's Winning the Cola Wars."

58. Grant and Ward, "A Better Model?"

59. "Historical Financials" section of entries for both Coca-Cola and PepsiCo, Hoover's Online, http://www. hoovers.com, accessed December 2005; Foust, with Byrnes, "Gone Flat"; Grant and Ward, "A Better Model?"

60. Sellers, "The Brand King's Challenge."

61. Foust, with Byrnes, "Gone Flat."

62. Caroline Wilbert, "Coke CEO Neville Isdell: Boss Confident About Strategy," *The Atlanta Journal-Constitution,* November 13, 2005, p. D1.

63. Chad Terhune, "In Switch, Pepsi Makes Diet Cola Its New Flagship," *The Wall Street Journal,* March 16, 2005, p. B1.

64. Rosie Mestel, "Soft Drink, Soda, Pop: Whatever You Call Them, These Sugar Drinks Are Getting Nutritional Heat," *The Evansville Courier,* September 26, 2005, p. D1; Scott Leith, "Obesity Weighs Heavily on Colas," *The Atlanta Journal-Constitution,* February 6, 2005, p. C1; Raja Mishra, "In Battle of Bulge, Soda Firms Defend Against Warning," *The Boston Globe,* November 28, 2004, p. A1.

65. Jeff Cioletti, "Weathering the Perfect Storm," *Beverage Aisle,* April 15, 2004, p. 23.

66. Melanie Warner, "Lines Are Drawn for Big Suit Over Sodas," *The New York Times,* December 7, 2005, p. C1.

67. Betsy McKay, "Soda Marketers Will Cut Back Sales to US Schools," *The Wall Street Journal,* August 17, 2005, p. B1.

68. Ward, "Coke Gets Real."

69. *Beverage Digest Fact Book 2005,* p. 51.

70. Stuart Elliott, "What's in a Name? Higher Sales, or That's the Hope of Some Soft Drink Makers Excising the Word 'Diet,'" *The New York Times,* December 20, 2004, p. C9; Scott Leith, "Refining Diet Drinks: Fewer Men Equate 'Low-Cal' with 'Girly,'" *The Atlanta Journal-Constitution,* February 16, 2005, p. C1.

71. *Beverage Digest Fact Book 2005,* p. 11; *Beverage Digest Fact Book 2001,* p. 11.

72. Herzog and Bloomgarden, "Coca-Cola Enterprises," pp. 36–37.

73. Grant and Ward, "A Better Model?"

74. Joanna Cosgrove, "The 2005 Soft Drink Report," *Beverage Industry,* March 2005, p. 22; Melanie Wells, "Pepsi's New Challenge," *Forbes,* January 10, 2003, p. 68; Grant and Ward, "A Better Model?"

75. *Beverage Digest Fact Book 2005,* pp. 104, 109, 184–195.

76. Scott Leith, "Coke Just So-So in Small Brands: Record Less Than Stellar in Noncarbonated Category," *The Atlanta Journal-Constitution,* June 13, 2004, p. G1.

77. Terhune and McKay, "Bottled Up: Behind Coke's Travails"; Leith, "Coke Just So-So in Small Brands"; Alan R. Elliott, "Energy Drinks Fuel Soda Field," *Investor's Business Daily,* May 23, 2005, p. A11.

78. Terhune, "CEO Says Things Aren't Going Better with Coke."

79. Grant and Ward, "A Better Model?"

80. *Beverage Digest Fact Book 2005,* pp. 116–118.

81. Ibid., p. 118; Chad Terhune, "Coke to Buy Danone's Stake in Bottled-Water Joint Venture," *The Wall Street Journal,* April 25, 2005, p. B4; Barbara Murray, "The Coca-Cola Company," Hoover's Online, http://www. hoovers.com, accessed November 2005.

82. Foust, with Byrnes, "Gone Flat"; Bonnie Herzog and Bloomgarden, "Pepsi Bottling Group," p. 23.

83. Santoli, "A New Formula for Coke."

84. Herzog and Bloomgarden, "Coca-Cola Enterprises," p. 17.

85. Casewriter conversation with industry insider, April 2006.

86. Scott Leith, "Coke, Bottler Work on Plan to Align Goals," *The Atlanta Journal-Constitution,* December 5, 2003, p. C1; Chad Terhune and Betsy McKay, "Coke Shelves Initiative of Ex-Chief," *The Wall Street Journal,* September 28, 2004, p. A3.

87. Chad Terhune, "Coke Bottler in Mexico Threatens to Cut Marketing," *The Wall Street Journal,* November 1, 2005, p. B5.

88. Herzog and Bloomgarden, "Pepsi Bottling Group," pp. 18, 20, 26.

89. *Beverage Digest Fact Book 2005,* pp. 66–68.

90. Herzog and Bloomgarden, "Pepsi Bottling Group," pp. 23–25.

91. Herzog and Bloomgarden, "Coca-Cola Enterprises," pp. 33–34; Richard Joy, "Foods and Nonalcoholic Beverages" (industry survey), Standard & Poor's, June 9, 2005, pp. 11–12.

92. Casewriter conversation with industry insider, April 2006.

93. Melanie Warner, "Making Room on Coke's Shelf Space," *The New York Times,* April 5, 2005, p. C1.

94. Chad Terhune, "Coke Readies New Ads to Boost Its Soda Sales," *The Wall Street Journal,* December 8, 2005, p. A3.

95. Scott Leith, "Designing the Next Big (or Small) Thing," *The Atlanta Journal-Constitution,* September 27, 2003, p. B1; "Fridge Packs Appear to Be Plus for Coke System," *Beverage Digest,* March 28, 2003, http://www. beverage-digest.com/editorial/030328.php, accessed December 2005.

96. "CSDs Have Most—and Proliferating—SKU's, but Number Is Small Relative to Volume," *Beverage Digest,* November 22, 2002, http://www.beverage-digest.com/edito-rial/021122.php, accessed December 2005; casewriter communication with industry analyst, November 2005.

97. Casewriter conversation with industry insider, April 2006.

98. Ward, "Coke Gets Real"; casewriter communication with industry analyst, November 2005.

99. Ward, "Coke Gets Real."

100. Sherri Day, "Summer May Bring a Bottled Water Price War," *The New York Times*, May 10, 2003, p. C1.

101. Betsy McKay, "Liquid Assets: In a Water Fight, Coke and Pepsi Try Opposite Tacks," *The Wall Street Journal*, April 18, 2002, p. A1.

102. Casewriter conversation with industry insider, April 2006.

103. "Water: Supermarkets Account for 50+% of Volume, Morgan Stanley Study Finds Low Brand Loyalty," *Beverage Digest*, June 7, 2002, http://www.beverage-digest.com/editorial/020607.php, accessed December 2005.

104. *Beverage Digest Fact Book 2005*, pp. 90–91.

105. Ibid., pp. 92–93.

106. John Huey, "The World's Best Brand," *Fortune*, May 31, 1993.

107. Paul Klebnikov, "Coke's Sinful World," *Forbes*, December 22, 2003, p. 86.

108. Ward, "Coke Gets Real."

109. *Beverage Digest Fact Book 2005*, p. 90.

110. Nikhil Deogun, "Burst Bubbles: Aggressive Push Abroad Dilutes Coke's Strength as Big Markets Stumble," *The Wall Street Journal*, February 8, 1999, p. A1.

111. Grant and Ward, "A Better Model?"

112. PepsiCo 2004 Annual Report, p. 60.

113. *Beverage Digest Fact Book 2005*, p. 90.

114. James Kanter, "European Court Sides with Coke Against Germany," *The Wall Street Journal*, December 15, 2004, p. 18.

115. Klebnikov, "Coke's Sinful World."

116. David Luhnow and Chad Terhune, "Latin Pop: A Low-Budget Cola Shakes Up Markets South of the Border," *The Wall Street Journal*, October 27, 2003, p. A1.

117. June Preston, "Things May Go Better for Coke amid Asia Crisis, Singapore Bottler Says," *Journal of Commerce*, June 29, 1998, p. A3.

118. Creswell and Schlosser, "Has Coke Lost Its Fizz?"; Ward, "Coke Gets Real."

119. Caroline Wilbert and Shelley Emling, "Obesity Weighs on Coke," *Atlanta Journal-Constitution*, October 27, 2005, p. A1.

120. Leslie Chang, Chad Terhune, and Betsy McKay, "As Global Growth Ebbs, Coke Makes Rural Push into China and India," *The Asian Wall Street Journal*, August 11, 2004, p. A1.

121. Betsy McKay, "Juiced Up: Pepsi Edges Past Coke, and It has Nothing to Do with Cola," *The Wall Street Journal*, November 6, 2000, p. A1.

Nancy Dai
Niraj Dawar
The University of Western Ontario

On July 7, 2002, Zong Qinghou, the general manager of the Wahaha Group (Wahaha), China's largest soft drink producer, was reviewing market data on Wahaha's Future Cola brand in his office in Hangzhou, Zhejiang Province. Wahaha Future Cola had been launched four years earlier to compete with products from Coca-Cola and PepsiCo, the dominant players in the category. At the launch, Zong and his management team had been tremendously energized by the opportunity to compete with some of the world's best companies. Four years later, despite the failure of several other domestic colas, Wahaha Future Cola and other Future Series carbonated drinks had achieved an impressive 18 percent of the carbonated drinks market in the first half of 2002. However, as Future Cola's share grew, Zong was preoccupied with how his multinational competitors would respond, how Wahaha should prepare for these responses, and how it should continue to increase its market share. Competition for share in the high-stakes market of the world's most populated country was intensifying.

Wahaha Group

COMPANY PROFILE. With 2001 sales revenue of RMB6.23 billion, and profits of RMB914 million,[1] the Wahaha Hangzhou Group Co. Ltd. consisted of more than 40 wholly-owned subsidiaries and majority holding companies in 23 provinces, autonomous regions and cities. With total assets of RMB6 billion and 14,000 employees, the group operated more than 68 advanced automated production lines at various locations. Unlike many other Chinese companies of its size, the group had a solid cash position and no long-term bank debt. Wahaha's 2002 target was to achieve sales revenues of RMB8 billion, and a profit of RMB1.3 billion. In the longer term, the Wahaha Group aimed to become a truly national, and even international, player. Specifically, it was working on establishing subsidiaries in most provinces, maintaining its leading position in water, milk drinks and

mixed congee, and on increasing its market share in carbonated beverages, tea and juice drinks.

In 2002, Wahaha competed in six major product categories: milk drinks, packaged water, carbonated drinks, tea and juice drinks, canned food and health-care products. For several years, its milk drink, packaged water and canned mixed congee had been leaders in their respective categories. For the first half of 2002, the total soft drink output for Wahaha was 1.83 million tons (1.66 billion litres), while its closest competitors—Coca-Cola and PepsiCo—sold 1.61 million tons (1.461 billion litres) and 0.76 million tons (0.689 billion litres), respectively. This was the first time that a domestic company's soft drink output had exceeded that of Coca-Cola in China. It was also an unusual situation for Coca-Cola that a local competitor had seemingly come out of nowhere to upstage the global giant. In a nation of 1.3 billion people, per capita consumption of Wahaha beverages in China was more than 10 bottles a year.

WAHAHA'S DEVELOPMENT. Wahaha was founded in 1987, when it began selling bottled soda water, ice cream and stationery to the children in Hangzhou, Zhejiang Province. Founder Zong Qinghou and two employees discovered in 1988 that although there were 38 companies nationwide producing nutritional drinks, none was specifically targeted toward children. The one-child policy had created a whole generation of "little emperors" who, due to their parents' and grandparents' indulgences, were fastidious with food, and presented a potentially huge opportunity. By some estimates there were 200 million such children in China. The company developed a nutritious drink

Nancy Dai prepared this case under the supervision of Professor Niraj Dawar solely to provide material for class discussion. The authors do not intend to illustrate either effective or ineffective handling of a managerial situation. The authors may have disguised certain names and other identifying information to protect confidentiality.

called the Wahaha Natrient Beverage for Children and aggressively pursued the children's market. (The brand Wahaha means "to make children happy.") The product was supported with the slogan "Drinking Wahaha boosts appetite." The product was an instant success, propelling corporate revenues to RMB400 million and profits to RMB70 million by 1990.

Management quickly realized that it was not easy to sustain growth with a single product that had low entry barriers and low technical content. Competitors followed close on the heels of Wahaha. Between 1992 and 1994, 3,000 companies entered the market for children's beverages. Zong decided to expand the product range, entering the fruit-flavored milk drinks market. At the time, a couple of companies had already launched fruit-flavored milk drinks, and the product had won market acceptance. Zong felt this was the best time to enter. In what was to become a pattern in several product categories, Wahaha was a fast follower that quickly ramped up production and achieved high retail coverage with its nationwide production facilities, well-known brand, and well-established distribution network. Its wide range of products made it competitive relative to other domestic producers who tended to have a narrow product line. By the end of 1991, Wahaha launched its fruit-flavored milk drink, followed quickly by Wahaha Milk enriched with vitamins A and D, and calcium. Its catchy advertising jingles rolled off the tongues of tots in many provinces. In 1996, amidst concerns over polluted tap water in several provinces, the company launched Wahaha purified water, which rapidly achieved leading market share, contributing to corporate sales revenues of over RMBI billion in that year.

Wahaha's brand extensions had aroused much debate among industry observers who held that Wahaha was mainly a children's brand and extending it to categories such as mixed congee and purified water would either not work, or would dilute the brand. Zong, while admitting the advantages of launching different brands for different product categories, held that it would spread the limited financial resources of most Chinese enterprises too thin. Wahaha's logic had been to continue to extend the brand into food and beverage categories in which there was no dominant player. For consumers, the connotation of the Wahaha brand broadened and came to represent health, wholesomeness, happiness, quality and reliability, and not just a brand for children's nutritious drinks. Results from the market rewarded and justified Wahaha's approach. After a series of brand extensions, Wahaha's sales revenue

exceeded RMB2 billion in 1997, and the revenue of Wahaha purified water and mixed congee exceeded RMB500 million and 100 million respectively. This was a rare achievement, even in China's rapidly growing food and beverage industry. In 1998, spurred by its success in other beverage categories, Wahaha decided to tackle the prize: the carbonated drinks market. Industry observers were skeptical and predicted that it would last no more than a few months on the market.

Corporate growth was powered not just by the launch of new products, but also through acquisitions, such as loss-making companies that were several times larger, but poorly managed. Acquisitions supported geographic expansion and allowed Wahaha to produce locally in various provincial markets, as well as to increase its market share and brand awareness in other provinces. By 2002, over a third of Wahaha's output was produced outside its home province.

WAHAHA'S JOINT VENTURES WITH DANONE. In 1996, despite Wahaha's excellent performance, management realized that it needed to scale its operations quickly and obtain world-class production technology if it was to survive competition from both local and multinational competitors. After careful consideration, it chose to partner with the giant French food company, Groupe Danone. The two companies established several production-oriented joint ventures. While Danone eventually held a 51 percent share of the joint ventures, Wahaha retained control of management and marketing. In 2002, among Wahaha Group's 42 companies and RMB3.5 billion registered capital, Danone's investment was 32 percent. With the injection of capital from Danone, Wahaha launched Wahaha Future Cola and introduced advanced production lines for bottling water, milk and tea. Prior to the joint venture, the annual increase in revenues and profits was about RMB100 million and RMBIO million respectively. Since 1996, both revenue and profit had grown even more rapidly (see Exhibit 1).

ZONG QINGHOU'S MANAGEMENT STYLE. Founder and general manager Zong Qinghou was a charismatic leader who liked to "put his eggs in the baskets he knew best." Like most of his generation of the Cultural Revolution, he spent 15 years in the countryside after finishing junior school. This experience taught him a lot about rural China. When he came back to his hometown, Hangzhou, he worked in a factory, first as a worker and then in sales. During this period, he

EXHIBIT 1
Wahaha Group Sales Revenue and Profit 1996 to 2001 (in RMB million)

Region %	1996	1997	1998	1999	2000	2001
Sales revenue	1,110	2,110	2,870	4,510	5,440	6,230
Profit	155	334	501	875	906	914
Profit margin	14%	16%	17%	19%	17%	15%

Source: Company files.

traveled extensively throughout China, deepening his knowledge of markets and consumers in various regions. He was 42 when he began his career as sales manager of the two person sales team at the factory. His job included delivering goods to retailers on his cycle.

When asked what made Wahaha so successful, Zong responded that the company understood the Chinese market well:

> Market research reports in China are not reliable. You pay the market research firms large amounts of money and you don't know where the money was spent. However, our own marketing people are our market research staff since we are always collecting information about the market, and we make decisions based on their understanding of the market.

Now in his late 50s, Zong worked long hours and still traveled more than 200 days every year "to keep a finger on the pulse of the market." He hosted most of the marketing meetings at Wahaha and participated in every product launch and marketing planning activity.

WAHAHA'S MARKETING. Marketing, research and development (R&D) and logistics management were centralized at headquarters, while the subsidiaries were engaged in production. Wahaha's marketing was clearly homegrown.

WAHAHA'S ADVERTISING. A typical new product launch followed a pattern established early on in Wahaha's history. In an early launch of Wahaha Natrient Beverage, Zong signed advertising deals worth several hundred thousand RMB with local television stations, exceeding even the company's cash reserves at the time. In its advertisement, Wahaha highlighted data from reports about children's malnutrition and endorsements from experts about Wahaha Natrient Beverage's nutritional benefits for children. On the strength of the advertising, Wahaha would convince the local government-controlled distribution companies to carry the product. If distributors hesitated, Wahaha's marketing staff would call every retailer and smaller distributor in the local yellow pages to inquire if they carried Wahaha Natrient Beverage. This created a buzz that usually resulted in the product being listed with the distribution companies.

In 2001, Wahaha was among the top 10 advertisers in China's US$11.2 billion advertising market, and the only beverage company in the group.[2] Wahaha's total advertising expenditures amounted to more than RMB500 million, with media buys accounting for 80 percent. Comparatively, Coca-Cola's 2001 media expense in China (including cinema, TV, radio, print, and outdoor) was US$19 million. Wahaha's television advertising was mainly intended to build brand awareness and recognition, while print advertising elaborated on product benefits and promotions. Wahaha spent 75 percent of its marketing budget on television advertising, and half of that was on CCTV Channel 1 (the national news channel). The remainder was spent on print media (5 percent), promotion (10 percent) and outdoor advertising (10 percent). Wahaha's advertising targeted the mass market, and not just the wealthier urban consumers. The prices of its products were usually lower than those of comparable products from its multinational competitors.

In addition to Wahaha's advertising, its sponsorship activities had helped build positive associations for its brand. Wahaha established Wahaha elementary school, Wahaha Children's Palace (a recreation center for children), Wahaha Children's Art Troupe and Wahaha Summer Camps to underscore its involvement in child development. In 2001, Wahaha held a campaign to celebrate Children's Day and Beijing's application to host the 2008 Summer Olympic Games.

Wahaha was also the first among Chinese companies to use celebrity product endorsement for its products. In 1996, Jinggangshan, a pop singer, was signed to endorse Wahaha purified water. Celebrity endorsement was also used for Wahaha Future Cola and Wahaha Tea series.

WAHAHA'S DISTRIBUTION. Key success factors for Wahaha were the unique relationships developed with distributors over the previous 10 years. In a vast country where logistics are notoriously difficult, Wahaha's network was able to quickly deliver its products, reaching even remote corners of China within days. Unlike many multinational and domestic companies which preferred to establish their own distribution networks, Wahaha focused on partnering with local distributors, and its initial promotional efforts on entry into a region included distributors rather than end consumers alone.

Partnerships with local distributors were not without problems. In particular, accounts receivable and bad debts were a perennial headache and the main reason why multinationals shunned this mode of distribution. In 1994, Wahaha concluded that the problem of accounts receivable was serious enough to jeopardize its growth and success. The company tackled the issue head-on by developing a radical new policy that ensured compliance and on-time payment by introducing incentives for channel members to play for long-term gain: distributors were required to pay an annual security deposit in advance and operate according to Wahaha's payment policy. In return, Wahaha would pay a higher-than-bank interest rate on the security deposit and offered discounts for early payment. At the end of the year, bonuses were awarded to distributors making prompt payments. The policy was replicated down the chain as distributors, in turn, developed secondary wholesalers, some of whom enjoyed preferential policies by paying security deposits to the distributors. It took Wahaha two years to implement the policy. In the process, a number of distributors that had low credibility dropped out of the system. Those that remained were more committed than ever to Wahaha.

Wahaha established offices in more than 30 provinces with sales staff coordinating operations with the distributors. Distributors were in charge of carrying inventory, providing funds and delivering to the retailers, and Wahaha's local offices supported them in retail coverage, inventory management, advertising and promotion. Wahaha established coordination teams to monitor prices in different areas to protect the interests of local distributors. Wahaha's staff collected information from the market and provided feedback to headquarters, which enabled the company to adjust its sales strategy and develop new products. Today, Wahaha 's 2,000 sales staff work closely with more than 1,000 influential distributors that have the credibility and infrastructure to sell large volumes. Loyalty and stability of the distributors are key, and bad debts have decreased substantially. In 2002, Wahaha began implementing an information system that would enable distributors and Wahaha to exchange information in real time.

The World Soft-Drink Industry

The term "soft drinks" refers to beverages that do not contain alcohol, and includes packaged water, carbonated drinks, juices and juice drinks, ready-to-drink tea, as well as sports and energy drinks.

In 2000, global soft drink consumption reached 320.2 billion litres. That total was split into 170 billion litres (53 percent) of carbonated drinks, 77 billion litres (24 percent) of packaged water, and the "other" category which included juices, ready-to-drink tea, sports and energy drinks, and miscellaneous drinks accounting for 73.2 billion litres (23 percent). Worldwide, the growth of carbonated drinks had been slowing in recent years from an average annual rate of 4 percent between 1994 and 2000 to a predicted rate of only 2 percent in 2003 (see Exhibit 2). These numbers masked fast growth in countries such as China and India, which compensated for declines in the more mature markets of North America and Europe. Packaged water was growing worldwide, in some markets due to consumer trends toward a healthier lifestyle, and in others due to the poor quality of tap water. The "other" category had great growth potential due to increased demand for more healthy, nutritious and tasty drinks. The size of this category had rapidly grown from 52.7 billion litres in 1994 to 73.2 billion litres in 2000. By 2003 volumes were forecast to reach 85.6 billion litres. Within this category, "ready-to-drink tea" had had the fastest growth since 1994 with an annual increase of over 11 percent and industry observers believed it still had plenty of untapped potential.

THE PLAYERS IN CHINA. The leading soft drink producers in the world included Coca-Cola, PepsiCo, Nestlé and Danone, and all four were also present in China. Globally, the first two were dominant in the carbonated category with more than 70 percent combined market share, while the latter two were strong in the ready-to-drink tea and water categories.

EXHIBIT 2

World Soft Drink Average Annual Growth Rate 1994 to 2003

Category	1994–2000	2001–2003
Carbonated drinks	4%	2%
Packaqed water	8%	6%
Other*	570%	530%
Juice and nectars	4.10%	4.20%
Non-carbonated drinks	4.90%	6.30%
Iced tea	11.70%	5.80%
Sports and energy drinks	6.40%	5.90%

'Other' category includes juice and nectars, still drinks, iced tea, sports and energy drinks.

Global Soft Drink Category Development (billions of litres)

Source: Canadean Ltd.

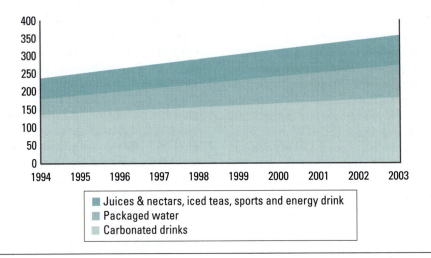

COCA-COLA Coca-Cola was the world's largest soft-drink company, and the fifth-largest food and beverage company. Its 2001 revenues were US$20.092 billion, with a net income of US$3.969 billion. The firm sold about 300 drink brands, including coffees, juices, sports drinks and teas in 200 nations. Its major brands included Coca-Cola Classic, Diet Coke, Sprite, Fanta (carbonated drinks), Minute Maid (juice), POWERade (sports drink) and Dasani (water). It distributed Danone's Evian water in North America and Danone's spring water brands in the United States. Beverage Partner Worldwide, its joint venture with Nestlé, S.A., marketed ready-to-drink coffee and tea. More than 60 percent of its sales revenues came from outside the United States. Coca-Cola's stated aim was to become an all around beverage company. In 2001,

water was the second largest contributor to its growth after carbonated drinks. Coca-Cola had recently instituted a "think local, act local, but leverage global" mandate to empower local decision-makers, in recognition of the need to both respond to local preferences and react to local competitors. In response, its local subsidiaries had launched a wide variety of drinks aimed at local needs.

Coca-Cola first opened bottling plants in Shanghai and Tianjin in 1927, which were shut after the communist revolution in 1949. In 1979, when Coca-Cola reentered China, following the re-establishment of relations between China and the United States, it became the first American consumer product to return to China. In 2000, it moved its marketing headquarters for China from Hong Kong to Shanghai. By 2002,

Coca-Cola had a total of 28 bottling plants in China, with a total investment of US$1.1 billion. In most of these joint ventures, Coca-Cola didn't have majority shareholding. Its soft drink output in China was 16 percent of the national total in 2001 and its carbonated drink output was about 35 percent of total carbonated drink output. China was the sixth largest market for the company worldwide. In addition to its global carbonated drink brands such as Coca-Cola, Diet Coke, Fanta and Sprite, the company also developed local brands such as Heaven and Earth (non-carbonated fruit juice, tea, water), Jinrneile (tea), Smart (fruit-flavored carbonated drink), Lanfeng (honey green tea) and Qoo (juice drink). In 2001, it launched its water brand "Sensation" (at the remarkably low wholesale price point of RMB0.50, while the market leader Wahaha water was selling at RMB0.90). In its advertising, the company included Chinese cultural icons such as windmills and dragons. Local film and sports stars were engaged as endorsers, including diver Fu Mingxia, the three-time Olympic gold medalist. It also sponsored the Coca-Cola Cup National Youth Soccer Tournament and the China national soccer teams at all levels. Coca-Cola also extended its sponsorship contracts with the International Olympic Committee up to 2008, which included US$1 billion in funding for the Beijing Games. In 2001, the total revenue for Coca-Cola China was about US$189 million and revenue from carbonated drinks was about US$186 million. However, the annual per capita consumption of Coca-Cola products in China was a meager eight servings (about 0.2268 litre per serving). Consumption was still a far cry from the average 415 servings consumed in the United States, 163 in Japan, 98 in Europe and 68 in South Korea.

PEPSICO After the merger with Quaker in 2001, PepsiCo became the fourth-largest food and beverage company in the world. Its 2001 total sales revenue of US$26.935 billion included beverage revenue and profit of US$10.44 billion and US$1.678 billion respectively. Forty-two of its sales were outside the United States. Its powerful soft drink brands included Pepsi-Cola, Diet Pepsi, Mountain Dew, 7UP, Miranda, Gatorade (sports drink), Tropicana (juice), Lipton teas and Aquafina (water).

In 1981, PepsiCo signed a deal with the Chinese government to establish a joint venture bottling plant in Shenzhen. By 2002, the company had invested a total of US$500 million in China in 14 bottling plants and employed close to 10,000 people. Unlike Coca-Cola, PepsiCo sought a majority share in the joint ventures. Its flagship carbonated drink brands in China were Pepsi-Cola, Pepsi Light, Pepsi Twist, 7UP, Miranda and Mountain Dew. It also owned local brands such as Asia, Arctic and Tianfu. Its non-carbonated drink brands in China included Gatorade and Dole (fruit juice). Its non-beverage brands included Lay's potato chips, Doritos and Cheetos. Its soft drink output in China was about 8 percent of the national total in 2001. According to A.C. Nielsen's market data in Asia, Pepsi-Cola was the most popular soft drink brand for young consumers, a reflection of its positioning for that demographic market. In its advertising in China, PepsiCo used popular entertainers such as Faye Wang, Guo Fuchen and Chen Huiling as endorsers. Despite its marketing efforts and popularity among China's youth, PepsiCo China had not been profitable during its 20 years in China: high marketing costs and conflicts with joint venture partners were holding the company back.[3]

NESTLÉ SA With revenues of CHF84.698 billion[4] (approximately US$56 billion) and profit of CHF6.681 billion (approximately US$4 billion) in 2001, Nestlé was the world's largest food and beverage company. Its major products included coffee, water, dairy products, breakfast cereals, culinary products, ice cream, frozen food, chocolate and confectionery, and pet care. Its major water brands included Nestlé Pure Life, Nestlé Aquarel, Perrier and Vittel. Other beverage brands included Nestea, Nesquik, Nescau, Milo, Carnation, Libby's and Cam. In 2001, Nestlé was the world leader in bottled water with a market share of 16.3 percent. Nestlé owned four of the top six water brands in the world.

Nestlé came to China in 1979. By 2002 it had established 14 fully owned enterprises, 19 joint ventures and one R&D center for a total investment of US$72 million. Its 2001 sales in China amounted to US$570 million. Due to the growth of packaged water and its profitability, Nestlé China aimed to be the market leader in this category. It established plants for producing packaged water in Tianjin and Shanghai and was expanding its own sales network to co-operate with distributors.

GROUPE DANONE The French company ranked sixth in the global food and beverage industry. In 2001, it had revenues of £14.470 billion (approximately US$14 billion), with net income of €132 million (approximately US$127.7 million). It operated in three core businesses: fresh dairy products, beverages and cereal biscuits and snacks. Its major brands included Danone and Dannon for fresh dairy products, Evian, Volvic and Aqua for mineral water, and LU for biscuits. Its leading position worldwide was based on a portfolio of major international brands and a solid presence in local markets (about 70 percent of global sales came from brands that were local market leaders in which Danone had shares). As part of a recent push toward globalization, the company had made about 40 acquisitions in Asia, Latin America, Central Europe, Africa and the Middle East.

Danone's major products in China included biscuits, water, yogurt and milk. Most of these products were sold under the Danone brand. In 1987, the company had begun operations in China by establishing the Guangzhou Danone Yogurt Company. This was followed in 1992 by the Shanghai Danone Biscuit Company. Since then, it had acquired a number of companies: in 1996 it purchased 63.2 percent of Haomen Beer, 54.2 percent of Wuhan Donghu Beer and its stake in the five joint ventures with Wahaha. In 1998 it owned 54.2 percent of Shenzhen Danone Yili Beverages Co. Ltd., and in 2000 it purchased 92 percent of Robust Group, one of the top 10 Chinese soft drink producers. In December 2000, it had acquired a 5 percent stake in Shanghai Bright Dairy, one of the top milk producers in China. It also purchased 50 percent of Meilin-Zhengguanghe Water Company and 10 percent of Zhengguanghe Online Shopping Company.

CHINA'S SOFT DRINK INDUSTRY. With the entry of multinationals into the Chinese market in the 1980s, marketing, advanced production technology and cutting-edge management expertise were injected into China's soft drink industry, spurring its development. Over the past 20 years, the industry had grown at an annual rate of over 21 percent, and annual output had increased from 0.288 million tons (261 million litres) in 1980 to 16.69 million tons (15.141 billion litres) in 2001 (see Exhibit 3). Per capita consumption increased from 0.3 litre per annum in 1982 to eight litres per annum in 2001, 27 times that of 1982. Total revenues exceeded RMB40 billion in 2000. In urban areas, soft drinks were no longer seen as an occasional luxury to be consumed only in restaurants and hotels, but a regularly consumed product. Drink package formats diversified to meet new consumption patterns, and now included cans, polyethylene terephtalate (PET) and paper packs.

China's soft drink industry had sped through three major development stages in a short time: the rise of carbonated drinks in the 1980s, packaged water in the 1990s and tea in the 2000s. In 2001, packaged water accounted for 40.6 percent of total sales, carbonated drinks for 27 percent and the "other" category for 32.4 percent. The fastest growing product was bottled tea because of its low-calorie, low-fat and low-sugar content, and

EXHIBIT 3

China's Soft Drink Output

Year	Soft Drink Output (in millions of tons)	Carbonated Drink Output (in millions of tons)	Carbonated Drinks as a Percentage of Total Soft Drinks
1994	6.29	3.14	50%
1995	9.82	5.21	53%
1996	8.84	4.29	49%
1997	10.69	4.92	46%
1998	12.00	5.40	45%
1999	11.86	4.27	36%
2000	14.91	4.62	31%
2001	16.69	4.57	27%

Source: The beverage industry.

convenience. It had a share of about 12 percent and an annual growth of 85 percent. It was predicted that juice and milk drinks would become the catalyst for growth in the next phase of development. Despite rapid growth, China's national per capita consumption was still only 20 percent of the world average and 33 percent of the United States average. Growth potential for all categories remained high. It was predicted that over the next 10 to 15 years, industry output would grow at an annual rate of about 10 percent, reaching 22.65 million tons (20.548 billion litres) in 2005, and 37 million tons (33.566 billion litres) by 2015. With China's entry into the World Trade Organization (WTO) in 2001, China's soft drink industry was expected to develop even more rapidly and competition was already intensifying as restrictions on foreign investment were lifted.

A number of large companies and brands were present on the national stage, yet the industry remained fragmented in comparison to developed markets. In 2001, the combined output of the top 10 domestic soft drink producers in China (see Exhibit 4) accounted for 40 percent of the national total.[5] With Coca-Cola China and PepsiCo China, the total output of the top players represented 63 percent of national output. In the 2000s, several of the top 10 companies were undergoing major changes: Jianlibao, a large domestic player, was in crisis; Danone invested in Wahaha, Robust and Meilin-Zhengguanghe; Xuri Group, the largest tea producer, failed in its competition with two iced-tea

brands from Taiwan (named Mr. Kon and President), which now held 75 percent share, with combined revenues of RMB3.5 billion. Nestlé, despite its leading position in the global tea market, did not do as well in China. Robust, in which Danone had a majority share, had its own problems. Five of its top executives resigned due to the company's failure to meet growth targets and because of differences of opinion on the future strategy of the company with Danone. Danone China's CEO took over the management role.

CONSUMERS. According to research conducted in 2001, the target customers for soft drinks were people in the 11 to 40 age group. Income and education level were positively related to soft drink purchases. When purchasing soft drinks, taste was a key criterion. In addition, young consumers were concerned with brand, lifestyle and fashion. Older consumers cared more about health and nutrition. Women and children preferred sweeter drinks, men and young consumers preferred a crisp taste, while older consumers preferred a light taste. Most consumers purchased soft drinks in supermarkets for reasons of price, choice, and the quality assurance the retailer provided. Drinks were also sold through convenience stores, ice cream shops and roadside stalls, especially those near residential areas and schools.

Marketing in the soft drink industry had changed in recent years. Prior to 1997, the emphasis had been

EXHIBIT 4

Top Ten Domestic Soft Drink Producers in China

Company	Major Soft Drink	Major Brand
Robust (Guangdong) Food & BeverageCo., Ltd.	non-carbonated drink	Robust
Guangdong Jianlibao Beverage Co., Ltd.	sport drink	Jianlibao
Shanghai Maling Aquarius (Group) Corporation	canned food, packaged water	Zhengguanghe
Beijing Huiyuan Juice Group Corporation	juice	Huiyuan
Hebei Xurishen Co. Ltd.	tea	Xurishen
Hebei Lolo Co. Ltd.	almond drink	Lolo
Hangzhou Wahaha Group Corporation	packaged water, carbonated drinks, tea, dairy drink	Wahaha Future
Hainan Coconut Palm Group Corporation	coconut milk	Coconut Palm
Shenzhen Danone Yili Beverage Co., Ltd.	mineral water	Yili
Cestbon Food & Beverage (shenzhen) Co., Ltd	distilled water	Cestbon

Source: China Soft Drink Industry Association.

on brand-building, and companies had spent heavily on advertising. However, with brand proliferation and several companies adopting similar positioning, distribution had become a key battleground for gaining competitive advantage.

Cola in China

Thanks to Coca-Cola and PepsiCo, cola was the most popular soft drink worldwide, with consumption amounting to 70 billion litres, and accounting for 20 percent of all soft drink sales. Cola sales were still on the rise, though its role in the overall soft drinks mix was diminishing.

In the early 1980s, before Coca-Cola and PepsiCo entered China, more than 10 domestic cola manufacturers produced cola, but with little marketing, revenues remained small. With the arrival of the two multinational giants, the local producers found it hard to compete, and gradually withdrew from the market or established joint bottling ventures with the two giants.

Coca-Cola's and PepsiCo's sales volumes rose in line with overall sales of cola until they dominated China's carbonated drink market. The two companies had replicated their global rivalry in China and were initially determined to seize market share from domestic cola producers, even at the cost of profitability. The headquarters of both companies in China co-ordinated the marketing efforts of the bottling plants. Both used heavy advertising and sponsoring to support their cola brands. By 2000, Coca-Cola had an average of 85 percent distribution penetration in cities, while PepsiCo stood at about 65 percent but was growing faster (3.7 percent growth rate versus Coca Coca's 1.3 percent).[6] Coca-Cola expanded its sales nationwide: it first targeted the 150 cities with a population greater than one million by establishing sales channels there. Next, it continued to roll out into cities with populations greater than 0.5 million, and so on. In comparison, PepsiCo focused on key markets and in cities such as Shanghai, Chongqing, Chengdu, Wuhan and Shenzhcn, where it had a higher share than its rival.

In 1998 some domestic soft drink producers, attracted by the rapidly growing market, launched their own cola brands. Among them were Wahaha Future Cola from Wahaha, and Fenhuang Cola from Guangzhou Fenhuang Food Company. Both advertised heavily on CCTV. Wahaha launched its Wahaha Future Cola brand during the soccer World Cup and utilized its well-established distribution channels. Fenhuang Cola signed up the famous martial arts actor Jackie Chan to endorse its brand. Both brands emphasized a "China's own cola" positioning, and were targeting smaller cities and the rural market where the two big foreign cola producers were comparatively weak. This revitalization of domestic cola brought other competitors into the fray, including Alishan Zhonghua Cola and Yanjing Cola in 2000, as well as Jianlibao's Huating Cola in 2001.

WAHAHA FUTURE COLA. By 1998, Wahaha had firmly established its production and distribution system, and its dominant position in non-carbonated drinks was secure. Wahaha could not, for long, neglect the carbonated market which represented almost half of the volume of the soft drink industry. Entering the market would provide a much better utilization of its distribution network, and leverage its marketing skills. But it would also mean direct competition with Coca-Cola and PepsiCo. In 1997, the total cola output in China was 1.36 million tons (1.234 billion litres) and Coca-Cola and PepsiCo held a combined market share of 80 percent. In 1998, Coca-Cola's total beverage output in China was two million tons and PepsiCo 0.8 million tons. Wahaha, despite its number one position among domestic producers, had a total output of 0.93 million tons. Coca-Cola's and PepsiCo's success against the domestic cola producers in the early stages and their strong brand name and sales network in big cities fanned a high entry barrier for new competitors.

Zong firmly believed local companies were capable of competing with the multinational players. He pointed to the computer industry, where domestic companies such as Legend were dominating the local market, and even building global brands. He pointed out that in the food and beverage industry where the technical requirements were relatively low and an understanding of domestic preferences was a distinct advantage, domestic companies had an edge. He concluded that the failure of domestic colas in the early stages was due to their lack of marketing and brand management skills, and that Wahaha had proven that it had these skills. As well, he believed some domestic producers did not want to compete with the multinationals because they lacked the confidence to compete against the giants. Confidence was not lacking at Wahaha.

Zong decided to target the rural market first because he knew and understood this market, and because it was not the focus of Coca-Cola and PepsiCo. He reasoned that cola had the potential to be a mass-market product, and the rural areas were where the mass market resided. The 1.1 billion people in the rural market were impossible to ignore. Over the years, China's rural population had become wealthier. In 2000, rural residents' average income was 36 percent of that of an urban resident (see Exhibit 5), but due to their large numbers, they accounted for two-thirds of national spending. A rural resident's spending on food and beverage totaled RMB820.52 a year, 42 percent that of an urban resident. Meanwhile, the development of mass communication had made the rural population more accessible, and exposed it to the outside world. Zong believed these trends represented an unparalleled and untapped opportunity.

To develop the product, Wahaha co-operated with R&D institutes and leading domestic flavor producers. To ensure that its cola would be of a high quality, Wahaha sought the advice of global beverage experts and conducted thousands of taste tests worldwide. Its taste was designed to be close to international colas, but a little bit sweeter and stronger to cater to the Chinese consumers' taste. In domestic blind taste tests, consumers preferred Wahaha Future Cola to other colas.

The name Wahaha Future Cola was put forward by Wahaha's employees. The Chinese characters of the brand meant "unusual," a reference to the unusual move of launching against entrenched and strong competitive rivals.

Wahaha did not intend to start a price war in the cola category, but it prepared to win such a war if one broke out. At launch, Wahaha offered three pack sizes, the same as Coca-Cola and PepsiCo: 355 ml, 500 ml and 1.25 litres. A standard unit case (12 bottles of 500 ml) of Wahaha Future Cola was priced at RMB19 (wholesale), RMB7 lower than Coca-Cola and Pepsi-Cola. This translated into a price difference of approximately RMB0.50 per bottle at retail. One reason for the lower price, Wahaha executives explained, was that Future Cola was aimed at the rural market which was more price-sensitive than the urban markets where the international competitors focused. Assessing potential competitive responses, Zong said:

> It is possible that Coca-Cola might reduce its price. But if it lowers the price per bottle of cola by RMB0.10, it will probably lose profit of about RMB0.5 billion; if it cuts price by RM0.50 it stands to lose RMB2.5 billion. If it is willing to do so, we are willing to follow.

Wahaha reasoned that its revenues from other products could support Future Cola through a price war. As it happened, Wahaha maintained the price difference with Coca-Cola and PepsiCo over the years despite the launch of new pack sizes (see Exhibit 6).

Wahaha supported the launch with an RMB33.9-million TV campaign, including RMB12.44 million spent on CCTV during the soccer World Cup. Simultaneously, Wahaha greatly increased its brand-building efforts. In 1998, total TV advertising of Wahaha reached RMB368.7 million, of which RMB65.18 million was devoted to Future Cola. CCTV's coverage (national, including rural areas) and credibility (as a domestic national voice) among consumers made it an excellent

EXHIBIT 5

Comparison of Urban Residents' and Rural Residents' Disposable Income in China

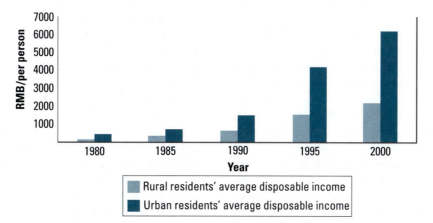

EXHIBIT 6

Retail Price Comparison of Various Pack Sizes in 2002 (in RMB)

Size	Coca-Cola	Pepsi-Cola	Wahaha Future Cola
355 ml	1.8–2.2	1.8–2.2	1.7–2.0
500 ml	2.2–2.5	2.2–2.5	1.9–2.2
600 ml	2.2–2.5	2.2–2.5	none
1.25 l	4.4–4.9	4.4–4.9	3.8
1.5 l	4.4–4.9	4.4–4.9	none
2 l	6.5	6.5	6.0–6.5
2.25 l	6.5	6.5	none

Note: Both Coca-Cola and Pepsi-Cola offered 600 ml, 1.5 l and 2.25 l at the same price as 500 ml, 1.25 l and 2 l as promotion prices.
Source: Company files .

channel to convey Wahaha Future Cola's brand image. According to a national survey, 61 percent of rural consumers said TV was their most important source of information and 33.8 percent said CCTV Channel 1 was the most frequently viewed channel. Favorite programs for rural residents included films, TV series and CCTV news. Prime advertising time was 7 p.m. to 10 p.m. It helped that Wahaha had been advertising on CCTV for 10 years and already had high brand awareness among rural consumers.

Wahaha relied on its nationwide distribution network to get the product to rural consumers. While Coca-Cola and PepsiCo had the advantage in large cities where chain stores and supermarkets accounted for half the grocery trade, Wahaha played on its strength in the countryside where the trade was fragmented, and reachable primarily through multi-layered wholesale markets. Distributors who had been working with Wahaha for years and who had benefited from Wahaha's remarkable growth supported the launch of the cola.

The initial success of the cola surprised even Wahaha. The company could not meet demand using its own bottling facilities and even resorted to outsourcing bottling to other bottlers. When Coca-Cola bottlers were approached, the answer was a firm "no." At the same time, many of Coca-Cola's distributors noticed that if they sold Wahaha Future Cola, Coca-Cola would stop supplying them and refuse end-of-year bonuses.[7]

On average, advertising expenses of Wahaha Future Cola comprised about 20 to 30 percent of the company's total advertising expenditure, adjusted for seasonal and promotional focus. Besides advertising on

CCTV and other local TV channels, Wahaha used outdoor advertising and point-of-sale advertising. In particular, to tackle the rural market, it used "wall advertising"—painting walls with advertising slogans—a cost-effective way to promote brand awareness. At busy roads and fairs, Wahaha set up large brand and slogan banners. It also sponsored traveling troupes that performed in rural markets and at fairs. In villages where there was no cinema, Wahaha sponsored traveling film shows. These activities catered to the needs of rural customers and quickly increased Wahaha Future Cola's awareness in the rural market.

In 2000, Yu Chen Qing, a pop singer from Taiwan, was signed on to endorse Wahaha Future Cola, while Coco Li Wen, another pop singer from Taiwan, endorsed the Future Lemon carbonated drink. In 2000 and 2001, Wahaha was the exclusive sponsor for CCTV's spring festival party, a program that attracted a mass audience, building national brand awareness.

In 2001, Wahaha Future Cola launched a new advertising slogan "Future Cola, the choice for happy occasions." To support this association, Wahaha provided free cola to wedding parties in some key markets. A co-promotion with liquor producers further reinforced the association.

Before the spring festival in 2002, Zong noticed that Coca-Cola changed its original paper case packaging to plastic wrap to save costs. Zong saw this as an opportunity to promote Wahaha Future Cola's paper packaging, which was easier to carry and looked better than plastic wrap. Sales staff promoted the paper case as a gift item for the festival, inserting posters of the image of the god of fortune in each case.

Wahaha Future Cola's focus on rural markets meant that 60 percent to 70 percent of total sales came from rural areas. In 2002, Wahaha launched carbonated drinks with fresh apple juice and orange juice. With the wider product range, it increased its sales efforts in supermarkets and big stores, and in larger cities.

During the same period, Coca-Cola and PepsiCo began to notice and respond to the domestic upstart, while continuing to compete with each other. In a few markets they offered their cola products at a lower price than Wahaha Future Cola. Meanwhile, they further localized their marketing. For example, Coca-Cola adjusted its advertising strategy and increased its advertising on CCTV. It also signed on pop singers from Taiwan and Hong Kong, Zhang Huimei and Xie Tingfeng, to endorse its brand. In 2001, to celebrate Beijing's victory in its bid to host the 2008 Olympic Games, Coca-Cola announced a new thematic pack design just 22 minutes after the news announcement. The following day the new design (in gold, integrating various architectural and sports themes in Beijing) was launched in key markets. In 2001 during the Spring Festival, Coca-Cola packs carried a picture of a traditional Chinese clay doll "A Fu" (a symbol of luck).

Coca-Cola and PepsiCo also began to actively develop the non-carbonated drink market while continuing to promote their carbonated products. Pepsi promoted non-carbonated drinks such as Dole (100 percent fruit juice) and Gatorade. Coca-Cola launched "Sensation" water in 2001 without any advertising support, and with a wholesale price that was 40 percent lower than Wahaha purified water in some regions. In 2002, it launched new 600 ml, 1.5 litre and 2.25 litre packages for its cola without increases in price over the 500 ml, 1.25 litre and two litre respectively. Coca-Cola also announced its intention to increase the number of bottling plants to 34 from 28 within five years, growing especially in the mainly rural western region.

Both Coca-Cola and PepsiCo were also working on their distribution policy, according to a report in *China Business*.[8] Coca-Cola and PepsiCo had never been directly involved in the sales of their products. Instead, their bottlers managed sales in their assigned territory, relying on distributors to cover areas their own systems could not serve. The two companies' practice was to set stringent sales targets for bottlers, and in turn bottlers would set targets for distributors. Bonuses were contingent on reaching these goals.

Distributors paid upfront for goods and couldn't return unsold merchandise. However, different wholesale prices in different regions and the incentive of the bonus resulted in distributors selling across provinces to achieve their sales targets, even though both companies had strict policies against cross-territory sales. Recognizing the problems of the current system, the two companies had recently redefined the roles of bottlers and distributors: distributors were in charge of carrying inventory and delivering to the retailer and their profit would come from the volume handled, but they no longer had any discretion over selling prices; bottlers were responsible for order taking, promotion and product display at the retail end, and retained ownership of the product until the retailer bought it. In comparison, Wahaha's sales company bought the products from its wholly-owned bottling subsidiaries and then coordinated sales and marketing on a national scale. Its sales company directly dealt with the distributors (see Exhibit 7). Coca-Cola and PepsiCo both made money from the sales of concentrate, thus limiting the potential profitability (and price flexibility) of third-party bottlers. Wahaha made money from the sales of the final product, as the production of concentrate and the final product was handled by its own subsidiaries. This gave Wahaha greater pricing flexibility in the field.

In 2002, PepsiCo encountered some problems with a local joint-venture partner. PepsiCo was applying to a commercial arbitration court in Stockholm to cancel its contracts with the joint-venture partner in Chengdu, Sichuan Province—a key Pepsi-Cola market. PepsiCo contended that it had been prevented from exercising its rights under the joint-venture contract, and alleged that there were major financial irregularities within the local company, while the latter accused PepsiCo China of bugging its phones. This was unprecedented in PepsiCo's 20 years in China. While PepsiCo was distracted by these internal problems, Coca-Cola was launching a campaign to seize market share in Sichuan and Chongqing—other key markets for PepsiCo.

In the meantime, Wahaha steadily increased sales and market share of Future Cola. Between 1998 and 2001, Wahaha Future series' sales volume increased from 73,800 tons (66.95 million litres) to 0.64 million tons (580 million litres), a share of 14 percent of the carbonated drink market (see Exhibit 8). In comparison, 2001 carbonated-drink sales for Coca-Cola and PepsiCo were 1.9 million tons (1.724 billion litres)

EXHIBIT 7

Comparison of Product Flow and Revenue Flow

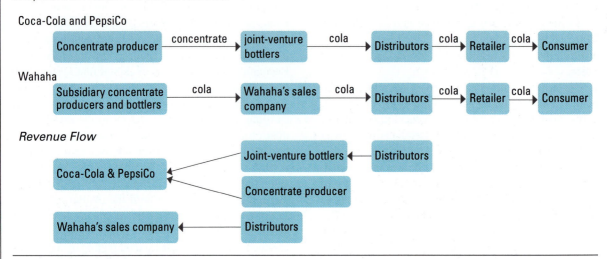

EXHIBIT 8

Comparison of Coca-Cola, Pepsico, and Wahaha's Carbonated Drink Sales

	1998		1999		2000		2001	
	Total (in tons)	Market Share	Total	Market Share	Total	Market Share	Total	Market Share
Coca-Cola	1,940,0	36%	2,040,0	48%	2,180,0	47%	1,920,0	42%
PepsiCo	760,0	14%	910,0	21%	1,090,0	24%	1,066,7	23%
Wahaha	73,8	1%	399,0	9%	480,0	10%	640,0	14%
China's total carbonated drink sales	5,400,0	100%	4,273,8	100%	4,620,0	100%	4,571.4	100%

and 1.07 million tons (971 million litres) respectively. In June 2002, Future series market share reached 18 percent, with sales revenues of RMB930 million. In some provinces such as Hunan, Xinjiang, Jiangxi and the three provinces in northern China, Future's market share was higher than that of Coca-Cola and Pepsi-Cola. In some provinces, Wahaha Future Cola was the only cola brand carried by retailers. In 2001, the Future brand was extended to tea drinks.

Coca-Cola now admitted that it faced competition from domestic companies. According to a *Wall Street Journal* article, Coca-Cola had been aggressively ramping up its sales efforts and "by opening more bottling plants and using recyclable bottles, it has brought the price down to one yuan for a single serving in remote towns."

During the past three years, Coke and its bottlers have been trying to map every supermarket, restaurant, barbershop or market stall where a can of soda might be consumed throughout much of China. Their army of more than 10,000 sales representatives makes regular visits, often on bicycle or foot, to each outlet to ensure there is enough in stock and to record how much was sold. All the information goes into a central database, updated daily, that gives Coke some of the most accurate consumer profiles available in China. Those data help Coke get closer to its customers, whether they are in large hypermarkets, spartan noodle shops or schools. . . . And in a strategy proven in markets such as Africa and India, Coke lets local distributors gradually own their own assets, whether these be tricycles used for deliveries or small refrigeration units.[9]

Wahaha, in the meantime, was planning on expanding its sales and marketing staff from 2,000 to 8,000 in 2002.

As Zong Qinghou reviewed the progress of Wahaha Future Cola, he knew that his strategy had allowed Wahaha to quickly become a player in the soft-drink business in China. As Coca-Cola and PepsiCo realized the threat from Chinese domestic cola producers and the vast market potential in the countryside, they would certainly take action to protect their position in the carbonated-drink market and tackle the rural market. Zong wondered what steps he should take next with Wahaha Future Cola and the carbonated-drink market. Meanwhile, changes in the soft drink industry also posed challenges for all participants. The rapid growth of new drink categories offered both opportunities and risks. As the general manager of China's number one soft drink producer, he also needed to consider competition in the rapidly growing non-carbonated drink market and the future growth of Wahaha.

Endnotes

1. An exchange rate of US$1 = RMB8.27 applied in 2002.

2. "China Market Racks Up Largest Ad Spending in Asia-Pacific," www1.chinadaily.com.cn/bw/2002–03–05/60571.html, March 12, 2002.

3. Yan Shi, "Pepsi's Business Model Encountering Trust Crisis in China," *Economic Observation*, April 24, 2002.

4. 1 U.S. dollar (US$) = 1.35 Swiss Francs (CHF).

5. Data from China Soft Drink Industry Association.

6. "An Analysis of the Competition Between Coca-Cola and PepsiCo in China," *China Business*, October 16, 2001. Market penetration refers to the percentage of consumers of a certain cola brand among total cola consumers.

7. Wu Xiaobo and Hu Honwei, *Extraordinary Marketing Strategy*, Zhejiang People's Publishing House, 2002, pp. 230–231.

8. Ma Qiang, "Comments on Banning the Association of PepsiCo's Bottlers," *China Business*, August 1, 2002.

9. Gebriet Kahn, "Coke Works Harder at Being The Real Thing in Hinterland," *Wall Street Journal*, November 26, 2002.

Fabiano Lopes, Alexandre Zimath, Andrea Maat, and Cel. Nivaldo Silva

WHILE TRAVELING TO an investor conference in Montreal, Canada, on Embraer's Legacy business jet, Mauricio Botelho, CEO of Embraer, reflected on his company's dramatic ascent to its position as the world's leading regional aircraft manufacturer. Since becoming a private company, Embraer had successfully introduced seven commercial aircraft models to the market, including its latest, the 118-seat EMBRAER 195. As the jet began its runway approach just a few miles from the headquarters of rival company Bombardier, Botelho pondered the potential competitive response to his company's recent attacks on the commercial aircraft market.

The U.S. Airline Industry

With the passing of the Airline Deregulation Act of 1978 by the U.S. Congress, government control of routes and fare pricing were eliminated, resulting in growth, increased competition, and the emergence of three new business models: major, regional, and low-cost carriers.

MAJOR CARRIERS. The distinguishing feature in the business model of a major carrier (or a "major") was the hub-and-spoke system. This system was based on central hubs to which feeder flights were directed. Passengers from the feeder flights transferred to numerous other flights provided at the hub to their final destinations.[1]

The enormous capital required to expand geographically was a substantial barrier to entry for new airlines. As low-cost and regional carriers primarily competed on price and local market convenience, the rationale for the majors' costly model lay largely on the improved customer loyalty generated by the convenience and reach of these airlines.

To further enhance breadth of service and increase the number of customers while limiting capital outlays, most majors turned to code-sharing and global alliances with other major and regional airlines. The major global alliances included Star Alliance, Sky Team, and One World.

REGIONAL CARRIERS. Regional airlines (or "regionals") operated short- and medium-haul scheduled airline service connecting smaller communities with larger cities and with the hubs of the major airlines. Although most were independently owned, several of the largest regional carriers were actually subsidiaries of the major airlines, including Atlantic Southwest, Comair (Delta), and AMR Eagle (American Airlines).

Many regionals benefited from arrangements with the majors, including code-sharing arrangements, scheduling assistance to ensure flight connections in majors' hubs, and the branding of a major airline.

With low-cost structure and improved service levels, regionals as a whole became the most profitable segment in the air carrier business. Regionals continued to replace turboprops on low-density routes and developed new routes that extended airline networks, enabling those carriers to serve unserved or underserved markets more cost-efficiently. Regionals were able to do that because newer, smaller jets were significantly faster than existing fleets of turboprop planes, had greater range, and burned less fuel (a major per-flight fixed cost). The regionals were the fastest-growing segment of commercial aviation and continued to serve a valuable segment of travelers unaddressed by low-cost and major carriers.

LOW-COST CARRIERS. Low-cost carriers (LCCs) offered airfares at a lower price than major and regional carriers. The largest LCCs included JetBlue, AirTran, Southwest Airlines, and America West, as well as new upstarts Song and Ted, which were owned by Delta and United, respectively.

Many of the LLCs started off as regionals, offering short-haul service connecting business and leisure travelers between high-volume destinations. By operating

This case was prepared by Fabiano Lopes, Alexandre Zimath, Andrea Maat, and revised by Cel. Nivaldo Silva, EADS Representative to Embraer, under the supervision of Ming-Jer Chen, Leslie E. Grayson Professor of Business Administration. It was written as a basis for class discussion rather than to illustrate effective or ineffective handling of an administrative situation. Copyright © 2007 by the University of Virginia Darden School Foundation, Charlottesville, VA. All rights reserved.

out of underutilized airports in those markets, the LLCs were able to keep a low profile. The largest LCCs were already operating nonstop transcontinental flights.

Contrary to the major airlines' hub-and-spoke system, LCCs generally operated a point-to-point route system. This feature was credited in the air carrier industry with providing higher levels in the quality of passenger service in terms of on-time departures and arrivals, limited lost luggage, etc. In order to effectively utilize the point-to-point system, LCCs offered service to the same general destinations as majors and regionals but used satellite airports, which were typically less congested than hub airports and charged lower fees.

LCCs limited their fleet of planes to one or two midsize, more fuel-efficient models, thus reducing training and maintenance costs. Moreover, by avoiding congested airports, LCCs were able to achieve faster turnaround times. The net effect was that planes were kept in the air longer, increasing the asset utilization. Additionally, LCCs tended to have lower labor costs because of the nonunion work force.

U.S. Market Conditions

The airline industry experienced uninterrupted growth in revenues throughout the 1990s. A weakening global economy, however, coupled with the September 11, 2001, terrorist attacks, had drastically reduced airline traffic by the end of 2001. As a result, the industry posted unprecedented losses of $7.7 billion for the year, as revenues dropped 13.5% from a record high of $93.6 billion in 2000. The slowdown continued into 2002 and 2003 as major airlines, faced with reduced sales, continued to reduce capacity and trim ranks. United Airlines, the second-largest airline in the world, filed for bankruptcy at the end of 2002.[2] The U.S. domestic available seat miles (ASM)[3] evolution (Exhibit 1) demonstrates the shift in capacity from majors to regionals and LCCs.

LCCs, whose cost structures were already tailored to the current fare environment, had not been affected as greatly as the majors. In fact, they continually reported profits even in the difficult post–September 11 environment.[4]

Market Conditions in Europe

In Europe, major airlines were faced with many of the same competitive issues as majors in the United States. Successful low-fare carriers exerted downward pressure on fares, and fall-off in passenger demand made it more difficult to maintain presence in existing

EXHIBIT 1

Embraer: Shaking up the Aircraft Manufacturing Market

Shifting Capacity among Business Models

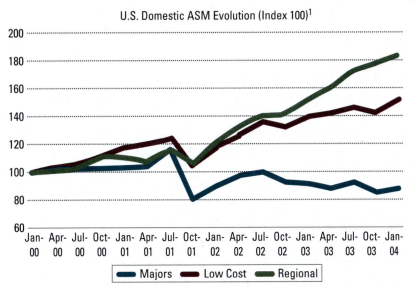

U.S. Domestic ASM Evolution (Index 100)[1]

Legend: Majors — Low Cost — Regional

[1] "Commercial Jets Market Assessment," http://www.embraer.com.br (accessed 10 November 2006).

markets, much less expand to new ones. Regional operators had softened the blow of the downturn. With their lower cost structures and greater flexibility, they had proven less vulnerable to outside market forces and capable of growth under adverse conditions.

The milestones in the airline industry for both the United States and Europe are presented in **Exhibits 2** and **3**.

It is important to highlight that these trends in the global airline industry were a key driver of the recent developments in the commercial aircraft industry.

The Commercial Aircraft Industry

OVERVIEW. Since most modern aircraft were incredibly complex (the Boeing 747, for example, had six million parts), a worldwide network of approximately 400 subcontractors was required to supply major structures and subassemblies, such as wings and fuselages, to manufacturers of finished aircraft. Those subcontractors, in turn, were supplied by up to 4,000 firms that manufactured components or raw materials. Parts that differentiated a product, or those strongly identified with a company, were usually produced in-house given their strategic and competitive importance.

A strong customer base and careful order-book management were needed to recoup the cost of developing new commercial or business jets. Standards for safety, quality, and value were crucial. Because of the capital-intensive nature of the industry, manufacturers needed to sell hundreds of units globally in order to break even on the design and manufacture of new aircraft.

The 1990s were years of consolidation in the aircraft industry. In 1997, two of the industry's largest producers, Boeing Company and McDonnell Douglas Corporation, merged. Other well-known companies,

---

EXHIBIT 2

Embraer: Shaking up the Aircraft Manufacturing Market

Milestones in the Airline Industry—United States[1]

HUB-AND-SPOKE

» U.S. Congress passes the Airline Deregulation Act of 1978, initiating a period of intense competition and paving the way for a new operational model, the hub-and-spoke system.

» Deregulation makes room for low-fare, point-to-point service expansion.

» By 1984, code-sharing alliances between major carriers and regional operators begin to be formed.

» Majors begin to rely more on low-cost regionals. Number of short-haul turboprop routes increase.

MARKET OUTSOURCING

» Regional jets are introduced in 1992.

» In 2002, U.S. orders for regional jets near 400. Turboprop orders collapse.

» Regional jet networks grow dramatically as majors shift routes to the lower-cost aircrafts and deploy them to expand into new markets.

» Regional jets become a crucial part of airline strategy to remain profitable in pre-September 11 downturn.

REGIONAL JETS

» Terrorist attacks in the United States on September 11, 2001, deliver a crippling blow to the airline industry.

» FAA enacts its Operational Evolution Plan.

» Airlines respond to plunging demand by cutting frequencies and trimming networks. Regional jets' ability to operate profitably with low load factors offset losses from mainlines operating with overcapacity.

» Regional jets used to complement or replace narrow-body aircraft on unprofitable short-haul routes.

[1] "2004–2023 Embraer Market Outlook."

EXHIBIT 3

Embraer: Shaking up the Aircraft Manufacturing Market

Milestones in the Airline Industry—Europe[1]

LIBERALIZATION IN EUROPE

>> European airlines evolved a hub-and-spoke system independently, primarily operating from each nation's capital city.

>> Europe takes a four-step approach to liberalization. The first phase is implemented in 1988.

>> Airlines begin to be restructured and privatized.

>> High labor costs in a competitive, deregulated environment force airlines to take drastic measures.

MARKET EXPANSION

>> Regional jets are introduced in 1992.

>> European airlines successfully deploy regional jets in the current established air transport system.

>> Regional jets replace many turboprops, but turboprops with 40-plus seats remain in service.

>> Low-fare carriers such as Ryanair and EasyJet see dramatic growth in RPK from 1995 to 2001.

REGIONAL JETS

>> The regional airline market in Europe averages 12% growth during the period from 1995 to 2002.

>> Terrorist attacks in the United States on September 11, 2001, deliver a crippling blow to the airline industry.

>> As in the United States, the regional jets' ability to adapt to different demand environments helps sustain allied majors through crisis.

[1] "2004–2023 Embraer Market Outlook."

---

such as Piper Aircraft Corporation and Fairchild Aircraft in the United States, as well as Fokker N.V. of the Netherlands, filed for bankruptcy during that period.

The market for commercial aircraft was typically divided into two product categories: narrow-body and wide-body aircraft. Narrow-body aircraft were single-aisle, short-range aircraft (up to 6,000 km or roughly 3,700 miles) that typically carried up to 200 passengers. Leading aircraft in that category were the Boeing 737, the Boeing 757, and the Airbus A-320. Wide-body aircraft were double-aisle, medium- to long-range aircraft (up to 14,000 km or roughly 8,700 miles) that could carry from 200 to 450 passengers. Leading aircraft in that category were the Boeing 747, the Boeing 777, and the Airbus A-300. Boeing and Airbus were the industry leaders in these segments.

REGIONAL JETS. The regional jets segment, which was included within the narrow-body category, was traditionally composed of aircraft that carried between 20 and 70 passengers. Bombardier and Embraer were the market leaders in this segment, which had

consistently expanded since 1992, when Bombardier introduced the first regional jet as a replacement for turboprop planes.

Even before regional jets became widely available, growth among regional airlines was consistently robust. Between 1971 and 1993, regional carriers outgrew the majors virtually every year. The expansion could be traced to two contributing factors. First, in the years leading up to 1978, many cities previously unserved had been introduced to air service, mainly on turboprop aircraft. Second, regional carriers in the years after the Deregulation Act of 1978 began to fill gaps in the ever-expanding hub-and-spoke networks of the majors.

By 1989, the majors changed their airline operations to increase the number of passengers flowing into the networks by adding capacity on its feeder routes, offering more destinations, and increasing frequency. It was a strategy that played against the strengths of regional turboprops, whose shorter range made them ineffective in reaching new markets.

The net effect was a surge in regional jet adoption and deployment, largely because of the replacement of turboprops on low-density routes and the development of new routes that extended airline networks. As the regional jets segment expanded, the capability of the jets themselves expanded to comprise roomy and cost-effective modern aircraft that flew up to 4,000 km (3,700 miles), enough to operate within most continents.

Based on expected growth of LCCs and regional carriers, as well as the aging of aircraft currently in use, the market for regional planes appeared to be poised for significant growth. Embraer had projected deliveries of 30- to 120-seat planes to total nearly 8,500 units over the next 20 years, representing a US$175 billion business. The United States was expected to generate 56% of this demand, while 19% of demand would come from Europe (Exhibit 4).

EMBRAER. In 2004, Embraer was the fourth-largest commercial airplane manufacturer in the world in terms of volume, behind Boeing, Airbus, and Bombardier. Airbus and Boeing led the market with deliveries of 320 and 285 commercial airplanes, respectively. In the regional market, Bombardier and Embraer demonstrated a close rivalry by achieving 158 and 148 deliveries, respectively (see Exhibit 5 for Embraer market share evolution).

Embraer, founded in 1969, was the product of an aeronautical technology center (CTA) that had been established in 1945 by Brazil's Ministry of Aeronautics. Together with Embraer, the CTA also generated one of the world's leading aeronautical engineering schools, the Aeronautical Technological Institute (ITA). Most of Embraer's aeronautical engineers had been hired out of ITA.

Moreover, Embraer's first great commercial success was the Bandeirante, a 15-seat plane with a design based on an eight-seat prototype assembled inside the CTA. Overall, 500 Bandeirantes were sold over a 10-year period. The first 80 were sold to the Brazilian military, as an indirect government support to the new enterprise.

From 1972 to 1983, Embraer introduced several small turboprop planes. Embraer's first international success, introduced in 1983, was the EMB 120 Brasilia, a 30-seat pressurized twin turboprop. In 2006, the Brasilia was still in production, with more than 350 planes operating worldwide. Embraer's jet era began in 1985 with the introduction of the AMX, a military jet developed in partnership with Aermacchi, an Italian aircraft manufacturer.

Embraer was privatized in December 1994 as part of President Fernando Henrique Cardoso's privatization program. Cia. Bozano, Simonsen (CBS), the leader of the consortium that took Embraer private, was a conglomerate with diversified investments in financial services, agriculture, real estate, and industrial products (see Exhibit 6 for Embraer's ownership structure).

In 1995, Embraer entered the commercial jet market with the introduction of its ERJ family. The ERJ 145 (introduced in 1995), ERJ 135 (introduced in 1998) and ERJ 140 (introduced in 2000) had a seating capacity of 50, 37, and 44 seats, respectively. Those planes were developed in accordance with Embraer's strategy of entering the 30- to 50-seat market to compete against Bombardier's Q-Series turboprop planes as well as its CRJ family of regional jets.

In 1999, while still celebrating the successful introduction of the ERJ family, Embraer began developing a new aircraft family that would serve the 70- to 120-seat market. In February 2002, the 70- to 78-seat EMBRAER 170 completed its first flight, taking off from São José dos Campos. In the following two years, Embraer completed the maiden flights of its 78- to 86-seat EMBRAER 175 as well as the 98- to 106-seat EMBRAER 190. To complete the family, in December 2004, the 108- to 118-seat EMBRAER 195 accomplished its first successful flight (see Exhibit 7 for a list of Embraer's products as of 2006).

THE 70- TO 120-SEAT MARKET. Several reasons motivated Embraer to manufacture 70- to 120-seat planes. First, Embraer identified a gap between capacity and demand for this range of planes. The absence of a true 70- to 120-seat jet family had forced airlines to deploy planes that were either too large or too small to operate efficiently in the intermediate-demand market. In 2002, 61% of flights in the United States departed the airport with loads appropriate for 70- to 110-seat aircraft.

Several trends in the airline industry also contributed to Embraer's interest in this segment. First, the continued growth of LCCs had created a shift in aircraft demand toward smaller, more efficient planes. In addition, the downturn in the airline industry that began with September 11, 2001, along with the resulting price wars, had highlighted the fact that the majors required a high-load factor to compete effectively against the LCCs. Furthermore, the increased volatility of passenger demand created a greater need for flexibility among airlines. As a result, the majors

EXHIBIT 4

Embraer: Shaking up the Aircraft Manufacturing Market

Market Outlook

Delivery Forecast by Segment and Region[1]			
30- to 120-seat Commercial Jet Category, World Deliveries by Seat Segment			
Segment	2004–13	2014–23	2004–23
30–60	1,150	1,450	2,600
61–90	1,300	1,600	2,900
91–120	1,250	1,700	2,950
Total	**3,700**	**4,750**	**8,450**

Deliveries by Region, 30- to 120-seat Segment			
Regions	2004–13	2014–23	2004–23
North America	2,245	2,495	4,740
Latin America	255	370	625
Europe	636	944	1,580
Africa & Middle East	154	236	390
China	240	395	635
Asia Pacific	170	310	480
Total	**3,700**	**4,750**	**8,450**

Deliveries by Region and Segment									
	30- to 60-seat Segment			61- to 90-seat Segment			91- to 120-seat Segment		
Regions	2004–13	2014–23	2004–23	2004–13	2014–23	2004–23	2004–13	2014–23	2004–23
North America	840	1,030	1,870	715	650	1,365	690	815	1,505
Latin America	25	70	95	90	130	220	140	170	310
Europe	85	152	237	263	424	687	288	368	656
Africa & Middle East	80	38	118	52	106	158	22	92	114
China	100	100	200	90	160	250	50	135	185
Asia Pacific	20	60	80	90	130	220	60	120	180
Total	**1,150**	**1,450**	**2,600**	**1,300**	**1,600**	**2,900**	**1,250**	**1,700**	**2,950**

[1] "2004–2023 Embraer Market Outlook."

EXHIBIT 5

Embraer: Shaking up the Aircraft Manufacturing Market

Embraer Market Share Evolution

30- to 60-seat Planes

Data source: http://www.embraer.com.br (accessed 10 November 2006).

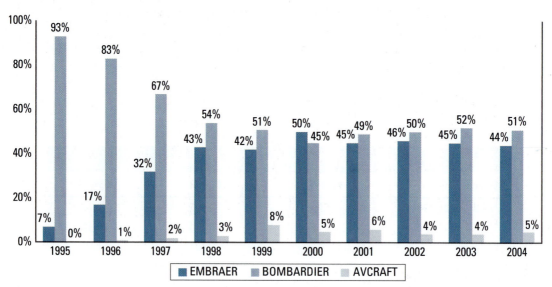

61- to 90-seat Planes

Data source: http://www.embraer.com.br (accessed 10 November 2006).

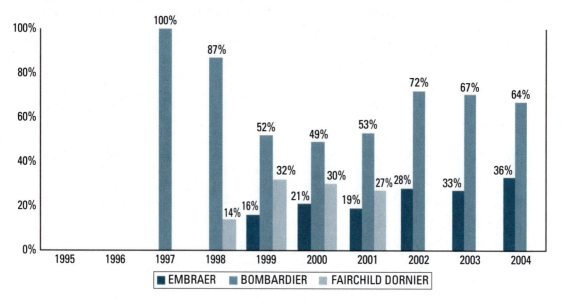

EXHIBIT 5 *(Continued)*

91- to 120-seat Planes

Data source: http://www.embraer.com.br (accessed 10 November 2006).

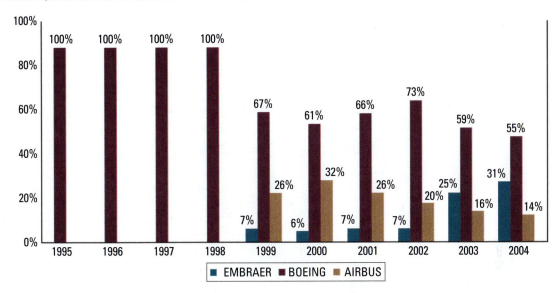

were becoming increasingly receptive to the notion of using smaller planes for short- to intermediate-range flights. As well, the financial problems experienced by the majors during this period had prompted their U.S.-based unions to relax clauses that limited the scope of their regional airlines to 50-seat jets. As a result, several airlines were beginning to expand regional operations to include planes with more than 70 seats.

Another key reason was related to aging fleets. More than one-third of the planes serving the 61- to 120-seat market were more than 20 years old. Those planes amounted to approximately 690 units, which would be gradually replaced within the next five to 10 years (see Exhibit 8 for details).

Embraer already delivered nine EMBRAER 170s to customers, including US Airways, which had broken in its new 170s with flights from Pittsburgh, Pennsylvania to Albany, New York on April 4, 2004. JetBlue Airways had 100 EMBRAER 190s on firm order—at a total cost of $3 billion—having chosen that model over the 107-seat Airbus A318. The total number of firm orders for the 170/190 family, as of December 2004, was 343.

BOMBARDIER. Founded in 1942 by Armand Bombardier as a snowmobile manufacturer, Bombardier has been publicly listed on the Toronto Stock Exchange since 1969, yet has remained under the majority control of the Bombardier family throughout the company's history. In the 1970s, Bombardier began to diversify into other transportation industries through acquisitions of various train, plane, bus, and boat manufacturers. Notable aerospace acquisitions included the purchases of Canadian aircraft manufacturer Canadair in 1986, business jet manufacturer Learjet Corporation in 1990, and de Havilland, manufacturer of the Dash-8 turboprop, in 1992.

In 1992, Bombardier entered the regional jet market with the launch of its 50-seat CRJ100/200. After Embraer's entry into that market in 1995, Bombardier began to face a significant erosion of its competitive position. Financial problems compounded the challenges posed by Embraer; they prevented Bombardier from launching major development projects outside of the CRJ family of jets. Instead, Bombardier raced to beat Embraer to the emerging 70- to 90-seat regional jet market by announcing in 1997 its plans to introduce the 64- to 75-seat CRJ700/705, a stretched version of the CRJ100/200. The CRJ700/705, first delivered in 2001, was followed by the 86- to 90-seat CRJ900, another stretched CRJ100/200, which was announced in 1999 and in service by 2003. In 2000, Bombardier's plans to develop a new generation jet that could have beaten Embraer to the 100-plus-seat

EXHIBIT 6

Embraer: Shaking up the Aircraft Manufacturing Market

Embraer Capital Structure

Data source: http://www.embraer.com.br (accessed 10 November 2006).

Common Shares (242,544,448 Shares)—33% of shares

BOVESPA Free Float,
19.20%

Cia. Bazano,
20%

European
Group,
20%

PREVI,
20%

SISTEL,
20%

Brazilian
Government,
0.80%

The European group includes: Thales (5.67%), Dassault (5.67%), Snecma (2.99%), and EADS (5.67%)

Preferred Shares (476,720,786 Shares) - 66% of Shares

NYSE,
56%

BOVESPA,
34.40%

BNDES,
9.60%

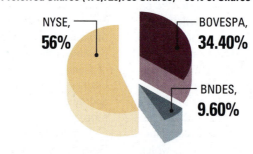

Total (719,265,234 Shares)

European
Group,
7.70%

Controlling
Shareholders,
32.60%

NYSE,
37.10%

Boves pa,
15.40%

BNDES,
6.90%

Brazilian
Government
0.30%

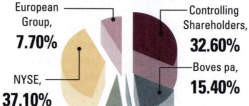

EXHIBIT 7

Embraer: Shaking up the Aircraft Manufacturing Market

Embraer's 2006 Product Mix

Commercial Aviation	Military Aviation	Corporate Aviation
EMB 120	Super Tucano	Legacy
ERJ 135	AMX	
ERJ 140	EMB 145 AEW&C	
ERJ 145	EMB 145 RS/AGS	
Embraer 170	P 99	
Embraer 175	Legacy	
Embraer 190		
Embraer 195		

Data source: http://www.embraer.com.br (accessed 10 November 2006).

EXHIBIT 8

Embraer: Shaking up the Aircraft Manufacturing Market

The 70- to 110-seat Capacity Gap

Data source: http://www.embraer.com.br (accessed 10 November 2006).

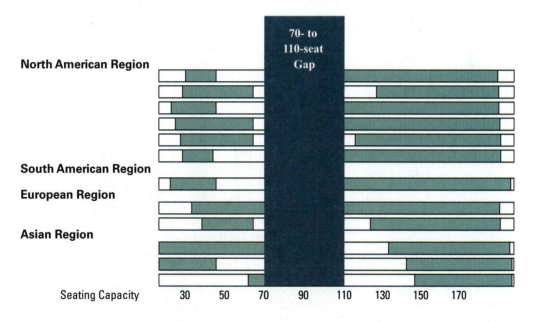

(continued)

EXHIBIT 8 *(Continued)*

How Overcapacity or Undercapacity Hurts the Bottom Line

Note: More than half of all U.S. domestic airlines operating narrow-body mainline aircraft have passenger loads better suited for 70- to 110-seat aircraft.

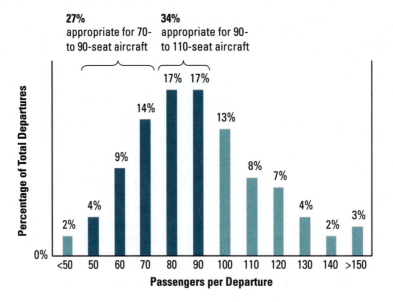

Seating Gap

Aircraft in Service (as of 2002)

Note: More than one-third of the world's jet fleet serving the 51- to 120-seat segment is more than 20 years old and should be retired in the coming years.

Data source: http://www.embraer.com.br (accessed 10 November 2006).

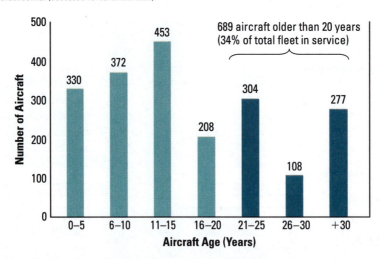

market were abandoned owing to financial constraints, and Bombardier was forced to continue relying on its existing platform.

After several years of escalating financial and business challenges, in 2003, Bombardier appointed former CN Railway CEO Paul Tellier as the company's president and CEO. Tellier quickly implemented a recapitalization program, featuring an equity issue and asset divestitures, to strengthen Bombardier's balance sheet and refocus on its aerospace and railcar businesses. The aerospace business continued to struggle, however, with 2005 production estimates for the 50-seat CRJ200 reduced from 98 to 54, as the market continued to migrate toward larger regional planes. Furthermore, the financial strength of airlines still interested in 50-seat jets, such as US Airways and Delta Airlines, continued to decline. In November 2004, Standard & Poor's and Moody's Investor Service downgraded Bombardier's credit rating to junk status. One month later, after less than two years on the job, Tellier was removed from his position as president and CEO of Bombardier. Replacing Tellier was Laurent Beaudoin, a member of Bombardier's founding family, chairman of Bombardier since 1979, and previously CEO of the company from 1979–1999. Beaudoin had reportedly pushed Tellier aside after disagreeing with his long-term vision for Bombardier.

The CSeries: The entrepreneurial Beaudoin was believed to be an enthusiastic supporter of the CSeries development project that began feasibility studies at Bombardier in 2004. The CSeries, a new family of three jets ranging from 110 to 135 seats, would serve as Bombardier's entry vehicle into the commercial jet market. Bombardier's board of directors was expected to decide in early 2005 whether to proceed with development efforts, with the objective of launching the project in spring of 2006 and delivering the first jet in 2010. The Canadian government, attracted to the opportunity to replace the thousands of jobs that had been lost because of the scaled-back production of Bombardier's CRJ200, had reportedly agreed to finance one-third of the expected $2 billion of capital costs associated with the prototype development. In exchange, Bombardier would commit to locating the CSeries manufacturing and development facilities in Canada.

The CSeries jets were expected to compete directly with Embraer's EMBRAER 190, Airbus's A318, and Boeing's 737-600. Bombardier claimed the CSeries would be the only jet specifically designed for the 110- to 135-seat market, as Embraer's 190 was an upward stretch from the 170, and Airbus's and Boeing's jets were downsized versions of their larger narrowbody jets. As a result, Bombardier claimed the CSeries would outperform each competing jet with respect to weight, size, or range. Bombardier expected the CSeries to achieve unmatched operating efficiency, reducing costs to 15% to 20% below the cost of operating competing planes.

Bombardier's recent hiring of former Boeing executive Gary Scott, who had previously worked on Boeing's development of the 737, to direct the CSeries program sparked conjecture in the Canadian press of a Bombardier plan to create a joint venture with Boeing. Bombardier called the reports "pure speculation," but Boeing Commercial Airplanes President Alan Mulally confirmed that his company had served as a "consultant" to Bombardier. A relationship with Boeing could add significant value to the CSeries, particularly if it allowed Bombardier to create cockpit commonality with Boeing's 737.

BOEING. Boeing was the world's second-largest manufacturer of large commercial jets behind Airbus, as well as the world's largest aerospace company, focusing on military aircraft, satellites, missile defense, human space flight, and launch systems and services. Since 2001, Boeing's commercial airplane sales had plummeted from 60% to 40% of Boeing sales. Boeing responded to that downturn by cutting costs, curtailing product development, and placing more emphasis on its military and space operations. In 2005, Boeing's commercial development efforts were primarily focused on the 787 Dreamliner, a super-efficient, long-range (9,500 km to 11,000 km, or 7,000 to 8,000 miles), 200- to 250-seat aircraft that was expected to be in service by 2008.

The smallest Boeing airplane in full-scale production as of 2005 was the 162- to 189-seat 737. Boeing announced in January 2005 that the 106- to 114-seat 717, which was inherited in Boeing's 1997 acquisition of McDonnell Douglas, would be taken out of production as soon as its existing orders were filled. Boeing cited insufficient demand as the reason for the decision, adding that the 717's market niche was simply too small for Boeing to continue serving. The 717 was considered by market analysts to be too big and heavy to operate efficiently relative to smaller regional jets such as Bombardier's CRJ900 and Embraer's EMBRAER 190. Furthermore, the 717 was an orphan product, with no cockpit or engine commonality with other Boeing jets, and had not received a great deal of marketing and development support from Boeing during its six years of production.

AIRBUS S.A.S. The world's largest commercial aircraft maker, Airbus, was 80% owned by the European Aeronautic Defense and Space Company (EADS), with U.K.-based BAE Systems controlling the remaining 20%. Airbus was founded in 1970 to address several European governments' wishes to have a European competitor in the aerospace industry. In 2005, Airbus was the manufacturer of the world's largest, lowest-cost, and longest-range aircraft. The company had recently been focused on the super-jumbo market, with the development of the 550-seat A380. In December 2004, however, Airbus announced plans to develop a midsized plane, the A350, to compete directly against Boeing's 787, seating 245 to 285 passengers.

Airbus's product line comprised four families: the single-aisle A320 family, the widebody A300/310 family, the long-range A330/340 family, and the new super-jumbo A380 family. Airbus's smallest airplane, the 318, was a 107- to 132-seat short-haul jet launched in 1999 to compete with Boeing's 717. The A318 benefited from a high degree of commonality with the entire A320 family in terms of airframes, on-board systems, cockpits, and handling characteristics, which meant that the entire family could be flown by the same pilots and maintained by the same engineers. Still, as a downsized version of the 150-seat A320, detractors considered the A318 to be larger and heavier than is desirable for jets in the 100-seat market.

Competitive History (1989–2005)

1989   Embraer began development of the ERJ 145.

1992   Bombardier entered the regional jet market with the 50-seat CRJ100/200, developed from the CL-601 Challenger business jet.

1993   Airbus launched development of the 120-seat A319.

1996   Embraer began delivering the ERJ 145.

1997   Embraer launched the 37-seat ERJ 135.

Bombardier announced plans to develop the 64- to 75-seat CRJ700/705.

1998   Embraer began delivering the ERJ 135.

1999   Bombardier began development of the 86- to 90-seat CRJ900.

Embraer launched development of the 44-seat ERJ 140 and launched its EMBRAER 170/190 family beginning with the development of the 70-seat EMBRAER 170.

Airbus launched development of the 107- to 132-seat A318.

After two years of discussion about government subsidies, Canada challenged the Brazilian subsidy program PROEX before the WTO. The WTO decided that the Brazilian PROEX was a prohibitive export program that had to be withdrawn. The value of the PROEX subsidy to Embraer was worth $1.4 billion. Following that, Canada chose to retaliate by imposing tariffs on the Brazilian exports including a temporary ban on Brazilian beef.

2000   Bombardier abandoned plans for development of a new 100-seat jet, the BRJ-X.

2001   Bombardier's CRJ700/705 began service.

2003   Bombardier's CRJ900 began service.

Embraer's EMBRAER 170 began service.

2004   Bombardier announced that it was studying the feasibility of a new jet family, the CSeries, which would serve the 110- to 135-seat market.

Embraer began delivery of the EMBRAER 175 and EMBRAER 190.

2005   Boeing announced plans to stop production of the 717 because of insufficient market demand.

The Decision

As he made final preparations for his upcoming investor presentation, Mauricio Botelho was concerned that Embraer still did not know what to expect from Bombardier, Boeing, and Airbus. How would they respond to Embraer's successful launch of its recent family of jets? Would Bombardier really follow through with its launch of the CSeries? Would Airbus and Boeing perceive the latest attacks by Embraer and Bombardier as attacks on their own families of jets? Most importantly, given Botelho's expectations of rivals' future competitive moves, what should Embraer do next to protect its position and influence its competitors' actions?

Endnotes

1. "Air Transportation," *Encyclopedia of Global Industries*, online edition, Thomson Gale, 2005. Reproduced in Business and Company Resource Center (Michigan: Gale Group, 2005), http://galenet.galegroup.com/servlet/BCRC.

2. "Air Transportation," *Encyclopedia of Global Industries*, Gale Research International Ltd., Pub ID: GE66 (1 December 2002).

3. Available seat miles (ASM) measure available passenger capacity.

4. "Airline Industry: A Business in Transition," Optimizing Air Travel Mini-Conference Presentation, Boston, Massachusets, 24 March 2004.

It's challenging. But UPS is all about global trade. Global trade is going to pull us out of this recession.

—UPS CEO SCOTT DAVIS IN A 2009 CNBC INTERVIEW

Marne L. Arthaud-Day
Kansas State University
Shreyasi Banerjee
Intel Corporation
Frank T. Rothaermel
Georgia Institute of Technology

IT HAD BEEN six months since Robin Page first walked into the Sandy Springs headquarters of United Parcel Service (UPS) and assumed her role as Chief Strategy Officer. Though she had been doing strategic analysis and planning for years, she felt an unusual amount of pressure to prove herself in this new position. Chief Executive Officer (CEO) Scott Davis had made it clear when he offered her the job that he had high expectations of what she could do for the company, and that he wanted to see concrete results by the end of the first year.

Ms. Page glanced at the pile of reports sitting on her desk, many of them describing recent international acquisitions and alliances. She knew that one of the reasons she had been Mr. Davis's top choice for the position was her extensive international experience. UPS already had a presence in more than 200 countries, but they wanted to penetrate those markets more deeply, especially the rapidly growing economies of Southeast Asia. Ms. Page had traveled extensively around the region both for work and for pleasure, and Mr. Davis was counting on her insights to help the company with its Asian expansion.

First and foremost on her mind was India. She remembered fondly a vacation she had taken there just a year or so ago, and how the city marketplaces had struck her as a unique mix of the modern and the ancient. People milled around everywhere, pushing their way through crowded streets, families piled on motor bikes weaving in and out of lanes of standstill traffic. Yet everywhere she looked, someone was talking on a cell phone, and modern buildings lined the horizon with names of multinational corporations from all over the world. An entrepreneurial spirit seemed to fill the air, with new businesses coming to life on a daily basis; for every venture that failed, two more sprouted up to claim its space. The country was awash with business opportunities amidst the clamor, congestion, and complexity that typified modern life in India's major cities like Mumbai, Delhi, and Bangalore. The sheer volume of people promised seemingly unlimited market potential.

Although UPS had established a footprint in India, it had yet to penetrate the market on the scale that Ms. Page and other UPS managers hoped for. They formed an alliance with Jet Air in 2005, which led to the opening of the first "UPS Store" in Mumbai and several other major cities. In 2008, UPS established a second alliance with AFL Private Ltd, gaining access to the logistics company's field stocking locations and significantly increasing its access points for international delivery. Since then, however, UPS's attention had shifted to other Asian markets like China and Malaysia, leaving India wide open to invading competitors. Sure enough, in UPS's absence, DHL acquired the Indian delivery company Blue Dart and had become the clear market leader in both the international and domestic segments. Today, DHL-Blue Dart had a combined market share three times higher than the next largest company.[1] Clearly, it was time to reformulate UPS's India strategy.

In many ways, the India situation reminded Ms. Page of when UPS first began to offer overnight delivery back in the 1980s. A major competitor (the U.S. Postal Service) dominated the marketplace, and

Professor Marne L. Arthaud-Day, Research Associate Shreyasi Banerjee (Industrial Engineer and Systems Analyst, Intel), and Professor Frank T. Rothaermel prepared this case from public sources. This case is developed for the purpose of class discussion. It is not intended to be used for any kind of endorsement, source of data, or depiction of efficient or inefficient management. © Arthaud-Day, Banerjee, and Rothaermel, 2013.

while UPS had strongholds in all of the major locations, the challenge was to figure out how to connect rural America to its major transportation hubs. UPS had promised overnight delivery between any two addresses in the United States, and they weren't joking. If a package needed to get to the base of the Grand Canyon, the plan was to drive the package on a dirt road for 50 miles from Valentine, Arizona, to the rim of the Canyon. A mule train operator would then take the letter over to the rocky final leg for a $35 charge to UPS. UPS would deliver the letter at a loss in order to maintain its commitment to overnight delivery. Ms. Page knew that vast regions of rural India still lacked adequate roadways, and she chuckled thinking that mule trains might not be such a far-fetched idea after all. Delivery at the local level was still very much a small business, especially in developing countries. It's like Kent Nelson, UPS's senior vice president for finance and customer service, said in a 1985 interview, "When you are in the package-delivery business, you are really in the pennies business. The trick is to have the pennies build up to be profitable."[2]

If UPS was to be a major player in the current "India Mania," the company would have to figure out the answers to several difficult questions. How unique was the Indian situation compared to other developing countries? UPS had been in business for over 100 years and had experience in over 200 worldwide marketplaces. Surely some of the lessons learned would transfer to India, but how could they determine which ones? Competitors already had a head start, so UPS could not afford to experiment based simply on trial and error. How should they go about tapping the extensive potential of one of the world's largest economies? How difficult would it be to streamline their supply and distribution chain given the lack of infrastructure development? With the size of India's population and the economy's rapid growth, the rewards for successfully addressing these issues were sizeable to say the least. Ms. Page sat down and started reviewing the pile of documents sitting on her desk, hoping the deals of the past would help her figure out the right path for UPS's future in India.

The UPS Story

The UPS saga has all the elements of a remarkable success story. Two teenage entrepreneurs in 1907 started what would one day become the world's largest package delivery company.

EARLY HISTORY. Claude Ryan and Jim Casey had a big idea and a small amount of debt capital. Working from a Seattle basement, they began running errands and carrying notes on foot, as well as making home deliveries for drugstore customers. As the arrival of new technologies such as the telephone and automobile led to a decrease in demand for messaging services, the company shifted its emphasis to delivering packages for retail stores. "Merchants Parcel Delivery" quickly built a strong reputation based on its personalized customer service and the care with which it handled every package.[3] The young enterprise changed its name to United Parcel Service in 1919 as it entered a golden period of domestic expansion. The word "United" was chosen to reflect that even as the company expanded into other cities like Oakland and Los Angeles, they still belonged to the same organization.

Throughout its early history, UPS functioned primarily as an intra-city delivery service, innovating in response to consumers' changing lifestyles and shopping patterns.[4] In the 1920s, UPS added several unique service features such as daily pick-ups, acceptance of C.O.D. payments, and multiple delivery attempts. It also developed a new conveyor belt system for handling packages.[5] When fuel shortages leading up to World War II caused retailers to curtail their delivery activities and encourage customers to carry their parcels home, UPS stepped up and expanded its retail store service.[6] After the war, as people migrated to the suburbs and bought cars that could hold their goods, UPS shifted its focus to the business-to-business segment.[7]

COMMON CARRIER RIGHTS. In the next phase of its expansion, UPS decided to pursue common carrier rights, meaning that it could deliver packages between both private and commercial customers. This was traditionally the domain of the U.S. Postal Service, as stipulated by the Interstate Commerce Commission and multiple state regulatory bodies. A series of legal battles ensued as UPS fought to expand its operating authority to all 48 states, a goal which it finally achieved in 1975. By 1978, UPS also provided nationwide air transport services, flying packages in the cargo bays of commercial airlines.[8]

UPS AIRLINES. In response to the deregulation of the airline industry, many established carriers trimmed flights during the 1980s, leading to reduced air freight capacity. UPS saw this as an opportunity to enter the air delivery business and began to acquire cargo jets. It offered next-day air service to 48 states by 1985, and in 1988, UPS Airlines was formally recognized by the Federal Aviation Administration. It was the fastest airline startup in FAA history, taking just over one year to get all systems into place.[9] Building on the success of its airline service, the company shifted from a national delivery company to a global footprint throughout the 1990s. UPS now provides delivery services to more than four billion people in over 200 countries.[10]

GOING PUBLIC. The latter half of the 1990s brought both major challenges and new business opportunities. In August 1997, the Teamsters Union led about 185,000 UPS workers on a strike. They wanted more union control of employee pension funds and objected to UPS's increasing use of part-time workers. UPS controlled about 80 percent of all package deliveries in the United States, so the repercussions of the 15-day strike for both the company and its customers were severe. UPS lost $650 million in business over a disagreement that then CEO James Kelly commented could have been worked out "without a strike."[11] UPS recovered quickly, however, and went public in 1999, almost 100 years after its conception. A report in *The New York Times* said, "Investors have greeted the new stock with an enthusiasm usually reserved for dot-com ventures whose founders' parents had not even been born by 1907."[12] In fact, the UPS IPO was the largest public offering to date. (See Exhibits 1 and 2 for UPS financial data.)

SYNCHRONIZED COMMERCE. In the meantime, UPS continued to redefine itself in response to changes in its external environment. No longer restricting its activities to delivery services, UPS sought to become a "solutions company" that offered services tailored to its customers' business process value chain.[13] It formed the UPS Logistics Group in 1995 to streamline service operations over its customer base, and UPS Capital in 1998 to provide financial products and services to help small businesses grow.[14] The company made about 30 acquisitions in total, including freight forwarders, customer clearers, and a bank for the efficient movement of goods, information, and financing along their supply and distribution network.[15] When a study by FutureBrand concluded that UPS had no terminology to explain their expanded business model to customers, they coined the term "Synchronized Commerce."[16]

By modifying its supply chain to streamline the flow between buyers and sellers, UPS was able to "synchronize" goods, information, and funds to deliver more products and services to its customers.

By the start of the new millennium, UPS was well on its way to becoming a full-service business.[17] In 2001, UPS acquired Mail Boxes Etc., then the world's largest franchisor of retail shipping, postal, and business service centers.[18] This strategic move enabled the company to target smaller businesses and increased its accessibility to residential and home-office customers. Over 3,000 Mail Boxes Etc. locations were re-branded as "The UPS Store," in the largest re-branding campaign in history. Mail Boxes Etc.'s CEO said that the initiative helped set lower maximum retail prices for UPS shipping. He added, "By pooling MBE's expertise in retail business services with UPS's expertise in shipping and other expanded capabilities, The UPS Store offers an extensive portfolio of products to our franchisees and their customers." Currently, "The UPS Store" and "Mail Boxes Etc." have over 4,800 locations in the United States, Canada, and India alone.[19]

Today, UPS maintains its focus on services as its core business while continually looking to grow new revenue sources. To ensure that the company keeps its strategic focus, former CEO Mike Eschew introduced the "Four Quadrant" growth strategy that "focuses on innovating existing business operations internally and externally, and, likewise, focuses innovation on new entrepreneurial ventures both internally and externally."[20] This strategy has helped to land UPS among the top 15 most respected companies and in the top 10 of all logistics companies worldwide (see Exhibits 3 and 4).

HUB AND SPOKE MODEL. UPS's delivery network is based on the hub and spoke model,[21] a centralized and integrated approach to logistics management.[22] It consists of a hub (the center), where packages are sent for consolidation, and spokes that link the hub to all other points in the system. UPS's rival, FedEx, pioneered the hub and spoke system in the U.S. domestic express delivery sector, and then extended it to its international operations. FedEx's first Asian hub was at Hangzhou Xiaoshan International Airport, located in east China's Zhejiang Province.[23] UPS transitioned from direct shipping to the hub and spoke system somewhat later than its major competitor, but has still benefitted from significant cost savings by doing so.

EXHIBIT 1

UPS Income Statement (U.S. $ in millions)

	Years Ended December 31,			
	2010	2009	2008	2007
Revenue	$49,545	$45,297	$51,486	$49,692
Operating Expenses:				
Compensation and benefits	26,324	25,640	26,063	31,745
Repairs and maintenance	1,131	1,075	1,194	1,157
Depreciation and amortization	1,792	1,747	1,814	1,745
Purchased transportation	6,640	5,379	6,550	5,902
Fuel	2,972	2,365	4,134	2,974
Other occupancy	939	985	1,027	958
Other expenses	3,873	4,305	5,322	4,633
Total Operating Expenses	43,671	41,496	46,104	49,114
Operating Profit	5,874	3,801	5,382	578
Other Income and (Expense):				
Investment income	3	10	75	99
Interest expense	(354)	(445)	(442)	(246)
Total Other Income and (Expense)	(351)	(435)	(367)	(147)
Income Before Income Taxes	5,523	3,366	5,015	431
Income Tax Expense	2,035	1,214	2,012	49
Net Income	3,488	2,152	3,003	382
Basic Earnings Per Share	$3.51	$2.16	$2.96	$0.36
Diluted Earnings Per Share	$3.48	$2.14	$2.94	$0.36

Source: SEC.gov.

EXHIBIT 2

UPS Consolidated Balance Sheets (U.S. $ in millions)

	December 31,			
	2010	2009	2008	2007
ASSETS				
Current Assets:				
Cash and cash equivalents	$ 3,370	$ 1,542	$ 507	$ 2,027
Marketable securities	711	558	542	577
Accounts receivable, net	5,627	5,369	5,547	6,084
Finance receivables, net	203	287	480	468
Deferred income tax assets	659	585	494	606

EXHIBIT 2 *(Continued)*

	December 31,			
	2010	**2009**	**2008**	**2007**
Income taxes receivable	287	266	167	1,256
Other current assets	712	668	1,108	742
Total Current Assets	11,569	9,275	8,845	11,760
Property, Plant and Equipment, Net	17,387	17,979	18,265	17,663
Goodwill	2,081	2,089	1,986	2,577
Intangible Assets, Net	599	596	511	628
Non-Current Finance Receivables, Net	288	337	476	431
Other Non-Current Assets	1,673	1,607	1,796	5,983
Total Assets	$33,597	$31,883	$31,879	$39,042
LIABILITIES AND SHAREOWNERS' EQUITY				
Current Liabilities:				
Current maturities of long-term debt and commercial paper	$ 355	$ 853	$ 2,074	$ 3,512
Accounts payable	1,974	1,766	1,855	1,819
Accrued wages and withholdings	1,505	1,416	1,436	1,414
Self-insurance reserves	725	757	732	704
Other current liabilities	1,343	1,447	1,720	2,391
Total Current Liabilities	5,902	6,239	7,817	9,840
Long-Term Debt	10,491	8,668	7,797	7,506
Pension and Postretirement Benefit Obligations	4,663	5,457	6,323	4,438
Deferred Income Tax Liabilities	1,870	1,293	588	2,620
Self-Insurance Reserves	1,809	1,732	1,710	1,651
Other Non-Current Liabilities	815	798	864	804
Shareowners' Equity:				
Class A common stock (285 and 314 shares issued in 2009 and 2008)	3	3	3	3
Class B common stock (711 and 684 shares issued in 2009 and 2008)	7	7	7	7
Additional paid-in capital	—	2	—	—
Retained earnings	14,164	12,745	12,412	14,186
Accumulated other comprehensive loss	(6,195)	(5,127)	(5,642)	(2,013)
Deferred compensation obligations	103	108	121	137
Less: Treasury stock (2 shares in 2009 and 2008)	(103)	(108)	(121)	(137)
Total Equity for Controlling Interests	7,979	7,630	6,780	12,183
Noncontrolling Interests	68	66	—	—
Total Shareowners' Equity	8,047	7,696	6,780	12,183
Total Liabilities and Shareowners' Equity	$33,597	$31,883	$31,879	$39,042

Source: SEC.gov.

EXHIBIT 3

The World's Most Respected Companies

Rank	Company	Mean
1.	Johnson and Johnson	4.15
2.	Berkshire Hathaway	3.98
3.	Procter & Gamble	3.92
4.	Apple	3.76
5.	Walmart Stores	3.75
6.	Exxon Mobil	3.74
7.	McDonald's	3.56
8.	Toyota Motors (Japan)	3.53
9.	Coca-Cola	3.47
10.	Cisco Systems	3.42
11.	United Parcel Service	3.42
12.	PepsiCo	3.35
13.	3M	3.29
14.	IBM	3.29
15.	Abbott Laboratories	3.22

Source: *Barron's* Magazine, 2009.

EXHIBIT 4

The Top 15 Global Logistics Companies

Rank	Company	2008 Revenues (million US$)	Base Country	Coverage
1	DHL Logistics	$39,900	Germany	Global
2	Kuehne + Nagel	$20,220	Switzerland	Global
3	DB Schenker Logistics	$12,503	Germany	Global
4	Geodis	$ 9,700	France	Global
5	CEVA Logistics	$ 9,523	Netherlands	Global
6	Panalpina	$ 8,394	Switzerland	Global
7	Altadis/Logista	$ 8,190	United Kingdom	Europe
8	C.H. Robinson Worldwide	$ 7,130	USA	Global
9	Agility Logistics	$ 6,316	Kuwait	Global
10	UPS Supply Chain Solutions	$ 6,293	USA	Global

Source: Traffic World, 2009.

UPS BRAND AND CULTURE. Claude Ryan and Jim Casey started UPS with the goal of providing the best service at the lowest rates. Jim's commitment to reliability, courtesy, neatness, and high ethical standards helped establish the values that continue to guide UPS today.[24] "They trust UPS, our technology and visibility tools. It's good to get there on time," said CEO Scott Davis, when asked what loyal customers think of the brand.[25]

Since its inception, UPS has stressed employee ownership as a way to get its people to feel responsible and involved. "We are all owners, that is a big part of enhancing culture. At some point, all of our employees have had a moment when they realize what it means to be a partner," said former UPS CEO Mike Eskew. The company cultivates further loyalty by following a "promote from within" principle. Over the years, many delivery workers and mail sorters have risen to management levels, including Eskew himself. Before serving as CEO from 2002 to 2007, Michael Eskew started as an industrial engineering manager in 1972 and worked his way up the ranks for 30 years.

India Mania

In a 2006 address, Dr. Manmohan Singh, the Prime Minister of India, declared, "We believe that India is now on a sustained path of high growth. We have developed a new model for service-led and technology-driven integration with the global economy."[26] As if on cue, India's GDP topped the $1 trillion mark in early April 2007, making it the 12th wealthiest nation in the world according to Swiss investment firm Credit Suisse.[27] India's GDP now stands at $1.16 trillion, with an annual growth rate of 7.9 percent even during the global financial crisis.[28] When asked about the biggest benefit of doing business in India, Steve Hochradel, Assistant VP of distribution for PBD Worldwide said, "India offers great growth opportunities, and it is easier to do business there than in many other international markets. India has a high population of English speakers, which makes it easy to enter the market, negotiate with vendors and partners, and set up operations."[29]

ECONOMIC REFORM. However, prosperity did not follow immediately after India's emergence from British control and establishment as an independent nation in 1947. For the first 40 years or so, the new socialist government took an extreme protectionist stance, structuring society on the basis of collective action as opposed to capitalist acquisitiveness. The License Raj represented the state's efforts to control all aspects of the economy. Elaborate permits and regulations were required to set up or run businesses, severely limiting their growth. Though there was economic discipline at the macro level and inflation was low compared to other developing countries, the Indian economy dragged along at a subsistence level with a low GDP per capita. Basic industries such as steel and textiles were conspicuous by their absence.[30]

The UPA (United Progressive Alliance), a coalition of political parties that constitutes the Government of India still today, is credited with opening up the economy. An economic crisis during the 1991 general election triggered the beginning of micro-economic liberalization. To rectify the situation, then–finance minister Dr. Manmohan Singh proposed changes such as repealing the "License Raj" and lifting a ban on foreign direct investment. The economy grew by 9 percent the following year as a result of these changes. The Manmohan Singh government showed further support for international trade through the achievement of two key foreign trade policy objectives in 2004: (1) to double India's percentage share of global merchandize trade in a five-year period; and (2) to use trade expansion for both employment generation and economic growth.[31] To expand upon these objectives, the government established several Special Economic Zones (SEZ Act, 2005) in 2006 to attract foreign and domestic investment. Companies operating in these zones receive significant tax benefits and face much simpler clearance and compliance procedures. India's worldwide trade is linked to the world economy. For example, with the recession hitting most of India's major trading partners like the United States, United Arab Emirates, and Singapore, export demand from India declined by 16 percent in January 2009.[32]

KEY INDUSTRIES. India boasts a technical work force of 4 million and trains 60,000 software engineers every year.[33] Combined with lower wages, these factors make India a prime source for information technology (IT) services and a choice business process outsourcing (BPO) destination. In turn, large-scale employment in the IT and BPO sectors has helped to create an upwardly mobile working class, driving increased purchasing/spending power for India's younger generations.

India's economic climate is highly dependent on the oil industry, which until recently has been closely regulated by the national government. An FICCI (Federation of Indian Chambers of Commerce and Industry) report found a strong positive correlation between the price of oil and commodity prices across different sectors of the Indian economy (with the exception of manufacturing, see Exhibit 5). This was largely due to the fact that political pressures ensured that the government absorbed a large part of the increase in oil prices. Public sector oil companies reported losses of approximately US$ 28 million per day on the sale of petroleum products at government-mandated prices. The government offset these losses by selling oil bonds, providing crude oil to state-owned oil retailers at discounted rates, and making periodic adjustments in retail oil prices.[34] In June 2010, the Indian government made a surprising announcement that it plans to deregulate the oil industry. This move is expected to drastically reduce India's fiscal deficit by shifting increased oil costs to the end consumer, and level the playing field between public and private sector oil companies.

TRANSPORTATION SECTOR. Transportation in India has undergone rapid development only in the last two decades. The onus of covering 1,269,210 square miles of land area and supporting a population of more than one billion (1,028,737,436) people makes the sustainable development of India's transportation sector difficult.[35] The Eleventh Five-Year plan, which detailed the latest plans for the Indian economy, projected that $500 billion was needed to achieve comprehensive growth in aviation, roads, railways, and waterways combined. The plan also proposed mobilization of resources from the private sector to complement government efforts.

India has 2.1 million miles of *roadways* that carry 80 percent of its total passengers and 65 percent of India's freight (see Exhibit 6). As of 2000, roughly 74 percent of India's rural population lacked adequate road access, while 40 percent of the existing roads lacked all-weather capability. As a result, the government plans to invest $70 billion in India's road infrastructure over the next few years;[36] $33 million has been dedicated to providing rural connectivity.[37] Developmental projects such as the Golden Quadrilateral Project are helping link India's four major metropolises (Delhi, Mumbai, Kolkata, and Chennai), while the Prime Minister's Rural Roads Program (PMGSY) aims to provide increased access to agricultural communities.

India's civil *aviation* industry was born in 1912 with the first air flight between Karachi and Delhi (see Exhibit 7). The government monopolized the industry for most of the 20th century through the state-owned Air India and Indian Airlines Corporation, until the passage of the "open sky" policy in April 1990 (effective as of 1994). Under "open sky," airlines could receive foreign direct investment of up to 49 percent, opening the market to a host of new players like Jet Airways and Sahara. Deccan Airlines was started by Captain Gopinath in August 2003 as a no-frills budget air service, becoming the first in the industry to fly to second-tier cities from major metropolitan areas.[38] However, after an initial period of rapid growth, the Indian airline industry fizzled around 2007. Today, the industry operates at fares below its costs and is weighed down by huge debt. When oil prices hit $75 a barrel in early 2009, the industry as a whole was expected to post a $9 billion loss. Major carriers like

EXHIBIT 5

The Impact of Oil Prices on Various Factors

International Oil Prices Per Barrel ($)	Increase in International Oil Prices (%)	Extent of Fall in Manufacturing Sector Growth (%)	Extent of Fall in GDP Growth (%)	Extent of Increase in WPI (%)
50	38.9	2.1	0.4	1.5
60	66.7	9.7	1.9	3.6
70	94.2	16.9	3.4	5.7
80	122.2	24.5	4.9	7.9

Source: Study on oil price impact, Federation of Indian Chambers of Commerce and Industry.

EXHIBIT 6

The Road Network in India, Showing Major Warehouse Hubs
Source: Cygnus Research and Consulting.

North and East

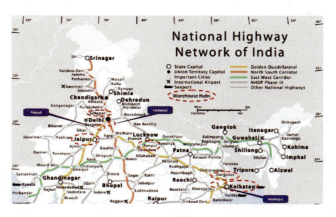

South and West

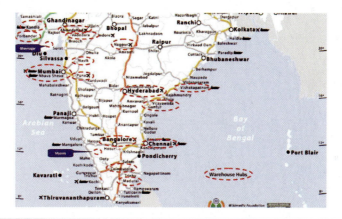

Indian, Jet, and Sahara have been forced to turn their full-service businesses into budget fleets by cutting down on frills, due to the government's refusal to provide bailouts.

While passenger airlines are suffering, the government has increased the maximum level of foreign direct investment in cargo carriers from 49 percent to 74 percent in order to attract overseas players to increase their network in India.[39] Research for Air Cargo India 2010 indicates that air cargo now comprises 19 percent of the total freight in India—the same amount as ocean and rail freight combined. Overall, aviation is expected to grow at a rate close to 25 percent in the next decade. Air cargo is expected to post a CAGR of 11.2 percent, expanding to more than three times its present size by 2025. Currently,

India has 126 functional airports, 12 of which are international and are managed by the Airport Authority of India (5 of these have been privatized for development). Pricing in the industry is directly dependent on high sales taxes on aviation turbine fuel (ATF) and high airport charges. Players in the industry also face major challenges in acquiring land, developing infrastructure, and other issues such as environmental clearance.

India's first *rail line* was set up as an experimental line during the Madras Presidency in 1836. Later, the British government encouraged development of a railway system to haul construction materials around the country, securing 9 million pounds from British companies in guarantees. In 1951, the Indian Railway was nationalized and integrated into one unit to form one of the largest rail networks in the world. Today, it has

EXHIBIT 7

The Air Network in India

Source: Pragati Infosoft Pvt Ltd, indiaeducation.net.

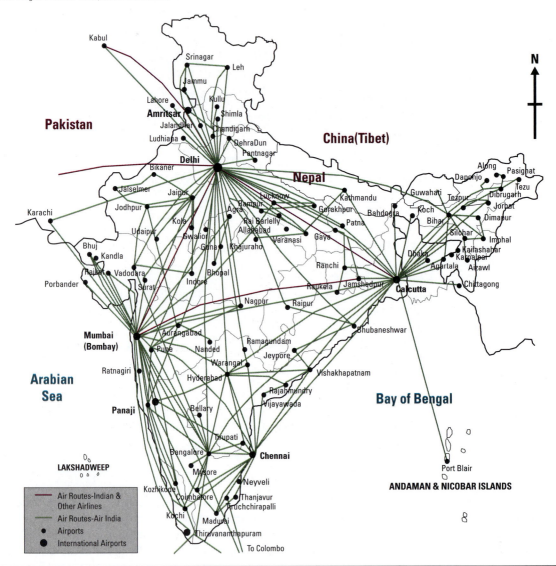

more than 7,500 railway stations connected by tracks spanning 39,233 miles that, most importantly, reach both metropolitan cities and rural villages.[40] Railroads in India carry over a million tons of freight every day (see Exhibit 8).

India has 12 major *seaports*, which account for about 90 percent of India's trade in terms of volume.[41] Inland, the presence of canals, rivers, backwaters, and creeks has facilitated the development of an extensive waterway network, maintained by the

Inland Waterways Authority of India. Ten of these inland waterways have potential significance at the national level. Although close to 5,700 miles can be used by mechanized crafts, freight transportation is limited to only 0.1 percent of the total inland traffic in India. The volume of cargo carried by Inland Waterways Transport has been declining consistently in recent years in favor of alternative modes of transportation.[42] Nevertheless, future development of the inland waterway system could bring economic as well

EXHIBIT 8

The Rail Network of India

Source: http://www.nationmaster.com/encyclopedia/Rail-transport-in-India

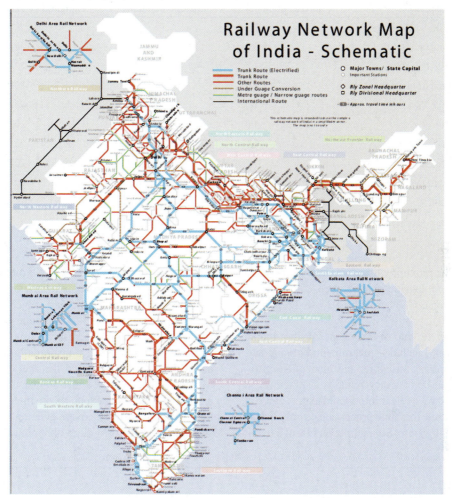

as environmental advantages, and under some conditions, may be the only feasible mode of carrying cargo.

Logistics Industry in India

A World Bank research paper sums up the Indian economic climate as having "a highly fragmented service industry. Outdated regulations, heavy government control, a constrained private sector, and largely inadequate infrastructure have curtailed efforts to improve trade logistics."[43] Despite these obstacles, the World Bank projects that the Indian logistics industry will grow at an annual rate of 15 percent to 20 percent, achieving revenues of $385 billion by 2015.[44] By 2013, approximately 110 logistics parks and 45,000,000 square feet of warehousing space are expected to be developed across the country by various logistics companies (see Exhibit 9). Tier-2 and tier-3 cities have become favorable destinations due to the availability of large pieces of land at lower prices, connectivity to multiple

EXHIBIT 9

Warehouse Capacity Plans of 3PL Players in India (in millions of square feet)

Company	Current Capacity	Planned Capacity	Expected by Year
TCI	7.5	10.0	2010
Safexpress	3.0	10.0	2010
DRS Logistics	1.5	5.0	2010
Indo Arya	2.0	3.5	2010
Blue Dart	1.0	2.0	2010
Gati	1.0	2.0	2009
TNT	0.5	2.0	2010
ProLogistics		7.5	2011
TranSmart		10.5	2013
Total	16.5	52.5	

Source: Industry, Centrum Research.

markets, and the proximity to industrial clusters. Such improvements in logistics capabilities could potentially spur national GDP growth to 11 to 12 percent (see Exhibit 10).

Impediments to the development of the Indian logistics industry include government bureaucracy, a fragmented market structure, and inadequate infrastructure. Indian bureaucracy remains a quagmire; it takes about 20 days to clear import and export cargo at India's ports, while the same process takes only 4 days on average in Singapore. Smaller players form a major part of the industry, and they are typically characterized by low capacity and poor technology. Meanwhile, the power supply is erratic and subject to prolonged outages in many parts of the country. All of these inefficiencies lead to increased costs. Compared to European countries, rail transportation in India costs about three times more and the average transit time by road is about three times longer. Airport charges and related operating expenses are the major contributors to the cost structure in the aviation segment, while shipping is plagued by high operating expenses, staff

EXHIBIT 10

Contribution of Logistics to India's GDP Growth

Source: Cygnus Research and Consulting.

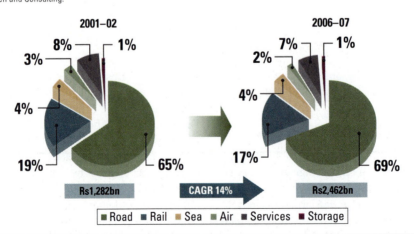

cost and depreciation.[45] In the Indian context, operating expenses generally exceed the costs of raw materials (see Exhibit 11).

A study by Cygnus Business Consulting and Research listed three main growth drivers for the Indian logistics industry in the near future. Since transportation accounts for over 40 percent of the total cost of production in India, growth in quality physical infrastructure is essential for improving the efficiency of the industry.[46] Secondly, the introduction of a Value Added Tax (VAT), a consumption tax levied on any value that is added to a product, has led to increased demand for integrated logistics solutions.[47] Manufacturers are seeking to reduce the number of independent warehouses spread over various regions to minimize unnecessary handling and processing (and thus their VAT burden). Lastly, globalization in the manufacturing sector has highlighted the need to

---

EXHIBIT 11

Cost Structure Analysis for Supply Chain Management (SCM) Companies

Source: BSE India; Cygnus Research.

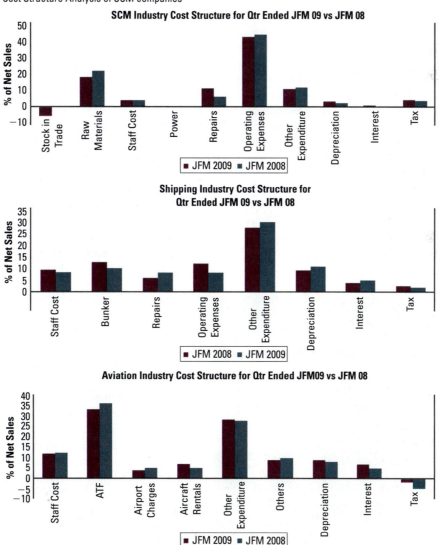

Cost Structure Analysis of SCM companies

integrate fragmented and independently operated functions (for example, transportation, warehousing, freight forwarding, and so on) in order to achieve greater efficiency (see Exhibit 12).[48] Despite strong potential, the Indian logistics sector currently comprises only about 2 percent of the estimated $5,000 billion global logistics industry.

Another potential growth driver is e-commerce and the associated increase in demand for shipping larger volumes of small packages direct to consumers. Online retailing has been somewhat slow to develop in India due to the lack of infrastructure. Many of the country's rural population of 700 million still lack Internet access, though Comat Technologies is actively working to establish Internet centers in villages with populations of more than 5,000. Other project collaborators include ICICI Bank, India's second-largest private bank, and Wyse Technologies, a manufacturer of computer terminal equipment.[49] Another barrier is that Indians value a personalized shopping experience and are not as discount-driven as the American consumer. Credit card transactions in India are not as secure as they are in other countries. Nevertheless, many analysts expect that India will warm up to the idea of Internet shopping as the technology infrastructure improves.

EXHIBIT 12

Trend Shift Toward "Integrated Supply Chain Models"

Source: Cygnus Research and Consulting.

UPS in the Asia–Pacific Region

UPS entered the Asia–Pacific market in 1986, by setting up a regional headquarters in Singapore. Today, the company's presence in the Asia–Pacific region spans more than 40 countries and territories, and employs more than 13,300 people. Additional air hubs are located in Hong Kong, Shenzhen, and Shanghai, China.

UPS's initial foray into India was its 2005 partnership with Jet Air. This agreement led to the opening of the first "UPS Store" in Mumbai, which also marked the brand's first expansion outside North America. The UPS Store was India's first full-service retail outlet to offer shipping, packaging, and other business services under one roof. Speaking at the official opening of a UPS Store in New Delhi in 2007, David Abney, then President of UPS International said, "India's role in the global economy continues to grow impressively . . . 'The UPS Store' will provide businesses as well as consumers a convenient channel to markets throughout the world."[50]

To better consolidate business processes and gain faster, more cost-effective outputs in India, UPS established a second alliance with AFL Private Ltd in 2008. AFL is a logistics service provider with a significant footprint in India. The alliance was mutually beneficial: UPS gained access to 130 of AFL's field stocking locations and increased its number of access points for international delivery customers from 26 to 200, while AFL gained access to UPS's export capabilities. UPS's penetration into the Asian markets deepened further with the incorporation of 101 additional field stocking locations in China into UPS's service parts logistics network.[51, 52] Globally, UPS maintains 1,000 such distribution centers to provide customer inventory and order management services in addition to core packaging services. Some of those facilities also house specialized contract services such as technical diagnostics and repair.

UPS continues to form alliances and collaborations with other local Asian companies to target different segments. For example, in May 2010, UPS formed an alliance with AliExpress, a subsidiary of the China-based Alibaba group. AliExpress is the world leader in e-commerce for small businesses and hosts the world's largest base of suppliers in the segment.[53] Jordan Colletta, VP of E-commerce and Marketing at UPS, explained the purpose of the agreement as follows: "Through our alliance with Alibaba, we hope to partner with more small and mid-sized Chinese businesses to simplify their logistics processes and connect them with new buyers and sellers worldwide."[54] Less than one month later, UPS formed another alliance with PosLaju, the leader in the Malaysian domestic courier business with a 27 percent market share. Together, the companies created PosLaju International Premium, which boasts money-back guaranteed overnight international delivery service to 215 Asian locations.[55]

Competition in India

India was proving to be one of the more difficult Asian markets to penetrate due to the sheer number of competitors. Currently, the subcontinent boasts more than 2,500 parcel carriers and courier services, all competing to differentiate themselves based on cost, speed, and territorial coverage. Larger players have a clear advantage with respect to infrastructure, business-consumer interface, and speed of delivery. Smaller or more local firms tend to have better access to local information and ease of penetration at the domestic level (see Exhibit 13 for market share data, Exhibit 14 for performance metrics, and Exhibit 15 for key success factors, respectively). These different

approaches are reflected in their respective investments in information systems: larger firms devote close to 20 percent of their development funds to information technology, compared to just over 7 percent for smaller firms.

Blue Dart-DHL Express is the clear market leader in both the international and domestic segments, with a combined market share three times higher than that of the nearest competitor.[56] Prior to its acquisition by DHL, Blue Dart had an 8 percent share in the non-document cargo and road freight sector. The next largest competitor in the international segment is TNT, which has double the market share of FedEx and UPS.[57] AFL, GATI, and First Flight are Blue Dart-DHL's main challengers in the domestic sector. See Exhibit 16 for a comparison of the stock performance of some of these key competitors.

Started in 1989, *GATI* has become a leader in express cargo delivery. With operations touching 603 out of 611 districts in India, GATI is one of the most sought-after freight carriers in the country.[58] The company covers 200,000 miles every day and claims to have brought India and the world closer by virtue of their "deeply entrenched network and domain knowledge." In recent years, GATI has diversified both its services and its geographic reach. GATI now offers distribution and supply chain management solutions as well as delivery services, and has spread across the Asian subcontinent. While expanding its international presence through the establishment of offices in Singapore, Hong Kong, China, and Sri Lanka, GATI continues to develop highly focused expertise in India-centric operations.

Of course, all of these private companies also compete against the *Indian Department of Posts*, the government-run postal service. The Department of Posts has the largest network of post boxes in the world, and close to 90 percent of this network spans rural India. The Department also offers express delivery through its Emergency Mail Service (EMS), which comprises 13 percent of the express market share in India.[59] The Post Office (Amendment) Bill of 2006 gives the Department a monopoly in the delivery of small letters and packages (weighing less than 0.66 lbs), limits foreign direct investment in the industry

---

EXHIBIT 13

Non-document Cargo and Road Freight,
Comprising 40 Percent of the Express Delivery Market

Source: Author's interview with logistics sector expert.

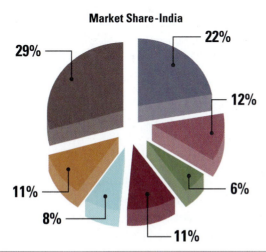

Market Share-India

- 22%
- 12%
- 6%
- 11%
- 8%
- 11%
- 29%

■ Safex (270 Cr) ■ XPS (150 Cr) ■ Speedage (70 Cr) ■ AFL (130 Cr)
■ Bluedart (100 Cr) ■ Gati (350 Cr) ■ OM, TVS etc (130 Cr)

EXHIBIT 14

Significant Dependency Relationships among Performance

Metrics and Key Success Factors

	Micro & Small Companies (78 responses)			All Companies (133 responses)		
	Independent variable	Type of relationship	p-value	Independent variable	Type of relationship	p-value
Revenue growth	Pricing of services	−	0.013	Coverage	+	0.007
				Breadth of services	+	0.028
				Client relations	+	0.034
				Integration of services	+	0.005
Profit growth	Experience	−	0.012	On-time delivery	−	0.029
				Coverage	+	0.029
				Breadth of services	+	0.027
	Integration of services	+	0.008	Integration of services	+	0.000
Shipment volume growth	Door-to-door service	+	0.039	Breadth of services	+	0.001
	Integration of services	−	0.019	Investment in information systems	+	0.002
Shipment value growth	Door-to-door service	−	0.007	Breadth of services	+	0.024
	Breadth of services	−	0.006	Client relations	+	0.001
				Human resources	+	0.003
Return on investments (ROI)	Door-to-door service	+	0.010	Coverage	+	0.000
	Coverage	+	0.025			
	Breadth of services	−	0.045	Integration of services	+	0.001
Return on assets (ROA)	On-time delivery	+	0.048	Coverage	+	0.001
				Integration of services	+	0.002
Customer satisfaction	Client relations	+	0.006	Reputation	+	0.015
				Credit facilities	+	0.021
				Client relations	+	0.039
	Investment in assets	−	0.030	Investment in information systems	−	0.046
				Human resources	+	0.023
Business relationship	Industry focus	−	0.015	Industry focus	−	0.019
	Client relations	+	0.002	Client relations	+	0.000
	Human resources	+	0.005	Human resources	+	0.000

EXHIBIT 14 *(Continued)*

	Micro & Small Companies (78 responses)			All Companies (133 responses)		
	Independent variable	Type of relationship	p-value	Independent variable	Type of relationship	p-value
Customer acquisition	Breadth of services	+	0.009	Coverage	+	0.000
	Industry focus	−	0.015	Experience	+	0.000
	Experience	+	0.015	Human resources	+	0.003
Grographic reach	Coverage	+	0.005	Coverage	+	0.001
	Industry focus	+	0.004	Industry focus	−	0.003
	Reputation	+	0.038	Investment in assets	+	0.001
	Client relations	−	0.006	Integration of services	+	0.000

Source: A Survey of Indian Express Delivery Providers, IIMC.

EXHIBIT 15

Comparative Study of Key Success Factors

	Cluster					
	Micro & Small		Medium		Large	
No. of Observations	78		15		7	
Key Success Factor	Rank	%	Rank	%	Rank	%
Door-to-door service	1	97.44	1	100	8	85.71
On-time delivery & reliablity	1	97.44	2	93.33	1	100
Coverage (national/international)	6	55.13	7	80	1	100
Breadth of service offerings	11	15.38	9	60	1	100
Focus on specific industries	12	11.54	14	6.67	13	57.14
Experience of service provider	5	88.46	2	93.33	11	71.43
Reputation of service provider	3	93.59	2	93.33	1	100
Competitive pricing of services	4	92.31	8	73.33	8	85.71
Extension of credit facilities	6	55.13	12	40	14	28.57
Relationship with customers	8	53.85	5	86.67	8	85.71
Investment in assets	12	11.54	11	46.67	1	100
Investment in information systems	9	38.46	5	86.67	1	100
Quality of human resources	9	38.46	10	53.33	11	71.43
Integration of services	14	5.13	13	26.67	1	100

Source: A Survey of Indian Express Delivery Providers, IIMC.

EXHIBIT 16

Comparative Study: Domestic vs. Global Market

Major Indian Domestic Players vs. the Sensex (Bombay Stock Exchange)

Source: Cygnus Consulting.

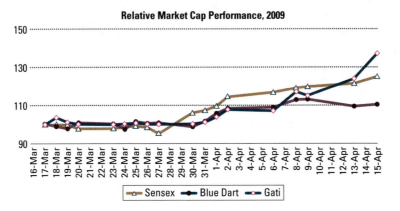

Relative Market Cap Performance, 2009

UPS vs. S&P 500 and Dow Jones Transportation Index

Source: UPS form 10K, Annual Report filed February 27, 2009.

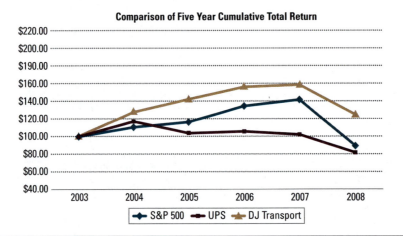

Comparison of Five Year Cumulative Total Return

to 49 percent, and requires all private carriers to participate in an expensive and cumbersome registration system. Every registered service provider with a turnover of $50,000 or more is required to deposit 10 percent of its annual turnover to a Universal Service Obligation Fund (USO Fund).[60] Despite its legal mandate, a survey of users of delivery services carried out by the Indian Institute of Management revealed that 60 percent of consumers did not use India Post. The 40 percent that did use it sent only letters or documents (but not packages). For all other shipments, customers preferred express delivery service providers for their reliability and accountability.

What Lies Ahead?

At the end of the day, Ms. Page gathered up the remaining reports, shut down her computer, and headed out to her car. She figured she'd catch up on some more "light" reading once she got home. At least she was starting to feel like she had a better sense of what UPS had done thus far, as well as some of the obstacles the company faced if they were to penetrate the Indian market more deeply. How could they take advantage of India's growth potential? Did UPS's strategy of promising delivery to "every address" in their area of reach make business sense in the Indian context? Was it possible to overcome the numerous challenges that this highly regulated yet underdeveloped economy presented?

Which global strategy should they apply? Could they decentralize decision making and adopt a strategy that would make it easier to incorporate the diverse local conditions of India? Which segment would prove to be most profitable: business-to-business, consumer-to-consumer, or the emerging business-to-consumer channel? How quickly would the advent of the new "credit-card generation" change the scope of e-commerce in the country? Once they decided what activities to pursue, what was the best means of accomplishing UPS's business objectives? Could they use their current strongholds to grow organically, or would additional alliances be a better way to go? Perhaps they should follow the model of DHL and pursue an acquisition instead. The dynamic business environment in India surely needed a dynamic strategy, and it was up to Ms. Page to figure out how to proceed from here . . .

Endnotes

1. Mitra, S. (2009), "A survey of Indian express delivery service providers," Indian Institute of Management Calcutta, May.

2. Berg, Eric N. (1985), "United Parcel extends its reach," *The New York Times,* June 9.

3. www.ups.com/content/corp/about/history/1929.html.

4. Hess, E. D., and R. Kazanjian (2006), *The search for organic growth.* Cambridge, UK: Cambridge University Press.

5. www.ups.com/content/corp/about/history/1929.html.

6. "Company history; About UPS," *UPS.com,* www.ups.com/content/corp/about/history/1980.html?WT.svl=SubNav.

7. www.pressroom.ups.com/About+UPS/Company+History/.

8. www.ups.com/content/corp/about/history/1980.html.

9. "Company history; About UPS," *UPS.com,* www.ups.com/content/corp/about/history/1990.html?WT.svl=SubNav.

10. Ibid.

11. "Teamsters end UPS strike," *CNN.com,* www.cnn.com/US/9708/20/ups.update.early/.

12. Leonhardt, D. (1999), "Returns to senders; Snail mail: It's alive! And it's mutating!" *The New York Times,* November 14, www.nytimes.com/1999/11/14/weekinreview/returns-to-senders-snail-mail-it-s-alive-and-it-s-mutating.html?ref=united_parcel_service_inc.

13. Hess, E. D., and R. Kazanjian (2006), "The search for organic growth."

14. www.ups.com/content/corp/about/history/1999.html?WT.svl=SubNav.

15. Hess, E. D., and R. Kazanjian (2006), "The search for organic growth."

16. UPS Media Kit, www.underconsideration.com/speakup_v2/ups_media_kit.pdf.

17. Hesseldahl, A. (2004), "Toshiba will have UPS fix its laptops," *Forbes.com,* www.forbes.com/2004/04/27/cx_ah_0427ups.html.

18. "Company history; About UPS," *UPS.com,* www.ups.com/content/corp/about/history/2002.html?WT.svl=SubNav.

19. "The UPS store debuts more than 3,000 strong," *The UPSStore.com Pressroom,* www.theupsstore.com/about/pressroom/pages/040703_press_release.aspx.

20. Hess, E. D., and R. Kazanjian (2006), "The search for organic growth."

21. "United Parcel Service," *Wikipedia.org,* http://en.wikipedia.org/wiki/United_Parcel_Service.

22. Hudson, S., "Success with hub and spoke distribution," Supply Chain Management, NCSU, http://scm.ncsu.edu/public/lessons/less031014.html.

23. "FedEx announces domestic express services in China," 2007 Press Releases, *Fedex.com,* http://fedex.com/cn_english/about/pressreleases/20070320_507.html.

24. "Company history; About UPS," *UPS.com,* www.ups.com/content/corp/about/history/.

25. UPS CEO Scott Davis in a 2009 CNBC interview, http://video.msn.com/?mkt=en-us&brand=money&vid=372a9fb9-1195-4a1c-93aa-1ad61bd526e4&playlist=videoByTag:tag:money_top_investing:ns:MSNmoney_Gallery:mk:us:vs:1&from=MSNmoney_ticker&tab=s216.

26. PM's address to Joint Session of the DIET, Press Information Bureau (India), December 14, 2006, www.pib.nic.in/release/release.asp?relid=23318.

27. Balogh, M., (2007). "Significant growth is crucial for India's economy," January 10, Credit Suisse, http://emagazine.credit-suisse.com/app/article/index.cfm?fuseaction=OpenArticle&aoid=200210&lang=EN.

28. "India GDP growth rate," *TradingEconomics,* July 5, 2010, www.tradingeconomics.com/Economics/GDP-Growth.aspx?Symbol=INR.

29. "UPS snapshot for small businesses: Doing business in India," http://pressroom.ups.com/pressroom/staticfiles/pdf/fact_sheets/India_Snapshot_for_Small_Businesses.pdf

30. Williamson, J., "The Rise of The Indian Economy," *www.unc.edu,* May 11, 2006, www.unc.edu/depts/diplomat/item/2006/0406/will/williamson_india.html.

31. Sharma, A. (2009), "India's Foreign Trade Policy 2009–2014," November 2, The Metropolitan Corporate Counsel, www.metrocorpcounsel.com/current.php?artType=view&EntryNo=10306.

32. ENAM Securities Logistics Update, March 2009.

33. "India information," Embassy of India, www.indianembassy.org/indiainfo/india_it.htm.

34. "Deregulation of oil prices—Yet another endeavor," *IndiQuest,* http://indiquest.wordpress.com/2009/06/30/deregulation-of-oil-prices-yet-another-endeavor/.

35. "Transport in India," *Wikipedia.org,* http://en.wikipedia.org/wiki/Transport_in_India.

36. "Indian road network," *Wikipedia.org,* http://en.wikipedia.org/wiki/Indian_Road_Network.

37. "Rural roads—A lifeline for villages in India," World Bank Publication, http://web.worldbank.org/WBSITE/EXTERNAL/ COUNTRIES/SOUTHASIAEXT/EXTSARREGTOPTRANSP ORT/0,,contentMDK:21755700~pagePK:34004173~piPK:340 03707~theSitePK:579598,00.html.

38. "Kingfisher Red," *Wikipedia.org,* http://en.wikipedia.org/ wiki/Kingfisher_Red.

39. "Research for Aircargo India 2010," www.stattimes.com/ aci2010/.

40. "Indian Railways Information System," www.indianrail. gov.in/abir.html.

41. "India: Transport and communications," *The Economist,* June 24, 2008, www.eiu.com/index. asp?layout=VWPrintVW3&article_id=1113483696&printer= printer&rf=0.

42. "Inland waterway transport," United Nations Economic and Social Commission for Asia and the Pacific, www.unescap.org/ttdw/Publications/TPTS_pubs/pub_2307/ pub_2307_ch11.pdf.

43. Peters, H. J., "India's growing conflict between trade and transport," Infrastructure and Urban Development Department, The World Bank, January 1990, www-wds. worldbank.org/external/default/WDSContentServer/IW3P/ IB/2000/02/24/000009265_3960929153437/Rendered/PDF/ multi_page.pdf.

44. www.tcil.com/pdfiifr/TCILar09_09_07_09.pdf.

45. Hesseldahl, A. (2004), "Toshiba will have UPS fix its laptops."

46. Cygnus Business Consulting and Research Pvt Limited, *Quarterly Performance Analysis of Companies (January–March 2009)*, Indian Logistics Industry.

47. "Value added tax," *Wikipedia.org,* http://en.wikipedia.org/ wiki/Value_added_tax.

48. www.tcil.com/pdfiifr/TCILar09_09_07_09.pdf.

49. Markoff, J. (2005), "Plan to connect rural India to the Internet," *The New York Times,* June 16, www.nytimes. com/2005/06/16/technology/16compute.html.

50. "First of its kind, one-stop retail outlet offers full range of business services to North India," press release, *UPS.com,* www.ups.com/content/in/en/about/news/press_releases/new_ delhi_ups_store.html.

51. Peters, H. J., "India's growing conflict between trade and transport," January 1990.

52. "UPS increases FSL presence in China," *Post and Parcel,* http://postandparcel.info/30941/markets/ ups-increases-fsl-presence-in-china/.

53. Home page, Alibaba.com, http://news.alibaba.com/spe-cials/aboutalibaba/index.html.

54. "UPS teams with AliExpress," *Atlanta Business Chronicle,* May 3, 2010, http://atlanta.bizjournals.com/atlanta/sto-ries/2010/05/03/daily23.html.

55. "PosLaju and UPS form alliance, *The New York Times,* July 5, 2010, http://markets.on.nytimes.com/research/stocks/ news/press_release.asp?docTag=201006031000BIZWIRE_ USPRX____BW5289&feedID=600&press_symbol=277628.

56. Mitra, S. (2009), "A survey of Indian express delivery ser-vice providers."

57. "Fast-growing Indian express market set for further con-solidation," press release, CEP Research, https://www.cep-research.com/export/sites/default/cepresearch/pages/custom/ press_release_articles/PI_06-09-21-CEP-Research.pdf.

58. These facts were collected in an author's interview with logistics industry expert, Supratem Ganguly.

59. Mitra, S. (2009), "A survey of Indian express delivery ser-vice providers."

60. "India together," www.indiatogether.org/2006/aug/law-poffice.htm.

Marne L. Arthaud-Day
Kansas State University

Frank T. Rothaermel
Georgia Institute of Technology

Wei Zhang
Georgia Institute of Technology

IT WAS ALMOST MIDNIGHT. Dr. Richard Scheller, Executive Vice President of Research and Early Development of Genentech, was sitting at his desk in the Grand Hotel Les Trois Rois, Basel, Switzerland. He had arrived in Switzerland earlier that afternoon, and spent the rest of the day finishing up the slides for his presentation to the Roche Executive Committee the next morning. Severin Schwan, CEO of Roche Group, was expecting Dr. Scheller to present his strategic plan on how to manage Genentech's R&D process and clinical pipeline. Roche had completed its acquisition of all remaining publicly held Genentech shares in 2009, cementing a corporate partnership that dated back to the 1980s. Roche believed that Genentech's legendary expertise in biotechnology could help propel the company to the forefront of personalized medicine.

Dr. Scheller's last meeting at Roche headquarters had not gone well. Many questions were raised regarding the recently failed clinical trial for the use of Avastin in early-stage colon cancer. Avastin was first approved for advanced colon cancer in 2004, and had since been approved for several other types of metastatic cancer. An antiangiogenesis agent, Avastin worked by blocking a protein called VEGF that tumors needed to form blood vessels and gain access to nutrients in order to grow.[1] One of Roche's main motivations for acquiring Genentech had been to obtain the rights to Avastin, and Roche was counting on extending its applications as a major part of its growth strategy. If positive, the clinical trial results could have led to billions more in Avastin sales, as well as primed the way for multiple other early-stage cancer indications. Instead, the negative results were a major setback, sending Roche shares down by 10 percent.

Severin Schwan's words from the last meeting at headquarters were still ringing in Scheller's head: "We need more efficiency in drug development, only an approved drug is a good drug." A failed Phase III clinical trial was a major "inefficiency" that Roche's executives did not want to see repeated. Phase III trials involved testing the effectiveness and safety of a new drug compared to existing treatments in anywhere from 1,000 to 3,000 patients, with costs exceeding $26,000 per patient.[2, 3] To make matters worse, a U.S. advisory panel had recently voted to revoke Avastin's approval for the treatment of advanced breast cancer, after two large Phase III trials revealed that Avastin provided no significant benefit in terms of survival. Patients and doctors were fighting to keep the product on the market, but the FDA rarely deviated from an advisory panel's recommendation, especially when the vote was 12 to 1.[4]

Despite this string of recent failures, Dr. Scheller continued to feel pressure from Roche to focus on the development of Phase III projects in order to bring more products to market. Things were different now that Roche owned Genentech outright and was not just a well-invested partner. Scheller missed some of his previous autonomy. He was not sure that reducing the resources dedicated to early drug discovery and reallocating them to the development of current Phase II and Phase III projects represented the best use of Genentech's talent. He believed strongly that early drug discovery research was the key to keeping the company's future product pipeline well stocked, and he feared the long-term implications of neglecting

Professors Marne Arthaud-Day, Frank T. Rothaermel, and Wei Zhang (PhD in Bioengineering) prepared this case from public sources. It was developed for the purpose of class discussion. We thank IMS Health for making various data reports available to us, and Dr. Christopher Boerner (formerly Director Avastin Franchise Strategy, Avastin Marketing, Genentech) for helpful comments and suggestions as well as for his presentation in the "Competing in the Health Sciences" course, Georgia Institute of Technology, April 9, 2010. This case is not intended to be used for any kind of endorsement, source of data, or depiction of efficient or inefficient management. © Arthaud-Day, Rothaermel, and Zhang, 2013.

this core capability to pursue more immediate returns. Finding the optimal strategic balance between generating novel therapies and pursuing further commercial applications of the discoveries already made was one of Scheller's most challenging tasks.

The Birth of Biotechnology

Medical biotechnology involves the use of cellular and biomolecular processes to develop new products with health care applications.[5] These so-called *biologics* differ from traditional, chemistry-based medicines (new chemical entities) in that they are derived from living cells and therefore have more complex structures. They may be composed of a variety of organic molecules, including sugars, proteins, or nucleic acids, or may be actual living cells or tissues derived from humans, animals, or microorganisms. Because of their biological nature, such products are more sensitive to heat and are susceptible to microbial contamination, making them more difficult to produce.[6] However, the specificity of DNA and the cellular processes upon which biologics are based means that they can be designed to address specific medical needs with fewer unintended side-effects, compared to traditional pharmaceuticals. (See Exhibit 1 for a comparison of biologics versus pharmaceuticals.)[7]

The theoretical groundwork for the emergence of the biotechnology industry dates back to Watson and Crick's discovery of the double helical structure of DNA in 1953. Twenty years later, a team led by Stanford University professor Stanley Cohen and University of California, San Francisco (UCSF) Professor Herbert Boyer (one of the eventual founders of Genentech) published its breakthrough research on recombinant DNA in the Proceedings of the National Academy of Sciences.[8] The development of recombinant DNA technology provided scientists with a simple but powerful method for isolating and amplifying any gene or DNA segment and moving it with controlled precision. This process allowed for the analysis of gene structure and function in simple and complex organisms, information that scientists then used to develop procedures for producing proteins, such as human insulin, in cell cultures under controlled conditions.[9]

On December 2, 1980, the U.S. Patent and Trademark Office issued the first major patent in the new biotechnology sector (U.S. Patent 4,237,224), one of the three patents subsequently known as the Cohen-Boyer recombinant DNA cloning patents. For his contribution, Cohen was entitled to one third of Stanford's licensing royalties on the three patents, but he decided to donate his share to the university. Boyer did not relinquish his personal share of patent royalties until he experienced strong pressure from UCSF. The university even threatened to conduct a detailed investigation of all sponsored research taking place on campus, making Boyer a target for personal hostility by his colleagues.[10] The three rDNA patents generated more than $250 million in licensing fees for Stanford University and UCSF before their expiration in 1997.

Recombinant DNA, along with several other biological breakthroughs (such as the discovery of monoclonal antibodies in 1975 by George Köhler and Caesar Milstein), revolutionized scientific approaches to drug development. Advances in fields like rational

---

EXHIBIT 1

Bio vs. Traditional: Advantages and Disadvantages of Biopharmaceuticals

Traditional Drugs	Biopharmaceuticals
Unspecific binding	Specific binding
Interactions with other drugs	Interactions rare
Carcinogenic substances possible	Not carcinogenic
Pharmacokinetics difficult	Breakdown is predictable for the most part
Immune reactions rare	Immunogenic effects possible
6% success rate in Phases I–III	25% success rate in Phases I–III
Development costs high, production costs low	Development costs low, production costs high
Theoretically, any target molecule can be reached	Target molecules limited, only outside the cell

Source: Modified from Roche Group (2006), *Biotechnology–New Ways in Medicine* (Basel, Switzerland), p. 36.

drug design, genomics, proteomics, RNA inference, and systems biology led to a host of new biologically based therapies, including vaccines, blood products, allergenics, somatic cells, gene therapy, tissues, and recombinant therapeutic proteins.[11] Consequently, treatment options have improved for more than 200 different diseases, including Alzheimer's, cancer, diabetes, multiple sclerosis, and AIDS.

Evolution of the Biotechnology Industry

Along with a host of new therapies, the birth of biotechnology led to the emergence of a powerful new business model for the commercialization of scientific intellectual property.[12] This model was based on three interrelated components: development of new technologies, venture capital and public equity markets, and a market for know-how. New biotechnology breakthroughs tended to be discovered in universities and other research institutes, which lacked the resources and knowledge needed to bring their innovations to market. Researchers therefore partnered with venture capital and private equity markets to provide the "fuel" to commercialize their new technologies. Development and marketing know-how was contributed to by large incumbent pharmaceutical firms in return for partial ownership of the new technology. Such partnerships provided the new ventures with a ready supply of financial capital to support ongoing research and development.

In a classical Schumpeterian swarm of new entry, the number of biotech startups exploded, reaching over 1,400. (See Exhibits 2 and 3 for the leading global biotech corporations.) Between 1994 and 2006, industry R&D expenditures tripled to $22.9 billion while revenues increased five-fold to $53.5 billion.[13] (See Exhibit 4 for U.S. biotech industry statistics.) In 2007, global prescription sales of biotech drugs increased 12.5 percent to more than $75 billion, nearly double the 6.4 percent growth rate of the global pharmaceutical market.[14] (See Exhibit 5 for global pharmaceutical sales from 2002 to 2009.) The range of biotech products and their therapeutic applications also steadily increased. By 2008, more than 200 new biologics had been approved for therapeutic use, with 400 more at various stages of clinical development.[15] Twenty-two biotech products generated sales exceeding $1 billion (the threshold to be considered a "blockbuster drug") in 2007, compared with just six products in 2002.[16] (See Exhibit 6 for a list of the leading global biotech products.)

EXHIBIT 2

Top 10 Companies by Global Sales of Biotech Drugs ($ millions, 2007)

Source: Data provided by IMS Health. The size of the global biotech market was $75 billion in 2007.

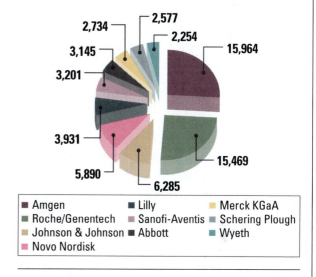

■ Amgen	■ Lilly	■ Merck KGaA
■ Roche/Genentech	■ Sanofi-Aventis	■ Schering Plough
■ Johnson & Johnson	■ Abbott	■ Wyeth
■ Novo Nordisk		

The double-digit growth in biotech revenues was only one side of the story, however. Only a small percentage of companies, like Amgen and Genentech, achieved commercial success. Many more biotechnology firms burned through significant amounts of capital (see Exhibit 7) without producing profits.[17] Moreover, while the industry as a whole continued to grow, growth rates appeared to be leveling off (see Exhibit 8). During the 2008–2009 recession, even the large biotech companies felt the pinch, while smaller firms struggled to survive. These numbers reflected the fact that the discovery and development of a new biologic was a long and costly process. Medical biotechnology was among the most research-intensive industries in the world; publicly traded U.S. biotech companies spent $27.1 billion in R&D in 2006.[18] The average drug development time increased from 12 to 15 years,[19] while mean development costs (excluding product launch and marketing expenses) nearly doubled from $800 million in 2000 to $1.5 billion in 2010.[20] Thus, biotechnology did not turn out to be quite the panacea for the bottom line that pharmaceutical companies once hoped.[21]

Facing empty product-development pipelines, expiring patents on their blockbuster drugs, and strong generic competition, the pharmaceutical industry as a whole was expected to lose as much as $65 billion from patent expiration by 2012 (see Exhibit 9). Given

EXHIBIT 3

World's Largest Biotech Companies (U.S. $ millions, 2003)

Many of the major healthcare companies are now also involved in the biotech sector. If these too are taken into account, the following picture emerges:

World's largest biotech companies by sales in 2003, in million US$		
1	Amgen (USA)	8,360
2	Genentech (USA)	3,300
3	Serono (Switzerland)	2,000
4	Biogen Idec (USA)	1,850[1]
5	Chiron (USA)	1,750
6	Genzyme (USA)	1,570
7	MedImmune (USA)	1,050
8	Invitrogen (USA)	780
9	Cephalon (USA)	710
10	Millenium (USA)	430

Source: Company reports

[1] Comparative figure after the merger of Biogen and Idec in Nov. 2003.

World's largest healthcare companies by sales of biotech products in 2003, in million US$		
1	Amgen	7,866
2	Roche Group including Genentech and Chugai	6,191
3	Johnson & Johnson	6,100
4	Novo Nordisk	3,561
5	Eli Lilly	3,043
6	Aventis	2,075
7	Wyeth	1,870
8	Schering-Plough	1,751
9	Serono	1,623
10	Baxter International	1,125
11	Biogen	1,057
12	Schering AG	1,035
13	Genzyme	879
14	MedImmune	780
15	GlaxoSmithKine	729
16	Bayer AG	563
17	Pfizer	481
18	Abbott Laboratories	397
19	Akzo Nobel	375
20	Kirin	355

Source: Evaluate Service.

Source: Roche Group (2006), *Biotechnology–New Ways in Medicine* (Basel, Switzerland), p. 16.

EXHIBIT 4

U.S. Biotech Industry Statistics: 1996–2006 (U.S. $ billions)

Year	2006	2005	2004	2003	2002	2001	2000	1999	1998	1997	1996
Sales	45.3	39.7	28.1	28.4	24.3	21.4	19.3	16.1	14.5	13.0	10.8
Revenues	53.5	48.5	43.8	39.2	29.6	29.6	26.7	22.3	20.2	17.4	14.6
R&D expense	22.9	16.6	19.6	17.9	20.5	15.7	14.2	10.7	10.6	9.0	7.9
Net loss	3.5	1.4	6.8	5.4	9.4	4.6	5.6	4.4	4.1	4.5	4.6
No. of public companies	336	331	331	314	318	342	339	300	316	317	294
No. of companies	1,452	1,475	1,346	1,473	1,466	1,457	1,379	1,273	1,311	1,274	1,287

Source: BIO, *Guide to Biotechnology*, p. 7. Original data from Ernst & Young LLP, annual biotechnology industry reports, 1995–2006. Financial data based primarily on fiscal-year financial statements of publicly traded companies.

EXHIBIT 5

Global Pharmaceutical Market, 2002–2009 (sales in U.S. $ billions)

Source: Data provided by IMS Health.

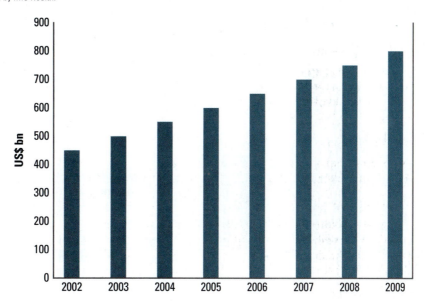

EXHIBIT 6

Leading Global Biotech Products in 2007

Top 10 Products	Sales U.S.$ millions	% Market Share 2007
Global Biotech Market	*75,120*	*100.0*
Enbrel	5,290	7.0
Aranesp	4,415	5.9
Remicade	4,220	5.6
Mabthera/Rituxan	3,714	4.9
Neulasta	3,556	4.7
Erypo/Procrit	3,291	4.4
Herceptin	3,255	4.3
Epogen	2,982	4.0
Avastin	2,790	3.8
Humira	2,790	3.7

Source: Data provided by IMS Health.

EXHIBIT 7

Revenue and Operating Income Before Depreciation (U.S. $ billions, 2004)

Source: Adapted from G. P. Pisano (2006), "Can science be a business? Lessons from biotech," *Harvard Business Review*, October.

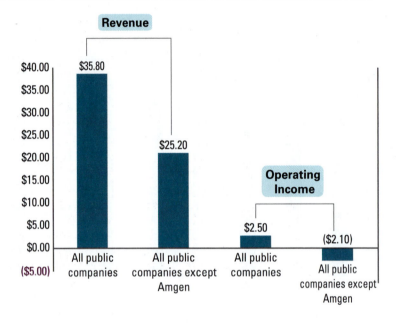

EXHIBIT 8

Biotech Market Size and Growth, 1998–2007

Source: Data provided by IMS Health.

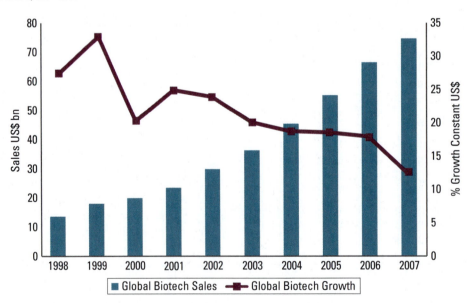

EXHIBIT 9

Projected Pharmaceutical Industry Revenue Losses due to Patent Expirations (U.S. $ billions)

Source: Data from Sanford C. Bernstein & Co.

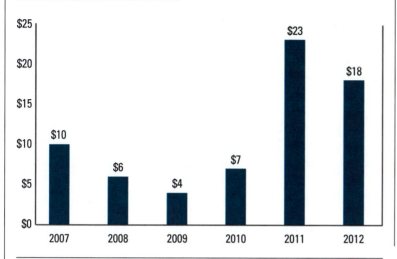

Biotech Wunderkind: Genentech

Genentech was founded in 1976 by the late venture capitalist Robert Swanson (MBA from MIT Sloan) and Herbert Boyer, a professor of biochemistry and biophysics at UCSF. After Boyer and Cohen published their breakthrough research on recombinant DNA in 1973, Swanson instantly recognized the new technology's commercial potential. He called Boyer to request a short meeting, which turned out to be three hours long. Swanson's enthusiasm and belief in the new technology was so persuasive that by the end of their conversation, Genentech was born. A few years after the company was founded, Genentech's scientists successfully produced the first therapeutic proteins by splicing human genes into fast-growing bacteria.[24]

Considered the creator of the biotechnology industry, Genentech's aim was to leverage the newly discovered rDNA technology to develop a new generation of therapeutics. Genentech's mission was to discover, develop, manufacture, and commercialize biotherapeutics using genetic engineering and other advanced technologies, with a focus on critical medical conditions in the areas of oncology, immunology, and tissue growth and repair. Prior to its acquisition by Roche in 2009, the company had built one of the leading product portfolios in the biotech industry, and had led in U.S. oncology sales since 2006. In 2008 (the company's last full year of independent operations), Genentech had revenues of $13.4 billion, more than double the amount ($6.6 billion) it had in 2005, and a net income of $3.4 billion. (See Exhibits 10 and 11 for Genentech financials.) Net U.S. product sales totaled $9.2 billion, an 11 percent increase from 2007. Product sales represented 78 percent of revenues, with royalties and contracts making up the remainder.

the more positive prognosis for biotechnology, big pharma firms readily established strategic alliances with biotech companies, hoping to share in their future profits. The first pharma-biotech agreement was formed between Eli Lilly and Genentech in 1978 to commercialize the new drug Humulin, a biotech-based human insulin. According to BioWorld, pharmaceutical and biotech companies formed 417 new partnerships in 2007 alone.[22]

Still other pharmaceutical firms sought to acquire their biotech partners in order to bring their innovative capabilities and new-product pipelines in-house. Novartis bought Chiron for $5.4 billion in 2006, AstraZeneca bought MedImmune for $15.6 billion in 2007, and Roche finalized its acquisition of Genentech in 2009. This flurry of biotech acquisitions formed part of a larger trend toward pharmaceutical industry consolidation, as companies vied for greater market power. Critics, however, were concerned that these mega-mergers would have a negative effect on R&D productivity and innovation in general. Increasing the amount of R&D did not necessarily make such research more productive. "On the contrary, it is very hard to manage science when you have huge teams of people," said Joseph Schlessinger, chairman of the department of pharmacology at Yale's School of Medicine and the founder of three biotechnology companies.[23]

DISCOVERY RESEARCH AND DRUG DEVELOPMENT. From its inception, Genentech's R&D activities focused on applying leading-edge scientific knowledge

EXHIBIT 10

Genentech Financials Leading Up to the Acquisition

YEARS ENDED DECEMBER 31 (in millions, except per-share stock price and employee data)	2008	2007	2006	2005	2004	2003	2002	2001	2000	1999	1998
TOTAL OPERATING REVENUE	$13,418	$11,724	$9,284	$6,633	$4,621	$3,300	$2,584	$2,044	$1,514	$1,292	$1,053
Product sales	10,531	9,443	7,640	5,488	3,749	2,621	2,164	1,743	1,278	1,039	718
Royalties	2,539	1,984	1,354	935	641	501	366	264	207	189	230
Contract revenue	348	297	290	210	231	178	54	37	29	64	105
TOTAL COSTS AND EXPENSES	$8,089	$7,495	$6,132	$4,712	$3,485	$2,495	$2,662	$1,896	$1,726	$2,730	$874
Cost of sales	1,744	1,571	1,181	1,011	673	480	442	354	365	286	139
Research and development	2,800	2,446	1,773	1,262	948	722	623	526	490	367	396
Marketing, general and administrative	2,405	2,256	2,014	1,435	1,088	795	546	447	367	367	299
Collaboration profit sharing	1,228	1,080	1,005	823	594	457	351	247	129	74	40
Write-off of in-process research and development-related acquisition	–	77	–	–	–	–	–	–	–	–	–
Gain on acquisition	–	(121)	–	–	–	–	–	–	–	–	–
Recurring amortization charges related to redemption and acquisition	172	132	105	123	145	154	156	322	375	198	–
Special items	(260)	54	54	58	37	(113)	544	–	–	1,438	–
Other income, net	$ 102	$ 197	$ 251	$ 92	$ 84	$ 92	$ 108	$ 135	$ 216	$ 78	$ 74
INCOME (LOSS) DATA											
Income (loss) pre-taxes and cumulative effect of accounting change	$ 5,431	$ 4,426	$3,403	$2,013	$1,220	$ 897	$ 30	$ 283	$ 4	$(1,360)	$ 253
Income tax provision (benefit)	2,004	1,657	1,290	734	435	287	(34)	127	20	(203)	71
Income (loss) before cumulative effect of accounting change	3,427	2,769	2,113	1,279	785	610	64	156	(16)	(1,157)	182
Cumulative effect of accounting change, net of tax	–	–	–	–	–	(47)	–	(6)	(58)	–	–
Net income (loss)	3,427	2,769	2,113	1,279	785	563	64	150	(74)	(1,157)	182
EARNINGS (LOSS) PER SHARE											
Basic: Earnings before cumulative effect of accounting change	$3.25	$2.63	$2.01	$1.21	$0.74	$0.59	$0.06	$0.15	$(0.02)	$(1.13)	$0.18
Cumulative effect of accounting change, net of tax	–	–	–	–	–	(0.05)	–	(0.01)	(0.05)	–	–
Net earnings per share	$3.25	$2.63	$2.01	$1.21	$0.74	$0.54	$0.06	$0.14	$(0.07)	$(1.13)	$0.18
Diluted: Earnings before cumulative effect of accounting change	$3.21	$2.59	$1.97	$1.18	$0.73	$0.58	$0.06	$0.15	$(0.02)	$(1.13)	$0.18
Cumulative effect of accounting change, net of tax	–	–	–	–	–	(0.05)	–	(0.01)	(0.05)	–	–
Net earnings per share	$3.21	$2.59	$1.97	$1.18	$0.73	$0.53	$0.06	$0.14	$(0.07)	$(1.13)	$0.18

EXHIBIT 10 *(Continued)*

YEARS ENDED DECEMBER 31
(in millions, except per-share stock price and employee data)

	2008	2007	2006	2005	2004	2003	2002	2001	2000	1999	1998
SELECTED BALANCE SHEET DATA											
Cash, cash equivalents, short-term investments, and long-term marketable debt and equity securities	$ 9,545	$ 6,065	$ 4,325	$ 3,814	$ 2,780	$ 2,935	$ 1,602	$ 2,865	$ 2,459	$ 1,957	$ 1,605
Accounts receivable	1,941	1,766	1,666	1,050	941	588	432	321	278	233	158
Inventories	1,299	1,493	1,178	703	590	470	394	357	266	275	149
Property, plant, and equipment, net	5,404	4,986	4,173	3,349	2,091	1,618	1,069	866	753	730	700
Goodwill	1,590	1,577	1,315	1,315	1,315	1,315	1,315	1,303	1,456	1,609	–
Other intangible assets	1,008	1,168	476	574	668	811	928	1,113	1,280	1,453	65
Other long-term assets	365	366	1,342	1,074	807	822	801	136	175	206	135
Total assets	21,787	18,940	14,842	12,147	9,403	8,759	6,776	7,162	6,739	6,561	2,868
Commercial paper	500	599	–	–	–	–	–	–	–	–	–
Total current liabilities	3,095	3,918	2,010	1,660	1,238	893	661	677	475	503	303
Long-term debt	2,329	2,402	2,204	2,083	412	412	–	–	150	150	150
Total liabilities	6,116	7,035	5,364	4,677	2,621	2,239	1,437	1,242	1,065	1,291	524
Total stockholders' equity	15,671	11,905	9,478	7,470	6,782	6,520	5,339	5,920	5,674	5,270	2,344
OTHER DATA											
Depreciation and amortization expense	$ 592	$ 492	$ 407	$ 370	$ 353	$ 295	$ 275	$ 428	$ 463	$ 281	$ 78
Capital expenditures	751	977	1,214	1,400	650	322	323	213	113	95	88
SHARE INFORMATION											
Shares used to compute basic earnings per share	1,053	1,053	1,053	1,055	1,055	1,035	1,038	1,054	1,044	1,026	1,007
Shares used to compute diluted earnings per share	1,067	1,069	1,073	1,081	1,079	1,058	1,049	1,071	1,044	1,026	1,039
Shares outstanding at year-end	1,053	1,052	1,053	1,054	1,047	1,049	1,026	1,057	1,051	1,032	1,017
PER SHARE DATA (Market Price)											
High	$99.14	$89.73	$95.16	$100.20	$68.25	$47.68	$27.58	$41.00	$61.25	$35.75	$9.97
Low	$65.60	$65.35	$75.58	$43.90	$41.00	$15.77	$12.55	$19.00	$21.13	$12.13	$7.41
Book value	$14.88	$11.32	$9.00	$7.09	$6.48	$6.21	$5.21	$5.60	$5.40	$5.10	$2.30
NUMBER OF EMPLOYEES AT YEAR-END	11,186	11,174	10,533	9,563	7,646	6,226	5,252	4,950	4,459	3,883	3,389

Source: Genentech 2008 Annual Report, pp. 16–19.

EXHIBIT 11

Genentech Financial Highlights (in millions, except per-share data)

Source: Genentech 2008 Annual Report, p. 13. See the 2008 Annual Report for more details.

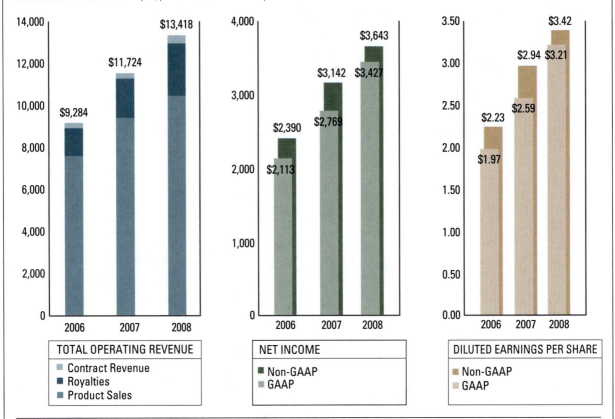

to discover and develop first- or best-in-class medicines. The company's research reputation attracted some of the best scientists in the world, who were encouraged not only to commit to projects associated with the company's strategic goals, but also to pursue projects of their own interest. The company viewed "individual creativity and initiative" as the driving force behind its numerous scientific breakthroughs. In total, there were approximately 1,100 researchers, scientists, and post-docs at Genentech, consistently publishing high-quality research papers in the top peer-reviewed scientific journals. Genentech's scientists held approximately 7,400 current patents and had about 6,250 patent applications pending worldwide.[25]

The Founders Research Center, a 275,000-square-foot facility, was opened in 1992 solely for biotechnology research in honor of the company's two founders, Swanson and Boyer. In 2001, the company expanded the Founders Research Center by 280,000 square

feet to celebrate Genentech's 25th anniversary. The 230,000-square-foot southern campus extension opened in 2007.[26] These facilities provided Genentech scientists a stimulating environment in an attractive setting, with numerous specialized laboratories and state-of-the-science equipment.

Genentech had a sophisticated set of selection criteria to move projects from discovery research into development, including scientific rationale, critical medical need, significant market opportunity, adequate market protection, and reasonable manufacturing economics. Once a new molecule entered the development phase, the process followed the guidelines prescribed by regulatory authorities (see Exhibit 12). Before testing a new medicine in humans, researchers conducted extensive preclinical investigations in cell lines and laboratory animals to determine its potential therapeutic targets, safety profile, and recommended starting dose. Phase I clinical trials served to examine

EXHIBIT 12

Drug Discovery and Development Process

Source: Roche 2009 Annual Report, p. 38.

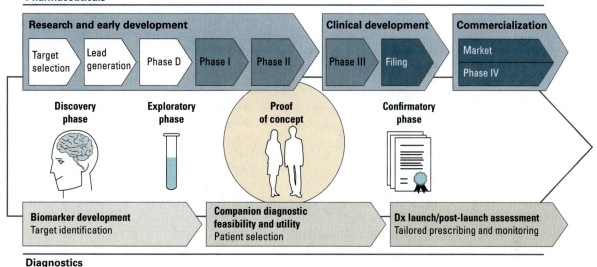

the safety of a drug and to determine appropriate dosage levels in humans. Phase II clinical trials provided a further assessment of safety and efficacy in humans over the short term, as well as helped establish parameters (e.g., dosage) for the longer-term Phase III trials. Phase III trials were designed to prove the efficacy and confirm the safety of the drug compared to the current standard of care. Once all phases of clinical testing were completed, Genentech applied to the Food and Drug Administration (FDA) for regulatory approval to market the medicine in the United States. Market approval in other countries followed a similar process.

GENENTECH'S PRODUCT PIPELINE. By 2008, Genentech's development pipeline included more than 100 projects across multiple therapeutic focus areas (see Exhibit 13). Oncology medicines were the main source of Genentech's revenue (around 70 percent of 2008 product sales). Genentech's best-selling product was Avastin (for multiple forms of advanced cancer), with $2.7 billion in annual sales. Its next-largest products were Rituxan (used to treat non-Hodgkin's lymphoma) and Herceptin (for certain types of breast cancer) with sales of $2.6 billion and $1.4 billion, respectively. (See Exhibit 14 for 2006–2008 product information.) Genentech's fourth cancer product,

Tarceva (for advanced non-small-cell lung and pancreatic cancers) had sales of $457 million in 2008.[27]

The market for cancer treatments was one of the largest and fastest-growing areas in the pharmaceutical industry. (See Exhibit 15 for leading global biotech therapy classes in 2007.) IMS Health forecasted that global sales of cancer drugs would grow at a compounded annual rate of 12 to 15 percent, reaching $75 to $80 billion by 2012.[28] This robust growth projection was due to numerous factors, including an aging population, the availability of new treatments, the unraveling of the genetics behind cancer, and the fact that cancer was a significant disease with many variations. The increased demand for oncology drugs represented a tremendous opportunity for Genentech to further increase revenues for its established cancer products. At the same time, Genentech scientists continued to perform basic research in identifying antigens that could serve as markers for novel therapeutic agents. Other areas of research aimed at new cancer drug discovery included the Human Epidermal Growth Factor Receptor (HER) pathway, angiogenesis, and apoptosis.

In immunology, Genentech had three products: Raptiva, Rituxan, and Xolair. Its tissue growth and repair products consisted of Activase, Cathflo Activase,

EXHIBIT 13

Genentech's Clinical Development Pipeline, 2008

PHASE 1		
ONCOLOGY	ABT-263	Chronic Lymphocytic Leukemia
		Lymphoid Malignancies
		Small Cell Lung Cancer
	Anti-NRP1	Cancer
	Apo2L/TRAIL	Colorectal Cancer
	Apomab	Colorectal Cancer
	Dacetuzumab (Anti-CD40)	Diffuse Large B-cell Lymphoma
		Multiple Myeloma
		Non-Hodgkin's Lymphoma
	GA101	Non-Hodgkin's Lymphoma
	IAP Antagonist	Cancer
	MEK Inhibitor	Cancer
	New Molecular Entity	Cancer
	New Molecular Entity	Cancer
	P13 Kinase Inhibitor	Cancer
	Trastuzumab-DM1 +Pertuzumab	HER2-Positive Metastatic Breast Cancer
IMMUNOLOGY	Anti-Beta7	Ulcerative Colitis
	Anti-CD4	Rheumatoid Arthritis
	Anti-OX40L	Asthma
	New Molecular Entity	Autoimmune Disease
TISSUE GROWTH AND REPAIR	Anti-oxLDL	Secondary Prevention of Cardiovascular Events
NEUROSCIENCE	Anti-Abeta	Alzheimer's Disease

PHASE 2		
ONCOLOGY	ABT-869	Advanced Renal Cell Carcinoma
		Advanced or Metastatic Hepatocellular Carcinoma
		First-line Metastatic Breast Cancer
		Second-Line Metastatic Colorectal Cancer
		Metastatic Non-small Cell Lung Cancer
	Apo2L/TRAIL	Indolent Relapsed Non-Hodgkin's Lymphoma
		First-Line Metastatic Non-small Cell Lung Cancer
	Apomab	Indolent Relapsed Non-Hodgkin's Lymphoma
		First-Line Metastatic Non-small Cell Lung Cancer
	Avastin	Extensive Small Cell Lung Cancer
		Non-Squamous, Non-small Cell Lung Cancer with Previously Treated CNS Metastases
		Relapsed Multiple Myeloma

EXHIBIT 13 *(Continued)*

PHASE 2		
	Dacetuzumab (Anti-CD40)	Relapsed Diffuse Large B-cell Lymphoma
		Second-Line Diffuse Large B-cell Lymphoma
	GA101	Relapsed or Refractory Hematologic Malignance
		Indolent Non-Hodgkin's Lymphoma
	Hedgehog Pathway Inhibitor	Advanced Basal Cell Carcinoma
		First-Line Metastatic Colorectal Cancer
		Ovarian Cancer Maintenance Therapy
	MetMAb	Second and Third-Line Metastatic Non-small Cell Lung Cancer
	Pertuzumab	Second-Line Metastatic Non-small Cell Lung Cancer
	Trastuzumab-DM1	First-Line HER2-Positive Metastatic Breast Cancer
		Second-Line HER2-Positive Metastatic Breast Cancer
		Third-Line HER2-Positive Metastatic Breast Cancer
IMMUNOLOGY	Anti-IF Nalpha	Systemic Lupus Erythematosus
	Anti-IL13	Asthma
	Ocrelizumab	Relapsed Remitting Multiple Sclerosis
	Xolair	Chronic Idiopathic Urticaria

PHASE 3		
ONCOLOGY	Avastin	Adjuvant Colon Cancer
		Adjuvant HER2-Negative Metastatic Breast Cancer
		Adjuvant HER2-Positive Metastatic Breast Cancer
		Adjuvant Non-small Cell Lung Cancer
		Diffuse Large B-cell Lymphoma
		First-Line Advanced Gastric Cancer
		First-Line HER2-Negative Metastatic Breast Cancer
		First-Line HER2-Positive Metastatic Breast Cancer
		First-Line Metastatic Ovarian Cancer
		Gastrointestinal Stromal Tumors
		High-Risk Carcinoid
		Hormone Refractory Prostate Cancer
		Newly Diagnosed Glioblastoma Multiforme
		Relapsed Platinum-Sensitive Ovarian Cancer
		Second-Line HER2-Negative Metastatic Breast Cancer

EXHIBIT 13 *(Continued)*

PHASE 3		
	Avastin +/− Tarceva Herceptin	First-Line Metastatic Non-Squamous, Non-Small Cell Lung Cancer
	Pertuzumab	Adjuvant HER2-Positive Breast Cancer (HERA 2-Year Treatment)
	Rituxan	First-Line HER2-Positive Metastatic Breast Cancer
	Tarceva	Platinum-Resistant Ovarian Cancer
	Trastuzumab-DM1	Follicular Non-Hodgkin's Lymphoma
IMMUNOLOGY	Ocrelizumab	Adjuvant Non-Small Cell Lung Cancer
		Second-Line HER2-Positive Metastatic Breast Cancer
	Rituxan	Lupus Nephritis
		Rheumatoid Arthritis
	Xolair	ANCA-Associated Vasculitis
		Lupus Nephritis
TISSUE GROWTH AND REPAIR	Lucentis	Asthma
		Liquid Formulation
	TNKase	Diabetic Macular Edema
		Retinal Vein Occlusion
		Central Venous Catheter Clearance
		Hemodialysis Catheter Clearance

FDA SUBMISSION PREP		
ONCOLOGY	Avastin	First-Line HER2-Negative Metastatic Breast Cancer
		(RIBBON-1 and AVADO)
	Rituxan	Previously Untreated Chronic Lymphocytic Leukemia
		Relapsed Chronic Lymphocytic Leukemia
IMMUNOLOGY	Tarceva	First-Line Maintenance Therapy for Advanced Non-Small Cell Lung Cancer
	Rituxan	Rheumatoid Arthritis (Radiographic Data)

AWAITING FDA ACTION		
ONCOLOGY	Avastin	First-Line Metastatic Renal Cell Carcinoma
		Previously Treated Glioblastoma
IMMUNOLOGY	Rituxan	Rheumatoid Arthritis DMARD-Inadequate Responders
	Xolair	Pediatric Asthma

Source: Genentech 2008 Annual Report, pp. 8–9.

EXHIBIT 14

Genentech's 2008 U.S. Product Sales ($ in millions)

Source: Genentech 2008 Annual Report, pp. 14–15.

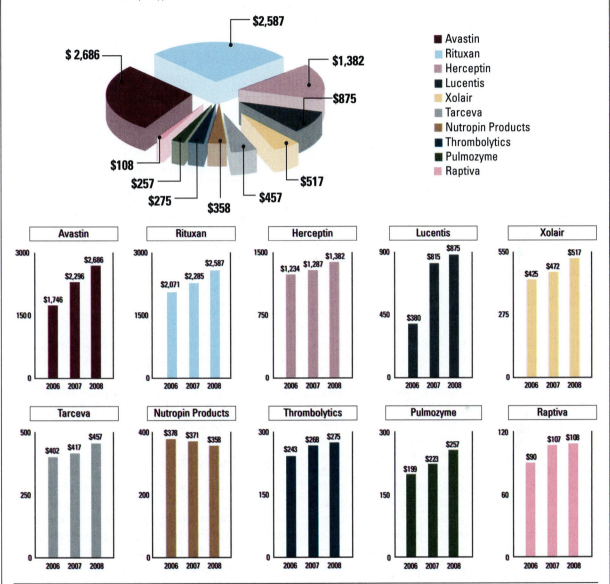

Lucentis, Nutropin AQ, and Pulmozyme. Both the immunology and tissue repair and growth markets were likewise growing rapidly, representing additional opportunities for Genentech's current product line. Leveraging their resources in immunology, Genentech researchers were also researching new mechanisms of innate and adaptive immunity. They hoped to translate their discoveries into new therapies for the treatment

of a broad range of diseases involving immune and inflammatory cells.

Despite Genentech's current market leadership and promising growth figures for the company's key market segments, Dr. Scheller recognized that the company was vulnerable in two main respects. First, both Avastin and Tarceva were brought to market in 2003. Since then, only two new products had received FDA

EXHIBIT 15

Global Biotech Leading Therapy Classes in 2007

Top 10 Therapy Classes	Sales (U.S. $ millions)	% Market Share
Global Biotech Market	**75,120**	**100**
Erythropoietins	12,872	17.1
Oncologics	11,365	15.1
Antidiabetics	10,231	13.6
Autoimmune Agents	8,357	11.1
Interferons	6,679	8.9
Immunostim Ag Ex Intfron	6,005	8.0
Immunosuppressive Agents	4,520	6.0
Growth Hormones	2,627	3.5
Blood Coagulation	2,433	3.2
Pure Vaccines	2,099	2.8
Total Top 10	**67,189**	**89.4**

Source: Data provided by IMS Health.

approval: Lucentis, for the treatment of neovascular (wet) age-related macular degeneration (AMD) in 2006; and Actemra, for rheumatoid arthritis, in 2010. (See Exhibit 16 for Genentech's medicine-approval timeline.) As evidenced by the time lag between recent product introductions, Genentech suffered from a lack of original drugs in its pipeline; the quality of the new therapies was excellent, but the firm needed to be producing more of them. Otherwise, a major problem with any of their flagship products could send Genentech's finances into a tailspin. Second, the company was reliant on the cancer market for a majority of its revenues, and high-priced cancer treatments were a prime target of health care reform. The degree to which the current positive growth rates for oncology products could be maintained was therefore quite uncertain.

Genentech had taken some important steps to address these issues. In March 2007, Genentech announced an internal stretch goal of advancing a total of 30 new molecular entities into clinical development by the end of 2010. According to its 2008 Annual Report, the company had eight new therapies in clinical trials by the end of the first year, though most were still in the area of oncology. Then in 2008, Genentech initiated early efforts in two new therapeutic

areas—neuroscience and infectious diseases—as a first step toward greater diversification. Dr. Scheller wondered how well Genentech's biotech capabilities would transfer to these new indications and at what point his scientists might start to feel that they were being spread too thin.

Buyout by Roche

Roche Holding Ltd. (headquartered in Basel, Switzerland) was one of the world's leading research-focused health care groups (see Exhibit 17 for Roche financials). Famous for discovering the blockbuster drug Valium, Roche operated in two segments, pharmaceutical and diagnostics, selling its products in more than 150 countries. As an innovator of products and services for the early detection, prevention, diagnosis, and treatment of diseases, Roche aimed at improving health and quality of life. Prior to the Genentech acquisition, the group's focused therapeutic areas included autoimmune diseases, inflammatory and metabolic disorders, and diseases of the central nervous system.

The Roche–Genentech relationship dated back to 1980 when Roche licensed the patents and know-how for interferon alpha-2a (Roferon-A) from its American partner. (See Exhibit 18 for the complete

EXHIBIT 16

Genentech Medicine-Approval Timeline, 2010

In 1998, Genentech licensed U.S. marketing and development rights to interferon gamma (including Actimmune) to Connetics Corporation. Thereafter, Connetics sublicensed, and then later assigned, all of its rights to InterMune Pharmaceuticals, Inc. Protropin manufacturing was discontinued at the end of 2002. Nutropin Depot commercialization was discontinued in June 2004.

On April 8, 2009, Genentech announced a phased voluntary withdrawal of the psoriasis drug Raptiva from the U.S. market.

Source: Genentech website, www.gene.com/gene/products/approvals-timeline.html.

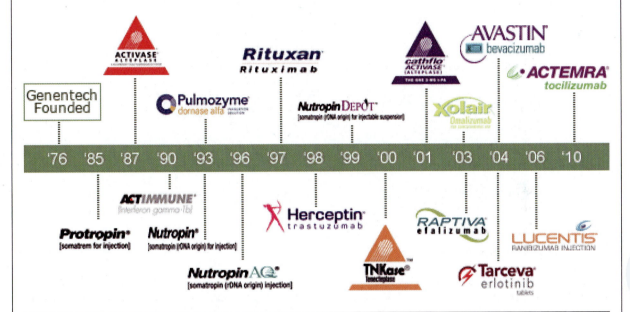

Roche–Genentech timeline.) Six years later, Roferon-A was one of the first biologics to receive FDA approval for the treatment of hairy cell leukemia, a cancer of the blood or bone marrow. Roche subsequently purchased 60 percent of Genentech in 1990, investing $2.1 billion in the new startup.[29] The deal was advantageous for both Roche and Genentech because it assured continued collaboration between the two companies. The companies agreed that Genentech would market its products domestically, while Roche would have the first option to market Genentech products internationally.

Almost 20 years later, on March 12, 2009, Roche and Genentech announced a final merger agreement under which Roche would acquire the remainder of Genentech's outstanding shares (44 percent) for $95.00 per share in cash, at a total valuation of $46.8 billion.[30] This 2009 purchase price amounted to a multiple of 22 times more than it paid for Genentech shares in 1990. The merger allowed Roche access to Genentech's top-selling drugs, including the blockbusters Avastin, MabThera, and Herceptin, all of which were outselling Roche's own drugs.[31] More importantly, Roche viewed the Genentech acquisition as central to its strategy of pursuing personalized medicine, which involved the use of molecular information to tailor medicines for specific patient populations. According to Roche CEO Severin Schwan, "personalized medicine means that we can develop drugs which are more effective, safer, and ultimately also more cost-effective."[32]

The combined company became the seventh-largest U.S. pharmaceutical company by market share, with expected annual revenues of $17 billion. Jointly, the companies employed approximately 17,500 workers in the United States, with a combined sales force of 3,000 people spanning several specialty areas.[33]

STRUCTURAL AND ORGANIZATIONAL CHANGES. After the merger, Roche's top executives decided to maintain Genentech as a wholly-owned subsidiary, which meant that it would continue operations as an independent research and early-development center within the larger Roche Group. Genentech also served

EXHIBIT 17

Roche Financials

Selected Income Statement Data (in millions CHF [Swiss francs], except per-share data)

	2010	2009	2008	2007	2006	2005	2004	2003	2002	2001	2000
Sales	47,473	49,051	45,617	46,133	42,041	35,511	31,273	31,220	29,453	29,163	28,672
Royalties and other operating income	1,694	2,100	2,287	2,243	1,466	1,447	1,737	1,335	1,381	—	232
Cost of sales	(13,293)	(14,615)	(13,661)	(13,743)	(10,616)	(9,270)	(7,182)	(8,315)	(8,432)	(8,339)	(9,163)
Marketing and distribution	(9,488)	(9,475)	(9,170)	(9,327)	(10,856)	(9,507)	(9,002)	(8,847)	(8,266)	(8,452)	(8,746)
Research and development	(10,026)	(9,874)	(8,845)	(8,385)	(6,589)	(5,672)	(5,093)	(4,766)	(4,257)	(3,893)	(3,950)
General and administration	(2,874)	(4,910)	(2,332)	(2,453)	(2,542)	(2,309)	(3,453)	(3,346)	(3,412)	(1,219)	(1,242)
Amortization and impairment of intangible assets					(1,174)	(1,011)	(1,026)	(1,013)	(1,019)	(2,476)	(2,621)
Operating profit before exceptional items	13,486	12,277	13,896	14,468	11,730	9,189	7,254	6,268	5,448	4,784	3,182
Amortization of goodwill							(579)	(497)	(501)	(777)	
Changes in group organization		(2,415)	(243)				2,304	(395)	(1,064)		3,949
Major legal cases		(320)	271		—	(356)		216	(2,548)	(760)	—
Operating profit	13,486	9,542	13,924	14,468	11,730	8,833	8,979	5,592	1,335	3,247	7,131
Associated companies	(3)		1	2	2	1	(43)	(44)	(34)	—	—
Financial income	557	792	1,123	1,805	1,829	1,313	908	0	663	1,515	2,337
Financing costs	(2,829)	(2,460)	(887)	(971)	(974)	(985)	(359)	(667)	—	—	—
Exceptional financing costs		(377)					0		(5,192)		
Profit before taxes	11,211	7,497	14,161	15,304	12,587	9,162	9,485	4,881	(3,228)	4,762	9,468
Income taxes	(2,320)	(2,870)	(3,317)	(3,867)	(3,436)	(2,284)	(2,345)	(1,445)	(839)	(1,038)	(2,272)
Income taxes on exceptional Items		1,148									
Profit from continuing business	8,891	5,775	10,844	11,437	9,151	6,878	7,140	3,436	(4,067)	3,724	7,196
Changes in accounting policies											1,395
Minority interests							(499)	(367)	41	(34)	33
Profit from discontinued businesses					20	(12)	0	0	0	7	23
Net income	8,891	5,775	10,844	11,437	9,171	6,866	6,641	3,069	(4,026)	3,697	8,647
Earnings per share and non-voting equity security											
Basic (CHF)	10.14	9.07	10.43	11.36	9.24	6.85	7.90	3.66	4.80	4.40	10.36
Diluted (CHF)	10.11	9.02	10.23	11.16	9.05	6.71	7.81	3.61	4.80	4.37	10.24

Selected Balance Sheet Data (in millions CHF)

	2010	2009	2008	2007	2006	2005	2004	2003	2002	2001	2000
Non-current assets											
Property, plant and equipment	16,729	17,697	18,190	17,832	16,417	15,097	12,408	12,494	13,434	15,052	13,785
Goodwill	7,722	8,261	8,353	6,835	5,914	6,132	5,532	5,206	5,057	14,943	
Intangible assets	5,133	6,005	7,121	6,346	5,469	6,256	6,340	6,945	7,786	186	15,870
Total non-current assets	**33,408**	**36,086**	**37,485**	**35,531**	**33,519**	**33,569**	**28,767**	**29,820**	**33,143**	**36,411**	**34,798**
Current assets											
Inventories	4,972	5,648	5,830	6,113	5,592	5,041	4,614	5,025	5,724	5,780	5,754
Accounts receivable	9,403	10,461	9,755	9,804	8,960	7,698	9,900	6,774	3,430	5,779	5,519
Marketable securities	9,060	16,107	15,856	20,447	21,121	16,657	10,394	10,819	12,395	21,412	18,086
Cash and cash equivalents	1,841	2,442	4,915	3,755	3,210	4,228	2,605	5,276	3,430	3,136	2,562
Total current assets	**27,612**	**38,479**	**38,604**	**42,834**	**40,895**	**35,626**	**29,679**	**29,666**	**30,852**	**38,875**	**34,737**
Total assets	**61,020**	**74,565**	**76,089**	**78,365**	**74,414**	**69,195**	**58,446**	**59,486**	**63,995**	**75,286**	**69,535**
Non-current liabilities											
Long-term debt	(27,857)	(36,143)	(2,972)	(3,834)	(6,199)	(9,322)	(7,077)	(10,246)	(14,167)	(16,395)	(16,167)
Other non-current liabilities	(337)	(416)	(459)	(723)	(585)	(806)	(961)	(1,054)	(504)	(490)	(402)
Total non-current liabilities	**(34,380)**	**(43,084)**	**(10,163)**	**(10,468)**	**(14,908)**	**(19,545)**	**(15,029)**	**(18,658)**	**(22,850)**	**(25,772)**	**(23,642)**
Current liabilities											
Short-term debt	(2,201)	(6,273)	(1,117)	(3,032)	(2,044)	(348)	(2,013)	(5,041)	(8,183)	(7,335)	(5,451)
Accounts payable	(2,068)	(2,300)	(2,017)	(1,861)	(2,213)	(2,373)	(1,844)	(1,700)	(1,787)	(1,710)	(2,215)
Accrued and other current liabilities	(6,526)	(9,398)	(5,973)	(5,829)	(5,645)	(5,127)	(4,107)	(3,667)	(3,395)	(4,034)	(3,350)
Total current liabilities	**(14,978)**	**(22,067)**	**(12,104)**	**(14,454)**	**(12,692)**	**(9,492)**	**(10,134)**	**(11,664)**	**(15,372)**	**(15,647)**	**(13,857)**
Total liabilities	**(49,358)**	**(65,151)**	**(22,267)**	**(24,922)**	**(27,600)**	**(29,037)**	**(25,163)**	**(30,322)**	**(38,222)**	**(41,419)**	**(37,499)**
Equity											
Capital and reserves attributable to Roche shareholders	9,469	7,366	44,479	45,483	39,444	33,334	27,998	23,570	20,810	28,973	27,608
Equity attributable to minority interests	2,193	2,048	9,343	7,960	7,370	6,824	5,285	5,594	4,963	4,894	4,428
Total equity	**11,662**	**9,414**	**53,822**	**53,443**	**46,814**	**40,158**	**33,283**	**29,164**	**25,773**	**33,867**	**32,036**

Source: Roche Annual Reports.

EXHIBIT 18

Genentech–Roche Relationship Chronology

1980

>> Genentech went public and raised $35 million with an offering that leapt from $35 a share to a high of $88 after less than an hour on the market. The event was one of the largest stock run-ups ever.

>> Genentech licensed patents and know-how for interferon alpha-2a (Roferon-A) to Hoffman-LaRoche, Inc. *

1986

>> Roferon-A — received approval from the FDA for the treatment of hairy cell leukemia.

1990

>> Genentech and Roche Holding Ltd. of Basel, Switzerland completed a $2.1 billion merger.

1995

>> Genentech announced an agreement with Roche Holding, Ltd. to extend for four years Roche's option to purchase the outstanding redeemable common stock of the company at a predetermined price that escalates quarterly up to $82.50 a share. As part of the agreement, Genentech began receiving royalties rather than recording European sales of Pulmozyme and Canadian sales of all Genentech products since Roche assumed responsibility for those sales.

1999

>> Roche exercised its option to cause Genentech to redeem all of its outstanding special common shares not owned by Roche. Roche announced its intent to publicly sell up to 19 percent of Genentech shares and continue Genentech as a publicly traded company with independent directors.

>> On July 20, after about a month-long hiatus due to the Roche redemption, Genentech returned to the New York Stock Exchange (NYSE) with a public reoffering of 22 million shares by Roche, in what is considered the largest public offering in the history of the U.S. health care industry. The stock closed the first day of trading at $127, over 31 percent above the public offering price of $97. This was also the first introduction of Genentech's new NYSE trading symbol, DNA.

>> Roche conducted a secondary offering of 20 million Genentech shares on October 20. The shares were priced at $143.50 per share, making it the largest secondary offering in U.S. history.

2000

>> Roche conducted a third offering of up to 19 million shares of Genentech stock at $163 per share.

2008

>> In July 2008, Genentech received a proposal from Roche to acquire all of the outstanding shares of Genentech stock not owned by Roche.

2009

>> In March 2009, Roche and Genentech announced that they had signed a merger agreement under which Roche would acquire the outstanding publicly held interest in Genentech for US$ 95.00 per share in cash, or a total payment of approximately US$ 46.8 billion, to equity holders of Genentech other than Roche.

Source: Adapted from the Genentech website at www.gene.com/gene/about/corporate/history/timeline.html.

---

* "Hoffman LaRoche and Genentech announce marketing agreement for Roferon-A: Genentech will market the drug to the U.S. oncology market," *PRNewswire*, January 8, 1997, www.thefreelibrary.com/Hoffmann-La+Roche+and+Genentech+Announce+Marketing+Agreement+for...-a019006166.

as the new name and headquarters of the companies' combined U.S. commercial operations, including support functions such as informatics and finance. Roche closed down its Palo Alto site, moving the virology unit to Genentech's campus in South San Francisco and relocating its inflammation group to Nutley, New Jersey. Genentech's late-stage development and manufacturing operations were combined with the global operations of Roche, in anticipation of significant scale benefits and operational synergies.[34]

Considerable leadership changes were made as well. Genentech's chairman and CEO Arthur Levinson and product development chief Susan Desmond-Hellmann left day-to-day operations but continued to function in an advisory capacity. David Ebersman, executive vice president and chief financial officer, and Steve Juelsgaard, executive vice president and chief compliance officer, also left Genentech. Pascal Soriot, previously responsible for commercial operations for Roche's pharma division, became the new CEO of Genentech. Richard Scheller continued to serve as executive vice president of Genentech research and early development, reporting directly to Roche Group CEO Severin Schwan.

CULTURAL CHANGES? Despite Roche's plan to maintain Genentech as an independent research and development center, there was some angst regarding the Genentech buyout. The biggest concern was whether or not Roche's top management would respect and nurture Genentech's informal and innovative culture.[35] The campus in South San Francisco felt more like a research university than corporate America. Executives preferred jeans over suits, and even wore lederhosen in honor of Roche's initial acquisition in 1990. In 2006, Genentech was voted as the best company to work for in the U.S. by *Fortune* magazine. This was not entirely surprising, given Genentech's history of providing generous employee perks such as day care for children and lavish employee get-togethers, the so-called "Ho-Hos." Insiders described Genentech as a place of "casual intensity."[36]

However, Roche Group CEO Severin Schwan was known for "being aggressive," and many were concerned about whether he would "be sensitive to the Genentech cultural differences."[37] Scheller still remembered the conversation between David Mott, former CEO of the biotech company MedImmune (which was acquired by Astra Zeneca), and former Roche Chairman Franz Humer in 2007. Mott compared the independent structure of MedImmune under Astra Zeneca with that of Genentech under Roche: "He [Humer] laughed at me and said, 'it will never work because if we owned all of Genentech we would kill it'; we wouldn't be able to resist tinkering and playing with it . . . ," Mott recalled.[38]

Multiple Challenges Ahead

Dr. Scheller recognized that the company faced multiple challenges ahead: the need to do comparative effectiveness research, increasing competition, and the threat of biogenerics.

COMPARATIVE EFFECTIVENESS RESEARCH. Another issue on Scheller's agenda for tomorrow's meeting was a discussion of the likely impact of the economic stimulus package approved by the U.S. Congress in 2009. The bill included $1.1 billion to perform Comparative Effectiveness Research (CER), which aimed to assess how various medical products and procedures compared with each other in terms of both effectiveness and cost.[39] CER was part of a broader movement to make science-based evidence the basis for medical practice (so-called "evidence-based medicine"). The bill's supporters believed that conducting CER could avoid unnecessary treatments and improve the quality of health care while lowering costs.

Passage of the stimulus package meant that the government would be involved in CER programs to a much greater extent. However, years of effort, both in the public and private sectors, had been invested in CER prior to the federal initiative. The Medicare Modernization Act of 2003 gave the federal Agency for Healthcare Research and Quality (AHRQ) a limited mandate to determine the clinical effectiveness and appropriateness of various medical products. The Blue Cross and Blue Shield Association's Technology Evaluation Center (TEC) had been engaged in technology assessment since 1985. Another related initiative was the Drug Effectiveness Review Project (DERP), a collaboration between public and private organizations that was housed at the Oregon Health & Science University.[40]

Outside the United States, CER programs were more established. The National Institute for Health and Clinical Excellence (NICE) in the United Kingdom was the most prominent example. Funded by the government, NICE provided guidance to the National Health Service (NHS), Britain's government-run health care system, about the effectiveness and cost of new therapies and diagnostic services. NHS determined coverage, while NICE played an advisory role. In 2008, NICE made a recommendation not to cover one of Genentech's cancer drugs, Tarceva, forcing the company to lower Tarceva's price significantly.[41]

This worried Scheller because Genentech's current and potential product portfolio was heavily focused on oncology medicines. In 2008, close to 70 percent of Genentech's sales came from its patent-protected, proprietary cancer drugs, which commanded premium prices. Avastin had sales of $2.7 billion in 2008 and cost $50,000 per year; Tarceva had sales of $457 million and cost $24,000 per year. However, several recent clinical trials had demonstrated little to no benefit in terms of survival time.[42] This could raise a red flag concerning the comparative effectiveness of these drugs. Should more disappointing results from CER trials come in, Genentech could lose coverage and be forced to cut prices on its blockbuster products, even in the United States.

INCREASING COMPETITION. At the same time, Genentech was facing increasing competition from established pharmaceutical companies, who viewed investments in biotechnology as a means to offset stagnating pharmaceutical sales.[43] (See Exhibits 19a and 19b for a list of the top 15 pharmaceutical companies and products by 2009 global sales.) GlaxoSmithKline produced Bexxar, which competed with Rituxan, and Tykerb (currently in clinical trials), which competed with Herceptin. Avastin's competitors include Erbitux by ImClone/Bristol-Myers Squibb (2008 sales of $749 million); Nexavar (2008 sales of $667.8 million) by Bayer/Onyx; Sutent (2008 sales of $847 million) by Pfizer; Gleevec (2008 sales of $950 million) by Novartis; and Vectibix (2008 sales

EXHIBIT 19a

Top Pharmaceutical Corporations by 2009 Global Sales (Total 2009 global sales of $752.02 billion)

Source: Data provided by IMS Health.

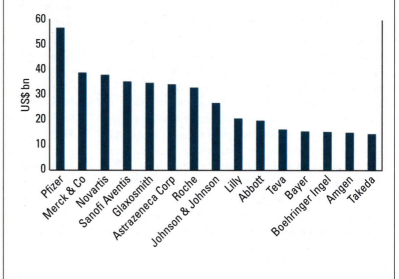

EXHIBIT 19b

Top Pharmaceutical Products by 2009 Global Sales (Total 2009 global sales of $752.02 billion)

Source: Data provided by IMS Health.

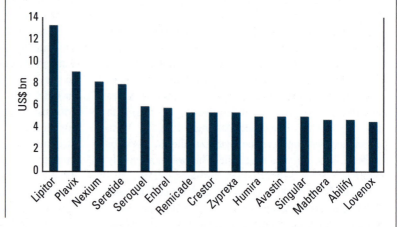

of $153 million) by Amgen. Macugen by Pfizer and Visudyne (2008 sales of $141.9 million) by Novartis were challenging the market for Lucentis. Meanwhile, Xolair faced competition from numerous inhaled corticosteroids.

Ironically, Genentech was also in danger of competing with itself. Scheller remembered how sales of Lucentis, a drug developed to treat an eye disease that causes blindness in the elderly, were threatened by off-label use of its older product, Avastin. Both Lucentis and Avastin had the effect of inhibiting a protein that initiates the growth of blood vessels, with applications in both cancer and macular degeneration. Some doctors believed that Avastin was "as effective, but less than one-tenth of the price of Lucentis."[44] The potential for cannibalization could pose a serious challenge for Genentech when developing new products based on the same biotechnology.

BIOGENERICS. Even more ominous was the specter of generic biologics looming on the horizon. Generics had long been the bane of pharmaceutical companies because generic companies would seek market approval for their copycat products as soon as the original period of patent exclusivity expired. Generic companies did not have to conduct clinical trials as long as they could establish that their product was "pharmaceutically equivalent" to the drug they wished to copy.[45] This resulted in drastically reduced development costs, which permitted them to charge significantly lower prices and dominate the market. In 2003, generic drugs comprised 54 percent of the pharmaceutical market; that figure leaped to 72 percent of total pharmaceutical sales in 2008.[46] By 2010, IMS Health forecasted that generics sales of pharmaceutical drugs would top $68 billion.[47]

However, the FDA had no parallel process for approving biogenerics, which were also called "biosimilars" or "follow-on biologics." While lobbyists for the generics industry proposed allowing biologics the same three- to five-year patent exclusivity as conventional drugs, biotechnology leaders argued that at least 14 years of protection were needed for them to recoup the high costs of development.[48] Others expressed concern that biologically engineered molecules would be too difficult to replicate accurately, without access to the original molecular clones, cell banks, and manufacturing processes. They pointed out that even minute differences in impurities or breakdown products could create a serious health hazard.[49]

Despite these reservations, President Obama signed the Biologics Price Competition and Innovation Act into law on March 23, 2010, as part of his health care reform legislation. This effectively amended the Public Health Service Act of 1944, allowing for an abbreviated approval pathway for biosimilars, much as the 1984 Hatch-Waxman Act had done for pharmaceuticals. Under the BPCI Act, sponsors could seek approval for a "biosimilar" product if they provided scientific data that it was "highly similar" and there were no "clinically meaningful differences" between the two products "in terms of safety, purity, and potency."[50] While the FDA had yet to develop a full implementation plan, one major difference compared to the process for pharmaceutical generics was that biogeneric sponsors would have to provide data from analytical, animal, and clinical studies, unless otherwise deemed to be unnecessary.[51]

A study by the Congressional Budget Office indicated that the federal government could save $6.6 billion over a 10-year period if biologics were granted 12 years of market exclusivity.[52] Generics manufacturers and the insurance industry likewise stood to gain considerably from the availability of biogeneric products. Biotechnology innovators like Roche and Genentech, on the other hand, were understandably apprehensive about how and when the new provisions would take effect.

A Balancing Act

In the new-product development process, *knowledge-generation* (or exploration) activity refers to the uncertain activities of discovering something new, or the "R" in the research and development process. *Knowledge-application* (or exploitation) activity refers to less-uncertain activities of commercializing the new knowledge generated through research, or the "D" in R&D.[53] Scheller and his counterparts at Roche were aware that research indicated firms needed to balance both knowledge-generation and knowledge-application activities in order to attain or sustain superior performance.[54, 55, 56, 57]

Scheller believed that Genentech's strong commitment to research was the fuel that had kept the product pipeline full, propelling the company forward all these years. Meanwhile, without late-stage development, Genentech's potential products could never mature over time and eventually reach their patients. Therefore, Scheller's "goal in setting strategy for the research department [was] to strike the optimal balance between basic biomedical research and translational research aimed at developing therapies for unmet medical needs."[58] Genentech reinvested more than $2.8 billion into research and development in 2008, approximately 21 percent of its operating revenues,[59] and significantly more than the pharmaceutical industry average.

Scheller had never faced more challenges when it came to allocating company resources to R&D. The answer was never as simple as a 50–50 split. Rather, it required ambidexterity, defined as the firm's ability to configure assets to compete in mature and emerging businesses, to find the optimal balance when engaging in both research and development.[60] Scheller wondered what that meant for Genentech, and how to achieve it.

Recent challenges were forcing him to consider new resource configurations in order to find a new "optimal" balance. With the failed clinical trial of Avastin, the pressure would keep coming from Roche to focus more on late-stage development. Scheller planned to direct more resources into the development of Phase II and Phase III projects, but he did have some doubts. The push for drug comparison trials, together with Genentech's major focus in oncology, also meant that Genentech needed to start focusing more on other therapeutic areas. Scheller was excited about the company's recent expansion into neuroscience and infectious disease. He also knew there was a lot more that could be done to increase the level of Genentech's product diversification: hire more talent in those other areas; give priority to those areas when picking projects to move forward in the pipeline; and favor them when it came to alliances and sourcing.

Scheller finished the last slide in his deck and glanced at the clock on his desk. It was five minutes past 2 a.m. He sat back in his chair and stretched his neck, thinking about the many challenges he faced in the board meeting that would commence in a few hours. He sincerely believed that it was the philosophy of deep commitment to excellent science that had made Genentech a success story. As a result, he feared that the most profound impact of the merger would come from whether or not the traditional Roche senior pharmaceutical management team could adapt to Genentech's science-driven and individualistic culture. Scheller had been asked a lot by Genentech employees about Roche's recent buyout, and whether this would mark the "end of Genentech as we know it."

Would Roche unintentionally kill the goose that laid the golden eggs by insisting that Genentech adopt their standardized business processes? Would reallocation of resources to more advanced stages of development cause Genentech's legendary scientists simply to walk away at their first opportunities? Could Genentech grab a significant slice of the market in areas other than oncology? Scheller looked outside the window at the lights near the Rhine River and wondered . . .

Glossary of Terms

Genetic engineering refers to the direct manipulation of an organism's gene. It is different than traditional breeding, where the organism's genes are manipulated indirectly. Genetic engineering uses the techniques of molecular cloning and transformation to alter the structure and characteristics of genes directly.

Genomics is the study of the genomes of organisms. The field includes intensive efforts to determine the entire DNA sequence of organisms and fine-scale genetic mapping efforts.

Monoclonal antibodies are monospecific antibodies that are identical because they are produced by one type of immune cell. The antibodies are all clones of a single parent cell. Given almost any substance, it is possible to create monoclonal antibodies that specifically bind to that substance; they can then serve to detect or purify that substance. This has become an important tool in biochemistry, molecular biology, and medicine.

Proteomics is the large-scale study of proteins, particularly their structures and functions. Proteins are vital parts of living organisms, as they are the main components of the physiological metabolic pathways of cells.

Rational drug design uses information about the structure of a drug receptor or one of its natural ligands to identify or create candidate drugs. The three-dimensional structure of a protein can be determined using methods such as X-ray crystallography or nuclear magnetic resonance spectroscopy. Knowing the structure of the receptor, researchers can either use powerful computer programs to search through databases and identify compounds that are most likely to interact with the receptor, or build molecules that are likely to interact with the receptor. These molecules can then be tested in the laboratory.

Recombinant DNA is DNA from one organism that has been recombined with DNA from another organism to form a new organism. In biotechnology, individual human genes are often isolated and combined with a "DNA transporter," such as a plasmid, and this recombinant plasmid is inserted into host cells so it can be cloned.

RNA interference (RNAi) is a system within living cells that helps control which genes are active and how active they are. Two types of small RNA molecules—microRNA (miRNA) and small interfering RNA (siRNA)—are central to RNA interference.

RNAs are the direct products of genes, and these small RNAs can bind to specific other RNAs and either increase or decrease their activity, for example by preventing a messenger RNA from producing a protein.

Endnotes

1 Alazraki, M. (2010), "Roche's Avastin fails in early-stage colon cancer study," *dailyfinance.com,* September 20, www.dailyfinance.com/story/company-news/avastin-cancer-drug-roche-fails-colon-study/19640322/.

2. "Understanding clinical trials," *clinicaltrials.gov,* http://clinicaltrials.gov/ct2/info/understand#Q18.

3. "Phase 3 clinical trial costs exceed $26,000 per patient," *LifeSciencesWorld*, October 13, 2006, www.lifesciencesworld.com/news/view/11080.

4. Walker, E. (2010), "Avastin not good for breast cancer, FDA panel says," *ABCNews.com*, July 20, 2010, http://abcnews.go.com/Health/OnCallPlusBreastCancerNews/avastin-breast-cancer-indication-panned-fda-panel/story?id=11209621&page=1.

5. "Guide to biotechnology 2008," Biotechnology Industry Organization, http://bio.org/speeches/pubs/er/BiotechGuide2008.pdf.

6. "What are 'biologics' questions and answers," U.S.A. Food and Drug Administration, www.fda.gov/AboutFDA/CentersOffices/CBER/ucm133077.htm.

7. "Guide to biotechnology 2008," Biotechnology Industry Organization.

8. Cohen, S. N., A.C.Y. Chang, H. W. Boyer, and R. B. Helling (1973), "Construction of biologically functional bacterial plasmids in vitro," *Proceedings of the National Academy of Sciences* 70: 3240–3244.

9. "Guide to biotechnology 2008," Biotechnology Industry Organization.

10. Hughe, S. (2001), "Making dollars out of DNA: The first major patent in biotechnology and the commercialization of molecular biology, 1974–1980," *Isis* 92: 541–575.

11. "What are 'biologics' questions and answers," U.S.A. Food and Drug Administration.

12. Pisano, G. P. (2006), "Can science be a business? Lessons from biotech," *Harvard Business Review*, October.

13. "Guide to biotechnology 2008," Biotechnology Industry Organization.

14. Gatyas, G. (2008), "IMS Health reports global biotech market sales grew 12.5 percent in 2007, exceeding $75 billion," *IMS Health*, June 17.

15. "Guide to biotechnology 2008," Biotechnology Industry Organization.

16. Gatyas, G. (2008), "IMS Health reports global biotech market sales grew 12.5 percent in 2007, exceeding $75 billion."

17. Pisano, G. P. (2006), "Can science be a business? Lessons from biotech."

18. "Biotechnology industry facts," Biotechnology Industry Organization.

19. "The fruits of genomics," Lehman Brothers and McKinsey & Company, January 30, 2001, p. 46.

20. Tyebjee, T., and J. Hardin (2004), "Biotech-pharma alliances," *Journal of Commercial Biotechnology*, June.

21. Pisano, G. P. (2006), "Can science be a business? Lessons from biotech."

22. "Guide to biotechnology 2008," Biotechnology Industry Organization.

23. "Pharma majors under merger pressure after Merck-Schering deal," www.domainb.com/industry/pharma/20090312_pharma.html.

24. Genentech Company Site, www.gene.com.

25. Ibid.

26. Ibid.

27. Genentech 2008 Annual Report.

28. Gatyas, G. (2008), "IMS Health forecasts continued double-digit annual growth of cancer therapeutics: Global sales expected to exceed $75 billion by 2012," *IMS Health*, May 15.

29. "Roche secures 96 pct of Genentech," *Forbes*, March 26, 2009, www.forbes.com/feeds/afx/2009/03/26/afx6215538.html.

30. "Roche and Genentech reach a friendly agreement to combine the two organizations and create a leader in healthcare innovation," *Fox Business*, from a Genentech press release, March 12, 2009, www.foxbusiness.com/story/markets/industries/health-care/roche-genentech-reach-friendly-agreement-combine-organizations-create-leader/.

31. "Swiss Roche embraces Genentech cool to keep drug pipeline lusty," *BusinessWeek*, July 1, 2010.

32. Greil, A. (2008), "Incoming Roche CEO sees growth in personalized medicine," *MarketWatch*, March 4, 2008. www.marketwatch.com/story/incoming-roche-ceo-sees-growth-in-personalized-medicine.

33. Roche Company Site, www.roche.com/media/media_releases.htm.

34. "Roche and Genentech reach a friendly agreement to combine the two organizations and create a leader in healthcare innovation," *Fox Business*.

35. "Swiss Roche embraces Genentech cool to keep drug pipeline lusty," *BusinessWeek*, July 1, 2010.

36. Ibid.

37. Erbes, A. (2009), "So here goes – Genentech under Roche management," WordPress.com Blogs about Genentech, April 15, 2009, http://en.wordpress.com/tag/genentech/.

38. Pethokoukis, J. (2009), "Roche's Humer said to have had Genentech buy doubts," *Reuters*, April 14, 2009, www.reuters.com/article/rbssHealthcareNews/idUSN1446175420090414.

39. Wechsler, J. (2009), "Comparative effectiveness research may shape treatment, coverage decisions," *Formulary*, May 1.

40. Ibid.

41. Carey, J. (2009), "Is Roche buying Genentech's IIIs?" *BusinessWeek*, March 12, 2009, www.businessweek.com/technology/content/mar2009/tc20090312_235221.htm.

42. Ibid.

43. "Genentech (DNA)," wikiinvest.com, www.wikinvest.com/wiki/Genentech.

44. Pollack, A. (2005), "Genentech in competition with itself on eye drug," *The New York Times*, September 27, 2005, www.nytimes.com/2005/09/27/business/27place.html?_r=1.

45. Voet, M. A. (2008), *The generic challenge: Understanding patents, FDA & pharmaceutical life-cycle management* (Boca Raton, FL: Brown Walker Press).

46. "National Sales Perspectives, National Prescription Audit," *IMS Health,* March 2009.

47. Gatyas, G., and C. Savage (2008), "IMS Health forecasts 4.5-5.5 percent growth for global pharmaceutical market in 2009, exceeding $820 billion," *IMS Health*, October 29.

48. Wangsness, L., and T. Wallack (2009), "Obama backing generic biologics," *The Boston Globe*, February 26, www.boston.com/business/healthcare/articles/2009/02/26/obama_backing_ generic_biologics/.

49. Biologic, http://en.wikipedia.org/wiki/Biologics.

50. "Implementation of the Biologics Price Competition and Innovation Act of 2009," U.S.A. Food and Drug Administration, www.fda.gov/Drugs/GuidanceComplianceRegulatoryInformation/ucm215089.htm.

51. Biologics Price Competition and Innovation Act of 2009, www.fda.gov/downloads/Drugs/GuidanceComplianceRegulatoryInformation/UCM216146.pdf.

52. Wangsness, L., and T. Wallack (2009), "Obama backing generic biologics."

53. Rothaermel, F. T., and D. L. Deeds (2004), "Exploration and exploitation alliances in biotechnology: A system of new product development," *Strategic Management Journal* 25 (3): 201–221.

54. Ibid.

55. Rothaermel, F. T., and M. T. Alexandre (2009), "Ambidexterity in technology sourcing: The moderating role of absorptive capacity," *Organization Science* 20 (4): 759–780.

56. Hoang, H., and F. T. Rothaermel (2010), "Leveraging internal and external experience: Exploration, exploitation, and R&D project performance," *Strategic Management Journal* 31 (7): 734–758.

57. O'Reilly, C. A., III, and M. L. Tushman (2007), "Ambidexterity as dynamic capability: Resolving the innovator's dilemma," *Research in Organizational Behavior* 28: 1–60.

58. Genentech Company Site, www.gene.com/gene/research/researchvision.html.

59. Genentech 2008 Annual Report.

60. O'Reilly, C. A., III, and M. L. Tushman (2007), "Ambidexterity as dynamic capability: Resolving the innovator's dilemma."

Robert M. Conroy

Introduction

The basic structure of corporate governance is that there is a set of representatives selected by the stakeholders, who in turn select management to run the corporation. While the basic structure is the same, the manner with which it gets implemented varies from country to country. The variation is in how "stakeholder" is defined and in the relationship between the supervisory board and management. Part of those differences is cultural, but a large part is due to historical happenstance. For example, the role of banks as stakeholders varies internationally. In the United States, banks play almost no role in the corporate governance of firms. In Japan and Germany, however, banks are major players. A good part of this was due to the way banks were chartered in the United States. U.S. banks were chartered by individual states and were prohibited from having branches in other states. In some cases, they could only have branches in a limited area within the state. At one point just before the stock market crash in 1929, there were over 17,000 commercial banks operating in the United States. Even in 1950, there were over 14,000 commercial banks in the United States, while Germany had a little over 200 and Japan only had about 85. This lack of a national banking system made using bond and equity markets more attractive in the United States versus the access to large banks that one found in Germany and Japan where banks provided most of the long-term financing. The consequence was that banks play a much larger role in corporate governance in Germany and Japan, than they do in the United States. This type of factor does not fully explain all the differences we see across markets, but it does represent the kind of indirect influence other types of decisions have.

In the sections which follow, we will explore some of the basic differences we see in the corporate governance structure across countries.

German Corporate Governance Structure

There are a number of different forms that business units can take in Germany. These include sole proprietorships, partnerships, cooperatives, and limited liability companies. The limited liability companies are closest to the U.S.–U.K. corporate form. The other forms do not have limited liability. There are two kinds of limited liability companies in the German economic system. The first and most numerous (over 438,000 in 1999) is the *gesellschaft mit beschränkter haftung* or GmbH. This is a partnership with limited liability. These firms usually do not issue shares, and transfer of ownership is difficult. The other form is *aktiengesellschaft* or AG. This is a limited liability company that issues shares. The proportion of total sales by each legal structure is shown in Table 1. It is obvious from Table 1 that the average size of the GmbH is much less than the AG, even though GmbHs do account for the largest proportion of total sales. Although there are some very large firms that maintain the GmbH structure, most large firms are AGs.

The corporate governance structure of the AG and the GmbH are somewhat different. For small GmbHs with fewer than 500 employees, there is a simple governance structure. The shareholders appoint a managing director, the *geschäftsführer*, who is responsible for the management of the firm. For GmbHs with over 500 employees and all AGs, there is a management board known as the *vorstand*. This group is jointly responsible for all aspects of the management of the firm. Separate from the *vorstand* is a supervisory board called the *aufsichtsrat*, which appoints the members of the *vorstand*, approves capital expenditures, strategic acquisitions, closures, and approval of the dividends. Of this list, appointing the members of the *vorstand* is the most important, since the *vorstand* is the group that will manage the firm. In the case of all GmbHs and AGs with less than 2,000 employees, the membership of the *aufsichtsrat* is made up of two-thirds shareholders' representatives and one-third employees/union representatives. For larger AGs with more than 2,000 employees, the proportion of shareholders to

DARDEN
BUSINESS PUBLISHING
UNIVERSITY*of*VIRGINIA

This note was prepared by Professor Robert M. Conroy. Copyright © 2002 by the University of Virginia Darden School Foundation, Charlottesville, VA. All rights reserved. *To order copies, send an e-mail to sales@dardenbusinesspublishing.com. No part of this publication may be reproduced, stored in a retrieval system, used in a spreadsheet, or transmitted in any form or by any means—electronic, mechanical, photocopying, recording, or otherwise—without the permission of the Darden School Foundation.*

TABLE 1

Proportion of Total Sales by Legal Structure

	1950	1972	1986	1999	
	%	%	%	%	Number
Limited Liability Companies					
Ag	17	19	21	20.73	3,951
GmbH	15	17	26	32.60	438,085
Non-limited Liability					
Partnerships	19	32	31	29.00	357,009
Sole proprietorship	37	24	15	12.89	982,527
Other	13	8	7	5.05	49,993
Total	100	100	100	100.00	1,831,565

employee representatives is 50:50 with a neutral individual as the chair. It is important to note that the employee/union representatives do include white-collar as well as blue-collar employees. To the extent that shareholders wish to limit the impact of employees, there is a substantial incentive for a large firm to remain under the GmbH form as long as possible.

The shareholder representatives on the *aufsichtsrat* are appointed for four years by the general meeting of the shareholders. This raises the question of just who are the shareholders. From Table 2, there is quite a bit of difference regarding which sector owns shares when

comparing the United States and Germany. The distinction is in the roles of banks and other enterprises. Historically, German corporations have received the majority of their outside funding from large banks. From their very beginnings, German banks operated as a combination of commercial bank, investment bank, and investment trust. They were planned primarily as institutions for the financing of industry.[1] The result was that as the association between the companies and the banks grew, German banks took on equity stakes in order to monitor the firm. Thus, in Table 2 we see banks holding over 10% of the shares in Germany.

TABLE 2

International Comparison of the Percentage of Total Shares in Circulation by Different Sectors: End of 1995

	United States %	Japan %	Germany %
Shareownership Profile			
Households	36.30	22.20	14.60
Enterprises	15.00	31.20	42.10
Public sector	0.00	0.50	4.30
Banks	0.20	13.30	10.30
Insurance & pension funds	31.30	10.80	12.40
Investment trusts & other financial institutions	13.00	11.70	7.60
Rest of the world	4.20	10.30	8.70
Total	100.00	100.00	100.00

Source: "Shares as financing and Investment Instruments," *Bundesbank Monthly Report* (January 1997).

It is interesting to note that the United States' banks hold essentially no shares.

In addition to banks holding shares, there is a tradition of crossholdings in Germany, which results in firms holding each other's shares. While most discussions focus on crossholdings in Japan, we actually find a large component of German AGs' shares are held by other firms. Consequently, we find a great deal of crossholding of shares between German firms. In these cases, it is common for two firms to each have a representative of the other firm on the supervisory board.

This ownership translates into representation on the supervisory board. However, it should be noted that banks have much more influence than their actual holding would represent. Because most shares of German AGs are bearer shares, there are complex rules that result in banks having control of a much larger share of the votes through proxies held for other shareholders. In fact, a study[2] of shareholder representatives on supervisory boards in 1979 noted that banks held over 16% of the shareholder seats on the supervisory board, but owned only about 10% of the outstanding shares.[3] Domestic non-bank firms had about 40% of the shareholder seats on the supervisory boards. This was roughly in the same proportion that domestic non-bank firms held outstanding shares. The consequence of all this is that the shareholder representation on the *aufsichtsrat*, or supervisory board, is heavily weighted toward banks and other firms.

Japanese Corporate Governance

There are three types of companies in Japan: commercial partnerships, limited partnerships, and limited companies. The limited companies, or *kabushiki kaisha*,[4] are the ones with limited liability and are the basic corporate form in Japan. While there are more than 2 million limited companies in Japan, there are only a little more than 2,000 that are actually quoted.

The governance structure of a Japanese corporation centers around the board of directors. Directors are appointed by a general meeting of the shareholders. The guidelines for the board of directors are that it shall decide the administration of affairs of the company and supervise the management. It is required to meet at least quarterly. In larger companies, the actual control of the company rests with its top management committee. In principle, there should be a separation between the board of directors and the top management committee, but in fact that is not the case for Japanese corporations. It is usually the case that the board of directors is composed of "insiders." These are full-time employees of the company. In 1992, over 75% of the members of the board of directors for Japanese firms were internal management appointees,[5] 20% were individuals from banks or other companies, and 5% would be classified as other. An obvious question is: Why do shareholders permit this lack of separation between the board and management? The reason has to do with the makeup of the shareholders.

There are strong historic reasons why Japanese firms have a particular ownership structure. Japan began to emerge as a modern nation sometime after 1860. During the next 50 years, Japan developed into a modern industrial state. This rapid industrialization was fostered and encouraged by the state. One consequence of the late industrialization of Japan was the opportunity to look for models that Japan could use to bring about rapid industrialization. Germany, which was also late in forming a modern, unified nation state was a model often used by Japan. One consequence of this is that Japan does have a structure of corporate ownership and governance that resembles the one found in Germany. At its base was the use of banks to fund industrial development and the mutual crossholding of corporate shares.

While the structure that existed before the end of World War II had significant impact on the structure of ownership, it was really the post-war experience that determined what we observe in Japan today. The Japanese banking system basically emerged from the American occupation unchanged. There were a small number of specialty banks focused on financing industrial development for the nation and an additional small number of banks, which formed strong relationships with particular industrial groups. These industrial groups existed before the war and were broken up during the American occupation between 1945 and 1952. By the 1960s these industrial groups had essentially reformed. In response to a threat of acquisitions by foreign firms, they exchanged shares with each other in order to create blocks of reliable shareholders. In 1949, only about 5.6% of the outstanding shares were held by business corporations.[6] By 1965, the percentage had increased to 18.4%.

Capital restrictions in the 1960s and early 1970s restricted firms to issuing new equity in the form of non-transferable par value rights offerings to existing shareholders. This resulted in a dramatic increase in the crossholdings. Since most individual shareholders did not have cash available, the fact that the rights offerings were not transferable resulted in most individual shareholders not being able to participate. Since other firms in the group did have enough liquidity to participate, the result was a dramatic increase in the levels of crossholdings between firms within a particular group. By 1975, the level of corporate ownership of shares had reached 26.3%. In the late 1990s, the level of crossholdings had decreased. For a number of reasons, many banks and group firms were making a concerted effort to reduce the level of crossholdings.

The result of all this is that a very large proportion of the shares of Japanese corporations are held in the hands of "stable shareholders." From Table 2, we see that about 44% of the outstanding shares are held by banks and other firms. For some firms the percentage of stable shareholding might exceed 70%. This level of stable shareholding and the degree to which one firm holds shares in another firm within an industrial group contributes to a significant degree to the independence of the management of Japanese firms. Traditionally, hostile takeovers in Japan are unknown. The stable shareholders support incumbent managers.

United States Corporate Governance

Like Japan, the United States has partnership and corporate entities. The main feature of the corporate form is its limited liability (i.e., investors are only liable for the amount of their investment). Unlike Japan or Germany where there is one national corporate or limited liability form, incorporation is by state in the United States. An entity can select the state in which it wishes to incorporate. While in principle the articles of incorporation are very similar, they are different enough that a large percentage of U.S. corporations choose the state of Delaware as the state of incorporation.

Even though there are some legal differences across states, corporate governance is fairly similar. The shareholders elect the board of directors, which in turn selects the chief executive officer (CEO) of the corporation. The CEO is responsible for the management of the corporation. The relationship between the board of directors and the CEO varies greatly in U.S. corporations. In the not too distant past, the board of directors was composed mainly of employees. There has been a tremendous change after a series of scandals in the 1970s. More recently, the majority of directors on boards are now made up of outside directors. The typical board for a large company will have about 12 board members. Exhibit 1 shows the makeup of the board of directors for the Coca-Cola Company for the year 2001. Out of the 12 members, CEO Douglas Draft is the only employee member of the board. Also listed on the exhibit are the main board committees on which Coca-Cola's members serve. The main duties of the board are as follows:

- Elect, evaluate, and oversee senior management;
- Administer to the corporation's business by allocating funds and reviewing corporate performance;
- Oversee corporate social responsibility;
- Ensure compliance with the law.

Shareholders elect the board. The makeup of corporate shareholders in the United States is quite different from that in either Japan or Germany. Table 2 shows that households make up the largest shareownership segment in the United States. The next largest is insurance and pension funds. Table 3 reports shareownership in the United States over time.[7] It is clear that the direct holdings of individuals have decreased dramatically over time, but the total shows much less of a decrease. This is due in large part to the growth in the use of mutual funds by households. The big change in the non-household sector is in the holdings by non-U.S. investors and the growth of the equity holdings of government pension funds. As of 1998, the main shareholders are individuals through either direct holdings, or indirect holding and pension funds. This is very different from either Japan or Germany, where banks and other corporations play a major role.

EXHIBIT 1

Corporate Governance in Three Economies: Germany, Japan, and the United States

Board of Directors for The Coca-Cola Company, 2001

Douglas N. Daft[3]: Board chair, board of directors, and CEO of The Coca-Cola Company.

Peter V. Ueberroth[1,4]: Board chair of the Contrarian Group, Inc. (a business management company) and co-chair of the Pebble Beach Company.

Sam Nunn[2,3]: Partner in the law firm of King & Spalding, and co-chair and CEO of Nuclear Threat Initiative.

Susan B. King[4,6]: Board chair of the Leadership Initiative of Duke University (non-profit consultants for leadership education).

James B. Williams[2,3]: Board chair of the executive committee, retired chair of the board of directors and CEO of SunTrust Banks, Inc.

James D. Robinson III[5,6]: Co-founder, board chair, and CEO of RRE Investors, LLC; general partner of RRE Ventures GP II, LLC (private information-technology venture investment firms); board chair of Violy, Byorum & Partners Holdings, LLC (a private financial advisory and investment banking firm); and president of JD Robinson, Inc.

Cathleen P. Black[1,4,6]: President of Hearst Magazines.

Paul F. Oreffice[2,4,5]: Retired chair of the board of directors and CEO of The Dow Chemical Company.

Herbert A. Allen[2,3]: President, CEO, director, and managing director of Allen & Company Incorporated (a privately held investment banking firm).

Donald F. McHenry[3,5,6]: Distinguished professor in the practice of diplomacy and international affairs at the School of Foreign Service at Georgetown University and president of the IRC Group, LLC.

Ronald W. Allen[1,3,5]: Consultant, advisory director, retired chair of the board of directors, president, and CEO of Delta Air Lines, Inc.

Warren E. Buffett[1,2]: Chair of the board of directors and CEO of Berkshire Hathaway Inc. (a diversified holding company).

[1] Audit committee.

[2] Finance committee.

[3] Executive committee.

[4] Compensation committee.

[5] Committee on directors.

[6] Public Issues & Diversity Review committee.

TABLE 3

Shareownership in the United States

	1950 %	1960 %	1970 %	1980 %	1990 %	1998 %
Direct household holdings	90.2	85.6	68.0	58.6	51.0	41.1
Indirect household holdings:						
Bank personal trusts & states	0.0	0.0	10.9	9.3	6.0	3.8
Life insurance companies	1.3	1.0	1.5	2.6	1.9	3.5

(continued)

TABLE 3 *(Continued)*

	1950 %	1960 %	1970 %	1980 %	1990 %	1998 %
Private pension funds	0.0	0.0	0.0	0.6	8.0	8.9
Mutual funds	2.0	3.5	4.1	2.1	5.1	11.3
Total indirect household holdings	**3.3**	**4.5**	**16.4**	**14.6**	**21.0**	**27.5**
Total household (direct & indirect)	**93.5**	**90.1**	**84.5**	**73.1**	**72.0**	**68.6**
Non-households:						
Outside U.S.	2.0	2.2	3.2	5.0	6.9	7.2
State & local government retirement plans	0.0	0.1	1.2	3.0	7.6	11.4
Private defined-benefit pension plans	0.8	3.9	8.0	14.9	8.8	5.6
Mutual funds not owned by households	0.0	0.0	0.6	0.7	1.5	5.0
Other non-household investors	3.7	3.6	2.5	3.2	3.2	2.2
Total non-household investors	**6.5**	**9.9**	**15.5**	**26.9**	**28.0**	**31.4**
Grand total	**100.0**	**100.0**	**100.0**	**100.0**	**100.0**	**100.0**

Source: NYSE Shareownership 2000, www.nyse.com.

ISSUES

- How do you think the management decisions are affected by the different corporate governance structures in each country?
- What should be the criteria for allocating capital within the corporation? Should it be the same in each country?
- How does globalization affect those structures?

Endnotes

1. For a more complete description of the role of banks in the industrial development of Germany, see G. Stolper, K. Häuser, K. Borchardt, *The German Economy 1870 to the Present*, trans. Toni Stolper (New York: Harcourt, Brace & World, Inc., 1967).

2. This figure is cited in Jeremy Edwards and Klaus Fischer, *Banks, Finance and Investment in Germany* (Cambridge: Cambridge University Press, 1994): 211. It is based on the work by E. Gerum, H. Steinmann, and W. Fees, *Der mitbestimmite Aufsichtsrat-eine empirsche Untersuchung* (Stuttgart: Poeschel Verlag, 1988): table D–3, 48.

3. Deutsches Aktieninstitut, *DAI Factbook* (1999): 8.1–8.2.

4. The exact English translation is stock companies.

5. Jonathan Charkham, *Keeping Good Company: A Study of Corporate Governance in Five Countries* (Oxford, U.K.: Clarendon Press, 1994): 85.

6. Complete data on shareholding in Japan can be found in the *2000 Shareownership Survey*, which is available at http://www.tse.or.jp/english/data/research/shareownership.html.

7. Note that the household sector includes assets held by non-profit institutions. At the end of 1996, these organizations accounted for about 5.3% of the direct household holdings. Deducting this from the numbers reported in Table 3 would place those totals in line with the lines reported in Table 2.

Lisa Stewart

I N JULY 2003, Pat Gnazzo, Vice President of Business Practices for United Technologies Corporation (UTC), sat at his desk in the company's Hartford, Connecticut, headquarters considering the challenge of integrating 46,000 new employees into UTC's global ethics and compliance program from the recently acquired Chubb plc, a United Kingdom–based leader in security and fire protection services. Although Gnazzo had faced many difficult issues since he had taken over business practices programs for UTC in 1995, this challenge was unique. Simultaneously integrating this volume of employees—who were situated in a variety of different cultures across the globe—would be a monumental task, especially since Chubb's ethics and compliance priorities were not on the level of UTC's. Gnazzo wondered where he should start.

History of UTC and Business Units[1]

United Technologies Corporation was a $31 billion global corporation made up of seven business units and a stand-alone research center, which supported research for all divisions. The business unit divisions were Carrier Corporation (climate control systems), Hamilton Sundstrand (airplane systems), Otis Elevator, Pratt & Whitney (airplane engines), Sikorsky (helicopters), UTC Power (hydrogen fuel cells), and the recently acquired Chubb (security and fire protection services). A global conglomerate with 205,700 employees after the Chubb acquisition (138,000 based outside of the United States), UTC had over 4,000 locations in approximately 62 countries and did business in more than 180 countries. In 2002, 55 percent of UTC's total revenues came from outside the United States, and its net income was $2.2 billion with assets totaling $29.1 billion. In March 2003, UTC ranked 49th on the Fortune 500 list of companies.

Many of UTC's long-standing business units were originally formed by business pioneers, whose names were still associated with the products. According to George David, chief executive officer (CEO) of UTC, "We invented every business we are in—and in a bunch of cases the name of the [business] is the name of the

person who did the invention."[2] Elisha Otis founded Otis Elevator in 1853; Willis H. Carrier invented air conditioning in 1902 and started Carrier Engineering in 1915; in 1920, Hamilton Aero Manufacturing was founded by Thomas Hamilton; Sundstrand Machine Tool Company by David Sundstrand in 1929; Igor Sikorsky founded Sikorsky Aero Engineering in 1923; and Pratt & Whitney Aircraft was incorporated in 1925. Chubb, a leader in security and fire protection services and UTC's newly acquired company, originated in 1818 in the United Kingdom when Charles and Jeremiah Chubb patented their prize-winning detector lock.

UTC had a long, complex history. United Aircraft and Transport was formed in 1929, when Boeing Airline & Transport joined forces with Hamilton, Sikorsky, Pratt & Whitney, Chance Vought, and Standard Steel Propeller. That same year, the Research Center, the corporation's central research laboratory, was established in Connecticut. Objections raised by the U.S. government in 1934 dissolved United Aircraft and Transport into three distinct units: Boeing Airplane Company, United Air Lines Transport, and United Aircraft Corporation. In 1975, United Aircraft Corporation changed its name to United Technologies Corporation, to more accurately reflect the broad nature of its business.

Defense Acquisition Scandals of the 1980s

UTC was and remains a major contractor to the U.S. government, including the Department of Defense. In the mid-1980s, the defense industry in the United States was embroiled in allegations of fraud, waste, and abuse. Reports of the military spending on wildly overpriced spare parts were prevalent in the media, including the memorable $640 toilet seats, $437 hammers, and the $748 spent for two pairs of pliers.[3] In June 1984, a Pentagon audit of the Defense Department's spare

Business Roundtable
Institute for Corporate Ethics

This case was prepared by Lisa Stewart, Program Manager for the Business Roundtable Institute for Corporate Ethics under the supervision of R. Edward Freeman, Elis and Signe Olsson Professor of Business Administration/Director of the Olsson Center/Academic Advisor of the Business Roundtable Institute for Corporate Ethics, and Jeanne Liedtka, Johnson & Higgins Associate Professor of Business Administration/Executive Director of the Batten Institute. Copyright © 2005 by the Business Roundtable Institute for Corporate Ethics (www.corporate-ethics.org). Reproduction and use for direct educational purposes permitted. All rights reserved.

parts purchases from October 1981 to September 1983 revealed that 36 percent of the 2,300 audited spare-parts purchases were either "unreasonably priced" or "potentially unreasonably priced."[4] In April 1985, the Pentagon's inspector general announced that 45 of the 100 biggest defense contractors were under investigation by the U.S. Department of Defense.[5]

One of UTC's divisions, Pratt & Whitney, faced allegations related to these acquisition scandals. In March 1985, Air Force Secretary Verne Orr wrote a letter asking Harry Gray, the chairman of UTC, to voluntarily repay $40 million in excess profits that Pratt & Whitney made on contracts over a six-year period.[6] Responding to the request, a Pratt & Whitney spokesperson asserted that the average earned profit on the contracts was 1.6 percent above the level "anticipated by the government at the outset." He contended that Pratt & Whitney's profits were not only reasonable, but they were also "consistent with the Department of Defense's own guidelines for profit objectives." Pratt & Whitney had "negotiated in good faith to deliver products at fixed prices, with the company assuming the risk of fluctuating costs," he added. Although UTC felt that no refund was justified, the spokesperson explained that the company had "offered to work with the government because its 'reputation as a major defense contractor [was] being questioned.'"

The Packard Commission

In July 1985, President Reagan responded to the defense management scandals by establishing a Blue Ribbon Commission known as the "Packard Commission" to conduct a study of the industry and to recommend a course of corrective action.[7] The commission examined a wide array of issues and strategies related to government dealings with defense contractors and found that inefficiency within the system was a far larger problem than fraud. The "well-publicized spare parts cases are only one relatively small aspect of a far costlier structural problem," the Packard Commission's final report noted. The report recommended that defense contractors "must promulgate and vigilantly enforce codes of ethics that address the unique problems and procedures incident to defense procurement. They must also develop and implement internal controls to monitor these codes of ethics and sensitive aspects of contract compliance." The commission called upon contractors to significantly improve efforts of self-governance.

Defense Industry Initiative

In 1986, a group of 32 defense contractors, including UTC, established the Defense Industry Initiative (DII), as a direct result of the requests of the commission and, more broadly, to the crisis in public perception. A study of public attitudes toward defense management presented to the Packard Commission indicated that industry contractors were "seen as especially culpable for waste and fraud in defense spending."[8] According to Pat Gnazzo, the DII originated when a group of defense representatives, including John "Jack" Welch, General Electric's board chair, decided that the industry needed a strong proactive response to the overall crisis in public trust. Welch invited the CEOs of several of GE's peer companies to discuss these issues as a group. The DII prescribed a detailed program of ethics education and voluntary compliance measures aimed at self-regulation. The program included six guidelines, referred to as the "Principles," to which all members of the initiative subscribed. (See Exhibit 1 for a list of the six principles.) The Principles, also detailed in the Packard Commission's report, outlined ways in which the members of the DII could cooperate on developing and maintaining ethical standards and practices, sharing their company's best practices within the group, and making commitments that each member company would self-regulate these issues.

Ethics and Compliance Regulations in the United States

Despite industry efforts to self-regulate, a 1988 Defense Department audit showed that overcharges to the government continued: almost $789 million or 47 percent of approximately $54 billion in military contracts.[9] Also in 1988, 34 of the 39 DII signatories were subject to over 200 investigations. Over 1,000 defense contractors were suspended from conducting business at some point in 1988 for a variety of ethical violations, "ranging from bribery and bid rigging to the manufacture of shoddy products and overcharging."

The U.S. government tried to increase the incentives for creating and implementing effective compliance programs. After years of data analysis and public hearings, the United States Sentencing Commission developed the Federal Sentencing Guidelines for Organizations (FSGO) in 1991.[10] The FSGO outlined broad standards of ethical behavior for corporations

EXHIBIT 1

United Technologies Corporation: Running a Global Ethics and Compliance Program

The DII Principles

The DII Principles were adopted at the time of the establishment of the DII in June 1986, and have been periodically reconfirmed. The Principles are:

(1) Each Signatory shall have and adhere to a written code of business conduct. The code establishes the high ethical values expected for all within the Signatory's organization.

(2) Each Signatory shall train all within the organization as to their personal responsibilities under the Code.

(3) Signatories shall encourage internal reporting of violations of the Code, with the promise of no retaliation for such reporting.

(4) Signatories have the obligation to self-govern by implementing controls to monitor compliance with federal procurement laws and by adopting procedures for voluntary disclosure of violations of federal procurement laws to appropriate authorities.

(5) Each Signatory shall have responsibility to each other to share their best practices in implementing the DII principles; each Signatory shall participate in an annual Best Practices Forum.

(6) Each Signatory shall be accountable to the public.

In addition to adopting and adhering to this set of principles of business ethics and conduct, Signatories have assumed a leading role in making the principles a standard for the entire defense industry, and a model for other industries.

Source: www.dii.org., excerpt from The Statement of DII Purpose and Organization; Defense Industry Initiative on Business Ethics and Conduct.

that applied to all organizations whether publicly or privately held. Deputy General Counsel for the Sentencing Commission Winthrop Swenson headed up the task force responsible for developing these guidelines. "The task force collected formal and informal comments from the public," Swenson explained, "and the defense industry representatives were the most vocal participants in this process."[11] As Swenson described, the defense contractors advocated the idea that self-regulating compliance and ethics programs should be key determinants in establishing punishments for violations. "The voice from the DII," he said, "helped to confirm and ratify the model that was being considered by the task force."

More than a decade after the original FSGO guidelines were established, the United States Congress passed the Sarbanes-Oxley Act of 2002 to provide additional government regulation of public companies' compliance to statutory and regulatory standards. Among other things, the act included a number of significant changes relating to the responsibilities of directors and officers, from reporting requirements to corporate governance obligations.

UTC's Ethics and Compliance Program [12]

In its quest to increase self-regulation of compliance issues in an increasingly government-regulated environment, UTC first published its Code of Ethics in 1990.[13] UTC adopted this broad-ranging code in order to articulate standards of conduct over and above compliance with legal requirements. Since then, the company has woven the Code of Ethics into the corporate culture through various business practices programs and detailed policies in the *UTC Corporate Policy Manual*. (See Exhibit 2 for a Code of Ethics excerpt.) In his introduction letter, CEO George David explained to UTC employees that "ethics and compliance are our joint responsibility." He continued, "We must have a spotless, perfect record, period. We're counting on each other."[14] UTC also incorporated five major company commitments, originally published in UTC's 2001 Annual Report, into the Code of Ethics.[15] The five company commitments were performance, pioneering innovation, personal development, social responsibility, and shareowner value. (See Exhibit 3

EXHIBIT 2

United Technologies Corporation: Running a Global Ethics and Compliance Program

Code of Ethics

Corporate Principles

United Technologies is committed to the highest standards of ethics and business conduct. This encompasses our relationship with our customers, our suppliers, our shareowners, our competitors, the communities in which we operate, and with each other as employees at every organizational level. These commitments and the responsibilities they entail are summarized here.

Our Customers

We are committed to providing high quality and value, fair prices, and honest transactions to those who use our products and services. We will deal both lawfully and ethically with all our customers.

Our Employees

We are committed to treating one another fairly and to maintaining employment practices based on equal opportunity for all employees. We will respect each other's privacy and treat each other with dignity and respect irrespective of age, race, color, sex, religion, or nationality. We are committed to providing safe and healthy working conditions and an atmosphere of open communication for all our employees.

Our Suppliers

We are committed to dealing fairly with our suppliers. We will emphasize fair competition, without discrimination or deception, in a manner consistent with long-lasting business relationships.

Our Shareowners

We are committed to providing a superior return to our shareowners and to protecting and improving the value of their investment through the prudent utilization of corporate resources and by observing the highest standards of legal and ethical conduct in all our business dealings.

Our Competitors

We are committed to competing vigorously and fairly for business and to basing our efforts solely on the merits of our competitive offerings.

Our Communities

We are committed to being a responsible corporate citizen of the worldwide communities in which we reside. We will abide by all national and local laws, and we will strive to improve the well-being of our communities through the encouragement of employee participation in civic affairs and through corporate philanthropy.

Standards of Conduct

Our Code of Ethics, comprised of our Corporate Principles and these Standards of Conduct, governs our business decisions and actions. The Code is an expression of fundamental values and represents a framework for decision-making. The Code is further explained and implemented in policy circulars and policies included in the Corporate Policy Manual. The integrity, reputation, and profitability of United Technologies ultimately depend upon the individual actions of our directors, officers, employees, representatives, agents, and consultants all over the world. Each is personally responsible and accountable for compliance with our Code. In addition, any representatives, agents, or consultants used by the Corporation shall be prohibited from acting on its behalf in any manner that is inconsistent with the standards of conduct applicable to employees under the Code of Ethics.

The following Standards of Conduct serve to assist in defining our ethical principles and are not all-encompassing. The Standards must be interpreted within the framework of the laws and mores of the jurisdictions in which we operate,

EXHIBIT 2 *(Continued)*

as well as in light of UTC policies and good common sense. Reasons such as "everyone does it" or "it's not illegal" are unacceptable as excuses for violating our Standards. We must each be mindful of avoiding at all times, on and off the job, circumstances and actions that give even the appearance of an impropriety or wrongdoing which could discredit the Corporation.

These Standards of Conduct will be enforced equitably at all organizational levels.

Source: www.utc.com., excerpt from UTC Code of Ethics.

EXHIBIT 3

United Technologies Corporation: Running a Global Ethics and Compliance Program

UTC Commitments

Performance

Our customers have a choice, and how we perform determines whether they choose us. We aim high, set ambitious goals and deliver results, and we use customer feedback to recalibrate when necessary. We move quickly and make timely, well-reasoned decisions because our future depends on them. We invest authority where it needs to be, in the hands of the people closest to the customer and the work.

Pioneering Innovation

We are a company of ideas that are nurtured by a commitment to research and development. The achievements of our founders—Willis Carrier, Charles and Jeremiah Chubb, Tom Hamilton, Elisha Otis, Fred Rentschler (who founded Pratt & Whitney), Igor Sikorsky, and David Sundstrand—inspire us to always reach for the next innovative and powerful and marketable idea. We seek and share ideas openly, and encourage diversity of experience and opinion.

Personal Development

Our employees' ideas and inspiration create opportunities constantly, and without limits. We improve continuously everything we do, as a company and as individuals. We support and pursue lifelong learning to expand our knowledge and capabilities and to engage with the world outside UTC. Confidence spurs us to take risks, to experiment, to cooperate with each other and, always, to learn from the consequences of our actions.

Social Responsibility

Successful businesses improve the human condition. We maintain the highest ethical, environmental and safety standards everywhere, and we encourage and celebrate our employees' active roles in their communities.

Shareowner Value

We are a preferred investment, because we meet aggressive targets whatever the economic environment. We communicate honestly and forthrightly to investors, and deliver consistently what we promise. We are a company of realists and optimists, and we project those values in everything we do.

Source: www.utc.com; excerpt from UTC Code of Ethics.

---

for details on those commitments.) An *Industry Week* article naming George David as "CEO of the Year" for 2002 credited those five commitments for guiding UTC's strong performance in 2001, during the U.S. recession.[16] The words were important, according to David, because "they focus on the present and future of UTC, while incorporating achievements and values of the past."[17]

Under the guidance of the Code of Ethics and UTC's commitments, UTC had two main ethics and compliance programs, serving specific, complementary functions. As Vice President of Business Practices, Pat Gnazzo oversaw both components: the Business Practices program and the Ombuds/DIALOG program. The Business Practices program was responsible for oversight of standards, beginning with corporate policies, training, assessments, and investigations. The Ombuds/DIALOG program was responsible for providing a confidential, anonymous avenue for employee communications.

UTC had distinguished itself from many other companies, Gnazzo explained, by fully institutionalizing its ethics and compliance programs, with a firm commitment to its success from top-level management. Ultimately, line management had responsibility. Rather than the typical pattern of declining infrastructure and authority he had observed in other companies' ethics programs, Gnazzo applauded UTC's commitment to providing the continued resources for the program and for maintaining the high-level of the Vice President of Business Practices within the reporting structure of the organization. (See Exhibit 4 for an overview of the structure of the Business Practices programs.)

The *UTC Corporate Policy Manual* clearly outlined that the Code of Ethics should serve as "a framework for decision-making" and that in addition to "compliance with the law," it also required "avoidance of conflicts of interest, integrity, and fair dealing."[18] The manual stated that "each director, officer, employee, and representative is personally responsible and accountable for meeting the requirements and standards of the code." UTC's chief executive officer and each business unit chief executive were "responsible for creating and fostering a culture of ethical business practices, encouraging open communications, and for instilling an awareness of and commitment to the Code of Ethics." In Gnazzo's view, management also viewed the ethics and compliance programs as a tool to protect the company's bottom line, guarding the corporation from individuals who may have acted either dishonestly or in their own self-interest. "Every manager at UTC knows that employees have an alternate channel to report a potential wrongdoing," as Gnazzo explained. [19]

UTC structured its programs so that the 206 Business Practices officers (BPO) were integrated throughout the corporation, in local business units, located in the various countries in which UTC operated. The BPOs all worked in other positions within the corporation, and the duties of the BPOs were in addition to their regular jobs. Employees approached BPOs for guidance and advice on business ethics issues, assistance with interpreting UTC's corporate policies, or general compliance issues. BPOs were also responsible for reinforcing the Code of Ethics through training and

EXHIBIT 4

United Technologies Corporation: Running a Global Ethics and Compliance Program

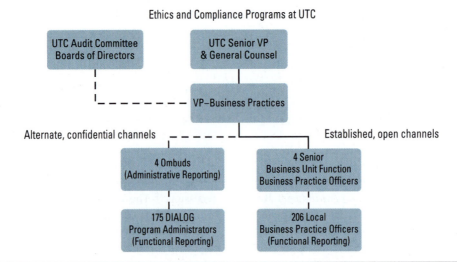

Ethics and Compliance Programs at UTC

communications, and they assisted with ethics and compliance reporting requirements. Although there were many difficulties in enforcing a single Code of Ethics across many countries and cultures, as Gnazzo noted, the basic rules of "don't lie; don't cheat; don't steal" seemed to translate into any culture's ethical beliefs.[20]

The other main component, the Ombuds program, was established at UTC in 1986 to allow employees an alternate, confidential means of raising ethical concerns, making suggestions, registering complaints, or asking for guidance in ethically unclear situations. Employees were still encouraged to resolve issues via the traditional routes of human resources or through their supervisors, but for employees who preferred a confidential channel, the Ombuds program provided an alternative. The four Ombuds, all long-term UTC employees with an average tenure of over 20 years, were assigned by geographic regions and assisted employees with complex ethical issues. Ombuds worked with employees over the phone, in person, or via the Internet. The Ombuds also trained and supervised approximately 175 DIALOG Program Administrators (DPAs), dispersed throughout the corporation, who, in addition to their full-time jobs, handled written inquiries to the DIALOG Program and assisted with the daily operations of a system for processing employee inquiries. Employees reached the DPAs via mail or a DIALOG website, where they chose a secure password that they could later use to return to the site for resolution on their inquiry. The DIALOG system was available to employees in 29 languages. Since the start of the Ombuds/DIALOG program, it had dealt with more than 10,000 Ombuds cases and over 60,000 DIALOG inquiries. Inquiries were varied and included issues ranging from questions about company policies to queries related to ethical business practices.

Chubb

Like its new parent company, Chubb also conducted business on multiple continents and in many countries around the globe.[21] The regional Chubb headquarters was located in Sydney (covering Australia and New Zealand), Hong Kong (covering all of Asia), Paris (covering all of continental Europe), London (covering England, Scotland, and South Africa), and Toronto (covering the United States, Canada, and Mexico).

All but about 1,000 of the approximately 46,000 Chubb employees worked outside of the United States.

When it acquired Chubb, UTC obtained not only security and fire protection systems, but also security guard employees who were widely dispersed in various buildings in the regions where Chubb operated, and who often had little affiliation with the central organization. Chubb had in prior years made hundreds of small acquisitions and was struggling with integration of a skilled, but geographically and culturally diverse, work force. The decentralized work force appeared to have weaker allegiances to Chubb than the typical UTC employee had to her or his UTC company. Further, a large number of Chubb managers had very short tenure with the company. Additionally, Chubb security guards reported directly to their assigned buildings, had little interaction with a central Chubb office, and had no access to the company's intranet or computer system.

In 1999, Pat Gnazzo had managed another large-scale integration of employees when UTC acquired Sundstrand, which later became part of Hamilton Sundstrand. According to Gnazzo, although the scope of the integrations was similar, the two situations were very different. Unlike Sundstrand, Chubb had a corporate culture prior to joining UTC that included no established ethics and compliance programs, so UTC's Business Practices team needed to instill the basics of why such a program was necessary and what it encompassed. Sundstrand, on the other hand, had a centrally connected and technically proficient work force and already had ethics and compliance self-regulation programs in place, so the focus during that integration was on strengthening the infrastructure and adding energy and resources to the existing programs.

Where to Start

With a well-established and highly trained network of Ombuds and Business Practices officers in place, Pat Gnazzo now faced the daunting task of simultaneously bringing 46,000 new Chubb employees into the UTC ethics and compliance system. Not only were these employees unfamiliar with a corporate ethics and compliance program, but Gnazzo and his team realized that UTC's standard methods of communication might be ineffective with the Chubb work force, which consisted primarily of security guards. Turning to his trusted team members for input and advice, Pat Gnazzo asked them, "Where should we start?"

Endnotes

1. The information in this section was gathered from the United Technologies Corporation website http://www.utc.com.

2. McClenahen, J.S. (2003), "UTC's master of principle," *Industry Week*, January 1.

3. "$437 hammers dent public support for military spending," *Seattle Times*, March 31, 1985.

4. Hiatt, F. (1984), "Pentagon concedes routine overpaying for its spare parts," *The Washington Post*, June 2.

5. Biddle, W. (1985), "45 of 100 biggest contractors being investigated, U.S. says," *The New York Times*, April 15.

6. Carrington, T. (1985), "U.S. suspends GE from defense work, asks it, Pratt & Whitney for repayments," *The Wall Street Journal*, March 29.

7. Information for this section was obtained from "A quest for excellence: Final report to the President by the President's Blue Ribbon Commission on Defense Management," chaired by David Packard, June 1986.

8. "U.S. national survey: Public attitudes on defense management," prepared by Market Opinion Research, *A Quest for Excellence Appendix, Final Report by the President's Blue Ribbon Commission on Defense Management,* Appendix L (June 1986).

9. Wrubel, R. (1989), "Addicted to fraud?" *Financial World Partners 1989*, June 27.

10. "An overview of the organizational guidelines," Paula Desio, Deputy General Counsel, United States Sentencing Commission; United States Sentencing Commission website at www.ussc.gov.

11. Telephone interview with Winthrop Swenson, October 4, 2004.

12. Unless otherwise noted, information in this section was gathered from a meeting with UTC Ombuds Consultant George Wratney on July 14, 2004, and from a telephone call with George Wratney and UTC Vice President of Business Practices Pat Gnazzo on August 19, 2004.

13. As part of its DII initiative, UTC in 1986 adopted a "policy statement on business ethics and conduct in contracting with the U. S. government." The policy statement remains in effect today.

14. UTC Code of Ethics, United Technologies Corporation website at www.utc.com.

15. *UTC World* 1 (2002).

16. McClenahen, J.S. (2003), "UTC's master of principle."

17. Ibid.

18. UTC Corporate Policy Manual, Section 36, Exhibit 1, Items 1–3 (February 1, 1993); revised March 11, 1993.

19. "Web-based ethics program encourages open communication," *Best Practices in HR* 774, October 2, 2004.

20. "Doing Things Right," video clip from UTC's website at www.utc.com.

21. Telephone interview with UTC Ombuds (Patti Lynch, Brian Nugent, Tom Neal, and Steve Cordery), UTC Ombuds Consultant George Wratney, and UTC Vice President of Business Practices Pat Gnazzo, November 22, 2004.

Frank T. Rothaermel
Georgia Institute of Technology

Alicia Horbaczewski
Merck & Co., Inc.

AUGUST 24, 2011. 6:05 A.M. At 1 Infinite Loop in Cupertino, California, Steve Jobs parked his Mercedes with no license plate at an odd angle in a handicap slot. Jobs was looking very thin, dressed in his typical uniform of a long-sleeved black turtleneck, blue jeans, and sneakers. He was a pancreatic cancer survivor. When he was first diagnosed in 2004, the doctors told him he had three to six months to live.[1] However, he turned out to have a rare form of pancreatic cancer that was treatable. "I had the surgery, and I'm fine now," he stated during his much-publicized commencement address for the Stanford graduating class of 2005.[2] Unfortunately, Jobs's cancer recurred, and he underwent a liver transplant in 2009, taking a six-month medical leave from his managerial responsibilities. His health problems had continued to plague him, forcing him to take a second medical leave starting in January 2011. Although Jobs had remained intimately involved with strategic decision making, and repeatedly assured shareholders that his health problems would not be a detriment to the company, the stock price had slipped as investors worried over the prospect of an Apple without Jobs at its helm. Apple had become such a close reflection of Jobs himself that the two hardly seemed distinguishable.

It seemed like just yesterday that Jobs had started Apple Computer, Inc. in his parents' garage in 1976. Thirty years later, he had succeeded in creating a fusion of computing, industrial design, and brand power that lead Apple to develop some of the most innovative products in the world, including the iPod, iPhone, and most recently, the iPad. In the process, Apple had become a household name. It dominated

Tim Cook, Apple CEO

a recent ranking of social brands, with the iPhone appearing at the top of the list, iTunes at number six, and the company itself ranked eighth.[3] Jobs was proud that he was credited with bringing life and inspiration to the company not once, but twice.

Jobs was in a hurry to start his day. He had a meeting scheduled at 10 a.m. with his board of directors to discuss the future of the company. He had to make an announcement that he had long dreaded: The time had come for him to step aside from the active management of the company and focus on his own health. Jobs hoped to remain as Chairman of the Board, to ensure that the culture of innovation that he helped instill would endure as the key to Apple's competitive success, no matter what uncertainties lay ahead. Meanwhile, Apple would need a new chief commander who would treat the company as Jobs did—not just as a passion, but as family, art, and above all, a place where people did not just work but changed the world.[4] Yet it would be difficult to find someone who could embody the image and culture of the company like Jobs did. To many, Apple was Steve Jobs, and Steve Jobs was Apple. Steve Jobs was more than a leader. He was a cult figure—a prophet of innovation. One employee even featured on his license plate the letters WWSJD—"What Would Steve Jobs Do?"[5]

When Jobs was 17, he read a quote that made a lasting impression on him: "If you live each day as if it was your last, someday you'll most certainly be right."[6] His recent bout with cancer proved to him that life was shorter than he ever expected. Having come so close to death and lived, Jobs could say with more certainty, "Death is very likely the single best invention of life. It is life's change agent. It clears out the old to make way for the new."[7] Change, and in particular the process of

Professor Frank T. Rothaermel and Research Associate Alicia Horbaczewski (GT MBA '10) prepared this case from public sources. This case is developed for the purpose of class discussion. It is not intended to be used for any kind of endorsement, source of data, or depiction of efficient or inefficient management. © by Rothaermel and Horbaczewski, 2013.

creative destruction, was the only constant Jobs had faith in, especially now.

The Creation of Apple, Inc.

In 1976, Steve Jobs and Steve Wozniak conceived the idea of a personal computer company and founded Apple Computer, Inc. (The word "Computer" was dropped in 2007 to reflect expansion from the personal computer market to consumer electronics in general.)[8] Only 21 years of age, Jobs had to sell his Volkswagen to get money to start the company. Jobs and Wozniak, then 26, began to assemble personal computers in Jobs's garage with a small group of friends. Soon after, they received additional financing to spur the growth of the company. In 1978, the Apple II, the first personal computer, was launched and sold for $666.66.[9] In December of that same year, Apple launched a successful IPO, making it a publicly traded company.

By 1980, Apple had released three improved versions of the personal computer, and its two founders Jobs and Wozniak had become multimillionaires. Then IBM entered the personal computer market in 1981 and quickly became a serious competitor. IBM's open architecture was easily imitable by other manufacturers and soon became the industry standard, giving rise to many more computer companies in the United States (e.g., Compaq and Dell) as well as in Taiwan, Korea, and other Asian countries. Even more threatening was the consortium between IBM, which specialized in the development of computer hardware, the newly formed Microsoft with its DOS operating system, and Intel with its expertise in memory and processors. By 1982, IBM had increased its profitability and market share substantially, and Apple's position was under attack.

"OBSESSED WITH DESIGN." Nonetheless, in just over 10 years Apple had grown into a $2 billion company with over 4,000 employees.[10] In 1984, Apple introduced its finest creation yet: the Macintosh. Jobs's curiosity and intuition had led him to become "notoriously obsessed with design and style." This passion began when Jobs dropped out of Reed College at the youthful age of 17. "The minute I dropped out, I could stop taking the required classes that didn't interest me, and begin dropping in on the ones that looked interesting," Jobs remembered.[11] He decided to take a calligraphy class to learn about serif and sans serif typefaces and what makes great typography: "It was beautiful, historical, artistically subtle in a way that science can't capture, and I found it fascinating. None of this had even a hope of any practical application in my life. But 10 years later, when we were designing the first Macintosh computer, it all came back to me. And we designed it all into the Mac. It was the first computer with beautiful typography."[12] Jobs firmly believed that if he had not dropped out of college and into that calligraphy class, the Mac would never have had multiple typefaces and proportionally spaced fonts. And, "since Windows just copied the Mac, it's likely that no personal computer would have them," if he had not made that decision.[13]

Although the Macintosh was the first personal computer applauded for unique industrial design and ease of use, it had a slower processor than IBM PCs and their clones, and very few compatible software programs due to Apple's closed proprietary operating system. As a result, the Mac was gradually pushed to the periphery as a niche player with customers mainly in education and graphic design. Apple's integrated value chain enabled the company to produce computers of very high quality, but placed the Macintosh at a price disadvantage as the growing consumer technology industry became increasingly commoditized.

NEW MARKETING GURU. In 1983, Jobs decided to bring on John Sculley to run the company with him. At the time, Sculley was a marketing guru from Pepsi whom Jobs "thought was very talented."[14] Sculley was responsible for the "Pepsi Challenge" and "Pepsi Generation" ad campaigns that helped Pepsi overtake Coca-Cola in market share for the first time in the history of the "Cola Wars." He had also turned around PepsiCo's failing food division by bringing in new management, improving product quality, and instituting new accounting and financial controls.[15]

Apple's innovative advertising tale started on January 22, 1984. During the third quarter of the Super Bowl that year, "one of the most famous television commercials of all time" was broadcast.[16] The ad was based on the dystopian society depicted by George Orwell in his novel *1984*. Hundreds of identical drones were shown listening to their larger-than-life dictator, whose black-and-white face was projected onto a screen in the middle of the room. Suddenly a beautiful woman, escaping capture from armed guards, threw a hammer at the screen which exploded in a technicolor display of dazzling light. The ad stated, "On January 24th, Apple Computer will introduce Macintosh. And you'll see why 1984 won't be like *1984*."[17] In this fashion, customers were introduced to Apple as the revolutionary, subversive, and rebellious company of the 1980s, ready to take on the tyrant of IBM.

For a while after John Sculley joined Apple, things went very well. But Jobs later recalled that "our visions of the future began to diverge and eventually we had a falling out."[18] Apple's core identity changed with Sculley in charge. The business strategy shifted from differentiation based on a premium product with a high price tag to producing a low-cost product with mass-market appeal. Sculley's new ambition for Apple was to compete directly with IBM in the household-computer market. Apple worked on bringing down the cost of manufacturing and formed alliances with Intel, Novell, and even its old nemesis, IBM. At the same time, Apple moved toward desktop publishing, multimedia, and peripherals. However, a series of major product flops, missed deadlines, and unrealistic earnings forecasts destroyed Apple's reputation. As a consequence, Apple's profitability continued on a downward slope. With dismal sales and declining net income, a power struggle erupted between Jobs and Sculley, who eventually succeeded in convincing Apple's board of directors to throw Jobs out of Apple in 1985.

HARD TIMES. To add insult to injury, Microsoft released its graphical user interface (GUI)–based operating system, Windows 3.0, in 1990, effectively cementing the Wintel standard with 90 percent market share in the PC industry. This was the powerful combination of a Windows operating system running on the x86 architecture chips made by Intel. Today, the x86 architecture is ubiquitous among computers, and a large amount of software supports the platform, including operating systems such as MS-DOS, Windows, Linux, BSD, Solaris, and Mac OS X. The innovator Apple had become a non-factor in the PC industry, retreating to ever-smaller niches of the market.

In June 1993, leadership changed hands again from Sculley to Michael Spindler. Spindler continued the company's focus on cost-cutting, but also made international growth a main objective. By 1995, Apple was spreading itself too thin across product lines and geographic markets. It had lost any strategic focus, and could not stop operating in the red.

Steve Jobs Returns

During this time, Jobs was starting over. "What had been the focus of my entire adult life was gone, and it was devastating."[19] Jobs had been fired very publicly from a company he had helped to create, and even considered leaving Silicon Valley for good.[20] Jobs later reminisced, "I didn't see it then, but it turned out that getting fired from Apple was the best thing that could have ever happened to me. The heaviness of being successful was replaced by the lightness of being a beginner again. . . . It freed me to enter one of the most creative periods of my life."[21] Had he in fact left Silicon Valley, he would not have founded two more of the most successful technology companies to date.

On February 3, 1986, Jobs founded Pixar Animation Studios. Since then, Pixar has earned ten Academy Awards, four Golden Globes and three Grammys, among many other awards. Pixar created the world's first completely computer-animated feature film, *Toy Story,* and is now the most successful animation studio in the world, with films like *A Bug's Life, Toy Story 2* and *3, Monsters Inc., Cars, Ratatouille, Finding Nemo, The Incredibles,* and *WALL-E*.

In 2006, Disney bought Pixar for $7.4 billion in a deal that also landed Jobs a seat on Disney's board of directors. "The addition of Pixar significantly enhances Disney animation, which is a critical creative engine for driving growth across our businesses," Disney CEO Robert Iger stated.[22] Jobs, the majority shareholder of Pixar at the time with 50.1 percent, became Disney's largest individual shareholder with 7 percent.[23] His holdings greatly exceeded those of the previous top shareholder of Disney, ex-CEO Michael Eisner who owned 1.7 percent, and even Disney's Director Emeritus Roy E. Disney, who owned less than 1 percent of the corporation's shares.[24]

Just one year prior to starting Pixar, Jobs had founded another computer company called NeXT, Inc., later known as NeXTSoftware, Inc. NeXT developed one of the first enterprise web application frameworks for the higher-education and business markets. In a bizarre twist of fate, Apple purchased NeXT on December 20, 1996, for $429 million.[25]

Earlier in 1996, Gilbert Amelio had replaced Spindler as CEO of Apple, which was reporting a mere $69 million in first-quarter revenues. Amelio's intention was to revive Apple's former strategy by focusing again on the premium-product market segment. Amelio made many changes at Apple, including terminating the IBM alliance and announcing massive layoffs of 30 percent of the company's total work force of 13,400.[26] With the acquisition of NeXT, Amelio also brought Jobs back as a part-time adviser to Apple. Despite all these measures, Apple's market share continued to tumble to just 3 percent worldwide.[27]

Apple experienced its worst year ever in 1997, and subsequently ousted Amelio due to crippling financial losses and a low stock price. Jobs was brought back as interim CEO in September of that same year. Thereafter, Steve Jobs succeeded in orchestrating one of the greatest corporate comebacks in modern-day history (see Exhibits 1 and 2 for financial performance data).

Restructuring Apple

When Steve Jobs returned to Apple in 1997, he was ready and eager to shake things up. In a meeting with Apple's top executives, after hearing all their explanations as to why Apple was performing poorly, Jobs infamously roared: "The products SUCK! There's no SEX in them anymore!"[28] Jobs swiftly refocused the company that he had helped start and discontinued several products such as the Newton PDA, the LaserWriter printer line, and the Apple QuickTake camera—all now collector items for Apple enthusiasts.

During this time of restructuring, Jobs outsourced manufacturing to Taiwan and scaled down the distribution system by ending relationships with smaller outlets. With Jobs's savvy insight for what consumers wanted, he launched a new, revolutionary website to sell Apple products directly to customers online. For the first time ever, he also opened Apple retail stores, tied to his build-to-order manufacturing strategy. Although these moves seemed risky at the time, all of these operational improvements helped to boost previously declining sales. For the first time since 1993, Apple once again became profitable in 1998.

Jobs also realized the necessity to make Apple's operating system more accessible for software providers. He switched everything to the open-source, UNIX-based operating system, Mac OS X. This proved to be a more stable operating environment and permitted the

EXHIBIT 1a

Apple's Consolidated Income Statement Data, 2004–2010

(in millions, except share and per-share amounts)		2010	2009	2008	2007	2006	2005	2004
Net sales		$65,225	$42,905	$37,479	$24,006	$19,315	$13,931	$8,279
Net income		14,013	8,235	6,119	3,496	1,989	1,328	266
Earnings per common share:								
	Basic	$15.41	$9.22	$6.94	$4.04	$2.36	$1.64	$0.36
	Diluted	15.15	9.08	6.78	3.93	2.27	1.55	0.34
Shares, '000' in computing EPS								
	Basic	909,461	893,016	881,592	864,595	844,058	808,439	743,180
	Diluted	924,712	907,005	902,139	889,292	877,526	856,878	774,776
Cash, cash equivalents, and short-term investments		$51,011	$33,992	$24,490	$15,386	$10,110	$8,261	$5,464
Total assets		$75,183	$47,501	$39,572	$25,347	$17,205	$11,516	$8,039
Long-term debt (including current maturities)		—	—	—	—	—	—	—
Total liabilities		$27,392	$15,861	$18,542	$10,815	$7,221	$4,088	$2,976
Shareholders' equity		$47,791	$31,640	$21,030	$14,532	$9,984	$7,428	$5,063

EXHIBIT 1b

Apple's Regional Sales, 2006–2010 (in millions)

Segment-wise Sales Breakup	2010		2009		2008		2007		2006
Net sales by operating segment		% increase		% increase		% increase		% increase	
Americas net sales	$24,498	29%	$18,981	15%	$16,447	38%	$11,907	26%	$ 9,415
Europe net sales	18,692	58%	11,810	28%	9,233	69%	5,469	34%	4,096
Japan net sales	3,981	75%	2,279	32%	1,728	59%	1,084	(10)%	1,211
Retail net sales	9,798	47%	6,656	(9)%	7,292	67%	4,362	34%	3,246
Other segments net sales (a)	8,256	160%	3,179	14%	2,791	59%	1,756	30%	1,347
Total net sales	$65,225	52%	$42,905	14%	$37,491	53%	$24,578	27%	$19,315
Unit sales by operating segment:									
Americas Mac unit sales	4,976	21%	4,120	4%	3,980	32%	3,019	24%	2,432
Europe Mac unit sales	3,859	36%	2,840	13%	2,519	39%	1,816	35%	1,346
Japan Mac unit sales	481	22%	395	2%	389	29%	302	(1)%	304
Retail Mac unit sales	2,846	35%	2,115	4%	2,034	47%	1,386	56%	886
Other segments Mac unit sales (a)	1,500	62%	926	17%	793	50%	528	58%	335
Total Mac unit sales	13,662	31%	10,396	7%	9,715	38%	7,051	33%	5,303

(a) Other segments include Asia Pacific and FileMaker.

Source: Apple Annual Reports 2006–2010.

EXHIBIT 1c

Net Sales by Product, 2006–2010

Net sales by product:	2010	2009	2008	2007	2006
Desktops (a)	$ 6,201	$ 4,324	$ 5,622	$ 4,023	$ 3,319
Portables (b)	11,278	9,535	8,732	6,313	4,056
Total Mac net sales	17,479	13,859	14,354	10,336	7,375
iPod	8,274	8,091	9,153	8,305	7,676
Other music related products and services (c)	4,948	4,036	3,340	2,496	1,885
iPhone and services (d)	25,179	13,033	6,742	630	—
iPad and related products (e)	4,958				
Peripherals and hardware (f)	1,814	1,475	1,694	1,303	1,100
Software and service sales (g)	2,573	2,411	2,208	1,508	1,279
Total net sales	$65,225	$42,905	$37,491	$24,006	$19,315

(a) Includes iMac, Mac mini, Mac Pro, Power Mac, and Xserve product lines.

(b) Includes MacBook, iBook, MacBook Air, MacBook Pro, and PowerBook product lines.

(c) Includes iTunes Store sales, iPod services, and Apple-branded and third-party iPod accessories.

(d) Includes revenue recognized from iPhone sales, carrier agreements, services, and Apple-branded and third-party iPhone accessories.

(e) Includes revenue recognized from iPad sales, services and Apple-branded and third-party iPad accessories.

(f) Includes sales of displays, wireless connectivity and networking solutions, and other hardware accessories.

(g) Includes sales of Apple-branded operating system and application software, third-party software, Mac and Internet services.

(continued)

EXHIBIT 1c *(Continued)*
Net Sales by Product 2006–2010

Unit sales by product:					
Desktops (a)	4,627	3,182	3,712	2,714	2,434
Portables (b)	9,035	7,214	6,003	4,337	2,869
Total Mac unit sales	13,662	10,396	9,715	7,051	5,303
Net sales per Mac unit sold (h)	$1,279	$1,333	$1,478	$1,466	$1,391
iPod unit sales	50,312	54,132	54,828	51,630	39,409
Net sales per iPod unit sold (h)	$164	$149	$167	$161	$195
iPhone units sold	39,989	20,731	11,627	1,389	—
iPad units sold	7,458				

(a) Includes iMac, Mac mini, Mac Pro, Power Mac, and Xserve product lines.

(b) Includes MacBook, iBook, MacBook Air, MacBook Pro, and PowerBook product lines.

(c) Includes iTunes Store sales, iPod services, and Apple-branded and third-party iPod accessories.

(d) Includes revenue recognized from iPhone sales, carrier agreements, services, and Apple-branded and third-party iPhone accessories.

(e) Includes revenue recognized from iPad sales, services and Apple-branded and third-party iPad accessories.

(f) Includes sales of displays, wireless connectivity and networking solutions, and other hardware accessories.

(g) Includes sales of Apple-branded operating system and application software, third-party software, Mac and Internet services.

(h) Derived by dividing total product-related net sales by total product-related unit sales.

Source: Apple Annual Reports 2006–2010.

EXHIBIT 2
Apple's Consolidated Balance Sheets, 2006–2010

Consolidated Balance Sheets					
(in millions)	25-Sep-10	26-Sep-09	27-Sep-08	29-Sep-07	30-Sep-06
ASSETS:					
Current assets:					
Cash and cash equivalents	$11,261	$5,263	$11,875	$9,352	$6,392
Short-term marketable securities	14,359	18,201	10,236	6,034	3,718
Accounts receivable, less allowances	5,510	3,361	2,422	1,637	1,252
Inventories	1,051	455	509	346	270
Deferred tax assets	1,636	1,135	1,447	782	607
Vendor nontrade receivables	4,414	1,696			
Other current assets	3,447	1,444	5,822	3,805	2,270
Total current assets	41,678	31,555	32,311	21,956	14,509
Long-term marketable securities	25,391	10,528	2,379		
Property, plant, and equipment, net	4,768	2,954	2,455	1,832	1,281
Goodwill	741	206	207	38	38
Acquired intangible assets, net	342	247	285	299	139
Other assets	2,263	2,011	1,935	1,222	1,238
Total assets	$75,183	$47,501	$39,572	$25,347	$17,205

Consolidated Balance Sheets					
(in millions)	25-Sep-10	26-Sep-09	27-Sep-08	29-Sep-07	30-Sep-06
LIABILITIES AND SHAREHOLDERS' EQUITY:					
Current liabilities:					
Accounts payable	$12,015	$5,601	$5,520	$4,970	$3,390
Accrued expenses	5,723	3,852	3,719	4,329	3,053
Deferred revenue	2,984	2,053	4,853		
Total current liabilities	20,722	11,506	14,092	9,299	6,443
Non-current liabilities:					
Deferred revenue–non-current	1,139	853	3,029		
Other non-current liabilities	5,531	3,502	1,421	1,516	778
Total liabilities	27,392	15,861	18,542	10,815	7,221
Commitments and contingencies					
Shareholders' equity:					
Common stock, no par value	10,668	8,210	7,177	5,368	4,355
Retained earnings	37,169	23,353	13,845	9,101	5,607
Accumulated other comprehensive (loss)/income	(46)	77	8	63	22
Total shareholders' equity	47,791	31,640	21,030	14,532	9,984
Total liabilities and shareholders' equity	$75,183	$47,501	$39,572	$25,347	$17,205

Source: Apple Annual Reports 2006–2010.

company to issue annual upgrades in response to customer feedback. In 2005, Apple completed this transition by switching from PowerPC to Intel processors, which meant that Apples could run not only the Mac OS X but also any operating systems that used the x86 architecture. This marked the beginning of a truly open era for Apple computers: They were now the most flexible as well as the most attractive. As a result, Apple's stock price rose from $6 in 2003 to over $80 in 2006, surpassing even Dell's market cap.[29] Dell's CEO, Michael Dell, was left retracting the words he had very publicly spat nine years prior, "If I ran Apple, I would shut it down and give the money back to shareholders."[30]

Jobs even formed an alliance with Apple's archrival Microsoft to release new versions of Microsoft Office for the Macintosh. In return, Microsoft made a $150 million investment in non-voting Apple stock.[31] Jobs, in a cell phone call with Gates said, "Bill, thank you. The world is a better place."[32]

Beyond changing the operating system, the most visible change Jobs instituted was leveraging industrial design to produce more aesthetically pleasing computers. Jobs almost instantly revitalized Apple's image by pushing the limits of technology and design. He appointed Jonathan Ive, a British designer, as head of Apple's in-house Industrial Design group (IDg). There have been several distinct design themes in Jobs and Ive's collaboration over the years: translucency, colors, minimalism, and dark aluminum. Ive has been credited with being the chief designer of the iMac, the aluminum and titanium PowerBook G4, the MacBook, unibody MacBook Pro, iPod, and iPhone.[33] Ive's work at Apple has won him a slew of awards and widespread recognition.

Jobs also started to brand Apple as a functionally appealing, hip alternative to other dull, clone-like computers in the market. Known for his candor, Steve Jobs once accused Michael Dell of making "un-innovative beige boxes."[34] Continuing in the same vein as the infamous 1984 television ad, Apple launched its "Think Different" campaign in 1997. The aim of the campaign was to reflect the culture of Apple, comprised of great people who think differently. The television advertisements featured major artists, scientists, and politicians who were seen as independent thinkers, including Albert Einstein, Martin Luther King, Jr., John Lennon, Thomas Edison, Amelia Earhart, Alfred Hitchcock, Pablo Picasso, and Jerry Seinfeld. Similarly, Apple's print advertisements had less to do with specific products, and everything do to with company image. They simply featured a portrait of one of the historic figures and a small Apple logo with the words "Think Different" in the bottom corner.

Apple's Culture

As early as 1983, Steve Jobs coined the following motto at an offsite retreat: "It's better to be a pirate than join the navy."[35] Jobs's Macintosh team had only 80 employees at the time, but already he sensed that they were developing the group-think mentality that he detested. In response to "Captain" Jobs's cry, programmers Steve Capps and Susan Kare painted a rainbow-colored Apple eye patch onto a pirate flag and hung it above the Macintosh building.[36] This iconic image became illustrative of Apple's unique corporate culture and also symbolic of Apple's first inspired slogan in the late 1970s, "Byte into an Apple."

According to its website, working at Apple was "less of a job, more of a calling."[37] Apple looked for employees who were on a mission to "change the world" and create "some of the best-loved technology on the planet."[38] Apple promoted itself to prospective candidates as "a whole different thing" with "corporate jobs without the corporate part."[39] Apple looked for people who were "smart, creative, up for any challenge, and incredibly excited about what they do. In other words, Apple people. You know, the kind of people you'd want to hang around with anyway."[40] Steve Jobs had been more than instrumental in developing Apple's envied corporate culture from its establishment. Employees typically worked 60 to 70 hours a week, and no one complained.

Apple has been thought of as putting Silicon Valley on the map with its hard-working but relaxed, casual atmosphere.[41] This characterization would be an impossible contradiction in most other corporations in the United States, but not at Apple. When Jobs returned to Apple in 1997, he became famous for his standard black turtleneck and jeans uniform, walking around the campus with, or sometimes without, his sneakers. Jobs even went barefoot to a 1999 meeting to settle a patent dispute with executives from Microsoft.[42] Jobs was the ultimate example of an "I'm-a-genius-and-I-don't-care" attitude. Apple employees embraced their hero and became convinced that with confidence and creativity, they, too, could become rich and leave a legacy—sans suit or shoes.

Apple's rebel spirit not only attracted a long-lasting appreciation from loyal employees, but also created an almost cult-like following among customers who appreciated Apple's propensity to think differently. Millions of people wanted to be seen as unique individuals, and hence, millions of people bought Apple products. The "Cult of Apple" was a group of rumored fanatical followers devoted to all things Apple, but "while there are many customers who eat, think, and breathe Apple, members of the Cult of Apple take their devotion one step further and *believe* in Apple."[43] The result was that Apple had a conspicuous horde-like following walking down the streets of every major city in the world with the signature white-ear buds of Apple products attached to their heads. Apple products became so trendy that other companies had to design their consumer electronics like Apple's to have a hope of selling. The loyalty of the Apple customers has served the company well, and now it is not just the die-hard fanatics who believe. Even people in the mainstream are becoming Apple converts.

Innovation at Apple

The one competency that has kept Apple on the cutting edge, all the way from startup to survival to success—and finally to profitability and industry envy—has been innovation. "Innovation distinguishes between a leader and a follower," Jobs repeatedly said.[44] Jobs believed that innovation is a process that can be cultivated and managed within an organization. It begins with idea generation, and then moves to idea adoption and development, and finally to idea implementation. All the while, the innovation process is being enabled by effective leadership and a supportive organizational culture.

Apple's top management was critical in nurturing an innovative organization because employees needed to know that they would not be reprimanded for making risky choices when attempting a creative project. A high tolerance for failure and calculated risk-taking is necessary for employees to feel comfortable bringing up new ideas in any organization.[45] Apple's workforce appeared to have embraced this attitude fully, as they proudly "[said] NO to 1,000 things."[46]

Compared to its competitors, Apple spent a minuscule 3.6 percent of revenues on research and development (R&D) for a grand total of $844 million in 2007. In contrast, Microsoft spent about 12.8 percent of annual revenues on R&D, equating to a whopping budget of $7.4 billion. Google similarly spent over 12.7 percent of annual revenues on R&D, for a total expenditure of $2.1 billion. (See Exhibit 3 for a list of R&D spending at selected technology companies.) Comparing the amount of money spent at Apple with that of other technology giants shows how effectively Apple's innovation process works, making possible a significant return on R&D investment. In fact, Jobs was known to say: "Innovation has nothing to do with how many R&D dollars you have. When Apple came up with the Mac, IBM was spending at least 100 times more on R&D. It's not about money. It's about the people you have, how you're led, and how much you 'get it.'"[47]

Apple's employees seemed to "get it," indeed. Apple was rated by *BusinessWeek* and Boston Consulting Group as the #1 Most Innovative Company in the world for several years in a row (see Exhibit 4).[48] This was quite a feat considering that Apple led both newer companies such as Google and Amazon, as well as more established firms like 3M and Procter & Gamble, in the rankings.

The iPod/iPhone/iPad Revolution

The big bang happened at Apple in October 2001 with the launch of the iPod, a portable digital music player based on the MP3 music format. The sleek design and smart graphical user interface bewitched consumers. The product was an instant hit, selling over 100 million units within six years.[49] The profitability of the iPod

---

EXHIBIT 3

R&D Spending at Selected Tech Companies, 2010 (in thousands)

Rank	Company	R&D, MOST RECENT	
		Four Quarters	Selected % of Revenue
1	Microsoft	$8,714,000	13.9
2	IBM	$5,820,000	6.08
3	Intel	$5,653,000	16.09
4	Cisco	$5,273,000	13.17
5	Oracle	$3,254,000	12.13
6	Google	$2,843,000	12.02
7	Hewlett-Packard	$2,819,027	2.46
8	SAP	$2,283,000	14.91
9	Apple	$1,782,000	2.70
10	Advanced Micro Devices	$1,721,000	31.85
11	EMC	$1,627,509	11.60
12	Yahoo	$1,210,168	18.73
13	Seagate	$ 877,000	7.70
14	Symantec	$ 857,000	14.32
15	Intuit	$ 566,232	13.69

Source: Adapted from Robert Hertzberg, "Top 50 Technology R&D Spenders," *CIO Zone*, www.ciozone.com/index.php/Editorial-Research/Top-50-Technology-R-D-Spenders.html.

EXHIBIT 4

Top 20 Companies on *Bloomberg Businessweek* 2010 Innovation Index

Rank	Company	Headquarters	Stock Returns 2006–2009 (in %)	Revenue Growth 2006–2009 (in %)	Margin Growth 2006–2009 (in %)
1	Apple	USA	35	30	29
2	Google	USA	10	31	2
3	Microsoft	USA	3	10	(4)
4	IBM	USA	12	2	11
5	Toyota Motor	JAPAN	(20)	(11)	NA
6	Amazon.Com	USA	51	29	6
7	LG Electronics	USA	31	16	707
8	BYD	CHINA	99	42	(1)
9	General Electric	USA	(22)	(1)	(25)
10	Sony	JAPAN	(19)	(5)	NA
11	Samsung Electronics	S. KOREA	10	17	(9)
12	Intel	USA	3	0	12
13	Ford Motor	USA	10	(12)	NA
14	Research In Motion	CANADA	17	75	(6)
15	Volkswagen	GERMANY	8	0	14
16	Hewlett-Packard	USA	9	8	9
17	Tata Group	INDIA	PRIVATE	PRIVATE	PRIVATE
18	BMW	GERMANY	(8)	0	NA
19	Coca-Cola	USA	9	9	1
20	Nintendo	JAPAN	(8)	22	3

Source: Adapted from *Bloomberg Businessweek*'s 50 Most Innovative Companies, http://bwnt.businessweek.com/interactive_reports/innovative_50_2009/?chan=magazine+channel_in%3A+inside+innovation.

was phenomenal, with margins estimated as high as 47.4 percent before freight, marketing, and other costs.[50]

In April 2003, Apple provided iTunes as a complement for the iPod. iTunes was the first online store from which customers could buy songs individually at 99 cents each, rather than purchasing entire albums for upward of $15 to $20 or downloading songs illegally. Within three days of launch, iTunes users had downloaded one million songs. By June 2008, iTunes had exceeded 5 billion downloads.[51] On February 25, 2010, which was coincidentally Steve Jobs's 55th birthday, Apple achieved the great milestone of 10 billion iTunes downloaded. Apple had seemingly effortlessly established itself as the newest icon of the digital age, revolutionizing the music industry and holding fast to its leadership position in the technology race.

In keeping with its iconoclastic reputation, Apple promoted its iPod as a stylish alternative to archetypal music technology products with the new "iPod People" campaign. Ads featured several silhouetted people with white headphones in their ears dancing against a colorful background. Apple advertising had always been creative by design, but its "iPod People" promotion brought in an unmistakable "coolness-factor" as the essence of the product. That desired attribute was directly transferred to the customer upon purchase.

THE IPHONE. In June 2007, Apple launched the iPhone, the third leg to Apple's innovation tripod, and soon Apple's share price passed the $100 mark.[52] The iPhone was a multifunction smartphone which provided the customer with a unique touch-based interface and a revolutionary operating system delivering a computer-based experience. According to Jobs, the iPhone was "the Internet in your pocket."[53] Apple partnered with AT&T to bring this device to the market and make it affordable for consumers. AT&T was happy to subsidize the phones, as long as it could ride the Apple wave of "coolness" and innovation.

One year later, Apple launched the iPhone 3G, which was advertised as twice as fast at half the price. The iPhone 3G supported all Microsoft document formats and had full support for a Microsoft Exchange server. Apple sold a record 6 million 3G iPhones in the first year, giving birth to a whole new generation of smartphones. In the summer of 2010, Apple released the iPhone 4 with built-in cameras and higher resolutions. In that same year, Apple had attained 17.4 percent of the smartphone market, with 82 percent sales growth since 2008. It had taken only two years for Apple to jump to second place behind Nokia, with 32.7 percent market share. Research in Motion, the maker of the BlackBerry, was third, with 15.3 percent.[54] Apple planned to introduce the 4G iPhone5 in the fall of 2011, this time allowing Verizon and Sprint, in addition to AT&T, to offer wireless services for the iPhone.[55]

In fact, Apple commanded such a following with its iPhone that even 10 percent of Microsoft employees used it, reopening the long-standing rivalry between the two companies. In September 2009, at a company-wide meeting in a sports stadium in Seattle, a Microsoft employee was using his iPhone to take photos of Microsoft CEO Steve Ballmer. Suddenly, "Mr. Ballmer snatched the iPhone out of the employee's hands, placed it on the ground, and pretended to stomp on it in front of thousands of Microsoft workers."[56] Afterward, Jobs sent an e-mail inquiring into this conspicuous iPhone use to a Microsoft spokesperson, who declined to comment.[57] Microsoft later announced its intention to release its own version of the smartphone—Windows Phone 7—in time for the 2010 winter-holiday season.[58]

THE IPAD. On January 25, 2010, Jobs took his biggest gamble yet with the announcement of the iPad, a multimedia, tablet-style computer designed to take the place of a pencil and pad of paper.[59] (See Exhibit 5 for a historical timeline of Apple's product introductions and net income.) During Jobs's keynote address introducing the iPad two days later, he praised his new invention as the "best browsing experience you've ever had. It's phenomenal! The Internet in your

---

EXHIBIT 5

Apple's Net Income ($ million) and Key Events over Time, 1981–2010

Source: Publicly available data.

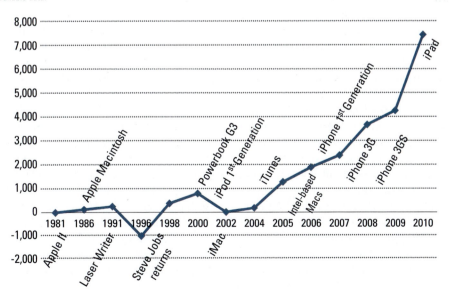

hands." Investors apparently shared Jobs's excitement, as Apple's stock price rose 15 percent after the iPad was unveiled.[60]

However, the idea of a keyboard-free, touch-screen portable computer tablet had been around for more than two decades. Apple had even launched its own Newton MessagePad in 1993, which became known less for its pioneering features and more for being ridiculed in "Doonesbury" for the software's problem in recognizing handwriting.[61] Upon returning to Apple in 1997, Jobs withdrew the Newton, which had become a commercial failure and a public relations embarrassment.[62] Competitors learned from Apple's Newton debacle and started to introduce improved products at a lower price, including Palm's Pilot, Handspring's Visor, and RIM's BlackBerry. Meanwhile, Jobs continuously scrapped all of Apple's new tablet prototypes for over a decade, because they reportedly "weren't good for anything except browsing the Web from the bathroom."[63]

Apple had come a long way since the Newton, evidenced by the fact that its iPad was the most highly anticipated gadget of 2010.[64] Jobs in his keynote address stated that "the iPad is our most advanced technology in a magical and revolutionary device at an unbelievable price."[65] The iPad was half an inch thick, weighed 1.5 pounds, and had a 9.7-inch "gorgeous, super-high quality display" and was "multitouch, super-responsive, and super-precise."[66] It had Wi-Fi wireless connectivity and was capable of browsing the web, e-mail, photos, video, music, games, and e-books. It operated much like the smaller iPhone and could run all 140,000 applications (apps) designed for the iPhone. Additionally, the iPad incorporated features like a calendar, photo manager, spreadsheets, and presentations to take on a more multimedia look.[67]

Given initial rumors that the iPad would cost anywhere from $700 to $1,000, customers were pleasantly surprised when it debuted at prices ranging from $499 up to $829. Many Apple fans remembered when Jobs famously spouted his disdain for the growing development of the notebook market: "We don't know how to make a $500 computer that's not a piece of junk."[68] However, customers had to pay an extra $30 a month to AT&T for the same always-on Internet access that the Kindle provided,[69] with an option to renew their subscription on a monthly basis. This arrangement represented a significant departure from the wireless industry's traditional carrier-centered

model, allowing Apple to extract more value while carriers bore more of the cost. On the other hand, AT&T did not subsidize the device, as it did with the iPhone, so this deal could potentially prove profitable for both parties.

Despite pent-up demand, it was estimated that the iPad would cannibalize the market for other Apple products, including the iPhone, iPod, and Mac notebooks, by around 10 percent.[70] To overcome this potential threat, Jobs would have to convince customers that they needed another gadget, in addition to their laptops and smartphones. Jobs believed there was room for a third category between the laptop and smartphone, but acknowledged that "it must do things far better than both existing devices." Jobs argued for the necessity of his iPad: "If it is not better at these tasks, then there is no reason for it being there."[71]

Yet critics pointed out that unlike the iPhone, the iPad lacked a built-in camera for taking photos. It also lacked the ability to play Flash-based content on websites, which accounted for 75 percent of video on the web, and it could run only one app on the screen at a time. While Jobs hailed the iPad as "a dream to type on,"[72] for many it was not as easy as a typical keyboard with tactile keys to feel. This caused many customers to express disappointment with the iPad as doing less than the iPhone, but on a bigger screen.[73] In March 2011, Steve Jobs in typical showman fashion, unveiled the iPad2, a thinner and sleeker but higher performing version of the original iPad. Moreover, the iPad2 now contained two cameras to facilitate online video chat.[74]

With the introduction of the iPad, Steve Jobs defined Apple as a mobile-devices company, competing against Sony, Samsung, and Nokia.[75] At the same time, Apple faced direct competition from other computer manufacturers, who were quick to jump on the iPad bandwagon, hoping to undercut Apple's price to gain market share. For example, Hewlett-Packard announced its own keyboardless computer called the "Slate," and Dell, Acer, and Sony were all refining their own versions of the tablet. In addition, the iPad was likely to face competition from the new mini-laptops or "netbooks" being offered by Apple's competitors for around $100.[76] These devices could perform all of the necessary functions needed for most personal, academic, and even professional needs. Nevertheless, Jobs did not appear to be too concerned: "The problem is netbooks aren't better at anything—they are just cheaper."[77]

Revolutionizing the Publishing Industry?

Because the iPad was capable of reading books, newspapers, and magazines, Jobs predicted that the iPad would reshape the publishing business much the way his iPod revolutionized the music industry.[78] The CEO of McGraw-Hill, Harold McGraw, expressed his agreement in an interview on CNBC saying, "We have 95 percent of all our materials on the e-book format. . . . So now with the tablet you're going to open up the higher-education market, the professional market. The tablet is going to be just really terrific!"[79] Technophiles envisioned that the iPad would "save the newspaper and book publishing industries, present another way to watch television and movies, play video games, and offer a visually rich way to enjoy the web and the expanding world of mobile applications."[80]

Many believed that the iPad represented the next technological innovation to replace Amazon's Kindle and Sony's Reader. Jobs described how Apple would take over Amazon's e-book market saying: "We're going to stand on its shoulders and go a bit further."[81] He started by announcing a new online store for electronic books called iBookstore along with new partnerships with major book publishers including the Hatchette Book Group, Macmillan, Penguin Group, HarperCollins, Simon & Schuster, and McGraw-Hill to provide e-book content for the iPad. The only publisher that did not sign on with the iPad was Random House. One reason why it held out is that publishers and authors would make lower revenues and royalties per book sold.

With few exceptions, the publishing industry was enthusiastic to tap into a market of 125 million Apple customers. "It is never wise to stand between a consumer and a preference for how they get their content," said John Makinson, CEO of Penguin.[82] Moreover, publishers detested Amazon's pricing model, which charged Kindle customers a standard $9.99 for each e-book, causing publishers to lose about $5 for each e-book sold. In contrast, the iBookstore set the maximum e-book price at the cost of printing the book, so publishers were able to charge anywhere from $12.99 to $14.99 for most titles.[83] Apple retained 30 percent of the sale price and returned the remaining 70 percent to the publishers. What publishers liked about the iPad deal was that they (and not Apple) got to determine the prices of e-content for end consumers. In addition, this deal gave publishers leverage to negotiate higher prices for their content with Amazon. It was even possible that publishers would withhold titles from Amazon if they did not agree to raise their prices. As a result, the competition between Apple and Amazon "is as intense a situation as the industry has ever had. . . . It's a huge chess match."[84]

Apple's Deep Executive Bench

After introducing the iPad, Jobs turned the presentation over to Scott Forstall, a computer science graduate from Stanford who came to Apple with NeXT computers. In a surprising step toward open innovation, Forstall announced that he was opening up his iPad code, making a new app-development kit available right away so that developers could begin building apps for the iPad. Perhaps symbolically, Jobs left the stage and Forstall sat in the same cushy chair Jobs had just occupied. Many in the audience speculated: Was this a signal that Forstall would replace Jobs as the next CEO of Apple?

While not addressing the succession question directly, Apple was quietly taking steps to ensure that its future was not as directly linked with Jobs playing such an active role in the company as he had in the past.[85] Apple investors were painfully aware of how any news regarding Jobs's health could affect Apple's stock price.[86]

After Jobs was initially diagnosed and treated for pancreatic cancer in 2004, rumors had continued to circulate about his health because of his gaunt appearance. Despite the fact that spokespeople for Apple repeated consistently that "Steve's health is robust,"[87] the media were not fully convinced. While *The New York Times* published a story citing Jobs's health issues as no more life-threatening than "a common bug," *Bloomberg* mistakenly published on August 28, 2008, a 2,500 word obituary of Jobs containing blank spaces for his age and cause of death.[88] Although *Bloomberg* promptly retracted the article, its accidental release only fueled the questions and rumors regarding Jobs's health.[89] Jobs, meanwhile, seemed to take all this speculation in stride. He even joked by quoting Mark Twain at a conference, "Reports of my death are greatly exaggerated."[90]

In April 2009, Jobs underwent a liver transplant at the Methodist University Hospital Transplant Institute in Memphis, Tennessee, and his prognosis was again "excellent."[91] A surgeon wrote: "Chances are Jobs will be fine, and will remain as cantankerous, arrogant, dictatorial, and wildly visionary as ever for many years to come."[92]

Nevertheless, when Jobs had announced his medical leave on January 14, 2009, Apple's stock took a $13 billion hit that same day, even though the public had known about his health problems for a long time. (See Exhibit 6 for Apple's stock price history.) While Jobs was away, Timothy Cook, head of worldwide sales and operations, ran the company. Cook was later awarded a bonus of $22 million, $5 million in cash and the rest in stock, for serving as interim CEO during Jobs's medical absence.[93]

Jobs returned on June 29, 2009, as the reigning CEO of Apple.[94] Apple refrained from making any official statements regarding Jobs's health, but Jobs held his first public appearance after almost a year in September 2009 to show investors that he was once again back, in charge, and healthier than ever. Jobs was dressed in his usual black turtleneck, jeans, and sneakers. The 54-year-old appeared enthusiastic, but still seemed very thin and spoke with a scratchy voice. Apple shares rose by 20 percent after Jobs's return, showing how deeply intertwined the company's health was with that of Jobs himself.[95]

Some Apple board members, however, did not think Jobs fulfilled his fiduciary responsibility to disclose the seriousness of his health problems in a timely and forthright manner. Jerome York, a long-time board member until his death in March 2010, as well as former CFO of Chrysler and IBM, stated in a 2009 *Wall Street Journal* interview that "he had strong feelings about the way Mr. Jobs handled disclosures about his leave for health reasons . . . he [Mr. York] almost resigned when told of the seriousness of Mr. Jobs's illness. Mr. Jobs should have publicly disclosed his health problem earlier."[96] York also said that he was disgusted by Jobs's concealment and added, "Frankly, I wish I had resigned then."[97]

EXHIBIT 6

Apple's Stock Price and NASDAQ, September 1984–November 2010

Source: Yahoo Inc.

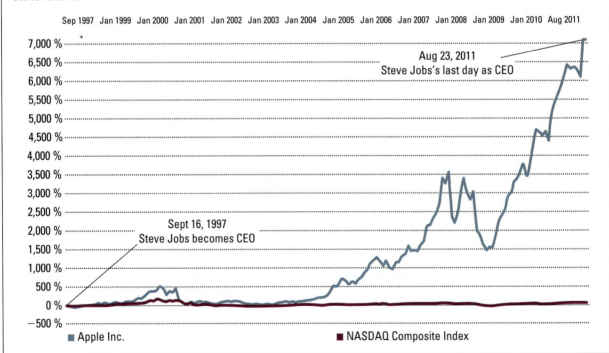

Jobs was a bit more proactive in announcing his second leave of absence in January 2011. The company released an e-mail sent to all employees, stating: "At my request, the board of directors has granted me a medical leave of absence so I can focus on my health. I will continue as CEO and be involved in major strategic decisions for the company."[98] Once again, it was Tim Cook who stepped into Jobs's shoes: "I have asked Tim Cook to be responsible for all of Apple's day-to-day operations. I have great confidence that Tim and the rest of the executive management team will do a terrific job executing the exciting plans we have in place for 2011."[99] Was this an implicit announcement that Tim Cook—with two terms as interim CEO—was Jobs's heir apparent?

Even without a major health crisis, Jobs and the board had a fiduciary responsibility to the shareholders to put a succession plan in place.[100] Fortunately, Apple had a deep executive bench:

- **Timothy Cook,** Chief Operating Officer. With an MBA from Duke University and a BS in Industrial Engineering from Auburn University, Tim was a low-profile, but high-impact executive at Apple. Tim's personality contrasted starkly with Jobs's; he displayed no ego and was much happier out of the limelight. Tim Cook served as CEO of the company when Jobs was on medical leave for pancreatic cancer.

- **Scott Forstall,** Senior Vice President, iPhone Software. With an MS in Computer Science and a BS in Symbolic Systems, both from Stanford University, Forstall came to Apple with NeXT computers. He was responsible for Mac OS X before being named vice president for iPhone software. He had spoken publicly at Apple's worldwide conferences.

- **Jonathan Ive,** Senior Vice President, Industrial Design. With a BS and an honorary doctorate from Newcastle Polytechnic in England, Ive was recognized as the man who designed the iPod and many more of Apple's most iconic products that had shaken up both the music and the electronics industry.

- **Phil Schiller,** Senior Vice President Worldwide Product Marketing. With a BS in Biology from Boston College, Schiller was a well-known public figure and showed up regularly on stage with Steve Jobs during keynotes to present new products. He was instrumental in marketing the iMac, iBook, iPod, and Mac OS X.

(For more details on the education and experience of these Apple executives, see http://www.apple.com/pr/bios/.)

Ron Johnson, who had been Senior Vice President, Retail, left Apple in June 2011 to become president (and ultimately CEO) of J.C. Penney. Under his direction, Apple's retail stores had achieved a record level of growth, exceeding $1 billion in annual sales within two years of their debut.

Challenges Ahead

Steve Jobs was feeling somewhat more cranky than usual as he walked into Apple headquarters. He could see the rebellious "think different" attitude on which he founded Apple's innovative culture weakening under the watch of his very own chosen MBA executives. He feared he had surrounded himself with business managers who thought similarly to the big tyrants IBM and Microsoft. Jobs wanted to remind himself and his leadership team to "Stay hungry. Stay foolish."[101]

Jobs had been described as both the best and the worst boss to work for. Many Apple employees had to readjust to Jobs's homecoming. They had grown accustomed to having a higher level of freedom over product development while Jobs was on leave, only to have him take it away upon his return.[102] While many were fiercely loyal and even in awe of Jobs's creative genius, they were also afraid of him. Jobs once criticized the work of an employee in an e-mail, saying, "Much of your information is incorrect," but he would not provide specifics.[103] He made them feel terrible and even made some cry. *Fortune* magazine wrote that Jobs was "considered one of Silicon Valley's leading egomaniacs."[104] Nor did he reserve his pronouncements only for Apple insiders. In an e-mail exchange with a blogger, Jobs asked, "What have you done that's so great? Do you create anything, or just criticize others [sic] work and belittle their motivations?"[105]

It was 10:12 a.m. when Jobs entered the conference room. Facing an anxious-looking board of directors, Jobs began to read a prepared statement:

To the Apple Board of Directors and the Apple Community:[106]

I have always said if there ever came a day when I could no longer meet my duties and expectations as Apple's CEO, I would be the first to let you know. Unfortunately, that day has come.

I hereby resign as CEO of Apple. I would like to serve, if the Board sees fit, as Chairman of the Board, director and Apple employee.

As far as my successor goes, I strongly recommend that we execute our succession plan and name Tim Cook as CEO of Apple.

I believe Apple's brightest and most innovative days are ahead of it. And I look forward to watching and contributing to its success in a new role.

I have made some of the best friends of my life at Apple, and I thank you all for the many years of being able to work alongside you.

Steve

On October 5, 2011, Steve Jobs lost his battle with cancer.

Endnotes

1. Jobs, S. (2005), "'You've got to find what you love,' Jobs says," *Stanford Report*, June 14.

2. Ibid.

3. "The Virtue 100: Top social brands of 2009," *Virtue.com*, accessed October 10, 2010; and http://Virtue.com/blog/2010/01/04/the-Virtue-100-top-social-brands-of-2009.

4. Jobs at Apple, www.apple.com/jobs/us/.

5. "Spotted: Ultimate Apple fanboy visits the mothership," *TechCrunch*, September 25, 2009.

6. Jobs, S. (2005), "'You've got to find what you love,' Jobs says."

7. Ibid.

8. "New mobile phone signals Apple's ambition," *The New York Times*, January 9, 2007.

9. Jobs, S., *Crunchbase*, www.crunchbase.com/person/steve-jobs.

10. Jobs, S. (2005), "'You've got to find what you love,' Jobs says."

11. Ibid.

12. Ibid.

13. Ibid.

14. Ibid.

15. Sculley, J., and J. A. Byrne (1987), *Odyssey: Pepsi to Apple* (New York: Harper & Row).

16. "DoubleTwist remakes Apple's classic 1984 ad with a new dictator: Steve Jobs," *TechCrunch*, September 29, 2009.

17. Text from Apple's TV ad during Super Bowl, January 22, 1984.

18. Jobs, S. (2005), "'You've got to find what you love,' Jobs says."

19. Ibid.

20. Ibid.

21. Ibid.

22. "Disney buys Pixar," *CNN Money*, January 25, 2006.

23. "Disney agrees to acquire Pixar in a $7 billion deal," *The New York Times*, January 25, 2006.

24. Ibid.

25. "Apple Computer, Inc. agrees to acquire NeXT Software Inc.," Apple Inc., December 20, 1996.

26. "Apple to trim jobs and its product line," *The New York Times*, March 15, 1997.

27. Yoffie, D. B., and R. Kim, (2010), "Apple Inc. in 2010 (9-710-467)," Harvard Business School, April 13.

28. "Steve Jobs' Magic Kingdom," *BusinessWeek*, February 2006.

29. "Dell: Apple should close shop," *CNET News*, October 6, 1997.

30. Ibid.

31. "Microsoft and Apple affirm commitment to build next generation software for Macintosh," Apple Inc., August 6, 1997.

32. *Time*, cover, September 12, 2006.

33. "Jonathan Ive and Apple win again." *BusinessWeek*, June 7, 2007.

34. "Look forward in anger," *The Economist*, March 18, 2010.

35. Hertzfeld, A., "Pirate flag," *Folklore*, August 1983. www.folklore.org/StoryView.py?story=Pirate_Flag.txt.

36. Ibid.

37. "Jobs at Apple," www.apple.com/jobs/us/.

38. Ibid.

39. Ibid.

40. Ibid.

41. "Growth by effort: The best company," *The Wise Nutrition*, December 2008.

42. "Apple and Microsoft: Jobs barefoot under a tree," *Computergram International*, January 26, 1999.

43. "Cult of Apple," *Uncyclopedia*, http://uncyclopedia.wikia.com/wiki/Cult_of_Apple.

44. Jobs, S., *Crunchbase*, www.crunchbase.com/person/steve-jobs.

45. Hill, C. W. L., and F. T. Rothaermel (2003), "The performance of incumbent firms in the face of radical technological innovation," *Academy of Management Review* 28 (2): 257–274.

46. "The seed of Apple's innovation," *BusinessWeek*, October 12, 2004.

47. "The second coming of Apple through a magical fusion of man—Steve Jobs—and company, Apple is becoming itself again: The little anticompany that could," *Fortune*, November 9, 1998.

48. "Is innovation too costly in hard times?" *BusinessWeek*, April 9, 2009.

49. "Apple enjoys ongoing iPod demand," *BBC News*, January 18, 2006.

50. "iPod tear-down suggests high Apple margins," *Apple Insider,* September 15, 2006.

51. "iTunes store tops five billion songs," Apple Inc., June 19, 2008.

52. "AAPL surges past $100, target at $140," *MacNN,* April 26, 2007.

53. "Apple's Jobs: Mobile Internet is terrible; iPhone delivers the real Internet," *Information Week,* May 31, 2007.

54. "iPhone sales double in 2009 as Apple claims third place in smartphone sales," *MacRumors.com,* February 23, 2010.

55. "Verizon wireless confident it's got muscle for iPhone," *The Wall Street Journal,* January 10, 2011.

56. "Forbidden fruit: Microsoft workers hide their iPhones," *The Wall Street Journal,* March 12, 2010.

57. Ibid.

58. Rothman, W., "Here come the Windows Phones," *msnbc. com,* www.msnbc.msn.com/id/39609748/?GT1=43001, accessed October 11, 2010.

59. "Apple takes big gamble on new iPad," *The Wall Street Journal,* January 25, 2010.

60. "Interest builds in Apple ahead of iPad's launch," *The Wall Street Journal,* March 20, 2010.

61. "Just a touch away, the elusive tablet PC," *The New York Times,* October 4, 2009.

62. Ibid.

63. "Apple to take tablet beyond bathroom Web browsing," *Apple Insider,* October 5, 2009.

64. "Just a touch away, the elusive tablet PC."

65. Jobs, S., Keynote address to introduce iPad, January 27, 2010, www.apple.com.

66. Ibid.

67. "The Microsofting of Apple," *The New York Times,* February 10, 2010.

68. "Jobs, back at Apple, focuses on new tablet," *The Wall Street Journal,* August 25, 2009.

69. "Apple takes big gamble on new iPad."

70. "iPhone sales double in 2009 as Apple claims third place in smartphone sales."

71. Jobs, S., Keynote address to introduce iPad.

72. Ibid.

73. "Apple's showman takes the stage," *The Wall Street Journal,* March 3, 2011.

74. "Apple takes big gamble on new iPad."

75. Jobs, S., Keynote address to introduce iPad.

76. "Apple says no to netbooks," *The New York Times,* April 24, 2009.

77. Jobs, S., Keynote address to introduce iPad.

78. "Apple sees money in old media," *The Wall Street Journal,* January 21, 2010.

79. "McGraw-Hill CEO confirms Apple tablet, iPhone OS based, going to be 'terrific,'" *MacRumors.com,* January 26, 2010.

80. "Just a touch away, the elusive tablet PC."

81. "Apple takes big gamble on new iPad."

82. "Books on iPad offer publishers a pricing edge," *The New York Times,* January 29, 2010.

83. Ibid.

84. "Apple tablet portends rewrite for publishers," *The Wall Street Journal,* January 27, 2010.

85. "Steve Jobs recovering after liver transplant," *CNN.com,* June 23, 2009.

86. Ibid.

87. "Apple's Cook gets $22 million bonus," *The Wall Street Journal,* March 13, 2010.

88. "Steve Jobs lives!" *InformationWeek,* August 11, 2006.

89. "Steve Jobs obituary published by Bloomberg," *The Daily Telegraph,* August 28, 2008.

90. Ibid.

91. "Apple posts 'Let's Rock' event video," *Macworld,* September 10, 2008.

92. "Steve Jobs recovering after liver transplant."

93. "Greatly exaggerated," *Daring Fireball,* September 11, 2008.

94. "On Apple's board, fewer independent voices," *The Wall Street Journal,* March 24, 2010.

95. Ibid.

96. "Jobs takes stage at Apple event," *The Wall Street Journal,* September 10, 2009.

97. Ibid.

98. http://www.apple.com/pr/library/2011/01/17Apple-Media-Advisory.html.

99. Ibid.

100. "Succession planning is a fiduciary responsibility," *The Rainmaker Group,* December 18, 2008.

101. Jobs, S. (2005), "'You've got to find what you love,' Jobs says."

102. "Jobs, back at Apple, focuses on new tablet."

103. Ibid.

104. "Steve Jobs' bad bet." *Fortune,* March 5, 2007.

105. "Steve Jobs indulges in email argument with Gawker writer," *Guardian.co.uk,* Technology Blog, May 15, 2010.

106. "Steve Jobs's resignation letter," *Forbes,* August 24, 2011, http://onforb.es/neJ4S0.

PHOTO CREDITS

COMPANY INDEX

Note: Page numbers followed by *n* indicate material in chapter endnotes and source notes. Page numbers beginning with C indicate material in case studies.

Note: Page numbers followed by *n* indicate material in chapter endnotes and source notes. Page numbers beginning with C indicate material in case studies.

SUBJECT INDEX

Note: Page numbers followed by *n* indicate material in chapter endnotes and source notes. Page numbers beginning with C indicate material in case studies.

A

Absorptive capacity, 190–191
Accounting data, 119–120
Accounting profit, 116
Accounting profitability, 114, 117–120, 123
Accounting Reform and Investor Protection Act of 2002 (SOX), 118, 339
Accounting scandals (fraud), 39, 43, 335
Acid-test (quick) ratio, 399
Acquisition and integration capability, 243
Acquisitions. *See* Mergers and acquisitions (M&A)
Activities
  core competencies and, 87
  in value chain, 96, 97
Activity ratios, 397
Administrative costs, 204, 214
Adverse selection, 344
Advertising
  competitive rivalry and, C368–C381
  as revenue source, C7–C8
AFI strategy framework, 1, 4, 19–21
  analysis, 40–41, 391
  formulation, 41–42, 392
  in strategic management. *See* Strategic management process
  strategy implementation, 41, 42, 43, 302–303, 392–393
  use in case analysis, 390
  use in scenario planning, 40–42, 43
Agency theory, 343–344, 352
Aircraft manufacturing
  case study: Embraer, C382–C394
  specialized equipment, C164–C166, C169–C171
Airframe-manufacturing industry, 63, 152
Airline industry
  case studies
    Embraer, C382–C394
    JetBlue Airways, C157–C174
  cost-leadership strategy in, 148
  economies of scale in, 151
  five forces model in, 68–70
  formalization in, 305
  horizontal integration in, 240
  mapping strategic groups, 75
  market conditions in, C383–C384
  mobility barriers in, 76–77
  oligopoly in, 179
  regional markets in, C382–C383
  resource-based view of, 90–91
  specialized equipment for, C164–C166, C169–C171
  strategic networks in, 254

Alliance champion, 253
Alliance leader, 253
Alliance management capability, 251–254, 259
  design and governance, 251–252
  partner selection and formation, 251
  post-formation management, 252–254
Alliance manager, 253
Ambidextrous organizational structure, 158–159, 311–312
Ambiguity
  causal, 104, 105, 321
  tolerance for, 279
Analysis
  of case studies. *See* Case analysis
  competitive analysis checklist, 69
  external. *See* External analysis
  internal. *See* Internal analysis
  of oligopolies, game theory in, 63
  stakeholder impact analysis, 337–341, 358
  strategy analysis *(A),* 20–21
  SWOT analysis, 105–106, 107
Analysis stage of AFI framework, 40–41, 391–392
Anti-dumping actions
  government duties, C335, C341
  litigation, C331
Apparel industry, 17
  case study: Geox, C87–C104
  shapewear, innovation in, 178
Architectural innovation, 182, 184
Artifacts, 318
Asian Tigers, 271
Assets
  complementary, 246–247, 375
  specialized, 213–214
  tangible or intangible, 120, 123
Auditors, 348–349
Automobile industry
  case studies
    barriers to entry: BYD, 55, 56, 77
    Tesla Motors, C32–C48, C50–C54
  competing technologies (minicase), 375
  competitive intensity in, 288
  complements in, 70–71
  customer service as value driver, 145, 146
  discontinuity in, 191
  disruptive innovation in, 184
  ecological concerns, 61
  equity alliances in, 250
  ERP systems in, 150
  globalization in, 274, 275

  organizational inertia in, 319
  parent-subsidiary relationships in, 209
  scope of competition in, 143
  strategic alliances in, 247–248
  strategic groups, 74
  United Auto Workers, 18–19, 66
Autonomous actions, 43

B

Baby boomers, 15
Backward integration, 67
Backward vertical integration, 212, 225
Balanced scorecard, 124–127
  advantages of, 126–127
  disadvantages of, 127
  elements of, 124–126
Balance of trade, 59
Bandwagon effects, 224
Banking industry
  case study: Bank of America, C175–C192
  external environment of, 57
  investment banking, 19–20
  leveraging core competencies, 219–220
  mergers and acquisitions in, 72
  microcredit, 15
  off-shore outsourcing in, 215
  shadow banks, C183, C186, C187
Bankruptcies, 39, 43, 68
Barriers to entry, 65–66, 72
  in auto industry, 55, 56
  case study: BYD, 55, 56, 77
  industry life cycle, 174
  overcoming, 183
  strategic groups, 76
Bathtub metaphor, 101–102
Benchmark comparisons, 5
Best-in-class practices, 9
Beverage industry. *See* Soft drink industry
BHAG (big hairy audacious goal), 128
Big Five personality test, 328
Big hairy audacious goal (BHAG), 128
Biotechnology industry
  birth and evolution of, C416–C421
  case studies
    Genentech/Roche, C415–C439
    Merck, C228–C247
Board independence, 345
Board of directors, 344–346
Bonded debt to equity ratio, 398
Book value of asset, 120
Book value per share ratio, 400